Essentials of Understanding Psychology

Second Canadian Edition

Robert S. Feldman
University of Massachusetts–Amherst

Joan E. Collins
Sheridan College

Judy M. Green
Sheridan College

 **McGraw-Hill Ryerson**

Toronto   Montréal   Boston   Burr Ridge, IL   Dubuque, IA   Madison, WI
St. Louis   Bangkok   Bogotá   Caracas   Kuala Lumpur   Lisbon   London
Mexico City   Milan   New Delhi   Santiago   Seoul   Singapore   Sydney   Taipei

ISBN-13: 978-0-07-093989-9
ISBN-10: 0-07-093989-6

2 3 4 5 6 7 8 9 10 CTPS 0 9 8 7

Printed and bound in China

Vice President, Editorial and Media Technology: Patrick Ferrier
Senior Sponsoring Editor: James Buchanan
Marketing Manager: Sharon Loeb
Developmental Editor: Darren Hick
Supervising Editor: Anne Nellis
Copy Editor: Dawn du Quesnay
Production Coordinators: Kelly Selleck/Paula Brown
Cover Design: Dianna Little
Interior Designer: Christopher Reese
Cover Image Credit: © Michael Mahovlich/Masterfile
Composition: Pronk&Associates
Printer: China Translation & Printing Services Ltd.

National Library of Canada Cataloguing in Publication

Feldman, Robert S. (Robert Stephen), 1947-
    Essentials of understanding psychology/Robert S. Feldman, Joan E. Collins,
Judy M. Green. -- 2nd Canadian ed.

Includes bibliographical references and indexes.

ISBN 0-07-093989-6

    1. Psychology. I. Collins, Joan E. II. Green, Judy, 1958- III. Title.

BF121.F338 2003   150   C2003-900051-6

About the Authors

Robert S. Feldman is Professor of Psychology at the University of Massachusetts at Amherst, where he is Director of Undergraduate Studies. He has also taught courses at Mount Holyoke College, Wesleyan University, and Virginia Commonwealth University. Professor Feldman is a fellow of both the American Psychological Association and the American Psychological Society. He is a winner of a Fulbright Senior Research Scholar and Lecturer award and has written some 100 scientific articles, book chapters, and books. His research interests encompass the development of non-verbal behavior in children and the social psychology of education, and his research has been supported by grants from the National Institute of Mental Health and the National Institute on Disabilities and Rehabilitation Research.

Joan Collins has spent most of her life in school. Her commitment to education has been inspired by the inscription above the front door of the college she attended at the University of Toronto, which reads "The Truth shall make you free." As a secondary school teacher teaching English, the most significant event she experienced was the discovery that a young student who sat at the front of the classroom could not read. Her awareness of student reading problems led her to develop a remedial reading program and later to write a thesis and a dissertation on reading.

Since 1988, Joan Collins has taught psychology at Sheridan College in Oakville, Ontario, at first to students in different daytime programs (Library Techniques, Computer Studies, Advertising, Applied Research, General Arts and Science) as well as to mature students in Continuing Education. Currently, she teaches a variety of psychology courses to General Arts and Science students. Joan Collins finds it very rewarding to introduce students to psychology and to see them discover that the subject matter is interesting, exciting, and relevant to everyday life.

Judy Green grew up in Montreal, Quebec, and graduated from Concordia University in that city. For more than ten years now, Judy Green has taught introductory psychology, social psychology and human development at Sheridan College in Oakville, Ontario. She has also taught at the American School in London (England). She and her colleague Joan Collins previously collaborated on the writing of *A Textbook of Social Psychology*, Brief Edition, with James Alcock, Bill Carment, and Stan Sadava.

Judy Green writes, "Working on this project has been most rewarding. With Robert Feldman's excellent book as a starting point, we expanded the representation of Canadian research, which has reinforced for me the knowledge that while psychology in Canada is unique in some respects, it has a great deal to offer on the world stage. Connecting with the very talented people who agreed to be featured in our 'Pathways' and 'Prologue' sections was a wonderful experience. We asked them to tell us about their journey . . . and we have been truly inspired by their achievements and their generosity of spirit."

To Ethel Radler, with love.

- Robert S. Feldman

To our students.

- Joan Collins

To Jim and Sarah with love.
And to Ian and Frances with gratitude.

- Judy Green

Contents in Brief

Contents

Chapter One

Introduction to Psychology 2

Chapter Two

The Biology Underlying Behaviour 42

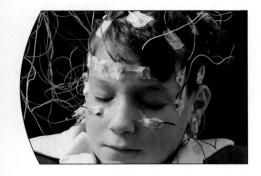

Chapter Three

Sensation and Perception   78

Chapter Four

States of Consciousness 120

Chapter Five

Learning   154

Chapter Six

Memory   186

Chapter Seven

Thinking, Language, and Intelligence 216

Chapter Eight

Motivation and Emotion   256

Chapter Nine

Development
288

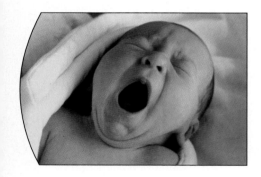

Chapter Ten

Personality
336

Chapter Eleven

Health Psychology: Stress, Coping, and Well-Being
368

Chapter Twelve

Psychological Disorders   394

Chapter Thirteen

Treatment of Psychological Disorders   428

Chapter Fourteen

Social Psychology
456

Preface

Estella Ramirez gained a better understanding of her mother's lifelong battle with major depression after learning about its possible causes in her introductory psychology course. She also developed a new appreciation for the struggles her mother faced in coping with this disorder.

As a new father, Phil Westport realized that he didn't know very much about infants, including his own daughter. He decided to take introductory psychology in part to learn more about child development. Applying what he learned in the course, Phil gained new insights into his daughter's behaviour and more confidence in his ability to be a good parent.

Joanne Chu is planning to become a special education teacher. Her aspirations have been fuelled by studying how people learn and how psychologists explain variations in intelligence in her introductory psychology course.

Tricia has always been curious about why people behave the way they do. While taking the introductory psychology course at college, Tricia found answers to many of her questions about people's behaviours. And she was intrigued with the strategies psychologists use to understand people and events. Tricia plans to further her education in psychology at university and to pursue a career in this field.

Psychology speaks with many voices to the diversity of students that we teach, offering a personal message to each one. To some, the discipline is a vehicle that can provide a better understanding of others' behaviour; for others it is a pathway to self-understanding. To some, psychology offers the potential of a future career; others are drawn to psychology because it gives them an opportunity for intellectual discovery.

Essentials of Understanding Psychology, Second Canadian Edition, is designed to present the discipline of psychology in a way that engages and excites students no matter what led them to take the introductory course or what level of motivation they initially bring to the course. It is designed to draw them into its way of looking at the world and to inform their understanding of psychological issues. The book provides a broad introduction to the essentials of the field of psychology, covering basic theories and research findings, as well as highlighting current applications outside the laboratory.

In revising *Essentials of Understanding Psychology,* we had six major goals:

1. To provide broad coverage of the field of psychology, introducing the theories, research, and applications that constitute the discipline.
2. To incorporate recent Canadian statistics and Canadian research, informing students of the exciting work being done by Canadian researchers.
3. To impel readers to think critically about psychological phenomena, particularly those that have an impact on their everyday lives.
4. To illustrate the substantial diversity both within the field of psychology and in society as a whole by presenting material that reflects the discipline's increasing concern with cultural, gender, racial, and ethnic issues.
5. To arouse intellectual curiosity and build an appreciation of how psychology can increase students' understanding of the world around them.
6. To engage readers in active learning with activities and thought-provoking questions.

In short, *Essentials of Understanding Psychology* is meant not only to expose readers to the content—and promise—of psychology, but also to do so in a way that will bring to life basic concepts and research findings, and sustain interest in the discipline long after they have completed their first encounter in the field.

Features of the Second Canadian Edition

Chapter Organization. Like the first Canadian edition of *Essentials of Understanding Psychology*, the second Canadian edition focuses on the essence of psychology, providing a broad introduction to the field. The book also shows how the field's theories and research have an impact on readers' everyday lives by emphasizing the applications of psychology.

There are, however, two major changes in chapter organization. First, an entire chapter has been devoted to health psychology in order to provide enhanced treatment of the topics of stress, coping, and well-being. College students are in a transitional stage in their lives, one marked by increasing responsibilities and demands. Many of them are also consciously accepting responsibility for their own health and well-being. The health psychology chapter provides readers with insight into effectively managing stress, the psychological aspects of illness and well-being, and the nature of the patient–physician relationship. The second major change involves repositioning the material on intelligence so that it is an integral part of the treatment of language, thinking, and problem solving. The most relevant concepts in intelligence have been retained, and placed within a chapter that provides an appropriate context for their discussion.

The flexibility of the book's organizational structure is considerable. Each chapter is divided into three or four manageable, self-contained units, allowing instructors to choose or omit sections in accordance with their syllabus or course outline. In addition, instructors may wish to teach the chapters in an order other than that indicated by the table of contents, and they may also choose to omit some chapters in order to give more attention to others.

Canadian Content. Canadian content is integrated seamlessly within the text and added to or featured in the chapter Prologues and the text's special boxes—Applying Psychology in the 21st Century, Becoming an Informed Consumer of Psychology, Exploring Diversity, Pathways Through Psychology, and Psychology at Work. Canadian statistics from the first edition have been revised and updated, if new information was available, to make the text relevant and current for Canadian students. Research by Canadian scholars is integrated throughout the text. The Canadian research in the text demonstrates the major contributions of Canadian scholars to the discussion of key issues in psychology today. More than 300 citations to Canadian research have been added, informing students of the exciting work being done by Canadian researchers. Canadians or events that occurred in Canada or have special relevance for Canadians are featured in 12 of the Prologues. Diversity and multiculturalism, significant themes in contemporary Canadian society, are featured in the Exploring Diversity boxes, and shape the discussion of relevant topics in the text. Five of the Exploring Diversity boxes have been written expressly for Canadian readers. These boxes focused on Aboriginal learning, linguistic variety, culture and the self, clinical practice and training, and ethnicity in Canada. All of the Pathways Through Psychology boxes and some of the Psychology at Work boxes profile Canadians. The Becoming an Informed Consumer of Psychology boxes are adapted to address the Canadian context. For example, information about the location of sleep centres in Canadian cities and about how to contact the Chronic Pain Association of Canada is provided in the boxes on improving sleep and managing pain. The extensive Canadian content is incorporated at all levels in the textbook.

Major Content Changes. This edition incorporates a significant amount of new and updated information, reflecting the advances in the field and the suggestions of reviewers. *Overall, more than a thousand new citations have been added, with most of those from articles and books published within the last three years.*

For instance, advances in such areas as evolutionary perspectives, brain and behaviour, mapping the human genome, cognition, emotions, and cultural approaches to psychological phenomena receive expanded or new coverage. In addition to the extensive updating, a broad range of new topics has been incorporated. The following sample of new and revised topics featured in this edition provides a good indication of the currency of the revision:

- Evolutionary perspectives (Chapter 1)
- The Human Genome Project and behavioural genetics (Chapter 2)
- Cochlear implants (Chapter 3)
- Visual processing and action (Chapter 3)
- PET scan data and psychoanalytic explanations of dreaming (Chapter 4)
- Stages of sleep (Chapter 4)
- Date rape drugs (Chapter 4)
- Effects of violent video games (Chapter 5)
- Spreading activation and associative models of memory (Chapter 6)
- Biological foundations of memory (Chapter 6)
- Being too smart for a job (Chapter 7)
- Beginning and fluent reading (Chapter 7)
- Emotional intelligence (Chapter 7)
- Intrinsic motivation (Chapter 8)
- Contemporary approaches to emotion (Chapter 8)
- Teratogens (Chapter 9)
- Hormone replacement therapy (Chapter 9)
- Self-perception and self-efficacy (Chapter 10)
- Cross-cultural assessment of personality (Chapter 10)
- Well-being and happiness (Chapter 11)
- Smoking (Chapter 11)
- Depression and ADHD (Chapter 12)
- St. John's wort (Chapter 13)
- Clinical training and practice in a multicultural society (Chapter 13)
- Industrial/organizational psychology (Chapter 14)
- Psychographics (Chapter 14)

Despite the extensive changes in this edition of *Essentials of Understanding Psychology*, one constant remains: the basic student-friendliness of the text. *Essentials of Understanding Psychology*, Second Canadian Edition, remains a textbook devoted to student success. In aiding students' efforts to master the body of material that the field of psychology encompasses, the book is designed to nurture students' excitement about psychology and keep that excitement alive throughout their lives.

The P.O.W.E.R. Learning System. The option of using a systematic study strategy, *P.O.W.E.R. Learning*, is built into the book. This systematic approach to learning and studying is based on five key steps (*P*repare, *O*rganize, *W*ork, *E*valuate, *R*ethink). Based on empirical research, *P.O.W.E.R Learning* systematizes the acquisition of new material by providing a learning framework. The system stresses the importance of learning objectives, self-evaluation, and critical thinking. The elements of *P.O.W.E.R Learning* can also be used with other learning systems such as *SQ3R*. (A more detailed description of the *P.O.W.E.R Learning* system follows in the Student Guide section of the Preface.)

Active Learning. Great care has been taken to select relevant and high-interest examples that motivate students to read as well as to explain key concepts. New to this edition, Chapter Activity boxes in every chapter invite students to interact with the material in the text. Also new to this edition, every chapter includes several exercises that require students to use the World Wide Web to identify and research information related to psychology.

Our prepublication research revealed that an increasing number of instructors find that the presentation of information in multiple modalities facilitates student mastery of the material. Consequently, this edition includes several features that speak to students' diverse learning styles. For example, there are more, and improved, figures. Each figure has been drawn to maximize clarity and pedagogical value, and many include annotations that draw attention to major points in the illustrations. Furthermore, there are additional photos, with captions that directly support learning. Photos have been carefully chosen to support the learning of key concepts, as well as for their visual impact. Captions have been improved and expanded, and many now include questions designed to promote critical thinking.

Learning Features. *The Second Canadian Edition* contains many features designed to help students learn, study, and master the text's content, including focus boxes on *Psychology at Work, Pathways Through Psychology*, and *Applying Psychology in the 21st Century*; special sections in each chapter on *Exploring Diversity* and *Becoming an Informed Consumer of Psychology; Looking Ahead* and *Looking Back* elements focusing on the key concepts in the chapters; and *PsychLinks, Prologues,* and *Epilogues* in each chapter. All of these features are fully described in the Student Guide section of the Preface, beginning on page xxv.

Integrated Resources

A complete, integrated multimedia package supports the second Canadian edition of *Essentials of Understanding Psychology.*

INTEGRATED MEDIA EDITION SUPPLEMENTS

*i*Learning Service Program

McGraw-Hill Ryerson offers a unique *i*Services package designed for Canadian faculty. Our mission is to equip providers of higher education with superior tools and resources required for excellence in teaching. For additional information, visit http://www.mcgrawhill.ca/highereducation/eservices/

The *i*ntegrator

Keyed to the chapters and topics of *Essentials of Understanding Psychology*, Second Canadian Edition, the *i*ntegrator ties together all of the elements in your resource package components—be it the Instructor's Manual, Test Bank, PowerPoint Slides, Online Learning Centre, Study Guide, or additional media supplements.

Learning Objects

To assist students and instructors alike, McGraw-Hill Ryerson has developed a library of learning objects, designed to provide an interactive, audio-visual learning environment for topics that prove challenging to students. Icons placed at the top of selected pages indicate that content on those pages is explored through Learning Objects. Visit the Online Learning Centre at http://www.mcgrawhill.ca/college/feldman for access to the Learning Objects, or through the *i*ntegrator to select Learning Objects by topic.

McGraw-Hill Media Resources for Teaching Psychology CD-ROM/DVD

Providing wide-ranging media resources across the field of psychology, from *Anagrams* (Thinking and Language), to *The Stroop Effect* (Sensation and Perception), to *Beautiful Minds: An Interview with John Nash and Son* (Psychological Disorders), this two-disc set provides over 60 topics, including 48 video segments from the Discovery Channel, as well as animations and activities.

Study to Go: A Mobile Learning Application for Palm and PocketPC

Do you use a handheld Personal Digital Assistant (PDA)? McGraw-Hill Ryserson's *Study to Go* application gives you the opportunity to study at any time, anywhere. And it's free for students using *Essentials of Understanding Psychology*! To download quizzes, key terms, and flashcards, visit the Online Learning Centre at http://www.mcgrawhill.ca/college/feldman.

FOR THE INSTRUCTOR

i-Learning Sales Specialist

Your *Integrated Learning Sales Specialist* is a McGraw-Hill Ryerson representative who has the experience, product knowledge, training, and support to help you assess and integrate any of the below-noted products, technology, and services into your course for optimum teaching and learning performance. Whether it's how to use our test bank software, helping your students improve their grades, or how to put your entire course online, your *i*-Learning Sales Specialist is there to help. Contact your local *i*-Learning Sales Specialist today to learn how to maximize all McGraw-Hill Ryerson resources!

Instructor's Manual

This thoroughly revised manual provides instructors of introductory psychology with all the tools and resources they need to present and enhance their course. The Instructor's Manual includes detailed chapter outlines; learning objectives; ideas for lectures, activities, and student projects; ready-to-use handouts; overhead masters; and multimedia references. Fully integrated with the *P.O.W.E.R. Learning* system, this manual has tips and activities that have a usefulness beyond any particular teaching approach.

Test Bank
The Test Bank has been thoroughly upgraded to reflect the new content in *Essentials of Understanding Psychology*, Second Canadian Edition. The Test Bank contains more than 2000 testing items, classified by cognitive type and level of difficulty, and keyed to the appropriate learning objective and section in the textbook. Items that test knowledge of material in the textbook's boxes are indicated for easy reference.

Computerized Test Bank
Available in a cross-platform format, in easy-to-use Brownstone Software, this CD-ROM makes all the items from the Test Bank easily available to instructors who wish to create their own tests. The test-generating program facilitates the selection of questions from the Test Bank and the printing of tests and answer keys, and also allows instructors to import questions from other sources.

Online Learning Centre
The Online Learning Centre for Instructors houses downloadable versions of the Instructor's Manual and PowerPoint slides, a variety of other text-specific instructor resources, including a bank of 145 images and access to our acclaimed customized Web site creation tool, PageOut! Visit us at http://www.mcgrawhill.ca/college/feldman.

Instructor's Resource CD-ROM
The CD-ROM contains every key instructor's resource in one flexible format. The Instructor's Manual, the Test Bank, PowerPoint presentations, and 145-item Image Bank are included.

In-Class Activities Manual for Instructors of Introductory Psychology
Geared to instructors of large introductory psychology courses, this activities manual covers every major topic in introductory psychology. Each activity includes a short description of the demonstration, the approximate time needed to complete the activity, the materials needed, step-by-step procedures, practical tips, and suggested readings related to the activity. The manual also includes advice and syllabi, what to consider when structuring your large section, how to select and manage a teaching assistant, and other key topics.

PowerWeb: Psychology
With *PowerWeb*, you'll have online access to current, carefully selected articles from the public press. The abridged version contains 20 online readings that are supported with well-researched links of interest and built-in assessment in the form of online quizzes and article reviews. An online search engine to connect with additional articles and an online *Instructor's Resource Guide* are also included. Contact your *i*-Learning Sales Specialist for details.

PowerWeb: Psychology 01/02, 31/e
This reader of public press articles explores the science of psychology; biological bases of behaviour; perceptual processes; learning and remembering; cognitive processes; emotion and motivation; development; personality processes; social processes; psychological disorders; and psychological treatments.

Taking Sides: Clashing Views on Controversial Psychological Issues, 11/e
This debate reader is designed to introduce students to controversies in psychology. The readings, which represent the arguments of leading psychologists and commentators, reflect a variety of viewpoints and have been selected for their liveliness and substance and because of their value in a debate framework. By requiring students to analyze opposing viewpoints and reach considered judgments, *Taking Sides* actively develops critical thinking skills.

Sources: Notable Sections in Psychology, 3/e
This volume contains approximately 40 selections of enduring intellectual value—classic articles, book excerpts, and research studies—that have shaped the study of psychology and our contemporary understanding of it.

FOR THE STUDENT

Study Guide

The *Study Guide* integrates the *P.O.W.E.R. Learning* system into a comprehensive review of the text material. Multiple-choice practice tests and essay questions allow students to gauge their understanding of the material. An answer key provides answers to all of the chapter's exercises, including feedback for all multiple-choice items. A list of activities and projects that encourage students to apply psychology to their daily lives is also included.

Online Learning Centre

The Student Online Learning Centre houses an array of chapter-by-chapter study tools, including detailed chapter outlines, concepts and learning objectives, key words, self-quizzes, essay questions, activities and projects, explanations of idiomatic expressions for ESL students, answers to *Epilogue* questions in the textbook, crossword puzzles, interesting Web links, and interactive exercises. Visit us at http://www.mcgrawhill.ca/college/feldman.

Making the Grade CD-ROM

This CD-ROM is designed to help students perform at their best. It contains practice quizzes for each text chapter, a learning styles assessment, study skills primer, guide to electronic research, and link to the text Web site.

New! In-Psych Student CD-ROM

In-Psych sets a new standard for introductory psychology multimedia. The CD-ROM is organized according to the textbook chapter outlines and features over 60 interactive exercises chosen to illustrate especially difficult core introductory psychology concepts. Each exercise showcases one of three types of media assets—an audio clip, a video clip, or a simulation—and includes a pretest, follow-up assignments, and Web resources. In-Psych also includes chapter quizzes, a student research guide, and an interactive timeline that puts events, key figures, and research in psychology in historical perspective.

WebQuester: Psychology

WebQuester is a series of online interactive exercises covering approximately 20 core topics in psychology. Each Web site includes 1 to 3 multiple-choice questions, short-answer questions, and essay questions. A 150-page *Guidebook to the Web* provides practical information and tips; topic areas include Searching the Web, Evaluating Information, Thinking Critically in the World of Information, and Computer Ethics.

Acknowledgments

One of the most important features of *Essentials of Understanding Psychology* is the involvement of both professionals and students in the review process. The Second Canadian Edition of *Essentials of Understanding Psychology* has relied heavily on—and profited substantially from—the advice of instructors and students from a wide range of backgrounds.

First, the manuscript was evaluated at several stages by Canadian academic reviewers, who served in their capacity as context experts and teachers of psychology, and helped ensure that the coverage and presentation was accurate, incorporated state-of-the-art research findings, and remained focused on the diverse needs of introductory psychology courses. They include the following:

Evelyn Kita
Niagara College

Joe Mior
Sir Sandford Fleming College

Jan Thompson
Sheridan College

Tom Hanrahan
Canadore College

Sharon Lowe
Sheridan College

Nicki Monahan
George Brown College

Malcolm Miller
Fanshawe College

Joe Ellis
Sir Sandford Fleming College

Jack Hirschberg
Vanier College

Marie Adams
Centennial College

Diane Malette
Loyalist College

Valerie Ringland
Algonquin College

David Langlotz
DeVry Institute of Technology

Jean Brown
Cambrian College

David English
Durham College

Angela Pind
Sir Sanford Fleming College

Des Quinn
Northern College

Yim Warrington
Algonquin College

We also wish to thank the reviewers of the manuscript and ancillaries of the US fifth edition of *Essentials of Understanding Psychology*, whose input was invaluable in giving shape to the development of the Canadian edition:

Marilyn Andrews
Hartnell College, California

Richard Baiardo
Evergreen Valley College, California

Louis Banderet
Northeastern University, Massachusetts

Carol Batt
Sacred Heart University, Connecticut

Manolya Bayar
Harford Community College, Maryland

Steven L. Berman
Florida International University, Florida

Kathleen Bey
Palm Beach Community College, Central Campus, Florida

David Bjorklund
Florida Atlantic University, Florida

Don Borden
Corning Community College, New York

Theresa Botts
Eastern Kentucky University

Deb Brihl
Valdosta State University, Georgia

Dominic Brucato
Miami-Dade Community College–North Campus, Florida

Richard Cavasina
California University of Pennsylvania

Linda Chaparro
Oxnard College, California

Carolyn Cohen
Massachusetts Bay Community College

Bob Conkright
Austin Community College, Cypress Campus, Texas

Natividad DeAnda
Los Medanos College, Pittsburg, California

Giselle Diaz
Palm Beach Community College, Florida

Karen Douglas
San Antonio College, Texas

Todd Farrar
Virginia College, Alabama

Aaron Fielder
Virginia College, Alabama

Stanley Fitch
El Camino College, California

Linda Flickinger
St. Clair County Community College, Michigan

Classie Foat
Skyline College, California

Tracy Forte
Potomac College, District of Columbia

Christopher Frost
Southwest Texas State University

Rod Gillis
University of Miami, Florida

Anthony Gordon
Contra Costa College, California

Joseph Hanak
Corning Community College, New York

Dave Harrison
Virginia Polytechnic Institute and State University, Virginia

Sarah Harrison
Evergreen Valley College, California

Milton Hatcher
Arkansas State University

Toni Haynes
Palm Beach Community College, South Campus, Florida

Alylene Hegar
Eastfield College, Texas

Lisa M. Henry
Loyola Marymount University, California

Kerry Hinkel
Valdosta State University, Georgia

Judith M. Horowitz
Medaille College, New York

Wayne Hren
Los Angeles Pierce College, California

Loreen Huffman
Missouri Southern State College

Robert Hutchinson
Modesto Junior College, California

Robert Hynes
Limestone College, South Carolina

Robert Jensen
California State University–Sacramento

Shirin Khosropour
Austin Community College, Pinnacle Campus, Texas

Norman E. Kinney
Southeast Missouri State University

W. Richard Krall
Gateway Community College, Arizona

Len Larsen
Eastfield College, Texas

Barbara Lusk
Collin County Community College, Texas

Joe Manganello
Gloucester County College, New Jersey

Michael R. Markham
Florida International University, Florida

Leslie Martin
La Sierra University, California

John Mastenbrook
Del Mar College, Texas

Dorothy L. Mercer
Eastern Kentucky University

Michael T. Miles
Palm Beach Community College, Central Campus, Florida

Richard Miller
Navarro College, Texas

Mindy Miserendino
Sacred Heart University, Connecticut

Gwen Murdock
Missouri Southern State College

Glen Musgrove
Broward Community College, Central Campus, Florida

Jerry Newell
Citrus Community College, California

Glenda Nichols
Tarrant County Junior College, South Campus, Texas

Sonya Nieves
Broward Community College, South Campus, Florida

Geri Olson
Sonoma State University, California

Carol Ponday
Los Angeles Pierce College, California

Ben Price
San Jose City College, California

Dan Quinn
Northeastern University, Massachusetts

Barbara Radigan
Community College of Allegheny County, Pennsylvania

Christopher K. Randall
Troy State University–Montgomery, Alabama

Kimberly Rector
Academy of Business College, Arizona

George Riday
Citrus College, California

MaryLou Robbins
San Jacinto College South Campus, Texas

Harry Saterfield
Foothill College, California

Karen Pitts Saenz
Houston Community College–Southeast, Texas

Nicole Schnopp-Wyatt
Pikeville College, Kentucky

Norman Schorr
Montgomery College–Rockville, Maryland

Bishop Scott
College of Alameda, California

Sharon Scott
South Plains College, Texas

Ann Shaver
Fairmont State College, West Virginia

Elizabeth Shaw
Texarkana College, Texas

Charlotte Simon
Montgomery College–Rockville, Maryland

Debjani Sinha
University of Cincinnati, Ohio

Nathan Slaughter
Merritt College, California

Jean Spaulding
Northwest College HCC, Texas

Mary Helen Spear
Prince George's Community College, Maryland

Brian Spillane
Antelope Valley College, California

Patricia Stephenson
Miami-Dade Community College–Kendall Campus, Florida

Janet Stubbs
Salem State College, Massachusetts

Robert Templeton
Palm Beach Community College, Central Campus, Florida

Donald Thompson
Troy State University–Montgomery, Alabama

Joe Tinnin
Richland College, Texas

Richard Townsend
Miami-Dade Community College, South Campus, Florida

Barbara Turner
Pasadena City College, California

Robin Vallacher
Florida Atlantic University, Florida

William Vasquez
Palo Alto College, California

Charles Verschoor
Miami-Dade Community College, Florida

Jean Volckmann
Pasadena City College, California

Gwen Walker
Los Angeles Mission College, California

Sandra Wilcox
California State University–Dominguez Hills, California

Matthew P. Winslow
Eastern Kentucky University

Stephen Wurst
State University of New York at Oswego

Andrea Zabel
Midland College, Texas

Another group of reviewers consisted of a panel of students who had used *Understanding Psychology* in their introductory psychology class. Over the course of a subsequent semester, they reviewed the entire book, literally line-by-line. Their insights, suggestions, and sometimes all-too-enthusiastic criticism were invaluable. The student review panel consisted of Cherilyn Johnson, Louis Meunier, Stacey Whitbourne, and Phil Zeyte.

Finally, dozens of students read parts of the manuscript to ensure that the material was clear and engaging. Their suggestions are incorporated throughout the text. We are grateful to all of these reviewers who provided their time and expertise to help ensure that *Essentials of Understanding Psychology* reflects the best that psychology has to offer.

* * *

Many people contributed to the development of the Second Canadian Edition of *Essentials of Understanding Psychology*. Robert Feldman again provided us with an excellent textbook to adapt for Canadian students. The McGraw-Hill Ryerson editorial and design teams have both been creative and supportive from start to finish. Our reviewers, colleagues, students, and the wonderful people who have provided a glimpse of psychology at work and in the academic world have all made valuable contributions.

We would like to thank everyone who sent us copies of their publications. We thank them, too, for their willingness to clarify information for us and for their good wishes. We thank Robert Feldman, Kimberly Cote, Meredyth Daneman, Eleanor Tegler-Gibson, and Jo-Anne Trigg for answering our questions.

We are grateful to the professors who served as reviewers for this edition. We appreciate their suggestions and the thoroughness with which they carried out the review process. We have made every effort to respond to their suggestions and believe that the book is better for this collaboration.

We would like to thank our students who used the first Canadian edition for their input. In particular, we thank them for giving us their impressions of the textbook boxes and for informing us about how they used these boxes to enhance learning, to maintain interest, and to gain useful insights into everyday concerns.

We thank the editorial team at McGraw-Hill Ryerson for their support and commitment to the development of this textbook. In particular, we would like to thank James Buchanan, Veronica Visentin, and Kelly Cochrane, Sponsoring Editors, for their support at various stages of this project. We are especially grateful to Darren Hick, our Developmental Editor, for his enthusiasm and guidance. He kept us in focus and on schedule. We also thank him for his participation in the writing process by contributing the profiles for Alexandra Kitty, Kavita Prakash, and Kevin Sweryd for the Psychology at Work boxes. Our Copy Editor, Dawn du Quesnay, was tireless in her pursuit of clarity, and we appreciate her enthusiastic support of the book.

We are also grateful to the McGraw-Hill Ryerson team responsible for design, production, marketing, and sales. The creative contributions made by Anne Nellis and Margaret Henderson, Supervising Editors, Stephanie Hess, Editorial Coordinator, Sharon Loeb, Marketing Manager, and Jeff Snook, Sales Manager, have been invaluable. We would also like to acknowledge the contribution of Lesley Mann as Senior Developmental Editor for the first edition; she got us off to a great start and saw us through a seamless transition to a new team.

Finally, we thank our families for their support and encouragement.

Joan E. Collins
Judy M. Green

Using *Essentials of Understanding Psychology:* A Guide for Students

The Second Canadian Edition of *Essentials of Understanding Psychology* has been designed to give students a better understanding of why people behave the way they do. It has been developed to provide insight into how and why psychologists conduct research, as well as the theories that guide their research. Finally, it has been created to acquaint students with the breadth of the field—to provide them with practical, useful information that they can employ both inside and outside of the classroom.

Use the Built-in Learning Aids

Each chapter in the text contains a wide selection of learning aids that will help you master the material. In addition, the book incorporates the *P.O.W.E.R. Learning* system. As we'll discuss in further detail later, the *P.O.W.E.R. Learning* system is based on a series of five steps: *P*repare, *O*rganize, *W*ork, *E*valuate, and *R*ethink. Each major section of a chapter starts with a *P*repare and *O*rganize segment, and—after you do the *W*ork of reading the section—ends with an *E*valuate and *R*ethink segment. Making use of the *P.O.W.E.R. Learning* system and the other built-in features will help you study more easily and effectively.

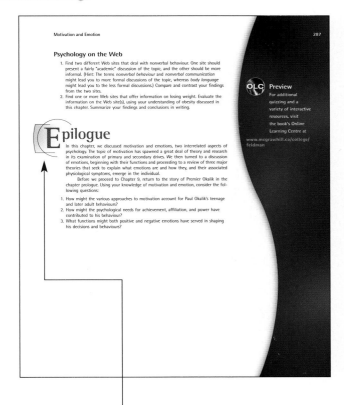

- **Prologue and Epilogue**
  Each chapter begins with a *Prologue* and ends with an *Epilogue*. The *Prologue* sets the stage for the chapter, providing a brief account of a real-life event that is relevant to the chapter content, and demonstrating why the material in the chapter is important. The *Epilogue* refers back to the *Prologue*, seeking to place it in the context of the chapter subject matter and asking questions designed to encourage you to think critically about what you've read.

- **Looking Ahead**
  The *Looking Ahead* section, which follows the *Prologue*, identifies the key themes and issues addressed in the chapter. It alerts you to what you'll have learned after reading and studying the chapter.

- **PsychLinks**
  These marginal icons provide a brief description and Web address of a Web site relevant to the material being discussed in the text. For your convenience, each *PsychLink* has a corresponding link on the *Essentials of Understanding Psychology* Web site (http://www.mcgrawhill.ca/college/feldman) that takes you directly to the site.

- **P.O.W.E.R.: Prepare and Organize segments**
  The *Prepare* section consists of learning objectives to help focus your thinking about the chapter content. (The same questions are used to organize the chapter summary at the end of the chapter.) The *Organize* section provides an outline of the material to orient you to the topics that will be covered.

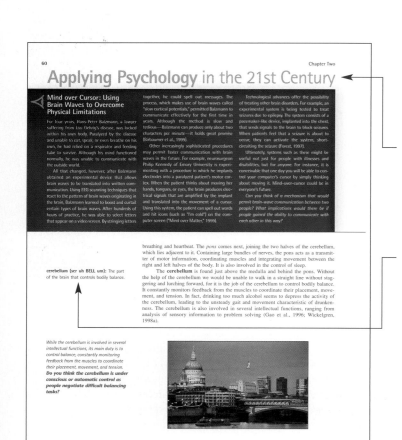

- **Applying Psychology in the 21st Century**
  These boxes describe psychological research that is being applied to everyday problems. Read them to understand how psychology promises to improve the human condition, in ways ranging from new approaches to treating psychological disorders to using brain waves to overcome physical disabilities.

- **Running Glossary**
  When a key term or concept appears in the text, it appears either in boldface or italics. Boldfaced words are of primary importance; italicized words are of secondary importance. Terms and concepts in bold are defined in the text where they are introduced and in the text margins, and in the end-of-book glossary. In addition, boldfaced terms are included in the page-referenced list of *Key Terms and Concepts* at the end of every chapter. You might want to highlight these terms with a marker.

Psychology at Work

Kevin Sweryd

Funeral Director, Manager

Education: B.A. psychology, University of Manitoba

Home: Winnipeg, Manitoba

Chapter Nine

In 1992, after finishing his B.A. in psychology at the University of Manitoba, Kevin Sweryd got a summer job at Bardal Funeral Home and Crematorium in Winnipeg. He got the job intending to save some money to pay for his master's degree. Over a decade later, however, Sweryd is still with Bardal—but now as a funeral director.

"This summer job was my first exposure to funeral service and I realized shortly after I started that there were many elements to the funeral director's position that were related to my studies in psychology."

Indeed, Sweryd's education has been fundamental in many aspects of his job: "My degree helped me to learn the skills I required to be able to listen to people, and observe behaviour in such a way that I am more able to effectively counsel them as to the options they have in arranging a personal and meaningful funeral service."

"There are occasions when people who are terminally ill come in to make their own arrangements prior to their deaths," says Sweryd. "In these cases, having an understanding of the stages of dying is invaluable. By understanding what stage or

Kevin Sweryd

> "In these cases, having an understanding of the stages of dying is invaluable."

stages they may be in while meeting with you, it can help as a funeral director to tailor the information you give them to meet their particular need in a way that they can understand it.

"Most often when I am meeting a family, however, the death has already occurred, and I do not see the classic Kübler-Ross stages, as people have progressed through them. However, there are stages of grieving that a family progresses through following a death. The grieving process mirrors the stages of death and dying in many ways, and having studied those stages, both in psychology classes and as a part of the training to become a funeral director, provides a much more in-depth understanding of the stages of grieving."

Although Sweryd never went on to get his master's degree, he feels his psychology degree is an invaluable asset. "The education experience you receive for a psychology degree provides you with many of the tools you need to be an effective funeral director. I would highly recommend this sort of educational background to anyone interested in funeral service, and would look on this type of education as a definite asset in considering someone for a position with our funeral home."

Memory Changes in Old Age: Are Older Adults Forgetful?

One of the characteristics most frequently attributed to late adulthood is forgetfulness. How accurate is this assumption?

Most evidence suggests that diminished memory is *not* an inevitable part of the aging process. For instance, research shows that in cultures where older adults are held in high esteem, such as in mainland China, older people are less likely to show memory losses than those living in cultures that expect older people's memory to decline. Similarly, when older people in Western societies are reminded of the advantages of age ("age brings wisdom"), they tend to do better on tests of memory (Levy & Langer, 1994; Levy, 1996).

Even when people do show memory declines during late adulthood, their deficits tend to be limited to particular types of memory. Losses tend to be limited to episodic memories, which relate to specific experiences about our lives. Other types of memories, such as semantic memories (memories of general knowledge and facts) and implicit memories (memories we are not consciously aware of) are largely unaffected by age (Graf, 1990; Russo & Parkin, 1993).

Declines in episodic memories can often be traced to changes in the lives of older adults. For instance, it is not surprising that a retired person who no longer faces the intellectual challenges encountered on the job might well be less practised in using memory or even be less motivated to remember things, leading to an apparent decline in memory. Even if their long-term memory declines, older adults can usually profit from compensatory efforts. When older adults learn to use the kinds of mnemonic strategies described in Chapter 6, they can not only prevent their long-term memory from deteriorating, but can actually improve it (Kotler-Cope & Camp, 1990; Verhaeghen, Marcoen, & Goossens, 1992; West, 1995).

328

- **Psychology at Work**
  These boxes present brief interviews with psychologists and other professionals who draw on psychological principles and findings in their work. These biographical sketches provide a glimpse of the broad range of professions that use psychology. They can help answer your questions on how to use your knowledge of psychology as you follow your own career path.

- **Pathways Through Psychology**
  Most of these boxes are about psychologists working at Canadian universities, but we have also included a profile of a psychological associate working for a school board, and a psychologist working in private practice. Each person has written his or her own profile, making it a truly personal and accessible portrait. These boxes can help you understand why people choose psychology as a career and what continues to motivate and fascinate them in their work.

Pathways Through Psychology

Wendy Josephson

Associate Professor of Psychology University of Winnipeg

Education: B.A., M.A., Ph.D. University of Manitoba

Home: Winnipeg, Manitoba

Chapter One

As an undergraduate student in psychology, I took my first course in social psychology from Bob Altemeyer, a wonderful classroom teacher and an inspiring researcher in the area of authoritarianism. I was captivated by social psychology from the very first lecture. Of all the disciplines and sub-disciplines I had encountered, I thought social psychology asked the best questions, and had very interesting answers. I still think that.

As a professor at a small undergraduate university, my work includes teaching courses in social and organizational psychology, research in the areas of violence and aggression, and service to the university and the community. Service to the university includes working on department or university committees and service to the community involves making my research useful to people outside the university world. For example, I have given talks to various educational, community, and industry groups including the Canadian Cable Television Association about the effects of television violence on children. I served as one of the academic advisers to Mediascope and the Children's Action Network. The project was to create a guide to help producers of children's educational television comply with U.S. federal requirements.

There are three accomplishments that I consider most important in my research: The first is a field experiment that I conducted on the effects of television violence on children's play behaviour, which was published in the *Journal of Personality and Social Psychology* in 1987. It demonstrated in a real-life setting that boys' aggressiveness toward each other could be significantly affected by having watched a violent television program, especially if there were other cues in their play setting that were associated with the TV violence.

Wendy Josephson

The second is the report that I wrote for the Department of Canadian Heritage in 1995. It reviewed the effects of television violence on children of different ages, and made suggestions for ways in which parents and the television industry could enhance the positive effects of television and reduce its negative effects.

The third is a study I'm doing now with my colleague Jocelyn Proulx, at the Prairie-based research network called RESOLVE (Research and Education for Solutions to Violence and Abuse). The Social Sciences and Humanities Research Council of Canada (SSHRC) has funded a project in which we provided activities from the Healthy Relationships dating-violence-prevention curriculum to grade seven, eight, and nine students in six Winnipeg schools over a three year period. We are currently evaluating the effects that the program had on students' knowledge, attitudes, and behaviour. This project is important because understanding how to prevent violence early in close relationships could have tremendous impact on individual and family happiness. It was also an opportunity to demonstrate that a lot could be accomplished in a collaboration among academic researchers, school divisions, government (Manitoba Culture, Heritage, and Citizenship) and community organizations (the Halifax group, Men for Change, which developed the Healthy Relationships program).

As a psychologist, I love to do research that answers interesting questions about human behaviour. But the work that is really important to me has to do more than just answer questions. I want the knowledge that is gained from my research to make a difference in people's lives.

Source: Wendy Josephson, Ph.D. University of Winnipeg wendy.josephson@uwinnipeg.ca

What is RESOLVE and why is the study that Dr. Josephson is doing here important?

(the participant, the victim, and four others), the average time was 166 seconds. Considering a simple yes/no measure of whether help was given confirms the elapsed-time pattern. Eighty-five percent of the participants in the 2-person-group condition helped, 62 percent in the 3-person-group condition, and only 31 percent in the 6-person-group condition helped.

Because these results are so straightforward, it seems clear that the original hypothesis was confirmed. However, Latané and Darley could not be sure that the results were truly meaningful until they determined whether the results represented a **significant outcome.** Through various statistical analyses, researchers can determine whether a numeric difference is meaningful or trivial. Only when differences between groups are large enough that statistical tests show them to be significant is it possible for researchers

significant outcome: Meaningful results that make it possible for researchers to feel confident that they have confirmed their hypotheses.

30

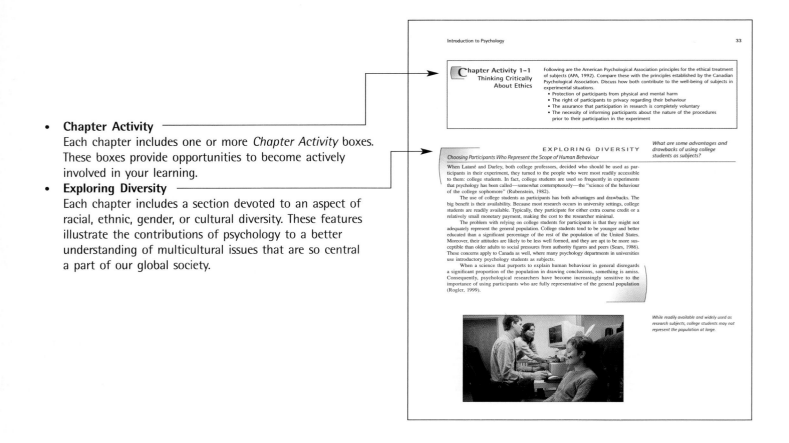

- **Chapter Activity**
  Each chapter includes one or more *Chapter Activity* boxes. These boxes provide opportunities to become actively involved in your learning.

- **Exploring Diversity**
  Each chapter includes a section devoted to an aspect of racial, ethnic, gender, or cultural diversity. These features illustrate the contributions of psychology to a better understanding of multicultural issues that are so central a part of our global society.

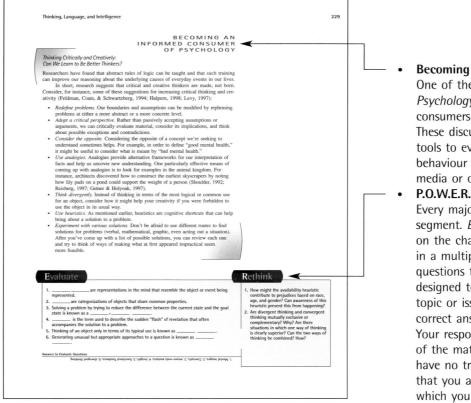

- **Becoming an Informed Consumer of Psychology**
  One of the major goals of *Essentials of Understanding Psychology* is to make readers more informed, critical consumers of information relating to psychological issues. These discussions, found in every chapter, give you the tools to evaluate information concerning human behaviour that you might hear or read about in the media or on the Web.

- **P.O.W.E.R.: Evaluate and Rethink segments**
  Every major section ends with an *Evaluate* and *Rethink* segment. *Evaluate* sections provide a series of questions on the chapter content that ask for concrete information, in a multiple-choice, fill-in, or true-false format. The questions that appear in the *Rethink* sections are designed to encourage you to think critically about a topic or issue, and they often have more than one correct answer. Answer *Evaluate* and *Rethink* questions! Your responses will indicate both your degree of mastery of the material and the depth of your knowledge. If you have no trouble with the questions, you can be confident that you are studying effectively. Use questions with which you have difficulty as a basis for further study.

States of Consciousness 151

What are the different states of consciousness?

- Consciousness is a person's awareness of the sensations, thoughts, and feelings at a given moment. It can vary from more active to more passive states. (p. 122)

What happens when we sleep, and what are the meaning and function of dreams?

- Using the electroencephalogram, or EEG, to study sleep, scientists have found that the brain is active throughout the night, and that sleep proceeds through a series of stages identified by unique patterns of brain waves. (p. 124)
- REM (rapid eye movement) sleep is characterized by an increase in heart rate, a rise in blood pressure, an increase in the rate of breathing and, in males, erections. Dreams occur during this stage. (p. 126)
- According to Freud, dreams have both a manifest content (their apparent story line) and a latent content (their true meaning). He suggested that the latent content provides a guide to a dreamer's unconscious, revealing unfulfilled wishes or desires. (p. 128)
- The dreams-for-survival theory suggests that information relevant to daily survival is reconsidered and reprocessed in dreams. Finally, the activation-synthesis theory proposes that dreams are a result of random electrical energy that stimulates

Looking **Back**

Key Terms and Concepts

consciousness (p. 122)	circadian rhythms (p. 132)
stage 1 sleep (p. 124)	daydreams (p. 133)
stage 2 sleep (p. 124)	hypnosis (p. 135)
stage 3 sleep (p. 125)	meditation (p. 137)
stage 4 sleep (p. 125)	psychoactive drugs (p. 140)
REM sleep (p. 126)	addictive drugs (p. 140)
unconscious wish fulfillment theory (p. 129)	stimulants (p. 141)
latent content of dreams (p. 129)	depressants (p. 144)
manifest content of dreams (p. 129)	narcotics (p. 147)
dreams-for-survival theory (p. 129)	hallucinogen (p. 148)
activation-synthesis theory (p. 130)	

Psychology on the Web

1. Find a resource on the Web that interprets dreams, and another that reports the results of scientific dream research. Compare the nature and content of the two sites in terms of the topics covered, reliability of information provided, and promises made about the use of the site and its information. Write a summary of what you found.
2. Find some sites on the Web that describe Canadian antidrug programs that are focused on school, family, and/or community settings. On the basis of the information at these sites and in the *Applying Psychology in the 21ˢᵗ Century* box in this chapter, explain how effective you think these programs would be.

States of Consciousness 153

Epilogue

In this chapter we discussed consciousness in its full range from active states to passive states. We focused especially on factors that affect consciousness, from natural factors like sleep, dreaming, and daydreaming, to more intentional ways of altering consciousness, including hypnosis, meditation, and drugs. We examined some of the reasons people seek to alter their consciousness, considered both uses and abuses of consciousness-altering strategies, and attempted to address some of the most dangerous ways people alter their consciousness.

Before we turn to the subject of learning in the next chapter, return briefly to the prologue in this chapter, about the death of five Quebec teenagers. Consider the following questions in light of your understanding of alcohol use and abuse.

1. Why would the police and others suspect that alcohol consumption may have contributed to the accident described in the prologue?
2. Why do people take risks such as combining drinking with driving?
3. What are some of the reasons why young people drink to excess?
4. How does alcohol affect the state of consciousness of users?

OLC Preview

For additional quizzing and a variety of interactive resources, visit the book's Online Learning Centre at www.mcgrawhill.ca/college/feldman

- **Looking Back**

  These end-of-chapter sections include four parts: a chapter summary, a list of *Key Terms and Concepts, Psychology on the Web,* and *OLC Preview.* The summary is organized around the *Prepare* questions from each major section. The *Key Terms and Concepts* list includes a page number where the term is first introduced in the chapter. To find its definition, you have two choices: turn to the margin of the page where the term is introduced, or consult the end-of-book glossary, which contains every *Key Term and Concept. Psychology on the Web* exercises take you online to help you learn more about topics covered in the chapter. The *OLC Preview* points you to the book Web site, where you can test your knowledge, do additional activities, and find interesting resources.

You'll find the same set of features in every chapter. Consequently, the book provides a set of familiar landmarks to help you chart your way through new material. This structure will help you organize each chapter's content, as well as learn and remember the material.

One final note: This text uses a reference citation style endorsed by the American Psychological Association (APA). According to APA style, citations include a name and date, typically set off in parentheses at the end of a sentence specifying the author of the work being cited and the year of publication—e.g., "(Anderson & Dill, 2000)." Each of these author-date citations refers to a book or article in the Reference List at the end of this book.

Using *P.O.W.E.R. Learning,* a Proven Strategy for Effective Study and Critical Thinking

Now that you are acquainted with the special features of *Essentials of Understanding Psychology* that are designed to help you understand and master this book's content, you should consider consistently applying the *P.O.W.E.R. Learning* system incorporated in the book. By using *P.O.W.E.R. Learning,* you can increase your ability to learn and retain information and to think critically, not only in your psychology course but in all academic subjects. As noted earlier, the *P.O.W.E.R. Learning* strategy includes five key steps: *P*repare, *O*rganize, *W*ork, *E*valuate, and *R*ethink. *P.O.W.E.R. Learning* systematizes the acquisition of new material by providing a learning framework. It stresses the importance of learning objectives and appropriate preparation prior to beginning to study, as well as the significance of self-evaluation and the incorporation of critical thinking into the learning process. Specifically, use of the *P.O.W.E.R. Learning* system entails the following steps:

- **Prepare.**   Before starting any journey, we need to know where we are headed. Academic journeys are no different; we need to know what our goals are. The *Prepare* stage consists of thinking about what we hope to attain from reading a particular section of the text by identifying specific goals that we seek to accomplish. In *Essentials of Understanding Psychology,* these goals are presented in the form of broad questions that start each major section.
- **Organize.**   Once we know what our goals are, we need to develop a route to accomplish those goals. The *Organize* stage involves developing a mental roadmap of where we are headed. *Essentials of Understanding Psychology* highlights the organization of each upcoming section. Read the outline to get an idea of what topics are covered and how they are organized.
- **Work.**   The heart of the *P.O.W.E.R. Learning* system entails actually reading and studying the material presented in the book. In some ways *Work* is the easy part, because if you have carried out the steps in the preparation and organization stage, you'll know where you're headed and how you'll get there. Of course it's not so simple—you'll need the motivation to conscientiously read and think about the material presented in the chapter. And remember, the main text isn't the only material that you need to read and think about. It's also important to read the boxes, the marginal glossary terms, and the special sections in order to gain a full understanding of the material, so be sure to include them as part of the *Work* of reading the chapter.
- **Evaluate.**   The fourth step, *Evaluate,* provides you with the opportunity to determine how effectively you have mastered the material. *Essentials of Understanding Psychology* has a series of questions at the end of each section that permit a rapid check of your understanding of the material. Evaluating your progress is essential to assessing your degree of mastery of the material.

- **Rethink.**   The final step in *P.O.W.E.R. Learning* involves critical thinking, which entails reanalyzing, reviewing, questioning, and challenging assumptions. It provides the opportunity to look at the big picture by thinking about how material fits with other information that you have already learned. Every major section of *Essentials of Understanding Psychology,* Second Canadian Edition, ends with a *Rethink* section that contains thought-provoking questions. Answering them will help you understand the material more fully and at a deeper level. If you want to maximize your potential to master the material in *Essentials of Understanding Psychology,* Second Canadian Edition, use *P.O.W.E.R. Learning!* Taking the time and effort to work through the steps of the system is a proven technique for understanding and learning the material.

Supplementing *P.O.W.E.R. Learning* with *SQ3R*

Although *P.O.W.E.R. Learning* is the learning strategy that is built into the book and consequently is the easiest to use, it is not the only system compatible with the book. For example, some readers may wish to supplement the *P.O.W.E.R. Learning* system with the *SQ3R* method, which includes a series of five steps, designated by the initials *S-Q-R-R-R.* The first step is to *survey* the material by reading the chapter outlines, chapter headings, figure captions, recaps, and *Looking Ahead* and *Looking Back* sections, providing yourself with an overview of the major points of the chapter. The next step—the *Q* in *SQ3R*—is to *question.* Formulate questions about the material—either aloud or in writing—prior to actually reading a section of the material. The queries posed in the *Prepare* sections and the *Evaluate* and *Rethink* questions that end each part of the chapter are also a good source of questions.

The next three steps in *SQ3R* ask you to *read, recite,* and *review* the material. *Read* carefully and, even more importantly, read actively and critically. While you are reading, answer the questions you have asked yourself. Critically evaluate material by considering the implications of what you are reading, thinking about possible exceptions and contradictions, and examining underlying assumptions. The *recite* step involves describing and explaining to yourself (or to a friend) the material you have just read and answering the questions you have posed earlier. Recite aloud; the recitation process helps to identify your degree of understanding of the material you have just read. Finally, *review* the material, looking it over, reading the *Looking Back* summaries, and answering the in-text review questions.

Some Final Comments

The *P.O.W.E.R. Learning* system (as well as *SQ3R*) provides a proven means of increasing your study effectiveness, yet you need not feel tied to a particular strategy. You might want to combine other elements into your own study system. For example, learning tips and strategies for critical thinking will be presented throughout *Essentials of Understanding Psychology,* such as in Chapter 6, where the use of mnemonics (memory techniques for organizing material to help its recall) is discussed. If these tactics help you to successfully master new material, stick with them.

By using the *P.O.W.E.R. Learning* system, you will maximize your understanding of the material in this book and will master techniques that will help you learn and think critically in all of your academic endeavours. More importantly, you will optimize your understanding of the field of psychology. It is worth the effort: the excitement, challenges, and promise that psychology holds for you are significant.

Essentials of
Understanding Psychology

Second Canadian Edition

Essentials of Understanding **Psychology**

Second Canadian Edition

Chapter One

Introduction to Psychology

Prologue

From Terrorism to Heroism

The attacks on the World Trade Towers and Pentagon raised a variety of psychological issues, ranging from efforts to explain the motivation of the attackers to the extraordinary bravery of the rescue workers.

September 11, 2001, began as a bright morning on the East Coast of the United States, filled with promise, but it soon turned into a day that would be remembered for the most deadly acts of terrorism the world had ever experienced.

Groups of terrorists hijacked four planes, levelled the World Trade Center towers, severely damaged the Pentagon, and caused the crash of another jetliner in Pennsylvania, killing just under 3000 people. Although the majority of the victims were Americans, citizens of 81 other countries lost their lives. This included 24 Canadians. For Americans and for people around the world it was a catastrophe of unprecedented scale. The scope of the carnage was so vast that people had difficulty comprehending it, let alone dealing with it.

In the midst of the tragedy, however, the best of humanity was also evident. Firefighters, paramedics, and other brave rescuers sifted through the rubble, putting themselves at risk as they sought to help. Thousands of people gave blood, seeking to aid those who were injured. And millions of citizens from the United States and around the world, who were far removed from the sites of the terrorist acts, made generous donations to help those whose lives had been shattered by the attacks.

Looking Ahead

The behaviours that were seen in the September 11 terrorist attacks and their aftermath—ranging from the deadly aggression of the terrorists to the selfless actions of those who came to the aid of the victims—raise many issues of a psychological nature. Consider, for example, how different kinds of psychologists would approach and examine the incident:

- Psychologists studying the biology underlying behaviour would consider changes in internal bodily activity as individuals dealt with the situation.
- Those psychologists who study learning and memory would examine what people remember of the incident afterward.
- Psychologists who study thinking processes would consider how people calculated what action to take during the crisis.
- Psychologists who focus on motivation would seek to explain the reasons behind the terrorists' actions.
- Developmental psychologists, who study growth and change throughout the life span, would ask how witnessing the incident would affect students' lives in the future.
- Health psychologists would examine the kinds of stress reactions and illnesses that might later occur as a result of the incident.
- Clinical and counselling psychologists would try to identify the most effective ways to help people cope with the loss of life.
- Social psychologists would attempt to explain the causes of aggression in society, as well as examine the humane and compassionate efforts of those who provided assistance during the incident.

Although the approaches taken by different types of psychologists in studying the impact of the attack are diverse, there is a common link: each represents a specialty area within the general field of study of **psychology**, the scientific study of behaviour and mental processes.

This definition seems straightforward, but its simplicity is deceptive. Most psychologists have answered these questions with the argument that the field should be receptive to a variety of viewpoints and approaches. Consequently, the phrase *behaviour and mental processes* in the definition of psychology must be understood to mean many things: It encompasses not just what people do, but also their thoughts, feelings, perceptions, reasoning processes, memories, and even the biological activities that maintain bodily functioning.

In order to "study" behaviour and mental processes, psychologists try to describe, explain, and predict human behaviour and mental processes. They also work to help change and improve the lives of people and the world in which they live. The use of scientific methods allows psychologists to find answers that are far more valid and legitimate than those resulting from mere intuition and speculation. And what a variety and range of questions psychologists seek to answer! Consider these examples: How long can we live without sleep? What is the best way to study? What is intelligence? What is normal sexual behaviour? Can people change their dysfunctional behaviour? Can aging be delayed? How does stress affect our lives? How can we reduce violence?

These questions provide just a hint of the various topics that we will encounter as we explore the field of psychology. Our discussions will take us through the range of what is known about behaviour and mental processes. At times, we will explore animal behaviour because it provides important clues about human behaviour. Many psychologists study non-human species in order to determine general laws of behaviour that pertain to *all* organisms. But we will always return to the everyday problems that confront human beings.

This book incorporates several features that illustrate how psychology can affect each of our lives. You will see how psychologists are applying what they have learned to resolve practical problems of daily life (*Applying Psychology in the 21st Century* boxes). You will meet people who have experienced firsthand how valuable a background in psychology can be in their professional lives (*Psychology at Work* boxes), and you will meet Canadian psychologists whose stories provide an inspiring example of the type of work that is being done in Canadian research (*Pathways Through Psychology* boxes). You will learn how psychology contributes to our understanding of the multicultural world in which we live (*Exploring Diversity* sections). And you will find material in each chapter that is intended to

psychology: The scientific study of behaviour and mental processes.

 **PsychLink**

Psychology organization home pages
www.mcgrawhill.ca/college/feldman

help you incorporate psychology into your everyday life (*Becoming an Informed Consumer of Psychology*).

This introductory chapter presents several topics central to an understanding of psychology. We begin our journey through the field of psychology by describing the different types of psychologists and the various roles they play. Next, we examine the major perspectives that guide the work psychologists do, and identify the major issues that underlie psychologists' views of the world and human behaviour. Finally, we examine how psychologists conduct research and the challenges they face.

Psychologists at Work

Prepare

What is the science of psychology?
What are the major specialties in the field of psychology?
Where do psychologists work?
How does psychology in Canada and the United States differ?

Organize

Psychologists at Work
    The Subfields of Psychology
    Working at Psychology
    Psychology in Canada and the United States

A month after losing his arm in an industrial accident, Henry Washington sits with his eyes closed as Hector Valdez, a research psychologist who studies the perception of touch, dribbles warm water on his cheek. Washington is startled as he reports feeling the water not only on his cheek, but running down his missing arm. The sensation is so strong that he checks to be sure that the arm is still missing.

***

Evelyn Poirier welcomes to her lab the Chow brothers, a pair of identical twins who were adopted by different families just after they were born. They have come to participate in her study examining similarities in the behavioural and personality traits of twins. By comparing twins who have lived together virtually all their lives to those who have been separated from birth, Poirier is seeking to determine the relative influence of heredity and experience on human behaviour.

***

Methodically—and painfully—recounting events that occurred in his youth, the college student discloses a childhood secret that he has revealed previously to no one. The listener, psychologist Jonnetta Pennybaker, responds with support, suggesting to him that his concern is in fact shared by many people.

***

A graduate-school student in China shows a group of university students a list of short proverbs, some of which contain two contradictory ideas ("too humble is half proud"), while others are more "linear" ("as the twig is bent, so grows the tree"). After learning which proverbs the Chinese students prefer, she then repeats the same study at a university in the United States. She finds that Chinese students prefer proverbs that contain two contradictory ideas, while U.S. students have the opposite preference (Peng & Nisbett, 1997).

***

Researchers provide four King pigeons with a choice of four pecking keys. All of these keys can potentially trigger the release of food. On any given trial, only one of these keys will actually trigger the release of food. Over a number of trials, the pigeons demonstrate that they know which key produces the food and concentrate their attention on that key. They also demonstrate memory that lasts up to 96 hours for which key had last produced food and return to that key first on the next trial (Wilson & Wilkie, 1993).

Each of these episodes describes work carried out by contemporary psychologists. Psychologists address extraordinarily different types of behaviour, ranging from the most basic biological processes to how people are affected by their culture.

Table 1-1 The Major Subfields of Psychology

Subfield	Description
Biopsychology	*Biopsychology* examines how biological structures and functions of the body affect behaviour.
Clinical psychology	*Clinical psychology* deals with the study, diagnosis, and treatment of psychological disorders.
Clinical neuropsychology	*Clinical neuropsychology* unites the areas of biopsychology and clinical psychology, focusing on the relationship between biological factors and psychological disorders.
Cognitive psychology	*Cognitive psychology* focuses on the study of higher mental processes.
Counselling psychology	*Counselling psychology* focuses primarily on educational, social, and career adjustment problems.
Cross-cultural psychology	*Cross-cultural psychology* investigates the similarities and differences in psychological functioning in and across various cultures and ethnic groups.
Developmental psychology	*Developmental psychology* examines how people grow and change from the moment of conception through death.
Educational psychology	*Educational psychology* is concerned with teaching and learning processes, such as the relationship between intelligence and school performance and the development of better teaching techniques.
Environmental psychology	*Environmental psychology* considers the relationship between people and their physical environment, including how our physical environment affects our emotions and the amount of stress we experience in a particular setting.
Evolutionary psychology	*Evolutionary psychology* considers how behaviour is influenced by our genetic inheritance from our ancestors.
Forensic psychology	*Forensic psychology* focuses on legal issues, such as deciding on criteria for determining whether a defendant was legally sane at the time a crime was committed.
Health psychology	*Health psychology* explores the relationship between psychological factors and physical ailments or disease.
Industrial/organizational psychology	*Industrial/organizational psychology* is concerned with the psychology of the workplace.
Personality psychology	*Personality psychology* focuses on the consistency in people's behaviour over time and the traits that differentiate one person from another.
Program evaluation	*Program evaluation* focuses on assessing large-scale programs, such as the Head Start preschool program, to determine whether they are effective in meeting their goals.
Psychology of women	*Psychology of women* focuses on issues such as discrimination against women, structural differences in women's and men's brains, and the causes of violence against women.
School psychology	*School psychology* is devoted to counselling children in elementary and secondary schools who have academic or emotional problems.
Social psychology	*Social psychology* is the study of how people's thoughts, feelings, and actions are affected by others.
Sport psychology	*Sport psychology* applies psychology to athletic activity and exercise.

The Subfields of Psychology: Psychology's Family Tree

The diversity of topical areas within psychology has resulted in the development of a number of subfields (described in Table 1-1). The subfields of psychology are like an extended family, with assorted nieces and nephews, aunts and uncles, and cousins who, although they might not interact on a day-to-day basis, are related to one another. The subfields of psychology are also related to one another because they share a common goal: understanding behaviour. Several basic questions about behaviour that are addressed by key subfields include the following:

PsychLink

Journey through biopsychology
www.mcgrawhill.ca/college/feldman

What Are the Biological Foundations of Behaviour?

In the most fundamental sense, people are biological organisms. *Biopsychology* is the subfield of psychology that specializes in the biological bases of behaviour. While they study a broad range of topics, biopsychologists focus on the operation of the brain and nervous system, considering how our body influences our behaviour. For example, they might examine the link between specific sites in the brain and the muscular tremors of people affected by Parkinson's disease (discussed in Chapter 2) or attempt to determine how our emotions are related to physical sensations (Chapter 8).

How Do People Sense, Perceive, Learn, and Think About the World?

If you have ever wondered how you learned to speak, how you solve problems, or how you remember material for your psychology test, a cognitive psychologist can answer your questions. *Cognitive psychology* focuses on higher mental processes, including thinking, memory, reasoning, problem solving, judging, decision making, and language (as we will discuss in Chapter 7).

What Are the Sources of Change and Stability in Behaviour Across the Life Span?

A baby producing her first smile . . . taking her first step . . . saying her first word. These universal milestones in development are also singularly special and unique for each person. *Developmental psychology* studies how people grow and change from the moment of conception through death (Chapter 9). *Personality psychology* focuses on the consistency in people's behaviour over time and the traits that differentiate one person from another (Chapter 10).

How Do Psychological Factors Affect Physical and Mental Health?

If you are frequently depressed, feel constant stress, or seek to overcome a fear that prevents you from carrying out your normal activities, your problems would interest a health psychologist. *Health psychology* explores the relationship between psychological factors and physical ailments or disease. For example, health psychologists are interested in how long-term stress (a psychological factor) can affect physical health and in identifying ways to promote behaviour that brings about good health (Chapter 11).

Clinical psychology deals with the study, diagnosis, and treatment of psychological disorders. Clinical psychologists are trained to diagnose and treat problems ranging from the everyday crises of life, such as unhappiness over the breakup of a relationship, to more extreme conditions, such as profound, lingering depression. Some clinical psychologists also research and investigate issues that range from identifying the early signs of psychological disturbance to studying the relationship between family communication patterns and psychological disorders (Chapters 12 and 13).

How Do Our Social Networks Affect Behaviour?

The complex networks of social interrelationships that are part of our world are the focus of study for a number of subfields of psychology. For example, *social psychology* is the study of how people's thoughts, feelings, and actions are affected by others. Social psychologists focus on such diverse topics as human aggression, liking and loving, persuasion, and conformity.

Cross-cultural psychology investigates the similarities and differences in psychological functioning in and across the various cultures and ethnic groups of the world. For example, cross-cultural psychologists examine how cultures differ in their

Cognitive psychologists study how people sense the world.
How do you think researchers adapt their techniques when working with children?

Health psychology
www.mcgrawhill.ca/college/feldman

Counselling psychologists who staff college centres advise students on career choices, methods of study, as well as strategies for coping with everyday adjustment problems.

use of punishment during child rearing, or why certain cultures view academic success as being determined mostly by hard work while others see it as being determined mostly by innate ability (J. G. Miller, 1999; Rosenzweig, 1999; Aycan, 2000).

How is Psychology Evolving?

As a science, psychology's boundaries are constantly growing. Two newer members of the field's family tree—clinical neuropsychology and evolutionary psychology—have sparked particular excitement, and debate, within psychology.

Clinical neuropsychology unites the areas of biopsychology and clinical psychology: It focuses on the relationship between biological factors and psychological disorders. Building on advances in our understanding of the structure and chemistry of the brain, the specialty is leading to promising new treatments for psychological disorders, as well as debates over the use of medication to control behaviour.

Evolutionary psychology considers how behaviour is influenced by our genetic inheritance from our ancestors. The evolutionary approach suggests that the chemical coding of information in our cells not only determines such traits as hair colour and race, but also holds the key to understanding a broad variety of behaviours that helped our ancestors survive and reproduce (Geary & Bjorklund, 2000).

Evolutionary concepts have been used to explain similarities in behaviour across cultures, such as the qualities desired in potential mates. However, such explanations have stirred up controversy by suggesting that many significant behaviours are wired into the human species as a result of evolution and occur automatically.

Working at Psychology

Help Wanted: Assistant professor at a college of arts, science, and technology. Teach undergraduate courses in introductory psychology and courses in specialty areas of cognitive psychology, perception, and learning. Strong commitment to quality teaching and student advising necessary. The candidate must also provide evidence of scholarship and research productivity.

Help Wanted: Industrial-organizational consulting psychologist. International firm is seeking psychologists for full-time career positions as consultants to management. Candidates must have the ability to establish a rapport with senior business executives and to help them find innovative, practical, and psychologically sound solutions to problems concerning people and organizations.

Help Wanted: Clinical psychologist. Ph.D., internship experience, and licence required. Comprehensive clinic seeks psychologist to work with children and adults providing individual and group therapy, psychological evaluations, crisis intervention, and development of behaviour treatment plans on multidisciplinary team. Broad experience with substance-abuse problems is desirable.

PsychLink
Industrial/organizational psychology
www.mcgrawhill.ca/college/feldman

As these advertisements suggest, psychologists are employed in a variety of settings. Most doctoral-level psychologists are employed by institutions of higher learning (universities and colleges) or are self-employed, usually working as private practitioners treating clients. Other work sites include hospitals, clinics, mental health centres, counselling centres, government human-services organizations, and schools (American Psychological Association [APA], 2000).

Why do so many psychologists work in academic settings? Because these are effective settings for the three major roles played by psychologists in society—teacher, scientist, and clinical practitioner. Many psychology professors are also actively involved in research or in serving clients. Whatever their particular job site, however, psychologists share a commitment to improving individual lives as well as society in general.

The Education of a Psychologist

How do people become psychologists? The most common route is a long one. Most psychologists in Canada and the United States have a doctorate (a *Ph.D.*). In the United States, psychologists may also earn a *Psy.D.* The Ph.D. is a research degree, requiring a dissertation based on an original investigation. The Psy.D. is obtained by psychologists who wish to focus on the treatment of psychological disorders. Both the Ph.D. and the Psy.D. typically take four or five years of work past the bachelor's level. Some fields of psychology involve education beyond the doctorate. For instance, doctoral-level clinical psychologists, who deal with people with psychological disorders, typically spend an additional year on an internship.

About a third of people working in the field of psychology have a master's degree as their highest degree, which is earned following two or three years of graduate work. Master's-level psychologists teach, conduct research under the supervision of a doctoral-level psychologist, or work in specialized programs dealing with drug abuse or crisis intervention. Some work in universities, government, and business, collecting and analyzing data.

An undergraduate major in psychology provides good preparation for a variety of occupations, although it does not allow professional work in psychology per se. For instance, many people in business, nursing, law, social work, and other professions report that an undergraduate background in psychology has proven invaluable in their careers. Some 20 percent of recipients of bachelor's degrees in psychology work in the social services or in some other form of public affairs. Furthermore, undergraduates who specialize in psychology typically have good analytical skills, are trained to think critically, and are able to synthesize and evaluate information well—skills that are held in high regard by employers in business, industry, and the government (APA, 2000).

Psychology in Canada and the United States

As a student of psychology in Canada, you might ask the question: is Canadian psychology the same as American psychology? The answer is yes it is and no it isn't.

In many ways Canadian and American psychology are the same. They share the same early history, starting with Wilhelm Wundt in 1879 (see "The Roots of Psychology" later in the chapter). They both have the same branches on the family tree; that is to say, they both have the same major areas of specialization and use the same perspectives (see "Today's Perspectives"). Canadian and American psychologists are interested in many of the same issues. They both practise psychology as science and both are held to a high standard of training and practice. They both have professional associations that support and regulate the work of psychology: The American Psychological Association (APA) in the United States (founded in 1892) and The Canadian Psychological Association (CPA) in Canada (founded in 1939) are the largest, but not the only ones.

In the beginning, there was little to distinguish Canadian from American psychology. Sometimes the same person is significant in the history of both academic communities. For example, an American, James Baldwin, teaching at the University of Toronto in the late 1800s and called "the first modern psychologist in Canada," was a founding member of the APA (Wright and Myers, 1982; Ferguson, 1993).

Although research and practice in both countries have much in common, there are some significant differences between them. For example, they differ in scale. The much larger population in the United States provides a larger research base. With many more universities, more research can be generated.

Another way in which Canadian and American psychology differ is in academic credentials. In Canada, most psychologists with a doctoral-level degree will have a Ph.D. In the U.S., psychologists might have a Ph.D. (for those whose focus is on research with original investigation) or a Psy.D. (for those who wish to focus on the treatment of psychological disorders). This is more than merely a difference in title. It underscores a very fundamental difference in the way that psychology is taught and practised. As both countries moved towards more applied psychology in the 1940s, they faced a division in their ranks between those psychologists who favoured academic (pure) psychology and those who were interested in applied research. In Canada, the emerging applied psychology remained rooted in the experimental, university, thesis-based model (Ph.D.) In the United States, there were more financial incentives to develop private teaching programs and the larger population could support such initiatives (Dobson, 1995; Goodman, 2000). This tradition in Canada of a strong experimental and empirical focus translated into a tendency for Canadian clinical psychologists, more than their American counterparts, to work from a behavioural or cognitive behavioural model (Hunsley & Lefebvre, 1990; Warner, 1991).

In both countries, because of their different historical, social, and cultural experiences, there are areas of special concern. In social psychology, as an example, both Canadian and American psychologists will study violence, but their experience of it may differ. Elaine Grandin and Eugen Lupri of the University of Calgary (1997) did a cross-national comparison of violence in Canada and the United States. They found significantly higher levels of "societal crime" in the United States and higher rates of intimate (couple) violence in Canada. In their study they identified a number of societal differences (e.g., more guns in the United States than Canada, and differences in what is socially acceptable to share about one's relationship) between the two countries. Their study presents a number of interesting findings and also points out some of the challenges of doing cross-cultural research.

Canada's universal health care system makes issues of health and well-being different from those in the United States. Canada's federal multicultural policy creates a potentially different experience around issues of ethnic diversity. Therefore, studies in these areas will produce a unique body of research. This knowledge is essential for those psychologists who are involved in program planning or evaluation.

In conclusion, it seems fair to say that, although the roots of Canadian and American psychology are the same and much research is easily transferable from one country to the other, psychology in these nations has evolved into two unique traditions based primarily on the difference in population size and historical and social experience in Canada and the United States.

Evaluate

1. Match each subfield of psychology with an issue or question posed below.

   a. Biopsychology

   b. Cognitive psychology

   c. Developmental psychology

   d. Personality psychology

   e. Health psychology

   f. Clinical psychology

   g. Counselling psychology

   1. Joan, a first-year college student, is panicking. She needs to learn better organizational skills and study habits to cope with the demands of college.

   2. At what age do children generally begin to acquire an emotional attachment to their fathers?

   3. It is thought that pornographic films that depict violence against women can prompt aggressive behaviour in some men.

   4. What chemicals are released in the human body as a result of a stressful event? What are their effects on behaviour?

   5. Luis is unique in his manner of responding to crisis situations, with an even temperament and a positive outlook.

   6. The teachers of 8-year-old Jack are concerned that he has recently begun to withdraw socially and show little interest in schoolwork.

   7. Janetta's job is demanding and stressful. She wonders if her lifestyle is making her more prone to certain illnesses, such as cancer and heart disease.

Rethink

1. Why might the study of twins who were raised together and twins who were not be helpful in distinguishing the effects of heredity and environment?

2. Suppose you know a 7-year-old child who is having problems learning to read and you want to help. Imagine that you can consult as many psychologists as you want to. How might each type of psychologist approach the problem?

h. Educational psychology

i. School psychology

j. Social psychology

k. Industrial/organizational psychology

8. A strong fear of crowds leads a young woman to seek treatment for her problem.

9. What mental strategies are involved in solving complex word problems?

10. What teaching methods most effectively motivate elementary school students to successfully accomplish academic tasks?

11. Jessica is asked to develop a management strategy that will encourage safer work practices in an assembly plant.

Answers to Evaluate Questions

1. a-4, b-9, c-2, d-5, e-7, f-8, g-1, h-10, i-6, j-3, k-11

A Science Evolves: The Past, the Present, and the Future

Prepare

What are the historical roots of the field of psychology?

What are the major approaches used by contemporary psychologists?

Organize

A Science Evolves
The Roots of Psychology
Today's Perspectives

Some half-million years ago, people assumed that psychological problems were caused by evil spirits. To allow these spirits to escape the person's body, ancient healers performed an operation called trephining. Trephining consisted of chipping away at a patient's skull with crude stone instruments until a hole was cut through the bone.

***

According to the seventeenth-century philosopher Descartes, nerves were hollow tubes through which "animal spirits" conducted impulses in the same way that water is transmitted through a pipe. When a person put a finger too close to a fire, heat was transmitted into the brain through the tubes.

***

Franz Josef Gall, an eighteenth-century physician, argued that a trained observer could discern intelligence, moral character, and other basic personality characteristics from the shape and number of bumps on a person's skull. His theory gave rise to the "science" of phrenology, employed by hundreds of devoted practitioners in the nineteenth century.

Though these explanations might sound far-fetched, in their own times they represented the most advanced thinking regarding what might be called the psychology of the era. Our understanding of behaviour has advanced tremendously since these earlier views were formulated, yet most of the advances have been recent—for, as sciences go, psychology is one of the "new kids on the block."

Psychology's roots can be traced back to the ancient Greeks and Romans, and philosophers argued for hundreds of years about some of the questions psychologists grapple with today. However, the formal beginning of psychology as a science is generally set at 1879, when Wilhelm Wundt established in Leipzig, Germany, the first experimental laboratory devoted to psychological phenomena. At about the same time, William James was setting up his laboratory in Cambridge, Massachusetts.

The Roots of Psychology

When Wilhelm Wundt set up the first psychology laboratory in 1879, his aim was to study the building blocks of the mind. He considered psychology to be the study of conscious experience, and he developed a perspective that came to be known as structuralism. **Structuralism** focused on the basic elements that constitute the foundation of perception, consciousness, thinking, emotions, and other kinds of mental states and activities.

structuralism: Wundt's approach, which focuses on the basic elements that form the foundation of thinking, consciousness, emotions, and other kinds of mental states and activities.

Wilhelm Wundt

William James

History of psychology
www.mcgrawhill.ca/college/feldman

introspection: A procedure used to study the structure of the mind, in which subjects are asked to describe in detail what they are experiencing when they are exposed to a stimulus.

functionalism: An early approach to psychology that concentrated on what the mind does—the functions of mental activity—and the role of behaviour in allowing people to adapt to their environments.

gestalt (geh SHTALLT) psychology: An approach to psychology that focuses on the organization of perception and thinking in a "whole" sense, rather than on the individual elements of perception.

To come to an understanding of how basic sensations combined to produce our perception of the world, Wundt and other structuralists used a procedure called **introspection** to study the mind. In introspection, people were presented with a stimulus—such as a bright green object or a sentence printed on a card—and were asked to describe, in their own words and in as much detail as they could manage, what they were experiencing. Wundt argued that, by analyzing the reports people offered of their reactions, psychologists could come to better understand the structure of the mind.

Over time, psychologists challenged Wundt's structuralism. They became increasingly dissatisfied with the assumption that introspection could unlock the fundamental elements of the mind. Introspection was not a truly scientific technique. There were few ways an outside observer could confirm the accuracy of others' introspections. Moreover, people had difficulty describing some kinds of inner experiences, such as emotional responses. Such drawbacks led to the evolution of new approaches, which largely supplanted structuralism.

However, the heritage of structuralism still exists. As we will see in Chapter 7, there has been a renewed interest in people's descriptions of their inner experience. Cognitive psychologists, who focus on higher mental processes such as thinking, memory, and problem solving, have developed innovative techniques that help us understand people's conscious experience and that overcome many of the difficulties inherent in introspection.

The main perspective that came to replace structuralism as psychology evolved is known as functionalism. Rather than focusing on the mind's components, **functionalism** concentrated on what the mind *does* and how behaviour *functions*. Functionalists, whose perspective became prominent in the early 1900s, asked what roles behaviour plays in allowing people to better adapt to their environments. Led by the American psychologist William James, the functionalists examined how behaviour allows people to satisfy their needs. The famous American educator John Dewey used functionalism to develop the field of school psychology, proposing ways to best meet students' educational needs.

Another important reaction to structuralism was the development of gestalt psychology in the early 1900s. **Gestalt psychology** is a perspective focusing on how perception is organized. Instead of considering the individual parts that make up thinking, gestalt psychologists took the opposite tack, concentrating on how people consider individual elements together as units or wholes. Their credo was "The whole is different from the sum of its parts," meaning that, when considered together, the basic elements that compose our perception of objects produce something greater and more meaningful than those individual elements alone. As we will see in Chapter 3, gestalt psychologists have made substantial contributions to our understanding of perception.

Women in Psychology: Pioneering Contributions

As in many scientific fields, societal constraints hindered women's participation during the early development of psychology. Despite the hurdles they faced, several women made major contributions to psychology, although until recently their contributions were largely overlooked. For example, Leta Stetter Hollingworth was one of the first psychologists to focus on child development and on women's issues. She collected data to refute the view, popular in the early 1900s, that women's abilities regularly declined during parts of the menstrual cycle (Benjamin & Shields, 1990; Hollingworth, 1943/1990; Denmark & Fernandez, 1993).

Karen Horney (pronounced "HORN-eye") focused on the social and cultural factors behind personality, and June Etta Downey spearheaded the study of personality traits and became the first woman to head a psychology department at a state university. Anna Freud (daughter of Sigmund Freud) also made notable contributions to the treatment of abnormal behaviour (Horney, 1937; Stevens & Gardner, 1982).

The 1930s and 1940s were years that saw women in increasing numbers take their places in teaching positions at Canadian universities. Reva Gerstein, who taught at the University of Toronto in the early 1940s, was to use her education in a career of service to Canada. Her work in the field of mental health won her a national award in 1987. Among her many accomplishments was the *Gerstein Report*, which provided a plan for deinstitutionalized psychiatric patients (Wright, 1993).

Brenda Milner

Brenda Milner is a distinguished pioneer in the field of neuropsychology. Her research at the Montreal Neurological Institute has contributed to our knowledge of learning, memory, and speech functions of the brain.

Despite the contributions of such women, psychology was largely a male-dominated field in its early years. However the number of women has been increasing rapidly in recent years. Consequently, when future historians of science write about psychology, they will be recording a history of men and women (Denmark, 1994).

Today's Perspectives

The women and the men who worked to build the foundations of psychology shared a common goal: to explain and understand behavior, using scientific methods. Seeking to achieve this same goal, the tens of thousands of psychologists who followed these early pioneers embraced—and often rejected—a variety of broad perspectives (Benjamin, 1997; Robins, Gosling, & Craik, 1999).

The various perspectives offer distinct outlooks and emphasize different factors. Just as we can use more than one map to find our way around a particular region—for instance, a map that shows roads and highways and another map that shows major landmarks—psychologists developed a variety of approaches to understanding behaviour. When considered jointly, the different perspectives provide the means to explain behaviour in its amazing variety.

Today, the field of psychology involves five major perspectives (summarized in Figure 1-1). Each of these broad perspectives emphasizes different aspects of behaviour and mental processes, and each takes our understanding of behaviour in a somewhat different direction.

The Biological Perspective: Blood, Sweat, and Fears

When we get down to the basics, human beings are animals made of skin and bones. The **biological perspective** considers how people and nonhumans function biologically: how individual nerve cells are joined together, how the inheritance of certain characteristics from parents and other ancestors influences behaviour, how the functioning of

Mary J. Wright, whose career in psychology has spanned 50 years, became the first woman president of the CPA in 1969. She has written extensively on the history of psychology in Canada.

biological perspective: The approach that views behaviour from the perspective of biological functioning.

The Major Perspectives of Psychology

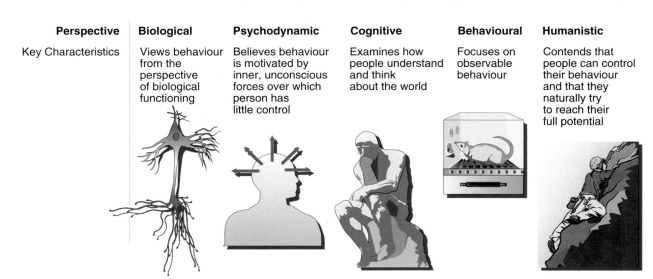

Perspective	Biological	Psychodynamic	Cognitive	Behavioural	Humanistic
Key Characteristics	Views behaviour from the perspective of biological functioning	Believes behaviour is motivated by inner, unconscious forces over which person has little control	Examines how people understand and think about the world	Focuses on observable behaviour	Contends that people can control their behaviour and that they naturally try to reach their full potential

Figure 1-1 The major perspectives used by psychologists.

Sigmund Freud

psychodynamic perspective: The approach based on the belief that behaviour is motivated by unconscious inner forces over which the individual has little control.

cognitive perspective: The approach that focuses on how people think, understand, and know about the world.

behavioural perspective: The approach that suggests that observable behaviour that can be measured objectively should be the focus of study.

the body affects hopes and fears, which behaviours are instinctual, and so forth. Even more complex kinds of behaviours, such as a baby's response to strangers, are viewed as having critical biological components by psychologists using the biological perspective. This perspective includes the study of heredity and evolution, and how heredity might influence behaviour.

Because every behaviour can at some level be broken down into its biological components, the biological perspective has broad appeal. Psychologists who subscribe to this perspective have made major contributions to the understanding and betterment of human life, ranging from developing cures for certain types of deafness to identifying medications to treat people with severe mental disorders.

The Psychodynamic Perspective: Understanding the Inner Person

To many people who have never taken a psychology course, psychology begins and ends with the psychodynamic perspective. Proponents of the **psychodynamic perspective** believe that behaviour is motivated by inner forces and conflicts about which we have little awareness or control. Dreams and slips of the tongue are viewed as indications of what a person is truly feeling within a seething cauldron of unconscious psychic activity.

The psychodynamic view is intimately linked with one individual: Sigmund Freud. Freud was a Viennese physician in the early 1900s whose ideas about unconscious determinants of behaviour had a revolutionary effect on twentieth-century thinking, not just in psychology but in related fields as well. Although some of the original principles of psychodynamic thinking have been roundly criticized, contemporary use of the perspective has provided a means not only to understand and treat some kinds of psychological disorders, but also to understand everyday phenomena such as prejudice and aggression.

The Cognitive Perspective: Identifying the Roots of Understanding

The route to understanding behaviour leads some psychologists straight into the mind. Evolving in part from structuralism, the **cognitive perspective** focuses on how people think, understand, and know about the world. The emphasis is on learning how people comprehend and represent the outside world within themselves, and how our ways of thinking about the world influence our behaviour.

Psychologists using the cognitive perspective often compare human thinking to the workings of a computer, considering how information is input, transformed, stored, and retrieved. In this view, thinking is *information processing*.

Psychologists relying on the cognitive perspective ask questions ranging from how people make decisions to whether a person can watch television and study at the same time. The common elements that link cognitive approaches are an emphasis on how people understand and think about the world and a concern to describe the patterns and irregularities in the operation of our minds.

The Behavioural Perspective: Observing the Outer Person

Whereas the biological, psychodynamic, and cognitive approaches look inside the organism to determine the causes of its behaviour, the behavioural perspective takes a very different approach. The **behavioural perspective** grew out of a rejection of psychology's early emphasis on the inner workings of the mind, suggesting instead that the field should focus on observable behaviour that can be measured objectively.

John B. Watson was the first major American psychologist to advocate a behavioural approach. Working in the 1920s, Watson was adamant in his view that one could gain a complete understanding of behaviour by studying and modifying the environment in which people operated. In fact, he believed rather optimistically that it was possible to elicit any desired sort of behaviour by controlling a person's environment. This philosophy is clear in his own words: "Give me a dozen healthy infants, well-formed, and my own specified world to bring them up in and I'll guarantee to take any one at random and train him to become any type of specialist I might select—doctor, lawyer, artist, merchant-chief, and yes, even beggar-man and thief, regardless of his talents, penchants, tendencies, abilities, vocations and race of his ancestors" (Watson, 1924). The behavioural perspective was later championed by B.F. Skinner, who until his death in 1990 was probably the best-known psychologist. Much of our understanding of how people learn new behaviours is based on the behavioural perspective.

As we will see, the behavioural perspective crops up along every byway of psychology. Along with its influence in the area of learning processes, this perspective has also made contributions in such diverse areas as treating mental disorders, curbing aggression, resolving sexual problems, and ending drug addiction.

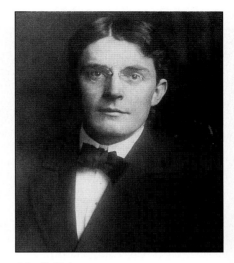

John B. Watson

The Humanistic Perspective: The Unique Qualities of Homo Sapiens

Rejecting the views that behaviour is determined largely by automatic biological forces, by unconscious processes, or by the environment, the **humanistic perspective** instead suggests that all individuals naturally strive to grow, develop, and be in control of their lives and behaviour. Humanistic psychologists maintain that each of us has the capacity to seek and reach fulfillment.

humanistic perspective: The approach that suggests that all individuals naturally strive to grow, develop, and be in control of their lives and behaviour.

According to Carl Rogers and Abraham Maslow, who were central figures in the development of the humanistic perspective, people will strive to reach their full potential if given the opportunity. The emphasis of the humanistic perspective is on *free will,* the ability to freely make decisions about one's own behaviour and life. The notion of free will stands in contrast to *determinism,* which sees behaviour as caused, or determined, by things beyond a person's control.

The humanistic perspective assumes that people have the ability to make their own choices about their behaviour rather than rely on societal standards. More than any other approach, it stresses the role of psychology in enriching people's lives and helping them to achieve self-fulfillment. The humanistic perspective has had an important influence on psychologists, reminding them of their commitment to the individual person in society.

It is important not to let the abstract qualities of the broad approaches we have discussed lull you into thinking that they are purely theoretical: These perspectives underlie ongoing work of a practical nature, as we will discuss throughout this book. As an introduction to the practical side of psychology, read the *Applying Psychology in the 21ˢᵗ Century* box.

Applying Psychology in the 21st Century

Psychology and the Reduction of Violence

A bomb explodes during the 1996 Olympics in Atlanta, killing one person and injuring dozens more. In 1996, a terrible tragedy plays itself out at Dunblane Primary School in Scotland, another in 1999 at Columbine High School in Colorado, and yet another in 2002 at a school in Erfurt, Germany. Violence is the reality we live with. No country—in fact no community—is immune to it. Violence invades our homes: Two young sisters are murdered in their suburban Toronto home. It invades our streets: A 14-year-old girl in British Columbia is viciously beaten and drowned by youth her own age. It invades our schools: One student is killed and another injured when an Alberta boy takes a gun to school.

In the aftermath of these events, we may feel disgusted, sad, or angry. We become fearful for ourselves and for our children. On the anniversary of the Columbine tragedy, dozens of Toronto schools were patrolled by uniformed police officers, and many parents kept children home because of fear of violence.

Yet violence is not going unchallenged, and psychology is playing a key role in efforts to reduce this social ill. Psychologists specializing in diverse areas and employing the major perspectives of the field are making a concerted effort to answer key questions relating to violence. These are some examples:

- *Is there a "cycle of violence" that perpetuates violent behaviour across generations?* According to the "cycle of violence" explanation, abuse and neglect during childhood make people more likely to abuse and neglect their own children (Widom, 1989). Research in developmental psychopathology by Muller and Diamond at York University (1999) found a relationship between physical maltreatment by both fathers and mothers and elevated levels of aggression in both sons and daughters, as early as preschool. They also found these patterns were consistent across generations.

  However, being abused does not inevitably lead to the abuse of one's own children. Current research is aimed at determining when a childhood history of abuse is most likely to result in adult violence, and how the cycle can be broken.

- *What are the effects of media violence?* Most social and developmental psychologists agree that observation of aggression in the media enhances the likelihood that viewers will act aggressively. In an extensive study done for the Department of Canadian Heritage, Wendy Josephson (1995) examined the effects of television violence on children of different ages. She found that although all ages are affected, preschoolers are particularly vulnerable. She and others have

Flowers and other tokens of sympathy at a school in Erfurt, Germany.

also found that observing media aggression serves to desensitize viewers to displays of aggression, leading them to react with passivity to actual incidents of aggression (Molitor & Hirsch, 1994; Josephson, 1995; Palermo, 1995).

Although television receives a lot of attention in this regard, some video games provide interactive violence, allowing people not only to observe violence but also to participate in it. One of the more popular games has players hitting, teasing, and abusing each other until they are driven sobbing out of the game. It has 25 000 registered users (Spencer, 2000).

- *What role do biological factors play in aggression?* Some psychologists have considered whether aggression is linked to biological factors. For instance, links have been identified between the presence of certain hormones and aggressive behaviour. This suggests the possibility that medical treatment might reduce violence in perpetrators (Dabbs, Hargrove, & Heusel, 1996; Davidson, Putnam, & Larson, 2000)

- *How can youth violence be reduced?* In Canada, the rate of young people charged with violent crimes is 77 percent higher than it was a decade ago. Of significant concern is the increasing violence reported for female youths (*Juristat*, 1999).

  A combination of factors such as a lack of nurturance; neglect and harsh treatment; frequent observation of violence; difficult life conditions; and poverty, prejudice, and discrimination result in higher rates of violence. Successful training programs have been designed to teach youth to respond to provocative situations without violence (Staub, 1996; Josephson et al., 1999; Spielman & Staub, 2000; Enserink, 2000b).

- *How can sexual aggression be reduced?* In 1998 there were over 21 000 reported cases of sexual assaults against Canadian women (Temblay, 1999). Psychologists from several different branches of the field— including specialists in clinical psychology, developmental psychology, and the psychology of women—have been working to devise ways of reducing sexually aggressive behaviour (Hall & Barongan, 1997).

Clearly, psychologists are playing important and quite varied roles in combatting violence. And violence is not the only societal problem to which psychologists are contributing their expertise in an effort to alleviate human suffering. As we will explore in *Applying Psychology in the 21st Century* boxes in every chapter, the basic principles of psychology are being used, as we move into the new century, to address a wide range of social problems.

Assuming that research on video games is confirmed, should violent video games be restricted to certain age groups? Should they be banned entirely? Why or why not?

Evaluate

1. Wundt described psychology as the study of conscious experience, a perspective he called
   _____.

2. Early psychologists studied the mind by asking people to describe what they were
   experiencing when exposed to various stimuli. This procedure was known as
   _____.

3. The statement, "In order to study human behaviour, we must consider the whole of
   perception rather than its component parts" might be made by a person subscribing to
   the _____ perspective.

4. Jeanne's therapist asks her to recount a violent dream she recently experienced in order to
   gain insight into the unconscious forces affecting her behaviour. Jeanne's therapist is
   working from a _____ perspective.

5. "We should study observable behaviour, not the suspected inner workings of the mind." This
   statement was most likely made by someone with which perspective:

   a. cognitive perspective

   b. biological perspective

   c. humanistic perspective

   d. behavioural perspective

6. "My therapist is wonderful! She always points out my positive traits. She dwells on my
   uniqueness and strength as an individual. I feel much more confident about myself—as if
   I'm really growing and reaching my potential." The therapist being described most likely
   practises from a _____ perspective.

Answers to Evaluate Questions

1. structuralism 2. introspection 3. gestalt 4. psychodynamic 5. d 6. humanistic

Rethink

1. How might today's major perspectives of psychology be related to the earliest perspectives, such as structuralism, functionalism, and gestalt psychology?

2. Select one of the five major perspectives in use today (biological, psychodynamic, cognitive, behavioural, or humanistic), and describe the sorts of research questions and studies that researchers using that perspective might pursue.

Psychology's Key Issues

As you consider the many subfields and perspectives that make up psychology, which range from a narrow focus on minute biochemical influences on behaviour to a broad focus on social behaviours, you might find yourself thinking that the discipline lacks cohesion. Yet the field is actually more unified than a first glimpse might suggest. For one thing, no matter what topical area a psychologist specializes in, he or she will rely on one of the five major perspectives. For example, a developmental psychologist who specializes in the study of children could make use of the cognitive perspective *or* the psychodynamic perspective *or* any of the other major perspectives.

Psychologists also agree on what the key issues of the field are. Although major arguments exist regarding how to best address and resolve these, psychology is a unified science because of this collective acknowledgment that these issues must be addressed in order for the field to advance.

As you contemplate these key issues (described below and summarized in Table 1-2), try not to think of them in "either/or" terms. Instead, consider the opposing viewpoints on each issue as opposite ends of a continuum, with the positions of individual psychologists typically falling somewhere between the two ends.

- *Nature (heredity) versus nurture (environment).* How much of our behaviour is due to heredity (or "nature") and how much is due to environment ("nurture"), and what is the interplay between the two forces? This question has deep philosophical and historical roots and it is a factor in many topics of psychology.

  A psychologist's take on this issue depends partly on which major perspective she or he subscribes to. For example, developmental psychologists, whose focus is on how people grow and change throughout the course of their lives, might be most interested in learning more about hereditary influences if

Prepare

What are psychology's key issues and controversies?

What is the future of psychology likely to hold?

Organize

Psychology's Key Issues
Psychology's Future

 **PsychLink**

Nature vs. nurture
www.mcgrawhill.ca/college/feldman

Table 1-2 Positions Taken by Psychologists Using the Major Perspectives of Psychology

Issue	PERSPECTIVE				
	Biological	**Psychodynamic**	**Cognitive**	**Behavioural**	**Humanistic**
Nature (heredity) vs. nurture (environment)	Nature (heredity)	Nature (heredity)	Both	Nurture (environment)	Nurture (environment)
Conscious vs. unconscious determinants of behaviour	Unconscious	Unconscious	Both	Conscious	Conscious
Observable behaviour vs. internal mental processes	Internal emphasis	Internal emphasis	Internal emphasis	Observable emphasis	Internal emphasis
Free will vs. determinism	Determinism	Determinism	Free will	Determinism	Free will
Individual differences vs. universal principles	Universal emphasis	Universal emphasis	Individual emphasis	Both	Individual emphasis

they were employing a biological perspective. On the other hand, developmental psychologists who are proponents of the behavioural perspective would be more likely to focus on environment.

- *Conscious versus unconscious causes of behaviour.* How much of our behaviour is produced by forces of which we are fully aware, and how much is due to unconscious activity—mental processes that are not accessible to the conscious mind? This question represents one of the great controversies in the field of psychology. For example, clinical psychologists adopting a psychodynamic perspective argue that much of abnormal behaviour is motivated by unconscious factors, whereas others employing the cognitive perspective suggest that abnormal behaviour is largely the result of faulty thinking processes. The specific approach taken has a clear impact on how abnormal behaviour is diagnosed and treated.

- *Observable behaviour versus internal mental processes.* Should psychology concentrate solely on behaviour that can be seen by outside observers? Or should it focus on unseen thinking processes? Some psychologists, particularly those relying on the behavioural perspective, contend that the only legitimate source of information for psychologists is behaviour that can be observed directly. Other psychologists, building on the cognitive perspective, argue that what goes on inside a person's mind is critical and that we cannot understand behaviour without concerning ourselves with mental processes.

- *Free will versus determinism.* How much of behaviour is a matter of *free will* (choices made freely by an individual), and how much is subject to *determinism,* the notion that behaviour is largely produced by factors beyond people's willful control? An issue long debated by philosophers, the free-will/determinism argument is also central to the field of psychology (Kimble, 1989; Hoeller, 1990). For example, some psychologists specializing in psychological disorders argue that people make intentional choices and that those who display so-called "abnormal behaviour" should be considered responsible for their actions. Other psychologists disagree and contend that such individuals are the victims of forces beyond their control. The position psychologists take on this issue has important implications for how they will treat abnormal behaviour, especially in deciding whether treatment should be forced on individuals who reject it.

- *Individual differences versus universal principles.* How much of our behaviour is a consequence of our unique and special qualities and how much reflects the culture and society in which we live? How much of our behaviour is universally human?

Members of different cultures attribute academic success to different factors.
How might different cultural perspectives affect the performance of Asian versus North American students?

Psychologists relying on the biological perspective tend to look for universal principles of behaviour, such as how our nervous system operates or the way certain hormones automatically prime us for sexual activity. Such psychologists concentrate on the similarities in our behavioural destinies despite vast differences in our upbringing. In contrast, psychologists employing the humanistic perspective focus more on the uniqueness of every individual. They consider how every person's behaviour is a reflection of distinct and special qualities.

The question of the degree to which psychologists can identify universal principles that apply to all people has taken on new significance in light of the tremendous demographic changes now occurring across the world, and is of special significance in Canada because of multiculturalism. As we discuss next, these and other changes raise new and critical issues for the discipline of psychology in the future.

Psychology's Future

We've examined psychology's foundations. But what does the future hold for the discipline? Although the course of scientific development is difficult to predict, several trends do seem likely to emerge in the near future:

- As its knowledge base grows, psychology will become increasingly specialized and new perspectives will evolve (Robins, Gosling, & Craik, 1999).
- More psychologists will focus on the prevention of psychological disorders rather than just on their treatment. Psychological treatment will become more available and socially acceptable as the number of psychologists increases (APA, 1999).
- Psychology's influence on issues of public interest will grow. The major problems of our time—such as violence, racial and ethnic prejudice, poverty, and environmental and technological disasters—have important psychological aspects, and it is likely that psychologists will make important practical contributions toward their resolution (Cialdini, 1997; Lerner, Fisher, & Weinberg, 2000).
- As the population of the United States and Canada becomes more diverse, issues of diversity—embodied in the study of racial, ethnic, linguistic, and cultural factors—will become more critical to psychologists providing services and doing research. The result will be a field that can provide an understanding of human behaviour in its broadest sense (Berry & Laponce, 1994; Gautier & Philips, 1997; J. G. Miller, 1999; Rosenzweig, 1999; Leong & Blustein, 2000).

 **PsychLink**
Cross-cultural psychology
www.mcgrawhill.ca/college/feldman

Evaluate

1. Which perspective suggests that abnormal behaviour is largely the result of unconscious forces?
2. "Psychologists should worry only about behaviour that is directly observable." This statement would most likely be made by a person using which psychological perspective?
3. Psychology is currently moving toward increased specialization. True or false?

Answers to Evaluate Questions

1. psychodynamic 2. behavioural 3. True

Rethink

1. "The fact that some businesses now promote their ability to help people 'expand their mind beyond virtual reality' shows the great progress psychology has made lately." Criticize this statement in light of what you know about professional psychology and pseudo-psychology.
2. How do some of the key issues identified in this chapter relate to law enforcement and criminal justice?

Prepare

What is the scientific method, and how do psychologists use theory and research to answer questions of interest?

What are the different research methods employed by psychologists?

How do psychologists establish cause-and-effect relationships in research studies?

Organize

Research in Psychology
   The Scientific Method
   Psychological Research

In an ambiguous situation, the presence of others behaving as if there is no emergency will indicate to the observer that help is not required.

Research in Psychology

Imagine that you are on a busy street and a fight breaks out. Nearby a young man is being beaten. Do you stop and help? Do you call the police? Do you walk right by? Do you watch and do nothing to intervene? Can you remember a situation where you saw someone in trouble and did nothing? Do you remember what you thought at the time? If you did nothing you are not alone. Bystander inaction is all too common.

Possibly the best known case of bystander inaction involved a young woman named Kitty Genovese, who was attacked by a man near an apartment building in New York City in the mid 1960s. At one point during the assault, which lasted 30 minutes, she managed to free herself and screamed, "Oh, my God, he stabbed me. Please help me!" In the stillness of the night, no fewer than 38 neighbours heard her screams. Windows opened and lights went on. One couple pulled chairs up to the window and turned off the lights so they could see better. Someone called out, "Let that girl alone." But shouts were not enough to scare off the killer. He chased her, stabbing her eight more times, and sexually molested her before leaving her to die. And how many of those 38 witnesses came to her aid? Not one person helped (Rogers & Eftimiades, 1995).

Bystander inaction happens in Canada as well. In 1973 a young woman of 18 was dragged down a Scarborough, Ontario, street. She was forced at knife-point to undress and was then raped in full view of people in the surrounding apartments. Like Kitty Genovese, no one came to her aid. There were no phone calls to the police (Alcock, Carment, & Sadava, 2000). Both of the cases above remain dismaying—and puzzling—examples of "bad Samaritanism." The general public, as well as psychologists, found it difficult to explain how so many people could stand by without coming to the aid of the victims.

One easy explanation, supplied by many editorial writers, was that the incidents could be attributed to the basic shortcomings of "human nature." But such an assumption is woefully inadequate. For one thing, there are numerous examples of people who have placed their own lives at risk to help others in dangerous situations.

Clearly, then, "human nature" encompasses a wide range of both negative and positive responses. Consequently, "it was human nature" is not a very satisfying explanation for the bystanders' unhelpful behaviour. The mystery of the lack of bystander intervention in both incidents remains unsolved.

Psychologists in particular puzzled over the problem for many years. After much research they finally reached an unexpected conclusion: Victims like Kitty Genovese and the Scarborough rape victim might well have been better off had there been just a few people who heard their cries for help rather than many. In fact, had there been just one bystander present in each instance, the chances of that person intervening might have been fairly high. For it turns out that the *fewer* witnesses present in situations like the two in question, the better the victim's chances of getting help.

How did psychologists come to such a curious conclusion? After all, logic and common sense clearly suggest that the presence of more bystanders would produce a greater likelihood that someone would help a person in need. This seeming contradiction—and the way psychologists resolved it—illustrates a central task for the field of psychology: the challenge of asking and answering questions of interest.

The Scientific Method

The challenge of posing appropriate questions and properly answering them has been met through reliance on the scientific method. The **scientific method** is the approach used by psychologists to systematically acquire knowledge and understanding about behaviour and other phenomena of interest. As illustrated in Figure 1-2, it consists of three main steps: (1) identifying questions of interest, (2) formulating an explanation, and (3) carrying out research designed to lend support to or refute the explanation.

Theories: Specifying Broad Explanations

In using the scientific method, psychologists start with the kinds of observations about behaviour we are all familiar with. If you have ever asked yourself why a particular teacher is so easily annoyed, why a friend is always late for appointments, or how your dog understands your commands, you have been formulating questions about behaviour. Psychologists, too, ask questions about the nature and causes of behaviour, and this questioning is the first step in the scientific method: identifying questions of interest.

Once a question has been identified, the next step in the scientific method involves developing theories to explain the phenomenon that has been observed. **Theories** are broad explanations and predictions concerning phenomena of interest. They provide a framework for understanding the relationships among a set of otherwise unorganized facts or principles.

All of us have developed our own informal theories of human behaviour, such as "People are basically good" or "People's behaviour is usually motivated by self-interest." However, psychologists' theories are more formal and focused. They are established on the basis of a careful study of the psychological literature to identify relevant research conducted and theories formulated previously, as well as psychologists' general knowledge of the field (Sternberg, 1990; Sternberg & Beall, 1991; McGuire, 1997).

Growing out of the diverse models of psychology, theories vary both in their breadth and in the level of detail they employ. For example, one theory might seek to

PsychLink

Guide for beginning researchers
www.mcgrawhill.ca/college/feldman

scientific method: The approach used by psychologists to systematically acquire knowledge and understanding about behaviour and other phenomena of interest.

theories: Broad explanations and predictions concerning phenomena of interest.

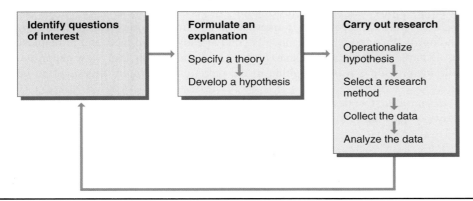

Figure 1–2 The scientific method, which encompasses the process of identifying, asking, and answering questions, is used by psychologists, and by researchers from every other scientific discipline, to come to an understanding about the world. What do you think are the advantages of this method?

THEORIES OF EVERYTHING

explain and predict as broad a phenomenon as emotional experience in general. A narrower theory might purport to predict how people display the emotion of fear nonverbally after receiving a threat. An even more specific theory might attempt to explain how the muscles of the face work together to produce expressions of fear.

Psychologists Bibb Latané and John Darley, responding specifically to the Kitty Genovese case, developed a theory based on a phenomenon they called *diffusion of responsibility* (Latané & Darley, 1970). According to their theory, the greater the number of bystanders or witnesses to an event that calls for helping behaviour, the more the responsibility for helping is perceived to be shared by all the bystanders. Because of this sense of shared responsibility, then, the more people present in an emergency situation, the less personal responsibility each person feels—and the less likely it is that any single person will come forward to help.

Hypotheses: Crafting Testable Predictions

hypothesis: A prediction, stemming from a theory, stated in a way that allows it to be tested.

Although such a theory makes sense, it represented only the beginning phase of Latané and Darley's investigative process. Their next step was to devise a way of testing their theory. To do this, they needed to create a hypothesis. A **hypothesis** is a prediction stated in a way that allows it to be tested. Hypotheses stem from theories; they help to test the underlying validity of theories.

In the same way as we develop our own broad theories about the world, we also construct hypotheses about events and behaviour. They can range from trivialities (such as why our English instructor wears those weird shirts) to more meaningful matters (such as what is the best way to study for a test). Although we rarely test these hypotheses systematically, we do try to determine whether they are right. Perhaps we try comparing two strategies: cramming the night before an exam versus spreading out our study over several nights. By assessing which approach yields better test performance, we have created a way to compare the two strategies.

Latané and Darley's hypothesis was a straightforward prediction from their more general theory of diffusion of responsibility: The more people who witness an emergency situation, the less likely it is that help will be given to a victim. They could, of course, have chosen another hypothesis (for instance, that people with greater skills related to emergency situations will not be affected by the presence of others), but their initial formulation seemed to offer the most direct test of the theory.

Psychologists rely on formal theories and hypotheses for many reasons. For one thing, theories and hypotheses allow psychologists to make sense of unorganized, separate observations and bits of information by permitting them to place the pieces within a structured and coherent framework. In addition, theories and hypotheses offer psychologists the opportunity to move beyond already known facts and principles and make deductions about as yet unexplained phenomena. In this way, theories and hypotheses provide a reasoned guide to the direction that future investigation ought to take.

In sum, then, theories and hypotheses help psychologists pose appropriate questions. But how are such questions answered? As we shall see, the answers come from research.

Psychological Research

Research, systematic inquiry aimed at the discovery of new knowledge, is a central ingredient of the scientific method in psychology. It provides the key to understanding the degree to which theories and hypotheses are accurate.

Just as we can apply different theories and hypotheses to explain the same phenomena, we can use a number of alternative methods to conduct research on the same problem (Ray, 2000). First, though, the hypothesis must be restated in a way that will allow it to be tested, a procedure known as operationalization. **Operationalization** is the process of translating a hypothesis into specific, testable procedures that can be measured and observed.

There is no single way to go about operationalizing a hypothesis; it depends on logic, the equipment and facilities available, the psychological model being employed, and ultimately the creativity of the researcher. For example, one researcher might develop a hypothesis in which she operationalizes "fear" as an increase in heart rate. In contrast, another psychologist might operationalize "fear" as a written response to the question, "How much fear are you experiencing at this moment?"

We will consider several of the major tools in the psychologist's research kit. As we discuss these research methods, keep in mind that their relevance extends beyond testing and evaluating theories and hypotheses in psychology. Even people who do not have degrees in psychology, for instance, often carry out elementary forms of research on their own. For example, a supervisor might need to evaluate an employee's performance; a physician might systematically test the effects of different dosages of a drug on a patient; a salesperson might compare different persuasive strategies. Each of these situations calls for the use of the research practices we are about to discuss.

Furthermore, a knowledge of the research methods used by psychologists permits us to better evaluate the research that others conduct. The media constantly bombard us with claims about research studies and findings. Knowledge of research methods allows us to sort out what is credible from what should be ignored. Finally, there is evidence that by studying some kinds of research methods in depth, people learn to reason more critically and effectively. Understanding the methods by which psychologists conduct research can enhance our ability to analyze and evaluate the situations we encounter in our everyday lives (Lehman, Lempert, & Nisbett, 1988; Shaughnessy, Zechmeister, & Zechmeister, 2000; Shadish, Cook, & Campbell, 2002).

Archival Research

Suppose that, like psychologists Latané and Darley, you were interested in finding out more about emergency situations in which bystanders did not provide help. One of the first places you might turn to would be historical accounts. By using newspaper records, for example, you might find support for the notion that a decrease in helping behaviour historically has accompanied an increase in the number of bystanders.

Using newspaper articles is an example of archival research. In **archival research,** existing data, such as census documents, college records, or newspaper clippings, are examined to test a hypothesis. For example, college records might be used to determine if there are gender differences in academic performance.

Archival research is a relatively inexpensive means of testing a hypothesis because someone else has already collected the basic data. Of course, the use of existing data has several drawbacks. For one thing, the data might not be in a form that allows the researcher to test a hypothesis fully. The information could be incomplete, or it could have been collected haphazardly (Stewart & Kamins, 1993).

Most archival research is hampered by the simple fact that records with the necessary information do not exist. In these instances, researchers often turn to another research method: naturalistic observation.

Naturalistic Observation

In **naturalistic observation,** the investigator simply observes some naturally occurring behaviour and does not make a change in the situation. For example, a researcher investigating helping behaviour might observe the kind of help given to victims in a high-crime area of a city. The important point to remember about naturalistic observation is that the researcher is passive and simply records what occurs (Erlandson et al., 1993; Adler & Adler, 1994; Schmidt, 1999).

operationalization: The process of translating a hypothesis into specific, testable procedures that can be measured and observed.

 **PsychLink**
Research methods
www.mcgrawhill.ca/college/feldman

archival research: Research in which existing data, such as census documents, college records, or newspaper clippings, are examined to test a hypothesis.

naturalistic observation: Research in which an investigator simply observes some naturally occurring behaviour and does not make a change in the situation.

Dian Fossey, a pioneer in the study of gorillas in their native habitat, relied on naturalistic observation for her research. ***What are the advantages of this approach?***

survey research: Research in which people chosen to represent some larger population are asked a series of questions about their behaviour, thoughts, or attitudes.

case study: An in-depth, intensive investigation of an individual or small group of people.

Although the advantage of naturalistic observation is obvious—we get a sample of what people do in their "natural habitat"—there is also an important drawback: the inability to control any of the factors of interest. For example, we might find so few naturally occurring instances of helping behaviour that we would be unable to draw any conclusions. Because naturalistic observation prevents researchers from making changes in a situation, they must wait until appropriate conditions occur. Furthermore, if people know that they are being watched, they might alter their reactions, producing behaviour that is not truly representative of the group in question.

Survey Research

There is no more straightforward way of finding out what people think, feel, and do than asking them directly. For this reason, surveys are an important research method. In **survey research**, a *sample* of people chosen to represent some larger group of interest (a *population*) are asked a series of questions about their behaviour, thoughts, or attitudes. Survey methods have become so sophisticated that even with a very small sample researchers are able to infer with great accuracy how a larger group would respond. For instance, a sample of just a few thousand voters is sufficient to predict within one or two percentage points who will win a presidential election—if the representative sample is chosen with care (Weisberg, Krosnick, & Bowen, 1996; Fink & Kosecoff, 1998).

Researchers investigating helping behaviour might conduct a survey by asking people to complete a questionnaire in which they indicate their reasons for not wanting to come forward to help another individual. Similarly, researchers interested in learning about sexual practices have carried out surveys to learn which practices are common and which are not, and to chart changing notions of sexual morality over the past several decades.

Asking people directly about their behaviour seems in some ways the most straightforward approach to understanding what people do, but survey research has several potential drawbacks. For one thing, people might give inaccurate responses because of memory lapses or because they don't want the researcher to know what they really believe about a particular issue. Moreover, people sometimes offer responses they think the researcher wants to hear—or, in just the opposite instance, responses they assume the researcher *doesn't* want to hear. Finally, if the sample of people who are surveyed are not representative of the broader population of interest, the results of the survey have little meaning.

"This is the New York 'Times' Business Poll again, Mr. Landau. Do you feel better or worse about the economy than you did twenty minutes ago?"

The Case Study

What is it that makes violent video games so appealing? Is there something in the personality or background of players that leads to the choice to play? Does playing these games increase aggressive behaviour? In order to answer these questions, psychologists might conduct a case study. In contrast to a survey, in which many people are studied, a **case study** is an in-depth, intensive investigation of an individual or a small group of people. Case studies often include *psychological testing,* a procedure in which a carefully designed set of questions is used to gain some insight into the personality of the individual or group being studied (Kvale, 1996; Sommer & Sommer, 1997; Gass et al., 2000).

When case studies are used as a research technique, the goal is often not only to learn about the few individuals being examined, but to use the insights gained from the study to improve our understanding of people in general. Sigmund Freud built his theories through case studies of individual patients. Similarly, case studies of suicide bombers might help identify those who are prone to violence.

Correlational Research

In using the research methods that we have described, researchers often wish to determine the relationship between two variables. **Variables** are behaviours, events, or other characteristics that can change, or vary, in some way. For example, we might want to find out if there is a relationship between the variable of religious service attendance and the variable of helpfulness in emergency situations. If we did find such a relationship, we could say that there was an association—or correlation—between attendance at religious services and helpfulness in emergencies.

In **correlational research**, the relationship between two sets of variables is examined to determine whether they are associated, or "correlated." The strength and direction of the relationship between the two variables is represented by a mathematical score, known as a *correlation* (or, more formally, a *correlation coefficient*), that can range from $+1.0$ to -1.0.

A *positive correlation* indicates that as the value of one variable increases, we can predict that the value of the other variable will also increase. For example, if we predict that the more that students study for a test, the higher their subsequent grades on the test will be, and that the less they study, the lower their test scores will be, we are expecting to find a positive correlation. (Higher values of the variable "amount of study time" would be associated with higher values of the variable "test score," and lower values of "amount of study time" would be associated with lower values of "test score.") The correlation, then, would be indicated by a positive number, and the stronger the association between studying and test scores, the closer the number would be to $+1.0$. For example, we might find a correlation of $+.85$ between test scores and amount of studying time, indicating a strong positive association.

On the other hand, a *negative correlation* tells us that as the value of one variable increases, the value of the other decreases. For instance, we might predict that as the number of hours spent studying increases, the number of hours spent in partying decreases. Here, we are expecting a negative correlation, ranging between 0 and -1.0. More studying is associated with less partying, and less studying is associated with more partying. The stronger the association between study and partying, the closer the correlation would be to -1.0. For instance, a correlation of $-.85$ would indicate a strong negative association between partying and studying.

Of course, it's quite possible that little or no relationship exists between two variables. For instance, we would probably not expect to find a relationship between number of study hours and height. Lack of a relationship would be indicated by a correlation close to 0. For example, if we found a correlation of $-.02$ or $+.03$, it would indicate that there is virtually no association between the two variables; knowing how much someone studies does not tell us anything about how tall he or she is.

When we find that two variables are strongly correlated with one another, it is tempting to presume that one variable causes the other. For example, if we find that more study time is associated with higher grades, we might guess that more studying *causes* higher grades. Although this is not a bad guess, it remains just a guess—because finding that two variables are correlated does not mean that there is a causal relationship between them. Although the strong correlation suggests that knowing how much a person studies can help us predict how she or he will do on a test, it does not mean that the studying caused the test performance. It might be, for instance, that people who are interested in the subject matter tend to study more than those who are less interested, and that the amount of interest, not the number of hours spent studying, predicts test performance. The mere fact that two variables occur together does not mean that one causes the other.

Another example illustrates the critical point that correlations tell us nothing about cause and effect but only provide a measure of the strength of a relationship between two variables. We might find that children who watch a lot of television programs featuring high levels of aggression are likely to demonstrate a relatively high degree of aggressive behaviour, and that those who watch few television shows that portray aggression are apt to exhibit a relatively low degree of such behaviour (see Figure 1-3). But we cannot say that the aggression is *caused* by the TV viewing, because several other explanations are possible.

variables: Behaviours, events, or other characteristics that can change, or vary, in some way.

correlational research: Research that examines the relationship between two sets of variables to determine whether they are associated, or "correlated."

 **PsychLink**

Correlational research designs
www.mcgrawhill.ca/college/feldman

Figure 1-3 If we find that frequent viewing of television programs having aggressive content is associated with high levels of aggressive behaviour, we might cite several plausible causes, as suggested in this figure. For example, choosing to watch shows with aggressive content could produce aggression *(a);* or being a highly aggressive person might cause one to choose to watch televised aggression *(b);* or having a high energy level might cause a person to *both* choose to watch aggressive shows and act aggressively *(c).* Correlational findings, then, do not permit us to determine causality. Can you think of a way to study the effects of televised aggression on aggressive behaviour that is not correlational?

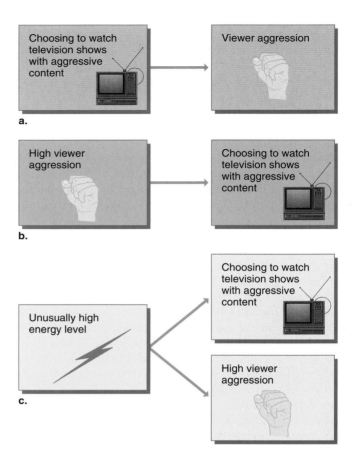

experiment: The investigation of the relationship between two (or more) variables by deliberately producing a change in one variable in a situation and observing the effects of that change on other aspects of the situation.

experimental manipulation: The change that an experimenter deliberately produces in a situation.

Many studies show that the observation of violence in the media is associated with aggression in viewers.

Can we conclude that the observation of violence causes aggression?

For instance, it could be that children who have an unusually high level of energy seek out programs with aggressive content *and* are more aggressive. The children's energy level, then, could be the true cause of the children's higher incidence of aggression. Finally, it is also possible that people who are already highly aggressive choose to watch shows with high aggressive content *because* they are aggressive. Clearly, then, any number of causal sequences are possible—none of which can be ruled out by correlational research.

The inability of correlational research to demonstrate cause-and-effect relationships is a crucial drawback to its use. There is, however, an alternative technique that does establish causality: the experiment.

Experimental Research

The *only* way psychologists can establish cause-and-effect relationships through research is by carrying out an experiment. In a formal **experiment**, the relationship between two (or more) variables is investigated by deliberately producing a change in one variable in a situation and observing the effects of that change on other aspects of the situation. In an experiment, then, the conditions required to study a question of interest are created by an experimenter, who deliberately makes a change in those conditions in order to observe the effects of that change.

The change that an experimenter deliberately produces in a situation is called the **experimental manipulation**. Experimental manipulations are used to detect relationships between different variables.

Several steps are involved in carrying out an experiment, but the process typically begins with the development of one or more hypotheses for the experiment to test. Recall, for example, the hypothesis derived by Latané and Darley to test their theory of helping behaviour: The more people who witness an emergency situation, the less likely it is that any of them will help the victim. We can trace the way these researchers designed an experiment to test this hypothesis.

Their first step was to operationalize the hypothesis by conceptualizing it in a way that could be tested. Doing so required that Latané and Darley take into account the fundamental principle of experimental research mentioned earlier. Experimenters must manipulate at least one variable in order to observe the effects of the manipulation on another variable. But the manipulation cannot be viewed by itself, in isolation; if a cause-and-effect relationship is to be established, the effects of the manipulation must be compared with the effects of no manipulation or a different kind of manipulation.

Experimental research requires, then, that the responses of at least two groups be compared with each other. One group will receive some special **treatment**—the manipulation implemented by the experimenter—and another group will receive either no treatment or a different treatment. Any group receiving a treatment is called an **experimental group**; a group that receives no treatment is called a **control group**. (In some experiments there are multiple experimental and control groups, each of which is compared with another.)

By employing both experimental and control groups in an experiment, researchers are able to rule out the possibility that something other than the experimental manipulation produced the results observed in the experiment. With no control group, we couldn't be sure that some other variable, such as the temperature at the time we were running the experiment, the colour of the experimenter's hair, or even the mere passage of time, wasn't causing the changes observed.

For example, consider a medical researcher who thinks she has invented a medicine that cures the common cold. To test her claim, she gives the medicine one day to a group of 20 people who have colds, and finds that 10 days later all of them are cured. Eureka? Not so fast. An observer viewing this flawed study might reasonably argue that the people would have gotten better even without the medicine. What the researcher obviously needed was a control group consisting of people with colds who *don't* get the medicine, and whose health is also checked 10 days later. Only if there is a difference between experimental and control groups can the effectiveness of the medicine be assessed. Through the use of control groups, then, researchers can isolate specific causes for their findings—and draw cause-and-effect inferences.

Returning to Latané and Darley's experiment, we note that the researchers needed a means of operationalizing their hypothesis in order to proceed. They decided they would create a false emergency situation that would appear to require the aid of a bystander. As their experimental manipulation, they decided to vary the number of bystanders present. They could have had just one experimental group with, say, two people present, and a control group for comparison purposes with just one person present. Instead, they settled on a more complex procedure involving three groups—consisting of two, three, and six people—that could be compared with one another.

Latané and Darley had now identified what is called the experimenter's independent variable. The **independent variable** is the variable that is manipulated by an experimenter. (You can think of the independent variable as being independent of the actions of those taking part in an experiment; it is controlled by the experimenter.) In the case of the Latané and Darley experiment, the independent variable was the number of people present, manipulated by the experimenters.

The next step was to decide how they were going to determine the effect that varying the number of bystanders had on the behaviour of those in the experiment. Crucial to every experiment is the **dependent variable**, the variable that is measured and is

In this experiment, preschoolers' reactions to the puppet are monitored.
Can you think of a hypothesis that might be tested in this way?

treatment: In an experiment, the manipulation implemented by the experimenter.

experimental group: Any group receiving a treatment in an experiment.

control group: A group that receives no treatment in an experiment.

 **PsychLink**

Two-group randomized experiment
www.mcgrawhill.ca/college/feldman

independent variable: The variable that is manipulated by an experimenter.

dependent variable: The variable that is measured and is expected to change as a result of changes caused by the experimenter's manipulation.

Bibb Latané and John Darley

random assignment to condition: A procedure in which participants are assigned to different experimental groups or "conditions" on the basis of chance and chance alone.

PsychLink

Random assignment explained
www.mcgrawhill.ca/college/feldman

expected to change as a result of changes caused by the experimenter's manipulation of the independent variable. The dependent variable is dependent on the actions of the *participants* or *subjects,* the people taking part in the experiment.

Latané and Darley had several possible choices for their dependent measure. One might have been a simple yes/no measure of the participants' helping behaviour. But the investigators also wanted a more precise analysis of helping behaviour. Consequently, they also measured the amount of time it took for a participant to provide help.

Latané and Darley now had all the necessary components of an experiment. The independent variable, manipulated by them, was the number of bystanders present in an emergency situation. The dependent variable was the measure of whether bystanders in each of the groups provided help and the amount of time it took them to do so. Consequently, like all experiments, this one had both an independent and a dependent variable. (To remember the difference, recall that a hypothesis predicts how a dependent variable *depends* on the manipulation of the independent variable.) *All* true experiments in psychology fit this straightforward model.

The Final Step: Random Assignment of Participants   To make the experiment a valid test of the hypothesis, the researchers needed to add a final step to the design: properly assigning participants to receive a particular treatment.

The significance of this step becomes clear when we examine various alternative procedures. For example, the experimenters might have assigned just males to the group with two bystanders, just females to the group with three bystanders, and both males and females to the group with six bystanders. Had they done so, however, any differences they found in helping behavior could not be attributed with any certainty solely to group size, because the differences might just as well be due to the composition of the group. A more reasonable procedure would be to ensure that each group had the same composition in terms of gender; then the researchers would be able to make comparisons across groups with considerably more accuracy.

Participants in each of the experimental groups ought to be comparable, and it is easy enough to create groups that are similar in terms of gender. The problem becomes a bit more tricky, though, when we consider other participant characteristics. How can we ensure that participants in each experimental group will be equally intelligent, extroverted, cooperative, and so forth, when the list of characteristics—any one of which could be important—is potentially endless?

The solution is a simple but elegant procedure called **random assignment to condition**: Participants are assigned to different experimental groups or "conditions" on the basis of chance and chance alone. The experimenter might, for instance, put the names of all potential participants into a hat and draw names to make assignments to specific groups. The advantage of this technique is that participant characteristics have an equal chance of being distributed across the various groups. By using random assignment, chances are that each of the groups will have approximately the same proportion of intelligent people, cooperative people, extroverted people, males and females, and so on.

The following set of key elements is important to keep in mind as you consider whether a research study is truly an experiment:

- An independent variable, the variable that is manipulated by the experimenter
- A dependent variable, the variable that is measured by the experimenter and expected to change as a result of the manipulation of the independent variable
- A procedure that randomly assigns participants to different experimental groups or "conditions" of the independent variable
- A hypothesis that predicts what effect the independent variable will have on the dependent variable.

Only if each of these elements is present can a research study be considered a true experiment in which cause-and-effect relationships can be determined. (For a summary of the different types of research we've discussed, see Table 1-3.)

Were Latané and Darley Right?   By now, you must be wondering whether Latané and Darley were right when they hypothesized that increasing the number of bystanders in an emergency situation would lower the degree of helping behaviour.

According to the results of the experiment they carried out, their hypothesis was right on target. To test the hypothesis, they used a laboratory setting in which participants were told that the purpose of the experiment was to hold a discussion about personal problems associated with college. The discussion was to be held over an intercom, supposedly to avoid the potential embarrassment of face-to-face contact. Chatting about personal problems was not, of course, the true purpose of the experiment, but participants were told that as a way of keeping their expectations about the experiment from biasing their behaviour. (Consider how they would have been affected if they had been told that their helping behaviour in emergencies was being tested. The experimenters could never have gotten an accurate assessment of what the participants would actually do in an emergency. By definition, emergencies are rarely announced in advance.)

The sizes of the discussion groups were two, three, and six people, which constituted the manipulation of the independent variable of group size. Participants were randomly assigned to these groups upon their arrival at the laboratory.

As the participants in each group were holding their discussion, they suddenly heard through the intercom one of the other participants (in reality a trained *confederate,* or employee, of the experimenters) having what sounded like an epileptic seizure and calling for help.

The participants' behaviour was now what counted. The dependent variable was the time that elapsed from the start of the "seizure" to the time a participant began trying to help the "victim." If six minutes went by without a participant's offering help, the experiment was ended.

As predicted by the hypothesis, the size of the group had a significant effect on whether a participant provided help (Latané & Darley, 1970). In the 2-person group (in which participants thought they were alone with the victim), the average elapsed time was 52 seconds; in the 3-person group (the participant, the victim, and one other person), the average elapsed time was 93 seconds; and in the 6-person group

Table 1-3 Research Strategies

	Correlational Research	Experimental Research
General Process	Researcher observes a previously existing situation but does not make a change in the situation	Researcher manipulates a situation in order to observe the outcome of the manipulation
Intended Result	Identifies associations between factors	Learns how changes in one variable cause changes in another variable
Type	Archival research (examines records to confirm hypothesis) Naturalistic observation (observation of naturally occurring behaviour, without making a change in the situation) Case study (intensive investigation of an individual or small group)	Experiment (investigator produces a change in one variable to observe the effects of that change on other variables)

Pathways Through Psychology

Wendy Josephson

Associate Professor of Psychology
University of Winnipeg

Education: B.A., M.A., Ph.D. University of Manitoba

Home: Winnipeg, Manitoba

Wendy Josephson

As an undergraduate student in psychology, I took my first course in social psychology from Bob Altemeyer, a wonderful classroom teacher and an inspiring researcher in the area of authoritarianism. I was captivated by social psychology from the very first lecture. Of all the disciplines and sub-disciplines I had encountered, I thought social psychology asked the best questions, and had very interesting answers. I still think that.

As a professor at a small undergraduate university, my work includes teaching courses in social and organizational psychology, research in the areas of violence and aggression, and service to the university and the community. Service to the university includes working on department or university committees and service to the community involves making my research useful to people outside the university world. For example, I have given talks to various educational, community, and industry groups including the Canadian Cable Television Association about the effects of television violence on children. I served as one of the academic advisers to Mediascope and the Children's Action Network. The project was to create a guide to help producers of children's educational television comply with U.S. federal requirements.

There are three accomplishments that I consider most important in my research: The first is a field experiment that I conducted on the effects of television violence on children's play behaviour, which was published in the *Journal of Personality and Social Psychology* in 1987. It demonstrated in a real-life setting that boys' aggressiveness toward each other could be significantly affected by having watched a violent television program, especially if there were other cues in their play setting that were associated with the TV violence.

The second is the report that I wrote for the Department of Canadian Heritage in 1995. It reviewed the effects of television violence on children of different ages, and made suggestions for ways in which parents and the television industry could enhance the positive effects of television and reduce its negative effects.

The third is a study I'm doing now with my colleague Jocelyn Proulx, at the Prairie-based research network called RESOLVE (Research and Education for Solutions to Violence and Abuse). The Social Sciences and Humanities Research Council of Canada (SSHRC) has funded a project in which we provided activities from the Healthy Relationships dating-violence-prevention curriculum to grade seven, eight, and nine students in six Winnipeg schools over a three year period. We are currently evaluating the effects that the program had on students' knowledge, attitudes, and behaviour. This project is important because understanding how to prevent violence early in close relationships could have tremendous impact on individual and family happiness. It was also an opportunity to demonstrate that a lot could be accomplished in a collaboration among academic researchers, school divisions, government (Manitoba Culture, Heritage, and Citizenship) and community organizations (the Halifax group, Men for Change, which developed the Healthy Relationships program).

As a psychologist, I love to do research that answers interesting questions about human behaviour. But the work that is really important to me has to do more than just answer questions. I want the knowledge that is gained from my research to make a difference in people's lives.

Source: Wendy Josephson, Ph.D. University of Winnipeg. wendy.josephson@uwinnipeg.ca

What is RESOLVE and why is the study that Dr. Josephson is doing here important?

(the participant, the victim, and four others), the average time was 166 seconds. Considering a simple yes/no measure of whether help was given confirms the elapsed-time pattern. Eighty-five percent of the participants in the 2-person-group condition helped, 62 percent in the 3-person-group condition helped, and only 31 percent in the 6-person-group condition helped.

Because these results are so straightforward, it seems clear that the original hypothesis was confirmed. However, Latané and Darley could not be sure that the results were truly meaningful until they determined whether the results represented a **significant outcome**. Through various statistical analyses, researchers can determine whether a numeric difference is meaningful or trivial. Only when differences between groups are large enough that statistical tests show them to be significant is it possible for researchers

significant outcome: Meaningful results that make it possible for researchers to feel confident that they have confirmed their hypotheses.

to confirm a hypothesis (Estes, 1997; Cwikel, Behar, & Rabson-Hare, 2000). For further information on statistics in psychology, visit the "Statistics Primer" at the Online Learning Centre for this text (http://www.mcgrawhill.ca/college/feldman).

Moving Beyond the Study   The Latané and Darley study contains all the elements of an experiment: an independent variable, a dependent variable, random assignment to conditions, and multiple experimental groups. Consequently, we can say with some confidence that group size *caused* changes in the degree of helping behaviour.

Of course, one experiment alone does not forever resolve the question of bystander intervention in emergencies. Psychologists require that findings be **replicated**, or repeated, sometimes using other procedures, in other settings, with other groups of participants, before full confidence can be placed in the validity of any single experiment. A procedure called *meta-analysis* permits psychologists to combine the results of many separate studies into one overall conclusion (Hunt, 1999).

In addition to replicating experimental results, psychologists need to test the limitations of their theories and hypotheses in order to determine under which specific circumstances they do and do not apply. It seems unlikely, for instance, that increasing the number of bystanders *always* results in less helping. Therefore it is critical to understand the conditions in which exceptions to this general rule occur. For example, we might speculate that in cases in which onlookers believe that a victim's difficulties could later affect them in some way, they will be more willing to help (Aronson, 1988). Testing this hypothesis (for which, in fact, there is some support) requires additional experimentation.

Like any science, then, psychology increases our understanding in small, incremental steps, with each step building upon previous work. The work is carried out on many fronts and involves many people—such as psychologist Wendy Josephson, who is doing research in the area of violence in children and violence prevention in youth (see the *Pathways Through Psychology* box on page 30).

replication: The repetition of research, sometimes using other procedures, settings, and other groups of participants, in order to increase confidence in prior findings.

Evaluate

1. An explanation about a phenomenon of interest is known as a _____.
2. An experimenter is interested in studying the relationship between hunger and aggression. He defines aggression as the number of times a participant will hit a punching bag. What is the process of defining this variable called?
3. Match the following forms of research to their definition:

   1. Archival research
   2. Naturalistic observation
   3. Survey research
   4. Case study

   a. Directly asking a sample of people questions about their behaviour
   b. Examining existing records to test a hypothesis
   c. Looking at behaviour in its true setting without intervening in the setting
   d. In-depth investigation of a person or small group

4. Match each of the following research methods with a problem basic to it:

   1. Archival research
   2. Naturalistic observation
   3. Survey research
   4. Case study

   a. Might not be able to generalize to the population at large.
   b. People's behaviour could change if they know they are being watched.
   c. The data might not exist or might be unusable.
   d. People might lie in order to present a good image.

5. A psychologist wants to study the effect of attractiveness on willingness to help a person with a math problem. Attractiveness would be the _____ variable, while amount of helping would be the _____ variable.

Rethink

1. Starting with the theory that diffusion of responsibility causes responsibility for helping to be shared among bystanders, Latané and Darley derived the hypothesis that the more people who witness an emergency situation, the less likely it is that help will be given to a victim. How many other hypotheses can you think of based on the same theory of diffusion of responsibility?

2. Can you describe how a researcher might use naturalistic observation, case study methods, and survey research to investigate gender differences in aggressive behaviour at the workplace? First state a hypothesis, then describe your research approaches. What positive and negative features does each method have?

Answers to Evaluate Questions

1. theory 2. Operationalization 3. 1. b; 2. c; 3. a 4. d; 4. 1. c; 2. b; 3. d; 4. a 5. independent; dependent

 **PsychLink**

Ethics in research
www.mcgrawhill.ca/college/feldman

informed consent: A document signed by participants affirming that they have been told the basic outlines of a research study and are aware of what their participation will involve.

Research Challenges: Exploring the Process

It is probably apparent by now that there are few simple formulas psychologists can follow as they carry out research. They must make choices about the type of study to conduct, the measures to take, and the most effective way to analyze the results. Even after they make these essential decisions, they must still consider several critical issues. We turn first to the most fundamental of these issues: ethics.

The Ethics of Research

Put yourself in the place of one of the participants in the Latané and Darley experiment. How would you feel when you learned that the person you thought was having a seizure was, in reality, a paid accomplice of the experimenter?

Although you might at first experience relief that there had been no real emergency, you might also feel some resentment that you had been deceived by the experimenter. And you might also experience concern that you had been placed in an unusual situation—one that might have dealt a blow to your self-esteem, depending on how you had behaved.

Most psychologists argue that the use of deception is sometimes necessary to prevent participants from being influenced by what they think the study's true purpose is. (If you knew that Latané and Darley were actually studying your helping behaviour, wouldn't you automatically have been tempted to intervene in the emergency?) To avoid such outcomes, researchers must occasionally use deception.

Nonetheless, because research has the potential to violate the rights of participants, psychologists are expected to adhere to a strict set of ethical guidelines aimed at protecting participants (Canadian Psychological Association, 1991). These guidelines are based on the following four principles:

- *Respect for the dignity of persons*: value for the intrinsic worth of the individual.
- *Responsible caring*: careful consideration that outcomes will not cause harm.
- *Integrity in relationships*: doing what is morally good for the profession.
- *Responsibility to society*: promoting the greatest good for society.

In both the United States (APA, 1992) and Canada (CPA, 1991) ethical guidelines do allow the use of deception. All experiments involving deception (in fact all experiments using human subjects) must be reviewed by the responsible agencies. In Canada, this process is carried out by the Ethics Review Board of the institution to which the researcher belongs. Guidelines for these boards come from the Social Sciences and Humanities Research Council of Canada, which serves as the national funding agency (Rosnow et al., 1993; Rosenthal, 1994; Kimmel, 1996; Dunbar, 1998; Stark, 1998).

One of the key ethical principles followed by psychologists is **informed consent**. Before participating in an experiment, participants must sign a document affirming that they have been told the basic outlines of the study and are aware of what their participation will involve, what risks the experiment may hold, and the fact that their participation is purely voluntary and may be terminated at any time. Furthermore, following participation in a study, participants must be given a *debriefing* in which they receive an explanation for the study and the procedures involved. The only time informed consent and a debriefing can be eliminated is in experiments in which the risks are minimal, as in a purely observational study on a street corner or in another public location (Koocher & Keith-Spiegel, 1998; Chastain & Landrum, 1999).

Chapter Activity 1-1
Thinking Critically About Ethics

Following are the American Psychological Association principles for the ethical treatment of subjects (APA, 1992). Compare these with the principles established by the Canadian Psychological Association. Discuss how both contribute to the well-being of subjects in experimental situations.

- Protection of participants from physical and mental harm
- The right of participants to privacy regarding their behaviour
- The assurance that participation in research is completely voluntary
- The necessity of informing participants about the nature of the procedures prior to their participation in the experiment

EXPLORING DIVERSITY

Choosing Participants Who Represent the Scope of Human Behaviour

What are some advantages and drawbacks of using college students as subjects?

When Latané and Darley, both college professors, decided who should be used as participants in their experiment, they turned to the people who were most readily accessible to them: college students. In fact, college students are used so frequently in experiments that psychology has been called—somewhat contemptuously—the "science of the behaviour of the college sophomore" (Rubenstein, 1982).

The use of college students as participants has both advantages and drawbacks. The big benefit is their availability. Because most research occurs in university settings, college students are readily available. Typically, they participate for either extra course credit or a relatively small monetary payment, making the cost to the researcher minimal.

The problem with relying on college students for participants is that they might not adequately represent the general population. College students tend to be younger and better educated than a significant percentage of the rest of the population of the United States. Moreover, their attitudes are likely to be less well formed, and they are apt to be more susceptible than older adults to social pressures from authority figures and peers (Sears, 1986). These concerns apply to Canada as well, where many psychology departments in universities use introductory psychology students as subjects.

When a science that purports to explain human behaviour in general disregards a significant proportion of the population in drawing conclusions, something is amiss. Consequently, psychological researchers have become increasingly sensitive to the importance of using participants who are fully representative of the general population (Rogler, 1999).

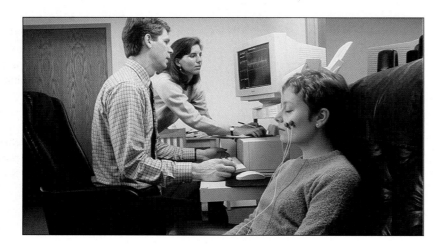

While readily available and widely used as research subjects, college students may not represent the population at large.

Researchers are increasingly sensitive to the importance of using participants in experiments who represent the general population.
Why do you think this is important?

Should Animals Be Used in Research?

Like those who work with humans, researchers who use animals in experiments have their own set of exacting guidelines to ensure that the animals do not suffer. Specifically, researchers must make every effort to minimize discomfort, illness, and pain, and procedures subjecting animals to distress may be used only when an alternative procedure is unavailable and when the research is justified by its prospective value. Moreover, there are federal regulations specifying how animals are to be housed, fed, and maintained. In Canada, animal welfare is governed under the Criminal Code. There are also two provincial acts that are specific to laboratory animals. However, the primary regulatory body for lab animals is the Canadian Council on Animal Care (CCAC), which was founded in 1968. Most of the universities and private institutions where animals are used hold a Certificate of Good Animal Practice from the CCAC. Those that did not would find it very difficult to obtain funding for research. Not only must researchers strive to avoid physical discomfort in the animals, they are also required to promote the *psychological* well-being of some species of animals—such as primates—that are used in research (Novak & Petto, 1991; APA, 1993; CPA, 1996).

Why should animals be used for research in the first place? Is it really possible to learn about human behaviour from the results of research employing rats, gerbils, and pigeons? The answer is that psychological research that does employ animals has

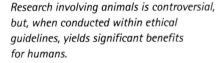

Research involving animals is controversial, but, when conducted within ethical guidelines, yields significant benefits for humans.

a different focus and is designed to answer different questions than research that uses humans. For example, the shorter life span of animals (rats live an average of two years) allows researchers to learn about the effects of aging in a much more rapid time frame than if they studied aging using human participants. Finally, some studies require large numbers of participants who share similar backgrounds or who have been exposed to particular environments—conditions that could not practically be met with human beings (Gallagher & Rapp, 1997; Mukerjee, 1997).

Research using animals has provided psychologists with information that has profoundly benefited humans. For instance, animal research furnished the keys to detecting eye disorders in children early enough to prevent permanent damage, communicating more effectively with severely retarded children, and reducing chronic pain in people, to name just a few results (APA, 1988; Botting & Morrison, 1997).

Despite the value of research that uses animals as participants, their use in psychological research is highly controversial. For example, some critics believe that animals have rights no less significant than those of humans, and that because animals are unable to consent to participation in studies, their use is unethical. Others say it is impossible to generalize from findings on nonhuman species to humans.

Because the issues involve complex moral and philosophical concerns, they are not easily resolved. As a consequence, review panels, which must approve all research before it is carried out, are particularly careful to ensure that research involving animals is conducted ethically (Plous, 1996a, 1996b; Barnard & Kaufman, 1997).

Threats to Experiments: Experimenter and Participant Expectations

Even the best-laid experimental plans are susceptible to **experimental bias**—factors that distort how the independent variable affects the dependent variable in an experiment. One of the most common forms of experimental bias is *experimenter expectations:* An experimenter unintentionally transmits cues to participants about the way they are expected to behave in a given experimental condition. The danger is that these expectations will bring about an "appropriate" behaviour—one that might not have otherwise occurred (Blanck, 1993; Rosnow & Rosenthal, 1994, 1997).

A related problem is *participant expectations* about appropriate behaviour. If you have ever been a participant in an experiment, you know that you quickly develop guesses about what is expected of you. In fact, it is typical for people to develop their own hypotheses about what the experimenter hopes to learn from the study. If participants form their own hypotheses, it might no longer be the experimental manipulation, but rather the participant's expectations, producing an effect.

To guard against participant expectations biasing the results of an experiment, the experimenter may try to disguise the true purpose of the experiment. Participants who do not know that helping behaviour is being studied, for example, are more apt to act in a "natural" way than they would if they knew.

In some experiments it is impossible to hide the actual purpose of the research. In cases such as these, other techniques are available. For example, suppose you were interested in testing the ability of a new drug to alleviate the symptoms of severe depression. If you simply gave the drug to half your participants and not to the other half, participants given the drug might report feeling less depressed merely because they knew they were getting a drug. Similarly, the participants who got nothing might report feeling no better because they knew that they were in a no-treatment control group.

To solve this problem, psychologists typically use a procedure in which all participants receive a treatment, but those in the control group receive only a **placebo**, a false treatment, such as a pill, "drug," or other substance, that has no significant chemical properties or active ingredient. Because members of both groups are kept in the dark as to whether they are getting a real or a false treatment, any differences that are found can be attributed to the quality of the drug and not to the possible psychological effects of being administered a pill or other substance (Kirsch, 1999; Enserink, 1999, 2000a).

 **PsychLink**

Ethical research using animals
www.mcgrawhill.ca/college/feldman

experimental bias: Factors that distort how the independent variable affects the dependent variable in an experiment.

placebo: A false treatment, such as a pill, "drug," or other substance, that has no significant chemical properties or active ingredient.

Psychology at Work

Alexandra Kitty

Journalist and Professor, Mohawk College

Education: B.A. in psychology, McMaster University; M.A. in journalism, University of Western Ontario

Home: Hamilton, Ontario

Alexandra Kitty

"A degree in psychology? What are you going to do with that?" Alexandra Kitty certainly heard this question a number of times as she pursued her undergraduate degree in psychology at McMaster University. For Kitty, though, there was no hesitation in her answer: "I want to be a psychologist." Things, however, do not always turn out as expected.

During her final semester as an undergraduate, Kitty wrote a letter to the CBS newsmagazine, *60 Minutes*, praising them for a story they had aired, adding some information to the letter she thought they already knew.

"It turned out they didn't know," Kitty says. "They called me one afternoon, and then asked me to conduct research for them on that very topic. I did and it was then that I decided that if *60 Minutes* thought that a Mac psych student had the right stuff to be in journalism, then who was I to argue?"

While employed as a reporter after graduation, Kitty also worked towards her master's degree in journalism from the University of Western Ontario. "I was the first student they ever admitted who had a degree in psychology," she remembers. "In fact, I was told no psych grad had ever applied."

Over the years, Kitty has found that her training in psychology has had a direct impact on her skills as a journalist: "Journalism and psychology go hand in hand, and I would strongly recommend that all journalists receive solid training in psychology to become stronger, more skeptical news gatherers, and better observers of the human condition."

"I learned that there are skills and advantages in life that only a psych degree can give you," says Kitty. "I learned how to research thoroughly and how to think critically. Many journalists have degrees in either English or political science, but these individuals will have a harder time understanding the scientific method and how to separate a useful source from a charlatan.

"McMaster University taught me to dig far deeper and look at all information through a critical eye: How reliable is the source of information? How credible is the expert or eyewitness? How reliable and valid is that study? Does that piece of data have any utility or is my source simply appealing to an authority figure?

"My psychology degree helped me learn how to thoroughly research and analyze data, two qualities that many journalists have difficulty with."

Kitty has since gone on to become a professor of language studies at Mohawk College, teaching courses in communication, research, reporting, and public speaking.

But there is still one more safeguard that a careful researcher must apply in an experiment such as this. To overcome the possibility that experimenter expectations will affect the participant, the person who administers the drug shouldn't know whether it is actually the true drug or the placebo. By keeping both the participant and the experimenter who interacts with the participant "blind" as to the nature of the drug that is being administered, researchers can more accurately assess the effects of the drug. This method is known as the *double-blind procedure*.

BECOMING AN INFORMED CONSUMER OF PSYCHOLOGY

How can we know when and if research is reliable?

Thinking Critically About Research

If you were about to purchase an automobile, it is unlikely that you would stop at the nearest car dealership and drive off with the first car a salesperson recommended. Instead, you would probably mull over the purchase, read about automobiles, consider the alternatives, talk to others about their experiences, and ultimately put in a fair amount of thought before you made such a major purchase.

In contrast, many of us are considerably less conscientious when we expend our intellectual, rather than financial, assets. People often jump to conclusions on the basis of incomplete and inaccurate information, and only rarely do they take the time to critically evaluate the research and data to which they are exposed.

 **PsychLink**

Links to ongoing research
www.mcgrawhill.ca/college/feldman

Because the field of psychology is based on an accumulated body of research, it is crucial for psychologists to scrutinize thoroughly the methods, results, and claims of researchers. Yet it is not just psychologists who need to know how to evaluate research critically; all of us are constantly exposed to the claims of others. Knowing how to approach research and data can be helpful in areas far beyond the realm of psychology.

Several basic questions can help us sort through what is valid and what is not. Among the most important questions to ask are the following:

- *What was the purpose of the research?* Research studies should evolve from a clearly specified theory. Furthermore, we must take into account the specific hypothesis that is being tested. Unless we know what hypothesis is being examined, it is not possible to judge how successful a study has been.
- *How well was the study conducted?* Consider who the participants were, how many were involved, what methods were employed, and what problems in collecting the data the researcher encountered. There are important differences, for example, between a case study that reports the anecdotes of a handful of respondents and a survey that collects data from several thousand people.
- *Are the results presented fairly?* It is necessary to assess statements based on the actual data they reflect and their logic. For instance, when the manufacturer of car X boasts that "no other car a has a better safety record than car X," this does not mean that car X is safer than every other car. It just means that no other car has been proved safer, though many other cars could be just as safe as car X.

These three basic questions can help you assess the validity of research findings you come across—both within and outside the field of psychology. The more you know how to evaluate research in general, the better you will be able to assess what the field of psychology has to offer.

Evaluate

1. Ethical research begins with the concept of informed consent. Before signing up to participate in an experiment, participants should be informed of
   a. The procedure of the study, stated generally.
   b. The risks that may be involved.
   c. Their right to withdraw at any time.
   d. All of the above
2. List three benefits of using animals in psychological research.
3. Deception is one means experimenters can use to try to eliminate participants' expectations. True or false?
4. A procedure in which neither participants nor experimenter knows whether participants are or are not receiving an actual treatment is known as the _____ procedure.
5. According to a report, a study has shown that men differ from women in their preference for ice cream flavours. This study was based on a sample of 2 men and 3 women. What might be wrong with this study?

Rethink

1. A pollster studies people's attitudes toward welfare programs by circulating a questionnaire via the Internet. Is this study likely to accurately reflect the views of the general population? Why or why not?
2. A researcher strongly believes that college professors tend to show female students less attention and respect in the classroom than they show male students. She sets up an experimental study involving observation of classrooms in different conditions. In explaining the study to the professors and students who will participate, what steps should the researcher take to eliminate experimental bias based on both experimenter expectations and participant expectations?

Answers to Evaluate Questions

1. d 2. (1) We can study some phenomena in animals more easily than we can in people, because with animal subjects we have greater control over environmental and genetic factors. (2) Large numbers of similar participants can be easily obtained. (3) We can look at generational effects much more easily in animals, because of their shorter life span, than we can with people. 3. True 4. double-blind 5. There are far too few participants. Without a larger sample, no valid conclusions can be drawn about ice cream preferences based on gender.

Looking Back

What is the science of psychology?

- Psychology is the scientific study of behaviour and mental processes, encompassing not just what people do, but their biological activities, feelings, perceptions, memory, reasoning, and thoughts. (p. 4)

What are the major subfields in the field of psychology?

- Biopsychologists focus on the biological basis of behaviour, whereas experimental psychologists study the processes of sensing, perceiving, learning, and thinking about the world. (p. 6)
- Cognitive psychology is the study of higher mental processes, including memory, knowing, thinking, reasoning, problem solving, judging, decision making, and language. (p. 7)
- Developmental psychologists study how people grow and change throughout the life span. (p. 7)
- Personality psychologists consider the consistency and change in an individual's behaviour as he or she moves through different situations, as well as the individual differences that distinguish one person's behaviour from another's when each is placed in the same situation. (p. 7)
- Health psychologists study psychological factors that affect physical disease; clinical psychologists consider the study, diagnosis, and treatment of psychological disorders. (p. 7)
- Social psychology is the study of how people's thoughts, feelings, and actions are affected by others. (p. 7)
- Cross-cultural psychologists examine the similarities and differences in psychological functioning across various cultures. The psychology of women concentrates on psychological factors relating to women's behaviour and development. (p. 7)

Where do psychologists work?

- Psychologists are employed in a variety of settings. Although the primary sites of employment are universities and colleges, many psychologists are found in hospitals, clinics, community mental health centres, and counselling centres. (p. 8)

What are the differences in psychology in Canada and the United States?

- Although psychology in Canada and the United States shares the same subfields and perspectives, the primary difference is one of scale. There is also a much stronger emphasis on applied psychology in the United States. Differences in social and cultural experiences have led to some differences in research interests. For example, there is a strong emphasis in Canada on research in multiculturalism and bilingualism. (p. 9).

What are the historical roots of the field of psychology?

- The foundations of psychology were established by Wilhelm Wundt in Germany in 1879. (p. 11)
- Early perspectives that guided the work of psychologists were structuralism, functionalism, and gestalt theory. (p. 11)

What are the major approaches used by contemporary psychologists?

- The biological approach focuses on the biological functioning of people and animals, considering the most basic components of behaviour. (p. 13)
- The psychodynamic perspective suggests that there are powerful, unconscious inner forces and conflicts that people have little or no awareness of and that are primary determinants of behaviour. (p. 14)
- Cognitive approaches to behaviour consider how people know, understand, and think about the world. (p. 14)
- The behavioural perspective deemphasizes internal processes and concentrates instead on observable behaviour, suggesting that an understanding and control of a person's environment is sufficient to fully explain and modify behaviour. (p. 14)
- The humanistic perspective emphasizes that people are uniquely inclined toward psychological growth and higher levels of functioning and that they will strive to reach their full potential. (p. 15)

What are psychology's key issues and controversies?

- Among the key issues are the questions of nature versus nurture, conscious versus unconscious determinants of behaviour, observable behaviour versus internal mental processes, free will versus determinism, and individual differences versus universal principles. (p. 17)

What is the future of psychology likely to hold?

- Psychology will become increasingly specialized, will pay increasing attention to prevention instead of just treatment, will become increasingly concerned with the public interest, and will take the growing diversity of the nation's population into account more fully. (p. 19)

What is the scientific method, and how do psychologists use theory and research to answer questions of interest?

- The scientific method is an approach psychologists use to understand the unknown. It consists of three steps: identifying questions of interest, formulating an explanation, and carrying out research that is designed to support the explanation. (p. 21)
- Research in psychology is guided by theories (broad explanations and predictions of phenomena of interest) and hypotheses (derivations of theories that are predictions stated in a way that allows them to be tested). (p. 22)

What are the different research methods employed by psychologists?

- Archival research uses existing records, such as old newspapers or other documents, to test a hypothesis. In naturalistic observation, the investigator acts mainly as an observer, making no change in a naturally occurring situation. In survey research, people are asked a series of questions about their behaviour, thoughts, or attitudes. The case study is an in-depth interview and examination of one person. (p. 23)
- These methods rely on correlational techniques, which describe associations between various variables but cannot determine cause-and-effect relationships. (p. 25)

How do psychologists establish cause-and-effect relationships in research studies?

- In a formal experiment, the relationship between variables is investigated by deliberately producing a change—called the experimental manipulation—in one of them and observing changes in the other. (p. 26)
- For a hypothesis to be tested, it must be operationalized: A researcher must translate the abstract concepts of the hypothesis into the actual procedures used in the study. (p. 27)
- In an experiment, at least two groups must be compared with each other to assess cause-and-effect relationships. The group receiving the treatment (the special procedure devised by the experimenter) is the experimental group; the second group (which receives no treatment) is the control group. There also may be multiple experimental groups; each of which is subjected to a different procedure and then compared with the others. (p. 27)
- The variable that experimenters manipulate is the independent variable. The variable that they measure and expect to change as a result of manipulation of the independent variable is called the dependent variable. (p. 27)
- In a formal experiment, participants must be assigned to treatment conditions randomly so that participant characteristics are evenly distributed across the different conditions. (p. 28)

What major issues underlie the process of conducting research?

- One of the key ethical principles followed by psychologists is that of informed consent. Participants must be informed, prior to participation, about the basic outline of the experiment and the risks and potential benefits of their participation. (p. 32)
- Although the use of college students as participants has the advantage of easy availability, there are drawbacks too. For instance, students do not necessarily represent the population as a whole. The use of animals as participants also has costs in terms of generalizability, although the benefits of using animals in research have been profound. (p. 33)
- Experiments are subject to a number of threats, or biases. Experimenter expectations can produce bias when an experimenter unintentionally transmits cues to participants about her or his expectations regarding their behaviour in a given experimental condition. Participant expectations can also bias an experiment. To help eliminate bias, researchers use placebos and double-blind procedures. (p. 35)

Key Terms and Concepts

psychology (p. 4)
structuralism (p. 11)
introspection (p. 12)
functionalism (p. 12)
gestalt psychology (p. 12)
biological perspective (p. 13)
psychodynamic perspective (p. 14)
cognitive perspective (p. 14)
behavioural perspective (p. 14)
humanistic perspective (p. 15)
scientific method (p. 21)
theories (p. 21)
hypothesis (p. 22)
operationalization (p. 23)
archival research (p. 23)
naturalistic observation (p. 23)
survey research (p. 24)

case study (p. 24)
variables (p. 25)
correlational research (p. 25)
experiment (p. 26)
experimental manipulation (p. 26)
treatment (p. 27)
experimental group (p. 27)
control group (p. 27)
independent variable (p. 27)
dependent variable (p. 27)
random assignment to condition (p. 28)
significant outcome (p. 30)
replication (p. 31)
informed consent (p. 32)
experimental bias (p. 35)
placebo (p. 35)

Psychology on the Web

1. Practise using several search strategies to find out more information on the Internet about one of the key issues in psychology (e.g., free will versus determinism, nature versus nurture, or conscious versus unconscious determinants of behaviour):
   a. Go to a "general purpose" search engine (such as Alta Vista at www.altavista.com).
   b. Go to a more specialized search engine (such as Yahoo's Psychology section, under the "Social Science" heading, at www.yahoo.com).
   c. Go to one of the more specialized psychology Web sites listed in PsychLinks on the *Essentials of Understanding Psychology* Web site (www.mcgrawhill.ca/college/feldman).

   Summarize and then compare the kind of information you have found through each strategy. List any useful Web sites you encounter in your searches.
2. Find a Web site that focuses on an important social issue (e.g., urban violence, gender differences in hiring or promotion, poverty) and locate descriptions of a research study about the issue. Evaluate the study by identifying the hypotheses that were tested, the methods used to test them, and the validity of the results reported.

For extra help in mastering the material in this chapter, see the integrator, practice quizzes, and other resources on the Online Learning Centre at

www.mcgrawhill.ca/college/feldman

Epilogue

The field of psychology, as we have seen, is broad and diverse. It encompasses many subfields and specialties practised in a variety of settings, with new subfields arising and coming to prominence all the time. Furthermore, we have seen that even within the various subfields of the field, it is possible to adopt several different approaches, including the biological, psychodynamic, cognitive, behavioural, and humanistic perspectives.

We have also seen that, for all its diversity, psychology is united in its use of the scientific method and its reliance on creating productive theories and crafting testable hypotheses. We've considered the basic methods psychologists use to conduct research studies, and we've explored some of the major challenges that psychologists have to deal with when conducting research, including ethical considerations, potential bias, and the question of significance.

Before we turn to a discussion of the biology that underlies behaviour, return for a moment to the opening prologue of this chapter, which discusses the terrorist attacks on New York and the Pentagon. In light of what you've learned about the branches, perspectives, and methods of psychology, consider the following questions:

1. How might a psychodynamic perspective explain why the terrorists decided to carry out suicide attacks? How would this explanation differ from the approach taken by a psychologist using the behavioural perspective?
2. Assume that two developmental psychologists are considering the effects of a child's observation of the attack on the World Trade Center towers on the child's later development. How would the questions and studies of interest to the psychologists differ if one employed the biological perspective and the other employed the behavioural perspective?
3. How might social psychologists explore the effects of watching news reports of the terrorist incident on viewers' later aggression?
4. How might researchers conduct an experiment to test a drug that they believe reduces aggression? What would the independent variable and dependent variable be in such an experiment?
5. How might clinical psychologists deal with increasing levels of depression and anxiety in the general population since September the 11th, 2001?

Chapter Two

The Biology Underlying Behaviour

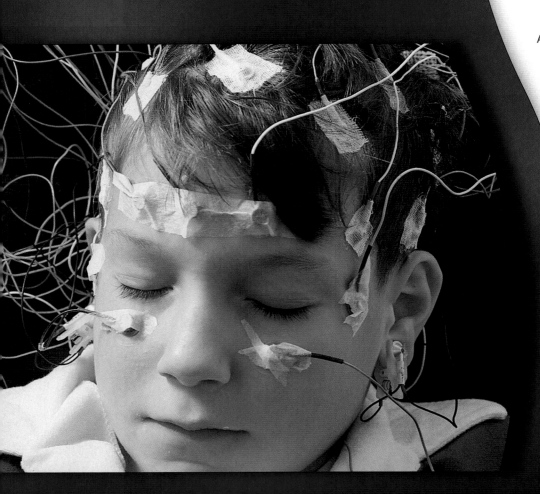

Michael J. Fox was freed of the worst symptoms of Parkinson's following an operation called a thalamotomy.

Prologue

The Fight of His Life

Michael J. Fox simply could not get out of the limousine. He and actress wife Tracy Pollan had just pulled up to the Beverly Hilton for the Golden Globe Awards, and the actor realized he was in serious trouble. Outside, reporters and photographers stood poised to greet the star of ABC's hit sitcom *Spin City*, but Fox, then 37, was in no shape to greet them. Like so many times before, his left arm and leg were shaking uncontrollably. Behind the limo's darkened windows, Pollan began squeezing Fox's hand and massaging his foot. But she could provide only temporary relief. For the tremors to fully subside, the couple would have to wait for his medication to kick in. Fox asked the driver to circle the block once. Then a second time. And a third. "He probably thought I was nuts," says Fox with a faint smile. "But I just couldn't get out of the car and let my arm go, or mumble, or shuffle" (Schneider & Gold, 1998, p. 136).

Looking Ahead

Fox's symptoms were produced by Parkinson's disease, a disorder marked by varying degrees of muscular rigidity and shaking. Parkinson's afflicts 1 in 300 people in Canada and the United States, with some 100 000 cases in Canada at present.

Happily, though, Fox was freed of the worst symptoms of the disease, following a painstaking four-hour operation called a thalamotomy. In this procedure, surgeons bored a hole into Fox's brain and located and destroyed misfiring brain cells.

The ability of surgeons to identify damaged portions of the brain and carry out repairs is little short of miraculous. But the greater miracle is the brain itself. As we shall see in this chapter, the brain, an organ roughly half the size of a loaf of bread, controls our behaviour through every waking and sleeping moment. The brain and the nerves that extend throughout the body constitute the human nervous system. Our movements, thoughts, hopes, aspirations, dreams—our very awareness that we are human—are all intimately related to this system.

Because of the importance of the nervous system in controlling behaviour, and because humans at their most basic level are biological beings, psychologists and researchers from other fields as diverse as computer science, zoology, and medicine have paid special attention to the biological underpinnings of behaviour. These experts are collectively called *neuroscientists* (Beatty, 2000). Much knowledge can be gained when researchers in these diverse fields work together. The Program in Neuroscience at the University of Toronto, as an example, includes researchers from 13 departments in four faculties (www.utoronto.ca/neurosci).

Psychologists who specialize in considering the ways in which biological structures and functions of the body affect behaviour are known as **biopsychologists (or behavioural neuroscientists)**. These specialists seek to answer questions such as these: What are the bases for voluntary and involuntary functioning of the body? How are messages communicated to and from the brain to other parts of the body? What is the physical structure of the brain, and how does this structure affect behaviour? Can the causes of psychological disorders be traced to biological factors, and how can such disorders be treated?

This chapter addresses such questions, focusing on the biological structures of the body that are of interest to biopsychologists. Initially, we discuss nerve cells, called neurons, which allow messages to travel through the brain and body; we learn that through their growing knowledge of neurons and the nervous system, psychologists are increasing their understanding of human behaviour and are uncovering important clues in their efforts to cure certain kinds of diseases. Then we turn to the structure and main divisions of the nervous system, explaining how they work to control voluntary and involuntary behaviours. In the process we also examine how the various parts of the nervous system operate together in emergency situations to produce lifesaving responses to danger.

Next, we consider the brain itself, examining its major structures and how these affect behaviour. We see how the brain controls movement, our senses, and our thought processes. We also consider the fascinating notion that the two halves of the brain might have different specialties and strengths. Finally, we examine the chemical messenger system of the body, the endocrine system.

As we discuss these biological processes, it is important to keep in mind the rationale for doing so: Our understanding of human behaviour cannot be complete without knowledge of the fundamentals of the brain and the rest of the nervous system. As we'll see in future chapters, biological factors have an important impact on our sensory experiences, states of consciousness, motivation and emotion, development throughout the life span, and physical and psychological health. Advances in biopsychology have paved the way for the creation of drugs and other treatments for psychological and physical disorders. In short, we cannot understand behaviour—the moods, motivations, goals, and desires that are central to the human condition—without an understanding of our biological makeup.

biopsychologists (or behavioural neuroscientists): Psychologists who specialize in considering the ways in which biological structures and functions of the body affect behaviour.

PsychLink

Description of neuropsychology
www.mcgrawhill.ca/college/feldman

Neurons: The Elements of Behaviour

If you have ever watched the precision with which a well-trained athlete or dancer executes a performance, you may have marvelled at the complexity—and wondrous abilities—of the human body. But even the most everyday tasks, such as picking up a pencil, writing, and speaking, require a sophisticated sequence of events that is itself truly impressive. For instance, the difference between saying the words *dime* and *time* rests primarily on whether the vocal cords are relaxed or tense during a period lasting no more than one one-hundredth of a second. Yet it is a distinction that almost everyone can make with ease.

The nervous system provides the pathways that permit us to carry out such precise activities. To understand how it is able to exert such exacting control over our bodies, we must begin by examining neurons, the most basic parts of the nervous system, and considering how nerve impulses are transmitted throughout the brain and body.

Prepare

Why do psychologists study the brain and nervous system?

What are the basic elements of the nervous system?

How does the nervous system communicate electrical and chemical messages from one part to another?

Organize

Neurons
> The Structure of the Neuron
> Firing the Neuron
> Where Neurons Meet
> Neurotransmitters

The Structure of the Neuron

The ability to play the piano, drive a car, or hit a tennis ball depends, at one level, merely on muscle coordination. But if we consider *how* the muscles involved in such activities are activated, we see that there are more fundamental processes involved. It is necessary for the body to provide messages to the muscles and to coordinate those messages, for the muscles to be able to produce the complex movements that characterize successful physical activity.

Such messages—as well as those that enable us to think, remember, and experience emotion—are passed through specialized cells called neurons. **Neurons**, or nerve cells, are the basic elements of the nervous system and have the ability to transmit messages to and from the brain and spinal cord. Their quantity is staggering—perhaps as many as one *trillion* neurons throughout the body are involved in the control of behaviour. Although there are several types of neurons, they all have a similar basic structure, as illustrated in Figure 2-1. Neurons have a cell body, containing a nucleus. The nucleus incorporates the inherited material that establishes how the cell will function. Neurons are physically held in place by **glial cells**, which provide nourishment and insulate them (Bear, Connors, & Paradiso, 2000).

In contrast to most other cells, however, neurons have a distinctive feature: the ability to communicate with other cells and transmit information, sometimes across relatively long distances. As you can see in Figure 2-1, neurons have clusters of fibres called **dendrites** at one end. These fibres, which look like the twisted branches of a tree, receive messages from other neurons. At the opposite end, neurons have a long, slim, tubelike extension called an **axon**, the part of the neuron that carries messages destined for other neurons. The axon is considerably longer than the rest of the neuron. Although most axons are several millimetres in length, some can be as long as a metre. Axons end in small bulges called **terminal buttons** that send messages to other neurons.

The messages that travel through the neuron are purely electrical in nature. Although there are exceptions, these electrical messages generally move across neurons as if they were travelling on a one-way street. They follow a route that begins with the dendrites, continues into the cell body, and leads ultimately down the tubelike extension, the axon. Dendrites, then, *d*etect messages from other neurons; *a*xons carry signals *a*way from the cell body.

To prevent messages from short-circuiting one another, axons must be insulated in some fashion (just as electrical wires must be insulated). In most axons and some dendrites as well, this is done with a **myelin sheath**, a protective coating of specialized fat and protein cells that wrap themselves around the axon.

The myelin sheath also serves to increase the velocity with which the electrical impulses travel through the axons. Those axons that carry the most important and most

neurons: Nerve cells that transmit messages to and from the brain and spinal cord.

glial cells: Cells that nourish and insulate neurons.

dendrites: A cluster of fibres at one end of a neuron that receive messages from other neurons.

axon: The part of the neuron that carries messages destined for other neurons.

terminal buttons: Small bulges at the end of axons that send messages to other neurons.

myelin sheath: Specialized cells of fat and protein that wrap themselves around the axon, providing a protective coating.

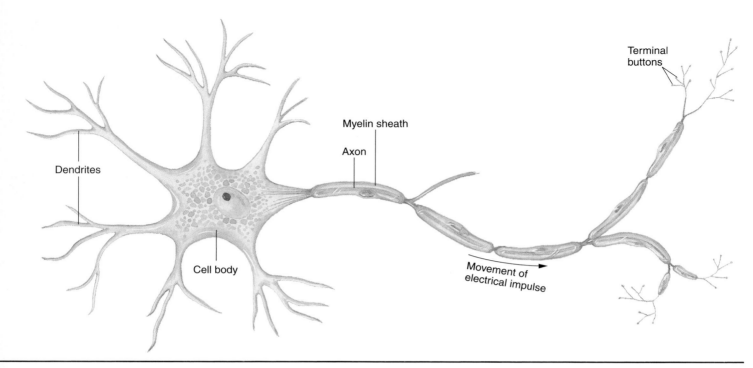

Figure 2-1 The primary components of the specialized cell called the neuron, the basic element of the nervous system (Van de Graaff, 2000). What advantages does the treelike structure of the neuron provide?

After K. Van De Graaff. Copyright © The McGraw-Hill Companies.

all-or-none law: The rule that neurons are either on or off.

resting state: The state in which there is a negative electrical charge of about −70 millivolts within the neuron.

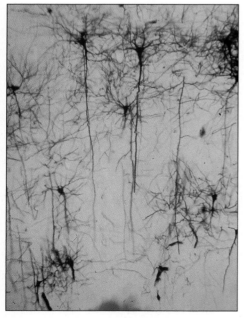

Taken with the aid of an electron microscope, this photograph shows cell bodies, dendrites, and axons in a cluster of neurons.

urgently required information have the greatest concentrations of myelin. If your hand touches a painfully hot stove, for example, the information regarding the pain is passed through axons in the hand and arm that have a relatively thick coating of myelin, speeding the message of pain to the brain. In certain diseases, such as multiple sclerosis, the myelin sheath surrounding the axon deteriorates, exposing parts of the axon that are normally covered. This short-circuits messages between the brain and muscles and results in symptoms such as the inability to walk, vision difficulties, and general muscle impairment.

Firing the Neuron

Like a gun, neurons either fire or don't fire; there is no in-between stage, just as pulling harder on a gun trigger doesn't make the bullet travel faster or move more surely. Similarly, neurons follow an **all-or-none law:** they are either on or off, with nothing in between the on or off state. Once triggered beyond a certain point by messages from the sense receptors or messages from other neurons, a neuron fires.

Before a neuron is triggered—that is, when it is in a **resting state**—it has a negative electrical charge of about −70 millivolts (a millivolt is one one-thousandth of a volt). However, when a message arrives, the cell walls in the neuron allow positively charged ions to rush in from outside the cell, at rates as high as 100 million ions per second. The sudden arrival of these positive ions causes the charge within that part of the cell to change momentarily from negative to positive. When the charge reaches a critical level, the "trigger" is pulled, and an electrical nerve impulse, known as an **action potential,** travels down the axon of the neuron like a flame moving along a fuse toward an explosive. After the passage of the impulse, positive ions are pumped out of the axon, and the neuron returns to its resting state and is prepared to fire again. (See Figures 2-2 and 2-3.)

These complex events can occur at dizzying speeds, although there is great variation among different neurons. The particular speed at which an action potential travels along an axon is determined by the axon's size and the thickness of its myelin

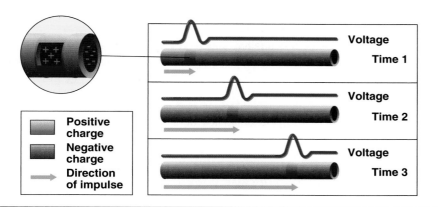

Figure 2-2 Movement of an action potential across an axon. Just prior to Time 1, positively charged ions enter the cell walls, changing the charge within that part of the cell from negative to positive. The action potential is thus triggered, travelling down the axon, as illustrated in the changes occurring from Time 1 to Time 3 (from top to bottom in this drawing). Following the passage of the action potential, positive ions are pumped out of the axon, restoring its charge to negative. The change in voltage illustrated at the top of the axon can be seen in greater detail in Figure 2-3.

sheath. Axons with small diameters carry impulses at about 3 kilometres per hour; longer and thicker ones can average speeds of more than 360 kilometres per hour.

Neurons differ not only in terms of how quickly an impulse moves across the axon, but in their potential rate of firing. Some neurons have the potential to fire as many as a thousand times per second; others have a maximum potential rate that is much lower. The intensity of a stimulus that provokes a neuron determines how much of this potential rate is reached. A strong stimulus, such as a bright light or a loud sound, leads to a higher rate of firing than a less intense stimulus does. It may also cause more neurons to fire. This provides the mechanism by which we can distinguish the tickle of a feather from the weight of someone standing on our toe.

The structure, operation, and functions of the neuron illustrate how fundamental biological aspects of the body underlie several primary psychological processes. Our understanding of the way we sense, perceive, and learn about the world would be greatly restricted without the information about the neuron that biopsychologists and other researchers have acquired.

action potential: An electric nerve impulse that travels through a neuron when it is set off by a "trigger," changing the neuron's charge from negative to positive.

PsychLink

The Myelin Project
www.mcgrawhill.ca/college/feldman

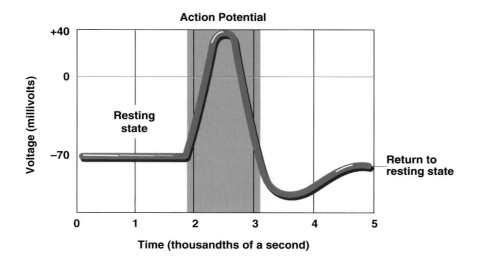

Figure 2-3 Changes in the electrical charge of a neuron during the passage of an action potential. In its normal resting state, a neuron has a negative charge of around −70 millivolts. When an action potential is triggered, however, the cell charge becomes positive, increasing to about +40 millivolts. Following the passage of the action potential, the charge becomes even more negative than it is in its typical state. It is not until the charge returns to its resting state that the neuron will be fully ready to be triggered once again.

Where Neurons Meet: Bridging the Gap

If you've ever looked inside a computer, you've seen that each part is physically connected to another. In contrast, evolution has produced a neural transmission system that at some points has no need for a structural connection between its components. Instead, a chemical connection bridges the gap, known as a synapse, between two neurons (see Figure 2-4). The **synapse** is the space between two neurons where the axon of a sending neuron communicates with the dendrites of a receiving neuron using chemical messages.

When a nerve impulse comes to the end of the axon and reaches a terminal button, the terminal button releases a chemical courier called a neurotransmitter. **Neurotransmitters** are chemicals that carry messages across the synapse to the dendrite (and sometimes the cell body) of a receiver neuron. Like a boat that ferries passengers across a river, these chemical messengers move toward the shorelines of other neurons. The chemical mode of message transmission that occurs between neurons is strikingly different from the means by which communication occurs inside neurons. It is important to remember, then, that although messages travel in electrical form *within* a neuron, they move *between* neurons through a chemical transmission system.

There are several types of neurotransmitters, and not all receiver neurons are capable of making use of the chemical message carried by a particular neurotransmitter. In the same way as a jigsaw puzzle piece can fit in only one specific location in a puzzle, so each kind of neurotransmitter has a distinctive configuration that allows it to fit into a specific type of receptor site on the receiving neuron (see Figure 2-4b). It is only when a neurotransmitter fits precisely into a receptor site that successful chemical communication is possible.

If a neurotransmitter does fit into a site on the receiving neuron, the chemical message it delivers is basically one of two types: excitatory or inhibitory. **Excitatory messages** make it more likely that a receiving neuron will fire and an action potential will travel down its axon. **Inhibitory messages**, in contrast, do just the opposite; they provide chemical information that prevents or decreases the likelihood that the receiving neuron will fire.

Because the dendrites of a neuron receive both excitatory and inhibitory messages simultaneously, the neuron must integrate the messages by using a kind of chemical calculator. If the concentration of excitatory messages is greater than the concentration of inhibitory ones, the neuron fires. On the other hand, if the inhibitory messages outweigh the excitatory ones, nothing happens, and the neuron remains in its resting state (Thomson, 1997; Miles, 2000).

If neurotransmitters remained at the site of the synapse, receptor neurons would be awash in a continual chemical bath, producing constant stimulation of the receptor neurons—and effective communication across the synapse would no longer be possible. To solve this problem, neurotransmitters are either deactivated by enzymes or—more frequently—reabsorbed by the terminal button in an example of chemical recycling called **reuptake**. Like a vacuum cleaner sucking up dust, neurons reabsorb the neurotransmitters that are now clogging the synapse. All this activity occurs at lightning speed, with the process taking just several milliseconds (Helmuth, 2000).

Neurotransmitters: Multitalented Chemical Couriers

Neurotransmitters are a particularly important link between the nervous system and behaviour. Not only are they important for maintaining vital brain and body functions, but a deficiency or an excess of a neurotransmitter can produce severe behaviour disorders. More than a hundred chemicals have been found to act as neurotransmitters, and biopsychologists believe that more may ultimately be identified (Purves et al., 1997; Penney, 2000).

Neurotransmitters vary significantly in terms of how strong their concentration must be to trigger a neuron to fire. Furthermore, the effects of a given neurotransmitter vary, depending on the area of the nervous system in which it is produced. The same

synapse: The space between two neurons where the axon of a sending neuron communicates with the dendrites of a receiving neuron using chemical messages.

PsychLink
All about synapses
www.mcgrawhill.ca/college/feldman

neurotransmitters: Chemicals that carry messages across the synapse to the dendrite (and sometimes the cell body) of a receiver neuron.

excitatory message: A chemical message that makes it more likely that a receiving neuron will fire and an action potential will travel down its axons.

inhibitory message: A chemical message that prevents a receiving neuron from firing.

reuptake: The reabsorption of neurotransmitters by a terminal button.

a.

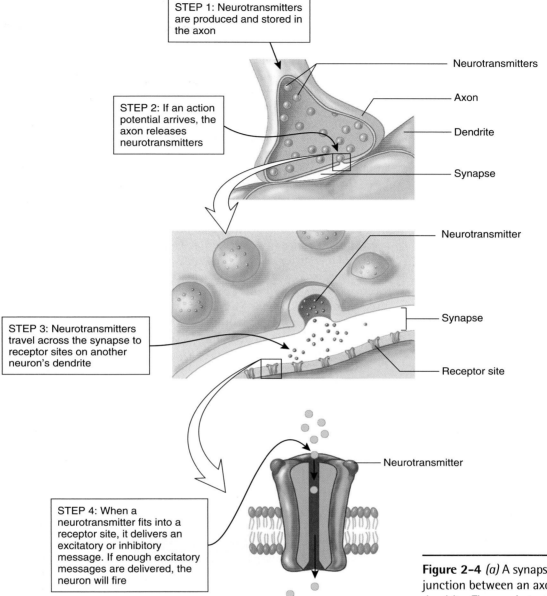

STEP 1: Neurotransmitters are produced and stored in the axon

Neurotransmitters

Axon

STEP 2: If an action potential arrives, the axon releases neurotransmitters

Dendrite

Synapse

Neurotransmitter

STEP 3: Neurotransmitters travel across the synapse to receptor sites on another neuron's dendrite

Synapse

Receptor site

Neurotransmitter

STEP 4: When a neurotransmitter fits into a receptor site, it delivers an excitatory or inhibitory message. If enough excitatory messages are delivered, the neuron will fire

Figure 2–4 *(a)* A synapse is the junction between an axon and a dendrite. The gap between the axon and the dendrite is bridged by chemicals called neurotransmitters (Mader, 2000). *(b)* Just as the pieces of a jigsaw puzzle can fit in only one specific location in a puzzle, each kind of neurotransmitter has a distinctive configuration that allows it to fit into a specific type of receptor cell (Johnson, 2000). Why is it advantageous for axons and dendrites to be linked by temporary chemical bridges rather than by the hard wiring typical of a radio connection or telephone hookup?

(a) After S. S. Mader. Copyright © The McGraw-Hill Companies.
(b) After G. B. Johnson. Copyright © The McGraw-Hill Companies.

b.

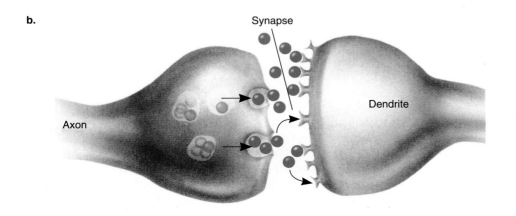

Synapse

Axon

Dendrite

neurotransmitter, then, can cause a neuron to fire when it is secreted in one part of the brain and can inhibit the firing of neurons when it is produced in another part. (The major neurotransmitters are described in Table 2-1.)

One of the most common neurotransmitters is *acetylcholine* (or *ACh,* its chemical symbol), which is found throughout the nervous system. ACh is involved in our every move, because—among other things—it transmits messages relating to our skeletal muscles. ACh is also involved in memory capabilities, and a diminished production of ACh might be related to Alzheimer's disease (Selkoe, 1997).

Another common excitatory neurotransmitter, *glutamate,* plays a role in memory. As we'll discuss in Chapter 6, memories appear to be produced by specific biochemical changes at particular synapses, and glutamate, along with other neurotransmitters, plays an important role in this process (Gibbs et al., 1996; Li et al., 1999; Bennett, 2000).

Gamma-amino butyric acid (GABA), found in both the brain and the spinal cord, appears to be the nervous system's primary inhibitory neurotransmitter. It moderates a variety of behaviours, ranging from eating to aggression. Several common substances, such as the tranquilizer Valium and alcohol, are effective because they permit GABA to operate more efficiently (Tabakoff & Hoffman, 1996).

Another major neurotransmitter is *dopamine (DA).* The discovery that certain drugs can have a marked effect on dopamine release has led to the development of effective treatments for a wide variety of physical and mental ailments. For instance, Parkinson's disease, from which actor Michael J. Fox suffers, is caused by a deficiency of dopamine in a particular part of the motor cortex of the brain. Techniques for increasing the production of dopamine in Parkinson's patients are proving effective (Schapira, 1999; LeWitt, 2000).

In other instances, *over*production of dopamine produces negative consequences. For example, researchers have hypothesized that the delusions and hallucinations associated with schizophrenia (see Chapter 12) are affected or perhaps caused by unusually high levels of dopamine. Dopamine follows a route known as the *mesolimbic pathway* from the midbrain of the brainstem to the limbic system (see Figure 2-10 on p. 59 and Figure 2-11 on p. 61). Drugs that block the reception of dopamine reduce the symptoms displayed by some people diagnosed with schizophrenia, as we will examine further in Chapters 12 and 13 (Kahn, Davidson, & Davis, 1996).

Table 2-1 Some Major Neurotransmitters

Name	Location	Effect	Function
Acetylcholine (ACh)	Brain, spinal cord, peripheral nervous system, especially some organs of the parasympathetic nervous system, myoneural junction	Excitatory in brain, myoneural junction, and autonomic nervous system; inhibitory elsewhere	Muscle movement; cognitive functioning
Glutamate	Brain, spinal cord	Excitatory	Memory
Gamma-amino butyric acid (GABA)	Brain, spinal cord	Main inhibitory neurotransmitter	Eating, aggression, sleeping
Dopamine (DA)	Brain	Inhibitory or excitatory	Muscle disorders, mental disorders, Parkinson's disease
Serotonin	Brain, spinal cord	Inhibitory	Sleeping, eating, mood, pain, depression
Norepinephrine	Brain, spinal cord, also as a hormone in adrenal gland	Inhibitory (gastrointestinal secretion) and excitatory (cardiac function—heart rate)	Increases mood, arousal, alleviates depression, active in stress response, raises blood pressure
Endorphins	Brain, spinal cord	Primarily inhibitory, except in hippocampus	Pain suppression, pleasurable feelings, appetites, placebos

Another neurotransmitter, *serotonin,* is associated with the regulation of sleep, eating, mood, and pain. A growing body of research points toward a broader role for serotonin, suggesting its involvement in such diverse behaviours as coping with stress, alcoholism, depression, suicide, impulsivity, and aggression (Smith, Williams, & Cowen, 2000).

Norepinephrine is a neurotransmitter associated with arousal and mood state. A lack of this neurotransmitter may contribute to depression. Research also that suggests that changes in the production of norepinephrine may be related to aging-related hypertension and depression. Norepinephrine is also produced as a stress hormone in the adrenal gland. In this capacity, it enables the flight-or-fight response. As a hormone it is also important for learning and memory (Lambert, Johansson, Agren, & Friberg, 2000; Supiano & Hogikyan, in press).

Endorphins, another class of neurotransmitter, are a family of chemicals produced by the brain that are similar in structure to painkilling drugs such as morphine. The production of endorphins seems to reflect the brain's effort to deal with pain. For instance, people who are afflicted with diseases that produce long-term, severe pain often develop large concentrations of endorphins in their brains—suggesting an effort by the brain to control the pain. Endorphins can also produce the euphoric feelings that runners sometimes experience after long runs. The exertion and perhaps even the pain involved in a long run stimulate the production of endorphins—ultimately resulting in what has been called "runner's high" (Kremer & Scully, 1994; Dishman, 1997).

Endorphin release might also explain other phenomena that have long puzzled psychologists. For example, acupuncture and placebos (pills or other substances that contain no actual drugs but that patients *believe* will make them better) might induce the release of endorphins, leading to the reduction of pain (Mikamo et al., 1994; Murray, 1995).

Evaluate

1. The _____ is the fundamental element of the nervous system.
2. Neurons receive information through their _____ and they send messages through their _____.
3. Just as electrical wires have an outer coating, so axons are insulated by a coating called the _____ _____.
4. The gap between two neurons is bridged by a chemical connection called a _____.
5. Endorphins are one kind of _____, the chemical "messengers" between neurons.

Answers to Evaluate Questions

1. neuron 2. dendrites; axons 3. myelin sheath 4. synapse 5. neurotransmitter

Rethink

1. Can you use your knowledge of psychological research methods to suggest how researchers can study the effects of neurotransmitters on human behaviour?
2. In what ways might endorphins help produce the placebo effect? Is there a difference between believing that one's pain is reduced and actually experiencing reduced pain? Why or why not?

The Nervous System

Given the complexity of individual neurons and the neurotransmission process, it should come as no surprise that the connections and structures formed by the neurons are complicated. Because just one neuron can be connected to 80 000 other neurons, the total number of possible connections is astonishing. For instance, estimates of the number of neural connections within the brain fall in the neighbourhood of 1 quadrillion—a 1 followed by 15 zeros; some experts put the number even higher (McGaugh, Weinberger, & Lynch, 1990; Estes, 1991; Eichenbaum, 1993).

Whatever the actual number of neural connections, the human nervous system has both a logic and an elegance. We turn now to its basic structures.

Prepare

In what way are the structures of the nervous system tied together?

Organize

The Nervous System
The Central and Peripheral Nervous Systems
The Evolutionary Foundations of the Nervous System
Behavioural Genetics

Figure 2–5 A schematic diagram of the relationship of the parts of the nervous system.

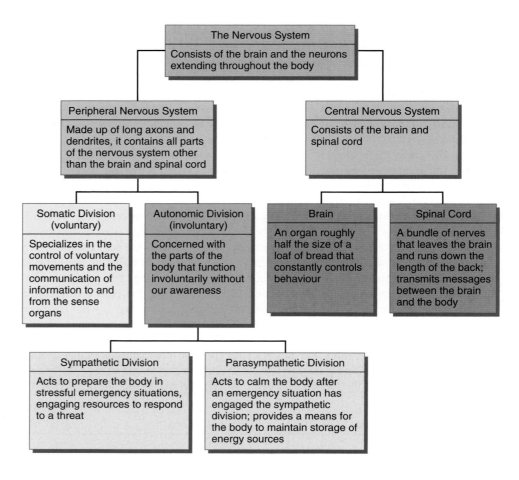

Figure 2–5 A schematic diagram of the relationship of the parts of the nervous system.

central nervous system (CNS): The system that includes the brain and spinal cord.

spinal cord: A bundle of nerves that leaves the brain and runs down the length of the back and is the main means for transmitting messages between the brain and the body.

reflexes: Automatic, involuntary responses to incoming stimuli.

sensory (afferent) neurons: Neurons that transmit information from the perimeter of the body to the central nervous system.

motor (efferent) neurons: Neurons that communicate information from the nervous system to muscles and glands of the body.

interneurons: Neurons that connect sensory and motor neurons, carrying messages between the two.

peripheral nervous system: The part of the nervous system that includes the autonomic and somatic subdivisions; made up of long axons and dendrites, it branches out from the spinal cord and brain and reaches the extremities of the body.

The Central and Peripheral Nervous Systems

As you can see from the schematic representation in Figure 2-5, the nervous system is divided into two main parts: the central nervous system and the peripheral nervous system. The **central nervous system (CNS)** is composed of the brain and spinal cord. The **spinal cord**, about the thickness of a pencil, contains a bundle of nerves that leaves the brain and runs down the length of the back (see Figure 2-6). It is the primary means for transmitting messages between the brain and the body.

However, the spinal cord is not just a communications conduit. It also controls some simple kinds of behaviours on its own, without any involvement of the brain. One example is the way your knee jerks forward when it is tapped with a rubber hammer. Such behaviours, called **reflexes**, are automatic, involuntary responses to incoming stimuli. Similarly, when you touch a hot stove and immediately withdraw your hand, a reflex is at work. Although the brain eventually analyzes and reacts to the situation ("Ouch—hot stove—pull away!"), the initial withdrawal is directed only by neurons in the spinal cord.

Three sorts of neurons are involved in reflexes. **Sensory (afferent) neurons** transmit information from the perimeter of the body to the central nervous system. **Motor (efferent) neurons** communicate information from the nervous system to muscles and glands of the body. **Interneurons** in the spinal cord connect sensory and motor neurons, carrying messages between the two.

The importance of the spinal cord and reflexes is illustrated by the outcome of accidents in which the cord is injured or severed. Actor Christopher Reeve, who was injured in a horse-riding accident, suffers from *quadriplegia*, a condition in which voluntary muscle movement below the neck is lost. In a less severe but still debilitating condition, *paraplegia*, people are unable to voluntarily move any muscles in the lower half of their body.

As suggested by its name, the **peripheral nervous system** branches out from the spinal cord and brain and reaches the extremities of the body. Made up of long axons and dendrites, the peripheral nervous system encompasses all parts of the nervous system other than the brain and spinal cord. There are two major divisions, the somatic division and the autonomic division, both of which connect the central nervous system with the sense organs, muscles, glands, and other organs. The **somatic division** specializes in the control of voluntary movements—such as the motion of the eyes to read this sentence or of the hand to turn this page—and the communication of information to and from the sense organs. On the other hand, the **autonomic division** is concerned with the parts of the body that keep us alive—the heart, blood vessels, glands, lungs, and other organs that function involuntarily without our awareness. As you are reading at this moment, the autonomic division of the peripheral nervous system is pumping blood through your body, pushing your lungs in and out, overseeing the digestion of the meal you had a few hours ago, and so on—all without a thought or care on your part.

Activating the Divisions of the Autonomic Nervous System

The autonomic division plays a particularly crucial role during emergency situations. Suppose as you are reading you suddenly sense that a stranger is watching you through the window. As you look up, you see the glint of something that just might be a knife. As confusion races through your mind and fear overcomes your attempts to think rationally, what happens to your body? If you are like most people, you react immediately on a physiological level. Your heart rate increases, you begin to sweat, and you develop goose bumps all over your body.

The physiological changes that occur result from the activation of one of the two parts that make up the autonomic division: the **sympathetic division**. The sympathetic division acts to prepare the body in stressful emergency situations, engaging all of the organism's resources to respond to a threat. This response often takes the form of "fight or flight." In contrast, the **parasympathetic division** acts to calm the body after the emergency situation is resolved. When you find, for instance, that the stranger at the window is actually your roommate who has lost his keys and is climbing in the window to avoid waking you, your parasympathetic division begins to predominate, lowering your heart rate, stopping your sweating, and returning your body to the state it was in prior to your fright. The parasympathetic division also provides a means for the body to maintain storage of energy sources such as fat and glycogen. The sympathetic and parasympathetic divisions work together to regulate many functions of the body (see Figure 2-7). For instance, sexual arousal is controlled by the parasympathetic division but sexual orgasm is a function of the sympathetic division.

The Evolutionary Foundations of the Nervous System

The complexities of the nervous system can be understood only by taking the course of evolution into consideration. The forerunner of the human nervous system is found in the earliest simple organisms to have a spinal cord.

Over millions of years, the front end of the spinal cord in these simple organisms became more specialized, and the organisms became capable of distinguishing between different kinds of stimuli and responding differently to them. Ultimately, the front end of the spinal cord evolved into what we would consider a primitive brain. At first, it had just three parts, devoted to close stimuli (such as smell), more distant stimuli (such as sights and sounds), and the ability to maintain balance and bodily coordination. In fact, many animals, such as fish, still have a nervous system that is structured in a roughly similar fashion (Merlin, 1993).

As a result of work dating back to the 1950s, Paul MacLean (head of the Brain Evolution and Behavior department of the U.S. National Institute of Mental Health) proposed the triune brain theory (1990). His notion is that the human brain evolved through three stages. The earliest stage, according to this theory, is the reptilian or old brain (resembling a large-headed golf club). On top of that, the mammalian or limbic brain

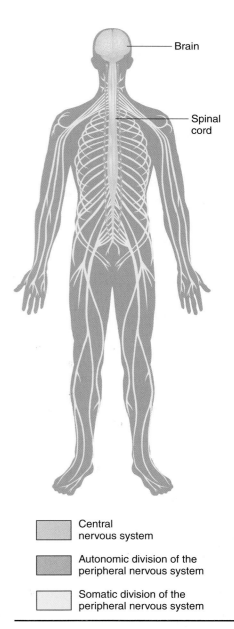

Brain

Spinal cord

Central nervous system

Autonomic division of the peripheral nervous system

Somatic division of the peripheral nervous system

Figure 2-6 The central nervous system—consisting of the brain and spinal cord—and the peripheral nervous system.

After E. Loftus and C. Wortmann. Copyright © The McGraw–Hill Companies.

somatic division: The part of the nervous system that specializes in the control of voluntary movements and the communication of information to and from the sense organs.

autonomic division: The part of the nervous system that controls involuntary movement (the actions of the heart, glands, lungs, and other organs).

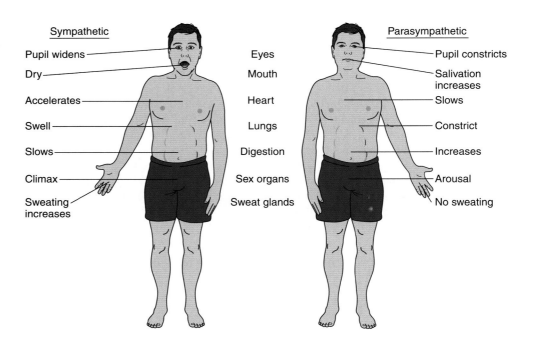

Figure 2-7 The major functions of the autonomic nervous system. The sympathetic division acts to prepare certain organs of the body for stressful emergency situations, and the parasympathetic division acts to calm the body after the emergency situation is resolved. Can you explain why each response of the sympathetic division might be useful in an emergency?

sympathetic division: The part of the autonomic division of the nervous system that acts to prepare the body in stressful emergency situations, engaging all the organism's resources to respond to a threat.

parasympathetic division: The part of the autonomic division of the nervous system that acts to calm the body after the emergency situation is resolved.

evolutionary psychology: The branch of psychology that seeks to identify behaviour patterns that result from our genetic inheritance from our ancestors.

 **PsychLink**

Human behavioural genetic data
www.mcgrawhill.ca/college/feldman

behavioural genetics: The study of the effects of heredity on behaviour.

 **PsychLink**

The Human Genome Project
www.mcgrawhill.ca/college/feldman

evolved (picture the golf club with a cover on it). The newest part of the brain to evolve is the cerebral cortex, which covers the other two and provides us with higher cognitive functions (see Figures 2-9 and 2-11 on pp. 59 and 61).

Evolutionary psychology is the branch of psychology that seeks to identify how behaviour is influenced and produced by the genetic inheritance from our ancestors. Its proponents argue that the course of evolution is reflected in the structure and functioning of the nervous system, and that evolutionary factors consequently have a significant influence on our everyday behaviour. Their work, and that of other scientists, has led to the development of a new field: behavioural genetics.

Behavioural Genetics

Our evolutionary heritage manifests itself through the structure and functioning of the nervous system, and through our behaviour as well. In the view of a blossoming new area of study, people's personality and behavioural habits are affected in part by their genetic heritage. **Behavioural genetics** is the study of the effects of heredity on behaviour. Behavioural genetics researchers are finding increasing evidence that cognitive abilities, personality traits, sexual orientation, and psychological disorders are determined to some extent by genetic factors (Funder, 1997; Craig et al., 2000).

Behavioural genetics gets to the heart of the nature-nurture issue that we first discussed in Chapter 1. Although no one would argue that our behaviour is *solely* determined by inherited factors, evidence collected by behavioural geneticists does suggest that our genetic inheritance predisposes us to respond in particular ways to our environment, and even to seek out particular kinds of environments. For instance, research indicates that genetic factors might be related to such diverse behaviour as level of family conflict, schizophrenia, learning disabilities, and general sociability (Elkins, McGue, & Iacono, 1997; Berrettini, 2000). Twin studies shed light on these issues. See Chapter 9 (p. 288) for a discussion of this important source of information.

Furthermore, important human characteristics and behaviours are related to the presence (or absence) of particular *genes,* the genetic material that controls the transmission of traits. For example, researchers have found evidence that novelty-seeking behaviour is determined, at least in part, by a certain gene.

Researchers have identified some 30 000 individual genes, each of which appears in a specific sequence on particular chromosomes. Scientists only recently succeeded in mapping these genes as part of a massive, multibillion-dollar project known as the Human Genome Project, which, after a decade of effort, identified the sequence of the 3 billion chemical pairs that make up the DNA in genes. By understanding the basic structure of the human *genome,* the "map" of humans' total genetic makeup, scientists are a giant step closer to understanding the biochemical recipes that direct human functioning (Human Genome Project, 2000; Pennisi, 2000).

Despite its relative infancy, the field of behavioural genetics has already made substantial contributions. By understanding the relationship between our genetic heritage and the structures of the nervous system, we are gaining new knowledge about the development of various behavioural difficulties, such as the psychological disorders we'll discuss in Chapter 12. Perhaps more importantly, behavioural genetics holds the promise of developing new treatment techniques to remedy genetic deficiencies that can lead to physical and psychological difficulties. For example, analysis of a drop of blood might tell a woman whether she has a form of breast cancer that is likely to be deadly or is treatable, and scientists might be able to analyze our children's genes to determine if they are susceptible to heart disease, as we'll discuss in detail in Chapter 9 (Risch & Merikangas, 1996; Haseltine, 1997; Begley, 2000).

We turn now to a consideration of the particular structures of the brain and the primary functions to which they are related. However, a caution is in order. Although we'll be discussing how specific brain areas are tied to specific behaviours, this approach is an oversimplification. No simple one-to-one correspondence between a distinct part of the brain and a particular behaviour exists. Instead, behaviour is produced by complex interconnections among sets of neurons located in many areas of the brain: Our behaviour, emotions, thoughts, hopes, and dreams are produced by a variety of neurons throughout the nervous system, working in concert (Grillner, 1996; Joseph, 1996; Sharma, Angelucci, & Sur, 2000).

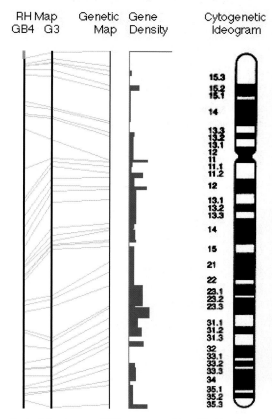

Chromosome 5: pTEL-D5S678

Part of the human DNA sequence, identified by the Human Genome Project, which has mapped the specific location and sequence of every gene.

Evaluate

1. If you should put your hand on a red–hot piece of metal, the immediate response of pulling it away would be an example of a(n) _____.
2. The central nervous system is composed of the _____ and _____ .
3. In the peripheral nervous system, the _____ division controls voluntary movements, whereas the _____ division controls organs that keep us alive and function without our awareness.
4. Maria saw a young boy run into the street and get hit by a car. When she got to the fallen child, she was in a state of panic. She was sweating and her heart was racing. Her biological state resulted from the activation of what division of the nervous system?

   a. Parasympathetic

   b. Central

   c. Sympathetic

5. The increasing complexity and hierarchy of the nervous system over millions of years is the subject of study for researchers working in the field of _____ _____.
6. The emerging field of _____ _____ studies how our genetic inheritance predisposes us to behave in certain ways.

Rethink

1. How might communication within the nervous system result in human consciousness?
2. How is the "fight or flight" response helpful to organisms in emergency situations?

Answers to Evaluate Questions

1. reflex 2. brain; spinal cord 3. somatic; autonomic 4. c 5. evolutionary psychology 6. behavioural genetics

---

Pathways Through Psychology

Julien Doyon

Professor in Cognitive Neuroscience, Université de Montréal

Adjunct professor in the Department of Neuropsychology, Montreal Neurological Institute, McGill University

Education: B.A., MA., Université Laval; Ph.D., McGill University

Home: Montréal, Québec

Julien Doyon

My interest in cognitive neuroscience began when I was doing my Ph.D. at McGill University and taking a course in adult assessment from Laughlin B. Taylor. This interest continued to develop while doing an internship practicum, learning how to do clinical assessments of patients with epilepsy who needed surgery of either the frontal or the temporal lobes. I really liked the clinical work and the research questions that could be pursued and asked Brenda Milner to supervise my thesis.

In my clinical practice, I conduct cognitive assessments of patients with a variety of neurological disorders. I also do work in the area of rehabilitation of motor skills. The main focus of my research is understanding and identifying the neural networks involved in learning a motor skill (e.g., playing the piano or playing golf). I am also interested in the plasticity of these networks and in understanding the brain structures involved at different phases of the learning process.

I believe that, in neuroscience, one must apply different techniques in order to find an answer. I thus use a multi-faceted approach in my work. In the case of motor-skill learning, I have carried out experiments looking at the effects of lesions to the brain (striatum and cerebellum, for example). A second line of inquiry consists of performing a series of brain imaging studies (PET and fMRI) in normal control subjects and patients with Parkinson's disease. A third line of inquiry involves the rat animal model, in which the effects of lesions to the cerebellum, striatum, or frontal cortex are assessed during both the learning of and retention of a motor sequence.

Basic research provides knowledge, which can then be applied to a clinical population. I have recently been using motor imagery as a means of keeping the neural circuits of stroke patients alive in order to improve their chances of recovery. If people produce a mental image of a motor activity the brain circuits for that movement are activated even if the actual performance is not possible at the time because of the stroke.

As a member and past president of both the Canadian Society for Brain, Behaviour and Cognitive Sciences and the International Society for Behavioural Neuroscience, I have had the opportunity to extend my network of collaborators and friends.

What has sustained my interest and provided me with a sense of accomplishment? I would say it would be my work towards understanding the brain structures mediating the learning of motor skills, and work on the neuropathophysiology underlying the cognitive and motor impairment in Parkinson's disease. I have also collaborated with Dr. Jeremy D. Schmahmann of the Massachusetts General Hospital of Harvard University to create a three-dimensional atlas of the human cerebellum. Researchers in the field of brain imaging can use this atlas to locate, with better precision, areas of the cerebellum active during a variety of cognitive and motor tasks.

I believe that brain research is both a fascinating and a necessary endeavour, especially when it allows us to increase our knowledge base and find better treatments for people with neurological disorders.

Source: Julien Doyon, Ph.D., Université de Montréal
julien@bic.mni.mcgill.ca

What work has Dr. Doyon done with stroke patients? Why is it so important?

The Brain

It is not much to look at. Soft, spongy, mottled, and pinkish-gray in colour, it can hardly be said to possess much in the way of physical beauty. Despite its physical appearance, however, it ranks as the greatest natural marvel we know of and possesses a beauty and sophistication all its own.

The object to which this description applies? The human brain. Our brain is responsible for our loftiest thoughts—and our most primitive urges. It is the overseer of the intricate workings of the human body. If one were to attempt to design a computer to mimic the range of capabilities of the brain, the task would be nearly impossible; in fact, it has proved difficult even to come close. The sheer quantity of nerve cells in the brain is enough to daunt even the most ambitious computer engineer. Many billions of nerve cells make up a structure weighing just 1.5 kilograms in the average adult. However, the most astounding thing about the brain is not its number of cells but its ability to allow human intellect to flourish as it guides our behaviour and thoughts.

Studying the Brain's Structure and Functions: Spying on the Brain

The brain has posed a continual challenge to those wishing to study it. For most of history, its examination was possible only after an individual was dead. Only then could the skull be opened and the brain cut into without serious injury. Although this was informative, such a limited procedure could hardly tell us much about the functioning of the healthy brain.

Today, however, important advances have been made in the study of the brain involving the use of brain scanning techniques. Using brain scanning, investigators can take a snapshot of the internal workings of the brain without doing surgery. One of the largest scientific communities in North America dedicated to imaging research is The McConnell Brain Imaging Centre of the Montreal Neurological Institute, McGill University, which brings together researchers from many disciplines, as a visit to their Web site shows (www.bic.mni.mcgill.ca). In use there are all of the major scanning techniques described below and illustrated in Figure 2-8.

- The *electroencephalogram (EEG)* records electrical activity in the brain through electrodes placed on the outside of the skull. Although traditionally the EEG could produce only a graph of electrical wave patterns, new techniques are now able to transform the brain's electrical activity into a pictorial representation of the brain that allows the diagnosis of such problems as epilepsy and learning disabilities.
- The *computerized axial tomography (CAT) scan* uses a computer to construct an image of the structures of the brain by combining thousands of separate X rays taken at slightly different angles. It is very useful for showing abnormalities in the structure of the brain, such as swelling and enlargement of certain parts, but does not provide information about brain activity.
- The *magnetic resonance imaging (MRI) scan* uses powerful magnets to produce three-dimensional images of body and brain structures. It is designed to show differences between normal and abnormal tissue throughout the body and is used to diagnose tumours of the pituitary gland and brain.

Prepare

How do researchers identify the major parts and functions of the brain?

What are the major parts of the brain, and for what behaviours is each part responsible?

How do the two halves of the brain operate interdependently?

How can an understanding of the nervous system help us find ways to relieve disease and pain?

Organize

The Brain
 Studying the Brain's Structure and Functions
 The Central Core
 The Limbic System
 The Cerebral Cortex
 Mending the Brain
 The Specialization of the Hemispheres
 The Split Brain
The Endocrine System

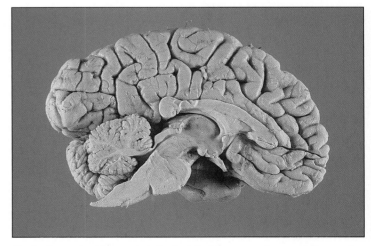

The brain may not be much to look at, but it represents one of the great marvels of human development.
Why do most scientists believe that it will be difficult, if not impossible, to duplicate the brain's abilities?

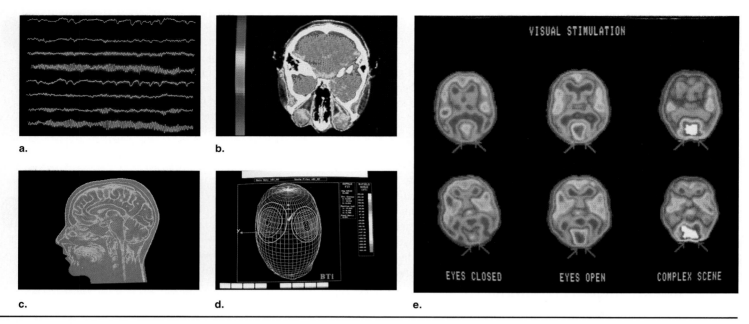

a.

b.

c.

d.

e.

Figure 2-8 Brain scans produced by different techniques. *(a)* A computer-produced EEG image. *(b)* This CAT scan shows the structures of the brain. *(c)* The MRI scan uses a magnetic field to detail the parts of the brain. *(d)* The SQUID scan shows the neural activity of the brain *(e)* The PET scan displays the functioning of the brain at a given moment and is sensitive to the person's activities.

 **PsychLink**

Numerous brain scans
www.mcgrawhill.ca/college/feldman

PsychLink

Information about NMR
www.mcgrawhill.ca/college/feldman

- The *functional magnetic resonance imaging (fMRI) scan* uses radio waves and powerful magnets to produce an image of brain activity while the patient performs particular tasks. The scan will show increased blood flow to the part of the brain responsible for the task. It is particularly valuable to identify parts of the brain to be avoided during surgery (for example, speech centres).
- The *superconducting quantum interference device (SQUID)* is sensitive to tiny changes in magnetic fields that occur when neurons fire. Using SQUID, researchers can pinpoint the location of neural activity.
- The *positron emission tomography (PET) scan* shows biochemical activity within the brain at a given moment in time. PET scans begin by injecting into the bloodstream a radioactive (but safe) liquid that makes its way to the brain. By locating radiation within the brain, a computer can determine which are the more active regions, providing a striking picture of the brain at work. PET is one of the tools used by Julien Doyon (see the *Pathways Through Psychology* box on p. 56) to study Parkinson's disease.

Each of these techniques offers exciting possibilities not only for the diagnosis and treatment of brain disease and injuries, but also for an increased understanding of the normal functioning of the brain. In addition, researchers are developing ways to combine separate scanning techniques (such as integrated, simultaneous PET and MRI scans) to produce even more effective portraits of the brain, such as three-dimensional reconstructions of the brain that can be used during surgery (Grimson et al., 1999).

Advances in brain scanning are also aiding the development of new methods for harnessing the brain's neural signals. We consider some of these intriguing findings in the *Applying Psychology in the 21st Century* box on page 60.

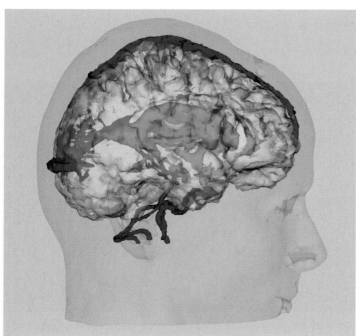

To get a better view of the brain, researchers are experimenting with various scanning techniques; this photo combines PET and MRI scans.

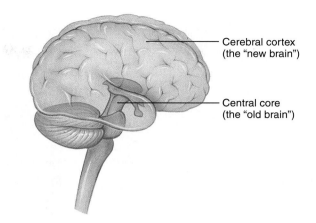

Cerebral cortex (the "new brain")

Central core (the "old brain")

Figure 2-9 The major divisions of the brain: the cerebral cortex and the central core.

After R. Seeley, et al. Copyright © The McGraw-Hill Companies.

The Central Core: Our "Old Brain"

Even though the capabilities of the human brain far exceed those of the brain of any other species we know of, it is not surprising that the basic functions that we share with more primitive animals, such as breathing, eating, and sleeping, are directed by a relatively primitive part of the brain. The portion of the brain known as the **central core** (see Figure 2-9) is quite similar to that found in all vertebrates (species with backbones). The central core is sometimes referred to as the "old brain" because its evolutionary underpinnings can be traced back some 500 million years to primitive structures found in nonhuman species.

If we were to move up the spinal cord from the base of the skull to locate the structures of the central core of the brain, the first part we would come to would be the *hindbrain,* which contains the medulla, pons, and cerebellum (see Figure 2-10). The *medulla* controls a number of critical body functions, the most important of which are

central core: The "old brain," which controls such basic functions as eating and sleeping and is common to all vertebrates.

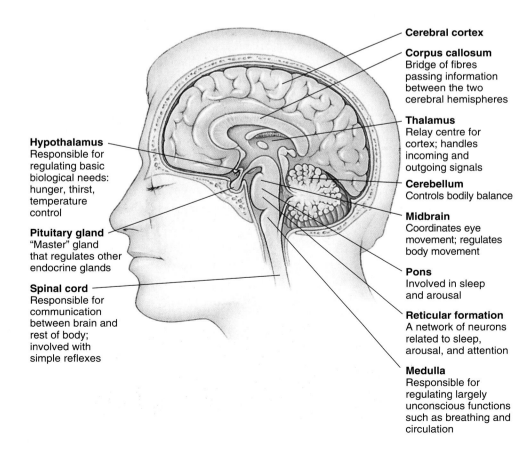

Cerebral cortex

Corpus callosum
Bridge of fibres passing information between the two cerebral hemispheres

Thalamus
Relay centre for cortex; handles incoming and outgoing signals

Cerebellum
Controls bodily balance

Midbrain
Coordinates eye movement; regulates body movement

Pons
Involved in sleep and arousal

Reticular formation
A network of neurons related to sleep, arousal, and attention

Medulla
Responsible for regulating largely unconscious functions such as breathing and circulation

Hypothalamus
Responsible for regulating basic biological needs: hunger, thirst, temperature control

Pituitary gland
"Master" gland that regulates other endocrine glands

Spinal cord
Responsible for communication between brain and rest of body; involved with simple reflexes

Figure 2-10 The major structures in the brain.

After G.B. Johnson. Copyright © The McGraw-Hill Companies.

Applying Psychology in the 21st Century

Mind over Cursor: Using Brain Waves to Overcome Physical Limitations

For four years, Hans-Peter Balzmann, a lawyer suffering from Lou Gehrig's disease, was locked within his own body. Paralyzed by the disease and unable to eat, speak, or even breathe on his own, he had relied on a respirator and feeding tube to survive. Although his mind functioned normally, he was unable to communicate with the outside world.

All that changed, however, after Balzmann obtained an experimental device that allows brain waves to be translated into written communication. Using EEG scanning techniques that react to the pattern of brain waves originating in the brain, Balzmann learned to boost and curtail certain types of brain waves. After hundreds of hours of practice, he was able to select letters that appear on a video screen. By stringing letters

together, he could spell out messages. The process, which makes use of brain waves called "slow cortical potentials," permitted Balzmann to communicate effectively for the first time in years. Although the method is slow and tedious—Balzmann can produce only about two characters per minute—it holds great promise (Birbaumer et al., 1999).

Other increasingly sophisticated procedures may permit faster communication with brain waves in the future. For example, neurosurgeon Philip Kennedy of Emory University is experimenting with a procedure in which he implants electrodes into a paralyzed patient's motor cortex. When the patient thinks about moving her hands, tongues, or eyes, the brain produces electrical signals that are amplified by the implant and translated into the movement of a cursor. Using this system, the patient can spell out words and hit icons (such as "I'm cold") on the computer screen ("Mind over Matter," 1999).

Technological advances offer the possibility of treating other brain disorders. For example, an experimental system is being tested to treat seizures due to epilepsy. The system consists of a pacemaker-like device, implanted into the chest, that sends signals to the brain to block seizures. When patients feel that a seizure is about to occur, they can activate the system, short-circuiting the seizure (Forest, 1997).

Ultimately, systems such as these might be useful not just for people with illnesses and disabilities, but for anyone. For instance, it is conceivable that one day you will be able to control your computer's cursor by simply thinking about moving it. Mind-over-cursor could be in everyone's future.

Can you think of a mechanism that would permit brain-wave communication between two people? What implications would there be if people gained the ability to communicate with each other in this way?

---

breathing and heartbeat. The *pons* comes next, joining the two halves of the cerebellum, which lies adjacent to it. Containing large bundles of nerves, the pons acts as a transmitter of motor information, coordinating muscles and integrating movement between the right and left halves of the body. It is also involved in the control of sleep.

cerebellum (ser uh BELL um): The part of the brain that controls bodily balance.

The **cerebellum** is found just above the medulla and behind the pons. Without the help of the cerebellum we would be unable to walk in a straight line without staggering and lurching forward, for it is the job of the cerebellum to control bodily balance. It constantly monitors feedback from the muscles to coordinate their placement, movement, and tension. In fact, drinking too much alcohol seems to depress the activity of the cerebellum, leading to the unsteady gait and movement characteristic of drunkenness. The cerebellum is also involved in several intellectual functions, ranging from analysis of sensory information to problem solving (Gao et al., 1996; Wickelgren, 1998a).

While the cerebellum is involved in several intellectual functions, its main duty is to control balance, constantly monitoring feedback from the muscles to coordinate their placement, movement, and tension. **Do you think the cerebellum is under conscious or automatic control as people negotiate difficult balancing tasks?**

The **reticular formation** extends from the medulla through the pons, passing through the middle section of the brain—or *midbrain*—and into the front-most part of the brain, called the *forebrain*. Like an ever-vigilant guard, the reticular formation is made up of groups of nerve cells that can immediately activate other parts of the brain to produce general bodily arousal. If you are startled by a loud noise, for example, your reticular formation can put you into a heightened state of awareness so you can determine whether a response is necessary. In addition, the reticular formation serves a different function when we are sleeping, seeming to filter out background stimuli to allow us to sleep undisturbed.

Hidden within the forebrain, the **thalamus** acts primarily as a busy relay station, mostly for information concerning the senses. Messages from the eyes, ears, and skin travel to the thalamus to be communicated upward to higher parts of the brain. The thalamus also integrates information from higher parts of the brain, sorting it out so that it can be sent to the cerebellum and medulla.

The **hypothalamus** is located just below the thalamus. Although tiny—about the size of a fingertip—the hypothalamus plays an inordinately important role. One of its major functions is to maintain *homeostasis,* a steady internal environment for the body. The hypothalamus helps maintain a constant body temperature and monitors the amount of nutrients stored in the cells. It also produces and regulates behaviour that is critical to the basic survival of the species, such as eating, self-protection, and sex.

reticular formation: The part of the brain from the medulla through the pons made up of groups of nerve cells that can immediately activate other parts of the brain to produce general bodily arousal.

thalamus: The part of the brain located in the middle of the central core that acts primarily as a busy relay station, mostly for information concerning the senses.

hypothalamus: A tiny part of the brain, located below the thalamus of the brain, that maintains homeostasis and produces and regulates vital, basic behaviour such as eating, drinking, and sexual behaviour.

The Limbic System: Beyond the Central Core

In an eerie view of the future, some science fiction writers have suggested that people will someday routinely have electrodes implanted in their brains. These electrodes will permit them to receive tiny shocks that produce the sensation of pleasure by stimulating certain centres of the brain. When they feel upset, people will simply activate their electrodes to achieve an immediate high.

Although farfetched, and ultimately improbable, such a futuristic fantasy is based on fact. The brain does have pleasure centres in several areas, including some in the **limbic system**. Consisting of a series of doughnut-shaped structures including the *amygdala, hippocampus,* and *fornix,* the limbic system borders the top of the central core and has connections with the cerebral cortex (see Figure 2-11).

limbic system: The part of the brain located outside the "new brain" that controls eating, aggression, and reproduction.

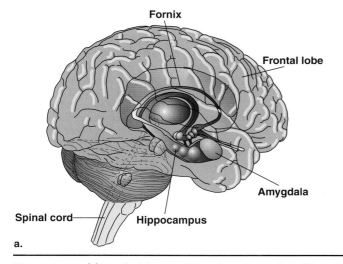
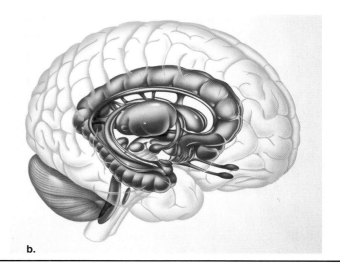

Figure 2-11 *(a)* The limbic system consists of a series of doughnut-shaped structures that are involved in self-preservation, learning, memory, and the experience of pleasure (After A. Schneider and B. Tarshih. Copyright © The McGraw-Hill Companies). *(b)* This computer-generated image provides another view of the limbic system (Courtesy of Dr. Robert B. Livingston, University of California-San Diego, and Philip J. Mercurio, Neurosciences Institute).

The structures of the limbic system jointly control a variety of basic functions relating to emotions and self-preservation, such as eating, aggression, and reproduction. Injury to the limbic system can produce striking changes in behaviour. It can turn animals that are usually docile and tame into belligerent savages. Conversely, those that are usually wild and uncontrollable might become meek and obedient (Bedard & Parsinger, 1995).

Research examining the effects of mild electric shocks to parts of the limbic system and other parts of the brain have produced some thought-provoking findings (Olds & Milner, 1954; Olds & Fobes, 1981). In one experiment, rats who pressed a bar received mild electric stimulation through an electrode implanted in their brain, which produced pleasurable feelings. Even starving rats on their way to food would stop to press the bar as many times as they could. Some rats would actually stimulate themselves literally thousands of times an hour—until they collapsed with fatigue (Routtenberg & Lindy, 1965).

The extraordinarily pleasurable quality of certain kinds of stimulation has also been experienced by humans, who, as part of treatment for certain kinds of brain disorders, have received electrical stimulation to certain areas of the limbic system. Although at a loss to describe just what it feels like, these people report the experience to be intensely pleasurable, similar in some respects to sexual orgasm.

The limbic system also plays an important role in learning and memory, a finding demonstrated in patients with epilepsy. In an attempt to stop their seizures, such patients have had portions of the limbic system removed. One unintended consequence of the surgery is that these individuals sometimes have difficulty learning and remembering new information.

The limbic system, then, is involved in several important functions, including self-preservation, learning, memory, and the experience of pleasure. These functions are hardly unique to humans; in fact, the limbic system is sometimes referred to as the "animal brain" because its structures and functions are so similar to those of other mammals. To identify the part of the brain that provides the complex and subtle capabilities that are uniquely human, we need to turn to another structure—the cerebral cortex.

Evaluate

1. _____ _____ is a procedure whereby a picture of the brain can be taken without opening the skull.
2. Match the name of each brain scan with the appropriate description:

   a. EEG
   b. CAT
   c. PET

   1. By locating radiation within the brain, a computer can provide a striking picture of brain activity.
   2. Electrodes placed around the skull record the electrical signals transmitted through the brain.
   3. A computer image combines thousands of X-ray pictures into one.

3. Control of such functions as breathing and sleep is located in the _____ _____.
4. Match the portion of the brain with its function:

   a. medulla
   b. pons
   c. cerebellum
   d. reticular formation

   1. Maintains breathing and heartbeat
   2. Controls bodily balance
   3. Coordinates and integrates muscle movements
   4. Activates other parts of the brain to produce general bodily arousal

5. The _____, a fingertip-sized portion of the brain, is responsible for the regulation of the body's internal environment.

Rethink

1. How would you answer the argument that "psychologists should leave the study of neurons and synapses and the nervous system to biologists"?
2. Before sophisticated brain-scanning techniques were developed, biopsychologists' understanding of the brain was largely based on the brains of people who had died. What limitations would this pose, and in what areas would you expect the most significant advances once brain-scanning techniques were possible?

Answers to Evaluate Questions

1. Brain scanning 2. a-2; b-3; c-1 3. central core or "old brain" 4. a-1; b-3; c-2; d-4 5. hypothalamus

The Cerebral Cortex: Our "New Brain"

As we have proceeded up the spinal cord and into the brain, our discussion has centred on areas of the brain that control functions similar to those found in less sophisticated organisms. But where, you may be asking, are the portions of the brain that enable humans to do what they do best, and that distinguish humans from all other animals? Those unique features of the human brain—indeed, the very capabilities that allow you to come up with such a question in the first place—are embodied in the ability to think, evaluate, and make complex judgments. The principal location of these abilities, along with many others, is the **cerebral cortex**.

The cerebral cortex is referred to as the "new brain" because of its relatively recent evolution. It consists of a mass of deeply folded, rippled, convoluted tissue that amounts to some 80 percent of the brain's total mass. Although only about 2 millimetres thick, it would, if flattened out, cover an area of more than 0.18 square metre. This configuration allows the surface area of the cortex to be considerably greater than if it were smoother and more uniformly packed into the skull. The uneven shape also permits a high level of integration of neurons, allowing sophisticated processing of information.

The cortex has four major sections, called **lobes**. If we take a side view of the brain, the *frontal lobes* lie at the front centre of the cortex, and the *parietal lobes* lie behind them. The *temporal lobes* are found in the lower centre of the cortex, with the *occipital lobes* lying behind them. These four sets of lobes are physically separated by deep grooves called sulci. Figure 2-12 shows the four areas.

Another way of describing the brain is by considering the functions associated with a given area. Figure 2-12 also shows the specialized regions within the lobes related to specific functions and areas of the body. Three major areas have been discovered: the motor areas, the sensory areas, and the association areas. Although we will discuss these areas as though they were separate and independent, keep in mind that this is an over-simplification. In most instances, behaviour is influenced simultaneously by several structures and areas within the brain, operating interdependently. Furthermore, even within a given area, additional subdivisions exist. Finally, when people suffer certain kinds of brain injury, uninjured portions of the brain can sometimes take over the functions that were previously handled by the damaged area. In short, the brain is extraordinarily adaptable (Gibbons, 1990; Sharma, Angelucci, & Sur, 2000).

cerebral cortex: The "new brain," responsible for the most sophisticated information processing in the brain; contains the lobes.

lobes: The four major sections of the cerebral cortex: frontal, parietal, temporal, and occipital.

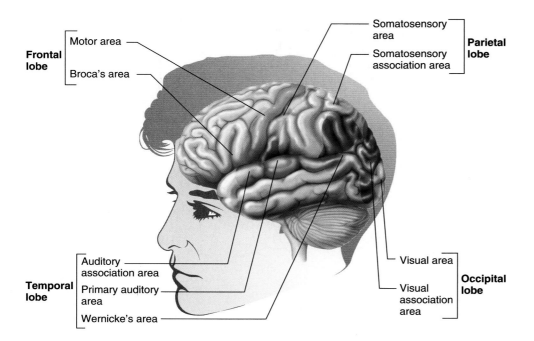

Figure 2–12 The cerebral cortex of the brain. The major physical *structures* of the cerebral cortex are called lobes. This figure also illustrates the *functions* associated with particular areas of the cerebral cortex.
Are any areas of the cerebral cortex present in nonhuman animals?

PsychLink

Information about lobes
www.mcgrawhill.ca/college/feldman

motor area: The part of the cortex that is largely responsible for the voluntary movement of particular parts of the body.

The Motor Area of the Cortex

If you look at the frontal lobe in Figure 2-12, you will see a shaded portion labelled the **motor area**. This part of the cortex is largely responsible for the voluntary movement of particular parts of the body. Every portion of the motor area corresponds to a specific locale within the body. If we were to insert an electrode into a particular part of the motor area of the cortex and apply mild electrical stimulation, there would be involuntary movement in the corresponding part of the body. If we moved to another part of the motor area and stimulated it, a different part of the body would move.

The motor area has been so well mapped that it is possible to devise the kind of schematic representation shown in Figure 2-13. Wilder Penfield, a neurosurgeon at the Montreal Neurological Institute, provided us with this knowledge. A map of motor function was critical to Penfield's work. He wanted to be sure not to interfere with critical functions in the process of performing brain surgery. During the course of surgery, he stimulated various areas of the cortex and recorded the parts of the patient's body that moved in response to the stimulation.

The model in Figure 2-13 shows the amount and relative location of cortical tissue that is used to produce movement in specific parts of the human body. As you can see, the control of body movements that are relatively large-scale and require little precision, such as movement of a knee or a hip, is centred in a very small space in the motor area. In contrast, movements that must be precise and delicate, such as facial expressions and finger movements, are controlled by a considerably larger portion of the motor area (Penfield & Rasmussen, 1950).

Figure 2-13 The correspondence between the amount and location of tissue in the brain's motor area and the specific body parts where movement is controlled by that tissue. Source: Penfield & Rasmussen, 1950.

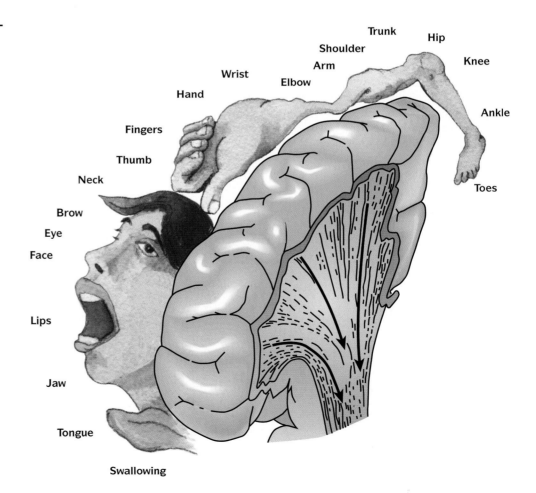

In short, the motor area of the cortex provides a guide to the degree of complexity and the importance of the motor capabilities of specific parts of the body. Keep in mind, however, that behaviour is produced by multiple sets of neurons in the nervous system, linked in elaborate ways. Like other behaviour, movement is produced through the coordinated firing of a complex variety of neurons, working together but not necessarily lined up neatly in the motor area of the cortex (Sanes et al., 1995; Batista et al., 1999; Kakei, Hoffman, & Strick, 1999).

The Sensory Area of the Cortex

Given the one-to-one correspondence between the motor area and the location of body movement, it is not surprising to find a similar relationship between specific portions of the **sensory area**, the site in the brain of the tissue that corresponds to each of the senses, and the senses themselves. Penfield also mapped this relationship. Because his patients were only under local anesthetic, they were able to report sensation to him as he probed the various areas of the cortex.

The sensory area of the cortex includes three regions: one that corresponds primarily to body sensations (including touch and pressure), one relating to sight, and a third relating to sound. For instance, the *somatosensory area* encompasses specific locations associated with the ability to perceive touch and pressure in a particular area of the body. As with the motor area, the amount of brain tissue related to a particular location on the body determines the degree of sensitivity of that location. The greater the space within the cortex, the more sensitive that area of the body (Penfield & Rasmussen, 1950). As you can see from the weird-looking individual in Figure 2-14, parts such as the fingers are related to proportionally more space in the somatosensory area and are the most sensitive.

The senses of sound and sight are also represented in specific areas of the cerebral cortex. An *auditory area* located in the temporal lobe is responsible for the sense of hearing. If the auditory area is stimulated electrically, a person will hear sounds such as clicks or hums. It also appears that particular locations within the auditory area respond to specific pitches (deCharms, Blake, & Merzenich, 1998; Klinke et al., 1999).

The *visual area* in the cortex, located in the occipital lobe, operates analogously to the other sensory areas. Stimulation by electrodes produces the experience of flashes of light or colours, suggesting that the raw sensory input of images from the eyes is received in this area of the brain and transformed into meaningful stimuli. The visual area also provides another example of how areas of the brain are intimately related to specific areas of the body: Particular areas of the eye's retina are related to a particular part of the cortex—with, as you might guess, more space in the brain given to the most sensitive portions of the retina (Martin et al., 1995; Miyashita, 1995).

sensory area: The site in the brain of the tissue that corresponds to each of the senses, with the degree of sensitivity relating to the amount of tissue.

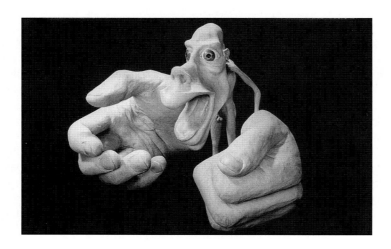

Figure 2-14 The greater the amount of tissue in the somatosensory area of the brain that is related to a specific body part, the more sensitive is that body part. If the size of our body parts reflected the corresponding amount of brain tissue, we would look like this strange creature.

*A model of the injury
sustained by Phineas Gage.*

association areas: One of the major areas of the brain; the site of the higher mental processes such as thought, language, memory, and speech.

PsychLink
Description of aphasia
www.mcgrawhill.ca/college/feldman

Broca's aphasia: Impaired speech function of language resulting from injury to the brain's association areas.
Wernicke's aphasia: Impaired understanding of language resulting from injury to the brain's association areas.

The Association Areas of the Cortex

Consider the following case:

> Twenty-five-year-old Phineas Gage, a railroad employee, was blasting rock one day in 1848 when an accidental explosion punched a 3-foot-long spike, about an inch in diameter, completely through his skull. The spike entered just under his left cheek, came out the top of his head, and flew into the air. Gage immediately suffered a series of convulsions, yet a few minutes later was talking with rescuers. In fact, he was able to walk up a long flight of stairs before receiving any medical attention. Amazingly, after a few weeks his wound healed, and he was physically close to his old self again. Mentally, however, there was a difference: Once a careful and hard-working person, Phineas now became enamored with wild schemes and was . . . irresponsible. As one of his physicians put it, ". . . His friends and acquaintances said he was 'no longer Gage'" (Harlow, 1869, p. 14).

What had happened to the old Gage? Although there is no way of knowing for sure—science being what it was in the 1800s—we can speculate that the accident injured the association areas of Gage's cerebral cortex. The **association areas** are generally considered to be the site of higher mental processes such as thinking, language, memory, and speech (Rowe et al., 2000).

The association areas take up a large proportion of the cerebral cortex. Most of our understanding of the association areas comes from patients who have suffered some type of brain injury. In some cases the injury stemmed from natural causes such as a tumour or a stroke, either of which would block certain blood vessels within the cerebral cortex. In other cases, accidents were the culprits, as was true with Phineas Gage. In any event, damage to these areas can result in unusual behavioural changes, indicating the importance of the association area to normal functioning (Herholz, 1995; Gannon et al., 1998).

Gage's case provides evidence that there are specialized areas for making rational decisions. When there is damage to these areas, people undergo personality changes that affect their ability to make moral judgments and process emotions. At the same time, people with damage in these areas can still be capable of reasoning logically, performing calculations, and recalling information (Damasio et al., 1994).

Apraxia and Aphasia   Injuries to other parts of the association areas can produce a condition known as *apraxia*. Apraxia occurs when an individual is unable to integrate activities in a rational or logical manner. The disorder is most evident when people are asked to carry out a sequence of behaviours requiring a degree of planning and foresight, suggesting that the association areas act as "master planners," or organizers of actions.

Injuries to the association areas of the brain can also produce *aphasia,* problems with language. In **Broca's aphasia** (caused by damage to the part of the brain first identified by a French physician, Paul Broca, in 1861), speech becomes halting, laborious, and often ungrammatical. The speaker is unable to find the right words, in a kind of tip-of-the-tongue phenomenon that we all experience from time to time. People with aphasia, though, grope for words almost constantly, eventually blurting out a kind of "verbal telegram." A phrase like "I put the book on the table" comes out as "I . . . put . . . book . . . table" (Cornell, Fromkin, & Mauner, 1993; Goodglass, 1993; Kirshner, 1995).

Wernicke's aphasia is a disorder named for Carl Wernicke, who identified it in the 1870s. Wernicke's aphasia produces difficulties both in understanding others' speech and in the production of language. The disorder is characterized by speech that sounds fluent but makes no sense. For instance, one patient, asked what brought him to a hospital, gave this rambling reply: "Boy, I'm sweating, I'm awful nervous, you know, once in a while I get caught up, I can't mention the tarripoi, a month ago, quite a little, I've done a lot well, I impose a lot, while, on the other hand, you know what I mean, I have to run around, look it over, trebbin and all that sort of stuff" (Gardner, 1975, p. 68).

Mending the Brain

Shortly after he was born, Jacob Stark's arms and legs started jerking every 20 minutes. Weeks later he could not focus his eyes on his mother's face. The diagnosis: uncontrollable epileptic seizures involving his entire brain.

His mother, Sally Stark, recalled: "When Jacob was two and a half months old, they said he would never learn to sit up, would never be able to feed himself. Nothing could be done to prevent profound retardation. They told us to take him home, love him and find an institution." (Blakeslee, 1992, C3).

Instead, the Starks brought Jacob to the University of California at Los Angeles for brain surgery when he was five months old. Surgeons removed 20 percent of his brain. The operation was a complete success. Three years later, Jacob seemed normal in every way, with no sign of seizures.

Jacob's surgery is representative of increasingly daring approaches in the treatment of brain disorders. It also illustrates how our growing understanding of the processes that underlie brain functioning can be translated into solutions to difficult problems.

The surgery that helped Jacob was based on the premise that the diseased part of his brain was producing seizures throughout the entire brain. Surgeons reasoned that if they removed the misfiring portion, the remaining parts of the brain, which appeared intact in PET scans, would take over and that Jacob could still lead a normal life.

Plasticity is the term used to explain the regenerative powers of the brain and nervous system. Although it has been known that the brain has the ability to shift functions to different locations following injury to a specific area or in cases of surgery, it had been assumed for decades that the neurons of the spinal cord and brain could never be replaced.

plasticity: The capacity of the brain to reorganize following injury (most common in children).

However, new evidence is beginning to suggest otherwise. For instance, researchers have found that the cells from the brains of adult mice can produce new neurons, at least in a test tube environment. Similarly, researchers have reported partial restoration of movement in rats who had a 5-millimetre-long gap in their spinal cords and, as a result, were unable to move their hind limbs. The researchers transplanted neurons from the peripheral nervous system into the gap, and subsequently the rats were able to flex their legs. One year after the operation, they were able to support themselves and move their legs, and examination of the neurons in the spinal cord showed significant regeneration around the area of the transplantation (Cheng, Cao, & Olson, 1996; McDonald, 1999; Blakeslee, 2000).

The future also holds promise for people who, like Michael J. Fox, suffer from the tremors and loss of motor control produced by Parkinson's disease. Because Parkinson's is caused by a gradual loss of cells that stimulate the production of dopamine in the brain, investigators reasoned that a procedure that increases the supply of dopamine might be effective. They seem to be on the right track. When certain cells from human fetuses are injected directly into the brains of Parkinson's sufferers, they seem to take root, stimulating dopamine production. For most of those who have undergone this procedure, the preliminary results are promising, with some patients showing great improvement. On the other hand, the technique remains experimental. According to the National Institute of Neurological Disorder and Stroke, this research has produced "insufficient benefit and unexpected complications," indicating that it should not be used widely without much more research (Kirschstein, 2000). It also raises some thorny ethical issues, given that the source of the implanted fetal tissue is aborted fetuses (Harvard Mental Health Letter, 2000; Pollack, 2000).

The Specialization of the Hemispheres: Two Brains or One?

The most recent development, at least in evolutionary terms, in the organization and operation of our brain probably occurred in the last million years: a specialization of the functions controlled by the two sides of the brain, which has symmetrical left and right halves.

hemispheres: The symmetrical left and right halves of the brain; each controls the side of the body opposite to it.

lateralization: The dominance of one hemisphere of the brain in specific functions.

What is a biological explanation for the gender differences in language development? An environmental example?

Specifically, the brain can be divided into two roughly similar mirror-image halves called **hemispheres**. Each hemisphere controls the side of the body opposite to its own location. The left hemisphere of the brain, then, generally controls the right side of the body, and the right hemisphere controls the left side of the body. Thus damage to the right side of the brain is typically indicated by functional difficulties in the left side of the body.

Despite the appearance of similarity between the two hemispheres of the brain, they are involved in somewhat different functions. It appears that certain activities are more likely to occur in one hemisphere than in the other. Early evidence for the functional differences between halves of the brain came from studies of people with aphasia. Researchers found that people with the speech difficulties characteristic of aphasia tended to have physical damage to the left hemisphere of the brain. In contrast, physical abnormalities in the right hemisphere of the brain tended to produce far fewer problems with language. This finding led researchers to conclude that for most people, language is **lateralized**, or located more in one hemisphere than in the other—in this case, in the left side of the brain (Grossi et al., 1996).

It now seems clear that the two hemispheres of the brain are somewhat specialized in terms of the functions they carry out. The left hemisphere concentrates more on tasks that require verbal competence, such as speaking, reading, thinking, and reasoning. The right hemisphere has its own strengths, particularly in nonverbal areas such as the understanding of spatial relationships, recognition of patterns and drawings, music, and emotional expression (Ornstein, 1998; Robertson & Ivry, 2000).

In addition, information is processed somewhat differently in the two hemispheres. The left hemisphere tends to consider information sequentially, one bit at a time; the right hemisphere tends to process information globally, considering it as a whole (Turkewitz, 1993; Banich & Heller, 1998).

On the other hand, it is important to keep in mind that the differences in specialization between the hemispheres are not great, and the degree and nature of lateralization vary from one person to another. If you are right-handed, control of language is probably concentrated more in your left hemisphere. If you are among the 10 percent of people who are left-handed or are ambidextrous (you use both hands interchangeably), it is much more likely that the language centres of your brain are located more in the right hemisphere or are divided equally between left and right hemispheres.

Researchers have also unearthed evidence that there may be subtle differences in brain lateralization patterns between males and females. In fact, some scientists have suggested that there are slight differences in the structure of the brain according to gender and culture. As we see next, such findings have led to a lively debate in the scientific community. Two Canadian neuroscientists, Doreen Kimura and Sandra Witelson, have figured prominently in this debate.

EXPLORING DIVERSITY

Human Diversity and the Brain

The interplay of biology and environment is particularly clear when we consider evidence suggesting that there are both sex and cultural differences in brain structure and function. Let's consider sex first. According to accumulating evidence, females and males show some intriguing differences in brain lateralization and weight, although the nature of those differences—and even their very existence—is a matter of considerable controversy (Kimura, 1992; Dorion et al., 2000).

We can be reasonably confident about some differences. For instance, most males tend to show greater lateralization of language in the left hemisphere. For them, language is clearly relegated largely to the left side of the brain. In contrast, women display less lateralization, with language abilities apt to be more evenly divided between the two hemispheres (Gur et al., 1982; Shaywitz et al., 1995; Kulynych et al., 1994). Such differences in brain lateralization could account, in part, for female superiority on certain

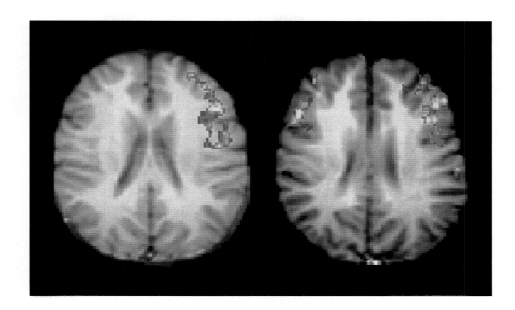

Figure 2-15 These composite MRI brain scans show the distribution of active areas in the brains of males *(left)* and females *(right)* during a verbal task involving rhyming. In males, activation is more lateralized, or confined, to the left hemisphere, while in females, activation is bilateralized, that is, occurring in both hemispheres of the brain.

(Source: B. A. Shaywitz et al., 1995. NMR/Yale Medical School)

measures of verbal skills, such as the onset and fluency of speech, and the fact that far more boys than girls have reading problems in elementary school (Kitterle, 1991).

Other research suggests that men's brains are somewhat bigger than women's brains, even after taking into account differences in body size. On the other hand, part of the *corpus callosum,* a bundle of fibres that connects the hemispheres of the brain, is proportionally larger in women than in men. Furthermore, some research suggests that women's brains have a higher proportion of the neurons that are actually involved in thinking than men's brains do (Witelson, 1995; Falk et al., 1999; Gur et al., 1999).

Men and women also might process information differently. For example, MRI brain scans of men sounding out words show activation of a small area of the left side of the brain, whereas women use areas on both sides of the brain (Shaywitz et al., 1995; see Figure 2-15). Similarly, PET brain scans of men and women while they are not engaged in mental activity show differences in the use of glucose (Gur et al., 1995; Gur, 1996).

The meaning of such sex differences is far from clear. Consider one possibility related to the differences that have been found in the proportional size of the corpus callosum: Its increased proportion in women might permit stronger connections to develop between those parts of the brain that control speech. In turn, this would explain why speech tends to emerge slightly earlier in girls than in boys.

Before we rush to such a conclusion, though, it is important to consider an alternative hypothesis: It is plausible that the earlier emergence of verbal abilities in girls is due to the fact that infant girls receive greater encouragement to verbalize than infant boys do. This greater early experience could foster growth of certain parts of the brain. Hence, physical brain differences might be a *reflection* of social and environmental influences, rather than a *cause* of the differences in men's and women's behaviour. At this point, it is impossible to confirm which of these two alternative hypotheses is correct.

The culture in which we are raised also might give rise to differences in brain lateralization. For example, native speakers of Japanese seem to process information regarding vowel sounds primarily in the brain's left hemisphere. In contrast, North and South Americans, Europeans, and individuals of Japanese ancestry who learn Japanese later in life handle vowel sounds principally in the right hemisphere.

The reason for this cultural difference in lateralization? One explanation could be that certain characteristics of the Japanese language, such as the ability to express complex ideas using only vowel sounds, result in the development of a specific type of brain lateralization in native speakers. Differences in lateralization could account for other dissimilarities between the ways native Japanese speakers and Westerners think about the world (Tsunoda, 1985).

In general, scientists are just beginning to understand the extent, nature, and meaning of sex and cultural differences in lateralization and brain structure. Furthermore, in evaluating the research on brain lateralization, it is important to keep in mind that the two hemispheres of the brain function interdependently in deciphering, interpreting, and reacting to the world.

The Split Brain: Exploring the Two Hemispheres

The patient, V. J., had suffered severe seizures. By cutting her corpus callosum, the fibrous portion of the brain that carries messages between the hemispheres, surgeons hoped to create a firebreak to prevent the seizures from spreading. The operation did decrease the frequency and severity of V. J.'s attacks. But V. J. developed an unexpected side effect: She lost the ability to write at will, although she could read and spell words aloud. (Strauss, 1998, p. 287)

People like V. J., whose corpus callosum has been surgically cut to stop seizures and who are therefore called **split-brain patients**, offer a rare opportunity for researchers investigating the independent functioning of the two hemispheres of the brain. For example, psychologist Roger Sperry—who won the Nobel Prize for his work—developed a number of ingenious techniques for studying how each hemisphere operated (Sperry, 1982; Baynes et al., 1998; Gazzaniga, 1998).

In one experimental procedure, blindfolded split-brain patients were allowed to touch an object with their right hand and were asked to name it. Because the right side of the body is connected to the left side of the brain—the hemisphere that is most responsible for language—the patient was able to name it. But if the blindfolded subjects touched the object with their left hand, they were not able to name it aloud. However, the information had registered: When the blindfold was taken off, subjects could pick out the objects that they had touched. Information can be learned and remembered, then, using only the right side of the brain. (By the way, unless you've had a split-brain operation, this experiment won't work with you, because the bundle of fibres connecting the two hemispheres of a normal brain immediately transfer the information from one hemisphere to the other.)

It is clear from experiments like this one that the right and left hemispheres of the brain specialize in handling different sorts of information. At the same time, it is important to realize that they are both capable of understanding, knowing, and being aware of the world, albeit in somewhat different ways. The two hemispheres, then, should be regarded as different in terms of the efficiency with which they process certain kinds of information, rather than as two entirely separate brains.

split-brain patient: A person who suffers from independent functioning of the two halves of the brain, as a result of which the sides of the body work in disharmony.

Chapter Activity 2–1
Hemispheric Specialization—Testing for Language Location

You will need a pencil or a piece of wooden dowel and a stopwatch if available.

The idea is to balance the pencil or dowel on the index finger of one hand and then the other while being silent and while performing a verbal task (e.g., spelling "psychology" backwards quickly). You will want to want to try this a number of times (perhaps three) with each hand to get an average for time for that hand.

Compare the results for each hand. Did the verbal task condition produce different results from the silent condition? For which hand, if any, was this true? Remember that the hand in question is controlled by the opposite hemisphere. If the verbal task made balancing more difficult on one side, perhaps it might suggest that the language processing in the controlling hemisphere was interfering with the balancing. This would suggest that language is predominately in that hemisphere.

You might look at the results for the class. Is there a gender difference? What do you think that a difference (or lack of one) means?

This activity is based on the work of Kemble, Filipi, & Gravlin (1985).

The Endocrine System: Of Chemicals and Glands

One aspect of the biopsychology of behaviour that we have not yet considered is the **endocrine system**, a chemical communication network that sends chemical messengers, in the form of hormones, throughout the body via the bloodstream. These **hormones** affect the functioning and growth of other parts of the body (Crapo, 1985; Kravitz, 1988).

Like neurotransmitters, hormones communicate chemical messages throughout the body, although the speed and mode of transmission are quite different. Whereas neural messages are measured in thousandths of a second, hormonal communications can take minutes to reach their destination. Furthermore, neural messages move across neurons in specific lines (as with wires strung along telephone poles), whereas hormones travel throughout the entire body, similar to the way radio waves transmit across the entire landscape. Just as radio waves evoke a response only when a radio is tuned to the correct station, so hormones flowing through the bloodstream activate only those cells that are receptive and "tuned" to the appropriate hormonal message.

Although endocrine glands are located throughout the body, as can be seen in Figure 2-16, major components of the endocrine system are located in the brain. They are the **pituitary gland**, and the hypothalamus which regulates it. The pituitary gland has sometimes been called the "master gland," because it controls the functioning of the rest of the endocrine system. But the pituitary gland is more than just the taskmaster of other glands; it has important functions in its own right. For instance, hormones secreted by the pituitary gland control growth. Extremely short people and unusually tall ones usually have pituitary gland abnormalities. Other endocrine glands affect emotional reactions, sexual urges, and energy levels.

Individual hormones can wear many hats, depending on circumstances. For example, the hormone oxytocin is at the root of many of life's satisfactions and pleasures. In new mothers, oxytocin produces an urge to nurse newborn offspring. The same hormone also seems to stimulate cuddling between species members. And, at least in rats, it encourages sexually active males to seek out females more passionately, and females to be more receptive to males' sexual advances (Angier, 1991).

endocrine system: A chemical communication network that sends messages throughout the body via the bloodstream.
hormones: Chemicals that circulate through the blood and affect the functioning or growth of other parts of the body.

pituitary gland: The "master gland," the major component of the endocrine system, which secretes hormones that control growth.

BECOMING AN INFORMED CONSUMER OF PSYCHOLOGY

Learning to Control Your Heart—and Mind—Through Biofeedback

What are some of the problems for which biofeedback provides successful treatment?

Tammy DeMichael was cruising along the New York State Thruway with her fiancé when he fell asleep at the wheel. The car slammed into the guardrail and flipped, leaving DeMichael with what the doctors called a "splattered C-6, 7"—a broken neck and crushed spinal cord.

After a year of exhaustive medical treatment, she still had no function or feeling in her arms and legs. "The experts said I'd be a quadriplegic for the rest of my life, able to move only from the neck up," she recalls. . . . But DeMichael proved the experts wrong. Today, feeling has returned to her limbs, her arm strength is normal or better, and she no longer uses a wheelchair. "I can walk about 60 feet with just a cane, and I can go almost anywhere with crutches," she says. (Morrow & Wolf, 1991, p. 64)

The key to DeMichael's astounding recovery: biofeedback. **Biofeedback** is a procedure in which a person learns to control through conscious thought internal physiological processes such as blood pressure, heart and respiration rate, skin temperature, sweating, and constriction of particular muscles. Although it had traditionally been thought that the heart, respiration rate, blood pressure, and other bodily functions were under the control of parts

biofeedback: A procedure in which a person learns to control through conscious thought internal physiological processes such as blood pressure, heart and respiration rate, skin temperature, sweating, and constriction of particular muscles.

Figure 2-16 Location and function of the major endocrine glands.
After S. S. Mader. Copyright © The McGraw-Hill Companies.

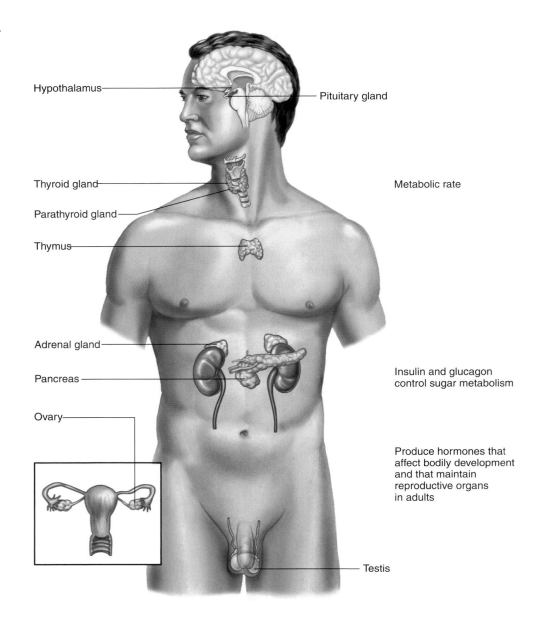

Hypothalamus

Pituitary gland

Thyroid gland

Metabolic rate

Parathyroid gland

Thymus

Adrenal gland

Pancreas

Insulin and glucagon control sugar metabolism

Ovary

Produce hormones that affect bodily development and that maintain reproductive organs in adults

Testis

of the brain over which we have no influence, psychologists have discovered that these responses are actually susceptible to voluntary control (Rau et al., 1996; Grimsley & Karriker, 1996; Bazell, 1998).

In biofeedback, a person is hooked up to electronic devices that provide continuous feedback relating to particular physiological responses. For instance, a person interested in controlling headaches through biofeedback might have electronic sensors placed on certain muscles on her head and learn to control the constriction and relaxation of those muscles. Later, after she mastered this training, when she felt a headache starting she could relax the relevant muscles and end the pain.

In DeMichael's case, biofeedback was effective because not all of the nervous system's connections between the brain and her legs were severed. Through biofeedback, she learned how to send messages to specific muscles, "ordering" them to move. Although it took more than a year, DeMichael was successful in restoring a large degree of her mobility.

Learning to control physiological processes through the use of biofeedback is not easy, but biofeedback has been employed with success in a variety of ailments, including emotional problems (such as anxiety, depression, phobias, tension headaches, insomnia, and hyperactivity); physical illnesses with a psychological component (such as asthma, high blood pressure, ulcers, muscle spasms, and migraine headaches); and physical problems (such as DeMichael's injuries, strokes, cerebral palsy, and, as we see in Figure 2-17, curvature of the spine).

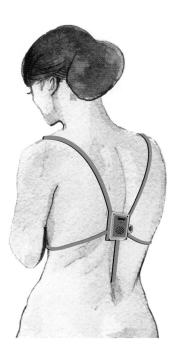

Figure 2–17 The traditional treatment for curvature of the spine employs an unsightly, cumbersome brace. In contrast, biofeedback treatment employs an unobtrusive set of straps attached to a small electronic device that produces tonal feedback when the patient is not standing straight. The person learns to maintain a position that gradually decreases the curvature of the spine until the device is no longer needed (Miller, 1985). What other disorders might biofeedback devices like this one help to treat?

Evaluate

1. A surgeon places an electrode on a portion of your brain and stimulates it. Immediately, your right wrist involuntarily twitches. The doctor has most likely stimulated a portion of the _____ area of your brain.
2. The _____ its corresponding space within the cortex, the more sensitive an area of the body is.
3. Each hemisphere controls the _____ side of the body.
4. Nonverbal realms, such as emotions and music, are controlled primarily by the _____ hemisphere of the brain, whereas the _____ hemisphere is more responsible for speaking and reading.
5. The left hemisphere tends to consider information _____, whereas the right hemisphere tends to process information _____.
6. As studies with split-brain patients have shown, information can be learned and remembered using only the nonverbal side of the brain. True or False?

Rethink

1. Suppose that abnormalities in an association area of the brain were linked through research to serious criminal behaviour. Would you be in favour of mandatory testing of individuals and surgery to repair or remove those abnormalities? Why or why not?

2. Could personal differences in people's specialization of right and left hemispheres be related to occupational success? For example, might an architect who relies on spatial skills have a different pattern of hemispheric specialization than a writer?

Answers to Evaluate Questions

1. motor 2. greater 3. opposite 4. right; left 5. sequentially; globally 6. True

Looking Back

Why do psychologists study the brain and nervous system?

- A full understanding of human behaviour requires knowledge of the biological influences underlying that behaviour. This chapter reviews what biopsychologists (psychologists who specialize in studying the effects of biological structures and functions on behaviour) have learned about the human nervous system. (p. 44)

What are the basic elements of the nervous system?

- Neurons, the most basic elements of the nervous system, allow nerve impulses to pass from one part of the body to another. Information generally follows a route that begins with the dendrites, continues into the cell body, and leads ultimately down the tubelike extension, the axon. (p. 45)

How does the nervous system communicate electrical and chemical messages from one part to another?

- Most axons are protected by a coating called the myelin sheath. When an axon receives a message to fire, it releases an action potential, an electrical charge that travels through the neuron. Neurons operate according to an all-or-none law: Either they are at rest or an action potential is moving through them. There is no in-between state. (p. 46)
- Once a neuron fires, nerve impulses are carried to other neurons through the production of chemical substances, neurotransmitters, that bridge the gaps—known as synapses—between neurons. Neurotransmitters are either excitatory (telling other neurons to fire), or inhibitory (preventing or decreasing the likelihood of other neurons firing). The major neurotransmitters include acetylcholine (ACh), which produces contractions of skeletal muscles, and dopamine, which has been linked to Parkinson's disease and certain mental disorders such as schizophrenia. (p. 48)
- Endorphins, another type of neurotransmitter, are related to the reduction of pain. Endorphins aid in the production of natural painkillers and are probably responsible for creating the kind of euphoria that joggers sometimes experience after running. (p. 51)

In what way are the structures of the nervous system tied together?

- The nervous system is made up of the central nervous system (the brain and spinal cord) and the peripheral nervous system (the remainder of the nervous system). The peripheral nervous system is made up of the somatic division, which controls voluntary movements and the communication of information to and from the sense organs, and the autonomic division, which controls involuntary functions such as those of the heart, blood vessels, and lungs. (p. 52)
- The autonomic division of the peripheral nervous system is further subdivided into the sympathetic and parasympathetic divisions. The sympathetic division prepares the body in emergency situations, and the parasympathetic division helps the body return to its typical resting state. (p. 53)
- Evolutionary psychology, the branch of psychology that seeks to identify behaviour patterns that are a result of our genetic inheritance, has led to increased understanding of the evolutionary basis of the structure and organization of the human nervous system. Behavioural genetics extends this study to include the evolutionary and hereditary bases of human personality traits and behaviour. (p. 53)

How do researchers identify the major parts and functions of the brain?

- Brain scans take a "snapshot" of the internal workings of the brain without having to cut surgically into a person's skull. Major brain-scanning techniques include the electroencephalogram (EEG), computerized axial tomography (CAT), the magnetic resonance imaging (MRI) scan, the functional magnetic resonance imaging (fMRI) scan, the superconducting quantum interference device (SQUID), and the positron emission tomography (PET) scan. (p. 57)

What are the major parts of the brain, and for which behaviours is each part responsible?

- The central core of the brain is made up of the medulla (which controls such functions as breathing and the heartbeat), the pons (which coordinates the muscles and the two sides of the body), the cerebellum (which controls balance), the reticular formation (which acts to heighten awareness in emergencies), the thalamus (which communicates sensory messages to and from the brain), and the hypothalamus (which maintains homeostasis, or body equilibrium, and regulates basic survival behaviours). The functions of the central core structures are similar to those found in other vertebrates. This part of the brain is sometimes referred to as the "old brain." Increasing evidence also suggests that female and male brains might differ in structure in minor ways. (p. 59)
- The cerebral cortex—the "new brain"—has areas that control voluntary movement (the motor area); the senses (the sensory area); and thinking, reasoning, speech, and memory (the association area). The limbic system, found on the border of the "old" and "new" brains, is associated with eating, reproduction, and the experiences of pleasure and pain. (p. 63)

How do the two halves of the brain operate interdependently?

- The brain is divided into left and right halves, or hemispheres, each of which generally controls the opposite side of the body. Each hemisphere can be thought of as specialized in the functions it carries out: The left is best at verbal tasks, such as logical reasoning, speaking, and reading; the right is best at nonverbal tasks, such as spatial perception, pattern recognition, and emotional expression. (p. 67)
- The endocrine system secretes hormones, allowing the brain to send messages throughout the nervous system via the bloodstream. A major component is the pituitary gland, which affects growth. (p. 71)

How can an understanding of the nervous system help us find ways to relieve disease and pain?

- Biofeedback is a procedure by which a person learns to control internal physiological processes. By controlling what were previously considered involuntary responses, people are able to relieve anxiety, tension, migraine headaches, and a wide range of other psychological and physical problems. (p. 71)

Key Terms and Concepts

biopsychologists (behavioural neuroscientists) (p. 44)

neurons (p. 45)

glial cells (p. 45)

dendrites (p. 45)

axon (p. 45)

For extra help in mastering the material in this chapter, see the integrator, practice quizzes, and other resources on the Online Learning Centre at

www.mcgrawhill.ca/college/feldman

Psychology on the Web

1. Biofeedback research is continuously changing and being applied to new areas of human functioning. Find at least two Web sites that discuss recent research on biofeedback and summarize the research and any findings it has produced. Include in your summary your own best estimate of future applications of this technique.
2. Find one or more Web sites on Parkinson's disease and learn more about this topic. Specifically, find reports of new treatments for Parkinson's that do not involve the use of fetal tissue. Write a summary of your findings.

Epilogue

This chapter has traced the ways in which biological structures and functions of the body affect behaviour. Starting with neurons, we considered each of the components of the nervous system, culminating in an examination of how the brain permits us to think, reason, speak, recall, and experience emotions—the hallmarks of being human.

Before we proceed to the next chapter, where we put our knowledge of the biology of behaviour to use in a look at sensation and perception, turn back for a moment to the prologue of this chapter, involving television and movie star Michael J. Fox. Consider the following questions.

1. Using what you now know about brain structures and functioning, can you explain what might have produced Fox's Parkinson's disease in the first place?
2. The operation used to treat Fox's disorder destroyed certain cells of his brain. Speculate about what part of the brain the operation might have involved.
3. Do you think biofeedback techniques could be used to control the symptoms of Parkinson's disease? Why or why not?

Chapter Three

Sensation and Perception

Prologue

Mae Brown: Without Sight and Sound

In June 1972, Mae Brown graduated from the University of Toronto, the first deaf-blind Canadian to earn a university degree. She went to work at the Canadian National Institute for the Blind as a counsellor for the deaf-blind, making contacts all over the world in order to develop and improve services for others who were both deaf and blind. Her career was cut short when she died at age 38.

Mae Brown

Mae's story began in May 1935 in Thunder Bay, Ontario. At birth, Mae had normal sight and hearing, but by the age of $2\frac{1}{2}$ years she developed visual problems. Speech and hearing problems developed later and by age 15 were so pronounced that she had to leave the regular school system.

At age 17, after a month of testing, doctors diagnosed the source of Mae's many problems (seizures, a stammer, poor vision, hearing, and balance) as neurofibramatosis. This is a rare disease in which tumours grow in the brain and interfere severely with its functioning. Surgery to save her life at age 17 caused deafness as well as the loss of the use of her facial muscles.

In spite of her problems, Mae was determined to live an independent life. In 1967, at 32 years of age, she was admitted to the University of Toronto at the Scarborough Campus. At university, her tutor and constant companion was Joan MacTavish. During lectures, Joan used English finger spelling to relay the lectures on Mae's hand. Joan described Mae's hands as her "highway to information" (MacTavish, 2001, p.163). Through finger spelling, Mae experienced the lectures as they occurred. Joan also taped the lectures, and later made notes from the tapes, which were transcribed into Braille. Mae finished her degree when she was 37 years old.

Mae lost her final battle against neurofibramatosis on November 3, 1973. Her experiences and those of her tutor Joan MacTavish were used in developing the Intervenor Program at George Brown College in Toronto. Intervenors are trained to act as the eyes and ears of people who are blind and deaf, helping them to communicate with others and assisting them in daily living so that they can be as independent as possible.

Source: MacTavish, 2001.

Looking Ahead

In this chapter we focus on the field of psychology that is concerned with the nature of the information our body takes in through its senses and with the way we interpret such information. Our ability to sense the stimuli in our environment is remarkable, enabling us to feel the gentlest of breezes, see flickering lights far away, and hear the soft murmuring of distant songbirds. We will explore both sensation and perception. Sensation encompasses the processes by which our sense organs receive information from the environment. Perception is the sorting out, interpretation, analysis, and integration of stimuli involving our sense organs and brain.

To a psychologist interested in understanding the causes of behaviour, sensation and perception are fundamental topics, because so much of our behaviour is a reflection of how we react to and interpret stimuli from the world around us. Questions ranging from "What processes enable us to see and hear?" to "How do we distinguish one person from another?" fall into the realm of sensation and perception.

Although perception clearly represents a step beyond sensation, in practice it is sometimes difficult to find the precise boundary between the two. The primary difference is that sensation can be thought of as an organism's first encounter with a raw sensory stimulus, whereas perception is the process by which the stimulus is interpreted, analyzed, and integrated with other sensory information. For example, if we were considering sensation, we might ask about the loudness of a ringing fire alarm. If we were considering perception, we might ask whether someone recognizes the ringing sound as an alarm and identifies its meaning. But both sensation and perception are necessary for transforming the physical world into our psychological reality.

This chapter begins with a discussion of the relationship between the characteristics of a physical stimulus and the kinds of sensory responses it produces. We then examine several of the major senses, including vision, hearing, balance, smell, taste, and the skin senses, which include touch and the experience of pain.

Next, the chapter explains how we organize the stimuli to which our sense organs are exposed. For instance, we consider a number of issues relating to perception, such as how we are able to perceive the world in three dimensions when our eyes are capable only of sensing two-dimensional images. Finally, we examine visual illusions, which provide us with important clues for understanding general perceptual mechanisms. As we explore these issues, we'll see how the senses work together to provide us with an integrated view and understanding of the world.

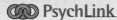

PsychLink

Perception demonstrations
www.mcgrawhill.ca/college/feldman

sensation: The processes by which our sense organs receive information from the environment.

perception: The sorting out, interpretation, analysis, and integration of stimuli involving our sense organs and brain.

Prepare

What is sensation, and how do psychologists study it?

What is the relationship between a physical stimulus and the kinds of sensory responses that result from it?

Organize

Sensing the World Around Us
  Absolute Thresholds
  Difference Thresholds
  Sensory Adaptation

Sensing the World Around Us

As Isabel sat down to Thanksgiving dinner, her father carried the turkey in on a tray and placed it squarely in the centre of the table. The noise level, already high from the talking and laughter of family members, grew louder still. As Isabel picked up her fork, the smell of the turkey reached her and she felt her stomach growl hungrily. The sight and sound of her family around the table, along with the smells and tastes of the holiday meal, made Isabel feel more relaxed than she had since starting school in the fall.

Put yourself in this setting and consider how different it might be if any one of your senses was not functioning. What if you were blind and deaf like Mae Brown? What if you were unable to see the faces of your family or the welcome shape of the golden-brown turkey? What if you had no sense of hearing and could not listen to the conversations of family members, or if you were unable to feel your stomach growl, smell the dinner, or taste the food? Clearly, you would experience the dinner very differently from someone whose sensory apparatus was intact.

Moreover, the sensations mentioned here barely scratch the surface of sensory experience. Although perhaps you were taught, as we were, that there are just five senses—sight, sound, taste, smell, and touch—this enumeration is too modest. Human sensory capabilities go well beyond the basic five senses. It is well established, for example, that we are sensitive not merely to touch, but to a considerably wider set of stimuli—pain, pressure, temperature, and vibration, to name a few. The ear is responsive to information that allows us not only to hear but also to keep our balance. Psychologists now believe there are at least a dozen distinct senses, all of which are interrelated.

To consider how psychologists understand the senses, and, more broadly, sensation and perception, we first need a basic working vocabulary. In formal terms, if any passing source of physical energy activates a sense organ, the energy is known as a stimulus. A **stimulus**, then, is energy that produces a response in a sense organ.

Stimuli vary in both type and intensity. Different types of stimuli activate different sense organs. For instance, we can differentiate light stimuli (which activate our sense of sight and allow us to see the colours of a tree in autumn) from sound stimuli (which, through our sense of hearing, permit us to hear the sounds of an orchestra).

Each sort of stimulus that is capable of activating a sense organ can also be considered in terms of its strength, or *intensity*. How intense a light stimulus needs to be before it is capable of being detected, or how much perfume a person must wear before it is noticed by others, are questions related to stimulus intensity.

The issue of how the intensity of a stimulus influences our sensory responses is considered in a branch of psychology known as psychophysics. **Psychophysics** is the study of the relationship between the physical aspects of stimuli and our psychological experience of them. Psychophysics played a central role in the development of the field of psychology, and many of the first psychologists studied issues related to psychophysics (Baird, 1997; Gescheider, 1997).

stimulus: Energy that produces a response in a sense organ.

psychophysics: The study of the relationship between the physical aspects of stimuli and our psychological experience of them.

absolute threshold: The smallest intensity of a stimulus that must be present for the stimulus to be detected.

 **PsychLink**

International Society for Psychophysics
www.mcgrawhill.ca/college/feldman

Absolute Thresholds: Detecting What's Out There

Just when does a stimulus become strong enough to be detected by our sense organs? The answer to this question requires an understanding of the concept of absolute threshold. An **absolute threshold** is the smallest intensity of a stimulus that must be present for it to be detected. Consider the following examples of absolute thresholds for the various senses (Galanter, 1962):

- *Sight:* A candle flame can be seen from 30 miles (about 50 kilometres) away on a dark, clear night.
- *Hearing:* The ticking of a watch can be heard 20 feet (6 metres) away under quiet conditions.
- *Taste:* Sugar can be tasted when 1 teaspoon is dissolved in 2 gallons of water (5 millimetres in 9 litres).
- *Smell:* Perfume can be detected when one drop is present in a three-room apartment.
- *Touch:* A bee's wing falling from a distance of 1 centimetre can be felt on the cheek.

Such thresholds permit our sensory apparatus to detect a wide range of sensory stimulation. In fact, the capabilities of our senses are so fine-tuned that we might have problems if they were any more sensitive. For instance, if our ears were just slightly more acute, we would be able to hear the sound of air molecules in our ears knocking into our eardrum—a phenomenon that would surely prove distracting and might even prevent us from hearing sounds outside our bodies.

Of course, the absolute thresholds we have been discussing are measured under ideal conditions. Normally our senses cannot detect stimulation quite as well because of the presence of noise. *Noise,* as defined by psychophysicists, is background stimulation that interferes with the perception of other stimuli. Hence, *noise* refers not just to auditory stimuli, but also to stimuli that affect the other senses. Picture a talkative group of people

Crowded conditions, sounds, and sights can all be considered as noise that interferes with sensation.
Can you think of other examples of noise that is not auditory in nature?

crammed into a small, crowded, smoke-filled room at a party. The din of the crowd makes it hard to hear individual voices, and the smoke makes it difficult to see, or even taste, the food. In this case, the smoke and crowded conditions would both be considered "noise" because they are both preventing sensation at more discriminating levels.

Difference Thresholds: Noticing Distinctions Between Stimuli

Suppose you wanted to choose the six best apples from a supermarket display—the biggest, reddest, and sweetest apples. One approach would be to systematically compare one apple with another until you were left with a few so similar that you could not tell the difference between them. At that point, it wouldn't matter which ones you chose.

Psychologists have discussed this comparison problem in terms of the **difference threshold**, the smallest level of stimulation required to sense that a *change* in stimulation has occurred. Put another way, the difference threshold is the minimum stimulation required to detect the difference between two stimuli, or a **just noticeable difference**.

The stimulus value that constitutes a just noticeable difference depends on the initial intensity of the stimulus. For instance, when the moon is visible during the late afternoon, it appears relatively dim—yet against a dark night sky, it seems quite bright.

The relationship between changes in the original value of a stimulus and the degree to which the change will be noticed forms one of the basic laws of psychophysics: Weber's law. **Weber's law** (with *Weber* pronounced "vay-ber") states that a just noticeable difference is a constant proportion of the intensity of an initial stimulus. For example, Weber found that the just noticeable difference for weight is 1:50. Consequently, it takes a 1-gram increase in a 50-gram weight to produce a noticeable difference, and it would take a 10-gram increase to produce a noticeable difference if the initial weight were 500 grams. In both cases, the same proportional increase is necessary to produce a just noticeable difference—1:50 = 10:500.

Sensory Adaptation: Turning Down Our Responses

You enter a bar, and the odour of cigarettes assaults you. A few minutes later, though, you barely notice the smell.

The reason you acclimate to the odour is sensory adaptation. **Adaptation** is an adjustment in sensory capacity following prolonged exposure to stimuli. Adaptation occurs as people become accustomed to a stimulus and change their frame of reference. In a sense, our brains mentally turn down the volume of the stimulation.

One example of adaptation is the decrease in sensitivity that occurs after repeated exposure to a strong stimulus. If you were to hear a loud tone over and over again, eventually it would begin to sound softer. Similarly, although jumping into a cold lake might be temporarily unpleasant, eventually we probably will get used to the temperature.

This apparent decline in sensitivity to sensory stimuli is due to the inability of the sensory nerve receptors to constantly fire off messages to the brain. Because these receptor cells are most responsive to *changes* in stimulation, constant stimulation is not effective in producing a reaction.

Judgments of sensory stimuli are also affected by the context in which the judgments are made. This is because judgments are made, not in isolation from other stimuli, but in terms of preceding sensory experience.

difference threshold: The smallest level of stimulation required to sense that a *change* in stimulation has occurred.

just noticeable difference: The minimum stimulation required to detect the difference between two stimuli.

Weber's law: One of the basic laws of psychophysics, that a just noticeable. difference is in constant proportion to the intensity of an initial stimulus.

 **PsychLink**

The fading dot
www.mcgrawhill.ca/college/feldman

adaptation: An adjustment in sensory capacity following prolonged exposure to stimuli.

1. _____ is the stimulation of the sense organs; _____ is the sorting out, interpretation, analysis, and integration of stimuli by our sense organs.
2. The term *absolute threshold* refers to the _____ intensity of a stimulus that must be present for the stimulus to be detected.
3. Weber discovered that in order for a difference between two stimuli to be perceptible, the stimuli must differ by at least a _____ proportion.
4. After completing a very difficult rock climb in the morning, Carmella found the afternoon climb unexpectedly easy. This case illustrates the phenomenon of _____.

Answers to Evaluate Questions

1. Sensation; perception 2. smallest 3. constant 4. adaptation

1. Do you think it is possible to have sensation without perception? Is it possible to have perception without sensation?
2. Do you think sensory adaptation is essential for everyday psychological functioning?

Vision: Shedding Light on the Eye

If, as poets say, the eyes provide a window to the soul, they also provide us with a window to the world. Our visual capabilities permit us to admire and react to scenes ranging from the beauty of a sunset to the configuration of our lover's face to the words written on the pages of a book.

Vision starts with light, the physical energy that stimulates the eye. Light is a form of electromagnetic radiation waves, which, as shown in Figure 3-1, are measured in wavelengths. The sizes of wavelengths correspond to different types of energy. The range of wavelengths that humans are sensitive to—called the *visual spectrum*—is relatively small. Many nonhuman species have different capabilities. For instance, some reptiles and fish sense energies of longer wavelengths than humans do, and certain insects sense energies of shorter wavelengths than humans do.

Prepare

What basic processes underlie the sense of vision?
How do we see colours?

Organize

Vision
    Illuminating the Structure of the Eye
    Colour Vision and Colour Blindness

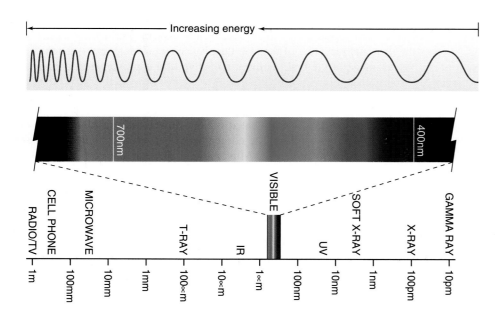

Figure 3–1 The visual spectrum—the range of wavelengths to which people are sensitive—is only a small part of the kinds of wavelengths present in our environment. Is it a benefit or disadvantage to our everyday lives that we aren't more sensitive to a broader range of visual stimuli? Why?

After R. Seeley, et al. Copyright © The McGraw-Hill Companies.

Figure 3–2 Although human vision is far more complicated than the most sophisticated camera, in some ways basic visual processes are analogous to those used in photography.

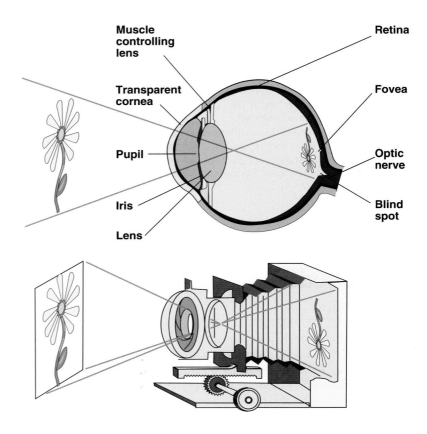

Muscle controlling lens

Transparent cornea

Pupil

Iris

Lens

Retina

Fovea

Optic nerve

Blind spot

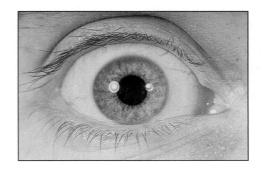

PsychLink
Visual perception
www.mcgrawhill.ca/college/feldman

Light waves coming from some object outside the body (imagine the light reflected off the flower in Figure 3-2) are sensed by the only organ that is capable of responding to the visual spectrum: the eye. Our eyes shape light into a form that can be used by the neurons that serve as messengers to the brain. The neurons themselves take up a relatively small percentage of the total eye. In other words, most of the eye is a mechanical device, analogous in many respects to a camera without film, as you can see in Figure 3-2.

Despite the similarities between the eye and a camera, vision involves processes that are far more complex and sophisticated than those of any camera. Furthermore, once the image reaches the neuronal receptors of the eye, the eye/camera analogy ends, for the processing of the visual image in the brain is more reflective of a computer than a camera.

Illuminating the Structure of the Eye

The ray of light we are tracing as it is reflected off the flower first travels through the *cornea,* a transparent, protective window. The cornea bends (or *refracts*) light as it passes through in order to more sharply focus it. After moving through the cornea, the light

Like the automatic lighting system on a camera, the human eye dilates to let in more light (left), *and contracts to block out light* (right).
Can humans adjust their ears to let in more or less sound in a similar manner?

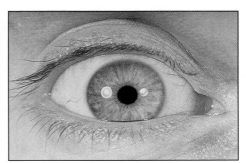

traverses the pupil. The *pupil* is a dark hole in the centre of the *iris,* the coloured part of the eye, which in humans ranges from a light blue to a dark brown. The size of the pupil opening depends on the amount of light in the environment. The dimmer the surroundings, the more the pupil opens in order to allow more light to enter.

Why shouldn't the pupil be opened completely all the time, thereby allowing the greatest amount of light into the eye? The answer relates to the basic physics of light. A small pupil greatly increases the range of distances at which objects are in focus. With a wide-open pupil, the range is relatively small, and details are harder to discern. The eye takes advantage of bright light by decreasing the size of the pupil and thereby becoming more discerning. In dim light the pupil expands to enable us to view the situation better— but at the expense of visual detail. (Perhaps one reason candlelight dinners are thought of as romantic is that the dim light prevents one from seeing the details of a partner's physical flaws.)

Once light passes through the pupil, it enters the *lens,* which is located directly behind the pupil. The lens acts to bend the rays of light so they are properly focused on the rear of the eye. The lens focuses light by changing its own thickness, a process called *accommodation.* The lens becomes flatter when viewing distant objects and rounder when looking at closer objects.

Reaching the Retina

Having travelled through the pupil and lens, our image of the flower finally reaches its ultimate destination in the eye—the **retina**. Here the electromagnetic energy of light is converted into the neural codes used by the brain. It is important to note that because of the physical properties of light, the image has reversed itself in travelling through the lens, and it reaches the retina upside down (relative to its original position). Although it might seem that this reversal would cause difficulties in understanding and moving about the world, this is not the case. The brain interprets the image in terms of its original position.

The retina consists of a thin layer of nerve cells at the back of the eyeball (see Figure 3-3). There are two kinds of light-sensitive receptor cells found in the retina. The names they have been given describe their shapes: rods and cones. **Rods** are thin, cylindrical receptor cells highly sensitive to light. **Cones** are cone-shaped, light-sensitive

retina: The part of the eye that converts the electromagnetic energy of light into useful information for the brain.

rods: Thin, cylindrical receptor cells in the retina that are highly sensitive to light.
cones: Cone-shaped, light-sensitive receptor cells in the retina that are responsible for sharp focus and colour perception, particularly in bright light.

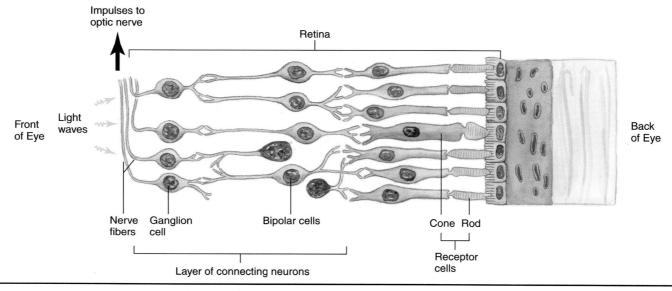

Figure 3-3 The basic cells of the eye. Light entering the eye travels through the ganglion and bipolar cells and strikes the light-sensitive rods and cones located at the back of the eye. The rods and cones then transmit nerve impulses to the brain via the bipolar and ganglion cells. *Processing in the eye is more complex in humans than in some other species. Can you think why?*
After D. Shier, et al. Copyright © The McGraw-Hill Companies.

receptor cells that are responsible for sharp focus and colour perception, particularly in bright light. The rods and cones are distributed unevenly throughout the retina. The greatest concentration of cones is on the part of the retina called the *fovea* (refer back to Figure 3-2). The fovea is a particularly sensitive region of the retina. If you want to focus in on something of particular interest, you will automatically try to centre the image from the lens onto the area of the fovea to see it more sharply.

The density of cones declines just outside the fovea, although cones are found throughout the retina in lower concentrations. On the other hand, there are no rods in the very centre of the fovea, but the density is greatest outside the fovea and then gradually declines toward the edges of the retina. Because the fovea covers only a small portion of the eye, there are fewer cones (about 7 million) than there are rods (about 125 million).

The rods and cones are not only structurally dissimilar, but they play distinctly different roles in vision. Cones are primarily responsible for the sharply focused perception of colour, particularly in brightly lit situations; rods are related to vision in dimly lit situations and are largely insensitive to colour and to details as sharp as those the cones are capable of recognizing. The rods play a key role in *peripheral vision*—seeing objects that are outside the main centre of focus—and in night vision.

Rods and cones also are involved in *dark adaptation,* the phenomenon of adjusting to dim light after being in brighter light. (Think of the experience of walking into a dark movie theatre and groping your way to a seat, but a few minutes later seeing the seats quite clearly.) The speed at which dark adaptation occurs is a result of the rate of change in the chemical composition of the rods and cones. Although the cones reach their greatest level of adaptation in just a few minutes, the rods take 15 minutes to reach the maximum level. The opposite phenomenon—*light adaptation,* or the process of adjusting to bright light after exposure to dim light—occurs much faster, taking only a minute or so.

Sending the Message from the Eye to the Brain

When light energy strikes the rods and cones, it starts a chain of events that transforms light into neural impulses that can be communicated to the brain. Even before the neural message reaches the brain, however, some initial coding of the visual information takes place.

What happens when light energy strikes the retina depends in part on whether it encounters a rod or a cone. Rods contain *rhodopsin,* a complex, reddish-purple substance whose composition changes chemically when energized by light. The substance found in cone receptors is different, but the principles are similar. Stimulation of the nerve cells in the eye triggers a neural response that is transmitted to other nerve cells, called *bipolar cells* and *ganglion cells,* leading to the brain.

Bipolar cells receive information directly from the rods and cones. This information is then communicated to the ganglion cells. Ganglion cells collect and summarize visual information, which is gathered and moved out of the back of the eyeball through a bundle of ganglion axons called the **optic nerve.**

Because the opening for the optic nerve passes through the retina, there are no rods or cones in the area, which creates a blind spot. Normally, however, this absence of nerve cells does not interfere with vision, because you automatically compensate for the missing part of your field of vision (Ramachandran, 1995; Churchland & Ramachandran, 1995). (To find your blind spot, see Chapter Activity 3-1.)

Once beyond the eye itself, the neural signals relating to the image move through the optic nerve. As the optic nerve leaves the eyeball, its path does not take the most direct route to the part of the brain right behind the eye. Instead, the optic nerves from each eye meet at a point roughly between the two eyes—called the *optic chiasm*—where each optic nerve then splits.

When the optic nerves split, the nerve impulses coming from the right half of each retina are sent to the right side of the brain, and the impulses arriving from the left half of each retina are sent to the left side of the brain. Because the image on the retinas is reversed and upside down, however, those images coming from the right half of each retina actually originated in the field of vision to the person's left, and images coming from the left half of each retina originated in the field of vision to the person's right

optic nerve: A bundle of ganglion axons that carry visual information from the eye to the brain.

PsychLink

Anatomy of the eye
www.mcgrawhill.ca/college/feldman

Chapter Activity 3–1
Find Your Blind Spot

FIGURE 3-4 To find your blind spot, close your right eye and look at the haunted house with your left eye. You will see the ghost on the periphery of your vision. Now, while staring at the house, move the page toward you. When the book is about 30 centimetres from your eye, the ghost will disappear. At this moment, the image of the ghost is falling on your blind spot.

But also notice how, when the page is at that distance, not only does the ghost seem to disappear, but the line seems to run continuously through the area where the ghost used to be. This shows how we automatically compensate for missing information by using nearby material to complete what is unseen. That's the reason you never notice the blind spot. What is missing is replaced by what is seen next to the blind spot. Can you think of any advantages that this tendency to provide missing information gives humans as a species?

(see Figure 3-5). In this way, our nervous system ultimately produces the phenomenon introduced in Chapter 2, in which each half of the brain is associated with the functioning of the opposite side of the body.

Processing the Visual Message

By the time a visual message reaches the brain, it has passed through several stages of processing. One of the initial sites is the ganglion cells. Each ganglion cell gathers information from a group of rods and cones in a particular area of the eye and compares the amount of light entering the centre of that area with the amount of light in the area around it. Some ganglion cells are activated by light in the centre (and darkness in the surrounding area). Other ganglion cells are activated when there is darkness in the centre and light in the surrounding areas. The ultimate effect of this process is to maximize the detection of variations in light and darkness. The neural image that is passed on to the brain, then, is an enhanced version of the actual visual stimulus outside the body.

The ultimate processing of visual images takes place in the visual cortex of the brain, and it is here that the most complex kinds of processing occur. Canadian psychologist David Hubel and Swedish psychologist Torsten Wiesel won the Nobel Prize for their discovery that many neurons in the cortex are extraordinarily specialized, being activated only by visual stimuli of a particular shape or pattern—a process known as **feature detection**. They found that some cells are activated only by lines of a particular width, shape, or orientation. Other cells are activated only by moving, as opposed to stationary, stimuli (Hubel & Wiesel, 1979; Patzwahl, Zanker, & Altenmuller, 1994).

feature detection: The activation of neurons in the cortex by visual stimuli of specific shapes or patterns.

More recent work has added to our knowledge of the complex ways in which visual information coming from individual neurons is combined and processed. For instance, according to Moutoussis and Zeki (1997), one system processes information for shapes, another processes colours, and other systems respond to movement, location, and depth. In Milner and Goodale's (1995) view, processing occurs in separate streams according to purposes such as identifying objects and tracking their movements, and these streams influence behaviour in a cooperative manner. For example, when an animal is hunting for live prey to eat, identifying is concerned with selecting the prey. Tracking the prey's movement is involved in pursuing it, which may lead to a reassessment of its desirability as a meal (refining the identification or possibly changing the identification) as well as an effort to facilitate the capture of the chosen prey.

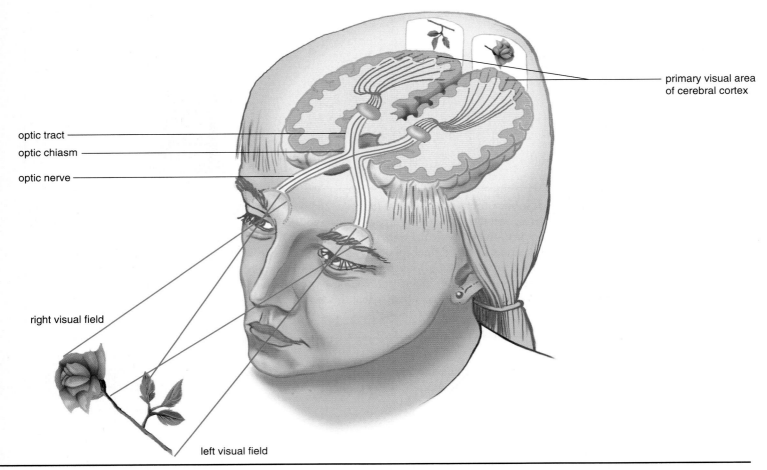

optic tract
optic chiasm
optic nerve

primary visual area
of cerebral cortex

right visual field

left visual field

Figure 3-5 Because the optic nerve coming from each eye splits at the optic chiasm, the image to a person's right is sent to the left side of the brain, and the image to the person's left is transmitted to the right side of the brain.

After S. S. Mader. Copyright © The McGraw-Hill Companies.

 **PsychLink**

Explanation of colour blindness
www.mcgrawhill.ca/college/feldman

Colour Vision and Colour Blindness: The Seven-Million-Colour Spectrum

Although the range of wavelengths to which humans are sensitive is relatively narrow, at least in comparison with the entire electromagnetic spectrum, the portion to which we are capable of responding still allows us great flexibility in sensing the world. Nowhere is this clearer than in terms of the number of colours we can discern. A person with normal colour vision is capable of distinguishing no less than seven million different colours (Bruce, Green, & Georgeson, 1997).

Although the variety of colours that people are generally able to distinguish is vast, there are certain individuals whose ability to perceive colour is quite limited—the colour-blind. Interestingly, the condition of these individuals has provided some of the most important clues for understanding how colour vision operates (Neitz, Neitz, & Kainz, 1996).

Before continuing, though, look at the photos shown in Figure 3-6. If you have difficulty seeing the differences among the series of photos, you may well be one of the few people—1 in 300 000 (Coren, Ward, & Enns, 1999)—who are completely colour-blind.

For most people with colour-blindness, the world looks quite dull. Red fire engines appear yellow, green grass seems yellow, and the three colours of a traffic light all look yellow. In fact, in the most common form of colour blindness, all red and green objects are seen as yellow. There are other forms of colour blindness as well, but they are quite rare. In yellow-blue blindness, people are unable to tell the difference between yellow and blue, and in the most extreme case an individual

a. b. c.

Figure 3-6 *(a)* To someone with normal vision, these hot-air balloons appear like this. *(b)* A person with red-green colour blindness would see the scene like this, in hues of blue and yellow. *(c)* A person who is blue-yellow blind, conversely, would see it in hues of red and green.

perceives no colour at all. To such a person the world looks something like the picture on a black-and-white television set.

To understand why some of us are colour-blind, it is necessary to consider the basics of colour vision. There appear to be two processes involved. The first process is explained by the **trichromatic theory of colour vision**. This theory suggests that there are three kinds of cones in the retina, each of which responds primarily to a specific range of wavelengths. One is most responsive to blue-violet colours, one to green, and the third to yellow-red (Brown & Wald, 1964). According to trichromatic theory, perception of colour is influenced by the relative strength with which each of the three kinds of cones is activated. If we see a blue sky, the blue-violet cones are primarily triggered, and the others show less activity. The trichromatic theory provides a straightforward explanation of colour-blindness. It suggests that one of the three cone systems malfunctions, and colours covered by that range are perceived improperly (Nathans et al., 1989).

However, there are phenomena that the trichromatic theory is less successful at explaining. For example, the theory does not explain what happens after you stare at something like the flag shown in Figure 3-7 for about a minute. Try Chapter Activity 3-2 on page 90. The afterimage experienced occurs because cells in the retina remain activated even when you are no longer staring at the original picture. This phenomenon also demonstrates that the trichromatic theory does not explain colour vision completely. Why should the colours in the afterimage be different from those in the original?

Because trichromatic processes do not provide a full explanation of colour vision, alternative explanations have been proposed. According to the **opponent-process theory of colour vision**, receptor cells are linked in pairs, working in opposition to each other. Specifically, there is a blue-yellow pairing, a red-green pairing, and a black-white pairing. If an object reflects light that contains more blue than yellow, it will stimulate the firing of the cells sensitive to blue, simultaneously discouraging or inhibiting the firing of receptor cells sensitive to yellow—and the object will appear blue. If, on the other hand, a light contains more yellow than blue, the cells that respond to yellow will be stimulated to fire while the blue ones are inhibited, and the object will appear yellow.

The opponent-process theory provides a good explanation for afterimages. When we stare at the green in the figure, for instance, our receptor cells for the green component of the green-red pairing become fatigued and are less able to respond to green stimuli. On the other hand, the receptor cells for the red part of the pair are not tired,

trichromatic theory of colour vision: The theory that there are three kinds of cones in the retina, each of which responds primarily to a specific range of wavelengths.

opponent-process theory of colour vision: The theory that receptor cells are linked in pairs, working in opposition to each other.

Chapter Activity 3-2
See an Afterimage

FIGURE 3-7 Stare at the dot in this flag for about a minute, and then look at the blank space underneath. Most people see an image of the traditional red and white Canadian flag. Where there was green, you'll see red, and where there was black, you'll see white. The phenomenon you have just experienced is called an *afterimage*.

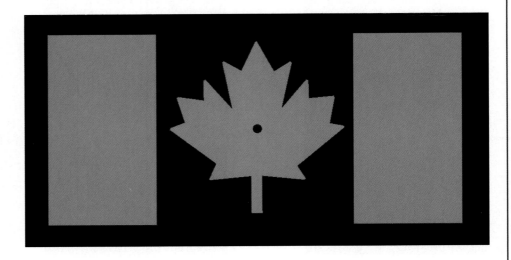

because they are not being stimulated. When we look at a white surface, the light reflected off it would normally stimulate both the green and the red receptors equally. But the fatigue of the green receptors prevents this from happening. They temporarily do not respond to the green, which makes the white light appear to be red. Because the black in the figure does the same thing relative to its specific opponent, white, the afterimage produces the opponent colours—for a while. The afterimage lasts only a short time, because the fatigue of the green receptors is soon overcome, and the white light begins to be perceived more accurately.

Both opponent processes and trichromatic mechanisms are at work in allowing us to see colour. However, they operate in different parts of the visual sensing system. Trichromatic processes work within the retina itself, whereas opponent mechanisms operate both in the retina and at later stages of neuronal processing (Leibovic, 1990; Gouras, 1991; de Valois & de Valois, 1993).

As we have gained more understanding of the processes that permit us to see, some psychologists have begun to develop new techniques to help overcome visual deficiencies in people with serious problems such as visual impairment or total blindness. One of the most promising devices is discussed in the *Applying Psychology in the 21ˢᵗ Century* box.

Applying Psychology in the 21st Century

▷ Bringing Sight to People with Blindness

At first sight, it looks like an off-centre ponytail flopping at the back of the head of a 62-year-old man named Jerry. But a closer look reveals that it is actually a bundle of wires entering Jerry's skull.

The purpose of the wires is to link a computer directly into Jerry's brain. The computer responds to a tiny pinhole camera mounted on one lens of a pair of sunglasses Jerry is wearing, along with an ultrasonic rangefinder mounted on the other lens. The camera and rangefinder send minute electrical charges through 68 electrodes implanted in a small area of the surface of Jerry's brain, allowing Jerry to perceive specks of light.

Admittedly, the kind of vision Jerry experiences is greatly limited. He is able to locate a mannequin in a room, find a black cap that is hanging on a wall, and place it on the head of the mannequin. He can also recognize five-centimetre letters from one and a half metres away.

Jerry (whose last name has not been divulged) is using an experimental device that may someday bring close to normal vision to people with blindness. Although in its current version the device permits Jerry to see only specks of flickering light, it is still sophisticated enough to permit him to perceive differences between light and dark areas (Dobelle, 2000).

Technological advances are providing other approaches to helping the blind. For instance, sensory perception psychologist Jack Loomis and colleagues are developing what they call a "personal guidance system" to help people with vision limitations move through their environment (Loomis et al., 1993; Golledge et al., 1998; Loomis, Golledge, & Klatzky, in press).

The system uses a positioning device linked to navigation satellites overhead that are able to map the ground with an accuracy of around a metre. Geographic information from the

Jerry, a 62-year-old man with blindness, is able to see as the result of electrodes implanted in his brain and connected to a camera mounted on a pair of glasses. A small computer on his hip permits him to read large letters and move around large objects in a room. Do you think modern technology will ever duplicate the functions of the human eye?

satellites is transmitted to an on-ground receiver and computer strapped to a person's back. The computer translates the geographic information into acoustic stimulation that is sent to one earphone or the other. The stimulation, which for now is just a code word, becomes softer or louder, depending on the direction the person is supposed to turn.

Klatzky and Loomis predict that future versions will go beyond a single code word to provide complete verbal directions, such as "go forward three metres, and then turn to the right." In addition, the computer will identify landmarks the person is passing by ("I'm the post office, and I'm six metres to your left"). Furthermore, the size of the backpack should shrink significantly, perhaps fitting into a pack around the waist.

Researchers predict that devices such as Jerry's electrodes and the personal guidance system will be commercially available within the next few years. Next on the horizon are electronic retinal implants, a kind of bionic eye, that will restore sight to people with damaged retinas. Some experts feel that such devices can be developed well before the end of the decade (Marcus, 1998; Eisenberg, 1999; Dobelle, 2000).

What psychological adjustments might be necessary when sight is restored for people who have been blind for their entire lives? Can you think of any disadvantages of the restoration of sight and why some blind individuals might decide not to have their sight restored?

Evaluate

1. Light entering the eye first passes through the _____, a protective window.
2. The structure that converts light into usable neural messages is called the _____.
3. A woman with blue eyes could be described as having blue pigment in her _____.
4. What is the process by which the thickness of the lens is changed in order to focus light properly?
5. The proper sequence of structures that light passes through in the eye is the _____, _____, _____, and _____.
6. Match each type of visual receptor with its function.

   a. Rods   1. Used for dim light, largely insensitive to colour.
   b. Cones   2. Detect colour, good in bright light.

7. Paco was to meet his girlfriend in the movie theatre. As was typical, he was late and the movie had begun. He stumbled down the aisle, barely able to see. Unfortunately, the woman he sat down beside and attempted to put his arm around was not his girlfriend. He sorely wished he had given his eyes a chance and waited for _____ adaptation to occur.
8. _____ theory states that there are three types of cones in the retina, each of which responds primarily to a different colour.

Answers to Evaluate Questions

1. cornea 2. retina 3. iris 4. Accommodation 5. cornea, pupil, lens, retina 6. a-1, b-2 7. dark 8. Trichromatic

Rethink

1. If the eye were constructed with a second lens that "unreversed" the image hitting the retina, do you think there would be changes in the way people perceive the world?
2. From an evolutionary standpoint, why might the eye have evolved so that the rods, which we rely on in low light, do not provide sharp images? Are there any advantages to this system?

Prepare

What role does the ear play in the senses of sound, motion, and balance?

How do smell and taste function?

What are the skin senses, and how do they relate to the experience of pain?

Organize

Hearing and the Other Senses
    Sensing Sound
    Smell and Taste
    The Skin Senses

Hearing and the Other Senses

The blast-off was easy compared with what the astronaut was experiencing now: space sickness. The constant nausea and vomiting were enough to make him wonder why he had worked so hard to become an astronaut. Even though he had been warned that there was a two-thirds chance that his first experience in space would cause these symptoms, he wasn't prepared for how terribly sick he really felt.

Whether or not the astronaut turns his rocket around and heads back to earth, his experience, a major problem for space travellers, is related to a basic sensory process centred in the ear: the sense of motion and balance. This sense allows people to navigate their bodies through the world and maintain an upright position without falling. Along with hearing, which is the process by which sound waves are translated into understandable and meaningful forms, the senses of motion and balance are the major functions of the ear.

Sensing Sound

Although many of us think primarily of the *outer ear* when we consider hearing, this part functions simply as a reverse megaphone, designed to collect and bring sounds into internal portions of the ear (see Figure 3-8). However, the location of the outer ears on different sides of the head helps with *sound localization,* the process by which we identify the location from which a sound is originating. Wave patterns in the air enter each ear at a slightly different time, permitting the brain to use the discrepancy to locate the sound's point of origin. In addition, the two outer ears delay or amplify sounds of particular frequencies to different degrees (Middlebrooks & Green, 1991; Yost, 1992; Konishi, 1993). High-frequency sounds seem louder to the ear that is nearer to the sound source. This occurs because the head interferes with the transmission of high-frequency sounds to the ear that is farther away from the sound source. The ear that is closer to the sound source receives more intense stimulation. The brain uses this difference in intensity as well as the difference in arrival times to localize sound.

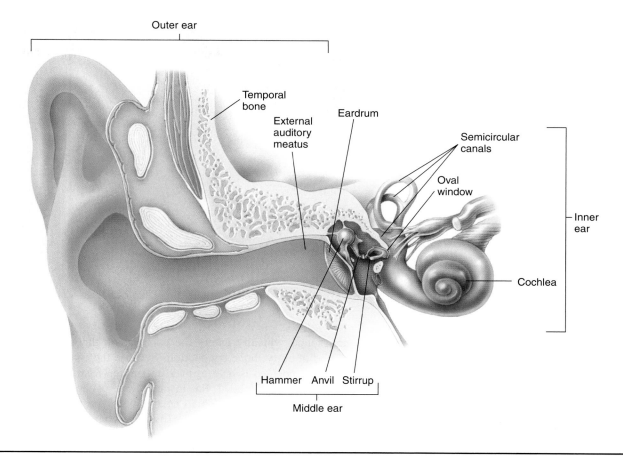

Figure 3-8 The ear.

After R. Seeley, et al. Copyright © The McGraw-Hill Companies.

Sound is the movement of air molecules brought about by the vibration of an object. Sounds travel through the air in wave patterns similar in shape to those made in water when a stone is thrown into a still pond. Sounds, arriving at the outer ear in the form of wave vibrations, are funnelled into the *auditory canal,* a tubelike passage that leads to the eardrum. The **eardrum** is aptly named because it operates like a miniature drum, vibrating when sound waves hit it. The more intense the sound, the more the eardrum vibrates. These vibrations are then transferred into the *middle ear,* a tiny chamber containing three bones (the *hammer,* the *anvil,* and the *stirrup*) that transmit vibrations to the *oval window,* a thin membrane leading to the inner ear. Because the hammer, anvil, and stirrup act as a set of levers, they not only transmit vibrations but increase their strength. Moreover, because the opening into the middle ear (the eardrum) is considerably larger than the opening out of it (the oval window), the force of sound waves on the oval window becomes amplified. The middle ear, then, acts as a tiny mechanical amplifier.

The *inner ear* is the portion of the ear that changes the sound vibrations into a form that allows them to be transmitted to the brain. It also contains the organs that allow us to locate our position and determine how we are moving through space. When sound enters the inner ear through the oval window, it moves into the **cochlea**, a coiled tube that looks something like a snail and is filled with fluid that can vibrate in response to sound. Inside the cochlea is the **basilar membrane**, a structure that runs through the centre of the cochlea, dividing it into an upper and a lower chamber. The basilar membrane is covered with **hair cells**. When these hair cells are bent by the vibrations entering the cochlea, a neural message is transmitted to the brain (Cho, 2000).

sound: The movement of air molecules brought about by the vibration of an object.

eardrum: The part of the ear that vibrates when sound waves hit it.

cochlea (KOKE lee uh): A coiled tube in the ear filled with fluid that vibrates in response to sound.

basilar membrane: A vibrating structure that runs through the centre of the cochlea, dividing it into an upper and a lower chamber, and containing sense receptors for sound.

hair cells: Tiny cells covering the basilar membrane that, when bent by vibrations entering the cochlea, transmit neural messages to the brain.

The eardrum is aptly named because it operates like a miniature drum, vibrating when sound waves hit it.

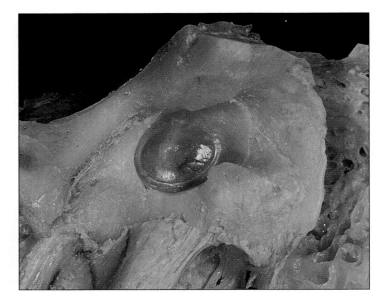

Although sound typically enters the cochlea via the oval window, there is an additional method of entry: bone conduction. Because the ear rests on a maze of bones within the skull, the cochlea is able to pick up subtle vibrations that travel across the bones from other parts of the head. For instance, one of the ways you hear your own voice is through bone conduction. This explains why you sound different to yourself than to other people who hear your voice. (Listen to yourself on a tape recorder sometime to hear what you *really* sound like!) The sound of your voice reaches you both through the air and via bone conduction and therefore sounds richer to you than to everyone else.

The Physical Aspects of Sound

As we mentioned earlier, what we refer to as sound is actually the physical movement of air molecules in regular, wavelike patterns caused by the vibration of an object (see Figure 3-9). Sometimes it is even possible to view these vibrations, as in the case of a stereo speaker that has no enclosure. If you have ever seen one, you know that, at least when the lowest notes are playing, you can see the speaker moving in and out. What is less obvious is what happens next: The speaker pushes air molecules into waves with the same pattern as its movement. These wave patterns soon reach your ear, although their strength has been weakened considerably during their travels. All other stimuli that produce sound work in essentially the same fashion, setting off wave patterns that move through the air to the ear. Air—or some other medium, such as water—is necessary to make the vibrations of objects reach us. This explains why there can be no sound in a vacuum.

PsychLink

Sound waves
www.mcgrawhill.ca/college/feldman

We are able to see the stereo speaker moving when low notes are played because of a primary characteristic of sound called frequency. *Frequency* is the number of wave cycles that occur in a second. With very low frequencies there are relatively few, and therefore slower, up-and-down wave cycles per second. These are visible to the naked eye as vibrations in the speaker. Low frequencies are translated into a sound that is very low in pitch. (*Pitch* is the characteristic that makes sound "high" or "low.") For example, the lowest frequency that humans are capable of hearing is 20 cycles per second. Higher frequencies translate into higher pitch. At the upper end of the sound spectrum, people can detect sounds with frequencies as high as 20 000 cycles per second (Coren, Ward & Enns, 1999).

Intensity or *amplitude* is a feature of wave patterns that allows us to distinguish between loud and soft sounds. Intensity is produced by the difference between the peaks

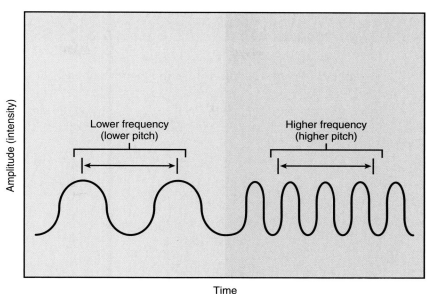

Figure 3-9 The waves produced by different stimuli are transmitted— usually through the air—in different patterns.
How do waves for low and high pitch differ?
After R. Seeley, et al. Copyright © The McGraw-Hill Companies.

and valleys of air pressure in a sound wave as it travels through the air. Waves with small peaks and valleys create less compression and expansion of molecules in the air through which the sound wave is travelling and produce soft sounds. Waves with larger peaks and valleys cause more intense changes in pressure in the air, and produce loud sounds.

We are sensitive to a broad range of sound intensity. The loudest sounds we are capable of hearing are about 10 million times as intense as the very weakest sound we can hear. This range is measured in *decibels*. When sounds get higher than 120 decibels, they become painful to the human ear.

Hearing Loss and Deaf Culture

The delicacy of the organs involved in hearing makes the ear vulnerable to damage. For instance, exposure to intense levels of sound—coming from events ranging from rock concerts to overly loud headphones—can eventually result in hearing loss, as the hair cells of the basilar membrane lose their elasticity and bend and flatten (see Table 3-1). Such hearing loss is often permanent.

Even without actual injury, many people eventually lose hearing acuity over the course of their lives. Ultimately, almost 10 percent of all individuals have some degree of hearing impairment. A small number of people, about 3000 Canadians, are both deaf and blind, as was Mae Brown, whose case was described in the chapter prologue.

Although minor hearing impairment can be treated with hearing aids that increase the volume of sounds reaching the ear, more drastic measures are necessary in more severe cases. Certain forms of deafness, produced by damage to the hair cells, can be treated through a *cochlear implant*. An implant consists of a tiny receiver inside the ear and an electrode that stimulates hair cells, controlled by a small external sound processor worn behind the ear.

Although the restoration of hearing to a deaf person may seem like an unquestionably positive achievement, some advocates for the deaf suggest otherwise, especially when it comes to deaf children. These critics suggest that deafness represents a legitimate culture—no better nor worse than the hearing culture—and that providing even limited hearing to deaf children robs them of their natural cultural heritage.

In North American deaf culture, the primary means of communication is American Sign Language (ASL), which is recognized as a legitimate language (Petitto, 2000). In Canada, there are also many other sign languages because deaf Canadians belong to many different cultures. For example, MacDougall (2001) found that in Nunavut, deaf people who have lived all their lives in the North use Inuit Sign Language (ISL), an

Table 3-1 Now Hear This

Various sounds, their decibel levels, and the amount of exposure that results in hearing damage

Sound	Decibel Level	Exposure Time Leading to Damage
Whispering	25 dB	
Library	30 dB	
Average home	50 dB	
Normal conversation	60 dB	
Washing machine	65 dB	
Car	70 dB	
Vacuum cleaner	70 dB	
Busy traffic	75 dB	
Alarm clock	80 dB	
Noisy restaurant	80 dB	
Average factory	85 dB	16 hours
Live rock music (moderately loud)	90 dB	8 hours
Screaming child	90 dB	8 hours
Subway train	100 dB	2 hours
Jackhammer	100 dB	2 hours
Helicopter	105 dB	1 hour
Sandblasting	110 dB	30 minutes
Auto horn	120 dB	7.5 minutes
Live rock music (loud)	130 dB	3.75 minutes
Air raid siren	130 dB	3.75 minutes
THRESHOLD OF PAIN	140 dB	Immediate damage
Jet engine	140 dB	Immediate damage
Rocket launching	180 dB	Immediate damage

indigenous signing system. However, deaf Inuit who have attended schools in the South use ASL and Manually Coded English finger spelling. Family members and others who interact frequently with deaf people use ISL to communicate with them. In the three communities MacDougall studied in depth, he observed that there was no stigma attached to deafness. In addition, people told him that the hearing Inuit used ISL to communicate not only with deaf people, but also with other hearing Inuit who spoke different dialects (MacDougall, 2001).

Sorting Out Theories of Sound

How are our brains able to sort out wavelengths of different frequencies and intensities? One clue comes from studies of the basilar membrane, the area within the cochlea that translates physical vibrations into neural impulses. It turns out that sounds affect different areas of the basilar membrane, depending on the frequency of the sound wave.

The part of the basilar membrane nearest the oval window is most sensitive to high-frequency sounds, and the part nearest the cochlea's inner end is most sensitive to low-frequency sounds. This finding has led to the **place theory of hearing**, which says that different areas of the basilar membrane respond to different frequencies.

On the other hand, place theory does not tell the full story of hearing, because very-low-frequency sounds trigger neurons across such a wide area of the basilar membrane that no single site is involved. Consequently, an additional explanation for hearing has been proposed: frequency theory. The **frequency theory of hearing** suggests that the entire basilar membrane acts like a microphone, vibrating as a whole in response to a sound. According to this explanation, the nerve receptors send out signals that are tied directly to the frequency (the number of wave crests per second) of the sounds to which we are exposed, with the number of nerve impulses being a direct function of the sound's frequency. Thus, the higher the pitch of a sound (and therefore the greater the frequency of its wave crests), the greater the number of nerve impulses that are transmitted up the auditory nerve to the brain.

Neither place theory nor frequency theory provides the full explanation for hearing (Luce, 1993; Hirsh & Watson, 1996). Place theory provides a better explanation for the sensing of high-frequency sounds, whereas frequency theory explains what happens when low-frequency sounds are encountered. Medium-frequency sounds incorporate both processes.

After an auditory message leaves the ear, it is transmitted to the auditory cortex of the brain through a complex series of neural interconnections. As the message is transmitted, it is communicated through neurons that respond to specific types of sounds. Within the auditory cortex itself, there are neurons that respond selectively to very specific sorts of sound features, such as clicks or whistles. Some neurons respond only to a specific pattern of sounds, such as a steady tone but not an intermittent one. Furthermore, specific neurons transfer information about a sound's location through their particular pattern of firing (Ahissar et al., 1992; Middlebrooks et al., 1994).

If we were to analyze the configuration of the cells in the auditory cortex, we would find that neighbouring cells are responsive to similar frequencies. The auditory cortex, then, provides us with a "map" of sound frequencies, just as the visual cortex furnishes a representation of the visual field.

Balance: The Ups and Downs of Life

Several structures of the ear are related more to our sense of balance than to our hearing. The **semicircular canals** of the inner ear consist of three tubes containing fluid that sloshes through them when the head moves, signalling rotational or angular movement to the brain. The pull on our bodies caused by the acceleration of forward, backward, or up-and-down motion, as well as the constant pull of gravity, is sensed by the **otoliths**, tiny, motion-sensitive crystals. When we move, these crystals shift like sands on a windy beach. The brain's inexperience in interpreting messages from the weightless otoliths is the cause of the space sickness commonly experienced by two-thirds of all space travellers (Flam, 1991; Stern & Koch, 1996).

Smell and Taste

Until he bit into a piece of raw cabbage on that February evening in 1997, Dr. Raymond Fowler had not thought much about the sense of taste.

The cabbage, part of a pasta dish he was preparing for his family's dinner, had an odd, burning taste, but he did not pay it much attention. Then a few minutes later, his daughter handed him a glass of cola, and he took a swallow. "It was like sulfuric acid," he said. "It was like the hottest thing you could imagine boring into your mouth." (Goode, 1999b, p. D1–D2)

place theory of hearing: The theory that different areas of the basilar membrane respond to different frequencies.

frequency theory of hearing: The theory that the entire basilar membrane acts like a microphone, vibrating as a whole in response to a sound.

semicircular canals: Three tubelike structures of the inner ear containing fluid that sloshes through them when the head moves, signalling rotational or angular movement to the brain.
otoliths: Tiny, motion-sensitive crystals within the semicircular canals that sense body acceleration.

Psychology at Work

Julia A. Mennella

Taste Researcher

Education: B.S., biology, Loyola University, Chicago; M.S., biology, DePaul University, Chicago; Ph.D., biopsychology, University of Chicago.

Home: Philadelphia

Julia Mennella

Researchers have long known that the senses of taste and smell are developed in the first months of a child's life, and that infants have strong positive and negative reactions to certain tastes and smells soon after birth. But recent discoveries have shown that taste and smell preferences can start even earlier—while a child is still in its mother's womb.

According to research conducted by psychologist Julia A. Mennella of the Monell Chemical Senses Center, a research laboratory in Philadelphia, the ability to detect certain tastes is present even before birth.

"Research has found that taste pores are functioning by the second trimester of pregnancy, and a child is born with a rich population of taste receptors," she noted. Furthermore, the flavours mothers consume prior to the birth of their babies affects children's preferences later in life. Mennella notes, "We found that babies who experienced a particular flavour in the amniotic fluid or, later, in their mother's milk, prefer that flavour when they start to eat solid foods."

One reason cultures favour certain kinds of diets and foods is due to the development of taste and smell at the earliest stages of life, according to Mennella.

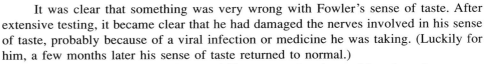

"One of the most enduring characteristics of people around the world are their food habits."

"One of the most enduring characteristics of people around the world are their food habits," Mennella said. "The food that a mother eats is one of the first mechanisms by which a baby learns about the food of a culture." She adds, "Mother's milk is like a flavour bridge that is enhancing the flavour experience before the child eats food from the table. Food is a celebration of a culture, and the baby is learning this even before tasting solid foods."

It was clear that something was very wrong with Fowler's sense of taste. After extensive testing, it became clear that he had damaged the nerves involved in his sense of taste, probably because of a viral infection or medicine he was taking. (Luckily for him, a few months later his sense of taste returned to normal.)

Even without disruptions in our ability to perceive the world such as those experienced by Fowler, we all know the important roles that taste and smell play. We'll consider these two senses next.

Smell

Although many animals have keener abilities to detect odours than we do, our sense of smell *(olfaction)* permits us to detect more than 10 000 separate smells. We also have a good memory for smells, and long-forgotten events and memories can be brought back with the mere whiff of an odour associated with the memory (Schab, 1991; Bartoshuk & Beauchamp, 1994; Gillyatt, 1997).

Results of "sniff tests" have shown that women generally have a better sense of smell than men (Engen, 1987). People also seem to have the ability to distinguish males from females on the basis of smell alone. In one experiment, blindfolded students, asked to sniff the breath of a female or male volunteer who was hidden from view, were able to distinguish the sex of the donor at better than chance levels. People can also distinguish happy from sad emotions by sniffing underarm smells (Doty et al., 1982; Haviland-Jones & Chen, 1999).

Our understanding of the mechanisms that underlie the sense of smell is just beginning to emerge. We do know that the sense of smell is sparked when the molecules of a substance enter the nasal passages and meet *olfactory cells,* the receptor cells of the nose, which are spread across the nasal cavity. More than 1000 separate types of receptor cells have been identified so far. Each of these cells is so specialized that it responds only to a small band of different odours. The responses of the separate olfactory cells are then transmitted to the olfactory bulbs located in the brain above the nasal cavity (see Figure 3-10). From here olfactory information is sent to several regions in the brain where it is combined into recognition of a particular smell (Buck & Axel, 1991; Rubin & Katz, 1999).

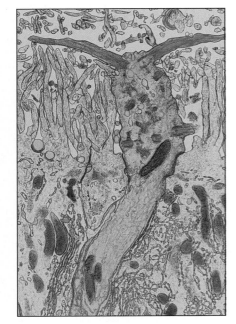

More than 1000 receptor cells, known as olfactory cells, are spread across the nasal cavity. The cells are specialized to react to particular odours.

Do you think it is possible to "train" the nose to pick up a greater number of odours?

There is increasing evidence that smell can also act as a hidden means of communication for humans. It has long been known that nonhumans release *pheromones,* pollen-like chemicals that produce a reaction in other members of a species, permitting the transmission of such messages as sexual availability. For instance, certain substances in the vaginal secretions of female monkeys contain pheromones that stimulate sexual interest in male monkeys (Holy, Dulac, & Meister, 2000).

Although it seems reasonable that humans might also communicate through the release of pheromones, the evidence is still scanty. Women's vaginal secretions contain chemicals similar to those found in monkeys, but in humans the smells do not seem to be related to sexual activity. On the other hand, the presence of these substances might explain why women who live together for long periods of time tend to start their menstrual cycles on the same day. In addition, women are able to identify their babies solely on the basis of smell just a few hours after birth (Porter, Cernich, & McLaughlin, 1983; Engen, 1987; Grammer, 1996).

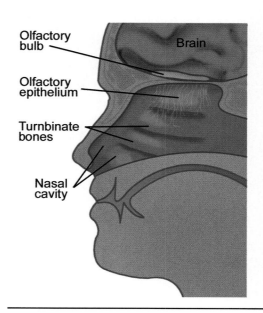

Figure 3–10 The olfactory system.

Taste

Unlike smell, which employs more than a thousand separate types of receptor cells, the sense of taste *(gustation)* seems to make do with only a handful of fundamental types of receptors. Most psychologists believe that there are just four basic receptor cells, which specialize in either sweet, sour, salty, or bitter flavours. Every other taste is simply a combination of these four basic qualities, in the same way that theprimary colours blend into a vast variety of shades and hues (McLaughlin & Margolskee, 1994).

The receptor cells for taste are located in roughly 10 000 *taste buds,* which are distributed across the tongue and other parts of the mouth and throat. The taste buds wear out and are replaced every ten days or so. That's a good thing, because if our taste buds weren't constantly reproducing, we'd lose the ability to taste after we'd accidentally burned our tongues.

Taste and smell
www.mcgrawhill.ca/college/feldman

The sense of taste differs significantly from one person to another, determined largely by genetic factors. Some people, dubbed "supertasters," are highly sensitive to taste; they have twice as many taste receptors as "nontasters," who are relatively insensitive to taste. Supertasters (who, for unknown reasons, are more likely to be female than male) find sweets sweeter, cream creamier, and spicy dishes spicier, and weaker concentrations of flavour are enough to satisfy any cravings they may have. On the other hand, because they aren't so sensitive to taste, nontasters may seek out relatively sweeter and fattier foods in order to maximize the taste. As a consequence, they may be prone to obesity (Bartoshuk & Drewnowski, 1997; Bartoshuk, 2000).

Most of the time our senses of smell and taste work together so that we can enjoy the flavours of food. For example, the flavour of a steak, an onion, or a vanilla pudding depends on our sense of smell as well as our sense of taste. You may recall that the last time you had a stuffy nose food lacked its usual appeal; smell did not contribute to the experience of flavour. And if you know someone who has lost the sense of smell, he or she will tell you that food does not taste good anymore. To learn more about research being done on taste and smell, see the *Psychology at Work* box on page 98.

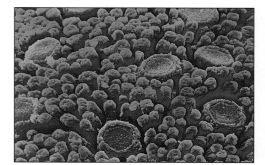

There are 10 000 taste buds spread across the tongue and other parts of the mouth. Taste buds wear out and are replaced every 10 days.
What would happen if taste buds were not regenerated?

The Skin Senses: Touch, Pressure, Temperature, and Pain

It started innocently, when Jennifer Darling hurt her right wrist during gym class. At first it seemed like a simple sprain. But even though the initial injury healed, the excruciating, burning pain accompanying it did not go away. Instead, it spread to her other arm, and then to her legs. The pain, which Jennifer described as similar to "a hot iron on your arm," was unbearable—and never stopped.

Pathways Through Psychology

Patrick J. McGrath

Pediatric Pain Researcher
Professor of Psychology, Pediatrics, Psychiatry and Biomedical Engineering, Dalhousie University
Psychologist, IWK Grace Health Centre

Education: 1st year undergraduate University of Ottawa; B.A., M.A. University of Saskatchewan; Ph.D. (Clinical Psychology) Queen's University, 1979

Home: Central Halifax with my wife, Anita Unruh, a professor of Occupational Therapy, our daughter Mika, our dog, Fergus, and Peaches, the rabbit.

Dr. Patrick J. McGrath with wife Dr. Anita Unruh, daughter Mika, and friend

I first became interested in psychology when, at age 9 or 10 years, I met a priest, Canice Connors, who was doing graduate work in psychology. My first year psychology professor at the University of Ottawa, Serge Piccinin, formally introduced me to psychology. I was strongly influenced by Chuck Jillings, a professor at the University of Regina, to see psychology as a way of helping people.

Interestingly, I did not like research until John Goodman, my boss at the Children's Hospital of Eastern Ontario in Ottawa, demanded that I do research. I wanted to keep my job and so I began with a small study of recurrent abdominal pain because several of my patients had that problem. All of the existing studies—which were not very good—said that this pain was caused by psychological factors. We found that recurrent Abdominal Pain was not due to psychological problems, although it causes many of them. Our research was almost always interdisciplinary and I always learned from my colleagues. I kept on doing research because of the challenge in helping to unravel the puzzle of pain, and the fact that research helps more children than I could ever see in clinic.

Today most of my time is spent in research. The Pediatric Pain Research Lab at Dalhousie University and the IWK Grace Health Centre is co-directed by Dr. Allan Finley, an anaesthetist, and myself.

Projects include research on event related potentials and pain, measurement of postoperative pain, phantom limb pain, pain in infants and children who have neurological damage, how infants and children learn about pain, and consciousness under anaesthesia. At the Hospital for Sick Children in Toronto we are doing studies on sickle cell pain. We also publish the *Pediatric Pain Letter*, a newsletter of abstracts and commentaries on pediatric pain, and host the International Forum on Pediatric Pain every two years.

What do I find most rewarding about my work? Teaching Introductory Psychology gives me an opportunity to spark students' interest in psychology. The graduate students that I teach help to keep me up-to-date on new developments. Our most important work has been in devising behavioural measures in pain and developing low-cost, distance-education type of treatments for pain. We have also been able to help health professionals realize that children's pain should not be ignored. And seeing patients in the pain service makes me appreciate how much more we have to learn. They are the reason we do the research.

Source: Patrick J. McGrath, Ph.D. Dalhousie University. <www.dal.ca/~pedpain>

Why did Dr. McGrath first become interested in psychology? What has he found most rewarding in his work on pain?

The source of Darling's pain turned out to be a rare condition known as "reflex sympathetic dystrophy syndrome," or RSDS for short. For a victim of RSDS, a stimulus as mild as a gentle breeze or the touch of a feather can produce agony. Even bright sunlight or a loud noise can trigger intense pain.

Pain like Darling's can be devastating. Yet a lack of pain can be equally bad. If you never experienced pain, for instance, you might not notice that your arm had brushed against a hot pan, and you would suffer a severe burn. Similarly, without the warning sign of abdominal pain that typically accompanies an inflamed appendix, your appendix might eventually rupture, spreading a fatal infection throughout your body.

skin senses: The senses that include touch, pressure, temperature, and pain.

In fact, all our **skin senses**—touch, pressure, temperature, and pain—play a critical role in survival, making us aware of potential danger to our bodies. Most of these senses operate through nerve receptor cells located at various depths throughout the skin, distributed unevenly throughout the body. For example, some areas, such as the fingertips, have many more receptor cells sensitive to touch and as a consequence are notably more sensitive than other areas of the body (Kreuger, 1989; see Figure 3-11).

Probably the most extensively researched skin sense is pain, and with good reason. In 1998–99, 12 percent of Canadians (approximately 3.5 million people) reported that they usually suffered from pain. The percent of pain sufferers is much higher in the elderly (30 percent) than in the very young (2 percent) (Statistics Canada, 2001). Chronic pain is most frequently associated with back problems, arthritis, or rheumatism. Most

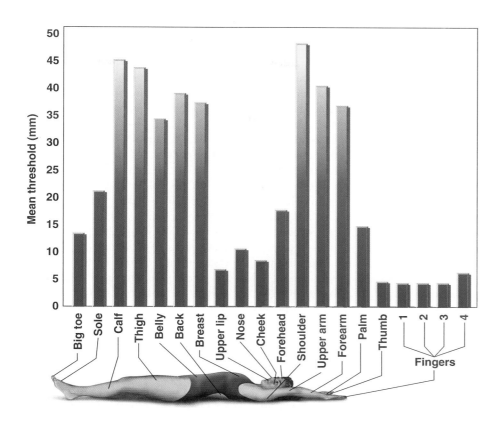

Figure 3-11 Skin sensitivity in various areas of the body. The shorter a line, the more sensitive a body part is. The fingers and thumb, lips, nose, cheeks, and big toe are the most sensitive.
Why do you think certain areas are more sensitive than others?
From Kenshalo, *The Skin Senses,* 1968. Courtesy of Charles C Thomas, Publisher, Ltd., Springfield, Illinois.

who suffer severe pain use analgesics (drugs that relieve pain), and consult their doctors approximately three times more frequently than those with no pain (Millar, 1996). To learn more about the experience and treatment of pain in children, see the *Pathways Through Psychology* box on p. 100 featuring Patrick McGrath. Dr. McGrath has recently received the Distinguished Career Award from the Canadian Pain Society and the Milbert E. Fordyke Clinical Investigator Award from the American Pain Society. In addition, he is currently the Killam Professor at Dalhousie University.

Pain is a response to a great variety of different kinds of stimuli. A light that is too bright can produce pain, and sound that is too loud can be painful. One explanation is that pain is an outcome of cell injury; when a cell is damaged, regardless of the source of damage, it releases a chemical called *substance P* that transmits pain messages to the brain.

But the experience of pain is not just a physical reaction to particular stimuli. For example, women report that the pain experienced in childbirth is moderated to some degree by the joyful nature of the situation. On the other hand, even a minor stimulus can produce the perception of strong pain if accompanied by anxiety (like a visit to the dentist). Clearly, then, pain is a perceptual response that depends heavily on our emotions and thoughts (Turk, 1994; Eccleston & Crombez, 1999; Gatchel & Weisberg, 2000).

According to the **gate-control theory of pain**, developed by Canadian psychologist Ronald Melzack and his colleague Patrick Wall (1965), a gate-like mechanism in the spinal column controls the flow of pain stimulation to the brain. Particular nerve receptors in the spinal cord lead to specific areas of the brain related to pain. When these receptors are activated because of some injury or problem with a part of the body, the "gate" to the brain is opened, allowing us to experience the sensation of pain.

gate-control theory of pain: The theory that a gate-like mechanism in the spinal column controls the flow of pain stimulation to the brain.

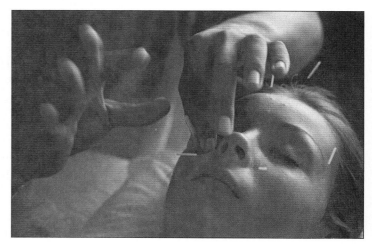

The ancient practice of acupuncture is still used in the 21st century.
How does the gate-control theory of pain explain how acupuncture works?

However, another set of neural receptors is able, when stimulated, to close the "gate" to the brain, thereby reducing the experience of pain. The gate can be shut in two different ways. First, other impulses can overwhelm the nerve pathways relating to pain, which are spread throughout the brain. In this case, nonpainful stimuli compete with and sometimes displace the neuronal message of pain, thereby shutting off the painful stimulus. This explains why rubbing the skin around an injury helps reduce pain (Wall & Melzack, 1989; Kakigi, Matsuda, & Kuroda, 1993).

Psychological factors account for the second way a gate can be shut. Depending on an individual's current emotions, interpretation of events, and previous experience, the brain can close a gate by sending a message down the spinal cord to an injured area, producing a reduction in or relief from pain. Thus soldiers who are injured in battle might experience no pain. The lack of pain probably occurs because a soldier experiences such relief at still being alive that the brain sends a signal to the injury site to shut down the pain gate (Turk, 1994; Gatchel & Weisberg, 2000).

Gate-control theory might explain the effectiveness of *acupuncture,* an ancient Chinese technique in which sharp needles are inserted into various parts of the body. The sensation from the needles might close the gateway to the brain, reducing the experience of pain. It is also possible that the body's own painkillers, the endorphins (discussed in Chapter 2), as well as positive and negative emotions, can play a role in opening and closing the gate (Murray, 1995; Bromm & Desmedt, 1995).

BECOMING AN INFORMED CONSUMER OF PSYCHOLOGY

Use your knowledge of pain to explain how these pain-management techniques work.

Managing Pain

Pain—whether it is a pounding, aching, stinging soreness or a burning feeling—is one sensation that cannot be easily overlooked. To fight pain, psychologists and medical specialists have devised several strategies. Among the most important approaches are these (Gatchel & Turk, 1996; Bazell, 1998; Keefe & France, 1999):

- *Medication.* Painkilling drugs are the most popular treatment in fighting pain. Drugs range from those that directly treat the source of the pain—such as reducing swelling in painful joints—to those that work on the symptoms of the pain. Medication can be in the form of pills, injections, or liquids. In a recent innovation, drugs are pumped directly into the spinal cord.
- *Nerve and brain stimulation.* Pain can sometimes be relieved when a low-voltage electric current is passed through the specific part of the body that is in pain. In even more severe cases, electrodes can be surgically implanted directly into the brain, and a handheld battery pack can stimulate nerve cells to provide direct relief (Garrison & Foreman, 1994; Walsh et al., 1995). This process is known as *transcutaneous electrical nerve stimulation,* or *TENS.*
- *Hypnosis.* For people who can be hypnotized, this method can greatly relieve pain (Holroyd, 1996; Spiegel, 1996c).
- *Biofeedback and relaxation techniques.* As we discussed in Chapter 2, biofeedback is a process through which people learn to control such "involuntary" functions as heartbeat and respiration. If the pain involves muscles, such as in tension headaches or back pain, biofeedback can be helpful when people are trained to relax their bodies systematically (Hermann, Kim, & Blanchard, 1995; National Institutes of Health, 1996).
- *Surgery.* In one of the most extreme methods, surgery can be used to cut certain nerve fibres that carry pain messages to the brain. Still, because of the danger that other bodily functions will be affected, surgery is a treatment of last resort, used most frequently with dying patients.
- *Cognitive restructuring.* People who continually say to themselves, "This pain will never stop," "The pain is ruining my life," or "I can't take it any more" are

likely to make their pain even worse. As we'll discuss in Chapter 13, by substituting more positive ways of thinking, people can increase their sense of control—and actually reduce the degree of pain they experience. Teaching people to rewrite the "script" that controls their reaction to pain through therapy can result in significant reductions in the perception of pain (Turk & Nash, 1993; Mufson, 1999).

If you wish to learn more about chronic pain, you can consult the North American Chronic Pain Association of Canada at 1-800-616-PAIN (7246). Their Web site is www.chronicpaincanada.org. From the Web site in the *Pathways Through Psychology* box you can locate information about pain in children.

Evaluate

1. The tubelike passage leading from the outer ear is known as the _____ _____.
2. The purpose of the eardrum is to protect the sensitive nerves underneath it. It serves no purpose in actual hearing. True or false?
3. The three middle ear bones transmit their sound to the _____.
4. The _____ theory of hearing states that the entire basilar membrane responds to a sound, vibrating more or less, depending on the nature of the sound.
5. The three fluid-filled tubes in the inner ear that are responsible for our sense of balance are known as the _____ _____.
6. The _____-_____ theory states that when certain skin receptors are activated as the result of an injury, a "pathway" to the brain is opened, allowing pain to be experienced.

Answers to Evaluate Questions

1. auditory canal 2. False; it vibrates when sound waves hit it, and transmits the sound. 3. oval window 4. frequency 5. semicircular canals 6. gate-control

Rethink

1. Much research is being conducted on repairing faulty sensory organs through such devices as personal guidance systems, eyeglasses, and so forth. Do you think that researchers should attempt to improve normal sensory capabilities beyond their "natural" range (e.g., make human visual or audio capabilities more sensitive than normal)? What benefits might this bring? What problems might it cause?
2. Why might sensitivity to pheromones have evolved differently in humans than in other species? What cultural factors might have played a role?

Perceptual Organization: Constructing Our View of the World

Take a moment and try Chapter Activity 3-3. If you examine the shapes in these figures, you will probably experience a shift in what you are seeing. The reason for these reversals is this: Because each figure is two-dimensional, the usual means we employ for distinguishing the *figure* (the object being perceived) from the *ground* (the background or spaces within the object) do not work.

The fact that we can look at the same figure in more than one way illustrates an important point. We do not just passively respond to visual stimuli that happen to fall on our retinas. Instead, we actively try to organize and make sense of what we see.

We turn now from a focus on the initial response to a stimulus (sensation) to what our minds make of that stimulus—perception. Perception is a constructive process by which we go beyond the stimuli that are presented to us and attempt to construct a meaningful situation (Haber, 1983; Kienker et al., 1986).

Prepare

What principles underlie our organization of the visual world, allowing us to make sense of our environment?

How are we able to perceive the world in three dimensions when our retinas are capable of sensing only two-dimensional images?

What clues do visual illusions give us about our understanding of general perceptual mechanisms?

Organize

Perceptual Organization: Constructing Our View of the World

The Gestalt Laws of Organization

Feature Analysis

Top-Down and Bottom-Up Processing

Visual Processing and Action

Perceptual Constancy

Depth Perception

Motion Perception

Perceptual Illusions

Subliminal Perception

Chapter Activity 3–3 Distinguish Figure from Ground

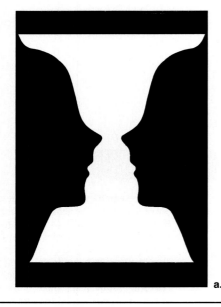 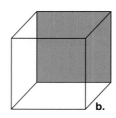 

a.   b.   c.

FIGURE 3-12 Look at the vase in Figure 3-12a. Or is it a vase? Take another look and you might see the profiles of two people. What is the white shape? Now look at the black part; what do you see? Look at Figure 3-12b. What do you see? Which way does the object face? When you focus on the white part of Figure 3-12c, what do you see? Look again; what is the black shape? When the usual cues we use to distinguish figure from ground are absent, we might shift back and forth between different views of the same figure. If you look at each of these objects long enough you'll probably experience a shift in what you're seeing. In (a), you can see either a vase or the profiles of two people. In (b), the shaded portion of the figure, called a Necker cube, can appear to be either the front or the back of the cube. Finally, in (c), you'll be able to see a face of a woman if you look at the drawing long enough.

The Gestalt Laws of Organization

Some of the most basic perceptual processes operate according to a series of principles that describe how we organize bits and pieces of information into meaningful wholes. These are known as **gestalt laws of organization**, set forth in the early 1900s by a group of German psychologists who studied patterns, or *gestalts* (Wertheimer, 1923). They discovered a number of important principles that are valid for visual (as well as auditory) stimuli, illustrated in Figure 3-13.

gestalt laws of organization: A series of principles that describe how we organize bits and pieces of information into meaningful wholes.

- *Closure.* Groupings are usually made in terms of enclosed or complete figures rather than open ones. We tend to ignore the breaks in Figure 3-13a and concentrate on the overall form.
- *Proximity.* Elements that are closer together are grouped together. As a result, we tend to see pairs of dots rather than a row of single dots, as in Figure 3-13b.
- *Similarity.* Elements that are similar in appearance are grouped together. We see, then, horizontal rows of circles and squares in Figure 3-13c instead of vertical mixed columns.
- *Simplicity.* In a general sense, the overriding gestalt principle is simplicity: When we observe a pattern, we perceive it in the most basic, straightforward manner that we can. For example, most of us see Figure 3-13d as a square with lines on two sides, rather than as the block letter *W* on top of the letter *M*. If we have a choice of interpretations, we generally opt for the simpler one.

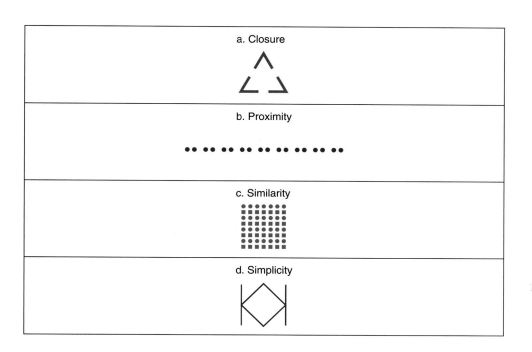

a. Closure

b. Proximity

c. Similarity

d. Simplicity

Figure 3-13 How we organize these bits and pieces of information into meaningful wholes is one of the most basic processes of perception known as the gestalt laws of organization.
Do you think any other species share this organizational tendency? How might we find out?

Although gestalt psychology no longer plays a prominent role in contemporary psychology, its legacy endures. For instance, one fundamental gestalt principle that remains influential is that two objects considered together form a whole that is different from the simple combination of the objects. Gestalt psychologists argued, quite convincingly, that the perception of stimuli in our environment goes well beyond the individual elements that we sense. Instead, it represents an active, constructive process carried out within the brain. There, bits and pieces of sensations are put together to make something more meaningful than the separate elements (Kriz, 1995; Humphreys & Müller, 2000; see Chapter Activity 3-4).

Chapter Activity 3–4
Perceive a "Whole"

FIGURE 3-14 At first it is difficult to see anything in this figure, but keep looking at it. Eventually you'll probably see a dog (James, 1966). The dog is a Dalmatian and his head is almost in the centre of the figure. The dog represents a *gestalt*, or perceptual whole, which is something greater than the sum of its individual elements.

AND FOR MY NEXT TRICK . . .

Falconer

feature analysis: A theory of perception according to which we perceive a shape, pattern, object, or scene by reacting first to the individual elements that make it up.

PsychLink

Feature analysis
www.mcgrawhill.ca/college/feldman

Feature Analysis: Focusing on the Parts of the Whole

A more recent approach to perception, **feature analysis**, considers how we perceive a shape, pattern, object, or scene by reacting first to the individual elements that make it up. These individual components are then used to understand the overall nature of what we are perceiving. Feature analysis begins with the evidence that individual neurons in the brain are sensitive to specific spatial configurations, such as angles, curves, shapes, and edges, as discussed earlier in the chapter. The presence of these neurons suggests that any stimulus can be broken down into a series of component features. For example, the letter *R* is a combination of a vertical line, a diagonal line, and a half circle (see Figure 3-15).

According to feature analysis, when we encounter a stimulus—such as a letter— our brain's perceptual processing system initially responds to its component parts. Each of these parts is compared with information about components that is stored in memory. When the specific components we perceive match up with a particular set of components that we have encountered previously, we are able to identify the stimulus (Spillmann & Werner, 1990; Ullman, 1996).

According to some research, the way we perceive complex objects is similar to how we perceive simple letters—viewing them in terms of their component elements. For instance, just 36 fundamental components seem to be capable of producing over 150 million objects—more than enough to describe the 30 000 separate objects that the average person can recognize (see Figure 3-16). Ultimately, these component features are combined into a representation of the whole object in the brain. This representation is compared to existing memories, thereby permitting us to identify the object (Biederman, 1987, 1990).

Psychologist Anne Treisman has a different perspective. She suggests that the perception of objects is best understood in terms of a two-stage process. In the *preattentive stage,* we focus on the physical features of a stimulus, such as its size, shape, colour, orientation, or direction of movement. This initial stage takes little or no conscious effort. In the *focused-attention stage,* we pay attention to particular features of an object, choosing and emphasizing features that were initially considered separately (Treisman, 1988, 1993).

For example, take a look at the two upside-down photos in Figure 3-17. Probably, your first impression is that you're viewing two similar photos of the Mona Lisa. But now look at them rightside up, and you'll be surprised to note that one of the photos has

Figure 3-15 According to feature analysis approaches to perception, we break down stimuli into their component parts and then compare these parts to information that is stored in memory. When we find a match, we are able to identify the stimulus. In this example, the process by which we recognize the letter *R* is illustrated (Goldstein, 1984).

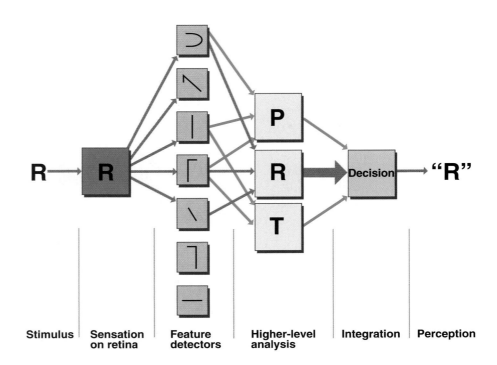

| Stimulus | Sensation on retina | Feature detectors | Higher-level analysis | Integration | Perception |

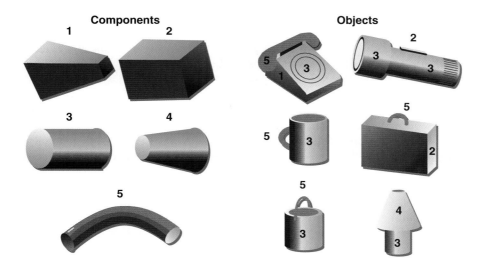

Figure 3-16 Components and simple objects created from them (adapted from Biederman, 1990).

distorted features. In Treisman's terms, your initial scanning of the photos took place at the preattentive stage. When you turned them over, however, you immediately progressed into the focused-attention stage, where you were able to more carefully consider the actual nature of the stimuli.

Treisman's two-stage model suggests that after preattentive processing we select and integrate stimulus information, producing a temporary representation that is compared with our existing knowledge. In the next section we turn to the question of how our knowledge guides perception.

Top-Down and Bottom-Up Processing

Ca- yo- re-d t-is –en-en-e, w-ic- ha- ev-ry –hi-d l-tt-r m-ss-ng? It probably won't take you too long to figure out that this says, "Can you read this sentence, which has every third letter missing?" You were able to read the sentence because of your prior reading experience, your knowledge of grammar and common English words, and your

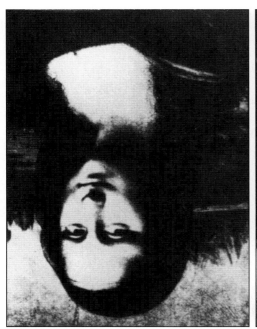 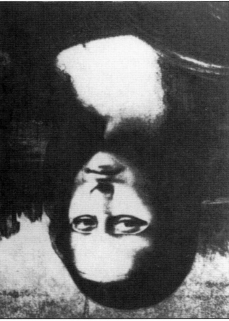

Figure 3-17 Double Mona Lisas? These pictures appear similar at first glance because only our preattentive process is active. When the pictures are seen upright, the true detail in the two faces is revealed (From Julesz, 1986).

top-down processing: Perception that is guided by higher-level knowledge, experience, expectations, and motivations.

bottom–up processing: Perception that consists of recognizing and processing information about the individual components of the stimuli.

expectations about the kinds of topics discussed in psychology books. This type of processing in which higher-level knowledge guides our perception is called **top-down processing**.

Top-down processing is illustrated by the importance of context in determining how we perceive objects (Biederman, 1981). Look, for example, at Figure 3-18. Most of us perceive that the first row consists of the letters A through F, while the second contains the numbers 10 through 14. But take a more careful look, and you'll see that the B and the 13 are identical. Clearly, our perception is affected by our expectations about the two sequences—even though the two stimuli are exactly the same.

Yet top-down processing cannot occur on its own. Even though top-down processing allows us to fill in the gaps in ambiguous and out-of-context stimuli, we would be unable to perceive the meaning of such stimuli without processing information about their individual components (**bottom-up processing**). Bottom-up processing is determined by observable characteristics of the stimulus input. It consists of recognizing and processing information about the individual components of stimuli. For example, we are more likely to notice a typographical error when our word perception is driven by bottom-up processing than when it is driven by top-down processing. In our perception of the world, bottom-up processing and top-down processing occur simultaneously and interact with each other.

Visual Processing and Action

Much of what we have described so far has to do with identifying objects and developing an internal representation of the world. According to Milner and Goodale (1995), this is only part of what visual processing is about. They argue that a second visual processing system is concerned with the relation between visual input and action, and is critically important for an organism's survival. Perceptual processing as it relates to actions is more finely tuned than perception concerned with establishing an internal representation of the world. For example, Milner and Goodale found that people adjust their aiming movements toward a target as the target shifts location without even being aware of the shifts. Of course, knowing where some things are is critical for our survival. In some situations, integrating information from different sensory modalities has been found to improve our ability to locate stimuli (Bell et al., 2001; Spence et al., 2001). Current research on multisensory integration and on the relation between perception and actions promises to add significantly to our understanding of perceptual processes. And it may also help us to more fully appreciate the difficulties faced by people like Mae Brown, who have profound deficits in more than one sensory system.

Perceptual Constancy

Consider what happens as you finish a conversation with a friend and she begins to walk away from you. As you watch her walk down the street, the image on your retina becomes smaller and smaller. Do you wonder why she is shrinking?

Of course not. Despite the very real change in the size of the retinal image, you factor into your thinking the knowledge that your friend is moving further away from you due to perceptual constancy. *Perceptual constancy* is a phenomenon in which physical objects are perceived as unvarying and consistent, despite changes in their appearance or in the physical environment.

Figure 3–18 The power of context is shown in this figure. Note how the B and the 13 are identical (Coren & Ward, 1989).

When the moon is near the horizon, we do not see it by itself and perceptual constancy leads us to take into account a misleading sense of distance.

One of the most dramatic examples of perceptual constancy involves the rising moon. When the moon first appears at night, close to the horizon, it seems to be huge—much larger than when it is high in the sky later in the evening. You may have thought that the apparent size of the moon was caused by the moon's being physically closer to the earth when it first appears. In fact, though, this is not the case at all.

Instead, the moon appears to be larger when it is close to the horizon primarily because of a misapplication of perceptual constancy. When the moon is near the horizon, the perceptual cues of intervening terrain and objects such as trees on the horizon produce a misleading sense of distance. Because perceptual constancy leads us to take that distance into account when we view the moon, we perceive the moon as relatively large. On the other hand, when the moon is high in the sky, we see it by itself, and perceptual constancy leads us to perceive it as relatively small. To prove this, try looking at the moon when it is relatively low on the horizon through a paper-towel tube; the moon will suddenly appear to "shrink" back to normal size (Coren & Aks, 1990; Coren, 1992b).

Although other factors help account for the moon illusion, perceptual constancy appears to be a primary ingredient in our susceptibility to the illusion. Furthermore, perceptual constancy occurs not just in terms of size (as with the moon illusion) but with shape and colour as well. Despite the varying images on our retina as a plane approaches, flies overhead, and disappears, we do not perceive the plane as changing shape (Coren & Aks, 1990; Suzuki, 1991).

Depth Perception: Translating 2-D to 3-D

As sophisticated as the retina is, the images projected onto it are flat and two-dimensional. Yet the world around us is three-dimensional, and we perceive it that way. How do we make the transformation from 2-D to 3-D?

The ability to view the world in three dimensions and to perceive distance—a skill known as *depth perception*—is due largely to the fact that we have two eyes (Regan, 1991). Because there is a certain distance between the eyes, a slightly different image reaches each retina. The brain then integrates these two images into one composite view. But it does not ignore the difference in images, which is known as *binocular disparity* (Howard & Rogers, 1995). The disparity allows the brain to estimate the distance of an object from us.

The fact that the discrepancy between the images in the two eyes varies according to the distance of objects that we view provides us with a means of determining distance. If we view two objects, and one is considerably closer to us than another, the retinal disparity will be relatively large and we will have a greater sense of depth between the two. On the other hand, if the two objects are a similar distance from us, the retinal disparity will be minor, and we will perceive them as being a similar distance from us.

Chapter Activity 3–5
Experience
Binocular Disparity
and Convergence

You can get a sense of binocular disparity for yourself. Hold a pencil at arm's length and look at it first with one eye and then with the other. There is little difference between the two views relative to the background. Now bring the pencil just 15 centimetres away from your face, and try the same thing. This time you will perceive a greater difference between the two views. This difference illustrates binocular disparity. Now bring the pencil even closer to your face. As you do so, you will likely experience some discomfort as your eye muscles turn your eyes inward. This discomfort makes you aware of convergence.

Another binocular cue for distance is *convergence*. Feedback to the brain from the eye muscles, indicating the extent to which the muscles are turning the eyes inward, provides information about distance from the visual stimulus. The more the eyes turn inward, the closer the object is; the less they turn inward, the farther away it is. See Chapter Activity 3-5 for a demonstration of binocular disparity and convergence.

In some cases, certain cues permit us to obtain a sense of depth and distance with just one eye (Burnham, 1983). These cues are known as *monocular cues*. One monocular cue—*motion parallax*—is the change in position of an object on the retina due to movement of the head. The brain is able to calculate the distance of the object by the amount of change in the retinal image. Similarly, experience has taught us that if two objects are the same size, the one that makes a smaller image on the retina is farther away than the one that provides a larger image—an example of the monocular cue of *relative size*. Also, if our view of an object is partially cut off by another object, we have learned that the partially seen object is further away from us *(interposition)*.

Anyone who has ever seen railroad tracks that seem to join together in the distance knows that distant objects appear to be closer together than nearer ones, a phenomenon called linear perspective. People use *linear perspective* as a monocular cue in estimating distance, allowing the two-dimensional image on the retina to record the three-dimensional world (Bruce, Green, & Georgeson, 1997; Dobbins et al., 1998). Finally, if you have ever looked down an old cobblestone street, you will remember that you could see all the details of the surface of the nearby cobblestones but fewer surface features of more distant cobblestones. This loss of detail in the distance is known as the *texture gradient*. See Chapter Activity 3-6 for a demonstration of monocular depth cues.

Motion Perception: As the World Turns

When a batter tries to hit a pitched ball, the most important factor is the motion of the ball. How is a batter able to judge the speed and location of a target that is moving at some 145 kilometres per hour?

The answer rests, in part, on several cues that provide us with relevant information about the perception of motion (Movshon & Newsome, 1992). For one thing, the movement of an object across the retina is typically perceived relative to some stable, unmoving background. Moreover, if the stimulus is heading toward us, the image on the retina will expand in size, filling more and more of the visual field. In such cases, we assume that the stimulus is approaching—and not that it is an expanding stimulus viewed at a constant distance.

It is not, however, just the movement of images across the retina that brings about the perception of motion. If it were, we would perceive the world as moving every time we moved our heads. Instead, one of the critical things we learn about perception is to factor information about head and eye movements along with information about changes in the retinal image.

Chapter Activity 3-6 Use Monocular Cues

Interposition:
Distance indicated by objects overlapping.

Linear Perspective:
Distance indicated by lines joining together.

Texture Gradient:
Distance indicated by clarity of detail.

How do the monocular cues pictured provide information about distance? How do artists use linear perspective?

Perceptual Illusions: The Deceptions of Perceptions

If you look carefully at the Parthenon, one of the most famous buildings of ancient Greece and still standing at the top of an Athens hill, you'll see that it was built with a bulge on one side. If it didn't have that bulge—and quite a few other "tricks" like it, such as columns that incline inward—it would look as if it were crooked and about to fall down. Instead, it appears to stand completely straight, at right angles to the ground.

The fact that the Parthenon appears to be completely upright is the result of a series of visual illusions. **Visual illusions** are physical stimuli that consistently produce errors in perception. In the case of the Parthenon, the building appears to be completely square, as illustrated in Figure 3-19a. However, had it been built that way, it would look to us as it does in Figure 3-19b. The reason for this is the illusion illustrated in 3-19c, which makes angles placed above a line appear as if they were bent. To offset the illusion, the Parthenon was constructed as in Figure 3-19d, with a slight upward curvature.

visual illusions: Physical stimuli that consistently produce errors in perception.

 **PsychLink**
Optical and sensory illusions
www.mcgrawhill.ca/college/feldman

Figure 3-19 In building the Parthenon, the Greeks constructed an architectural wonder that looks perfectly straight, with right angles at every corner, as in *(a)*. However, if it had been built with completely true right angles, it would have looked as it does in *(b)*, due to the visual illusion illustrated in *(c)*. To compensate for this illusion, the Parthenon was designed to have a slight upward curvature, as shown in *(d)* (Coren & Ward, 1989, p. 5).

b.

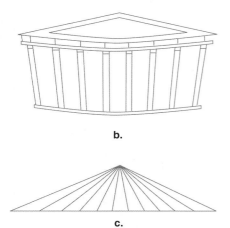

c.

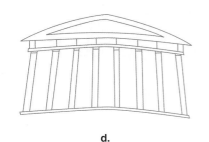

d.

a.

Such perceptual insights did not stop with the Greeks. Modern-day architects and designers also take visual distortions into account in their planning. For example, the New Orleans Superdome makes use of several visual tricks. Its seats vary in colour throughout the stadium to give the appearance, from a distance, that there is always a full house. The carpeting in some of the sloping halls has stripes that make people slow their pace by producing the perception that they are moving faster than they actually are. The same illusion is used at toll booths on superhighways. Stripes painted on the pavement in front of the toll booths make drivers feel that they are moving more rapidly than they actually are and cause them to decelerate quickly.

These illusions are examples of many that consistently fool the eye. Another, illustrated in Figure 3-20, is called the *Müller-Lyer illusion*. Although the two lines are the same length, the one with the arrow tips pointing inward (Figure 3-20a, top) appears to be longer than the one with the arrow tips pointing outward (Figure 3-20a, bottom).

Although all kinds of explanations for visual illusions have been suggested, most concentrate either on the physical operation of the eye or on our misinterpretation of the visual stimulus. For example, one explanation for the Müller-Lyer illusion is that eye movements are greater when the arrow tips point inward, making us perceive the line as longer than when the arrow tips face outward. In contrast, a different explanation for the illusion suggests that we unconsciously attribute particular significance to each of the lines (Gregory, 1978; Redding & Hawley, 1993). When we see the top line in Figure 3-20a, we tend to perceive it as if it were the inside corner of a room extending away from us, as illustrated in Figure 3-20b. On the other hand, when we view the bottom line in Figure 3-20a, we perceive it as the relatively close outside corner of a rectangular object such as the building corner in Figure 3-20c. Because previous experience leads us to assume that the outside corner is closer than the inside corner, we make the further assumption that the inside corner must therefore be larger.

Despite the complexity of the latter explanation, a good deal of evidence supports it. For instance, cross-cultural studies show that people raised in areas where there are few right angles—such as the Zulu in Africa—are much less susceptible to the illusion than people who grow up where most structures are built using right angles and rectangles (Segall, Campbell, & Herskovits, 1966).

a.   b.   c.

Figure 3-20 In the Müller-Lyer illusion *(a)*, the upper horizontal line appears longer than the lower one. One explanation for the Müller-Lyer illusion suggests that the line with arrow points directed inward is to be interpreted as the inside corner of a rectangular room extending away from us *(b)*, and the line with arrow points directed outward is viewed as the relatively close corner of a rectangular object, such as the building corner in *(c)*. Our previous experience with distance cues leads us to assume that the outside corner is closer than the inside corner and that the inside corner must therefore be longer.

EXPLORING DIVERSITY

Culture and Perception

How might cultural differences in perception influence the way archaeologists interpret some of their findings?

The particular culture in which we are raised has clear consequences for how we perceive the world (Berry et al., 1992). Consider the drawing in Figure 3-21. Sometimes called the "devil's tuning fork," it is likely to produce a mind-boggling effect, as the centre tine of the fork alternates between appearing and disappearing.

Now try to reproduce the drawing on a piece of paper. Chances are that the task is nearly impossible for you—unless you are a member of an African tribe with little exposure to Western cultures. For such individuals, the task is simple; they have no trouble reproducing the figure. The reason seems to be that Western people automatically interpret the drawing as something that cannot exist in three dimensions, and they are therefore inhibited from reproducing it. The African tribal members, on the other hand, do not make the assumption that the figure is "impossible" and instead view it in two dimensions, which enables them to copy the figure with ease (Deregowski, 1973).

Cultural differences are also reflected in depth perception. A Western viewer of Figure 3-22 would interpret the hunter in the drawing as aiming for the antelope in the foreground, while an elephant stands under the tree in the background. A member of an isolated African tribe, however, interprets the scene very differently by assuming that the hunter is aiming at the elephant. Westerners use the difference in sizes between the two animals as a cue that the elephant is farther away than the antelope (Hudson, 1960).

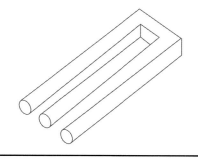

Figure 3-21 The "devil's tuning fork" has three prongs . . . or does it have two?

Figure 3–22 Is the man aiming for the elephant or the antelope? Westerners assume that the differences in size between the two animals indicate that the elephant is farther away, and therefore the man is aiming for the antelope. On the other hand, members of some African tribes, not used to depth cues in two-dimensional drawings, assume that the man is aiming for the elephant. (The drawing is based on Deregowski, 1973.) Do you think Westerners, who view the picture in three dimensions, could explain what they see to someone who views the scene in two dimensions and eventually get them to view it in three dimensions?

PsychLink

Analysis of subliminal influence
www.mcgrawhill.ca/college/feldman

The misinterpretations created by visual illusions are ultimately due, then, to errors in both fundamental visual processing and the way the brain interprets the information it receives. But visual illusions, by illustrating something fundamental about perception, become more than mere psychological curiosities. There is a basic connection between our prior knowledge, needs, motivations, and expectations about how the world is put together and the way we perceive it. Our view of the world is very much a function, then, of fundamental psychological factors. Furthermore, each person perceives the environment in a way that is unique and special—a fact that allows each of us to make our own special contribution to the world.

Subliminal Perception

Can stimuli that we're not even aware we've been exposed to change our behaviour in a significant way? Probably not.

Subliminal perception refers to the perception of messages about which we have no awareness. The stimulus could be a word, a sound, or even a smell that activates the sensory system, but that is not intense enough for a person to report having experienced it. For example, in some studies people are exposed to a descriptive label—called a *prime*—about a person (such as the word *smart* or *happy*) so briefly that they cannot report seeing the label. Later, however, they form impressions that are influenced by the content of the prime. Somehow, they have been influenced by the prime that they say they couldn't see, providing some evidence for subliminal perception (Bargh & Pietromonaco, 1982; Greenwald, Draine, & Abrams, 1996). Merikle and Daneman (1996) found that patients remembered specific information following surgery as long as testing occurred within 36 hours.

Yet does this mean that subliminal messages can actually lead to significant changes in attitudes or behaviour? Most research suggests not. Although we are able to perceive at least some kinds of information of which we are unaware, no evidence demonstrates that subliminal messages can change our attitudes or behaviour in any substantial way (Greenwald et al., 1991).

Extrasensory Perception (ESP)

Given the lack of evidence for subliminal perception, psychologists are even more skeptical of reports of *extrasensory perception,* or *ESP*—perception that does not involve our known senses. Most psychologists reject the existence of ESP, asserting that there is no sound documentation that the phenomenon exists (Alcock, 1981, 1987, 1998; Swets & Bjork, 1990; Hyman, 1994).

However, an ongoing debate in the last decade in one of the most prestigious psychology journals, *Psychological Bulletin,* has heightened interest in the area. According to proponents of ESP, reliable evidence exists for an "anomalous process of information transfer," or *psi* (Bem & Honorton, 1994). These researchers, who painstakingly reviewed considerable evidence, argue that a cumulative body of research shows reliable support for the existence of psi.

However, their conclusion has been challenged on several counts. For example, critics suggest that the research methodology was inadequate, and that the experiments supporting psi are flawed (Hyman, 1994; Milton & Wiseman, 1999).

Because of questions about the quality of the research, as well as a lack of any credible theoretical explanation for how extrasensory perception might take place, most psychologists continue to believe that there is no reliable scientific support for ESP. Still, the exchanges in *Psychological Bulletin* are likely to heighten the debate. More importantly, the renewed interest in ESP among psychologists is likely to inspire more research, which is the only way that the issue can be resolved.

∞ PsychLink

Extrasensory perception
www.mcgrawhill.ca/college/feldman

Evaluate

1. Match each of the following organizational laws with its meaning:

   a. Closure
   b. Proximity
   c. Similarity
   d. Simplicity

   1. Elements close together are grouped together.
   2. Patterns are perceived in the most basic, direct manner possible.
   3. Groupings are made in terms of complete figures.
   4. Elements similar in appearance are grouped together.

2. _____ analysis deals with the way in which we break an object down into its component pieces in order to understand it.

3. Processing that involves higher functions such as expectations and motivations is known as _____, while processing that recognizes the individual components of a stimulus is known as _____.

4. When a car passes you on the road and appears to shrink as it gets farther away, the phenomenon of _____ permits you to realize that the car is not in fact getting smaller.

5. _____ is the ability to view the world in three dimensions instead of two.

6. The eyes use a technique known as _____, which makes use of the differing images each eye sees to give three dimensions to sight.

7. Match the monocular cues with their definitions.

   a. Relative size
   b. Linear perspective
   c. Motion parallax

   1. Straight lines seem to join together as they become more distant.
   2. An object changes position on the retina as the head moves.
   3. If two objects are the same size, the one producing the smaller retinal image is farther away.

Rethink

1. Can you think of examples of the combined use of top-down and bottom-up processing in everyday life? Is one type of processing superior to the other?

2. In what ways do painters represent three-dimensional scenes in two dimensions on a canvas? Do you think artists in non-Western cultures use the same or different principles to represent three-dimensionality? Why?

Answers to Evaluate Questions

1. a-3; b-1; c-4; d-2 **2.** Feature **3.** Top-down; bottom-up **4.** perceptual constancy **5.** depth perception **6.** binocular disparity **7.** a-3; b-1; c-2

Looking Back

What is sensation, and how do psychologists study it?

- Sensation is the stimulation of the sense organs that comes from our initial encounter with stimuli (forms of energy that activate a sense organ). In contrast, perception is the process by which we sort out, interpret, analyze, and integrate stimuli to which our senses are exposed. (p. 80)

What is the relationship between a physical stimulus and the kinds of sensory responses that result from it?

- The absolute threshold is the smallest amount of physical intensity at which a stimulus can be detected. Although under ideal conditions absolute thresholds are extraordinarily sensitive, the presence of noise (background stimuli that interfere with other stimuli) reduces detection capabilities. (p. 81)
- Difference thresholds relate to the smallest level of stimulation required to sense that a change in stimulation has occurred, with a just noticeable difference being the minimum stimulation required to detect the difference between two stimuli. According to Weber's law, a just noticeable difference is a constant proportion of the intensity of an initial stimulus. (p. 82)
- Sensory adaptation occurs when we become accustomed to a constant stimulus and change our evaluation of it. Repeated exposure to a stimulus results in an apparent decline in sensitivity to it. (p. 82)

What basic processes underlie the sense of vision?

- Human sensory experience goes well beyond the traditional five senses, although most is known about just two: vision and hearing. Vision depends on sensitivity to light, electromagnetic waves that are reflected off objects outside the body. The eye shapes the light into an image that is transformed into nerve impulses and interpreted by the brain. (p. 83)
- When light first enters the eye, it travels through the cornea and then traverses the pupil, a dark hole in the centre of the iris. The size of the pupil opening adjusts according to the amount of light entering the eye. Light then enters the lens, which, by a process called accommodation, acts to focus light rays onto the rear of the eye. On the rear of the eye is the retina, composed of light-sensitive nerve cells called rods and cones. Because of the phenomenon of adaptation, it takes time to adjust to situations that are darker than the previous environment. (p. 84)
- The visual information gathered by the rods and cones is transferred via bipolar and ganglion cells through the optic nerve, which leads to the optic chiasm— the point where the optic nerve splits. Because the image on the retina is reversed and upside down, images from the right half of the retina actually originated in the field of vision to the left of the person, and vice versa. (p. 85)

How do we see colours?

- Colour vision seems to be based on two processes described by the trichromatic theory and the opponent-process theory. The trichromatic theory suggests that there are three kinds of cones in the retina, each of which is responsive to a certain range of colours. The opponent-process theory presumes pairs of different types of cells in the eye. These cells work in opposition to each other. (p. 88)

What role does the ear play in the senses of sound, motion, and balance?

- Sound, motion, and balance are centred in the ear. Sounds, in the form of vibrating air waves, enter through the outer ear and travel through the auditory canal until they reach the eardrum. The vibrations of the eardrum are transmitted into the middle ear, which consists of three bones: the hammer, the anvil, and the stirrup. These bones transmit vibrations to the oval window. In the inner ear, vibrations move into the cochlea, which encloses the basilar membrane. Hair cells on the basilar membrane change the mechanical energy of sound waves into nerve impulses that are transmitted to the brain. The ear is also involved in the sense of balance and motion. (p. 92)

- Sound has a number of important characteristics, including frequency and intensity. The place theory of hearing and the frequency theory of hearing explain the processes by which we distinguish sounds of varying frequency and intensity. (p. 95)

How do smell and taste function?

- Smell employs olfactory cells (the receptor cells of the nose), and taste is centred in the tongue's taste buds. (p. 97)

What are the skin senses, and how do they relate to the experience of pain?

- The skin senses are responsible for the experiences of touch, pressure, temperature, and pain. Gate-control theory suggests that particular nerve receptors lead to specific areas of the brain related to pain. When these receptors are activated, a "gate" to the brain is opened, allowing the sensation of pain to be experienced. In addition, another set of receptors closes the gate when stimulated, thereby reducing the experience of pain. Endorphins might also affect the operation of the gate. (p. 99)
- Among the techniques used most frequently to alleviate pain are administration of drugs, hypnosis, biofeedback, relaxation techniques, surgery, nerve and brain stimulation, and psychotherapy. (p. 102)

What principles underlie our organization of the visual world, allowing us to make sense of our environment?

- Work on figure-ground distinctions shows that perception is a constructive process in which people go beyond the stimuli that are physically present and try to construct a meaningful situation. Perception follows the gestalt laws of organization, a series of principles by which we organize bits and pieces of information into meaningful wholes, known as gestalts. Among the most important laws are closure, proximity, similarity, and simplicity. (p. 103)
- Feature analysis pertains to how we consider a shape, pattern, object, or scene in terms of the individual elements that make it up. These component features are then combined into a representation of the whole object in the brain. Finally, this combination of features is compared against existing memories, permitting identification of the object. (p. 106)
- Processing of perceptual stimuli occurs in both a top-down and a bottom-up fashion. In top-down processing, perception is guided by higher-level knowledge, experience, expectations, and motivations. In bottom-up processing, perception involves recognizing and processing information about the individual components of stimuli. (p. 107)
- Perceptual constancy permits us to perceive stimuli as unvarying and consistent, despite changes in the environment or the appearance of the objects being perceived. Perceptual constancy occurs in terms of size, shape, and colour constancy. (p. 108)

How are we able to perceive the world in three dimensions when our retinas are capable of sensing only two-dimensional images?

- Depth perception is the ability to perceive distance and to view the world in three dimensions, even though the images projected on our retinas are two-dimensional. We are able to judge depth and distance as a result of binocular disparity and monocular cues, such as motion parallax, the relative size of images on the retina, and linear perspective. (p. 109)
- Motion perception depends on several cues. They include the perceived movement of an object across our retina and information about how the head and eyes are moving. (p. 110)

What clues do visual illusions give us about our understanding of general perceptual mechanisms?

- Visual illusions are physical stimuli that consistently produce errors in perception, causing judgments that do not accurately reflect the physical reality of the stimulus. One of the best-known illusions is the Müller-Lyer illusion. (p. 111)
- Visual illusions are usually the result of errors in the brain's interpretation of visual stimuli. Furthermore, culture clearly affects how we perceive the world. (p. 112)
- Subliminal perception refers to the perception of messages about which we have no awareness. The reality of the phenomenon, as well as of ESP, is open to question and debate. (p. 115)

Key Terms and Concepts

sensation (p. 80)
perception (p. 80)
stimulus (p. 81)
psychophysics (p. 81)
absolute threshold (p. 81)
difference threshold (p. 82)
just noticeable difference (p. 82)
Weber's law (p. 82)
adaptation (p. 82)
retina (p. 85)
rods (p. 85)
cones (p. 85)
optic nerve (p. 86)
feature detection (p. 87)
trichromatic theory of colour vision (p. 89)
opponent-process theory of colour vision (p. 89)

sound (p. 93)
eardrum (p. 93)
cochlea (p. 93)
basilar membrane (p. 93)
hair cells (p. 93)
place theory of hearing (p. 97)
frequency theory of hearing (p. 97)
semicircular canals (p. 97)
otoliths (p. 97)
skin senses (p. 100)
gate-control theory of pain (p. 101)
gestalt laws of organization (p. 104)
feature analysis (p. 106)
top-down processing (p. 108)
bottom-up processing (p. 108)
visual illusions (p. 111)

Psychology on the Web

1. Select one topic of personal interest to you that was mentioned in this chapter (e.g., psi, cochlear implants, visual/optical illusions). Find one "serious" or scientific Web site and one "popular" or commercial Web site with information about your chosen topic. Compare the type, level, and reliability of the information that you find on each site. Write a summary of your findings.
2. Are there more gestalt laws of organization than the four discussed in this chapter (i.e., closure, proximity, similarity, and simplicity)? Find the answer to this question on the Web and write a summary of any additional gestalt laws you find.

pilogue

In this chapter we have noted the important distinction between sensation and perception, and we have examined the processes that underlie both of them. We've seen how external stimuli evoke sensory responses, and how our different senses process the information contained in those responses. We also have focused on the physical structure and internal workings of the individual senses, including vision, hearing, balance, smell, taste, and the skin senses, and we've explored how our brains organize and process sensory information to construct a consistent, integrated picture of the world around us.

Before we proceed to a discussion of consciousness in the next chapter, let's return to the opening prologue of this chapter. Consider the story of Mae Brown and answer the following questions, using your knowledge of sensation and perception.

1. Can you think of any ways Mae Brown might have compensated for her poor vision during childhood?
2. What do you think happens to speech, if anything, when a formerly hearing person such as Mae Brown becomes deaf?
3. How do you think starting out with both good vision and hearing may have affected Mae's ability to handle her later profound sensory deficits?
4. How do you think Mae's life would have turned out if she had chosen to belong exclusively to the deaf culture rather than to also participate in the hearing world?

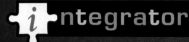

For extra help in mastering the material in this chapter, see the integrator, practice quizzes, and other resources on the Online Learning Centre at

www.mcgrawhill.ca/college/ feldman

Chapter Four

States of Consciousness

Prologue

The Last Summer Party

The teens' car being pulled from the quarry.

One summer night in June 2001, five teens died when the car in which they were riding plunged into a water-filled quarry near Sherbrooke, Quebec. The quarry was a popular rendezvous spot where young people went to build bonfires and drink. The dead teens included two young women and three young men, all aged 15 to 18 years. A sixth person, the 21-year-old driver, escaped with minor injuries. According to provincial police, speed was not a factor in the accident. However, a sample of the driver's blood was taken to be tested for alcohol.

Source: Picard, 2001.

Looking Ahead

Drinking alcohol is common in our society. People sometimes take their first drink in the middle elementary school years. Next to caffeine, alcohol is the drug most frequently used by Canadians. Each year many people die from complications of alcohol and drug overdoses, and more become addicted to various kinds of drugs.

What leads people to use alcohol and other types of drugs to alter their normal states of consciousness? More generally, what *is* consciousness, and how does normal waking consciousness relate to states of consciousness such as sleep, hypnotic trances, or drug-induced experiences? In this chapter, we consider these questions.

Consciousness is the awareness of the sensations, thoughts, and feelings being experienced at a given moment. Consciousness is our subjective understanding of both the environment around us and our private internal world, unobservable to outsiders.

Consciousness is generally divided into two broad states: waking consciousness and altered states of consciousness, although the boundary between the two types is not always clear. In *waking consciousness,* we are awake and aware of our thoughts, emotions, and perceptions. In more active states of waking consciousness, we systematically carry out mental activity, focusing our thoughts and absorbing the world around us. In more passive states of waking consciousness, thoughts and images come to us more spontaneously; we might drift from one thought to another (Velmans, 2000).

When we enter an *altered state of consciousness,* our mental state differs significantly from waking consciousness. Some altered states of consciousness, such as sleeping and dreaming, occur naturally. Others, such as those induced by drug use or hypnosis, are triggered by deliberate attempts to alter one's state of consciousness.

Because consciousness is so personal a phenomenon, psychologists have sometimes been reluctant to study it. After all, who can say that your consciousness is similar to or, for that matter, different from anyone else's? In fact, early psychologists suggested that the study of consciousness was out of bounds for the discipline. They argued that because consciousness could be understood only by relying on the "unscientific" introspections of experimental participants about what they were experiencing at a given moment, its study was best left to disciplines such as philosophy.

However, contemporary psychologists reject the view that the study of consciousness is unsuitable for the field of psychology. Instead, they argue that several approaches permit the scientific study of consciousness. For example, biopsychologists can measure brain-wave patterns under conditions of consciousness ranging from sleep to waking to hypnotic trances. Moreover, new understanding of the chemistry of drugs such as marijuana and alcohol has provided insights into the way they produce their pleasurable—as well as adverse—effects (Shear, 1997; Damasio, 1999; Sommerhof, 2000).

Another impetus for the study of consciousness is the realization that people in many different cultures routinely seek ways to alter their states of consciousness. Across a variety of cultures, variations in states of consciousness share some basic characteristics (Ludwig, 1969; Martindale, 1981). One is an alteration in thinking, which may become shallow, illogical, or otherwise different from normal. In addition, people's sense of time can become disturbed, and their perceptions of the world and of themselves might be changed. They might experience a loss of self-control. Finally, they might feel a sense of *ineffability*—the inability to understand an experience rationally or describe it in words.

This chapter considers several states of consciousness, beginning with two that we have all experienced: sleeping and dreaming. Next, we turn to states of consciousness found under conditions of hypnosis and meditation. Finally, we examine drug-induced states of consciousness.

consciousness: The awareness of the sensations, thoughts, and feelings being experienced at a given moment.

 **PsychLink**

Information on consciousness
www.mcgrawhill.ca/college/feldman

Sleep
Learning Object
at http://www.mcgrawhill.ca/college/feldman

Sleep and Dreams

The crowd roared as running back Donald Dorff, age 67, took the pitch from his quarterback and accelerated smoothly across the artificial turf. As Dorff braked and pivoted to cut back over a tackle, a huge defensive lineman loomed in his path. One hundred twenty pounds of pluck, Dorff did not hesitate. But let the retired grocery merchandiser from Golden Valley, Minnesota, tell it:

"There was a 280-pound tackle waiting for me, so I decided to give him my shoulder. When I came to, I was on the floor in my bedroom. I had smashed into the dresser and knocked everything off it and broke the mirror and just made one heck of a mess. It was 1:30 A.M." (Long, 1987, p. 787)

Dorff, it turned out, was suffering from a rare condition (called *REM sleep behaviour disorder*) in which the mechanism that usually shuts down bodily movement during dreams does not function properly. People with the malady have been known to hit others, smash windows, punch holes in walls—all while fast asleep.

Luckily, Dorff's problem had a happy ending. With the help of clonazepam, a drug that suppresses movement during dreams, his malady vanished, permitting him to sleep through the night undisturbed.

Despite the success of Dorff's treatment, many unanswered questions about sleep remain, along with a considerable number of myths. (Try testing your own knowledge of sleep and dreams by answering the questions in Chapter Activity 4-1.)

Prepare

What are the different states of consciousness?

What happens when we sleep, and what are the meaning and function of dreams?

What are the major sleep disorders and how can they be treated?

How much do we daydream?

Organize

Sleep and Dreams
  The Stages of Sleep
  REM Sleep
  Why Do We Sleep, and How Much Sleep Is Necessary?
  The Function and Meaning of Dreaming
  Sleep Disturbances
  Circadian Rhythms
  Daydreams

Chapter Activity 4–1 Sleep Quiz

Although sleeping is something we all do for a significant part of our lives, myths and misconceptions about the topic abound. To test your own knowledge of sleep and dreams, try answering the following questions before reading further.

_____ 1. Some people never dream. *True or false?*

_____ 2. Most dreams are caused by bodily sensations such as an upset stomach. *True or false?*

_____ 3. It has been proved that people need eight hours of sleep to maintain mental health. *True or false?*

_____ 4. When people do not recall their dreams, it is probably because they are secretly trying to forget them. *True or false?*

_____ 5. Depriving someone of sleep will invariably cause the individual to become mentally imbalanced. *True or false?*

_____ 6. If we lose some sleep, we will eventually make up all the lost sleep the next night or another night. *True or false?*

_____ 7. No one has been able to go for more than 48 hours without sleep. *True or false?*

_____ 8. Everyone is able to sleep and breathe at the same time. *True or false?*

_____ 9. Sleep enables the brain to rest, because little brain activity takes place during sleep. *True or false?*

_____ 10. Drugs have been proved to provide a long-term cure for sleeping difficulties. *True or false?*

Scoring: This is an easy set of questions to score, for every item is false. But don't lose any sleep if you missed them; they were chosen to represent the most common myths regarding sleep.

Best friends having a nap.

The Stages of Sleep

Most of us consider sleep a time of tranquility, as we set aside the tensions of the day and spend the night in uneventful slumber. However, a closer look at sleep shows that a good deal of activity occurs throughout the night, and that what at first appears to be a unitary state is, in fact, quite diverse (Broughton & Ogilvie, 1992).

Much of our knowledge of what happens during sleep comes from the *electroencephalogram*, or *EEG*, a measurement of electrical activity within the brain (see Chapter 2). When probes from an EEG machine are attached to the surface of a sleeping person's scalp and face, it becomes clear that the brain is active throughout the night. It produces electrical discharges with systematic, wavelike patterns that change in height (or amplitude) and speed (or frequency) in regular sequences. Instruments that measure muscle and eye movements also reveal a good deal of physical activity.

During a night's sleep, people pass through cycles of sleep stages. Each cycle, which lasts for about 90 minutes, is composed of four non-REM stages and a REM stage. Each stage has unique brain wave patterns, as shown in Figure 4-1, as well as other characteristic features.

Non-REM Sleep Stages

non-REM sleep stages:

stage 1 sleep: The state of transition between wakefulness and sleep, characterized by relatively rapid, low-voltage brain waves.

stage 2 sleep: A sleep deeper than that of stage 1, characterized by a slower, more regular wave pattern, along with momentary interruptions of "sleep spindles".

stage 3 sleep: A sleep characterized by slow brain waves, with greater peaks and valleys in the wave pattern.

stage 4 sleep: The deepest stage of sleep, during which we are least responsive to outside stimulation.

When people first go to sleep, they move from a waking state into a sleep onset period called **stage 1 sleep**. This stage is marked by changes in respiration and muscle activity, and by rapid low-voltage brain waves (Ogilvie, 1995). During wakefulness, people generate characteristic changes in the electrical activity of the brain, called *event-related potentials* (ERPs) when external stimuli are present. Kimberly Cote (at Brock University in St. Catharines) and her colleagues found that people generated these ERPs less often during stage 1 sleep than during wakefulness. They also found that in stage 1 sleep, as compared to the waking state, ERPs were less pronounced over the frontal regions of the brain and more pronounced over the parietal regions. They concluded that stage 1 consists of two substages, one when the sleeper is aware of the external environment and another when the sleeper is not (Cote et al., 2002).

As sleep becomes deeper, people enter **stage 2 sleep**, which makes up about half of the total sleep of people in their twenties. During this stage people no longer show any awareness of the external environment (Cote, de Lugt, & Campbell, 2002). Brain waves are

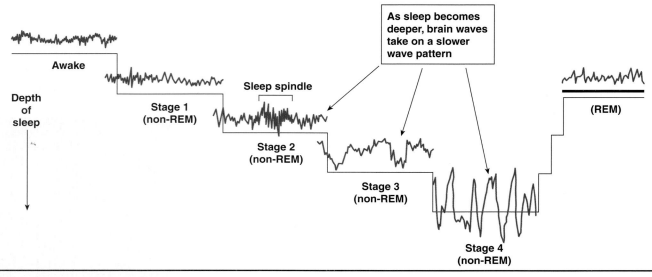

Figure 4-1 Brain-wave patterns (measured by an EEG apparatus) vary significantly during the different stages of sleep (Hobson, 1989). As sleep moves from stage 1 through stage 4, brain waves become slower.

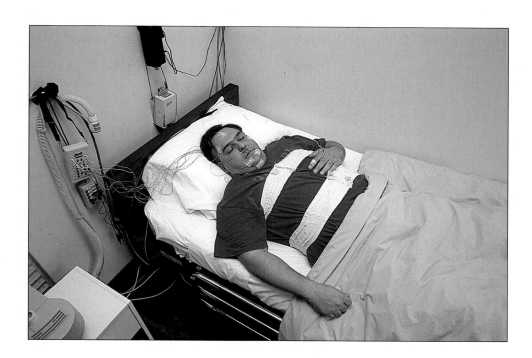

This man's physiological responses during sleep are being studied at the Sleep Disorders Centre in Toronto.

characteristically slower and are interrupted by bursts of sharply pointed, spiky waves called *sleep spindles*. The sleep spindles may occur as a consequence of the inhibition of information processing caused by neurons in the thalamus (Cote & Campbell, 2000).

As people drift into **stage 3 sleep**, the next stage of sleep, the brain waves become slower, with higher peaks and lower valleys in the wave pattern. By the time sleepers arrive at **stage 4 sleep**, the pattern is even slower and more regular, and people are least responsive to outside stimulation.

As you can see in Figure 4-2, during the first half of the night, our sleep is dominated by stages 3 and 4. The last half is characterized by lighter stages of sleep—as well as the phase of sleep during which dreams occur, as we discuss next (Dement & Wolpert, 1958). In addition to passing through regular transitions between stages of sleep, then, people tend to sleep less and less deeply over the course of the night.

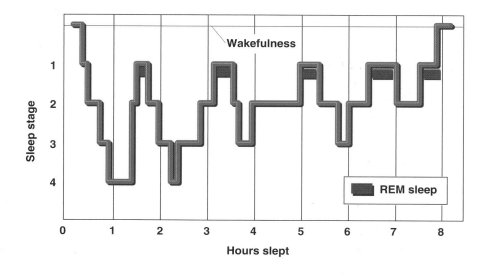

Figure 4-2 During the night, the typical sleeper passes through all four stages of sleep and several REM periods. *Would waking someone be more difficult during the first half of the night, or the second half? Why?*
From E. Hartman, *The Biology of Dreaming*, 1967. Courtesy of Charles C Thomas, Publisher, Ltd., Springfield, Illinois.

Pathways Through Psychology

Robert D. Ogilvie

Sleep Researcher
Brock University, St. Catharines, Ontario

Education: B.A., Carleton University; M.A., Hollins College, Virginia; Ph.D., Cambridge University

Robert D. Ogilvie

Although I'm officially a psychologist by training, I think of myself as a sleep researcher—because that's what I do when I'm not teaching here at Brock University in St. Catharines.

My interest in sleep began almost accidentally in graduate school where I wrote an essay on the effects of sleep and sleep deprivation on early mammalian development. (Try to imagine a world without sleep—it's as essential as air and water.) I soon decided to make sleep the focus of my doctoral work.

Sleep was a relatively new area of study in the late '60s and '70s, when I began to study it, and it was interdisciplinary. Psychologists, psychiatrists, biologists, neurologists, and many others were drawn, like me, to study sleep and dreaming in the years after Aserinsky and Kleitman discovered the link between REM sleep and dreaming. They gave us the first tools with which to link the psychology (dreams and thoughts) and the physiology (rapid eye movements [REM] and brain-wave activity) of sleep! This was incredibly exciting and challenging, for it pointed towards a whole new emerging field—one which I've watched and helped to develop.

Now, after 30 years, the knowledge base is solid enough to support a whole new discipline—sleep disorders medicine. Contributing to this creative, dynamic enterprise is amazingly rewarding. I've developed my own expertise within the sleep field: I study the process of falling asleep. As we shift from waking to sleeping mode, our brains and conscious processes undergo a wider array of changes than can be seen at any other time. Studying this transition period can teach us lots about both waking and sleeping.

First, my students and I studied the sequence of changes in brain and behaviour as sleep began in normal sleepers. We found that waking and sleeping systems overlap considerably, and different systems give conflicting signals as to when they themselves have "fallen asleep." For instance, when you are very drowsy and your eyes are closed, slow rolling eye movements begin and last throughout the wake-to-sleep transition.

Next, we began to study sleep onset in people with sleep problems, and soon saw that normal, insomniac, and narcoleptic sleepers entered sleep quite differently. We are presently looking to see whether these different patterns are unique enough to be of diagnostic value.

Why do I do these weird studies, watching others go to sleep? First, as I've mentioned, it is really exciting to place one or two pieces of the sleep jig-saw together in this huge collaborative adventure we call the science of sleep. Second, being a member of this scientific team is rewarding too. I've met fascinating people the world over at sleep conferences. And in the final analysis, being a sleep researcher is simply an important part of who I am.

Source: Robert D. Ogilvie, Ph.D. Brock University. <www.psyc.brocku.ca/~rogilvie/ sleep.htm>

Why has Dr. Ogilvie been most interested in studying the process of falling asleep?

REM Sleep

REM sleep: Sleep stage characterized by increased heart rate, blood pressure, and breathing rate; decreased muscle tone; rapid eye movements; and the experience of dreaming.

Several times a night, something curious happens. The sleeper's heart rate increases and becomes irregular, blood pressure rises, and breathing rate increases. The sleeper may also show signs of sexual arousal; males, even male infants, have erections and females can have vaginal secretions. The eyes move rapidly back and forth, and up and down. The sleeper has entered **REM sleep**, the rapid eye movement stage. In addition to rapid eye movements, this stage is characterized by increased heart rate, blood pressure, and breathing rate; decreased muscle tone; and the experience of dreaming. Since this is the period when most dreams occur, some researchers suggest that the rapid eye movements may be caused by the sleeper watching the action of dreams (Dement, 1979; Kelly, 1991). Another peculiar feature of REM sleep is that during this stage, we may be able to detect some external stimuli without being aware of doing so (Cote, Etienne, & Campbell, 2001).

There is good reason to believe that REM sleep serves important functions. REM sleep occupies about 20 percent of adult sleeping time, proportionately more in infants, and less in seniors. People who have been deprived of this type of sleep show a REM-rebound effect, in which they have longer REM periods, making up for the loss. Numerous researchers have found evidence for the role of REM sleep in information processing. For example, Cote and her colleagues measured ERPs in the parietal lobes of sleepers during REM sleep, which suggested sleepers might be updating memory after detecting external stimuli (Cote, Etienne, & Campbell, 2001).

To read about a psychologist who has been a sleep researcher during his academic career, see the *Pathways Through Psychology* box on p. 126 featuring Robert Ogilvie. Dr. Ogilvie has recently retired, and Dr. Kimberly Cote, whose work we have cited frequently in this chapter, is now the Director of the Brock University Sleep Research Laboratory.

Why Do We Sleep, and How Much Sleep Is Necessary?

Sleep is a requirement for normal human functioning. It is reasonable to expect that our bodies would require a tranquil "rest and relaxation" period in order to revitalize themselves. Some researchers, using an evolutionary perspective, suggest that sleep permitted our ancestors to conserve energy at night, a time when food was relatively hard to come by. Still, this explanation is speculative, and although we know that *some* sleep is necessary, we don't fully know why we must sleep (Webb, 1992; Porkka-Heiskanen et al., 1997).

Scientists have been unable to establish just how much sleep is absolutely required. For instance, today most people sleep seven to eight hours each night, but they sleep three hours a night *less* than people did a hundred years ago. In addition, there is wide variability among individuals, with some people needing as little as three hours. Sleep requirements also vary over the course of a lifetime: As they age, people generally need less and less sleep (see Figures 4-3 and 4-4).

People who participate in sleep deprivation experiments, in which they are kept awake for stretches as long as 200 hours, show no lasting effects. It's no fun—they feel weary and irritable, can't concentrate, and show a loss of creativity, even after only minor deprivation. They also show a decline in logical reasoning ability. However, after being allowed to sleep normally, they bounce back quickly and are able to perform at predeprivation levels after just a few days (Dement, 1976; Webb, 1992; Dinges et al., 1997).

Those of us who worry, then, that long hours of study, work, or perhaps partying are ruining our health should feel heartened. As far as anyone can tell, most people suffer no permanent consequences of such temporary sleep deprivation. At the same time, though, a lack of sleep can make us feel edgy, slow our reaction time, and lower our performance on academic tasks. In addition, we put ourselves, and others, at risk when we carry out routine activities, such as driving, when we're very sleepy. Most single-vehicle accidents occur between two and six o'clock in the morning (Caldwell, 2001).

PsychLink

Basics of sleep behaviour
www.mcgrawhill.ca/college/feldman

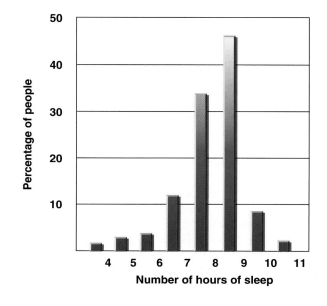

Figure 4–3 Although most people report sleeping between eight and nine hours per night, the amount varies a great deal (Borbely, 1996).
Where would you place yourself on this graph, and why do you think you need more or less sleep than others?

Figure 4-4 Over the course of their life span, people sleep less (Roffwarg, Muzio, & Dement, 1996).

Approximately what percent of a night's sleep is occupied by REM sleep for a newborn? For people in their twenties? How does the proportion of REM sleep change across the lifespan?

Reprinted with permission from H. P. Roffwarg, J. N. Munzio and W. C. Dement, "Ontogenci Development of the Human Sleep-Dream Cycle," *Science,* 152, pp. 604–619, 1966. Copyright © 1966 American Association for the Advancement of Science.

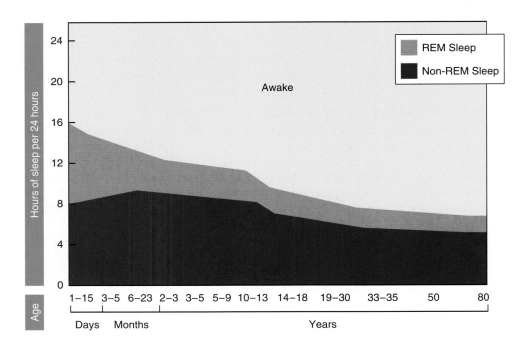

"I've got it again, Larry ... an eerie feeling like there's something on top of the bed."

The Function and Meaning of Dreaming

I was sitting at my desk when I remembered that this was the day of my chemistry final! I was terrified, because I hadn't studied a bit for it. In fact, I had missed every lecture all semester. In a panic, I began running across campus desperately searching for the classroom, to which I'd never been. It was hopeless; I knew I was going to fail and flunk out of college.

If you have had a similar dream—a surprisingly common dream among people involved in academic pursuits—you know how utterly convincing are the panic and fear that the events in the dream can bring about. *Nightmares,* unusually frightening dreams, occur fairly often. In one survey, almost half of a group of college students who kept records of their dreams over a two-week period reported having at least one nightmare. This works out to some 24 nightmares per person each year, on average (Wood & Bootzin, 1990; Berquier & Ashton, 1992; Tan & Hicks, 1995).

On the other hand, most of the 150 000 dreams the average person experiences by the age of 70 are much less dramatic (Snyder, 1970; Webb, 1992). They typically encompass such everyday events as going to the supermarket, working at the office, or preparing a meal. Students dream about going to class; professors dream about lecturing. Dental patients dream of getting their teeth drilled; dentists dream of drilling the wrong tooth. The English take tea with the Queen in their dreams; in the United States, people go to a bar with the president (Solomon, 1993; Potheraju & Soper, 1995; Domhoff, 1996).

But what, if anything, do all these dreams mean? Whether dreams have a specific significance and function is a question that scientists have considered for many years, and they have developed several alternative theories.

Do Dreams Represent Unconscious Wish Fulfillment?

Sigmund Freud viewed dreams as a guide to the unconscious (Freud, 1900). In his **unconscious wish fulfillment theory,** he proposed that dreams represented unconscious wishes that dreamers desire to see fulfilled. However, because these wishes are threatening to the dreamer's conscious awareness, the actual wishes—called the **latent content of dreams**—are disguised. The true subject and meaning of a dream, then, may have little to do with its overt story line, which Freud called the **manifest content of dreams**.

To Freud, it was important to pierce the armour of a dream's manifest content to understand its true meaning. To do this, Freud tried to get people to discuss their dreams, associating symbols in the dreams to events in the past. He also suggested that certain common symbols with universal meanings appear in dreams. For example, to Freud, dreams in which the person is flying symbolize a wish for sexual intercourse. (See Table 4-1 for other common symbols.)

Today, many psychologists reject Freud's view that dreams typically represent unconscious wishes and that particular objects and events in a dream are symbolic. Instead, they believe that the direct, overt action of a dream is the focal point of its meaning. For example, a dream in which we are walking down a long hallway to take an exam for which we haven't studied does not relate to unconscious, unacceptable wishes. Instead, it simply might mean we are concerned about an impending test. Even more complex dreams can often be interpreted in terms of everyday concerns and stress (Domhoff, 1996; Nikles et al., 1998).

Moreover, we now know that some dreams reflect events occurring in the dreamer's environment as he or she is sleeping. For example, sleeping participants in one experiment were sprayed with water while they were dreaming. These unlucky volunteers reported more dreams involving water than a comparison group of participants who were left to sleep undisturbed (Dement & Wolpert, 1958).

Dreams-for-Survival Theory

According to the **dreams-for-survival theory,** dreams permit information that is critical for our daily survival to be reconsidered and reprocessed during sleep. Dreaming is seen as an inheritance from our animal ancestors, whose small brains were unable to sift sufficient information during waking hours. Consequently, dreaming provided a mechanism that permitted the processing of information 24 hours a day.

According to this theory, dreams represent concerns about our daily lives, illustrating our uncertainties, indecisions, ideas, and desires. Dreams are seen, then, as consistent with everyday living. Rather than being disguised wishes, as Freud suggested, they would represent key concerns growing out of our daily experiences (Pavlides & Winson, 1989; Winson, 1990).

Research supports the dreams-for-survival theory, suggesting that certain dreams permit people to focus on and consolidate memories, particularly dreams that pertain to "how-to-do-it" memories related to motor skills. For instance, in one experiment,

unconscious wish fulfillment theory: Sigmund Freud's theory that dreams represent unconscious wishes that dreamers desire to fulfill.

latent content of dreams: According to Freud, the "disguised" or real meanings of dreams, hidden by more obvious subjects.

manifest content of dreams: According to Freud, the overt story line of dreams.

 **PsychLink**

Comprehensive information on dreams
www.mcgrawhill.ca/college/feldman

dreams-for-survival theory: The theory that dreams permit information that is critical for our daily survival to be reconsidered and reprocessed during sleep.

Table 4–1 Dream Symbolism, According to Freud	
Symbol (Manifest Content of Dream)	**Interpretation (Latent Content)**
Climbing up a stairway, crossing a bridge, riding an elevator, flying in an airplane, walking down a long hallway, entering a room, train travelling through a tunnel	Sexual intercourse
Apples, peaches, grapefruits	Breasts
Bullets, fire, snakes, sticks, umbrellas, guns, hoses, knives	Male sex organs
Ovens, boxes, tunnels, closets, caves, bottles, ships	Female sex organs

Freud suggested that certain common symbols with universal meanings appear in dreams. According to his symbolism, a plane flying across the sky might represent the dreamer's wish for sexual intercourse. Can this claim be proved?

Freud suggested that certain common symbols with universal meanings appear in dreams. According to his symbolism, a plane flying across the sky might represent the dreamer's wish for sexual intercourse. Can this claim be proved?

activation–synthesis theory: Hobson's theory that the brain produces random electrical energy during REM sleep that stimulates memories lodged in various portions of the brain.

participants learned a visual memory task late in the day. They were then sent to bed, but awakened at certain times during the night. When they were awakened at times that did not interrupt dreaming, their performance on the memory task typically improved the next day. But when they were awakened during rapid eye movement (REM) sleep—the stage of sleep when people dream—their performance declined. The conclusion: Dreaming can play a role in helping us remember material to which we have been previously exposed (Karni et al., 1992, 1994).

Activation-Synthesis Theory

According to psychiatrist J. Allan Hobson, who proposed **activation-synthesis theory**, the brain produces random electrical energy during REM sleep, possibly due to changes in the production of particular neurotransmitters. This electrical energy randomly stimulates memories lodged in various portions of the brain. Because we have a need to make sense of our world, even while asleep, the brain takes these chaotic memories and weaves them into a logical story line, filling in the gaps to produce a rational scenario (Hobson, 1996; Porte & Hobson, 1996).

Yet Hobson does not entirely reject the view that dreams reflect unconscious wishes. He suggests that the particular scenario a dreamer produces is not just random but instead is a clue to the dreamer's fears, emotions, and concerns. Hence, what starts out as a random process culminates in something meaningful.

Dream Theories in Perspective

The range of theories about dreaming (summarized in Table 4-2) clearly illustrates that dream researchers have yet to agree on the fundamental meaning of dreams. Furthermore, new research is suggesting that the different approaches might be closer together than originally thought.

For instance, according to work by Allen Braun and colleagues, the parts of the brain associated with emotions and visual imagery are strongly activated during REM sleep. Using PET scans that show brain activity, Braun's research team found that the limbic and paralimbic regions of the brain, which are associated with emotion and motivation, are particularly active during REM sleep. At the same time, the association areas of the prefrontal cortex, which control logical analysis and attention, are inactive during REM sleep (Braun et al., 1998; see Figure 4-5).

The results can be viewed as consistent with several aspects of Freudian theory. For example, the high activation of emotional and motivational centres of the brain during dreaming makes it more plausible that dreams might reflect unconscious wishes and instinctual needs, just as Freud suggested. Similarly, the fact that the areas of the brain responsible for emotions are highly active, while the brain regions responsible for

Table 4-2 Three Views of Dreams

Theory	Basic Explanation	Meaning of Dreams	Is Meaning of Dream Disguised?
Unconscious wish fulfillment theory (Freud)	Dreams represent unconscious wishes the dreamer wants to fulfill	Latent content reveals unconscious wishes	Yes, by manifest content of dreams
Dreams-for-survival theory	Information relevant to daily survival is reconsidered and reprocessed	Clues to everyday concerns about survival	Not necessarily
Activation-synthesis theory (Hobson)	Dreams are the result of random activation of various memories, which are tied together in a logical story line	Dream scenario that is constructed is related to dreamer's concerns	Not necessarily

rational thought are offline during REM sleep, suggests that the ego and superego are dormant, permitting unconscious thoughts to dominate.

On the other hand, critics of Freudian explanations for dreams disagree that the new research findings necessarily support Freud. There is still no evidence that the meaning of dreams is hidden behind symbols found in the storyline of the dream. Furthermore, just because areas of the brain involved with motivation and emotion are activated during REM sleep does not prove that dreams relate to hidden motivations and emotions of the dreamer.

One thing is clear: Despite the advances in our understanding of the biological aspects of dreaming, the debate about the meaning of dreams is not yet resolved. But Freud would probably take satisfaction in the fact that almost a hundred years after he published his first book on the meaning of dreams, scientists are still debating his theory.

Sleep Disturbances: Slumbering Problems

At one time or another, almost all of us have difficulty sleeping—a condition known as *insomnia.* It could be due to a particular situation, such as the breakup of a relationship or the loss of a job. Some cases of insomnia, however, have no obvious cause. Some people are unable to fall asleep easily, or they go to sleep readily but wake up frequently during the night. Insomnia is a problem that afflicts about a quarter of the population of the United States (Hauri, 1991; Pressman & Orr, 1997). About one million Canadians over the age of 11 used sleeping pills in 1997 (Health Canada, 1999).

Interestingly, some people who *think* they have sleeping problems are mistaken. For example, researchers in sleep laboratories have found that some people who report being up all night actually fall asleep in 30 minutes and stay asleep all night. Furthermore, some people with insomnia accurately recall sounds that they heard while they were asleep, which gives them the impression that they were actually awake during the night. In fact, some researchers suggest that future drugs for insomnia could function by changing people's *perceptions* of how much they have slept, rather than by making them sleep more (Engle-Friedman, Baker, & Bootzin, 1985; Klinkenborg, 1997).

Other sleep problems are less common than insomnia, although they are still widespread. For instance, one million Canadians and some 20 million Americans suffer from *sleep apnea,* a condition in which a person has difficulty breathing while sleeping. The result is disturbed, fitful sleep, as the person is constantly reawakened when the lack of oxygen becomes great enough to trigger a waking response. Some people with apnea wake as many as 500 times during the course of a night, although they might not even be aware that they have wakened. Not surprisingly, such disturbed sleep results in complaints of fatigue the next day. Sleep apnea might also account for *sudden infant death syndrome (SIDS),* a mysterious killer of seemingly normal infants who die while sleeping (Ball et al., 1997).

Narcolepsy is uncontrollable sleeping that occurs for short periods while awake. No matter what the activity—holding a heated conversation, exercising, or driving—the

PsychLink

Sleep disorders information
www.mcgrawhill.ca/college/feldman

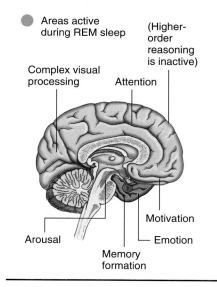

Areas active during REM sleep

(Higher-order reasoning is inactive)

Complex visual processing

Attention

Motivation

Emotion

Arousal

Memory formation

Figure 4-5 New research has found that those parts of the brain that are associated with emotions and visual imagery are strongly activated during REM sleep.
Why might this be the case?

narcoleptic will suddenly fall asleep. People with narcolepsy go directly from wakefulness to REM sleep, skipping the other stages. The causes of narcolepsy are not known, although there could be a genetic component because narcolepsy runs in some families (Siegel, 2000).

We know relatively little about sleeptalking and sleepwalking, two sleep disturbances that are usually harmless. Both occur during stage 4 sleep and are more frequent in children than in adults. Sleeptalkers and sleepwalkers usually have a vague consciousness of the world around them, and a sleepwalker might be able to walk with agility around obstructions in a crowded room. Unless a sleepwalker wanders into a dangerous environment, sleepwalking typically poses little risk (Hobson & Silverstri, 1999; Swanson, 1999).

Circadian Rhythms: Life Cycles

The fact that we cycle back and forth between wakefulness and sleep is one example of our body's circadian rhythms. **Circadian rhythms** (from the Latin *circa diem*, or "around a day") are biological processes that occur repeatedly on approximately a 24-hour cycle. Sleep and waking, for instance, occur naturally to the beat of an internal pacemaker that works on a cycle of about 24 hours. Several other bodily functions, such as body temperature and the female menstrual cycle, also work on circadian rhythms (Oren & Terman, 1998; Czeisler et al., 1999; Young, 2000).

Circadian cycles are complex. For instance, sleepiness occurs not just in the evening, but throughout the day in regular patterns. As you can see in Figure 4-6, most of us tend to get drowsy in midafternoon—regardless of whether we have eaten a heavy lunch. By making an afternoon siesta part of their everyday habit, people in several cultures take advantage of the body's natural inclination to sleep at this time (Dement, 1989; Ogilvie & Harsh, 1994).

An internal pacemaker or clock mechanism for organizing many circadian rhythms is located in an area of the hypothalamus known as the *suprachiasmatic nucleus*. When Martin Ralph at the University of Toronto transplanted the suprachiasmatic nuclei from a mutant stream of hamsters having a 21-hour cycle into normal hamsters, he found that the normal hamsters changed to a 21-hour cycle (Ralph & Lehman, 1991). Other means of altering circadian rhythms include changing the rats' exposure to light (Arvanitogiannis, 1999) and varying hamsters' times for exercise or feeding or both (Mistlberger, 1991).

circadian rhythms: Biological processes that occur repeatedly on approximately a 24-hour cycle.

PsychLink

Circadian rhythms
www.mcgrawhill.ca/college/feldman

Figure 4-6 These are the times of day that people report feeling the sleepiest (during periods when they are normally awake and trying to stay alert) (Dement, 1989).

What implications does this information have for the workplace? For schools and colleges?

From W. C. Dement, in D. F. Dinges and Broughton (eds.), Sleep and Alertness: Chronobiological, Behavioral, and Medical Aspects of Napping, 1989. Reprinted with permission of Lippincott, Wiliams and Wilkins Publishers.

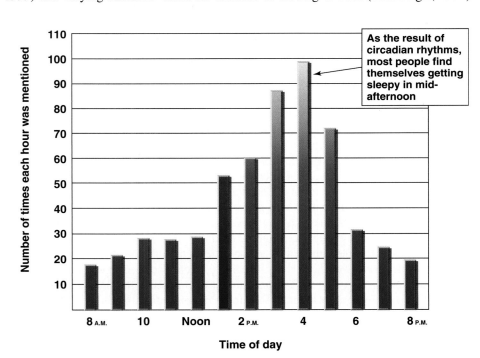

As the result of circadian rhythms, most people find themselves getting sleepy in mid-afternoon

As mentioned above, the relative amount of light and darkness, which differs with the seasons of the year, plays a role in determining circadian rhythms. In fact, some people experience *seasonal affective disorder,* a form of severe depression in which feelings of despair and hopelessness increase during the winter and lift during the rest of the year. The disorder appears to be a result of the brevity and gloom of winter days. Psychologists have found that several hours of daily exposure to bright lights is sometimes sufficient to improve the mood of those with the disorder (Sack et al., 1990; Roush, 1995; Oren & Terman, 1998).

Circadian rhythms explain the difficulty people have in flying through multiple time zones—the phenomenon of *jet lag.* Pilots, as well as others who must work on constantly changing time shifts (police officers and physicians), must fight their internal clocks. The result can be fatigue, irritability, and, even worse, outright error. In fact, an analysis of major disasters caused by human error finds that many, such as the Exxon *Valdez* oil spill in Alaska and the Chernobyl nuclear reactor accident, occurred late at night (Mapes, 1990; Moore-Ede, 1993). Researchers have found that administration of the hormone melatonin may help shift workers deal with night shifts (Folkhard et al., 1993).

Daydreams: Dreams Without Sleep

It is the stuff of magic: Our past mistakes can be wiped out and the future filled with noteworthy accomplishments. Fame, happiness, and wealth can be ours. In the next moment, though, the most horrible of tragedies can occur, leaving us devastated, alone, and penniless.

The source of these scenarios is **daydreams**, fantasies that people construct while awake. Unlike dreaming that occurs while sleeping, daydreams are more under people's control. Therefore their content is often more closely related to immediate events in the environment than is the content of the dreams that occur during sleep. Although they might include sexual content, daydreams also pertain to other activities or events that are relevant to a person's life.

Daydreams are a typical part of waking consciousness, even though our awareness of the environment around us declines while we are daydreaming. People vary considerably in the amount of daydreaming they do. For example, around 2 to 4 percent of the population spend at least half their free time fantasizing. Although most people daydream much less frequently, almost everyone fantasizes to some degree. Studies that ask people to identify what they are doing at random times during the day have shown that they are daydreaming about 10 percent of the time. As for the content of fantasies, most concern such mundane, ordinary events as paying the telephone bill, picking up the groceries, or solving a romantic problem (Singer, 1975; Lynn & Rhue, 1988; Lynn et al., 1996).

Frequent daydreaming might seem to suggest psychological difficulties, but there appears to be little relationship between psychological disturbance and daydreaming. Except in those rare cases in which a daydreamer is unable to distinguish a fantasy from reality (a mark of serious problems, as we discuss in Chapter 12), daydreaming seems to be a normal part of waking consciousness. Indeed, fantasy can contribute to the psychological well-being of some people by enhancing their creativity and by permitting them to use their imagination to understand what other people are experiencing (Lynn & Rhue, 1988; Pihlgren, Gidycz, & Lynn, 1993; Lynn et al., 1996).

Daydreams are fantasies that people construct while they are awake.
What are the similarities and differences between daydreams and night dreams?

daydreams: Fantasies that people construct while awake.

BECOMING AN INFORMED CONSUMER OF PSYCHOLOGY

Sleeping Better

What are some strategies you might use to sleep better?

Do you have trouble sleeping? You're not alone. About 35 percent of North American adults suffer from insomnia. Seventeen percent consider their insomnia to be a serious problem because it is so frequent and disruptive (Coren, 1996). For those of us who spend hours tossing and turning in bed, psychologists studying sleep disturbances have a number of suggestions for overcoming insomnia (National Institutes of Health, 1996b; Kupfer & Reynolds, 1997; Scharf, 1999), including these:

- *Exercise during the day (at least six hours before bedtime) and avoid naps.* Not surprisingly, it helps to be tired before going to sleep! Moreover, learning systematic relaxation techniques and biofeedback (see Chapter 2) can help you unwind from the day's stresses and tensions (Lehrer, 1996).
- *Choose a regular bedtime and stick to it.* Adhering to a habitual schedule helps your internal timing mechanisms regulate your body more effectively.
- *Don't use your bed as an all-purpose area.* Leave studying, reading, eating, watching TV, and other recreational activities to some other part of your living quarters. If you follow this advice, your bed will become a cue for sleeping.
- *Avoid drinks with caffeine after lunch.* The effects of beverages such as coffee, tea, and some soft drinks can linger for as long as 8 to 12 hours after they are consumed.
- *Drink a glass of warm milk at bedtime.* Your grandparents were right when they dispensed this advice: Milk contains the chemical tryptophan, which helps people fall asleep.
- *Avoid sleeping pills.* Although some prescription pills can be temporarily effective, in the long run they can cause more harm than good because they disrupt the normal sleep cycle (Haimov & Lavie, 1996; Zhdanova, Lynch, & Wurtman, 1997).
- *Try* not *to sleep.* This approach works because people often have difficulty falling asleep because they are trying so hard. A better strategy is to go to bed only when you feel tired. If you don't get to sleep within ten minutes, leave the bedroom and do something else, returning to bed only when you feel sleepy. Continue this process all night if necessary. But get up at your usual hour in the morning, and don't take any naps during the day. After three or four weeks, most people become conditioned to associate their beds with sleep—and fall asleep rapidly at night (Seltzer, 1986; Ubell, 1993; Sloan et al., 1993).

For long-term problems with sleep, you might consider visiting a sleep disorders centre. A list of some sleep centres in cities across Canada can be found on the Internet at http://swdca.org/can-labs2.html.

Evaluate

1. _____ is the term used to describe our understanding of the world external to us, as well as our own internal world.
2. A great deal of neural activity goes on during sleep. True or false?
3. Dreams occur in _____ sleep.
4. _____ _____ are internal bodily processes that occur on a daily cycle.
5. Freud's theory of unconscious _____ _____ states that the actual wishes that an individual expresses in dreams are disguised because they are threatening to the person's conscious awareness.
6. Match the theory of dreaming with its definition.

1. Activation-synthesis theory	a. Dreams permit important information to be reprocessed during sleep.
2. Dreams-for-survival theory	b. The manifest content of dreams disguises the latent content of the dreams.
3. Dreams as wish fulfillment	c. Electrical energy stimulates random memories, which are woven together to produce dreams.

7. Match the sleep problem with its definition.

1. Insomnia	a. Condition that makes breathing while sleeping difficult
2. Narcolepsy	b. Difficulty in sleeping
3. Sleep apnea	c. Uncontrollable need to sleep during the day

Rethink

1. How would studying the sleep patterns of nonhuman species potentially help us figure out which of the theories of dreaming provides the best account of the functions of dreaming?

2. Suppose that a new "miracle pill" is developed that will allow a person to function with only one hour of sleep per night. However, because a night's sleep is so short, a person who takes the pill will never dream again. Knowing what you do about the functions of sleep and dreaming, what would be some advantages and drawbacks of such a pill from a personal standpoint? Would you take such a pill?

Answers to Evaluate Questions

1. Consciousness 2. True 3. REM 4. Circadian rhythms 5. wish fulfillment 6. 1-c; 2-a; 3-b 7. 1-b; 2-c; 3-a

Hypnosis and Meditation

Prepare

Are hypnotized people in a different state of consciousness?

What are the effects of meditation?

Organize

Hypnosis and Meditation

   Hypnosis

   Meditation

You are feeling relaxed and drowsy. You are getting sleepier and sleepier. Your body is becoming limp. Now you are starting to become warm, at ease, more comfortable. Your eyelids are feeling heavier and heavier. Your eyes are closing; you can't keep them open any more. You are totally relaxed.

Now, as you listen to my voice, do exactly as I say. Place your hands above your head. You will find they are getting heavier and heavier—so heavy you can barely keep them up. In fact, although you are straining as hard as you can, you will be unable to hold them up any longer.

An observer watching the above scene would notice a curious phenomenon occurring. Many of the people listening to the voice would, one by one, drop their arms to their sides, as if they were holding heavy lead weights. The reason for this strange behaviour? The people have been hypnotized.

It is only recently that hypnotism has become an area considered worthy of scientific investigation. In part, the initial rejection of hypnosis relates to its bizarre eighteenth-century origins: Franz Mesmer's arguing that a form of "animal magnetism" could influence people and cure their illnesses. After a commission headed by Benjamin Franklin discredited the phenomenon, it fell into disrepute, only to rise again to respectability in the nineteenth century. But even today, as we will see, the nature of hypnosis is a matter of controversy.

Hypnosis: A Trance-Forming Experience?

People under **hypnosis** are in a trancelike state of heightened susceptibility to the suggestions of others. In some respects, it appears that they are asleep. Yet other aspects of their behaviour contradict this notion, for these people are attentive to the hypnotist's suggestions and might carry out bizarre or silly suggestions.

Despite their compliance when hypnotized, people do not lose all will of their own. They will not suddenly become antisocial or self-destructive. They will not reveal hidden truths about themselves, and they are capable of lying when hypnotized. Moreover, people cannot be hypnotized against their will—despite popular misconceptions (Gwynn & Spanos, 1996).

There are wide variations in people's susceptibility to hypnosis. About 5 to 20 percent of the population cannot be hypnotized at all, and some 15 percent are very easily hypnotized. Most people fall somewhere in between. Moreover, the ease with which a person is hypnotized is related to a number of other characteristics. People who are readily hypnotized are also easily absorbed while reading books or listening to music, becoming unaware of what is happening around them, and they often spend

hypnosis: A trancelike state of heightened susceptibility to the suggestions of others.

Despite common misconceptions, people such as these cannot be hypnotized against their will, nor do they lose all will of their own.
In what ways is hypnosis beneficial?

an unusual amount of time daydreaming. In sum, then, they show a high ability to concentrate and to become completely absorbed in what they are doing (Rhue, Lynn, & Kirsch, 1993; Weitzenhoffer, 1999).

A Different State of Consciousness?

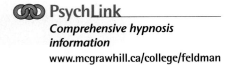

PsychLink

Comprehensive hypnosis information
www.mcgrawhill.ca/college/feldman

The question of whether hypnosis is a state of consciousness that is qualitatively different from normal waking consciousness is controversial. Psychologist Ernest Hilgard presented one side of the argument when he argued convincingly that hypnosis is a state of consciousness that differs significantly from other states. He contended that particular behaviours clearly differentiate hypnosis from other states, including higher suggestibility, increased ability to recall and construct images, and the acceptance of suggestions that clearly contradict reality. Moreover, changes in electrical activity in the brain are associated with hypnosis, supporting the position that hypnosis is a state of consciousness different from normal waking (Hilgard, 1975; Graffin, Ray, & Lundy, 1995).

On the other side of the controversy were theorists who rejected the notion that hypnosis is a significantly different state of consciousness from normal waking consciousness. They argued that altered brain-wave patterns are not sufficient to demonstrate a qualitative difference, given that no other specific physiological changes occur when a person is in a trance. Furthermore, little support exists for the contention that adults can accurately recall memories of childhood events while hypnotized. Such evidence suggests that there is nothing qualitatively special about the hypnotic trance (Spanos et al., 1993; Kirsch & Lynn, 1998).

There is increasing agreement that the controversy over the nature of hypnosis has led to extreme positions on both sides of the issue (Kirsch & Lynn, 1995). More recent approaches suggest that the hypnotic state might best be viewed as lying along a continuum, in which hypnosis is neither a totally different state of consciousness nor totally similar to normal waking consciousness.

As arguments about the true nature of hypnosis continue, though, one thing is clear: Hypnosis has been successfully used to solve practical human problems. In fact, psychologists working in many different areas have found hypnosis to be a reliable, effective tool (Rhue, Lynn, & Kirsch, 1993). Among the range of applications are the following:

- *Controlling pain.* Patients suffering from chronic pain might be given the suggestion, while hypnotized, that their pain is eliminated or reduced. Hypnosis has proved to be particularly useful during childbirth and dental procedures (Oster, 1994; Mairs, 1995; Barber, 1996).
- *Reducing smoking.* Although it hasn't been successful in stopping drug and alcohol abuse, hypnosis sometimes helps people stop smoking through hypnotic suggestions that the taste and smell of cigarettes are unpleasant (Erickson, Hershman, & Secter, 1990; Spiegel et al., 1993).
- *Treating psychological disorders.* Hypnosis sometimes is used during treatment for psychological disorders. For example, hypnosis may be employed to heighten relaxation, reduce anxiety, increase expectations of success, or modify self-defeating thoughts (Fromm & Nash, 1992).
- *Assisting in law enforcement.* Witnesses and victims are sometimes better able to recall details of a crime when hypnotized. In one case, a witness to the kidnapping of a group of California schoolchildren was placed under hypnosis and was able to recall all but one digit of the licence number on the kidnapper's vehicle (Geiselman et al., 1985). On the other hand, sometimes hypnotic recollections are inaccurate, and the legal status of hypnosis is unresolved (Gibson, 1995; Lynn et al., 1997; Baker, 1998).
- *Improving athletic performance.* Athletes sometimes turn to hypnosis to improve their performance. For example, baseball player Mark McGwire used hypnotism to increase his concentration when batting, with considerable success (Udolf, 1981; Stanton, 1994; Edgette & Edgette, 1995).

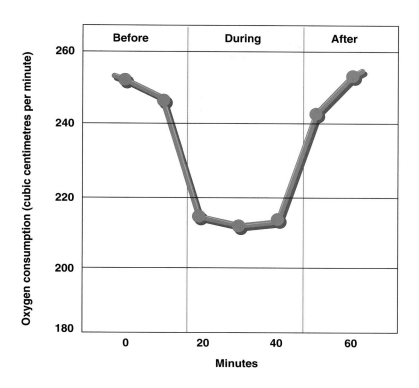

Figure 4-7 The body's use of oxygen declines significantly during meditation (Benson, 1993).
Why do you thnk this happens?

Meditation: Regulating Our Own State of Consciousness

When traditional practitioners of the ancient Eastern religion Zen Buddhism want to achieve greater spiritual insight, they turn to a technique that has been used for centuries to alter their state of consciousness: meditation.

Meditation is a learned technique for refocusing attention that brings about an altered state of consciousness. Meditation often consists of the repetition of a *mantra*—a sound, word, or syllable—over and over. In other forms of meditation, the focus is on a picture, flame, or specific part of the body. Regardless of the nature of the particular initial stimulus, the key to the procedure is concentrating on it so thoroughly that the meditator becomes unaware of any outside stimulation and reaches a different state of consciousness.

Following meditation, people report feeling thoroughly relaxed. They sometimes relate that they have gained new insights into themselves and the problems they are facing. The long-term practice of meditation can even improve health due to the biological changes it produces. For example, oxygen usage decreases, heart rate and blood pressure decline, and brain-wave patterns can change (Wallace & Benson, 1972; Holmes, 1985; Jevning et al., 1996; Zamarra et al., 1996; see Figure 4-7).

Anyone can meditate by using a few simple procedures. The fundamentals include sitting in a quiet room with eyes closed, breathing deeply and rhythmically, and repeating a word or sound—such as the word *one*—over and over. Practised twice a day for 20 minutes, the technique is effective in bringing about relaxation (Benson & Friedman, 1985; Benson, 1993; Benson et al., 1994).

 **PsychLinks**

Transcendental meditation research
www.mcgrawhill.ca/college/feldman

meditation: A learned technique for refocusing attention that brings about an altered state of consciousness.

EXPLORING DIVERSITY
Cross-Cultural Routes to Altered States of Consciousness

Why are there cultural differences in methods used to alter consciousness?

- A group of Native American Sioux sit naked in a steaming sweat lodge, as a medicine man throws water on sizzling rocks to send billows of scalding steam into the air.

- Aztec priests smear themselves with a mixture of crushed poisonous herbs, hairy black worms, scorpions, and lizards. Sometimes they drink the potion.
- A devout sixteenth-century Hasidic Jew lies across the tombstone of a celebrated scholar. As he murmurs the name of God repeatedly, he seeks to be possessed by the soul of the dead wise man's spirit. If successful, he will attain a mystical state, and the deceased's words will flow out of his mouth.

Each of these rituals has a common goal: suspension from the bonds of everyday awareness and access to an altered state of consciousness (Furst, 1977; Fine, 1994). Although they might seem exotic from the vantage point of many Western cultures, these rituals represent an apparently universal effort to alter consciousness. According to recent studies, television, videogames, and virtual reality games or devices can alter consciousness (Preston, 1998).

Some scholars suggest that the quest to alter consciousness represents a basic human desire (Siegel, 1989). Whether or not one accepts such an extreme view, it is clear that different cultures have developed their own unique forms of consciousness-altering activities. Similarly, when we discuss psychological disorders in Chapter 12, we will see that what is deemed "abnormal" behaviour varies considerably from one culture to another.

Of course, realizing that efforts to produce altered states of consciousness are widespread throughout the world's societies does not answer a fundamental question: Is the experience of *un*altered states of consciousness similar across different cultures?

There are two possible responses to this question. Because humans share basic biological commonalties in the ways their brains and bodies are wired, we might assume that the fundamental experience of consciousness is similar across cultures. As a result, we could suppose that consciousness shows some basic similarities across cultures.

On the other hand, cultures can differ greatly in how they interpret and view certain aspects of consciousness. For example, people in different cultures might experience the passage of time differently: One study found that Mexicans view time as passing more slowly than other North Americans do (Diaz-Guerrero, 1979).

Whatever the true nature of consciousness and regardless of why people seek to alter it, it is clear that people often seek the means to alter their everyday experience of the world. In some cases that need becomes overwhelming, as we see next when we consider the use of drugs.

Evaluate

1. _____ is a state of heightened susceptibility to the suggestions of others.
2. A friend tells you, "I once heard of a person who was murdered by being hypnotized and then told to jump from the Golden Gate Bridge!" Could such a thing have happened? Why or why not?
3. _____ is a learned technique for refocusing attention to bring about an altered state of consciousness.
4. Leslie repeats a unique sound, known as a _____, when she engages in meditation.

Answers to Evaluate Questions

1. Hypnosis 2. No; people who are hypnotized cannot be made to perform self-destructive acts. 3. Meditation 4. mantra

Rethink

1. What sorts of mental functioning does hypnosis appear to affect most strongly? Do you think it might have more effect on the left or right hemisphere of the brain, or would it affect both equally? Why?
2. Meditation produces several physical and psychological benefits. Does this suggest that we are physically and mentally burdened in our normal state of waking consciousness? Why?

Drug Use: The Highs and Lows of Consciousness

Green Bay Packers quarterback Brett Favre can tell you exactly when he changed his life, even if he doesn't remember it. It was 6 P.M. on February 27, and Favre was in his room at Bellin Hospital in Green Bay, Wisconsin, recovering from ankle surgery. A nurse was about to reinsert his IV, and the oft-injured quarterback was rolling his eyes in resignation at his longtime girlfriend, Deanna Tynes, and their 7-year-old daughter, Brittany. Then suddenly he went into convulsions. "His whole body was jerking around, his lip was folded under," says Deanna, 27, who screamed to the nurse to stop him from swallowing his tongue. Asked a terrified Brittany: "Mom, is he going to die?"

In a sense, just the opposite happened. When Favre, 26, regained consciousness minutes later, he awakened to a central fact of his life: He was an addict in need of help. For the previous five months, Favre had been taking the painkiller Vicodin—first to help him deal with a season's worth of injuries and then as a crutch for coping with fame. Doctors could not pinpoint the cause of the seizure, but it seemed clear to Favre that it was related to his dependency on the prescription drug. Three months later he checked into the Menninger Clinic in Topeka, Kansas, for six weeks of rehab. (Plummer & Pick, 1996, p. 129)

Brett Favre was successful in his personal war on drugs: He became free of painkillers and later was able to lead his team to triumph in the Super Bowl. Others, though, are not so lucky. Each year, thousands of people die from complications of drug overdoses, and many more are addicted to various kinds of drugs.

Drugs are a part of almost everyone's life. From infancy on, most people take vitamins, aspirin, cold-relief medicine, and the like. In a recent Canadian survey, 70 percent of respondents reported using aspirin during the month before the survey (Canadian Centre for Substance Abuse, 1995). North Americans use four tons of aspirin in a year (Jackson, 2002). However, these drugs rarely produce an altered state of consciousness (Dortch, 1996).

Prepare

What are the major classifications of drugs, and what are their effects?

Organize

Drug Use: The Highs and Lows of Consciousness
Stimulants
Depressants
Narcotics
Hallucinogens

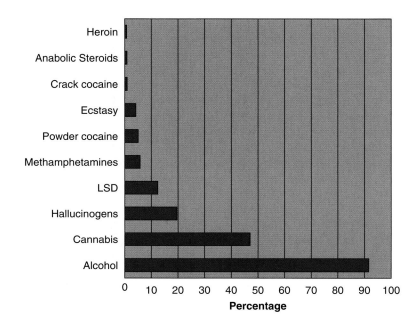

Figure 4-8 Percentages of Canadian university undergraduates reporting use of various drugs at least once. (Based on Gliksman et al., 2000). Although 92 percent had tried alcohol at least once, 87 percent drank alcohol in the year prior to the survey. *Can you think of some reasons why alcohol consumption is so prevalent among students?*

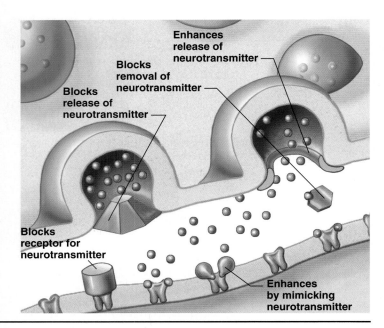

Figure 4-9 Different drugs affect different parts of the nervous system and brain and each drug functions in one of these specific ways.

After S. S. Mader. Copyright © The McGraw-Hill Companies.

psychoactive drugs: Drugs that influence a person's emotions, perceptions, and behaviour.

addictive drugs: Drugs that produce a biological or psychological dependence in the user; withdrawal from them leads to a craving for the drug that in some cases can be nearly irresistible.

⊕ PsychLink

Information on addiction
www.mcgrawhill.ca/college/feldman

On the other hand, some substances, known as psychoactive drugs, lead to an altered state of consciousness. **Psychoactive drugs** influence a person's emotions, perceptions, and behaviour. Yet even these drugs are common in most of our lives. If you have ever had a cup of coffee or sipped a beer, you have taken a psychoactive drug.

Many Canadian university students have used drugs at some point in their lives (see Figure 4-8). In a 1998 survey of undergraduates at universities across Canada, 92 percent of the sample reported use of alcohol, followed by 47 percent for cannabis, 20 percent for hallucinogens and 12 percent for LSD. Smaller but significant proportions used methamphetamines (6 percent), cocaine (5 percent), and ecstasy (4 percent). The drugs least used were crack, anabolic steroids, and heroin (less than 1 percent each). Cigarettes were used daily or occasionally by 23 percent of the sample (Gliksman et al., 2000).

Of course, drugs vary widely in the effects they have on users, in part because they affect the nervous system in very different ways. Some drugs alter the limbic system, others affect the operation of specific neurotransmitters across the synapses of neurons (see Chapter 2). For example, some drugs and other substances block or enhance the release of neurotransmitters. *Botulinum* toxin, a poison found in badly preserved food, blocks the release of acetylcholine. Alcohol, cocaine, and THC (tetrahydrocannabinol, the active ingredient in marijuana) enhance the release of dopamine. Black widow spider venom triggers the release of acetylcholine. Some drugs block the receipt or removal of a neurotransmitter. Antipsychotic drugs used to reduce symptoms of schizophrenia (e.g., chlorpromazine, clozapine) block dopamine receptors. Curare, a plant-derived poison used on arrow tips by some South American aboriginals, blocks acetylcholine receptors and causes paralysis and death. Still other drugs, such as nicotine and morphine, mimic the effects of neurotransmitters (see Figure 4-9).

The most dangerous drugs are addictive. **Addictive drugs** produce a biological or psychological dependence in the user, and withdrawal from them leads to a craving for the drug that, in some cases, can be nearly irresistible. Addictions can be *biologically based,* in which case the body becomes so accustomed to functioning in the presence of a drug that it cannot function in its absence. Or, addictions can be *psychologically based,* in which case people believe that they need the drug in order to respond to the stresses of daily living. Although we generally associate addiction with drugs such as heroin, everyday sorts of drugs like caffeine (found in coffee) and nicotine (found in cigarettes) have addictive aspects as well.

We know surprisingly little about the underlying causes of addiction. One of the problems in identifying the causes is that different drugs (such as alcohol and cocaine) affect the brain in very different ways—and yet can be equally addicting. Furthermore, it takes longer to become addicted to some drugs than to others, even though the ultimate consequences of addiction can be equally grave (Wickelgren, 1998b; Thombs, 1999).

Why do people take drugs in the first place? There are many reasons, ranging from the perceived pleasure of the experience itself, to the escape a drug-induced high affords from the everyday pressures of life, to an attempt to achieve a religious or spiritual state. But other factors, ones that have little to do with the nature of the experience itself, also lead people to try drugs (McDowell & Spitz, 1999).

For instance, the alleged drug use of well-known athletes and film stars (such as Ross Rebagliati and Robert Downey, Jr.), the easy availability of some illegal drugs, and peer pressure all play a role in the decision to use drugs. In some cases, the motive is simply the thrill of trying something new. Finally, the sense of helplessness experienced

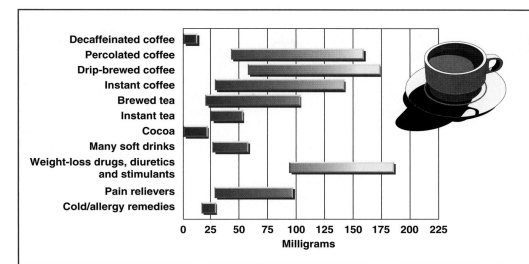

FIGURE 4-10 This chart shows the range of caffeine found in common foods and drinks (*New York Times*, 1991). Use the information to assess your caffeine consumption. Daily average consumption per person is about 240 mg in Canada and 200 mg in the U.S.

by poor, unemployed individuals trapped in lives of poverty might lead them to try drugs as a way of escaping the bleakness of their lives. Regardless of the forces that lead a person to begin using drugs, drug addiction is among the most difficult of all behaviours to modify, even with extensive treatment (Dupre et al., 1995; Tucker, Donovan, & Marlatt, 1999).

Because of the difficulty in treating drug problems, there is little disagreement that the best hope for dealing with the overall societal problem of substance abuse is to prevent people from becoming involved with drugs in the first place. However, developing effective programs for preventing substance use and related problems among youth is challenging. In the *Applying Psychology in the 21st Century* box, we consider some of the effective programs in Canada.

Stimulants: Drug Highs

It's one o'clock in the morning, and you still haven't finished reading the last chapter of the text on which you will be tested in the morning. Feeling exhausted, you turn to the one thing that might help you stay awake for the next two hours: a cup of strong, black coffee.

If you have ever found yourself in such a position, you have been relying on a major **stimulant**, caffeine, to stay awake. *Caffeine* is one of a number of stimulants that affect the central nervous system by causing a rise in heart rate, blood pressure, and muscular tension. Caffeine is present not only in coffee; it is an important ingredient in tea, soft drinks, and chocolate as well (see Chapter Activity 4-2).

Caffeine produces several reactions. The major behavioural effects of caffeine are an increase in attentiveness and a decrease in reaction time. Caffeine can also bring about an improvement in mood, most likely by mimicking the effects of a natural brain chemical, adenosine. Too much caffeine, however, can result in nervousness and insomnia. People can build up a biological dependence on the drug. If they suddenly stop drinking coffee, they might experience headaches or depression. Many people who drink large amounts of coffee on weekdays have headaches on weekends because of a sudden drop in the amount of caffeine they are consuming (Silverman et al., 1992; Silverman, Mumford, & Griffiths, 1994; James, 1997).

Nicotine, found in cigarettes, is another common stimulant. The soothing effects of nicotine help explain why cigarette smoking is addictive. Smokers develop a dependence on nicotine, and those who suddenly stop smoking develop strong cravings for the drug. This is not surprising: nicotine activates neuronal mechanisms similar to those activated by cocaine, which, as we see next, is also highly addictive (Murray, 1990; Pich et al., 1997). (We will discuss smoking in greater detail in Chapter 11 when we consider health psychology.)

stimulants: Drugs that affect the central nervous system by causing a rise in heart rate, blood pressure, and muscular tension.

Applying Psychology in the 21st Century

Finding Antidrug Programs that Work

Substance abuse among young people and the problems associated with it have increased significantly in recent years. And so have the strategies and programs aimed at lessening or preventing the abuse and the problems. But how do we know which programs are effective?

Research indicates that substance abuse typically starts early in life, and so this is clearly the time to begin prevention education. Since Canadians must attend school until age 16, our schools provide a captive audience. The issue is how to reach this audience. One effective approach is based on the common though narrow view that students start to use consciousness-altering substances simply because of peer pressure. This approach acknowledges the power of peer influence, and uses it as a tool in delivering effective information and skills-training programs (Roberts et al., 2001). Youth Assisting Peers is a program aimed at grade nine students in which senior students provide information and share opinions with younger students. Its goals are to dispel myths about substance abuse, to provide information (especially harm-reduction messages), and to address the

An antidrug program meeting.

concerns of ninth graders. Another program, Parents Against Drugs, is a parent-sponsored peer-education program in which trained high school students conduct sessions with eighth graders, focusing on examining and making choices about the use of alcohol and drugs.

Other programs strive for accountability by focusing their delivery on at-risk students. For example, in Opening Doors, the target group consists of those who are likely to experience problems with low school achievement, violent behaviour, truancy, and drug use. Secondary target groups include parents and members of the school community at large because of their

impact on students. The Rural and Northern Youth Intervention Strategy of Manitoba provides counselling to help young people assess the effects of alcohol and drugs on their health, social relations, and other areas of their lives, and promotes discussion of youth issues generally. Let 'Em Go is a program aimed at empowerment and reduction of drug use in marginalized youth. Street youth are involved in the development and delivery of the program. The Strengthening Families Program, which targets not only at-risk youth, but also their families, has received favourable evaluations for its use in both Canada and the United States (Kumpfer & Alvarado, 1995; Roberts et al., 2001).

Common themes in program evaluations are that antidrug programs that work involve youth actively at all levels (in planning, implementation, and as targets) and are supported by the larger community. Another important criterion for success is that programs demonstrate an understanding of how young people view substance use. In addition, the suitability of program materials and delivery strategies for young people at various stages of growth and development help to determine program success. Cost and program sustainability are also important factors (Roberts et al., 2001).

Cocaine

Although its use has declined over the last decade, the stimulant *cocaine* and its derivative, crack, are still a serious concern. Cocaine is inhaled or "snorted" through the nose, smoked, or injected directly into the bloodstream. It is rapidly absorbed into the body and takes effect almost immediately.

During the late nineteenth century, and even into the early twentieth century, cocaine was used in numerous home remedies and medicines.

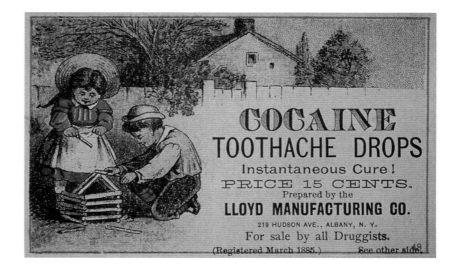

Table 4–3 Drugs and Their Effects

Drug	Street Name	Effects	Withdrawal Symptoms	Adverse/Overdose Reactions
Stimulants				
Cocaine	Coke, blow, snow, lady, crack	Increased confidence, mood elevation, sense of energy and alertness, decreased appetite, anxiety, irritability, insomnia, transient drowsiness, delayed orgasm	Apathy, general fatigue, prolonged sleep, depression, disorientation, suicidal thoughts, agitated motor activity, irritability, bizarre dreams	Elevated blood pressure, increase in body temperature, face-picking, suspiciousness, bizarre and repetitious behaviour, vivid hallucinations, convulsions, possible death
Amphetamines Benzedrine Dexedrine	Speed Speed			
Depressants				
Alcohol	Booze	Anxiety reduction, impulsiveness, dramatic mood swings, bizarre thoughts, suicidal behaviour, slurred speech, disorientation, slowed mental and physical functioning, limited attention span	Weakness, restlessness, nausea and vomiting, headaches, nightmares, irritability, depression, acute anxiety, hallucinations, seizures, possible death	Confusion, decreased response to pain, shallow respiration, dilated pupils, weak and rapid pulse, coma, possible death
Barbiturates Nembutal Seconal Phenobarbital	Yellowjackets, yellows Reds			
Rohypnol	Roofies, rope, "date rape drug"	Muscle relaxation, amnesia, sleep	Seizures	Seizures, coma, incapacitation, inability to resist sexual assault
Narcotics				
Heroin	H, hombre, junk, smack, dope, crap, horse	Anxiety and pain reduction, apathy, difficulty in concentration, slowed speech, decreased physical activity, drooling, itching, euphoria, nausea	Anxiety, vomiting, sneezing, diarrhea, lower back pain, watery eyes, runny nose, yawning, irritability, tremors, panic, chills and sweating, cramps	Depressed levels of consciousness, low blood pressure, rapid heart rate, shallow breathing, convulsions, coma, possible death
Morphine	Drugstore dope, cube, first line, mud			
Hallucinogens				
Cannabis Marijuana Hashish Hash oil	Bhang, kif, ganja, dope, grass, pot, smoke, hemp, joint, weed, bone, Mary Jane, herb, tea	Euphoria, relaxed inhibitions, increased appetite, disoriented behaviour	Hyperactivity, insomnia, decreased appetite, anxiety	Severe reactions are rare but include panic, paranoia, fatigue, bizarre and dangerous behaviour, decreased testosterone over long term; immune-system effects
MDMA	Ecstasy	Heightened sense of oneself and insight, feelings of peace, empathy, energy	Not reported	Increase in body temperature, possible memory difficulties
LSD	Acid, quasey, microdot, white lightning	Heightened aesthetic responses; vision and depth distortion; heightened sensitivity to faces and gestures; magnified feelings; paranoia; panic; euphoria	Not reported	Nausea and chills; increased pulse, temperature, and blood pressure; slow, deep breathing; loss of appetite; insomnia; bizarre, dangerous behaviour

When used in relatively small quantities, cocaine produces feelings of profound psychological well-being, increased confidence, and alertness. Cocaine produces this "high" through the neurotransmitter dopamine. As you'll recall from Chapter 2, dopamine is one of the chemicals that transmit between neurons messages related to ordinary feelings of pleasure. Normally when dopamine is released, excess amounts of the neurotransmitter are reabsorbed by the releasing neuron. However, when cocaine enters the brain, it blocks reabsorption of leftover dopamine. As a result, the brain is flooded with dopamine-produced pleasurable sensations (Landry, 1997; Bolla, Cadet, & London, 1998; see Table 4-3 for a summary of the effects of cocaine and other illegal drugs.)

PsychLink

Factline on cocaine
www.mcgrawhill.ca/college/feldman

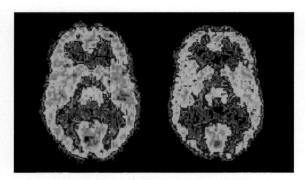

On the left is a PET scan of a normal, awake brain. On the right is a PET scan of a cocaine abuser's brain. The scans indicate where cocaine use has affected the brain's use of glucose. The red areas indicate the highest level of glucose use, yellow a lower level, and blue the lowest. The lack of red in the scan on the right shows that the brain is not using glucose nearly as efficiently.

However, there is a steep price to be paid for the pleasurable effects of cocaine. The drug is psychologically and physically addictive, and users can grow obsessed with obtaining it. Cocaine addicts indulge in binge use, administering the drug every 10 to 30 minutes if it is available. During these binges, they think of nothing but cocaine; eating, sleeping, family, friends, money, and even survival have no importance. Their lives become tied to the drug. Over time, users deteriorate mentally and physically. In extreme cases, cocaine can cause hallucinations—a common one is of insects crawling over one's body (Pottieger et al., 1992; Crits-Christoph et al., 1999).

In Canada, the percent of the population who have tried cocaine at least once is highest in 25- to 34-year-olds (8 percent), followed by 20- to 24-year-olds (5 percent) (Single et al., 1999). Given the strength of cocaine, withdrawal from the drug is difficult. Although the reported use of cocaine among Canadian high school students is 5 percent or less, the drug is still a major problem because there is evidence of sharply increasing use in recent years. For example, reported use has increased in Nova Scotia from 3 percent (1991) to 5 percent (1998), in New Brunswick from 3 percent (1992) to 4 percent (1998), and in Ontario from 2 percent (1993) to 4 percent (2001) (Barceló, Jones, & Grobe, 1998; Adlaf & Paglia, 2001). Use among street youths is much higher (Roberts et al., 2001).

Amphetamines

Amphetamines are strong stimulants, such as Dexedrine and Benzedrine, popularly known as "speed." When their use soared in the 1970s, the phrase "speed kills" became prevalent as the drugs caused an increasing number of deaths. Although amphetamine use has declined from its 1970s peak, many drug experts believe that speed would quickly resurface in large quantities if cocaine supplies were interrupted.

In small quantities, amphetamines—which stimulate the central nervous system—bring about a sense of energy and alertness, talkativeness, heightened confidence, and a mood "high." They increase concentration and reduce fatigue. Amphetamines also cause a loss of appetite, increased anxiety, and irritability. When taken over long periods of time, amphetamines can cause feelings of being persecuted by others, as well as a general sense of suspiciousness. People taking amphetamines can lose interest in sex. If taken in too large a quantity, amphetamines overstimulate the central nervous system to such an extent that convulsions and death can occur.

Amphetamines (shown here greatly magnified) are strong stimulants that increase alertness and energy and provide a sense of heightened confidence.

Depressants: Drug Lows

depressants: Drugs that slow down the nervous system.

In contrast to the initial effect of stimulants, which is an increase in arousal of the central nervous system, the effect of **depressants** is to impede the nervous system by causing neurons to fire more slowly. Small doses result in at least temporary feelings of *intoxication*—drunkenness—along with a sense of euphoria and joy. When large amounts are taken, however, speech becomes slurred and muscle control becomes disjointed, making motion difficult. Ultimately, heavy users can lose consciousness entirely.

Alcohol

The most common depressant is *alcohol*. In 1996–97, Canadians drank almost 2 billion litres of beer, 253 million litres of wine, and 130 million litres of spirits. Overall, 42 percent of drinkers reported at least one episode of heavy drinking (consuming 5 or more drinks on a single occasion) during the year, and 6 percent reported drinking heavily on a weekly basis. The percentages for heavy drinking were highest for young people aged 20 to 24 years. In this age group, 68 percent reported a single occasion of heavy drinking and 13 percent reported heavy drinking on a weekly basis

Most alcohol consumers are casual users. The effects of alcohol vary significantly, depending on who is drinking it and the setting in which they are drinking.
If alcohol were a newly discovered drug, do you think its sale would be legal?

(Single et al., 1999; Statistics Canada, 1998a). Heavy drinking is also reported by provincial drug use surveys (Barceló, Jones, & Grobe, 1998; Patton et al., 2001; Adlaf & Paglia, 2001) and by the Canadian Campus Survey, a nationwide survey of university students (Gliksman et al., 2000). See Figure 4-11.

Students have reported a range of problems related to drinking such as personal injury, regretting actions, memory loss, poor academic performance, missing class, and trouble with the law. Of particular concern is the relation between alcoholic consumption and high-risk behaviours such as driving under the influence of alcohol and unplanned sex (MacDonald, Zanna, & Fong, 1996).

Although alcohol consumption is widespread, significant gender and cultural variations exist in its use. For example, women are typically somewhat lighter drinkers than men are (Single et al., 1999), although the gap between the sexes for high school students is small or nonexistent. On average, male university students drink more often and have a higher weekly alcohol intake than female university students (Gliksman et al., 2000). Women are usually more susceptible to the effects of alcohol, because of differences in blood volume and body fat that permit more alcohol to go directly into the bloodstream (Galanter, 1995; National Center on Addiction and Substance Abuse, 1996; Blume, 1998).

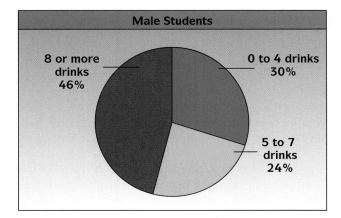
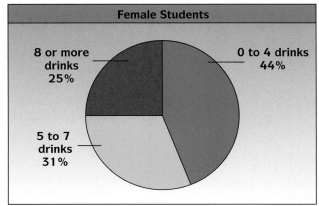

Figure 4–11 Drinking patterns of Canadian university students. The figure shows the percents of male and female students who abstained or drank moderately (0 to 4 drinks), drank heavily (5 to 7 drinks), and drank very heavily (8 or more drinks) on a single occasion during the autumn of 1998. Based on Gliksman et al., 2000.

Figure 4–12 The effects of alcohol. The quantities represent only rough benchmarks; the effects vary significantly depending on an individual's weight, height, recent food intake, genetic factors, and even a person's psychological state.

Number of drinks consumed in 2 hours	Alcohol in blood, percentage	Typical effects
2	0.05	Judgment, thought, and restraint weakened; tension released, giving carefree sensation
3	0.08	Tensions and inhibitions of everyday life lessened; cheerfulness
4	0.10	Voluntary motor action affected, making hand and arm movements, walk, and speech clumsy
7	0.20	Severe impairment—staggering, loud, incoherent, emotionally unstable,100 times greater traffic risk; exuberance and aggressive inclinations magnified
9	0.30	Deeper areas of brain affected, with stimulus-response and understanding confused; stuporous; blurred vision
12	0.40	Incapable of voluntary action, sleepy, difficult to arouse; equivalent of surgical anesthesia
15	0.50	Comatose; centres controlling breathing and heartbeat anesthetized; death increasingly probable

Note: A drink refers to a typical 341 mL (12-ounce) bottle of beer, a 43 mL (1.5-ounce) shot of hard liquor, or a 142 mL (5-ounce) glass of wine.

There are also ethnic differences in alcohol consumption. For example, people of East Asian backgrounds who live in the United States tend to drink significantly less than Caucasians or African Americans, and their incidence of alcohol-related problems is lower. It could be that physical reactions to drinking, which can include sweating, a quickened heartbeat, and flushing, are more unpleasant for East Asians than for other groups (Akutsu et al., 1989; Smith & Lin, 1996; Garcia-Andrade, Wall, & Ehlers, 1997).

Although alcohol is a depressant, most people claim that it increases their sense of sociability and well-being. The discrepancy between the actual and the perceived effects of alcohol lies in the initial effects it produces in the majority of individuals who use it: release of tension and stress, feelings of happiness, and loss of inhibitions (Steele & Southwick, 1985; Josephs & Steele, 1990; Steele & Josephs, 1990; Sayette, 1993). As the dose of alcohol increases, however, the depressive effects become more pronounced (see Figure 4-12). People might feel emotionally and physically unstable. They also show

PsychLink

Alcohol and alcoholism information
www.mcgrawhill.ca/college/feldman

poor judgment and might act aggressively. Moreover, their memories are impaired, brain processing of spatial information is diminished, and speech becomes slurred and incoherent. Eventually they might fall into a stupor and pass out. If they drink enough alcohol in a short time, they can die of alcohol poisoning (Bushman, 1993; Matthews et al., 1996; Chin & Pisoni, 1997).

Why some people continue to consume alcohol even though it causes serious difficulties is not clear. There is some evidence of a genetic influence on alcoholism, but not all alcoholics have close relatives who are alcoholics. In these cases environmental stressors are suspected of playing a larger role (Pennisi, 1997a; McGue, 1999). According to interaction theory, alcoholism develops as a result of interaction between person variables and features of the environment. For example, persons prone to experience anxiety are likely to become alcoholics if alcohol is readily available (Sadava, 1987). In young adults problem drinking is multidimensional (DeCourville & Sadava, 1997). It involves the frequency and amount of alcohol consumption, coping functions and adverse consequences of alcohol use, and the individual's perceptions that his or her drinking is problematic. DeCourville and Sadava's model identifies problem drinkers whose consumption is frequent and high, and is associated with adverse consequences, as well as those whose consumption is low, and also has severe consequences. Some alcoholics rely on alcohol to function in their daily lives, and quickly build up a tolerance to the effects of alcohol. They must drink progressively more in order to experience the positive feelings alcohol produces (Galanter & Kleber, 1999). Other alcoholics drink inconsistently, but occasionally go on sporadic binges, consuming large quantities and becoming violent and aggressive. Although their excessive drinking episodes are relatively infrequent and therefore do not seem to be too serious, when these episodes occur they are accompanied by devastating outcomes.

Even legal drugs, when used improperly, can lead to addiction.

Barbiturates

Barbiturates, which include such drugs as Nembutal, Seconal, and Phenobarbital, are another form of depressant. Frequently prescribed by physicians to induce sleep or to reduce stress, barbiturates produce a sense of relaxation. Yet they also are psychologically and physically addictive, and the combination of barbiturates with alcohol can be deadly because it relaxes the muscles of the diaphragm to such an extent that the user stops breathing.

Rohypnol

Rohypnol is frequently called the "date rape drug," because when it is mixed with alcohol it can prevent victims from resisting sexual assault. Sometimes people who are unknowingly given the drug are so incapacitated that they have no memory of the assault.

narcotics: Drugs that increase relaxation and relieve pain and anxiety.

Narcotics: Relieving Pain and Anxiety

Narcotics are drugs that increase relaxation and relieve pain and anxiety. *Codeine,* as well as two of the most powerful narcotics, *morphine* and *heroin,* are derived from the opium poppy. Codeine is probably the most frequently used narcotic because it is combined with other drugs, such as the painkillers Aspirin and Tylenol, that are very widely used. Although morphine is used medically to control severe pain, heroin is illegal in Canada and the United States. This has not prevented its use.

Heroin users usually inject the drug directly into their veins with a hypodermic needle. The immediate effect has been described as a "rush" of positive feeling, similar in some respects to a sexual orgasm—and just as difficult to describe. After the rush, a heroin user experiences a sense of well-being and peacefulness that lasts three to five hours. When the effects of the drug wear off, however, the user feels extreme anxiety and a desperate desire

The use of heroin creates a cycle of biological and physical dependence. Combined with the strong positive feelings produced by the drug, this makes heroin addiction especially difficult to cure.

Figure 4–13 This chart shows the trends in prevalence of use of marijuana and Ecstasy for Ontario students in grades 7 to OAC (Based on Adlaf et al., 2001).

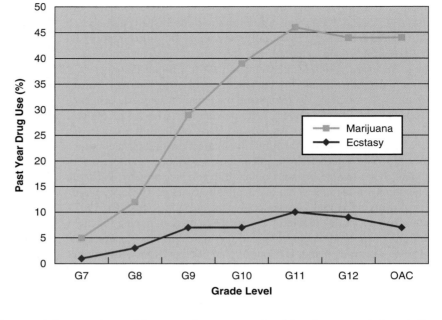

to repeat the experience. Moreover, larger amounts of heroin are needed each time to produce the same pleasurable effect. This leads to a cycle of biological and psychological addiction: The user is constantly either shooting up or attempting to obtain ever-increasing amounts of the drug. Eventually, the life of the addict revolves around heroin.

Because of the powerful positive feelings the drug produces, heroin addiction is particularly difficult to cure. One treatment that has shown some success is the use of methadone. *Methadone* is a synthetic chemical that satisfies a heroin user's physiological cravings for the drug without providing the "high" that accompanies heroin. When heroin users are placed on regular doses of methadone they might be able to function relatively normally. The use of methadone has one substantial drawback, however. Although it can eliminate the psychological dependence on heroin, it replaces the biological addiction to heroin with a biological addiction to methadone. Researchers are attempting to find nonaddictive chemical substitutes for heroin, as well as substitutes for other addictive drugs, that do not replace one addiction with another (Waldrop, 1989; Sinclair, 1990; Pulvirenti & Koob, 1994).

hallucinogen: A drug that is capable of producing hallucinations, or changes in the perceptual process.

Hallucinogens: Psychedelic Drugs

What do mushrooms, jimsonweed, and morning glories have in common? Besides being fairly common plants, each can be the source of a powerful **hallucinogen**, a drug that is capable of producing hallucinations, or changes in the perceptual process.

The most common hallucinogen in widespread use today is *marijuana,* whose active ingredient—tetrahydrocannabinol (THC)—is found in a common weed, cannabis. Marijuana is typically smoked in cigarettes or pipes, although it can be cooked and eaten. Recent provincial drug-use surveys found that 30 percent or more of high school students in Manitoba, Ontario, New Brunswick, Nova Scotia, and Newfoundland reported using marijuana during the previous year (Patton et al., 2001; Adlaf & Paglia, 2001; Barceló, Jones, & Grobe, 1998). Among university students, 29 percent reported marijuana use during the year prior to the survey (Gliksman et al., 2000). (See Figure 4-13 for a comparison of marijuana and Ecstasy use by Ontario high school students.)

The effects of marijuana vary from person to person, but they typically consist of feelings of euphoria and general well-being. Sensory experiences seem more vivid and intense, and a person's sense of self-importance seems

What are the effects of a hallucinogen on thinking? Artists have tried to depict the hallucinogenic experience, as in this yarn painting.

to grow. Memory can be impaired, causing the user to feel pleasantly "spaced out." On the other hand, the effects are not universally positive. Individuals who use marijuana when feeling depressed can end up even more depressed, because the drug tends to magnify both good and bad feelings.

There are clear risks associated with long-term, heavy marijuana use. Although marijuana does not seem to produce addiction by itself, some evidence suggests that there are similarities in the way marijuana and drugs such as cocaine and heroin affect the brain. Furthermore, there is some evidence that heavy use at least temporarily decreases the production of the male sex hormone testosterone, potentially affecting sexual activity and sperm count (DiChiara & Reinhart, 1997; Iversen, 2000).

In addition, marijuana smoked during pregnancy has lasting effects on children who are exposed prenatally. Heavy use also diminishes the ability of the immune system to fight off germs and increases stress on the heart, although it is unclear how strong these effects are. There is one unquestionably negative consequence of smoking marijuana: The smoke damages the lungs much the way cigarette smoke does, producing an increased likelihood of developing cancer and other lung diseases (Julien, 1995; "Marijuana as Medicine," 1997).

Despite the possible dangers of marijuana use, there is little scientific evidence for the popular belief that users "graduate" from marijuana to more dangerous drugs. Furthermore, the use of marijuana is routine in certain cultures. For instance, some people in Jamaica habitually drink a marijuana-based tea for religious purposes. In addition, marijuana has several medical uses; it can prevent nausea from chemotherapy, treat some AIDS symptoms, and relieve muscle spasms for people with spinal cord injuries. In a controversial move, several U.S. states have made the use of the drug legal if it is prescribed by a physician—although it remains illegal under U.S. federal law (Brookhiser, 1997; Iverson, 2000). In Canada, a new medicinal marijuana law was passed on July 30, 2001. The new regulations allow people suffering from serious illness to use marijuana for medicinal purposes and to grow marijuana or have someone grow it for them.

MDMA (Ecstasy) and LSD

MDMA ("Ecstasy") and *lysergic acid diethylamide* (LSD, or "acid") fall into the category of hallucinogens. Both drugs affect the operation of the neurotransmitter serotonin in the brain, altering brain-cell activity and perception (Aghajanian, 1994; Cloud, 2000).

Ecstasy users report a sense of peacefulness and calm, increased empathy and connection with others, and feeling relaxed yet energetic. Although the data are not conclusive, some researchers have found declines in memory and performance on intellectual tasks for Ecstasy users, and such findings suggest that there can be long-term changes in serotonin receptors in the brain (McCann et al., 1999).

LSD produces vivid hallucinations. Perceptions of colours, sounds, and shapes are altered so much that even the most mundane experience—such as looking at the knots in a wooden table—can seem moving and exciting. Time perception is distorted, and objects and people might be viewed in a new way, with some users reporting that LSD increases their understanding of the world. For others, however, the experience brought on by LSD can be terrifying, particularly if users have had emotional difficulties in the past. Furthermore, people can experience flashbacks—hallucinations that start suddenly, long after they stopped using the drug.

PsychLink

Information on marijuana
www.mcgrawhill.ca/college/feldman

BECOMING AN INFORMED CONSUMER OF PSYCHOLOGY

Identifying Drug and Alcohol Problems

How do these signs of drug and alcohol problems show that use has become abuse?

In a society bombarded with commercials for drugs that are guaranteed to do everything from cure the common cold to give new life to "tired blood," it is no wonder that drug-related problems are a major social issue. Yet many people with drug and alcohol problems deny they have them, and even close friends and family members can fail to realize when occasional social use of drugs or alcohol has turned into abuse.

Certain signs, however, indicate when use becomes abuse (Archambault, 1992; National Institute on Drug Abuse, 2000). Among them:

- Always getting high to have a good time
- Being high more often than not
- Getting high to get oneself going
- Going to work or class while high
- Missing or being unprepared for class or work because you were high
- Feeling bad later about something you said or did while high
- Driving a car while high
- Coming in conflict with the law because of drugs
- Doing something while high that you wouldn't otherwise do
- Being high in nonsocial, solitary situations
- Being unable to stop getting high
- Feeling a need for a drink or a drug to get through the day
- Becoming physically unhealthy
- Failing at school or on the job
- Thinking about liquor or drugs all the time
- Avoiding family or friends while using liquor or drugs

Any combination of these symptoms should be sufficient to alert you to the potential of a serious drug problem. Because drug and alcohol dependence are almost impossible to cure on one's own, people who suspect that they have a problem should seek immediate attention from a psychologist, physician, or counsellor.

You can also get help from Alcoholics Anonymous or Narcotics Anonymous. Your local telephone book will have a listing for each of these groups. Finally, you can get information about treatment programs and facilities across Canada from the Canadian Centre on Substance Abuse. You can contact them by phone at (613) 235-4048, fax (613) 235-8101, or mail (75 Albert Street, Suite 300, Ottawa, Ontario, K1P 5E7), or get information from their Web site (www.ccsa.ca).

Evaluate

1. Drugs that affect a person's consciousness are referred to as _____.
2. Match the type of drug to an example of that type.
   1. Narcotic—a pain reliever   a. LSD
   2. Amphetamine—a strong stimulant   b. Heroin
   3. Hallucinogen—capable of producing c. Dexedrine or speed
      hallucinations
3. Classify each drug listed as a stimulant (S), depressant (D), hallucinogen (H), or narcotic (N).
   1. Nicotine _____
   2. Cocaine _____
   3. Alcohol _____
   4. Morphine _____
   5. Marijuana _____
4. The effects of LSD can recur long after the drug has been taken. True or false?
5. _____ is a drug that has been used to treat people with heroin addiction.

Answers to Evaluate Questions

1. psychoactive 2. 1-b; 2-c; 3-a 3. 1-S; 2-S; 3-D; 4-N; 5-H 4. True 5. Methadone

Rethink

1. Why do you think people in almost every culture use psychoactive drugs and search for altered states of consciousness?
2. People often use the word *addiction* loosely, speaking of an addiction to candy or a television show. Can you explain the difference between this type of "addiction" and a true physiological addiction? Is there a difference between this type of "addiction" and a psychological addiction?

What are the different states of consciousness?

- Consciousness is a person's awareness of the sensations, thoughts, and feelings at a given moment. It can vary from more active to more passive states. (p. 122)

What happens when we sleep, and what are the meaning and function of dreams?

- Using the electroencephalogram, or EEG, to study sleep, scientists have found that the brain is active throughout the night, and that sleep proceeds through a series of stages identified by unique patterns of brain waves. (p. 124)
- REM (rapid eye movement) sleep is characterized by an increase in heart rate, a rise in blood pressure, an increase in the rate of breathing and, in males, erections. Dreams occur during this stage. (p. 126)
- According to Freud, dreams have both a manifest content (their apparent story line) and a latent content (their true meaning). He suggested that the latent content provides a guide to a dreamer's unconscious, revealing unfulfilled wishes or desires. (p. 128)
- The dreams-for-survival theory suggests that information relevant to daily survival is reconsidered and reprocessed in dreams. Finally, the activation-synthesis theory proposes that dreams are a result of random electrical energy that stimulates different memories, which are then woven into a coherent story line. (p. 129)

What are the major sleep disorders and how can they be treated?

- Insomnia is a sleep disorder characterized by difficulty sleeping. Sleep apnea is a condition in which people have difficulty sleeping and breathing at the same time. People with narcolepsy have an uncontrollable urge to sleep. Sleepwalking and sleeptalking are relatively harmless. (p. 131)
- Psychologists and sleep researchers advise people with insomnia to increase exercise during the day, avoid caffeine and sleeping pills, drink a glass of warm milk before bedtime, and try *not* to go to sleep. (p. 133)

How much do we daydream?

- Daydreaming may occur 10 percent of the time, although wide individual differences exist in the amount of time devoted to it. (p. 133)

Are hypnotized people in a different state of consciousness?

- Hypnosis produces a state of heightened susceptibility to the suggestions of the hypnotist. Under hypnosis, significant behavioural changes occur, including increased concentration and suggestibility, heightened ability to recall and construct images, lack of initiative, and acceptance of suggestions that clearly contradict reality. (p. 135)

What are the effects of meditation?

- Meditation is a learned technique for refocusing attention that brings about an altered state of consciousness. (p. 137)
- Different cultures have developed their own unique ways to alter states of consciousness. (p. 137)

Looking Back

What are the major classifications of drugs, and what are their effects?

- Drugs can produce an altered state of consciousness. However, they vary in how dangerous they are and in whether or not they are addictive, producing a physical or psychological dependence. Drug addiction is one of the most difficult behaviours to modify. (p. 140)
- Stimulants cause arousal in the central nervous system. Two common stimulants are caffeine (found in coffee, tea, and soft drinks) and nicotine (found in cigarettes). More dangerous are cocaine and amphetamines, or "speed." In large quantities they can overload the central nervous system, leading to convulsions and death. (p. 141)
- Depressants decrease arousal in the central nervous system, causing the neurons to fire more slowly. They can cause intoxication along with feelings of euphoria. The most common depressants are alcohol and barbiturates. (p. 145)
- Alcohol is the most frequently used depressant. Its initial effects of released tension and positive feelings yield to depressive effects as the dose of alcohol increases. Both genetic causes and environmental stressors can lead to alcoholism. (p. 145)
- Morphine and heroin are narcotics, drugs that produce relaxation and relieve pain and anxiety. Because of their addictive qualities, morphine and heroin are particularly dangerous. (p. 147)
- Hallucinogens are drugs that produce hallucinations or other changes in perception. The most frequently used hallucinogen is marijuana, which has several long-term risks. Two other hallucinogens are LSD and Ecstasy. (p. 148)
- A number of signals indicate when drug use becomes drug abuse. A person who suspects that he or she has a drug problem should get professional help. People are almost never capable of solving drug problems on their own. (p. 149)

Key Terms and Concepts

consciousness (p. 122)
stage 1 sleep (p. 124)
stage 2 sleep (p. 124)
stage 3 sleep (p. 125)
stage 4 sleep (p. 125)
REM sleep (p. 126)
unconscious wish fulfillment theory (p. 129)
latent content of dreams (p. 129)
manifest content of dreams (p. 129)
dreams-for-survival theory (p. 129)
activation-synthesis theory (p. 130)

circadian rhythms (p. 132)
daydreams (p. 133)
hypnosis (p. 135)
meditation (p. 137)
psychoactive drugs (p. 140)
addictive drugs (p. 140)
stimulants (p. 141)
depressants (p. 144)
narcotics (p. 147)
hallucinogen (p. 148)

Psychology on the Web

1. Find a resource on the Web that interprets dreams, and another that reports the results of scientific dream research. Compare the nature and content of the two sites in terms of the topics covered, reliability of information provided, and promises made about the use of the site and its information. Write a summary of what you found.
2. Find some sites on the Web that describe Canadian antidrug programs that are focused on school, family, and/or community settings. On the basis of the information at these sites and in the *Applying Psychology in the 21st Century* box in this chapter, explain how effective you think these programs would be.

Epilogue

In this chapter we discussed consciousness in its full range from active states to passive states. We focused especially on factors that affect consciousness, from natural factors like sleep, dreaming, and daydreaming, to more intentional ways of altering consciousness, including hypnosis, meditation, and drugs. We examined some of the reasons people seek to alter their consciousness, considered both uses and abuses of consciousness-altering strategies, and attempted to address some of the most dangerous ways people alter their consciousness.

Before we turn to the subject of learning in the next chapter, return briefly to the prologue in this chapter, about the death of five Quebec teenagers. Consider the following questions in light of your understanding of alcohol use and abuse.

1. Why would the police and others suspect that alcohol consumption may have contributed to the accident described in the prologue?
2. Why do people take risks such as combining drinking with driving?
3 What are some of the reasons why young people drink to excess?
4. How does alcohol affect the state of consciousness of users?

For extra help in mastering the material in this chapter, see the integrator, practice quizzes, and other resources on the Online Learning Centre at

www.mcgrawhill.ca/college/ feldman

Chapter Five

Learning

Prologue

A Friend Named Pippa

Pippa is a wonderful friend and companion, gentle, loyal and unselfishly giving of time and affection. She is ever ready to help, and in return, she asks for little.

Jean Little with Ritz, Pippa's predecessor. Seeing Eye dogs can be trained to carry out surprisingly sophisticated tasks using the basic principles of learning.

Pippa, a 6-year-old yellow Lab, is a guide dog. She is trained to be a helpmate to her owner, Jean Little, a beloved and award-winning author who has entertained and inspired Canadian children for over 30 years. Little, who has been legally blind for all of her adult life, does all of the things that you would expect of a well-known author. She travels a lot, often on planes, to schools and conferences. She attends ball games (Pippa is a great Jays fan). Whether she is on a country lane or on the streets of New York, Pippa is always there a few steps ahead of her.

Pippa's trainers, using praise as a reward, taught her to respond to specific commands. Little, who has had two other guide dogs, Zepher and Ritz, since 1982, has spent a number of weeks learning how to work with each one at The Seeing Eye School where they were trained. She needed to learn what signals would produce the desired responses in the dogs.

At home and out of harness, Pippa is a pet. In harness, she is all business, totally in control and responsible for her owner's safety. Pippa seems to know that her owner is dependent on her in a way that is different from her sighted trainers. Of Pippa, Little says, "She guides better than a person and she also provides a bridge to the sighted world." People who might hesitate approaching someone who is blind find that the dog provides a way of opening the channels of communication.

Source: Jean Little

Looking Ahead

The expertise developed by both Pippa and Jean Little is the result of painstaking training procedures—the same ones that are at work in each of our lives, illustrated by our ability to write or read a book, drive a car, play Scrabble, study for a test, or perform any of the numerous activities that make up our daily routine. Like Little and her dog, each of us must acquire and refine our skills and abilities through learning.

Learning is a fundamental topic for psychologists and plays a central role in almost every specialty area of psychology, as we will see throughout this book. For example, a psychologist studying perception might ask, "How do we learn that people who look small from a distance are far away and not simply tiny?" A developmental psychologist might inquire, "How do babies learn to distinguish their mothers from other people?" A clinical psychologist might wonder, "Why do some people learn to be afraid when they see a spider?" A social psychologist might ask, "How do we learn to believe that we've fallen in love?" Each of these questions, although drawn from very different fields of psychology, can be answered only through an understanding of basic learning processes.

What do we mean by learning? Although psychologists have identified a number of different types of learning, a general definition encompasses them all: Learning is a relatively permanent change in behaviour brought about by experience.

To understand learning, we need to return to the nature–nurture issue we first discussed in Chapter 1. Specifically, we must distinguish between performance changes due to *maturation* and changes brought about by experience. (Maturation is the nature part of the nature–nurture question; experience is the nurture part.) For instance, children become better tennis players as they grow older partially because their strength increases with their size—a maturational phenomenon. Maturational changes need to be differentiated from improvements due to practice, which indicate that learning has taken place.

Similarly, we must distinguish short-term changes in behaviour that are due to factors other than learning, such as declines in performance resulting from fatigue or lack of effort, from performance changes that are due to actual learning. For example, if Venus Williams performs poorly in a tennis game because of tension or fatigue, this does not mean that she has not learned to play correctly or has forgotten how to play well.

In short, we begin this chapter by examining the type of learning that explains responses ranging from a dog salivating when it hears its owner opening a can of dog food to the emotions we feel when our national anthem is played. We then discuss other theories that consider how learning is a consequence of rewarding circumstances. Finally, we examine approaches that focus on the cognitive aspects of learning.

learning: A relatively permanent change in behaviour brought about by experience.

 **PsychLink**

Theories on learning
www.mcgrawhill.ca/college/feldman

Prepare

What is learning?
How do we learn to form associations
between stimuli and responses?

Organize

Classical Conditioning
  The Basics of Classical Conditioning
  Applying Conditioning Principles to Human
    Behaviour
  Extinction
  Generalization and Discrimination
  Beyond Traditional Classical Conditioning

Classical Conditioning

Does the mere sight of the golden arches in front of McDonald's make you feel pangs of hunger and think about hamburgers? If it does, then you are displaying an elementary form of learning called classical conditioning. Classical conditioning helps explain such diverse phenomena as crying at the sight of a bride walking down the aisle, fearing the dark, and falling in love.

The Basics of Classical Conditioning

Ivan Pavlov, a Russian physiologist, never intended to do psychological research. In 1904 he won the Nobel Prize for his work on digestion, testimony to his contribution to that field. Yet Pavlov is remembered not for his physiological research, but for his experiments on basic learning processes—work that he began quite accidentally (Windholz, 1997).

Pavlov had been studying the secretion of stomach acids and salivation in dogs in response to the ingestion of varying amounts and kinds of food. While doing so, he observed a curious phenomenon: Sometimes stomach secretions and salivation would begin in the dogs when they had not yet eaten any food. The mere sight of the experimenter who normally brought the food, or even the sound of the experimenter's footsteps, was enough to produce salivation in the dogs. Pavlov's genius was his ability to recognize the implications of this discovery. He saw that the dogs were responding not only on the basis of a biological need (hunger), but also as a result of learning—or, as it came to be called, classical conditioning. **Classical conditioning** is a type of learning in which a neutral stimulus (such as the experimenter's footsteps) comes to bring about a response after it is paired with a stimulus (such as food) that naturally brings about that response.

To demonstrate and analyze classical conditioning, Pavlov conducted a series of experiments (Pavlov, 1927). In one, he attached a tube to the salivary gland of a dog, which would allow him to measure precisely the dog's salivation. He then rang a bell and, just a few seconds later, presented the dog with meat. This

Ivan Pavlov (centre) developed the principles of classical conditioning.

pairing occurred repeatedly and was carefully planned so that each time exactly the same amount of time elapsed between the presentation of the bell and the meat. At first the dog would salivate only when the meat itself was presented, but soon it began to salivate at the sound of the bell. In fact, even when Pavlov stopped presenting the meat, the dog still salivated after hearing the sound. The dog had been classically conditioned to salivate to the bell.

As you can see in Figure 5-1, the basic processes of classical conditioning that underlie Pavlov's discovery are straightforward, although the terminology he chose is not simple. Consider first the diagram in Figure 5-1a. Before conditioning, there are two unrelated stimuli: the ringing of a bell and meat. We know that normally the ringing of a bell does not lead to salivation but to some irrelevant response, such as perking up the ears or perhaps a startle reaction. The bell is therefore called the **neutral stimulus** because it is a stimulus that, before conditioning, does not naturally bring about the response we are interested in. We also have meat, which, because of the biological makeup of the dog, naturally leads to salivation—the response that we are interested in conditioning. The meat is considered an **unconditioned stimulus**, or **UCS**, because food placed in a dog's mouth automatically causes salivation to occur. The response that the meat elicits (salivation) is called an **unconditioned response**, or **UCR**—a natural, innate response that is not associated with previous learning. Unconditioned responses are always brought about by the presence of unconditioned stimuli.

Figure 5-1b illustrates what happens during conditioning. The bell is rung just before each presentation of the meat. The goal of conditioning is for the bell to become associated with the unconditioned stimulus (meat) and therefore to bring about the same sort of response as the unconditioned stimulus. During this period, salivation gradually increases each time the bell is rung, until the bell alone causes the dog to salivate.

When conditioning is complete, the bell has evolved from a neutral stimulus to what is now called a **conditioned stimulus**, or **CS**. At this time, salivation that occurs as a response to the conditioned stimulus (bell) is considered a **conditioned response**, or **CR**. This situation is depicted in Figure 5-1c. After conditioning, then, the conditioned stimulus evokes the conditioned response.

The sequence and timing of the presentation of the unconditioned stimulus and the conditioned stimulus are particularly important (Rescorla, 1988; Wasserman & Miller, 1997). Like a malfunctioning warning light at a railroad crossing that goes on after the train has passed by, a neutral stimulus that *follows* an unconditioned stimulus has little chance of becoming a conditioned stimulus. On the other hand, just as a warning light works best if it goes on right before a train passes, a neutral stimulus that is presented *just before* the unconditioned stimulus is most apt to result in successful conditioning. Research has shown that conditioning is most effective if the neutral stimulus (which will become a conditioned stimulus) precedes the unconditioned stimulus by between a half-second and several seconds, depending on what kind of response is being conditioned.

classical conditioning: A type of learning in which a neutral stimulus comes to bring about a response after it is paired with a stimulus that naturally brings about that response.

neutral stimulus: A stimulus that, before conditioning, does not naturally bring about the response of interest.

unconditioned stimulus (UCS): A stimulus that brings about an automatic or unlearned response.

unconditioned response (UCR): A response that is natural and needs no training (e.g., salivation at the smell of food).

conditioned stimulus (CS): A once-neutral stimulus that has been paired with an unconditioned stimulus to bring about a response formerly caused only by the unconditioned stimulus.

conditioned response (CR): A response that, after conditioning, follows a previously neutral stimulus (e.g., salivation at the ringing of a bell).

Figure 5-1 The basic process of classical conditioning. *(a)* Prior to conditioning, the ringing of a bell does not bring about salivation—making the bell a neutral stimulus. On the other hand, meat naturally brings about salivation, making the meat an unconditioned stimulus and salivation an unconditioned response. *(b)* During conditioning, the bell is rung just before the presentation of the meat. *(c)* Eventually, the ringing of the bell alone brings about salivation. We can now say that conditioning has been accomplished: The previously neutral stimulus of the bell is now considered a conditioned stimulus that brings about the conditioned response of salivation.

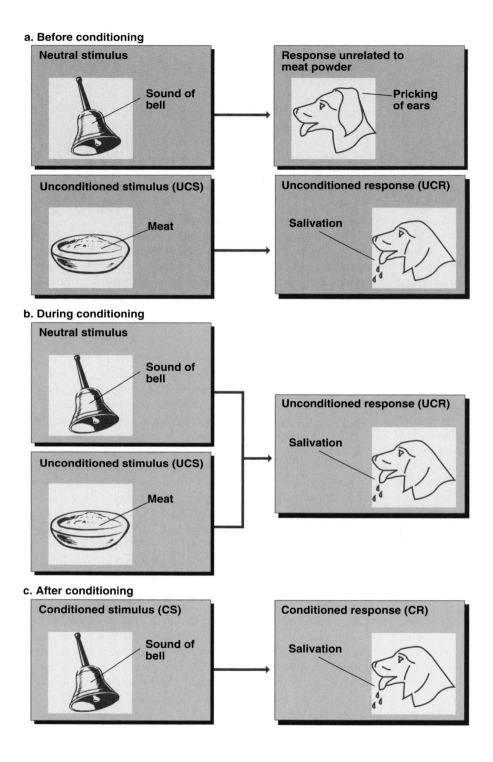

Although the terminology Pavlov used to describe classical conditioning might at first seem confusing, the following summary rules can help make the relationships between stimuli and responses easier to understand and remember:

- An *un*conditioned stimulus leads to an *un*conditioned response.
- *Un*conditioned stimulus–*un*conditioned response pairings are *un*learned and *un*trained.
- During conditioning, a previously neutral stimulus is transformed into the conditioned stimulus.

- A conditioned stimulus leads to a conditioned response, and a conditioned stimulus–conditioned response pairing is a consequence of learning and training.
- An unconditioned response and a conditioned response are similar (such as salivation in the example described earlier), but the conditioned response is learned, whereas the unconditioned response occurs naturally.

Applying Conditioning Principles to Human Behaviour

PsychLink

Classical conditioning
www.mcgrawhill.ca/college/feldman

Although the initial conditioning experiments were carried out with animals, classical conditioning principles were soon found to explain many aspects of everyday human behaviour. Recall, for instance, the earlier illustration of how people might experience hunger pangs at the sight of McDonald's golden arches. The cause of this reaction is classical conditioning: The previously neutral arches have become associated with the food inside the restaurant (the unconditioned stimulus), causing the arches to become a conditioned stimulus that brings about the conditioned response of hunger.

Emotional responses are particularly likely to be learned through classical conditioning processes. For instance, how do some of us develop fears of mice, spiders, and other creatures that are typically harmless? In a now-famous case study designed to show that classical conditioning was at the root of such fears, an 11-month-old infant named Albert, who initially showed no fear of rats, heard a loud noise just as he was shown a rat (Watson & Rayner, 1920). The noise (the unconditioned stimulus) evoked fear (the unconditioned response). After just a few pairings of noise and rat, Albert began to show fear of the rat by itself. The rat, then, had become a CS that brought about the CR, fear. Similarly, the pairing of the appearance of certain species (such as mice or spiders) with the fearful comments of an adult may cause children to develop the same fears their parents have. (By the way, we don't know what happened to the unfortunate Albert, and Watson, the experimenter, has been condemned for using ethically questionable procedures.)

Learning via classical conditioning also occurs during adulthood. For example, you might not go to a dentist as often as you should because of prior associations of dentists and pain. Or you might have a particular fondness for the smell of a certain perfume or aftershave lotion because the feelings and thoughts of an early lover come rushing back whenever you encounter it. Classical conditioning, then, explains many of the reactions we have to stimuli in the world around us (Woodruff-Pak, 1999).

Extinction

What do you think would happen if a dog who had become classically conditioned to salivate at the ringing of a bell never again received food when the bell was rung? The answer lies in one of the basic phenomena of learning: extinction. **Extinction** occurs when a previously conditioned response decreases in frequency and eventually disappears.

To produce extinction, one needs to end the association between conditioned and unconditioned stimuli. For instance, if we had trained a dog to salivate at the ringing of a bell, we could produce extinction by ceasing to provide meat after the bell was rung. At first the dog would continue to salivate when it heard the bell, but after a few such instances, the amount of salivation would probably decline, and the dog would eventually stop responding to the bell altogether. At that point, we could say that the response had been extinguished. In sum, extinction occurs when the conditioned stimulus is repeatedly presented without the unconditioned stimulus. We should keep in mind that extinction can be a helpful phenomenon. Consider, for instance, what it would be like if the fear you experienced while watching *The Blair Witch Project* never was extinguished. You might well tremble with fright every time you entered any wooded area.

As we will describe in Chapter 13, psychologists have treated people with irrational fears, or phobias, by using a form of therapy called systematic desensitization. The goal of *systematic desensitization* is to bring about the extinction of the phobia. For example, a therapist using systematic desensitization for a client who is afraid of dogs might repeatedly expose the client to dogs, starting with a less frightening aspect (a photo

extinction: The decrease in frequency, and eventual disappearance, of a previously conditioned response; one of the basic phenomena of learning.

of a cute dog) and moving toward more feared ones (such as an actual encounter with an unfamiliar dog). As the anticipated negative consequences of exposure to the dog (e.g., being jumped on or bitten) do not occur, the fear eventually becomes extinguished.

Once a conditioned response has been extinguished, has it vanished forever? Not necessarily. Pavlov discovered this when he returned to his dog a few days after the conditioned behaviour had seemingly been extinguished. If he rang a bell, the dog once again salivated—an effect known as **spontaneous recovery**, or the reemergence of an extinguished conditioned response after a period of rest.

Spontaneous recovery helps explain why it is so hard to overcome drug addictions. For example, cocaine addicts who are thought to be "cured" could experience an irresistible impulse to use the drug again if they are subsequently confronted by a stimulus with strong connections to the drug, such as a white powder (O'Brien et al., 1992; Drummond et al., 1995).

Generalization and Discrimination

Despite differences in colour and shape, to most of us a rose is a rose is a rose. The pleasure we experience at the beauty, smell, and grace of the flower is similar for different types of roses. Pavlov noticed a similar phenomenon. His dogs often salivated not only at the ringing of the bell that was used during their original conditioning but at the sound of a buzzer as well.

Such behaviour is the result of stimulus generalization. **Stimulus generalization** takes place when a conditioned response follows a stimulus that is similar to the original conditioned stimulus. The greater the similarity between the two stimuli, the greater the likelihood of stimulus generalization. Baby Albert, who, as we mentioned earlier, was conditioned to be fearful of rats, was later found to be afraid of other furry white things as well. He was fearful of white rabbits, white fur coats, and even a white Santa Claus mask. On the other hand, according to the principle of stimulus generalization, it is unlikely that he would have been afraid of a black dog, because its colour would differentiate it sufficiently from the original fear-evoking stimulus.

The conditioned response elicited by the new stimulus is usually not as intense as the original conditioned response, although the more similar the new stimulus is to the old one, the more similar the new response will be. It is unlikely, then, that Albert's fear of the Santa Claus mask was as great as his learned fear of a rat. Still, stimulus generalization permits us to know, for example, that we ought to brake at all red lights, even if there are minor variations in size, shape, and shade.

If two stimuli are sufficiently distinct from one another so that one evokes a conditioned response but the other does not, we can say that stimulus discrimination has occurred. **Stimulus discrimination** is the ability to differentiate between stimuli. For example, the ability to discriminate between a red and a green traffic light prevents us from getting mowed down by oncoming traffic at intersections.

Beyond Traditional Classical Conditioning: Challenging Basic Assumptions

Although Pavlov hypothesized that all learning is nothing more than long strings of conditioned responses, this notion has not been supported by subsequent research. It turns out that classical conditioning provides us with only a partial explanation of how people and animals learn and that Pavlov was wrong in some of his basic assumptions (Risley & Rescorla, 1972; Hollis, 1997).

For example, according to Pavlov, the process of linking stimuli and responses occurs in a mechanistic, unthinking way. In contrast to this perspective, learning theorists influenced by cognitive psychology have argued that learners actively develop an understanding and expectancy about which particular unconditioned stimuli are matched with specific conditioned stimuli. A ringing bell, for instance, gives a dog something to

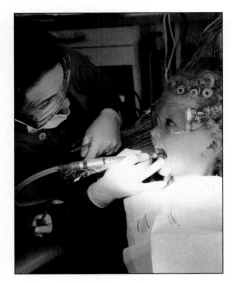

Because of a previous unpleasant experience, a person may expect a similar occurrence when faced with a comparable situation in the future, a process known as stimulus generalization.
Can you think of ways this process is used in everyday life?

spontaneous recovery: The reemergence of an extinguished conditioned response after a period of rest.

stimulus generalization: A response to a stimulus that is similar to but different from a conditioned stimulus; the more similar the two stimuli, the more likely generalization is to occur.

stimulus discrimination: The ability to differentiate between stimuli.

Because of prior experience with meat that had been laced with a mild poison, this coyote does not obey its natural instincts and ignores what otherwise would be a tasty meal.
What principles of classical conditioning does this phenomenon contradict?

think about: the impending arrival of food (Rescorla, 1988; Clark & Squire, 1998; Woodruff-Pak, 1999).

Traditional explanations of how classical conditioning operates have also been challenged by learning psychologist John Garcia, whose research was initially concerned with the effects of exposure to nuclear radiation on laboratory animals. In the course of his experiments, he realized that rats placed in a radiation chamber drank almost no water, even though in their home cage they drank eagerly. The most obvious explanation—that it had something to do with the radiation—was soon ruled out. Garcia found that even when the radiation was not turned on, the rats still drank little or no water in the radiation chamber (Garcia, Hankins, & Rusiniak, 1974; Garcia, 1990).

Initially puzzled by the rats' behaviour, Garcia eventually figured out that the drinking cups in the radiation chamber were made of plastic, thereby giving the water an unusual, plastic-like taste. In contrast, drinking cups in the home cage were made of glass and left no abnormal taste.

As a result, the plastic-tasting water had become repeatedly paired with illness brought on by exposure to radiation, and that had led the rats to form a classically conditioned association. The process began with the radiation acting as an unconditioned stimulus evoking the unconditioned response of sickness. With repeated pairings, the plastic-tasting water had become a conditioned stimulus that evoked the conditioned response of sickness.

This finding violated one of the basic rules of classical conditioning—that an unconditioned stimulus should *immediately* follow a conditioned stimulus for optimal conditioning to occur. Instead, Garcia's findings showed that conditioning could occur even when there was an interval of as long as eight hours between exposure to the conditioned stimulus and the response of sickness. Furthermore, the conditioning persisted over very long periods and sometimes occurred after just one exposure to water that was followed later on by illness.

These findings have had important practical implications. For example, to prevent coyotes from killing their sheep, some ranchers now routinely lace a sheep carcass with a drug and leave the carcass in a place where coyotes will find it. The drug temporarily makes the coyotes quite ill, but it does not permanently harm them. After just one exposure to a drug-laden sheep carcass, coyotes avoid sheep, which are normally one of their primary natural victims (Gustavson et al., 1974).

Evaluate

1. _____ involves changes brought about by experience, whereas maturation describes changes due to biological development.

2. _____ is the name of the scientist responsible for discovering the learning phenomenon known as _____ conditioning, in which an organism learns a response to a stimulus to which it would not normally respond.

Refer to the passage below to answer questions 3 through 6:

The last three times little Theresa visited Dr. Lopez for checkups, he administered a painful preventive immunization shot that left her in tears. Today, when her mother takes her for another checkup, Theresa begins to sob as soon as she comes face-to-face with Dr. Lopez, even before he has had a chance to say hello.

3. The painful shot that Theresa received during each visit was a(n) _____ _____, which elicited the _____ _____, her tears.

4. Dr. Lopez is upset because his presence has become a _____ _____ for Theresa's crying.

5. Fortunately, Dr. Lopez gave Theresa no more shots for quite some time. Over that time she gradually stopped crying and even came to like him. _____ had occurred.

6. _____ _____ occurs when a stimulus that is fairly similar to the conditioned stimulus produces the same response.

7. On the other hand, _____ _____ occurs when there is no response to a stimulus that is slightly distinct from the conditioned stimulus.

Answers to Evaluate Questions

1. Learning 2. Pavlov; classical 3. unconditioned stimulus; unconditioned response 4. conditioned stimulus 5. Extinction 6. Stimulus generalization 7. stimulus discrimination

Rethink

1. Can you think of ways that classical conditioning is used by politicians? advertisers? moviemakers? Do ethical issues arise from any of these uses?

2. Is it likely that Albert, Watson's experimental subject, went through life afraid of Santa Claus? Describe what probably happened to prevent this.

Prepare

What is the role of reward and punishment in learning?

Organize

Operant Conditioning
Thorndike's Law of Effect
The Basics of Operant Conditioning
Positive Reinforcers, Negative Reinforcers, and Punishment
The Pros and Cons of Punishment
Shaping
Schedules of Reinforcement
Discrimination and Generalization in Operant Conditioning
Superstitious Behaviour
Biological Constraints on Learning

operant conditioning: Learning in which a voluntary response is strengthened or weakened, depending on its favourable or unfavourable consequences.

Operant Conditioning

Very good.... What a clever idea.... Fantastic.... I agree.... Thank you.... Excellent.... Super.... You get an A.... I'm impressed.... Let me give you a hug.... You're getting a raise.... Have a cookie.... You look great.... I love you....

Few of us mind being the recipient of any of the above comments. But what is especially noteworthy about them is that each of these simple statements can be used, through a process known as operant conditioning, to bring about powerful changes in behaviour and to teach the most complex tasks. Operant conditioning is the basis for many of the most important kinds of human, and animal, learning.

Operant conditioning is learning in which a voluntary response is strengthened or weakened, depending on its favourable or unfavourable consequences. Unlike classical conditioning, in which the original behaviours are the natural, biological responses to the presence of some stimulus such as food, water, or pain, operant conditioning applies to voluntary responses, which an organism performs deliberately, to produce a desirable outcome. The term *operant* emphasizes this point: The organism *operates* on its environment to produce some desirable result. For example, operant conditioning is at work when we learn that toiling industriously can bring about a raise, or that studying hard results in good grades.

As with classical conditioning, the basis for understanding operant conditioning was laid by work with animals. We turn now to some of that early research, which began with a simple inquiry into the behaviour of cats.

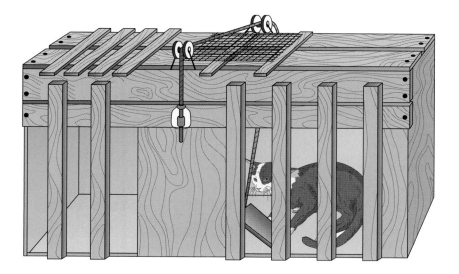

Figure 5-2 Edward L. Thorndike devised this puzzle box to study the process by which a cat learns to press a paddle to escape the box and receive food. Do you think Thorndike's work has relevance to the question of why humans voluntarily solve puzzles, such as crossword puzzles and jigsaw puzzles? Do they receive any rewards?

Thorndike's Law of Effect

If you placed a hungry cat in a cage and then put a small piece of food outside of it, just beyond the cat's reach, chances are the cat would eagerly search for a way out of the cage. The cat might first claw at the sides or push against an opening. Suppose, though, that you had rigged things so that the cat could escape by stepping on a small paddle that released the latch to the door of the cage (see Figure 5-2). Eventually, as it moved around the cage, the cat would happen to step on the paddle, the door would open, and the cat would eat the food.

What would happen if you then returned the cat to the box? The next time, it would probably take a little less time for the cat to step on the paddle and escape. After a few trials, the cat would deliberately step on the paddle as soon as it was placed in the cage. What would have occurred, according to Edward L. Thorndike (1932), who studied this situation extensively, was that the cat would have learned that pressing the paddle was associated with the desirable consequence of getting food. Thorndike summarized that relationship by formulating the *law of effect:* that responses that lead to satisfying consequences are more likely to be repeated, and responses followed by negative outcomes are less likely to be repeated.

Thorndike believed that the law of effect operated as automatically as leaves fall off a tree in autumn. It was not necessary for an organism to understand that there was a link between a response and a reward. Instead, Thorndike believed, over time and through experience the organism would make a direct connection between the stimulus and the response without any awareness that the connection existed.

The Basics of Operant Conditioning

Thorndike's early research served as the foundation for the work of one of the century's most influential psychologists, B. F. Skinner, who died in 1990. You may have heard of the Skinner box (shown in one form in Figure 5-3), a chamber with a highly controlled environment used to study operant conditioning processes with laboratory animals. Whereas Thorndike's goal was to get his cats to learn to obtain food by leaving the box, animals in a Skinner box learn to obtain food by operating in their environment within the box. Skinner became interested in specifying how behaviour varied as a result of alterations in the environment.

Skinner, whose work went far beyond perfecting Thorndike's earlier apparatus, is considered the inspiration for a whole generation of psychologists studying operant

B. F. Skinner, who was the founding father of operant conditioning, developed what came to be called the "Skinner box."
In what ways has Skinner's research contributed to the study of learning?

Figure 5–3 A Skinner box, used to study operant conditioning. Laboratory animals learn to press the lever in order to obtain food, which is delivered in the tray.

Lever

Food dispenser

conditioning (Delprato & Midgley, 1992; Bjork, 1993; Keehn, 1996). To illustrate Skinner's contribution, let's consider what happens to a pigeon in the typical Skinner box.

Suppose you want to teach a hungry pigeon to peck a key that is located in its box. At first the pigeon will wander around the box, exploring the environment in a relatively random fashion. At some point, however, it will probably peck the key by chance, and when it does, it will receive a food pellet. The first time this happens, the pigeon will not learn the connection between pecking and receiving food and will continue to explore the box. Sooner or later the pigeon will again peck the key and receive a pellet, and in time the frequency of the pecking response will increase. Eventually, the pigeon will peck the key continually until it satisfies its hunger, thereby demonstrating that it has learned that the receipt of food is contingent on pecking the key.

Reinforcing Desired Behaviour

Skinner called the process that leads the pigeon to continue pecking the key "reinforcement." **Reinforcement** is the process by which a stimulus increases the probability that a preceding behaviour will be repeated. In other words, pecking is more likely to occur again due to the stimulus of food.

In a situation such as this one, the food is called a reinforcer. A **reinforcer** is any stimulus that increases the probability that a preceding behaviour will occur again. Hence, food is a reinforcer because it increases the probability that the behaviour of pecking the key (formally referred to as the *response* of pecking) will take place.

reinforcement: The process by which a stimulus increases the probability that a preceding behaviour will be repeated.
reinforcer: Any stimulus that increases the probability that a preceding behaviour will occur again.

What kind of stimuli can act as reinforcers? Bonuses, toys, and good grades can serve as reinforcers—if they strengthen the probability of the response that occurred before their introduction. In each case, it is critical that the organism learn that the delivery of the reinforcer is contingent on the response occurring in the first place.

Of course, we are not born knowing that a dollar can buy us a candy bar. Rather, through experience we learn that money is a valuable commodity because of its association with stimuli, such as food and drink, that are naturally reinforcing. This fact suggests a distinction between primary reinforcers and secondary reinforcers. A *primary reinforcer* satisfies some biological need and works naturally, regardless of a person's prior experience. Food for the hungry person, warmth for the cold person, and relief for the person in pain would all be classified as primary reinforcers. A *secondary reinforcer,* in contrast, is a stimulus that becomes reinforcing because of its association with a primary reinforcer. For

"Oh, not bad. The light comes on, I press the bar, they write me a check. How about you?"

instance, we know that money is valuable because we have learned that it allows us to obtain other desirable objects, including primary reinforcers such as food and shelter. Money thus becomes a secondary reinforcer.

What makes something a reinforcer depends on individual preferences. Though a Hershey bar could act as a reinforcer for one person, an individual who dislikes chocolate might find a dollar more desirable. The only way we can know if a stimulus is a reinforcer for a given organism is to observe whether the frequency of a previously occurring behaviour increases after the presentation of the stimulus. (For a further discussion of the applications of reinforcement and other psychological approaches to learning, see the *Psychology at Work* box.)

Positive Reinforcers, Negative Reinforcers, and Punishment

In many respects, reinforcers can be thought of in terms of rewards; both a reinforcer and a reward increase the probability that a preceding response will occur again. But the term *reward* is limited to *positive* occurrences, and this is where it differs from a reinforcer—for it turns out that reinforcers can be positive or negative.

A **positive reinforcer** is a stimulus *added* to the environment that brings about an increase in a preceding response. If food, water, money, or praise is provided following

PsychLink

Positive and negative reinforcers
www.mcgrawhill.ca/college/feldman

positive reinforcer: A stimulus added to the environment that brings about an increase in a preceding response.

Psychology at Work

Lynne Calero

Dolphin Research Center, Grassy Key, Florida

Education: B.A. in psychology, George Washington University

Home: Big Pine Key, Florida

Lynne Calero

Many people have read about the possible connections between dolphins and humans in terms of both behaviour and intellect, but for more than a decade Lynne Calero has seen these similarities firsthand.

An employee of the Dolphin Research Center in Grassy Key, Florida, Calero received her primary exposure to psychology as an under-graduate major at George Washington University in Washington, D.C. "Our facility is a research education facility in which we do training to educate the public, as well as monitoring individual animals' health," she says.

In training dolphins, Calero makes use of the basic principles of learning. "The whole basis of the training done with dolphins and sea lions is operant conditioning and positive reinforcement," she notes.

For instance, one specific type of training aims at getting dolphins to present their tail flukes, thereby permitting medical tests that require

> "Our facility is a research education facility in which we do training to educate the public, as well as monitoring individual animals' health."

blood samples. "All the animals first learn the basics, such as responding to a whistle. The whistle becomes connected with feeding, giving attention, or a back rub.

"From there we gradually get them to position alongside of the dock," she explains, "followed by a series of approximations, as in training with any behaviour. With each step we get closer to the tail flukes until the dolphin allows us to hold onto the flukes above the water surface."

Younger dolphins are easier to train, and it takes only a month of training before they will present their flukes.

To Calero, this is one example of the unusual intelligence of dolphins. "Certainly their brain anatomy is very complicated. Overall, my impression is that dolphins are incredibly intelligent, as well as being intensely intuitive."

> "Overall, my impression is that dolphins are incredibly intelligent, as well as being intensely intuitive and wise."

Table 5-1 Types of Reinforcement and Punishment

| | EFFECT ON BEHAVIOUR | |
Procedure	Increases	Decreases
Presentation of stimulus	*Positive reinforcement* *Example:* Giving a raise for good performance *Result: Increase* in frequency of response (good performance)	*Positive punishment* *Example:* Giving a spanking following misbehaviour *Result: Decrease* in frequency of response (misbehaviour)
Removal of stimulus	*Negative reinforcement* *Example:* Terminating a headache by taking aspirin *Result: Increase* in frequency of response (taking aspirin)	*Negative punishment* *Example:* Removal of favourite toy after misbehaviour *Result: Decrease* in frequency of response (misbehaviour)

negative reinforcer: An unpleasant stimulus whose removal leads to an increase in the probability that a preceding response will occur again in the future.

punishment: A stimulus that decreases the probability that a previous behaviour will occur again.

a response, it is more likely that that response will occur again in the future. The paycheque that workers get at the end of the week, for example, increases the likelihood that they will return to their jobs the following week.

In contrast, a **negative reinforcer** refers to an unpleasant stimulus whose *removal* from the environment leads to an increase in the probability that a preceding response will occur again in the future. For example, if you have cold symptoms (an unpleasant stimulus) that are relieved when you take medicine, you are more likely to take the medicine when you experience such symptoms again. Taking medicine, then, is negatively reinforcing, because it removes the unpleasant cold symptoms. Similarly, if the radio volume is so loud that it hurts your ears, you are likely to find that turning it down relieves the problem. Lowering the volume is negatively reinforcing and you are more apt to repeat the action in the future. Negative reinforcement, then, teaches the individual that taking an action removes a negative condition that exists in the environment. Like positive reinforcers, negative reinforcers increase the likelihood that preceding behaviours will be repeated.

It is important to note that negative reinforcement is not the same as punishment. **Punishment** refers to a stimulus that *decreases* the probability that a prior behaviour will occur again. Unlike negative reinforcement, which produces an *increase* in behaviour, punishment reduces the likelihood of a prior response. If we receive a shock that is meant to decrease a certain behaviour, then, we are receiving punishment; but if we are already receiving a shock and do something to stop that shock, the behaviour that stops the shock is considered to be negatively reinforced. In the first case, the specific behaviour is apt to decrease because of the punishment; in the second, it is likely to increase because of the negative reinforcement.

There are two types of punishment: positive punishment and negative punishment, just as there is positive and negative reinforcement. (In both cases, "positive" means adding something, whereas "negative" means removing something.) *Positive punishment* weakens a response through the application of an unpleasant stimulus. For instance, spanking a child for misbehaving or ten years in jail for committing a crime is positive punishment. In contrast, *negative punishment* consists of the removal of something pleasant. For instance, when a teenager is told she is "grounded" and will no longer be able to use the family car because of her poor grades, or when an employee is informed that he has been demoted with a cut in pay because of poor job evaluations, negative punishment is being administered. Both positive and negative punishment result in a decrease in the likelihood that a prior behaviour will be repeated.

The distinctions between the two types of punishment, as well as positive and negative reinforcement, might seem confusing initially, but the following rules (and the summary in Table 5-1) can help you to distinguish these concepts from one another:

- Reinforcement *increases* the frequency of the behaviour preceding it; punishment *decreases* the frequency of the behaviour preceding it.
- The *application* of a *positive* stimulus brings about an increase in the frequency of behaviour and is referred to as positive reinforcement; the *application* of a *negative* stimulus decreases or reduces the frequency of behaviour and is called positive punishment.
- The *removal* of a *negative* stimulus that results in an increase in the frequency of behaviour is termed negative reinforcement; the *removal* of a *positive* stimulus that decreases the frequency of behaviour is called negative punishment.

The Pros and Cons of Punishment: Why Reinforcement Beats Punishment

Numerous articles on punishment www.mcgrawhill.ca/college/feldman

Is punishment an effective way to modify behaviour? Punishment often presents the quickest route to changing behaviour that, if allowed to continue, might be dangerous to an individual. For instance, a parent might not have a second chance to warn a child not to run into a busy street, so punishing the first incidence of this behaviour might prove to be wise.

The subject of punishment is not an insignificant one. Seventy-five percent of Canadian parents use physical discipline in an effort to alter or control the behaviour of their children. A study conducted in Toronto and Winnipeg in 1992 provided insight on parents' attitudes about the acceptability and the value of physical punishment. The primary reason cited for using punishment as an acceptable response was if the child was putting themselves in danger or hitting others. The finding that "more than one-third of respondents believe that hitting a child is an appropriate way in which to teach a child not to hit others" certainly raises some interesting questions. Another significant finding was that only one-fifth of the sample believed that punishment reliably brought about the desired result of behaviour change (Durrant, 1996). If four-fifths of the sample believed that punishment was not effective, it certainly raises the question: why use it?

Several disadvantages make the routine use of punishment questionable. For one thing, punishment is frequently ineffective, particularly if it is not delivered shortly after the undesired behaviour or if the individual is able to leave the setting in which the punishment is being given. An employee who is reprimanded by the boss might quit; a teenager who loses the use of the family car might borrow a friend's instead. In such instances, the initial behaviour that is being punished might be replaced by one that is even less desirable.

Even worse, physical punishment can convey to the recipient the idea that physical aggression is permissible and perhaps even desirable. A father who yells at and hits his son for misbehaving teaches the son that aggression is an appropriate, adult response. The son might soon copy his father's behaviour by acting aggressively toward others. In addition, physical punishment is often administered by people who are themselves angry or enraged. It is unlikely that individuals in such an emotional state will be able to think through what they are doing or control carefully the degree of punishment they are inflicting. Ultimately, those who resort to physical punishment run the risk that they will grow to be feared. Punishment can also reduce the self-esteem of recipients unless they can understand the reasons for it.

Finally, punishment does not convey any information about what an alternative, more appropriate behaviour might be. To be useful in bringing about more desirable behaviour in the future, punishment must be accompanied by specific information about the behaviour that is being punished, along with specific suggestions concerning a more desirable behaviour. Punishing a child for staring out the window in school could merely lead her to stare at the floor instead. Unless we teach her appropriate ways to respond, we have merely managed to substitute one undesirable behaviour for another. If punishment is not followed up with reinforcement for subsequent behaviour that is more appropriate, little will be accomplished.

In short, reinforcing desired behaviour is a more appropriate technique for modifying behaviour than using punishment. Both in and out of the scientific arena, then, reinforcement usually beats punishment (Sulzer-Azaroff & Mayer, 1991; Seppa, 1996).

Shaping: Reinforcing What Doesn't Come Naturally

Consider the difficulty of using operant conditioning to teach people to repair an automobile transmission. If you had to wait until they chanced to fix a transmission perfectly before you provided them with reinforcement, the Model T might be back in style long before they mastered the repair process.

There are many complex behaviours, ranging from auto repair to zither playing, which we would not expect to occur naturally as part of anyone's spontaneous behaviour. In cases such as these, in which there might otherwise be no opportunity to provide reinforcement for the particular behaviour (since it never occurs in the first place), a procedure known as shaping is used. **Shaping** is the process of teaching a complex behaviour by rewarding closer and closer approximations of the desired behaviour. In shaping, any behaviour that is at all similar to the behaviour you want the person to learn is reinforced at first. Later, you reinforce only responses that are closer to the behaviour you ultimately want to teach. Finally, you reinforce only the desired response. Each step in shaping, then, moves only slightly beyond the previously learned behaviour, permitting the person to link the new step to the behaviour learned earlier.

Shaping allows even lower animals to learn complex responses that would never occur naturally, ranging from lions trained to jump through hoops to seeing-eye dogs such as Pippa, mentioned in the prologue of this chapter, learning to navigate complex environments. Shaping also underlies the learning of many complex human skills. For instance, the organization of most textbooks is based on the principles of shaping. Typically, information is presented so that new material builds on previously learned concepts or skills. Thus the concept of shaping could not be presented in this chapter until we had discussed the more basic principles of operant learning.

Schedules of Reinforcement: Timing Life's Rewards

The world would be a different place if poker players never played cards again after their first losing hand, fishermen returned to shore as soon as they missed a catch, or door-to-door salespeople turned in their samples after their first experience of being turned away. The fact that such unreinforced behaviours continue, often with great frequency and persistence, illustrates that reinforcement need not be received continually in order for behaviour to be learned and maintained. In fact, behaviour that is reinforced only occasionally can ultimately be learned better than behaviour that is always reinforced.

When we refer to the frequency and timing of reinforcement following desired behaviour, we are talking about **schedules of reinforcement**. Behaviour that is reinforced every time it occurs is said to be on a **continuous reinforcement schedule**; if it is reinforced some but not all of the time, it is on a **partial reinforcement schedule**. Although learning occurs more rapidly under a continuous reinforcement schedule, behaviour lasts longer after reinforcement stops when it is learned under a partial reinforcement schedule.

Why should partial reinforcement schedules result in stronger, longer-lasting learning than continuous reinforcement schedules? We can answer the question by examining how we might behave when using a candy vending machine compared with a Las Vegas slot machine. When we use a vending machine, prior experience has taught us that every time we put in the appropriate amount of money, the reinforcement, a candy bar, ought to be delivered. In other words, the schedule of reinforcement is continuous. In comparison, a slot machine offers a partial reinforcement schedule. We have learned that after putting in our cash, most of the time we will not receive anything in return. At the same time, though, we know that we will occasionally win something.

Now suppose that, unbeknownst to us, both the candy vending machine and the slot machine are broken, so that neither one is able to dispense anything. It would not be very

shaping: The process of teaching a complex behaviour by rewarding closer and closer approximations to the desired behaviour.

schedules of reinforcement: The frequency and timing of reinforcement following desired behaviour.
continuous reinforcement schedule: Reinforcement of behaviour every time it occurs.
partial reinforcement schedule: Reinforcement of behaviour some but not all of the time.

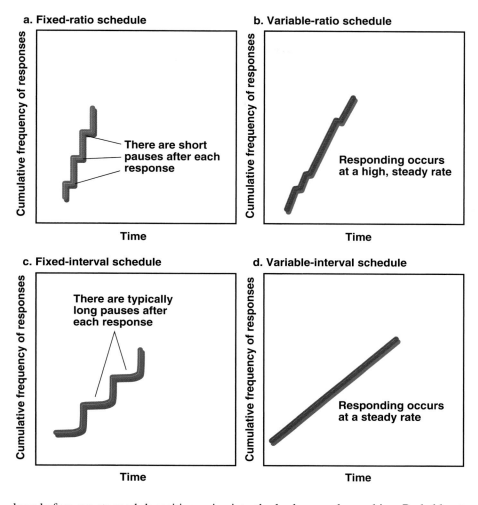

a. Fixed-ratio schedule

Cumulative frequency of responses

There are short pauses after each response

Time

b. Variable-ratio schedule

Cumulative frequency of responses

Responding occurs at a high, steady rate

Time

c. Fixed-interval schedule

Cumulative frequency of responses

There are typically long pauses after each response

Time

d. Variable-interval schedule

Cumulative frequency of responses

Responding occurs at a steady rate

Time

Figure 5-4 Typical outcomes of different reinforcement schedules. *(a)* In a fixed-ratio schedule, short pauses occur following each response. Because the more responses, the more reinforcement, fixed-ratio schedules produce a high rate of responding. *(b)* In a variable-ratio schedule, responding also occurs at a high rate. *(c)* A fixed-interval schedule produces lower rates of responding, especially just after reinforcement has been presented, since the organism learns that a specified time period must elapse between reinforcement. *(d)* A variable-interval schedule produces a fairly steady stream of responses.

long before we stopped depositing coins into the broken candy machine. Probably at most we would try only two or three times before leaving the machine in disgust. But the story would be quite different with the broken slot machine. Here, we would drop in money for a considerably longer time, even though there would be no payoff.

In formal terms, we can see the difference between the two reinforcement schedules: Partial reinforcement schedules (such as those provided by slot machines) maintain performance longer than continuous reinforcement schedules (such as those established in candy vending machines) before extinction—the disappearance of the conditioned response—occurs.

Certain kinds of partial reinforcement schedules produce stronger and lengthier responding before extinction than others. Although many different partial reinforcement schedules have been examined, they can most readily be put into two categories: schedules that consider the *number of responses* made before reinforcement is given, called fixed-ratio and variable-ratio schedules, and those that consider the *amount of time* that elapses before reinforcement is provided, called fixed-interval and variable-interval schedules.

Fixed- and Variable-Ratio Schedules

In a **fixed-ratio schedule**, reinforcement is given only after a certain number of responses. For instance, a pigeon might receive a food pellet every tenth time it pecked a key; here, the ratio would be 1:10. Similarly, garment workers are generally paid on fixed-ratio schedules: They receive several dollars for every blouse they sew. Because a greater rate of production means more reinforcement, people on fixed-ratio schedules are apt to work as quickly as possible (see Figure 5-4).

fixed-ratio schedule: A schedule whereby reinforcement is given only after a certain number of responses are made.

variable–ratio schedule: A schedule whereby reinforcement occurs after a varying number of responses rather than after a fixed number.

In a **variable-ratio schedule**, reinforcement occurs after a varying number of responses rather than after a fixed number. A good example of a variable-ratio schedule is a telephone salesperson's job. She might make a sale during the third, eighth, ninth, and twentieth calls without being successful during any call in between. Although the number of responses that must be made before making a sale varies, it averages out to a 20 percent success rate. Under these circumstances, you might expect that the salesperson would try to make as many calls as possible in as short a time as possible. This is the case with all variable-ratio schedules, which lead to a high rate of response and resistance to extinction.

Fixed- and Variable-Interval Schedules: The Passage of Time

In contrast to fixed- and variable-ratio schedules, in which the crucial factor is the number of responses, fixed-*interval* and variable-*interval* schedules focus on the amount of *time* that has elapsed since a person or animal was rewarded. One example of a fixed-interval schedule is a weekly paycheque. For people who receive regular, weekly paycheques, it typically makes relatively little difference exactly how much they produce in a given week.

fixed–interval schedule: A schedule that provides reinforcement for a response only if a fixed time period has elapsed, making overall rates of response relatively low.

Because a **fixed-interval schedule** provides reinforcement for a response only if a fixed time period has elapsed, overall rates of response are relatively low. This is especially true in the period just after reinforcement when the time before another reinforcement is relatively great. Students' study habits often exemplify this reality. If the periods between exams are relatively long (meaning that the opportunity for reinforcement for good performance is fairly infrequent), students often study minimally or not at all until the day of the exam draws near. Just before the exam, however, students begin to cram for it, signalling a rapid increase in the rate of their studying response. As you might expect, immediately following the exam there is a rapid decline in the rate of responding, with few people opening a book the day after a test.

variable–interval schedule: A schedule whereby the time between reinforcements varies around some average rather than being fixed.

One way to decrease the delay in responding that occurs just after reinforcement, and to maintain the desired behaviour more consistently throughout an interval, is to use a variable-interval schedule. In a **variable-interval schedule**, the time between reinforcements varies around some average rather than being fixed. For example, a professor who gives surprise quizzes that vary from one every three days to one every three weeks, averaging one every two weeks, is using a variable-interval schedule. Compared to the study habits we observed with a fixed-interval schedule, students' study habits under such a variable-interval schedule would most likely be very different. Students would be apt to study more regularly since they would never know when the next surprise quiz was coming. Variable-interval schedules, in general, are more likely to produce relatively steady rates of responding than fixed-interval schedules, with responses that take longer to extinguish after reinforcement ends.

Nomar Garciaparra, like many baseball players, goes through a ritual of superstitious behaviours before batting. **How can his actions be explained in terms of the principles of reinforcement?**

Discrimination and Generalization in Operant Conditioning

It does not take a child long to learn that a red light at an intersection means stop and a green light indicates that it is permissible to continue. Just as in classical conditioning, then, operant learning involves the phenomena of discrimination and generalization.

The process by which people learn to discriminate stimuli is known as stimulus control training. In *stimulus control training,* a behaviour is reinforced in the presence of a specific stimulus, but not in its absence. For example, one of the most difficult discriminations many people face is determining when someone's friendliness is not mere friendliness, but a signal of romantic interest. People learn to make the discrimination by observing the presence of certain nonverbal cues—such as increased eye contact and touching—that indicate romantic interest. When such cues are absent, people learn that no romantic interest is indicated. In this case, the nonverbal cue acts as a discriminative stimulus, one to which an organism learns to respond during stimulus control training. A *discriminative stimulus* signals the likelihood that reinforcement will follow a response. For example, if you wait until your roommate is in a good mood before you ask to borrow her favourite compact disc, your behaviour can be said to be under stimulus control because you can discriminate between her moods.

Just as in classical conditioning, the phenomenon of stimulus generalization, in which an organism learns a response to one stimulus and then applies it to other stimuli, is also found in operant conditioning. If you have learned that being polite produces the reinforcement of getting your way in a certain situation, you are likely to generalize your response to other situations. Sometimes, though, generalization can have unfortunate consequences, such as when people behave negatively toward all members of a racial group because they have had an unpleasant experience with one member of that group.

Superstitious Behaviour

Have you ever knocked on wood after speaking about good fortune? After spilling salt, do you quickly throw a pinch over your left shoulder? Do you have a lucky pen that you take to all exams? To learning psychologists, such rituals are examples of *superstitious behaviour*.

Superstitious behaviour can be explained in terms of learning and reinforcement. As we have seen, behaviour that is followed by a reinforcer tends to be strengthened. Occasionally, however, the behaviour that occurs prior to the reinforcement is entirely coincidental. Still, an association is made between the behaviour and reinforcement.

Imagine, for instance, that a baseball player taps his bat against the ground three times in a row just prior to getting a single. The hit is, of course, coincidental to the batter's tapping the ground, but the player might see it as somehow related. Because the player makes this association, he might tap the ground three times every time he is at bat in the future. And because he will be at least partially reinforced for this behaviour—batters usually get a hit 25 percent of the time—his tapping behaviour will be maintained, as a superstitious behaviour (Van Ginkel, 1990; Matute, 1994, 1995).

Biological Constraints on Learning: You Can't Teach an Old Dog Just Any Trick

Psychologists Keller and Marian Breland were pleased with their idea: As consultants to a professional animal trainer, they came up with the notion of having a pig place a wooden disk into a piggy bank. With their experience in training animals through operant conditioning, they thought the task would be easy to teach, given that it was certainly well within the range of the pig's physical capabilities. Yet every time they tried out the procedure, it failed. Upon viewing the disk, the pigs were willing to do nothing but root the wooden disk along the ground. Apparently, the pigs were biologically programmed to push stimuli in the shape of disks along the ground.

Their lack of swine success led the Brelands to substitute a raccoon. Although the procedure worked fine with one disk, when two disks were used, the raccoon refused

PsychLink

Psychology of superstition
www.mcgrawhill.ca/college/feldman

Biological constraints make it nearly impossible for animals to learn certain behaviours. Here, psychologist Marian Breland Bailey attempts to overcome the natural limitations that inhibit the success of conditioning in this rooster.

Chapter Two

Pathways Through Psychology

Catharine Rankin

Associate Professor of Psychology, University of British Columbia

Education: B.A., M.A., University of Guelph; B.Ed., University of Western Ontario; Ph.D. (biopsychology) City University of New York

Home: Vancouver, British Columbia

Catharine Rankin

I have always been interested in science, starting with my fossil collection in grade 3. In university I divided my time between psychology and biology. My honours project was a study of seal behaviour; my master's was in cognitive psychology. I then took time out of academics, and did a bachelor of education degree, and taught grades 4 and 5 in Toronto for two years.

I left there to do a Ph.D. in biopsychology at the City University of New York, where I studied the African electric catfish in the Animal Behaviour Program at Hunter College and the American Museum of Natural History. As I learned more about behaviour, I found myself asking more and more questions about mechanisms. I always wanted to know why and how the animals did what they did.

One summer I took a course at Woods Hole Marine Biological Laboratory called "Neural Systems and Behaviour." It was all about how nervous systems produced behaviour. I was particularly fascinated by the research that used invertebrates to study the biological basis of learning and memory. I decided to pursue that area of research. After finishing my Ph.D. on the electric catfish, I went to Yale University to do post-doctoral research on learning in the marine mollusc *Aplysia californica* in the laboratory of Dr. Thomas Carew.

When I came to UBC to set up my own lab, I ended up choosing an even simpler animal to study. My research is on the biological basis of learning and memory in the nematode worm *C. elegans*. This tiny (1 millimetre) worm has only 302 neurons! (Humans have over a trillion neurons—it is impossible to understand what every neuron in a human is doing when it learns. We hope that we can figure out what every neuron in *C. elegans* is doing when it learns.) I am very excited about research—it is like solving a great mystery. It always feels like the next answer is just around the corner. However, the challenge in research is that every answer leads to more questions! It is very satisfying to understand behaviour enough to be able to predict what an animal is going to do.

Research done by my students and me has demonstrated that this simple worm can learn (it shows habituation, that is, it learns not to respond to stimuli that are repeated, but are not important). It also can remember training for at least 24 hours (not bad for a worm that only lives about 12 days). We have used a laser to kill single neurons and then have studied the role of those neurons in habituation. Through this technique we have identified the neurons important for the response we study. We have also studied genetic mutations in *C. elegans* to try to understand what genes are involved in learning and memory. Since *C. elegans* shows habituation in exactly the same way as all other animals, including humans, it is my hope that by understanding the mechanisms of habituation in the worm, I can shed light on mechanisms of human learning. In additon, many human disorders, such as schizophrenia, include deficits in habituation. Understanding the genes that play a role in habituation in the worm may help to understand these human genetic disorders.

Source: Catharine Rankin, Ph.D. University of British Columbia crankin@cortex.psych.ubc.ca

Why is study of this particular little worm important to psychology?

to deposit either of them and instead rubbed the two together, as if it were washing them. Once again, it appeared that the disks evoked biologically innate behaviours that were impossible to replace through even the most exhaustive training (Breland & Breland, 1961).

The Brelands' difficulties illustrate an important point: Not all behaviours can be trained in all species equally well. Instead, there are *biological constraints,* built-in limitations, in the ability of animals to learn particular behaviours. In some cases, an organism will have a special predisposition that will aid in its learning a behaviour (such as pecking behaviours in pigeons); in other cases, biological constraints will act to prevent or inhibit an organism from learning a behaviour. In either instance, it is clear that animals have specialized learning mechanisms that influence how readily both classical and operant conditioning influence their behaviour, and each species is biologically primed to develop particular kinds of associations and to have a difficult time in learning others (Hollis, 1984).

Sometimes researchers are surprised at unexpected behaviour. Dr. Catherine Rankin and her students (see the *Pathways Through Psychology* box) work with a tiny worm that has demonstrated an ability to learn.

Evaluate

1. _____ conditioning describes learning that occurs as a result of reinforcement.
2. Match the type of operant learning with its definition:

   1. An unpleasant stimulus is presented to decrease behaviour
   2. An unpleasant stimulus is removed to increase behaviour
   3. A pleasant stimulus is presented to increase behaviour
   4. A pleasant stimulus is removed to decrease behaviour

   a. Positive reinforcement
   b. Negative reinforcement
   c. Positive punishment
   d. Negative punishment

3. Sandy had had a rough day, and his son's noisemaking was not helping him relax. Not wanting to resort to scolding, Sandy told his son in a serious manner that he was very tired and would like the boy to play quietly for an hour. This approach worked. For Sandy, the change in his son's behaviour was

   a. positively reinforcing.
   b. negatively reinforcing.

4. In a _____ reinforcement schedule, behaviour is reinforced some of the time, while in a _____ reinforcement schedule, behaviour is reinforced all the time.

5. Match the type of reinforcement schedule with its definition.

   1. Reinforcement occurs after a set time period
   2. Reinforcement occurs after a set number of responses
   3. Reinforcement occurs after a varying time period
   4. Reinforcement occurs after a varying number of responses

   a. Fixed-ratio
   b. Variable-interval
   c. Fixed-interval
   d. Variable-ratio

6. Fixed reinforcement schedules produce greater resistance to extinction than variable reinforcement schedules. True or false?

Answers to Evaluate Questions

1. Operant 2. 1-c, 2-b, 3-a, 4-d 3. b 4. partial; continuous 5. 1-c, 2-a, 3-b, 4-d 6. False; variable ratios are more resistant to extinction.

Rethink

1. How might operant conditioning be used to address serious personal concerns, such as smoking and unhealthy eating?
2. How might you go about "curing" superstitious behaviour, such as the rituals people engage in before examinations or athletic competitions? Should we try to extinguish such behaviour?

Cognitive Approaches to Learning

Consider what happens when people learn to drive a car. They don't just get behind the wheel and stumble around until they randomly put the key into the ignition, and later, after many false starts, accidentally manage to get the car to move forward, thereby receiving positive reinforcement. Instead, they already know the basic elements of driving from prior experience as passengers.

Clearly, not all learning is due to the unthinking, mechanical, and automatic acquisition of associations between stimuli and responses, as in classical conditioning, or the presentation of reinforcement, as in operant conditioning. In fact, instances such as learning to drive a car imply that some kinds of learning must involve higher-order processes in which people's thoughts and memories and the way they process information account for their responses.

Psychologists who view learning in terms of the thought processes, or cognitions, that underlie it use **cognitive learning theory**. Although psychologists using the cognitive learning perspective do not deny the importance of classical and

Prepare

What is the role of cognition and thought in learning?

What are some practical methods for bringing about behaviour change, both in ourselves and in others?

Organize

Cognitive Approaches to Learning

Latent Learning

Observational Learning

Violence on Television and in Movies

The Unresolved Controversy of Cognitive Learning Theory

cognitive learning theory:
The study of the thought processes that underlie learning.

operant conditioning, they have developed approaches that focus on the unseen mental processes that occur during learning, rather than concentrating solely on external stimuli, responses, and reinforcements. In other words, according to cognitive learning theory, people develop an expectation that they will receive a reinforcer upon making a response.

Support for the view that the development of expectations is critical to our understanding of cognitive learning also comes from studies of animal cognition. These studies have examined, among other things, temporal cognition (Wilkie et al., 1997), spatial cognition (Shettleworth & Hampton, 1998), and memory (Brodbeck & Shettleworth, 1995). Marcia Spetch of the University of Alberta conducts extensive research on the cognitive behaviour of both animals and humans. Some studies have presented similar tasks to both pigeons and humans: requiring that they use landmarks to locate a hidden goal. Both similarities and differences in search strategies were examined (Spetch, 1995; Spetch, Cheng, & MacDonald, 1996; Spetch et al., 1997).

Latent and observational learning provide the evidence for this view, so we turn now to a discussion of these two types of learning.

Latent Learning

latent learning: Learning in which a new behaviour is acquired but is not demonstrated until reinforcement is provided.

Some of the most direct evidence regarding cognitive processes comes from a series of experiments that revealed a type of cognitive learning called latent learning. In **latent learning**, a new behaviour is learned but not demonstrated until reinforcement

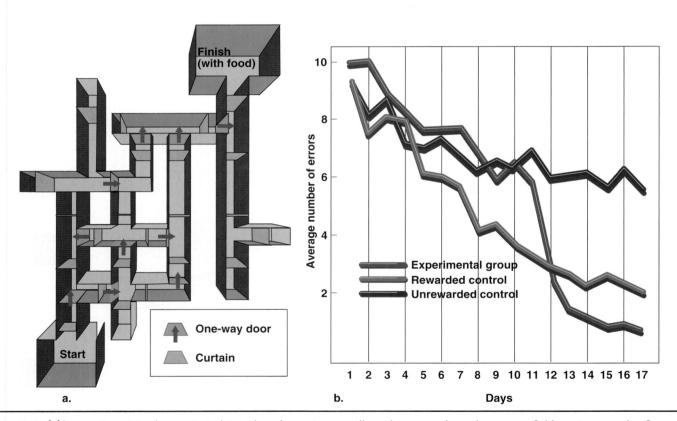

a.

b.

Figure 5-5 *(a)* In an attempt to demonstrate latent learning, rats were allowed to roam through a maze of this sort once a day for seventeen days. *(b)* Those rats that were never rewarded (the unrewarded control condition) consistently made the most errors, whereas those that received food at the finish every day (the rewarded control condition) consistently made far fewer errors. But the results also showed latent learning: Rats that were initially unrewarded but began to be rewarded only after the tenth day (the experimental group) showed an immediate reduction in errors and soon became similar to the error rate of the rats that had been consistently rewarded. According to cognitive learning theorists, the reduction in errors indicates that the rats had developed a cognitive map—a mental representation—of the maze (Tolman & Honzik, 1930).
Can you think of other examples of latent learning?

is provided for displaying it (Tolman & Honzik, 1930). In the studies, psychologists examined the behaviour of rats in a maze such as the one shown in Figure 5-5a. In one representative experiment, a group of rats was allowed to wander around the maze once a day for seventeen days without ever receiving any reward. Understandably, these rats made many errors and spent a relatively long time reaching the end of the maze. A second group, however, was always given food at the end of the maze. Not surprisingly, these rats learned to run quickly and directly to the food box, making few errors.

A third group of rats started out in the same situation as the unrewarded rats, but only for the first ten days. On the eleventh day, a critical experimental manipulation was introduced: From that point on, the rats in this group were given food for completing the maze. The results of this manipulation were dramatic, as you can see from the graph in Figure 5-5b. The previously unrewarded rats, who had earlier seemed to wander about aimlessly, showed such reductions in running time and declines in error rates that their performance almost immediately matched that of the group that had received rewards from the start.

cognitive map: A mental representation of spatial locations and directions.

To cognitive theorists, it seemed clear that the unrewarded rats had learned the layout of the maze early in their explorations; they just never displayed their latent learning until the reinforcement was offered. Instead, the rats seemed to develop a **cognitive map** of the maze—a mental representation of spatial locations and directions.

People, too, develop cognitive maps of their surroundings, based primarily on particular landmarks. When they first encounter a new environment, their maps tend to rely on specific paths—such as the directions we might give someone unfamiliar with an area: "Turn right at the stop sign, make a left at the bridge, and then go up the hill." However, as people become more familiar with an area, they develop an overall conception of it, which has been called an abstract cognitive map. Using such a map, they are eventually able to take shortcuts as they develop a broad understanding of the area (Garling, 1989; Gale et al., 1990; Plumert et al., 1995).

The possibility that we develop our cognitive maps through latent learning presents something of a problem for strict operant conditioning theorists. If we consider the results of Tolman's maze experiment, for instance, it is unclear what the specific reinforcement was that permitted the rats that initially received no reward to learn about the layout of the maze, because there was no obvious reinforcer present. Instead, the results support a cognitive view of learning, in which learning might have resulted in changes in unobservable mental processes.

Observational Learning: Learning Through Imitation

Let's return for a moment to the case of a person learning to drive. How can we account for instances in which an individual with no direct experience in carrying out a particular behaviour learns the behaviour and then performs it? To answer this question, psychologists have proposed another form of cognitive learning: observational learning.

According to psychologist Albert Bandura and colleagues, a major part of human learning consists of **observational learning**, which they define as learning through observing the behaviour of another person called a *model* (Bandura, 1977). Bandura and his colleagues demonstrated rather dramatically the ability of models to stimulate learning. In what is now considered a classic experiment, young children saw a film of an adult wildly hitting a large inflatable punching toy called a Bobo doll (Bandura, Ross, & Ross, 1963a, 1963b). Later the children were given the opportunity to play with the Bobo doll themselves and, sure enough, most displayed the same kind of behaviour, in some cases mimicking the aggressive behaviour almost identically.

Not only negative behaviours are acquired through observational learning. In one experiment, for example, children who were afraid of dogs were exposed to a model—dubbed the Fearless Peer—playing with a dog (Bandura, Grusec, & Menlove, 1967).

PsychLink
Observational learning
www.mcgrawhill.ca/college/feldman

observational learning: Learning through observing the behaviour of another person called a *model*.

As this boy watches his father, he is engaging in observational learning.
How does observational learning contribute to defining gender roles?

Albert Bandura examined the principles of observational learning.

Following exposure, childern who had observed the model were considerably more likely to approach a strange dog than children who hadnot viewed the Fearless Peer.

According to Bandura, observational learning takes place in four steps: (1) paying attention and perceiving the most critical features of another person's behaviour; (2) remembering the behaviour; (3) reproducing the action; and (4) being motivated to learn and carry out the behaviour. Instead of learning occurring through trial and error, then, with successes being reinforced and failures punished, many important skills are learned through observational processes (Bandura, 1986).

Observational learning is particularly important in acquiring skills for which shaping is inappropriate. Piloting an airplane and performing brain surgery, for example, are behaviours that could hardly be learned using trial-and-error methods without grave cost—literally—to those involved in the learning.

Not all behaviour that we witness is learned or carried out, of course. One crucial factor that determines whether we later imitate a model is the consequences of the model's behaviour. If we observe a friend being rewarded for putting more time into her studies by receiving higher grades, we are more likely to imitate her behaviour than if her behaviour only results in her being stressed and tired. Models who are rewarded for behaving in a particular way are more apt to be mimicked than models who receive punishment. Interestingly, though, observing the punishment of a model does not necessarily stop observers from learning the behaviour. Observers can still describe the model's behaviour—they are just less apt to perform it (Bandura, 1977, 1986, 1994).

Observational learning is central to a number of important issues relating to the extent to which people learn by simply watching the behaviour of others. For instance, the degree to which observation of aggression in the media produces subsequent aggression on the part of viewers is a crucial—and controversial—question, as we discuss next.

Violence on Television and in Movies: Does the Media's Message Matter?

The daughter of a judge from a politically prominent family runs off with her ne'er-do-well boyfriend. They drop LSD and watch, over and over, the ultraviolent Oliver Stone movie "Natural Born Killers," about a young couple who take drugs and kill people for pleasure. One afternoon, out joyriding in rural Mississippi, the boy suggests [according to the girl] "finding an isolated farmhouse and doing a home invasion, robbing a family and killing them, leaving no witnesses . . . as if he was fantasizing from the movie 'Natural Born Killers.'" At a cotton gin on a lonely highway, the boyfriend guns down an innocent citizen, a devoted husband of 40 years, just for the thrill of it. . . . The next day the boy says to the girl, "It's your turn." That night, wearing a hooded poncho, she shoots a convenience-store clerk in cold blood, leaving the mother of three children paralyzed below the neck.
(A. G. Miller, 1999, p. 176)

The aftermath of the killers' shooting spree may have a profound effect not just on the individuals directly involved, but on the motion picture industry, because the family of one of the victims sued the film's director and producers for millions of dollars. Although legal experts suggest that the lawsuit is unlikely to succeed, it raises a critical issue: Does observation of violence and antisocial acts in the media lead viewers to behave in similar ways? Because research on modelling shows that people frequently learn and imitate the aggression that they observe, this question is among the most important being addressed by social psychologists. For example, a 1994 study on weapons use in Canadian schools found that sensationalized violence in the media, although not the only factor, was certainly a contributing factor to weapons (primarily knives) being carried and used in schools (Ministry of the Solicitor General, 1994).

Applying Psychology in the 21st Century

Does Virtual Aggression Lead to Actual Aggression?

Blood flows freely as still-warm corpses lie on the ground. Potential victims beg for mercy, while others moan in pain. Some people catch fire before they are mowed down, falling to the ground, dead.

This is just some of the continual violence that characterizes the computer game Postal. In the game, trigger-happy players act out the role of Postal Dude, who shoots at everything—and everyone—in his path. Like Doom, a favourite game of one of the Columbine High School killers, Postal allows players their choice of a variety of weapons of carnage.

Postal and Doom are just two of many highly realistic, involving, and violent video games now on the market. In fact, one survey found that almost 80 percent of the most popular games involved aggression, with one-fifth of them involving violence against women (Dietz, 1998).

Can playing games like Postal and Doom lead to actual aggression? Increasing research evidence suggests that it might. According to a recent series of studies by psychologists Craig Anderson and Karen Dill (2000), playing violent video games is associated with later aggressive behaviour. In one study, for example, they found that college students who frequently played violent video games were more likely to have been involved in delinquent behaviour and aggression. Frequent players also had lower academic achievement.

On the other hand, such results do not show that playing violent games *causes* delinquency, aggression, and lower academic performance; the research only found that the various variables were *associated with* one another. To explore the question of whether violent game play actually caused aggression, Anderson and Dill subsequently conducted a short-term laboratory study. In it, they had participants in an experiment play either a violent video game (Wolfenstein 3D) or one that was nonviolent (Myst). The results were clear: Exposure to the graphically violent video game increased aggressive thoughts and actual aggression.

The finding of a link between playing violent video games and aggressive behaviour is consistent with findings from other studies, and it makes sense in light of the research on the consequences of exposure to violence in the media. In fact, the effects of playing video games could be even greater than the effects of merely watching an aggressive television program,

While research has shown that a link exists between playing violent video games and aggressive thoughts and behaviour, it has not shown that game playing causes delinquency, real-world aggression, or lower academic achievement. Do you think a definite causal connection will ever be found?

because video games teach something that the mere observation of violence does not: the motor skills involved in aggression. By actually firing virtual weapons at people and objects appearing on the screen, game players presumably hone the skills that would make them more effective in using actual weapons (Cooper & Mackie, 1986; D. Cohen, 1996; Griffiths, 1997).

If a conclusive causal link between playing violent video games and subsequent aggressive acts were established, would you support a ban on such games? Why or why not?

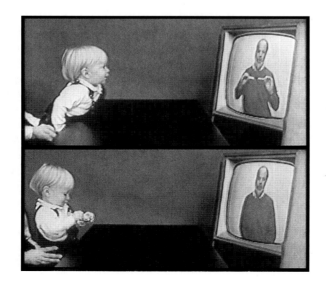

Illustrating observational learning, this infant observes an adult on the television and then is able to imitate his behaviour. Learning has obviously occurred through the mere observation of the television model.

PsychLink

Violence in the media
www.mcgrawhill.ca/college/feldman

Certainly, the amount of violence in the mass media is enormous. Between the ages of 5 and 15, the average Canadian or American child is exposed to no fewer than 13 000 violent deaths on television; the number of fights and aggressive sequences that children view is still higher (Mifflin, 1998). In an extensive study done for the Department of Canadian Heritage, Wendy Josephson (see the *Pathways Through Psychology* box in Chapter 1) examined the effects of television violence on children of different ages. She found that although children of all ages are affected, preschoolers are particularly vulnerable (Josephson, 1995).

Most experts agree that watching high levels of media violence make viewers more susceptible to acting aggressively—for several reasons. For one thing, viewing violence seems to lower inhibitions against the performance of aggression—watching television portrayals of violence makes aggression seem a legitimate response to particular situations. Viewing violence also can distort our understanding of the meaning of others' behaviour, predisposing us to view even nonaggressive acts by others as aggressive. Finally, a continual diet of aggression can leave us desensitized to violence, and what previously would have repelled us now produces little emotional response. Our sense of the pain and suffering brought about by aggression might be diminished (Berkowitz, 1993; Josephson, 1995; Berkowitz & LePage, 1996; Huesmann & Moise, 1996).

Of course, the media are not the only source of aggressive models. For example, many computer and video games involve a significant amount of graphic violence. Does exposure to such violence affect players? For an answer, consider the research findings described in the *Applying Psychology in the 21st Century* box on p.177.

EXPLORING DIVERSITY

Does Culture Influence How We Learn?

Why does formal, content-based education present problems for Aboriginal students outside urban areas? What educational system would help to ensure better retention of students?

Do the differences in teaching approaches between cultures affect how people learn? According to one school of thought, learners develop *learning styles*, characteristic ways of approaching material, based on their cultural background and unique pattern of abilities (Anderson & Adams, 1992; Milgram, Dunn, & Price, 1993; Chi-Ching & Noi, 1994; Furnham, 1995; Sternberg & Grigorenko, 1997).

The issue of cultural background and learning styles is at the heart of the attempts to transform Aboriginal education in Canada. Aboriginal peoples, including First Nations, Métis, and Inuit, are struggling to create for their children an Aboriginal education system to replace years of Eurocentric, government-mandated (formal) education. This goes far beyond simply reviving Aboriginal languages and cultures, although they are important.

In a study of Inuit education, Arlene Stairs (1995) explains that there are two different models of education. She uses the Inuit term *isumaqsayuq* to denote an Aboriginal educational system that includes knowledge based on real-world, practical experience, shared and passed on from those with more experience to the young. Embedded in this knowledge are group identity and values. In contrast, she refers to *ilisayuq* as a formal system of education based on abstraction, verbal ability, and preparation for some future endeavour.

Her contention is that the more formal way of transmitting knowledge or educating students runs counter to Aboriginal learning styles and in fact disadvantages Aboriginal students. Their learning style, especially for those outside of urban centres, is based on repeating practical skills in a variety of settings. These are skills of experience and survival, like hunting and fishing. They are skills that put the group ahead of the individual and will ultimately help to define the person's role in the social community. In a formal classroom, where more individualistic behaviour is valued, a learning style that is based on cooperation and experience may be misinterpreted as "inattention or even cheating" and may not produce the desired learning outcomes required by a formal education system (Stairs, 1995).

This will naturally have an impact on retention. Aboriginal student retention is a challenging issue. It is impacted by far more than learning styles. It also varies dramatically from one jurisdiction to another. In Ontario, for example, retention rates vary from 90 percent in urban centres to as low as 9 percent in more remote parts of the province (Mackay & Myles, 1995).

The challenge for Aboriginal educators is to find a way to transmit the knowledge provided by the formal system using a model of delivery that respects an alternate (*isumaqsayuq*) learning style. This is particularly important for mathematics and science, so that Aboriginal students are not limited in their opportunities in a technologically diverse world.

Of course, this is not an easy thing to do. One such attempt has been made in northern Alaska, where the *qargi* (a traditional community house where the youth learned from their elders) is being transformed into a "school." In this school, Aboriginal teachers work with community elders to educate the young. Formal learning, in a subject such as mathematics, is applied to real life situations, for example building a boat (Stairs, 1995).

The conclusion that members of particular ethnic and gender groups have similar learning styles is controversial. Because there is so much diversity within each particular racial and ethnic group, critics argue that generalizations about learning styles cannot be used to predict the style of any single individual, regardless of group membership. Instead, they suggest that it is more fruitful to concentrate on determining each individual's particular learning style and pattern of academic and social strengths.

The Unresolved Controversy of Cognitive Learning Theory

The degree to which learning is based on unseen internal factors rather than on external factors remains one of the major issues dividing learning theorists today. Both classical conditioning and operant conditioning theories consider learning in terms of external stimuli and responses—a kind of "black box" analysis in which all that matters are the observable features of the environment, not what goes on inside a person's head. To the cognitive learning theorists, such an analysis misses the mark. Instead, they argue that what is crucial is the mental activity—the thoughts and expectations—that takes place inside the head.

Regardless of how the theoretical controversies are resolved, research on learning has allowed psychologists to make important advances in such areas as the treatment of psychological disorders (discussed in Chapter 13), and—as we see next—in suggesting solutions to everyday problems.

BECOMING AN INFORMED CONSUMER OF PSYCHOLOGY

Using Behaviour Analysis and Behaviour Modification

How does learning theory explain the success of behaviour modification?

A couple who had been living together for three years began to fight more and more frequently. The issues of disagreement ranged from the seemingly petty, such as who was going to do the dishes, to the more profound, such as the quality of their love life and whether they found each other interesting. Disturbed about this increasingly unpleasant pattern of interaction, the couple went to a behaviour analyst, a psychologist who specialized in behaviour-modification techniques. After interviewing each of them alone and then speaking to them together, he asked them to keep a detailed written record of their interactions over the next two weeks—focusing in particular on the events that preceded their arguments.

When they returned two weeks later, he carefully went over the records with them. In doing so, he noticed a pattern that the couple themselves had observed after they had started keeping their records: Each of their arguments had occurred just after one or the other had left some household chore undone. For instance, the woman would go into a fury when she came home from work and found that the man, a student, had left his dirty lunch dishes on the table and had not even started dinner preparations. The man would get angry when he found the woman's clothes draped on the only chair in the bedroom. He insisted it was her responsibility to pick up after herself.

PsychLink
Journal of Applied Behaviour Analysis
www.mcgrawhill.ca/college/feldman

Using the data that the couple had collected, the behaviour analyst devised a system for the couple to try out. He asked them to list all of the chores that could possibly arise and assign each one a point value depending on how long it took to complete. Then he had them divide the chores equally according to total points and agree in a written contract to fulfill the ones assigned to them. If either failed to carry out one of the assigned chores, he or she would have to place $1 per point in a fund for the other to spend. They also agreed to a program of verbal praise, promising to verbally reward each other for completing a chore.

Although skeptical about the value of such a program, the couple agreed to try it for a month and to keep careful records of the number of arguments they had during this period. To their surprise, the number of arguments declined rapidly, and even the more basic issues in their relationship seemed on the way to being resolved.

The case described here provides an illustration of **behaviour modification**, a formalized technique for promoting the frequency of desirable behaviours and decreasing the incidence of unwanted ones. Using the basic principles of learning theory, behaviour-modification techniques have proved to be helpful in a variety of situations. People with severe mental retardation have learned the rudiments of language and, for the first time in their lives, have started dressing and feeding themselves. Behaviour modification has also helped people lose weight, give up smoking, and behave more safely (Bellack, Hersen, & Kazdin, 1990; Sulzer-Azaroff & Mayer, 1991; Malott, Whaley, & Malott, 1993; Walter, Vaughan, & Wynder, 1994).

The techniques used by behaviour analysts are as varied as the list of processes that modify behaviour. These include reinforcement scheduling, shaping, generalization training, discrimination training, and extinction. Participants in a behaviour-change program do, however, typically follow a series of similar basic steps. These steps include:

- *Identify goals and target behaviours.* The first step is to define "desired behaviour." Is it an increase in time spent studying? a decrease in weight? an increase in the use of language? a reduction in the amount of aggression displayed by a child? The goals must be stated in observable terms and lead to specific targets. For instance, a goal might be "to increase study time," with the target behaviour "to study at least two hours per day on weekdays and an hour on Saturdays."
- *Design a data-recording system and record preliminary data.* To determine whether behaviour has changed, it is necessary to collect data before any changes are made in the situation. This information provides a baseline against which future changes can be measured.
- *Select a behaviour-change strategy.* The most crucial step is to select an appropriate strategy. Because all the principles of learning can be employed to bring about behaviour change, a "package" of treatments is normally used. This might include the systematic use of positive reinforcement for desired behaviour (verbal praise or something more tangible, such as food), as well as a program of extinction for undesirable behaviour (ignoring a child who throws a tantrum). Selecting the right reinforcers is critical; it could be necessary to experiment a bit to find out what is important to a given individual. It is best for participants to avoid threats, because these are merely punishing and ultimately not very effective in bringing about long-term changes in behaviour.
- *Implement the program.* The next step is to institute the program. Probably the most important aspect of program implementation is consistency. It is also important to make sure that one is reinforcing the behaviour one wants to reinforce. For example, suppose a mother wants her daughter to spend more time on her homework, but as soon as the child sits down to study, she asks for a snack. If the mother gets one for her, she is likely to be reinforcing her daughter's delaying tactic, not her studying. Instead, the mother might tell her child that she will provide her with a snack after a certain time interval has gone by during which she has studied—thereby using the snack as a reinforcement for studying.
- *Keep careful records after the program is implemented.* Another crucial task is record keeping. If the target behaviours are not monitored, there is no way of

behaviour modification: A formalized technique for promoting the frequency of desirable behaviours and decreasing the incidence of unwanted ones.

PsychLink

Behavioural analysis issues
www.mcgrawhill.ca/college/feldman

knowing whether the program has been successful. Participants are advised not to rely on memory, because memory lapses are all too frequent.

- *Evaluate and alter the ongoing program.* Finally, the results of the program should be compared with baseline, pre-implementation data to determine its effectiveness. If successful, the procedures employed can gradually be phased out. For instance, if the program called for reinforcing every instance of picking up one's clothes from the bedroom floor, the reinforcement schedule could be modified to a fixed-ratio schedule in which every third instance was reinforced. On the other hand, if the program has not been successful in bringing about the desired behaviour change, consideration of other approaches might be advisable.

Behaviour-change techniques based on these general principles have enjoyed wide success and have proved to be one of the most powerful means of modifying behaviour (Greenwood et al., 1992). Clearly, it is possible to employ the basic notions of learning theory to improve our own lives.

Evaluate

1. Cognitive learning theorists are concerned only with overt behaviour, not with its internal causes. True or false?

2. In cognitive learning theory, it is assumed that people develop an _____ about receiving a reinforcer when they behave a certain way.

3. In _____ learning, a new behaviour is learned but is not shown until appropriate reinforcement is presented.

4. Bandura's theory of _____ learning states that people learn through watching a _____ — another person displaying the behaviour of interest.

5. A man wishes to quit smoking. Upon the advice of a psychologist, he begins a program in which he sets goals for his withdrawal, carefully records his progress, and rewards himself for not smoking during a certain period of time. What type of program is he following?

Answers to Evaluate Questions

1. False: cognitive learning theorists are primarily concerned with mental processes 2. expectation 3. latent 4. observational; model 5. Behaviour modification

Rethink

1. What is the relationship between a model (in Bandura's sense) and a role model (as the term is used popularly)? Celebrities often complain that their actions should not be scrutinized closely because they do not want to be role models. How would you respond?

2. The desire to make education more relevant for Aboriginal children in Canada has educators proposing that education should be based on the existing cultural and practical experience of the students and not simply on abstract theories and principles. Could other educational systems benefit from this model?

Looking Back

What is learning?

- Learning, a relatively permanent change in behaviour due to experience, is a basic topic of psychology. However, learning must be assessed indirectly by observing performance. (p. 156)

How do we learn to form associations between stimuli and responses?

- One major form of learning is classical conditioning, which occurs when a neutral stimulus—one that brings about no relevant response—is repeatedly paired with a stimulus (called an unconditioned stimulus) that brings about a natural, untrained response. (p. 156)
- Conditioning occurs when the neutral stimulus is repeatedly presented just before the unconditioned stimulus. After repeated pairings, the neutral stimulus brings about the same response as the unconditioned stimulus. When this occurs, the neutral stimulus has become a conditioned stimulus, and the response a conditioned response. (p. 157)
- Learning is not always permanent. Extinction occurs when a previously learned response decreases in frequency and eventually disappears. (p. 159)
- Stimulus generalization occurs when a conditioned response follows a stimulus that is similar to, but not the same as, the original conditioned stimulus. The converse phenomenon, stimulus discrimination, occurs when an organism learns to distinguish between stimuli. (p. 160)

What is the role of reward and punishment in learning?

- A second major form of learning is operant conditioning. According to B. F. Skinner, the major mechanism underlying learning is reinforcement, the process by which a stimulus increases the probability that a preceding behaviour will be repeated. (p. 162)
- Primary reinforcers involve rewards that are naturally effective without prior exposure because they satisfy a biological need. Secondary reinforcers begin to act as if they were primary reinforcers through frequent pairings with a primary reinforcer. (p. 164)
- Positive reinforcers are stimuli that are added to the environment and lead to an increase in a preceding response. Negative reinforcers are stimuli that remove something unpleasant from the environment, leading to an increase in the preceding response. (p. 165)
- Punishment decreases the probability that a prior behaviour will occur. Positive punishment weakens a response through the application of an unpleasant stimulus, while negative punishment weakens a response by the removal of something positive. In contrast to reinforcement, in which the goal is to increase the incidence of behaviour, punishment is meant to decrease or suppress behaviour. (p. 167)
- Shaping is a process for teaching complex behaviours by rewarding closer and closer approximations of the desired final behaviour. (p. 168)
- Schedules and patterns of reinforcement affect the strength and duration of learning. Generally, partial reinforcement schedules—in which reinforcers are not delivered on every trial—produce stronger and longer-lasting learning than continuous reinforcement schedules. (p. 168)
- Among the major categories of reinforcement schedules are fixed- and variable-ratio schedules, which are based on the number of responses made, and fixed- and variable-interval schedules, which are based on the time interval that elapses before reinforcement is provided. (p. 169)
- Generalization and discrimination operate in operant conditioning as well as classical conditioning. (p. 170)

- Superstitious behaviour results from the mistaken belief that particular ideas, objects, or behaviour will cause certain events to occur. (p. 171)
- There are biological constraints, or built-in limitations, on the ability of an organism to learn. Because of these constraints, certain behaviours will be relatively easy to learn, whereas other behaviours will be either difficult or impossible to learn. (p. 171)

What is the role of cognition and thought in learning?

- Cognitive approaches consider learning in terms of thought processes or cognition. Phenomena such as latent learning—in which a new behaviour is learned but not performed until reinforcement is provided for its performance—and the apparent development of cognitive maps support cognitive approaches. Learning also occurs through observation of the behaviour of models. (p. 173)
- The major factor that determines whether an observed behaviour will actually be performed is the nature of reinforcement or punishment a model receives. (p. 175)
- Learning styles are characteristic ways of approaching material, based on a person's cultural background and unique pattern of abilities. It is hoped that developing educational strategies that take this into account will impact favourably on Aboriginal student retention. (p. 178)

What are some practical methods for bringing about behaviour change, both in ourselves and in others?

- Behaviour modification is a method for formally using the principles of learning theory to promote the frequency of desired behaviours and to decrease or eliminate unwanted ones. (p. 180)

Key Terms and Concepts

learning (p. 156)
classical conditioning (p. 157)
neutral stimulus (p. 157)
unconditioned stimulus (UCS) (p. 157)
unconditioned response (UCR) (p. 157)
conditioned stimulus (CS) (p. 157)
conditioned response (CR) (p. 157)
extinction (p. 159)
spontaneous recovery (p. 160)
stimulus generalization (p. 160)
stimulus discrimination (p. 160)
operant conditioning (p. 162)
reinforcement (p. 164)
reinforcer (p. 164)
positive reinforcer (p. 165)

negative reinforcer (p. 166)
punishment (p. 166)
shaping (p. 168)
schedules of reinforcement (p. 168)
continuous reinforcement schedule (p. 168)
partial reinforcement schedule (p. 168)
fixed-ratio schedule (p. 169)
variable-ratio schedule (p. 170)
fixed-interval schedule (p. 170)
variable-interval schedule (p. 170)
cognitive learning theory (p. 173)
latent learning (p. 174)
cognitive map (p. 175)
observational learning (p. 175)
behaviour modification (p. 180)

Psychology on the Web

1. B. F. Skinner had an impact on society and thought that is only hinted at in this chapter. Find additional information on the Web about Skinner's life and influence. See if you can find out about his ideas for an ideal, utopian society based on the principles of conditioning and behaviourism. Write a summary of what you find.

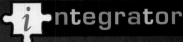

For extra help in mastering the material in this chapter, see the integrator, practice quizzes, and other resources on the Online Learning Centre at

www.mcgrawhill.ca/college/feldman

2. Select a topic discussed in this chapter that is of interest to you (e.g., superstition, teaching complex behaviours by shaping, violence in video games, behaviour modification, etc.). Find at least two sources of information on the Web about your topic and summarize the results of your quest. It may be most helpful to find two different approaches to your topic and compare them.

3. Behavioural therapy is based on learning theory. Aversive therapy derives from classical conditioning. Search the Web for examples of how aversive therapy is used. What are the ethical issues raised by this type of therapy especially as it concerns autistic children? What do you think about the use of this type of therapy?

Epilogue

In this chapter we have discussed several kinds of learning, ranging from classical conditioning, which depends on the existence of natural stimulus-response pairings, to operant conditioning, in which reinforcement is used to increase desired behaviour. These approaches to learning focus on outward, behavioural learning processes. We have also been introduced to more cognitive approaches to learning, which focus on mental processes and enable learning.

We have also noted that learning is affected by culture and individual differences, with individual learning styles potentially affecting the ways in which people learn most effectively. Finally, we saw some ways in which our learning about learning can be put to practical use, through such means as behaviour modification programs designed to decrease negative behaviours and increase positive ones.

Before proceeding to the next chapter—on memory—return to the prologue of this chapter and consider the following questions in relation to Pippa, the helpful dog who served Jean Little.

1. Is Pippa's learning primarily an example of classical conditioning, operant conditioning, or cognitive learning? Why?

2. Do you think punishment would be an effective teaching strategy for Pippa? Why?

3. In what way would shaping have been used to teach Pippa some of the more complex behaviours seeing-eye dogs must perform?

Chapter Six

Memory

THE UNKNOWN SOLDIER

Prologue

Philip Staufen: Man With No Past

In November 1999, a young man woke up in a Toronto hospital. On his wrist was a hospital bracelet with the name Philip Staufen and the birth date June 7, 1975. He was unable to talk or walk, and he had a broken nose. He didn't remember what had happened to cause his injuries; in fact, he didn't remember anything of his past. He was diagnosed with post-concussion global amnesia.

In June 2001, Philip Staufen still had not regained his memory. He wasn't even sure whether the name Philip Staufen and the birth date on the hospital bracelet were his. He was unemployed because he did not have a social insurance number. And he could not leave Canada to find work or search for his identity because the government dismissed his petition for a birth certificate.

As of August 2002, several suggestions had been made regarding Staufen's identity, but none of the leads put forward had been confirmed. No publicized solution or satisfactory conclusion to his story was available.

Looking Ahead

Philip Staufen's experience is certainly out of the ordinary. His story shocks, but it also reminds us that we often take memory for granted, forgetting the critical role it plays in our daily lives.

Stories like this illustrate not only the important role memory plays in our lives, but also its fragility. Memory allows us to retrieve a vast amount of information. We are able to remember the name of a friend we haven't talked with for years and to recall details of a picture that hung in our childhood bedroom. At the same time, though, memory failures are common. We forget where we left the keys to the car and fail to answer an exam question about material we studied only a few hours earlier.

In this chapter, we consider the nature of memory. We examine how information is stored and retrieved. We discuss approaches that suggest there are several separate types of memory, and we explain how each type is believed to function in a somewhat different fashion. We also consider the biological foundation of memory. We examine the problems of retrieving information from memory, the accuracy of memories, and the reasons information is sometimes forgotten. Finally, we discuss some practical means of increasing memory capacity.

Prepare

What is memory?
Are there different kinds of memory?
What are the biological bases of memory?

Organize

Encoding, Storage, and Retrieval of Memory
  Memory Storehouses
  Contemporary Approaches to Memory
  The Biological Bases of Memory

 **PsychLink**

Reports on memory
www.mcgrawhill.ca/college/feldman

memory: The process by which we encode, store, and retrieve information.

Encoding, Storage, and Retrieval of Memory

You are playing a game of Trivial Pursuit, and winning the game comes down to one question: On what body of water is Bombay located?

As you rack your brain for the answer, several fundamental processes relating to memory come into play. Perhaps you have never been exposed to information regarding Bombay's location, or if you have been exposed to it, perhaps it didn't register in a meaningful way. In other words, your difficulty in answering the question might be traced to the initial encoding stage of memory. *Encoding* refers to the process by which information is initially recorded in a form usable to memory.

On the other hand, even if you had been exposed to the information and originally knew the name of the body of water, you might still be unable to recall it during the game because of a failure in the retention process. Memory specialists speak of *storage,* the maintenance of material saved in the memory system. If the material is not stored adequately, it cannot be recalled later.

Memory also depends on a third process: retrieval. In *retrieval,* material in memory storage is located, brought into awareness, and used. Your failure to recall Bombay's location, then, could rest on your inability to retrieve information that you learned earlier.

In sum, psychologists consider **memory** as the process by which we encode, store, and retrieve information (see Figure 6-1). Each of the three parts of this definition—encoding, storage, and retrieval—represents a different process. You can think of these processes as analogous to the functions of a computer's keyboard (encoding), disk (storage), and screen (retrieval). Only if all three processes have operated will you experience success and be able to recall the body of water on which Bombay is located: the Arabian Sea.

However, before continuing, we should keep in mind the value of memory *failures.* Forgetting is essential to the proper functioning of memory. The ability to forget inconsequential details about experiences, people, and objects helps us to avoid being burdened and distracted by immense stores of meaningless data. Furthermore, forgetting permits us to form general impressions and recollections. For example, the reason our friends consistently look familiar to us is because of our ability to forget their clothing, facial blemishes, and other transient features that change from one occasion to the next. Instead, our memories are based on a summary of various critical features—a far more economical use of our memory capabilities. Forgetting unnecessary information, then, is as essential to the proper functioning of memory as is remembering more important material.

Figure 6–1 Memory is built on three basic processes—encoding, storage, and retrieval—that are analogous to the functions of a computer's keyboard, disk, and screen. The analogy is not perfect, however, because human memory is less precise than a computer's. How might you modify the analogy to make it more accurate?

Memory Storehouses: The Modal Model

One of the most influential theories of memory was developed by Atkinson and Shiffrin (1968, 1971). According to the Atkinson and Shiffrin model, memory consists of three memory storehouses and a set of processes that determine the transfer of information from one storehouse to another. The storehouses vary in terms of their capacity and the length of time they retain information. This model was so common and generated so much research that it has been called the *modal model* (Murdock, 1974).

As shown in Figure 6-2, the first storehouse, **sensory memory**, refers to the initial, momentary storage of information, lasting only an instant. Information is recorded by the person's sensory system as an exact replica of the stimulus. In a second storehouse or stage, **short-term memory** holds information for 15 to 25 seconds. The third storehouse is **long-term memory**. Information is stored in long-term memory on a relatively permanent basis, although it might be difficult to retrieve.

Although we'll be discussing the three types of memory as separate memory stores, keep in mind that these are not mini-warehouses located in particular portions of the brain. Instead, they represent three different types of memory systems with different characteristics. Furthermore, although the three-part model of memory dominated the field of memory research for several decades, recent studies have suggested several newer models, as we'll discuss later. Still, considering memory in terms of three major kinds of stores provides us with a useful framework for understanding how information is both recalled and forgotten.

sensory memory: The initial, momentary storage of information, lasting only an instant.

short-term memory: Memory that holds information for 15 to 25 seconds.

long-term memory: Memory that stores information on a relatively permanent basis.

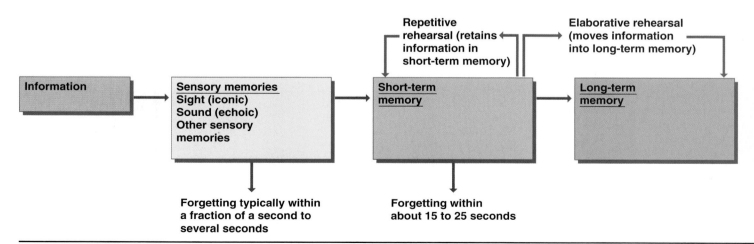

Figure 6–2 In this three-stage model of memory, information initially recorded by the person's sensory system enters sensory memory, which momentarily holds the information. It then moves to short-term memory, which stores the information for 15 to 25 seconds. Finally, the information can move into long-term memory, which is relatively permanent. Whether the information moves from short-term to long-term memory depends on the kind and amount of rehearsal of the material that is carried out (After Atkinson & Shifrin, 1968).

PsychLink

Theory of sensory memory
www.mcgrawhill.ca/college/feldman

iconic memory: Memory of information from our visual system.
echoic memory: Memory of auditory information coming from the ears.

Sensory Memory

A momentary flash of lightning, the sound of a twig snapping, and the sting of a pinprick all represent stimulation of exceedingly brief duration, but they might nonetheless provide important information that can require some response. Such stimuli are initially—and briefly—stored in sensory memory, the first repository of the information that the world presents to us. Actually, the term *sensory memory* denotes several types of sensory memories, each related to a different source of sensory information. There is **iconic memory**, which reflects information from our visual system; **echoic memory**, which stores auditory information coming from the ears; and corresponding memories for each of the other senses.

Regardless of the individual subtypes, sensory memory in general is able to store information for only a very short time. If information does not pass to short-term memory, it is lost for good. For instance, iconic memory lasts for one-quarter to one-third of a second, although if the initial stimulus is very bright, the image might last a little longer. Echoic memory typically fades within two or three seconds. However, despite the brief duration of sensory memory, its precision is high: Sensory memory can store an almost exact replica of each stimulus to which it is exposed (Darwin, Turvey, & Crowder, 1972; Long & Beaton, 1982; Sams et al., 1993).

If the storage in sensory memory is so brief, it would seem almost impossible to find evidence for its existence; new information would constantly be replacing older information, even before a person could report its presence. Not until psychologist George Sperling (1960) conducted a series of clever and now-classic studies was sensory memory well understood. Sperling briefly exposed people to a series of 12 letters arranged in the following pattern:

$$\begin{matrix} F & T & Y & C \\ K & D & N & L \\ Y & W & B & M \end{matrix}$$

When exposed to this pattern of letters for just one-twentieth of a second, most people could accurately recall only four or five of the letters. Although they knew that they had seen more, the memory of these letters had faded by the time they reported the first few letters. It was possible, then, that the information had initially been accurately stored in sensory memory, but during the time it took to verbalize the first four or five letters the memory of the other letters faded.

To test that possibility, Sperling conducted an experiment in which a high, medium, or low tone sounded just after a person had been exposed to the full pattern of letters. People were told to report the letters in the highest line if a high tone were sounded, the middle line if the medium tone occurred, or the lowest line at the sound of the low tone. Because the tone occurred after the exposure, people had to rely on their memory to report the correct row.

A momentary flash of lightning leaves a sensory visual memory, a fleeting but exact replica of the stimulus that fades rapidly.

The results of the study clearly showed that people had been storing the complete pattern in memory. They were accurate in their recollection of the letters in the line that had been indicated by the tone, regardless of whether it was the top, middle, or bottom line. Obviously, *all* the lines they had seen had been stored in sensory memory. Despite its rapid loss, then, the information in sensory memory was an accurate representation of what people had seen.

By gradually lengthening the time between the presentation of the visual pattern and the tone, Sperling was able to determine with some accuracy the length of time that information was stored in sensory memory. The ability to recall a particular row of the pattern when a tone was sounded declined progressively as the period between visual exposure and tone increased. The decline continued with recall reaching chance level at about one-half of a second. Sperling concluded that the entire visual image was stored in sensory memory for one-quarter to one-third of a second.

In sum, sensory memory operates as a kind of snapshot that stores information—of a visual, auditory, or other sensory nature—for a brief moment in time. But it is as if each snapshot, immediately after being taken, is destroyed and replaced with a new one. Unless the information in the snapshot is transferred to some other type of memory, it is lost.

Short-Term Memory: Giving Memory Meaning

Because the information that is stored briefly in our sensory memory consists of representations of raw sensory stimuli, it is not meaningful to us. For us to make sense of it and to allow for the possibility of long-term retention, the information must be transferred to the next stage of memory, short-term memory.

The specific process by which sensory memories are transformed into short-term memories is not yet clear. Some theorists suggest that the information is first translated into graphical representations or images, and others hypothesize that the transfer occurs when the sensory stimuli are changed to words (Baddeley & Wilson, 1985). Information is held in short-term memory for about 15 to 25 seconds unless it is rehearsed. Craik and Lockhart (1972) refer to the deliberate repetition of information intended to maintain it in short-term memory as rote rehearsal or maintenance rehearsal. For example, if you look up a telephone number in a directory, and then have to walk across a room to get to a phone, you will probably repeat the number in your head (using an "inner voice") to maintain the number in short-term memory until you can make the phone call.

Another feature of short-term memory is that it has a very limited capacity. According to Miller (1956), the limit is seven (plus or minus two) items or "chunks" of information. A **chunk** is a meaningful grouping of stimuli that can be stored as a unit in short-term memory. Chunks could be individual letters, as in the following list:

CNQMWNT

But a chunk might also consist of larger categories, such as words or other meaningful units. For example, consider the following list of 21 letters:

CBCNAFTATVOCNBCTVRCMP

Because the list exceeds seven chunks, it is difficult to recall the letters after one exposure. But suppose they were presented to you as follows:

CBC NAFTA TVO CN BCTV RCMP

In this case, even though there are still 21 letters, you'd be able to store them in short-term memory, because they represent only six chunks.

Chunks can vary in size from single letters or numbers to categories that are far more complicated. The specific nature of what constitutes a chunk varies according to one's past experience. You can see this for yourself by trying an experiment that was first carried out as a comparison between expert and inexperienced chess players, illustrated in Chapter Activity 6-1 (deGroot, 1966; Schneider et al., 1993; Gobet & Simon, 1996).

An artist must repeatedly view the subject of a painting in order to capture the image as viewed, using both short-term and long-term memory.

Why do you think people tend to close their eyes when recalling a scene or picture?

 **PsychLink**

Short-term memory demonstration
www.mcgrawhill.ca/college/feldman

chunk: A meaningful grouping of stimuli that can be stored as a unit in short-term memory.

Chapter Activity 6–1 Chunks in Memory

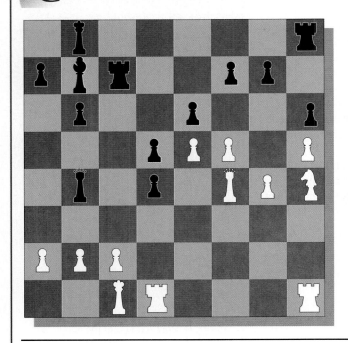

FIGURE 6-3 Examine the chessboard containing the chess pieces for about five seconds. Then, after covering up the board, try to reproduce the position of the pieces on the blank chessboard. Unless you are an experienced chess player, you are likely to have great difficulty carrying out such a task. Yet chess masters—the kind who win tournaments—do quite well (deGroot, 1966). They are able to reproduce correctly 90 percent of the pieces on the board. In comparison, inexperienced chess players are typically able to reproduce only 40 percent of the board properly. The chess masters do not have superior memories in other respects; they generally test normally on other measures of memory. What they can do better than others is see the board in terms of chunks or meaningful units and reproduce the position of the chess pieces by using these units.

Rehearsal

Although it is possible to remember seven or so relatively complicated sets of information entering short-term memory, the information, as indicated above, does not last there for long without rehearsal. According to University of Toronto memory researchers Craik and Lockhart (1972), there are two kinds of **rehearsal**: repetition rehearsal and elaborative rehearsal. *Repetition rehearsal* keeps information active in short-term memory. Consider again the earlier example of repeating a phone number while walking from a phone directory to a telephone. This repetition keeps the number current in short-term memory, but it will not necessarily transfer it to long-term memory. As soon as we stop dialing, the number is likely to be replaced by other information and will be completely forgotten.

Elaborative rehearsal, on the other hand, effectively transfers information to long-term memory. As the name implies, the process of elaborative rehearsal involves elaborating on material by working with or processing its meaning. It occurs when the material is considered and organized. Organizing the information might include expanding it to make it fit a logical framework, linking it to another memory, or transforming it in some other way. For example, a list of vegetables to be purchased at a store could be woven together in memory as items being used to prepare a salad; they could be linked to an earlier shopping trip, or they could be thought of in terms of the farm where they were grown. The concept of elaboration will be considered in more detail later in the chapter in the section on levels-of-processing theory.

rehearsal: The repetition or elaboration of information that has entered short-term memory.

We can deliberately organize material in a way that increases the likelihood that it will be remembered. By using organizational strategies called *mnemonics* (pronounced "neh MON ix"), we can vastly improve our retention of information. For instance, when a beginning musician learns that the spaces on the music staff spell the word *FACE*, or when we learn the rhyme "Thirty days hath September, April, June, and November...," we are using mnemonics (Mastropieri & Scruggs, 1991; Bellezza, Six, & Phillips, 1992; Schoen, 1996; Goldstein et al., 1996; Carney et al., 2000).

Long-Term Memory: The Final Storehouse

Material that makes its way from short-term memory to long-term memory enters a storehouse of almost unlimited capacity. Like a new file we save on our hard drive, the information in long-term memory is filed and coded so that we can retrieve it when we need it.

Evidence of the existence of long-term memory, as distinct from short-term memory, comes from a number of sources. For example, people with certain kinds of brain damage have no lasting recall of new information following the damage, although information about people and events stored in memory prior to the injury remains intact (Milner, 1966). Because information that was encoded and stored before the injury can be recalled and because short-term memory following the injury appears to be operational—new material can be recalled for a very brief period—we can infer that there are two distinct types of memory, one for short-term and one for long-term storage.

Results from laboratory experiments are also consistent with the notion of separate short- and long-term memories. For example, in one set of studies people were asked to recall a relatively small amount of information (such as a set of three letters). Then, to prevent practice of the initial information, participants were required to recite some extraneous material aloud, such as counting backward by threes (Brown, 1958; Peterson & Peterson, 1959). By varying the amount of time between presentation of the initial material and the need for its recall, investigators found that recall was quite good when the interval was very short but declined rapidly thereafter. After 15 seconds had gone by, recall hovered at around 10 percent of the material initially presented.

Apparently the distraction of counting backward prevented almost all the initial material from reaching long-term memory. Initial recall was good because it was coming from short-term memory, but these memories were lost at a rapid rate. Eventually, all that could be recalled was the small amount of material that had made its way into long-term storage despite the distraction of counting backward.

 **PsychLink**

Long-term memory article
www.mcgrawhill.ca/college/feldman

Contemporary Approaches to Memory: Working Memory, Levels of Processing, Long-Term Memory Modules, and Associative Models of Memory

So far, we have relied on the traditional model of memory, which suggests that the processing of information in memory proceeds in three sequential stages: starting with sensory memory, advancing to short-term memory, and potentially ending in long-term memory. However, many contemporary approaches suggest that this traditional model provides an incomplete account of memory. For instance, rather than information being processed sequentially from sensory to short-term to long-term memory stores (a *serial* process), increasing evidence suggests that the brain processes information simultaneously in different memory components (a *parallel* process). These views are exemplified by the approaches to short- and long-term memory that we consider next.

Working Memory

Rather than seeing short-term memory as an independent way-station through which memories travel, some theorists conceive of short-term memory as an information-processing system known as working memory. **Working memory** is an active "workspace" in which information is retrieved and manipulated, and in which information is held through rehearsal (Baddeley, 1992, 1993, 1995a, 1995b; see Figure 6-4).

In this view, working memory contains a *central executive* processor, which is involved in reasoning and decision making. The central executive coordinates two distinct storage-and-rehearsal systems: the visual store and the verbal store. The *visual store* specializes in visual and spatial information, and the *verbal store* is responsible for holding and manipulating material relating to speech, words, and numbers (Della Sala et al., 1995; Baddeley, 1996; Logie & Gilhooly, 1998).

Working memory permits us to briefly maintain information in an active state so that we can do something with the information. For instance, we use working memory when we're doing a multistep arithmetic problem in our heads, storing the result of one calculation while getting ready to move to the next stage. We make use of working memory when we look at the price tag on something, calculate the sales tax, and then the total we will have to pay.

Some researchers suspect that a breakdown in the central executive might result in the memory losses that are characteristic of Alzheimer's disease, the progressively degenerative disorder that produces loss of memory and confusion (Cherry, Buckwalter, & Henderson, 1996). (We'll discuss Alzheimer's disease and other memory disorders at greater length later in this chapter.)

Levels of Processing

According to **levels-of-processing theory**, memory reflects the thoroughness with which new material is analyzed (Craik & Lockhart, 1972; Craik, 1990). Processing exists on a continuum from shallow (superficial) to deeper (thorough) levels of analysis. Because we do not pay close attention to much of the information to which we are exposed, typically only shallow processing takes place, and we forget the material almost immediately. However, information to which we pay greater attention is processed more thoroughly and is more likely to be remembered.

Characteristic types of analysis are associated with three levels of processing (Craik & Tulving, 1975). At shallow levels, information is processed in terms of its physical and sensory aspects. For example, if we are required to decide whether a word appears in

working memory: An active "workspace" in which information is retrieved and manipulated, and in which information is held through rehearsal.

levels-of-processing theory: The theory of memory that emphasizes the degree to which new material is mentally analyzed.

Figure 6-4 Working memory is an active "workspace" in which information is retrieved and manipulated, and in which information is held through rehearsal (Gathercole & Baddeley, 1993). It consists of a "central executive" that coordinates the visual store (which concentrates on visual and spatial information) and the verbal store (concentrating on speech, words, and numbers).

How are you using your working memory as you read?

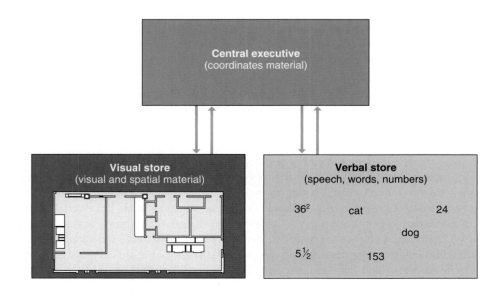

uppercase or lowercase letters we attend only to the physical characteristics; the processing is shallow and the associated recall is poor. On the other hand, if we have to decide whether one word rhymes with another word, we analyze it acoustically at an intermediate level of processing. For instance, when processing the word *dog* at an intermediate level, we may note that it rhymes with *fog* but not with *car*. At the deepest level, information is analyzed semantically in terms of its meaning and its associations with other related concepts. When processing *dog* semantically at the deepest level, we may think about various breeds of dogs or ways in which dogs are similar to or different from cats.

In short, the main idea of levels-of-processing theory is that memory depends on how material has been processed.

The ability to remember specific skills and the order in which they are used is known as procedural memory.
If driving involves our procedural memory, is it safe to use a cell phone while driving?

Long-Term Memory Modules

Although long-term memory was initially viewed as a single entity, most research now suggests that it is composed of different components, memory modules, or systems. For instance, some researchers have distinguished between declarative and nondeclarative memory (Eichenbaum, 1997; Schacter, Wagner, & Buckner, 2000). **Declarative memory** is memory for factual information: names, faces, dates, and the like. Information or knowledge about the world is stored in declarative memory. It includes both general knowledge of the sort acquired through schooling (*semantic memory*), and more personal knowledge such as information about events we have experienced personally (*episodic memory*). In contrast, **nondeclarative memory** is memory for skills, habits, and the products of conditioning. Memory for acquired skills such as how to ride a bike is called *procedural memory*. Information about things is stored in declarative memory; information regarding how to do things is stored in nondeclarative memory.

Endel Tulving (1985, 1993, 2000), a University of Toronto memory researcher, has conceptualized episodic, semantic, and procedural memories as three distinct memory systems that have evolved over time. In his view, **procedural memory** is the most basic system because it involves "blueprints" for behaviours that allow any organism that can learn to adapt to the environment. **Semantic memory** is more specialized knowledge of the world. **Episodic memory** is the most specialized, since it involves memories for specific episodes in the past that have personal relevance. Our memories of what we have done and the kinds of experiences we have had constitute episodic memory. Consequently, when we recall our first date, the time we fell off our bicycle, or what we felt like when we graduated from high school, we are recalling episodic memories. Figure 6-5 shows the different types of long-term memory.

Episodic memories can be surprisingly detailed. Consider, for instance, how you'd respond if you were asked to identify what you were doing on a specific day two years ago. Impossible? You might think otherwise as you read the following exchange between a researcher and a participant in a study who was asked, in a memory experiment, what he was doing "on Monday afternoon in the third week of September two years ago."

> PARTICIPANT: Come on. How should I know?
> EXPERIMENTER: Just try it anyhow.
> PARTICIPANT: OK. Let's see: Two years ago . . . I would be in high school in Pittsburgh. . . . That would be my senior year. Third week in September—that's just after summer—that would be the fall term. . . . Let me see. I think I had chemistry lab on Mondays. I don't know. I was probably in chemistry lab. Wait a minute—that would be the second week of school. I remember he started off with the atomic table—a big

declarative memory: Memory for factual information: names, faces, dates, and the like; information about things.
nondeclarative memory: Memory for skills, habits, and the products of conditioning; information about how to do things.
procedural memory: Memory for skills and habits, such as riding a bike or hitting a baseball.

semantic memory: Memory for general knowledge and facts about the world, as well as memory for the rules of logic that are used to deduce other facts.
episodic memory: Memory for the biographical details of our individual lives.

In addition to procedural memory, driving a car also involves what is known as declarative or explicit memory, which permits us to remember how to get to our destination.

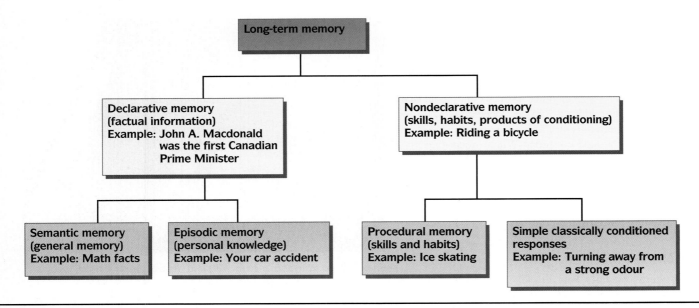

Figure 6-5 Long-term memory can be subdivided into several different types. What type of long-term memory is involved in your recollection of the moment you first arrived on your campus at the start of college?

fancy chart. I thought he was crazy trying to make us memorize that thing. You know, I think I can remember sitting . . . (Lindsay & Norman, 1977)

Episodic memory, then, can provide information from events that happened long in the past (Reynolds & Takooshian, 1988). But semantic memory is no less impressive, permitting us to dredge up tens of thousands of facts ranging from the date of our birthday to the knowledge that $1 is less than $5.

Associative Models of Memory

Our ability to recall detailed information has led some memory researchers to view memory primarily in terms of associations between different pieces of information. **Associative models of memory** suggest that memory consists of mental representations of clusters of interconnected information (e.g., Collins & Quillian, 1969; Collins & Loftus, 1975).

Consider, for example, Figure 6-6, which shows some of the relationships in memory relating to the concept "animal." Associative memory models suggest that thinking about a particular concept leads to recall of related concepts. For example, seeing a bird in the distance could activate our recollections of "robin," which in turn might activate recall of related concepts such as "eats worms" and "has a red breast." Activating one memory triggers the activation of related memories in a process known as *spreading activation*.

According to Murdock (1974, 1999), memory depends on our use of three types of information: order, item, and associative. For example, when we try to identify people in an old school photo, we use order information about when the event pictured occurred. We use item information about the specific identities of the people in the photograph. In addition, we use more general information that we may associate with the people and event pictured. In our effort to remember the people in the photograph, we integrate the three types of information.

Associative memory models help account for **priming**, a phenomenon in which exposure to a word or concept (called a *prime*) later makes it easier to recall related information. The typical experiment designed to illustrate priming helps clarify the phenomenon. In priming experiments, participants are rapidly exposed to a stimulus such as

associative models of memory: Models suggesting that memory consists of mental representations of clusters of interconnected information.

priming: A phenomenon in which exposure to a word or concept (called a *prime*) later makes it easier to recall related information, even when one has no conscious memory of the word or concept.

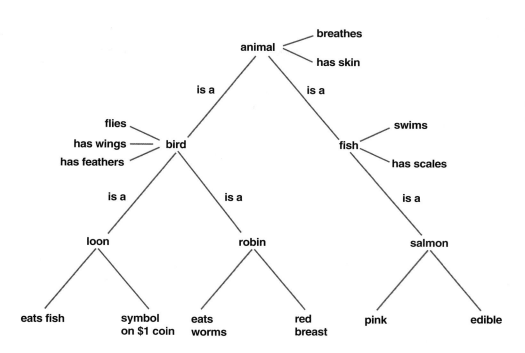

Figure 6-6 Associative models suggest that semantic memory consists of relationships between pieces of information, such as those relating to the concept of "animal," shown in this figure (After Collins & Quillian, 1969).

a word, an object, or perhaps a drawing of a face. The second phase of the experiment is held after an interval ranging from several seconds to several months. At that point, participants are exposed to incomplete perceptual information that is related to the first stimulus, and they are asked whether they recognize it. For example, the new material might consist of the first letter of a word that had been presented earlier, or a part of a face that had been shown earlier. If participants are able to identify the stimulus more readily than they identify stimuli that have not been presented earlier, priming has taken place.

Priming occurs even when participants report no conscious awareness of having been exposed to a stimulus earlier (Tulving & Schacter, 1990; Toth & Reingold, 1996; Schacter, 1998). For instance, studies have found that people who are anesthetized during surgery can sometimes recall snippets of information that they heard during surgery—even though they have no conscious recollection of the information (Kihlstrom et al., 1990; Sebel, Bonke, & Winogard, 1993; Merikle & Daneman, 1996).

The discovery that people have memories about which they are unaware has been an important one. It has led to speculation that two forms of memory, explicit and implicit, might exist side-by-side. **Explicit memory** refers to intentional or conscious recollection of information. When we try to remember a name or date that we have encountered or learned about previously, we are using explicit memory. In contrast, **implicit memory** refers to memories people are not consciously aware of, but that can affect their subsequent performance and behaviour. Skills that operate automatically and without thinking, such as jumping out of the path of an automobile coming toward us as we walk down the side of a road, are stored in implicit memory. Similarly, a feeling of vague dislike for an acquaintance, when we don't know why we have that feeling, could be a reflection of implicit memories. Our expectations and behaviour after surgery may reflect a conversation that occurred in the operating room when we were anesthetized. There have been some studies on this issue, but the results are not conclusive (Merikle & Daneman, 1996, 1998; Schacter, 1996). In short, when an event that we are unable to consciously recall affects our behaviour, implicit memory is at work (Graf & Masson, 1993; Schacter, Chiu, & Ochsner, 1993; Schacter, 1994, 1995; Underwood, 1996; Tulving, 2000).

explicit memory: Intentional or conscious recollection of information.

implicit memory: Memories people are not consciously aware of, but that can affect their subsequent performance and behaviour.

Implicit memory issues
www.mcgrawhill.ca/college/feldman

The Multiple Models of Memory

We've seen that the way that memory is viewed has been expanded from the three-stage model of memory. Although the traditional view of memory has not been rejected, contemporary views take a broader approach, considering memory in terms of multiple interdependent systems, operating simultaneously, that are responsible for different types of recall. Moreover, greater emphasis has been placed on working memory, in an effort to determine how different types of information can be simultaneously stored and processed.

You might be asking which of these views of memory is most accurate. It's a fair question, but one that is not easily answered at this point. More than most areas of psychology, memory has attracted a great deal of theorizing, and it is probably too early to tell—let alone remember—which of the multiple models proposed by different memory psychologists gives us the most accurate characterization of memory (Collins et al., 1993; Searleman & Herrmann, 1994; Wolters, 1995; Bjork & Bjork, 1996; Conway, 1997). All of the models of memory discussed so far were developed by psychologists working within the cognitive perspective. In the last part of the section on contemporary approaches to memory, we will turn our attention to memory studied from the biological perspective.

The Biological Bases of Memory

What are the biological foundations of memory? One answer comes from work on *long-term potentiation*, which shows that certain neural pathways become easily excited while a new response is being learned. At the same time, changes occur in the number of synapses between neurons as the dendrites branch out to receive messages. These changes reflect a process called *consolidation*, in which memories become fixed and stable in long-term memory. Consolidation takes time; it can continue for days and even years (Johnston, 1997; McGaugh, 2000).

The location of *memory traces*, the physical record of memory in the brain, depends on the nature of the material being learned and the specific neural systems that process it. Information storage seems to be linked to sites where processing occurs. A stimulus is processed in terms of its sensory aspects (e.g., visual, auditory, and tactile) by several processing systems, and the resultant memory traces are distributed throughout the brain (Desimone, 1992; Squire, 1993; Brewer et al., 1998).

A study by Petersen and Fiez (1993) illustrates the activation of several brain areas during a simple task. Participants were given a list of nouns, and were required to read each one aloud, and after doing so, to respond with a related verb. For example, after reading *dog*, a person might respond *bark*. The brain areas activated during this experiment are shown in the left and right PET scans in Figure 6-7. When the task was repeated using the same nouns several times, the areas of activation shifted, as the middle PET scan shows. These findings suggest that memory also is distributed in the brain in terms of its function.

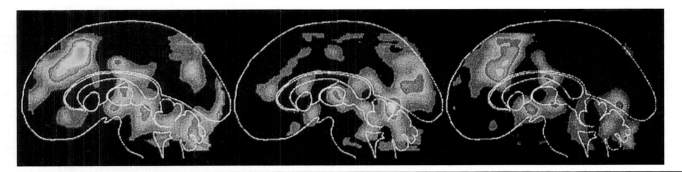

Figure 6-7 PET scans of a subject in an experiment who was first asked to read a list of nouns and produce a related verb (*left scan*). When asked to carry out the task repeatedly with the same list of nouns, different areas of the brain became active (*centre*). However, when the subject was given a new list of nouns, the regions of the brain that were initially involved became reactivated (*right*) (Peterson, 1993).

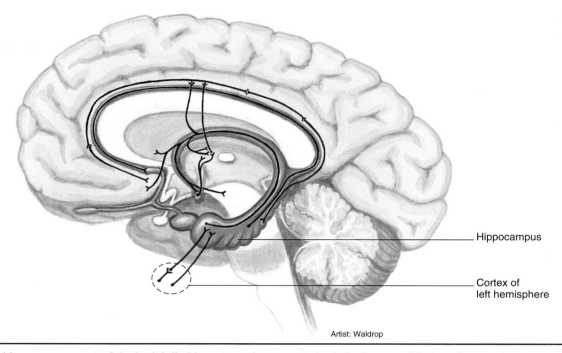

Hippocampus

Cortex of
left hemisphere

Artist: Waldrop

Figure 6-8 The hippocampus, part of the brain's limbic system, plays a central role in the consolidation of memories.
After K. Van De Graaff. Copyright © The McGraw-Hill Companies.

Certain areas and structures in the brain seem to specialize in different types of memory activities. For example, working memory related to spatial tasks appears to reside in the frontal cortex (Smith & Jonides, 1999; Smith, 2000). The frontal lobes are involved in searches for information with a temporal organization (Smith, 1985, as cited in Milner, Petrides, & Smith, 1985). The frontal lobes also guide other retrieval searches and the organization of retrieval output (Moscovitch, 1992, 1994). Retrieval of contextual information (such as where, when, and how something occurred) depends on the frontal lobes, whereas retrieval of items (such as faces) depends on the temporal lobes (Cabeza et al., 1997; Graham & Cabeza, 2001). In addition to encoding faces, the right temporal lobes are important in learning and recalling spatial locations and in memory for music and its characteristics. The left temporal lobes are involved in processing speech sounds and recalling verbal material (Smith & Bigel, 2000). The hippocampus (see Figure 6-8) is involved in both initial encoding and consolidation of memories (Tulving & Craik, 2000; Burgess et al., 2001).

Evaluate

1. Match the type of memory with its definition:
   1. Long-term memory
   2. Short-term memory
   3. Sensory memory

   a. Holds information 15 to 25 seconds
   b. Relatively permanent storage
   c. Direct representation of a stimulus

2. A _____ is a meaningful group of stimuli that can be stored together in short-term memory.

3. _____ are strategies used to organize information for retrieval.

4. There appear to be two types of long-term memory: _____ memory, for knowledge and facts, and _____ memory, for skills, habits, and conditioned responses.

5. _____ models of memory state that long-term memory is stored as associations between pieces of information.

Rethink

1. It is a truism that "you never forget how to ride a bicycle." Why might this be so? Where is information about bicycle riding stored? What happens when a person has to retrieve that information after not using it for a long time?

2. Priming often occurs without conscious awareness. How might this effect be used by advertisers and others to promote their products? What ethical principles are involved? Can you think of a way to protect yourself from unethical advertisers?

Answers to Evaluate Questions

1. 1-b; 2-a; 3-c 2. chunk 3. Mnemonics 4. declarative; nondeclarative 5. Associative

Recalling Long-Term Memories

An hour after his job interview, Ricardo was sitting in a coffee shop, telling his friend Laura how well it had gone, when the woman who had interviewed him walked in. "Well, hello, Ricardo. How are you doing?" Trying to make a good impression, Ricardo began to make introductions, but suddenly realized he could not remember the name of the interviewer. Stammering, he desperately searched his memory, but to no avail. "I *know* her name," he thought to himself, "but here I am, looking like a fool. I can kiss this job goodbye."

Have you ever tried to remember someone's name, convinced that you knew it, but were unable to recall it no matter how hard you tried? This common occurrence—known as the **tip-of-the-tongue phenomenon**—exemplifies the difficulties that can occur in retrieving information stored in long-term memory (Smith, 1994; Riefer, Keveri, & Kramer, 1995; Schwartz et al., 2000).

Retrieval Cues

tip-of-the-tongue phenomenon: The inability to recall information that one realizes one knows—a result of the difficulty of retrieving information from long-term memory.

One reason recall is not perfect is the sheer quantity of recollections stored in long-term memory. Although the issue is far from settled, many psychologists have suggested that the material that makes its way to long-term memory is relatively permanent (Tulving & Psotka, 1971). If they are correct, this suggests that the capacity of long-term memory is vast, given the broad range of people's experiences and educational backgrounds. For instance, if you are like the average college student, your vocabulary includes some 50 000 words, you know hundreds of mathematical "facts," and you are able to conjure up images—such as the way your childhood home looked—with no trouble at all. In fact, simply cataloguing all your memories would probably take years of work.

How do we sort through this vast array of material and retrieve specific information at the appropriate time? One of the major ways is through the use of retrieval cues. A *retrieval cue* is a stimulus that allows us to recall more easily information that is located in long-term memory (Tulving & Thompson, 1973; Ratcliff & McKoon, 1989). It could be a word, an emotion, a sound; whatever the specific cue, a memory will suddenly come to mind when the retrieval cue is present. For example, the smell of roasting turkey might evoke memories of Thanksgiving or family gatherings (Schab & Crowder, 1995).

Retrieval cues guide people through the information stored in long-term memory in much the same way as the cards in an old-fashioned card catalogue guided people through a library, or a search engine like Yahoo! guides people through the World Wide Web. They are particularly important when we are making an effort to *recall* information, as opposed to being asked to *recognize* material stored in memory. In *recall,* a specific piece of information must be retrieved—such as that needed to answer a fill-in-the-blank question or write an essay on a test. In contrast, *recognition* occurs when people are presented with a stimulus and asked whether they have been exposed to it previously, or are asked to identify it from a list of alternatives.

As you might guess, recall is generally a more difficult task than recognition (the task in Chapter Activity 6-2 is more difficult than the task in Chapter Activity 6-3). Recall is more difficult because it consists of a series of processes: a search through memory, retrieval of potentially relevant information, and then a decision regarding whether or not the information you have found is accurate. If the information appears correct, the search is over, but if it does not, the search must continue. The facility with which we recall information is extremely important. For instance, it is critical in our ability to comprehend textbooks like

The tip-of-the-tongue phenomenon is especially frustrating in situations in which a person cannot recall the name of someone he or she has just met. **Can you think of ways to avoid this common occurrence?**

Chapter Activity 6–2
Recall

FIGURE 6-9 Try to recall the names of these characters. Because it is a recall task, it is relatively difficult.

this one (Hannon & Daneman, 2001a, 2001b). It is also the key to proficiency in mental arithmetic (Hewlett, 2001). On the other hand, recognition is simpler because it involves fewer steps (Anderson & Bower, 1972; Miserando, 1991).

Encoding Processes

The use of retrieval cues assumes we have the information in memory. But what if we never encoded it in the first place? If we didn't, obviously we will have no memory to retrieve. As you read the preceding page, did you pay enough attention to really process the information? Recall the levels-of-processing theory discussed earlier: If you really thought about the text as you read it, chances are you will recall the information quite well.

Levels-of-processing theory has considerable practical implications. For example, the depth at which information is processed (or *encoded*) is critical when learning and studying course material. Rote memorization of a list of key terms for a test is unlikely to produce long-term recollection of information, because it involves only a shallow level of processing or encoding. In contrast, thinking about the meanings of the terms and reflecting on how they relate to other information you know (semantic encoding) is a far more effective route to long-term retention.

Answer this recognition question:

Which of the following are the names of the seven dwarfs in the Disney movie *Snow White and the Seven Dwarfs*?

Goofy	Bashful
Sleepy	Meanie
Smarty	Doc
Scaredy	Happy
Dopey	Angry
Grumpy	Sneezy
Wheezy	Crazy

Chapter Activity 6–3
Recognize

FIGURE 6-10 The recognition problem posed on the left is considerably easier than the recall task in the previous activity.

 PsychLink
Role of flashbulb memories
www.mcgrawhill.ca/college/feldman

flashbulb memories: Memories of a specific, important, or surprising event that are so vivid, they are like a snapshot of the event.

Flashbulb Memories

Where were you on September 11, 2001? You may draw a blank until this piece of information is added: that was the day that terrorists attacked the World Trade Center in New York City and the Pentagon in Washington, D.C.

You probably have little trouble recalling your exact location and a variety of trivial details about your surroundings when you heard the news. The reason is a phenomenon known as flashbulb memory. **Flashbulb memories** are memories of a specific, important, or surprising event that are so vivid, they are like a snapshot of the event.

Several types of flashbulb memories are common among college students, including involvement in a car accident, meeting one's roommate for the first time, and the night of high school graduation (Rubin, 1985; see Chapter Activity 6-4).

Of course, flashbulb memories do not contain every detail of an original scene. For instance, you may recall your exact location and what you were doing when you first heard the news that planes had crashed into the World Trade Center in New York on September 11, 2001. But you may not remember the name of the news reporter from whom you first heard the news.

Flashbulb memories illustrate a more general phenomenon about memory: Memories that are exceptional are more easily retrieved (although not necessarily accurately) than those relating to events that are commonplace. The more distinctive a stimulus, then, the more likely we are to recall it later (von Restorff, 1933; Winningham, Hyman, & Dinnel, 2000).

Chapter Activity 6–4
Recall Flashbulb Memories

FIGURE 6-11 These are the most common flashbulb memories, based on a survey of American college students (Rubin, 1985). Make a list of some of your own flashbulb memories. What characteristics of flashbulb memories do they possess?

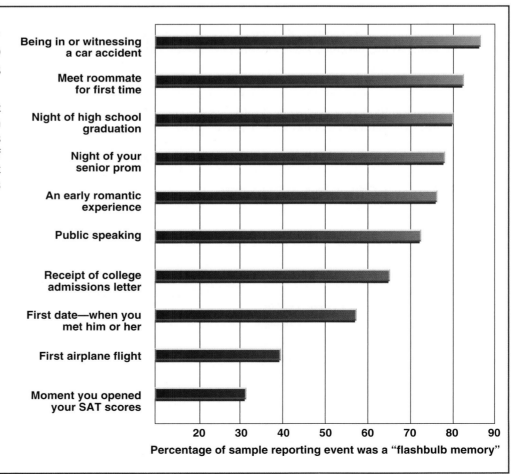

Constructive Processes in Memory: Rebuilding the Past

As we have seen, although it is clear that we can have detailed recollections of significant and distinctive events, it is difficult to gauge the accuracy of such memories. In fact, it is apparent that our memories reflect, at least in part, **constructive processes**, processes in which memories are influenced by the meaning that we give to events. When we retrieve information, then, the memory that is produced is affected not just by the direct prior experience we have had with the stimulus, but by our guesses and inferences about its meaning as well.

The notion that memory is based on constructive processes was first put forward by Sir Frederic Bartlett, a British psychologist. He suggested that people tend to remember information in terms of **schemas**, organized bodies of information stored in memory that bias the way new information is interpreted, stored, and recalled (Bartlett, 1932). Our reliance on schemas means that memories often consist of a general reconstruction of previous experience. Bartlett argued that schemas are based not only on the specific material to which people are exposed, but also on their understanding of the situation, their expectations about the situation, and their awareness of the motivations underlying the behaviour of others.

One of the earliest demonstrations of schemas came from a classic study that involved a procedure similar to the children's game of "telephone," in which information from memory is passed sequentially from one person to another. In the study, a participant viewed a drawing of a variety of people of differing racial and ethnic backgrounds on a subway car, one of whom—a white person—was shown with a razor in his hand (Allport & Postman, 1958). The first participant was asked to describe the drawing to someone else without looking back at it. Then that person was asked to describe it to another person (without looking at the drawing), and then the process was repeated with still one more participant.

The report of the last person differed in significant, yet systematic, ways from the initial drawing. Specifically, many people described the drawing as depicting a black person with a knife—an incorrect recollection. The transformation of the Caucasian's razor into an a black person's knife clearly indicates that participants held a schema that included the unwarranted prejudice that blacks are more violent than Caucasians and thus more apt to be holding a knife.

In short, our expectations and knowledge affect the reliability of our memories (Katz, 1989; Ross & Newby, 1996; McDonald & Hirt, 1997). Sometimes the imperfections of people's recollections can have profound implications, as we see when we consider memory in the legal realm.

Memory in the Courtroom: The Eyewitness on Trial

The inadequate memories of witnesses cost Thomas Sophonow four years of his life. It was a case of mistaken identity; witnesses said they saw Sophonow flee from the doughnut shop where 16-year-old Barbara Stopppel was murdered in 1981. After three trials and two convictions, he was released in 1985. But it was not until June 2000 that the Winnipeg police announced that the results of recent DNA tests cleared Sophonow of suspicion.

Guy Paul Morin was sentenced to life imprisonment in 1992 for the murder of Christine Jessop. Among the factors that contributed to his wrongful conviction was the fact that the victim's mother mistakenly identified a voice crying for help outside her home as belonging to Morin. The prosecution claimed that the cry for help was motivated by Morin's feelings of guilt. Morin, like Sophonow, was wrongfully convicted and later cleared on the basis of DNA evidence (Yarmey, 2001).

Unfortunately, Sophonow and Morin are only two of more than 20 individuals wrongfully convicted for serious crimes in Canada. Research on eyewitness identification of suspects, as well as on their memory for other details of crimes, has shown that witnesses are apt to make errors in recalling details of criminal activity (Miller, 2000; Wells et al., 2000). One finding that may seem surprising at first is that eyewitnesses are

constructive processes: Processes in which memories are influenced by the meaning we give to events.

schemas: Organized bodies of information stored in memory that bias the way new information is interpreted, stored, and recalled.

particularly likely to make misidentifications if the lineup does not contain individuals who are similar in appearance to the suspected culprit. If there are people who resemble the suspect in the lineup, witnesses may consider the identity much more carefully and therefore be less likely to make a mistake. Also, eyewitnesses tend to underestimate the influences of lighting and observation time on perception and memory for an event (Lindsay, 1994).

Elizabeth Loftus has argued that eyewitnesses recall, like other recall, is subject to the effects of reconstruction in memory (Loftus, 1979). In particular, Loftus demonstrated that the specific wording of questions can influence recall. In one experiment, participants were shown a film of two cars crashing into each other. Participants who were asked how fast the two cars were going when they *smashed* into each other gave faster estimates (an average of 65.7 kilometres per hour, or 40.8 miles per hour) than those asked how fast the cars were going when they *contacted* each other (51.2 kilometres per hour, or 31.8 miles per hour) (Loftus & Palmer, 1974; see Figure 6-12).

The wording of questions is particularly problematic when children are interviewed. Carole Peterson at Memorial University has found that preschoolers who watched a staged incident while taking part in craft activities were more accurate in answering Yes/No questions when the correct answer was yes than when it was no, indicating a response bias toward saying yes. No response bias was found on multiple choice questions. Children answered questions beginning with "what," "where," "when," and "who," which asked for specific details, with a high level of accuracy. Peterson and her colleagues also found that 2- to 11-year-old children remembered central details of an injury experience that required emergency hospital care better than less important details of the injury scene and the treatment (Peterson, 1999; Peterson & Whalen, 2001). These studies demonstrate that the accuracy of children's memories depends on the kind of information and the type of questions used. In a review of studies on children's memory for autobiographical events, Peterson (2001) concluded that children as young as two years of age can recall highly salient personal experiences when questioned appropriately, and that they need to be explicitly trained to say "I don't know" when that applies.

In her review of the literature on child witnesses, Andrea Welder (2000) at the University of Calgary concluded that children can give accurate and reliable testimony when interviewers use a warm and non-intimidating style to ask questions that are unbiased and open-ended. John Yuille at the University of British Columbia has also extensively

Figure 6-12 After viewing an accident involving two cars, subjects were asked to estimate the speed of the collision. Estimates varied substantially, depending on the way the question was worded (Loftus & Palmer, 1974). *Do you think the questions influenced encoding or retrieval of information about the accident?*

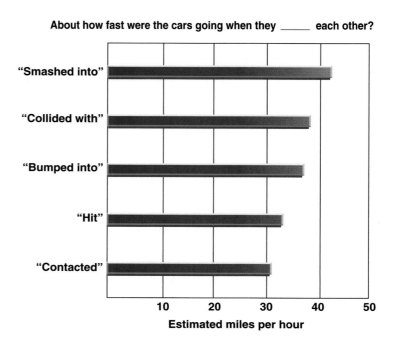

Applying Psychology in the 21st Century

Repressed Memories: Truth or Fiction?

Guilty of murder in the first degree.

That was the jury's verdict in the case of George Franklin, Sr., who was charged with murdering his daughter's playmate. But this case was different from most other murder cases: It was based on memories that had been repressed for 20 years. Franklin's daughter claimed that she had forgotten everything she had once known about her father's crime until two years earlier, when she began to have flashbacks of the event. Gradually, though, the memories became clearer in her mind, until she recalled her father lifting a rock over his head and then seeing her friend lying on the ground, covered with blood. On the basis of her memories, her father was convicted—but then later cleared of the crime following an appeal of the conviction.

Although the prosecutor and jury clearly believed Franklin's daughter, there is good reason to question the validity of *repressed memories,* recollections of events that are initially so shocking that the mind responds by pushing them into the unconscious. Supporters of the notion of repressed memory (who draw on Freud's psychoanalytic theory, first discussed in Chapter 1) suggest that such memories can remain hidden, possibly throughout a person's lifetime, unless they are triggered by some current circumstance, such as the probing that occurs during psychological therapy.

However, memory researcher Elizabeth Loftus (1997, 1998) maintains that so-called repressed memories can well be inaccurate or even wholly false—representing *false memory.* For example, false memories develop when people are unable

As the result of testimony from Eileen Franklin, based on repressed memory, her father was found guilty of murder. The validity of repressed memory, especially in investigating crimes, remains controversial. Can you think of a test to tell whether a recovered memory is accurate or not?

to recall the source of a memory of a particular event about which they have only vague recollections. When the source of the memory becomes unclear or ambiguous, people become confused about whether they actually experienced the event or whether they imagined it. Ultimately, people come to believe that the event actually occurred (Schacter, 1999a; Clancy et al., 2000).

In fact, some therapists have been accused of accidentally encouraging people who come to them with psychological difficulties to recreate false chronicles of childhood sexual experiences (Belicki et al., 1993). Furthermore, the publicity surrounding well-publicized declarations of supposed repressed memories, such as those of people who claim to be the victims of satanic rituals, makes the possibility of repressed memories seem more legitimate and ultimately might

prime people to recall "memories" of events that never happened (Lynn, 1997).

The controversy regarding the legitimacy of repressed memories is unlikely to be resolved soon. Many psychologists, particularly those who provide therapy, give great weight to the reality of repressed memories. On the other side of the issue are many memory researchers, who maintain that there is no scientific support for the existence of such memories. The challenge for those on both sides of the issue is to distinguish truth from fiction (Brown & Pope, 1996; Pezdek & Banks, 1996; Loftus, 1997; Walcott, 2000).

Can you think of any way to determine which details of a repressed memory are true and which are false? How do you think attorneys and psychologists go about establishing the accuracy or inaccuracy of repressed memories of allegedly criminal actions?

---

studied the complexities of eliciting and assessing children's statements. He has developed a procedure for interviewing children that has been adopted in most Canadian provinces (Yuille, 1988, 1997; Marxsen, Yuille, & Nisbett, 1995).

As the preceding discussion indicates, memory for events is a complex phenomenon influenced by many different factors. Cases like those of Thomas Sophonow and Guy Paul Morin demonstrate the costs of mistaken identification. In the United States, mistaken identifications account for more wrongful convictions than all the other causes (Yarmey, 2001). Daniel Yarmey suggests that expert eyewitnesses in Canadian courts can help jurors better understand the factors that affect eyewitness testimony so that they will be able to make better decisions.

The question of the accuracy of memories becomes even more complex, however, when we consider the triggering of memories of events that people at first don't even recall happening. As we discuss in the *Applying Psychology in the 21st Century* box, this issue has raised considerable controversy.

PsychLink

False memory discussion

www.mcgrawhill.ca/college/feldman

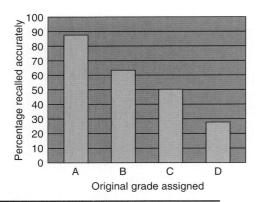

Figure 6-13 We distort memories for unpleasant events. For example, college students are much more likely to accurately recall their good grades, while inaccurately recalling their poor ones (Bahrick, Hall, & Berger, 1996). Now that you know this, how well do you think you can recall your own high school grades?

autobiographical memories: Our recollections of circumstances and episodes from our own lives.

Which aspects of memory seem to be universal, and which differ according to culture?

Autobiographical Memory: Where Past Meets Present

Your memory of experiences in your own past might well be a fiction—or at least a distortion of what actually occurred. The same constructive processes that act to make us inaccurately recall the behaviour of others also reduce the accuracy of autobiographical memories. **Autobiographical memories** are our recollections of circumstances and episodes from our own lives. Autobiographical memories encompass the episodic memories we hold about ourselves (Stein et al., 1997; Rubin, 1999).

For example, we tend to forget information about our past that is incompatible with how we currently see ourselves. One study found that adults who were well adjusted but who had been treated for emotional problems during the early years of their lives tended to forget important but troubling childhood events, such as being in foster care. College students tend to misremember their bad grades—but remember their good ones (see Figure 6-13; Robbins, 1988; Bahrick, Hall, & Berger, 1996; Stein et al., 1996).

It is not just certain kinds of events that are distorted; particular periods of life are remembered more easily than others. For example, adults do not remember early childhood very well. The earliest events adults can usually recall tend to have occurred between their third and sixth birthdays. In one study, Darryl Bruce and his colleagues at St. Mary's University asked people to describe two kinds of early experiences: an event that they knew had happened to them (because of family stories, etc.) but could not remember, and another event that they could remember. Using the ages for these two events, they found earliest memories occurred at 4.64 years of age (Bruce, Dolan, & Phillips-Grant, 2000). In another study, children who were visited five years after an injury event recalled the main details of the event with over 80 percent accuracy, even if they had been only three years old when the event occurred (Peterson & Whalen, 2001). At the other end of the lifespan, when people reach old age, they remember periods of life in which they experienced major transitions, such as attending college or working at their first job, better than their middle-age years (Rubin, 1985; Newcombe et al., 2000).

EXPLORING DIVERSITY

Are There Cross-Cultural Differences in Memory?

Travellers who have visited areas of the world in which there is no written language often have returned with tales of people with phenomenal memories. For instance, storytellers in some preliterate cultures can recount long chronicles that recall the names and activities of people over many generations. These feats initially led experts to argue that people in preliterate societies develop a different, and perhaps better, type of memory than those in cultures that employ a written language. They suggested that in a society that lacks writing, people are motivated to accurately recall information, particularly information relating to tribal histories and traditions that would be lost if they were not passed down orally from one generation to another (Bartlett, 1932; Cole & Gay, 1972; Rubin, 1995).

However, more recent approaches to cultural differences suggest a different conclusion. For one thing, preliterate peoples don't have an exclusive claim on amazing memory feats. For instance, some Hebrew scholars memorize thousands of pages of text and can recall the locations of particular words on the page. Similarly, poetry singers in the former Yugoslavia can recall thousands of lines of poetry. Even in cultures in which written language exists, then, astounding feats of memory are possible (Neisser, 1982).

Cultural differences in the age of earliest memory have also been observed. In one study, researchers found that adults' first memories occurred at an earlier age in Caucasians than in Asians. And New Zealand Maoris had the earliest first memories with events remembered occurring on average at 30 months of age (Mac-Donald et al., 2000, as cited in Peterson, 2001).

Storytellers in many cultures can recount hundreds of years of history in vivid detail. Research has found that this amazing ability is due less to basic memory processes than to the ways in which they acquire and retain information.

Memory researchers now suggest that there are both similarities and differences in memory across cultures. Basic memory processes such as short-term memory capacity and the structure of long-term memory—the "hardware" of memory—are universal and operate similarly in people of all cultures (Wagner, 1981). In contrast, differences can be seen in how information is acquired and rehearsed—the "software" of memory. Culture determines how people frame information initially, how much they practise learning and recalling it, and the strategies they use to try to recall it.

Evaluate

1. While with a group of friends at a dance, Eva bumps into a man she dated last month. When she tries to introduce him to her friends, she cannot remember his name. What is the term for this?
2. _____ is used when a person is asked to retrieve a specific item from memory.
3. Your mother's friend tells you, "I know exactly where I was and what I was doing when I heard that John Lennon died." What phenomenon explains this type of recollection?
4. The same person could probably also accurately describe in detail what she was wearing when she heard about John Lennon's death, right down to the colour of her shoes. True or false?
5. _____ are organized bodies of information stored in memory that bias the way new information is interpreted, stored, and recalled.
6. _____ - _____ - _____ theory states that the more a person analyzes a statement, the more likely he or she is to remember it later.

Answers to Evaluate Questions

1. Tip-of-the-tongue phenomenon 2. Recall 3. Flashbulb memory 4. False; small details probably won't be remembered through flashbulb memory. 5. Schemas 6. Levels-of-processing

Rethink

1. How do schemas help people process information during encoding, storage, and retrieval? In what ways are they helpful? Can they contribute to inaccurate autobiographical memories?
2. How might courtroom procedure be improved, based on what you've learned about memory errors and biases?

Forgetting: When Memory Fails

He could remember, quite literally, nothing—nothing, that is, that had happened since the loss of his brain's temporal lobes and hippocampus during experimental surgery to reduce epileptic seizures. Until that time, his memory had been quite normal. But after the operation he was unable to recall anything for more than a few minutes, and then the memory was seemingly lost forever. He did not remember his address, or the name of the person to whom he was talking. He would read the same magazine over and over again. According to his own description, his life was like waking from a dream and being unable to know where he was or how he got there. (Milner, 1966)

Prepare

Why do we forget information?
What are the major memory impairments?

Organize

Forgetting
Proactive and Retroactive Interference
Memory Dysfunctions

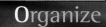

As this case illustrates, a person without a normal memory faces severe difficulties. All of us who have experienced even routine instances of forgetting—such as not remembering an acquaintance's name or a fact on a test—understand the very real consequences of memory failure.

The first attempts to study forgetting were made by German psychologist Hermann Ebbinghaus about a hundred years ago. Using himself as the only participant in his study, he memorized lists of three-letter nonsense syllables—meaningless sets of two consonants with a vowel in between, such as *FIW* and *BOZ*. By measuring how easy it was to relearn a given list of words after varying periods of time had passed since initial learning, he found that forgetting occurred systematically, as shown in Figure 6-14. As the figure indicates, the most rapid forgetting occurs in the first nine hours, and particularly in the first hour. After nine hours, the rate of forgetting slows and declines little, even after the passage of many days.

Despite his primitive methods, Ebbinghaus's study had an important influence on subsequent research, and his basic conclusions have been upheld (Wixted & Ebbesen, 1991). There is almost always a strong initial decline in memory, followed by a more

Figure 6-14 In his classic work, Ebbinghaus found that the most rapid forgetting occurs in the first nine hours after exposure to new material. However, the rate of forgetting then slows down and declines very little even after many days have passed (Ebbinghaus, 1885). Check your own memory: What were you doing exactly two hours ago? What were you doing last Tuesday at 5 P.M.? Which information is easier to retrieve?

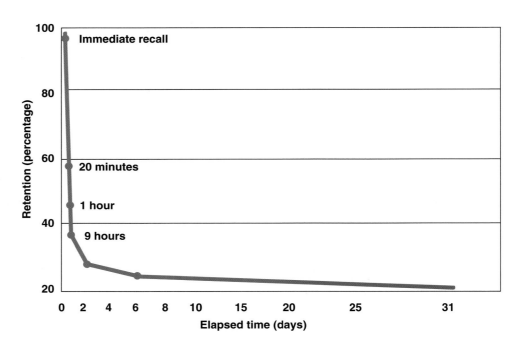

decay: The loss of information in memory through its nonuse.

memory trace: A physical change in the brain that occurs when new material is learned.

interference: The phenomenon by which information in memory displaces or blocks out other information, preventing its recall.

gradual drop over time. Furthermore, relearning of previously mastered material is almost always faster than starting from scratch, whether the material is academic information or a motor skill such as serving a tennis ball.

Why do we forget? Two major processes account for memory failures: decay and interference. **Decay** is the loss of information through nonuse. This explanation for forgetting assumes that when new material is learned, a **memory trace**—a physical change in the brain—appears. In decay, the trace simply fades away with nothing left behind, because of the mere passage of time.

Although there is evidence that decay does occur, this does not seem to be the complete explanation for forgetting. Often there is no relationship between how long ago a person was exposed to information and how well it is recalled. If decay explained all forgetting, we would expect that the longer the time between the initial learning of information and our attempt to recall it, the harder it would be to remember it, because there would be more time for the memory trace to decay. Yet people who take several consecutive tests on the same material often recall more of the initial information when taking later tests than they did on earlier tests. If decay were operating, we would expect the opposite to occur (Payne, 1986).

Because decay does not fully account for forgetting, memory specialists have proposed an additional mechanism: **interference**. In interference, information in memory displaces or blocks out other information, preventing its recall.

To distinguish between decay and interference, think of the two processes in terms of a row of books on a library shelf. In decay, the old books are constantly crumbling and rotting away, leaving room for new arrivals. In interference, new books knock the old ones off the shelf, where they become inaccessible.

Most research suggests that interference is the key process in forgetting (Mel'nikov, 1993; Bower, Thompson, & Tulving, 1994). We mainly forget things because new memories interfere with the retrieval of old ones, not because the memory trace has decayed.

Proactive and Retroactive Interference: The Before and After of Forgetting

There are actually two sorts of interference that influence forgetting: proactive and retroactive. In *proactive interference,* information learned earlier interferes with recall of newer material. Suppose, as a student of foreign languages, you first learned French in grade 10, and then in grade 11 you took Spanish. When in grade 12 you took a college achievement test in Spanish, you might have found you had difficulty recalling the Spanish translation of a word because all you could think of was its French equivalent.

On the other hand, *retroactive interference* refers to difficulty in recall of information because of later exposure to different material. If, for example, you have difficulty on a French achievement test because of your more recent exposure to Spanish, retroactive interference is the culprit (see Figure 6-15). One way to remember the difference between proactive and retroactive interference is to keep in mind that *pro*active interference progresses in time—the past interferes with the present—whereas *retro*active interference retrogresses in time, working backward as the present interferes with the past.

Although the concepts of proactive and retroactive interference suggest why material might be forgotten, they still do not explain whether forgetting due to interference is caused by actual loss or modification of information, or by problems in the retrieval of information. Most research suggests that material that has apparently been lost because of interference can eventually be recalled if appropriate stimuli are presented (Tulving & Psotka, 1971; Anderson, 1981), but the question has not been fully answered.

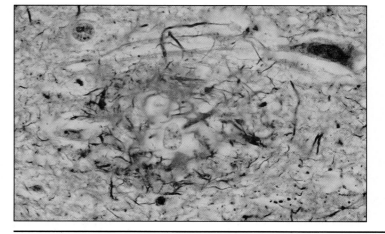

Figure 6-15 Proactive interference occurs when material learned earlier interferes with recall of newer material. In this example, studying French before studying Spanish interferes with performance on a Spanish test. In contrast, retroactive interference exists when material learned after initial exposure to other material interferes with the recall of the first material. In this case, retroactive interference occurs when recall of French is impaired because of later exposure to Spanish.

Memory Dysfunctions: Afflictions of Forgetting

First you notice that you're always misplacing things, or that common nouns are evading you as stubbornly as the names of new acquaintances. Pretty soon you're forgetting appointments and getting flustered when you drive in traffic. On bad days you find you can't hold numbers in your mind long enough to dial the phone. You try valiantly to conceal your lapses, but they become ever more glaring. You crash your car. You spend whole mornings struggling to dress yourself properly. And even as you lose the ability to read or play the piano, you're painfully aware of what's happening to you. (Cowley, 2000, p. 46)

The problem is *Alzheimer's disease,* an illness that includes among its symptoms severe memory problems. In Canada, Alzheimer's disease affects 1 percent of people aged 65 to 74, 7 percent of those aged 75 to 84, and 26 percent of those aged 85 and over (Canadian Study of Health and Aging Working Group, 1994).

In its initial stages, Alzheimer's symptoms appear as simple forgetfulness of things like appointments and birthdays. As the disease progresses, memory loss becomes more profound, and even the simplest tasks—such as how to dial a telephone—are forgotten. Ultimately, victims can lose their ability to speak or comprehend language, and physical deterioration sets in, leading to death.

The causes of Alzheimer's disease are not fully understood. However, increasing evidence suggests that it results from an

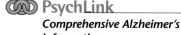
PsychLink

Comprehensive Alzheimer's information
www.mcgrawhill.ca/college/feldman

Figure 6-16 These tangles of neurons are characteristic of the damage found in the brains of people with Alzheimer's disease.

Pathways Through Psychology

Holly Tuokko

Associate Director, Centre on Aging
Associate Professor, Department of
Psychology
University of Victoria, British Columbia

Education: B.A., M.A., Lakehead University; Ph.D., University of Victoria

Home: Victoria

Holly Tuokko

When I began university, I don't think there was such a thing as geriatric neuropsychology and yet somehow I ended up writing a textbook in this field, *An Assessment Guide to Geriatric Neuropsychology*, in 1998. This book brings together neuropsychological information of special relevance for those working with older adults. It provides useful summary information on normative data, approaches to assessment, and diagnostic issues specific to geriatric populations, and fills a gap in the available resources for clinicians.

I first became interested in neuropsychology when I worked as a summer student at an institution for mentally handicapped persons after completing first year university. As part of the orientation week, the various reasons why people may be mentally handicapped were discussed. This opened my eyes to the connection between the brain and behaviour. Throughout my university training, I continued to be fascinated by brain-behaviour connections and I sought instruction and jobs in settings providing care to persons with mental health problems. After completing my master's degree in clinical psychology at Lakehead University, I worked on research projects with learning disabled children and discovered the growing field of neuropsychology.

After completing my Ph.D., I accepted a position at the Clinic for Alzheimer's Disease and Related Disorders, a research centre affiliated with the University of British Columbia. There I spent 10 years as a scientist/practitioner performing clinical neuropsychological assessment and conducting research on issues related to the identification and care of persons with dementia. This research has included test development and generation of normative data for older adults on a variety of neuropsychological measures. I moved to a mental health outreach team three years before returning to the University of Victoria with the Centre on Aging, an interdisciplinary applied research centre.

At present, I am the Associate Director of the Centre on Aging at the University of Victoria. I teach courses in the Department of Psychology on adult development and aging, health psychology, and dysfunctional development and aging. My primary research area is mental health and aging. I am conducting rigorous, applied research around issues related to the mental health of older adults. The current focus of my research is the evolution of cognitive disorders in older adults and the impact of these disorders on functional competencies. Specific competencies of interest are driving, financial management, and the types of understanding necessary to consent to health care and to consent to receive assistance.

I served as a steering committee member on a national epidemiological study examining issues related to the prevalence of cognitive impairment in older Canadians, the Canadian Study of Health and Aging (CSHA). My major contribution was to facilitate the development of a neuropsychological assessment as part of the clinical examination component of this study. This is the first study of its kind to examine neuropsychological functioning of older adults in detail. By being involved in the CSHA, I was able to advocate for and demonstrate the importance of neuropsychology in understanding the cognitive disorders affecting older adults. Neuropsychology has much to contribute to this field.

Source: Holly Tuokko, Ph.D. R.Psych.
University of Victoria
<www.coag.uvic.ca/TuokkoBioframes.htm>

How can neuropsychological assessment benefit seniors?

inherited susceptibility to a defect in the production of the protein beta amyloid, necessary for the maintenance of nerve cell connections. When the manufacture of beta amyloid goes awry, large clumps of cells grow that trigger inflammation and the deterioration of nerve cells in the brain (Barinaga, 1999; Cowley, 2000; Cooper et al., 2000; see Figure 6-16). See the *Pathways Through Psychology* box on Holly Tuokko to read about a Canadian psychologist with a special interest in the neuropsychological assessment of cognitive functioning in older adults.

Alzheimer's disease is just one of several memory dysfunctions that plague their victims. Another is *amnesia,* memory loss that occurs without other mental difficulties. The story of Philip Staufen described in the chapter prologue illustrates the devastating effect of amnesia. Without memory of his past, he was unable to give his lawyer the information needed to establish his identity. Attempts to find his birth record and match his fingerprints failed in Canada, the British Isles, and Germany.

There are several kinds of amnesia. In *retrograde amnesia,* memory is lost for occurrences prior to a certain event. Usually, lost memories gradually reappear, although full restoration can take as long as several years. In certain cases, some memories are lost forever (Eich et al., 1997; Kapur, 1999). The case of KC, who sustained a head injury during a motorcycle accident and suffered a loss of memory for events that occurred prior to the accident, is a classic example of retrograde amnesia (Tulving, Hayman, & McDonald, 1991).

A second type of amnesia is exemplified by people who remember nothing of their current activities. In *anterograde amnesia,* loss of memory occurs for events following an injury. Information cannot be transferred from short-term to long-term memory, resulting in the inability to remember anything other than what was in long-term storage prior to the accident.

Amnesia is also displayed by people who suffer from *Korsakoff's syndrome,* a disease afflicting long-term alcoholics. Although many of their intellectual abilities might be intact, Korsakoff's sufferers display a strange array of symptoms, including hallucinations and repetition of the same story over and over again.

Fortunately, most of us have intact memories, and the occasional failures we do suffer might be preferable to having a perfect memory. Consider, for instance, the case of a man who had total recall. After reading passages of the *Divine Comedy* in Italian—a language he did not speak—he was able to repeat them from memory even some 15 years later. He could memorize lists of 50 unrelated words and recall them at will more than a decade later. He could even repeat the same list of words backward, if asked (Luria, 1968).

Such a skill might at first seem to be enviable, but it actually presented quite a problem. The man's memory became a jumble of lists of words, numbers, and names, and when he tried to relax, his mind was filled with images. Even reading was difficult, because every word evoked a flood of thoughts from the past that interfered with his ability to understand the meaning of what he was reading.

BECOMING AN INFORMED CONSUMER OF PSYCHOLOGY

How will you use these suggestions in your daily life?

Improving Your Memory

Apart from the advantages of forgetting, say, a bad date, most of us still would like to find ways to improve our memories. Is it possible to find practical ways to increase our recall of information? Most definitely. Research has revealed a number of strategies that can be used to help us develop better memories (West, 1995; Herrmann et al., 1996; VanLehn, 1996). Among the best:

- *The keyword technique.* Suppose you are taking a foreign language class and need to learn vocabulary words. You can try using the *keyword technique,* in which a foreign word is paired with a common English word that has a similar *sound.* This English word is known as the keyword. For example, to remember the Spanish word for duck (*pato,* pronounced *pot-o*), you might choose the keyword *pot;* for the Spanish word for horse (*caballo,* pronounced *cob-eye-yo*), the keyword might be *eye.*

    Once you have thought of a keyword, imagine the Spanish word "interacting" with the English keyword. For instance, you might envision a duck taking a bath in a pot to remember the word *pato,* or a horse with a large, bulging eye in the center of its head to recall *caballo.* This technique has produced considerably superior results in learning foreign language vocabulary than more traditional techniques involving memorization of the words themselves (Pressley, 1987; Gruneberg & Pascoe, 1996; Carney & Levin, 1998).

- *Encoding specificity.* Some research suggests that we remember information best in an environment that is the same as or similar to where we initially learned it. This phenomenon is known as *encoding specificity* (Tulving & Thompson, 1973). You might do better on a test, then, if you study in the classroom where the test will be given. On the other hand, if you must take a test in a different room from the one in which you studied, don't despair: The features of the test itself, such as the wording of the test questions, are sometimes so powerful that they overwhelm the

PsychLink

Improving memory
www.mcgrawhill.ca/college/feldman

subtler cues relating to the original encoding of the material (Bjork & Richardson-Klarehn, 1989).

- *Organization cues*. Many of life's important recall tasks involve texts that you have read. One proven technique for improving recall of written material is to organize the material in memory as you read it for the first time—one of the rationales for the *P.O.W.E.R. Learning* (prepare-organize-work-evaluate-rethink) system incorporated into this book.

  Organize your reading by using any advance information you have about the content of the material (the *prepare* questions in this book) and about its organization (outlined in the *organize* sections). This activity will enable you to make connections and see relationships among the various facts, and to process the material at a deeper level, which in turn will later aid recall.

- *Effective note-taking*. "Less is more" is perhaps the best advice for taking lecture notes that facilitate recall. Rather than trying to jot down every detail of a lecture, it is better to listen and think about the material, and take down the main points. In effective note taking, thinking about the material initially is more important than writing it down. This is one reason borrowing someone else's notes is a bad proposition, because you will have no framework in memory that you can use to understand them (Feldman, 2000).

- *Practise and rehearse*. Although practice does not necessarily make perfect, it helps. By studying and rehearsing material past initial mastery—a process called *overlearning*—people are able to show better long-term recall than if they stop practising after their initial learning of the material. Keep in mind that, as research clearly demonstrates, fatigue and other factors prevent long practice sessions from being as effective as distributed practice.

- *Don't believe claims about drugs that improve memory*. Advertisements for One-A-Day vitamins with ginkgo biloba or Quanterra Mental Sharpness Product would have you believe that taking a drug could improve your memory. Not so, according to results of studies. No research has shown that commercial memory enhancers are effective (Meier, 1999). Save your money!

Evaluate

1. If, after learning the history of the Middle East for a class two years ago, you now find yourself unable to recall what you learned, you are experiencing memory _____, caused by nonuse.

2. Difficulty in accessing a memory because of the presence of other information is known as _____.

3. _____ interference occurs when material is difficult to retrieve because of exposure to later material. _____ interference refers to the difficulty in retrieving material due to the interference of previous material.

4. Match the following memory disorders with the correct information:

   1. Affects alcoholics; can result in hallucinations   a. Alzheimer's disease

   2. Memory loss occurring without other mental problems   b. Korsakoff's syndrome

   3. Beta amyloid defect; progressive forgetting and   c. Amnesia
      physical deterioration

Answers to Evaluate Questions

1. decay 2. interference 3. Retroactive; Proactive 4. 1-b; 2-c; 3-a

Rethink

1. Does the phenomenon of interference help explain the unreliability of autobiographical memory? Why?

2. How might findings on the biological mechanisms of memory aid in the treatment of memory disorders such as amnesia?

What is memory?

- Memory is the process by which we encode, store, and retrieve information. There are three basic kinds of memory storage: sensory memory, short-term memory, and long-term memory. (p. 188)

Are there different kinds of memory?

- Sensory memory, corresponding to each of the sensory systems, is the first place where information is saved, although the memories are very brief. Despite their brevity, sensory memories are precise, storing a nearly exact replica of each stimulus to which a person is exposed. (p. 190)
- Roughly seven (plus or minus two) chunks of information are capable of being transferred and held in short-term memory. Information in short-term memory is held from 15 to 25 seconds and, if not transferred to long-term memory, is lost. (p. 191)
- Memories are transferred into long-term storage through rehearsal. If memories are transferred into long-term memory, they become relatively permanent. (p. 192)
- Some theorists view short-term memory as a three-part working memory, an active "workspace" in which information is retrieved and manipulated, and held through rehearsal. In this view, there is a central executive, which coordinates the material to focus on during reasoning and decision making, and two subcomponents: the visual store and the verbal store. (p. 194)
- The levels-of-processing approach to memory suggests that the way in which information is initially perceived and analyzed determines the success with which the information is recalled. The deeper the initial processing, the greater the recall of the material. (p. 194)
- Newer memory models view long-term memory in terms of memory modules, each of which is related to separate memory systems in the brain. For instance, we can distinguish between declarative memory and nondeclarative memory. Declarative memory is further divided into episodic memory and semantic memory. (p. 195)
- Associative models of memory suggest that memory consists of mental representations of clusters of interconnected information. (p. 196)
- Explicit memory refers to intentional or conscious recollection of information. In contrast, implicit memory refers to memories of which people are not consciously aware, but which can affect subsequent performance and behaviour. (p. 197)

What are the biological bases of memory?

- Changes in neural pathways consolidate memories in long-term memory. (p. 198)
- Memories are distributed throughout the brain, depending on what processing systems are used. (p. 198)
- Certain areas and structures in the brain specialize in different types of memory activities. (p. 199)
- The hippocampus is involved in both initial encoding and consolidation of memories. (p. 199)

What causes difficulties and failures in remembering?

- The tip-of-the-tongue phenomenon refers to the experience of trying in vain to remember information that one is certain one knows. A major strategy for successfully recalling information is to use retrieval cues. (p. 200)
- Flashbulb memories are memories centred around a specific, important event. Flashbulb memories illustrate the broader point that the more distinctive a memory, the more easily it can be retrieved. (p. 202)

- Memory is a constructive process in which we relate memories to the meaning, guesses, and expectations that we give to the events the memory represents. Specific information is recalled in terms of schemas, organized bodies of information stored in memory that bias the way new information is interpreted, stored, and recalled. (p. 203)
- Eyewitnesses of crimes are apt to make substantial errors when they try to recall details of criminal activity. The problem of memory reliability becomes even more acute when the witnesses are children. (p. 203)
- Autobiographical memory, which refers to memories of circumstances and episodes from our own lives, is influenced by constructive processes. (p. 206)

Why do we forget information?

- Two major processes account for memory failures: decay and interference. Interference seems to be the major cause of forgetting. There are two sorts of interference: proactive interference and retroactive interference. (p. 207)

What are the major memory impairments?

- Among the memory dysfunctions are Alzheimer's disease, which leads to a progressive loss of memory, and amnesia, a memory loss that occurs without other mental difficulties and that can take two forms: retrograde amnesia and anterograde amnesia. Korsakoff's syndrome is a disease that afflicts long-term alcoholics, resulting in memory impairment. (p. 209)
- Among the techniques for improving memory are the keyword technique to memorize foreign language vocabulary; using the encoding specificity phenomenon; organizing text material and lecture notes; and practice and rehearsal, leading to overlearning. (p. 211)

Key Terms and Concepts

memory (p. 188)
sensory memory (p. 189)
short-term memory (p. 189)
long-term memory (p. 189)
iconic memory (p. 190)
echoic memory (p. 190)
chunk (p. 191)
rehearsal (p. 192)
working memory (p. 194)
levels-of-processing theory (p. 194)
declarative memory (p. 195)
nondeclarative memory (p. 195)
procedural memory (p. 195)
semantic memory (p. 195)

episodic memory (p. 195)
associative models of memory (p. 196)
priming (p. 196)
explicit memory (p. 197)
implicit memory (p. 197)
tip-of-the-tongue phenomenon (p. 200)
flashbulb memories (p. 202)
constructive processes (p. 203)
schemas (p. 203)
autobiographical memories (p. 206)
decay (p. 208)
memory trace (p. 208)
interference (p. 208)

Psychology on the Web

1. The study of repressed memories can lead down unusual pathways—even more unusual than the criminal investigation pathway we discussed in this chapter. Two other areas in which repressed memories play a large part are alien abduction and reincarnation. Find two sources on the Web that deal with one of these issues— one supportive and one skeptical. Read what they say and relate it to your knowledge of memory. Summarize your findings and indicate which side of the controversy your study of memory leads you to favour.

2. Memory is a topic of serious interest to psychologists, but it is also a source of amusement. Find a Web site that focuses on the amusing side of memory (such as memory games, tests of recall, or lists of mnemonics; hint: there's even a mnemonics generator out there!). Write down the address of any interesting sites you encounter and summarize what you find there.

Epilogue

In this chapter we have taken a look at memory. We noted that memory comprises the processes of encoding, storage, and retrieval, and we saw that memory can be regarded as having different components. We also encountered several phenomena relating to memory, including the tip-of-the-tongue phenomenon and flashbulb memories. Above all we observed that memory is a constructive process by which interpretations, expectations, and guesses contribute to the nature of our memories.

Before we move on to the next chapter, return briefly to the prologue of this chapter, in which we encountered Philip Staufen and his lost memories of his past. Consider the following questions in light of what you know about memory.

1. Philip Staufen was diagnosed with post-concussion global amnesia. What features of retrograde amnesia did he exhibit?
2. How would Staufen's life following his concussion have differed if he had suffered from anterograde amnesia?
3. How might investigators use Staufen's case to answer questions about the biological bases of memory? Assuming that Staufen gave his consent to PET scans and other means of looking inside his cerebral cortex, what sorts of questions might be explored?

integrator

For extra help in mastering the material in this chapter, see the integrator, practice quizzes, and other resources on the Online Learning Centre at

www.mcgrawhill.ca/college/feldman

Chapter Seven

Thinking, Language, and Intelligence

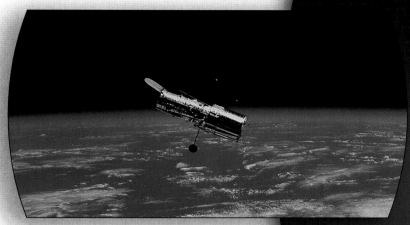

Many situations require problem-solving skills. The repair of the Hubble space telescope, however, demanded an extraordinary degree of problem-solving effort, which eventually led to a triumphant success.

Prologue

Housecall in Space

In April 1990, the Hubble Space Telescope, a huge astronomical observatory designed to answer questions about our universe and other galaxies, was put into space by the Canadarm. Hubble was supposed to send back pictures of objects as far away as 14 billion light years. Imagine the disappointment when the first pictures to arrive were blurry.

The problem turned out to be a tiny flaw; the telescope's primary mirror had been ground too flat at the edge. NASA engineers pondered the problem for months, devising and discarding one potential solution after another. Finally they developed a daring solution. They decided to send the Canadarm with a crew to install several new mirrors between the telescope's primary mirror and its other instruments. Canadarm captured Hubble and then moved the crew into position, supporting them while they installed the new mirrors and made other repairs. Then Canadarm redeployed Hubble.

It was not until the first photos were beamed back to Earth that the NASA engineers knew their solution had worked. These photos provided spectacular views of galaxies millions of light years from Earth.

Looking Ahead

The repair of the Hubble telescope proved to be a moment of problem-solving triumph for the NASA engineers on the ground, as well as the astronauts in space. Overcoming the obstacles to a solution while working under enormous pressure, they had succeeded in solving a difficult and risky problem. Their success illustrates how intelligent and thoughtful effort can lead to solutions in the face of formidable challenges.

Their accomplishment also raises a number of issues of central importance to psychologists: How do people use information to devise innovative solutions to problems? How do people think about, understand, and, through language, describe the world? And what is the nature of the intelligence that permits people to learn about, understand, and adapt to their surroundings?

In this chapter we focus on thinking, language, and intelligence. Each of these topics is central to **cognitive psychology**, the branch of psychology that focuses on the study of higher mental processes, including thinking, language, memory, problem solving, knowing, reasoning, judging, and decision making.

We begin by considering concepts, the building blocks of thinking. We examine different strategies for approaching problems, means of generating solutions, and ways of making judgments about the usefulness and accuracy of solutions.

Next we turn to the way we communicate with others: language. We consider how language is developed and acquired, its basic characteristics, and the relationship between language and thought.

Finally, we examine intelligence. We consider the challenges involved in defining and measuring intelligence, and examine the two groups displaying extremes of intelligence: people with mental retardation and the gifted. We also explore what are probably the two most controversial issues surrounding intelligence: the degree to which intelligence is influenced by heredity and the environment, and whether traditional tests of intelligence are biased toward the dominant cultural groups in society.

cognitive psychology: The branch of psychology that focuses on the study of mental processes.

Prepare

What is thinking?

What processes underlie decision making?

How do people approach and solve problems?

What are the major obstacles to problem solving?

Organize

Thinking
> Mental Images
> Concepts
> Solving Problems

thinking: The manipulation of mental representations of information.

mental images: Representations in the mind of an object or event.

Thinking

What are you thinking?

The mere ability to pose such a question underscores the distinctive nature of the human ability to think. No other species contemplates, analyzes, recollects, or plans as humans do. Understanding what thinking is, however, goes beyond knowing that we think.

Psychologists define **thinking** as the manipulation of mental representations of information. The representation may be in the form of a word, a visual image, a sound, or data in any other modality. The function of thinking is to transform that representation of information into new and different forms for the purposes of answering questions, solving problems, or reaching goals.

The nature of the fundamental elements involved in thinking is becoming increasingly well understood. We begin by considering our use of mental images and concepts, the building blocks of thought.

Mental Images: Examining the Mind's Eye

Think of your best friend.

Chances are that you "see" some kind of visual image when asked to think of her or him—or any other person or object, for that matter. To some cognitive psychologists, such mental images constitute a major part of thinking.

Mental images are representations in the mind in the form of an object or event. They are not just visual representations; your ability to "hear" a tune in your head also relies on a mental image. In fact, it might be that every sensory modality produces corresponding mental images (Paivio, 1971, 1975; Kosslyn et al., 1990; Kosslyn & Shin, 1994).

Research has found that our representations of mental images have many of the properties of the actual perception of objects. For example, it takes longer to scan mental images of large objects than of small ones, just as the eye takes longer to scan an actual large object than an actual small one. Similarly, we are able to manipulate and rotate mental images of objects, just as we are able to manipulate and rotate physical objects themselves (Kosslyn, 1981; Cooper & Shepard, 1984; Denis & Greenbaum, 1991; Brandimonte, Hitch, & Bishop, 1992; Sharps, Price, & Williams, 1994; Shepard et al., 2000; see Chapter Activity 7-1).

The production of mental images has been heralded by some as a way to improve various skills. For instance, many athletes use mental imagery in training. Basketball players might visualize themselves taking a foul shot, watching the ball, and hearing the swish as it goes through the net (May, 1989; Issac & Marks, 1994). Systematic evaluations of the use of mental imagery by athletes suggest that it provides a means for improving performance in sports (Druckman & Bjork, 1991).

Concepts: Categorizing the World

If someone asked you what is in your kitchen cabinet, you might answer with a detailed list of items ("a jar of peanut butter, three boxes of macaroni and cheese, six unmatched dinner plates," and so forth). More likely, though, you would respond by using some broader categories, such as "food" and "dishes."

The use of such categories reflects the operation of concepts. **Concepts** are categorizations of objects, events, or people that share common properties. By employing concepts, we are able to organize complex phenomena into simpler, and therefore more easily usable, cognitive categories (Margolis & Laurence, 1999).

concepts: Categorizations of objects, events, or people that share common properties.

PsychLink

Imagery and cognition
www.mcgrawhill.ca/college/feldman

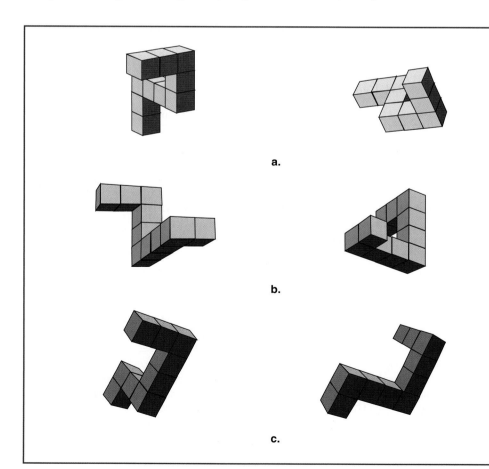

a.

b.

c.

Chapter Activity 7-1
Rotate Mental Images

FIGURE 7-1 Try to mentally rotate one of each pair of patterns to see if it is the same as the other member of the pair. It's likely that the further you have to mentally rotate a pattern, the longer it will take to decide if the patterns match one another (Based on Shepard & Metzler, 1971.) Does this mean that it will take you longer to visualize a map of the world than a map of Canada? Why or why not?

Reprinted with permission from R. Shepard and J. Metzler, "Mental Rotation of Three Dimensional Objects," *Science,* 171, pp. 701–703, 1971. Copyright © 1971 American Association for the Advancement of Science.

Concepts allow us to classify newly encountered objects on the basis of our past experience. For example, we can surmise that a small rectangular box with buttons that is on a chair near a television is probably a remote control—even if we have never encountered that specific brand before. Ultimately, concepts influence behaviour; we would assume, for instance, that it might be appropriate to pet an animal after determining that it is a dog, whereas we would behave differently after classifying the animal as a wolf.

When cognitive psychologists first studied concepts, they focused on those that were clearly defined by a unique set of properties or features. For example, an equilateral triangle is a closed shape that has three sides of equal length. If an object has these characteristics, it is an equilateral triangle; if it does not, then it is not an equilateral triangle.

prototypes: Typical, highly representative examples of a concept.

Other concepts—often those with the most relevance to our everyday lives—are more ambiguous and difficult to define. For instance, objects that fall under concepts such as "table" or "bird" share a set of general, relatively loose characteristic features, rather than unique, clearly defined properties that distinguish an example of the concept from a nonexample. When we consider these more ambiguous concepts, we usually think in terms of examples called prototypes. **Prototypes** are typical, highly representative examples of a concept. For instance, a prototype of the concept "bird" is a robin. Relatively high agreement exists among people in a particular culture as to which examples of a concept are prototypes, as well as which examples are not. For instance, most people in Western cultures consider cars and trucks good examples of vehicles, and elevators and wheelbarrows poor examples. Consequently, cars and trucks are Western prototypes of the concept "vehicle."

Concepts enable us to think about and understand more readily the complex world in which we live. For example, the judgments we make about the reasons for other people's behaviour are based on the ways in which we classify their behaviour. Our evaluations of a person who washes her hands 20 times a day could vary, depending on whether we place her behaviour within the conceptual framework of health care worker or mental patient. Similarly, physicians make diagnoses by drawing upon concepts and prototypes of symptoms that they learned about in medical school.

Algorithms and Heuristics

When faced with a decision, we often seek help from various kinds of cognitive shortcuts, known as algorithms and heuristics. An **algorithm** is a rule that, if applied appropriately, guarantees a solution to a problem. We can use an algorithm even if we cannot understand why it works. For example, you may know that the length of the third side of a right triangle can be found using the formula $a^2 + b^2 = c^2$, although you might not have the foggiest notion of the mathematical principles behind the formula.

algorithm: A rule that, if applied appropriately, guarantees a solution to a problem.

For the many problems and decisions for which no algorithm is available, we can often get help from heuristics. A **heuristic** is a cognitive shortcut that might lead to a solution. Heuristics enhance the likelihood of finding a solution but, unlike algorithms, they cannot ensure it (Nisbett et al., 1993).

heuristic: A cognitive shortcut that might lead to a solution.

Although heuristics often help people solve problems and make decisions, certain kinds of heuristics can lead to inaccurate conclusions. For example, we sometimes use the *availability heuristic,* which involves judging the probability of an event by how easily the event can be recalled. According to this heuristic, we assume that events we remember easily are likely to have occurred more frequently in the past—and are more likely to occur in the future—than those that are harder to remember. For instance, people are usually more afraid of dying in a plane crash than in an auto accident, despite statistics clearly showing that airplane travel is safer than auto travel. The reason is that plane crashes receive more publicity than car crashes, and are therefore more easily remembered (Slovic, Fischhoff, & Lichtenstien, 1976; Schwarz et al., 1991).

PsychLink

Explanation of heuristics
www.mcgrawhill.ca/college/feldman

Solving Problems

According to an old legend, a group of Vietnamese monks are guardians of three towers on which sit 64 golden rings. The monks believe that if they succeed in moving the rings from the first tower to the third according to a series of rigid rules, the world as we know it will come to an end. (Should you prefer that the world remain in its present state, there's no need for immediate concern: the puzzle is so complex that it will take about a trillion years to reach a solution.)

In a simpler version of the task facing the monks, which has come to be known as the Tower of Hanoi puzzle, three disks are placed on three posts in the order shown in Chapter Activity 7-2.

Why are cognitive psychologists interested in the Tower of Hanoi problem? The answer is that the way people go about solving this puzzle and simpler ones like it helps illuminate the processes by which people solve complex problems. For example, psychologists have found that problem solving typically involves three major steps: preparation for the creation of solutions, production of solutions, and evaluation of solutions that have been generated (Sternberg & Frensch, 1991).

Preparation: Understanding and Diagnosing Problems

When approaching a problem like the Tower of Hanoi, most people begin by trying to ensure that they thoroughly understand the problem. If the problem is a novel one, they are likely to pay particular attention to any restrictions placed on coming up with a solution as well as the initial status of the components of the problem. If the problem is familiar, they are apt to spend considerably less time in this stage.

Problems typically sort into the three categories exemplified in Chapter Activity 7-3: arrangement, inducing structure, and transformation (Greeno, 1978; Spitz, 1987). The three types require somewhat different kinds of psychological skills and knowledge to solve.

- *Arrangement problems* require that a group of elements be rearranged or recombined in a way that will satisfy a given criterion. Usually there are several different possible arrangements, only one or a few of which will produce a solution. Anagram problems and jigsaw puzzles are arrangement problems.
- In *problems of inducing structure,* a person must identify the relationships that exist among the elements presented and construct a new relationship among them. It is necessary to determine not only the relationships among the elements,

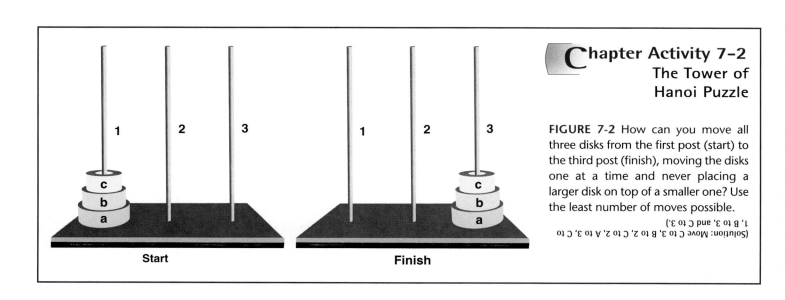

Chapter Activity 7–2
The Tower of Hanoi Puzzle

FIGURE 7-2 How can you move all three disks from the first post (start) to the third post (finish), moving the disks one at a time and never placing a larger disk on top of a smaller one? Use the least number of moves possible.

(Solution: Move C to 3, B to 2, C to 2, A to 3, C to 1, B to 3, and C to 3.)

Chapter Activity 7-3
Solve Different Types of Problems

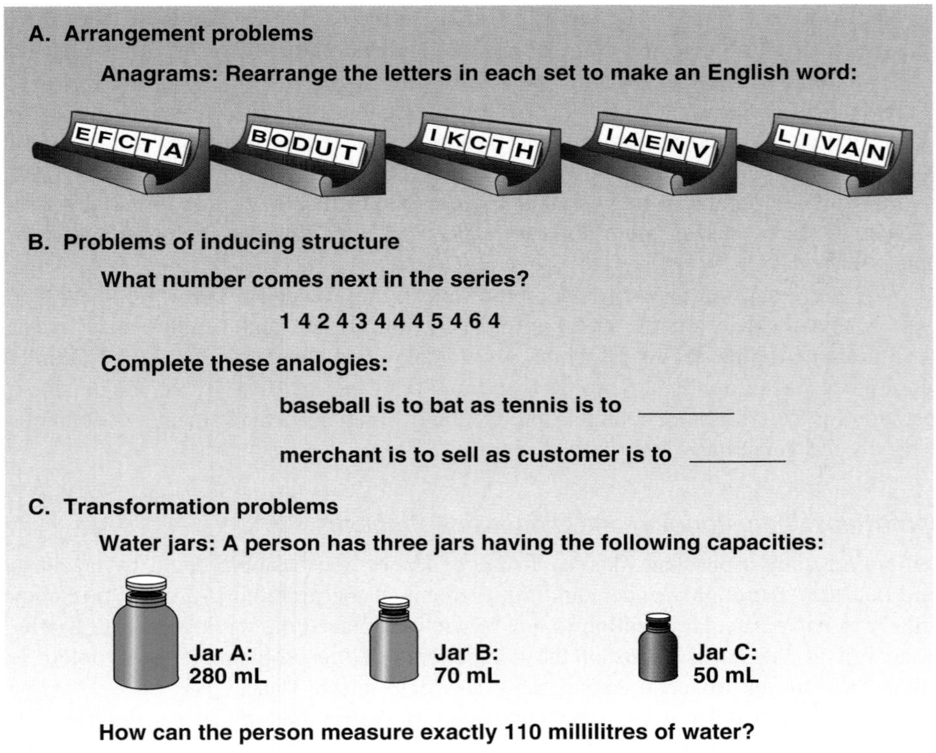

FIGURE 7-3 The major categories of problems: (a) arrangement, (b) inducing structure, and (c) transformation. (Bourne et al., 1986; hobbit problem: Solso, 1991, p. 448. Solutions appear below.)

Source: Poncini, M. (1990). *Brain Fitness.* New York: Random House; Bourne, L.E., Dominowski, R.L., Loftus, E.F., & Healy, A.F. (1986). Cognitive processes (2nd ed.). Englewood Cliffs, NJ: Prentice-Hall; and Solso, R.L. (1991). Cognitive psychology, 3rd. ed. Needham Heights, MA: Allyn & Bacon. p. 448

Answers:

Arrangement problems: FACET, DOUBT, THICK, NAIVE, ANVIL; Problems of inducing structure: 7; racquet, buy; Transformation problems: Fill jar A, empty into jar B once and into jar C twice. What remains in jar A is 110 millilitres.

A. Arrangement problems

Anagrams: Rearrange the letters in each set to make an English word:

EFCTA BODUT IKCTH IAENV LIVAN

B. Problems of inducing structure

What number comes next in the series?

1 4 2 4 3 4 4 4 5 4 6 4

Complete these analogies:

baseball is to bat as tennis is to _____

merchant is to sell as customer is to _____

C. Transformation problems

Water jars: A person has three jars having the following capacities:

Jar A: 280 mL   Jar B: 70 mL   Jar C: 50 mL

How can the person measure exactly 110 millilitres of water?

---

but the structure and size of the elements. In the example shown in Figure 7-3b, a person must first determine that the solution requires the numbers to be considered in pairs (14-24-34-44-54-64). Only after that part of the problem is identified can the solution rule (the first number of each pair increases by one, while the second number remains the same) be determined.

- *Transformation problems* consist of an initial state, a goal state, and a series of methods for changing the initial state into the goal state. For example, in the Tower of Hanoi problem, the initial state is the original configuration; the goal state consists of the three disks on the third peg; and the method consists of the rules for moving the disks.

Whether the problem is one of arrangement, inducing structure, or transformation, the initial stage of understanding and diagnosing is critical in problem solving because it allows us to develop our own cognitive representation of the problem and to place it within a personal framework. The problem may be divided into subparts or some information may be ignored as we try to simplify the task. Winnowing out nonessential information is often a critical step in problem solving.

A crucial aspect of the initial encounter with a problem is how we represent it to ourselves and organize the information presented to us (Brown & Walter, 1993; Davidson, Deuser, & Sternberg, 1994). Our ability to represent a problem—and the kind of solution we eventually come to—is affected by the way a problem is phrased, or *framed*. Suppose, for example, that you are a cancer patient having to choose between surgery or radiation, and you are given the two sets of options shown in Figure 7-4 (Tversky & Kahneman, 1987). When the options were framed in terms of the likelihood of survival, only 18 percent of participants in a study chose radiation over surgery. However, when the choice was framed in terms of the likelihood of dying, 44 percent chose radiation over surgery—even though the outcomes are identical in both sets of framing conditions.

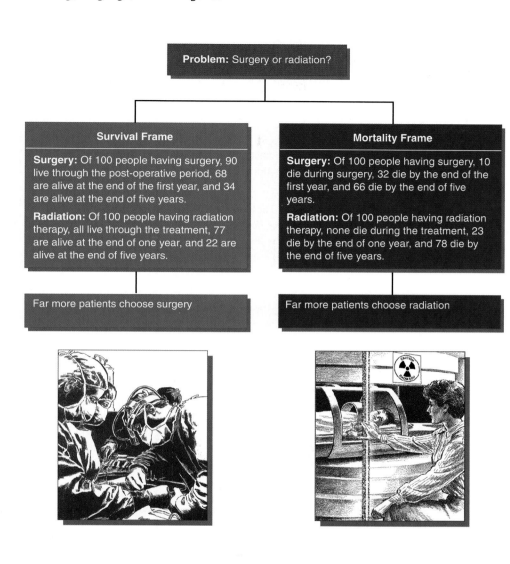

Problem: Surgery or radiation?

Survival Frame

Surgery: Of 100 people having surgery, 90 live through the post-operative period, 68 are alive at the end of the first year, and 34 are alive at the end of five years.

Radiation: Of 100 people having radiation therapy, all live through the treatment, 77 are alive at the end of one year, and 22 are alive at the end of five years.

Far more patients choose surgery

Mortality Frame

Surgery: Of 100 people having surgery, 10 die during surgery, 32 die by the end of the first year, and 66 die by the end of five years.

Radiation: Of 100 people having radiation therapy, none die during the treatment, 23 die by the end of one year, and 78 die by the end of five years.

Far more patients choose radiation

Figure 7–4 A decision is often affected by the way a problem is framed. *How did framing influence the decisions made in this study? Can you think of other examples of framing influencing decisions?*

Production: Generating Solutions.

If a problem is relatively simple, a direct solution might already be stored in long-term memory; then all that is necessary is to retrieve the appropriate information. If the solution cannot be retrieved or is not known, we must instigate a process by which possible solutions can be generated and compared with information in long- and short-term memory.

At the most primitive level, solutions to problems can be obtained through trial and error. Thomas Edison was able to invent the lightbulb only because he tried thousands of different kinds of materials for a filament before he found one that worked (carbon). The difficulty with trial and error, of course, is that some problems are so complicated it would take a lifetime to try out every possibility. For example, according to one estimate, there are some 10^{120} possible sequences of chess moves.

In place of trial and error, complex problem solving often involves the use of heuristics, which, as we discussed earlier, are cognitive shortcuts that can lead the way to solutions. Probably the most frequently applied heuristic is a means-end analysis. In a **means-end analysis**, people repeatedly test for differences between the desired outcome and what currently exists. Consider this simple example (Newell & Simon, 1972):

> I want to take my son to nursery school. What's the difference between what I have and what I want? One of distance. What changes distance? My automobile. My automobile won't work. What is needed to make it work? A new battery. What has new batteries? An auto repair shop. . . .

means–ends analysis: Repeated testing for differences between the desired outcome and what currently exists.

In such a means-end analysis, each step brings the problem-solver closer to a resolution. Although this strategy is often effective, a means-end analysis can be counterproductive for a problem that requires indirect steps that temporarily *increase* the discrepancy between a current state and the solution. For example, sometimes the fastest route to a summit requires a mountain climber to backtrack temporarily; a means-end approach—which implies that the mountain climber should always forge ahead and upward—will be ineffective in such instances.

Furthermore, for some problems, the best approach is working backward, by focusing on the goal rather than on the starting point of the problem. Consider, for example, the water lily problem:

> Water lilies are growing on Blue Lake. The water lilies grow rapidly, so that the amount of water surface covered by lilies *doubles* every 24 hours.
>
> On the first day of summer, there was just one water lily. On the 90th day of the summer, the lake was entirely covered. On what day was the lake *half covered?*
> (Reisberg, 1997)

If you start searching for a solution to the problem by thinking about the initial state on Day 1 (one water lily) and move forward from there, you're facing a daunting task of trial-and-error estimation. But try taking a different approach: Start with Day 90, when the entire lake was covered with lilies. Given that the lilies double their coverage daily, on the prior day only half the lake was covered. The answer, then, is Day 89, a solution found by working backward (Bourne et al., 1986; Hunt, 1994).

For some problems, the easiest way to solve them is to divide them into intermediate steps, or *subgoals,* and solve each of those steps. Still other solutions seem to come in a sudden burst of comprehension. Just after World War I, German psychologist Wolfgang Köhler examined learning and problem-solving processes in chimps (Köhler, 1927). In his studies, Köhler exposed chimps to challenging situations in which the elements of the solution were all present; all that was needed was for the chimps to put them together.

For example, in one series of studies, chimps were kept in a cage in which boxes and sticks were strewn about, with a bunch of tantalizing bananas hanging from the ceiling out of reach. Initially, the chimps engaged in a variety of trial-and-error attempts to get the bananas: They would throw the sticks at the bananas, jump from one of the boxes, or leap wildly from the ground. Frequently, they would seem to give up in frustration, leaving the bananas dangling temptingly overhead. But then, in what seemed like a sudden revelation, they would abandon whatever activity they were involved in, stand on a box, and reach the bananas with a stick. Köhler called the cognitive processes underlying the chimps' behaviour **insight**, a sudden awareness of the relationships among various elements that had previously appeared to be unrelated to one another.

Although Köhler emphasized the apparent suddenness with which solutions were revealed, subsequent research has shown that prior experience and initial trial-and-error practice in problem solving are prerequisites for "insight" (Metcalfe, 1986; Ansburg & Dominowski, 2000).

Judgment: Evaluating the Solutions

The final step in problem solving is judging the adequacy of a solution. Often this is a simple matter: If there is a clear solution, as in the Tower of Hanoi problem, we will know immediately whether we have been successful.

If the solution is less concrete or if there is no single correct solution, evaluating solutions becomes more difficult. In such instances, we must decide which solution alternative is best. Unfortunately, we are often inaccurate in estimating the quality of our own ideas (Johnson, Parrott, & Stratton, 1968). For instance, a team of drug researchers working for a particular company might feel that their remedy for an illness is superior to all others, overestimating the likelihood of success and belittling the approaches of competing companies.

PsychLink
Means-end analysis technique
www.mcgrawhill.ca/college/feldman

insight: A sudden awareness of the relationships among various elements that had previously appeared to be independent of one another.

PsychLink
Köhler and insight research
www.mcgrawhill.ca/college/feldman

a.

b.

c.

In an impressive display of insight, Sultan, one of the chimpanzees in Köhler's experiments in problem solving, sees a bunch of bananas that is out of his reach (a). He then carries over several crates (b), stacks them, and stands on them to reach the bananas (c).
What sorts of problem-solving strategies do you think chimpanzees use in their natural habitat?

Theoretically, if the heuristics and information we rely on to make decisions are appropriate and valid, we can make accurate choices among problem solutions. However, as we see next, there are several kinds of obstacles to and biases in problem solving that affect the quality of the decisions and judgments we make.

Impediments to Solutions: Why Is Problem Solving Such a Problem?

Consider the following problem-solving test (Duncker, 1945):

> You are presented with a set of tacks, candles, and matches in small boxes, and told your goal is to place three candles at eye level on a nearby door, so that wax will not drip on the floor as the candles burn [see Chapter Activity 7-4]. How would you approach this challenge?

If you have difficulty solving the problem, you are not alone. Most people are unable to solve it when it is presented in the manner illustrated in Figure 7-5, in which the objects are located *inside* the boxes. However, if the objects were presented *beside* the boxes, just resting on the table, chances are you would solve the problem much more readily—which, in case you are wondering, requires tacking the boxes to the door and then placing the candles inside them (see Figure 7-7).

The difficulty you probably encountered in solving the problem stems from its presentation and relates to the fact that you were misled at the initial preparation stage. Actually, significant obstacles to problem solving exist at each of the three major stages. As a person confronts a problem and considers various solutions, a number of factors hinder the development of creative, appropriate, and accurate solutions.

THE FAR SIDE® **BY GARY LARSON**

The Far Side® by Gary Larson © 1981 FarWorks, Inc. All Rights Reserved. Used with permission.

Chapter Activity 7–4
Creative Problem Solving

FIGURE 7-5 The problem here is to place three candles at eye level on a nearby door so that the wax will not drip on the floor as the candles burn—using only material in the figure. For a solution, see Figure 7-7.

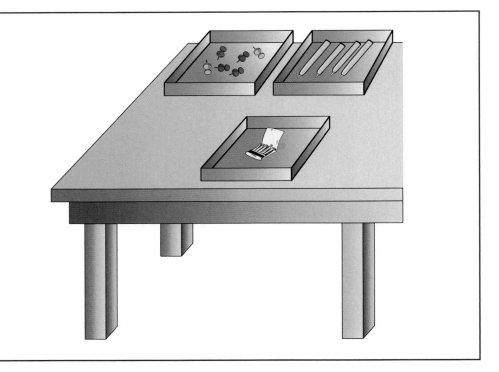

functional fixedness: The tendency to think of an object only in terms of its typical use.

mental set: The tendency for old patterns of problem solving to persist.

- *Functional fixedness.* The reason most people experience difficulty with the candle problem is a phenomenon known as **functional fixedness**, the tendency to think of an object only in terms of its typical use. For instance, functional fixedness probably leads you to think of the book you are holding in your hands as something to read, as opposed to its value as a doorstop or as kindling for a fire. In the candle problem, functional fixedness occurs because the objects are first presented inside the boxes, which are then seen simply as containers for the objects they hold rather than as a potential part of the solution.
- *Mental set.* Functional fixedness is an example of a broader phenomenon known as **mental set**, the tendency for old patterns of problem solving to persist. This phenomenon was demonstrated in a classic experiment carried out by Abraham Luchins (1946). As you can see in Chapter Activity 7-5, the object of the task is to use the containers in each row to measure out the designated amount of liquid. (Try it yourself to get a sense of the power of mental set before moving on.)

  If you have tried to solve the problem, you know that the first five parts are all solved in the same way: Fill the largest container (B) and from it fill the middle-size container (A) once and the smallest container (C) two times. What is left in B is the designated amount. (Stated as a formula, it is B − A − 2C.) The demonstration of mental set comes with the sixth part of the problem, a point at which you probably encountered some difficulty. If you are like most people, you tried the formula and were perplexed when it failed. Chances are, in fact, that you missed the simple (but different) solution to the problem, which merely involves subtracting C from A. Interestingly, those people who were given problem 6 *first* had no difficulty with it at all.
- *Inaccurate evaluation of solutions.* When the nuclear power plant at Three Mile Island in Pennsylvania suffered its malfunction in 1979, a disaster that almost led to a nuclear meltdown, the plant operators were faced with solving a problem of the most serious kind. Several monitors indicated contradictory information about the source of the problem: One suggested that the pressure

Given containers with these capacities (in millilitres)

a   b   c

	a	b	c	Obtain
1.	21	127	3	100
2.	14	163	25	99
3.	18	43	10	5
4.	9	42	6	21
5.	20	59	4	31
6.	28	76	3	25

Chapter Activity 7–5
Encounter Mental Set

FIGURE 7-6 Try this classic demonstration, which illustrates the importance of mental set in problem solving. The objective is to use the containers in each row to measure out the designated amount of liquid. After you figure out the solution for the first five rows, you'll likely have trouble with the sixth row—even though the solution is actually easier. In fact, if you had tried to solve the problem in the sixth row first, you probably would have no difficulty at all.

was too high, leading to the danger of an explosion; others indicated that the pressure was too low, which could lead to a meltdown. Although the pressure was in fact too low, the supervisors on duty relied on the one monitor—which was faulty—that suggested the pressure was too high. Once they had made their decision and acted upon it, they ignored the contradictory evidence from the other monitors (Wickens, 1984).

One reason for the operators' mistake is the *confirmation bias,* in which initial hypotheses are favoured and contradictory information supporting alternative hypotheses or solutions is ignored. Even when we find evidence that contradicts a solution we have chosen, we are apt to stick with our original hypothesis.

Creativity and Problem Solving

Despite obstacles to problem solving, many people are adept at coming up with creative solutions to problems. One of the enduring questions that cognitive psychologists have sought to answer is what factors underlie **creativity**, the combining of responses or ideas in novel ways.

Although identifying the stages of problem solving helps us understand how people approach and solve problems, it does little to explain why some people come up with better solutions than others. For instance, the possible solutions to even the simplest of problems often show wide discrepancies. Consider, for example, how you might respond to the question "How many uses can you think of for a newspaper?"

Now compare your own solution with this one proposed by a 10-year-old boy:

> You can read it, write on it, lay it down and paint a picture on it. . . . You could put
> it on your door for decoration, put it in the garbage can, put it on a chair if the chair
> is messy. If you have a puppy, you put newspaper in its box or put it in your
> backyard for the dog to play with. When you build something and you don't want
> anyone to see it, put newspaper around it. Put newspaper on the floor if you have no

creativity: The combining of responses or ideas in novel ways.

Figure 7-7 A solution to the problem posed in Chapter Activity 7-4 involves tacking the boxes to the door and placing the candles in the boxes.

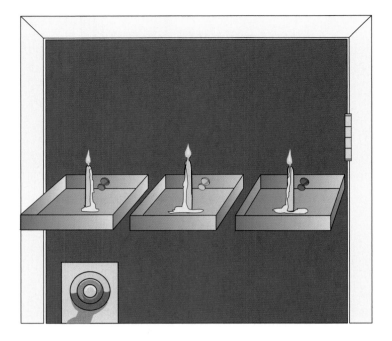

mattress, use it to pick up something hot, use it to stop bleeding, or to catch the drips from drying clothes. You can use a newspaper for curtains, put it in your shoe to cover what is hurting your foot, make a kite out of it, shade a light that is too bright. You can wrap fish in it, wipe windows, or wrap money in it. . . . You put washed shoes in newspaper, wipe eyeglasses with it, put it under a dripping sink, put a plant on it, make a paper bowl out of it, use it for a hat if it is raining, tie it on your feet for slippers. You can put it on the sand if you had no towel, use it for bases in baseball, make paper airplanes with it, use it as a dustpan when you sweep, ball it up for the cat to play with, wrap your hands in it if it is cold. (Ward, Kogan, & Pankove, 1972)

This list obviously shows extraordinary creativity. Unfortunately, it has proved to be considerably easier to identify *examples* of creativity than to determine its sources. Several factors, however, seem to be associated with creativity (Csikszentmihalyi, 1997; Ward, Smith, & Vaid, 1997; Root-Bernstein & Root-Bernstein, 1999).

One of these factors is divergent thinking. **Divergent thinking** is the ability to generate unusual, yet nonetheless appropriate, responses to problems or questions. This type of thinking contrasts with **convergent thinking**, which produces responses that are based primarily on knowledge and logic. For instance, someone relying on convergent thinking answers "You read it" to the query "What do you do with a newspaper?" In contrast, "You use it as a dustpan" is a more divergent—and creative—response (Baer, 1993; Runco & Sakamoto, 1993; Finke, 1995).

Another aspect of creativity is *cognitive complexity,* the preference for elaborate, intricate, and complex stimuli and thinking patterns. Similarly, creative people often have a wider range of interests and are more independent and more interested in philosophical or abstract problems than are less creative individuals (Barron, 1990).

One factor that is *not* closely related to creativity is intelligence. Researchers consistently find that creativity is only slightly related to school grades and intelligence, when intelligence is measured using traditional intelligence tests (Hong, Milgram, & Gorsky, 1995; Sternberg & O'Hara, 2000).

divergent thinking: The ability to generate unusual, yet nonetheless appropriate, responses to problems or questions.
convergent thinking: The ability to produce responses that are based primarily on knowledge and logic.

Creativity and innovation
www.mcgrawhill.ca/college/feldman

BECOMING AN
INFORMED CONSUMER
OF PSYCHOLOGY

Thinking Critically and Creatively: Can We Learn to Be Better Thinkers?

Researchers have found that abstract rules of logic can be taught and that such training can improve our reasoning about the underlying causes of everyday events in our lives.

In short, research suggests that critical and creative thinkers are made, not born. Consider, for instance, some of these suggestions for increasing critical thinking and creativity (Feldman, Coats, & Schwartzberg, 1994; Halpern, 1998; Levy, 1997):

- *Redefine problems.* Our boundaries and assumptions can be modified by rephrasing problems at either a more abstract or a more concrete level.
- *Adopt a critical perspective.* Rather than passively accepting assumptions or arguments, we can critically evaluate material, consider its implications, and think about possible exceptions and contradictions.
- *Consider the opposite.* Considering the opposite of a concept we're seeking to understand sometimes helps. For example, in order to define "good mental health," it might be useful to consider what is meant by "bad mental health."
- *Use analogies.* Analogies provide alternative frameworks for our interpretation of facts and help us uncover new understanding. One particularly effective means of coming up with analogies is to look for examples in the animal kingdom. For instance, architects discovered how to construct the earliest skyscrapers by noting how lily pads on a pond could support the weight of a person (Shoulder, 1992; Reisberg, 1997; Getner & Holyoak, 1997).
- *Think divergently.* Instead of thinking in terms of the most logical or common use for an object, consider how it might help your creativity if you were forbidden to use the object in its usual way.
- *Use heuristics.* As mentioned earlier, heuristics are cognitive shortcuts that can help bring about a solution to a problem.
- *Experiment with various solutions.* Don't be afraid to use different routes to find solutions for problems (verbal, mathematical, graphic, even acting out a situation). After you've come up with a list of possible solutions, you can review each one and try to think of ways of making what at first appeared impractical seem more feasible.

Evaluate

1. _____ _____ are representations in the mind that resemble the object or event being represented.
2. _____ are categorizations of objects that share common properties.
3. Solving a problem by trying to reduce the difference between the current state and the goal state is known as a _____-_____ _____.
4. _____ is the term used to describe the sudden "flash" of revelation that often accompanies the solution to a problem.
5. Thinking of an object only in terms of its typical use is known as _____ _____.
6. Generating unusual but appropriate approaches to a question is known as _____ _____.

Rethink

1. How might the availability heuristic contribute to prejudices based on race, age, and gender? Can awareness of this heuristic prevent this from happening?
2. Are divergent thinking and convergent thinking mutually exclusive or complementary? Why? Are there situations in which one way of thinking is clearly superior? Can the two ways of thinking be combined? How?

Answers to Evaluate Questions

1. Mental images; 2. Concepts; 3. means-ends analysis; 4. Insight; 5. functional fixedness; 6. divergent thinking.

language: The communication of information through symbols arranged according to systematic rules.

grammar: The system of rules that determine how our thoughts can be expressed.

phonology: The study of the sound system in language.

phonemes: The smallest basic sound units.

syntax: The rules that indicate how words and phrases can be combined to form sentences.

semantics: The rules governing the meaning of words and sentences.

Language

'Twas brillig, and the slithy toves
Did gyre and gimble in the wabe:
All mimsy were the borogoves,
And the mome raths outgrabe.

Although few of us have ever come face to face with a tove, we have little difficulty in discerning that in Lewis Carroll's (1872) poem "Jabberwocky," the expression *slithy toves* contains an adjective, *slithy,* and the noun it modifies, *toves.*

Our ability to make sense out of nonsense, if the nonsense follows typical rules of language, illustrates both the sophistication of human language capabilities and the complexity of the cognitive processes that underlie the development and use of language. The use of **language**—the communication of information through symbols arranged according to systematic rules—clearly is an important cognitive ability, one that is indispensable for communicating with others. Not only is language central to communication, it is also closely tied to how we think about and understand the world. It is not surprising, then, that psychologists have devoted considerable attention to studying the topic of language (Forrester, 1996; Velichkovsky & Rumbaugh, 1996; Barrett, 1999; Owens, 2001).

Grammar: Language's Language

To understand how language develops and its relationship to thought, we first need to review some of the formal elements that constitute language. The basic structure of language rests on grammar. **Grammar** is the system of rules that determine how our thoughts can be expressed.

Grammar involves three major components of language: phonology, syntax, and semantics. **Phonology** is the study of the sound system in language (i.e., rules that determine which sound sequences occur in words). The smallest units of sound that can affect meaning of speech are called **phonemes**. For instance, *a* in *fat* and the *a* in *fate* are two different phonemes in English (Vihman, 1996; Baddeley, Gathercole, & Pagano, 1998).

Although English speakers use just 42 basic phonemes to produce words, the basic phonemes of other languages range from as few as 15 to as many as 85 (Akmajian, Demers, & Harnish, 1984). Differences in phonemes are one reason people have difficulty learning other languages: For example, to the Japanese speaker, whose native language does not have an *r* phoneme, English words such as roar present some difficulty.

Syntax refers to the rules governing how words and phrases can be combined to form sentences. Every language has intricate rules that guide the order in which words may be strung together to communicate meaning. English speakers have no difficulty recognizing that *Radio down the turn* is not an appropriate sequence, while *Turn down the radio* is. The importance of appropriate syntax is demonstrated in English by the changes in meaning that are caused by the different word orders in the following three utterances: "John kidnapped the boy," "John, the kidnapped boy," and "The boy kidnapped John" (Lasnik, 1990).

The third major component of language is semantics. **Semantics** refers to the rules governing the meaning of words and sentences (Larson, 1990; Hipkiss, 1995; O'Grady & Dobrovolsky, 1996). Semantic rules allow us to use words to convey the subtlest of nuances. For instance, we are able to make the distinction between "The truck hit Laura" (which we would likely say if we had just seen the vehicle hitting Laura) and "Laura was hit by a truck" (which we would probably say if asked why Laura was missing class while she recuperated).

Despite the complexities of language, most of us acquire the basics of grammar without even being aware that we have learned its rules (Pinker, 1994). Moreover, although we might have difficulty explicitly stating the rules of grammar that we use, our linguistic abilities are so sophisticated that they enable us to utter an infinite number of different statements. We now consider how such abilities are acquired.

Language Development: Developing a Way with Words

To parents, the sounds of their infant babbling and cooing are music to their ears (except, perhaps, at three o'clock in the morning). These sounds also serve an important function: They mark the first step on the road to the development of language.

Children **babble**—make speechlike but meaningless sounds—from around the age of 3 months through 1 year. While they babble they may produce, at one time or another, any of the sounds found in all languages, not just the ones to which they are exposed. Even deaf children display their own form of babbling: Infants who are unable to hear and who are exposed to sign language from birth "babble," but they do it with their hands (Pettito & Marentette, 1991; Pettito, 1993; Meier & Willerman, 1995).

Babbling increasingly reflects the specific language that is being spoken in an infant's environment, initially in terms of pitch and tone, and eventually in terms of specific sounds. Some theorists suggest there is a *critical period* for language development early in life, in which a child is particularly sensitive to language cues and during which language is most easily acquired. In fact, children who are not exposed to language during this critical period have great difficulty in later overcoming their early deficit (Kuhl et al., 1992; Blake & de Boysson-Bardies, 1992; de Boysson-Bardies & Halle, 1994).

By the time the child is approximately 1 year old, sounds that are not in the language to which the infant is exposed disappear from the child's utterances (Werker, 1989). It is then a short step to the production of actual words. In English, these are typically short words that start with a consonant such as *b, d, m, p,* or *t*—which helps to explain why *mama* and *dada* are so often among babies' first words. Of course, even before they produce their first words, children are capable of understanding a fair amount of the language they hear. Language comprehension precedes language production.

After the age of 1 year, children begin to learn more complicated forms of language. They produce two-word combinations, which become the building blocks of sentences, and the number of different words they are capable of using increases sharply. By the age of 2 years, the average child has a vocabulary of more than 50 words. Just six months later, that vocabulary has grown to several hundred words. At that time, children can produce short sentences, although they use **telegraphic speech**—sentences that sound as if they were part of a telegram, in which words not critical to the message are left out. Rather than saying, "I showed you the book," a child using telegraphic speech might say, "I show book"; and "I am drawing a dog" might become "Drawing dog." As children get older, of course, their use of telegraphic speech declines and their sentences become increasingly complex (Blake, Quartaro, & Onorati, 1993).

By age 3, children learn to make plurals by adding *-s* to nouns and to form the past tense by adding *-ed* to verbs. This ability also leads to errors, because children tend to apply rules too inflexibly. This phenomenon is known as **overgeneralization**, whereby children apply rules even when the application results in an error. Thus, although it is correct to say "He walked" for the past tense of *walk,* the *-ed* rule doesn't work quite so well when children say "He runned" for the past tense of *run* (Marcus, 1996).

Children acquire most of the basic rules of language by age 5. However, a full vocabulary and the ability to comprehend and use subtle grammatical rules are not attained until later. For example, a 5-year-old boy who is shown a blindfolded doll and is asked, "Is the doll easy or hard to see?" would have great difficulty responding to the question. In fact, if he were asked to make the doll easier to see, he would probably try to remove the doll's blindfold. By 8 years of age, children have little difficulty understanding the question, realizing that the doll's blindfold has nothing to do with an observer's ability to see the doll (Chomsky, 1969).

babble: To make speechlike but meaningless sounds; usually done by children from the ages of around 3 months through 1 year.

telegraphic speech: Sentences that sound as if they were part of a telegram, in which words not critical to the message are left out.

overgeneralization: The phenomenon whereby children apply rules even when the application results in an error.

A syllable in signed language, similar to this, is found in the manual babbling of deaf infants. Corresponding verbal syllables are found in the spoken babbling of hearing infants. The similarities in language structure suggest that language has biological roots.

Understanding Language Acquisition: Identifying the Roots of Language

Anyone who spends even a little time with children will notice the enormous strides they make in language development throughout childhood. However, the reasons for this rapid growth are far from obvious. Two major explanations have been offered, one based on learning theory and the other on innate processes.

The rapidity of early language development has led many psychologists to argue that humans are biologically predisposed to learn language. Noam Chomsky suggests that the human brain has a neural system, the **language acquisition device**, that permits us to understand and produce language (Chomsky, 1968, 1978, 1991). This biological approach is supported by the existence of universal stages in language acquisition described in the preceding section. Deaf children, as well as hearing children, go through these stages (Petitto, 2000). Children all over the world go through the same steps in learning language. Also, the types of errors they make, such as overgeneralizations, are characteristic of children's speech but not adults' speech.

The second approach, the **learning-theory approach**, suggests that language is learned according to the principles of learning discussed in Chapter 5 (Skinner, 1957). This approach is supported by research that shows that the more parents speak to their young children, the more proficient the children become in language usage. In addition, higher levels of linguistic sophistication in parents' speech to their young children are related to a greater rate of vocabulary growth, vocabulary usage, and even general intellectual achievement by the time the children are 3 years of age (Hart & Risley, 1997).

With the passage of time it has become apparent that neither approach can wholly explain language acquisition. To read about second language acquisition, see the *Pathways Through Psychology* box on Fred Genesee, and the *Exploring Diversity* box on linguistic variety.

Understanding Reading Acquisition: Beginning and Fluent Reading

In early reading instruction, Canadian teachers have used the whole language approach, the basic skills approach, or a combination of the two. The **whole language approach** stresses the use of whole and meaningful materials, whereas the **basic skills approach** emphasizes the recognition of words in isolation. In the whole language approach instructional materials are whole, meaningful passages of text. Word identification and comprehension are derived from context. For example, a common classroom activity involves having children develop a story orally. The teacher prints the story as the children compose it, and then the children read it. The basic skills approach depends on learning the rules for translating the visual symbols into spoken words (spelling-to-sound correspondences). Children learn to segment words into sound units and also to blend segments into words. The whole language approach emphasizes top-down processing, whereas the basic skills approach emphasizes bottom-up processing. (See Chapter 3, p. 108.)

Research by Betty Ann Levy (at McMaster University) indicates that both basic skills and whole language approaches contribute to reading acquisition, but in different ways. Levy and Lysynchuk (1997) instructed one group of beginning readers in the acquisition of an initial word set or reading vocabulary using the whole language approach. They instructed another group of beginning readers by the basic skills approach, using strategies such as segmentation of words into syllables and blending of word segments into whole words. They found that the word set was learned more quickly and accurately by readers instructed by the basic skills approach than by the whole language approach.

In addition to the acquisition of reading vocabulary, the generalization of word recognition skills to new words and the comprehension of sentences and stories are important goals in beginning reading instruction. In the study mentioned in the preceding paragraph, Levy and Lysynchuk found that the thoroughness with which children learned the initial word set determined how well they read new words. In another study, Levy, Abello, and Lysynchuk (1997) gave children practice in single-word reading so that they would develop fluency in word recognition. Children given this practice read

language acquisition device: A hypothesized neural system of the brain that permits understanding of language.

learning-theory approach: The theory suggesting that language acquisition follows the principles of reinforcement and conditioning.

PsychLink

Language acquisition
www.mcgrawhill.ca/college/feldman

whole language approach: An approach to early reading instruction that stresses the use of whole and meaningful materials.
basic skills approach: An approach to early reading instruction that emphasizes the recognition of words in isolation.

"He's pretty good at rote categorization and single-object relational tasks, but he's not so hot at differentiating between representational and associational signs, and he's very weak on syntax."

stories containing the practised words more quickly and with better comprehension than children who did not receive single-word reading practice. These findings imply that when word recognition is fluent, more processing resources are available for comprehension.

Reading experiences provided by instructional strategies are used differently by good and poor readers to improve reading subskills. For example, poor readers learn individual words when they read stories. They use story reading to practise word recognition skills. In contrast, good readers practise and improve comprehension processes when they read stories (Faulkner & Levy, 1994). Findings such as these indicate that instructional strategies contribute to different aspects of reading acquisition and development (Levy, 2000).

In older students, learning from textbooks depends on both text format and learner characteristics. For example, Rukavina and Daneman (1996) found that a text format that structures information according to how students will need to use it aided learning. Working memory capacity and relative sophistication in ideas about the nature of knowledge also influenced learning. Readers who have less efficient memory strategies read text more superficially than readers with better memory strategies (Hannon & Daneman, 2001a). In adult readers, working memory strategies and ability to access and use information in long-term memory predict reading comprehension (Hannon & Daneman, 2001b).

The Influence of Language on Thinking: Do Inuit Have More Words for Snow Than Texans Have?

Do Inuit living in the frigid Arctic have a more expansive vocabulary for discussing snow than people living in warmer climates?

It makes sense that they might, and arguments that the Inuit language (Inuktitut) has many more words than English for snow have been made since the early 1900s. In 1956, linguist Benjamin Lee Whorf put forward the *linguistic relativity hypothesis*. According to this view, language shapes and produces thought (Whorf, 1956; Lucy, 1992, 1996; Smith, 1996).

Let's consider another possibility, however. Suppose that, instead of language being the *cause* of certain ways of thinking, thought *produces* language. The only reason to expect that Inuktitut might have more words for snow than English is that snow is considerably more relevant to Inuit than it is to people in other cultures.

Which view is correct? Most recent research refutes the linguistic relativity hypothesis and suggests, instead, that thought generally influences language—and not the other way around (Brown, 1986; Pinker, 1990; McFadyen, 1996).

Do Animals Use Language?

A question that has long puzzled psychologists is this: Is language uniquely human, or are other animals also able to acquire it? It is clear that many animals communicate with one another: fiddler crabs wave their claws to signal, bees dance to indicate the direction in which food will be found, certain birds say "zick, zick" during courtship and "kia" when they are about to fly away. But researchers have yet to demonstrate conclusively that animals use true language, which is characterized in part by the ability to produce and communicate new and unique meanings following a formal grammar.

Psychologists have, however, been able to teach chimps to communicate at surprisingly high levels. For instance, a chimp named Washoe learned to make signs for 132 words and was able to combine signs into simple sentences after four years of training. Even more impressively, Kanzi, a pygmy chimpanzee, has linguistic skills that some psychologists claim are close to those of a 2-year-old human being (Gardner & Gardner, 1969; Savage-Rumbaugh et al., 1993).

Despite the skills displayed by primates such as Kanzi, critics contend that the language they use still lacks the grammar and the complex and novel constructions that characterize the realm of human capabilities. Furthermore, firm evidence is lacking that animals are able to recognize and respond to the mental states of others of their species, an important aspect of human communication (Seidenberg & Pettito, 1987; Seyfarth & Cheney, 1992, 1996). Most evidence supports the contention that humans are better equipped than animals to produce and organize language in the form of meaningful sentences (Savage-Rumbaugh & Brakke, 1996).

Pathways Through Psychology

Fred Genesee

Professor
Department of Psychology
McGill University

Education: B.A., University of Western Ontario; M.A., Ph.D., McGill University

Home: Montreal

Fred Genesee

My interest in language began when I was an undergraduate; I did an Honours project on lateralization of language functions in the brain. During my first years at McGill I became interested in language acquisition, and in particular, second language acquisition in children. My interest in this topic arose from my belief that studying children acquiring language was a good way to examine biological factors that influence language learning. Focusing on second language acquisition was a way of examining the limits of the brain to learn language. I was also interested in developmental aspects of language because I wanted to examine how language impacts other aspects of development—social, cognitive, and even educational. For me, language is not only a biological endowment of human beings but a tool that influences diverse aspects of our lives. Language is undoubtedly the most complex accomplishment of human development and I continue to be fascinated by how this miraculous feat of childhood occurs. Bilingual acquisition is even more miraculous since bilingual children acquire two, or more, languages while monolingual children acquire one.

In my early research, I conducted numerous evaluations of second language immersion programs in Canada, and some in the U.S. I was concerned with the impact of immersion on students' first and second language development, their academic achievement, and their sociocultural development (e.g., attitudes towards themselves and others). This research led me to an interest in the pedagogy of second language instruction and I have written numerous articles and several books that seek to inform second language educators about the implications of research and theory for language teaching and learning in school. Much of what I do in the educational domain now encompasses education for language minority students (ESL) as well as language majority students, who were my original interest. My work has broadened to include consultation and collaboration with educators and policymakers around the world who are concerned with helping school-age children become bilingual—for example in Spain, Estonia, Japan, Germany. Educators and policymakers worldwide are increasingly adopting educational programs that will promote bilingualism among their students so that they can advance professionally, socioculturally, and economically. The global village is here and multilingualism is essential.

My research on second language immersion programs has shown that students who come to school speaking society's majority language can be educated effectively through the use of a second language without negative effects on their first language development or their academic achievement. My research has also shown that majority group students with characteristics that normally put them at risk for failure in school can also benefit from immersion in a second language. This research is often consulted by other researchers and professional educators.

My recent research focuses on preschool children who grow up learning two languages from birth—most of this work has examined French-English bilingual children. We carefully collect language samples from children and analyze transcriptions of their language in order to describe how they become bilingual and to test out various theories or hypotheses. For example, we are examining whether bilingual children go through the same milestones at the same rate in language development as monolingual children, and how they come to know when to use which language with whom.

My research on bilingual acquisition has shown that, from the one-word stage, bilingual children have differentiated linguistic systems and can use their developing languages differentially and appropriately in a variety of contexts. My work has also shown that child bilingual code-mixing (the use of words and structures from two languages in the same sentence) reveals linguistic, cognitive and communicative capacities that are truly unique to bilinguals and speaks to their developing competence.

Many people are skeptical about raising children bilingually. My interest in bilingual acquisition is motivated in part by my academic desire to contribute to theories of language acquisition, but also by my desire to demystify the misperceptions that people often have about bilingual acquisition. I regularly meet with groups who take care of bilingual children and share with them my and others' research so that they can make better decisions in their work with these children. I view myself as a science-broker—someone who translates research and theory into terms that are meaningful and useful to professionals, practitioners, and laypersons.

Source: Fred Genesee, Ph.D. McGill University.
<www.psych.mcgill.ca/faculty/genesee.html>

What are some misconceptions people have about second language learning? What are some benefits of bilingualism and multilingualism?

EXPLORING DIVERSITY

Linguistic Variety

In Canada we have two official languages, French and English, which reflect the founding nations of our country. Eighty-four percent of Canadians have English (60 percent) or French (24 percent) as their mother tongue (Statistics Canada, 1996b, 1999a). The remaining portion of the population shows great diversity in language, having one of about a dozen European or Asian languages or an equal number of Aboriginal languages as their mother tongue.

The most common language spoken by Canadians, other than English or French, is Chinese (used by 2.5 percent of the population), followed by Italian (1.8 percent) and German (1.6 percent). Most Chinese speakers live in Ontario and British Columbia. Most Italian and German speakers live in Ontario.

The most frequently spoken Aboriginal languages are Cree and Inuktitut. Cree is spoken by almost 10 percent of the Aboriginal population, mostly those living in the Prairie provinces. Inuktitut is spoken by a much smaller percent of Aboriginals (3.4 percent) who live mainly in the Northwest Territories or Quebec.

An increasing number of Canadians (about 17 percent) speaks more than one language fluently. Among parents and educators there is considerable interest in providing second language instruction in an effort to increase bilingualism. French-immersion programs developed by psychologists at McGill University (Lambert & Tucker, 1972; Genesee, 1984; Cenoz & Genesee, 1998) have served as pedagogical models in other Canadian provinces, and in other countries (e.g., Germany, Switzerland, Japan, and the United States).

Research findings show that bilinguals have some distinct advantages compared to monolinguals. For example, they solve problems with greater flexibility and creativity (Bochner, 1996). Bilingual children perform better than monolingual children on both verbal and nonverbal tests of intelligence (Lambert & Anisfeld, 1969; Lambert & Peal, 1972; Hakuta & Garcia, 1989). In addition, young bilingual children have a more fully developed metalinguistic awareness (awareness and knowledge of the characteristics of language), that gives them a distinct advantage in learning to read (Bialystok, 1997; Bialystok & Herman, 1999; Segalowitz, 1997).

Besides English and French, what languages are most commonly used by Canadians?

Evaluate

1. Match the component of grammar with its definition:
   1. Syntax
   2. Phonology
   3. Semantics

   a. Rules showing how words can be combined into sentences
   b. Rules governing the meaning of words and sentences
   c. The study of the sound system in language

2. Language production and language comprehension develop in infants at about the same time. True or false?

3. _____ _____ refers to the phenomenon in which young children omit nonessential portions of sentences.

4. A child knows that adding -ed to certain words puts them in the past tense. As a result, instead of saying "He came," the child says "He comed." This is an example of _____.

5. _____ theory assumes that language acquisition is based on principles of operant conditioning and shaping.

6. Chomsky argues that language acquisition is an innate ability tied to the structure of the brain. True or false?

Rethink

1. Why is overgeneralization seen as an argument against a strict learning-theory approach to explaining language acquisition?

2. Does the ability of infants who are deaf to use manual babbling support or contradict the view that language is innate in humans? Why?

Answers to Evaluate Questions

1. 1-a, 2-c, 3-b; 2. False; language comprehension precedes language production; 3. Telegraphic speech; 4. Overgeneralization; 5. Learning; 6. True.

Prepare

- How do psychologists characterize and define intelligence?
- What are the major approaches to measuring intelligence?
- How can the extremes of intelligence be characterized?
- Are traditional IQ tests culturally biased?
- To what degree is intelligence influenced by the environment and to what degree is it influenced by heredity?

Organize

Intelligence
    Measuring Intelligence
    Are There Different Kinds of Intelligence?
    Variations in Intellectual Ability
    Individual Differences in Intelligence

 **PsychLink**

Evolution of intelligence
www.mcgrawhill.ca/college/feldman

intelligence: The capacity to understand the world, think rationally, and use resources effectively when faced with challenges.

intelligence tests: Tests devised to identify a person's level of intelligence.

Intelligence

It is typical for members of the Trukese, a small tribe in the South Pacific, to sail a hundred miles in open ocean waters. Although their destination may be just a small dot of land less than a mile wide, the Trukese are able to sail unerringly toward it without the aid of a compass, chronometer, sextant, or any of the other sailing tools that are indispensable to modern western navigation. They are able to sail accurately, even when prevailing winds do not allow a direct approach to the island and they must take a zigzag course. (Gladwin, 1964)

How are the Trukese able to navigate so effectively? If you asked them, they could not explain it. They might tell you that they take into account the rising and setting of the stars and the appearance, sound, and feel of the waves against the side of the boat. But at any given moment as they are sailing along, they could not identify their position or say why they are doing what they are doing. Nor could they explain the navigational theory underlying their sailing technique.

Some might say the inability of the Trukese to explain in Western terms how their sailing technique works is a sign of primitive or even unintelligent behaviour. In fact, if we made Trukese sailors take a Western standardized test of navigational knowledge and theory, or, for that matter, a traditional test of intelligence, they may do poorly on it. Yet, as a practical matter, it is not possible to accuse the Trukese of being unintelligent: Despite their inability to explain how they do it, they are able to navigate successfully through the open ocean waters.

Trukese navigation points out the difficulty in coming to grips with what is meant by intelligence. To a Westerner, travelling in a straight line along the most direct and quickest route using a sextant and other navigational tools is likely to represent the most "intelligent" kind of behaviour; to this person, a zigzag course, based on the "feel" of the waves, would not seem very reasonable. To the Trukese, who are accustomed to their own system of navigation, however, the use of complicated navigational tools might seem so overly complex and unnecessary that they might think of Western navigators as lacking in intelligence.

It is clear that the term *intelligence* can take on many different meanings. A person who lives in a remote part of the Australian outback might differentiate between more intelligent and less intelligent people in terms of their success at mastering hunting skills. To someone living in the heart of urban Miami, intelligence might be exemplified by being "streetwise" or by business success.

Each of these conceptions of intelligence is reasonable. Each represents an instance in which more intelligent people are better able to use the resources of their environment than less intelligent people are, a distinction that is presumably basic to any definition of intelligence. Yet it is also clear that these conceptions involve very different views of intelligence.

The definition of intelligence that psychologists employ contains some of the same elements found in the layperson's conception. To psychologists, **intelligence** is the capacity to understand the world, think rationally, and use resources effectively when faced with challenges (Wechsler, 1975).

Unfortunately, neither laypersons' nor psychologists' conception of intelligence is of much help when it comes to distinguishing, with any degree of precision, more intelligent people from less intelligent ones. To overcome this problem, psychologists who study intelligence have focused much of their attention on the development of **intelligence tests**, and have relied on such tests to identify a person's level of intelligence. These tests have proven to be of great benefit in identifying students in need of special attention in school, in diagnosing cognitive difficulties, and in helping people make optimal educational and vocational choices. At the same time, their use has proven quite controversial, raising important social and educational issues.

Measuring Intelligence

The forerunner of the modern IQ test was based on the uncomplicated, but completely wrong, assumption that the size and shape of a person's head could be used as an objective measure of intelligence. The idea was put forward by Sir Francis Galton (1822–1911), an eminent English scientist whose ideas in other domains proved to be considerably better than his notions about intelligence. Although Galton's theory proved wrong on virtually every count, it did have at least one desirable result: He was the first to suggest that intelligence could be quantified and measured in an objective manner.

The first legitimate intelligence tests were developed by Alfred Binet (1857–1911). His tests followed a simple premise: If performance on certain tasks or test items improved with *chronological*, or physical, age, then performance could be used to distinguish more intelligent people from less intelligent ones within a particular age group. Using this principle, Binet, a French psychologist, devised the first formal intelligence test, which was designed to identify the "dullest" students in the Paris school system in order to provide them with remedial aid.

Binet began by presenting tasks to same-age students who had been labelled "bright" or "dull" by their teachers. If a task could be completed by the bright students but not by the dull ones, he retained the task as a proper test item; otherwise it was discarded. In the end he came up with a test that distinguished between the bright and dull groups, and—with further work—one that distinguished among children in different age groups (Binet & Simon, 1916).

On the basis of the Binet test, children were assigned a score relating to their **mental age**, the average age of individuals who achieve a particular level of performance on a test. For example, if the average 8-year-old answered, say, 45 items correctly on a test, anyone who answered 45 items correctly would be assigned a mental age of 8 years. Consequently, whether the person scoring 45 on the test was 20 years old or 5 years old, each would have the same mental age of 8 years.

Assigning a mental age to students provided an indication of their general level of performance. However, it did not allow for adequate comparisons among people of different chronological ages. By using mental age alone, for instance, we might assume that a 20-year-old responding at an 18-year-old's level would be as bright as a 5-year-old answering at a 3-year-old's level, when actually the 5-year-old would be displaying a much greater *relative* degree of slowness.

A solution to the problem came in the form of the **intelligence quotient**, or **IQ**, a score that takes into account an individual's mental *and* chronological ages. In the following formula for calculating IQ scores, *MA* stands for mental age and *CA* for chronological age:

$$\text{IQ score} = \frac{\text{MA}}{\text{CA}} \times 100$$

Using this formula, we can return to the earlier example of a 20-year-old performing at a mental age of 18 and calculate an IQ score of $(18/20) \times 100 = 90$. In contrast, the 5-year-old performing at a mental age of 3 comes out with a considerably lower IQ score: $(3/5) \times 100 = 60$.

Anyone who has a mental age equal to his or her chronological age will have an IQ equal to 100. People with a mental age that is greater than their chronological age will have IQs that exceed 100.

Although the basic principles behind the calculation of an IQ score still hold, IQ scores actually are figured in a different manner today and are known as *deviation IQ scores*. First, the average test score for everyone of the same age who takes the test is determined, and this average score is assigned an IQ of 100. Then, with the aid of statistical techniques that calculate the differences (or "deviations") between each score and the average, IQ scores are assigned.

As you can see in Figure 7-8, approximately two-thirds of all individuals fall within 15 IQ points above and below the average score of 100. As scores increase or fall beyond that range, the percentage of people in a category falls considerably.

PsychLink
Gardner's Essay on IQ
www.mcgrawhill.ca/college/feldman

mental age: The average age of individuals who achieve a particular level of performance on a test.

intelligence quotient (IQ): A score that takes into account an individual's mental *and* chronological ages.

IQ Tests: Gauging Intelligence

Remnants of Binet's original intelligence test are still with us, although it has been revised in significant ways. Now in its fourth edition and called the *Stanford-Binet IV,* the test consists of a series of items that vary in nature according to the age of the person being tested (Hagen, Sattler, & Thorndike, 1985; Thorndike, Hagan, & Sattler, 1986). For example, young children are asked to copy figures or answer questions about everyday activities. Older people are asked to solve analogies, explain proverbs, and describe similarities that underlie sets of words.

The test is administered orally. An examiner begins by finding a mental age level at which the person is able to answer all questions correctly, and then moves on to successively more difficult problems. When a mental age level is reached at which no items can be answered, the test is over. By examining the pattern of correct and incorrect responses, the examiner is able to compute an IQ score for the person being tested. In addition, the Stanford-Binet provides separate subscores, providing clues to a test-taker's particular strengths and weaknesses.

The other IQ test frequently used in North America was devised by psychologist David Wechsler and is known as the *Wechsler Adult Intelligence Scale—III,* or, more commonly, the *WAIS-III.* There is also a children's version, the *Wechsler Intelligence Scale for Children—III,* or *WISC-III.* Both the WAIS-III and the WISC-III have two major parts: a verbal scale and a performance (or nonverbal) scale. As you can see from the sample questions in Figure 7-9, the two scales include questions of very different types. Verbal tasks consist of more traditional kinds of problems, including vocabulary definition and comprehension of various concepts. In contrast, the performance (nonverbal) part involves the timed assembly of small objects and arranging pictures in a logical order. By providing separate scores, the WAIS-III and WISC-III give a more precise picture of a person's specific abilities than other IQ tests (Kaufman & Lichtenberger, 1999).

Because the Stanford-Binet, WAIS-III, and WISC-III all require individualized, one-on-one administration, it is relatively difficult and time-consuming to administer and score them on a large-scale basis. Consequently, there are now a number of IQ tests that allow group administration. Rather than having one examiner ask one person at a time to respond to individual items, group IQ tests are strictly paper-and-pencil measures, in which those taking the tests read the questions and provide their answers in writing. The primary advantage of group tests is their ease of administration (Anastasi & Urbina, 1997).

Figure 7-8 The average and most frequent IQ score is 100, and 68 percent of all people are within a 30-point range centred on 100. Some 95 percent of the population have scores that are within 30 points above or below 100, and 99.7 percent have scores that are between 55 and 145.

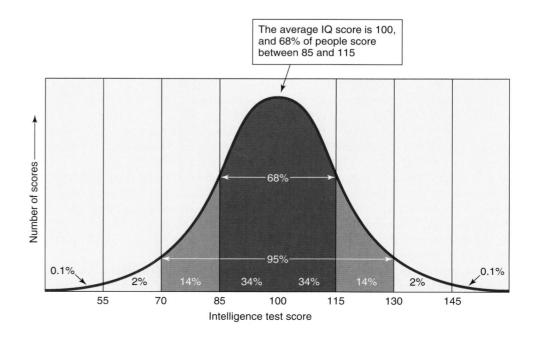

There are, however, sacrifices made in group testing which, in some cases, may outweigh the benefits. For instance, group tests generally offer fewer kinds of questions than tests administered individually. Furthermore, people may be more motivated to perform at their highest ability level when working on a one-to-one basis with a test administrator than they are in a group. Finally, in some cases it is simply impossible to employ group tests, particularly with young children or people with unusually low IQ (Aiken, 1996).

Achievement and Aptitude Tests

IQ tests are not the only kind of tests that you may have taken during the course of your schooling. Two other kinds of tests, related to intelligence but designed to measure somewhat

Types of Items Found on the Wechsler Intelligence Scales for Children—III (WISC-III)

Name	Goal of Item	Example
Verbal scale		
Information	To assess general information	Where does milk come from?
Comprehension	To test understanding and evaluation of social norms and past experience	Why do we put food in the refrigerator?
Arithmetic	To assess math reasoning through verbal problems	Stacy had two crayons and the teacher gave her two more. How many did she have altogether?
Similarities	To test understanding of how objects or concepts are alike, tapping abstract reasoning	In what way are cows and horses alike?
Performance Scale		
Digit symbol	To assess speed of learning	Match symbols to numbers using the key 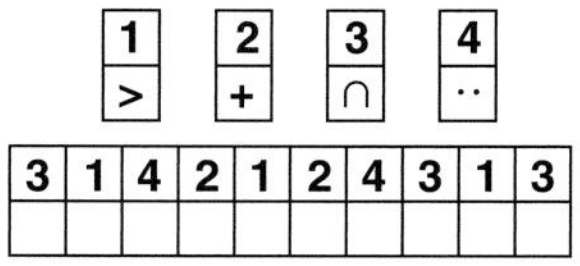
Picture completion	To identify missing parts, testing visual memory and attention	Identify what is missing 
Object assembly	To test understanding of relationship of parts to wholes	Put pieces together to form a whole 

Figure 7–9 Typical kinds of items found on the verbal and performance (nonverbal) scales of the Wechsler Intelligence Scales for Children—III (WISC-III).

achievement test: A test designed to determine a person's level of knowledge in a given subject area.

different phenomena, are achievement tests and aptitude tests. An **achievement test** is a test designed to determine a person's level of knowledge in a given subject area. In Canadian schools these tests are given routinely at least three times, usually in grades three, five, and eight, though the exact grades when the tests are administered differ from province to province. Rather than measuring general ability, as an intelligence test does, an achievement test concentrates on the specific material that a person has learned. Ministries of education in all provinces and territories are requiring standardized testing in the foundation skills of reading comprehension and mathematics at various grade levels. High school students sometimes take specialized achievement tests in particular areas such as world history or chemistry as a college entrance requirement.

aptitude test: A test designed to predict a person's ability in a particular area or line of work.

An **aptitude test** is designed to predict a person's ability in a particular area or line of work. In the process of pursuing admission to university, American students, and Canadian students applying to universities in the United States, take one of the best known aptitude tests: the Scholastic Achievement Test (SAT). The SAT is meant to predict how well people will do in university, and the scores have proven over the years to be moderately correlated with university grades.

Aptitude and achievement tests are not restricted to application to academic institutions. Air traffic control is one of many training programs for which applicants are expected to take the appropriate aptitude test to evaluate their potential for success. Lawyers must pass an achievement test (in the form of the bar exam) in order to practise law.

Although in theory the distinction between aptitude and achievement tests is precise, it is difficult to develop an aptitude test that does not rely at least in part on past achievement. (For more on how tests are used, see the *Applying Psychology in the 21ˢᵗ Century* box.)

Reliability and Validity: Taking the Measure of Tests

reliability: The concept that tests measure consistently what they are trying to measure.
validity: The concept that tests actually measure what they are supposed to measure.

When we use a ruler, we expect to get the same length for a centimetre as the last time we used it. When we weigh ourselves on the bathroom scale, we hope that the variations we see on the scale are due to changes in our weight and not to errors on the part of the scale (unless the change in weight is in an unwanted direction!).

In the same way, we hope that psychological tests have **reliability**—that they measure consistently what they are trying to measure. We need to be sure that each time we administer the test, a test-taker will achieve the same results—assuming that nothing about the person has changed relevant to what is being measured (a type of reliability called *test-retest reliability*).

Suppose, for instance, that when you first took the SAT exams you scored a 400 on the verbal section of the test. Then, after taking the test again a few months later, you scored a 700. Upon receiving your new score, you might well stop celebrating for a moment to question whether the test is reliable, for it is unlikely that your abilities could have changed enough to raise your score by 300 points.

But suppose your score changed hardly at all, and both times you received a score of about 400. You couldn't complain about a lack of reliability. However, if you knew your verbal skills were above average, you might be concerned that the test did not adequately measure what it was supposed to measure—the question has now become one of validity rather than reliability. A test has **validity** when it actually measures what it is supposed to measure.

Applying Psychology in the 21st Century

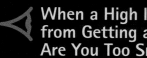

◁ **When a High IQ Keeps You from Getting a Job: Are You Too Smart for the Job You Want?**

Wanted: one not-so-smart police officer.

Although that's not how the advertisement for police officers in New London, Connecticut, put it, it might as well have. The official hiring policy prevents people who score too low or too *high* on an employment test administered by the town to be considered for a position as police officer (Allen, 1999; see Figure 7-10).

The hiring standards came to light during a three-year court battle, in which an applicant for a position as police officer was refused even an interview. The reason was that he scored 33 out of 50 on an exam used by the police department to screen applicants, and anyone who scored above 27 was considered too skilled to do a good job as a police officer.

The screening test used by the police department has been utilized by 40 000 employers throughout the United States and has been given to 125 million people since it was first devised. It is designed to give a range of scores for people who are likely to be successful in a given profession, with the range depending on the nature of the specific job. Although not a traditional IQ measure, the test gauges learning ability, skill in understanding instructions, and problem-solving potential (Wonderlic, 2000).

The rationale for excluding applicants who score too high, according to the New London police department, is that much police work is routine. As a consequence, highly intelligent police officers become bored and leave the job soon after they have received their expensive initial training.

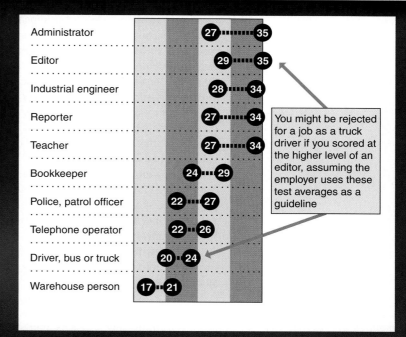

Figure 7-10 Based on a scale from 1 to 50, these are suggested minimum and maximum scores for selected professions as determined by a preemployment test developed by a private human resources firm. (Source: Wonderlic, Inc., 1999.)

Critics of the police department's position point out that it takes considerable intelligence to deal with complex situations faced by police officers, such as complicated social situations involving families. Furthermore, some decisions must be made instantly and under enormous pressure—in these situations intelligence would clearly be of benefit. Furthermore, one could argue that it is better to have frequent turnover of intelligent workers, rather than be saddled with not-so-intelligent employees for long periods.

Despite these criticisms, courts have ruled that employers have the right to exclude potential workers on the basis of being too skilled, as long as the guidelines are uniformly applied to all job seekers. As a consequence, job applicants have a new worry to add to their anxieties—that they might score too high on a job test.

How do you think employers established that some scores on the tests described above were too high for certain jobs? Do you think it is reasonable to exclude people from certain jobs on the basis of high test scores? Why?

Considering the widespread use of the SAT in the university admission process in the United States, its validity is extremely important. Some researchers have questioned whether test-takers' strategies influence the validity of the reading portion of the SAT. For example, Katz et al. (1990) questioned its validity because they found that test-takers performed at better than chance level even when they did not see the test passages. Daneman and Hannon (2001) conducted a study using University of Toronto students, who, like most Canadian university students, have not taken the SAT. In experimental conditions in which participants read the SAT passages and answered the questions, scores on another reading test (Nelson-Denny) were the best predictor of SAT reading scores. These results indicate that the two tests were measuring the same thing, thus demonstrating the validity of the SAT reading test. In addition, Daneman and Hannon also investigated the

PsychLink

Reliability and validity discussion
www.mcgrawhill.ca/college/feldman

validity of the SAT reading test in an experimental condition in which participants did not have access to the test passages to read them, but still were required to answer the questions on them. These participants, like those who had the opportunity to read the passages, also did the Nelson-Denny reading test and a test of working-memory that measured verbal reasoning and inferential skills. In this condition, the scores on the working-memory test were the best predictor of SAT reading scores. These results suggest that when test-takers guessed at the answers to the SAT reading test, they were using verbal reasoning and inferential skills that are important for reading comprehension. Thus, in a very broad sense, the SAT reading test appeared to have validity even when participants were simply guessing at answers. (Incidentally, Daneman and Hannon also found that the strategy that produced the best SAT reading scores was to read each passage in advance and then reread it to answer the questions.)

Knowing that a test is reliable is no guarantee that it is also valid. For instance, Sir Francis Galton assumed that skull size was related to intelligence, and he was able to measure skull size with great reliability. However, the measure of skull size was not valid—it had nothing to do with intelligence. In this case, then, we have reliability without validity.

On the other hand, if a test is unreliable, it cannot be valid. Assuming that all other factors—motivation to score well, knowledge of the material, health, and so forth—are similar, if a person scores high the first time he or she takes a specific test and low the second time, the test cannot be measuring what it is supposed to measure. Therefore, the test is both unreliable and not valid.

Assuming that a test is both valid and reliable, one further step is necessary in order to interpret the meaning of a particular test-taker's score: the establishment of norms. **Norms** are standards of test performance that permit the comparison of one person's score on the test to the scores of others who have taken the same test. For example, a norm permits test-takers to know that they have scored, say, in the top 15 percent of those who have taken the test previously. Tests for which norms have been developed are known as *standardized tests*.

The basic scheme for developing norms is for test designers to calculate the average score achieved by a particular group of people for whom the test is designed. The test designers can then determine the extent to which each person's score differs from the scores of the others who have taken the test in the past. Test-takers are then able to consider the meaning of their raw scores relative to the scores of others who have taken the test, giving them a qualitative sense of their performance. Of course, the people used to determine norms must be representative of the individuals to whom the test is directed.

norms: Standards of test performance that permit the comparison of one person's score on the test to the scores of others who have taken the same test.

Adaptive Testing: Using Computers to Assess Performance Ensuring that tests are reliable and valid, and are based on appropriate norms, has become even more critical with the introduction of computers to administer standardized tests. In the new computerized version of the SAT, not only are test questions viewed and answered on a computer, but the test itself is individualized. Using *adaptive testing,* students do not necessarily receive identical sets of test questions. Instead, the computer first presents a randomly selected question of moderate difficulty. If the test-taker answers it correctly, the computer will then present a randomly chosen item of slightly greater difficulty. If the answer is wrong, then the computer will present a slightly easier item. Each question becomes slightly harder or easier than the question preceding it, depending on whether the previous response is correct. Ultimately, the greater the number of difficult questions answered correctly, the higher the score.

Are There Different Kinds of Intelligence?

Although Binet's procedure for measuring intelligence, exemplified by the modern Stanford-Binet and WAIS-III intelligence tests, remains one of the most frequently employed, some theorists argue that it lacks an underlying conception of what intelligence is. To Binet and his followers, intelligence was generally conceived of as a direct reflection of a person's score on his or her test. That was an eminently practical approach, but it depended not on an understanding of the nature of intelligence but primarily on comparing one person's performance with that of others. For this reason, the intelligence tests of Binet and his successors do little to increase our understanding of what intelligence is; they merely measure behaviour assumed to exemplify intelligence.

One central question addressed by researchers is whether intelligence is a single, unitary factor, or whether it is made up of multiple components. Early psychologists interested in intelligence assumed that there was a single, general factor for mental ability, which they called **g**, or the **g-factor** (Spearman, 1927). This general intelligence factor was thought to underlie performance on every aspect of intelligence, and it was the g-factor that was presumably being measured on tests of intelligence (Jensen, 1998; Mackintosh, 1998).

g or g-factor: The single, general factor for mental ability, assumed to underlie intelligence in some early theories of intelligence.

Fluid and Crystallized Intelligence

More recently, some psychologists have suggested that there are really two different kinds of intelligence: fluid intelligence and crystallized intelligence (Cattell, 1967, 1987). **Fluid intelligence** reflects information-processing capabilities, reasoning, and memory. If we were asked to group a series of letters according to some criterion, or to remember a set of numbers, we would be using fluid intelligence.

In contrast, **crystallized intelligence** is the accumulation of information, skills, and strategies that people have learned through experience and that they can apply in problem-solving situations. We would be likely to rely on crystallized intelligence, for instance, if we were asked to participate in a discussion about the solution to the causes of poverty, a task that allows us to draw upon our own past experiences and knowledge of the world. The differences between fluid and crystallized intelligence become particularly evident in the elderly, who—as we will discuss further in Chapter 9—show declines in fluid, but not crystallized, intelligence (Schaie, 1993, 1994; Schretlen et al., 2000).

fluid intelligence: Intelligence that reflects information-processing capabilities, reasoning, and memory.
crystallized intelligence: The accumulation of information, skills, and strategies learned through experience and that can be applied in problem-solving situations.

Other theoreticians conceive of intelligence as encompassing even more components. For example, Louis Thurstone (1938) suggested there were seven factors, which he called primary mental abilities, and J. P. Guilford (1985) said there were 150!

Gardner's Multiple Intelligences: The Many Ways of Showing Intelligence

In his consideration of intelligence, psychologist Howard Gardner has taken an approach that is very different from traditional thinking about the topic. Gardner argues that rather than asking "How smart are you?" we should be asking a different question: "How are you smart?" In answering the latter question, Gardner has developed a theory of *multiple intelligences* that has become quite influential (Chen & Gardner, 1997).

Gardner argues that we have eight forms of intelligence (described in Figure 7-11), each relatively independent of the others. He suggests that each of the multiple intelligences is linked to an independent system in the brain (Gardner, 1997, 1999). Each of us has the same eight kinds of intelligence, although in different degrees. Gardner suggests that these separate intelligences do not operate in isolation. Normally, any activity encompasses several kinds of intelligence working together.

Is Information Processing Intelligence?

One of the newer contributions to understanding intelligence comes from the work of cognitive psychologists who use an *information-processing approach*. They assert that the way people store material in memory and use the material to solve intellectual tasks provides the most accurate measure of intelligence. Consequently, rather than focusing on the structure of intelligence or its underlying content or dimensions, information processing approaches examine the *processes* involved in producing intelligent behaviour (Sternberg, 1990; Deary & Stough, 1996; Embretson, 1996).

"To be perfectly frank, I'm not nearly as smart as you seem to think I am."

1. Musical intelligence (skills in tasks involving music). Case example:

When he was 3, Yehudi Menuhin was smuggled into the San Francisco Orchestra concerts by his parents. The sound of Louis Persinger's violin so entranced the youngster that he insisted on a violin for his birthday and Louis Persinger as his teacher. He got them both. By the time he was 10 years old, Menuhin was an international performer.

2. Bodily kinesthetic intelligence (skills in using the whole body or various portions of it in the solution of problems or in the construction of products or displays, exemplified by dancers, athletes, actors, and surgeons). Case example:

Fifteen-year-old Babe Ruth played third base. During one game, his team's pitcher was doing very poorly and Babe loudly criticized him from third base. Brother Matthias, the coach, called out, "Ruth, if you know so much about it, *you* pitch!" Babe was surprised and embarrassed because he had never pitched before, but Brother Matthias insisted. Ruth said later that at the very moment he took the pitcher's mound, he *knew* he was supposed to be a pitcher.

3. Logical-mathematical intelligence (skills in problem-solving and scientific thinking). Case example:

Barbara McClintock won the Nobel Prize in medicine for her work in microbiology. She describes one of her breakthroughs, which came after thinking about a problem for half an hour . . .: "Suddenly I jumped and ran back to the (corn) field. At the top of the field (the others were still at the bottom) I shouted, 'Eureka, I have it!' "

4. Linguistic intelligence (skills involved in the production and use of language). Case example:

At the age of 10, T. S. Eliot created a magazine called *Fireside,* to which he was the sole contributor. In a three-day period during his winter vacation, he created eight complete issues.

5. Spatial intelligence (skills involving spatial configurations, such as those used by artists and architects). Case example:

Natives of the Caroline Islands navigate at sea without instruments. During the actual trip, the navigator must envision mentally a reference island as it passes under a particular star and from that he computes the number of segments completed, the proportion of the trip remaining, and any corrections in heading.

6. Interpersonal intelligence (skills in interacting with others, such as sensitivity to the moods, temperaments, motivations, and intentions of others). Case example:

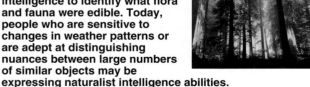

When Anne Sullivan began instructing the deaf and blind Helen Keller, her task was one that had eluded others for years. Yet, just two weeks after beginning her work with Keller, Sullivan achieved a great success. In her words, "My heart is singing with joy this morning. A miracle has happened! The wild little creature of two weeks ago has been transformed into a gentle child."

7. Intrapersonal intelligence (knowledge of the internal aspects of oneself; access to one's own feelings and emotions). Case example:

In her essay "A Sketch of the Past," Virginia Woolf displays deep insight into her own inner life through these lines, describing her reaction to several specific memories from her childhood that still, in adulthood, shock her: "Though I still have the peculiarity that I receive these sudden shocks, they are now always welcome; after the first surprise, I always feel instantly that they are particularly valuable. And so I go on to suppose that the shock-receiving capacity is what makes me a writer."

8. Naturalist intelligence (ability to identify and classify patterns in nature). Case example:

During prehistoric times, hunter/gatherers would rely on naturalist intelligence to identify what flora and fauna were edible. Today, people who are sensitive to changes in weather patterns or are adept at distinguishing nuances between large numbers of similar objects may be expressing naturalist intelligence abilities.

Figure 7-11 Howard Gardner believes that there are eight major kinds of intelligences, corresponding to abilities in different domains. *In what area does your greatest intelligence reside, and why do you think you have particular strengths in that area?* (Adapted from Gardner, 2000).

For example, research shows that people with high IQ scores spend more time on the initial encoding stages of problems, identifying parts of a problem and retrieving relevant information from long-term memory, than do people with lower scores. This initial emphasis on recalling relevant information pays off in the end; those who use this approach are more successful in finding solutions than those who spend relatively less time on the initial stages (Sternberg, 1982, 1990; Deary & Stough, 1996).

Other information-processing approaches examine sheer speed of processing. For example, research shows that the speed with which people are able to retrieve information from memory is related to verbal intelligence. In general, people with higher IQ scores react more quickly on a variety of information-processing tasks, ranging from reactions to flashing lights to distinguishing between letters. The speed of information processing, then, may underlie differences in intelligence (Hunt, 1983; Deary & Stough, 1996; Siegler, 1998).

Practical Intelligence and Emotional Intelligence: Toward a More Intelligent View of Intelligence

According to psychologist Robert Sternberg, the most useful measure of intelligence is represented by **practical intelligence**, intelligence related to overall success in living. Noting that traditional tests were designed to relate to academic success, Sternberg points to evidence showing that IQ does not relate particularly well to *career* success (McClelland, 1993). Specifically, although successful business executives usually score at least moderately well on IQ tests, the rate at which they advance and their ultimate business achievements are only minimally associated with their specific IQ scores (Sternberg, 1998, 2000; Wagner, 1997, 2000).

Sternberg argues that career success requires a type of intelligence very different from academic success. Whereas academic success is based on knowledge of a particular information base obtained from reading and listening, practical intelligence is learned mainly through observation of others' behaviour. People who are high in practical intelligence are able to learn general norms and principles and apply them appropriately. Consequently, practical intelligence tests measure the ability to employ broad principles in solving everyday problems (Sternberg et al., 1995; Polk, 1997; see Chapter Activity 7-6).

Some psychologists broaden the concept of practical intelligence even further beyond the intellectual realm and consider intelligence involving emotions. The concept of emotional intelligence was introduced by Peter Salovey and John Mayer (1990). By **emotional intelligence** they meant the ability to understand emotions in oneself and others and to regulate emotions in order to make life better. The concept was popularized by Daniel Goleman, who wrote the best-selling book *Emotional Intelligence: Why It Can Matter More Than IQ* (1995). According to Goleman, there are five domains in emotional intelligence: knowing one's emotions, managing or regulating emotions, using emotion to motivate oneself, recognizing and understanding emotions in others, and handling relationships. In his view, how we function in these domains affects our personal relationships, our degree of job success, and our health. He also believes that the development and exercise of higher levels of emotional intelligence is crucial to the welfare of society at large (Goleman, 1995, 1998).

Another psychologist who is interested in applying the theory of emotional intelligence is Steven Stein, a Canadian clinical psychologist. Stein distinguishes intrapersonal aspects of emotional intelligence (such as being emotionally self-aware, and using emotions as motivators) from interpersonal aspects (such as recognizing and understanding emotions in others). He has been particularly interested in applying emotional intelligence in problem solving, fulfilling social responsibilities, managing mood and stress, and promoting one's sense of happiness and general well-being (Stein & Book, 2000). Table 7-1 presents a summary of the different approaches to intelligence used by psychologists.

Variations in Intellectual Ability

Both those individuals with low IQs and those with unusually high IQs require special attention if they are to reach their full potential.

PsychLink
Multiple intelligences
www.mcgrawhill.ca/college/feldman

practical intelligence: Intelligence related to overall success in living.

PsychLink
Triarchic theory of intelligence
www.mcgrawhill.ca/college/feldman

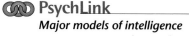
PsychLink
Major models of intelligence
www.mcgrawhill.ca/college/feldman

emotional intelligence: The ability to understand emotions in oneself and others and to regulate emotions in order to make life better.

Chapter Activity 7–6
Measuring Practical Intelligence

FIGURE 7-12 Most standard tests of intelligence primarily measure analytical skills, while more comprehensive tests measure creative and practical abilities as well (Sternberg 2000, pg. 399).

Reprinted with permission from R. J. Sternberg, "The Holey Grail of General Intelligence," *Science*, 289, pp. 399–401, 2000. Copyright 2000 American Association for the Advancement of Science.

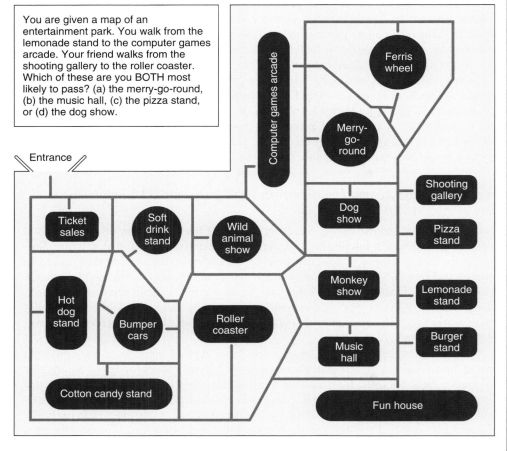

You are given a map of an entertainment park. You walk from the lemonade stand to the computer games arcade. Your friend walks from the shooting gallery to the roller coaster. Which of these are you BOTH most likely to pass? (a) the merry-go-round, (b) the music hall, (c) the pizza stand, or (d) the dog show.

Intellectual Disability and Mental Retardation

intellectual disability: An impaired ability to learn.

mental retardation: Having significantly below-average intellectual functioning accompanied by limitations in at least two areas of adaptive functioning.

Although sometimes thought of as a rare phenomenon, **intellectual disability** occurs in 1 to 3 percent of the population. There is wide variation among those labelled as having intellectual disability, which is an impaired ability to learn.

In the United States, the American Association on Mental Retardation (AAMR) has developed an inclusive definition of **mental retardation** (a term used in the United States, but no longer commonly used in Canada, where terms such as *intellectual disability*

Table 7-1 Major Approaches to Intelligence

Approach	Characteristics
IQ tests	General measures of intelligence
Fluid and crystallized intelligence	Fluid intelligence relates to reasoning, memory, and information-processing capabilities; crystallized intelligence relates to information, skills, and strategies learned through experience
Gardner's multiple intelligences	Eight independent forms of intelligence
Information-processing approaches	Intelligence is reflected in the ways people store and use material to solve intellectual tasks
Practical intelligence	Intelligence in terms of nonacademic, career, and personal success
Emotional intelligence	Intelligence that provides an understanding of what other people are feeling and experiencing, and permits us to respond appropriately to others' needs

and *developmental disability* are preferred.) According to this definition, mental retardation exists when there is significantly below-average intellectual functioning, plus limitations in at least two areas of adaptive functioning involving communication skills, social skills, community involvement, self-care, self-direction, ability to live independently, health and safety, academics, or leisure and work (AAMR, 1992; Burack, Hodapp, & Zigler, 1998). Most people with mental retardation (about 90 percent) are classified as having *mild retardation* (IQs from 55 to 69) because of their mild deficits. They can be taught to work and function with little special attention. Those with *moderate retardation* (IQs of 40 to 54) have early obvious deficits with language and motor skills lagging behind those of peers, require moderate supervision throughout their lives, and can hold simple jobs as adults. Those with *profound retardation* (IQs below 25) are generally unable to function independently and require institutional treatment throughout their lives (Durkin & Stein, 1996; Negrin & Capute, 1996; Detterman, Gabriel, & Ruthsatz, 2000).

In Canada, provincial ministries of education have established guidelines for classifying those with intellectual disability. For example, in Ontario two broad categories are commonly used. Those with *intellectual disability* have comparatively mild deficits (poor daily living and social skills, but functional reading and mathematics skills). They can benefit from a modified educational program. Those with *developmental disability* have profound disability (moderate to severe intellectual deficits as well as physical challenges in the most severe cases). They may require an alternative individualized educational program.

What are the causes of intellectual disability? In nearly one-third of the cases there is an identifiable biological reason. The most common biological cause is *Down Syndrome,* which involves the presence of an extra chromosome. Other biological causes include abnormality in the structure of a chromosome, birth complications such as temporary lack of oxygen, and fetal alcohol syndrome (Simonoff, Bolton, & Rutter, 1996; Selikowitz, 1997). Intellectual disability may also be caused by environmental factors such as extreme poverty or deprivation, or a combination of environmental and genetic factors.

In the last several decades, important advances in the care and treatment of the intellectually disabled have been made. Prior to that, the philosophy was to segregate the intellectually disabled into special education classes, where students could learn at their own pace along with other handicapped students. Isolation and social stigma were inherent characteristics of special education classes. In the United States, change was initiated by the passage of a federal law in 1975, Public Law 94-142: Education for All Handicapped Children. According to this law, intellectually disabled people are entitled to a full education *in the least restricted environment*. This law had far-ranging effects in Canada as well: It gave motivation and support to similar initiatives here. Interestingly, Saskatchewan and Nova Scotia already had mandatory legislation in place in 1971 and 1973 respectively. Mandatory legislation for Ontario came in 1980. These laws aided the implementation of *mainstreaming* (Hocutt, 1996; Weber & Bennett, 1999). As other provinces passed similar laws, mainstreaming became the norm in Canadian education. The philosophy behind mainstreaming suggests that integration of individuals with mental retardation into regular classrooms will improve their educational opportunities, increase their social acceptance, and facilitate their integration into society as a whole.

The Intellectually Gifted

Another group of people—the intellectually gifted—are as different from those with average intelligence as are individuals who are intellectually disabled, although in a different manner. Composing 2 to 4 percent of the population, the **intellectually gifted** have IQ scores higher than 130.

Although the stereotype associated with the gifted suggests that they are awkward, shy, social misfits unable to get along well with peers, most research indicates that just the opposite is true. Most intellectually gifted individuals are outgoing, well-adjusted, popular people who are able to do most things better than the average person (Li, 1995; Harden, 2000; Winner, 1997, 2000).

PsychLink
NADS Homepage
www.mcgrawhill.ca/college/feldman

intellectually gifted: The 2 to 4 percent of the population who have IQ scores greater than 130.

For example, in a long-term study by psychologist Lewis Terman that started in the early 1920s and is still going on, 1500 children who had IQ scores above 140 were followed and examined periodically over the next 60 years (Terman & Oden, 1947; Sears, 1977). From the start, members of this group were more physically, academically, and socially capable than their nongifted peers. They were generally healthier, taller, heavier, and stronger than average. Not surprisingly, they did better in school as well. They also showed better social adjustment than average. And all these advantages paid off in terms of career success: As a group, the gifted received more awards and distinctions, earned higher incomes, and made more contributions in art and literature than typical individuals. For example, by the time the members of the group were 40 years old, they had collectively written more than 90 books, 375 plays and short stories, and 2000 articles, and had registered more than 200 patents. Perhaps most important, they reported greater satisfaction in life than the nongifted.

Of course, not every member of the group Terman studied was successful. Furthermore, high intelligence is not a homogeneous quality; a person with a high overall IQ is not necessarily gifted in every academic subject, but might excel in just one or two. A high IQ, then, is no universal guarantee of success (Shurkin, 1992; Winner, 2000).

Individual Differences in Intelligence: Hereditary and Environmental Determinants

Consider the following multiple-choice question:

Kwang is often washed with a pleck tied to a:
(a) rundel
(b) flink
(c) pove
(d) quirj

If you found this kind of item on an intelligence test, you would probably complain that the test was totally absurd and had nothing to do with your intelligence or anyone else's—and rightly so. How could anyone be expected to respond to items presented in a language that is so unfamiliar?

Yet to some people, even more reasonable questions can appear just as nonsensical. Consider, for example, a child who has been raised in a city who is asked about procedures for milking cows, or a child raised in a rural area who is asked about subway ticketing procedures. Obviously, the previous experience of the test-takers would affect their ability to answer correctly. If such questions were included on an IQ test, a critic could rightly contend that the test had more to do with prior experience than with intelligence.

Although IQ tests do not include questions that are so clearly dependent on prior knowledge as questions about cows and subways, the background and experiences of test-takers do have the potential to affect results. In fact, the issue of devising fair intelligence tests that measure knowledge unrelated to culture and family background and experience is central to explaining an important and persistent finding: Members of certain racial and cultural groups consistently score lower on traditional intelligence tests than members of other groups (MacKenzie, 1984; Humphreys, 1992). For example, as a group, blacks tend to average 10 to 15 IQ points lower than whites. Does this reflect a true difference in intelligence, or are the questions biased in the kinds of knowledge they test? Clearly, if whites perform better because of their greater familiarity with the kind of information that is being tested, their higher IQ scores are not necessarily an indication that they are more intelligent than members of other groups.

There is good reason to believe that some standardized IQ tests contain elements that discriminate against minorities whose experiences differ from those of the white majority. In Canada, this is particularly evident when standardized tests are used with Aboriginal youth. To address this situation for the Cree of James Bay, Mawhinney and his collaborators from the Cree people developed the Cree Picture Vocabulary Test

PsychLink

Gifted Children Information
www.mcgrawhill.ca/college/feldman

(Mawhinney, 1983). The test was designed to suit the Cree experience and it was administered in their language.

In an attempt to produce a **culture-fair IQ test**, one that does not discriminate against members of any minority group, psychologists have tried to devise test items that assess experiences common to all cultures or do not depend upon language usage. However, test makers have found this difficult to do, because past experiences, attitudes, and values almost always have an impact on respondents' answers. For example, children raised in Western cultures group things based on what they *are* (such as putting *dog* and *fish* into the category of *animal*). In contrast, members of the Kpelle tribe in Africa see intelligence demonstrated by grouping things according to what they *do* (grouping *fish* with *swim*). Similarly, U.S. children asked to memorize the position of objects on a chessboard perform better than African children living in remote villages if household objects familiar to the U.S. children are used. But if rocks are used instead of household objects, the African children do better. In short, it is difficult to produce a test that is truly culture-fair (Anastasi, 1988; Samuda, 1998; Sandoval et al., 1998).

The extent to which hereditary and environmental factors influence intelligence continues to be a controversial issue. Many researchers argue that intelligence in general shows a high degree of **heritability**, a measure of the degree to which a characteristic is related to genetic, inherited factors (e.g., Bouchard et al., 1990; Plomin & Petrill, 1997; Grigorenko, 2000). As can be seen in Figure 7-13, the closer the genetic link between two people, the greater the correspondence of their IQ scores. Those who argue that heredity has a less pronounced influence on intelligence point out that it is difficult, if not impossible, to distinguish hereditary from environmental influences. For example, a well-intentioned first grade teacher asks a child perceived to be "less intelligent" less challenging questions, thereby contributing to a less stimulating environment. In this instance the teacher seems to have assumed that the child was born with a certain level of ability and that he or she is incapable of dealing with challenging questions. However, by not asking challenging questions the teacher is unwittingly shaping the environment so that it does not facilitate intellectual development. We are left wondering to what extent innate factors and environmental influences account for the child's demonstrated intellectual ability. For information on a related concept, see the discussion of the self-fulfilling prophecy in Chapter 14, p. 473. University of Alberta researcher Douglas Wahlsten has concluded that it is impossible to determine the exact effects of heredity and environment on human intelligence (Gottlieb, Wahlsten, & Lickliter, 1998).

culture-fair IQ test: A test that does not discriminate against members of any minority group.

Culture-fair IQ test
www.mcgrawhill.ca/college/feldman

heritability: A measure of the degree to which a characteristic is related to genetic, inherited factors.

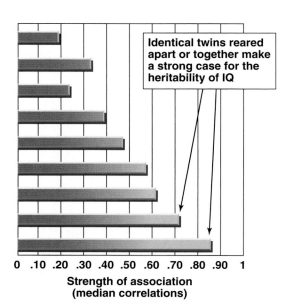

Figure 7-13 Summary findings on IQ and closeness of genetic relationship. The bars indicate the median correlations found across studies, while the percentages indicate the degree of genetic overlap within the relationship. Note, for example, that the median correlation for unrelated people reared apart is quite low, while the correlation for identical twins reared together is substantially higher. In general, the more similar the genetic and environmental background of two people, the greater the correlation (Adapted from Bouchard & McGue, 1981).

Figure 7-14 Although average IQ scores have increased steadily during the 1900s—a phenomenon known as the Flynn effect—the reason for the rise is not at all clear.

Do you think this trend is likely to continue in the 21st century?

(Source: Horgan, 1995, p. 12.)

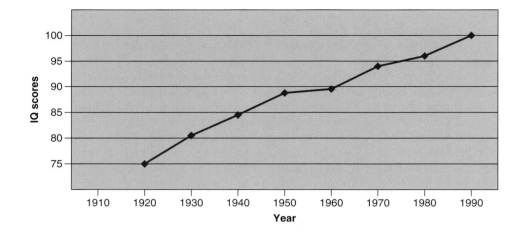

The more critical question to ask, then, is not whether hereditary or environmental factors primarily underlie intelligence, but whether there is anything we can do to maximize the intellectual development of each individual. If we can find ways to do this, we will be able to make changes in the environment—which might take the form of enriched home and school environments—that can lead each person to reach her or his potential.

Figure 7-14 demonstrates that IQ scores in general have been increasing steadily since 1900. While it may be tempting to interpret these data as indicative of the evolution of people into a more intelligent species, the time is too short for such an evolution to have occurred. The improvement of scores is more likely due to better nutrition, better parenting, improvement in education, improvement in the social environment, increases in skills related to technological change, or some combination of these factors. Improvements in these areas may help individuals maximize their intellectual development.

Evaluate

1. _____ is a measure of intelligence that takes into account both a person's chronological and mental ages.
2. _____ tests predict a person's ability in a specific area, whereas _____ tests determine the specific level of knowledge in an area.
3. _____ _____ is a disorder caused by an extra chromosome that is responsible for some cases of intellectual disability.
4. People with high intelligence are generally shy and socially withdrawn. True or false?
5. A_____-_____test tries to use only questions appropriate to all people taking the test.
6. Intelligence can be seen as a combination of_____and_____factors.

Answers to Evaluate Questions

1. IQ; 2. Aptitude; achievement; 3. Down syndrome; 4. False; the gifted are generally more socially adept than persons with lower IQ scores; 5. culture-fair; 6. hereditary; environmental.

Rethink

1. Job interviews are really a kind of test. In what ways does a job interview resemble an aptitude test? an achievement test? Do you think job interviews can be shown to have validity? reliability?
2. Why do you think negative stereotypes persist of gifted individuals and people who are intellectually disabled, even in the face of contrary evidence? How can these stereotypes be changed?

What is thinking?

- Cognitive psychology encompasses the higher mental processes, including the way people know and understand the world, process information, make decisions and judgments, and describe their knowledge and understanding to others. (p. 218)
- Thinking is the manipulation of mental representations of information. Thinking transforms such representations into novel and different forms, permitting people to answer questions, solve problems, or reach goals. (p. 218)
- Mental images are representations in the mind that resemble the object or event being represented. (p. 218)
- Concepts are categorizations of objects, events, or people that share common properties. Prototypes are representative examples of concepts. (p. 219)

What processes underlie decision making?

- Decisions can sometimes (but not always) be improved through the use of algorithms and heuristics. Algorithms are rules that, if applied appropriately, guarantee a solution; heuristics are cognitive shortcuts that might lead to a solution but are not guaranteed to do so. (p. 220)

How do people approach and solve problems?

- Problem solving typically involves three major steps: preparation, production of solutions, and evaluation of solutions that have been generated. (p. 221)
- A crucial aspect of the preparation stage is the representation and organization of the problem. (p. 221)
- In the production stage, people try to generate solutions. The solutions to some problems may already be in long-term memory. Some problems can be solved through simple trial and error; more complex problems require the use of algorithms and heuristics. (p. 221)
- In arrangement problems, a group of elements must be rearranged or recombined in a way that will satisfy a certain criterion. In problems of inducing structure, a person must identify the relationships among the elements presented and construct a new relationship among them. Finally, transformation problems consist of an initial state, a goal state, and a series of methods for changing the initial state into the goal state. (p. 221)
- In a means-end analysis, a person will repeatedly test for differences between the desired outcome and what currently exists, trying each time to come closer to the goal. (p. 223)
- Köhler's research with chimpanzees illustrates insight, a sudden awareness of the relationships among elements that had previously seemed unrelated. (p. 224)

What are the major obstacles to problem solving?

- Several factors hinder effective problem solving. Functional fixedness is an example of a broader phenomenon known as mental set. Mental set is the tendency for old patterns of problem solving to persist. The inappropriate use of algorithms and heuristics can also act as an obstacle to the production of solutions. Confirmation bias, in which initial hypotheses are favoured, can hinder the accurate evaluation of solutions to problems. (p. 225)
- Creativity is combining responses or ideas in novel ways. Creativity is related to divergent thinking (the ability to respond with unusual, but still appropriate, responses to problems or questions) and cognitive complexity. (p. 227)

How do people use language?

- Language is the communication of information through symbols arranged according to systematic rules. All languages have a grammar—a system of rules that determines how thoughts can be expressed—that encompasses the three major components of language: phonology, syntax, and semantics. (p. 230)

How does language develop?

- Language production, preceded by language comprehension, develops out of babbling, which leads to the production of actual words. After age 1 year, children begin to use two-word combinations and their vocabulary increases, using telegraphic speech, in which words not critical to the message are dropped. By the age of 5, acquisition of language rules is relatively complete. (p. 231)
- Learning theorists suggest that language is acquired through reinforcement and conditioning. In contrast, Chomsky suggests that there is an innate language acquisition device that guides the development of language. (p. 232)
- The linguistic relativity hypothesis suggests that language shapes and can determine the way people think about the world. Most evidence suggests that although language does not determine thought, it does affect the way information is stored in memory and how well it can be retrieved. (p. 233)
- The degree to which language is a uniquely human skill remains controversial. Although some psychologists contend that certain primates communicate at a high level but nonetheless do not use language, others suggest that they truly understand and produce language in much the same way as humans do. (p. 233)

How do psychologists characterize and define intelligence?

- Because intelligence can take many forms, defining it is challenging. One commonly accepted view is that intelligence is the capacity to understand the world, think rationally, and use resources effectively when faced with challenges. (p. 236)

What are the major approaches to measuring intelligence?

- Intelligence tests are used to measure intelligence. Traditionally, such tests have compared a person's mental age and chronological age to yield an IQ, or intelligence quotient, score. (p. 236)
- Specific tests of intelligence include the Stanford-Binet test, the Wechsler Adult Intelligence Scale—III (WAIS-III), and the Wechsler Intelligence Scale for Children—III (WISC-III). Achievement tests and aptitude tests are other types of standardized tests. (p. 238)
- Tests are expected to be both reliable and valid. Reliability is the consistency with which a test measures what it is trying to measure. A test has validity when it actually measures what it is supposed to measure. (p. 240)
- The earliest psychologists assumed that there was a general factor for mental ability called g. However, later psychologists disputed the view that intelligence was unidimensional. (p. 243)
- Some researchers suggest that there are two kinds of intelligence: fluid intelligence and crystallized intelligence. Gardner's theory of multiple intelligences proposes that there are eight spheres of intelligence: musical, bodily kinesthetic, logical-mathematical, linguistic, spatial, interpersonal, intrapersonal, and naturalist. (p. 243)

- Information-processing approaches suggest that intelligence should be conceptualized as the way in which people represent and use material cognitively. Rather than focusing on the structure of intelligence, this approach examines the processes underlying intelligent behaviour. (p. 243)
- Practical intelligence is intelligence related to overall success in living. Emotional intelligence is the set of skills that underlie the accurate assessment, evaluation, expression, and regulation of emotions. (p. 245)

How can the extremes of intelligence be characterized?

- At the two extremes of intelligence are individuals with intellectual disability and the intellectually gifted. (p. 246)
- About one-third of the cases of intellectual disability have a known biological cause; Down syndrome is the most common. (p. 247)
- There have been a number of advances in educating both people with intellectual disability and the intellectually gifted. In mainstreaming, individuals with intellectual disability are integrated into regular education classrooms as much as possible. In full inclusion, all students, even those with the most severe educational disabilities, are integrated into regular classes. (p. 247)

Are traditional IQ tests culturally biased?

- Traditional intelligence tests have frequently been criticized for being biased in favour of the white middle-class population. This controversy has led to attempts to devise culture-fair tests, IQ measures that avoid questions that depend on a particular cultural background. (p. 248)
- The issue of environmental and genetic influences on intelligence continues to be a major controversy. (p. 249)

To what degree is intelligence influenced by the environment and to what degree is it influenced by heredity?

- Attempting to distinguish environmental from hereditary factors in intelligence is probably futile and certainly misguided. It is more critical to ask what can be done to maximize the intellectual development of each individual. (p. 249)

Key Terms and Concepts

cognitive psychology (p. 218)
thinking (p. 218)
mental images (p. 218)
concepts (p. 219)
prototypes (p. 220)
algorithm (p. 220)
heuristic (p. 220)
means-end analysis (p. 223)
insight (p. 224)
functional fixedness (p. 226)
mental set (p. 226)
creativity (p. 227)
divergent thinking (p. 228)
convergent thinking (p. 228)
language (p. 230)

grammar (p. 230)
phonology (p. 230)
phonemes (p. 230)
syntax (p. 230)
semantics (p. 230)
babble (p. 231)
telegraphic speech (p. 231)
overgeneralization (p. 231)
language acquisition device (p. 232)
learning-theory approach (p. 232)
whole language approach (p. 232)
basic skills approach (p. 232)
intelligence (p. 236)
intelligence tests (p. 236)
mental age (p. 237)

Psychology on the Web

1. Aside from mental images of sights and sounds, are there mental representations that correspond to the other senses? See if you can answer this question by searching the Web. Summarize your findings in writing.

2. Do animals think? What evidence is there on either side of this question? Find on the Web at least one example of research and/or argument on each side of this question. Summarize your findings and use your knowledge of cognitive psychology to state your position on this question.

3. Many sites on the Web permit you to assess your IQ. Take at least two such tests and compare (a) your results, (b) what mental qualities seemed to be tested on the test, and (c) your impression of the reliability and validity of the tests. Write up your conclusions.

4. Find a way to assess at least one other of your multiple intelligences (i.e., one not tested by the IQ tests you took) on the Web. What sort of intelligence was the test supposed to be testing? What sorts of items were included? How valid and reliable do you think it was, both in and of itself and compared with the IQ tests you took? Summarize your findings in writing.

Epilogue

The topics in this chapter occupy a central place in the field of psychology. We first examined thinking and problem solving, focusing on the importance of mental images and concepts and identifying the steps commonly involved in solving problems. We discussed language, describing the components of grammar and tracing language development in children. Finally, we considered intelligence. Some of the most heated discussions in all of psychology are focused around this topic, engaging educators, policymakers, politicians, and psychologists alike. The issues include the very meaning of intelligence, its measurement, individual extremes of intelligence, and, finally, the heredity/environment question.

Before we proceed to the next chapter, turn back to the Prologue, where we looked at the ability of NASA scientists to figure out how to restore vision to the damaged Hubble space telescope. Consider the following questions in light of what you have learned about problem solving, creativity, and intelligence.

1. How might the concepts of functional fixedness and mental set have hindered figuring out a solution to the Hubble problem?

2. Do you believe a computer could have created the solution to the Hubble problem, or is there something special about human intelligence that is superior to computer problem solving? Why?

3. Do you think the concept of insight was involved in determining the solution to the repair of the telescope? How?

4. In what ways do you think divergent and convergent thinking are involved in the processes of problem solving?

Chapter Eight

Motivation and Emotion

Prologue

A Change in Direction

Paul Okalik

The brief biography of Premier Paul Okalik, which is available on the Nunavut government homepage, reads like a problem-free success story. Okalik was born in 1964 in Pangnirtung, and lived in this isolated Inuit community until he moved to Iqaluit to go to high school. Later he moved to Ottawa to attend Carleton University, where he earned a degree in political science and Canadian studies. In 1997 he graduated with a degree in law from Ottawa University. He was called to the bar and elected as a representative in the first Legislative Assembly of Nunavut in February 1999, just before becoming Premier. He is married and has two children, Shasta and Jordan. And he accomplished all this by his 35th birthday.

But there's another side to Paul Okalik's story. At 17, he was drinking heavily and in so much trouble at school that he was expelled. When he was caught trying to break into a post office to steal alcohol, he was put in jail. Boredom, confusion, addiction, and a general lack of purpose characterized his life as a teenager. After his release from jail, he drifted aimlessly from one job to another.

At age 20, Okalik reached a turning point. He was hired to do research for the negotiators working on the Nunavut land claim, the largest land claim in Canadian history. As a member of the negotiating team, he developed self-confidence and faith in himself. Finally he was receptive to positive influences. His parents' lifestyle demonstrated the quality of life he could have without drinking. He promised his mother he would try to improve his life. What he learned about traditional Inuit culture from his grandmother's teachings became a source of pride. He wanted to give back to his community and returned to school, beginning the path that would eventually lead him to the Premier's office.

Today, as Premier, Okalik represents both Inuit and non-Inuit who have come to live in Nunavut. As a speaker of Inuktitut, English, and French, he sees himself as a bridge between the diverse elements in Canada's newest territory.

Looking Ahead

What motivation lay behind Paul Okalik's change from a troubled teenager to an adult leader in society? Was it fear of the consequences of his teenage lifestyle? Or was it a desire for power? Or was it the satisfaction of achieving increasingly challenging goals?

In this chapter, we consider the issues that can help answer such questions, as we address the topic of motivation and the related area of emotion. **Motivation** concerns the factors that direct and energize the behaviour of humans and other organisms.

Psychologists who study motivation seek to discover the particular desired goals—the *motives*—that underlie behaviour. Motives are exemplified in behaviour as basic as drinking to satisfy thirst or as inconsequential as taking a stroll to get exercise. To the psychologist specializing in the study of motivation, underlying motives are assumed to steer one's choice of activities.

The study of motivation, then, consists of identifying why people seek to do the things they do. Psychologists studying motivation ask questions such as these: Why do people choose particular goals for which to strive? What specific motives direct behaviour? What individual differences in motivation account for the variability in people's behaviour? How can we motivate people to behave in particular ways, such as eating certain foods, quitting smoking, or engaging in safer sexual practices?

Whereas motivation is concerned with the forces that direct future behaviour, emotion pertains to the feelings we experience throughout the course of our lives. The study of emotions focuses on our internal experiences at any given moment. Most of us have felt a variety of emotions: happiness at getting an A on a difficult exam, sadness brought about by the death of a loved one, anger at being treated unfairly. Because emotions not only motivate our behaviour but can also reflect our underlying motivation, they play an important role in our lives.

We begin this chapter by focusing on the major conceptions of motivation, discussing how the different motives and needs people experience jointly affect behaviour. We consider motives that are biologically based and universal in the animal kingdom, such as hunger and sex, as well as motives that are unique to humans, like the needs for achievement, affiliation, and power.

We then turn to the nature of emotional experience. We consider the roles and functions that emotions play in people's lives, discussing a number of theories meant to explain how people understand which emotion they are experiencing at a given moment. Finally, the chapter ends with a look at some contemporary approaches to emotion.

motivation: The factors that direct and energize the behaviour of humans and other organisms.

Prepare

How does motivation direct and energize behaviour?

Organize

Explaining Motivation
   Instinct Approaches
   Drive-Reduction Approaches
   Arousal Approaches
   Incentive Approaches
   Cognitive Approaches
   Maslow's Hierarchy
   Applying the Different Approaches
      to Motivation

Explaining Motivation

In just a moment, John Thompson's life changed. That's all it took for him to slip against a piece of farm equipment, which instantly ripped off both his arms.

In the moments following the accident, Thompson demonstrated incredible bravery. Despite his pain and shock, he ran 400 feet to his house. After managing to open the door, he ran inside and dialed for help with a pen gripped in his teeth. When emergency crews arrived 30 minutes later, he told them where to find ice and plastic bags so that his severed arms could be packed for possible surgical reattachment. Thompson's rescuers came none too soon: By the time surgery could start, he had lost half his blood. (Nelson, 1992)

Amazingly, John Thompson's surgery to reattach his arms was a success, and he recovered from his ordeal. But how can we account for his enormous motivation to stay alive?

Like many questions involving motivation, this one has no single answer; biological, cognitive, and social factors combined to fuel his will to survive. The complexity of motivation has led to the development of a variety of conceptual approaches to its understanding. Although they vary in the degree to which they focus on biological, cognitive, and social factors, all seek to explain the energy that guides people's behaviour in particular directions.

Instinct Approaches: Born to Be Motivated

When psychologists first sought to explain motivation, they turned to **instincts**, inborn patterns of behaviour that are biologically determined rather than learned. According to instinct approaches to motivation, people and animals are born with preprogrammed sets of behaviours essential to their survival. These instincts provide the energy that channels behaviour in appropriate directions. Hence, sex might be explained as a response to an instinct for reproduction, and exploratory behaviour might be viewed as motivated by an instinct to examine one's territory.

There are several difficulties with such a conception, however. For one thing, there is no agreement on what, or even how many, primary instincts exist. One early psychologist, William McDougall (1908), suggested that there are 18 instincts. Other theorists came up with even more—with one sociologist (Bernard, 1924) claiming that there are exactly 5759 distinct instincts!

Furthermore, explanations based on the concept of instincts do not go very far in explaining *why* a specific pattern of behaviour, and not others, has appeared in a given species. In addition, although it is clear that a significant amount of animal behaviour is based on instincts, the variety and complexity of human behaviour, much of which is learned, cannot be seen as instinctual.

As a result of these shortcomings, newer explanations have replaced conceptions of motivation based on instincts. However, instinct approaches still play a role in certain theories, particularly those based on the evolutionary approach we discussed in Chapter 1. Furthermore, in later chapters we will discuss Freud's work, which suggests that instinctual drives of sex and aggression motivate behaviour.

Drive–Reduction Approaches: Satisfying Our Needs

After rejecting instinct theory, psychologists first proposed simple drive-reduction theories of motivation in its place (Hull, 1943). **Drive-reduction approaches** suggest that when people lack some basic biological requirement such as water, a drive to obtain that requirement (in this case, the thirst drive) is produced.

To understand this approach, we need to begin with the concept of drive. A **drive** is motivational tension, or arousal, that energizes behaviour in order to fulfill some need. Many basic kinds of drives, such as hunger, thirst, sleepiness, and sex, are related to biological needs of the body or of the species as a whole. These are called *primary drives.* Primary drives contrast with *secondary drives,* in which no obvious biological need is being fulfilled. The needs involved in secondary drives are created by prior experience and learning. As we will discuss later, some people have strong needs to achieve academically and in their careers. We can say that their achievement need is reflected in a secondary drive that motivates their behaviour.

We usually try to satisfy a primary drive by reducing the need underlying it. For example, we become hungry after not eating for a few hours and might raid the refrigerator, especially if our next scheduled meal is not imminent. If the weather turns cold, we put on extra clothing or raise the setting on the thermostat to keep warm. If our body needs liquids in order to function properly, we experience thirst and seek out water.

Homeostasis

The reason for such behaviour is homeostasis, a basic motivational phenomenon underlying primary drives. **Homeostasis** is the body's tendency to maintain a steady internal state. Homeostasis operates through feedback loops that bring deviations in body functioning back to a more optimal state, similar to the way a thermostat and furnace work in a home heating system to maintain a steady temperature. Receptor cells throughout the body constantly monitor factors such as temperature and nutrient levels, and when deviations from the ideal state occur, the body adjusts in an effort to return to an optimal state. Many of our fundamental needs, including the need for food, water, stable body temperature, and sleep, operate via homeostasis.

instincts: Inborn patterns of behaviour that are biologically determined rather than learned.

 **PsychLink**
Motivation and emotion information
www.mcgrawhill.ca/college/feldman

drive-reduction approaches to motivation: A theory suggesting that when people lack some basic biological requirement such as water, a drive to obtain that requirement (in this case, the thirst drive) is produced.
drive: Motivational tension, or arousal, that energizes behaviour in order to fulfill some need.

homeostasis: The body's tendency to maintain a steady internal state.

Although drive-reduction theories provide a good explanation of how primary drives motivate behaviour, they are inadequate when it comes to explaining behaviours in which the goal is not to reduce a drive, but rather to maintain or even to increase a particular level of excitement or arousal. For instance, some behaviours seem to be motivated by nothing more than curiosity, such as rushing to check e-mail messages. Similarly, many people seek thrills through such activities as riding a roller coaster and steering a raft down the rapids of a river. Such behaviours certainly don't suggest that people seek to reduce drives, as drive-reduction approaches would indicate (Mineka & Hendersen, 1985; Loewenstein, 1994).

Both curiosity and thrill-seeking behaviour, then, shed doubt on drive-reduction approaches as a complete explanation for motivation. In both cases, rather than seeking to reduce an underlying drive, people appear to be motivated to *increase* their overall level of stimulation and activity. To explain this phenomenon, psychologists have devised an alternative: arousal approaches to motivation.

Arousal Approaches: Beyond Drive Reduction

arousal approaches to motivation: The belief that we try to maintain a certain level of stimulation and activity, increasing or reducing them as necessary.

Arousal approaches seek to explain behaviour in which the goal is to maintain or increase excitement (Berlyne, 1967; Brehm & Self, 1989). According to **arousal approaches to motivation**, each of us tries to maintain a certain level of stimulation and activity. As with the drive-reduction model, if our stimulation and activity levels become too high, we try to reduce them. But in contrast to the drive-reduction model, the arousal model also suggests that if the levels of stimulation and activity are too low, we will try to *increase* them by seeking stimulation.

People vary widely in the optimal level of arousal that they seek out, with some people seeking out especially high levels of arousal. For example, psychologists have hypothesized that individuals such as comic John Belushi, daredevil Evel Knievel, and bank robbers Bonnie and Clyde exhibited a particularly high need for arousal. You can get a sense of your own preferred level of stimulation by completing the questionnaire in Chapter Activity 8-1 (Zuckerman, 1991, 1994; Farley, 1986).

Incentive Approaches: Motivation's Pull

incentive approaches to motivation: The theory suggesting that motivation stems from the desire to obtain valued external goals, or incentives.

When a luscious dessert is brought to the table after a filling meal, its appeal has little or nothing to do with internal drives or with the maintenance of arousal. Rather, if we choose to eat the dessert, such behaviour is motivated by the external stimulus of the dessert itself, which acts as an anticipated reward. This reward, in motivational terms, is an *incentive*.

Incentive approaches to motivation suggest that motivation stems from the desire to obtain valued external goals, or incentives. In this view, the desirable properties of external stimuli—be they grades, money, affection, food, or sex—account for a person's motivation.

Although the theory explains why we might succumb to an incentive (like a mouth-watering dessert) even though internal cues (like hunger) are lacking, it does not provide a complete explanation of motivation, since organisms seek to fulfill needs even when incentives are not apparent. Consequently, many psychologists believe that the internal drives proposed by drive-reduction theory work in tandem with the external incentives of incentive theory to "push" and "pull" behaviour, respectively. Thus, at the same time as we seek to satisfy our underlying hunger needs (the push of drive-reduction theory), we are drawn to food that appears particularly appetizing (the pull of incentive theory). Rather than contradicting each other, then, drives and incentives can work together in motivating behaviour (Petri, 1996).

Cognitive Approaches: The Thoughts Behind Motivation

cognitive approaches to motivation: The theory suggesting that motivation is a product of people's thoughts and expectations—their cognitions.

Cognitive approaches to motivation suggest that motivation is a product of people's thoughts, expectations, and goals—their cognitions. For instance, the degree to which people are motivated to study for a test is based on their expectation of how well studying will pay off in terms of a good grade (Wigfield & Eccles, 2000).

Chapter Activity 8–1 Do You Seek Out Sensation?

TABLE 8-1 How much stimulation do you crave in your everyday life? You will have an idea after you complete the following questionnaire, which lists some items from a scale designed to assess your sensation-seeking tendencies. Circle either *A* or *B* in each pair of statements.

1. *A* I would like a job that requires a lot of travelling.
   B I would prefer a job in one location.

2. *A* I am invigorated by a brisk, cold day.
   B I can't wait to get indoors on a cold day.

3. *A* I get bored seeing the same old faces.
   B I like the comfortable familiarity of everyday friends.

4. *A* I would prefer living in an ideal society in which everyone was safe, secure, and happy.
   B I would have preferred living in the unsettled days of our history.

5. *A* I sometimes like to do things that are a little frightening.
   B A sensible person avoids activities that are dangerous.

6. *A* I would not like to be hypnotized.
   B I would like to have the experience of being hypnotized.

7. *A* The most important goal of life is to live it to the fullest and to experience as much as possible.
   B The most important goal of life is to find peace and happiness.

8. *A* I would like to try parachute jumping.
   B I would never want to try jumping out of a plane, with or without a parachute.

9. *A* I enter cold water gradually, giving myself time to get used to it.
   B I like to dive or jump right into the ocean or a cold pool.

10. *A* When I go on a vacation, I prefer the comfort of a good room and bed.
    B When I go on a vacation, I prefer the change of camping out.

11. *A* I prefer people who are emotionally expressive, even if they are a bit unstable.
    B I prefer people who are calm and even-tempered.

12. *A* A good painting should shock or jolt the senses.
    B A good painting should give one a feeling of peace and security.

13. *A* People who ride motorcycles must have some kind of unconscious need to hurt themselves.
    B I would like to drive or ride a motorcycle.

Scoring Give yourself one point for each of the following responses: 1*A*, 2*A*, 3*A*, 4*B*, 5*A*, 6*B*, 7*A*, 8*A*, 9*B*, 10*B*, 11*A*, 12*A*, 13*B*. Find your total score by adding up the number of points and then use the following scoring key:

0–3 very low sensation seeking

4–5 low

6–9 average

10–11 high

12–13 very high

Keep in mind, of course, that this short questionnaire, for which the scoring is based on the results of college students who have taken it, provides only a rough estimate of your sensation-seeking tendencies. Moreover, as people get older, their sensation-seeking scores tend to decrease. Still, the questionnaire will at least give you an indication of how your sensation-seeking tendencies compare with those of others.

(Source: Zuckerman, 1978, 1994)

Cognitive theories of motivation draw a key distinction between intrinsic and extrinsic motivation. *Intrinsic motivation* causes us to participate in an activity for our own enjoyment, rather than for any concrete, tangible reward. In contrast, *extrinsic motivation* causes us to do something for money, a grade, or some other concrete, tangible reward. For example, when a physician works long hours because she loves medicine, intrinsic motivation is prompting her; if she works hard in order to make a lot of money, extrinsic motivation underlies her efforts (Rawsthorne & Elliot, 1999; Ryan & Deci, 2000).

We are more apt to persevere, work harder, and produce work of higher quality when motivation for a task is intrinsic rather than extrinsic. In fact, providing rewards might cause intrinsic motivation to decline and extrinsic motivation to increase, although this view is controversial (Deci, Koestner, & Ryan, 1999; Eisenberger, Pierce, & Cameron, 1999; Sansone & Harackiewicz, 2000).

In a dramatic demonstration of the differing effects of rewards on motivation, researchers promised a group of nursery school students a reward for drawing with magic markers (an activity for which they had previously shown high motivation). The reward reduced their enthusiasm for the task, for they later showed considerably less zeal for drawing (Lepper & Greene, 1978). It was as if the promise of reward undermined their intrinsic interest in drawing.

Such research suggests the importance of promoting intrinsic motivation and indicates that providing extrinsic rewards (or even just calling attention to them) can undermine the effort and quality of performance. Parents might think twice, then, about offering their children monetary rewards for getting good report cards. Instead, research on intrinsic motivation suggests that better results would come from reminding them of the pleasures that can come from learning and mastering a body of knowledge (Deci, Koestner, & Ryan, 1999: Lepper, Henderlong, & Gingras, 1999). See Chapter Activity 8-2 for an example of what intrinsic motivation can accomplish.

Maslow's Hierarchy: Ordering Motivational Needs

What do Eleanor Roosevelt, Abraham Lincoln, and Albert Einstein have in common? The common thread, according to a model of motivation devised by psychologist Abraham Maslow, is that each of them fulfilled the highest levels of motivational needs underlying human behaviour.

Maslow's hierarchy explained
www.mcgrawhill.ca/college/feldman

Maslow's model considers different motivational needs to be ordered in a hierarchy, and it suggests that before more sophisticated, higher-order needs can be met, certain primary needs must be satisfied (Maslow, 1970, 1987). The model can be conceptualized as a pyramid (see Figure 8-1) in which the more basic needs are at the bottom and the higher-level needs are at the top.

The most basic needs are primary drives: needs for water, food, sleep, sex, and the like. To move up the hierarchy, a person must have these basic physiological needs met. Safety needs come next in the hierarchy; Maslow suggests that people need a safe, secure environment in order to function effectively. Physiological and safety needs compose the lower-order needs.

Chapter Activity 8–2
Gina's Invention

Gina Gallant, a Prince George, B.C., teenager, was curious. She knew that plastics take up too much space in landfill sites. And she knew that in trying to make new types of asphalt for roads, people had tried to use peculiar substances like glass and rubber. Gina wanted to find out if plastics could be used to make asphalt. She started by saving milk cartons and grinding them up in a blender, and eventually she produced a new type of asphalt. In 2001, she entered her invention in the Canada Wide Science Fair, and won in the junior engineering category.

How does this story about a British Columbia teenager illustrate some of the concepts of cognitive approaches to motivation? What other views of motivation may help to explain the reasons for Gina's behaviour?

SELF-
ACTUALIZATION
A state of self-
fulfillment

ESTEEM
The need to develop a sense
of self-worth

LOVE AND BELONGINGNESS
The need to obtain and give affection

SAFETY NEEDS
The need for a safe and secure environment

PHYSIOLOGICAL NEEDS
The primary drives: needs for water, food, sleep, and sex

Figure 8-1 Maslow's hierarchy shows how our motivation progresses up the pyramid from a basis in the broadest, most fundamental biological needs to higher-order ones (After Maslow, 1970). Do you agree that lower-order needs must be satisfied before higher-order needs? Do hermits and monks who attempt to achieve spiritual needs while denying basic physical needs contradict Maslow's hierarchy?

From A. Maslow, *Motivation and Personality* 3/e, Copyright © 1970. Reproduced by permission of Pearson Education, Inc., Upper Saddle River, New Jersey.

Only when the basic lower-order needs are met in a generally satisfactory manner can a person consider fulfilling higher-order needs, such as the need for love and a sense of belonging, esteem, and self-actualization. Love and belongingness needs include the need to obtain and give affection and to be a contributing member of some group or society. After these needs are fulfilled, the person strives for esteem. In Maslow's thinking, esteem relates to the need to develop a sense of self-worth by knowing that others are aware of one's competence and value.

Once these four sets of needs are fulfilled—no easy task—the person is able to strive for the highest-level need, self-actualization. **Self-actualization** is a state of self-fulfillment in which people realize their highest potential in their own unique way. Although at first Maslow suggested that self-actualization occurred in only a few, famous individuals, he later expanded the concept to encompass everyday people. For example, a parent with excellent nurturing skills who raises a family, a teacher who year after year creates an environment that maximizes students' opportunities for success, and an artist who realizes her creative potential might all be self-actualized. In a sense, achieving self-actualization produces a decline in the striving and yearning for greater fulfillment that marks most people's lives and instead provides a sense of satisfaction with the current state of affairs (Jones & Crandall, 1991).

Although research has been unable to validate the specific ordering of Maslow's stages, and it is difficult to measure self-actualization objectively, Maslow's model is important for two reasons: It highlights the complexity of human needs, and it emphasizes that until more basic biological needs are met, people will be relatively unconcerned with higher-order needs. For example, if people are hungry, their first interest will be in obtaining food; they will not be concerned with such needs as love and self-esteem (Weiss, 1991; Neher, 1991).

PsychLink
Maslow's self-actualization
www.mcgrawhill.ca/college/feldman

self-actualization: A state of self-fulfillment in which people realize their highest potential in their own unique way.

Pathways Through Psychology

Tara K. MacDonald

**Assistant Professor of Psychology
Department of Psychology
Queen's University, Kingston, Ontario**

Education: B.A., University of Western Ontario;
Ph.D., University of Waterloo

Home: Kingston, Ontario

Tara K. MacDonald

As a first-year university student, I had actually intended to pursue an undergraduate degree in English, but found psychology so interesting and exciting that I decided to switch majors. I was especially curious about experimental social psychology—I thought that it was fascinating to learn about clever experiments in the laboratory and the field that were designed to "capture" phenomena that were so interesting and important. I decided to go to graduate school in social psychology. I was interested in the "attitude-behaviour problem," the question of why people do not always engage in behaviours that are consistent with their attitudes and intentions. This is an interesting and potentially important question. For example, most people report very negative attitudes and intentions toward the behaviour of drinking and driving, but unfortunately, statistics show that all too often, people do decide to engage in this risky behaviour.

Dr. Mark Zanna, Dr. Geoffrey Fong, and I conducted an initial set of laboratory and field experiments in which we demonstrated that alcohol causes people to be more likely to report intentions to drink and drive. In other experiments, we found that alcohol intoxication also causes people to be more likely to report intentions to engage in unprotected sexual intercourse.

We interpreted our findings as being consistent with Alcohol Myopia, a theory posited by Claude Steele and Robert Josephs in 1990. According to this theory, alcohol intoxication limits people from attending to all of the different cues in the environment, and so intoxicated people are likely to focus on, and act on, the most apparent cues. Interestingly, the alcohol myopia hypothesis suggests that if cues that would deter risky behaviour are highly salient, then alcohol intoxication should be associated with more cautious intentions and

behaviour. Indeed, in our most recent research, we have found that when the dangers of unprotected sexual intercourse are made salient, then intoxicated people are less likely than sober people to intend to have unprotected sex.

I enjoy this area of research because it is theoretically interesting, as we are studying how alcohol affects decision making, and finding that the story is more complicated than most people think. A popular belief is that alcohol simply causes disinhibition; thus, one would expect that alcohol would always lead to risky behaviour. In contrast, we find that alcohol causes people to be highly influenced by the cues in the environment. If cues that emphasize risk are apparent, then alcohol leads to risky intentions; if cues that emphasize caution are apparent, then alcohol leads to more cautious intentions. Also, this research has practical value: it can be applied to efforts to reduce the incidence of risky and costly behaviours associated with alcohol intoxication.

I feel very fortunate to work as a researcher and teacher in a university environment. The job is demanding, to be sure, but it is also very rewarding. I enjoy conducting research and exploring problems that are interesting to me, and then sharing my findings with others through conference presentations and journal publications. I also enjoy teaching psychology—it's a challenge to find ways to present the material so that it is interesting, entertaining, and memorable. Finally, I believe that training future researchers is a very important aspect of my career.

Source: Tara K. MacDonald, Ph.D., Queen's University <psyc.queensu.ca/faculty/macdonald/tara.html>

How have Professor MacDonald's research findings helped to explain why people's behaviours are not always consistent with their intentions?

Applying the Different Approaches to Motivation

The various theories of motivation provide us with several different perspectives on motivation. It often is useful to employ more than one approach in order to understand motivation in a particular instance.

Consider, for example, John Thompson's brave determination after his farm accident (described earlier in the chapter). From the drive-reduction perspective, he was motivated to get medical help in order to end the pain that followed his accident. And from a cognitive perspective, his expectation that surgeons could reattach his arms led him to take action that would maximize the chances of recovery.

In short, applying multiple approaches to motivation to a given situation provides a broader understanding than we might obtain by employing only a single approach. We'll see this fact again as we proceed to consider specific motives—such as the needs for food, achievement, affiliation, and power—where we will draw upon several of the theories to provide us with the fullest account of what motivates our behaviour.

The relationship between motivation and behaviour is often very complex. To read about a psychologist whose current research focuses on the question of why people's behaviours are not always consistent with their attitudes and intentions, see the *Pathways Through Psychology* box on Tara MacDonald. In 2001, MacDonald received the New Investigator Award from the Canadian Institutes of Health Research.

Evaluate

1. _____ are forces that guide a person's behaviour in a certain direction.
2. Biologically determined, inborn patterns of behaviour are known as_____.
3. Your psychology professor tells you, "Explaining behaviour is easy! When we lack something we are motivated to get it." Which approach to motivation does your professor subscribe to?
4. By drinking water after running a marathon, a runner tries to keep his or her body at an optimal level of functioning. This process is called_____.
5. I help an elderly person across the street because doing a good deed makes me feel good. What type of motivation is at work here? What type of motivation would be at work if I were to help an elderly man across the street because he paid me $20?
6. According to Maslow, a person with no job, no home, and no friends can become self-actualized. True or false?

Answers to Evaluate Questions

1. Motives 2. instincts 3. Drive reduction 4. homeostasis 5. Intrinsic; Extrinsic 6. False; lower-order needs must be fulfilled before self-actualization can occur.

Rethink

1. Which approaches to motivation are most commonly used in the workplace? How might each approach be used to design employment policies that can sustain or increase motivation?
2. A writer who works all day composing copy for an advertising firm has a hard time keeping her mind on her work and continually watches the clock. After work she turns to a collection of stories she is creating and writes long into the night, completely forgetful of the clock. What ideas from your reading on motivation help to explain this phenomenon?

Human Needs and Motivation: Eat, Drink, and Be Daring

As a sophomore at the University of California, Santa Cruz, Lisa Arndt followed a menu of her own making: For breakfast she ate cereal or fruit, with 10 diet pills and 50 chocolate-flavored laxatives. Lunch was a salad or sandwich; dinner: chicken and rice. But it was the feast that followed that Arndt relished most. Almost every night at about 9 P.M., she would retreat to her room and eat an entire small pizza and a whole batch of cookies. Then she'd wait for the day's laxatives to take effect. "It was extremely painful," says Arndt of those days in 1992. "But I was that desperate to make up for my bingeing. I was terrified of fat the way other people are afraid of lions or guns." (Hubbard, O'Neill, & Cheakalos, 1999, p. 59)

Lisa suffers from an eating disorder. These disorders, which usually appear during adolescence, can bring about extraordinary declines in weight and other physical deterioration. They are extremely dangerous, sometimes resulting in death.

Why are Lisa and others like her subject to such disordered eating, revolving around the motivation to avoid weight gain at all costs? And why do so many other people engage in overeating, leading to obesity?

To answer these questions, we must consider some of the specific kinds of needs that underlie behaviour. In this section, we will examine several of the most important human needs. We'll begin with hunger and sex, the primary drives that have received the most attention from researchers, and then turn to secondary drives—those uniquely human strivings, based on learned needs and past experience, that help explain why people strive to achieve, to affiliate with others, and to seek power over others.

Prepare

What biological and social factors underlie hunger?

What are the varieties of sexual behaviour?

How are needs relating to achievement, affiliation, and power motivation exhibited?

Organize

Human Needs and Motivation
    The Motivation Behind Hunger and Eating
    Sexual Motivation
    The Need for Achievement
    The Need for Affiliation
    The Need for Power

overweight: Having a BMI of 27 or higher.

obesity: The state of being more than 20 percent above the average weight for a person of one's height.

The Motivation Behind Hunger and Eating

Thirty percent of Canadians aged 15 or older are overweight and 47 percent have some excess weight. **Overweight** is defined as having a Body Mass Index (BMI) of 27 or higher, where BMI = weight (in kilograms)/height(in metres squared). For example, someone who weighs 60 kilograms and is 1.65 metres tall has a BMI of 22 (60 ÷ 1.65^2). "Some excess weight" is defined as having a BMI of 25 or higher. Canadians are more likely to be overweight if they are male and over 25 years of age (Statistics Canada, 1999b). According to one recent study, 25 percent of Canadian children are seriously overweight and face possible health problems (CBC News Online, 2002). More than half the people in the United States are overweight, and more than a fifth are so overweight that they have **obesity**, body weight that is more than 20 percent above the average weight for a person of their height. And the rest of the world is not far behind: the prevalence of obesity around the globe is so great that the World Health Organization has said it has reached epidemic proportions (National Center for Health Statistics, 1994; Taubes, 1998).

Perceptions of ideal weight and body shape vary significantly across different cultures and, within Western cultures, from one time period to another. For instance, many contemporary Western cultures stress the importance of slimness in women. However, for most of the twentieth century—except for a period in the 1920s and the most recent decades—the ideal female figure was relatively full. Even today, weight standards differ among different cultural groups. For instance, in the United States, blacks generally judge heavier women more positively than whites do (Silverstein et al., 1986; Hebl & Heatherton, 1998; Rosenthal, 1999).

Regardless of societal standards relating to appearance and weight, there is no question that being overweight is a major health risk. However, controlling weight is complicated, because eating behaviour involves a variety of mechanisms, which are not generally well understood. Researchers at the University of British Columbia have found that people's incorrect beliefs about hunger and eating could promote overeating and obesity (Assanand et al., 1998). In our discussion of what motivates people to eat, we'll start with the biological aspects of eating.

Biological Factors in the Regulation of Hunger

In contrast to human beings, nonhuman species are unlikely to become obese. Internal mechanisms regulate not only the quantity of their food intake, but also the kind of food they desire. For example, rats that have been deprived of particular foods seek out alternatives that contain the specific nutrients their diet is lacking, and animals given the choice of a wide variety of foods choose a well-balanced diet (Rozin, 1977; Bouchard & Bray, 1996; Woods et al., 2000).

The mechanisms by which organisms know whether they require food or should stop eating are complex. It's not just a matter of an empty stomach causing hunger pangs and a full one alleviating hunger. (Even people whose stomachs have been removed still experience the sensation of hunger.) One important factor is changes in the chemical composition of the blood. In particular, changes in levels of glucose, a kind of sugar, regulate feelings of hunger (Inglefinger, 1944; Rodin, 1985; Campfield et al., 1996).

Glucose levels are monitored by the brain's *hypothalamus,* a tiny brain structure we first discussed in Chapter 2. Increasing evidence suggests that the hypothalamus is the organ primarily responsible for monitoring food intake. Injury to the hypothalamus has radical consequences for eating behaviour, depending upon the site of the injury. For example, rats whose *lateral hypothalamus* is damaged might literally starve to death. They refuse food when offered and, unless they are force-fed, eventually die. Rats with an injury to the *ventromedial hypothalamus* display the opposite problem: extreme overeating. Rats with this injury can increase in weight by as much as 400 percent. Similar phenomena occur in humans who have tumours of the hypothalamus (Rolls, 1994; Woods et al., 1998).

Although the hypothalamus clearly plays an important role in regulating food intake, exactly how it operates is still unclear. One hypothesis is that injury to the hypothalamus affects the weight set point by which food intake is regulated. According to

Cultural influences on eating habits vary tremendously. Grasshoppers, red agave worms, and excamola may be considered a delicacy in Mexico, but most people in Canada would feel differently.
Have you ever overcome your culture-based dislike of a food after exposure to another culture's eating habits?

this hypothesis, the **weight set point** is the particular level of weight that the body strives to maintain. Acting as a kind of internal weight thermostat, the hypothalamus calls for either greater or less food intake (Nisbett, 1972; Capaldi, 1996; Woods et al., 2000).

In most cases, the hypothalamus does a good job. People who are not monitoring their weight show only minor weight fluctuations, in spite of substantial day-to-day variations in how much they eat and exercise. However, injury to the hypothalamus drastically raises or lowers the weight set point, and the organism then strives to meet its internal goal by increasing or decreasing its food consumption.

The weight set point is determined at least partly by genetic factors. People seem destined through heredity to have a particular **metabolism**, the rate at which food is converted to energy and expended by the body. People with a high metabolic rate are able to eat virtually as much as they want without gaining weight, whereas people with a low metabolic rate might eat literally half as much and yet gain weight readily (Woods et al., 1998).

weight set point: The particular level of weight that the body strives to maintain.

metabolism: The rate at which food is converted to energy and expended by the body.

Social Factors in Eating

You've just finished a full meal and are completely stuffed. Suddenly, your host announces with great fanfare that he will be serving his "house specialty" dessert, bananas flambé, and that he has spent the better part of the afternoon preparing it. Even though you are full and don't even like bananas, you accept a serving of his dessert and eat it all.

Clearly, internal biological factors do not provide the full explanation for our eating behaviour. External social factors, based on societal rules and conventions and on what we have learned about appropriate eating behaviour, also play an important role. Take, for example, the simple fact that people customarily eat breakfast, lunch, and dinner at approximately the same times every day. Because we are accustomed to eating on schedule every day, we tend to feel hungry as the usual hour approaches, sometimes quite independently of what our internal cues are telling us.

Similarly, we tend to put roughly the same amount of food on our plates every day, even though the amount of exercise we may have had, and consequently our need for energy replenishment, varies from day to day. We also tend to prefer particular foods over others. Rats and dogs might be a delicacy in certain Asian cultures, but few people in Western cultures find them appealing, despite their potentially high nutritional value. In sum, cultural influences and our own individual habits play an important role in determining when, what, and how much we eat (Boaks, Popplewell, & Burton, 1987; Rozin, 1990; Booth, 1994; Capaldi, 1996).

"Gee, I had no idea you were married to a supermodel."

Other social factors are related to our eating behaviour as well. Some of us head toward the refrigerator after a difficult day, seeking solace in a pint of Heath Bar Crunch ice cream. Why? Perhaps when we were children, our parents gave us food when we were upset. Eventually, we might have learned, through the basic mechanisms of classical and operant conditioning, to associate food with comfort and consolation. Similarly, we might learn that eating, by focusing our attention on immediate pleasures, provides an escape from unpleasant thoughts. As a consequence, we might eat when we experience distress (Heatherton, Herman, & Polivy, 1992; McManus & Waller, 1995; Hill & Peters, 1998).

The Roots of Obesity

Given that eating behaviour is influenced by both biological and social factors, determining the causes of obesity has proved to be a challenging task. Researchers have followed several paths.

Some psychologists suggest that obesity is produced by oversensitivity to external eating cues based on social factors, coupled with insensitivity to internal hunger cues. Others argue that overweight people have higher set points than people of normal weight. Because their set points are unusually high, their attempts to lose weight by eating less can make them especially sensitive to external, food-related cues and therefore more apt to eat, perpetuating their obesity (Nisbett, 1968; Schachter, 1971; Hill & Peters, 1998).

But why would some people's weight set points be higher than others? One possible explanation relates to the size and number of fat cells in the body, which increase as a function of weight increase. Because the set-point level appears to reflect the number of fat cells a person has, any increase in weight—which produces a rise in fat cells—might raise the set point. According to the weight-set-point hypothesis, having too many fat cells can make the set point become "stuck" at a higher level than is desirable. Under such circumstances, losing weight is difficult, because one is constantly at odds with one's own internal set point when dieting (Leibel, Rosenbaum & Hirsch, 1995; Freedman, 1995).

Not everyone agrees with the set point explanation for obesity. Set-point theory can account for low numbers of obese individuals in terms of pathological deviations in their feeding systems. However, the theory cannot account for the high incidence of overeating and obesity in some populations (Assanand et al., 1998). Some researchers suggest there is a *settling point,* determined by a combination of our genetic heritage and the nature of the environment in which we live. If high-fat foods are prevalent in our environment, and we are genetically predisposed to obesity, then we settle into an equilibrium that maintains relatively high weight. On the other hand, if our environment is nutritionally healthier, genetic predispositions to obesity will not be triggered, and we will settle into an equilibrium in which our weight is lower (Gibbs, 1996; Comuzzie & Allison, 1998).

According to an evolutionary view, the mammalian feeding system has evolved with preferences for sweet, salty, and fatty foods. These tastes in nature are associated with foods having high levels of essential vitamins and minerals, as well as calories that provide enough energy for future needs (Pinel, Assanand, & Lehman, 2000). In industrialized societies these taste preferences are readily satisfied by many highly accessible prepared foods.

Eating Disorders

One of the most devastating weight-related disorders is anorexia nervosa. **Anorexia nervosa** is a severe eating disorder in which people refuse to eat, while denying that their behaviour and appearance—which can become skeletonlike—are unusual. Some 10 percent of anorexics literally starve themselves to death.

Anorexia nervosa afflicts mainly females between the ages of 12 and 40, although both men and women of any age can develop it. People with the disorder typically come from stable homes, and they are often successful, attractive, and relatively affluent. The disorder often occurs following serious dieting, which somehow gets out of control. Life begins to revolve around food: Although people with the disorder eat little themselves, they might cook for others, go shopping for food frequently, or collect cookbooks (Lask & Bryant-Waugh, 1999; Rosen, 1999).

anorexia nervosa: A severe eating disorder in which people may refuse to eat, while denying that their behaviour and appearance—which can become skeletonlike—are unusual.

Despite looking skeleton-like to others, people with the weight disorder anorexia nervosa see themselves as overweight.

A related problem, **bulimia**, from which Lisa Arndt (described earlier) suffered, is a disorder in which people binge on large quantities of food. They might consume an entire tub of ice cream and a whole pie in a single sitting. Following such a binge, sufferers often induce vomiting or take laxatives to rid themselves of the food—behaviour known as purging. Chronic dieting may lead to bingeing, which is considered to be a disruption in dieting in the form of a breakdown of restraints (Polivy & Herman, 1985; Heatherton & Polivy, 1992). Constant bingeing-and-purging cycles and the use of drugs to induce vomiting or diarrhea can lead to heart failure. Often, though, the weight of a person suffering from bulimia remains normal.

Eating disorders have increased rapidly during the last 50 years. Some of this increase may be attributed to greater awareness of eating disorders. However, they are becoming a growing problem. Prevalence estimates range from 3 to 10 percent of females aged 15 to 29 years (Polivy & Herman, 2002).

What are the causes of anorexia nervosa and bulimia? Some researchers suspect there is a biological cause such as a chemical imbalance in the hypothalamus or pituitary gland, perhaps brought on by genetic factors. Others believe that these disorders are rooted in societal preference for slenderness and the parallel notion that being obese is undesirable—a serious problem, since obsession with excessive thinness can lead to chronic dieting and serious health risks (McFarlane, Polivy, & McCabe, 1999). As countries become more developed and Westernized, and dieting becomes more popular, eating disorders increase. Another possible cause is that people with eating disorders may see their efforts to control their weight as opportunities to succeed at something. Early on in the course of eating disorders, restricting food intake leads to emotional gratification, and purging following bingeing produces emotional relief. In later stages of eating disorders, however, these efforts produce negative emotions and behaviours such as anxiety, depression, guilt, and possibly suicide (Coren & Hewitt, 1998; Polivy & Herman, 2002). Finally, some psychologists suggest that the disorders occur as a consequence of overdemanding parents or other family problems (Schneider, 1996; Horesh et al., 1996; Walsh & Devlin, 1998).

The complete explanation for anorexia nervosa or bulimia remains elusive. The disorders probably stem from both biological and social causes. In their review of research on the development of eating disorders, Polivy and Herman (2002) conclude that the necessary factors for the development of eating disorders appear to be body dissatisfaction, negative emotion, low self-esteem, social factors, and personality features. Successful treatment is likely to encompass several strategies, including therapy and dietary changes (Walsh & Devlin, 1998; Gilbert, 2000; Miller & Mizes, 2000).

bulimia: A disorder in which a person binges on incredibly large quantities of food, then purges by vomiting or by using laxatives.

BECOMING AN INFORMED CONSUMER OF PSYCHOLOGY

Dieting and Losing Weight Successfully

Which of these suggestions about dieting would you find most useful? Why?

For most of us, dieting is a losing battle: Most people who diet eventually regain the weight they have lost, so they try again and get caught in a seemingly endless cycle of weight loss and gain (Lowe, 1993). Given what we know about the causes of obesity, this is not entirely surprising, because so many factors affect eating behaviour and weight.

According to diet experts, there are several things to keep in mind when trying to lose weight (Gurin, 1989; "How to Lose Weight and Keep It Off," 1990; "Dieting and Weight Loss," 1993):

- *There is no easy route to weight control.* You will have to make permanent changes in your life in order to lose weight without gaining it back. The most obvious strategy, cutting down on the amount of food you eat, is just the first step toward a lifetime commitment to changing your eating habits. You must consider the nutrient content, as well as the overall quantity of food that you consume.

- *Set reasonable goals.* Know how much weight you want to lose before you start to diet. Don't try to lose too much weight too quickly or you may doom yourself to failure.

- *Exercise.* When you exercise, you burn fat stored in your body, which is used as fuel for muscles. As this fat is used, you will probably lose weight. Almost any activity helps burn calories. The weight-set-point hypothesis suggests another advantage to moderate exercise: It might lower your set point. Although there is some dispute about just how much exercise is sufficient to lower weight, most experts recommend at least 30 consecutive minutes of moderate exercise at least three times a week. (If nothing else, the release of endorphins following exercise— discussed in Chapter 2—will make you feel better even if you don't lose weight.)
- *Decrease the influence of external, social stimuli on your eating behaviour.* For instance, serve yourself smaller portions of food, and leave the table before you see what is being served for dessert. Don't even buy snack foods such as nachos or potato chips; if they're not readily available in the kitchen cupboard, you're not apt to eat them. Wrap foods in the refrigerator in aluminum foil so you cannot see the contents to avoid being tempted every time you open the refrigerator.
- *Avoid fad diets.* No matter how popular they are at a given time, extreme diets, including liquid diets, usually don't work in the long run and can be dangerous to your health.
- *Maintain good eating habits.* When you have reached your desired weight, maintain the habits built up while dieting to avoid gaining back the weight you have lost.
- *Don't feel guilty!* Above all, don't feel guilty if you don't succeed in losing weight. Given the evidence that obesity may be genetically determined, the inability to lose weight should not be seen as a moral failing. Indeed, you are in good company, for some 90 to 95 percent of dieters put back the weight they have lost (Bennett & Gurin, 1982; Fritsch, 1999).

In light of how difficult it can be to lose weight, psychologists Janet Polivy and C. Peter Herman suggest—paradoxically—that the best approach might be to avoid dieting in the first place. They recommend that people eat what they really want to eat, even if this means indulging in candy or ice cream every so often. In turn, this freedom to eat anything can reduce binge eating, which is more likely to occur when people feel that bingeing is their only opportunity to eat what they really wish to eat. Even a relatively small weight loss is better than none: Just a 5- to 7-kilogram drop in body weight can decrease the major health risks associated with obesity (Polivy & Herman, 1991; Foreyt & Goodrick, 1994; Bruce & Wilfley, 1996).

Sexual Motivation: The Facts of Life

Anyone who has seen two dogs mating knows that sexual behaviour has a biological basis. Dogs' sexual behaviour appears to occur spontaneously, without much prompting from others. A number of genetically controlled factors influence the sexual behaviour of nonhuman animals. For instance, animal behaviour is affected by the presence of certain hormones in the blood, and many female animals are receptive to sexual advances only at certain relatively limited periods of time during the year.

Human sexual behaviour, by comparison, is more complicated, although the underlying biology is not all that different from that of related species. In males, for example, the *testes* begin to secrete **androgens**, male sex hormones, at puberty. Not only do androgens produce male secondary sex characteristics, such as the growth of body hair and a deepening of the voice, they also increase the sex drive. Because the level of androgen production by the testes is fairly constant, males are capable of (and interested in) sexual activities without any regard to biological cycles. Given the proper stimuli leading to arousal, male sexual behaviour can occur (Goldstein, 2000).

Females show a different pattern. When they reach maturity at puberty, the two *ovaries* begin to produce **estrogen** and **progesterone**, female sex hormones. However, these hormones are not produced consistently; instead, their production follows a cyclical pattern. The greatest output occurs during **ovulation**, when an egg is released from

androgens: Male sex hormones secreted by the testes.

estrogen: Female sex hormone.
progesterone: Female sex hormone.
ovulation: The point at which an egg is released from the ovaries.

the ovaries, making the chances of fertilization by a sperm cell highest. In nonhumans, the period around ovulation is the only time the female is receptive to sex, but humans are different: females can be receptive to sex throughout their cycles, depending on the external stimuli they encounter (Hoon, Bruce, & Kinchloe, 1982).

Though biological factors "prime" people for sex, it takes more than hormones to motivate and produce sexual behaviour (McClintock & Herdt, 1996). In animals the presence of a partner who provides arousing stimuli leads to sexual activity. Humans are considerably more versatile; not only other people, but nearly any object, sight, smell, sound, or other stimulus can lead to sexual excitement. Because of prior associations, then, people might be turned on sexually by the smell of Chanel No. 5 or Brut or the sound of a favourite song hummed softly in their ear. The reaction to a specific, potentially arousing stimulus, as we shall see, is highly individual—what turns on one person could do just the opposite for another.

Sexual fantasies also play an important role in producing sexual arousal. Not only do people have fantasies of a sexual nature during their everyday activities, but about 60 percent of all people have fantasies during sexual intercourse. Interestingly, such fantasies often include having sex with someone other than one's partner of the moment.

Men's and women's fantasies differ little from each other in terms of content or quantity (Jones & Barlow, 1990). One recent study of Canadian university students found that the most common themes involved intimacy and romance (Hyde et al., 2000). It is important to note that having a particular fantasy does not mean that one has a desire to fulfill it in the real world.

Masturbation: Solitary Sex

If you were to listen to physicians many years ago, you would have been told that **masturbation**—sexual self-stimulation, often by using the hand to rub the genitals—would lead to a wide variety of physical and mental disorders, ranging from hairy palms to insanity. Had they been correct, however, most of us would be wearing gloves to hide the sight of our hair-covered palms—for masturbation is one of the most frequently practised sexual activities. Some 94 percent of all males and 63 percent of all females have masturbated at least once, and among college students the frequency ranges from "never" to "several times a day" (Hunt, 1974; Houston, 1981; Michael et al., 1994).

Men and women typically begin to masturbate for the first time at different ages. Furthermore, men masturbate considerably more often than women, although there are differences in frequency according to age. For instance, male masturbation is most frequent in the early teens and then declines, whereas females both begin and reach a maximum frequency later (Oliver & Hyde, 1993).

Although masturbation is often thought of as an activity to engage in only if no other sexual outlets are available, this is not the reality. Close to three-quarters of married men (aged 20 to 40) report masturbating an average of 24 times a year, and 68 percent of married women in the same age group masturbate an average of 10 times a year (Hunt, 1974; Michael et al., 1994).

Despite the high incidence of masturbation, attitudes toward it still reflect some of the negative views of yesteryear. However, most experts on sex view masturbation not only as a healthy, legitimate—and harmless—sexual activity, but also as a means of learning about one's own sexuality.

Heterosexuality

People often believe that the first time they have sexual intercourse they have achieved one of life's major milestones. However, **heterosexuality**—sexual attraction and behaviour directed to the opposite sex—consists of far more than intercourse. Kissing, petting, caressing, massaging, and other forms of sex play are all components of heterosexual behaviour. Still, the focus of sex researchers has been on the act of intercourse, particularly in terms of its first occurrence and its frequency.

⟨⟨⟩⟩ PsychLink
Sexual fantasies
www.mcgrawhill.ca/college/feldman

masturbation: Sexual self-stimulation.

heterosexuals: People who are sexually attracted to persons of the opposite sex.

Premarital Sex   Until fairly recently, premarital sexual intercourse was considered one of the major taboos of our society, at least for women. Traditionally, women have been warned by society that "nice girls don't do it"; men have been told that although premarital sex is OK for them, they should make sure they marry virgins. This view, that premarital sex is permissible for males but not for females, is called the **double standard**.

double standard: The view that premarital sex is permissible for males but not for females.

Although as recently as the 1960s the majority of adult North Americans believed that premarital sex was always wrong, since that time there has been a dramatic change in public opinion. Changes in attitudes toward premarital sex were matched by changes in actual rates of premarital sexual activity during the same period. For instance, the most recent figures show that just over one-half of women between the ages of 15 and 19 have had premarital sexual intercourse. These figures are close to double the number of women in the same age range who in 1970 reported having had intercourse. Clearly, the trend over the last several decades has been toward more women engaging in premarital sexual activity (Singh & Carroch, 1999).

Males, too, are having more premarital sexual intercourse, although the increase has not been as dramatic as for females—probably because the rates for males were higher to begin with. For instance, the first surveys of premarital intercourse carried out in the 1940s showed an incidence of 84 percent across males of all ages; recent figures put the figure at closer to 95 percent. Moreover, the average age of males' first sexual experience has also been declining steadily. Approximately half of all males in Canada and the United States have had sexual intercourse by the age of 17 or 18. Over 80 percent have had intercourse by the time they reach 19 or 20 (Arena, 1984; Centers for Disease Control, 1992; Singh et al., 2000; Hyde et al., 2000).

Marital Sex   To judge by the number of articles about sex in marriage, one would think that sexual behaviour is the number one standard by which marital bliss is measured. Married couples are often concerned that they are having too little sex, too much sex, or the wrong kind of sex (Sprecher & McKinney, 1993).

Although many different dimensions have been used to consider sex in marriage, one is certainly the frequency of sexual intercourse. What is typical? As with most other types of sexual activity, there is no easy answer because there are such wide variations in patterns between individuals. We do know that 50 percent of Canadian married couples report having sexual intercourse at least once a week, and 14 percent do so two or three times a month (Barrett et al., 1997). In the United States, 36 percent of married couples have intercourse two or three times a week and 43 percent have it a few times a month (Michael et al., 1994). With increasing age and length of marriage, the frequency of intercourse declines. Still, sex continues into late adulthood, with almost half of people reporting they engage in sexual activity at least once a month and that its quality is high (Michael et al., 1994).

extramarital sex: Sexual activity between a married person and someone who is not his or her spouse.

Although early research suggested that **extramarital sex** is widespread, apparently this is not true. In both Canada and the United States, adultery is the exception, not the rule. Most married men (86 percent in Canada and 75 percent in the United States) and married women (93 percent in Canada and 85 percent in the United States) have never been unfaithful (Barrett et al., 1997; Michael et al., 1994). Furthermore, according to the Macleans/Global Television Network's year-end poll in 2000, only 13 percent of Canadian women and 36 percent of Canadian men reported having had 6 or more sexual partners in their entire lifetime (O'Hara, 2000). In the United States, the median number of sex partners, inside and outside of marriage, since the age of 18 for men was 6, and for women 2. Accompanying these numbers is a high, consistent degree of disapproval of extramarital sex, with 9 out of 10 people saying that it is "always" or "almost always" wrong (Michael et al., 1994; Westera & Bennett, 1994; Calmes, 1998).

Homosexuality and Bisexuality

homosexuals: Persons who are sexually attracted to people of their own sex.
bisexuals: Persons who are sexually attracted to people of the same sex *and* people of the opposite sex.

Homosexuals are sexually attracted to people of their own sex; **bisexuals** are sexually attracted to people of the same sex *and* people of the opposite sex. (Many male homosexuals prefer the term *gay* and female homosexuals the label *lesbian,* because they refer to a broader array of attitudes and lifestyle than the term *homosexual,* which focuses on the sexual act.)

The number of people who choose same-sex sexual partners at one time or another is considerable. Estimates suggest that around 20 to 25 percent of males and about 15 percent of females have had at least one homosexual experience during adulthood. The exact number of people who identify themselves as exclusively homosexual has proven difficult to gauge, with some estimates as low as 1.1 percent and some as high as 10 percent. Most experts suggest that between 5 and 10 percent of both men and women are exclusively homosexual during extended periods of their lives (Hunt, 1974; Sells, 1994; Firestein, 1996).

Although many people view homosexuality and heterosexuality as completely distinct sexual orientations, the issue is not that simple. Pioneering sex researcher Alfred Kinsey acknowledged this when he considered sexual orientation in terms of a scale or continuum, with "exclusively homosexual" at one end and "exclusively heterosexual" at the other. In the middle were people who showed both homosexual and heterosexual behaviour. Kinsey's approach suggests that sexual orientation is dependent on a person's sexual feelings and behaviours and romantic feelings (Weinberg, Williams, & Pryor, 1991).

Extensive research has found that bisexuals and homosexuals enjoy the same overall degree of mental and physical health as heterosexuals.

What determines people's sexual orientation? Although there are a number of theories, none has proved completely satisfactory. Biological explanations for sexual orientation suggest that there may be genetic or hormonal causes. Evidence for a genetic origin of sexual orientation comes from studies of identical twins, which have found that when one twin identified himself or herself as a homosexual, the occurrence of homosexuality in the other twin was higher than in the general population. This was the case even for twins who were separated early in life and therefore were not necessarily raised in similar social environments (Hamer et al., 1993; Turner, 1995; Bailey et al., 1997).

Furthermore, there is some evidence that differences in brain structures might be related to sexual orientation. For instance, the anterior hypothalamus, an area of the brain that governs sexual behaviour, has a different structure in male homosexuals than in male heterosexuals. Similarly, other research shows that, compared with heterosexual men or women, homosexual men have a larger anterior commissure, which is a bundle of neurons connecting the right and left hemispheres of the brain (LeVay, 1991, 1993; Harrison, Everall, & Catalan, 1994; Byne, 1996). Sandra Witelson (McMaster University) has found different patterns of functional cerebral asymmetry in gay men and lesbian women compared with heterosexuals (McCormick & Witelson, 1994).

However, research into biological causes for sexual orientation is not conclusive, given that most findings are based on only small samples of individuals. Still, the possibility is real that inherited or biological factors predispose people to their sexual orientations, if certain environmental conditions are met (Bailey & Pillard, 1994; Gladue, 1995; Looy, 1995; Bailey, 1995; Rice et al., 1999).

Other theories of sexual orientation have focused on childhood and family background. Freud believed that homosexuality occurred as a result of inappropriate identification with the opposite-sex parent during development. He and other psychoanalysts have suggested that the nature of the parent–child relationship can lead to homosexuality, and that male homosexuals frequently have overprotective, dominant mothers and passive, ineffective fathers (Freud, 1922/1959; Bieber et al., 1962; Bailey & Zucker, 1995).

The problem with such theories is that there are probably as many homosexuals who were not subjected to the influence of such family dynamics as there are homosexuals who were. The evidence does not support explanations that rely on child-rearing practices or on the nature of the family structure (Bell & Weinberg, 1978; Isay, 1990).

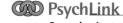 PsychLink

Sexual orientation information
www.mcgrawhill.ca/college/feldman

Most experts suspect that a combination of biological and environmental factors is at work in sexual orientation. Alfred Kinsey's approach suggests that sexual orientation is dependent on a person's sexual feelings and behaviours and romantic feelings.

Another explanation for sexual orientation rests on learning theory (Masters & Johnson, 1979). According to this view, sexual orientation is learned through rewards and punishments in much the same way that we might learn to prefer swimming over tennis. For example, a young adolescent who has an unpleasant heterosexual experience might learn to link unpleasant associations with the opposite sex. If that same person has a rewarding, pleasant homosexual experience, homosexuality might be incorporated into his or her sexual fantasies. If such fantasies are then used during later sexual activities—such as masturbation—they could be positively reinforced through orgasm, and the association of homosexual behaviour and sexual pleasure might eventually cause homosexuality to become the preferred form of sexual behaviour.

Although the learning theory explanation is plausible, several difficulties rule it out as a definitive explanation. Because our society tends to hold homosexuality in low esteem, one ought to expect that the punishments involved in homosexual behaviour would outweigh the rewards attached to it. Furthermore, children growing up with a homosexual parent are statistically unlikely to become homosexual, thus contradicting the notion that homosexual behaviour might be learned from others (Victor & Fish, 1995; Golombok & Tasker, 1996).

Given the difficulty in finding a consistent explanation, the majority of researchers reject the notion that any single factor produces sexual orientation. Most experts suspect that a combination of biological and environmental factors is at work (McWhirter, Sanders, & Reinisch, 1990; Greene & Herek, 1994; Bem, 1996).

Although we don't know at this point exactly why people develop a particular sexual orientation, one thing is clear: There is no relationship between sexual orientation and psychological adjustment. Bisexuals and homosexuals enjoy the same overall degree of mental and physical health as heterosexuals do. They hold equivalent ranges and types of attitudes about themselves, independent of sexual orientation. For such reasons, the American Psychological Association and most other mental health organizations have endorsed efforts to reduce discrimination against gays and lesbians, such as efforts to revoke the ban against homosexuals in the military (Herek, 1993; Shawver, 1995; Perez, DeBord, & Bieschke, 2000).

Why do people have such different views on female circumcision?

EXPLORING DIVERSITY

Female Circumcision: A Celebration of Culture—or Genital Mutilation?

On a late-summer night in Washington, D.C., one young Ethiopian immigrant confides to another, "Mother says she will do it anyway, herself—when I'm out of the house—if I don't agree to get it done soon…. She says she will take a razor blade and do it." (Burstyn, 1995, p. 28)

In Dakar, an office manager at a large European airline returned home at the end of his working day to find his two little daughters lying on the bed terrified. His wife's aunt had come with the excisist and had circumcised the girls against his and his wife's wishes. His wife could do nothing to prevent it; they didn't even have a phone. (Armstrong, 1998)

Waris Dirie was just an innocent child of 5 when she begged her mother to let her be circumcised like virtually all females in Somalia…. Months later her awful wish came true. As her mother held her down crying, a gypsy performed the circumcision using a dirty, dull razor and no anesthetic. She sewed the wound with thorns and thread. "It's not a pain you forget," says Dirie, in a whisper. (Cheakalos & Heyn, 1998, p. 149)

Female circumcision, or female genital mutilation, as the procedure is also called, is one of the most controversial operations in the world. In one form of the procedure, the outer layer of skin over the clitoris is removed. Approximately 100 to 135 million women and girls worldwide have undergone some form of this operation (Burstyn, 1995; Amnesty International, 1998). Most of these women live in Africa, the Middle East, or Asia. For instance, more than 90 percent of Nigerian women were circumcised during childhood, and most of these intend to circumcise their daughters. In some cases the surgery is more extensive; additional parts of the female genitals are removed and most of the remaining edges sewn together with thorns, catgut, or sewing thread (Ebomoyi, 1987; Rosenthal, 1993; French, 1997; Aikman, n.d.).

Those who practise female circumcision say it upholds an ancient societal tradition, no different from other cultural customs. Its purpose, they say, is to preserve virginity before marriage, to keep women faithful to their husbands after marriage, and to enhance a woman's beauty. Proponents believe that it differs little from the Western practice of male circumcision, in which the foreskin of the penis is surgically removed soon after birth (hence the name female circumcision).

Critics, on the other hand, argue that female circumcision is nothing less than female genital mutilation, and that it is a gross violation of human rights. It can lead to constant pain and infection, depending on the nature of the surgery. Because the procedure is traditionally conducted without anesthetic, using a razor blade, sawtooth knife, or glass, it can be physically traumatic (Dugger, 1996).

This procedure is forbidden by law in Western nations such as Canada, Britain, Denmark, Belgium, the United States, Sweden, and Switzerland (Burstyn, 1995; Robinson, 1998). In the United States, according to federal law, the penalty for performing the surgery on anyone under the age of 18 is five years' imprisonment. In Canada, not only is the procedure banned, but the Canadian Criminal Code protects children (who are citizens or landed immigrants) from being taken to another country for the surgery. Medical associations in most Canadian provinces have strict penalties against female circumcision and reinfibulation (sewing the vagina nearly shut after childbirth) (Burstyn, 1995; Robinson, 1998). In several jurisdictions women have been granted refugee status on the grounds that they or their daughters would be at risk for female circumcision in their homeland. For example, in Canada in 1993, a Somali woman who fled her country to protect her daughter from the procedure was granted refugee status (Amnesty International, 1998).

PsychLink

Female circumcision
www.mcgrawhill.ca/college/feldman

The Need for Achievement: Striving for Success

Though hunger might be one of the most potent primary drives in our day-to-day lives, we are also motivated by powerful secondary drives that have no clear biological basis (McClelland, 1985; Geen, 1984, 1995). Among the most prominent of these is the need for achievement.

The **need for achievement** is a stable, learned characteristic in which satisfaction is obtained by striving for and attaining a level of excellence (McClelland et al., 1953). People with a high need for achievement seek out situations in which they can compete against some standard—be it grades, money, or winning at a game—and prove themselves successful. But they are not indiscriminate when it comes to picking their challenges: They tend to avoid situations in which success will come too easily (which would be unchallenging) and situations in which success is unlikely. Instead, people high in achievement motivation are apt to choose tasks that are of intermediate difficulty.

In contrast, people with low achievement motivation tend to be motivated primarily by a desire to avoid failure. As a result, they seek out easy tasks, being sure to avoid failure, or they seek out very difficult tasks for which failure has no negative implications because almost anyone would fail at them. People with a high fear of failure will stay away from tasks of intermediate difficulty, because they might fail where others have been successful (Atkinson & Feather, 1966; Sorrentino, Hewitt, & Raso-Knott, 1992; Elliot & Church, 1997).

need for achievement: A stable, learned characteristic in which satisfaction is obtained by striving for and attaining a level of excellence.

The outcomes of a high need for achievement are generally positive, at least in a success-oriented society such as our own (Heckhausen, Schmalt, & Schneider, 1985; Spence, 1985). For instance, people motivated by a high need for achievement are more likely to attend college than their low-achievement counterparts, and once in college they tend to receive higher grades in classes that are related to their future careers (Atkinson & Raynor, 1974). Furthermore, high achievement motivation is associated with future economic and occupational success (McClelland, 1985).

Measuring Achievement Motivation

How can we measure a person's need for achievement? The technique used most frequently is to administer a *Thematic Apperception Test (TAT)* (Spangler, 1992). In the TAT, people are shown a series of ambiguous pictures, such as the one in Figure 8-2. They are told to write a story that describes what is happening, who the people are, what led to the situation, what the people are thinking or wanting, and what will happen next. A standard scoring system is then used to determine the amount of achievement imagery in people's stories. For example, someone who writes a story in which the main character is striving to beat an opponent, studying in order to do well at some task, or working hard in order to get a promotion shows clear signs of an achievement orientation. It is assumed that the inclusion of such achievement-related imagery in their stories indicates an unusually high degree of concern with—and therefore a relatively strong need for—achievement.

need for affiliation: An interest in establishing and maintaining relationships with other people.

need for power: A tendency to seek impact, control, or influence over others, and to be seen as a powerful individual.

The Need for Affiliation: Striving for Friendship

Few of us choose to lead our lives as hermits. Why?

One main reason is that most people have a **need for affiliation**, an interest in establishing and maintaining relationships with other people. Individuals with a high need for affiliation write TAT stories that emphasize the desire to maintain or reinstate friendships and show concern over being rejected by friends.

People who are higher in affiliation needs are particularly sensitive to relationships with others. They desire to be with their friends more of the time, and alone less often, than people who are lower in the need for affiliation (O'Connor & Rosenblood, 1996). However, gender is a greater determinant of how much time is actually spent with friends: Regardless of their affiliative orientation, female students spend significantly more time with their friends and less time alone than male students do (Wong & Csikszentmihalyi, 1991).

The Need for Power: Striving for Impact on Others

If your fantasies include being elected Prime Minister of Canada or running Microsoft, they could be reflecting a high need for power. The **need for power**—a tendency to seek impact, control, or influence over others, and to be seen as a powerful individual—is an additional type of motivation (Winter, 1973, 1987).

As you might expect, people with a strong need for power are more apt to belong to organizations and seek office than those low in the need for power. They are also apt to be in professions in which their power needs can be fulfilled, such as business management and—you may or may not be surprised—teaching (Jenkins, 1994). In addition, they seek to display the trappings of power. Even in college, they are more apt to collect prestigious possessions, such as stereos and sports cars.

There are some significant sex differences in the display of need for power. Men who are high in power needs tend to show unusually high levels of aggression, drink heavily, act in a sexually exploitative manner, and participate more frequently in competitive sports. In contrast, women display their power needs in a more restrained manner, congruent with traditional societal constraints on women's behaviour. Women high in the need for power are more apt than men to channel their power needs in a socially responsible manner, such as by showing concern for others or displaying highly nurturant behaviour (Winter, 1988).

Figure 8-2 This ambiguous picture is similar to those used in the Thematic Apperception test to determine people's underlying motivation (© 1943 by the President and Fellows of Harvard College; 1971 by Henry A. Murray). What do you see? Do you think your response is related to your motivation?

Evaluate

1. Match the following terms with their definitions:

   1. Hypothalamus
   2. Lateral hypothalamic damage
   3. Ventromedial hypothalamic damage

   a. Leads to refusal of food and starvation
   b. Responsible for monitoring food intake
   c. Causes extreme overeating

2. The_____ _____ _____is the particular level of weight the body strives to maintain.

3. _____is the rate at which energy is produced and expended by the body.

4. Although the incidence of masturbation among young adults is high, once men and women become involved in intimate relationships, they typically cease masturbating. True or false?

5. The increase in premarital sex in recent years has been greater for women than for men. True or false?

6. Julio is the type of person who constantly strives for excellence. He feels intense satisfaction when he is able to master a new task. Julio most likely has a high need for_____.

7. Debbie's Thematic Apperception Test (TAT) story depicts a young girl who is rejected by one of her peers and seeks to regain her friendship. What major type of motivation is Debbie displaying in her story?

   a. Need for achievement
   b. Need for motivation
   c. Need for affiliation
   d. Need for power

Answers to Evaluate Questions

1. 1-b; 2-a; 3-c 2. weight set point 3. Metabolism 4. False 5. True 6. achievement 7. c

Rethink

1. In what ways do societal expectations, expressed by television shows and commercials, contribute to both obesity and excessive concern about weight loss? How could television contribute to better eating habits and attitudes toward weight? Should it be required to do so?

2. Can traits such as need for achievement, need for power, and need for affiliation be used to select workers for jobs? What other criteria, both motivational and personal, would have to be considered when making such a selection?

Understanding Emotional Experiences

Karl Andrews held in his hands the envelope he had been waiting for. It could be the ticket to his future: an offer of admission to his first-choice college. But what was it going to say? He knew it could go either way; his grades were pretty good, and he had been involved in some extracurricular activities; but his SAT scores had been not-so-terrific. He felt so nervous that his hands shook as he opened the thin envelope (not a good sign, he thought). Here it comes. "Dear Mr. Andrews," it read. "The Trustees of the University are pleased to admit you...." That was all he needed to see. With a whoop of excitement, Karl found himself jumping up and down gleefully. A rush of emotion overcame him as it sank in that he had, in fact, been accepted. He was on his way.

At one time or another, all of us have experienced the strong feelings that accompany both very pleasant and very negative experiences. Perhaps it was the thrill of getting a sought-after job, the joy of being in love, the sorrow over someone's death, or the anguish of inadvertently hurting someone. Moreover, we experience such reactions on a less intense level throughout our daily lives: the pleasure of a friendship, the enjoyment of a movie, or the embarrassment of breaking a borrowed item.

Despite the varied nature of these feelings, they all are emotions. Although everyone has an idea of what an emotion is, formally defining the concept has proved to be an elusive task. We'll use a general definition: **Emotions** are feelings that generally have both physiological and cognitive elements and that influence behaviour.

Prepare

What are emotions, and how do we experience them?
What are the functions of emotions?

Organize

Understanding Emotional Experiences
The Functions of Emotions
Determining the Range of Emotions
The Roots of Emotions
The James–Lange Theory
The Cannon–Bard Theory
The Schachter–Singer Theory
Contemporary Perspectives on Emotion

emotions: Feelings that generally have both physiological and cognitive elements and that influence behaviour.

Think, for example, about how it feels to be happy. First, we obviously experience a feeling that we can differentiate from other emotions. It is likely that we also experience some identifiable physical changes in our body: Perhaps our heart rate increases, or—like Karl Andrews—we find ourselves "jumping for joy." Finally, the emotion probably encompasses cognitive elements: Our understanding and evaluation of the meaning of what is happening prompts our feelings of happiness.

It is also possible, however, to experience an emotion without the presence of cognitive elements. For instance, we might react emotionally to an unusual or novel situation (such as encountering a person who, for no apparent reason, makes us feel uncomfortable, without cognitively understanding why).

Some psychologists argue that there are entirely separate systems governing cognitive responses and emotional responses. One current controversy is whether the emotional response is predominant over the cognitive response or vice versa. Some theorists suggest that we first respond to a situation with an emotional reaction, and later try to understand it (Zajonc, 1985; Zajonc & McIntosh, 1992; Murphy & Zajonc, 1993). For example, we might enjoy a complex modern symphony without at first understanding it or knowing why we like it.

In contrast, other theorists propose that people first develop cognitions about a situation and then react emotionally. This school of thought suggests that it is necessary for us to first think about and understand a stimulus or situation, relating it to what we already know, before we can react on an emotional level (Lazarus, 1991a, 1991b, 1994, 1995).

Both sides of this debate can cite research to support their viewpoints, and so the question is far from resolved. It may be the case that the sequence varies from situation to situation, with emotions predominating in some instances and cognitive processes occurring first in others. What both sides do agree on is that we can experience emotions that involve little or no conscious thought. We might not know why we're afraid of mice, understanding that objectively they represent no danger, but still be frightened out of our wits when we see them (Lewis & Haviland-Jones, 2000).

PsychLink

Emotions and emotional intelligence
www.mcgrawhill.ca/college/feldman

The Functions of Emotions

Imagine what it would be like if we didn't experience emotion—no depths of despair, no depression, no remorse, but at the same time no happiness, joy, or love. Obviously life might be considerably less satisfying, and even dull, if we lacked the capacity to sense and express emotion.

But do emotions serve any purpose beyond making life interesting? Indeed they do. Psychologists have identified a number of important roles that emotions play in our daily lives (Scherer, 1984, 1994; Averill, 1994; Oatley & Jenkins, 1996; Greenberg & Paivio, 1997). Among the most important daily functions of emotions:

- *Preparing us for action.* Emotions act as a link between events in our environment and our responses. For example, if we see an angry dog charging toward us, the emotional reaction (fear) is associated with physiological arousal of the sympathetic division of the autonomic nervous system (see Chapter 2). The role of the sympathetic division is to prepare us for emergency action, which presumably will get us moving out of the dog's way—quickly.
- *Shaping our future behaviour.* Emotions help us learn information that improves our chances of making appropriate responses in the future. For example, the emotional response that occurs when we experience something unpleasant—such as the threatening dog—teaches us to avoid similar circumstances in the future. Similarly, pleasant emotions act as reinforcement for our prior behaviour and therefore are apt to lead us to seek out similar situations in the future.
- *Helping us interact more effectively with others.* The emotions we experience are frequently obvious to observers, as they are communicated through our verbal and nonverbal behaviours. These behaviours can act as a signal to observers, allowing them to better understand what we are experiencing and to predict our future behaviour. In turn, this promotes more effective and appropriate social interaction.

Determining the Range of Emotions: Labelling Our Feelings

If we were to try to list the words in the English language that have been used for emotions, we would end up with at least 500 examples (Averill, 1975). The list would range from such obvious entries as *happiness* and *fear* to less common ones, such as *adventurousness* and *pensiveness.*

One challenge for psychologists has been to try to sort through this list in order to identify the most important, fundamental emotions. The issue of cataloguing emotions has been hotly contested, and various emotion theorists have come up with different lists, depending on how they define the concept of emotion. In fact, some reject the question entirely, saying that *no* set of emotions should be singled out as most basic, and that emotions are best understood by breaking them down into their component parts. Other researchers argue that it is best to look at emotions in terms of a hierarchy, dividing them into positive and negative categories, and then organizing them into increasingly narrower subcategories (see Fischer, Shaver, & Carnochan, 1990; Carroll & Russell, 1997; Figure 8-3).

Still, most researchers suggest that a list of basic emotions would include, at the minimum, happiness, anger, fear, sadness, and disgust. Other lists are broader, including such emotions as surprise, contempt, guilt, and joy (Plutchik, 1980; Ortony & Turner, 1990; Russell, 1991a; Ekman, 1994a; Shweder, 1994).

One difficulty in finding a definitive basic set of emotions is that cultures differ substantially in how they describe emotions. For instance, Germans report experiencing *schadenfreude,* a feeling of pleasure over another person's difficulties, whereas the Japanese experience *hagaii,* a mood of vulnerable heartache coloured by frustration. In Tahiti, people experience *musu,* a feeling of reluctance to yield to unreasonable demands made by one's parents.

Finding *schadenfreude, hagaii,* and *musu* in a particular culture doesn't mean that inhabitants of other cultures are incapable of experiencing such emotions, of course. It does suggest, though, that the existence of a linguistic category to describe a particular emotion may make it easier to discuss, contemplate, and perhaps experience the emotion (Russell, 1991a; Mesquita & Frijda, 1992; Russell & Sato, 1995).

PsychLink

Culture and emotions
www.mcgrawhill.ca/college/feldman

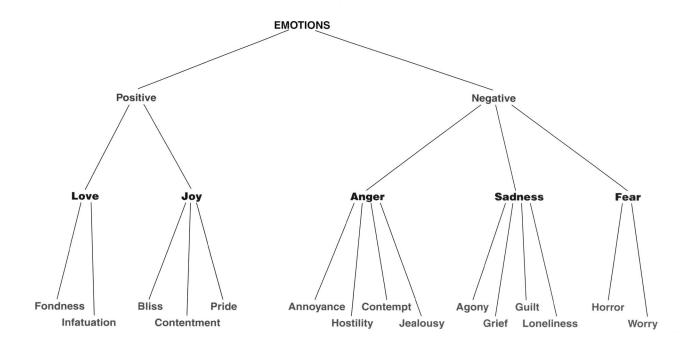

Figure 8–3 One approach to organizing emotions is to use a hierarchy, in which emotions are divided into increasingly narrow subcategories (Adapted from Fischer, Shaver, & Carnochan, 1990).

The Roots of Emotions

I've never been so angry before; I feel my heart pounding, and I'm trembling all over. . . . I don't know how I'll get through the performance. I feel like my stomach is filled with butterflies. . . . That was quite a mistake I made! My face must be incredibly red. . . . When I heard the footsteps in the night I was so frightened that I couldn't catch my breath.

If you examine our language, you will find that there are literally dozens of ways to describe how we feel when we experience an emotion, and that the language we use to describe emotions is, for the most part, based on the physical symptoms that are associated with a particular emotional experience (Koveces, 1987).

Consider, for instance, the experience of fear. Pretend that it is late one New Year's Eve. You are walking down a dark road, and you hear a stranger approaching behind you. It is clear that he is not trying to hurry by but is coming directly toward you. You think of what you will do if the stranger attempts to rob you—or worse, hurt you in some way.

While these thoughts are running through your head, something rather dramatic will be happening to your body. The most likely reactions, which are associated with activation of the autonomic nervous system (see Chapter 2), include an increase in your rate of breathing, an acceleration of your heart, a widening of your pupils (to increase visual sensitivity), and a dryness in your mouth as the functioning of your salivary glands, and in fact of your entire digestive system, ceases. At the same time, though, your sweat glands will likely increase their activity, since increased sweating will help you rid yourself of excess heat developed by any emergency activity in which you engage.

Of course, all these physiological changes are likely to occur without your awareness. At the same time, though, the emotional experience accompanying them will be obvious to you: You would most surely report feeling fearful.

Although it is relatively easy to describe the general physical reactions that accompany emotions, the specific role that these physiological responses play in the experience of emotions has proved to be a major puzzle for psychologists. As we shall see, some theorists suggest that there are specific bodily reactions that *cause* us to experience a particular emotion—we experience fear, for instance, *because* our heart is pounding and we are breathing deeply. In contrast, other theorists suggest that the physiological reaction is the *result* of the experience of an emotion. In this view, we experience fear, and this emotional experience causes our heart to pound and our breathing to deepen.

The James–Lange Theory: Do Gut Reactions Equal Emotions?

To William James and Carl Lange, who were among the first researchers to explore the nature of emotions, emotional experience is, very simply, a reaction to instinctive bodily events that occur as a response to some situation or event in the environment. This view is summarized in James's statement, "we feel sorry because we cry, angry because we strike, afraid because we tremble" (James, 1890).

James and Lange took the view that the instinctive response of crying over a loss leads us to feel sorrow; that striking out at someone who frustrates us results in our feeling anger; that trembling at a menacing threat causes us to feel fear. They suggested that for every major emotion there is an accompanying physiological or "gut" reaction of internal organs—called a *visceral experience*. It is this specific pattern of visceral response that leads us to label the emotional experience.

In sum, James and Lange proposed that we experience emotions as a result of physiological changes that produce specific sensations. In turn, these sensations are interpreted by the brain as particular kinds of emotional experiences (see Chapter Activity 8-3). This view has come to be called the **James-Lange theory of emotion** (Izard, 1990; Laird & Bresler, 1990).

The James-Lange theory has some serious drawbacks, however. For the theory to be valid, visceral changes would have to occur at a relatively rapid pace, because we experience some emotions—such as fear upon hearing a stranger rapidly approaching

James–Lange theory of emotion: The belief that emotional experience is a reaction to bodily events occurring as a result of an external situation ("I feel sad because I am crying").

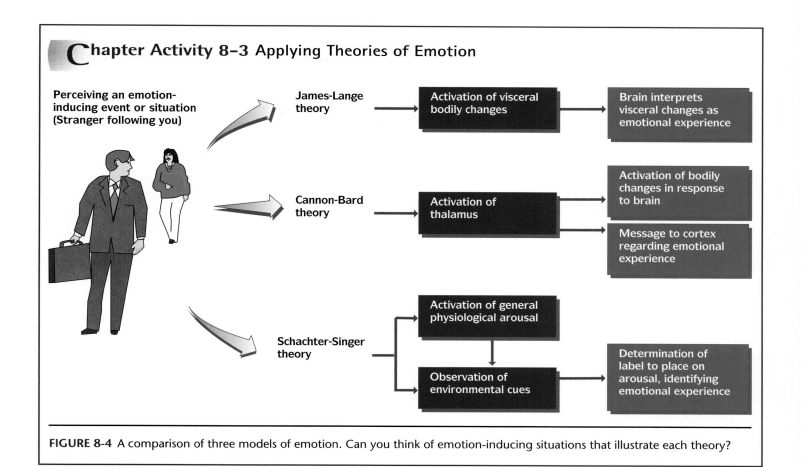

Chapter Activity 8–3 Applying Theories of Emotion

Perceiving an emotion-inducing event or situation (Stranger following you)

James-Lange theory → Activation of visceral bodily changes → Brain interprets visceral changes as emotional experience

Cannon-Bard theory → Activation of thalamus → Activation of bodily changes in response to brain / Message to cortex regarding emotional experience

Schachter-Singer theory → Activation of general physiological arousal / Observation of environmental cues → Determination of label to place on arousal, identifying emotional experience

FIGURE 8-4 A comparison of three models of emotion. Can you think of emotion-inducing situations that illustrate each theory?

on a dark night—almost instantaneously. Yet emotional experiences frequently occur even before there is time for certain physiological changes to be set into motion. Because of the slowness with which some visceral changes take place, it is hard to see how they could be the source of immediate emotional experience.

The James-Lange theory poses another difficulty: Physiological arousal does not invariably produce emotional experience. For example, a person who is jogging has an increased heartbeat and respiration rate, as well as many of the other physiological changes associated with certain emotions. Yet joggers do not typically think of such changes in terms of emotions. There cannot be a one-to-one correspondence, then, between visceral changes and emotional experience. Visceral changes by themselves may not be sufficient to produce emotion.

Finally, our internal organs produce a relatively limited range of sensations. Although some types of physiological changes are associated with specific emotional experiences (Levenson et al., 1992; Levenson, 1992; Davidson et al., 1994), it is difficult to imagine how the range of emotions that people are capable of experiencing could be the result of unique visceral changes. Many emotions are actually associated with relatively similar sorts of visceral changes, a fact that contradicts the James-Lange theory.

The Cannon–Bard Theory: Physiological Reactions as the Result of Emotions

In response to the difficulties inherent in the James-Lange theory, Walter Cannon, and later Philip Bard, suggested an alternative view. In what has come to be known as the **Cannon-Bard theory of emotion**, they proposed the model illustrated in the second part of Figure 8-4 (Cannon, 1929). The major thrust of the theory is to reject the view that physiological arousal alone leads to the perception of emotion. Instead, the theory assumes that both physiological arousal *and* the emotional experience are produced simultaneously by the same nerve stimulus, which Cannon and Bard suggested emanates from the brain's thalamus.

Cannon–Bard theory of emotion: The belief that both physiological and emotional arousal are produced simultaneously by the same nerve stimulus.

The theory states that after an emotion-producing stimulus is perceived, the thalamus is the initial site of the emotional response. In turn, the thalamus sends a signal to the autonomic nervous system, thereby producing a visceral response. At the same time, the thalamus communicates a message to the cerebral cortex regarding the nature of the emotion being experienced. Hence, it is not necessary for different emotions to have unique physiological patterns associated with them—as long as the message sent to the cerebral cortex differs according to the specific emotion.

The Cannon-Bard theory seems to have been accurate in its rejection of the view that physiological arousal alone accounts for emotions. However, more recent research has led to some important modifications of the theory. As you may recall from Chapter 2, we now understand that it is the hypothalamus and the limbic system, and not the thalamus, that play a major role in emotional experience. In addition, the simultaneity of the physiological and emotional responses, which is a fundamental assumption of the theory, has yet to be conclusively demonstrated (Pribram, 1984). This ambiguity has allowed room for yet another theory of emotions: the Schachter-Singer theory.

The Schachter–Singer Theory: Emotions as Labels

Suppose that, as you were being followed down a dark street on New Year's Eve, you noticed a man being followed by a shady figure on the other side of the street. Now assume that instead of reacting with fear, the man begins to laugh and act gleeful. Might the reactions of this other individual be sufficient to lay your fears to rest? Might you, in fact, decide there is nothing to fear, and get into the spirit of the evening by beginning to feel happiness and glee yourself?

According to an explanation that focuses on the role of cognition, the **Schachter-Singer theory of emotion**, this might very well happen. This approach to explaining emotions emphasizes that we identify the emotion we are experiencing by observing our environment and comparing ourselves with others (Schachter & Singer, 1962).

A classic experiment found evidence for this hypothesis. In the study, participants were told that they would receive an injection of a vitamin. In reality, they were given epinephrine, a drug that causes an increase in physiological arousal, including higher heart and respiration rates and a reddening of the face, responses that typically occur during strong emotional reactions. Participants in both groups were then individually placed in a situation where a confederate of the experimenter acted in one of two ways. In one condition, he acted angry and hostile, while in the other condition he behaved as if he were exuberantly happy.

The purpose of the experiment was to determine how the participants would react emotionally to the confederate's behaviour. When they were asked to describe their own emotional state at the end of the experiment, those participants exposed to the angry confederate reported that they felt angry, whereas those exposed to the happy confederate reported feeling happy. In sum, the results suggest that participants turned to the environment and the behaviour of others for an explanation of the physiological arousal they were experiencing.

The results of the Schachter-Singer experiment, then, supported a cognitive view of emotions, in which emotions are determined jointly by a relatively nonspecific kind of physiological arousal *and* the labelling of the arousal based on cues from the environment (refer to the third part of Figure 8-4).

Although later research has found that arousal is not as nonspecific as Schachter and Singer assumed, it is clear that arousal can magnify, and be mistaken for, many emotions. For example, in one experiment, men who crossed a swaying 450-foot suspension bridge spanning a deep canyon were more attracted to a woman they encountered at the other end than those who crossed a stable bridge spanning a shallow stream. Apparently, the men who crossed the frightening bridge attributed their subsequent high arousal to the woman, rather than to the swaying bridge (Dutton & Aron, 1974; Reisenzein, 1983; Leventhal & Tomarken, 1986).

Schachter–Singer theory of emotion: The belief that emotions are determined jointly by a nonspecific kind of physiological arousal and its interpretation, based on environmental cues.

This is Capilano River Bridge (BC), the high, swaying suspension bridge that was used to increase the physiological arousal of male subjects.

In short, the Schachter-Singer theory of emotions is important because of its suggestion that, at least under some circumstances, emotional experiences are a joint function of physiological arousal and the labelling of that arousal. When the source of physiological arousal is unclear, we may look to our surroundings to determine just what it is we are experiencing.

Contemporary Perspectives on Emotion

When Schachter and Singer carried out their groundbreaking experiment in the early 1960s, they were relatively limited in the ways that they could evaluate the physiology that accompanies emotion. However, advances in the measurement of the nervous system and other parts of the body have allowed researchers to examine more closely the biological responses that are involved in emotion. As a result, contemporary research on emotion is pointing to a revision of earlier views that physiological responses associated with emotions are undifferentiated. Instead, evidence is growing that specific patterns of biological arousal are associated with individual emotions (Davidson, 1994; Levenson, 1994; Franks & Smith, 1999).

For instance, researchers have found that specific emotions produce activation of very different portions of the brain. In one study using PET brain scans, participants were asked to recall either events that made them feel sad, such as deaths and funerals, or events that were happy, such as weddings and births. They also looked at photos of faces that were happy or sad. The results were clear: Happiness was related to a decrease in activity in certain areas of the cerebral cortex, and sadness was associated with increases in activity in particular portions of the cortex (see Figure 8-5). Ultimately, it might be possible to map particular emotions to specific sites in the brain (George et al., 1995).

Other approaches to emotion have also evolved, and Canadian psychologists have developed a number of these theories. James Russell developed a model that represents the structure of emotional experience and indicates relationships between specific emotions, a view he called a *circumplex model* (Russell, 1980). More recently he has developed a prototypical approach to emotion concepts that suggests we identify and understand emotions by assessing their resemblance to best examples of emotions (Russell, 1991b; Russell & Fehr, 1994). Keith Oatley has examined social, cognitive, and experiential aspects of emotions (Oatley & Johnson-Laird, 1987; Oatley, 1992; Oatley & Duncan, 1994). Winter and Kuiper have developed a self-schema model of emotion, which accounts well for the variety of emotional responses people make to a given situation (Winter & Kuiper, 1997; Kirsh & Kuiper, 2002). Beginning with the idea that people vary greatly in their self-schemata (views of self), Winter and Kuiper argue that these differences result in very different evaluations of events and emotional responses to them.

Why are theories of emotion so plentiful? The answer is that emotions are such complex phenomena, encompassing both biological and cognitive aspects, that no single theory has been able to fully explain all facets of emotional experience. For each of the approaches, there is contradictory evidence of one sort or another, and therefore no theory has proved invariably accurate in its predictions.

To read about attempts to apply our knowledge of emotions to a practical problem, see the *Applying Psychology in the 21st Century* box on p. 284.

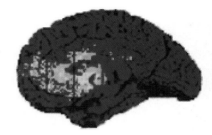
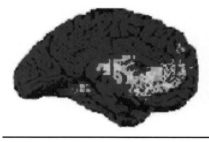

Figure 8-5 Experiencing different emotions activates particular areas of the brain. These scans, showing two views of the brain, indicate brain activity that occurs during the experience of sadness, as compared with situations in which no emotion is being experienced (Courtesy of Mark George, NIMH).

PsychLink

The emotional brain
www.mcgrawhill.ca/college/feldman

Applying Psychology in the 21st Century

The Truth About Lies: Do Lie Detectors Work?

Aldrich Ames was given routine lie detector tests periodically by his employer, the U.S. Central Intelligence Agency. On every occasion he passed the test. Yet at the very same time his truthfulness was being vouched for by the lie detector, he was involved in high-level spying for the Russians.

No surprise, at least among researchers who study the validity of lie detector test results. Repeatedly, lie detectors have proved to be unreliable indicators of lying.

A lie detector, or *polygraph,* is an electronic device designed to expose people who are telling lies. The basic assumption behind the apparatus is straightforward: The autonomic nervous system of people who are not being truthful becomes aroused as their emotionality increases. Polygraphs are designed to detect the physiological changes that are indicative of this arousal.

Actually, a number of separate physiological functions are measured simultaneously by a lie detector, including changes in breathing pattern, heart rate, blood pressure, and sweating. In theory, polygraph operators ask a series of questions, some of which they know will elicit verifiable, truthful responses. For instance, they might ask a person to provide his or her name and address. Then, when more critical questions

are answered, operators can observe the nature of the physiological changes that occur. Answers whose accompanying physiological responses deviate significantly from those accompanying truthful responses are assumed to be false (Reicherter, 1997).

That's the theory, at least. The reality is something different: There is no foolproof technique for assessing the extent of the physiological changes that can indicate a lie. Even truthful responses can elicit physiological arousal, if the question is emotion-laden (Waid & Orne, 1982). How many innocent people accused of a murder, for instance, would *not* respond emotionally when asked whether they committed the crime, since they know that their future may hang in the balance?

One further drawback of lie detector tests is that people are capable of fooling the polygraph. For instance, biofeedback techniques (see Chapter 2) can be employed to produce emotional responses to accompany even truthful statements, meaning that the polygraph operator will be unable to differentiate between honest and dishonest responses. Even biting one's tongue or hiding a tack in a shoe and pressing on it as each question is answered could be sufficient to produce physiological arousal during each response, making truthful and deceptive responses indistinguishable (Honts, Raskin, & Kircher, 1987; Honts & Kircher, 1994; Sleek, 1998).

Because of these sources of error, lie detector operators often make mistakes when trying to judge another person's honesty. The American Psychological Association has adopted a resolution stating that the evidence for the effectiveness of polygraphs "is still unsatisfactory." Even the major proponent of the use of polygraphs—the American Polygraph Association—admits an error rate between 4 and 13 percent, and critics suggest that research has shown that the actual rate is closer to 30 percent. Using such evidence, U.S. federal law bars employers from using polygraphs as screening devices for most jobs (Iacono, 1991; Saxe, 1994; Iacono & Lykken, 1997).

In short, there are good reasons to doubt that polygraph tests can determine accurately whether someone is lying. For now, then, you can be assured that any secrets you might harbour will remain hidden: No one has yet identified a foolproof way to distinguish people who are telling the truth from those who are lying (Saxe, 1994; Alliger, Lilienfeld, & Mitchell, 1996).

Techniques for "fooling" lie detectors focus on artificially elevating emotional responses so that truthful and untruthful responses display similar patterns of emotionality. Do you think a lack of emotional response would therefore indicate truthfulness? Or is it possible to defeat a lie detector by depressing (rather than elevating) one's emotional response?

Evaluate

1. Emotions are always accompanied by a cognitive response. True or false?
2. The_____-_____theory of emotions states that emotions are a response to bodily reactions to events.
3. According to the_____-_____theory of emotion, both an emotional response and physiological arousal are produced simultaneously by the same nerve stimulus.
4. Your friend—a psychology major—tells you, "I was at a party last night. During the course of the evening, my general level of arousal increased. Since I was at a party where people were enjoying themselves, I assume I must have felt happy." What theory of emotion does your friend subscribe to?
5. The_____or "lie detector" is an instrument used to measure physiological responses associated with answers to questions.

Answers to Evaluate Questions

1. False; emotions may occur without a cognitive response. 2. James-Lange 4. Cannon-Bard 5. Schachter-Singer 6. polygraph

Rethink

1. Many people enjoy watching movies, sporting events, and music performances in crowded theatres and arenas more than they like watching them at home alone. Which theory of emotions might help explain this? How?
2. If researchers learned how to control emotional responses so that targeted emotions could be caused or prevented, what ethical concerns might arise? Under what circumstances, if any, should such techniques be used?

How does motivation direct and energize behaviour?

- Motivation relates to the factors that direct and energize behaviour. Drive is the motivational tension that energizes behaviour to fulfill a need. Primary drives relate to basic biological needs. Secondary drives are those in which no obvious biological need is fulfilled. (p. 258)
- Motivational drives often operate under the principle of homeostasis, the maintenance of a steady internal state. (p. 259)
- A number of broad approaches to motivation move beyond explanations that rely on instincts. Drive-reduction approaches, though useful for primary drives, are inadequate for explaining behaviour in which the goal is not to reduce a drive but to maintain or even increase excitement or arousal. In contrast, arousal approaches suggest that we try to maintain a particular level of stimulation and activity. (p. 260)
- Incentive approaches focus on the positive aspects of the environment that direct and energize behaviour. Finally, cognitive approaches focus on the role of thoughts, expectations, and understanding of the world in producing motivation. Cognitive approaches draw a distinction between intrinsic and extrinsic motivation. (p. 260)
- Maslow's hierarchy of needs suggests that there are five needs: physiological, safety, love and belongingness, esteem, and self-actualization. (p. 262)

What biological and social factors underlie hunger?

- Eating behaviour is subject to homeostasis, because most people's weight stays within a relatively stable range. The brain's hypothalamus is central to the regulation of food intake. (p. 265)
- Social factors also play a role in the regulation of eating, determining when, what, and how much one eats. An oversensitivity to social cues and an insensitivity to internal cues might also be related to obesity. In addition, obesity could be caused by an unusually high weight set point—the weight at which the body attempts to maintain homeostasis—and genetic factors. (p. 267)

What are the varieties of sexual behaviour?

- Although biological factors, such as the presence of androgens (male sex hormones) and estrogen and progesterone (female sex hormones) prime people for sex, almost any kind of stimulus can produce sexual arousal, depending on a person's prior experience. (p. 270)
- The frequency of masturbation is high, particularly for males. Attitudes toward masturbation are now increasingly liberal. (p. 271)
- Heterosexuality, or sexual attraction to people of the opposite sex, is the most common sexual orientation. In terms of premarital sex, the double standard, in which premarital sex is thought to be more permissible for men than for women, has declined. For many people, the double standard has been replaced by endorsement of "permissiveness with affection," the view that premarital intercourse is permissible if it occurs in the context of a loving and committed relationship. (p. 271)
- The frequency of marital sex varies widely. However, younger couples tend to have sexual intercourse more frequently than older couples. In addition, most men and women do not engage in extramarital sex. (p. 272)
- Homosexuals are sexually attracted to people of their own sex; bisexuals are sexually attracted to people of the same sex and people of the opposite sex. No explanation of sexual orientation has been confirmed; possibilities include genetic or biological factors, childhood and family influences, and prior learning experiences and conditioning. (p. 272)

How are needs relating to achievement, affiliation, and power motivation exhibited?

- Need for achievement refers to the stable, learned characteristic in which a person strives to attain a level of excellence. Need for achievement is usually measured through the Thematic Apperception Test (TAT), a series of pictures about which a person writes a story. (p. 275)
- The need for affiliation is a concern with establishing and maintaining relationships with others, whereas the need for power is a tendency to seek to exert an impact on others. (p. 276)

What are emotions, and how do we experience them?

- Emotions are broadly defined as feelings that can affect behaviour and generally have both a physiological and a cognitive component. There is debate over whether there are separate systems that govern cognitive and emotional responses, and whether one has primacy over the other. (p. 277)

What are the functions of emotions?

- Several theories explain emotions. The James-Lange theory suggests that emotional experience is a reaction to bodily, or visceral, changes that occur as a response to an environmental event and are interpreted as an emotional response. (p. 280)
- In contrast, the Cannon-Bard theory contends that both physiological arousal *and* an emotional experience are produced simultaneously by the same nerve stimulus and that the visceral experience itself does not necessarily differ among differing emotions. (p. 281)
- The Schachter-Singer theory suggests that emotions are determined jointly by a relatively nonspecific physiological arousal and the subsequent labelling of that arousal, using cues from the environment to determine how others are behaving in the same situation. (p. 282)
- The most recent approaches to emotions focus on their biological and cognitive aspects. (p. 283)

Key Terms and Concepts

motivation (p. 258)
instincts (p. 259)
drive-reduction approaches to motivation (p. 259)
drive (p. 259)
homeostasis (p. 259)
arousal approaches to motivation (p. 260)
incentive approaches to motivation (p. 260)
cognitive approaches to motivation (p. 260)
self-actualization (p. 263)
overweight (p. 266)
obesity (p. 266)
weight set point (p. 267)
metabolism (p. 267)
anorexia nervosa (p. 268)
bulimia (p. 269)
androgens (p. 270)

estrogen (p. 270)
progesterone (p. 270)
ovulation (p. 270)
masturbation (p. 271)
heterosexuality (p. 271)
double standard (p. 272)
extramarital sex (p. 272)
homosexuals (p. 272)
bisexuals (p. 272)
need for achievement (p. 275)
need for affiliation (p. 276)
need for power (p. 276)
emotions (p. 277)
James-Lange theory of emotion (p. 280)
Cannon-Bard theory of emotion (p. 281)
Schachter-Singer theory of emotion (p. 282)

Psychology on the Web

1. Find two different Web sites that deal with nonverbal behaviour. One site should present a fairly "academic" discussion of the topic, and the other should be more informal. (Hint: The terms *nonverbal behaviour* and *nonverbal communication* might lead you to more formal discussions of the topic, whereas *body language* might lead you to the less formal discussions.) Compare and contrast your findings from the two sites.

2. Find one or more Web sites that offer information on losing weight. Evaluate the information on the Web site(s), using your understanding of obesity discussed in this chapter. Summarize your findings and conclusions in writing.

Epilogue

In this chapter, we discussed motivation and emotions, two interrelated aspects of psychology. The topic of motivation has spawned a great deal of theory and research in its examination of primary and secondary drives. We then turned to a discussion of emotions, beginning with their functions and proceeding to a review of three major theories that seek to explain what emotions are and how they, and their associated physiological symptoms, emerge in the individual.

   Before we proceed to Chapter 9, return to the story of Premier Okalik in the chapter prologue. Using your knowledge of motivation and emotion, consider the following questions:

1. How might the various approaches to motivation account for Paul Okalik's teenage and later adult behaviours?
2. How might the psychological needs for achievement, affiliation, and power have contributed to his behaviour?
3. What functions might both positive and negative emotions have served in shaping his decisions and behaviours?

OLC

integrator

For extra help in mastering the material in this chapter, see the integrator, practice quizzes, and other resources on the Online Learning Centre at

www.mcgrawhill.ca/college/ feldman

Chapter Nine

Development

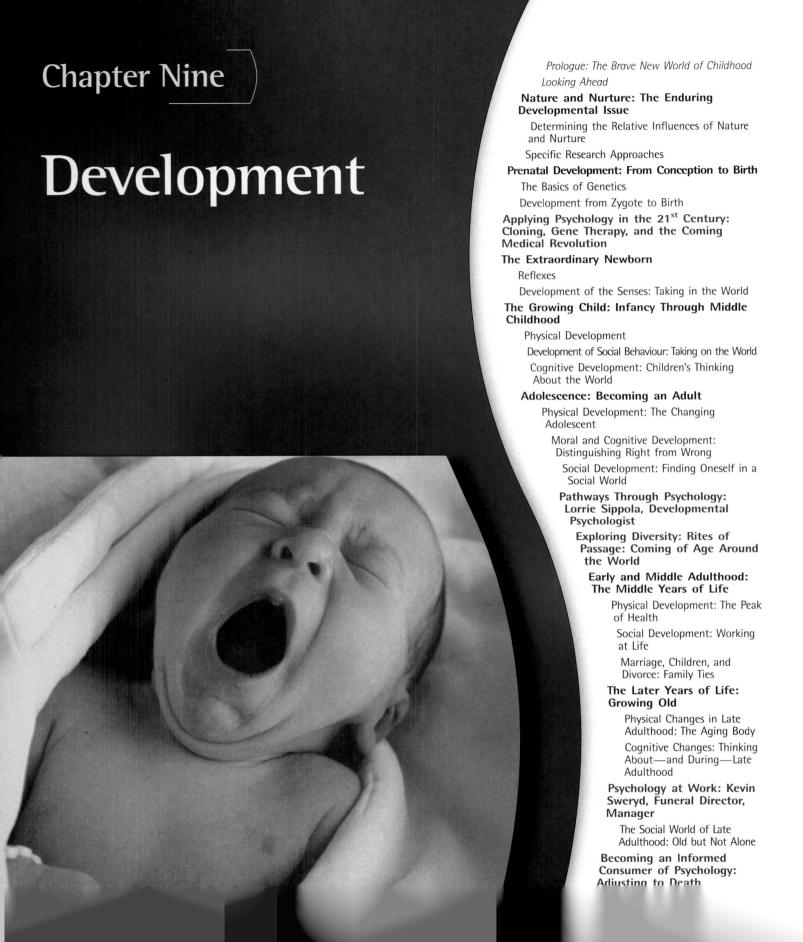

Elizabeth Carr

Prologue

The Brave New World of Childhood

A few years ago, when Elizabeth Carr's class was learning how an egg combines with sperm in the mother's body to create a child, she felt compelled to interrupt.

"I piped up to say that not all babies are conceived like that and explained about sperm and eggs and petri dishes," said Elizabeth . . . , the first child in the United States born through in vitro fertilization.

Because her mother's landmark pregnancy was documented in great detail by a film crew, Elizabeth has seen pictures of the egg and sperm that united to become her, the petri dish where she was conceived, the embryonic blob of cells that grew into the bubbly young woman who now plays field hockey and sings in the school chorus. . . .

Elizabeth . . . said that her parents—whose egg and sperm joined in a petri dish at the Jones Institute for Reproductive Medicine in Norfolk, Virginia—have always made it clear that she was created differently from other children. Although she said she had faced taunts of "test tube baby" or "weirdo" a few times at school, she said she had never felt resentful about her conception. "I'm so grateful that they went through all this to have me" (Rosenthal, 1996, A1, B8).

Looking Ahead

Now a bubbly teenager, Elizabeth is just "one of a crowd," as her mother predicted when she was born—a crowd of some 60 000 children in the United States who were born only thanks to the technology of in vitro fertilization (Goldberg, 1999).

Welcome to the brave new world of childhood—or rather, one of the brave new worlds. From new ways of conceiving children to learning how to raise children most sensibly, the issues involved in human development touch each of us.

These issues, along with many others, are addressed by **developmental psychology**, the branch of psychology that studies the patterns of growth and change occurring throughout life. In large part, developmental psychologists study the interaction between the unfolding of biologically predetermined patterns of behaviour and a constantly changing, dynamic environment. They ask how our genetic background affects our behaviour throughout our lives and whether our potential is limited by heredity. Similarly, they are committed to understanding how the environment works with—or against—our genetic capabilities, how the world we live in affects our development, and how we can be encouraged to reach our full potential.

More than other psychologists, developmental psychologists consider the day-to-day patterns and changes in behaviour that occur across the life span. This chapter deals broadly with the entire life cycle, beginning with conception, moving through birth, infancy, and childhood, exploring adolescence and adulthood, and finally proceeding to old age and death.

We begin our discussion of development by examining the approaches used to study the environmental and genetic factors—the nature-nurture issue. Then we consider the very start of development, beginning with conception and the nine months of life prior to birth. We describe both genetic and environmental influences on the unborn individual, and how these can affect behaviour throughout the remainder of the life cycle.

Next, we examine the physical and perceptual developments that occur after birth, witnessing the enormous and rapid growth that takes place during the early stages of life. We also focus on the developing child's social world, indicating what draws the child into relationships with others and membership in society. Finally, we discuss cognitive growth during infancy and childhood, tracing changes in the ways children think about the world.

We then examine development from adolescence through young adulthood, middle age, and old age. Our discussion of adolescence focuses on some of the major physical, emotional, and cognitive changes that occur during this transition from childhood to adulthood. Next, we consider early and middle adulthood, stages in which people are at the peak of their physical and intellectual abilities. We discuss the developmental changes people undergo during these periods and their relationship to work, families, and social changes that occur as a consequence of the aging process, and we see that aging can bring about both improvements and declines in various kinds of functioning. We end with a discussion of the ways people prepare themselves for death.

developmental psychology: The branch of psychology that studies the patterns of growth and change occurring throughout life.

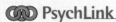 **PsychLink**

Theories of child development
www.mcgrawhill.ca/college/feldman

Prepare

How do psychologists study the influences of hereditary and environmental factors in development?

What is the nature of development prior to birth?

What factors affect a child during the mother's pregnancy?

Organize

Nature and Nurture
   Determining the Relative Influences of Nature and Nurture
   Specific Research Approaches

Prenatal Development
   The Basics of Genetics
   Development from Zygote to Birth

Nature and Nurture: The Enduring Developmental Issue

How many bald, 198-centimetre, 114-kilogram volunteer fire fighters are there in New Jersey who wear droopy mustaches, aviator-style eyeglasses, and a key ring on the right side of the belt?

The answer is: two. Gerald Levey and Mark Newman are identical twins, separated at birth. Each twin did not even know the other existed until they were reunited—in a fire station—by a fellow fire fighter who knew Newman and was startled to see Levey at a fire fighters' convention.

The lives of the twins, although separate, took remarkably similar paths. Levey went to college, studying forestry; Newman planned to study forestry in college but instead took a job trimming trees. Both had jobs in supermarkets. One has a job installing sprinkler systems; the other installed fire alarms.

Both men are unmarried and find the same kind of woman attractive: "tall, slender, long hair." They share similar hobbies, enjoying hunting, fishing, going to the beach, and watching old John Wayne movies and professional wrestling. Both like Chinese food and drink the same brand of beer. Their mannerisms are also similar—for example, each one throws his head back when he laughs. And, of course, there is one more thing: They share a passion for fighting fires.

Gerald Levey and Mark Newman

The similarities we see in twins Gerald Levey and Mark Newman vividly raise one of the fundamental questions posed by developmental psychologists: How can we distinguish between the causes of behaviour that are *environmental* (i.e., due to the influence of parents, siblings, family, friends, schooling, nutrition, and all the other experiences to which a child is exposed) and those causes that are *hereditary* (those based on the genetic makeup of an individual that influence growth and development throughout life)? This question, which we explored when we considered intelligence in Chapter 7, is known as the **nature-nurture issue**. In this context, nature refers to hereditary factors, and nurture to environmental influences.

Discussion on nature vs. nurture
www.mcgrawhill.ca/college/feldman

nature–nurture issue: The issue of the degree to which environment and heredity influence behaviour and development.

Although the question was first posed as a nature-*versus*-nurture issue, developmental psychologists today agree that *both* nature and nurture interact to produce specific developmental patterns and outcomes. Consequently, the question has evolved to *how and to what degree* environment and heredity both produce their effects. No one grows up free of environmental influences, nor does anyone develop without being affected by his or her inherited *genetic makeup.* However, the debate over the comparative influence of the two factors remains active, with different approaches and theories of development emphasizing the environment or heredity to a greater or lesser degree (Scarr, 1996; Saudino, 1997; de Waal, 1999).

For example, some developmental theories stress the role of learning in producing changes in behaviour in the developing child, relying on the basic principles of learning discussed in Chapter 5. Such theories emphasize the role of environment in accounting for development. In contrast, other approaches emphasize the influence of one's physiological makeup and functioning on development. Such theories stress the role of heredity and *maturation*—the unfolding of biologically predetermined patterns of behaviour—in producing developmental change. Maturation can be seen, for instance, in the development of sex characteristics (such as breasts or body hair) that occurs at the start of adolescence. Furthermore, developmental psychologists have been influenced by the work of behavioural geneticists, who study the effects of heredity on behaviour, and the theories of evolutionary psychologists, whose goal is to identify behaviour patterns that are a result of our genetic inheritance from our ancestors. Both behavioural geneticists and evolutionary psychologists have highlighted the importance of heredity in influencing our behaviour (Bjorklund, 1997).

However, developmental psychologists of different theoretical persuasions agree on some points. It seems clear that genetic factors not only provide the potential for particular behaviours or traits to emerge, but also place limitations on the emergence of such behaviour or traits. For instance, heredity defines people's general level of intelligence, setting an upper limit which—regardless of the quality of the environment—people usually do not exceed. Heredity also provides limits on physical abilities; humans simply cannot run at a speed of 100 kilometres per hour, nor will they grow to be three metres tall, no matter what the quality of their environment (Plomin, 1990; Plomin & McClearn, 1993; Steen, 1996).

Table 9-1 lists some of the characteristics that are most affected by heredity. As you consider these items, keep in mind that these characteristics are not *entirely* determined by heredity, but that environmental factors also play a role.

In fact, in most instances, environmental factors play a critical role in enabling people to develop the capabilities that their genetic background makes possible. Had Roberta Bondar

Table 9-1 Characteristics Influenced Significantly by Genetic Factors

Physical Characteristics	Intellectual Characteristics	Emotional Characteristics and Disorders
Height	Memory	Shyness
Weight	Intelligence	Extraversion
Obesity	Age of language acquisition	Emotionality
Tone of voice	Reading disability	Neuroticism
Blood pressure	Mental retardation	Schizophrenia
Tooth decay		Anxiety
Athletic ability		Alcoholism
Firmness of handshake		
Age of death		
Activity level		

not had the opportunity to develop her physical abilities and the education to provide her with the intellectual skills to fulfill her potential, it is unlikely that she would have been Canada's first woman in space. Similarly, it is unlikely that the great athlete and basketball star Michael Jordan would have developed outstanding physical skill if he had not been raised in an environment that nurtured his innate talent and gave him the opportunity to train and perfect his natural abilities.

It is clear that the relationship between heredity and environment is far from simple. As a consequence, developmental psychologists typically take an *interactionist* position on the nature-nurture issue, suggesting that a combination of hereditary and environmental factors influences development. The challenge facing developmental psychologists is to identify the relative strength of each of these influences on the individual, as well as the specific changes that occur over the course of development (Plomin & Neiderhiser, 1992; Wozniak & Fischer, 1993; Saudino & Plomin, 1996).

Determining the Relative Influences of Nature and Nurture

Developmental psychologists use several approaches to determine the relative influence of genetic and environmental factors on behaviour. For example, researchers can experimentally control the genetic makeup of laboratory animals by carefully breeding them for specific traits; and by observing animals with identical genetic makeup in varied environments, researchers can ascertain the effects of particular kinds of environmental stimulation. Although generalizing the findings of nonhuman research to a human population must be done only with care, findings from animal research provide important information that, for ethical reasons, could not be obtained by using human participants.

identical twins: Twins who are genetically identical.

Human twins also are an important source of information about the relative effects of genetic and environmental factors. If **identical twins** (those who are genetically identical) display different patterns of development, such differences have to be attributed to variations in the environment in which the twins were raised. The most useful data come from identical twins (such as Gerald Levey and Mark Newman) who are adopted at birth by different sets of adoptive parents and raised apart in differing environments. Studies of nontwin siblings who are raised in totally different environments also shed some light on the issue. Because they have relatively similar genetic makeups, siblings who show similarities as adults provide strong evidence for the importance of heredity (Lykken et al., 1993; Gottesman, 1997; McClearn et al., 1997).

It is also possible to take the opposite tack. Instead of concentrating on genetically similar people raised in different environments, we could consider people raised in similar environments who are genetically dissimilar. If we find, for example, that two adopted children—genetically dissimilar but raised in the same family—develop similarly, we have evidence for the importance of environmental influences on development. Moreover, it is possible to carry out research involving genetically dissimilar animals; by experimentally varying the environment in which they are raised, we can determine the influence of environmental factors (independent of heredity) on development (Segal, 1993; Vernon et al., 1997).

Specific Research Approaches

Because of the unique demands of measuring behavioural change across different ages, developmental researchers have designed several unique methodologies. In the most frequently used, **cross-sectional research**, people of different ages are compared at the same point in time. Cross-sectional studies provide information about differences in development between different age groups.

cross-sectional research: A research method in which people of different ages are compared at the same point in time.

Suppose, for instance, we were interested in the development of intellectual ability in adulthood. To carry out a cross-sectional study, we might compare a sample of 25-, 45-, and 65-year-olds on an IQ test. We then can determine whether average IQ test scores differ in each age group.

Cross-sectional research has limitations, however. For instance, we cannot be sure that the IQ score differences we might find in our example are due to age differences alone. Instead, they might reflect cohort differences in educational attainment. A *cohort* is a group of people who grow up at similar times, in similar places, and under similar conditions. In the case of IQ differences, any age differences we find in a cross-sectional study could reflect educational differences among the cohorts studied: People in the older age group might belong to a cohort that was less likely to attend college than those in the younger groups.

One way around the problem is to employ the second major research strategy used by developmental psychologists: a longitudinal study. In **longitudinal research**, the behaviour of one or more participants is traced as the participants age. Longitudinal studies assess *change* in intellectual ability over time, unlike cross-sectional studies, which assess *differences* among groups of people.

longitudinal research: A research method that investigates behaviour as participants age.

For instance, consider how we might investigate intellectual development during adulthood using a longitudinal research strategy. First, we might give IQ tests to a group of 25-year-olds. We'd then come back to the same people 20 years later and retest them at age 45. Finally, we'd return to them once more when they were 65 years old and test them again.

By examining changes over several points in time, we can clearly see how individuals develop. Unfortunately, longitudinal research requires an enormous expenditure of time (as the researcher waits for the participants to get older), and participants who begin a study at an early age might drop out, move away, or even die as the research continues. Moreover, participants who take the same test at several points in time can become "testwise" and perform better each time they take it, having become more familiar with the test.

To make up for the limitations in cross-sectional and longitudinal research, investigators have devised an alternative strategy. Known as **cross-sequential research**, it combines cross-sectional and longitudinal approaches by taking a number of different age groups and examining them over several points in time. For example, investigators might use a group of 3-, 5-, and 7-year-olds, examining them every six months for a period of several years. This technique allows the developmental psychologist to tease out the effects of age changes themselves from other possibly influential factors.

cross-sequential research: A research method that combines cross-sectional and longitudinal research by considering a number of different age groups and examining them over several points in time.

Prenatal Development: From Conception to Birth

Our understanding of the biology of *conception*—when a male's sperm cell penetrates a female's egg cell—makes it no less of a miracle. At that single moment, an individual's genetic endowment is established for the rest of her or his life.

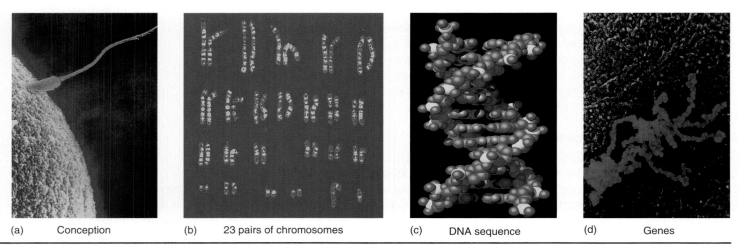

| (a) Conception | (b) 23 pairs of chromosomes | (c) DNA sequence | (d) Genes |

Figure 9-1 Every individual's characteristics are determined by the individual's specific genetic information. At the moment of conception *(a)*, humans receive 23 pairs of chromosomes *(b)*, half from the mother and half from the father. These chromosomes are made up of coils of DNA *(c)*. Each chromosome contains thousands of genes *(d)* that "program" the future development of the body.

The Basics of Genetics

chromosomes: Rod-shaped structures that contain the basic hereditary information.

genes: The parts of the chromosomes through which genetic information is transmitted.

The one-cell entity that is established at conception contains 23 pairs of **chromosomes**, rod-shaped structures that contain the basic hereditary information. One member of each pair is from the mother and the other is from the father.

Each chromosome contains thousands of **genes**—smaller units through which genetic information is transmitted. Either individually or in combination, genes produce the particular characteristics of each person. Composed of sequences of *DNA (deoxyribonucleic acid)* molecules, genes are the biological equivalent of "software" that programs the future development of all parts of the body's hardware. Humans have some 30 000 different genes (see Figure 9-1).

Some genes are responsible for the development of systems common to all members of the human species—the heart, circulatory system, brain, lungs, and so forth; others control the characteristics that make each human unique, such as facial configuration, height, eye colour, and the like. The child's sex is also determined by a particular combination of genes. Specifically, a child inherits an X chromosome from its mother, and either an X or Y chromosome from its father. A child with an XX combination is female; a child with an XY combination is male. Male development is triggered by a single gene on the Y chromosome, and without the presence of that specific gene, the individual will develop as a female.

As behavioural geneticists are increasingly discovering, genes are also at least partially responsible for a wide variety of personal characteristics, encompassing cognitive abilities, personality traits, and psychological disorders. Of course, few of these characteristics are determined by a single gene. Instead, most traits are the result of a combination of multiple genes, which operate together with environmental influences (Gilger, 1996; Pillard, 1996; Rieder, Kaufmann, & Knowles, 1996; Funder, 1997).

To better understand how genes influence human characteristics and behaviour, scientists have mapped the specific location and sequence of every human gene in the massive, multiyear Human Genome Project (first discussed in Chapter 2). As you can see by reading the *Applying Psychology in the 21st Century* box, the Human Genome Project is likely to produce a revolution in health care, as scientists identify the particular genes that are responsible for various disorders.

PsychLink

Publications on genetics
www.mcgrawhill.ca/college/feldman

Development from Zygote to Birth

zygote: The new cell formed by the union of an egg and sperm.

When the egg becomes fertilized by the sperm, the result is a one-celled entity called a **zygote** that immediately begins to develop. The zygote starts out as a microscopic speck. Three days after fertilization, though, the zygote increases to around 32 cells,

Applying Psychology in the 21st Century

Cloning, Gene Therapy, and the Coming Medical Revolution

As he chats with the young mother, the doctor flicks a cotton swab into the mouth of her infant son, collecting a small sample of mucus from inside his cheek. In the back room of his office, he inserts the sample into a machine, which extracts DNA from the mucus cells and compares it with the genetic material on a dime-size chip. Minutes later, a computer printer begins to spit out a list of the infant's genes. Fortunately, all but a few of the genes are labeled "normal." It is those few that the doctor discusses as he explains the results to the mother. "Your son's genetic inheritance is generally good," he says, "but he is somewhat predisposed to skin lesions. So starting right away, he should be protected against excessive exposure to the sun." And the doctor warns, "he may well be susceptible to cardiovascular disease later in life. To lessen his risk, after about age two he should begin a lifelong low-fat, high-fiber diet." (Jaroff, 1996, p. 24)

This view of a visit to a pediatrician's office is not so futuristic, for it could become reality within the next few decades. Our increasing understanding of genetics is leading not only to the identification of risk factors in children, but also to the development of new treatments for everything from serious physical illnesses, such as cancer, to psychological disorders like schizophrenia and depression.

This potential medical revolution has been heralded, in part, by an unlikely achievement: the birth of Dolly, a rather ordinary looking sheep with an extraordinary genetic background. Dolly was the first animal to be cloned from the cells of an adult sheep, making her an exact genetic replica of her "parent." Dolly was soon followed by a menagerie of cloned animals, each genetically identical to another member of its species (Pennisi, 1997c; Kolata, 1998).

Dolly, the first adult mammal to be cloned. Is it possible for Dolly to have a different "personality" than her clone?

The ability of scientists to produce clones raises new possibilities of correcting genetic flaws, not only in sheep and other animals, but in humans, and it accelerates the pace of developments in the new field of gene therapy. In *gene therapy*, genes are introduced into existing cells in order to prevent or cure a disorder. For instance, genes targeted to treat a particular disease can be injected into a patient's blood stream. When the genes reach the site of the problem—such as a cancerous tumour—the new genes provide existing cells with a set of new instructions that modify their functioning, thereby potentially curing the disease. It also might be possible to "harvest" defective cells from a child prior to birth. These cells could be treated by gene therapy and reintroduced into the unborn child, thereby repairing the defect (Kmiec, 1999; Levy, 2000; Yan, Kinzler, & Vogelstein, 2000).

Some forms of gene therapy are already in use, and the number of diseases treated by gene therapy is growing. For example, such disorders as AIDS, cystic fibrosis, and rheumatoid arthritis are promising candidates for gene therapy (Weiner, 2000).

Cloning advances are likely to continue to raise significant ethical issues. In one radical possibility, cloning might be employed if both a husband and wife were infertile. In such a case, they might consider cloning one or the other of themselves in order to have at least one child who was genetically similar (in this case, genetically identical) to one of them. The ethical and moral issues of such a procedure, of course, are profound—but the rapid advances in cloning and gene therapy suggest they need to be dealt with now (Angier, 1999; Gordon, 1999; Shiels et al., 1999; Wright, 1999).

Would you choose to be genetically tested so that you could know your susceptibility to future genetic diseases? What if you learned that you had a genetic disorder that was likely to shorten your life?

and within a week it has grown to 100 to 150 cells. These first two weeks are known as the *germinal period*.

Two weeks after conception, the developing individual enters the *embryonic period*, which lasts from week 2 through week 8, and he or she is now called an **embryo**. As the embryo develops through an intricate, preprogrammed process of cell division, it grows 10 000 times larger by 4 weeks of age, attaining a length of about half a centimetre. At this point it has developed a rudimentary beating heart, brain, and intestinal tract, and a number of other rudimentary organs. Although all these organs are at a primitive stage of development, they are clearly recognizable. Moreover, by 8 weeks, the embryo is about two and a half centimetres long, and has arms, legs, and a face that are discernible.

From 8 weeks and continuing until birth, the developing individual enters the *fetal period* and is now called a **fetus**. At the start of this period, it begins to respond to touch; it bends its fingers when touched on the hand. At 16 to 18 weeks, the baby's movements

embryo: A developed zygote that has a rudimentary heart, brain, and other organs.

fetus: A developing child, from 8 weeks after conception until birth.

become strong enough for the mother to sense. At the same time, hair might begin to grow on the baby's head, and the facial features become similar to those the child will display at birth. The major organs begin functioning, although the fetus could not yet be kept alive outside the mother. In addition, a lifetime's worth of brain neurons are produced—although it is unclear whether the brain is capable of thinking at this early stage.

By 24 weeks, the fetus has many of the characteristics it will display as a newborn. In fact, when an infant is born prematurely at this age, it can open and close its eyes; suck; cry; look up, down, and around; and even grasp objects placed in its hands, although it is still unable to survive for long outside the mother.

age of viability: The point at which the fetus can survive if born prematurely.

The fetus continues to develop prior to birth. It begins to grow fatty deposits under the skin and it gains weight. The fetus reaches the **age of viability**, the point at which it can survive if born prematurely, at about 24 weeks, although through advances in medical technology this crucial age is getting earlier. At 28 weeks, the fetus weighs less than 1.5 kilograms and is about 40 centimetres long. It might be capable of learning: One study found that the infants of mothers who had repeatedly read aloud the Dr. Seuss story *The Cat in the Hat* prior to birth preferred the sound of that particular story over other stories after they were born (Spence & DeCasper, 1982).

Darwin Muir of Queens University, a leading expert in the field of infant research, took part in some innovative research designed to investigate development in the womb. He and his colleagues found that responses to external stimuli were related to maturation. For example, acceleration of the heartbeat and movement of the fetus in response to vibration were found to develop at different ages. Acceleration of the heart rate occurred at 29 weeks' gestation, while response with body movement occurred at 26 weeks' gestation. Understanding this stage of development could well shed light on newborn behaviour (Kisilevsky, Muir, & Low, 2000).

As they develop prior to birth, children pass through several *critical periods,* times during development when specific events have their greatest impact. For example, children are particularly sensitive to environmental influences such as drugs during certain certain critical periods before birth. If they are exposed to the drug before or after the critical period, it might have relatively little impact, but if exposure comes during a critical period, its impact will be maximized. Critical periods can also occur after birth; some language specialists suggest, for instance, that there is a period where children are particularly receptive to language (Bornstein & Bruner, 1989; Eisen, Field, & Larson, 1991; Shatz, 1992).

In the final weeks of pregnancy, the fetus continues to gain weight and grow. At the end of the normal 38 weeks of pregnancy, the fetus typically weighs around 3 kilograms and is about 50 centimetres in length.

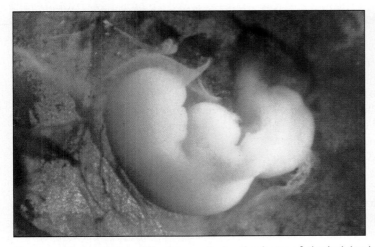
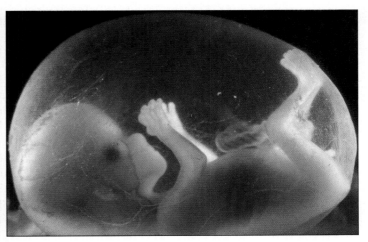

These remarkable photos of live fetuses display the degree of physical development at 4 and 15 weeks.

Genetic Influences on the Fetus

The process of fetal growth that we have just described reflects normal development, which occurs in 95 to 98 percent of all pregnancies. Some people are less fortunate, for in the remaining 2 to 5 percent of cases, children are born with serious birth defects. A major cause of such defects is faulty genes or chromosomes. Here are some of the most common genetic and chromosomal difficulties.

- *Phenylketonuria (PKU).* A child born with the inherited disease phenylketonuria cannot produce an enzyme that is required for normal development. This results in an accumulation of poisons that eventually cause profound mental retardation. The disease is treatable, however, if caught early enough. In Canada, all infants today are routinely tested for PKU, and children with the disorder can be placed on a special diet that allows them to develop normally.
- *Sickle-cell anemia.* About 10 percent of black people have the possibility of passing on sickle-cell anemia, a disease that gets its name from the abnormal shape of the victims' red blood cells. Children with the disease might have poor appetites, swollen stomachs, and yellowish eyes; they frequently die during childhood.
- *Tay-Sachs disease.* Children born with Tay-Sachs disease, a disorder that most often afflicts Jews of eastern European ancestry, usually die by the age of 3 or 4 because of the body's inability to break down fat. If both parents carry the genetic defect producing the fatal illness, their child has a one-in-four chance of being born with the disease (Navon & Proia, 1989).
- *Down syndrome.* Down syndrome, a cause of mental retardation, occurs when the zygote receives an extra chromosome at the moment of conception, causing retardation. Down syndrome is often related to the mother's age; mothers over 35 and younger than 18, in particular, stand a higher risk than other women of having a child with the syndrome. Down syndrome occurs in approximately 1 in 700 births in Canada.

PsychLink
Sickle-cell anemia information
www.mcgrawhill.ca/college/feldman

PsychLink
Canadian Down Syndrome Society
www.mcgrawhill.ca/college/feldman

Prenatal Environmental Influences

Genetic factors are not the only causes of difficulties in fetal development. Environmental influences—the *nurture* part of the nature-nurture equation—also affect the fetus. Some of the most profound consequences are brought about by **teratogens**, environmental agents such as drugs, chemicals, viruses, or other factors that produce birth defects. Among the major prenatal environmental influences on the fetus:

- *Mother's nutrition and emotional state.* What a mother eats during her pregnancy can have important implications for the health of her baby. Mothers who are seriously undernourished cannot provide adequate nutrition to the growing baby, and they are likely to give birth to underweight babies. Poorly nourished babies are also more susceptible to disease, and a lack of nourishment can adversely affect mental development (Adams & Parker, 1990; Ricciuti, 1993; Sigman, 1995).

   Moreover, the mother's emotional state affects the baby. Mothers who are anxious and tense during the last months of their pregnancies are more apt to have infants who are irritable and who sleep and eat poorly. The reason? One hypothesis is that the autonomic nervous system of the fetus becomes especially sensitive as a result of the chemical changes produced by the mother's emotional state (Kagan, Kearsley, & Zelazo, 1978).
- *Mother's illness.* Several diseases that have a relatively minor effect on the mother's health can have devastating consequences for the developing fetus if contracted during the early part of a woman's pregnancy. For example, rubella (German measles), syphilis, diabetes, and high blood pressure can permanently harm the fetus. The virus that causes AIDS can also be passed from mother to child prior to birth. The virus can also be passed on through breast-feeding after birth (Heyward & Curran, 1988; Health Canada, 1996).

teratogens: Environmental agents such as drugs, chemicals, viruses, or other factors that produce birth defects.

- *Mother's use of drugs.* Mothers who take illegal and physically addictive drugs such as cocaine run the risk of giving birth to babies who are similarly addicted. Their newborns suffer painful withdrawal symptoms after birth and sometimes have permanent physical and mental impairment. Even legal drugs taken by pregnant women (who might not know that they have become pregnant) can have a tragic effect. For example, drugs such as the acne medicine Acutane can produce fetal abnormalities (Hannigan et al., 1999; Streissguth et al., 1999; Ikonomidou et al., 2000).

- *Alcohol and nicotine use.* Alcohol and nicotine are dangerous to fetal development. For example, *fetal alcohol syndrome,* a condition resulting in mental and growth retardation, has been found in the children of mothers who consumed heavy or sometimes even moderate amounts of alcohol during pregnancy. Pregnant mothers who smoke also put their children at considerable risk (DiFranza & Lew, 1995; Mills, 1999; Ness et al., 1999).

A number of other environmental factors have an impact upon the child prior to and during birth (see Table 9-2). It is important to keep in mind, however, that although we have been discussing the influences of genetics and environment separately, neither factor works alone. Furthermore, despite the emphasis here on some of the ways development can go wrong, the vast majority of pregnancies develop without difficulty. And in most instances, subsequent child development also proceeds normally, as we discuss next.

Table 9-2 Environmental Factors Affecting Prenatal Development

Factor	Possible Effect
Rubella (German measles)	Blindness, deafness, heart abnormalities, stillbirth
Syphilis	Mental retardation, physical deformities, maternal miscarriage
Addictive drugs	Low birth weight, addiction of infant to drug, with possible death, after birth, from withdrawal
Smoking	Premature birth, low birth weight and length
Alcohol	Mental retardation, lower-than-average birth weight, small head, limb deformities
Radiation from X rays	Physical deformities, mental retardation
Inadequate diet	Reduction in growth of brain, smaller-than-average weight and length at birth
Mother's age—younger than 18 at birth of child	Premature birth, increased incidence of Down syndrome
Mother's age—older than 35 at birth of child	Increased incidence of Down syndrome
DES (diethylstilbestrol)	Reproductive difficulties and increased incidence of genital cancer in children of mothers who were given DES during pregnancy to prevent miscarriage
AIDS	Possible spread of AIDS virus to infant; facial deformities; growth failure

1. Developmental psychologists are interested in the effects of both _____ and _____ on development.
2. Environment and heredity both influence development, with genetic potentials generally establishing limits on environmental influences. True or false?
3. By observing genetically similar animals in differing environments, we can increase our understanding of the influences of hereditary and environmental factors in humans. True or false?
4. _____ research studies the same individuals over a period of time, whereas _____-_____ research studies people of different ages at the same time.
5. Match the following terms with their definition:

   1. Zygote
   2. Gene
   3. Chromosome

   a. Smallest unit through which genetic information is passed
   b. Fertilized egg
   c. Rod-shaped structure containing genetic information

6. Specific kinds of growth must take place during a _____ period if the embryo is to develop normally.

Answers to Evaluate Questions

1. heredity (or nature); environment (or nurture) 2. True 3. True 4. Longitudinal; cross-sectional 5. 1–b; 2–a; 3–c 6. critical

1. What sort of policy might you create for notifying persons who have genetically based disorders that can be identified by genetic testing? Would your policy treat potentially fatal disorders differently from less serious ones? Would it make a distinction between treatable and untreatable disorders?
2. Given the possible effects of the environment on the developing child, do you think expectant mothers should be subject to legal prosecution for their use of alcohol and other drugs that can seriously harm their unborn children? Defend your position.

The Extraordinary Newborn

His head was molded into a long melon shape and came to a point at the back. . . . He was covered with a thick greasy white material known as "vernix," which made him slippery to hold. In addition to a shock of black hair on his head, his body was covered with dark, fine hair known as "lanugo." His ears, his back, his shoulders, and even his cheeks were furry. . . . His skin was wrinkled and quite loose. . . . His ears were pressed to his head in unusual positions—one ear was matted firmly forward on his cheek. His nose was flattened and pushed to one side. (Brazelton, 1969, p. 3)

Although the description hardly fits that of the adorable babies seen in advertisements, we are in fact talking about a normal, completely developed child just after the moment of birth. Called a **neonate**, the newborn presents itself to the world in a form that hardly meets the standards of beauty against which we typically measure babies. Yet ask any parent: No sight is more beautiful or exciting than the first glimpse of their newborn.

The neonate's strange appearance is brought about by a number of factors. The trip through its mother's birth canal might have squeezed the incompletely formed bones of the skull together and squashed the nose into the head. *Vernix,* its white, greasy covering, is secreted to protect its skin prior to birth, and it might have *lanugo,* a soft fuzz, over its entire body for a similar purpose. Its eyelids could be puffy with an accumulation of fluids because of its upside-down position during birth.

All this changes during the first two weeks of life as the neonate takes on a more familiar appearance. Even more impressive are the capabilities the neonate begins to display from the time it is born—capabilities that grow at an astounding rate over the ensuing months.

What are the major competencies of newborns?

What are the milestones of physical and social development during childhood?

The Extraordinary Newborn
   Reflexes
   Development of the Senses
The Growing Child
   Physical Development
   Development of Social Behaviour

neonate: A newborn child.

PsychLink

Birthing process
www.mcgrawhill.ca/college/feldman

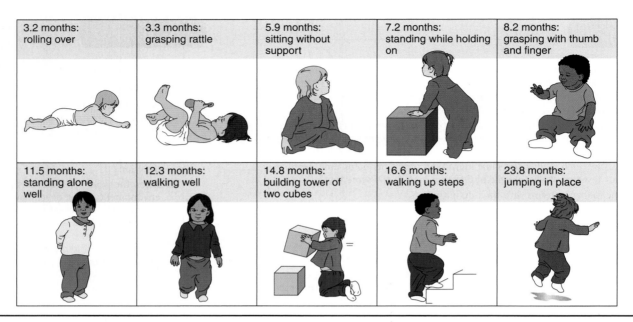

Figure 9-2 Although at birth the neonate is capable of only jerky, limited voluntary movements, during the first year of life the ability to move independently grows enormously. The ages indicate the time when 50 percent of children are able to perform each skill. Remember, however, that when each skill appears varies considerably. For example, 25 percent of children are able to walk well at 11 months, and by 15 months, 90 percent of children are walking well (Frankenburg et al., 1992).

Reflexes

reflexes: Unlearned, involuntary responses that occur automatically in the presence of certain stimuli.

The neonate is born with a number of **reflexes**—unlearned, involuntary responses that occur automatically in the presence of certain stimuli. Many of these reflexes are critical for survival and unfold naturally as a part of an infant's ongoing maturation. The *rooting reflex,* for instance, causes neonates to turn their heads toward things that touch their cheeks—such as the mother's nipple or a bottle. Similarly, a *sucking reflex* prompts the infant to suck at things that touch its lips. Among its other reflexes are a *gag reflex* (to clear its throat); the *startle reflex* (a series of movements in which the infant flings out its arms, fans its fingers, and arches its back in response to a sudden noise); and the *Babinski reflex* (the baby's toes fan out when the outer edge of the sole of its foot is stroked).

These primitive reflexes are lost after the first few months of life and replaced by more complex and organized behaviours. Although at birth the neonate is capable of only jerky, limited voluntary movements, during the first year of life the ability to move independently grows enormously. The typical baby is able to roll over by the age of 3 months; it can sit without support at 6 months, stand alone at about $11\frac{1}{2}$ months, and walk by the time it is just over a year old. Not only does the ability to make large-scale movements improve during this time, but fine-muscle movements also become increasingly sophisticated (as illustrated in Figure 9-2).

Development of the Senses: Taking in the World

When proud parents pick up their neonate and peer into its eyes, is the child able to return their gaze? Although it was thought for some time that newborns could see only a hazy blur, most current findings indicate that the capabilities of neonates are far more impressive. Although their eyes have limited capacity to focus on objects that are not within 18 to 20 centimetres of their face, neonates are able to follow objects moving within their field of vision. They also show the rudiments of depth perception, as they react by raising their hands when an object appears to be moving rapidly toward the face (Gelman & Au, 1996; Maurer et al., 1999).

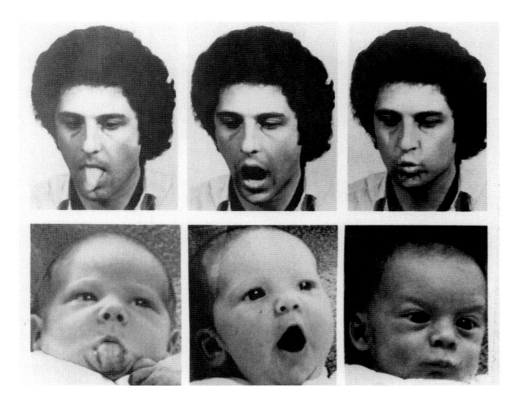

Figure 9-3 This newborn infant is clearly imitating the expressions of the adult model in these amazing photos. How does this ability contribute to social development?

You might think that it would be hard to figure out just how well neonates are able to see, given that their lack of both language and reading ability clearly prevents them from saying what direction the *E* on a vision chart is facing. However, a number of ingenious methods, relying on the newborn's biological responses and innate reflexes, have been devised to test perceptual skills (Koop, 1994; Atkinson, 1995).

For instance, infants who are shown a novel stimulus typically pay close attention to it, and, as a consequence, their heart rates increase. But if they are repeatedly shown the same stimulus, their attention to it decreases, as indicated by a return to a slower heart rate. This phenomenon is known as **habituation**, the decrease in the response to a stimulus that occurs after repeated presentations of the same stimulus. By studying habituation, developmental psychologists can tell when a stimulus can be detected and discriminated by a child too young to speak (Peterzell, 1993).

Researchers have developed a number of other methods for measuring neonate and infant perception. One technique involves babies sucking on a nipple attached to a computer. Changes in the rate and vigour of sucking are taken to show that babies can perceive variations in stimuli. Other approaches include examining babies' eye movements and observing which way babies move their heads when presented with a visual stimulus (George, 1999).

Using such research techniques, we now know that infants' visual perception is remarkably sophisticated from birth. At birth, babies show preferences for patterns with contours and edges over less distinct patterns, indicating that they are capable of responding to the configuration of stimuli. Furthermore, even newborns are aware of size constancy, apparently sensitive to the phenomenon that objects stay the same size even though the image on the retina changes size as the distance between the object and the retina varies (Slater, Mattock, & Brown, 1990; Slater, 1996).

In fact, neonates have the ability to discriminate facial expressions—and even to imitate them. As you can see in Figure 9-3, newborns exposed to particular facial expressions are able to produce a good imitation of the adult's expression. Even very young infants, then, can respond to the emotions and moods revealed by their caregivers' facial

habituation: The decrease in the response to a stimulus that occurs after repeated presentations of the same stimulus.

expressions. This capability provides the foundation for social interactional skills in children (Meltzoff, 1996; Mumme, Fernald, & Herrera, 1996).

Other visual abilities grow rapidly after birth. By the end of their first month, babies can distinguish some colours from others, and after 4 months they can readily focus on near or far objects. In fact, from 1 to 3 months infants are much more interested in visual patterns than auditory stimuli (Muir, Humphrey, & Humphrey, 1994). By 3 months infants can discriminate between their mother's face and that of a stranger (Barrera & Maurer, 1981). By 4 or 5 months, they are able to recognize two- and three-dimensional objects, and they can perceive the gestalt organizing principles that we discussed in Chapter 3. Furthermore, there are rapid improvements in perceptual abilities: Sensitivity to visual stimuli, for instance, becomes three to four times greater at 1 year of age than it was at birth (Slater, 1996; Vital-Durand, Atkinson, & Braddick, 1996).

In addition to vision, infants' other sensory capabilities are quite impressive. Newborns can distinguish different sounds to the point of being able to recognize their own mothers' voices at the age of 3 days. They are also capable of making subtle perceptual distinctions that underlie the language abilities described in Chapter 7. For example, at 2 days of age, infants are able to distinguish between their native tongue and foreign languages, and they can discriminate between such closely related sounds as *ba* and *pa* when they are 4 days old. By 6 months of age, they are capable of discriminating virtually any difference in sound that is relevant to the production of language. Moreover, they are capable of discriminating different tastes and smells at a very early age. There even seems to be something of a built-in sweet tooth: Neonates prefer liquids that have been sweetened with sugar over unsweetened liquids (Bornstein & Arterberry, 1999).

The Growing Child: Infancy Through Middle Childhood

It was during the windy days of March that the problem in the day care center first arose. Its source: 10-month-old Russell Ruud. Otherwise a model of decorum, Russell had somehow learned how to unzip the Velcro chin strap to his winter hat. He would remove the hat whenever he got the urge, seemingly oblivious to the potential health problems that might follow.

But that was just the start of the real difficulty. To the chagrin of the teachers in the day care center, not to speak of the children's parents, soon other children were following his lead, removing their own caps at will.

Russell's mother, made aware of the anarchy at the day care center—and the other parents' distress over Russell's behaviour—pleaded innocent. "I never showed Russell how to unzip the Velcro," claimed his mother, Judith Ruud, an economist with the Congressional Budget Office in Washington, D.C. "He learned by trial and error, and the other kids saw him do it one day when they were getting dressed for an outing." (Goleman, 1993, C10)

At the age of 10 months, Russell is asserting his personality, illustrating the tremendous growth that occurs in a variety of domains during the first year of life. Throughout the remainder of childhood, as children move from infancy into middle childhood and the start of adolescence around age 11 or 12, children develop physically, socially, and cognitively in extraordinary ways. In the remainder of this chapter, we'll consider this development.

Physical Development

The most obvious sign of development is children's physical growth. During the first year of life, children typically triple their weight, and their height increases by about half. This

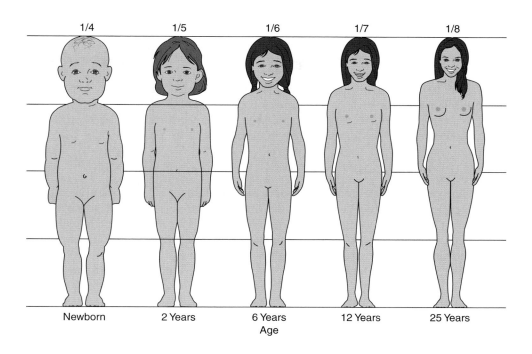

| 1/4 | 1/5 | 1/6 | 1/7 | 1/8 |

Newborn · 2 Years · 6 Years · 12 Years · 25 Years

Age

Figure 9-4 As development progresses, the relative size of the head, in relation to the rest of the body, decreases until adulthood is reached. Why do you think the head starts out so large?

rapid growth slows down as the child gets older—think how gigantic adults would be if that rate of growth were constant—and the average rate of growth from age 3 to the beginning of adolescence, around age 13, is a gain of about 2.2 kilograms and 7.5 centimetres a year.

The physical changes that occur as children develop are not just a matter of increasing growth; the comparative sizes of the various body parts change dramatically as children age. As you can see in Figure 9-4, the head of the newborn is disproportionately large. However, the head soon becomes more proportional in size to the rest of the body as growth occurs mainly in the trunk and legs.

Development of Social Behaviour: Taking on the World

As anyone who has seen an infant smiling at the sight of her or his mother can guess, at the same time as infants are growing physically and honing their perceptual abilities, they are also developing socially. The nature of a child's early social development provides the foundation for social relationships that will last a lifetime.

Attachment, the positive emotional bond that develops between a child and a particular individual, is the most important form of social development that occurs during infancy. The earliest studies of attachment were carried out by animal ethologist Konrad Lorenz (1966). Lorenz focused on newborn goslings, who under normal circumstances instinctively follow their mother, the first moving object to which they are exposed after birth. Lorenz found that goslings whose eggs were raised in an incubator and who viewed him immediately after hatching would follow his every movement, as if he were their mother. He labelled this process *imprinting,* behaviour that takes place during a critical period and involves attachment to the first moving object that is observed.

Our understanding of attachment made progress when psychologist Harry Harlow, in a classic study, gave infant monkeys the choice of cuddling a wire "mother" that provided milk, or a soft, terry-cloth "mother" that was warm but did not provide milk. Their choice was clear: They spent most of their time clinging to the warm cloth "monkey," although they made occasional forays to the wire monkey to nurse (Harlow & Zimmerman, 1959). It was obvious that the cloth monkey provided greater comfort to the infants; milk alone was insufficient to create attachment (see Figure 9-5).

Building on this pioneering work with nonhumans, developmental psychologists have suggested that human attachment grows through the responsiveness of infants'

attachment: The positive emotional bond that develops between a child and a particular individual.

PsychLink

Attachment theory and research
www.mcgrawhill.ca/college/feldman

caregivers to the signals the babies provide, such as cries, smiles, reaching, and clinging. The greater the responsiveness of the caregiver to the child's signals, the more likely it is that the child will become securely attached. Full attachment eventually develops as a result of a complex series of interactions between caregiver and child (Bell & Ainsworth, 1972). In the course of these interactions, the infant plays as critical and active a role as the caregiver in the formation of the bond. Infants who respond positively to a caregiver produce more positive behaviour on the part of the caregiver, which in turn produces an even stronger degree of attachment in the child.

Measuring Attachment

Developmental psychologists have devised a quick and direct way of measuring attachment. Developed by Mary Ainsworth, the *Ainsworth strange situation* consists of a sequence of events involving a child and (typically) his or her mother. Initially, the mother and baby enter an unfamiliar room, and the mother permits the baby to explore while she sits down. An adult stranger then enters the room, after which the mother leaves. The mother then returns, and the stranger leaves. The mother then once again leaves the baby alone, and the stranger returns. Finally, the stranger leaves, and the mother returns (Ainsworth et al., 1978).

Babies' reactions to the experimental situation vary drastically, depending, according to Ainsworth, on their degree of attachment to the mother. One-year-old children who are *securely attached* employ the mother as a kind of home base, exploring independently but returning to her occasionally. When she leaves, they exhibit distress, and they go to her when she returns. *Avoidant* children do not cry when the mother leaves, but they seem to avoid her when she returns, as if they were indifferent to her. *Ambivalent* children display anxiety before they are separated and are upset when the mother leaves, but they might show ambivalent reactions to her return, such as seeking close contact but simultaneously hitting and kicking her. A fourth reaction is *disorganized-disoriented;* these children show inconsistent, often contradictory behaviour.

The nature of attachment between children and their mothers has far-reaching consequences for later development. For example, children who are securely attached to their mothers tend to be more socially and emotionally competent than their less securely attached peers, and they are viewed as more cooperative, capable, and playful. Furthermore, research has found that children who are securely attached at age 1 show fewer psychological difficulties when they grow older than do avoidant or ambivalent youngsters (Lewis et al., 1984; Ainsworth & Bowlby, 1991; Greenberg, 1997).

On the other hand, children who lack secure attachment do not always have difficulties later in life, and being securely attached at an early age does not guarantee good adjustment later. Furthermore, some cultures foster higher levels of secure attachment than others. In short, attachment style is related to the social environment that children encounter as they are growing up (Hamilton, 2000; Lewis, Feiring, & Rosenthal, 2000; Waters, Hamilton, & Wienfield, 2000). Benoit and Parker (2000) studied triads made up of grandmother, mother and infant. In 65 percent of these triads, the grandmother-mother attachment style corresponded to the mother-infant style.

The Father's Role

Although early developmental research focused largely on the mother-child relation, more recent research has highlighted the father's role in parenting. With good reason: The number of fathers who are primary caregivers for their children has grown significantly, and fathers play an increasing role in their children's lives. For example, in Canada and the United States, in almost 20 percent of families with children, the father is the parent who stays at

Figure 9-5 Although the wire "mother" dispensed milk to the hungry infant monkey, the soft, terry cloth "mother" was preferred (Harry Harlow Primate Laboratory/University of Wisconsin). Do you think human babies would react the same way? What does this tell us about attachment?

home caring for preschoolers (Parke, 1996; U.S. Bureau of the Census, 1997; Walker & Henning, 1997).

When fathers interact with their children, their play is often different from that of mothers. Fathers engage in more physical, rough-and-tumble sorts of activities, whereas mothers play more verbally oriented and traditional games such as peekaboo. Despite such behavioural differences, attachment between fathers and children can be similar to attachment between mothers and children. In fact, children are capable of forming multiple attachments simultaneously (Lamb, 1982; Larson, Richards, & Perry-Jenkins, 1994; Genuis & Violato, 2000).

"Please, Jason. Don't you want to grow up to be an autonomous person?"

Social Relationships with Peers

By the time they are 2 years old, children start to become less dependent on their parents and more self-reliant, increasingly preferring to play with friends. During childhood there is a preference for friendships with same sex peers. This will change in adolescence to more positive attitudes towards friendships with other sex peers (Sippola, Bukowski, & Noll, 1997). Initially, play is relatively independent: Even though they might be sitting side by side, 2-year-olds pay more attention to toys than to one another when playing. Later, however, children actively interact, modifying one another's behaviour and later exchanging roles during play (Bukowski, Newcomb, & Hartup, 1996).

As children reach school age, their social interactions begin to follow set patterns, and become more frequent. They might engage in elaborate games involving teams and rigid rules. This play serves purposes other than mere enjoyment. It allows children to become increasingly competent in their social interactions with others. Through play they learn to take the perspective of other people and to infer others' thoughts and feelings, even when these are not directly expressed (Asher & Parker, 1991; Cohen, 1993).

In short, social interaction helps children interpret the meaning of others' behaviour and develop the capacity to respond appropriately. Furthermore, children learn physical and emotional self-control: They learn to avoid hitting a playmate who wins at a game, to be polite, and to control their emotional displays and facial expressions (e.g., smiling even when receiving a disappointing gift). Situations that provide children with opportunities for social interaction, then, can enhance their social development (Feldman, 1982, 1993; Crick & Dodge, 1994; Fox, 1994).

The Consequences of Day Care

Research on the importance of social interaction is corroborated by work that examines the benefits of day care, which is an important part of an increasing number of children's lives. In Canada, 40 percent of all children under the age of 5 are cared for by people other than their parents. Twenty percent of these children are cared for in a day-care centre (Statistics Canada, 1996).

Do out-of-the-home child-care arrangements benefit children's development? If they are of high quality, they can. According to the results of a large study supported by the U.S. National Institute of Child Health and Development (NICHD), children who attend high-quality child-care centres might not only do as well as children who stay at home with their parents, but in some respects might do better. Children in child care are generally more considerate and sociable than other children, and they interact more positively with teachers. They can also be more compliant and regulate their own behaviour more effectively, and their mothers show increased sensitivity to their children (Lamb, 1996; NICHD Early Child Care Research Network, 1997, 1998, 1999; Childcare Resource and Research Unit, University of Toronto, 1998).

In addition, especially for children from poor or disadvantaged homes, child care in specially enriched environments—those with many toys, books, a variety of children, and high-quality care providers—often is more intellectually stimulating than the home environment. Such child care can lead to increased intellectual achievement, demonstrated in higher IQ scores and better language development. In fact, children in child-care centres

Table 9-3 The Four Main Parenting Styles

Parenting Style	Parent Behaviour	Children's Behaviour
Authoritarian	Rigid, punitive, strict standards	Unsociable, unfriendly, withdrawn
Permissive	Lax, inconsistent, undemanding	Immature, moody, dependent, low self-control
Authoritative	Firm, sets limits and goals, uses reasoning, encourages independence	Good social skills, likable, self-reliant, independent
Uninvolved	Detached emotionally, sees role as only providing food, clothing, and shelter	Indifferent, rejecting behaviour

Source: Baumrind, 1971.

are sometimes found to score higher on tests of cognitive abilities than children who are cared for by their mothers or by sitters or home day-care providers, and these effects last into adulthood (Wilgoren, 1999; Burchinal et al., 2000).

On the other hand, the outcomes of child care are not universally positive. Children can feel less secure when they are placed in low-quality child care or in multiple child-care arrangements. Furthermore, although the findings are not consistent, some research suggests that infants who are involved in outside care more than 20 hours a week in their first year show less secure attachment to their mothers than those who have not been in day care (Belsky & Rovine, 1988; NICHD Early Child Care Research Network, 1997, 1999).

The key to the success of day care is its quality. High-quality day care produces benefits; low-quality day care provides little or no gain, and can even hinder children's development. In short, significant benefits result from the social interaction and intellectual stimulation provided by high-quality day-care centres—particularly for children from impoverished environments (Harvey, 1999; Burchinal et al., 2000; Campbell, Lamb, & Hwang, 2000).

Parenting Styles and Social Development

Parents' child-rearing practices are critical in shaping their children's social competence. According to classic research by developmental psychologist Diana Baumrind, there are four main parenting styles. **Authoritarian parents** are rigid and punitive and value unquestioning obedience from their children. They have strict standards and discourage expressions of disagreement. **Permissive parents** give their children relaxed or inconsistent direction and, although warm, require little of them. In contrast, **authoritative parents** are firm, setting limits for their children. As the children get older, these parents try to reason with and explain things to them. They also set clear goals and encourage their children's independence. Finally, **uninvolved parents** show little interest in their children. They are emotionally detached, and they view parenting as nothing more than providing food, clothing, and shelter for children. In its most extreme form, uninvolved parents are guilty of neglect, a form of child abuse (Baumrind, 1971, 1980). Table 9-3 summarizes the four parenting styles.

As you might expect, the four parenting styles seem to produce very different kinds of behaviour in children (although there are, of course, many exceptions). Children of authoritarian parents tend to be unsociable, unfriendly, and relatively withdrawn. Permissive parents' children tends to be immature, moody, and dependent and have low self-control. The children of authoritative parents fare best: Their social skills are high—they are likable, self-reliant, independent, and cooperative. Worst off are children of uninvolved parents; they feel unloved and emotionally detached, and their physical and cognitive development is impeded (Howes, Galinsky, & Kontos, 1998; Saarni, 1999).

PsychLink
Comprehensive information on parenting
www.mcgrawhill.ca/college/feldman

authoritarian parents: Parents who are rigid and punitive and value unquestioning obedience from their children.
permissive parents: Parents who give their children lax or inconsistent direction and, although warm, require little of them.
authoritative parents: Parents who are firm, set clear limits, reason with their children, and explain things to them.
uninvolved parents: Parents who show little interest in their children and are emotionally detached from them.

Before we rush to congratulate authoritative parents and condemn authoritarian, permissive, and uninvolved ones, it is important to note that many nonauthoritative parents produce children who are perfectly well adjusted. Moreover, as we'll discuss further in Chapter 10, children are born with a particular **temperament**—a basic, innate disposition. Some children are naturally easy-going and cheerful, whereas others are irritable and fussy. The kind of temperament a baby is born with might tend to elicit a particular parenting style (Goldsmith & Harman, 1994; Kendler, 1996; Chess, 1997). In a study of infant-care decisions and attachment security, McKim and colleagues (1999) gathered information on 189 families in the Ottawa-Carleton area. Among other things, this research found that children with difficult temperaments had less secure attachment to their mothers than did infants with less difficult temperaments. This lack of attachment was found to be mediated when these infants had a significant part of their care outside the home. This improvement was beneficial to both mother and infant.

temperament: Basic, innate disposition.

Furthermore, the findings regarding child-rearing styles apply primarily to North American society, with its emphasis on children learning to be independent and not relying too heavily on their parents. In contrast, Japanese parents encourage dependence in order to promote the values of cooperation and community life. These differences in cultural values result in very different philosophies of child rearing. For example, Japanese mothers believe it is a punishment to make a young child sleep alone, so many children sleep next to their mothers throughout infancy and toddlerhood (Kagan, Kearsley, & Zelazo, 1978; Miyake, Chen, & Campos, 1985; Kawasaki et al., 1994).

In sum, a child's upbringing is a consequence of the child-rearing philosophy parents hold, the specific practices they use, and the nature of their own and their child's personality. As is the case with other aspects of development, then, behaviour is a function of a complex interaction of environmental and genetic factors.

Erikson's Theory of Psychosocial Development

In trying to trace the course of social development, some theorists have considered how society and culture present challenges that change as the individual matures. Following this path, psychoanalyst Erik Erikson developed one of the most comprehensive theories of social development. According to Erikson (1963), the developmental changes occurring throughout our lives can be viewed as a series of eight stages of psychosocial development, of which four occur during childhood. **Psychosocial development** involves changes in our interactions and understanding of one another as well as in our knowledge and understanding of ourselves as members of society.

psychosocial development: Development of individuals' interactions and understanding of each other and of their knowledge and understanding of themselves as members of society.

Erikson suggests that passage through each of the stages necessitates resolution of a crisis or conflict. Accordingly, each of Erikson's stages is represented as a pairing of the most positive and most negative aspects of the crisis of the period. Although each crisis is never resolved entirely—life becomes increasingly complicated as we grow older—it needs to be resolved sufficiently so that we are equipped to deal with demands made during the following stage of development.

In the first stage of psychosocial development, the **trust-versus-mistrust stage** (birth to $1\frac{1}{2}$ years), infants develop feelings of trust if their physical requirements and psychological needs for attachment are consistently met and their interactions with the world are generally positive. On the other hand, inconsistent care and unpleasant interactions with others can lead to the development of mistrust and leave the infant unable to meet the challenges required in the next stage of development.

trust-versus-mistrust stage: According to Erikson, the first stage of psychosocial development, occurring from birth to 18 months of age, during which time infants develop feelings of trust or lack of trust.

In the second stage, the **autonomy-versus-shame-and-doubt stage** ($1\frac{1}{2}$ to 3 years), toddlers develop independence and autonomy if exploration and freedom are encouraged, or they experience shame, self-doubt, and unhappiness if they are overly restricted and protected. According to Erikson, the key to the development of autonomy during this period is for the child's caregivers to provide the appropriate amount of control. If parents provide too much control, children will be unable to assert themselves and develop their own sense of control over their environment; if parents provide too little control, children themselves become overly demanding and controlling.

autonomy-versus-shame-and-doubt stage: The period during which, according to Erikson, toddlers (ages 18 months to 3 years) develop independence and autonomy if exploration and freedom are encouraged, or shame and self-doubt if they are restricted and overprotected.

initiative–versus–guilt stage: According to Erikson, the period during which children ages 3 to 6 years experience conflict between independence of action and the sometimes negative results of that action.

industry–versus–inferiority stage: According to Erikson, the last stage of childhood, during which children aged 6 to 12 years either develop positive social interactions with others or feel inadequate and become less sociable.

The next crisis that children face is that of the **initiative-versus-guilt stage** (ages 3 to 6). In this stage, the major conflict is between children's desire to act independently and the guilt that comes from the unintended and unexpected consequences of their behaviour. Children in this period come to understand that they are persons in their own right, and they begin to make decisions about their behaviour. If parents react positively to their child's attempts at independence, they help their child resolve the initiative-versus-guilt crisis positively.

The fourth and last stage of childhood is the **industry-versus-inferiority stage** (ages 6 to 12). During this period, successful psychosocial development is characterized by increasing competency in all areas, including social interactions and academic skills. In contrast, difficulties in this stage lead to feelings of failure and inadequacy.

Erikson's theory suggests that psychosocial development continues throughout life, and he proposes that there are four more crises to face past childhood (which we discuss later in this chapter). Although his theory has been criticized on several grounds—such as the imprecision of the concepts he employs and his greater emphasis on male development than female development—it remains influential and is one of the few theories that encompass the entire life span.

Evaluate

1. Researchers studying newborns use _____, or the decrease in the response to a stimulus that occurs after repeated presentations of the same stimulus, as an indicator of a baby's interest.
2. The emotional bond that develops between a child and its caregiver is known as _____.
3. Children develop an attachment to their mothers only; the father's role is important, but children do not become attached to their fathers. True or false?
4. Match the parenting style with its definition:

   1. Permissive
   2. Authoritative
   3. Authoritarian
   4. Uninvolved

   a. Rigid; highly punitive; demand obedience
   b. Give little direction; lax on obedience
   c. Firm but fair; try to explain their decisions
   d. Emotionally detached and unloving

5. Erikson's theory of _____ development involves a series of eight stages, each of which must be resolved in order for a person to develop optimally.

Answers to Evaluate Questions

5. psychosocial
1. habituation 2. attachment 3. False; attachment to a father can be as strong as attachment to a mother 4. 1-b; 2-c; 3-a; 4-d

Rethink

1. In what ways might the infant's major reflexes—the rooting, sucking, gagging, startle, and Babinski reflexes—have had survival value, from an evolutionary perspective? Does the infant's ability to mimic the facial expressions of adults have a similar value?

2. Do you think the growing trend toward greater parental involvement by fathers will have effects on the child-rearing styles to which children are exposed? Will it affect attachment? Psychosocial development? Why or why not?

Prepare

How does cognitive development proceed during childhood?

Organize

Cognitive Development

Cognitive Development: Children's Thinking About the World

Suppose you had two drinking glasses of different shapes—one short and broad, and one tall and thin. Now imagine that you filled the short, broad one with pop about halfway and then poured the liquid from that glass into the tall one. The pop appears to fill about three-quarters of the second glass. If someone asked you whether there was more pop in the second glass than there had been in the first, what would you say?

You might think that such a simple question hardly deserves an answer; of course there is no difference in the amount of pop in the two glasses. However, most 4-year-olds would be likely to say that there is more pop in the second glass. If you then poured the soda back into the short glass, they would say there is now less pop than there was in the taller glass.

Why are young children confused by this problem? The reason is not immediately obvious. Anyone who has observed preschoolers must be impressed by how far they have progressed from the early stages of development. They speak with ease, know the alphabet, count, play complex games, use CD players, tell stories, and communicate quite ably. Yet, despite this seeming sophistication, there are deep gaps in children's understanding of the world. Some theorists have suggested that children are incapable of understanding certain ideas and concepts until they reach a particular stage of **cognitive development**—the process by which a child's understanding of the world changes as a function of age and experience. In contrast to the theories of physical and social development discussed earlier (such as those of Erikson), theories of cognitive development seek to explain the quantitative and qualitative intellectual advances that occur during development.

cognitive development: The process by which a child's understanding of the world changes as a function of age and experience.

Piaget's Theory of Cognitive Development

No theory of cognitive development has had more impact than that of Swiss psychologist Jean Piaget. Piaget believed that cognitive development begins with trying to make sense of our experience and the world around us. We begin this process as children by constructing concepts that Piaget termed **schemas**. Schemas are a type of prototype, and over the years we develop many, from what a cat is to how to tie our shoes to who is the perfect mate.

schemas: Concepts that allow us to organize and make sense of our world.

Piaget further proposed that new information we encounter is interpreted in relation to existing schemas. He used the term **assimilate** for this process. For this reason, a young child may call all small, furry animals "kitty." However, as her experience grows, she will learn to **accommodate** or alter schemas to allow for this new knowledge. She will then differentiate between the kitty, and say, a bunny.

assimilate: To interpret new information by assigning it to existing schemas.
accommodate: To alter existing schemas to allow for new knowledge or experience.

According to Piaget (1970), children throughout the world proceed through a series of four stages in a fixed order. He maintained that these stages differ not only in the *quantity* of information acquired at each stage, but also in the *quality* of knowledge and understanding. Taking an interactionist point of view, he suggested that movement from one stage to the next occurred when the child reached an appropriate level of maturation *and* was exposed to relevant types of experiences. Without such experiences, children were assumed to be incapable of reaching their highest level of cognitive growth.

Piaget's four stages are the sensorimotor, preoperational, concrete operational, and formal operational stages (see Table 9-4). Let's examine each of them and the approximate ages they span.

 **PsychLink**
Theory of cognitive development
www.mcgrawhill.ca/college/feldman

Sensorimotor Stage: Birth to 2 Years During the **sensorimotor stage**, children's understanding of the world is based primarily on touching, sucking, chewing, shaking, and manipulating objects. In the initial part of this stage, children have relatively little competence in representing the environment using images, language, or other kinds of symbols. Consequently, infants have no awareness of objects or people that are not immediately present

sensorimotor stage: According to Piaget, the stage from birth to 2 years, during which a child has little competence in representing the environment using images, language, or other symbols.

Table 9-4 Piaget's Stages of Cognitive Development

Stage	Approximate Age Range	Major Characteristics
Sensorimotor	Birth–2 years	Development of object permanence, development of motor skills, little or no capacity for symbolic representation
Preoperational	2–7 years	Development of language and symbolic thinking, egocentric thinking
Concrete operational	7–12 years	Development of conservation, mastery of concept of reversibility
Formal operational	12–adulthood	Development of logical and abstract thinking

object permanence: The awareness that objects—and people—continue to exist even if they are out of sight.

at a given moment, lacking what Piaget calls **object permanence**. Object permanence is the awareness that objects—and people—continue to exist even if they are out of sight.

How can we know that infants lack object permanence? Although we cannot ask them, we can observe their reactions when a toy that they are playing with is hidden under a blanket. Until the age of about 9 months, children will make no attempt to locate the toy. However, soon after this age they will begin to search actively for the object when it is hidden, indicating that they have developed a mental representation of the toy. Object permanence, then, is a critical development during the sensorimotor stage.

preoperational stage: According to Piaget, the period from 2 to 7 years of age which is characterized by language development.

Preoperational Stage: 2 to 7 Years The most important development during the **preoperational stage** is the use of language, which we described in more detail in Chapter 7. Children develop internal representational systems that allow them to describe people, events, and feelings. They even use symbols in play, pretending, for example, that a book pushed across the floor is a car.

Although children's thinking is more advanced in this stage than in the earlier sensorimotor stage, it is still qualitatively inferior to that of adults. We see this when we observe the preoperational child using **egocentric thought**, a way of thinking in which the child views the world entirely from her or his own perspective. Preoperational children think that everyone shares their own perspective and knowledge. Thus, children's stories and explanations to adults can be maddeningly uninformative, as they are described without any context. For example, a preoperational child might start a story with "He wouldn't let me go," neglecting to mention who "he" is or where the storyteller wanted to go. Egocentric thinking is also seen when children at the preoperational stage play hiding games. For instance, 3-year-olds frequently hide with their faces against a wall, covering their eyes—although they are still in plain view. It seems to them that if *they* cannot see, no one else will be able to see them, because they assume that others share their view.

egocentric thought: A way of thinking in which the child views the world entirely from his or her own perspective.

principle of conservation: The knowledge that the quantity of a substance remains the same even though its shape or other aspects of its physical appearance might change.

concrete operational stage: According to Piaget, the period from 7 to 12 years of age, which is characterized by logical thought and a loss of egocentrism.

Another characteristic of preoperational children is demonstrated by their inability to understand the **principle of conservation**, which is the knowledge that quantity can remain the same when shape and other aspects of physical appearance change. Children who have not mastered this concept do not know, for instance, that the amount or volume of a substance (such as a lump of clay) does not change when its shape or configuration is changed. The question about pouring liquid between two glasses—one short and broad, the other tall and thin—with which we began our discussion of cognitive development illustrates this point quite clearly. Children who do not understand the principle of conservation invariably state that the amount of liquid changes as it is poured back and forth. They cannot comprehend that a transformation in appearance does not imply a transformation in amount. Instead, it seems just as reasonable to the child that there is a change in quantity as it does to the adult that there is no change.

There are a number of other ways, some quite startling, in which their failure to understand the principle of conservation affects children's responses. Research demonstrates that principles that are obvious to and unquestioned by adults can be completely misunderstood by children during the preoperational period, and that it is not until the next stage of cognitive development that children grasp the concept of conservation. (Several examples of conservation are illustrated in Figure 9-6.)

Children who have not mastered the principle of conservation assume that the volume of a liquid increases when it is poured from a short, wide container to a tall, thin one. **What other tasks might a child under 7 have difficulty comprehending?**

Concrete Operational Stage: 7 to 12 Years The beginning of the **concrete operational stage** is marked by mastery of the principle of conservation. However, there are still some aspects of conservation—such as conservation of weight and volume—that are not fully understood for a number of years.

During the concrete operational stage, children develop the ability to think in a more logical manner, and they begin to overcome some of the egocentrism characteristic of the preoperational period. One of the major principles that children grasp during this stage is reversibility, the idea that some changes can be undone by reversing an earlier action. For example, they can understand that when a ball of clay is rolled into a long sausage shape, it is possible to recreate

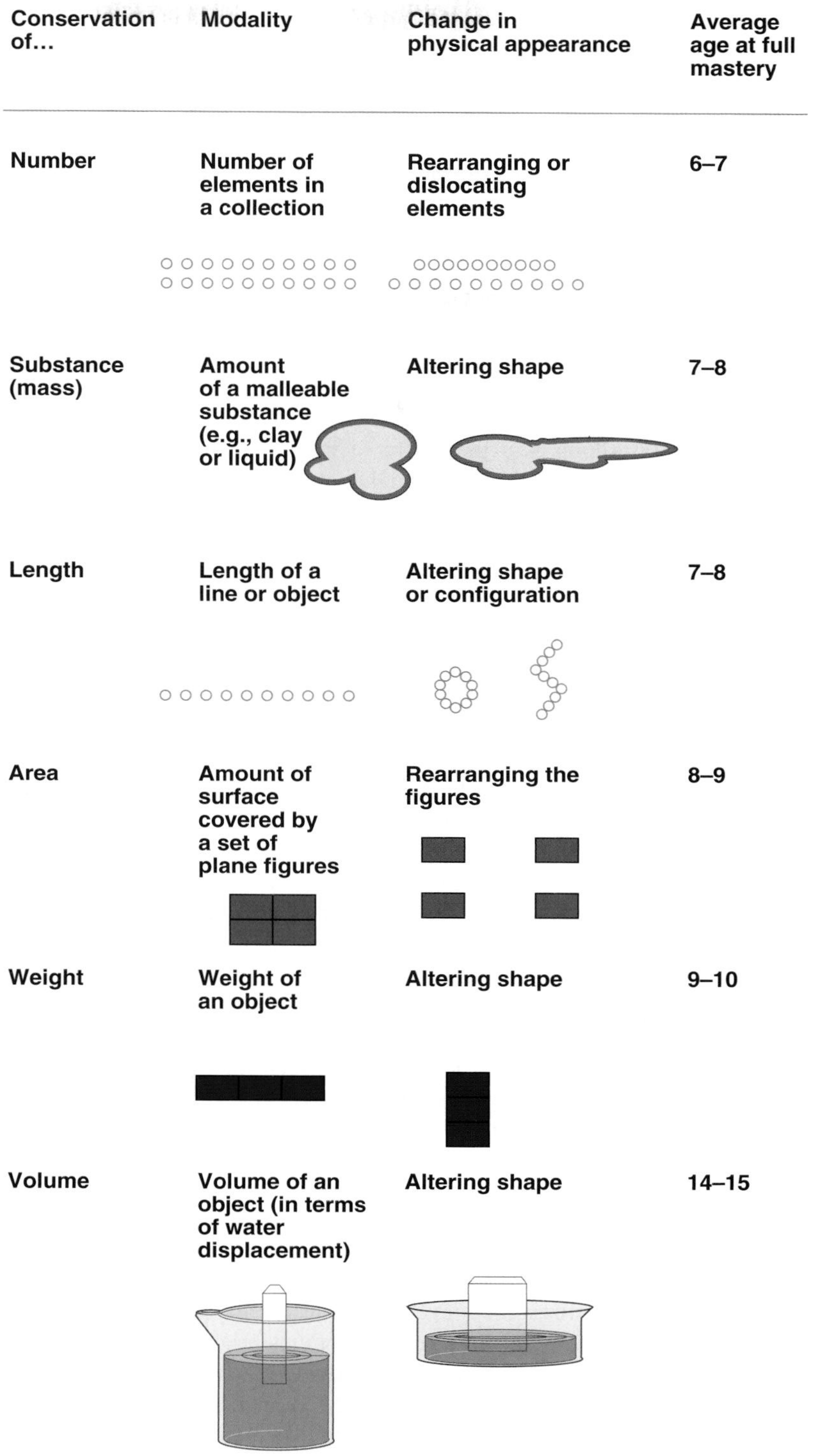

Conservation of...	Modality	Change in physical appearance	Average age at full mastery
Number	Number of elements in a collection	Rearranging or dislocating elements	6–7
Substance (mass)	Amount of a malleable substance (e.g., clay or liquid)	Altering shape	7–8
Length	Length of a line or object	Altering shape or configuration	7–8
Area	Amount of surface covered by a set of plane figures	Rearranging the figures	8–9
Weight	Weight of an object	Altering shape	9–10
Volume	Volume of an object (in terms of water displacement)	Altering shape	14–15

Figure 9-6 These tests are frequently used to assess whether children have learned the principle of conservation across a variety of dimensions (Adapted from Schickendanz, Schickendanz, & Forsyth, 1982).
Do you think children in the preoperational stage can be taught to avoid conservation mistakes before the typical age of mastery?
From Judith A. Schickendanz, David I. Schickendanz, Peggy D. Forsyth, and G. Alfred Forsyth, *Understanding Children and Adolescents,* 4th Edition. Copyright © 2001. Reprinted by permission of Allyn & Bacon.

the original ball by reversing the action. They can even conceptualize this principle in their heads, without having to see the action performed before them.

Although children make important advances in their logical capabilities during the concrete operational stage, there is still one major limitation in their thinking: They are largely bound to the concrete, physical reality of the world. For the most part, they have difficulty understanding questions of an abstract or hypothetical nature.

formal operational stage: According to Piaget, the period from age 12 to adulthood, which is characterized by abstract thought.

Formal Operational Stage: 12 Years to Adulthood   The **formal operational stage** produces a new kind of thinking that is abstract, formal, and logical. Thinking is no longer tied to events observed in the environment but makes use of logical techniques to solve problems.

The emergence of formal operational thinking is illustrated by how children approach the "pendulum problem," devised by Piaget (Piaget & Inhelder, 1958). The problem solver is asked to figure out what determines how fast a pendulum swings. Is it the length of the string, the weight of the pendulum, or the force with which the pendulum is pushed? (For the record, the answer is the length of the string.)

Children in the concrete operational stage approach the problem haphazardly, without a logical or rational plan of action. For example, they might simultaneously change the length of the string *and* the weight on the string *and* the force with which they push the pendulum. Because they are varying all factors at once, they are unable to tell which factor is the critical one. In contrast, people in the formal operational stage approach the problem systematically. Acting as if they were scientists conducting an experiment, they examine the effects of changes in just one variable at a time. This ability to rule out competing possibilities is characteristic of formal operational thought.

Although formal operational thought emerges during the teenage years, many individuals use this type of thinking infrequently. Moreover, it appears that many people never reach this stage at all; most studies show that only 40 to 60 percent of college students and adults fully reach it, with some estimates running as low as 25 percent in the general population. In addition, in certain cultures—particularly those that are less technologically sophisticated than most Western societies—almost no one reaches the formal operational stage (Chandler, 1976; Keating & Clark, 1980; Super, 1980).

Stages Versus Continuous Development: Was Piaget Right?   No other theorist has given us as comprehensive a theory of cognitive development as Piaget. Still, many contemporary theorists suggest that a better explanation of how children develop cognitively can be provided by theories that do not subscribe to a stage approach. For instance, children are not always consistent in their performance of tasks that—if Piaget's theory were accurate—ought to be performed equally well at a given stage (Siegler, 1994).

Furthermore, some developmental psychologists suggest that cognitive development proceeds in a more continuous fashion than Piaget's stage theory implies. They propose that cognitive development is primarily quantitative in nature, rather than qualitative. They argue that although there are differences in when, how, and to what extent a child is capable of using given cognitive abilities—reflecting quantitative changes—the underlying cognitive processes change relatively little with age (Gelman & Baillargeon, 1983; Case & Okamoto, 1996).

Piaget also underestimated the age at which infants and children are able to understand specific concepts and principles; in fact, they seem to be more sophisticated in their cognitive abilities than Piaget believed. For instance, some evidence suggests that infants as young as 5 months have rudimentary mathematical skills (Wynn, 1995, 2000).

Despite such criticisms, most developmental psychologists agree that, although the processes that underlie changes in cognitive abilities might not unfold in the manner suggested by his theory, Piaget has generally provided us with an accurate account of age-related changes in cognitive development. Moreover, the influence of his theory has been enormous. For example, Piaget suggests that increases in cognitive performance cannot be attained unless both cognitive readiness brought about by maturation *and* appropriate environmental stimulation are present. This view has been influential in determining the nature and structure of children's education, which needs to take into account both cognitive readiness and appropriate teaching strategies.

Information-Processing Approaches: Charting Children's Mental Programs

If cognitive development does not proceed as a series of stages, as Piaget suggested, what *does* underlie the enormous growth in children's cognitive abilities that is apparent

PsychLink

Challenge to Piaget's views
www.mcgrawhill.ca/college/feldman

Jean Piaget

to even the most untutored eye? To many developmental psychologists, changes in **information processing**—the ways people take in, use, and store information—account for cognitive development (Siegler, 1998).

According to this approach, quantitative changes occur in children's ability to organize and manipulate information. From this perspective, children become increasingly adept at information processing, much as a computer program might become more sophisticated as a programmer modifies it on the basis of experience. Information-processing approaches consider the kinds of "mental programs" children invoke when approaching problems (Reyna, 1997).

Several significant changes occur in children's information-processing capabilities. For one thing, speed of processing increases with age, as some abilities become more automatic. The speed at which stimuli can be scanned, recognized, and compared with other stimuli increases with age. With increasing age, children can pay attention to stimuli longer and discriminate between different stimuli more readily, and they are less easily distracted (Jensen & Neff, 1993; Mayr, Kliegl, & Krampe, 1996; Miller & Vernon, 1997).

Memory also improves dramatically with age. You may recall from Chapter 6 that adults are able to keep seven, plus or minus two, chunks of information in short-term memory. In contrast, preschoolers can hold only two or three chunks; 5-year-olds can hold four; and 7-year-olds can hold five. The size of chunks also grows with age, as does the sophistication and organization of knowledge stored in memory. Still, memory capabilities are impressive at a very early age: Even before they can speak, infants can remember for months events in which they were active participants, according to recent research (Bjorklund, 1985; Rovee-Collier, 1993; Bauer, 1996; see Figure 9-7).

Finally, improvement in information processing is tied to advances in **metacognition**, an awareness and understanding of one's own cognitive processes. Metacognition involves the planning, monitoring, and revising of cognitive strategies. Younger children, who lack an awareness of their own cognitive processes, are often ignorant of their incapabilities. Thus, when they misunderstand others, they might fail to recognize their own errors. It is only later, when metacognitive abilities become more sophisticated, that children are able to know when they *don't* understand. Such increasing sophistication reflects a change in children's *theory of mind,* their knowledge and beliefs about the way the mind operates (Flavell, 1993; Chandler & Lalonde, 1996; Taylor, 1996).

information processing: The ways people take in, use, and store information.

metacognition: An awareness and understanding of one's own cognitive processes.

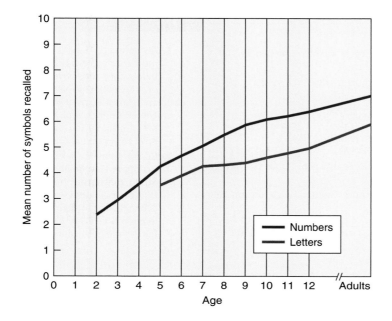

Figure 9-7 Memory span increases with age for both numbers and letters (Dempster, 1981).

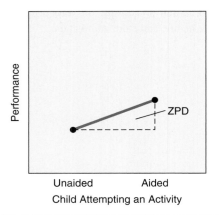

Figure 9-8 Zone of proximal development (ZPD).

zone of proximal development (ZPD): According to Vygotsky, the range between what a child is able to accomplish unaided and what he or she is able to accomplish with the help of a more advanced peer or teacher.

Discussion of Vygotsky's theory
www.mcgrawhill.ca/college/feldman

Vygotsky's View of Cognitive Development: Considering Culture

According to Russian developmental psychologist Lev Vygotsky, the culture in which we are raised has an important influence on our cognitive development. In Vygotsky's view, which is increasingly influential, the focus on individual performance of both Piagetian and information-processing approaches is misplaced. Instead, Vygotsky holds, we cannot understand cognitive development without taking into account the social aspects of learning (Vygotsky, 1926/1997; Beilin, 1996; Daniels, 1996).

Vygotsky argues that cognitive development occurs as a consequence of social interactions in which children work with others to jointly solve problems. Through such interactions, children increase their cognitive skills and gain the ability to function intellectually on their own. More specifically, children's cognitive abilities increase when they are exposed to information that falls within their zone of proximal development. The **zone of proximal development**, or **ZPD**, is the range between what the child is able to accomplish unaided and what he or she is able to accomplish with the help of a more advanced peer or other teacher. When children encounter information that falls within the ZPD, they are able to increase their understanding or master a new task. On the other hand, if the information lies outside children's ZPD, they will not be able to master it (Blank & White, 1999; see Figure 9-8).

In short, cognitive development occurs when parents, teachers, or skilled peers assist the child by presenting information that is both new and within the ZPD. This type of assistance is called *scaffolding* (Wood, Bruner, & Ross, 1976). When we put up a scaffold around a building to construct it, the scaffolding must suit the stage of the construction process. There is no value to having a scaffold 10 stories high if the building is only two stories high. In a similar way, scaffolding as a support for a child's learning and problem solving must be appropriate to the child's developmental stage and ability. The result will be an expanded ZPD in which the child has increased what he or she is able to do unaided and can demonstrate strengthened overall cognitive ability (Bruner, 1983; Steward, 1995).

More than other approaches to cognitive development, Vygotsky's theory considers how the specific cultural and social context of society affects intellectual growth. How a child understands the world is seen as an outgrowth of interactions with parents, peers, and other members of the child's culture. Furthermore, as we see next, cultural influences on cognitive development also result in significant differences in scholastic success.

Evaluate

1. _____ suggested four stages of cognitive development, each of which is dependent on maturational and environmental factors.

2. Match the stage of development with the thinking style characteristic of the stage:

   1. Egocentric thought   a. Sensorimotor
   2. Object permanence   b. Formal operational
   3. Abstract reasoning   c. Preoperational
   4. Conservation; reversibility   d. Concrete operational

3. Current research suggests that child development might proceed in a continuous fashion, rather than in stages as suggested by Piaget. True or false?

4. _____-_____ theories of development suggest that how children handle information is critical to their development.

5. According to Vygotsky, information that is within a child's _____ ____ _____ _____ is most likely to result in cognitive development.

Rethink

1. According to Piaget's theory, children must reach a certain level of maturity before they can learn particular kinds of information. What might be the pros and cons of exposing a child to more complex material at an early age? What might information–processing theory have to say about this?

2. Do you think the widespread use of IQ testing in Canada and the United States contributes to parents' views that their children's academic success is largely due to their children's innate intelligence? Why? Would it be possible (or desirable) to change this view?

Answers to Evaluate Questions

1. Piaget 2. 1-c; 2-a; 3-b; 4-d 3. True 4. Information-processing 5. zone of proximal development

Adolescence: Becoming an Adult

Prepare

What major physical, social, and cognitive transitions characterize adolescence?

Organize

Adolescence
   Physical Development
   Moral and Cognitive Development
   Social Development

Diana Leary, Age 17: "The school is divided into different groups of kids: the break-dancers, the people who listen to heavy metal, the pretty girls, the ravers and the hip-hop people. But there's no pressure to be in one group or another. If a person is a break-dancer, they can still chill with the ravers. I'm a hip-hopper. We wear baggy jeans and sweatshirts. But if I'm really good friends with a person in the heavy-metal group, I can go chill with them and it's just like, whatever." (Gordon et al., 1999, p. 48)

Trevor Kelson, Age 15: "Keep the Hell Out of My Room!" says a sign on Trevor's bedroom wall, just above an unmade bed, a desk littered with dirty T-shirts and candy wrappers, and a floor covered with clothes. Is there a carpet? "Somewhere," he says with a grin. "I think it's gold." (Fields-Meyer, 1995, p. 53)

Lauren Barry, Age 18: "I went to a National Honor Society induction. The parents were just staring at me. I think they couldn't believe someone with pink hair could be smart. I want to be a high-school teacher, but I'm afraid that, based on my appearance, they won't hire me." (Gordon et al., 1999, p. 47)

Although Diana, Trevor, and Lauren have never met, they share anxieties that are common to adolescence—concerns about friends, parents, appearance, independence, and their futures. **Adolescence**, the developmental stage between childhood and adulthood, is a crucial period. It is a time of profound changes and, occasionally, turmoil. Considerable biological change occurs as adolescents attain sexual and physical maturity. At the same time, these physiological changes are rivalled by important social, emotional, and cognitive changes that occur as adolescents strive for independence and move toward adulthood.

Because many years of schooling precede most people's entry into the workforce in Western societies, the stage of adolescence is a fairly lengthy one, beginning just before the teenage years and ending just after them. No longer children, but considered by society to be not quite adults, adolescents face a period of rapid physical, cognitive, and social change that affects them for the rest of their lives.

Adolescents' development is also being affected by dramatic changes taking place in society. Twenty percent of all children in Canada will spend all or some of their childhood and adolescence in single-parent families. Furthermore, adolescents spend considerably less time with their parents, and more with their peers, than they did several decades ago.

adolescence: The developmental stage between childhood and adulthood.

PsychLink

Adolescent directory
www.mcgrawhill.ca/college/feldman

Physical Development: The Changing Adolescent

If you think back to the start of your own adolescence, it is likely that the most dramatic changes you remember are of a physical nature. A spurt in height, the growth of breasts in girls, deepening voices in boys, the development of body hair, and intense sexual feelings are a source of curiosity, interest, and sometimes embarrassment for individuals entering adolescence.

The physical changes that occur at the start of adolescence are largely a result of the secretion of various hormones (see Chapter 2), and they affect virtually every aspect of the adolescent's life. Not since infancy has development been so dramatic. Weight and height increase rapidly due to a growth spurt that typically begins around age 10 for girls and age 12 for boys. Adolescents might grow as much as 13 centimetres in one year.

Diana Leary and her mother, Kathryn.

Although puberty begins around age 11 or 12 for girls and 13 or 14 for boys, there are wide variations. What are some advantages and disadvantages of early puberty?

puberty: The period during which maturation of the sexual organs occurs, beginning at about age 11 or 12 for girls and 13 or 14 for boys.

Puberty, the period when the sexual organs mature, begins at about age 11 or 12 for girls and 13 or 14 for boys. However, there are wide variations. For example, some girls begin to menstruate as early as age 8 or 9 or as late as age 16. In both boys and girls, sexual *attraction* to others begins even before the maturation of the sexual organs, at around the age of 10 (Eveleth & Tanner, 1976; Tanner, 1990; McClintock & Herdt, 1996).

Significant cultural and situational variations occur in the timing of first menstruation. For example, the average Lumi girl in New Guinea does not begin menstruating until she is 18. In Western cultures, the average age at which adolescents reach sexual maturity has been steadily decreasing over the last century, most likely a result of improved nutrition and medical care (Dreyer, 1982).

The age when they enter puberty has important implications for the way adolescents feel about themselves—as well as how others treat them. Early-maturing boys have a distinct advantage over later-maturing boys. They do better in athletics, are generally more popular with peers, and have more positive self-concepts. On the other hand, they are more likely to have difficulties at school, to commit minor acts of delinquency, and to become involved with alcohol abuse. One reason for such behaviour seems to be that early-maturing boys are more likely to become friends with older, and therefore more influential, boys, who might lead them into age-inappropriate activities. On balance, though, the consequences of early maturation for boys are basically positive; early maturers, compared to later maturers, are typically somewhat more responsible and cooperative in later life (Duncan et al., 1985; Peterson, 1985; Anderson & Magnusson, 1990).

The picture is different for girls. Although early-maturing girls are more sought after as dates and have better self-esteem than later-maturing girls, some of the consequences of their early physical maturation can be less positive. For example, early breast development can set them apart from their peers and be a source of ridicule (Simmons & Blyth, 1987; Ge, Conger, & Elder, 1996).

Late maturation can produce certain psychological difficulties for both boys and girls. Boys who are smaller and less coordinated than their more mature peers tend to be ridiculed and seen as less attractive, and in time they might come to view themselves in the same way. Similarly, late-maturing girls are at a disadvantage in junior high and early high school. They hold relatively low social status, and they might be overlooked in dating. On the other hand, late-maturing girls report greater satisfaction with their bodies later in high school and college, because late maturers tend to be relatively tall and slim—closer to the current societal ideal of female beauty (Apter et al., 1981; Clarke-Stewart & Friedman, 1987).

Clearly, the rate at which their physical changes occur can affect the way adolescents are viewed by others and how they view themselves. Just as important as physical changes, however, are the psychological and social changes that unfold during adolescence.

Moral and Cognitive Development: Distinguishing Right from Wrong

In a European country, a woman is near death from a special kind of cancer. The one drug that the doctors think might save her is a medicine that a medical researcher has recently discovered. The drug is expensive to make, and the researcher is charging ten times the cost, or $5000, for a small dose. The sick woman's husband, Henry, approaches everyone he knows in hopes of borrowing money, but he can get together only about $2500. He tells the researcher that his wife is dying and asks him to lower the price of the drug or let him pay later. The researcher says, "No, I discovered the drug and I'm going to make money from it." Henry is desperate and considers stealing the drug for his wife.

What would you tell Henry to do?

Kohlberg's Theory of Moral Development

In the view of psychologist Lawrence Kohlberg, the advice you give Henry is a reflection of your level of moral development. According to Kohlberg, people pass through a series of stages in the evolution of their sense of justice and in the kind of reasoning they use to make moral judgments (Kohlberg, 1984). Largely because of the various cognitive limitations that Piaget described, preadolescent children tend to think either in terms of concrete, unvarying rules ("It is always wrong to steal" or "I'll be punished if I steal") or in terms of the rules of society ("Good people don't steal" or "What if everyone stole?").

Adolescents, however, are capable of reasoning on a higher plane, having typically reached Piaget's formal operational stage of cognitive development. Because they are able to comprehend broad moral principles, they can understand that morality is not always black and white and that conflict can exist between two sets of socially accepted standards.

Kohlberg (1984) suggests that the changes occurring in moral reasoning can be understood best as a three-level sequence (see Table 9-5). His theory assumes that people move through the levels in a fixed order, and that they are not capable of reaching the highest level until about the age of 13—primarily because of limitations in cognitive development before then. However, many people never reach the highest level of moral reasoning. In fact, Kohlberg found that only a relatively small percentage of adults rise above the second level of his model (Kohlberg & Ryncarz, 1990).

Although Kohlberg's theory has had a substantial influence on our understanding of moral development, the research support is mixed. One difficulty with the theory is that it pertains to moral *judgments,* not moral *behaviour.* Knowing right from wrong does not mean that we will always act in accordance with our judgments. In addition, the theory is primarily applicable to Western society and its moral code; cross-cultural research conducted in cultures with different moral systems suggests that Kohlberg's theory is not necessarily relevant there (Kurtines & Gewirtz, 1995; Coles, 1997; Damon, 1999).

Moral Development in Females

One glaring shortcoming of Kohlberg's research is that he used primarily male participants. Furthermore, psychologist Carol Gilligan (1982, 1987, 1993) argues that because of their distinctive socialization experiences, there is a fundamental difference in how

PsychLink

Kohlberg's theory of moral development
www.mcgrawhill.ca/college/feldman

Table 9-5 Kohlberg's Levels of Moral Reasoning

Level	SAMPLE MORAL REASONING OF SUBJECTS	
	In Favour of Stealing the Drug	**Against Stealing the Drug**
Level 1 Preconventional morality: At this level, the concrete interests of the individual are considered in terms of rewards and punishments.	"If you let your wife die, you will get in trouble. You'll be blamed for not spending the money to save her, and there'll be an investigation of you and the druggist for your wife's death."	"You shouldn't steal the drug because you'll be caught and sent to jail if you do. If you do get away, your conscience will bother you thinking how the police will catch up with you at any minute."
Level 2 Conventional morality: At this level, people approach moral problems as members of society. They are interested in pleasing others by acting as good members of society.	"If you let your wife die, you'll never be able to look anybody in the face again."	"After you steal the drug, you'll feel bad thinking how you've brought dishonour on your family and yourself; you won't be able to face anyone again."
Level 3 Postconventional morality: At this level, people use moral principles which are seen as broader than those of any particular society.	"If you don't steal the drug, and if you let your wife die, you'll always condemn yourself for it afterward. You won't be blamed and you'll have lived up to the outside rule of the law but you won't have lived up to your own standards of conscience."	"If you steal the drug, you won't be blamed by other people, but you'll condemn yourself because you won't have lived up to your own conscience and standards of honesty."

women and men view moral behaviour. According to Gilligan, men view morality primarily in terms of broad principles, such as justice and fairness. In contrast, women see it in terms of responsibility toward individuals and willingness to make sacrifices to help a specific individual within the context of a particular relationship. Compassion for individuals is a more salient factor in moral behaviour for women than it is for men (Gilligan, Ward, & Taylor, 1988; Gilligan, Lyons, & Hanmer, 1990).

Because Kohlberg's model conceives of moral behaviour largely in terms of abstract principles such as justice, Gilligan finds it inadequate for describing the moral development of females. She suggests that women's morality is centred on individual well-being and social relationships—a morality of *caring*. In her view, the highest levels of morality are represented by compassionate concern for the welfare of others.

Other research has questioned whether there is a difference in the development of men's and women's morality (Hoff-Sommers, 2000). Lawrence Walker of the University of British Columbia (1984) examined over 80 studies, which included 108 samples and over 8000 subjects. These studies were chosen because they included both males and females and were examining sex differences in moral reasoning. Included are some of Gilligan's studies. In his conclusion he states "… contrary to the prevailing stereotype, very few sex differences in moral development have been found" (p. 688). Concerns raised by Hoff-Sommers (2000) have opened a dialogue between her and Carol Gilligan (Hoff-Sommers, 2000). The controversy will undoubtedly continue.

Social Development: Finding Oneself in a Social World

"Who am I?" "How do I fit into the world?" "What is life all about?"

Questions such as these assume particular significance during the teenage years, as adolescents seek to find their place in the broader social world. As we will see, this quest takes adolescents along several routes.

Erikson's Theory of Psychosocial Development: The Search for Identity

Erikson's theory of psychosocial development emphasizes the search for identity during the adolescent years. As noted earlier, psychosocial development encompasses changes in people's understanding of themselves, one another, and the world around them during the course of development (Erikson, 1963).

The fifth stage of Erikson's theory (summarized, with the other stages, in Table 9-6) is labelled the **identity-versus-role-confusion stage** and encompasses adolescence. This stage is a time of major testing, as people try to determine what is unique and special about themselves. They attempt to discover who they are, what their strengths are, and what kinds of roles they are best suited to play for the rest of their lives—in short, their **identity**. Confusion over the most appropriate role to follow in life can lead to lack of a stable identity, adoption of a socially unacceptable role such as that of a social deviant, or difficulty in maintaining close personal relationships later in life (Kahn et al., 1985; Archer & Waterman, 1994; Kidwell et al., 1995; Brendgen, Vitaro, & Bukowski, 2000).

During the identity-versus-role-confusion period, pressures to identify what one wants to do with one's life are acutely felt. Because these pressures come at a time of major physical changes as well as important changes in what society expects of them, adolescents can find the period particularly difficult. The identity-versus-role-confusion stage has another important characteristic: a decline in reliance on adults for information, with a shift toward using the peer group as a source of social judgments. The peer group becomes increasingly important, enabling adolescents to form close, adultlike relationships and helping them clarify their personal identities. According to Erikson, the identity-versus-role-confusion stage during adolescence marks a pivotal point in

PsychLink
Gilligan vs. Kohlberg
www.mcgrawhill.ca/college/feldman

identity-versus-role-confusion stage: According to Erikson, a time in adolescence of major testing to determine one's unique qualities.

identity: The distinguishing character of the individual: who each of us is, what our roles are, and what we are capable of.

According to Erikson's theory, during the identity-versus-role confusion stage, adolescents seek to determine what is special and unique about themselves.

psychosocial development, paving the way for continued growth and the future development of personal relationships.

During early adulthood, people enter the **intimacy-versus-isolation stage**. Spanning the period of early adulthood (from post-adolescence to the early thirties), the focus is on developing close relationships with others. Difficulties during this stage result in feelings of loneliness and a fear of relationships with others, but successful resolution of the crises of this stage results in the possibility of forming relationships that are intimate on a physical, intellectual, and emotional level.

Development continues during middle adulthood as people enter the **generativity-versus-stagnation stage**. Generativity is the ability to contribute to one's family, community, work, and society, assisting the development of the younger generation. Success in this stage results in positive feelings about the continuity of life; difficulties lead to feelings that one's activities are trivial, a sense of stagnation, or feeling that one has done nothing for upcoming generations. In fact, the person who has not successfully resolved the identity crisis of adolescence might still be floundering in middle adulthood to find an appropriate career.

Finally, the last stage of psychosocial development, the period of **ego-integrity-versus-despair**, comprises later adulthood and continues until death. Success in resolving the difficulties presented by this stage of life is signified by a sense of accomplishment; difficulties result in regret over what might have been achieved but was not.

One of the most noteworthy aspects of Erikson's theory is its suggestion that development does not stop at adolescence but continues throughout adulthood, a view that a substantial amount of research now confirms. For instance, a 22-year study by psychologist Susan Whitbourne found considerable support for the fundamentals of Erikson's theory, determining that psychosocial development continues through adolescence and adulthood. In sum, adolescence is not an endpoint but rather a way-station on the path of psychosocial development (Whitbourne et al., 1992; McAdams et al., 1997).

Stormy Adolescence: Myth or Reality?

Does puberty invariably foreshadow a stormy, rebellious period of adolescence?

At one time most children entering adolescence were thought to be beginning a period fraught with stress and unhappiness. However, psychologists are now finding that this characterization is largely a myth, that most young people pass through adolescence without appreciable turmoil in their lives, and that parents speak easily—and fairly often—with their children about a variety of topics (Steinberg, 1993; Klein, 1998; van Wel, Linssen, & Abma, 2000).

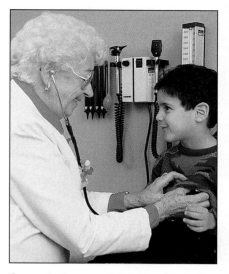

Success in the generativity-versus-stagnation stage results in positive feelings about the continuity of life, while difficulties lead to feelings of triviality regarding one's activities and a sense of stagnation.

intimacy–versus–isolation stage: According to Erikson, a period during early adulthood that focuses on developing close relationships.

generativity–versus–stagnation stage: According to Erikson, a period in middle adulthood during which we take stock of our contributions to family and society.

ego-integrity–versus–despair stage: According to Erikson, a period from late adulthood until death during which we review our life's accomplishments and failures.

Table 9-6 A Summary of Erikson's Stages

Stage	Approximate Age	Positive Outcomes	Negative Outcomes
1. Trust-vs.-mistrust	Birth–1½ years	Feelings of trust from environmental support	Fear and concern regarding others
2. Autonomy-vs.-shame-and-doubt	1½–3 years	Self-sufficiency if exploration is encouraged	Doubts about self, lack of independence
3. Initiative-vs.-guilt	3–6 years	Discovery of ways to initiate actions	Guilt from actions and thoughts
4. Industry-vs.-inferiority	6–12 years	Development of sense of competence	Feelings of inferiority, no sense of mastery
5. Identity-vs.-role-confusion	Adolescence	Awareness of uniqueness of self, knowledge of role to be followed	Inability to identify appropriate roles in life
6. Intimacy-vs.-isolation	Early adulthood	Development of loving, sexual relationships and close friendships	Fear of relationships with others
7. Generativity-vs.-stagnation	Middle adulthood	Sense of contribution to continuity of life	Trivialization of one's activities
8. Ego-integrity-vs.-despair	Late adulthood	Sense of unity in life's accomplishments	Regret over lost opportunities of life

Pathways Through Psychology

Lorrie K. Sippola

Assistant Professor, University of Saskatchewan

Education: B.A. M.A. Ph.D. Concordia University, Montreal

Home: Saskatoon, Saskatchewan

Lorrie K. Sippola and Kita

My interest in adolescent development stems primarily from earlier intervention work with young offenders and, later, with adult male sexual offenders in the criminal justice system. At the time, clinical literature suggested that early developmental challenges were contributing factors to criminal behaviour and sexual deviance. From my perspective, then, it made sense to work from a preventative model, which focuses on understanding the factors contributing to development of a particular outcome. This perspective is in contrast to an intervention model that focuses on treating outcome after onset. From my clinical experiences, adolescence appeared to be a crucial stage of development for various behaviours. In particular, relationships during this period of development seemed to provide a window of opportunity for change. From my own observations, positive relational experiences in adolescence seemed to provide opportunities to repair damage from earlier experiences. Alternatively, challenging relationships during this time seemed to contribute to the onset of particular problems. The road to my current career was not a straight path with clearly defined goals and aspirations. But, eventually, these ideas led me to study the role of interpersonal relationships in adolescent development.

Currently, we know little about the development of healthy, intimate, relationships between romantic partners. Much of the research in the area has focused on factors predicting early onset of intercourse or teenage pregnancy. I'm interested in extending this work by examining platonic but emotionally engaged relationships between boys and girls and how these relationships change over time. To do this, students in my lab and I pursue the following questions: What are the features of adolescent cross-sex friendships? How are these relationships similar to and different from relationships with same-sex peers? How does gender influence adolescents' experience of cross-sex relationships and how do cross-sex relationships influence adolescents' understanding of the concept of gender?

The question regarding important accomplishments is a difficult one to answer. I guess the obvious ones would be winning awards for my dissertation, receiving a post-doctoral fellowship to continue my training at Radcliffe College at Harvard University, and recently receiving external funding for two longitudinal projects that are currently ongoing in Saskatoon. These awards reflect recognition for my research from my peers. This is always satisfying. However, I have recently become involved in a research project at an inner-city high school. Sharing my research skills to address questions raised by the teachers, guidance counsellors, and social workers at the school has been most rewarding. These educators have taught me a great deal about how basic, developmental science can be used to address real-world problems. This has been an important and meaningful personal and professional experience.

Source: Lorrie K. Sippola, Ph.D., University of Saskatchewan http://www.usask.ca/psychology/faculty/lsippola.htm

What are the research questions that Dr. Sippola is interested in?

PsychLink

Teenage suicide
www.mcgrawhill.ca/college/feldman

This is not to say that adolescence is completely calm. In most families, there is clearly a rise in the amount of arguing and bickering that goes on. Young teenagers, as part of their search for identity, tend to experience a degree of tension between their attempts to become independent from their parents and their actual dependence on them. They might experiment with a range of behaviours, flirting with a variety of activities that their parents, and even society as a whole, find objectionable. Happily, though, for the majority of families such tensions tend to stabilize during middle adolescence—around age 15 or 16—and eventually decline around age 18 (Eccles, Lord, & Roeser, 1996; Gullotta, Adams, & Markstrom, 1999).

One reason for the increase in discord during adolescence appears to be the protracted period in which children stay at home with their parents. In prior historical periods—and in some nonwestern cultures today—children leave home immediately after puberty and are considered adults. Today, however, sexually mature adolescents might spend as many as seven or eight years with their parents. Current statistics even hint at an extension of the conflicts of adolescence beyond the teenage years for a significant number of people. Some one-third of all unmarried men and one-fifth of unmarried women between the ages of 25 and 34 continue to reside with their parents (Steinberg, 1989; Gross, 1991).

Another source of strife with parents lies in the way adolescents think. Adolescence fosters *adolescent egocentrism,* a state of self-absorption in which adolescents view the world from their own point of view. Egocentrism leads adolescents to be highly critical of authority figures, unwilling to accept criticism, and quick to fault others. It also makes them believe that they are the centre of everyone else's attention, leading to considerable self-consciousness. Furthermore, they develop *personal fables,* the view that what happens to them is unique, exceptional, and shared by no one else. Such personal fables can make adolescents feel invulnerable to the risks that threaten others (Elkind, 1967, 1985; Klacynski, 1997).

Adolescence also introduces a variety of stresses outside the home. These stresses include, among other things, the move from elementary to high school and relationships with friends and peers, which can be particularly volatile. Many adolescents hold part-time jobs, increasing the demands of school, work, and social activities on their time. Such stressors can lead to tensions at home (Steinberg & Dornbusch, 1991; Cotterell, 1996). Lorrie Sippola, featured in the *Pathways Through Psychology* box, works to understand adolescent relationships through her research.

EXPLORING DIVERSITY

Rites of Passage: Coming of Age Around the World

It is not easy for male members of the Awa tribe in New Guinea to make the transition from childhood to adulthood. First come whippings, in which the boys are hit with sticks and prickly branches, both for their own past misdeeds and in honour of those tribesmen who were killed in warfare. In the next phase of the ritual, adults jab sharpened sticks into the boys' nostrils. Then they force a $1\frac{1}{2}$-metre length of vine into the boys' throats, until they gag and vomit. Finally, tribesmen cut the boys' genitals, causing severe bleeding.

Although the rites that mark the coming-of-age of boys in the Awa sound horrifying to Westerners, they are comparable to those in other cultures. In some cultures, rites require kneeling on hot coals without displaying pain. In others, girls must toss wads of burning cotton from hand to hand and allow themselves to be bitten by hundreds of ants (Selsky, 1997).

Other cultures have less fearsome, although no less important, ceremonies that mark the passage from childhood to adulthood. For instance, when a girl first menstruates in traditional Apache tribes, the event is marked by dawn-to-dusk chanting. Western religions, too, have several types of celebrations, including bar and bat mitzvahs at age 13 for Jewish boys and girls and confirmation ceremonies for children in many Christian denominations (Myerhoff, 1982; Dunham, Kidwell, & Wilson, 1986; Delaney, 1995; Rakoff, 1995).

In most societies, males, but not females, are the focus of coming-of-age ceremonies. The renowned anthropologist Margaret Mead remarked, only partly in jest, that the preponderance of male ceremonies might reflect that "the worry that boys will not grow up to be men is much more widespread than that girls will not grow up to be women" (Mead, 1949, p. 195). Or it might be that men traditionally have higher status than women, and therefore their transition into adulthood is regarded as more important.

However, there is another explanation for why most cultures place greater emphasis on male rites than female rites. For females, the transition from childhood is marked by a definite, biological event: menstruation. For males, no single event pinpoints entry into adulthood, so they are forced to rely on culturally determined rituals to acknowledge that they have become adults (Chodorow, 1978; Bird & Melville, 1994).

What are some of the reasons given for most cultures placing a greater emphasis on rites of passage for males than for females?

Evaluate

1. _____ is the period during which the sexual organs begin to mature.
2. Delayed maturation typically provides both males and females with a social advantage. True or false?
3. _____ proposed a set of three levels of moral development ranging from reasoning based on rewards and punishments to abstract thinking involving concepts of justice.
4. Erikson believed that, during adolescence, people must search for _____, and that during early adulthood the major task is _____.

Answers to Evaluate Questions

1. Puberty 2. False; both male and female adolescents suffer if they mature late. 3. Kohlberg 4. identity; intimacy

Rethink

1. In what ways do school cultures help or hurt teenage students who are going through adolescence? What school policies might benefit early-maturing girls and late-maturing boys? Would same-sex schools help, as some have argued?
2. Many cultures have "rites of passage" that officially recognize young people as adults. Do you think such rites can be beneficial? Does Canada have any such rites? Would setting up an official designation that one has achieved "adult" status have benefits?

Prepare

What are the principal kinds of physical, social, and intellectual changes that occur in early and middle adulthood, and what are their causes?

Organize

Early and Middle Adulthood
    Physical Development
    Social Development
    Marriage, Children, and Divorce

Early and Middle Adulthood: The Middle Years of Life

Psychologists generally consider early adulthood to begin around age 20 and last until about age 40 to 45, with middle adulthood beginning then and continuing until around age 65. Despite the enormous importance of these periods of life in terms of both the accomplishments that occur within them and their overall length (together they span some 45 years), they have been studied less than any other stage. One reason is that the physical changes that occur during these periods are less apparent and more gradual than changes during other periods of the life span. In addition, the social changes that arise during this period are so diverse that they defy simple categorization. However, developmental psychologists have recently begun to focus on early and middle adulthood, particularly on the social changes in the family and women's careers.

Physical Development: The Peak of Health

For most people, early adulthood marks the peak of physical health. From about 18 to 25 years of age, people's strength is greatest, their reflexes are quickest, and their chances of dying from disease are quite slim. Moreover, reproductive capabilities are at their highest level.

Around age 25, the body starts to become slightly less efficient and more susceptible to disease. Overall, however, ill health remains the exception; most people stay remarkably healthy during early adulthood. (Can you think of any machine other than the body that can operate without pause for so long a period?)

During middle adulthood, people gradually become aware of changes in their bodies. Many people begin to put on weight (although this can be avoided through exercise). Furthermore, the sense organs gradually become less sensitive, and it takes more time to react to stimuli. But generally, the physical declines that do occur during middle adulthood are minor and often unnoticeable (DiGiovanna, 1994).

The major biological change during middle adulthood pertains to reproductive capabilities. During their late forties or early fifties, on average, women begin **menopause**, a process in which they stop menstruating and become infertile. Because menopause is accompanied by a significant reduction in the production of estrogen, a female hormone, menopausal women sometimes experience symptoms such as hot flashes, sudden sensations of heat. However, many symptoms can be treated through

menopause: The point at which women stop menstruating and are no longer fertile.

hormone replacement therapy (HRT), in which the hormones estrogen and progesterone are taken. However, estrogen replacement therapy poses several dangers, such as an increase in the risk of breast cancer. The uncertainties make the routine use of HRT controversial (LaVecchia, 1996; Swan, 1997).

Menopause was once blamed for a variety of psychological symptoms, including depression and memory loss. However, such difficulties, if they do occur, might be caused by women's expectations about reaching an "old" age in a society that highly values youth.

Furthermore, women's reactions to menopause vary significantly across cultures. According to anthropologist Yewoubdar Beyene, the more a society values old age, the less difficulty its women have during menopause. In a study of women in Mayan villages, she found that women looked forward to menopause, because they then stopped having children. In addition, they didn't even experience some of the classic symptoms of menopause; hot flashes, for example, were unheard of. It is clear that a society's attitudes affect how women experience menopause (Ballinger, 1981; Beyene, 1989; Beck, 1992; Figueiras & Marteau, 1995; Mingo, Herman, & Jasperse, 2000).

For men, the aging process during middle adulthood is somewhat subtler. There are no physiological signals of increasing age equivalent to the end of menstruation in women. In fact, men remain fertile and are capable of fathering children until well into old age. On the other hand, some gradual physical declines occur: Sperm production decreases and the frequency of orgasm tends to decline. Once again, though, most psychological difficulties associated with these changes are due not so much to physical deterioration as to societal glorification of youthfulness.

Women's reactions to menopause vary significantly across cultures, and, according to one study, the more a society values old age, the less difficulty its women have during menopause.
Why do you think this would be the case?

 PsychLink

Medical information on menopause
www.mcgrawhill.ca/college/feldman

Social Development: Working at Life

Whereas physical changes during adulthood reflect development of a quantitative nature, social developmental transitions are more profound. During this period people typically launch themselves into careers, marriage, and families.

The entry into early adulthood is usually marked by leaving one's childhood home and entering the world of work. People envision the accomplishments they desire in life and make career choices. Their lives often become centred on their careers, which form an important part of their identity (Vaillant & Vaillant, 1990; Levinson, 1990, 1992).

In their early forties, however, people might begin to question their lives as they enter a period called the *midlife transition*. The idea that life will end at some point becomes increasingly influential in their thinking, and they might question their past accomplishments (Gould, 1978). As they face signs of physical aging and feel dissatisfaction with their lives, some individuals experience what has been popularly labelled a *midlife crisis*.

For most people, though, the passage into middle age is relatively calm. Most 40-year-olds view their lives and accomplishments positively enough to proceed relatively smoothly through midlife, and the forties and fifties are often a particularly rewarding period of life. Rather than looking to the future, people concentrate on the present, and their involvement with their families, friends, and other social groups takes on new importance. A major developmental thrust of this period of life is coming to terms with one's circumstances (Whitbourne, 1999).

Finally, during the last stages of adulthood people become more accepting of others and their lives, and less concerned about issues or problems that once bothered them. People come to accept the realization that death is inevitable, and they try to understand their accomplishments in terms of the broader meaning of life. Although people might for the first time begin to label themselves as "old," many also develop a sense of wisdom and feel freer to enjoy life (Gould, 1978; Karp, 1988, 1991).

Marriage, Children, and Divorce: Family Ties

In the typical fairy tale, a dashing young man and a beautiful young woman marry, have children, and live happily ever after. However, such a scenario does not match the realities of love and marriage in the twenty-first century. Today, it is just as likely that the woman and man would first live together, then get married and have children, but ultimately end up getting divorced.

The percentage of unmarried couples in Canadian and U.S. households has increased dramatically over the last two decades. At the same time, the average age at which marriage takes place is higher than at any time since the turn of the century (in Canada, 27 years of age for women, and 30 years of age for men.) These changes have been dramatic, and they suggest that the institution of marriage has changed considerably from earlier historical periods.

When people do marry, the probability of divorce is high, particularly for younger couples. Thirty-seven percent of all Canadian marriages end in divorce. Moreover, the rise in divorce is not just a North American phenomenon: The divorce rate has accelerated over the last several decades in most industrialized countries except Japan and Italy (Cherlin, 1993; Ahrons, 1995).

According to the 1996 Census (Statistics Canada, 1996b), there are 7.8 million families in Canada. Sixty-five percent of these families have children. Changes in marriage and divorce trends have led to an increase in lone-parent families. Fifteen percent of children live in lone-parent families. Eighty percent of lone-parent families are headed by women. This is a phenomenon that is consistent across racial and ethnic groups throughout the industrialized world (Burns & Scott, 1994).

What are the consequences for children living in homes with only one parent? Single-parent families are often economically less well off, diminishing children's opportunities. Many single parents are unable to find good child care, and they feel psychological stress and sometimes guilt over the child-care arrangements they must make for economic reasons. Time is always at a premium in single-parent families (Hetherington, 1999; Wallerstein, Lewis, & Blakeslee, 2000). Furthermore, for children of divorce, the parents' separation is often a painful experience that can make it difficult for the children to establish close relationships later in life. Children might blame themselves for the breakup or feel pressure to take sides. Most evidence, however, suggests that children from single-parent families are no less well adjusted than those from two-parent families. In fact, children can be more successful growing up in a harmonious single-parent family than in a two-parent family in which the parents are engaged in continuous conflict with one another (Harold et al., 1997; Kelly, 1999; Clarke-Stewart et al., 2000).

PsychLink

Children and divorce
www.mcgrawhill.ca/college/feldman

The Changing Roles of Men and Women: The Time of Their Lives

One of the major changes in family life in the last two decades has been the evolution of the roles played by men and women. More women than ever before act simultaneously as wives, mothers, and wage earners—in contrast to women in traditional marriages, in which the husband is the sole wage earner and the wife assumes primary responsibility for care of the home and children.

In Canada, close to 80 percent of all married women with school-age children are now employed outside the home, and 69 percent of mothers with children under 6 are working (Statistics Canada, 1996b). Most married working women are not free of household responsibilities. Even in marriages in which the spouses hold jobs that have similar status and require similar hours, the distribution of household tasks between husbands and wives has not changed substantially. Working wives are still more likely to view themselves as responsible for traditional homemaking tasks such as cooking and cleaning. In contrast, husbands still view themselves as responsible primarily for such household tasks as repairing broken appliances, putting up screens in the summer, and doing yard work (Perry-Jenkins, 1993; Ganong & Coleman, 1999).

Women's "Second Shift"   The number of hours put in by working mothers can be staggering. One survey found that employed mothers of children under 3 years of age worked an average of 90 hours per week! Sociologist Arlie Hochschild refers to the additional work experienced by women as the "second shift." According to her analysis of American statistics, employed mothers put in an extra month of 24-hour days during the course of a year. Similar patterns are seen in many developing societies throughout the world, with women working at full-time jobs and also having primary responsibilities for child care. Studies in Canada show that women spend 32.5 hours on household work compared to 18.1 hours a week for men (Hochschild, 1990; Hochschild, Machung, & Pringle, 1995; Mednick, 1993; Vanier Institute, 1997).

Consequently, rather than women's careers being a substitute for household work, they usually are an addition to the role of homemaker. It is not surprising that some wives feel resentment toward husbands who spend less time on child care and housework than the wives had expected before the birth of their children (Williams & McCullers, 1983; Ruble et al., 1988; Crouter et al., 1999; Stier & Lewin-Epstein, 2000).

Evaluate

1. Emotional and psychological changes that sometimes accompany menopause are probably not due to menopause itself. True or false?
2. Rob recently turned 40 and surveyed his goals and accomplishments to date. Although he has accomplished a lot, he realized that many of his goals will not be met in his lifetime. This stage is called a _____ _____.
3. It is typically in the best interests of children for their parents to remain in a stormy marriage until the children move away from home. True or false?
4. In households where the partners have similar jobs, the usual division of labour is the same as in "traditional" households where the husband works and the wife stays at home. True or false?

Answers to Evaluate Questions

1. True 2. midlife transition, 3. False; a stable one-parent home is generally preferable to a two-parent home filled with conflict. 4. True

Rethink

1. How do you think popular culture contributes to the midlife crisis experienced by some people as they reach their forties? What sorts of cultural changes might ease the midlife crisis or make the phenomenon less prevalent?
2. Given the current divorce rate and the number of households in which both parents work, do you think it is reasonable to still think in terms of a "traditional" household in which the father is the breadwinner and the wife is a homemaker? What problems might such a definition cause for children whose homes do not match this definition?

The Later Years of Life: Growing Old

Prepare

How does the reality of old age differ from the stereotypes about the period?

How can we adjust to death?

Organize

The Later Years of Life
    Physical Changes in Late Adulthood
    Cognitive Changes
    The Social World of Late Adulthood

I've always enjoyed doing things in the mountains—hiking or, more recently, active cliff-climbing. When climbing a route of any difficulty at all, it's absolutely necessary to become entirely absorbed in what you're doing. You look for a crack that you can put your hand in. You have to think about whether the foothold over there will leave you in balance or not. Otherwise you can get trapped in a difficult situation. And if you don't remember where you put your hands or feet a few minutes before, then it's very difficult to climb down.

The more difficult the climb, the more absorbing it is. The climbs I really remember are the ones I had to work on. Maybe a particular section where it took two or three tries before I found the right combination of moves that got me up easily—and, preferably, elegantly. It's a wonderful exhilaration to get to the top and sit down and perhaps have lunch and look out over the landscape and be so grateful that it's still possible for me to do that sort of thing. (Lyman Spitzer, age 74, quoted in Kotre & Hall, 1990, pp. 358–359)

 **PsychLink**

Aging process information
www.mcgrawhill.ca/college/feldman

 **PsychLink**

Information on aging
www.mcgrawhill.ca/college/feldman

genetic preprogramming theories of aging: Theories that hold that there is a built-in time limit to the reproduction of human cells, and that after a certain time they are no longer able to divide.

wear-and-tear theories of aging: Theories that hold that the mechanical functions of the body simply stop working efficiently when we are old.

If you can't quite picture a 74-year-old climbing rocks, some rethinking of your view of old age might well be in order. In spite of the societal stereotype of old age as a time of inactivity and physical and mental decline, *gerontologists*, specialists who study aging, are beginning to paint quite a different portrait of late adulthood.

By focusing on the period of life that starts at around age 65, gerontologists are making important contributions to clarifying the capabilities of older adults. Their work is demonstrating that significant developmental processes continue even during old age. And as life expectancy increases, the number of people who reach older adulthood will continue to grow substantially. Consequently, developing an understanding of late adulthood has become a critical priority for psychologists (Birren, 1996; Moody, 2000).

Physical Changes in Late Adulthood: The Aging Body

Napping, eating, walking, conversing. It probably doesn't surprise you that these relatively nonstrenuous activities represent the typical pastimes of late adulthood. But what is striking about this list is that these activities are identical to the most common leisure activities reported in a survey of college students. Although the students cited more active pursuits—such as sailing and playing basketball—as their favourite activities, in actuality they engaged in such sports relatively infrequently, spending most of their free time napping, eating, walking, and conversing (Harper, 1978).

Although the leisure activities in which older adults engage might not differ all that much from those of younger people, many physical changes are, of course, brought about by the aging process. The most obvious are those of appearance—hair thinning and turning gray, skin wrinkling and folding, and sometimes a slight loss of height as the thickness of the disks between vertebrae in the spine decreases—but there are also subtler changes in the body's biological functioning (DiGiovanna, 1994).

For example, sensory capabilities decrease as a result of aging: Vision, hearing, smell, and taste become less sensitive. Reaction time slows, and there are changes in physical stamina. Because oxygen intake and heart-pumping ability decline, the body is unable to replenish lost nutrients as quickly—and therefore the rebound from physical activity is slower. Of course, none of these changes begins suddenly at age 65. Gradual declines in some kinds of functioning start earlier. In late adulthood, however, these changes become more apparent (Schneider & Rowe, 1996; Whitbourne, 2000).

What are the reasons for these physical declines? **Genetic preprogramming theories of aging** suggest that there is a built-in time limit to the reproduction of human cells. These theories suggest that after a certain time cells stop dividing or become harmful to the body—as if a kind of automatic self-destruct button has been pushed. In contrast, **wear-and-tear theories of aging** suggest that the mechanical functions of the body simply stop working efficiently as people age. Waste by-products of energy production eventually accumulate, and mistakes are made when cells divide. Eventually the body, in effect, wears out, just like an old automobile (Hayflick, 1994; Ly et al., 2000).

Evidence exists to support both the genetic preprogramming view and the wear-and-tear view, and perhaps both processes contribute to natural aging. It is clear, however, that physical aging is not a disease, but rather a natural biological process. Many physical functions do not decline with age. For example, sex remains pleasurable well into old age (although the frequency of sexual activity decreases), and some people report that the pleasure they derive from sex increases during late adulthood (Olshansky, Carnes, & Cassel, 1990; Gelfand, 2000).

Cognitive Changes: Thinking About—and During—Late Adulthood

At one time, many gerontologists would have agreed with the popular view that older adults are forgetful and confused. Today, however, most research tells us that this is far from an accurate assessment of older people's capabilities.

One reason for the change in view is the availability of more sophisticated research techniques for studying cognitive changes that occur in late adulthood. For example, if we were to give a group of older adults an IQ test, we might find that the average score is lower than the score achieved by a group of younger people. We might conclude that this signifies a decline in intelligence. Yet if we looked a little closer at the specific test, we might find that such a conclusion is unwarranted. For instance, many IQ tests include portions based on physical performance (such as arranging a group of blocks) or on speed. In such cases, poorer performance on the IQ test might be due to decrements in reaction time—a physical decline that accompanies old age and has little or nothing to do with the intellectual capabilities of older adults (Schaie, 1991).

Other difficulties hamper research into cognitive functioning during late adulthood. For example, many older people are less healthy than younger ones; when only *healthy* older adults are compared to healthy younger adults, intellectual differences are far less evident. Furthermore, the average number of years in school is often lower in older adults (for historical reasons) than in the younger ones, and older adults can be less motivated to perform well on intelligence tests than younger people. Finally, traditional IQ tests might be inappropriate measures of intelligence in late adulthood. Older adults sometimes perform better on tests of practical intelligence (of the sort we discussed in Chapter 7) than younger individuals do (Cornelius & Caspi, 1987; Willis & Schaie, 1994; Kausler, 1994).

Still, there are some declines in intellectual functioning during late adulthood, although the pattern of age differences is not uniform for different types of cognitive abilities (see Figure 9-9). In general, skills relating to *fluid intelligence* (which involves reasoning, memory, and information processing) do show declines in old age. On the other hand, skills relating to *crystallized intelligence* (intelligence based on the accumulation of information, skills, and problem-solving strategies) remain steady and in some cases actually improve (Schaie, 1993, 1994; Powell & Whitla, 1994; Salthouse, 1996).

Even when changes in intellectual functioning do occur during late adulthood, people often are able to compensate for any decline. They can still learn what they want to; it might just take more time. Furthermore, when older adults learn strategies for dealing with new problems, this can prevent declines in their performance (Willis & Nesselroade, 1990; Coffey et al., 1999).

Many people remain active and vigorous during late adulthood, as exemplified by this participant in the Senior Olympics.

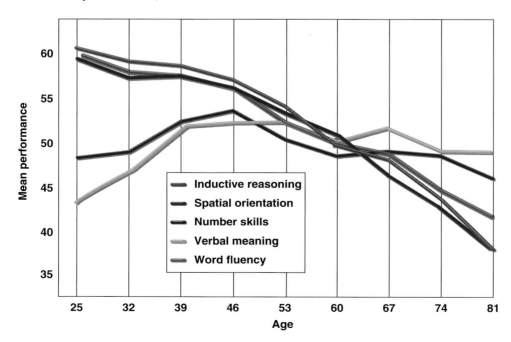

Figure 9-9 Age-related changes in intellectual skills vary according to the specific cognitive ability in question (Schaie, 1994).

Psychology at Work

Kevin Sweryd

Funeral Director, Manager

Education: B.A., psychology, University of Manitoba

Home: Winnipeg, Manitoba

Kevin Sweryd

In 1992, after finishing his B.A. in psychology at the University of Manitoba, Kevin Sweryd got a summer job at Bardal Funeral Home and Crematorium in Winnipeg. He got the job intending to save some money to pay for his master's degree. Over a decade later, however, Sweryd is still with Bardal—but now as a funeral director.

"This summer job was my first exposure to funeral service and I realized shortly after I started that there were many elements to the funeral director's position that were related to my studies in psychology."

Indeed, Sweryd's education has been fundamental in many aspects of his job: "My degree helped me to learn the skills I required to be able to listen to people, and observe behaviour in such a way that I am more able to effectively counsel them as to the options they have in arranging a personal and meaningful funeral service."

"There are occasions when people who are terminally ill come in to make their own arrangements prior to their deaths," says Sweryd. "In these cases, having an understanding of the stages of dying is invaluable. By understanding what stage or stages they may be in while meeting with you, it can help as a funeral director to tailor the information you give them to meet their particular need in a way that they can understand it.

"Most often when I am meeting a family, however, the death has already occurred, and I do not see the classic Kübler-Ross stages, as people have progressed through them. However, there are stages of grieving that a family progresses through following a death. The grieving process mirrors the stages of death and dying in many ways, and having studied those stages, both in psychology classes and as a part of the training to become a funeral director, provides a much more in-depth understanding of the stages of grieving."

Although Sweryd never went on to get his master's degree, he feels his psychology degree is an invaluable asset. "The education experience you receive for a psychology degree provides you with many of the tools you need to be an effective funeral director. I would highly recommend this sort of educational background to anyone interested in funeral service, and would look on this type of education as a definite asset in considering someone for a position with our funeral home."

> "In these cases, having an understanding of the stages of dying is invaluable."

Memory Changes in Old Age: Are Older Adults Forgetful?

One of the characteristics most frequently attributed to late adulthood is forgetfulness. How accurate is this assumption?

Most evidence suggests that diminished memory is *not* an inevitable part of the aging process. For instance, research shows that in cultures where older adults are held in high esteem, such as in mainland China, older people are less likely to show memory losses than those living in cultures that expect older people's memory to decline. Similarly, when older people in Western societies are reminded of the advantages of age ("age brings wisdom"), they tend to do better on tests of memory (Levy & Langer, 1994; Levy, 1996).

Even when people do show memory declines during late adulthood, their deficits tend to be limited to particular types of memory. Losses tend to be limited to episodic memories, which relate to specific experiences about our lives. Other types of memories, such as semantic memories (memories of general knowledge and facts) and implicit memories (memories we are not consciously aware of) are largely unaffected by age (Graf, 1990; Russo & Parkin, 1993).

Declines in episodic memories can often be traced to changes in the lives of older adults. For instance, it is not surprising that a retired person who no longer faces the intellectual challenges encountered on the job might well be less practised in using memory or even be less motivated to remember things, leading to an apparent decline in memory. Even if their long-term memory declines, older adults can usually profit from compensatory efforts. When older adults learn to use the kinds of mnemonic strategies described in Chapter 6, they can not only prevent their long-term memory from deteriorating, but can actually improve it (Kotler-Cope & Camp, 1990; Verhaeghen, Marcoen, & Goossens, 1992; West, 1995).

In the past, older adults with severe cases of memory decline, accompanied by other cognitive difficulties, were viewed as suffering from senility. *Senility* is a broad, imprecise term typically applied to older adults who experience progressive deterioration of mental abilities, including memory loss, disorientation to time and place, and general confusion. Though senility was once thought to be an inevitable state that accompanies aging, the label senile is now viewed by gerontologists as having outlived its usefulness. Rather than senility being the cause of certain symptoms, the symptoms are deemed to be caused by some other factor.

Some cases of memory loss, however, are produced by actual disease. For instance, *Alzheimer's disease* is a progressive brain disorder, discussed in Chapter 7, that leads to a gradual and irreversible decline in cognitive abilities. In other cases, the declines are caused by temporary anxiety and depression, which can be successfully treated, or might even be due to overmedication. The danger is that people suffering such symptoms will be labelled "senile" and left untreated, thereby continuing their decline—even though treatment would have been beneficial (Selkoe, 1997).

During late adulthood, people can find fulfillment through their contributions to their community and society by working with others.

In sum, most declines in cognitive functioning in old age are not inevitable. The key to maintaining cognitive skills might lie in intellectual stimulation. Like the rest of us, older adults need a stimulating environment in order to hone and maintain their skills.

The Social World of Late Adulthood: Old but Not Alone

Just as the view that mental declines are an inevitable outcome of old age has proved to be wrong, so has the view that old age inevitably brings loneliness. Most people in late adulthood see themselves as functioning members of society; only a small minority report that loneliness is a serious problem (Binstock & George, 1996).

There is no single way to age successfully. According to the **disengagement theory of aging**, aging produces a gradual withdrawal from the world on physical, psychological, and social levels (Cummings & Henry, 1961). But such disengagement serves an important purpose, providing the opportunity for increased reflectiveness and decreased emotional investment in others at a time of life when social relationships will inevitably be ended by death.

An alternative view of aging is presented by the **activity theory of aging**, which suggests that the people who age most successfully are those who maintain the interests, activities, and level of social interaction they experienced during middle adulthood (Blau, 1973). Albert Kozma of Memorial University in Newfoundland has done extensive research on aging. In terms of physical activity, walking is correlated with reduction of depression and organized exercise programs with increased happiness. This may well be related to the social as well as the physical aspects of the activity (Kozma, Stones, & McNeil, 1991).

Both disengagement and activity can lead to successful aging. Not all people in late adulthood need a life filled with activities and social interaction to be happy; as in every stage of life, there are those who are just as satisfied leading a relatively inactive, solitary existence. There are vast individual differences in how people cope with the aging process.

Regardless of whether people become disengaged or maintain their activities from earlier stages of life, most engage in a process of **life review**, in which they examine and evaluate their lives. Remembering and reconsidering what has occurred in the past, many people in late adulthood come to a better understanding of themselves, sometimes resolving lingering problems and conflicts, and face their lives with greater wisdom and serenity.

Clearly, people in late adulthood are not just marking time until death. Rather, old age is a time of continued growth and development, as important as any other period of life (Butler et al., 1990; Harlow & Cantor, 1996).

disengagement theory of aging: A theory that holds that aging is a gradual withdrawal from the world on physical, psychological, and social levels.

activity theory of aging: A theory that holds that the elderly who age most successfully are those who maintain the interests and activities they had during middle age.

life review: The process in which people in late adulthood examine and evaluate their lives.

What are the five stages that people may go through when they are facing their own death?

Adjusting to Death

At some time in our lives, we all face death—certainly our own, as well as the deaths of friends, loved ones, and even strangers. Although there is nothing more inevitable in life, death remains a frightening, emotion-laden topic. Certainly, little is more stressful than the death of a loved one or the contemplation of our own imminent death, and preparing for death is one of our most crucial developmental tasks (Aiken, 2001).

Not too long ago, talk of death was taboo. The topic was never mentioned to dying people, and gerontologists had little to say about it. That changed, however, with the pioneering work of Elisabeth Kübler-Ross (1969), who brought the subject of death into the open with her observation that those facing impending death tend to move through five broad stages:

- *Denial.* In this first stage, people resist the idea that they are dying. Even if told that their chances for survival are small, they refuse to admit that they are facing death.
- *Anger.* After moving beyond the denial stage, dying people become angry—angry at people around them who are in good health, angry at medical professionals for being ineffective, angry at God.
- *Bargaining.* Anger leads to bargaining, in which the dying try to think of ways to postpone death. They might decide to dedicate their lives to religion if God saves them; they might say, "If only I can live to see my son married, I will accept death then."
- *Depression.* When dying people come to feel that bargaining is of no use, they move to the next stage: depression. They realize that their lives really are coming to an end, leading to what Kübler-Ross calls "preparatory grief" for their own death.
- *Acceptance.* In this last stage, people accept impending death. Usually they are unemotional and uncommunicative; it is as if they have made peace with themselves and are expecting death with no bitterness.

It is important to keep in mind that not everyone experiences each of these stages in the same way and some people may not go through them all. In fact, Kübler-Ross's stages pertain only to people who are fully aware that they are dying and have the time to evaluate their impending death. Furthermore, there are vast differences in how specific individuals react to impending death. The specific cause and duration of dying, as well as the person's sex, age, and personality and the type of support received from family and friends, all have an impact on how people respond to death (Zautra, Reich, & Guarnaccia, 1990; Stroebe, Stroebe, & Hansson, 1993).

Few of us enjoy contemplating death. Yet awareness of its psychological aspects and consequences can make its inevitable arrival less anxiety-producing and perhaps more understandable.

PsychLink

Death and dying in America
www.mcgrawhill.ca/college/feldman

Evaluate

1. _____ _____ theories suggest that there is a maximum time limit in which cells are able to reproduce. This time limit explains the eventual breakdown of the body during old age.

2. In contrast to the above theories, _____ - _____ - _____ theories state that the body simply becomes less efficient as time passes.

3. Lower IQ test scores during late adulthood do not necessarily mean a decrease in intelligence. True or false?

4. During old age, a person's _____ intelligence continues to increase, through _____ intelligence might decline.

5. Lavinia feels that, in her old age, she has gradually decreased her social contacts and has become more self-oriented. A proponent of _____ theory interprets the situation as a result of Lavinia's not maintaining her past interests. A supporter of _____ theory views her behaviour in a more positive light, suggesting that it is a natural process accompanied by enhanced reflectiveness and declining emotional investment.

6. In Kübler-Ross's _____ stage, people resist the idea of death. In the _____ stage, they attempt to make deals to avoid death, and in the _____ stage, they passively await death.

Answers to Evaluate Questions

1. Genetic preprogramming 2. wear-and-tear 3. True 4. crystallized; fluid 5. activity; disengagement 6. denial; bargaining; acceptance

Rethink

1. Is the possibility that life might be extended for several decades a mixed blessing? What societal consequences might an extended life span bring about?

2. It has been found that people in late adulthood require intellectual stimulation. Does this have implications for the societies in which older people live? In what way might stereotypes about older individuals contribute to their isolation and lack of intellectual stimulation?

Looking Back

How do psychologists study the influences of hereditary and environmental factors in development?

- Developmental psychology is the branch of psychology that studies growth and change throughout life. One fundamental question is how much developmental change is due to heredity and how much is due to environment—the nature-nurture issue. Heredity seems to define the upper limits of our growth and change, whereas the environment affects the degree to which the upper limits are reached. (p. 290)
- Cross-sectional research compares people of different ages with one another at the same point in time. Longitudinal research traces the behaviour of one or more participants as the participants become older. Finally, cross-sequential research combines the two methods by taking several different age groups and examining them over several points in time. (p. 293)

What is the nature of development prior to birth?

- At the moment of conception, a male's sperm cell and a female's egg cell unite, with each contributing to the new individual's genetic makeup. The union of sperm and egg produces a zygote, which contains 23 pairs of chromosomes—with one member of each pair coming from the father and the other from the mother. Each chromosome contains genes, through which genetic information is transmitted. Genes, which are composed of DNA sequences, are the "software" that programs the future development of the body's hardware. (p. 294)
- Genes affect not only physical attributes but also a wide array of personal characteristics, such as cognitive abilities, personality traits, and psychological disorders. (p. 294)
- After 2 weeks the zygote becomes an embryo. By 8 weeks, the embryo has become a fetus and is responsive to touch and other stimulation. At about 24 weeks it reaches the age of viability, which means it might survive if born prematurely. A fetus is normally born after 38 weeks of pregnancy, weighing around 3 kilograms and measuring about 50 centimetres. (p. 295)

What factors affect a child during the mother's pregnancy?

- Genetic abnormalities produce birth defects such as phenylketonuria (PKU), sickle-cell anemia, Tay-Sachs disease, and Down syndrome. Among the prenatal environmental influences on fetal growth are the mother's nutrition, illnesses, drug intake, and birth complications. (p. 297)

What are the major competencies of newborns?

- Newborns, or neonates, have rooting, sucking, gag, startle, and Babinski reflexes. (p. 299)
- Sensory abilities also increase rapidly; infants can distinguish colour, depth, sound, tastes, and smells relatively soon after birth. (p. 300)

What are the milestones of physical and social development during childhood?

- After birth, physical development is rapid; children typically triple their weight in their first year. (p. 302)
- Social development in infancy is marked by the phenomenon of attachment—the positive emotional bond between a child and a particular individual. Attachment is measured in the laboratory using the Ainsworth strange situation and is related to later social and emotional adjustment. (p. 303)

- As children become older, the nature of their social interactions with peers changes. Initially children play relatively independently, but their play becomes increasingly cooperative. (p. 305)
- The different child-rearing styles include authoritarian, permissive, authoritative, and uninvolved. (p. 306)
- According to Erikson, eight stages of psychosocial development involve people's changing interactions and understanding of themselves and others. During childhood, the four stages are trust versus mistrust (birth to 18 months), autonomy versus shame and doubt (18 months to 3 years), initiative versus guilt (3 to 6 years), and industry versus inferiority (6 to 12 years). (p. 307)

How does cognitive development proceed during childhood?

- Piaget's theory suggests that cognitive development proceeds through four stages in which qualitative changes occur in thinking: the sensorimotor stage (birth to 2 years), the preoperational stage (2 to 7 years), the concrete operational stage (7 to 12 years), and the formal operational period (12 years to adulthood). (p. 308)
- Although Piaget's theory has had an enormous influence, some theorists suggest that development is more continuous and that the changes occurring within and between stages are reflective of quantitative advances in cognitive development rather than qualitative changes in thinking. (p. 312)
- Information-processing approaches suggest that quantitative changes occur in children's ability to organize and manipulate information about the world, such as significant increases in speed of processing, attention span, and memory. In addition, there are advances in metacognition, the awareness and understanding of one's own cognitive processes. (p. 312)
- Vygotsky argued that children's cognitive development occurs as a consequence of social interactions in which children and others work together to solve problems. (p. 314)

What major physical, social, and cognitive transitions characterize adolescence?

- Adolescence, the developmental stage between childhood and adulthood, is marked by the onset of puberty, or sexual maturation. The age at which they enter puberty affects how people view themselves and how they are seen by others. (p. 315)
- Moral judgments during adolescence increase in sophistication, according to Kohlberg's three-level model. Although Kohlberg's levels are an adequate description of males' moral judgments, Gilligan suggests that women view morality in terms of caring for individuals rather than in terms of broad, general principles of justice. (p. 317)
- According to Erikson's model of psychosocial development, adolescence can be accompanied by an identity crisis. Adolescence is followed by three stages of psychosocial development that cover the remainder of the life span. (p. 318)

What are the principal kinds of physical, social, and intellectual changes that occur in early and middle adulthood, and what are their causes?

- Early adulthood marks the peak of physical health. Physical changes occur relatively gradually in men and women during early and middle adulthood. (p. 322)
- One major physical change occurs at the end of middle adulthood for women: They begin menopause, after which they are no longer fertile. (p. 322)
- During middle adulthood, people typically experience a midlife transition in which the notion that life is not unending becomes more important. In some

cases this can lead to a midlife crisis, although the passage into middle age is typically relatively calm. (p. 323)

- As aging continues during middle adulthood, people realize in their fifties that their lives and accomplishments are fairly well set, and they try to come to terms with them. (p. 323)

- The most important developmental milestones of adulthood include marriage, family changes, and divorce. Another important determinant of adult development is work. (p. 323)

How does the reality of old age differ from the stereotypes about the period?

- Old age can bring marked physical declines, caused by genetic preprogramming or physical wear and tear. Although the activities of people in late adulthood are not all that different from those of younger people, older adults do experience declines in reaction time, sensory abilities, and physical stamina. (p. 326)

- Intellectual declines are not an inevitable part of aging. Fluid intelligence does decline with age, and long-term memory abilities are sometimes impaired. In contrast, crystallized intelligence shows slight increases with age, and short-term memory remains at about the same level. (p. 326)

- Disengagement theory sees successful aging as a process accompanied by gradual withdrawal from the physical, psychological, and social worlds. In contrast, activity theory suggests that the maintenance of interests and activities from earlier years leads to successful aging. (p. 329)

How can we adjust to death?

- According to Kübler-Ross, dying people move through five stages as they face death: denial, anger, bargaining, depression, and acceptance. (p. 330)

Key Terms and Concepts

developmental psychology (p. 290)
nature–nurture issue (p. 291)
identical twins (p. 292)
cross-sectional research (p. 293)
longitudinal research (p. 293)
cross-sequential research (p. 293)
chromosomes (p. 294)
genes (p. 294)
zygote (p. 294)
embryo (p. 295)
fetus (p. 295)
age of viability (p. 296)
teratogens (p. 297)
neonate (p. 299)
reflexes (p. 300)
habituation (p. 301)
attachment (p. 303)
authoritarian parents (p. 306)
permissive parents (p. 306)
authoritative parents (p. 306)
uninvolved parents (p. 306)
temperament (p. 307)
psychosocial development (p. 307)

trust-versus-mistrust stage (p. 307)
autonomy-versus-shame-and-doubt
    stage (p. 307)
initiative-versus-guilt stage (p. 308)
industry-versus-inferiority stage (p. 308)
cognitive development (p. 309)
schemas (p. 309)
assimilate (p. 309)
accommodate (p. 309)
sensorimotor stage (p. 309)
object permanence (p. 310)
preoperational stage (p. 310)
egocentric thought (p. 310)
principle of conservation (p. 310)
concrete operational stage (p. 310)
formal operational stage (p. 312)
information processing (p. 313)
metacognition (p. 313)
zone of proximal development (ZPD) (p. 314)
adolescence (p. 315)
puberty (p. 316)
identity-versus-role-confusion stage (p. 318)
identity (p. 318)

Psychology on the Web

1. On the Web, check out the current status of the Human Genome Project. Find a picture of part of the genetic map the project is creating, download it, and print it out. Summarize the current status of the project.
2. Find different answers to the question "Why do people die?" Search the Web for scientific, philosophical, and spiritual/religious answers. Write a summary in which you compare the different approaches to this question. Does the thinking in any one realm influence the thinking in the others? How?

Epilogue

We have traced major events in human development across the life span, including changes in physical, social, and cognitive abilities. It is clear that children advance rapidly after birth in all these areas, developing abilities upon which they build further in adolescence and later life. We also observed that development continues throughout the life span, even into old age.

As we explored each area of development, we encountered anew the nature-nurture issue, concluding in every significant instance that both nature and nurture contribute to a person's development of skills, personality, and interactions. Specifically, our genetic inheritance—nature—lays down general boundaries within which we can advance and grow, and our environment helps determine the extent to which we take advantage of our potential.

Our consideration of development included a look at the major theories of development, especially Erik Erikson's theory of psychosocial development, Jean Piaget's theory of cognitive development, and Lev Vygotsky's theory of cognitive development, Kohlberg's theory of moral development, and Gilligan's corresponding theory for women.

Before proceeding to the next chapter, turn once again to the prologue that introduced this one, on Elizabeth Carr, who was conceived using in vitro fertilization. Using your knowledge of human development, consider the following questions.

1. Do you think there is any way Elizabeth Carr's birth, infancy, and development differ from those of her classmates who were not conceived through in vitro fertilization? Why or why not?
2. How would you design a longitudinal study of the development of individuals who were conceived through in vitro fertilization? What sorts of questions would this type of study help you answer?
3. What sorts of questions could you examine through a cross-sectional study? A cross-sequential study?
4. If a future Elizabeth Carr were *cloned* from one of her parents, do you think she would turn out to be exactly like that parent, or different in some ways? Why?

For extra help in mastering the material in this chapter, see the integrator, practice quizzes, and other resources on the Online Learning Centre at

www.mcgrawhill.ca/college/feldman

Chapter Ten

Personality

Anna Mae Pictou-Aquash was found shot to death in 1976. The person or persons responsible remain unidentified, and more questions about who Anna Mae was have been raised than answered in the ensuing investigation.

Prologue

Who Was Anna Mae?

Anna Mae Pictou-Aquash was born on the Pictou Landing Mi'kmaq Reserve in Nova Scotia. She attended local schools until the end of ninth grade. She moved to Boston in her late teens, worked in an autoplant and a sewing factory, married another Mi'kmaq, and had two children, Denise and Deborah. Her daughters remember her as a loving mother and a woman with many interests. One of these interests involved teaching at Native centres in Boston.

Anna Mae rose rapidly in the American Indian Movement (AIM). Sometimes she took her young daughters to participate in marches and demonstrations. At one point she left the girls with a relative in Boston while she and the man who became her second husband, Nogeeshik Aquash, travelled west to the Badlands of South Dakota, moving supplies (including firearms) past law officers to members of the AIM. She travelled throughout various parts of Canada and the United States, made friends and enemies within the AIM, and had several run-ins with the law.

Anna Mae was shot to death and her body was found in 1976 on the Pine Ridge Reservation in South Dakota. Rumours sprang up shortly afterwards. According to some, AIM members who thought she was an FBI informant shot her; according to others, persons who were connected to the FBI killed her.

Looking Ahead

Was Anna Mae a loving mother of two daughters who was simply determined to live her life according to what she considered to be her rights? Or was she an activist who was determined to raise the consciousness of Americans in an effort to improve the lot of her people? Or was she a fugitive from the law who refused to respect and abide by it?

Many people, like Anna Mae, have different sides to their personalities, appearing one way to some people and quite differently to others. At the same time, you probably know people whose behaviour is so consistent that you can easily predict how they are going to behave, no matter what the situation.

Psychologists who specialize in personality seek to understand the characteristic ways in which people behave. Personality is the pattern of enduring characteristics that differentiates a person—those patterns of behaviours that make each of us unique. It is also personality that leads us to act consistently and predictably in different situations and over extended periods of time.

In this chapter we consider a number of approaches to personality. We begin with the earliest comprehensive theory: Freud's psychoanalytic theory. Next, we turn to more recent theories of personality. We consider approaches that concentrate on identifying the most fundamental personality traits; on theories that view personality as a set of learned behaviours; on biological and evolutionary perspectives on personality; and on approaches, known as humanistic theories, that highlight the uniquely human aspects of personality. We end our discussion by focusing on how personality is measured and how personality tests can be used.

personality: The pattern of enduring characteristics that differentiates a person—the patterns of behaviours that make each individual unique.

Prepare

How do psychologists define and use the concept of personality?

What do the theories of Freud and his successors tell us about the structure and development of personality?

Organize

Psychoanalytic Approaches to Personality
    Freud's Psychoanalytic Theory
    The Neo-Freudian Psychoanalysts

Psychoanalytic Approaches to Personality

The college student was intent on making a good first impression on an attractive woman he had spotted across a crowded room at a party. As he walked toward her, he mulled over a line he had heard in an old movie the night before: "I don't believe we've been properly introduced yet." To his horror, what came out was a bit different. After threading his way through the crowded room, he finally reached the woman and blurted out, "I don't believe we've been properly seduced yet."

Although this student's error might seem to be merely an embarrassing slip of the tongue, according to one group of personality theorists—*psychoanalysts*—such a mistake is not an error at all (Motley, 1987). Instead, it illustrates one way our behaviour is triggered by forces within personality of which we are not aware. These hidden drives, shaped by childhood experiences, play an important role in energizing and directing our everyday behaviour.

Freud's Psychoanalytic Theory

psychoanalytic theory: Freud's theory that unconscious forces act as determinants of personality.

unconscious: A part of the personality of which a person is not aware, and which is a potential determinant of behaviour.

Sigmund Freud, an Austrian physician, originated **psychoanalytic theory** in the early 1900s. Freud believed that conscious experience was just the tip of our psychological makeup and experience. In fact, he thought that much of our behaviour is motivated by the **unconscious**, a part of the personality of which a person is not aware.

Like the unseen mass of a floating iceberg, the material in the unconscious far surpasses in quantity the information of which we are aware. Freud argued that to understand personality, it is necessary to expose what is in the unconscious. But because the unconscious disguises the meaning of the material it holds, the content of the unconscious cannot be observed directly. It is therefore necessary to interpret clues to the unconscious—slips of the tongue, fantasies, and dreams—in order to understand the unconscious processes that direct behaviour. A slip of the tongue such as the one quoted earlier (sometimes termed a *Freudian slip*) might be interpreted as revealing the speaker's unconscious sexual desires.

To Freud, much of our personality is determined by our unconscious. Some of the unconscious is made up of the *preconscious,* which contains material that is not threatening and is easily brought to mind, such as the knowledge that 2 + 2 = 4. But deeper in the unconscious are instinctual drives, the wishes, desires, demands, and needs that are hidden from conscious awareness because of the conflicts and pain they would cause us if they were part of our everyday lives. The unconscious provides a "safe haven" for our recollections of threatening events.

Structuring Personality: Id, Ego, and Superego

To describe the structure of personality, Freud developed a comprehensive theory, which held that personality consists of three separate but interacting components: the id, the ego, and the superego. Freud suggested that the three structures can be diagrammed to show how they are related to the conscious and the unconscious (see Figure 10-1).

Although it might appear that Freud is describing the three components of personality as actual physical structures in the nervous system, they are not. Instead, they represent abstract conceptions of a general *model* of personality that describes the interaction of forces that motivate behaviour.

If personality consisted only of primitive, instinctual cravings and longings, it would have just one component: the id. The **id** is the raw, unorganized, inborn part of personality. From the time of birth, the id attempts to reduce tension created by primitive drives related to hunger, sex, aggression, and irrational impulses. These drives are fuelled by "psychic energy" or *libido* as Freud called it.

The id operates according to the *pleasure principle,* in which the goal is the immediate reduction of tension and the maximization of satisfaction. However, reality prevents the fulfillment of the demands of the pleasure principle in most cases: We cannot always eat when we are hungry, and we can discharge our sexual drives only when time, place— and partner—are willing. To account for this fact of life, Freud suggested a second component of personality, which he called the ego.

The **ego** strives to balance the desires of the id and the realities of the objective, outside world. In contrast to the pleasure-seeking nature of the id, the ego operates according to the *reality principle,* in which instinctual energy is restrained in order to maintain the safety of the individual and help integrate the person into society. In a sense, then, the ego is the "executive" of personality: It makes decisions, controls actions, and allows thinking and problem solving of a higher order than the id's capabilities permit.

The **superego,** the final personality structure to develop, represents social right and wrong as taught and modelled by a person's parents, teachers, and other significant individuals. The superego has two components, the *conscience* and the *ego-ideal.* The conscience prevents us from behaving in a morally improper way by making us feel guilty if we do wrong, and the ego-ideal, which represents the "perfect person" that we wish we were, motivates us to do what is morally right. The superego helps us control impulses coming from the id, making our behaviour less selfish and more virtuous.

The superego and id share an important feature: Both are unrealistic, in that they do not consider the practical realities imposed by society. The superego, if left to operate without restraint, would create perfectionists, unable to make the compromises that life requires. Similarly, an unrestrained id would create a primitive, pleasure-seeking, thoughtless individual, seeking to fulfill every desire without delay. As a result, the ego must compromise between the demands of the superego and the demands of the id.

Developing Personality: A Stage Approach

Freud also provided us with a view of how personality develops in childhood through a series of stages. The sequence he proposed is noteworthy because it explains how experiences and difficulties during a particular childhood stage might predict specific characteristics in adult personality. The theory is also unique in focusing each stage on the major biological function that Freud assumed to be the focus of pleasure in that stage (see Table 10-1).

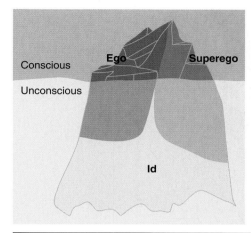

Figure 10-1 In Freud's model of personality, there are three major components: the id, the ego, and the superego. As the iceberg analogy shows, only a small portion of personality is conscious. Why do you think that only the ego and superego have conscious components?

id: The raw, unorganized, inborn part of personality, whose sole purpose is to reduce tension created by primitive drives related to hunger, sex, aggression, and irrational impulses.

ego: The part of the personality that provides a buffer between the id and the outside world.

superego: According to Freud, the final personality structure to develop; it represents society's standards of right and wrong as handed down by a person's parents, teachers, and other important figures.

PsychLink
Freud's works
www.mcgrawhill.ca/college/feldman

Table 10-1 Freud's Stages of Personality Development

Stage	Age	Major Characteristics
Oral	Birth to 12–18 months	Interest in oral gratification from sucking, eating, mouthing, biting
Anal	12–18 months to 3 years	Gratification from expelling and withholding feces; coming to terms with society's controls relating to toilet training
Phallic	3 to 5–6 years	Interest in the genitals; coming to terms with Oedipal conflict, leading to identification with same-sex parent
Latency	5–6 years to adolescence	Sexual concerns largely unimportant
Genital	Adolescence to adulthood	Reemergence of sexual interests and establishment of mature sexual relationships

oral stage: According to Freud, a stage from birth to 12 to 18 months, in which an infant's centre of pleasure is the mouth.

fixation: Conflicts or concerns that persist beyond the developmental period in which they first occur.

anal stage: According to Freud, a stage from 12 to 18 months to 3 years of age, in which a child's pleasure is centred on the anus.

phallic stage: According to Freud, a period beginning around age 3 during which a child's interest focuses on the genitals.

Oedipus conflict: A child's sexual interest in his or her opposite-sex parent, typically resolved through identification with the same-sex parent.

identification: The process of trying to be like another person as much as possible, imitating that person's behaviour and adopting similar beliefs and values.

In the first stage of development, called the **oral stage**, the baby's mouth is the focal point of pleasure. During the first 12 to 18 months of life, children suck, mouth, and bite anything that will fit into their mouths. To Freud, this behaviour suggested that the mouth is the primary site of a kind of sexual pleasure. Infants who are either overly indulged (perhaps by being fed every time they cried) or frustrated in their search for oral gratification might become fixated at this stage. **Fixation** refers to conflicts or concerns that persist beyond the developmental period in which they first occur. Such conflicts can be due to one's needs being either ignored or overly indulged during the earlier period. For example, fixation might occur if an infant's oral needs were constantly immediately gratified at the first sign of hunger. Fixation at the oral stage might produce an adult who is unusually interested in oral activities—eating, talking, smoking—or who shows symbolic sorts of oral interests: being either "bitingly" sarcastic or very gullible ("swallowing" anything).

From around 12 to 18 months until 3 years of age—where the emphasis in Western cultures is on toilet training—the child enters the **anal stage**. At this point, the major source of pleasure changes from the mouth to the anal region, and children obtain considerable pleasure from both retention and expulsion of feces. If toilet training is particularly demanding, the result may be fixation. Freud suggested that adults who are fixated in the anal stage might show unusual rigidity, orderliness, punctuality—or extreme disorderliness or sloppiness.

At about age 3, the **phallic stage** begins, at which point there is another major shift in the primary source of pleasure for the child. This time, interest focuses on the genitals and the pleasures derived from fondling them. This is also the stage of one of the most important points of personality development, according to Freudian theory: the **Oedipus conflict**. As children focus their attention on their genitals, the differences between female and male anatomy become more salient. Furthermore, at this time, according to Freud, the male unconsciously begins to develop sexual interests in his mother, starts to see his father as a rival, and harbours a wish to kill his father—as Oedipus did in the ancient Greek tragedy. But because he views his father as too powerful, he develops a fear of retaliation in the form of "castration anxiety." Ultimately, this fear becomes so powerful that the child represses his desires for his mother and instead identifies with his father. **Identification** is the process of trying to be like another person as much as possible, imitating that person's behaviour and adopting similar beliefs and values. By identifying with his father, a son seeks to obtain a woman like his unattainable mother.

For girls, the process is different. Freud reasoned that girls begin to experience sexual arousal toward their fathers and—in a suggestion that was later to bring serious accusations that he viewed women as inferior to men—that they begin to experience *penis envy:* they wish, said Freud, that they had an anatomical part that, at least to Freud, seems "missing" in girls. Blaming their mothers for their lack of a penis, girls come to believe that their mothers are responsible for their "castration." As with males, though, they find that in order to resolve such unacceptable feelings, they must identify with the same-sex parent by behaving like her and adopting her attitudes and values. In this way, a girl's identification with her mother is completed.

At this point, the Oedipus conflict is said to be resolved, and Freudian theory assumes that both males and females move on to the next stage of development. If difficulties arise during this period, however, all sorts of problems are thought to occur, including improper sex-role behaviour and the failure to develop a conscience.

Following the resolution of the Oedipus conflict, typically at around age 5 or 6, children move into the **latency period**, which lasts until puberty. During this period, sexual interests become dormant, even in the unconscious. Then, during adolescence, sexual feelings reemerge, marking the start of the final period, the **genital stage**, which extends until death. The focus during the genital stage is on mature, adult sexuality, which Freud defined as sexual intercourse.

Imitating a person's behaviour and adopting similar beliefs and values is part of Freud's concept of identification.
How can this concept be applied to the definition of gender roles? Is identification similar in all cultures?

latency period: According to Freud, the period between the phallic stage and puberty during which children temporarily put aside their sexual interests.
genital stage: According to Freud, the period from puberty until death, marked by mature sexual behaviour (i.e., sexual intercourse).

Defence Mechanisms

Freud's efforts to describe and theorize about the underlying dynamics of personality and its development were motivated by very practical problems that his patients faced in dealing with *anxiety,* an intense, negative emotional experience. According to Freud, anxiety is a danger signal to the ego. Although anxiety can arise from realistic fears—such as seeing a poisonous snake about to strike—it can also occur in the form of *neurotic anxiety,* in which irrational impulses emanating from the id threaten to burst through and become uncontrollable.

Because anxiety, obviously, is unpleasant, Freud believed that people develop a range of defence mechanisms to deal with it. **Defence mechanisms** are unconscious strategies people use to reduce anxiety by concealing its source from themselves and others.

The primary defence mechanism is *repression,* in which unacceptable or unpleasant id impulses are pushed back into the unconscious. Repression is the most direct method of dealing with anxiety; instead of handling an anxiety-producing impulse on a conscious level, one simply ignores it. For example, a college student who feels hatred for her mother might repress these personally and socially unacceptable feelings. The feelings remain lodged within the unconscious, because acknowledging them would provoke anxiety. Similarly, memories of childhood abuse can be repressed (discussed in Chapter 6). Although such memories might not be consciously recalled, they can affect later behaviour, and they can be revealed through dreams, slips of the tongue, or symbolically in some other fashion.

If repression is ineffective in keeping anxiety at bay, other defence mechanisms might be used. Freud, and later his daughter Anna Freud (who became a well-known psychoanalyst herself), formulated an extensive list of potential defence mechanisms; the major ones are summarized in Table 10-2 (Cooper, 1989; Conte & Plutchik, 1995; Basch, 1996).

All of us employ defence mechanisms to some degree (try Chapter Activity 10-1), according to Freudian theory, and they can serve a useful purpose by protecting us from unpleasant information. Yet some people use them to such an extent that they must constantly direct a large amount of psychic energy toward hiding and rechannelling unacceptable impulses. This makes everyday living difficult. The result is a mental disorder produced by anxiety—what Freud called "neurosis" (a term rarely used by psychologists today, although it endures in everyday conversation).

defence mechanisms: Unconscious strategies people use to reduce anxiety by concealing the source of the anxiety from themselves and others.

TABLE 10-2 Freud's Defence Mechanisms

Defence Mechanism	Explanation	Example
Repression	Unacceptable or unpleasant impulses are pushed back into the unconscious.	A woman is unable to recall that she was raped.
Regression	People behave as if they were at an earlier stage of development.	A boss has a temper tantrum when an employee makes a mistake.
Displacement	The expression of an unwanted feeling or thought is redirected from a more threatening, powerful person to a weaker one.	A brother yells at his younger sister after a teacher gives him a bad grade.
Rationalization	People distort reality in order to justify something that has happened.	A person who is passed over for an award says she didn't really want it in the first place.
Denial	People refuse to accept or acknowledge an anxiety-producing piece of information.	A student refuses to believe that he has flunked a course.
Projection	People attribute unwanted impulses and feelings to someone else.	A man who is angry at his father acts lovingly to his father but complains that his father is angry with him.
Sublimation	People divert unwanted impulses into socially approved thoughts, feelings, or behaviours.	A person with strong feelings of aggression becomes a soldier.
Reaction formation	Unconscious impulses are expressed as their opposite in consciousness.	A mother who unconsciously resents her child acts in an overly loving way to the child.

Chapter Activity 10–1
Using Defence Mechanisms

Think of some situations in which you have used defence mechanisms. Why did you do so? What was the outcome?

PsychLink

Questioning Freud's theories
www.mcgrawhill.ca/college/feldman

Evaluating Freud's Legacy

Freud's theory has had a significant impact on the field of psychology—and even more broadly on Western philosophy and literature. The ideas of the unconscious, defence mechanisms, and childhood roots of adult psychological difficulties have become accepted by many. Furthermore, Freud's emphasis on the unconscious has been partially supported by current research on dreams (Chapter 4) and implicit memory (Chapter 6), and it has generated an important method of treating psychological disturbances, as we will discuss in Chapter 13 (Westen, 1998; Westen & Gabbard, 1999; Kihlstrom, 1999).

On the other hand, personality psychologists have levelled significant criticisms against the theory. Among the most compelling is the lack of scientific data to support the theory. Although individual case studies *seem* supportive, we lack conclusive evidence showing that the personality is structured and operates along the lines Freud laid out. This is partly due to the fact that Freud's conception of personality is built on unobservable abstract concepts. Moreover, it is difficult to predict how certain developmental difficulties will be displayed in the adult. For instance, a person who is fixated at the anal stage might, according to Freud, be unusually messy—or unusually neat. Freud's theory offers us no way to predict which way the difficulty will be exhibited (Macmillan, 1991; Crews, 1996).

Finally, Freud made his observations—admittedly insightful ones—and derived his theory from a limited population. His theory was based almost entirely on upper-class Austrian women living in the strict, puritanical era of the early 1900s. How far one can generalize beyond this population is a matter of considerable debate. For instance, in some Pacific Island societies, the role of disciplinarian is played by a mother's oldest brother, not the father. In such a culture, it is unreasonable to argue that the Oedipus conflict would progress in the same way as in Freud's Austrian society, where the father typically was the major disciplinarian. In short, a cross-cultural perspective raises questions about the universality of Freud's view of personality development (Doi, 1990; Brislin, 1993; Altman, 1996).

The Neo-Freudian Psychoanalysts

One important outgrowth of Freud's theorizing was the work done by a series of successors who were trained in traditional Freudian theory but who later rejected some of its major points. These theorists are known as **neo-Freudian psychoanalysts**.

The neo-Freudians placed greater emphasis than Freud on the functions of the ego, suggesting that it had more control than the id over day-to-day activities, and less emphasis on sex as a driving force in people's lives. They also paid greater attention to social factors and the effects of society and culture on personality development.

Jung's Collective Unconscious

One of the most influential neo-Freudians, Carl Jung (pronounced "Yoong"), rejected the notion of the primary importance of unconscious sexual urges. Instead he looked at the primitive urges of the unconscious more positively, suggesting that people had a **collective unconscious**, a set of influences we inherit from our own relatives, the whole human race, and even nonhuman animal ancestors from the distant past. According to Jung, this collective unconscious is shared by everyone and is displayed in behaviour that is common across diverse cultures—such as love of mother, belief in a supreme being, and even behaviour as specific as fear of snakes.

Jung went on to propose that the collective unconscious contains *archetypes,* universal symbolic representations of a particular person, object, or experience (Jung, 1961). For instance, a mother archetype, which contains reflections of our ancestors' relationships with mother figures, is suggested by the prevalence of mothers in art, religion, literature, and mythology. (Think of the Virgin Mary, Earth Mother, wicked stepmothers of fairy tales, Mother's Day, and so forth!) Jung also suggested that men possess an unconscious feminine archetype (anima) affecting how they behave, and that women have a male archetype (animus) that colours their behaviour.

To Jung, archetypes play an important role in determining our day-to-day reactions, attitudes, and values. For instance, Jung might argue that the popularity of the *Star Wars* movies is due to their use of broad archetypes of good (such as Luke Skywalker) and evil (such as Darth Vader).

Adler and the Other Neo-Freudians

Alfred Adler, another important neo-Freudian psychoanalyst, also considered Freudian theory's emphasis on sexual needs to be misplaced. Adler proposed instead that the primary human motivation is a striving for superiority, not in terms of superiority over others, but as a quest to achieve self-improvement and perfection.

According to Adler, when adults have not been able to overcome the feelings of inferiority that they developed as children, when they were small and limited in their knowledge about the world, they develop an **inferiority complex**. Early social relationships with parents have an important effect on how well children are able to outgrow feelings of personal inferiority and instead orient themselves toward attaining more socially useful goals, such as improving society.

neo-Freudian psychoanalysts: Psychoanalysts who were trained in traditional Freudian theory but who later rejected some of its major points.

collective unconscious: A set of influences we inherit from our own particular ancestors, the whole human race, and even animal ancestors from the distant evolutionary past.

inferiority complex: According to Adler, a complex developed by adults who have not been able to overcome the feelings of inferiority they developed as children, when they were small and limited in their knowledge about the world.

PsychLink

Jung's theory
www.mcgrawhill.ca/college/feldman

In Jungian terms, Darth Vader and Luke Skywalker are archetypes, or universally recognizable symbols of good and evil.

Other neo-Freudians, such as Erik Erikson (whose theory we discussed in Chapter 9), Freud's own daughter Anna Freud, and Karen Horney (1937), also focused less than Freud on inborn sexual and aggressive drives and more on the social and cultural factors behind personality. Horney (pronounced "HORN-eye") was one of the first psychologists to champion women's issues. She suggested that personality develops in terms of social relationships and depends particularly on the relationship between parents and child and how well the child's needs are met. She rejected Freud's suggestion that women have penis envy, asserting that what women envy most in men is not their anatomy but the independence, success, and freedom that women are often denied.

Evaluate

1. _____ theory states that behaviour is motivated primarily by unconscious forces.
2. Match each section of the personality (according to Freud) with its description:

    1. Ego
    2. Id
    3. Superego

    a. Determines right from wrong on the basis of cultural standards.
    b. Operates according to the "reality principle"; redirects energy to integrate the person into society.
    c. Seeks to reduce tension brought on by primitive drives.

3. Within the superego, the _____-_____ motivates us to do what is right, and the _____ restrains us from doing what is unacceptable.
4. Which of the following represents the proper order of personality development according to Freud?

    a. Oral, phallic, latency, anal, genital
    b. Anal, oral, phallic, genital, latency
    c. Oral, anal, phallic, latency, genital
    d. Latency, phallic, anal, genital, oral

5. In the resolution of the _____ complex, Freud believed, boys learn to repress their desire for their mother and identify with their father.
6. _____ _____ is the term Freud used to describe unconscious strategies used to reduce anxiety.

Answers to Evaluate Questions

1. Psychoanalytic 2. 1-b; 2-c; 3-a 3. ego-ideal; conscience 4. c 5. Oedipus 6. Defence mechanisms

Rethink

1. Can you think of ways in which Freud's theories of unconscious motivations are commonly used in popular culture? How accurately do you think such popular uses of Freudian theories reflect Freud's ideas?
2. What are some examples of archetypes in addition to those mentioned in this chapter? In what ways are archetypes similar to and different from stereotypes?

Prepare

What are the major aspects of trait, learning, biological and evolutionary, and humanistic approaches to personality?

Organize

Other Major Approaches to Personality
  Trait Approaches
  Learning Approaches
  Biological and Evolutionary Approaches
  Humanistic Approaches
  Comparing Approaches to Personality

Other Major Approaches to Personality: In Search of Human Uniqueness

"Tell me about Nelson," said Johnetta.

"Oh, he's just terrific. He's the friendliest guy I know—goes out of his way to be nice to everyone. He hardly ever gets mad. He's just so even-tempered, no matter what's happening. And he's really smart, too. About the only thing I don't like is that he's always in such a hurry to get things done. He seems to have boundless energy, much more than I have."

"He sounds great to me, especially in comparison to Rico," replied Johnetta. "He is so self-centred and arrogant it drives me crazy. I sometimes wonder why I ever started going out with him."

Friendly. Even-tempered. Smart. Energetic. Self-centred. Arrogant.

The interchange above lists a series of trait characterizations of the boyfriends being discussed. In fact, much of our own, personal understanding of the reasons behind others' behaviour is based on the premise that people possess certain traits that are consistent across different situations. For example, we generally assume that a person who is outgoing and sociable in one situation will be outgoing and sociable in other situations (Gilbert et al., 1992; Gilbert, Miller, & Ross, 1998).

A number of formal theories of personality employ variations of this approach. We turn now to a discussion of these and other personality approaches, each of which provides an alternative to the psychoanalytic emphasis on unconscious processes in determining behaviour.

Trait Approaches: Placing Labels on Personality

If someone were to ask you to characterize another person, it is probable that—like the two people in the conversation just presented—you would come up with a list of that individual's personal qualities, as you see them. But how would you know which of these qualities are most important to an understanding of that person's behaviour? For example, we could list qualities that describe Anna Mae Pictou-Aquash, the subject of the prologue of this chapter (e.g., mother, warrior, and activist), but how could we determine which characteristics best describe her personality?

Personality psychologists have asked similar questions themselves. To answer them, they have developed a model of personality known as **trait theory**. **Traits** are enduring dimensions of personality characteristics along which people differ: Trait theorists do not assume that some people have a trait and others do not; rather, they propose that all people possess certain traits, but that each person possesses a given trait to a given degree that can be quantified, and that people can differ in the degree to which they have a trait. For instance, you might be relatively friendly, whereas I might be relatively unfriendly. We both have a "friendliness" trait, although your degree of "friendliness" might be higher than mine. The major challenge for trait theorists taking this approach has been to identify the specific primary traits necessary to describe personality. As we shall see, different theorists have come up with surprisingly different sets of traits.

trait theory: A model of personality that seeks to identify the basic traits necessary to describe personality.

traits Enduring dimensions of personality characteristics along which people differ.

Allport's Trait Theory: Identifying the Basics

When personality psychologist Gordon Allport systematically pored over an unabridged dictionary, he came up with some 18 000 separate terms that could be used to describe personality. Although he was able to pare down the list to a mere 4500 descriptors after eliminating words with the same meaning, he was obviously still left with a problem crucial to all trait approaches: Which of these were the most basic?

Allport answered this question by suggesting that there are three basic categories of traits: cardinal, central, and secondary (Allport, 1961, 1966). A *cardinal trait* is a single characteristic that directs most of a person's activities. For example, a totally selfless woman might direct all her energy toward humanitarian activities; an intensely power-hungry person might be driven by an all-consuming need for control.

Most people, however, do not develop a single, comprehensive cardinal trait. Instead, they possess a handful of central traits that make up the core of personality. *Central traits,* such as honesty and sociability, are the major characteristics of an individual; most people have five to ten central traits. Finally, *secondary traits* are characteristics that affect an individual's behaviour in fewer situations and are less influential than central or cardinal traits. For instance, a reluctance to eat meat or a love of modern art would be considered secondary traits.

Cattell, Eysenck, and the Big Five: Factoring Out Personality

More recent attempts to identify primary traits have centred on a statistical technique known as factor analysis. *Factor analysis* is a method of summarizing the relationships among a large number of variables into fewer, more general patterns. For example, a personality researcher might administer a questionnaire to many participants, asking them to describe themselves by referring to an extensive list of traits. By statistically combining responses and computing which traits are associated with one another in the same person, a researcher can identify the most fundamental patterns or combinations of traits—called factors—that underlie participants' responses.

Using factor analysis, personality psychologist Raymond Cattell (1965) suggested that 16 pairs of *source traits* represent the basic dimensions of personality. Using these source traits, he developed the Sixteen Personality Factor Questionnaire, or 16 PF, a measure that provides scores for each of the source traits. Figure 10-2 shows the pattern of average scores on each of the source traits for three different groups of participants—airplane pilots, creative artists, and writers (Cattell, Cattell, & Cattell, 1993).

Another trait theorist, psychologist Hans Eysenck (1975, 1994a; Eysenck et al., 1992), also used factor analysis to identify patterns of traits, but he came to a very different conclusion about the nature of personality. He found that personality could best be described in terms of just three major dimensions: *extraversion, neuroticism,* and *psychoticism.* The extraversion dimension relates to the degree of sociability; the neurotic dimension encompasses emotional stability; psychoticism refers to the degree to which reality is distorted. By evaluating people along these three dimensions, Eysenck has been able to predict behaviour accurately in a variety of types of situations. Figure 10-3 illustrates specific traits associated with each of the dimensions.

The most influential trait approach today contends that five broad trait factors—called the "Big Five"—lie at the core of personality. The five factors are *openness to experience, conscientiousness, extraversion, agreeableness,* and *neuroticism* (emotional stability). (These are described in Table 10-3. The characteristics listed on the right portray people who would measure high on each factor. The words on the left describe people who would measure low on each factor. You can remember the five factors using the mnemonic *OCEAN,* representing the first letter of each trait).

The Big Five factors emerge quite consistently in different populations of individuals, including children, college students, older adults, and speakers of different languages. Furthermore, cross-cultural research conducted in countries as diverse as Canada, Finland, Poland, and the Philippines is also supportive. In short, although the evidence

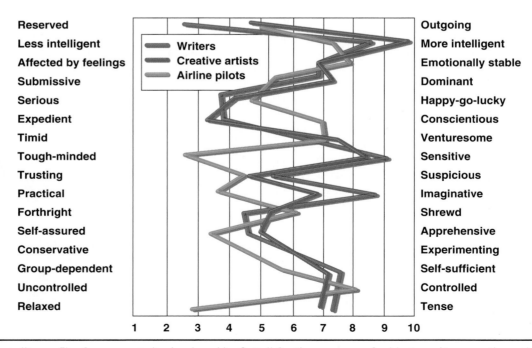

Figure 10-2 Personality profiles for source traits developed by Cattell for three groups of subjects: writers, creative artists, and airline pilots. The average score for the general population is between 4.5 and 6.5 on each scale (Cattell, Eber, & Tatsuoka, 1970). On what traits do airline pilots and writers differ most? How do these differences contribute to their chosen work?

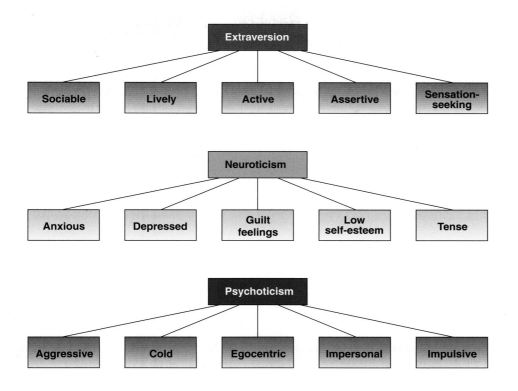

Figure 10-3 According to Eysenck, personality could best be described in terms of just three major dimensions; extraversion, neuroticism, and psychoticism. Eysenck has been able to predict behaviour accurately in a variety of types of situations by evaluating people along these three dimensions (Eysenck, 1990). How do you think an airline pilot would score on Eysenck's scale?

is not conclusive, a growing consensus exists that the "Big Five" represent the best description of personality.

Still, the debate over the specific number and kinds of traits that are fundamental to personality remains a lively one (McCrae & Costa, 1999; John & Srivastava, 1999; Saggino, 2000). For instance, Ashton and his colleagues have recently argued that there is a sixth major dimension, honesty, and supported their view with evidence from several cultures (Ashton et al., 2000; Ashton & Lee, 2001). Other researchers have also suggested that there is a sixth main factor, but they do not agree on what it is (Jackson et al., 1996; Cheung & Leung, 1998). In addition, some disagreement about the components or facets of the major factors exists. For example, is the key element in extraversion social attention (Ashton et al., 2002) or reward sensitivity (Lucas et al., 2000)?

Evaluating Trait Approaches to Personality

Trait approaches have several virtues. They provide a clear, straightforward explanation of people's behavioural consistencies. Traits are useful in studying people's everyday lives (Wiggins & Pincus, 1992). For example, in their review article of research on self-enhancement and its implications for the workplace, Robins and Paulhus (2001) point out that the trait of self-enhancement has both advantages and disadvantages in the work-place. Self-enhancers tend to perceive and describe themselves in overly positive terms. They make good first impressions and they are likely to succeed in jobs where the ability to connect with new contacts is important. They are also likely to do well in positions where a belief in the importance of one's own ideas is adaptive or advantageous, since success seems to come more easily where there is a "good fit" between personal characteristics and job requirements. However, their manipulative behaviour and pushing for recognition may interfere with group cooperation and productivity as well as with building relationships with subordinates. And their good first impressions tend to deteriorate into unfavourable later impressions. Furthermore, traits allow us to readily compare one person with another. Because of these advantages, trait approaches to personality have had an important practical influence on the development of several personality measures discussed later in this chapter (Funder, 1991; Wiggins, 1997).

Table 10-3 The Big Five Personality Factors and Dimensions of Sample Traits

Openness to experience	
Commonplace	Wide interests
Narrow interests	Imaginative
Simple	Intelligent
Shallow	Original

Conscientiousness	
Careless	Organized
Disorderly	Thorough
Frivolous	Planful
Irresponsible	Efficient

Extraversion	
Quiet	Talkative
Reserved	Assertive
Shy	Active
Silent	Energetic

Agreeableness	
Fault-finding	Sympathetic
Cold	Kind
Unfriendly	Appreciative
Quarrelsome	Affectionate

Neuroticism	
Stable	Tense
Calm	Anxious
Contented	Nervous
Unemotional	Moody

Source: Adapted from Pervin (1990), Chapter 3.

On the other hand, trait approaches have some drawbacks. A fundamental problem for some psychologists is that traits label or describe personality, but they do not explain it. Describing someone as altruistic does not tell why that person helps others or the reasons for helping in a particular situation. Other researchers (Paunonen & Ashton, 2001a; Paunonen et al., 2001) have pointed out that reliance on measures of the Big Five factors without also assessing their component traits is unwise because it may result in decreased understanding of behaviour and decreased ability to predict behaviour. Paunonen and Ashton (2001b) found that measures of the needs for achievement and understanding (component traits) were better indicators of academic performance than measures of conscientiousness and openness to experience (Big Five traits). Similarly, Ashton and his colleagues (Ashton et al., 1995) found that sociability and impulse control (component traits) were better predictors of fun-seeking behaviours (e.g., party-going, sports participation) than extraversion and conscientiousness (Big Five traits).

Learning Approaches: We Are What We've Learned

The psychoanalytic and trait approaches we've discussed concentrate on the "inner" person—the stormy fury of an unobservable but powerful id or a hypothetical but critical set of traits. In contrast, learning approaches to personality focus on the "outer" person. To a strict learning theorist, personality is simply the sum of learned responses to the external environment—internal events such as thoughts, feelings, and motivations are irrelevant. Although they don't deny the existence of personality, learning theorists say that it is best understood by looking at features of a person's environment.

According to the most influential of the learning theorists, B. F. Skinner (whom we discussed first in terms of operant conditioning in Chapter 5), personality is a collection of learned behaviour patterns (Skinner, 1975). Similarities in responses across different situations are caused by similar patterns of reinforcement that have been received in such situations in the past. If I am sociable both at parties and at meetings, it is because I have been reinforced previously for displaying social behaviours—not because I am fulfilling some unconscious wish based on experiences during my childhood or because I have an internal trait of sociability.

Strict learning theorists such as Skinner are less interested in the consistencies in behaviour across situations, however, than in ways of modifying behaviour. Their view is that humans are infinitely changeable through the process of learning new behaviour patterns. If one is able to control and modify the patterns of reinforcers in a situation, behaviour that other theorists would view as stable and unyielding can be changed and ultimately improved. Learning theorists are optimistic in their attitudes about the potential for resolving personal and societal problems through treatment strategies based on learning theory—methods we will discuss in Chapter 13.

Social Cognitive Approaches to Personality

social cognitive approaches to personality: The theory that emphasizes the influence of a person's cognitions—thoughts, feelings, expectations, and values—in determining personality.

Not all learning theories of personality take such a strict view in rejecting the importance of what is "inside" the person by focusing solely on the "outside." Unlike other learning approaches to personality, **social cognitive approaches** emphasize the influence of a person's cognitions—thoughts, feelings, expectations, and values—in determining personality. For example, knowing more about Anna Mae Pictou-Aquash's thoughts, feelings, expectations and values would help us to understand her complex personality and lifestyle.

According to Albert Bandura, one of the main proponents of the social-cognitive perspective, external factors (e.g., rewards, punishments), internal factors (e.g., thoughts, expectations), and behaviour are all parts of an interacting system. Changes in any one of the parts will influence the other two. For example, consequences of a behaviour will affect our beliefs and expectations as well as the likelihood of repeating the behaviour. This model of personality is called *reciprocal determinism* (see Figure 10-4).

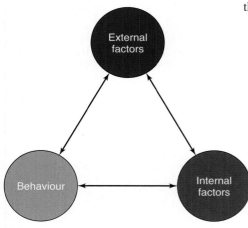

Figure 10–4 Bandura's reciprocal determinism model of personality.

One of Bandura's most important contributions to psychology is his work on the concept of *observational learning*. Through the mechanism of observational learning, people learn by viewing the actions of others and observing their consequences (Bandura, 1986, 1999). People are able to foresee the possible outcomes of behaviours in a given setting without actually having to carry them out.

For instance, as we first discussed in Chapter 5, children who view a model behaving in, say, an aggressive manner tend to copy the behaviour if the consequences of the model's behaviour are seen to be positive. If, on the other hand, the model's aggressive behaviour has resulted in no consequences or negative consequences, children are considerably less likely to act aggressively. According to social cognitive approaches, personality thus develops by repeated observation of the behaviour of others.

Bandura places particular emphasis on the role played by *self-efficacy,* belief in one's own personal capabilities. Self-efficacy underlies people's faith in their ability to carry out a particular behaviour or produce a desired outcome. People with high self-efficacy have higher aspirations and greater persistence in working to attain goals, and ultimately achieve greater success, than those with lower self-efficacy (Scheier & Carver, 1992; Bandura, 1997, 1999).

How do we develop self-efficacy? One way is by paying close attention to our prior successes and failures. If we try snowboarding and experience little success, we'll be less likely to try it again. However, if our initial efforts appear promising, we'll be more likely to attempt it again. Direct reinforcement and encouragement from others also play a role in developing self-efficacy (Bandura, 1988; Jenkins & Gortner, 1998).

Compared to other learning theories of personality, social cognitive approaches are distinctive in their emphasis on the reciprocity between individuals and their environment. These approaches assume not only that the environment affects personality, but also that people's behaviour and personalities give "feedback" to and modify the environment (Bandura, 1999, 2000).

Our behaviour also reflects the view we have of ourselves and our valuations of the various parts of our personality. *Self-esteem* is the component of personality that encompasses our positive and negative self-evaluations. Although people have a general level of self-esteem, it is not unidimensional. Specifically, we could see ourselves positively in one domain but negatively in others. For example, a good student might have high self-esteem in academic domains but more negative self-esteem in athletic areas (Moretti & Higgins, 1990; Baumeister, 1998).

Self-esteem has strong cultural components. For example, having high *relationship harmony*—a sense of success in forming close bonds with other people—is more important to self-esteem in Asian cultures than in more individualistic Western societies (Kwan, Bond, & Singelis, 1997).

Although almost everyone goes through periods of low self-esteem (after, for instance, an undeniable failure), some people are chronically low in self-esteem. For them, failure seems to be an inevitable part of life. Low self-esteem can lead to a cycle of failure, in which past failure breeds future failure. For example, consider students with low self-esteem who are studying for a test. Because of their low self-esteem, they expect to do poorly on the test. In turn, this raises their anxiety level, making it increasingly difficult to study and perhaps even leading them to work less hard. Because of these attitudes, the ultimate outcome is that they do, in fact, do badly on the test. Ultimately, this failure reinforces their low self-esteem, and the cycle is perpetuated, as illustrated in Figure 10-5.

In short, low self-esteem can lead to a self-destructive cycle of failure. On the other hand, high self-esteem can also be of concern. As you can see in the *Applying Psychology in the 21st Century* box on p. 351, high self-esteem, particularly if it is unwarranted, can produce problems.

Self-efficacy, the belief in one's own personal capabilities, leads to higher aspirations and greater persistence.

PsychLink
Self-efficacy and culture
www.mcgrawhill.ca/college/feldman

Evaluating Learning Approaches to Personality

Because they ignore the internal processes that are uniquely human, traditional learning theorists such as Skinner have been accused of so oversimplifying personality that the

Figure 10-5 The cycle of low self-esteem begins with an individual who has low self-esteem. The person will have low performance expectations and expect to fail a test, thereby producing anxiety and reduced effort. As a result, the person will actually fail, which in turn reinforces the low self-esteem.

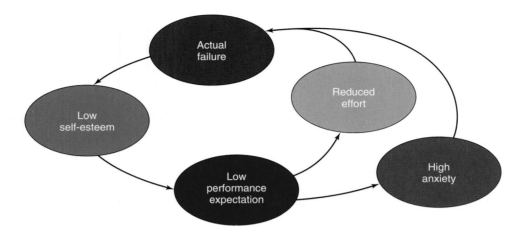

biological and evolutionary approaches to personality: The theory that important components of personality are inherited.

concept becomes meaningless. In the eyes of their critics, reducing behaviour to a series of stimuli and responses, and excluding thoughts and feelings from the realm of personality, leaves behaviourists practising an unrealistic and inadequate form of science.

Of course, some of these criticisms are blunted by social cognitive approaches, which explicitly consider the role of cognitive processes in personality. Still, learning approaches tend to share a highly *deterministic* view of human behaviour, seeing it as shaped primarily by forces beyond the control of the individual. According to some critics, determinism disregards our ability to pilot our own courses through life.

On the other hand, learning approaches have had a major impact in a variety of ways. For one thing, they have helped make the study of personality an objective, scientific venture by focusing on observable behaviour and environment. In addition, they have produced important, successful means of treating personality disorders. The degree of success these treatments have enjoyed is testimony to the merits of learning theory approaches to personality.

Biological and Evolutionary Approaches: Are We Born with Personality?

Do we inherit our personality?

That's the question raised by **biological and evolutionary approaches to personality**, which suggest that important components of personality are inherited. Building on the work of behavioural geneticists (first discussed in Chapter 2), researchers using biological and evolutionary approaches argue that personality is determined at least in part by particular combinations of genes, in much the same way that our height is largely a result of genetic contributions from our ancestors (Plomin & McClearn, 1993; Buss, 1999).

The importance of genetic factors in personality has been illustrated by studies of twins. For instance, personality psychologists Auke Tellegen and colleagues at the University of Minnesota examined the personality traits of pairs of twins who were genetically identical but raised apart from each other (Tellegen et al., 1988). Results indicated that in major respects the twins were quite similar in personality. However, some traits were more influenced by heredity than others. For example, social potency had particularly strong genetic components, whereas social closeness had relatively weak genetic components (see Figure 10-6 on p. 352).

In a study of the sources of personality differences in identical twins and siblings, Canadian psychologist Philip Vernon and his colleagues found that extraversion and openness were highly heritable personality traits. Autonomy was the least heritable of the Big Five factors, and both heredity and environmental factors influenced neuroticism and conscientiousness (Vernon et al., 1997). In another twin study out of the University of British Columbia, Kerry Jang and John Livesley and their colleagues found that genetic influences as well as environmental factors contribute to individual differences in the character traits that make up the Big Five factors (Jang et al., 1998).

Applying Psychology in the 21st Century

Can Unjustified High Self-Esteem Lead to Violence?

One societal belief widely held at the start of the twenty-first century is that we should do everything we can to nurture people's self-esteem. High self-esteem is usually viewed as a forerunner of success and accomplishment, and low self-esteem is seen as a problem to be remedied.

But not everyone agrees. According to psychologists Brad Bushman and Roy Baumeister (1998), not only can high self-esteem be psychologically damaging to the person who holds it—it can lead to violence if that self-esteem is unjustified by actual accomplishments. These researchers suggest not only that some people who turn to violence see themselves in a positive light, but that their positive view of themselves is exaggerated. Even in the face of events that would typically lead to lower self-esteem—such as school or work failure—such individuals maintain positive views of themselves, and ultimately this unwarrantedly positive self-esteem leads to violence.

This view of violent personalities suggests that when people with unjustified high self-esteem (a condition known as *narcissism*) feel challenged, or threatened by others, they react vigorously—and often violently—by seeking to maintain their positive view of themselves. In contrast, people with lower self-esteem who are challenged or threatened simply see the challenge or threat as confirming their lower self-esteem; and those with high, but justified, self-esteem are able to ignore challenges and threats (Baumeister, Bushman, & Campbell, 2000).

Results of experiments support this view. For example, Bushman and Baumeister (1998) asked participants in a study to write an essay, which, for some, was greatly criticized. The participants then were asked to play a game that gave them the opportunity to blast loud noise at an opponent—a measure of aggression. The results showed that participants with high unjustified narcissistic self-esteem who had been criticized showed significantly more aggression to their opponents than those with justified high self-esteem.

These findings have direct relevance to social programs that uncritically aim to raise self-esteem. Feel-good messages that seek to instill higher self-esteem in everyone ("We're all special" and "We applaud ourselves") might be off the target, leading people to develop unwarranted high self-esteem. Instead, parents, schools, and community institutions should seek to provide opportunities for people to earn self-esteem through their actual achievements (Begley, 1998b).

Are there particular social groups for which the issue of self-esteem is of particular importance? For example, what might be the consequences if a politician—say, a presidential candidate—had unjustified high self-esteem?

Furthermore, it is increasingly clear that the roots of adult personality emerge at the earliest periods of life. Infants are born with a particular **temperament**, a basic, innate disposition. Temperament encompasses several dimensions, including general activity level and mood. For instance, some individuals are quite active, while others are relatively calm; some are relatively easygoing, while others are irritable, easily upset, and difficult to soothe. Temperament is quite consistent, with significant stability from infancy well into adolescence (Caspi et al., 1995; Clark & Watson, 1999; Molfese & Molfese, 2000). Some research on the genetic basis of personality at different ages suggests that the genetic contribution to personality traits increases with age (Jang et al., 1996).

Some researchers believe that specific genes are related to personality. For example, people with a longer version of a dopamine-4 receptor gene are more likely to be thrill seekers than those without such a gene. These thrill seekers tend to be extroverted, impulsive, quick-tempered, and always on the prowl for excitement and novel situations (Benjamin et al., 1996). Some genetic researchers are studying the extent to which specific genetic factors affect two or more personality characteristics. For instance, variations in the serotonin transporter gene have been found to partially account for the relationship between neuroticism and agreeableness (Jang et al., 2001).

Does the identification of specific genes linked to personality, coupled with the discovery that aspects of our temperaments are established before birth, mean that we are destined to have certain types of personalities? Hardly. First, it is unlikely that any single gene is linked to a specific trait. For instance, the dopamine-4 receptor accounts for only about 10 percent of the variation in novelty seeking between different individuals. The rest of the variation is accounted for by other genes and environmental factors (Angier, 1996).

More importantly, genes and the environment never work in isolation. As we saw in our discussions of the heritability of intelligence (Chapter 7) and the nature-nurture issue (Chapter 9), it is impossible to completely divorce genetic factors from environmental factors. Although studies of identical twins raised in different environments are helpful, they are

temperament: A basic, innate disposition that emerges early in life.

Figure 10-6 The roots of personality. The percentages indicate the degree to which 11 personality characteristics reflect the influence of heredity.

Source: Tellegen et al., 1988.

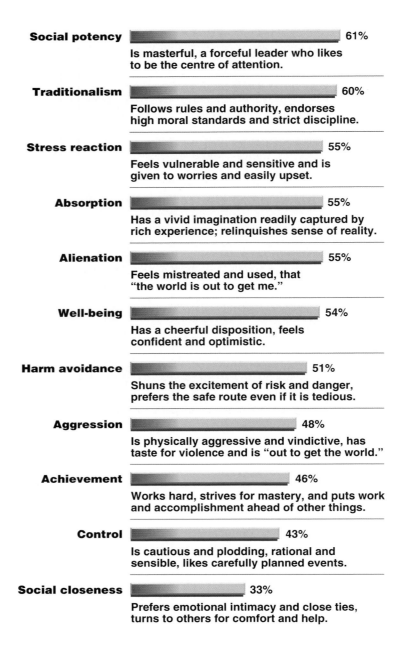

Social potency — 61%
Is masterful, a forceful leader who likes to be the centre of attention.

Traditionalism — 60%
Follows rules and authority, endorses high moral standards and strict discipline.

Stress reaction — 55%
Feels vulnerable and sensitive and is given to worries and easily upset.

Absorption — 55%
Has a vivid imagination readily captured by rich experience; relinquishes sense of reality.

Alienation — 55%
Feels mistreated and used, that "the world is out to get me."

Well-being — 54%
Has a cheerful disposition, feels confident and optimistic.

Harm avoidance — 51%
Shuns the excitement of risk and danger, prefers the safe route even if it is tedious.

Aggression — 48%
Is physically aggressive and vindictive, has taste for violence and is "out to get the world."

Achievement — 46%
Works hard, strives for mastery, and puts work and accomplishment ahead of other things.

Control — 43%
Is cautious and plodding, rational and sensible, likes carefully planned events.

Social closeness — 33%
Prefers emotional intimacy and close ties, turns to others for comfort and help.

not definitive, because it is impossible to fully assess and control environmental factors. Furthermore, estimates of the influence of genetics are just that—estimates—and they apply to groups, not individuals. Consequently, findings such as those shown in Figure 10-6 must be regarded as approximations.

Finally, even if more genes are found to be linked to specific personality characteristics, genes still cannot be viewed as the sole cause of personality. For one thing, genetically determined characteristics might not be expressed if they are not "turned on" by particular environmental experiences. Furthermore, the appearance of behaviours produced by genes in some ways might create a particular environment. For instance, a cheerful, smiley baby might lead her parents to smile more and act more responsive, thereby creating an environment that is supportive and pleasant. On the other hand, the parents of a cranky, fussy baby might be less inclined to smile at the child, leading to an environment that is less supportive or pleasant. In a sense, then, genes not only influence a person's behaviour—they also help produce the environment in which the person is raised (Scarr, 1992, 1993; Plomin & Caspi, 1999).

Although an increasing number of personality theorists are taking biological and evolutionary factors into account, no comprehensive, unified theory that considers biological and evolutionary factors is widely accepted. Still, it is clear that certain personality traits have substantial genetic components and that heredity and environment interact to determine personality (Buss, 1999; Plomin & Caspi, 1999).

Humanistic Approaches: The Uniqueness of You

Where, in all these approaches to personality, is there an explanation for the saintliness of a Mother Teresa, the creativity of a Michelangelo, the brilliance and perseverance of an Einstein? An understanding of such unique individuals—as well as more ordinary sorts of people who share some of the same attributes—comes from humanistic theory.

According to humanistic theorists, all of the approaches to personality that we have discussed share a fundamental misperception in their views of human nature. Instead of seeing people as controlled by unconscious, unseen forces (as do psychoanalytic approaches), a set of stable traits (trait approaches), situational reinforcements and punishments (learning theory), or inherited factors (biological and evolutionary approaches), **humanistic approaches** argue that people are basically good and tend to grow to higher levels of functioning—and that this conscious, self-motivated ability to change and improve, along with people's unique creative impulses, makes up the core of personality.

The major proponent of the humanistic point of view is Carl Rogers (1971). Rogers suggests that people have a need for positive regard that reflects a universal requirement to be loved and respected. Because others provide this positive regard, we grow dependent on them. We begin to see and judge ourselves through the eyes of other people, relying on their values.

According to Rogers, one outgrowth of placing importance on the opinions of others is that there can be a conflict between people's actual experiences and their *self-concepts,* or self-impressions. If the discrepancies are minor, so are the consequences. But great discrepancies will lead to psychological disturbances in daily functioning, such as the experience of frequent anxiety.

Rogers suggests that one way of overcoming the discrepancy between experience and self-concept is through receiving unconditional positive regard from another person—such as a friend, spouse, or therapist. As we will discuss in Chapter 13, **unconditional positive regard** is an attitude of acceptance and respect on the part of an observer, no matter what the other person says or does. This acceptance, says Rogers, allows people the opportunity to evolve and grow both cognitively and emotionally and to develop more realistic self-concepts. You might have experienced the power of unconditional positive regard when you opened up to someone, revealing embarrassing secrets because you knew the listener would still love and respect you, even after hearing the worst about you.

On the other hand, if you receive *conditional positive regard,* others' view of you is dependent on your behaviour. Others will withdraw their love and acceptance if you do something they don't approve of. The result is a discrepancy between your true self and what others wish you would be, leading you to feel anxiety and frustration (see Figure 10-7).

To Rogers and other humanistic personality theorists such as Abraham Maslow (whose theory of motivation we discussed in Chapter 8), the ultimate goal of personality growth is self-actualization. **Self-actualization** is a state of self-fulfillment in which people realize their highest potential. To reach this state, people's everyday experience and their self-concept must closely match. People who are self-actualized accept themselves as they are in reality, which enables them to achieve happiness and fulfillment. They are open to new experiences, accepting of others, and independent (Ford, 1991).

"*So, while extortion, racketeering, and murder may be bad acts, they don't make you a bad person.*"

 **PsychLink**
Humanistic psychology
www.mcgrawhill.ca/college/feldman

humanistic approaches to personality: The theory that people are basically good and tend to grow to higher levels of functioning.

unconditional positive regard: An attitude of acceptance and respect on the part of an observer, no matter what the other person says or does.

self-actualization: According to Rogers, a state of self-fulfillment in which people realize their highest potential.

Pathways Through Psychology

Romin Tafarodi

Assistant Professor of Psychology University of Toronto, Toronto, Ontario

Education: B.A., University of Waterloo; Ph.D., University of Texas at Austin

Home: Toronto

Romin Tafarodi

My interest in psychology stems from a childhood tendency to think too much about why I am who I am and do what I do. By the time I reached adulthood, I realized that the answers to those questions might also apply to understanding others. I've always been fascinated by our ability to conceive of ourselves as persons and why this ability becomes a blessing for some but a curse for others.

I came from a small family and was a bit of a loner growing up. When in the company of others, I tended to be acutely aware of their presence and its influence on my behaviour. My interest in social dynamics as causes and consequences of personality is an outgrowth of this early awareness. As a child, I was uncomfortable with the idea that we are self-made, autonomous agents. Rather, I felt that genetics and social experience were the building blocks of personality. Moreover, because personality itself is really nothing more than consistency in behaviour, I concluded that the real causes of what we do cannot be found in our experience of choice. I've maintained that position ever since, although at times I've wished that I believed otherwise. I suppose I was attracted to science in part because it is a haven for unrepentant determinists. As I've always been much more interested in people than in plants, animals, or inanimate objects, psychology was the natural choice. Psychology is a relatively young science and I'm often struck by how little we really know about the mind. This realization is more exciting than discouraging, as it presents the possibility of major theoretical advances in the near future. It is this promise that inspires me.

My parents were Iranian immigrants who struggled to build a new life for themselves in Canada. The challenges of their cultural transition became a major theme in my life and led to interests that are reflected in my work on cross-cultural differences in self-identity. Much of my research to date has focused on the attitude that people hold toward themselves—their self-esteem. I have proposed that self-esteem, even in its most generalized form, consists of two distinct aspects, one involving the perception of power, or efficacy, and the other the perception of goodness, or social worth. Conceiving of self-esteem as two-dimensional helps us better understand those who see themselves as competent yet worthless, or incompetent yet worthy. Given that the two dimensions have distinct origins and sensitivities, it also helps us predict how different types of life events, and changing cultural conditions, impact self-esteem. Such knowledge may prove useful in treating those who suffer from self-esteem problems and for promoting the development of healthy self-esteem in children and adolescents. Though researchers continue to disagree on what self-esteem is, where it comes from, and what it affects, nearly all see it as a central feature of personality and perhaps our most important attitude. The consensus assures me that I'm at least working in the right area. I'm currently looking at how choice, distinctiveness, family dynamics, and cultural conditions affect self-esteem and other aspects of self-identity.

Source: Romin Tafarodi, Ph.D., University of Toronto. <psych.utoronto.ca/~tafarodi>

According to Dr. Tafarodi, what are the two aspects of self-esteem? What are some advantages of having a two-dimensional view of self-esteem?

Figure 10-7 According to the humanistic view of Carl Rogers, people have a basic need to be loved and respected. If you have unconditional positive regard from others, you will develop more realistic self-concepts, but if the response is conditional it may lead to anxiety and frustration.

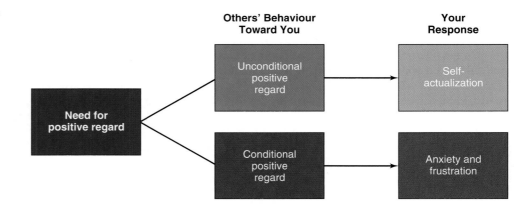

Evaluating Humanistic Approaches

An important contribution of humanistic approaches has been to highlight the uniqueness of individuals. They have focused considerable attention and research on various aspects of the self. See the *Pathways Through Psychology* box to read about Romin Tafarodi, a Canadian psychologist whose research concerns the self, particularly self-esteem. Humanistic theories have also guided the development of a significant form of therapy. (See Chapter 13 for humanistic approaches to psychotherapy.)

Humanistic approaches have been criticized because verifying their basic assumptions is very difficult. For example, the assumption that people are basically "good" is unverifiable. In addition, some critics have questioned whether unconditional positive regard does, in fact, lead to greater personality adjustment. Humanistic approaches have also been criticized for using nonscientific values to build supposedly scientific theories.

Comparing Approaches to Personality

Given the multiple approaches we have discussed, you could be wondering which of the theories provides the most accurate description of personality. This question cannot be answered precisely. Each theory is built on different assumptions and focuses on somewhat different aspects of personality (see Table 10-4 for a comparison). Given the complexity of every individual, it seems reasonable that personality can be viewed from a number of perspectives simultaneously (Pervin & John, 1999).

Table 10-4 Comparing Approaches to Personality

Theoretical Approach and Major Theorists	Conscious Versus Unconscious Determinants of Personality	Nature (Hereditary Factors) Versus Nurture (Environmental Factors)	Free Will Versus Determinism	Stability Versus Modifiability
Psychoanalytic (Freud)	Emphasizes the unconscious	Stresses innate, inherited structure of personality while emphasizing importance of adulthood experience	Stresses determinism, the view that behaviour is directed and caused by factors outside one's control	Emphasizes the stability of characteristics throughout a person's life
Trait (Allport, Cattell, Eysenck)	Disregards both conscious and unconscious	Approaches vary	Stresses determinism, the view that behaviour is directed and caused by factors outside one's control	Emphasizes the stability of characteristics throughout a person's life
Learning (Skinner, Bandura)	Disregards both conscious and unconscious	Focuses on the environment	Stresses determinism, the view that behaviour is directed and caused by factors outside one's control	Stresses that personality remains flexible and resilient throughout one's life
Biological and Evolutionary (Tellegen)	Disregards both conscious and unconscious	Stresses the innate, inherited determinants of personality	Stresses determinism, the view that behaviour is directed and caused by factors outside one's control	Emphasizes the stability of characteristics throughout a person's life
Humanistic (Rogers, Maslow)	Stresses the conscious more than unconscious	Stresses the interaction between both nature and nurture	Stresses the freedom of individuals to make their own choices	Stresses that personality remains flexible and resilient throughout one's life

Evaluate

1. Carl's determination to succeed is the dominant force in all his activities and relationships. According to Gordon Allport's theory, this is an example of a _____ trait. In contrast, Cindy's fondness for old western movies is an example of a _____ trait.

2. A person who enjoys such activities as parties and hang gliding might be described by Eysenck as high on what trait?

3. Proponents of which approach to personality would be most likely to agree with the statement "Personality can be thought of as learned responses to a person's upbringing and environment"?

   a. Humanistic approaches

   b. Biological and evolutionary approaches

   c. Learning approaches

   d. Trait approaches

4. A person who would make the statement "I know I can't do it" would be rated by Bandura as low on _____-_____.

5. Which approach to personality emphasizes the innate goodness of people and their desire to grow?

   a. Humanistic

   b. Psychoanalytic

   c. Learning

   d. Biological and evolutionary

Answers to Evaluate Questions

1. cardinal; secondary 2. Extraversion 3. c 4. self-efficacy 5. a

Rethink

1. If personality traits are merely descriptive and not explanatory, of what use are they? Can assigning a trait to a person be harmful—or helpful? Why or why not?

2. In what ways are Cattell's 16 source traits, Eysenck's three dimensions, and the "Big Five" factors similar, and in what ways are they different? Which traits seem to appear in all three schemes (under one name or another), and which are unique to one scheme? Is this significant?

Prepare

How can we most accurately assess personality?

What are the major types of personality measures?

Organize

Assessing Personality
   Self-Report Measures of Personality
   Projective Methods
   Behavioural Assessment
   Cross-Cultural Assessment of Personality

 **PsychLink**

Personality tests
www.mcgrawhill.ca/college/feldman

Assessing Personality: Determining What Makes Us Special

You have a need for other people to like and admire you.

You have a tendency to be critical of yourself.

You have a great deal of unused potential that you have not turned to your advantage.

Although you have some personality weaknesses, you are generally able to compensate for them.

Relating to members of the opposite sex has presented problems to you.

Although you appear to others to be disciplined and self-controlled, you tend to be anxious and insecure inside.

At times you have serious doubts as to whether you have made the right decision or done the right thing.

You prefer a certain amount of change and variety and become dissatisfied when hemmed in by restrictions and limitations.

You do not accept others' statements without satisfactory proof.

You have found it unwise to be too frank in revealing yourself to others.

If you think these statements provide a surprisingly accurate account of your personality, you are not alone: Most college students think that the descriptions are tailored just to them. In fact, the statements are intentionally designed to be so vague as to apply to just about anyone (Forer, 1949; Russo, 1981).

The ease with which we can agree with such imprecise statements underscores the difficulty in coming up with accurate and meaningful assessments of people's personalities (Johnson et al., 1985; Prince & Guastello, 1990). Just as trait theorists were faced with the problem of determining the most critical and important traits, psychologists interested in assessing personality must be able to define the most meaningful ways to discriminate between one person's personality and another's. To do this, they use **psychological tests**, standard measures devised to assess behaviour objectively. Such tests are used by psychologists to help people make decisions about their lives and understand more about themselves. They are also employed by researchers interested in the causes and consequences of personality (Groth-Marnat, 1990, 1996; Matarazzo, 1992; Kaplan & Saccuzzo, 1997; Aiken, 1997).

Like the intelligence assessments that we discussed in Chapter 7, all psychological tests must have reliability and validity. *Reliability,* you may recall, refers to the measurement consistency of a test. If a test is reliable, it yields the same result each time it is administered to a given person or group. In contrast, unreliable tests give different results each time they are administered.

Tests also must be valid in order to draw meaningful conclusions. Tests have *validity* when they actually measure what they are designed to measure. If a test is constructed to measure sociability, for instance, we need to know that it actually measures sociability and not some other trait.

Finally, psychological tests are based on *norms,* standards of test performance that permit the comparison of one person's score on the test to the scores of others who have taken the same test. For example, a norm permits test-takers who have received a particular score on a test to know that they have scored in the top 10 percent of all those who have taken the test.

Norms are established by administering a particular test to a large number of people and determining the typical scores. It is then possible to compare a single person's score to the scores of the group, providing a comparative measure of test performance against the performance of others who have taken the test.

The establishment of appropriate norms is not a simple endeavour. For instance, the specific group that is employed to determine norms for a test has a profound effect on how an individual's performance is evaluated. In fact, as we discuss next, the process of establishing norms can take on political overtones.

psychological tests: Standard measures devised to assess behaviour objectively and used by psychologists to help people make decisions about their lives and understand more about themselves.

What are some cultural differences in self-views? Why are these differences important? How do you think cultural differences affect the validity of personality tests?

EXPLORING DIVERSITY

How Much of Your Self Is Cultural?

As we have seen in this chapter, a common question addressed by the various perspectives on personality is "How do people view themselves?" In fact, research on the self accounts for a large proportion of research published in personality journals (Endler & Speer, 1998). As our interaction with people from different parts of the world increases, an interesting question that arises is whether the self-view held by Westerners is shared by other cultures or merely reflective of a concept inherent in our culture.

A little over a decade ago, Hazel Markus (an American psychologist) and Shinobu Kitayama (a Japanese psychologist) published their famous paper on the self and culture (Markus & Kitayama, 1991). They eloquently described strikingly different self-views in Eastern and Western cultures. Their paper, which was widely read, focused attention on differences between Western and Asian self-views. The Western self is an individualistic self, composed of unique and stable characteristics that are largely independent of situations. In contrast, the Eastern self is composed of changing characteristics whose existence depends largely on the social roles inherent in situations. Whereas knowing oneself is critically important in Western culture, knowing the demands of various social roles is essential in Eastern culture.

The existence of these differences in self-views has important implications for the application of concepts and findings in personality and social psychology. For example, one of the most thoroughly researched topics in social psychology is cognitive dissonance, which emphasizes the desire for consistency among an individual's cognitions and behaviours (see Chapter 14). However, research findings in East Asia typically do not support cognitive dissonance theory (Heine & Lehman, 1997).

The consistency and even the extent to which people define and articulate beliefs about themselves (known as self-concept clarity) depends on the culture in which they live. For instance, in one study Canadian university students were found to exhibit more self-concept clarity than their counterparts in Japan (Campbell et al., 1996).

According to Stephen Heine (University of British Columbia) and his colleagues, the need to view oneself positively "is easily the most common and consensually endorsed assumption in research on the self" (Heine et al., 1999, p. 766). These researchers have found evidence for self-enhancing strategies that serve to maintain a positive self-view (e.g., ignoring or discounting criticism) in North Americans, and evidence for self-effacement (self-criticism and acceptance of negative information about the self) in East Asians (Heine et al., 1999, 2001a, 2001b). They suggest that East Asians may take criticism more seriously because it provides information that will assist them to successfully fulfill a social role and fit into a social group. Other researchers have found that Hong Kong Chinese also show more self-effacement than North Americans do. However, there is evidence of inconsistencies in the degree of self-effacement. Hong Kong Chinese showed more self-effacement related to communal than other dimensions of personality (Yik et al., 1998). For example, they showed self-effacement in rating themselves on characteristics such as sociability, application, and helpfulness, but not on openness to experience, intellect, or assertiveness.

These findings about Asian self-effacement and acceptance of negative self-relevant information do not necessarily indicate that people in Asian cultures like themselves less. Romin Tafarodi argues that collectivist cultures foster the development of one aspect of self-esteem, self-liking. Comparing questionnaire responses by Chinese and American college students, Tafarodi and Swann (1996) found that Chinese students scored higher in the self-liking aspect of self-esteem and lower in the self-competence aspect than the Americans.

Together, these findings argue in favour of the view that we need to take culture into account when conceptualizing and measuring aspects of the self.

Self-Report Measures of Personality

If someone wanted to assess your personality, one possible approach would be to extensively interview you about the most important events of your childhood, your social relationships, and your successes and failures. Obviously, though, such a technique would be extraordinarily costly in time and effort.

It is also unnecessary. Just as physicians draw only a small sample of your blood to test it, psychologists can utilize **self-report measures** that ask people about a relatively small sample of their behaviour. This sampling of self-report data is then used to infer the presence of particular personality characteristics (Conoley & Impara, 1997).

One of the best examples of a self-report measure, and the most frequently used personality test, is the **Minnesota Multiphasic Personality Inventory-2 (MMPI-2)**. Although the original purpose of the measure was to differentiate people with specific sorts of psychological difficulties from those without disturbances, it has been found to predict a variety of other behaviours. For instance, MMPI scores have been shown to be good predictors of whether college students will marry within 10 years and whether they will get an advanced degree. Police departments use the test to measure whether police officers are prone to use their weapons. Psychologists in Russia administer a modified form of the MMPI to their astronauts and Olympic athletes (Butcher, 1995, 1999; Craig, 1999; Friedman et al., 2000).

The test itself consists of a series of 567 items to which a person responds "true," "false," or "cannot say." The questions cover a variety of issues, ranging from mood ("I feel useless at times") to opinions ("People should try to understand their dreams") to physical and psychological health ("I am bothered by an upset stomach several times a week" and "I have strange and peculiar thoughts"). There are no right or wrong answers. The test yields scores on separate subscales, and the interpretation of results depends on the pattern of these subscale scores.

self-report measures: A method of gathering data about people by asking them questions about a sample of their behaviour.

Minnesota Multiphasic Personality Inventory-2 (MMPI-2): A test used to identify people with psychological difficulties as well as to predict such behaviour as job performance.

PsychLink

MMPI-2
www.mcgrawhill.ca/college/feldman

How did the authors of the MMPI determine what specific patterns of responses indicate? The procedure they used is typical of personality test construction—a process known as **test standardization**. To create the test, groups of psychiatric patients with a specific diagnosis, such as depression or schizophrenia, were asked to complete a large number of items. The test authors then determined which items best differentiated members of these groups from a comparison group of normal participants, and these specific items were included in the final version of the test. By systematically carrying out this procedure on groups with different diagnoses, the test authors were able to devise a number of subscales that identified different forms of abnormal behaviour (see Figure 10-8).

When the MMPI is used for the purposes for which it was devised—identification of personality disorders—it does a reasonably good job. However, like other personality tests, it can be abused. For example, employers who use it as a job-screening tool may lack the skill required for interpretation of results. Overlap between the individual scales makes interpretation of their scores difficult. In sum, although the MMPI remains the most widely used personality test and has been translated into more than a hundred languages, it must be used with caution (Greene & Clopton, 1994; Graham, 1999; Holden, 2000). A problem common to self-report measures is that people may give false answers, intentionally or otherwise. The MMPI has a "lie scale" that indicates when people are falsifying answers (Butcher et al., 1990; Butcher, 1999; Graham, 1999). For self-report measures that do not include a "lie scale," an effective strategy for detecting faking is to measure reaction times. Holden and Hibbs (1995) found that participants who were instructed to answer so as to "look good" took longer than honest participants who made unfavourable responses.

test standardization: A technique used to validate questions in personality tests by studying the responses of people with known diagnoses.

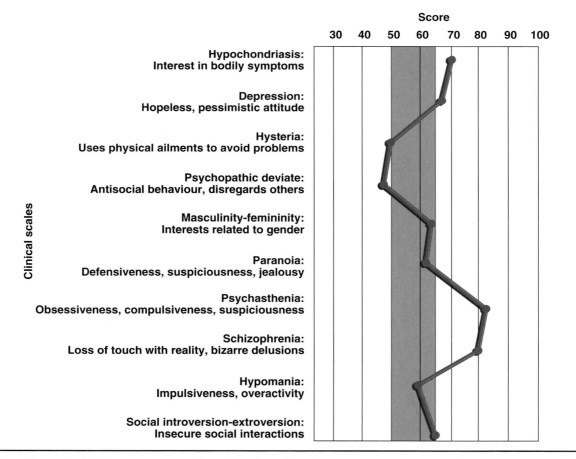

Figure 10–8 A profile on the MMPI-2 of a person who suffers from obsessional anxiety, social withdrawal, and delusional thinking.

Based on R. P. Halgin and S. K. Whitbourne, *Abnormal Psychology*, 1994, Harcourt Brace and Minnesota Multiphasic Personality Inventory 2, University of Minnesota.

Projective Methods

If you were shown one of the shapes presented in Chapter Activity 10-2 and asked what it represented to you, you might not think that your impressions would mean very much. But to a psychoanalytic theoretician, your responses to such an ambiguous figure would provide valuable clues to the state of your unconscious, and ultimately to your general personality characteristics.

The shape in the figure is representative of inkblots used in **projective personality tests**, in which a person is shown an ambiguous stimulus and asked to describe it or tell a story about it. The responses are then considered to be "projections" of what the person is like.

The best-known projective test is the **Rorschach test**. Devised by Swiss psychiatrist Hermann Rorschach (1924), the test consists of showing a series of symmetrical stimuli, similar to the ones in Chapter Activity 10-2, to people who are then asked what the figures represent to them. Their responses are recorded, and through a complex set of clinical judgments on the part of the examiner, people are classified into different personality types. For instance, respondents who see a bear in one inkblot are thought to have a strong degree of emotional control, according to the rules developed by Rorschach (Aronow, Reznikoff, & Moreland, 1994; Weiner, 1998).

The **Thematic Apperception Test (TAT)** is another well-known projective test. As we noted when we discussed achievement motivation in Chapter 8, the TAT consists of a series of pictures about which a person is asked to write a story. The stories are then used to draw inferences about the writer's personality characteristics (Cramer, 1996; Kelly, 1997).

Tests with stimuli as ambiguous as the Rorschach and TAT require particular skill and care in their interpretation—too much, in many critics' estimation. The Rorschach, in particular, has been criticized for requiring too much inference on the part of the examiner, and attempts to standardize scoring have frequently failed. Furthermore, many critics complain that the Rorschach does not provide much valid information about underlying personality traits. Despite such problems, both the Rorschach and the TAT are widely used, particularly in clinical settings, and their proponents suggest that their reliability and validity are great enough to provide useful inferences about personality (Bornstein, 1996; Weiner, 1998; Meyer, 2000).

projective personality test: A test in which a person is shown an ambiguous stimulus and asked to describe it or tell a story about it.

Rorschach test: A test by developed by Swiss psychiatrist Hermann Rorschach that consists of showing a series of symmetrical stimuli to people and then asking them to say what the figures represent to them.

Thematic Apperception Test (TAT): A test consisting of a series of ambiguous pictures about which the person is asked to write a story.

Chapter Activity 10–2 What's in an Inkblot?

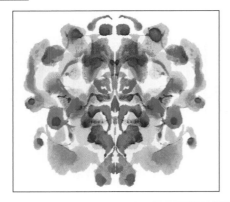  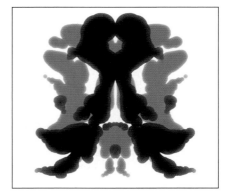

FIGURE 10-9 These inkblots are similar to the type used in the Rorschach personality test (Alloy, Jacobson, & Acocella, 1999). What do you see in these inkblots?

Figure 10-9a after L. B. Alloy, N. S. Jackson & J. Acocella. Copyright © The McGraw-Hill Companies.

Behavioural Assessment

If you were a psychologist subscribing to a learning approach to personality, you would be likely to object to the indirect nature of projective tests. You would instead be more apt to use **behavioural assessment**—direct measures of an individual's behaviour used to describe characteristics indicative of personality. As with observational research (discussed in Chapter 1), behavioural assessment can be carried out naturalistically by observing people in their own settings: in the workplace, at home, or in school. It can also be carried out in the laboratory, under controlled conditions in which a psychologist sets up a situation and observes an individual's behaviour.

Regardless of the setting in which behaviour is observed, an effort is made to ensure that behavioural assessment is carried out objectively, quantifying behaviour as much as possible. For example, an observer might record the number of social contacts a person initiates, the number of questions asked, or the number of aggressive acts. Another method is to measure the duration of events: the duration of a temper tantrum in a child, the length of a conversation, the amount of time spent working, or the time spent in cooperative behaviour.

Behavioural assessment is particularly appropriate for observing—and eventually remedying—specific behavioural difficulties, such as increasing socialization in shy children. It provides a means of assessing the specific nature and incidence of a problem and subsequently allows psychologists to determine whether intervention techniques have been successful.

Behavioural assessment techniques based on learning theories of personality have also made important contributions to the treatment of certain kinds of psychological difficulties. Indeed, the knowledge of normal personality provided by the theories we have discussed throughout this chapter has led to significant advances in our understanding and treatment of both physical and psychological disorders.

Cross–Cultural Assessment of Personality

Cross-cultural assessment of personality poses a number of challenges, not the least of which is the language barrier. To overcome these difficulties, psychologists at the University of Western Ontario, together with their colleagues in other countries, have used both a verbal self-report measure and a nonverbal measure in cross-cultural research. Douglas Jackson developed the verbal measure, the Personality Research Form (PRF). Sampo Paunonen and Douglas Jackson (University of Western Ontario) and Mirja Keinonen (University of Helsinki) developed the Nonverbal Personality Questionnaire (NPQ). This test has 136 line drawings of a person engaging in various trait-related behaviours. Respondents indicate the likelihood that they would engage in behaviours similar to those pictured (Paunonen et al., 1990). See Figure 10-10 for two sample NPQ drawings.

Paunonen and his colleagues used these tests to assess personality in seven countries, including Canada, Finland, Poland, Germany, Russia, China (Hong Kong), and Korea (Paunonen et al., 1992, 1996; Lee at al., 2000). The use of both a verbal and a nonverbal measure is advantageous because each measure alone has some problems. On the one hand, translating tests is difficult because of a lack of correspondence between words, idioms, and grammar across languages. Subtle differences in content of test items may occur. On the other hand, in constructing a nonverbal test, it is difficult to represent all traits in pictorial format. Also, some aspects of a trait can be better represented in pictures than other aspects (Ashton et al., 1998).

Recently, Paunonen, Ashton, and Jackson (2001) have developed the Five-Factor Nonverbal Personality Questionnaire (FF-NPQ), a nonverbal measure of the Big Five factors, which is intended for use in cross-cultural research. Using self-report measures on which people rate themselves in different cultures must be done cautiously (Heine et al., 2002). People from different cultures have different reference groups or standards when rating themselves, which may result in distortions in comparisons between cultures.

behavioural assessment: Direct measures of an individual's behaviour used to describe characteristics indicative of personality.

 **PsychLink**

Behavioural assessment
www.mcgrawhill.ca/college/feldman

Figure 10-10 Sample Nonverbal Personality Questionnaire items depicting aggressive behaviour (A) and thrill-seeking behaviour (B).

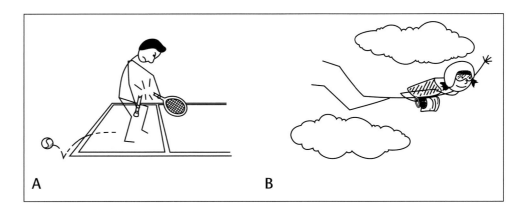

A   B

What types of personality tests and other information do you think employers and placement agencies should use? Why?

Although projective tests such as the Rorschach test and the Thematic Apperception Test (TAT) are frequently employed in testing situations, their reliability and validity have been questioned.

BECOMING AN
INFORMED CONSUMER
OF PSYCHOLOGY

Assessing Personality Assessments

Wanted: People with "kinetic energy," "emotional maturity," and the ability to "deal with large numbers of people in a fairly chaotic situation."

Although this job description might seem most appropriate for the job of co-host of *Wheel of Fortune,* in actuality it is part of an advertisement for managers for American Multi-Cinema's theatres (Dentzer, 1986). To find people with such qualities, AMC has developed a battery of personality measures for job applicants to complete. In developing its own tests, AMC joined scores of companies, ranging from General Motors to J. C. Penney, that employ personality tests to help determine who gets hired (Hogan, Hogan, & Roberts, 1996).

Individuals, too, have come to depend on personality testing. Many organizations will—for a hefty fee—administer a battery of personality tests that claim to steer people toward a career for which their personality is particularly suited. When considering the results of such personality testing, either in the role of potential employee, employer, or consumer of testing services, you should keep several points in mind:

- *Understand what the test claims to measure.* Standard personality measures are accompanied by information that discusses how the test was developed, to whom it is most applicable, and how the results should be interpreted. Read any explanations of the test; it will help you understand the meaning of any results.
- *Make no decision based only on the results of any one test.* Test results should be interpreted in the context of other information—academic records, social interests, and home and community activities.
- *Remember that test results are not always accurate.* The results can be in error; the test might be unreliable or invalid. You might, for example, have had a "bad day" when you took the test, or the person scoring and interpreting the test might have made a mistake. You should not place undue stock in the results of the single administration of any test.

- *Critically evaluate the information at Internet sites presenting online personality tests in the same manner as you would assess any information online.* In particular, consider the credibility and expertise of the source as well as the reasons for offering the tests. For more information see the last PsychLink for this chapter (p. 361), as well as the Internet Primer available on the Online Learning Centre.

In sum, it is important to keep in mind the complexity of human behaviour—particularly your own. No one test can provide an understanding of the intricacies of someone's personality without considering a good deal more information than can be provided in a single testing session.

Evaluate

1. _____ is the consistency of a personality test, while _____ is the ability of a test to actually measure what it is designed to measure.
2. _____ are standards used to compare scores of different people taking the same test.
3. Tests such as the MMPI-2, in which a small sample of behaviour is assessed to determine larger trends, are examples of
   a. cross-sectional tests
   b. projective tests
   c. achievement tests
   d. self-report tests
4. A person shown a picture and asked to make up a story about it would be taking a _____ personality test.

Answers to Evaluate Questions

1. Reliability, validity 2. Norms 3. d 4. projective

Rethink

1. What do you think are some of the problems that developers and interpreters of self-report personality tests must deal with in their effort to provide useful information about test-takers? Why is a "lie scale" included on such measures?
2. Should personality tests be used for personnel decisions? Should they be used for other social purposes, such as identifying individuals at risk for certain types of personality disorders? What sorts of policies would you devise to ensure that such tests were used ethically?

How do psychologists define and use the concept of personality?

- Personality is the pattern of enduring characteristics that differentiates a person—those patterns of behaviours that make each person unique. (p. 338)

What do the theories of Freud and his successors tell us about the structure and development of personality?

- According to psychoanalysts, much behaviour is caused by unconscious parts of personality, of which we are unaware. (p. 338)
- According to Freud's theory, personality is composed of the id, the ego, and the superego. The id is the unorganized, inborn part of personality whose purpose is to immediately reduce tensions relating to hunger, sex, aggression, and other primitive impulses. The ego restrains instinctual energy in order to maintain the safety of the individual and to help the person to be a member of society. The superego represents social right and wrong and consists of the conscience and the ego-ideal. (p. 339)
- Freud's psychoanalytic theory says that personality develops through a series of stages, each of which is associated with a primary biological function. (p. 340)
- Defence mechanisms are unconscious strategies for dealing with anxiety related to impulses from the id. (p. 341)
- Freud's psychoanalytic theory has provoked a number of criticisms, especially focusing on its lack of supportive scientific data, the theory's inadequacy in making predictions, and its reliance on a highly restricted population. (p. 342)
- Neo-Freudian psychoanalytic theorists built on Freud's work, although they placed greater emphasis on the role of the ego and paid greater attention to social factors in determining behaviour. (p. 343)

What are the major aspects of trait, learning, biological and evolutionary, and humanistic approaches to personality?

- Trait approaches have tried to identify the most basic and relatively enduring dimensions along which people differ from one another—dimensions known as traits. (p. 345)
- Learning approaches to personality concentrate on observable behaviour. To the strict learning theorist, personality is the sum of learned responses to the external environment. (p. 348)
- Social cognitive approaches concentrate on the role of cognitions in determining personality and pay particular attention to how self-efficacy determines behaviour. (p. 348)
- Biological and evolutionary approaches to personality focus on the inheritance of personality characteristics. (p. 350)
- Humanistic approaches assume that people are basically good. They consider the core of personality in terms of a person's ability to change and improve. (p. 353)
- The major personality approaches differ substantially from one another, which could reflect both their focus on different aspects of personality and the overall complexity of personality. (p. 355)

How can we most accurately assess personality?

- Psychological tests such as the MMPI are standard assessment tools that are intended to objectively measure behaviour. They must be reliable, measuring what they are trying to measure consistently, and valid, measuring what they are supposed to measure. (p. 356)

What are the major types of personality measures?

- Self-report measures ask people about a sample range of their behaviours. These reports are used to infer the presence of particular personality characteristics. (p. 358)
- Projective personality tests (such as the Rorschach and Thematic Apperception Test) present an ambiguous stimulus; the observer's responses are then used to infer information about the observer. (p. 360)
- Behavioural assessment is based on the principles of learning theory. It employs direct measurement of an individual's behaviour to determine characteristics related to personality. (p. 361)

Key Terms and Concepts

personality (p. 338)

psychoanalytic theory (p. 338)

unconscious (p. 338)

id (p. 339)

ego (p. 339)

superego (p. 339)

oral stage (p. 340)

fixation (p. 340)

anal stage (p. 340)

phallic stage (p. 340)

Oedipus conflict (p. 340)

identification (p. 340)

latency period (p. 341)

genital stage (p. 341)

defence mechanisms (p. 341)

neo-Freudian psychoanalysts (p. 343)

collective unconscious (p. 343)

inferiority complex (p. 343)

trait theory (p. 345)

traits (p. 345)

social cognitive approaches to personality (p. 348)

biological and evolutionary approaches to personality (p. 350)

temperament (p. 351)

humanistic approaches to personality (p. 353)

unconditional positive regard (p. 353)

self-actualization (p. 353)

psychological tests (p. 357)

self-report measures (p. 358)

Minnesota Multiphasic Personality Inventory-2 (MMPI-2) (p. 358)

test standardization (p. 359)

projective personality test (p. 360)

Rorschach test (p. 360)

Thematic Apperception Test (TAT) (p. 360)

behavioural assessment (p. 361)

Psychology on the Web

1. Sigmund Freud is one of the towering figures of psychology, with an influence far beyond his psychoanalytic work. Find further information on the Web about Freud. Pick one aspect of his work or influence (e.g., on therapy, medicine, literature, film, culture and society, etc.) and summarize in writing what you have found, including your attitude toward your findings.
2. Find a Web site that links to personality tests and take one or two tests—remembering to take them with skepticism. For each test, summarize in writing the aspects of personality that were tested, the theoretical approach that the test appeared to be based on, and your assessment of the trustworthiness of the information you received.

Epilogue

In this chapter, we have discussed the different ways in which psychologists have interpreted the development and structure of personality. The perspectives we've examined range from Freud's analysis of personality, based primarily on internal, unconscious factors, to the externally based view of personality as a learned set of traits and actions that is championed by the learning theorists. We have also noted that there are many ways to interpret personality, and that there is no consensus on what are the key traits central to personality.

Before proceeding to the topic of health psychology in the next chapter, return to the prologue of this chapter and consider the case of Anna Mae. Use your understanding of personality to consider the following questions.

1. What are some of Anna Mae's conflicting characteristics and behaviours? How would learning approaches to personality account for these differences?
2. How would psychoanalytic theory account for some of Anna Mae's behaviours?
3. Would a personality profile of Anna Mae administered during the time she was at home with her young children have been different from one administered after she became heavily involved in the American Indian Movement?

Chapter Eleven

Health Psychology:
Stress, Coping, and Well-Being

Prologue

So Much to Do, So Little Time to Do It

Jasmine and her three children have been in Canada for a year. Her husband is still working in South America, but he hopes to come to Canada eventually to join his family. He wants to provide well for them and hesitates to leave his job. Jasmine is getting

Feeling pressured by time and the responsibility of completing a large number of tasks can take both a physical and a psychological toll on one's well-being.

used to managing on her own. Sometimes making decisions about her children is really challenging because she has difficulty understanding the new social world her children have entered.

Five days a week Jasmine gets up very early to attend college. She arrives home again just in time to prepare dinner. After dinner, she supervises her children's homework. Then she does laundry, cleaning and other household chores. Finally, she turns to reading, assignments, and the studying she must do to succeed in her college program.

It's not hard to guess what Jasmine was experiencing every morning: stress. For people like her—and that probably includes most of us—the intensity of juggling multiple roles leads to feelings of never having sufficient time, and, in some cases, takes a toll on both physical and psychological well-being.

Stress, and ways of coping with it, have long been central topics of interest to psychologists. However, in recent years the focus has broadened as psychology has come to view stress in the broader context of a new subfield known as health psychology. **Health psychology** investigates the psychological factors related to wellness and illness, including the prevention, diagnosis, and treatment of medical problems. Health psychologists are also concerned with issues of prevention: how health problems such as heart disease and stress can be avoided by more healthful behaviour.

Health psychologists take a decisive stand on the enduring mind/body issue that philosophers have debated since the time of the ancient Greeks (a debate that psychologists later joined in on and that we first considered in Chapter 1). In their view, the mind and body are clearly linked, and are not two distinct systems (Sternberg, 2000).

The primary link between mind and body is the immune system, the complex of organs, glands, and cells that constitutes our line of defence in fighting disease. The growing field of **psychoneuroimmunology (PNI)** is the study of the relationships among psychological factors, the immune system, and the brain. PNI has led to discoveries such as the existence of an association between one's emotional state and the success of the immune system in fighting disease (Baum, Revenson, & Singer, 2000).

In sum, health psychologists view the mind and the body as two parts of a whole human being that cannot be considered independently. This more recent view marks a sharp departure from earlier thinking. Previously, disease was seen as a purely biological phenomenon, and psychological factors were of little interest to most health care workers. In the early twentieth century, the primary causes of death were short-term infections, from which one either rapidly recovered or died. Now, however, the major causes of death, such as heart disease, cancer, and diabetes, are chronic illnesses that often cannot be cured and that can linger for years, posing significant psychological issues (Delahanty & Baum, 2000).

In this chapter we discuss how psychological factors affect health. We first focus on the causes and consequences of stress and ways of coping with it. Next, we explore the psychological aspects of several major health problems, including heart disease, cancer, and ailments resulting from smoking. Finally, we examine the ways in which patient–physician interactions influence our health, and offer suggestions for increasing people's adherence to behaviour that will improve their well-being.

health psychology: The branch of psychology that investigates the psychological factors related to wellness and illness, including the prevention, diagnosis, and treatment of medical problems.

psychoneuroimmunology (PNI): The study of the relationships among psychological factors, the immune system, and the brain.

Prepare

How is health psychology a union between medicine and psychology?

What is stress, how does it affect us, and how can we best cope with it?

Organize

Stress and Coping
  Stress
  Coping with Stress

Stress and Coping

Tara Knox's day began badly: She slept through her alarm and had to skip breakfast in order to catch the bus to campus. Then, when she went to the library to catch up on the reading she had to do before taking a test the next day, the article she needed was missing. The librarian told her that replacing it would take 24 hours. Feeling exasperated, she walked to the computer lab to print out the paper she had completed the night before. However, she couldn't get the computer to read her disk. Although she searched for someone to help her, she was unable to find anyone who seemed to know any more than she did.

It was only 9:42 A.M., and all Tara could think about was how much stress she felt.

Stress: Reacting to Threat and Challenge

Most of us need little introduction to the phenomenon of **stress**, the response to events that threaten or challenge a person. Two-thirds of Canadians aged 18 to 24 years report experiencing some life stress (Statistics Canada, 2000). Whether it be an exam deadline,

stress: The response to events that are threatening or challenging.

a family problem, or even a cumulative series of events such as those faced by Tara Knox or Jasmine's stressful lifestyle, life is full of circumstances and events, known as *stressors,* that produce threats to our well-being. Even pleasant events—such as planning a party— can produce stress, although negative events result in greater detrimental consequences than positive ones.

All of us face stress in our lives. Some health psychologists believe that daily life actually involves a series of repeated sequences of perceiving a threat, considering ways to cope with it, and ultimately adapting to the threat, with greater or lesser success. Although adaptation is often minor and occurs without our awareness, adaptation requires major effort when stress is more severe or longer lasting. Ultimately, our attempts to overcome stress can produce biological and psychological responses that result in health problems.

The High Cost of Stress

Stress can take its toll in many ways. Often the most immediate reaction to stress is biological. Exposure to stressors generates a rise in certain hormones secreted by the adrenal glands, an increase in heart rate and blood pressure, and changes in how well the skin conducts electrical impulses. On a short-term basis, these responses can be adaptive because they produce an "emergency reaction" in which the body prepares to defend itself through activation of the sympathetic nervous system (see Chapter 2). These responses can allow more effective coping with the stressful situation (Akil & Morano, 1996; McEwen, 1998).

However, continued exposure to stress results in a decline in the body's overall level of biological functioning due to the constant secretion of stress-related hormones. Over time, stressful reactions can promote deterioration of bodily tissues such as blood vessels and the heart. Ultimately, we become more susceptible to disease as our ability to fight off infection is lowered (Sapolsky, 1996; Shapiro, 1996; McCabe et al., 2000).

In fact, an entire class of physical problems, known as **psychophysiological disorders**, may result from stress. Once referred to as *psychosomatic disorders* (a term dropped because it implied that the disorders were somehow unreal), psychophysiological disorders are actual medical problems influenced by an interaction of psychological, emotional, and physical difficulties. Among the common psychophysiological disorders are headaches, backaches, indigestion, skin problems, and high blood pressure. Stress has even been linked to the common cold (S. Cohen, 1996; Rice, 2000).

On a psychological level, high levels of stress prevent people from adequately coping with life. Their view of the environment can become clouded (e.g., a minor criticism made by a friend is blown out of proportion). Moreover, at the greatest levels of stress, emotional responses can be so extreme that people are unable to act at all. People under a lot of stress also become less able to deal with new stressors. The ability to contend with future stress, then, declines as a result of past stress.

In short, stress affects us in multiple ways. It can increase the risk that we will become ill; it can directly produce illness; it can make us less able to recover from a disease; and it can reduce our ability to cope with future stress. (For a measure of stress in your life, complete the questionnaire in Chapter Activity 11-1.)

The General Adaptation Syndrome Model: The Course of Stress

The effects of stress are illustrated in a model devised by Hans Selye (pronounced "SELL-yay"), a Canadian physician who was a pioneering stress theorist (Selye, 1976, 1993). This model, the **general adaptation syndrome (GAS)**, suggests that the same set of physiological reactions to stress occurs regardless of the particular cause of stress.

The model has three phases. The first stage, the *alarm and mobilization stage,* occurs when people become aware of the presence of a stressor. On a biological level, the sympathetic nervous system (Chapter 2) becomes energized, helping to cope initially with the stressor.

PsychLink
Stress management
www.mcgrawhill.ca/college/feldman

psychophysiological disorders: Medical problems influenced by an interaction of psychological, emotional, and physical difficulties.

general adaptation syndrome (GAS): A theory developed by Selye that suggests that a person's response to stress consists of three stages: alarm and mobilization, resistance, and exhaustion.

Chapter Activity 11–1 How Stressful is Your Life?

Test your level of stress by answering these questions, and adding the score from each box. Questions apply to the last month only. A key below will help you determine the extent of your stress.

1. How often have you been upset because of something that happened unexpectedly?

   0=never, 1=almost never, 2=sometimes, 3=fairly often, 4=very often

2. How often have you felt that you were unable to control the important things in your life?

   0=never, 1=almost never, 2=sometimes, 3=fairly often, 4=very often

3. How often have you felt nervous and "stressed"?

   0=never, 1=almost never, 2=sometimes, 3=fairly often, 4=very often

4. How often have you felt confident about your ability to handle your personal problems?

   0=never, 1=almost never, 2=sometimes, 3=fairly often, 4=very often

5. How often have you felt that things were going your way?

   0=never, 1=almost never, 2=sometimes, 3=fairly often, 4=very often

6. How often have you been able to control irritations in your life?

   0=never, 1=almost never, 2=sometimes, 3=fairly often, 4=very often

7. How often have you found that you could not cope with all the things that you had to do?

   0=never, 1=almost never, 2=sometimes, 3=fairly often, 4=very often

8. How often have you felt that you were on top of things?

   0=never, 1=almost never, 2=sometimes, 3=fairly often, 4=very often

9. How often have you been angered because of things that were outside your control?

   0=never, 1=almost never, 2=sometimes, 3=fairly often, 4=very often

10. How often have you felt difficulties were piling up so high that you could not overcome them?

    0=never, 1=almost never, 2=sometimes, 3=fairly often, 4=very often

How You Measure Up:

Stress levels vary among individuals—compare your total score to the averages below:

AGE		GENDER	
18-29	14.2	Men	12.1
30-44	13.0	Women	13.7
45-54	12.6		
55-64	11.9		
65 & over	12.0		

MARITAL STATUS	
Widowed	12.6
Married or living with	12.4
Single or never wed	14.1
Divorced	14.7
Separated	16.6

Source: Cohen, 1999.

However, if the stressor persists, people move into the next stage of the model. In the *resistance stage*, people prepare themselves to fight the stressor. During resistance, people use a variety of means to cope with the stressor—sometimes successfully—but at a cost of some degree of physical or psychological general well-being.

If resistance is inadequate, people enter the last stage of the model, the *exhaustion stage*. During the exhaustion stage, a person's ability to adapt to the stressor declines to the point where negative consequences of stress appear: physical illness, psychological symptoms in the form of an inability to concentrate, heightened irritability, or, in severe instances, disorientation and a loss of touch with reality. In a sense, people wear out, and their physical reserves are taxed to the limit.

How do people move out of the third stage after they have entered it? Exhaustion sometimes enables people to avoid the stressor. For example, people who become ill from overwork might be excused from their duties for a time, giving them a temporary respite from their responsibilities. At least for a time, then, the immediate stress is reduced.

The GAS model has had a substantial impact on our understanding of stress. By suggesting that the exhaustion of resources in the third stage of the model produces biological damage, it has provided a specific explanation of how stress can lead to illness. Furthermore, the model can be applied to both people and nonhuman species.

Contemporary health psychologists specializing in psychoneuroimmunology have taken a broader approach than the GAS. Focusing on the outcomes of stress, they have identified three main consequences (see Figure 11-1). First, stress has direct physiological results, including an increase in blood pressure, increased hormonal activity, and an overall decline in the functioning of the immune system. Second, stress leads people to engage in behaviour that is harmful to their health, including increased use of nicotine, drugs, and alcohol, poor eating habits, and decreased sleep. Stress influences the circumstances under which people drink as well as the way they drink in specific situations (McCreary & Sadava, 1998). Finally, stress produces indirect consequences that result in declines in health: a failure to obtain health care and decreased compliance with medical advice (Baum, 1994; McCabe et al., 2000).

The Nature of Stressors: My Stress Is Your Pleasure

As noted above, the general adaptation syndrome model is useful in explaining how people respond to stress, but it is not specific about what constitutes a stressor for a given person. Although certain kinds of events, such as the death of a loved one or participation in combat during a war, are universally stressful, other situations might or might not be stressful to a particular person (Fleming, Baum, & Singer, 1984; Pledge, 1992; Affleck et al., 1994; Krohne, 1996).

Consider, for instance, bungee jumping. Some of us would find jumping off a bridge attached to a slender rubber tether extremely stressful. However, there are those who see such an activity as challenging and fun-filled. Whether or not bungee jumping is stressful depends in part, then, on individual perceptions of the activity.

For people to consider an event to be stressful, they must perceive it as threatening and must lack the resources to deal with it effectively (Folkman et al., 1986). Consequently, the same event might at times be stressful and at other times provoke no stressful reaction at all. For instance, a young man might experience stress when he is turned down for a date—if he attributes the refusal to his unattractiveness or unworthiness. But if he attributes it to some factor unrelated to his self-esteem, such as a previous commitment by the person he asked, the experience of being refused might create no stress at all. Hence, our interpretation of events plays an important role in the determination of what is stressful.

The severity of stress is greatest when important goals are threatened, the threat is immediate, or the anticipation of a threatening event extends over a long period. For example, members of minority groups who feel they are potentially the targets of racist behaviour experience significant stress (Clark et al., 1999).

PsychLink

Posttraumatic stress disorder
www.mcgrawhill.ca/college/feldman

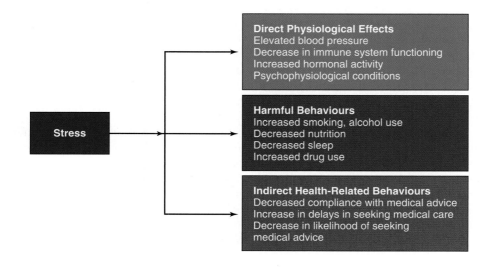

Figure 11-1 Three major types of consequences result from stress: direct physiological effects, harmful behaviours, and indirect health-related behaviours.

Source: Adapted from Baum, 1994.

Psychology at Work

Kavita Prakash

Sports Psychology Consultant and Professor

Education: BSc, MSc, University of Ottawa; Ph.D. candidate, Carleton University

Home: Ottawa, Ontario

Kavita Prakash

When Kavita Prakash was 6 years old, she took up figure skating. Little did she realize how important a part this would play in her career and her education decades later. Prakash eventually moved from skating to coaching, at the same time pursuing her undergraduate degree in psychology. She immediately saw applications: "I coached for five years," says Prakash, "and realized that the mental aspect of the sport was crucial for success."

Prakash completed her B.Sc., and moved on to pursue her master's degree. "When I conducted my master's thesis in sports psychology, I used some skaters in one of the Ottawa clubs as my subjects," she notes. "The club phoned me about a year later to see if I was interested in working with the athletes on a regular basis."

Prakash took up the offer, and became a sports psychology consultant. "Everything I teach my athletes is based on psychological theories," says Prakash. "I feel that mental training provides the athlete with the missing link in their training," she says. "Without learning about sports psychology and effective training methods, they are really only training from the neck down. By incorporating mental techniques, they are training their entire body.

"My skaters range in age from 9 to 19. The number of stressors they have to deal with is incredible. They all go to school full time and then train for about 20 hours a week on top of this. If athletes are exposed to ineffective ways of coping with stress in their home environment, I strongly believe that these habits will be their dominant response under pressure. As a consultant, I try to find opportunities during daily training sessions to train new dominant responses that will help to facilitate performance. I try to teach my skaters how to take something stressful and break it down into manageable pieces so that they feel more in control again."

Prakash has managed to balance both of her interests, finding applications from one to the other as she goes. Currently finishing her Ph.D. in social psychology and working as a professor of psychology at Heritage College in Hull, Quebec, Prakash continues to consult as a sports psychologist. "I love both of these jobs," she says. "I feel that I now have the best of both worlds."

> "I coached for five years," says Prakash, "and realized that the mental aspect of the sport was crucial for success."

> "Without learning about sports psychology and effective training methods, they are really only training from the neck down."

---

cataclysmic events: Strong stressors that occur suddenly, affecting many people at once (e.g., natural disasters).

Categorizing Stressors

What kinds of events tend to be seen as stressful? There are three general classes of such events: cataclysmic events, personal stressors, and background stressors.

Cataclysmic events are strong stressors that occur suddenly and typically affect many people simultaneously. Natural disasters (e.g., the Quebec ice storm of 1998; the Pine Lake, Alberta, tornado of 2000; the Alberta forest fires of 2002) and catastrophic events (e.g., the Holocaust of World War II; the attacks on the World Trade Center in 2001) are examples of cataclysmic events that can affect many people simultaneously.

Although it might seem that cataclysmic events would produce potent, lingering stress, this is not always true. Sometimes cataclysmic events produce less stress in the long run than events that initially are not as devastating. One reason is that some cataclysmic events have a clear resolution that allows people to move on to the future, believing the worst is over. Also, victims of major catastrophes may share their experiences, offering each other social support (Kaniasty & Norris, 1995; Hobfoll, 1996).

posttraumatic stress disorder (PTSD): A phenomenon in which people who have been exposed to traumatic events reexperience the original stress event and associated feelings in a variety of ways, including vivid flashbacks or dreams.

On the other hand, some victims of major catastrophes experience **posttraumatic stress disorder (PTSD)**. Exposure to a traumatic event (either personally or through association with those who did experience the event) is the defining characteristic of PTSD. Thus, not only victims but also families of victims, rescue workers and others whose jobs expose them to traumatic events may experience PTSD. Symptoms include reexperiencing the events in the form of flashbacks or dreams, sleep disturbances, memory problems, survivor guilt, emotional bluntness, depression, social problems, and substance abuse (Lamerson & Kelloway, 1996; Baranowsky et al., 1998; Brunet et al., 2001).

We usually think of PTSD in relation to combat victims. Depending on which statistics one accepts, between 5 and 60 percent of the veterans of the Vietnam War suffer from PTSD. The suicide rate for Vietnam veterans is as much as 25 percent higher than for the general American population (Friedman & Marsella, 1996; Wilson & Keane, 1996; Davidson, 2000). Canadian Forces assigned to peacekeeping operations also are regularly exposed to combat conditions, for example, in the former Yugoslavia (Lamerson & Kelloway, 1996). In addition, their situation is complicated by the frequency and duration of missions as well as by role conflict between peacekeeper and traditional soldier. (See the *Applying Psychology in the 21st Century* box in Chapter 12 to read about a senior Canadian military officer who suffers from PTSD.)

The second major category of stressor is the personal stressor. **Personal stressors** include major life events such as the death of a parent or spouse, the loss of one's job, a major personal failure, or a diagnosis of a life-threatening illness. Immigration to Canada may have been a personal stressor for Jasmine, who was described in the chapter prologue. Typically, personal stressors produce an immediate major reaction that soon tapers off. For example, stress arising from the death of a loved one tends to be greatest just after the time of death, but people begin to feel less stress and are better able to cope with the loss after the passage of time. In some cases, though, the effects of stress are lingering. Victims of rape sometimes suffer consequences long after the event, facing major difficulties in adjustment.

Standing in a long line at a bank and getting stuck in a traffic jam are examples of the third major category of stressor: **background stressors** or, more informally, *daily hassles*. These are the minor irritations of life that we all face time and time again: delays, noisy cars and trucks, broken appliances, other people's irritating behaviour, and so on. No doubt, like most other people, Jasmine experiences minor irritations as she goes about her many daily activities. Another type of background stressor is a long-term, chronic problem, such as experiencing dissatisfaction with school or job, being in an unhappy relationship, or living in crowded quarters without privacy (Lazarus & Cohen, 1977; van Eck, Nicolson, & Berkhof, 1998).

By themselves, daily hassles do not require much coping or even a response on the part of the individual, although they certainly do produce unpleasant emotions and moods. Yet daily hassles add up—and ultimately they can produce as great a toll as a single, more stressful incident. In fact, the number of daily hassles that people face is associated with psychological symptoms and health problems such as flu, sore throat, and backaches (Chamberlain & Zika, 1990; Roberts, 1995). Some of us associate overwork with the build-up of daily hassles, and many of us in Canada feel that we are overworked. However, a recent survey of people in 32 countries indicated that the average workweek for full-time employees is 42.2 hours for Canadians and longer for full-time employees in 28 other countries (Galt, 2001a). It may be that our perceptions of overwork and mounting daily hassles reflect a determination to include work, other responsibilities, and leisure activities in our lifestyles.

The flip side of hassles are **uplifts**, those minor positive events that make one feel good—even if only temporarily. Uplifts range from relating well to a companion to finding one's surroundings pleasing. What is especially intriguing about uplifts is that they are associated with people's psychological health in just the opposite way that hassles are: The greater the number of uplifts experienced, the fewer the psychological symptoms people later report.

Learned Helplessness

Have you ever faced an intolerable situation that you just couldn't resolve, where you finally just gave up and accepted things the way they were? This example illustrates one of the possible consequences of being in an environment in which control over a situation is not possible—a state that produces learned helplessness. According to psychologist Martin Seligman, **learned helplessness** occurs when people conclude that unpleasant or aversive stimuli cannot be controlled—a view of the world that becomes so

The Pine Lake, Alberta, tornado of 2000, was a cataclysmic event that caused severe, though in most cases short-term, stress in thousands of people.
Why is this type of stress generally less dangerous than many others?

personal stressors: Major life events, such as the death of a family member, that have immediate negative consequences that usually fade with time.

background stressors: Everyday annoyances, such as being stuck in traffic, that cause minor irritations that can have long-term ill effects if they continue or are compounded by other stressful events.

uplifts: Minor positive events that make one feel good.

learned helplessness: A state in which people conclude that unpleasant or aversive stimuli cannot be controlled—a view of the world that becomes so ingrained that they cease trying to remedy their aversive circumstances, even if they actually could exert some influence on them.

Everyone confronts daily hassles, or background stressors, at some point.
At what point do daily hassles become more than mere irritants?

ingrained that they cease trying to remedy the aversive circumstances, even if they actually can exert some influence (Seligman, 1975; Peterson, Maier, & Seligman, 1993).

Take, for example, what often happens to elderly persons when they are placed in nursing homes or hospitals. One of the most striking features of their new environment is that they are no longer independent: They do not have control over the most basic activities in their lives. They are told what and when to eat, and told when they may watch TV or participate in recreational activities. In addition, their sleeping schedules are arranged by someone else. It is not hard to see how this loss of control can have negative effects upon people suddenly placed, often reluctantly, in such a situation.

The results of this loss of control and the ensuing stress are frequently poorer health and even a likelihood of earlier death. These outcomes were confirmed in a classic experiment conducted in a nursing home where elderly residents in one group were encouraged to make more choices and take greater control of their day-to-day activities (Langer & Janis, 1979). As a result, members of the group were more active and happier than a comparison group of residents who were encouraged to let the nursing home staff take care of them. Moreover, an analysis of the residents' medical records revealed that six months after the experiment, the group encouraged to be self-sufficient showed significantly greater health improvement than the comparison group. Eighteen months after the experiment began, only 15 percent of the "independent" group had died—compared with 30 percent of the comparison group.

Other research confirms that learned helplessness has negative consequences, and not just for elderly people. People of all ages report more physical symptoms and depression when they perceive that they have little or no control than when they feel a sense of control over a situation (Rodin, 1986; Joiner & Wagner, 1995; Shnek et al., 1995).

Coping with Stress

Stress is a normal part of life—and not necessarily a completely bad part. For example, without stress, we might not be sufficiently motivated to complete the activities we need to accomplish. However, it is also clear that too much stress can take its toll on both physical and psychological health. How do people deal with stress? Is there a way to reduce its negative effects?

The efforts to control, reduce, or learn to tolerate the threats that lead to stress are known as **coping**. We habitually use certain coping responses to help ourselves deal with stress. Most of the time, we're not aware of these responses—just as we might be unaware of the minor stressors of life until they build up to sufficiently aversive levels (Snyder, 1999).

One means of dealing with stress that occurs on an unconscious level is the use of defence mechanisms. As we discussed in Chapter 10, **defence mechanisms** are reactions that maintain a person's sense of control and self-worth by distorting or denying the actual nature of the situation. For example, one study examined California students who lived in dormitories close to a geological fault. Those who lived in dorms that were rated as being unlikely to withstand an earthquake were significantly more likely to doubt experts' predictions of an impending earthquake than were those who lived in safer structures (Lehman & Taylor, 1988).

Another defence mechanism used to cope with stress is *emotional insulation,* in which a person stops experiencing any emotions at all, thereby remaining unaffected and unmoved by both positive and negative experiences. The problem with defence mechanisms, of course, is that they do not deal with reality but merely hide the problem.

People also use other, more direct and potentially more positive means for coping with stress. Specifically, coping strategies fall into two categories: emotion-focused coping and problem-focused coping. In *emotion-focused coping,* people try to manage

coping: Efforts to control, reduce, or learn to tolerate the threats that lead to stress.

defence mechanisms: Unconscious strategies people use to reduce anxiety by concealing its source from themselves and others.

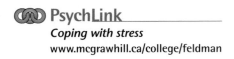
PsychLink
Coping with stress
www.mcgrawhill.ca/college/feldman

their emotions in the face of stress, seeking to change the way they feel about or perceive a problem. Examples of emotion-focused strategies include denial, avoidance, and accepting sympathy from others. These strategies may be adaptive or maladaptive, depending on the situation in which they are used (Zeidner & Saklofske, 1996). For example, avoiding a difficult situation until we can decide how to deal with it effectively is usually beneficial. However, habitually avoiding a situation instead of engaging in problem solving in order to resolve an interpersonal issue is maladaptive. *Problem-focused coping* attempts to modify the stressful problem or source of the stress. Problem-focused strategies lead to changes in behaviour or to the development of a plan of action to deal with stress. Starting a study group to improve poor classroom performance is an example of problem-focused coping.

In most stressful incidents, people employ *both* emotion-focused and problem-focused strategies. Norman Endler (York University) recently developed a multidimensional interaction model of stress and anxiety (Endler, 1997). According to this model, stressful events, coping strategies, and the consequences of stressful events all interact with each other. In general, people use emotion-focused strategies more frequently when they perceive circumstances as being unchangeable, and problem-focused approaches more often in situations they see as relatively modifiable (Lazarus, 1999; Stanton & Frantz, 1999; Folkman & Moskowitz, 2000). Cross-cultural research shows that there are both similarities and differences between cultures with respect to how people perceive and respond to stressful events. For example, Indian and Canadian university students are similar in their use of problem-focused strategies, but different in their use of emotion-focused strategies (Sinha et al., 2000).

Recently, some researchers have turned their attention to the potential of leisure for coping with stress. Leisure coping involves both leisure-coping beliefs (our beliefs about the effectiveness of chosen leisure activities in dealing with stressful situations) and leisure-coping strategies (the situation-specific use of leisure activities to combat stress) (Iwasaki & Mannell, 2000). Results of a study involving 85 Canadian university students who kept a stress log for two weeks demonstrated that both leisure-coping beliefs and strategies contributed to effectiveness of coping, satisfaction with coping outcomes, and stress reduction (Iwasaki, 2001).

Coping Style: The Hardy Personality

Most of us cope with stress in a characteristic manner, employing a *coping style* that represents our general tendency to deal with stress in a specific way. For example, you may know people who habitually react to even the smallest amount of stress with hysteria, and others who calmly confront even the greatest stress in an unflappable manner. These kinds of people clearly have quite different coping styles (Taylor, 1991; Taylor & Aspinwall, 1996). The Coping Inventory for Stressful Situations is a measure of preferred coping styles that was developed in Canada by Endler and Parker (1993). It assesses problem-focused, emotion-focused, and avoidance coping strategies.

Among those who cope with stress most successfully are people with the coping style of **hardiness**, a personality characteristic associated with a lower rate of stress-related illness. It consists of three components (Kobasa, 1979; Gentry & Kobasa, 1984):

hardiness: A personality characteristic associated with a lower rate of stress-related illness, consisting of three components: commitment, challenge, and control.

- *Commitment.* Commitment is a tendency to throw ourselves into whatever we are doing with a sense that our activities are important and meaningful.
- *Challenge.* Hardy people believe that change, rather than stability, is the standard condition of life. To them, the anticipation of change is an incentive rather than a threat to their security.
- *Control.* Hardy people feel a sense of control—they believe that they can influence the events in their lives.

Hardy individuals approach stress optimistically and take direct action, changing stressful events into less threatening ones. As a consequence, hardiness acts as a defence against stress-related illness (Wiebe, 1991; Solcova & Tomanek, 1994; Kobasa et al., 1994).

Pathways Through Psychology

Jo-Anne Trigg

Supervisor of Special Services, Halton District School Board, Burlington, Ontario

Education: B.A. (psychology), University of Toronto; M.A., (applied child development), University of Guelph; Registered Psychological Associate, College of Psychologists of Ontario

Home: Oakville, Ontario

Jo-Anne Trigg

I work within the Student Services Department of the Halton Board, where the primary responsibility is the education of students with special needs. The role is varied and includes case management and problem solving for children who have serious learning and behaviour problems. There is co-ordination of a Behaviour Action Team, and supervision of a special services team which consists of child and youth counsellors, social workers, psychoeducational consultants, and speech and language pathologists. I also consult two classes of students who have serious behaviour problems and require a special setting. I am involved with decisions regarding allocation of resources and staff, policy development, and staff development.

Over the years there have been many opportunities to develop areas of interest and therefore some expertise. For example, I had the opportunity to work with a committee of staff from the school board and representatives from the broader community to develop a protocol for assessment of Attention Deficit Hyperactivity Disorder (ADHD), and a manual for schools on this condition. Resources were researched and purchased for schools, and inservice on ADHD was conducted.

I have an ongoing interest in the area of autism, which developed when increasing numbers of students with this developmental disorder were entering school and there was little known about

it. I have been able to learn more about this condition through training opportunities, reading, and working closely with families and the community. The training has taken me to North Carolina, where I had the opportunity to meet teachers, parents, and other professionals from all over the world. A most fulfilling role was to participate with a group of dedicated parents in the formation of the Halton Chapter of the Autism Society. Recently I chaired a task force made up of board staff, community partners, and parents. The report, which made recommendations about the services and programmes required for students with autism, will hopefully direct our planning over the next several years.

I am fortunate to work within an organization and with people who have encouraged me both professionally and personally. In addition, the parents and kids I have met along the way have been instrumental in making my career in psychology a fulfilling one.

Source: Jo-Anne Trigg, M.A., Halton District School Board

What issues challenge the students that Jo–Anne Trigg and her colleagues at Halton Board work with? What are some of the stresses experienced by special needs students? What are some stresses and satisfactions associated with the work Jo-Anne Trigg does?

Social Support: Turning to Others

social support: A mutual network of caring, interested others.

Our relationships with others also help us cope with stress. Researchers have found that **social support**, the knowledge that we are part of a mutual network of caring, interested others, enables us to cope better with the stress we do undergo (Uchino, Uno, & Holt-Lunstad, 1999; McCabe et al., 2000).

Social and emotional support helps in dealing with stress in several ways. For instance, such support demonstrates that the person is an important and valued member of a social network, and other people can provide information and advice about appropriate ways of dealing with stress (Hobfoll et al., 1996; Lepore, Ragan, & Jones, 2000). People can also provide actual goods and services to help others in stressful situations: by supplying a person whose house has burned down with temporary living quarters, helping a student who is experiencing stress study for a test, and so on (Croyle & Hunt, 1991; Peirce et al., 1996).

Furthermore, the social support available in close relationships can moderate or prevent some inappropriate ways of handling stress. In one study, young adults who were not involved in intimate relationships were found to be more prone to problem drinking than those in committed relationships. Over time, unattached young adults tended to increase alcoholic consumption, whereas those involved in intimate relationships tended to reduce their alcoholic consumption (Sadava & Pak, 1994).

"Today, we examined our life style, we evaluated our diet and our exercise program, and we also assessed our behavioral patterns. Then we felt we needed a drink."

Surprisingly, the benefits of social support are not limited to the comfort provided by other humans. One study found that owners of pets were less likely than those without pets to require medical care following exposure to stressors. Dogs, in particular, helped diminish the effects of stress (Siegel, 1990, 1993).

BECOMING AN
INFORMED CONSUMER
OF PSYCHOLOGY

Why is it so important to develop strategies for coping with stress?

Effective Coping Strategies

What are the most effective ways to deal with stress? There is no universal solution, of course, because effective coping depends on the nature of the stressor and the degree to which it is possible to control it. Still, researchers have developed some general guidelines (Holahan & Moos, 1990; McCain & Smith, 1994; Zeidner & Endler, 1996; Aspinwall & Taylor, 1997):

- *Turn threat into challenge.* When a stressful situation might be controllable, the best coping strategy is to treat the situation as a challenge, focusing on ways to control it. For instance, if you experience stress because your car is always breaking down, you might take an evening course in auto mechanics and learn to deal directly with the car's problems.
- *Make a threatening situation less threatening.* When a stressful situation seems to be uncontrollable, a different approach must be taken. It is possible to change your appraisal of the situation, to view it in a different light, and to modify your attitudes toward it. The old truism "Look for the silver lining in every cloud" is supported by research (Silver & Wortman, 1980; Taylor & Aspinwall, 1996; Salovey et al., 2000). A sense of humour also helps by acting as a buffer against stress (Martin, 1996). Humour can also facilitate changing pessimism to optimism (Lefcourt, 2001).
- *Change your goals.* When faced with an uncontrollable situation, a reasonable strategy is to adopt new goals that are practical in view of the particular situation. For example, a dancer who has been in an automobile accident and has lost full use of her legs might replace her aspiration to a career in dance with the goal of becoming a dance instructor.
- *Take physical action.* Changing your physiological reaction to stress can help you cope. For example, biofeedback, discussed in Chapter 2, can alter your basic physiological processes, allowing you to reduce your blood pressure, heart rate, and other consequences of heightened stress. Exercise can also be effective in reducing stress. Regular exercise improves your overall health and can even reduce your risk for certain diseases. Finally, exercise can give you a sense of control over your body and a feeling of accomplishment (Thune et al., 1997; Barinaga, 1997; Langreth, 2000).
- *Prepare for stress before it happens.* A final strategy for coping with stress is *proactive coping:* anticipating and preparing for stress *before* you encounter it. Through proactive coping, you can ready yourself for upcoming stressful events and thereby reduce their negative consequences (Aspinwall & Taylor, 1997).

Evaluate

1. _____ is defined as a response to challenging or threatening events.
2. Match each portion of the GAS with its definition
   1. Alarm
   2. Exhaustion
   3. Resistance

   a. The ability to adapt to stress diminishes; symptoms appear
   b. Activation of the sympathetic nervous system
   c. Various strategies are used to cope with a stressor
3. Stressors that affect a single person and produce an immediate major reaction are known as
   a. Personal stressors
   b. Psychic stressors
   c. Cataclysmic stressors
   d. Daily stressors
4. People with the personality characteristic of _____ seem to be more able to successfully combat stressors.

Answers to Evaluate Questions

1. Stress 2. 1–b; 2–a; 3–c 3. a 4. hardiness

Rethink

1. Why are cataclysmic stressors less stressful in the long run than other types of stressors? Does the reason relate to the coping phenomenon known as social support? How?
2. Given what you know about coping strategies, how would you train people to avoid stress in their everyday lives? How would you use this information with a group of Canadian peacekeepers suffering from posttraumatic stress disorder?

Prepare

How do psychological factors affect such health-related problems as coronary heart disease, cancer, and smoking?

Organize

Psychological Aspects of Illness and Well-Being
  The A's and B's of Coronary Heart Disease
  Psychological Aspects of Cancer
  Smoking
  Well-Being and Happiness

Psychological Aspects of Illness and Well-Being

Once a week they meet to talk, to cry, sometimes to laugh together. "Is the pain still worse in the mornings?" Margaret asks Kate today.

A petite, graceful woman in her late forties, Kate shakes her head no. "It's getting bad all the time," she says in a voice raw with worry and fatigue. A few weeks ago she learned that the cancer that began in her breast had spread into her bones. Since then she's hardly slept. She knows, as do the other women in the group, that her prognosis isn't good. "Sometimes I'm afraid I'm not going to do that well because it all came on so fast," she tells them. "It's like being in the ocean and the waves are just coming too fast, and you can't get your breath."

They nod in tacit understanding, eight women sitting in a loose circle of chairs here in a small, sparely furnished room at Stanford University Medical Center. They know. All of them have been diagnosed with recurrent breast cancer. . . .

They gather here each Wednesday afternoon to talk with each other and to listen. It's a chance to discuss their fears and find some small comfort, a time to feel they're not alone. And in some way that no one has been able to explain, it may be keeping them alive. (Jaret, 1992, p. 87)

As recently as two decades ago, most psychologists and health-care providers would have scoffed at the notion that a discussion group could improve a cancer patient's chances of survival. Today, however, such methods have gained increasing respectability.

Growing evidence suggests that psychological factors have a substantial impact, both on major health problems that were once seen in purely physiological terms and on our everyday sense of health, well-being, and happiness. A recent Canadian public health policy report emphasizes the importance of lifestyle in relation to health and well-being (Federal, Provincial and Territory Advisory Committee on Population Health, 1999). Among young Canadian adults, employment status as well as lifestyle factors (e.g., health behaviours, driving practices) have been found to influence health (Sadava et al., 2000). "Being satisfactorily employed is health-enhancing, and those who lack satisfactory employment, both those who are unemployed and those who are underemployed in terms of the nature or the hours of their work, suffer by comparison" (Sadava et al., 2000, p. 559).

We'll consider the psychological components of three major health problems—heart disease, cancer, and smoking—and then consider the nature of people's well-being and happiness.

The A's and B's of Coronary Heart Disease

Have you ever seethed impatiently at being caught behind a slow-moving vehicle, or felt anger and frustration at not finding material you needed at the library?

Many of us experience these sorts of feelings at one time or another, but for some people they represent a pervasive, characteristic set of personality traits (of the type discussed in Chapter 10) known as the **Type A behaviour pattern**. Type A individuals are competitive, show a continual sense of urgency about time, are aggressive, exhibit a driven quality regarding their work, engage in "multitasking," and are hostile, both verbally and nonverbally—especially when interrupted while trying to complete a task. On the other hand, people who show the **Type B behaviour pattern** are more cooperative, far less competitive, not especially time-oriented, and not usually aggressive, driven, or hostile. Although people are typically not "pure" Type A's or Type B's, showing instead a combination of both behaviour types, they generally do fall into one category or the other (Rosenman, 1990; Strube, 1990; see Chapter Activity 11-2).

The Type A behaviour pattern is linked to coronary heart disease. Studies have found that men who display the Type A pattern develop coronary heart disease twice as often and suffer significantly more fatal heart attacks compared with those classified as having the Type B pattern. Moreover, the Type A pattern predicts who is going to develop heart disease at least as well as—and independently of—any other single factor, including

Type A behaviour pattern: A pattern of behaviour characterized by competitiveness, impatience, tendency toward frustration, and hostility.

Type B behaviour pattern: A pattern of behaviour characterized by cooperation, patience, noncompetitiveness, and nonaggression.

 **PsychLink**

Type A personality
www.mcgrawhill.ca/college/feldman

Chapter Activity 11–2 Type Yourself

To get an idea of whether you have the characteristics of a Type A or Type B personality, answer the following questions:

1. When you listen to someone talking and this person takes too long to come to the point, how often do you feel like hurrying the person along?

   _____Frequently
   _____Occasionally
   _____Never

2. Do you ever set deadlines or quotas for yourself at work or at home?

   _____No
   _____Yes, but only occasionally
   _____Yes, once a week or more

3. Would people you know well agree that you tend to get irritated easily?

   _____Definitely yes
   _____Probably yes
   _____Probably no
   _____Definitely no

4. Would people who know you well agree that you tend to do most things in a hurry?

   _____Definitely yes
   _____Probably yes
   _____Probably no
   _____Definitely no

Scoring: The more frequently your answers reflect affirmative responses, the more Type A characteristics you hold.

From Jenkins, Zyzsndki & Rosenman, "Coronary-Prone Behavior: One Pattern or Several?" *Psychosomatic Medicine*, 40, pp. 25–43, 1979. Reprinted with permission of Lippincott, Williams and Wilkins Publishers.

Most people can be classified as primarily either Type A or Type B. Type A's tend to be competitive, time-oriented, aggressive, driven, and hostile— and to be more vulnerable to coronary heart disease than Type B's. Are there types of careers where Type A personalities are more successful than Type B's? Why?

age, blood pressure, smoking habits, and cholesterol levels in the body (Rosenman et al., 1976; Rosenman et al., 1994; Wielgosz & Nolan, 2000).

Current research suggests that not every component of the Type A behaviour pattern is linked to coronary heart disease. Hostility and anger seem to be the key factors, though other negative emotions, such as depression and low self-esteem, are now also thought to be related to heart attacks (Mittleman et al., 1995; McCabe et al., 2000; Williams, Paton, et al., 2000).

Why is Type A behaviour, and hostility and anger in particular, linked to coronary heart disease? The most convincing theory is that the Type A behaviour pattern produces excessive physiological arousal. This arousal, in turn, results in increased production of the hormones epinephrine and norepinephrine, as well as increased heart rate and blood pressure. Such exaggerated physiological responsivity ultimately produces an increased incidence of coronary heart disease (Blascovich & Katkin, 1993; Sundin et al., 1995).

It's important to keep in mind that not everyone who displays Type A behaviours is destined to have coronary heart disease. For one thing, a firm association between Type A behaviours and coronary heart disease has not been established for women; most studies have been done on males, not females. Furthermore, the evidence relating Type A behaviour and coronary heart disease is correlational. Consequently, as we first discussed in Chapter 1, we cannot say for sure whether Type A behaviour *causes* heart disease or whether, instead, some other factor causes both heart disease and Type A behaviour. In fact, rather than focusing on Type A behaviour as the cause of heart disease, it might make more sense to ask whether Type B behaviour *prevents* heart disease (Powell, Shaker, & Jones, 1993; Orth-Gomér, Chesney, & Wenger, 1996).

Psychological Aspects of Cancer

Hardly any disease is more feared than cancer. Most people think of cancer in terms of lingering pain, and being diagnosed with the disease is typically viewed as receiving a death sentence.

Although a diagnosis of cancer is not as grim as you might at first suspect—several kinds of cancer have a high cure rate if detected early enough—cancer remains the second leading cause of death after coronary heart disease. Recent statistics show that 28 percent of deaths in Canada in 1999 were due to cancer, compared with 36 percent due to cardiovascular disease (Statistics Canada, 2002a). The precise trigger for cancer is not well understood, but the process by which the disease spreads is straightforward. Certain cells in the body become altered and multiply rapidly and in an uncontrolled fashion. As these cells grow, they form tumours, which, if left unchecked, suck nutrients from healthy cells and bodily tissue, ultimately destroying the body's ability to function properly.

Although the processes involved in the spread of cancer are basically physiological, accumulating evidence suggests that the emotional responses of cancer patients to their disease can have a critical effect on its course. For example, one experiment found that people who adopt a fighting spirit are more likely to recover than those who pessimistically suffer and resign themselves to death (Pettingale et al., 1985). Female breast cancer patients who stoically accepted their fate and felt they faced a hopeless situation had lower survival rates than patients who responded with a fighting spirit and felt they could overcome the disease. (See Figure 11-2.)

On the other hand, other research contradicts the notion that the course of cancer is affected by patients' attitudes and emotions. For example, some findings show that although a "fighting spirit" leads to better coping, the long-term survival rate is no better than for patients with a less positive attitude (Watson et al., 1999).

Despite the contradictory evidence, health psychologists believe that patients' emotions might at least partially determine the course of their disease. For example, psychologists specializing in psychoneuroimmunology suggest that a patient's emotional state affects the immune system, the body's natural defences that fight disease. Our bodies produce *lymphocytes,* specialized white blood cells that fight disease, at an extraordinary rate—some 10 million every few seconds—and it is possible that emotions affect this production. In the case of cancer, for instance, it is possible that positive emotional responses might help generate specialized "killer" cells that help control the size and spread of cancerous tumours. Conversely, negative emotions might suppress the ability of the same kinds of cells to fight tumours (Andersen, Kiecolt-Glaser, & Glaser, 1994; Seligman, 1995; Schedlowski & Tewes, 1999).

Other research suggests that "joy" (mental resilience and vigour) is related to the likelihood of survival of patients with recurrent breast cancer. Similarly, cancer patients who are characteristically optimistic report less distress throughout the course of their treatment (Levy et al., 1988; Carver et al., 2000).

Is a particular personality type linked to cancer? Some findings suggest that cancer patients are less emotionally reactive, suppress anger, and lack outlets for emotional release. However, the data are still too tentative and inconsistent to suggest firm conclusions about a link between personality characteristics and cancer. Certainly there is no conclusive evidence that people who develop cancer would not have done so if they had had a different personality or more positive attitudes (Smith, 1988; Zevon & Corn, 1990; Holland, 1996).

What is increasingly clear, however, is that certain types of psychological therapy have the potential to extend the lives of cancer patients. One study found that women with breast cancer who received psychological treatment lived at least a year and a half longer, and experienced less anxiety and pain, than women who did not participate in therapy. Research on patients with other health problems, such as heart disease, also finds that therapy can be beneficial, both psychologically and medically (Spiegel, 1993, 1996a; Galavotti et al., 1997; Frasure-Smith, Lesperance, & Talajic, 2000).

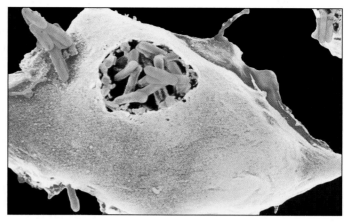

The ability to fight off disease is related to psychological factors. Here a cell from the body's immune system engulfs and destroys disease-producing bacteria.

PsychLink

Stress and cancer
www.mcgrawhill.ca/college/feldman

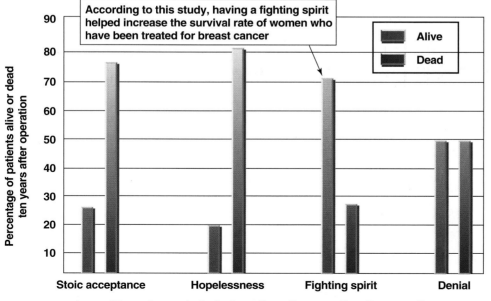

Figure 11-2 The relationship between women's psychological response to breast cancer three months after surgery and their survival ten years after the operation (Pettingale et al., 1985). *What implications do these findings have for the treatment of people with cancer?*

Smoking

Since the passage of the Canadian Tobacco Act in 1997, packages of tobacco products must bear warning labels containing information about the product's emissions and associated health hazards and effects. For example, some cigarette packages state that each year 45 000 Canadians die from tobacco use. Currently, cigarette packages also have alarming pictures accompanying the warning labels. Some health groups (such as the Canadian Cancer Society, the Heart and Stroke Foundation, and the Canadian Medical Association) question the effectiveness of these warning labels and are urging the federal government to target tobacco companies instead of smokers in the campaign to reduce smoking (Picard, 2002). Smoking is linked to cancer, heart attacks, strokes, bronchitis, emphysema, and a host of other serious illnesses. In part because of exposure to smoking, Aboriginal children worldwide are at greater risk for lower respiratory tract infections than non-Aboriginal children. Researchers calculated that Inuit preschoolers on Baffin Island are 48 times as likely to require hospitalization for such infections as the general population (Mahoney, 2001). Worldwide, 3 million people die prematurely each year due to the effects of smoking (Heishman, Kozlowki, & Henningfield, 1997; Kawachi et al., 1997; Noble, 1999).

Why do people smoke, despite all the evidence that it is bad for their health? It is not that they are unaware of the link between smoking and disease; surveys show that most *smokers* agree with the statement "Cigarette smoking frequently causes disease and death." And almost three-quarters of the 48 million smokers in the United States say they would like to quit (Centers for Disease Control, 1994; Wetter et al., 1998). According to a recent Canadian survey (Health Canada, 2001), half of the daily smokers surveyed had tried to quit smoking; 38 percent had made one to three attempts to quit and another 12 percent had made four or more attempts.

Heredity seems to partly determine whether people will become smokers, how much they will smoke, and how easily they can quit. Genetics also influences how susceptible people are to the harmful effects of smoking. For instance, there is an almost 50 percent higher rate of lung cancer in black smokers than in white smokers. This difference could be due to genetically produced variations in the efficiency with which enzymes are able to reduce the effects of the cancer-causing chemicals in tobacco smoke (Pomerlau, 1995; Heath & Madden, 1995; Richie, 1994).

On the other hand, although genetics plays a role in smoking, most research suggests that environmental factors are the primary cause of the habit. Smokers might at first see smoking as sophisticated or as helping them perform calmly under stressful situations. In addition, smoking a cigarette is sometimes viewed as a "rite of passage" for adolescents, undertaken at the urging of friends and viewed as a sign of growing up (Grube, Rokeach, & Getzlaf, 1990; Koval et al., 2000; Wagner & Atkins, 2000).

But ultimately, smoking becomes a habit. In Canada, 22 percent of the population aged 12 years and over smoke daily (Statistics Canada, 2000). People begin to label themselves smokers, and smoking becomes part of their self-concept. Moreover, they become dependent on the physiological effects of smoking, because nicotine, a primary ingredient of tobacco, is highly addictive. Ultimately, a complex relationship develops among smoking, nicotine levels, and the smoker's emotional state, in which a certain nicotine level becomes associated with a positive emotional state. As a result, people smoke in an effort to regulate *both* emotional states and nicotine levels in the blood (Leventhal & Cleary, 1980; Gilbert, 1995).

Quitting Smoking

Because smoking has both psychological and biological components, few habits are as difficult to break. Long-term successful treatment typically occurs in just 15 percent of those trying to stop

Changes in society's attitudes, and strong anti-smoking campaigns, can go a long way toward reducing tobacco use.

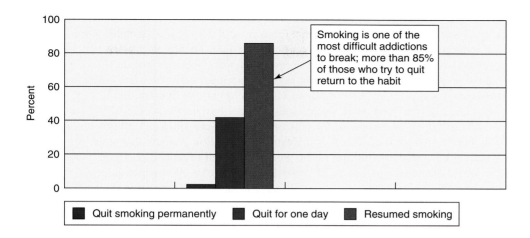

Figure 11-3 The difficulty of quitting smoking is evident in this graph. More than 85 percent of those who tried to quit returned to smoking.
Why do you think so many people return to smoking?
Morbidity and Mortality Weekly Report, July 9, 1993, Center for Disease Control.

smoking, and once smoking becomes a habit, it is as hard to stop as an addiction to cocaine or heroin. In fact, some of the biochemical reactions to nicotine are similar to reactions to cocaine, amphetamines, and morphine. Many people try to quit and fail, as you can see in Figure 11-3 (Glassman & Koob, 1996; Piasecki et al., 1997; National Council on Aging, 2000).

Among the most effective tools for ending the smoking habit are drugs that replace the nicotine found in cigarettes. Whether in the form of gum, patches, nasal sprays, or inhalers, these products provide a dose of nicotine that reduces dependence on cigarettes. Another approach is exemplified by the drug Zyban, which, rather than replacing nicotine, raises dopamine levels in the brain, thereby reducing the desire to smoke (Rock, 1999).

Behavioural strategies that view smoking as a learned habit and concentrate on changing the smoking response can also be effective. Initial "cure" rates of 60 percent have been reported, and one year after treatment more than half of those who quit have not resumed smoking. Counselling, either individually or in groups, also increases the rate of success in breaking the habit. The best treatment seems to be a combination of nicotine replacement *and* counselling. What doesn't work? Going it alone: Only 5 percent of smokers who quit cold-turkey on their own are successful (Wetter et al., 1998; Rock, 1999; Noble, 1999).

In the long term, the most effective way to reduce smoking could be changes in societal norms and attitudes toward the habit. Legislation banning smoking in public places such as college buildings and restaurants supports a negative view of smoking.

EXPLORING DIVERSITY

Hucksters of Death: Promoting Smoking Throughout the World

In Dresden, Germany, three women in miniskirts offer passers-by a pack of Lucky Strikes and a leaflet that reads: "You just got hold of a nice piece of America." Says a local doctor, "Adolescents time and again receive cigarettes at such promotions."

A Jeep decorated with the Camel logo pulls up to a high school in Buenos Aires. A woman begins handing out free cigarettes to 15- and 16-year-olds during their lunch recess.

At a video arcade in Taipei, free American cigarettes are strewn atop each game. At a disco filled with high school students, free packs of Salems are on each table. (Ecenbarger, 1993, p. 50)

As the number of smokers has declined in the United States, cigarette manufacturers have turned to new markets in an effort to increase the number of people who smoke. They have set their sights on other parts of the world, where they see a fertile market of nonsmokers (Sesser, 1993). In the process, they have employed some dubious marketing

Do developed countries have a responsibility for combatting the promotion of smoking in developing countries? Why or why not?

Smoking and health
www.mcgrawhill.ca/college/feldman

techniques. Although they must often sell cigarettes more cheaply abroad than in the United States, the number of potential smokers still makes it financially worthwhile for the tobacco companies. For instance, in 1995, China opened its market of 298 million smokers—more than the entire U.S. population—to American brands (Hass, 1994). As can be seen in Figure 11-4, overseas sales have surged since the mid 1980s, as sales in the United States have declined (Bartecchi, MacKenzie, & Schrier, 1995).

Clearly, the push into worldwide markets has been successful. In some Latin American cities, as many as 50 percent of teenagers smoke. Children as young as 7 smoke in Hong Kong. The World Health Organization predicts that smoking will prematurely kill some 200 million of the world's children (Ecenbarger, 1993). According to the World Health Organization, at present, more than 10 000 people die every day from smoking. By the year 2020, tobacco will become the world's largest single health problem, causing an estimated 8.4 million deaths annually, and this number will increase to an estimated 10 million deaths annually by 2030. Furthermore, since tobacco use is declining in developed countries and increasing rapidly in developing countries, a disproportionate number of deaths will occur in developing regions of the world (World Health Organization, n.d.). Clearly, smoking is one of the world's greatest health problems.

Well-Being and Happiness

What makes for a good life?

Philosophers and theologians have pondered this question for centuries, and now health psychologists are turning their spotlight on it. They are doing so by investigating **subjective well-being**, people's evaluations of their lives in terms of both their thoughts and emotions. Considered another way, subjective well-being is the measure of how happy people are (Diener, 2000).

Research on subjective well-being shows that happy people share several characteristics (Myers & Diener, 1996; Myers, 2000):

- *Happy people have high self-esteem.* Particularly in Western cultures, which emphasize the importance of individuality, people who are happy like themselves. They see themselves as more intelligent and better able to get along with others than the average person.

subjective well-being: People's evaluations of their lives in terms of both their thoughts and their emotions; how happy people are.

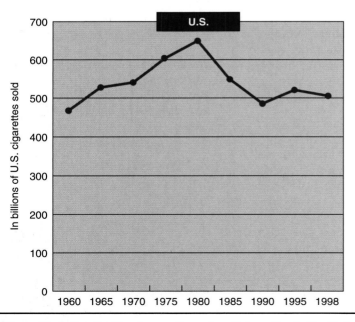

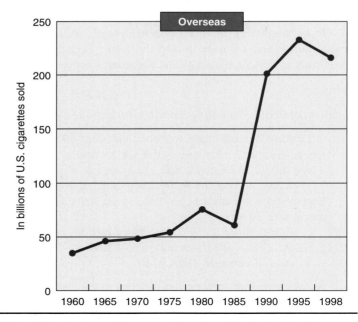

Figure 11–4 Despite the plummeting sales of cigarettes in the United States, the number sold overseas has dramatically increased. *How can these differences be accounted for?*

Source: U.S. Department of Agriculture, 1998.

Applying Psychology in the 21st Century

If You Won the Lottery, Would You Be Happier?

Probably not.

At least that's the implication of an increasing body of research on subjective well-being. This research shows that although winning the lottery brings an initial surge in happiness, a year later winners' level of happiness seems to return to what it was before. The converse phenomenon occurs for people who have suffered serious injuries in accidents: Despite an initial decline in happiness, most victims return to their prior levels of happiness over time (Diener et al., 1999).

Why is the level of subjective well-being so stable? One explanation is that people have a general "set point" for happiness, a marker that establishes the tone for one's life. Although a particular event (a surprise promotion or a job loss, for example) might temporarily elevate or depress one's mood, ultimately people return to their usual general level of happiness.

Although it is not certain how people's happiness set points are initially established, some evidence suggests that genetic factors play a role. Specifically, identical twins who grow up in widely different circumstances turn out to have quite similar levels of happiness (Diener & Diener, 1996; Lykken & Tellegen, 1996; Kahneman, Diener, & Schwarz, 1998).

Most people's well-being set point is relatively high. For example, some 30 percent

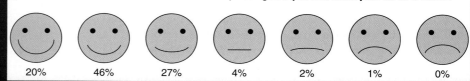

Faces Scale: "Which face comes closest to expressing how you feel about your life as a whole?"

20%   46%   27%   4%   2%   1%   0%

Figure 11–5 Most people in the U.S. rate themselves very happy; only a small percentage indicate that they are not happy (Myers, 2000).

of people in the United States rate themselves as "very happy," and only one in ten rate themselves as "not too happy." Most people declare themselves to be "pretty happy." Such feelings are graphically confirmed by people asked to place themselves on the measure of happiness illustrated in Figure 11-5. The scale clearly illustrates that most people view their lives quite positively.

Similar results are found when people are asked to compare themselves to others. For example, when asked "Who of the following people do you think is the happiest?" survey respondents answered "Oprah Winfrey" (23 percent), "Bill Gates" (7 percent), "the Pope" (12 percent), "Chelsea Clinton" (3 percent), and "yourself" (49 percent), with 6 percent saying they didn't know (Black & McCafferty, 1998).

Demographic groups don't differ much from each other on this measure. Men and women report being equally happy, and African

Americans are only slightly less likely than white Americans to rate themselves as "very happy." Furthermore, happiness is hardly unique to U.S. culture. Even countries that are far from economically prosperous have, on the whole, happy residents (Myers & Diener, 1996; Mroczek & Kolarz, 1998; Schkade & Kahneman, 1998; Staudinger, Fleeson, & Baltes, 1999; Diener, 2000).

The bottom line: Money does *not* seem to buy happiness. Despite the ups and downs of life, most people tend to be reasonably happy, and they adapt to the trials and tribulations—and joys and delights—of life by returning to a steady-state level of happiness.

Why do you think people consistently rate themselves happier than they rate wealthy and powerful people like Oprah Winfrey and Bill Gates? Do you think Winfrey and Gates would agree?

- *Happy people have a firm sense of control.* They feel more in control of events in their lives, unlike people who feel they are the pawns of others and who experience learned helplessness.
- *Happy individuals are optimistic.* Their optimism permits them to persevere at tasks and ultimately to achieve more. Their health is also better (Peterson, 2000).
- *Happy people like to be around other people.* They tend to be extroverted and have a supportive network of close relationships.

Perhaps most important, most people are at least moderately happy most of the time. Canadians who enjoy their jobs are generally happier than those who do not, and this is particularly true for women (Galt, 2001b). However, workaholics are much less likely to say they are happy and much more likely than others to experience frequent stress (Kemeny, 2002). In both national and international surveys, people living in a wide variety of circumstances report being happy. Furthermore—as we consider in the *Applying Psychology in the 21st Century* box—winning the lottery probably won't make you happy. According to a variety of findings, happiness can't be bought.

Evaluate

1. Type_____behaviour is characterized by cooperativeness and by being easy-going, whereas Type_____behaviour is characterized by aggression and competitiveness.
2. Type A behaviour is known to directly cause heart attacks. True or false?
3. A cancer patient's attitude and emotions might affect that person's_____system, helping or hindering their fight against the disease.
4. Smokers use smoking to regulate both their nicotine levels and their emotional states. True or false?

Answers to Evaluate Questions

1. B; A 2. False; Type A behaviour is related to a higher incidence of coronary heart disease, but does not necessarily directly cause it. 3. immune 4. True

Rethink

1. Do you think Type A or Type B behaviour is more widely encouraged in Canada and the United States? Why?
2. If money doesn't buy happiness, what *can* you do to make yourself happier? As you answer, consider the research findings on stress and coping, as well as our discussion of emotions in Chapter 8.

Prepare

How do our interactions with physicians affect our health and adherence to medical treatment?

Organize

Psychological Factors Related to Physical Illness
    Physician–Patient Communication
    Adhering to Physicians' Recommendations

PsychLink
Physician communication
www.mcgrawhill.ca/college/feldman

Psychological Factors Related to Physical Illness: Going to the Doctor

When Stuart Grinspoon first noticed the small lump in his arm, he assumed it was just a bruise from the football game he had played the previous week. But as he thought about it more, he considered more serious possibilities and decided that he better get it checked out at the university health service. The visit was less than satisfactory. A shy person, Stuart felt embarrassed talking about his medical condition. Even worse, after answering a string of questions, he couldn't even understand the physician's diagnosis, and was too embarrassed to ask for clarification.

Stuart Grinspoon's attitudes toward health care are shared by many of us. Good medical care does not depend just on physical exams and prescribing a treatment. Several psychological factors are involved in determining the success of a health care provider's effectiveness in diagnosing and treating medical problems.

Physician–Patient Communication

Many patients are reluctant to describe their symptoms to their physicians. But this is a common problem. They believe that a skilled physician will easily be able to identify a patient's problems through a thorough physical examination, the way a good mechanic diagnoses car problems. But diagnosing a medical problem is both a science and an art—one in which physicians are not always successful (Leigh & Reiser, 1980; Mentzer & Snyder, 1982; Konrad, 1994).

One source of physician–patient communication difficulties is that physicians have relatively high social prestige and power, which can intimidate patients. Patients might also be reluctant to volunteer information that could cast them in a bad light, and physicians might not be skilled at encouraging their patients to provide information. Physicians often dominate the interview with questions of a technical nature, whereas patients tend to attempt to communicate a personal sense of their illness and the impact it is having on their lives. Add to these communication problems the embarrassment many people feel in discussing personal matters (Beckman & Frankel, 1984; Goleman, 1988). These communication difficulties can prevent providers from understanding the extent of the difficulties that led the patients to seek medical care in the first place (Parrott, Duncan, & Duggan, 2000; see Table 11-1).

The view held by many patients that physicians are "all-knowing" can also result in serious communication problems. For instance, many patients do not understand their treatment, yet fail to ask their physicians for a clearer explanation of a prescribed course of action. About half of all patients are unable to accurately report how long they are to continue taking a medication prescribed for them, and about a quarter do not even know the purpose of the drug. In fact, some patients are not even sure, as they are about to be rolled into the operating room, why they are having surgery (Svarstad, 1976; Atkinson, 1997)!

Another reason for patient–physician communication difficulties is that the information that must be communicated can be too technical for patients who lack fundamental knowledge about the human body and basic medical practices. In response to this problem, some health care providers routinely use baby talk (calling patients "honey" or telling them to go "night-night") and assume that patients are unable to understand even simple information (Whitbourne & Wills, 1993; DiMatteo, 1997; Basset et al., 1998).

Cultural values and expectations also contribute to communication barriers between patients and their physicians, as can language barriers when the patient and the physician do not speak the same native language. Furthermore, medical practices differ between cultures, and medical practitioners need to be familiar with a patient's culture if they are going to be successful in getting the patient to comply with medical recommendations (Bush & Osterweis, 1978; Dressler & Oths, 1997; Whaley, 2000).

Adhering to Physicians' Recommendations

One serious major consequence of patient–physician communication difficulties is a lack of adherence to medical advice: Surveys show that perhaps as many as 85 percent of patients do not fully comply with their physician's advice. In fact, some estimates suggest that almost three-quarters of the prescriptions for medicine are not followed properly, at a cost of $100 billion each year (Kaplan, Sallis, & Patterson, 1993; Hammond & Lambert, 1994a, 1994b; Zuger, 1998).

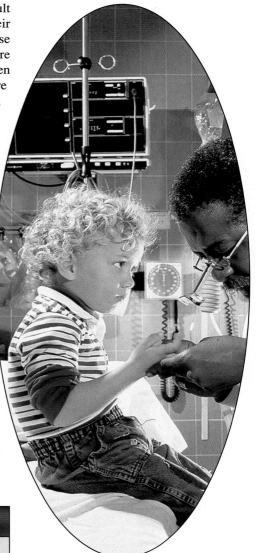

Good health care combines trust on the part of the patient with empathy and understanding on the part of the physician.

Table 11-1 A Patient Talks to Her Physician

The following excerpt from a case study used at the Harvard Medical School is an example of poor interviewing technique on the part of the physician.

Patient: I can hardly drink water.
Doctor: Um hum.
Patient: Remember when it started? . . . It was pains in my head. It must have been then.
Doctor: Um hum.
Patient: I don't know what it is. The doctor looked at it . . . said something about glands.
Doctor: Ok. Um hum, aside from this, how have you been feeling?
Patient: Terrible.
Doctor: Yeah.
Patient: Tired . . . there's pains . . . I don't know what it is.
Doctor: Ok. . . . Fevers or chills?
Patient: No.
Doctor: Ok. . . . Have you been sick to your stomach or anything?
Patient: (Sniffles, crying) I don't know what's going on. I get up in the morning tired. The only time I feel good . . . maybe like around suppertime . . . and everything (crying) and still the same thing.
Doctor: Um hum. You're getting the nausea before you eat or after? (Goleman, 1988, p. B16)

Although the frequent "um hums" suggest that the physician is listening to the patient, in fact they do not encourage the patient to disclose more pertinent details. Even more, late in the interview, the physician ignores the patient's emotional distress and coldly continues through the list of questions.

Forms of Patient Nonadherence

Nonadherence can take many forms. Patients might fail to show up for scheduled appointments. They might not follow diets or might not give up smoking. They might discontinue medication during treatment; sometimes, they don't take prescribed medicine at all. Patients also might practise *creative nonadherence,* in which they modify a treatment prescribed by a physician, relying instead on their own medical judgment and experience. (Weintraub, 1976; Taylor, 1995).

Nonadherence is sometimes the result of psychological reactance. **Reactance** is a negative emotional and cognitive reaction to a restriction of one's freedom. People who experience reactance feel hostility and anger and may act in a way that worsens their medical condition. For instance, a man who develops reactance to a strict diet might eat even more than he did before his diet was restricted (Brehm & Brehm, 1981; Rhodewalt & Fairfield, 1991).

reactance: A negative emotional and cognitive reaction to a restriction of one's freedom that can be associated with medical regimens.

 **PsychLink**

Physician–patient rapport
www.mcgrawhill.ca/college/feldman

Increasing Adherence

Although adherence to a physician's advice does not guarantee that the patient's medical problems will go away, it does optimize the possibility that the patient's condition will improve. What, then, can physicians do to produce greater adherence on the part of their patients? One strategy is to provide clear instructions to patients regarding drug regimens. Another is for physicians to maintain good, warm relationships with patients (Cramer, 1995; Cheney, 1996).

Physicians who provide clear, honest communication with their patients also produce greater adherence. Patients who are well informed and like their physicians have greater confidence in their physician's medical expertise, which in turn leads them to have less anxiety and better medical outcomes. Overall, then, a positive relationship with one's physician brings with it the potential for substantial health benefits (Kaplan, Sallis, & Patterson, 1993; Wyshak & Barsky, 1995).

Evaluate

1. Many health psychologists believe that the biggest problem in health care is:
   a. incompetent health care providers.
   b. rising health care costs.
   c. lack of communication between physician and patient.
   d. scarcity of medical research funding.
2. Patients are more likely to adhere to a physician's advice if:
   a. they are satisfied with and friendly toward their physician.
   b. the physician is female.
   c. they have a critical illness.
   d. the physician is a specialist as opposed to a general practitioner.
3. A good physician should be able to:
   a. make an accurate diagnosis on the basis of a physical examination alone.
   b. provide information and advice in technical terms.
   c. explain to the patient every decision that is made in her or his care, without considering patient input.
   d. provide good medical skills and sufficient information to the patient.

Rethink

1. Do you think stress plays a role in communication difficulties between physicians and patients? Why?
2. You are given the job of instructing a group of medical school students on "Physician/Patient Interactions." How would you set up your class, and what kind of information would you provide?

Answers to Evaluate Questions

1. c 2. a 3. d

How is health psychology a union between medicine and psychology?

- The field of health psychology considers how psychology can be applied to the prevention, diagnosis, and treatment of medical problems. (p. 370)

What is stress, how does it affect us, and how can we best cope with it?

- Stress is a response to threatening or challenging environmental conditions. People encounter both positive and negative stressors—circumstances that produce stress. (p. 370)
- Stress produces immediate physiological reactions. In the short term, these reactions can be adaptive, but in the long term they can have negative consequences, including the development of psychophysiological disorders. (p. 371)
- The consequences of stress can be explained in part by Selye's general adaptation syndrome (GAS), which suggests that there are three stages in stress responses: alarm and mobilization, resistance, and exhaustion. (p. 371)
- The way a person interprets an environmental circumstance affects whether that person will consider it to be stressful. Still, there are general classes of events that provoke stress: cataclysmic events, personal stressors, and background stressors or daily hassles. (p. 373)
- Stress can be reduced by developing a sense of control over one's circumstances. Some people, though, develop a state of learned helplessness. (p. 375)
- Coping with stress can take a number of forms, including the unconscious use of defence mechanisms and the use of emotion-focused or problem-focused coping strategies. (p. 376)

How do psychological factors affect such health-related problems as coronary heart disease, cancer, and smoking?

- Coronary heart disease is linked to a specific type of behaviour pattern known as Type A. Type A individuals tend to be competitive, show a sense of time urgency and hurriedness, be hostile and aggressive, and be driven. (p. 381)
- There is increasing evidence that a patient's attitudes and emotional responses can affect the course of that patient's disease through links to the immune system. (p. 382)
- Smoking, the leading preventable cause of health problems, has proved to be difficult to control, even though most smokers are aware of the dangerous consequences of smoking. (p. 384)
- Subjective well-being, the measure of how happy people are, is highest in people with high self-esteem, a sense of control, optimism, and a supportive network of close relationships. (p. 386)

How do our interactions with physicians affect our health and adherence to medical treatment?

- Although patients often expect physicians to make a diagnosis from only a physical examination, communicating one's problem to the physician is equally critical. (p. 388)
- Many patients find it difficult to communicate openly with their physicians because of the high social prestige of physicians and the technical nature of medical information. (p. 388)

For extra help in mastering the material in this chapter, see the integrator, practice quizzes, and other resources on the Online Learning Centre at

www.mcgrawhill.ca/college/ feldman

Key Terms and Concepts

health psychology (p. 370)

psychoneuroimmunology (PNI) (p. 370)

stress (p. 370)

psychophysiological disorders (p. 371)

general adaptation syndrome (GAS) (p. 371)

cataclysmic events (p. 374)

posttraumatic stress disorder (PTSD) (p. 374)

personal stressors (p. 375)

background stressors (p. 375)

uplifts (p. 375)

learned helplessness (p. 375)

coping (p. 376)

defence mechanisms (p. 376)

hardiness (p. 377)

social support (p. 378)

Type A behaviour pattern (p. 381)

Type B behaviour pattern (p. 381)

subjective well-being (p. 386)

reactance (p. 390)

Psychology on the Web

1. Find three or more Web sites that deal with stress reduction. Gather at least five techniques for reducing stress and summarize them. Write a critique and evaluation of these techniques, using the information you learned about stress in this chapter. Which ones seem to have a sound basis in psychological theory and/or research?

2. Are you a Type A personality or a Type B? Find two Web sites offering tests that claim to provide the answer. Summarize in writing the nature of each test and compare the results you received from each one.

Epilogue

In this chapter we have explored an important area in which psychology and physiology intersect. We've seen how the emotional and psychological experience of stress can lead to physical symptoms of illness, how personality factors can be related to major health problems, and how psychological factors can interfere with effective communications between physician and patient. We've also looked at the other side of the coin, noting that some relatively simple strategies can help us control stress, affect our illness, and improve our interactions with our physicians.

Turn back to the prologue of this chapter, about Jasmine, and use your understanding of health psychology and stress to consider these questions.

1. Which of Jasmine's stressors are personal and which are background stressors?
2. What uplifts are likely to occur during Jasmine's day?
3. How might Jasmine use problem-solving strategies to cope with some of her stressors?
4. Are there any of Jasmine's stressors that might be handled well by emotion-focused strategies? Why or why not?
5. How could Jasmine build a support network?

Chapter Twelve

Psychological Disorders

Lori Schiller, who suffered from schizophrenia, is now a peer counsellor at a mental health centre and a member of the Board of Directors of the U. S. National Alliance for the Mentally Ill.

Prologue

Lori Schiller

Lori Schiller thinks it all began one night at summer camp when she was 15.

Suddenly, she was hearing voices. "You must die! Die! Die!" they screamed. The voices drove her from her bunk, out into the dark, where she thought she could escape. Camp officials found her jumping frantically on a trampoline, screaming. "I thought I was possessed," says Schiller, now 33. Terrified, she told no one about the voices when she first heard them. The camp sent her home sick. Says Nancy Schiller, her mother: "We thought she had the flu...."

Voices had begun sliding down the telephone wire; they were assaulting her from the TV screen. "The people on TV were telling me it was my responsibility to save the world, and if I didn't I would be killed," she says....

Her behaviour became erratic, wilder. On a whim one day, she hopped into her car, drove four hours home to Scarsdale, changed her mind and drove back. She went sky diving. She got stopped by police for speeding. She had fits of hysterical laughter....

As time went on, Lori had more and more trouble concentrating, and more difficulty in controlling her impulses, one of which was to commit suicide. "I used to sit in the library, up all these stairs, and think about jumping," she recalls. Finally, in her senior year, she told her parents she "had problems" and asked to see a counsellor. (Bennett, 1992, pp. A1, A10)

Looking Ahead

Although she initially managed to hide her disorder from everyone, Lori Schiller was losing her grip on reality. Less than a year after she graduated from college, her parents convinced her to get treatment. She would spend the next decade in and out of institutions, suffering from schizophrenia, one of the most severe psychological disorders.

Happily, today Schiller is a leader in the mental health field. But her case raises several questions. What caused her disorder? Were genetic factors involved, or were stressors in her life primarily responsible? Were there signs that others should have noticed earlier? Could her schizophrenia have been prevented? What were the specific symptoms of her psychological disorder? And, more generally, how do we distinguish normal from abnormal behaviour, and how can Lori's behaviour be categorized and classified to pinpoint the specific nature of her problem?

We address some of the issues raised by Lori Schiller's case in this and the following chapter. We begin by discussing the subtle distinctions between normal and abnormal behaviour. We examine the various approaches that have been used to explain psychological disorders, ranging from explanations based on superstition to those based on more scientific approaches.

The heart of the chapter consists of a description of the various types of psychological disorders. Using a classification system employed by mental health practitioners, we examine the most significant kinds of disorders. The chapter also includes a discussion of how you can evaluate your own behaviour to determine whether it is advisable for you to seek help from a mental health professional.

Prepare

How can we distinguish normal from abnormal behaviour?

What are the major perspectives on psychological disorders used by mental health professionals?

What classification system is used to categorize psychological disorders?

Organize

Normal Versus Abnormal
   Defining Abnormality
   Perspectives on Abnormality
   Classifying Abnormal Behaviour

 **PsychLink**

Information on disorders
www.mcgrawhill.ca/college/feldman

Normal Versus Abnormal: Making the Distinction

> Universally that person's acumen is esteemed very little perceptive concerning whatsoever matters are being held as most profitable by mortals with sapience endowed to be studied who is ignorant of that which the most in doctrine erudite and certainly by reason of that in them high mind's ornament deserving of veneration constantly maintain when by general consent they affirm that other circumstances being equal by no exterior splendour is the prosperity of a nation. . . .

It would be easy to conclude that these words were the musings of a madman. The passage does not seem to make any sense at all. But literary scholars would disagree. This passage is from James Joyce's classic *Ulysses* (Joyce, 1934, p. 377), which has beeen hailed as one of the major works of twentieth-century literature.

As this example illustrates, a casual examination of a person's writing is insufficient to determine the degree to which he or she is "normal." But even when we consider more extensive samples of a person's behaviour, we find that there might be only a fine line between behaviour that is considered normal and that which is considered abnormal.

Defining Abnormality

Because of the difficulty in distinguishing normal from abnormal behaviour, psychologists have struggled to devise a precise, scientific definition of "abnormal behavior." For instance, consider the following definitions, each of which has its advantages and disadvantages:

- *Abnormality as deviation from the average.* To employ this statistics-based approach, we simply observe what behaviours are rare or infrequent in a given society or culture and label these deviations from the norm "abnormal."

  The difficulty with such a definition is that some behaviours that are statistically rare clearly do not lend themselves to classification as abnormal. If most people prefer to have cornflakes for breakfast, but you prefer raisin bran, this hardly makes your behaviour abnormal. Similarly, based on such a concept of abnormality a person who has an unusually high IQ would be categorized as abnormal simply because a high IQ is statistically rare. A definition of abnormality that rests on deviation from the average, then, is insufficient.

- *Abnormality as deviation from the ideal.* An alternative approach considers abnormality in relation to the standard toward which most people are striving—the ideal. This sort of definition considers behaviour abnormal if it deviates enough from some kind of ideal or cultural standard. However, because society has so few standards on which people agree, and the standards that do arise tend to change over time and vary across cultures, the deviation-from-the-ideal approach is inadequate.

- *Abnormality as a sense of personal discomfort.* A more useful definition concentrates on the psychological consequences of the behaviour for the individual. In this approach, behaviour is considered abnormal if it produces a sense of personal distress, anxiety, or guilt in an individual—or if it is harmful to others in some way.

  Even a definition that relies on personal discomfort has its drawbacks, though. For instance, people with some particularly severe forms of mental disturbance report feeling wonderful, even though their behaviour seems bizarre to others. Most of us would consider their behaviour abnormal even though they feel a personal state of well-being.

- *Abnormality as the inability to function effectively.* Most people are able to feed themselves, hold a job, get along with others, and in general live as productive members of society. Yet there are those who are unable to adjust to the demands of society or function effectively.

  According to this view of abnormality, people who are unable to function effectively and adapt to the demands of society are abnormal. For example, an unemployed, homeless woman living on the street might be considered unable to function effectively, so her behaviour would be viewed as abnormal even if she had chosen to live this way. Her inability to adapt to the requirements of society is what makes her "abnormal," according to this approach.

- *Abnormality as a legal concept.* In one of Canada's most high profile trials, Paul Bernardo was found guilty of sexual assault and two counts of first degree murder and sentenced as a dangerous offender to an indeterminate jail term (Pillitteri, 2002). To most people, the horrendous crimes committed by Bernardo are abnormal. However, by law he was considered mentally fit to stand trial.

  In Canada, fitness to stand trial has two components. People may be found, upon psychiatric examination, to be unfit to stand trial if, because of mental illness, they are unable to understand the court proceedings. If they are found fit to stand trial they may be found "not criminally responsible due to mental disorder." In each province there is a provincial review board that appoints a multi-disciplinary team made up of both legal and health care professionals to decide these matters. In either case, if people are found to be "not fit" or "not responsible," they are usually placed in the care of a psychiatric facility. Bernardo was legally both fit to stand trial and to take responsibility for his crimes.

  The term that we are more familiar with is *not guilty by reason of insanity.* Insanity refers to the person's mental state at the time the crime was committed. It is a legal term, not a psychological one, and refers to whether the person knew what he was doing was wrong and if he was unable to control his actions at the time the crime was committed.

  The insanity defence has a long history, dating from the mid 1800s when Daniel M'Naughten killed a political assistant while attempting to murder the Prime Minister of Great Britain. He believed that the man was persecuting him. The test used to establish the sanity of a defendant at the time the crime was committed was termed the *M'Naughten rule* (American Psychiatric Association, 1996).

PsychLink
Fitness to stand trial
www.mcgrawhill.ca/college/feldman

A person who deviates from the average or standards of society may be regarded as psychologically abnormal; yet the justice system deemed Paul Bernardo, convicted of rape and two gruesome murders, sane and deserving of legal punishment.
Why are psychological and legal definitions of abnormality so different?

Psychology at Work

Margaret H. Coggins

**Senior Research Psychologist,
United States Secret Service**

Education: B.A., psychology, Dickinson College;
M.A., Ph.D., psychology, Catholic University

Home: Reston, Virginia

Margaret H. Coggins

Protecting the president of the United States is the responsibility of the Secret Service, whose agents must be ready at an instant to aid and defend the U.S. leader. And while many agents are literally at the president's side every moment, others—such as psychologist Margaret Coggins—work for his or her safety in the background.

Coggins works closely with agents in the field and with mental health professionals to ensure the safety of U.S. leaders.

"The nature of my work consists of research, liaison, and training and educational work. All are tied to the Secret Service's protective mission," Coggins explained.

"The research program is designed to help the agency better understand the risk factors for violence that may be directed toward the people we protect, as well as helping to prevent and minimize any risk that is out there," she said.

Agents in the field not only must be vigilant in watching people, but must also be knowledgeable about the state of mind of people wishing to harm U.S. leaders or their families. Coggins works to identify the motivations and behaviours of those who are potentially threatening.

"Many of the individuals who come to the attention of the Secret Service are those who have active symptoms of a psychiatric disorder or are found to have a history of mental disorder," she said. "We conduct research on the cases that come to the attention of the Secret Service so we can get a better grasp on the types of behaviours, threats, and motivations. Some people communicate threats but are not likely to do harm, while a few others do pose serious threats."

Bringing together law enforcement with mental health and behavioural science is a major commitment for Coggins. As a result, her staff works closely with mental health specialists to manage the treatment of clients whose behaviour could be threatening to people under Secret Service protection.

"One main area of our research has to do with the general understanding and awareness in the mental health community about our protective mission," she noted. "We share some of the same goals, and we have to make the right decisions."

> "We conduct research on the cases that come to the attention of the Secret Service so we can get a better grasp on the types of behaviours, threats, and motivations."

Identifying Normal and Abnormal Behaviour: Drawing the Line

Clearly, none of the previous definitions is broad enough to cover all instances of abnormal behaviour. Consequently, the distinction between normal and abnormal behaviour often remains ambiguous even to trained professionals. Furthermore, what is viewed as abnormal behaviour depends largely on cultural expectations for "normal" behaviour in a particular society (Scheff, 1999).

Probably the best way to deal with this imprecision is to view abnormal and normal behaviour as marking two ends of a continuum rather than as absolute states. Behaviour would then be evaluated in terms of gradations, ranging from completely normal functioning to extremely abnormal behaviour. Behaviour typically falls somewhere between these two extremes. (To learn about someone who deals with life-and-death issues involving the potential for disordered behaviour, see the *Psychology at Work* box.)

Perspectives on Abnormality: From Superstition to Science

For much of the past, abnormal behaviour was linked to superstition and witchcraft. People displaying abnormal behaviour were accused of being possessed by the devil or some sort of demonic god. Authorities felt justified in "treating" abnormal behaviour by attempting to drive out the source of the problem. This typically involved whipping, immersion in hot water, starvation, or other forms of torture in which the cure was often worse than the affliction (Howells & Osborn, 1984; Berrios, 1996).

Contemporary approaches take a more enlightened view. Today, there are six major perspectives on psychological disorders. These perspectives suggest not only different causes of abnormal behaviour but also, as we shall see in the next chapter, different treatment approaches. Furthermore, some are more applicable to particular disorders than others. Table 12-1 summarizes the perspectives and how each can be applied to the case of Lori Schiller described in the prologue to this chapter.

Table 12-1 Perspectives on Psychological Disorder

In considering the case of Lori Schiller, discussed in the prologue to this chapter, we can employ each of the different perspectives on abnormal behaviour. Note, however, that given the nature of her psychological disorder, some of the perspectives are more applicable than others.

Perspective	Description	Possible Application of Perspective to Schiller's Case
Medical perspective	Assumes that physiological causes are at the root of psychological disorders	Examine Schiller for medical problems, such as brain tumour, chemical imbalance in the brain, or disease
Psychoanalytic perspective	Argues that psychological disorders stem from childhood conflicts	Seek out information about Schiller's past, considering possible childhood conflicts
Behavioural perspective	Assumes that abnormal behaviours are learned responses	Concentrate on rewards and punishments for Schiller's behaviour, and identify environmental stimuli that reinforce her behaviour
Cognitive perspective	Assumes that cognitions (people's thoughts and beliefs) are central to psychological disorders	Focus on Schiller's perceptions of herself and her environment
Humanistic perspective	Emphasizes people's responsibility for their own behaviour and the need to self-actualize	Consider Schiller's behaviour in terms of her choices and efforts to reach her potential
Sociocultural perspective	Assumes that behaviour is shaped by family, society, and culture	Focus on how societal demands contributed to Schiller's disorder

The Medical Perspective

When people display the symptoms of tuberculosis, we generally find the tuberculin germ in their body tissue. In the same way, the **medical perspective** suggests that when an individual displays symptoms of abnormal behaviour, the fundamental cause will be found in a physical examination of the individual, which might reveal a hormonal imbalance, a chemical deficiency, or a brain injury. Indeed, when we speak of mental "illness," "symptoms" of abnormal behaviour, and mental "hospitals," we are using terminology associated with the medical perspective.

Because many abnormal behaviours have been linked to biological causes, the medical perspective is a reasonable approach. Yet serious criticisms have been levelled against it. For one thing, there are many forms of abnormal behaviour for which no biological cause has been identified. In addition, some critics have argued that the use of the term *illness* implies that people displaying abnormal behaviour are not responsible for their actions (Szasz, 1982, 1994).

Still, recent advances in our understanding of the biological bases of behaviour have supported the importance of considering physiological factors in abnormal behaviour. For instance, we'll see later in this chapter that some of the most severe forms of psychological disturbance, such as major depression and schizophrenia, are influenced by genetic factors and neurotransmitters (Resnick, 1992; Brunner et al., 1993; Crow, 1995; Petronis & Kennedy, 1995).

medical perspective: The perspective that the root cause of abnormal behaviour will be found in a physical examination of the individual, which might reveal a hormonal imbalance, a chemical deficiency, or a brain injury.

The Psychoanalytic Perspective

Whereas the medical perspective suggests that biological causes are at the root of abnormal behaviour, the **psychoanalytic perspective** holds that abnormal behaviour stems from childhood conflicts over opposing wishes regarding sex and aggression. As we discussed in Chapter 10, Freud believed that children pass through a series of stages in which sexual and aggressive impulses take different forms and produce conflicts that require resolution—and that if these childhood conflicts are not dealt with successfully, they remain unresolved in the unconscious and eventually bring about abnormal behaviour during adulthood.

psychoanalytic perspective: The perspective that abnormal behaviour stems from childhood conflicts over opposing wishes regarding sex and aggression.

To understand the roots of people's disordered behaviour, the psychoanalytic perspective scrutinizes their early life history. However, because there is no conclusive way of linking people's childhood experiences with the abnormal behaviours they display as adults, we can never be sure that the causes suggested by psychoanalytic theory are accurate. Moreover, psychoanalytic theory paints a picture of people as having relatively little control over their behaviour, because much of it is taken to be guided by unconscious impulses.

On the other hand, the contributions of psychoanalytic theory have been significant. More than any other approach to abnormal behaviour, this perspective highlights the fact that people can have a rich, involved inner life and that prior experiences can have a profound effect on current psychological functioning (Horgan, 1996).

The Behavioural Perspective

behavioural perspective: The perspective that looks at the behaviour itself as the problem.

Both the medical and psychoanalytic perspectives look at abnormal behaviours as *symptoms* of some underlying problem. In contrast, the **behavioural perspective** looks at the behaviour itself as the problem. Using the principles of learning theory discussed in Chapter 5, behavioural theorists see both normal and abnormal behaviours as responses to a set of stimuli, responses that have been learned through past experience and that are guided in the present by stimuli in the individual's environment. To explain why abnormal behaviour occurs, one must analyze how an abnormal behaviour has been learned and observe the circumstances in which it is displayed.

The emphasis on observable behaviour is both the greatest strength and the greatest weakness of the behavioural approach to abnormal behaviour. The behavioural perspective is the most precise and objective approach for examining behavioural displays of particular disorders, such as attention deficit hyperactivity disorder (ADHD), which we'll consider later in this chapter. At the same time, though, critics charge that the perspective ignores the rich inner world of thoughts, attitudes, and emotions that can contribute to abnormal behaviour.

The Cognitive Perspective

cognitive perspective: The perspective that people's thoughts and beliefs are a central component of abnormal behaviour.

The medical, psychoanalytic, and behavioural perspectives view people's behaviour as being caused by factors largely beyond their control. To many critics, however, people's thoughts cannot be ignored.

In response to such concerns, some psychologists employ a **cognitive perspective**. Rather than considering only external behaviour, as in traditional behavioural approaches, the cognitive approach assumes that *cognitions* (people's thoughts and beliefs) are central to a person's abnormal behaviour. A primary goal of treatment using the cognitive perspective is to explicitly teach new, more adaptive ways of thinking.

For instance, suppose that whenever she takes an exam, a student forms the erroneous cognition "Doing well on this exam is crucial to my entire future." Through therapy, such a person might be taught to hold the more realistic, and less anxiety-producing, thought: "My entire future is not dependent on this one exam." By changing cognitions in this way, psychologists working within a cognitive framework seek to help people free themselves from thoughts and behaviours that are potentially maladaptive. This perspective has been criticized for its emphasis on thought processes, which does not take into account the emotional aspects of a person's situation.

The Humanistic Perspective

humanistic perspective: The perspective that emphasizes people's responsibility for their own behaviour, even when such behaviour is abnormal.

Psychologists who subscribe to the **humanistic perspective** emphasize the responsibility that people have for their own behaviour, even when such behaviour is seen as abnormal. The humanistic perspective—growing out of the work of Rogers and Maslow (see Chapter 10)—concentrates on what is uniquely human, viewing people as basically rational, oriented toward a social world, and motivated to seek self-actualization (Rogers, 1980).

Humanistic approaches focus on the relationship between the individual and society, considering how people view themselves in relation to others and see their place in the world. People are viewed as having an awareness of life and of themselves that leads them to search for meaning and self-worth. Rather than assuming that a "cure" is required, the humanistic perspective suggests that individuals can, by and large, set their own limits of what is acceptable behaviour. As long as they are not hurting others and do not feel personal distress, people should be free to choose what behaviours to engage in.

Although the humanistic perspective has been criticized for its reliance on unscientific, unverifiable information and its vague, almost philosophical, formulations, it offers a distinctive view of abnormal behaviour. The perspective stresses the unique aspects of being human and provides a number of important suggestions for helping those with psychological problems.

"First off, you're not a nut. You're a legume."

The Sociocultural Perspective

The **sociocultural perspective** assumes that people's behaviour—both normal and abnormal—is shaped by the kind of family group, society, and culture in which they live. According to this view, the nature of one's relationships with others may support abnormal behaviours and even cause them to occur. Consequently, the kinds of stresses and conflicts people experience as part of their daily interactions with others in their environment can promote and maintain abnormal behaviour.

Statistical support for the position that sociocultural factors shape abnormal behaviour can be found in the fact that some kinds of abnormal behaviour are far more prevalent among certain social groups than others. For instance, women are twice as likely as men to suffer from depression. Some other high-risk groups for depression are people who are seriously ill or recently bereaved. Increasing numbers of Canadian children, it is estimated at up to 26 percent, suffer from mental health problems. Furthermore, poor economic times tend to be linked to general declines in psychological functioning, and social problems such as homelessness are associated with psychological disorders (Feightner, 1994; Nelson et al., 1996; Kiesler, 1999).

On the other hand, alternative explanations abound for the association between abnormal behaviour and social factors. For example, men may be less likely than women, and poorer people less likely than wealthier, to seek help. Furthermore, sociocultural explanations provide relatively little in the way of direct guidance for the treatment of individuals showing mental disturbance, since the focus is on broader societal factors (Nelson et al., 1996; Paniagua, 2000).

sociocultural perspective: The perspective that people's behaviour—both normal and abnormal—is shaped by the kind of family group, society, and culture in which they live.

Classifying Abnormal Behaviour: The ABCs of the *DSM*

Crazy. Whacked. Mental. Loony. Insane. Neurotic. Psycho. Strange. Demented. Odd. Possessed.

Society has long placed labels on people who display abnormal behaviour. Unfortunately, most of the time these labels have reflected intolerance and have been used with little thought to what the label signifies.

Providing appropriate and specific names and classifications for abnormal behaviour has presented a major challenge to psychologists. It is not too hard to understand why, given the difficulties discussed earlier in simply distinguishing normal from abnormal behaviour. Yet classification systems are necessary in order to be able to describe and ultimately to diagnose abnormal behaviour.

Table 12-2 Major *DSM-IV* Diagnostic Categories

The following list of disorders represents the major categories from the *DSM-IV*. This is only a partial list of the over 200 disorders found in the *DSM-IV*.

Disorder	Subcategories
Anxiety (problems in which anxiety impedes daily functioning)	Generalized anxiety disorder, panic disorder, phobic disorder, obsessive-compulsive disorder, post-traumatic stress disorder
Somatoform (psychological difficulties displayed through physical problems)	Hypochondriasis, conversion disorder
Dissociative (the splitting apart of crucial parts of personality that are usually integrated)	Dissociative identity disorder (multiple personality), dissociative amnesia, dissociative fugue
Mood (emotions of depression or euphoria that are so strong they intrude on everyday living)	Major depression, bipolar disorder
Schizophrenia (declines in functioning, thought and language disturbances, perception disorders, emotional disturbances, and withdrawal from others)	Disorganized, paranoid, catatonic, undifferentiated, residual
Personality (problems that create little personal distress but lead to an inability to function as a normal member of society)	Antisocial (sociopathic) personality disorder, narcissistic personality disorder
Sexual (problems related to sexual arousal from unusual objects or problems related to sexual functioning)	Paraphilia, sexual dysfunction
Substance-related (problems related to drug dependence and abuse)	Alcohol, cocaine, hallucinogens, marijuana
Delirium, dementia, amnesia, and other cognitive disorders	

The DSM-IV: *Determining Diagnostic Distinctions*

Over the years many different classification systems have been used. Some have been more useful than others, and some have been more accepted than others by mental health workers. Today, however, one standard system, devised by the American Psychiatric Association, is employed by most professionals in Canada and the United States to diagnose and classify abnormal behaviour. This classification system is presented in the ***Diagnostic and Statistical Manual of Mental Disorders*, Fourth Edition *(DSM-IV)*** (American Psychiatric Association, 1994).

The *DSM-IV* presents comprehensive and relatively precise definitions for more than 200 diagnostic categories. By following the criteria presented in the system, diagnosticians can clearly describe the specific problem an individual is experiencing. (Table 12-2 provides a brief outline of the major diagnostic categories.)

One noteworthy feature of the *DSM-IV* is that it is designed to be primarily descriptive and tries to avoid suggesting an underlying cause for an individual's behaviour and problems. Hence, the term *neurotic*—a label that is commonly used by people in their everyday descriptions of abnormal behaviour—is not listed as a *DSM-IV* category. The reason is that the term *neurotic* comes directly from Freud's theory of personality. Because the term refers to problems associated with a specific cause and theoretical approach, neurosis is no longer listed as a category.

Diagnostic and Statistical Manual of Mental Disorders, **Fourth Edition** *(DSM-IV):* The manual of the American Psychiatric Association that presents the diagnostic system used by most Canadian and U.S. mental health professionals to diagnose and classify abnormal behaviour.

The *DSM-IV* has the advantage, then, of providing a descriptive system that does not specify a cause or reason behind the problem. Instead, it paints a picture of the behaviour that is being displayed. Why should this be important? For one thing, it allows communication between mental health professionals of diverse backgrounds and approaches. In addition, precise descriptive classification enables researchers to make progress in exploring the causes of a problem. If displays of an abnormal behaviour cannot be reliably described, researchers will be hard-pressed to find ways of investigating the disorder. Finally, the *DSM-IV* provides a kind of conceptual shorthand through which professionals can describe the behaviors that tend to occur together in an individual (Frances, First, & Pincus, 1995; Halling & Goldfarb, 1996).

Conning the Classifiers: The Shortcomings of the DSM-IV

PsychLink

Symptoms of disorders
www.mcgrawhill.ca/college/feldman

When clinical psychologist David Rosenhan and eight colleagues sought admission to separate mental hospitals across the United States in the 1970s, each stated that they were hearing voices—"unclear voices" that said "empty," "hollow," and "thud"—and each was immediately admitted to the hospital (Rosenhan, 1973).

However, the truth was that they were conducting a study, and none of them was actually hearing voices. Aside from these misrepresentations, *everything* else they did and said was their true behaviour, including the responses they gave during extensive admission interviews and answers to the battery of tests they were asked to complete. In fact, as soon as they were admitted, they said they no longer heard any voices. In short, each of the pseudo-patients acted in a "normal" way.

We might assume that Rosenhan and his colleagues would be quickly discovered as the impostors they were, but they were not. Instead, each of them was diagnosed as severely abnormal on the basis of observed behaviour. Most were labelled as suffering from schizophrenia, and they were kept in the hospital from 3 to 52 days, with the average stay being 19 days. Even when they were discharged, most of the "patients" left with the label *schizophrenia—in remission,* implying that the abnormal behaviour had only temporarily subsided and could recur at any time. Most disturbing of all, none of the pseudo-patients was identified by the staff of the hospitals as an impostor—although some of the real patients figured out the ruse.

The results of Rosenhan's classic study illustrate the fact that labelling individuals powerfully influences how their actions are perceived and interpreted. It also points out that determining who is psychologically disordered is not always a clear-cut, accurate process.

Although the *DSM-IV* was developed to provide more accurate and consistent determinations of psychological disorders, it has not been entirely successful. For instance, critics charge that it relies too much on the medical perspective on psychological disorders. It was drawn up by psychiatrists—who are physicians—and some condemn it for viewing psychological disorders primarily in terms of symptoms of some underlying physiological disorder. Moreover, critics suggest that the *DSM-IV* sorts people into inflexible, all-or-none categories, ignoring the degree to which a person displays psychologically disordered behaviour.

Other concerns with the *DSM-IV* are more subtle, but equally important. For instance, some critics argue that labelling an individual "abnormal" attaches a lifetime stigma to that person that is dehumanizing. Furthermore, after an initial diagnosis is made, other diagnostic possibilities might be overlooked by mental health professionals, who concentrate on the initial diagnostic category (Szasz, 1961, 1994; Kirk, 1992).

Still, despite the drawbacks inherent in any labelling system, the *DSM-IV* has had an important influence on how mental health professionals approach psychological disorders. It has increased both the reliability and the validity of diagnostic categorization, and it gives us a logical way to organize our examination of the major types of mental disturbance, to which we turn next.

Evaluate

1. One problem in defining abnormal behaviour is that:

   a. statistically rare behaviour might not be abnormal.

   b. not all abnormalities are accompanied by feelings of discomfort.

   c. cultural standards are too general to use as a measuring tool.

   d. all of the above.

2. If abnormality is defined as experiencing personal discomfort or causing harm to others, which of the following people is most likely to need treatment?

   a. An executive who is afraid to accept a promotion because it would require moving from his ground-floor office to the top floor of a tall office building.

   b. A woman who decides to quit her job and chooses, with great pleasure, to live on the street in order to live a "simpler life."

   c. A man who believes that friendly spacemen visit his house every Thursday, and is glad for their company.

   d. A photographer who enjoys living with nineteen cats in a small apartment.

3. Virginia's mother thinks that Virginia's behaviour is clearly abnormal because, despite being offered admission to medical school, Virginia decides to become a waitress instead. What approach is Virginia's mother using to define abnormal behaviour?

4. Which of the following is a strong argument against the medical perspective?

   a. Physiological abnormalities are almost always impossible to identify.

   b. There is no conclusive way to link past experience and behaviour.

   c. The medical perspective rests too heavily on the effects of nutrition.

   d. Assigning behaviour to a physical problem takes responsibility away from the individual for changing his or her behaviour.

5. Cheryl is painfully shy. According to the behavioural perspective, the best way to deal with her "abnormal" behaviour is to

   a. treat the underlying physical problem.

   b. use the principles of learning theory to modify her shy behaviour.

   c. express a great deal of caring.

   d. uncover her negative past experiences through hypnosis.

Answers to Evaluate Questions

1. d 2. a 3. Deviation from the ideal 4. d 5. b

Rethink

1. Imagine that an acquaintance of yours was recently arrested for shoplifting a $3 pen. What sorts of questions and issues would be raised by proponents of *each* of these perspectives on abnormality: medical, psychoanalytic, behavioural, cognitive, humanistic, and sociocultural?

2. Do you agree or disagree that the *DSM* should be updated every several years? What makes abnormal behaviour so variable? Why can't there be one, unchanging definition of abnormal behaviour?

Prepare

What are the major psychological disorders?

Organize

Major Disorders
  Anxiety Disorders
  Somatoform Disorders
  Dissociative Disorders

Major Disorders

Sally experienced her first panic attack out of the blue, 3 weeks after completing her senior year in college. She had just finished a job interview and was meeting some friends for dinner. In the restaurant, she began to feel dizzy. Within a few seconds, her heart was pounding, and she was feeling breathless, as though she might pass out. Her friends noticed that she did not look well and offered to drive her home. Sally suggested they stop at the hospital emergency room instead. Although she felt better by the time they arrived at the hospital, and tests indicated nothing wrong, Sally experienced a similar episode a week later while at a movie. . . .

Her attacks became more and more frequent. Before long, she was having several attacks per week. In addition, she constantly worried about having attacks. She began to avoid exercise and other activities that produced physical sensations. She also noticed the attacks were worse when she was alone. She began to avoid driving, shopping in large stores, and eating in all restaurants. Some weeks she avoided leaving the house completely. (Antony, Brown, & Barlow, 1992, p. 79)

Sally suffered from panic disorder, one of the specific psychological disorders we'll be considering in the remainder of this chapter. Keep in mind that the chapter will present psychological disorders in a dispassionate and clinical way. However it is important to remember that people with these disorders suffer not only from their illness but also struggle daily to cope in a world that presents many challenges and barriers. For family members, it is painful to see those they love in such pain. The challenge we all face is to help break down the barriers of ignorance. An understanding of these disorders is a good place to start, but the understanding should also be accompanied by compassion.

Anxiety Disorders

A study of psychiatric disorders done in Edmonton found that 11.2 percent of the population experienced an anxiety disorder at some point in their lifetime, with most of these (7.2 percent) suffering from specific phobias (Bland, Newman, and Orn, 1988). Gender also appears to be a factor: A study done by the Ontario Ministry of Health (1994) found that 9 percent of men and 16 percent of women had suffered anxiety disorders in the previous 12 months (Antony & Swinson, 1996).

All of us, at one time or another, experience *anxiety,* a feeling of apprehension or tension, in reaction to stressful situations. There is nothing "wrong" with such anxiety. Anxiety is a normal reaction to stress that often helps, rather than hinders, our daily functioning. Without some anxiety, for instance, most of us probably would not be terribly motivated to study hard, undergo physical exams, or spend long hours at our jobs.

But some people experience anxiety for no clear reason. When anxiety occurs without external justification and begins to affect a person's daily functioning, it is considered a psychological problem known as an **anxiety disorder**. We'll discuss four types of anxiety disorders: phobic disorder, panic disorder, generalized anxiety disorder, and obsessive-compulsive disorder.

anxiety disorder: Anxiety with no obvious external cause that impairs daily functioning.

Phobic Disorder

Claustrophobia. Acrophobia. Xenophobia. Although these sound like characters in a Greek tragedy, they are actually members of a class of psychological disorders known as phobias. **Phobias** are intense, irrational fears of specific objects or situations. For example, claustrophobia is a fear of enclosed places, acrophobia is a fear of high places, and xenophobia is a fear of strangers. Although the objective danger posed by an anxiety-producing stimulus (which can be just about anthing, as you can see from the list in Table 12-3) is typically small or nonexistent, to the individual suffering from the phobia the danger is great, and a full-blown panic attack can follow exposure to the stimulus. Phobic disorders differ from generalized anxiety disorders and panic disorders in that there is a specific, identifiable stimulus that sets off the anxiety reaction.

phobias: Intense, irrational fears of specific objects or situations.

Phobias might have only a minor impact if those who suffer from them can avoid the stimuli that trigger the fear. If one is not a professional firefighter or tightrope walker, for example, a fear of heights might have little impact on one's daily life. On the other hand, a fear of strangers presents a more serious problem. In one extreme case, a Washington woman suffering from xenophobia left her home just three times in 30 years—once to visit her family, once for a medical operation, and once to purchase ice cream for a dying companion (Adler, 1984).

Agoraphobia is the fear of open spaces and public places. Depending on its severity, it can seriously affect a person's ability to do ordinary activities that most of us take for granted.

What sort of behaviour-modification approaches might be used to deal with agoraphobia?

Table 12-3 Giving Fear a Proper Name

Phobia	Trigger	Phobia	Trigger	Phobia	Trigger
Acrophobia	Heights	Brontophobia	Thunder	Numerophobia	Numbers
Aerophobia	Flying	Claustrophobia	Closed Spaces	Nyctophobia	Darkness
Agoraphobia	Public spaces	Cynophobia	Dogs	Ochlophobia	Crowds
Ailurophobia	Cats	Dementophobia	Insanity	Ophidiophobia	Snakes
Amaxophobia	Vehicles, driving	Gephyrophobia	Bridges	Ornithophobia	Birds
Anthophobia	Flowers	Herpetophobia	Reptiles	Phonophobia	Speaking out loud
Anthrophobia	People	Hydrophobia	Water	Pyrophobia	Fire
Aquaphobia	Water	Mikrophobia	Germs	Thanatophobia	Death
Arachnophobia	Spiders	Murophobia	Mice	Trichophobia	Hair
Astraphobia	Lightning	Mysophobia	Dirt or germs	Xenophobia	Strangers

Panic Disorder

panic disorder: Anxiety that reveals itself in the form of panic attacks that last from a few seconds to as long as several hours.

In another type of anxiety disorder, **panic disorder**, *panic attacks* occur that last from a few seconds to several hours. Unlike phobias, which are brought about by specific objects or situations, panic disorders are not triggered by any identifiable stimulus. Instead, during an attack, such as the ones experienced by Sally in the case described earlier, anxiety suddenly—and often without warning—rises to a peak, and the individual feels a sense of impending, unavoidable doom. Although symptoms differ from person to person, they might include heart palpitations, shortness of breath, unusual amounts of sweating, faintness and dizziness, an urge to urinate, gastric sensations, and—in extreme cases—a sense of imminent death. After such an attack, it is no wonder that people tend to feel exhausted (Rachman & deSilva, 1996; Pollack & Marzol, 2000).

Panic attacks seemingly come out of nowhere and are unconnected to any specific stimulus. Because they don't know what triggers their feelings of panic, victims of panic attacks can become fearful of going places. Panic disorder may be accompanied by *agoraphobia,* the fear of being in a situation in which escape is difficult, and in which help for a possible panic attack would not be available. People with extreme cases of agoraphobia never leave their homes (Cox et al., 1994; Cox, Endler, & Swinson, 1995; Langs et al., 2000).

Generalized Anxiety Disorder

generalized anxiety disorder: Long-term, persistent anxiety and worry.

People with **generalized anxiety disorder** experience long-term, persistent anxiety and worry. Sometimes their concerns are directed toward identifiable issues involving such things as family, money, work, and health. In other cases, though, people with the disorder feel that something dreadful is about to happen but can't identify what it is, experiencing "free-floating" anxiety.

Because of their persistent anxiety, they cannot concentrate, cannot set their worry and fears aside, and their lives become centred around their worry. Their anxiety can eventually result in medical problems. Because of heightened muscle tension and arousal, individuals with generalized anxiety disorder can begin to experience headaches, dizziness, heart palpitations, or insomnia.

Obsessive-Compulsive Disorder

obsessive-compulsive disorder: A disorder characterized by obsessions or compulsions.
obsession: A persistent, unwanted thought or idea that keeps recurring.

People with **obsessive-compulsive disorder** are plagued by unwanted thoughts (obsessions) or feel that they must carry out some actions (compulsions) against their will.

An **obsession** is a persistent, unwanted thought or idea that keeps recurring. For example, a student might be unable to stop thinking that she has neglected to put her name on a test. A man might go on vacation and wonder the whole time whether he locked his house. In each case, the thought or idea is unwanted and difficult to put out of mind. Of course, many of us suffer from mild obsessions from time to time, but usually such thoughts persist only for a short period. For people with serious obsessions, however, the thoughts persist for days or months and can consist of bizarre, troubling images.

As part of an obsessive-compulsive disorder, people might also experience **compulsions**, irresistible urges to repeatedly carry out some act that seems strange and unreasonable, even to them. Whatever the compulsive behaviour, these people experience extreme anxiety if they cannot carry it out, even if it is something they want to stop. The acts involved could be relatively trivial, such as repeatedly checking the stove to make sure all the burners are turned off, or more unusual, such as continuously washing oneself (Rachman & Hodgson, 1980; Carter, Pauls, & Leckman, 1995). For example, consider this case report of a 27-year-old woman with a cleaning ritual:

> Bess would first remove all of her clothing in a preestablished sequence. She would lay out each article of clothing at specific spots on her bed, and examine each one for any indications of "contamination." She would then thoroughly scrub her body, starting at her feet and working meticulously up to the top of her head, using certain washcloths for certain areas of her body. Any articles of clothing that appeared to have been "contaminated" were thrown into the laundry. Clean clothing was put in the spots that were vacant. She would then dress herself in the opposite order from which she took the clothes off. (Meyer & Osborne, 1987, p. 156)

Unfortunately for those experiencing an obsessive-compulsive disorder, little or no reduction in anxiety results from carrying out a compulsive ritual. People with severe cases lead lives filled with unrelenting tension (Bouchard, Rhéaume, & Ladouceur, 1999; Goodman, Rudorfer, & Maser, 1999).

The Causes of Anxiety Disorders

No one cause fully explains all cases of anxiety disorders, and each of the perspectives on abnormal behaviour that we discussed earlier has something to say about their causes. However, the medical, behavioural, and cognitive perspectives have been particularly influential in psychologists' thinking about anxiety disorders.

Biological approaches, derived from the medical perspective, have shown that genetic factors play a role in anxiety disorders. For example, if one identical twin has panic disorder, there is a 30 percent chance that the other twin will have it also. Furthermore, recent research shows that a person's characteristic level of anxiety is related to a specific gene that is involved in the production of the neurotransmitter serotonin. This work is consistent with findings indicating that certain chemical deficiencies in the brain appear to produce some kinds of anxiety disorder (Lesch et al., 1996; Rieder, Kaufmann, & Knowles, 1996).

Psychologists employing the behavioural perspective have taken a different approach, emphasizing environmental factors. They consider anxiety to be a learned response to stress. For instance, suppose a young girl is bitten by a dog. When she next sees a dog, she is frightened and runs away—a behaviour that relieves her anxiety and thereby reinforces her avoidance behaviour. After repeated encounters with dogs in which she is reinforced for her avoidance behaviour, she might develop a full-fledged phobia regarding dogs. (Environmental stress is a significant factor in posttraumatic stress disorder, discussed in the *Applying Psychology in the 21st Century* box.)

Finally, the cognitive perspective suggests that anxiety disorders are an outgrowth of inappropriate and inaccurate cognitions about circumstances in the person's world. For example, a person with an anxiety disorder might view any friendly puppy as a ferocious and savage pit bull, or might see an air disaster looming whenever she or he is in the vicinity of an airplane. According to the cognitive perspective, people's maladaptive thoughts about the world are at the root of anxiety disorders.

compulsion: An irresistible urge to repeatedly carry out some act that seems strange and unreasonable.

PsychLink

Causes of anxiety disorders
www.mcgrawhill.ca/college/feldman

somatoform disorder: Psychological difficulties that take on a physical (somatic) form, but for which there is no medical cause.

hypochondriasis: A disorder involving having a constant fear of illness and a preoccupation with one's health.

conversion disorder: A major somatoform disorder that involves an actual physical disturbance, such as the inability to use a sensory organ or the complete or partial inability to move an arm or leg.

Somatoform Disorders

Somatoform disorders are psychological difficulties that take on a physical (somatic) form, but for which there is no medical cause. Even though an individual with a somatoform disorder reports physical symptoms, no biological cause exists, or, if there is a medical problem, the person's reaction is greatly exaggerated.

One type of somatoform disorder is **hypochondriasis**, in which people have a constant fear of illness and a preoccupation with their health, taking everyday aches and pains to be symptoms of some dread disease. The "symptoms" are not faked; instead, hypochondriasis is the misinterpretation of these ordinary sensations as evidence of some dread disease—often in the face of inarguable medical evidence to the contrary (Noyes et al., 1993; Cantor & Fallon, 1996; Lautenbacher & Rollman, 1999).

Another somatoform disorder is conversion disorder. Unlike hypochondriasis, in which there is no actual physical problem, **conversion disorders** involve an actual physical disturbance—such as the inability to see or hear, or to move an arm or leg—but the *cause* of the physical disturbance is purely psychological. There is no biological reason for the problem. Some of Freud's classic cases involved conversion disorders. For instance, one patient of Freud's was suddenly unable to use her arm, without any apparent physiological cause. Later, just as abruptly, she regained its use.

Conversion disorders often have a rapid onset. People wake up one morning blind or deaf, or they experience numbness that is restricted to a certain part of the body. Someone's hand, for example, might become entirely numb, while an area above the wrist, controlled by the same nerves, remains sensitive to touch—something that is biologically implausible. Such a condition is referred to as "glove anesthesia," because the area that is numb is the part of the hand that would be covered by a glove, and not a region related to pathways of the nervous system (see Figure 12-1).

One of the most surprising characteristics of people with conversion disorders is their lack of concern over symptoms that most of us would find very anxiety-producing. Most sighted people would be panic-stricken if they suddenly went blind. For a person in good health to suddenly go blind and react to this with bland dispassion (with *la belle indifférence,* a French phrase meaning "beautiful indifference") hardly seems appropriate.

Dissociative Disorders

The topic of the classic movie *The Three Faces of Eve* and the book *Sybil* (about a girl who allegedly had 16 personalities) represents a class of disorders that are among the most dramatic: dissociative disorders. **Dissociative disorders** are characterized by the separation (or dissociation) of critical parts of personality that are normally integrated and work together. People who dissociate key parts of their personality are able to prevent disturbing memories or perceptions from reaching their conscious awareness, thereby reducing their anxiety (Ross et al., 1990; Putnam, 1995a; Spiegel, 1996b).

There are several dissociative disorders, and all are rare. A person with **dissociative identity disorder** (or **multiple personality**) displays characteristics of two or more distinct personalities. Each personality has a unique set of likes and dislikes and its own reactions to situations. Some people with multiple personalities even carry several pairs of glasses because their vision changes with each personality. Moreover, each individual personality can be well adjusted when considered on its own (Ross, 1996; Kluft, 1996).

The problem, of course, is that there is only one body available to the various personalities, forcing the personalities to take turns. Because there can be strong variations in personalities, the person's behaviour—considered as a whole—can appear very inconsistent. For instance, in the

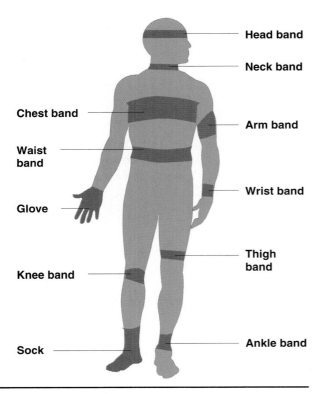

Head band
Neck band
Chest band
Arm band
Waist band
Wrist band
Glove
Thigh band
Knee band
Ankle band
Sock

Figure 12-1 Conversion disorders sometimes produce numbness in particular isolated areas of the body (indicated by the shaded areas of the figure). For instance, in glove anesthesia, the area of the body covered by a glove is numb. However, the condition is biologically implausible because of the nerves involved, suggesting that the problem is the result of a psychological disorder rather than actual nerve damage.

Applying Psychology in the 21st Century

Erasing the Stigma of Psychological Disorders

"A great soldier, a great patriot, a great humanitarian" who bears a great burden.

These remarks by Art Eggleton, then Canada's Defence Minister, were delivered in recognition of the career of Lt. General Roméo Dallaire, who resigned after a 35-year career in the Canadian Forces. Dallaire, who retired early for medical reasons, refers to himself as "a casualty of Rwanda, an injured officer of the Rwandan war." As the commanding officer of a United Nations' peacekeeping mission to Rwanda in 1994, Dallaire and his troops were helpless in the face of the massive genocide which occurred. It is estimated that up to one million people died, including thousands of women and children, as well as a number of peacekeepers.

The injury suffered by Dallaire was not caused by a bullet but by the terrible things he saw and was unable to do anything about. He, like as many as 10 percent of Canadian soldiers, suffers from an anxiety disorder known as posttraumatic stress disorder (PTSD) (Thompson, 2000).

Research done on peacekeeping stress at the University of Guelph (Lamerson & Kelloway, 1996) cites the work of Everly (1989) and Everly and Mitchell (1992) as identifying PTSD as "the most severe and disabling variation of occupational stress known." Lamerson and Kelloway (1996) believe that Canadian peacekeepers may be particularly vulnerable because of the frequency with which they are sent on these missions. Also, peacekeepers operate under very stringent guidelines that add to already heightened stress. Being in a war zone, often shot at, and not able to take action creates what

Lt. General Roméo Dallaire is fighting to overcome posttraumatic stress disorder.

the authors term a "multiplicative effect" for stress.

PTSD has many symptoms. They include inability to sleep, memory problems, survivor guilt, emotional numbness, reliving the trauma, headaches, digestive problems, and substance abuse. Depression may develop. Work and family situations may become a casualty. The cost on a personal and organizational level is extremely high (Lamerson & Kelloway, 1996).

For a number of years Dallaire was in denial, believing that hard work would erase the terrible memories. This effort, accompanied by an inability to eat or sleep properly, led to total collapse. Daillaire talks about anger and depres-

sion so severe that he could not function. He finds the dark and silence difficult. Unexpected flashbacks occur—something as simple as bushes at the side of the road can appear to become piles of corpses. In a moment of great dispair, General Dallaire attempted suicide. He survived, and with the support of his family and professional help he is attempting to put his life back together. Of the professional support he has received he says, "you literally cannot get out of this without professional help. There is absolutely no way." (Thompson, 2000).

By being so open about his condition Dallaire joins other well-known individuals who are beginning to admit publicly that they suffer from a serious psychological disorder—and who, in the process, are helping to erase the stigma attached to abnormal behaviour. For instance, Academy Award–winner Rod Steiger has lectured about his eight years of depression, which he describes as producing pain so searing that it "skins you alive." Singer Naomi Judd suffered from panic attacks that made it difficult to leave home. Ted Turner, who founded CNN and Turner Broadcasting, has discussed suffering from bipolar disorder. American Secretary of State General Colin Powell, when asked at a news conference about his wife's rumoured depression, replied "My wife has depression. It's not a family secret. It is very easily controlled with proper medication, just as my blood pressure is."

Such public admissions, as well as raising awareness, often are a force for social change. For example, General Dallaire continues to encourage the Canadian military to improve support for personnel suffering from PTSD (Thompson, 2000).

Why are peacekeepers at such high risk for posttraumatic stress disorder?

---

famous case portrayed in *The Three Faces of Eve,* the meek, bland Eve White provided a stunning contrast to the dominant and carefree Eve Black (Sizemore, 1989).

A person with **dissociative amnesia** has significant, selective memory loss. Dissociative amnesia is unlike simple amnesia, which, as we discussed in Chapter 6, involves an actual loss of information from memory, typically due to a physiological cause. In cases of dissociative amnesia, the "forgotten" material is still present in memory—it simply cannot be recalled. The term *repressed memories* is sometimes used to describe the lost memories of dissociative amnesia.

In the most severe forms, individuals cannot recall their names, are unable to recognize parents and other relatives, and do not know their addresses. In other respects, though, they might appear quite normal. Apart from an inability to remember certain facts about themselves, they might be able to recall skills and abilities that they developed

dissociative disorder: Psychological dysfunctions characterized by the separation of critical personality facets that are normally integrated; this reduces anxiety by repressing disturbing thoughts or memories.

dissociative identity disorder (multiple personality): A disorder in which a person displays characteristics of two or more distinct personalities.

dissociative amnesia: A disorder in which the person has significant, selective memory loss.

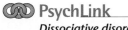

PsychLink

Dissociative disorders
www.mcgrawhill.ca/college/feldman

"Jane Doe," who suffered from dissociative amnesia, was found wandering in a Florida park, unable to recall who she was or anything about her past.

dissociative fugue: A form of amnesia in which people take sudden, impulsive trips, sometimes assuming a new identity.

earlier. For instance, a chef might not remember where he grew up or received training, but might still be able to prepare gourmet meals.

In some cases of dissociative amnesia, the memory loss is quite profound. For example, a woman—dubbed Jane Doe by her rescuers—was found by a Florida park ranger in the early 1980s. Incoherent, thin, and only partially clothed, Doe was unable to recall her name, her past, and even how to read and write. On the basis of her accent, authorities thought the woman was from Illinois, and interviews conducted while she was given tranquilizing drugs revealed that she had had a Catholic education. However, the childhood memories she revealed were so universal that her background could not be further pinpointed. In a desperate attempt to rediscover her identity, she appeared on the television show *Good Morning America,* and ultimately a couple from Roselle, Illinois, whose daughter had moved to Florida, stepped forward, saying that they were her parents. However, Jane Doe never regained her memory (Carson, Butcher, & Coleman, 1992).

A more unusual form of amnesia is a condition known as **dissociative fugue**. In this state, people take sudden, impulsive trips, sometimes assuming a new identity. After a period of time—days, months, or sometimes even years—they suddenly realize that they are in a strange place and completely forget the period that they had spent wandering. Their last memories are from the time just before they entered the fugue state. Disociative fugue is very rare and in some cases may be undiagnosed multiple personality disorder (Ross, 1994).

What the dissociative disorders have in common is that they allow people to escape from some anxiety-producing situation. Either the person produces a new personality to deal with stress, or the situation that caused the stress is forgotten or left behind as the individual journeys to some new—and perhaps less anxiety-producing—environment (Spiegel & Cardena, 1991; Putnam, 1995b).

Evaluate

1. Kathy is terrified of elevators. She is likely to be suffering from
   a. an obsessive-compulsive disorder
   b. a phobic disorder
   c. a panic disorder
   d. a generalized anxiety disorder
2. Carmen described an incident in which her anxiety suddenly rose to a peak and she felt a sense of impending doom. Carmen had experienced a(n) _____ _____.
3. Troubling thoughts that persist for days or months are known as
   a. obsessions
   b. compulsions
   c. rituals
   d. panic attacks
4. An overpowering urge to carry out a strange ritual is called a(n) _____.
5. In what major way does conversion disorder differ from hypochondriasis?
6. The separation of the personality, providing escape from stressful situations, is the key factor in _____ disorders.

Rethink

1. What cultural factors might contribute to the rate of anxiety disorders found in a culture? What perspectives on psychological disorders would best explain cultural contributions to anxiety disorders?
2. Do you think the behavioural perspective would be effective in dealing with dissociative disorders? Why or why not? Which perspective do you think would be most promising for this type of disorder?

Answers to Evaluate Questions

1. b. 2. panic attack 3. a 4., compulsion 5. In conversion disorder, an actual physical disturbance is present. 6. dissociative

Mood Disorders

> I do not care for anything. . . . I do not care to walk, for walking is too strenuous. I do not care to lie down, for I should either have to remain lying, and I do not care to do that, or I should have to get up again, and I do not care to do that either. . . . I do not care at all.

We all experience mood swings. Sometimes we are happy, perhaps even euphoric; at other times we feel upset, saddened, or depressed. Such changes in mood are a normal part of everyday life. In some people, however, moods are so pronounced and lingering—like the feelings described above by philosopher Søren Kierkegaard—that they interfere with the ability to function effectively. In extreme cases a mood can become life-threatening, and in others it can cause the person to lose touch with reality. Situations such as these represent **mood disorders**, disturbances in emotional feelings strong enough to impair everyday living.

Major Depression

Queen Victoria. Mark Twain. Sigmund Freud. The common link among these people? Each suffered from periodic attacks of *major depression,* one of the most common mood disorders. A major study for 1996–97 released by Health Canada in 1999 reported that 4 percent of Canadians 12 years of age and older had reported a major episode of depression. This is equivalent to one million people. Of this number, 45 percent were in a depressed state for 5 to 26 weeks. Based on an interview, this study identified people who were likely to be identified as depressed but who were not presently under treatment.

Women are twice as likely to experience major depression as men. The group with the highest rate of depression (8 to 9 percent) in Canada is young women aged 15 to 19. For both sexes, depression is more likely at younger ages. However, as people get older, their periods of depression tend to last longer, from a low of 5 weeks for 12- to 19-year olds, to a high of 10.3 weeks for those aged 75 and older (Health Canada, 1999). The rate of depression is going up throughout the world. Results of in-depth interviews conducted in Canada, the United States, Puerto Rico, Taiwan, Lebanon, Italy, Germany, and France confirm this trend. In fact, in some countries, the likelihood that individuals will suffer major depression at some point in their lives is three times higher than it was for earlier generations. In addition, people are developing major depression at increasingly early ages (Compas, Ey, & Grant, 1993; Weissman & Olfson, 1995; Beckham & Leber, 1997; Culbertson, 1997).

Of course, some depression is normal following the breakup of a long-term relationship, the death of a loved one, or the loss of a job. It is even normal following less serious problems, like doing badly on a test or finding that a romantic partner has forgotten one's birthday.

People who suffer from **major depression** experience similar sorts of feelings, but with much greater severity. They might feel useless, worthless, and lonely and might despair over the future. They might experience difficulty with concentration, decision making, and relationships. Moreover, they might experience such problems for months or even years. They might cry uncontrollably or have sleep disturbances, and they are at risk for suicide. The depth of such behaviour and the length of time it lasts are the hallmarks of major depression. (Chapter Activity 12-1 provides an assessment for depression.)

Mania and Bipolar Disorders

Depression leads to the depths of despair; mania leads to emotional heights. **Mania** is an extended state of intense, wild elation. People experiencing mania feel intense happiness, power, invulnerability, and energy. Consider, for example, the following description of an individual who suffered from *bipolar disorder:*

mood disorder: Disturbances in emotional feelings strong enough to interfere with everyday living.

 **PsychLink**

Major depressive disorders
www.mcgrawhill.ca/college/feldman

major depression: A severe form of depression that interferes with concentration, decision making, and sociability.

mania: An extended state of intense, wild elation.

Chapter Activity 12–1 A Test for Depression

This test was distributed by mental health organizations during National Depression Screening Day in the early 1990s, a nationwide event that sought to identify people who suffered from depression severe enough to warrant psychological intervention. On the day of the screening, the organizations received some 30 000 inquiries (Hill, 1992).

To complete the questionnaire, count the number of statements with which you agree:

1. I feel downhearted, blue, and sad.

2. I don't enjoy the things that I used to.

3. I feel that others would be better off if I were dead.

4. I feel that I am not useful or needed.

5. I notice that I am losing weight.

6. I have trouble sleeping through the night.

7. I am restless and can't keep still.

8. My mind isn't as clear as it used to be.

9. I get tired for no reason.

10. I feel hopeless about the future.

Scoring If you agree with at least five of the statements, including either item 1 or 2, and if you have had these symptoms for at least two weeks, help from a professional is strongly recommended. If you answer yes to number 3, you should get help immediately.

---

hypomanic: Someone who experiences mood disturbances characterized by elevated energy and activity level, of shorter duration than a manic episode, without psychotic characteristics.

During my depression I was quite introspective. As a **hypomanic**, however, I didn't stop to analyze my thoughts, feelings, or behaviour. I was much too busy and didn't always stop to think about what I was doing…At times I seemed to have lost my sense of judgment. This was quite different from my usual pattern of behaviour, but I was not aware of the discrepancy. (Endler, 1982, p.86)

The above excerpt was written by Dr. Norman Endler, a clinical psychologist and a psychology professor. His book, *Holiday of Darkness*, is the story of his battle with bipolar disorder. It is a book that is both a text on depressive illness and the story of a personal journey. He addresses with great honesty his feelings, the stigma of mental illness, and the powerful healing force of his therapy and his family.

bipolar disorder: A disorder in which a person alternates between periods of euphoric feelings of mania and periods of depression.

A person who sequentially experiences periods of mania and depression has **bipolar disorder** (or, as it used to be known, manic-depressive disorder). The swings between highs and lows might occur as frequently as a few days apart or they might alternate over a period of years. The periods of depression usually are longer than the periods of mania.

Ironically, some of society's most creative individuals have suffered from bipolar disorder. The imagination, drive, excitement, and energy of their manic periods fuel their creativity. For instance, historical analysis of his music shows that composer Robert Schumann was most prolific during his periodic episodes of mania. His output dropped off drastically during his periods of depression (see Figure 12-2). On the other hand, the high output associated with mania does not necessarily lead to higher quality: Schumann created some of his greatest works when he was not manic (Jamison, 1995; Week & James, 1995; Ludwig, 1996).

PsychLink
Bipolar disorder
www.mcgrawhill.ca/college/feldman

Causes of Mood Disorders

Because they are a major mental health problem, mood disorders—and, in particular, depression—have received a good deal of study. Several approaches have been used to explain mood disorders. Psychoanalytic approaches, for example, see depression

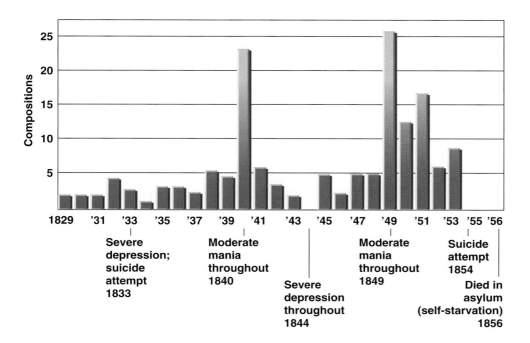

Figure 12–2 The number of pieces written by composer Robert Schumann in a given year is related to his periods of depression and mania (Slater & Meyer, 1959; reprinted in Jamison, 1993). *Why do you think mania might be associated with creative productivity in some people?*

as the result of feelings of loss (real or potential) or of anger directed at oneself. One psychoanalytic approach sees depression as produced by the loss or threatened loss of a parent early in life; another sees depression as caused by people feeling responsible for the bad things that happen to them and directing their anger inward.

On the other hand, convincing evidence has been found that both bipolar disorder and major depression may have genetic and biochemical roots. Heredity is known to play a role in bipolar disorder: the affliction clearly runs in some families. Furthermore, several neurotransmitters, including serotonin and norepinephrine, appear to play a role in depression (Delgado & Moreno, 2000; Leonard, 2000; Vogel, 2000).

Some explanations for mood disorders are based on cognitive factors. For example, psychologist Martin Seligman suggests that depression is largely a response to learned helplessness. *Learned helplessness* is a learned expectation that one cannot control the events in one's life and there is no escape from one's situation. People with these expectations simply give up fighting negative events and submit to them, and develop depression. Other theorists go a step further, suggesting that depression is a result of *hopelessness,* a combination of learned helplessness and an expectation that negative outcomes in one's life are inevitable (Peterson, Maier, & Seligman, 1993; Nunn, 1996; Alloy, Abramson, & Francis, 1999).

Clinical psychologist Aaron Beck has proposed that faulty cognitions underlie people's depressed feelings. Specifically, his cognitive theory of depression suggests that depressed individuals typically view themselves as life's losers, blaming themselves whenever anything goes wrong. By focusing on the negative side of situations, they feel inept and unable to act constructively to change their environment. In sum, their negative cognitions lead to feelings of depression (Sacco & Beck, 1995; Wright & Beck, 1996).

Building on the work of Beck, Canadian researchers have made significant contributions to the cognitive model of depression, with a focus on negative self-schemas. Research suggests that knowledge, stored in stable units called *schemas,* influences the selection and interpretation of future information. Depressed people appear to have more negative self-schemas and access them more readily than do non-depressed people. Although it is

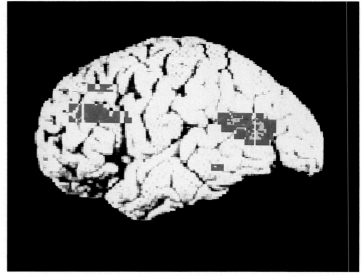

The functioning of several areas of the brain is involved in producing the symptoms of depression.

not possible to say that these schemas cause depression, they might help to maintain it (Segal & Vella, 1990; Segal et al., 1995; Rector, Segal, & Gemar, 1998).

In a study that used a narrative report, a group of psychiatric patients at a Calgary hospital were found to employ one of four distinct strategies to deflect the responsibility for their condition away from themselves. Unlike the traditional findings of cognitive research, with an emphasis on negative self-schemas, this study found the participants blamed others or circumstances for their situation (Drew, Dobson, & Stam, 1999).

The most recent explanation of depression is drawn from evolutionary psychology. In this view, depression is an adaptive response to pursuing goals that are unattainable. When people fruitlessly pursue an ever-elusive goal, depression kicks in, ending pursuit of the goal. Ultimately, when the depression lifts, people can turn to other, more reasonable goals. In this view, depression serves a positive function, in the long run increasing the chances of survival for particular individuals, who can then pass the behaviour to their offspring. Such reasoning, of course, is highly speculative (Nesse, 2000).

The various theories of depression have still not provided a complete answer to an elusive question that has dogged researchers: Why is the incidence of depression twice as high for women as for men? One explanation is that women experience more stress than men at certain points in their lives—such as when a woman must simultaneously earn a living and be the primary caregiver for her children. In addition, women have a higher risk for physical and sexual abuse, typically earn lower wages than men, report greater unhappiness with their marriages, and generally experience chronic negative circumstances (Joiner & Coyne, 1999; Nolen-Hoeksema, Larson, & Grayson, 1999).

But biological factors could also explain some women's depression. For example, 25 to 50 percent of women who take oral contraceptives report symptoms of depression, and depression that occurs following the birth of a child is linked to hormonal changes (Strickland, 1992).

As yet, researchers have discovered no definitive solutions to the puzzle of depression. Many alternative explanations are offered, and most likely mood disorders are caused by a complex interaction of several factors.

Schizophrenia

PsychLinks
Schizophrenia
www.mcgrawhill.ca/college/feldman

MYTH: Schizophrenia is split personality or multiple personality disorder.

FACT: Schizophrenia is often confused with split personality. They are NOT the same thing. The confusion arose because the word *schizophrenia* comes from two Greek roots meaning "split mind." The splitting or fragmentation referred to is the breakdown of an individual's thinking and feeling processes, not a division of the person into two separate personalities. The popular use of the word "schizophrenic" to describe a mixture of contradictory qualities is completely different from the correct psychiatric use of the term (The World Psychiatric Association Program to Fight Stigma Due to Schizophrenia, 2002).

Schizophrenia is one of the most severe forms of mental disturbance. In Canada, 1 percent of the population suffers from schizophrenia. According to the Schizophrenia Society of Canada (1998), schizophrenic patients occupy more hospital beds than patients with any other disorder except cardiovascular disease. They are also in many respects the least likely to recover from their psychological difficulties.

Schizophrenia refers to a class of disorders involving severe distortions of reality. Thinking, perception, and emotion might deteriorate; there might be a withdrawal from social interaction; and there might be displays of bizarre behaviour. Although several types of schizophrenia have been observed (see Table 12-4), the distinctions between them are not always clear-cut (Bentall, 1992; Cannon, 1998). Moreover, the symptoms displayed by persons with schizophrenia can vary considerably over time, and people with schizophrenia can have significantly different symptoms even though they are labelled with the same diagnostic category. Nonetheless, a number of characteristics reliably distinguish schizophrenia from other disorders:

schizophrenia: A class of disorders involving severe distortions of reality.

Table 12-4 The Major Types of Schizophrenia

Type	Symptoms
Disorganized (hebephrenic) schizophrenia	Inappropriate laughter and giggling, silliness, incoherent speech, infantile behaviour, strange and sometimes obscene behaviour
Paranoid schizophrenia	Delusions and hallucinations of persecution or of greatness, loss of judgment, erratic and unpredictable behaviour
Catatonic schizophrenia	Major disturbances in movement; in some phases, loss of all motion, with patient frozen into a single position, remaining that way for hours and sometimes even days; in other phases, hyperactivity and wild, sometimes violent, movement
Undifferentiated schizophrenia	Variable mixture of major symptoms of schizophrenia; classification used for patients who cannot be typed into any of the more specific categories
Residual schizophrenia	Minor signs of schizophrenia following a more serious episode

- *Decline from a previous level of functioning.* The individual can no longer carry out activities he or she was once able to do.
- *Disturbances of thought and language.* People with schizophrenia use logic and language in peculiar ways. Their thinking often does not make sense, and their information processing is frequently faulty. They also do not follow conventional linguistic rules (Penn et al., 1997). Consider, for example, the following response to the question "Why do you think people believe in God?"

> Uh, let's, I don't know why, let's see, balloon travel. He holds it up for you, the balloon. He don't let you fall out, your little legs sticking down through the clouds. He's down to the smokestack, looking through the smoke trying to get the balloon gassed up you know. Way they're flying on top that way, legs sticking out. I don't know, looking down on the ground, heck, that'd make you so dizzy you just stay and sleep you know, hold down and sleep there. I used to be sleep outdoors, you know, sleep outdoors instead of going home. (Chapman & Chapman, 1973, p. 3)

As this selection illustrates, although the basic grammatical structure may be intact, the substance of thinking characteristic of schizophrenia is illogical, garbled, and lacking in meaningful content.

- *Delusions.* People with schizophrenia often have *delusions,* firmly held, unshakable beliefs with no basis in reality. Most commonly, they believe that they are being controlled by someone else, that they are being persecuted by others, or that their thoughts are being broadcast so that others are able to know what they are thinking.
- *Perceptual disorders.* People with schizophrenia do not perceive the world as most other people do. They might see, hear, or smell things differently than others do (see Figure 12-3), and they do not have a normal sense of their bodies. For instance, they could have difficulty determining where their own bodies stop and the rest of the world begins (Ritzler & Rosenbaum, 1974). They might also have *hallucinations,* perceiving things that do not actually exist (McGuire, Shah, & Murray, 1993; Ruppin, Reggia, & Horn, 1996; Reichman & Rabins, 1996).

Figure 12–3 These drawings of cats were made by an artist who suffered from schizophrenia.

- *Emotional disturbances.* People with schizophrenia sometimes show a bland lack of emotional response to even the most dramatic events. Or they might display emotion that is inappropriate to a situation. For example, a person with schizophrenia might laugh uproariously at a funeral or might react with anger when being helped by someone.
- *Withdrawal.* People with schizophrenia tend to have little interest in others. They tend not to socialize or hold real conversations with others, although they might talk *at* another person. In the most extreme cases they do not even acknowledge the presence of other people, appearing to be in their own isolated world.

The symptoms of schizophrenia follow two primary courses. In *process schizophrenia,* the symptoms develop relatively early in life, slowly and subtly. There could be a gradual withdrawal from the world, excessive daydreaming, and a blunting of emotion, until eventually the disorder reaches the point where others cannot overlook it. In other cases, known as *reactive schizophrenia,* the onset of symptoms is sudden and conspicuous. The treatment outlook for reactive schizophrenia is relatively favourable; process schizophrenia has proved to be much more difficult to treat.

A relatively recent addition to the classifications for schizophrenia distinguishes *positive-symptom schizophrenia* from *negative-symptom schizophrenia* (Fenton & McGlashan, 1994; Tandon, 1995; Hafner & Maurer, 1995). Positive-symptom schizophrenia is indicated by the presence of disordered behaviour such as hallucinations, delusions, and extremes of emotionality. In contrast, negative-symptom schizophrenia involves an absence or loss of normal functioning, such as social withdrawal or blunted emotions. The distinction is becoming increasingly important because it suggests that two different underlying processes might explain the roots of schizophrenia—which remains one of the greatest mysteries facing psychologists who deal with disordered behaviour (Fenton & McGlashan, 1991; Heinrichs, 1993).

Solving the Puzzle of Schizophrenia: Biological Causes

Although it is clear that schizophrenic behaviour departs radically from normal behaviour, its causes are less apparent. It does appear, however, that schizophrenia has both biological and environmental origins.

Let's first consider the evidence pointing to a biological cause of schizophrenia. Because schizophrenia is more common in some families than in others, genetic factors seem to be involved in producing at least a susceptibility to or readiness for developing schizophrenia. For example, research has shown that the closer the genetic link between a person with schizophrenia and another individual, the higher the likelihood that the other person will develop schizophrenia (see Table 12-5; Gottesman & Moldin, 1998; Brzustowicz et al., 2000).

On the other hand, if genetics alone were responsible, the chance that the identical twin of a schizophrenic would have schizophrenia would be 100 percent instead of 48 percent (Table 12-5), because identical twins are genetically identical. Moreover, research that has sought to find a link between schizophrenia and a particular gene has been only partly successful. However, researchers feel that they are getting closer. In early 2000, Anne Bassett of the University of Toronto announced that she and her colleagues, a team of Canadians and Americans, had identified the chromosome on which they believe they will find the gene for schizophrenia. The subjects were 304 Canadians from families that appeared to have an inherited predisposition for the disorder. Although this research is promising, Basset believes that more than one gene is probably involved, as well as environmental factors (Vallis, 2000). Other researchers agree that schizophrenia is produced by more than genetic factors alone (Franzek & Beckmann, 1996; Lenzenweger & Dworkin, 1998).

One of the most intriguing biological hypotheses to explain schizophrenia is that the brains of victims harbour either a biochemical imbalance or a structural abnormality. For example, the *dopamine hypothesis* is that schizophrenia occurs when there is excess activity in the areas of the brain that use dopamine as a neurotransmitter. This hypothesis

Table 12-5 Risk of Developing Schizophrenia, Based on Genetic Relatedness to a Person with Schizophrenia

Relationship	Genetic Relatedness, %	Risk of Developing Schizophrenia, %
Identical twin	100	48
Child of two schizophrenic parents	100	46
Fraternal twin	50	17
Offspring of one schizophrenic parent	50	17
Sibling	50	9
Nephew or niece	25	4
Spouse	0	2
Unrelated person	0	1

Source: Gottesman, 1991.

came to light after the discovery that drugs that block dopamine action in brain pathways can be highly effective in reducing the symptoms of schizophrenia. Other research suggests that dopamine might operate in conjunction with other neurotransmitters such as serotonin (Seeman, 1993; Kapur & Remington, 1996; Abi-Dargham et al., 1997).

Some biological explanations propose that there are structural abnormalities in the brains of people with schizophrenia, perhaps due to exposure to a virus during prenatal development. For example, some research has found abnormal neural circuits in the cortex and limbic system of individuals with schizophrenia. Consistent with such research, different brain functioning has been found in people with schizophrenia compared to those without the disorder (Andreasen et al., 1994; Akbarian et al., 1996; Brown et al., 1996; Lenzenweger & Dworkin, 1998; see Figure 12-4).

Environmental Perspectives on Schizophrenia

Although biological factors provide some pieces of the puzzle of schizophrenia, we still need to consider past and current experiences in the environments of people who develop the disturbance. For instance, theories that look to the emotional and communication patterns of families of people with schizophrenia suggest that schizophrenia is affected by high levels of expressed emotion. *Expressed emotion* is an interaction style characterized by criticism, hostility, and emotional intrusiveness by family members. Other researchers suggest that faulty communication patterns lie at the heart of schizophrenia (Weisman et al., 1993; Mueser et al., 1993; Bayer, 1996; Linszen et al., 1997).

Psychologists who take a cognitive perspective on schizophrenia look for cognitive causes for disordered schizophrenic thinking. Some suggest that schizophrenia is the result of *overattention* to stimuli in the environment. Rather than being able to screen out unimportant or inconsequential stimuli and focus on the most important things in the environment, people with schizophrenia might be excessively receptive to virtually everything in their environment. This overloads their information-processing capabilities, which eventually break down. Other cognitivists argue that schizophrenia is the result of *underattention* to certain stimuli: people with schizophrenia fail to focus on important stimuli sufficiently, and pay attention to other, less important information in their surroundings (Braff, 1993).

Although it is plausible that overattention and underattention are related to different forms of schizophrenia, these phenomena do not explain the origins of such information-processing disorders. Consequently, cognitive approaches—like other environmental explanations—are not the full explanation of the disorder.

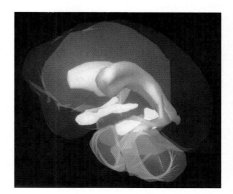

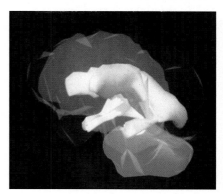

Figure 12-4 Structural changes in the brain have been found in people with schizophrenia. In the first MRI reconstruction of the brain of a patient with schizophrenia, the hippocampus (yellow) is shrunken, and the ventricles (gray) are enlarged and fluid-filled. In contrast, the lower MRI of a brain of a person without the disorder appears structurally different.

Source: N. C. Andreasen, University of Iowa.

Pathways Through Psychology

Sylvia Geist

Community and Clinical Psychologist, Geist Family Centre, Toronto, Ontario

Education: B.A. York University; M.Ed., Ed.D. University of Toronto
Registered Psychologist (C. Psych.), Province of Ontario

Home: Toronto, Ontario

Sylvia Geist

My interest in psychological disorders or mental illnesses was sparked in 1980 when I began to listen to families attending the family support group at the Centre for Addiction and Mental Health (formerly the Clarke Institute of Psychiatry). It was there that I first learned about the devastating consequences of these brain disorders on individuals and their families. Their voices became the focus of my doctoral dissertation, entitled "Impact of Schizophrenia on the Family: A Voyage Through Turbulence." My research highlighted the families as reactors to mental illness and not as causes of the illness. This shift in thinking contrasted with the literature at the time that discussed mental illness as the result of family dynamics or faulty parenting. My thesis was published as a video, which is being used as an educational and training tool for professionals and families.

I have held various employment positions at the Centre for Addiction and Mental Health (at what was formerly known as the Queen Street Mental Health Centre). As a psychometrist, I provided case management and clinical services to persons with serious mental illnesses and as an administrator of a community clinic of the Centre I developed and implemented (within a multi-disciplinary team) community rehabilitation programs. I created a family pyschoeducational program and facilitated a support group for families whose loved ones were patients of the hospital. As a volunteer I actively participated for many years in the Schizophrenia Society of Ontario. Later, as President of the Schizophrenia Society of Canada, I was able to advocate for the improvement of services and to work towards the elimination of the stigma that keeps mental illnesses "in the closet." I am continually involved in advocacy activities as founding and past Chairperson of the Canadian Alliance of Mental Illness and Mental Health (CAMIMH), an alliance of five national organizations whose mandate is to place mental illnesses and mental health as a priority on Canadian political and social agendas.

My understanding of mental illnesses was formed from a number of perspectives gleaned from these positions. Over my 20 years of working in the field, I have had the privilege of receiving several awards for my work and have had the opportunity to work with many dedicated individuals (researchers, professionals, families, politicians, media, etc). The recent opening of the Geist Family Centre (in Toronto) which focuses on services for mental illnesses and mental health, is a continuation of my work as a community and clinical psychologist. My belief that I could make a difference in the quality of life of "marginalized" Canadian citizens has made my career as a psychologist both meaningful and sustaining.

Source: Sylvia Geist, Ed.D., C. Psych., Geist Family Centre
E-mail: sylvia@geistfamilycentre.com

What was the focus of Dr. Geist's early research on schizophrenia?

The Multiple Causes of Schizophrenia

We have seen that several different biological and environmental factors are related to schizophrenia. It is likely, then, that not just one but several causes jointly explain the onset of the disorder. The predominant approach used today, the *predisposition model of schizophrenia,* considers a number of factors simultaneously. This model suggests that individuals might inherit a predisposition or an inborn sensitivity to schizophrenia that makes them particularly vulnerable to stressful factors in the environment. The stressors can vary—social rejection or dysfunctional family communication patterns—but if they are strong enough and are coupled with a genetic predisposition, the result will be the onset of schizophrenia. Similarly, if the genetic predisposition is strong enough, schizophrenia can occur even when the environmental stressors are relatively weak.

In short, schizophrenia is associated with several kinds of biological and environmental factors and is produced by a combination of interrelated variables (Lenzenweger & Dworkin, 1998; McDonald & Murray, 2000; Meltzer, 2000). (To read about a researcher who has worked with families of schizophrenic patients, see the *Pathways Through Psychology* box.)

Personality Disorders

Canada's most notorious and reviled criminal is Clifford Olson, a serial murderer sentenced in January 1982 to life imprisonment for the torture and killing of eleven boys and girls. These crimes were the latest and most despicable in a string of antisocial and criminal acts extending back to his early childhood. Although some psychopaths are not violent and few are as brutal as he is, Olson is the prototypical psychopath.

.... In the years since his imprisonment Olson has continued to bring grief to the families of his victims by sending them letters with comments about the murders of their children. He has never shown any guilt or remorse for his depredations....
(Hare, 1993, p. 132)

Olson is a clear example of a person with a personality disorder. **Personality disorders** are different from the other problems we have discussed in this chapter, because people with these psychological maladjustments feel little personal distress. In fact, people with personality disorders frequently lead seemingly normal lives. However, just below the surface lies a set of inflexible, maladaptive personality traits that do not permit them to function appropriately as members of society (Clarkin & Lenzenweger, 1996; Millon & Davis, 1996; Millon & Davis, 1999).

The best-known type of personality disorder is **antisocial personality disorder** (sometimes referred to as sociopathic personality). Individuals with this disturbance show no regard for the moral and ethical rules of society or the rights of others. Although they are intelligent and likable (at least at first), upon closer examination they turn out to be manipulative and deceptive. Moreover, they lack any feelings of guilt or anxiety over their wrongdoings. When people with antisocial personality disorder injure others, they understand intellectually that they have caused the harm but feel no remorse (Lykken, 1995).

People with antisocial personalities are often impulsive, and they are unable to tolerate frustration. They can be extremely manipulative. They also can have excellent social skills, being charming, engaging, and highly persuasive. Some of the best con men have antisocial personalities. Although many psychopaths end up in prison for criminal activity, many live out their lives in the community, bringing personal and economic pain to those with whom they interact (Hare, 1993).

What causes such an unusual constellation of problems? Many factors have been suggested, ranging from a biologically induced inability to appropriately experience emotions to problems in family relationships. For example, many people with antisocial behaviour come from a home in which a parent has died or left, or where they have been treated with a lack of affection, a lack of consistency in discipline, or outright rejection. Other explanations concentrate on sociocultural factors, because an unusually high proportion of people with antisocial personalities come from lower socioeconomic groups. Still, no one has been able to pinpoint the specific causes of antisocial personalities, and it is likely that some combination of factors is responsible (Nigg & Goldsmith, 1994; Hare, Hart, & Harpur, 1991; Rosenstein & Horowitz, 1996).

There is very little evidence that treatment has any effect on psychopathic behaviour (Hare, 1993). Recognized as a world authority on psychopaths, Robert Hare of the University of British Columbia was approached by the Canadian government to design a treatment and management program for psychopaths. He brought together a group of international experts and has devised an experimental treatment plan. Believing that attempts to develop empathy or conscience are futile, the program will focus on intensive and tightly controlled efforts to foster a sense of responsibility. Clients will be encouraged to meet their needs in a more socially acceptable way, on the premise that their self-interest is not being well served in jail. Hare (1993) does caution that even this program may not help psychopaths who are not in custody, as their behaviour cannot be controlled.

People with **borderline personality disorder** have difficulty developing a secure sense of who they are. As a consequence, they tend to rely on relationships with others to define their identity. The problem with this strategy is that rejections are devastating.

personality disorder: A mental disorder characterized by a set of inflexible, maladaptive personality traits that keep a person from functioning properly in society.

antisocial personality disorder: A disorder in which individuals tend to display no regard for the moral and ethical rules of society or the rights of others.

 **PsychLink**

Antisocial personality
www.mcgrawhill.ca/college/feldman

borderline personality disorder: A disorder in which individuals have difficulty developing a secure sense of who they are.

narcissistic personality disorder: A personality disturbance characterized by an exaggerated sense of self-importance.

People with this disorder are distrustful of others and have difficulty controlling their anger, and their emotional volatility leads them to impulsive and self-destructive behaviour. Individuals with borderline personality disorder often feel empty and alone. They might form intense, sudden, one-sided relationships, demanding the attention of another person and then feeling angered when they don't receive it (Horwitz et al., 1996).

Another example of a personality disturbance is **narcissistic personality disorder**, characterized by an exaggerated sense of self-importance. People with this disorder expect special treatment from others, and at the same time disregard others' feelings. One of the main attributes of the narcissistic personality is an inability to experience empathy for other people.

There are several other categories of personality disorder, ranging in severity from individuals who might simply be regarded by others as eccentric, obnoxious, or difficult, to people who criminally endanger others. Although they are not out of touch with reality in the way that people with schizophrenia are, people with personality disorders live on the fringes of society (Millon et al., 2000).

Attention Deficit Hyperactivity Disorder (ADHD)

attention deficit hyperactivity disorder (ADHD): A learning disability marked by inattention, impulsiveness, a low tolerance for frustration, and a great deal of inappropriate activity.

You'll find one in almost every elementary school classroom: a student who can't sit still, has trouble concentrating, and is constantly fidgeting. The cause, quite often, is **attention deficit hyperactivity disorder**, or **ADHD**, a disorder marked by inattention, impulsiveness, a low tolerance for frustration, and generally a great deal of inappropriate activity. Although all children show such behaviour some of the time, it is so frequent in children diagnosed with ADHD that it interferes with their everyday functioning (Barkley, 1998b; Silver, 1999; Brown, 2000).

ADHD is a disorder that has been estimated to affect 5 to 7 percent of school-aged children in Canada, with 4 to 5 percent of those being boys. Children diagnosed with this disorder require a great deal of understanding from parents, who play a critical role in helping their children by setting appropriate guidelines for their behaviour and by helping them work through educational and social issues.

The cause of ADHD is not known, although most experts feel that it is produced by dysfunctions in the nervous system. For example, one theory suggests that ADHD is caused by unusually low levels of arousal in the central nervous system. To compensate, children with ADHD seek out stimulation in order to increase their arousal. Still, such theories are speculative. Furthermore, because many children occasionally show behaviours characteristic of ADHD, it is often misdiagnosed. It is the frequency and persistence of the symptoms of ADHD that allow for a correct diagnosis, which can only be done by a trained professional (Hinshaw et al., 1997; Barkley, 1998a, 1998b).

Evaluate

1. States of extreme euphoria and energy paired with severe depression characterize _____ disorder.
2. _____ schizophrenia is characterized by symptoms that are sudden and of easily identifiable onset, whereas _____ schizophrenia develops gradually over a person's lifespan.
3. The _____ _____ states that schizophrenia might be caused by an excess of certain neurotransmitters in the brain.
4. Which of the following theories states that schizophrenia is caused by the combination of a genetic predisposition and environmental stressors?
   a. Learned inattention theory
   b. Predisposition model
   c. Learned helplessness theory

Answers to Evaluate Questions

1. bipolar 2. Reactive; process 3. dopamine hypothesis 4. b

Rethink

1. Do any of the explanations of schizophrenia offer the promise of a treatment or cure of the disorder? Do any of the explanations permit us to predict who will be affected by the disorder? How is explanation different from treatment and prediction?
2. Personality disorders are often not apparent to others, and many people with these problems seem to live basically normal lives without being a threat to others. If these people can function well in society, why should they be considered psychologically disordered?

Beyond the Major Disorders: Abnormal Behaviour in Perspective

Prepare

What indicators signal a need for the help of a mental health practitioner?

Organize

Beyond the Major Disorders
The Prevalence of Psychological Disorders

The various forms of abnormal behaviour described in the *DSM-IV* cover much wider ground than we have been able to discuss in this chapter. Some we have considered in earlier chapters, such as *psychoactive substance-use disorder,* in which problems arise from the abuse of drugs (Chapter 4); and *eating disorders* (Chapter 8). Another important class of disorders that we have previously touched upon is *organic mental disorders.* These are problems that have a purely biological basis. There are other disorders we have not mentioned at all, and each of the classes we have discussed can be divided into several subcategories.

Keep in mind that the specific natures of the disorders included in the *DSM-IV* are reflections of today's Western cultures. The classification system is a snapshot of how its authors viewed mental disorder when the *DSM-IV* was published in 1994. In fact, the development of the latest version of the *DSM* was a source of great debate, in part reflecting social issues.

For example, two disorders were particularly controversial during the revision process. One, the category "self-defeating personality disorder," was ultimately removed from the appendix, where it had appeared in the previous revision. The label *self-defeating personality disorder* was meant to apply to people who neither leave nor take other action regarding relationships in which they receive unpleasant and demeaning treatment. It was typically applied to people who remained in abusive relationships. Although some clinicians argued that it was a valid category, applicable to patients they observed in their clinical practice, it lacked adequate research support. Furthermore, some critics complained that use of the label condemned targets of abuse for their plight—a blame-the-victim phenomenon. For these reasons, the category was removed from the manual.

A second and even more controversial category was "premenstrual dysphoric disorder": severe, incapacitating mood changes or depression related to a woman's menstrual cycle. Some critics argued that the classification simply labelled normal female behaviour as a disorder. Former U.S. Surgeon General Antonia Novello suggested that what "in women is called PMS [premenstrual syndrome, a similar classification] in men is called healthy aggression and initiative" (Cotton, 1993, p. 13). Advocates for including the disorder prevailed, however, and "premenstrual dysphoric disorder" appears in the appendix of *DSM-IV* (Hartung & Widiger, 1998).

Such controversies underline the fact that our understanding of abnormal behaviour is a reflection of the society and culture in which we live. Future revisions of *DSM* might include a different catalogue of disorders. Even now, other cultures might well include a list of disorders that look very different from the list that appears in the current *DSM,* as we discuss next.

PsychLink
PMS vs. PMDD
www.mcgrawhill.ca/college/feldman

What is important to keep in mind regarding the relationship between the DSM and culture?

EXPLORING DIVERSITY

The DSM and Culture—and the Culture of the DSM

In most people's estimation, a person who hears voices of the recently deceased is probably a victim of some psychological disturbance. Yet some Plains Indians routinely hear the voices of the dead calling to them from the afterlife.

This is but one example of the role culture plays in the labelling of behaviour as "abnormal." In fact, of all the major adult disorders identified in the *DSM,* just four are found across all cultures of the world: schizophrenia, bipolar disorder, major depression, and anxiety disorders. *All* the rest are particular to North America and Western Europe (Kleinman, 1996; López & Guarnaccia, 2000; Cohen, Slomkowski, & Robins, 1999).

Take, for instance, anorexia nervosa, first discussed in Chapter 8. Anorexia nervosa is a disorder in which people, particularly young women, develop inaccurate views of their body appearance, become obsessed with their weight, and refuse to eat, sometimes starving to death. This disorder appears only in cultures holding the societal standard that slender female bodies are most desirable. Most of the world does not have this standard, and likewise does not have anorexia nervosa. Interestingly, there is no anorexia nervosa in all of Asia, with two exceptions: the upper and upper-middle classes of Japan and Hong Kong, where Western influence tends to be great. It is also noteworthy that anorexia nervosa is a fairly recent disorder even in Western cultures. In the 1600s and 1700s it did not occur because the ideal female body in Western cultures at that time was plump.

Similarly, dissociative identity disorder (multiple personality) makes sense as a problem only in societies where a sense of self is fairly concrete. In India, the self is based more on external factors that are relatively independent of the person. There, when an individual displays symptoms of what people in a Western society would call dissociative identity disorder, it is assumed that the person is possessed either by demons (and has a malady) or by gods (and does not need treatment).

Other cultures have disorders that do not appear in the West. For example, in Malaysia, a behaviour called "amok" is characterized by a wild outburst in which a person, usually quiet and withdrawn, kills or severely injures another. "Koro" is a condition in Southeast Asian males who develop an intense panic that their penis is about to withdraw into their abdomen. Finally, a disorder sometimes found among children in the Andean mountains is "susto," in which those afflicted are apathetic, unable to sleep, depressed, and anxious. This condition is brought on by fear that the soul will be lost because of contact with the supernatural, such as witches or the evil eye (Berry et al., 1992; Stix, 1996).

In sum, we should not assume that the *DSM* provides the final word on psychological disorders. The disorders it includes are very much a creation and function of Western cultures at a particular moment in time, and its categories should not be seen as universally applicable.

PsychLink
Dissociative identity disorder
www.mcgrawhill.ca/college/feldman

The Prevalence of Psychological Disorders

How common are the kinds of psychological disorders we've been discussing? In Canada we get an idea of the numbers from reports of psychiatric hospitalization. Health Canada predicts that there will be 18 million hospital patient days per year for mental disorders by 2002–03. This is an increase of two-thirds since 1982–83 (Stephens, 1998). In Canada, education and occupational status are highly correlated with mental health. Unemployment and disability are related to psychological disorders. Social support is another significant factor. Canadians with the lowest levels of support are six times more likely to have mental health problems.

Hospitalization rates vary according to type of psychological disorder. Figure 12-5 presents major categories based on the International Classification of Diseases, 9th revision. Each category includes many disorders. For example, affective disorders (which include, among others, bipolar disorder and major depressive disorder) account for 25 percent of hospitalizations. Schizophrenia accounts for 15 percent and neurotic and personality disorders

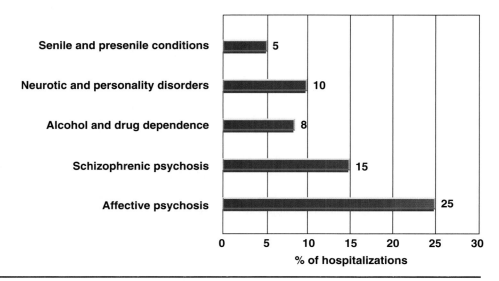

Figure 12-5 The percentage of hospitalizations for selected mental disorders in Canada, 1999-2000.

Source: Canadian Institute for Health Information. (Note: the categories are based on the International Classification of Diseases, 9th revision.)

(which include, among others, obsessive-compulsive disorders and paranoid personality disorder) account for 10 percent (Canadian Institute for Health Information, 2002).

Poor mental health is very costly, first on a personal level in terms of suffering, and then on a national or provincial level in terms of dollars spent. Mental health care in Canada costs $7.8 billion dollars a year. Of this, approximately $5 billion goes to direct costs (drugs, physicians, hospitals, and research). Figure 12-6 shows the breakdown of these expenditures. The rest of the money goes to pay indirect costs such as premature death and long- and short-term disability (Stephens, 1998).

It is important to keep in mind that we have only presented Canadian statistics on the prevalence of psychological disorders and that other cultures may differ significantly. For instance, cross-cultural surveys show that the incidence of major depression varies significantly from one culture to another. The probability of suffering at least one episode of depression is only 1.5 percent in Taiwan and 2.9 percent in Korea, compared to 11.6 percent in New Zealand and 16.4 percent in France. Such notable differences underscore the importance of considering the cultural context of psychological disorders (Weissman et al., 1996).

The prevalence figures for Canada suggest that psychological disorders are far from rare, and yet significant prejudice and discrimination are directed toward people with psychological disorders. The stigma (a label that leads people to be seen as different and therefore defective) against people who experience a psychological disorder remains real.

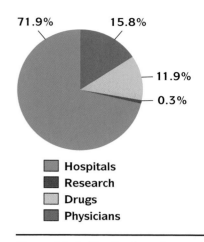

71.9%   15.8%
                    11.9%
                     0.3%

■ Hospitals
■ Research
□ Drugs
■ Physicians

Figure 12-6 Distribution of direct costs for mental health care in Canada.

Source: Health Canada, Economic Burden of Illness in Canada, 1993.

BECOMING AN INFORMED CONSUMER OF PSYCHOLOGY

Deciding When You Need Help

Should we assume that every time we feel anxious or upset we should seek professional help? Why or why not?

After you consider the range and variety of psychological disturbances that can afflict people, it would not be surprising if you began to feel that you are suffering from one (or more) of the problems we have discussed. In fact, there is a name for this perception: *medical student's disease.* Although in the present case it might more aptly be labelled "psychology student's disease," the basic symptoms are the same: feeling that you suffer from the problems you are studying.

Most often, of course, your concerns will be unwarranted. As we have discussed, the differences between normal and abnormal behaviour are often so fuzzy that it is easy to jump to the conclusion that one has the symptoms that are involved in serious forms of mental disturbance.

Before coming to such a conclusion, though, it is important to reflect on the fact that over time we all experience a wide range of emotions, and it is not unusual to feel deeply unhappy, to fantasize about bizarre situations, or to feel anxiety about the circumstances of one's life. It is the persistence, depth, and consistency of such behaviour that set abnormal reactions apart from normal ones. If you have not previously had serious doubts about the normality of your behaviour, reading about others' psychological disorders is probably not a strong reason for you to reevaluate your earlier self-confidence.

On the other hand, many people do have problems that merit concern, and it is important for them to consider the possibility that they might need professional help. Following is a list of symptoms that can arise when the normal problems of everyday living escalate beyond your ability to deal with them yourself (Engler & Goleman, 1992):

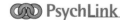 **PsychLink**

International Classification of Diseases
www.mcgrawhill.ca/college/feldman

- Long-term feelings of distress that interfere with your sense of well-being, competence, and ability to function effectively in daily activities
- Occasions in which you experience overwhelmingly high stress, accompanied by feelings of inability to cope with the situation
- Prolonged depression or feelings of hopelessness, particularly when they do not have any clear cause (such as the death of someone close)
- Withdrawal from other people
- A chronic physical problem for which no physical cause can be determined
- A fear or phobia that prevents you from engaging in everyday activities

- Feelings that other people are out to get you or are talking about and plotting against you
- The inability to interact effectively with others, preventing the development of friendships and loving relationships

This list offers a rough set of guidelines for determining when you might need to seek professional help. In such situations, the least reasonable approach would be to pore over the psychological disorders we have discussed in an attempt to pigeonhole yourself into a specific category. A more reasonable strategy is to consider seeking professional help—a possibility that we discuss in the next chapter.

Evaluate

1. The latest version of the *DSM* is considered to be the conclusive guideline on defining mental disorders. True or False?

2. _____ _____ _____, characterized by severe, incapacitating mood changes or depression related to a woman's menstrual cycle, was eventually added to the appendix of the *DSM-IV* despite controversy surrounding its inclusion.

3. Match the disorder with the place where it is most commonly found

   1. amok   a. Southeast Asia
   2. anorexia nervosa   b. Malaysia
   3. Susto   c. North America
   4. Koro   d. Andean Mountains

4. In Canada, statistics on psychological disorders come from reports on psychiatric _____.

Answers to Evaluate Questions

1. False: the development of the latest version of the DSM was a source of great controversy, in part reflecting issues that divide society. 2. Premenstrual dysphoric disorder 3. 1b, 2c, 3d, 4a 4. hospitalization

Rethink

1. Why is inclusion in the *DSM-IV* of "borderline" disorders such as self-defeating personality disorder and premenstrual dysphoric disorder so controversial and political? What disadvantages does inclusion bring? Does inclusion bring any benefits?

2. What societal changes would have to occur for psychological disorders to be regarded as the equivalent of appendicitis or another treatable physical disorder? Do you think a person who has been treated for a psychological disorder could become prime minister of Canada? Should such a person become prime minister?

How can we distinguish normal from abnormal behaviour?

- Definitions of abnormality include deviation from the average, deviation from the ideal, abnormality as a sense of personal discomfort, inability to function effectively, and legal conceptions. (p. 396)
- No single definition is totally adequate, suggesting that abnormal and normal behaviour should be considered in terms of a continuum. (p. 398)

What are the major perspectives on psychological disorders used by mental health professionals?

- The medical perspective views abnormality as a symptom of an underlying disease that requires a cure. (p. 399)
- Psychoanalytic perspectives see abnormal behaviour as caused by conflicts in the unconscious produced by past experience. (p. 399)
- Behavioural approaches view abnormal behaviour not as a symptom of some underlying problem, but as the problem itself. To resolve the problem, one must change the behaviour. (p. 400)
- The cognitive approach sees abnormal behaviour as the result of faulty cognitions. In this view, abnormal behaviour can be remedied through a change in cognitions (thoughts and beliefs). (p. 400)
- Humanistic approaches view people as rational and motivated to get along with others; abnormal behaviour is seen as a result of difficulty in fulfilling one's needs. (p. 400)
- Sociocultural approaches view abnormal behaviour in terms of difficulties arising from family and other social relationships. (p. 401)

What classification system is used to categorize psychological disorders?

- In the United States and Canada, the most widely used system for classifying psychological disorders is the *DSM-IV*—the *Diagnostic and Statistical Manual of Mental Disorders,* Fourth Edition. (p. 401)

What are the major psychological disorders?

- Anxiety disorders are present when a person experiences so much anxiety that it affects daily functioning. Specific types of anxiety disorders include phobic disorder, panic disorder, generalized anxiety disorder, and obsessive-compulsive disorder. (p. 405)
- Somatoform disorders are psychological difficulties that take on a physical (somatic) form, but for which there is no medical cause. Examples are hypochondriasis and conversion disorders. (p. 408)
- Dissociative disorders are marked by the separation, or dissociation, of crucial parts of personality that are usually integrated. The major kinds of dissociative disorders are dissociative identity disorder (multiple personality), dissociative amnesia, and dissociative fugue. (p. 408)

What are the most severe forms of psychological disorders?

- Mood disorders are characterized by emotional states of depression or euphoria so strong that they intrude on everyday living. They include major depression and bipolar disorder. (p. 411)
- Schizophrenia is one of the severest forms of mental illness. Symptoms of schizophrenia include declines in functioning, thought and language disturbances, perceptual disorders, emotional disturbance, and withdrawal from others. (p. 414)

- Strong evidence links schizophrenia to genetic, biochemical, and environmental factors. According to the predisposition model, interactions among these kinds of factors produce the disorder. (p. 416)
- People with personality disorders feel little or no personal distress, but they do suffer from an inability to function as normal members of society. The best-known types of personality disorders are antisocial personality disorder, borderline personality disorder, and narcissistic personality. (p. 419)
- Attention deficit hyperactivity disorder (ADHD), which is marked by inattention, impulsiveness, a low tolerance for frustration, and inappropriate activity, has become a commonly diagnosed (and sometimes misdiagnosed) disorder, particularly among schoolchildren. (p. 420)

What indicators signal a need for the help of a mental health practitioner?

- There are many other categories of disorders, including sexual disorders, psychoactive substance-use disorders, and organic mental disorders. There are significant cultural differences in the nature and prevalence of psychological disorders. (p. 421)
- Students of psychology are susceptible to the same sort of "disease" that afflicts medical students: the perception that they suffer from the problems they are studying. (p. 423)
- The signals that indicate a need for professional help include long-term feelings of psychological distress, feelings of inability to cope with stress, withdrawal from other people, prolonged feelings of hopelessness, chronic physical problems with no apparent causes, phobias and compulsions, paranoia, and an inability to interact with others. (p. 423)

Key Terms and Concepts

medical perspective (p. 399)
psychoanalytic perspective (p. 399)
behavioural perspective (p. 400)
cognitive perspective (p. 400)
humanistic perspective (p. 400)
sociocultural perspective (p. 401)
Diagnostic and Statistical Manual of Mental Disorders, Fourth Edition *(DSM-IV)* (p. 402)
anxiety disorder (p. 405)
phobias (p. 405)
panic disorder (p. 406)
generalized anxiety disorder (p. 406)
obsessive-compulsive disorder (p. 406)
obsession (p. 406)
compulsion (p. 407)
somatoform disorder (p. 408)
hypochondriasis (p. 408)

conversion disorder (p. 408)
dissociative disorder (p. 409)
dissociative identity disorder (multiple personality) (p. 409)
dissociative amnesia (p. 409)
dissociative fugue (p. 410)
mood disorder (p. 411)
major depression (p. 411)
mania (p. 411)
hypomanic (p. 412)
bipolar disorder (p. 412)
schizophrenia (p. 414)
personality disorder (p. 419)
antisocial personality disorder (p. 419)
borderline personality disorder (p. 419)
narcissistic personality disorder (p. 420)
attention deficit hyperactivity disorder (ADHD) (p. 420)

Psychology on the Web

1. On the Web, consulting at least two sources, research what advice and help is available for family and friends who are providing help and support for people suffering with schizophrenia. How accessible and helpful is this information?
2. Find information on the Web about the controversy surrounding dissociative (or multiple) personality disorder. Summarize both sides of the controversy. Using your knowledge of psychology, state your own opinions on the matter.

Epilogue

In this chapter, we discussed a few of the many types of psychological disorders to which people are prone, noting the difficulty that psychologists and physicians have in clearly differentiating normal from abnormal behaviour, and looking at some of the approaches that have been taken to explain and treat psychological disorders. We took note of what is currently the most commonly used classification scheme (the *DSM-IV*), and we examined some of the most prevalent forms of psychological disorders. To gain a perspective on the topic of psychological disorders, we discussed the surprisingly broad incidence of psychological disorders in North American society and the cultural nature of such disorders.

Before we proceed to focus on treatment of such disorders, turn back to the chapter prologue, where you read about Lori Schiller. Using the knowledge you gained from this chapter, consider the following questions.

1. Schiller was diagnosed as suffering from schizophrenia. What elements of her behaviour seem to fit the description of schizophrenia provided by the *DSM-IV* (and summarized in Table 12-2)?
2. From which type of schizophrenia (disorganized, paranoid, catatonic, undifferentiated, or residual; see Table 12-4) do you think Schiller was probably suffering? Why?
3. Which perspective (medical, psychoanalytic, behavioural, cognitive, humanistic, or sociocultural) do you think provides the best explanation of Schiller's case? Could two or more approaches be used together?
4. Were there signs of psychological disorder in Schiller's actions during adolescence? Why do you think Schiller's family failed to notice that she needed help? Why do you think it took so long for Schiller to tell her parents she had problems?

integrator

For extra help in mastering the material in this chapter, see the integrator, practice quizzes, and other resources on the Online Learning Centre at

www.mcgrawhill.ca/college/ feldman

Chapter Thirteen

Treatment of Psychological Disorders

Prologue

Dr. Norman Endler: Darkness and Beyond

Dr. Norman Endler

In the summer of 1976, Professor Norman Endler was 45 years old and at the height of his career. He was head of the Psychology Department at York University, a psychiatric consultant at two Toronto hospitals, and an author of numerous journal articles and books. During the next year it became clear that something was very wrong. In June 1977, he sought psychiatric help.

At first, Dr. Endler was diagnosed with unipolar depression, and was given antidepressants plus tranquilizers. He had negative thoughts toward taking pills and difficulty accepting the diagnosis. He developed serious side effects to several types of antidepressants (e.g., dangerously high blood pressure). He also developed a secondary depression with some paranoid-like symptoms, felt grossly incompetent and worthless, and became convinced that he would never recover. As summer wore on, he made no progress. Finally, because drug therapy was not working, his psychiatrist gave him a choice between two undesirable alternatives: hospitalization or ECT. He chose ECT. He responded well to the treatments, and soon resumed his usual professional duties and other activities.

His first depression was followed by a second depression, more antidepressants, lithium, and more ECT (to which he did not respond quite as well as his first course of treatments). The diagnosis was later changed to a bipolar disorder (which is also a mood disorder). Dr. Endler suffered another mild depressive episode and also had two heart attacks. However, by the time he had finished writing the revised edition of his book, *Holiday of Darkness*, in August 1989, he had been living free of depressive symptoms for eight years. With the publication of his book and the many interviews and speaking engagements in which he participated, he demonstrated that a high-profile academic clinical psychologist could continue in a successful professional, social, and family life without repercussions from the stigma associated with having a psychological disorder. He had struggled through the darkness and beyond it. Dr. Endler is currently a Fellow of the Royal Society of Canada and a Distinguished Research Professor (Emeritus) at York University.

Looking Ahead

In his book, Norman Endler shares details of his experience with depression and the treatments he received. In describing both drug and electroconvulsive therapies, he portrays the complex nature of modern treatment for depression. Although treatment approaches for psychological disorders vary considerably, ranging from one-meeting, informal counselling sessions to long-term drug therapy, all have a common objective: relief from a psychological disorder, with the ultimate aim of enabling individuals to achieve rich, meaningful, and fulfilling lives.

In this chapter, we explore a number of basic issues related to the treatment of abnormal behaviour: How do we treat people with psychological disorders? Who is the most appropriate person to provide treatment? Is one form of therapy better than another?

Most of this chapter focuses on the various approaches used by providers of treatment for psychological disturbances. Despite their diversity, these approaches fall into two main categories: psychologically based therapy and biologically based therapy. Psychologically based therapy, or **psychotherapy**, is treatment in which a trained professional—a therapist—uses psychological techniques to help someone overcome psychological difficulties and disorders, resolve problems in living, or bring about personal growth. In psychotherapy, the goal is to produce psychological change in a person (called a "client" or "patient") as a result of discussions and interactions with the therapist. In contrast, **biomedical therapy** relies on drugs and other medical procedures to improve psychological functioning.

As we describe the various approaches to therapy, keep in mind that although the distinctions might seem clear-cut, there is a good deal of overlap among the classifications and procedures employed. In fact, many therapists today use a variety of methods with a given person, in what is referred to as an *eclectic approach to therapy*. Assuming that psychological disorders are often the product of both psychological and biological processes, eclectic therapists will draw from several perspectives simultaneously, in an effort to address both the psychological and the biological aspects of a person's problems (Wachtel & Messer, 1997; Nathan & Gorman, 1997).

psychotherapy: Treatment in which a trained professional—a therapist—uses psychological techniques to help someone overcome psychological difficulties and disorders, resolve problems in living, or bring about personal growth.

biomedical therapy: Therapy that relies on drugs and other medical procedures to improve psychological functioning.

Prepare

What are the goals of psychologically and biologically based treatment approaches?
What are the basic kinds of psychotherapies?

Organize

Psychotherapy
    Psychodynamic Approaches to Therapy
    Behavioural Approaches to Therapy
    Cognitive Approaches to Therapy

Psychotherapy: Psychological Approaches to Treatment

There are some 400 different varieties of psychotherapy. Although diverse in many respects, all psychological approaches see treatment as a way of solving psychological problems by modifying people's behaviour and helping them gain a better understanding of themselves and their past, present, and future.

Given the variety of psychological approaches, it is not surprising that the people who provide therapy vary considerably in their educational backgrounds and training (see Table 13-1). Many have doctoral degrees in psychology (meaning that they have attended graduate school, learned clinical and research techniques, and held an internship). But therapy is also provided by people in fields allied with psychology, such as psychiatry and social work.

Regardless of their specific training, almost all psychotherapists employ one of four major approaches to therapy—psychodynamic, behavioural, cognitive, and humanistic—each of which is based on the models of personality and abnormal behaviour discussed in Chapters 10 and 12. We'll consider each in turn.

Psychodynamic Approaches to Therapy

Psychodynamic therapy is based on the premise, first suggested by Freud that the primary sources of abnormal behaviour are unresolved past conflicts and the possibility that unacceptable unconscious impulses might enter consciousness. To guard against this anxiety-provoking possibility, individuals employ *defence mechanisms,* psychological strategies to protect themselves from these unconscious impulses (see Chapter 10).

psychodynamic therapy: First suggested by Freud, therapy based on the premise that the primary sources of abnormal behaviour are unresolved past conflicts and the possibility that unacceptable unconscious impulses will enter consciousness.

Table 13-1 Getting Help from the Right Person

Clinical psychologists

Ph.D.s who have also completed a postgraduate internship. They specialize in assessment and treatment of psychological difficulties

Counselling psychologists

Psychologists with Ph.D. or Ed.D. who typically treat day-to-day adjustment problems, often in a university mental health clinic

Psychiatrists

M.D.s with postgraduate training in abnormal behaviour. Because they can prescribe medication, they often treat the most severe disorders

Psychoanalysts

Either M.D.s or psychologists who specialize in psychoanalysis, the treatment technique first developed by Freud

Clinical or **Psychiatric Social Workers**

Professionals with a master's degree and specialized training who may provide therapy, usually regarding common family and personal problems

Each of these trained professionals could be expected to give helpful advice and direction. However, the nature of the problem a person is experiencing may make one or another more appropriate. For example, a person who is suffering from a severe disturbance and who has lost touch with reality will typically require some sort of biologically based drug therapy. In that case, a psychiatrist—who is a physician—would be the professional of choice. On the other hand, those suffering from milder disorders, such as difficulty in adjusting to the death of a family member, have a broader choice that might include any of the professionals listed above. The decision can be made easier by initial consultations with professionals in mental health facilities in communities, colleges, and health organizations, who can provide guidance in selecting an appropriate therapist.

The most common defence mechanism is repression, in which threatening conflicts and impulses are pushed back into the unconscious. However, because unacceptable conflicts and impulses can never be completely buried, some of the anxiety associated with them can produce abnormal behaviour in the form of what Freud called *neurotic symptoms.*

How does one rid oneself of the anxiety produced by unconscious, unwanted impulses and drives? To Freud, the answer was to confront the conflicts and impulses by bringing them out of the unconscious part of the mind and into the conscious part. Freud assumed that this technique would reduce anxiety stemming from past conflicts and that the patient could then participate in his or her daily life more effectively.

Freud's development of "talking cures" is likely to be acknowledged as his greatest contribution to medical science (Murray et al., 2000). Basically, the technique consists of leading patients to consider and discuss in detail their past experiences from the time of their first memories. The process assumes that the person will eventually stumble upon the anxiety-producing conflicts. They will then be able to "work through" these difficulties.

Psychoanalysis: Freud's Therapy

Classic Freudian psychodynamic therapy, called **psychoanalysis**, tends to be a lengthy and expensive affair. Patients typically meet with their therapists for an hour a day, four to six days a week, for several years. In their sessions, they often use a technique developed by Freud called *free association.* Patients are told to say aloud whatever comes to mind, regardless of its apparent irrelevance or senselessness, and analysts attempt to recognize and label the connections between what is being said and the patient's unconscious. Therapists also use *dream interpretation,* examining dreams to find clues to unconscious conflicts and problems (first discussed in Chapter 4). Moving beyond the surface description of a dream (the *manifest content*), therapists seek to find

PsychLink

What is psychotherapy?
www.mcgrawhill.ca/college/feldman

psychoanalysis: Psychodynamic therapy that involves frequent sessions and can last for many years.

Freud's psychoanalytic therapy is an intensive, lengthy process that includes techniques such as free association and dream interpretation. **What are some advantages and disadvantages of psychoanalysis compared to other approaches?**

its underlying meaning (the *latent content*), thereby revealing the true unconscious meaning of the dream (Galatzer-Levy & Cohler, 1997).

The processes of free association and dream interpretation do not always move forward easily. The same unconscious forces that initially produced repression can work to keep past difficulties out of the conscious, producing resistance. *Resistance* is an inability or unwillingness to discuss or reveal particular memories, thoughts, or motivations. Resistance can be expressed in a number of ways. For instance, patients might be discussing a childhood memory and suddenly forget what they were saying, or they might completely change the subject. It is the therapist's job to pick up instances of resistance and to interpret their meaning, as well as to ensure that patients return to the subject—which is likely to hold difficult or painful memories for them.

Because of the close, almost intimate interaction between patient and psychoanalyst, the relationship between the two often becomes emotionally charged and takes on a complexity unlike most others. Patients might eventually perceive the analyst as symbolic of significant others in their past, perhaps a parent or a lover, and apply some of their feelings for that person to the analyst—a phenomenon known as *transference* (Mann, 1997).

Transference can be used by a therapist to help the patient recreate past relationships that were psychologically difficult. For instance, if a patient undergoing transference views her therapist as symbolic of her father—with whom she had a difficult relationship—the patient and therapist might "redo" an earlier interaction, this time including more positive aspects. Through this process, conflicts regarding the real father might be resolved—something that is beginning to happen in the following therapy session:

> Sandy: My father . . . never took any interest in any of us. . . . It was my mother—rest her soul—who loved us, not our father. He worked her to death. Lord, I miss her. . . . I must sound angry at my father. Don't you think I have a right to be angry?
> Therapist: Do you think you have a right to be angry?
> Sandy: Of course, I do! Why are you questioning me? You don't believe me, do you?
> Therapist: You want me to believe you.
> Sandy: I don't care whether you believe me or not. . . . I know what you're thinking—you think I'm crazy—you must be laughing at me—I'll probably be a case in your next book! You're just sitting there—smirking—making me feel like a bad person—thinking I'm wrong for being mad, that I have no right to be mad.
> Therapist: Just like your father.
> Sandy: Yes, you're just like my father.—Oh my God! Just now—I—I—thought I was talking to him. (Sue, Sue, & Sue, 1990, pp. 514–515)

Contemporary Alternatives to Psychoanalysis

Few people have the time, money, or patience required for years of traditional psychoanalysis. Moreover, no conclusive evidence shows that psychoanalysis, as originally conceived by Freud, works better than other, more contemporary versions of psychodynamic therapy. Today, for instance, psychodynamic therapy tends to be shorter, usually lasting no longer than three months or 20 sessions (DeLuca, Grayston, & Romano, 1999). The therapist takes a more active role than Freud would have liked, controlling the course of therapy and prodding and advising the patient with considerable directness. Finally, there is less emphasis on a patient's past history and childhood. Instead, the therapist concentrates on an individual's current relationships, emotions, and specific complaints ("Brief Psychodynamic Therapy," 1994; Greenberg & Paivio, 1997).

Even with its current modifications, psychodynamic therapy has its critics. In its longer versions, it can be relatively time-consuming and expensive, especially in comparison with other forms of psychotherapy that we will discuss later. Furthermore, patients who are less articulate might not do as well as those who are more verbal.

Ultimately, the most important concern about psychodynamic treatment is whether it actually works, and here we find no simple answer. Psychodynamic treatment techniques have been controversial since Freud introduced them. Part of the problem is the difficulty in establishing whether or not patients have improved following psychodynamic therapy. One must depend on reports from the therapist or the patients themselves, reports that are obviously open to bias and subjective interpretation.

Critics have questioned the entire theoretical basis of psychodynamic theory, maintaining that there is no proof that such constructs as the unconscious exist. Despite the considerable criticism, though, the psychodynamic treatment approach has remained viable. To proponents, it not only provides effective treatment in many cases of psychological disturbance, but also permits the potential development of an unusual degree of insight into one's life (Barber & Lane, 1995; Clay, 2000).

Behavioural Approaches to Therapy

Perhaps, as a child, you were rewarded by your parents with an ice cream cone when you were especially good . . . or sent to your room if you misbehaved. As we saw in Chapter 5, the principles behind such a child-rearing strategy are valid: Good behaviour is maintained by reinforcement, and unwanted behaviour can be eliminated by punishment.

These principles represent the basic underpinnings of **behavioural treatment approaches**. Building upon the basic processes of learning, behavioural treatment approaches make this fundamental assumption: Both abnormal behaviour and normal behaviour are *learned*. People who display abnormal behaviour have either failed to learn the skills needed to cope with the problems of everyday living or have acquired faulty skills and patterns that are being maintained through some form of reinforcement. To modify abnormal behaviour, then, behavioural approaches propose that people must learn new behaviour to replace their maladaptive behaviour patterns (Bergin & Garfield, 1994; Agras & Berkowitz, 1996).

To behavioural psychologists, it is not necessary to delve into people's pasts or their psyches. Rather than viewing abnormal behaviour as a symptom of some underlying problem, they consider the abnormal behaviour itself as the problem in need of modification. Changing people's behaviour to allow them to function more effectively solves the problem—with no need for concern about the underlying cause. In this view, then, if you can change abnormal behaviour, you've cured the problem.

Aversive Conditioning Techniques

Suppose you bite into your favourite candy bar and find that it is not only infested with ants, but that you've swallowed a bunch of them. You immediately become sick to your stomach and throw up. Your long-term reaction? You never eat that kind of candy bar again, and it might be months before you eat any type of candy.

This simple example demonstrates how classical conditioning might be used to modify behaviour. Recall from our discussion in Chapter 5 that when a stimulus that naturally evokes a negative response (such as an unpleasant taste or a puff of air in the face) is paired with a previously neutral stimulus (such as the sound of a tone), the neutral stimulus can come to elicit a similar negative reaction by itself. Using this procedure, we can create unpleasant reactions to stimuli that an individual previously enjoyed—possibly to excess. The technique, known as *aversive conditioning,* has been used to treat alcoholism, drug abuse, and smoking.

PsychLink

Benefits of psychotherapy
www.mcgrawhill.ca/college/feldman

behavioural treatment approaches: Treatment approaches that build upon the basic processes of learning, such as reinforcement and extinction.

Behavioural approaches to treatment would seek to modify the behaviour of this couple, rather than focusing on the underlying causes of the behaviour.

Chapter Activity 13–1 **Producing the Relaxation Response**

Step 1. Pick a focus word or short phrase that's firmly rooted in your personal belief system. For example, a nonreligious individual might choose a neutral word like one or peace or love. A Christian person desiring to use a prayer could pick the opening words of Psalm 23. *The Lord is my shepherd*; a Jewish person could choose *Shalom*.

Step 2. Sit quietly in a comfortable position.

Step 3. Close your eyes.

Step 4. Relax your muscles.

Step 5. Breathe slowly and naturally, repeating your focus word or phrase silently as you exhale.

Step 6. Throughout, assume a passive attitude. Don't worry about how well you're doing. When other thoughts come to mind, simply say to yourself, "Oh, well," and gently return to the repetition.

Step 7. Continue for 10 to 20 minutes. You may open your eyes to check the time, but do not use an alarm. When you finish, sit quietly for a minute or so, at first with your eyes closed and later with your eyes open. Then do not stand for one or two minutes.

Step 8. Practise the technique once or twice a day.

The basic procedure in aversive conditioning is relatively straightforward. For example, a person with a drinking problem might be given an alcoholic drink along with a drug that causes severe nausea and vomiting. After these two are paired a few times, the alcohol alone becomes associated with the vomiting and becomes less appealing.

Although aversion therapy works reasonably well to inhibit substance-abuse problems such as alcoholism and certain kinds of sexual disorders, its long-term effectiveness is questionable. There are also important ethical concerns about aversion techniques that employ such potent stimuli as electric shock, which are used only in the most extreme cases, such as self-mutilation. It is clear, though, that aversion therapy is an important procedure for eliminating maladaptive responses for some period of time—a respite that provides, even if only temporarily, the opportunity to encourage more adaptive behaviour patterns (Yuskauskas, 1992).

Systematic Desensitization

The most successful treatment based on classical conditioning is systematic desensitization. **Systematic desensitization** is a technique in which gradual exposure to an anxiety-producing stimulus is paired with relaxation in order to extinguish the response of anxiety (Wolpe, 1990; St. Onge, 1995a).

Suppose, for instance, you were extremely afraid of flying. The very thought of being in an airplane made you begin to sweat and shake, and you'd never even been able to get yourself near enough to an airport to know how you'd react if you actually had to fly somewhere. If systematic desensitization were used to treat your problem, you would first be trained in relaxation techniques by a behaviour therapist (try Chapter Activity 13-1), learning to relax your body fully—a highly pleasant state, as you might imagine.

The next step would involve the construction of a *hierarchy of fears*—a list, in order of increasing severity, of the things that are associated with your fears. For instance, your hierarchy might resemble this one:

1. Watching a plane fly overhead
2. Going to an airport
3. Buying a ticket
4. Stepping into the plane
5. Seeing the plane door close
6. Having the plane taxi down the runway
7. Taking off
8. Being in the air

systematic desensitization: A behavioural technique in which gradual exposure to anxiety-producing stimuli is paired with relaxation in order to extinguish the response of anxiety.

These participants in a systematic desensitization program have worked to overcome their fear of flying and are about to "graduate" by taking a brief flight. **In what ways is this approach based on classical conditioning?**

Once this hierarchy had been developed and you had learned relaxation techniques, the two sets of responses would be associated with each other. To do this, your therapist might ask you to put yourself into a relaxed state and then to imagine yourself in the first situation identified in your hierarchy. After you were able to consider that first step while remaining relaxed, you would move on to the next situation, eventually moving up the hierarchy in gradual stages until you could imagine yourself being in the air without experiencing anxiety. Ultimately, you would be asked to make a visit to an airport and later to take a flight.

Systematic desensitization has proved to be an effective treatment for a number of problems, including phobias, anxiety disorders, and even impotence and fear of sexual contact. In short, we *can* learn to enjoy the things we once feared (Mendez & Garcia, 1996; Rachman, 1990, 1991, 1997).

PsychLink

Treating fear of flying
www.mcgrawhill.ca/college/feldman

Operant Conditioning Techniques

Behavioural approaches using operant conditioning techniques (which demonstrate the effects of rewards and punishments on future behaviour) are based on the notion that we should reward people for carrying out desirable behaviour and extinguish behaviour that we wish to eliminate, by either ignoring it or punishing it (Kazdin, 1994).

One example of the systematic application of operant conditioning principles is the *token system,* whereby a person is rewarded for desired behaviour with a token such as a poker chip or some kind of play money. Although it is most frequently employed in institutional settings for individuals with relatively serious problems, the system is not unlike what parents do when they give children money for being well behaved—money that they can later exchange for something they want. The desired behaviour might range from such simple things as keeping one's room neat to personal grooming or interacting with other people. In institutions, tokens can be exchanged for some object or activity, such as snacks, new clothes, or viewing a movie.

Contingency contracting, a variant of the more extensive token system, has proved quite effective in producing behaviour modification. In *contingency contracting,* a written agreement is drawn up between therapist and client (or teacher and student, or parent and child). The contract states a series of behavioural goals that the client hopes to achieve. It also specifies the positive consequences for the client if the goals are reached—usually some explicit reward such as money or additional privileges. Contracts frequently state negative consequences if the goals are not met. For example, clients who are trying to quit smoking might write out a cheque to a cause they have no interest in supporting (for instance, the Maple Leaf Gun Club if they are strong gun control supporters). If the client smokes on a given day, the therapist would mail the cheque.

Behaviour therapists also make use of *observational learning,* the process in which the behaviour of other people is modelled, to systematically teach people new skills and ways of handling their fears and anxieties. For example, modelling helps teach basic social skills such as maintaining eye contact during conversation or acting assertively. Similarly, children with dog phobias have been able to overcome their fears by watching another child—called the "Fearless Peer"—repeatedly walk up to a dog, touch it, pet it, and finally play with it. Modelling, then, can play an effective role in resolving some kinds of behaviour difficulties, especially if the model is rewarded for her or his behaviour (Bandura, Grusec, & Menlove, 1967; St. Onge, 1995b).

How Does Behaviour Therapy Stack Up?

Behaviour therapy works particularly well for phobias and compulsions, for establishing control over impulses, and for learning complex social skills to replace maladaptive behaviour. More than any of the other therapeutic techniques, it has produced methods that can be employed by nonprofessionals to change their own behaviour. Moreover, it tends to be economical in terms of time, because it is directed toward the solution of carefully defined problems (Wilson & Agras, 1992).

Behaviour therapy has its disadvantages. It is not particularly successful in treating deep depression or personality disorders (Brody, 1990). And, because it emphasizes changing external behaviour, people do not necessarily gain insight into their thoughts and expectations that might be fostering their maladaptive behaviour. Finally, behaviour therapy has less success in the long term than in the short term. Because of such concerns, some psychologists have turned to cognitive approaches.

Cognitive Approaches to Therapy

If you assumed that faulty, maladaptive cognitions lie at the heart of psychological disorders, wouldn't the most direct treatment route be to teach people new, more adaptive modes of thinking? The answer is yes, according to psychologists who take a cognitive approach to treatment.

cognitive treatment approaches:
Approaches to treatment that teach people to think in more adaptive ways by changing their dysfunctional cognitions about the world and themselves.
cognitive–behavioural approach: An approach used by cognitive therapists that attempts to change the way people think through the use of basic principles of learning.

Cognitive treatment approaches teach people to think in more adaptive ways by changing their dysfunctional cognitions about the world and themselves. For example, changing faulty beliefs and perceptions of self-efficacy has been found to be effective in treating anxiety disorders (Gauthier, 1999). Strategies that rely on information processing and basic principles of learning are called the **cognitive-behavioural approach** (Beck, 1991). Developing effective cognitive-behavioural interventions depends on a thorough understanding of cognitive functioning characteristic of the disorders being treated. Keith Dobson of the University of Calgary and David Dozois of the University of Western Ontario have found that depressed people not only encode negative self-relevant information better, but that they have a more interconnected memory organization for negative than for positive self-relevant information (Dozois & Dobson, 2001).

Cognitive treatment approaches are relatively short-term. For example, in the treatment of depression, 20 sessions of behavioural activation (monitoring of daily activities, engagement in tasks associated with pleasure and mastery, building skills required for success in specific situations, etc.) have been found to be as effective as more complete versions of cognitive-behavioural therapy (Jacobson et al., 1996; Gortner et al., 1998).

One of the best examples of cognitive treatment is rational-emotive behaviour therapy. **Rational-emotive behaviour therapy** attempts to restructure a person's belief system into a more realistic, rational, and logical set of views. According to psychologist Albert Ellis (1999), many people lead unhappy lives and suffer from psychological disorders because they harbour such irrational, unrealistic ideas as these:

rational-emotive behaviour therapy:
A form of therapy that attempts to restructure a person's belief system into a more realistic, rational, and logical set of views.

- That it is necessary to have the love or approval of virtually every significant other person for everything we do

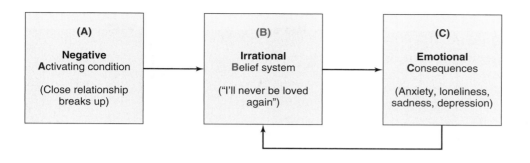

Figure 13-1 In the A-B-C model of rational-emotive behaviour therapy, negative activating conditions (A) lead to the activation of an irrational belief system (B), that leads to emotional consequences (C). Those emotional consequences then feed back and support the belief system.
At what steps in the model could change occur due to rational-emotive behaviour therapy?

- That we should be thoroughly competent, adequate, and successful in all possible respects if we are to consider ourselves worthwhile

Such irrational beliefs trigger negative emotions, which in turn support the irrational beliefs, leading to a self-defeating cycle. Ellis calls it the A-B-C model, in which negative activating conditions (A) lead to the activation of an irrational belief system (B), that in turn leads to emotional consequences (C). For example, if a person goes through the breakup of a close relationship (A) and holds the irrational belief (B) "I'll never be loved again," this triggers negative emotions (C) that in turn feed back into support of the irrational belief (see Figure 13-1).

The goal of rational-emotive behaviour therapy is to help clients eliminate the maladaptive cognitions and adopt more effective thinking. To accomplish this goal, therapists take an active, directive role during therapy, openly challenging patterns of thought that appear to be dysfunctional. Consider this example:

Martha: The basic problem is that I'm worried about my family. I'm worried about money. And I never seem to be able to relax.

Therapist: Why are you worried about your family? . . . What's to be concerned about? They have certain demands which you don't want to adhere to.

Martha: I was brought up to think that I mustn't be selfish.

Therapist: Oh, we'll have to knock that out of your head!

Martha: My mother feels that I shouldn't have left home—that my place is with them. There are nagging doubts about what I should—

Therapist: Why are there doubts? Why *should* you?

Martha: I think it's a feeling I was brought up with that you always have to give of yourself. If you think of yourself, you're wrong.

Therapist: That's a *belief*. Why do you have to keep believing that—at *your* age? You believed a lot of superstitions when you were younger. Why do you have to retain them? Your parents indoctrinated you with this nonsense, because that's *their* belief. . . . Who needs that philosophy? All it's gotten you, so far, is guilt. (Ellis, 1974, pp. 233–286)

By poking holes in Martha's reasoning, the therapist is attempting to help her adopt a more realistic view of herself and her circumstances (Ellis & Dryden, 1997; Dryden, 1999).

Another form of therapy that builds on a cognitive perspective is that of Aaron Beck (Beck, 1991, 1995). Like rational-emotive behaviour therapy, the basic goal of Beck's *cognitive therapy* is to change people's illogical thoughts about themselves and the world. However, Beck's cognitive therapy is considerably less confrontational and challenging than rational-emotive behaviour

"To this day, I can hear my mother's voice—harsh, accusing. 'Lost your mittens? You naughty kittens! Then you shall have no pie!'"

Applying Psychology in the 21st Century

Beating the Video Lottery Terminals (VLTs): Problem Gambling and its Treatment

In 2000, Canadians spent an average of $424 per person on gambling compared to $130 per person in 1992. In 2001, the net revenue for government-run lotteries, VLTs, and casinos was more than $10.7 billion, four times the 1992 level (Statistics Canada, 2002b). VLTs are a major problem for pathological gamblers (Hodgins & el-Guebaly, 2000; Hodgins et al., 2001). There is widespread concern internationally about VLT gambling because VLTs are readily available and playing them may be especially addictive (Hodgins et al., 2002).

Many explanations have been offered as to why people gamble (Inter-Provincial Task Force on Problem Gambling, 1999). According to psychodynamic models, people gamble to cope with

conflict or heal a deep emotional wound. Trait approaches link gambling to traits such as the desire for control, and the needs for dominance and achievement. Biological models have emphasized variables such as EEG waves, arousal, plasma endorphin levels, and chemical imbalances in the brain. Behavioural models have focused on the reinforcing aspects of gambling such as the arousal of winning and the powerful control of the partial reinforcement schedule. Cognitive models have stressed irrational thought processes that support gambling behaviour (for example, the illusion of control).

The treatment for gambling is as varied as the models that describe it. For a number of years, Robert Ladouceur (University of Laval) and his colleagues have researched gambling behaviours and their treatment (Ladouceur et al., 1994; Ladouceur & Mireault, 1988; Bujold

et al., 1994). Effective treatment has emphasized cognitive and behavioural strategies, such as the correction of misperceptions about gambling, problem-solving training, social-skills training, and relapse prevention (Sylvain et al., 1997; Ladouceur et al., 1998).

David Hodgins (University of Calgary) has been particularly interested in reasons for quitting and recovery from gambling. He and his colleagues have found that gamblers decide to quit for many different reasons. The most frequently stated reasons are negative emotions (such as guilt or depression), financial reasons, and family influences. About one-third of their research participants related their decision to quit to a particular critical incident (Hodgins & el-Guebaly, 2000; Hodgins et al., in press).

Hodgins and his colleagues have demonstrated that a motivational interview combined with a workbook is an effective intervention. The motivational interview emphasizes the advantages of quitting and involves participants in a discussion that assesses their situation and strategies that seem most promising. The workbook focuses on self-assessment, goal setting, cognitive-behavioural strategies, and preventing and coping with relapse. This type of intervention is promising because it responds to many gamblers' wish to handle their problem independently, and it can be offered to people in remote areas (Hodgins & Makarchuk, 1997; Hodgins et al., 2001; Hodgins et al., 2002).

How is gambling likely to disrupt life at home and at work? Can you think of reasons for quitting gambling other than those mentioned?

Trying to beat the VLT. Research shows that this may be a particularly addictive form of gambling.

therapy. Instead of actively arguing with clients about their dysfunctional cognitions, the therapist is more apt to play the role of teacher. Clients are urged to obtain information on their own that will lead them to discard their inaccurate thinking. During the course of treatment, clients are helped to discover ways of thinking more appropriately about themselves and others (Alford & Beck, 1997; Greenberg, 2000; Rosen, 2000).

Cognitive approaches to therapy have proved successful in dealing with a broad range of disorders. For example, they have been successfully applied to pathological gambling (Sylvain et al., 1997; Ladouceur et al., 1998), depression (Hurst & Genest, 1995), and anxiety disorders (Rachman, 1994; Pelletier et al., 1995; Dugas et al., 1996). To read more about problem gambling and its treatment, see the *Applying Psychology in the 21st Century* box.

Evaluate

1. Match the following kinds of mental health practitioners with the appropriate description
   1. Psychiatrist
   2. Clinical psychologist
   3. Counselling psychologist
   4. Psychoanalyst

   a. Ph.D. specializing in treatment of psychological disorders
   b. Professional specializing in Freudian therapy techniques
   c. M.D. trained in abnormal behaviour
   d. Ph.D. specializing in adjustment of day-to-day problems

2. According to Freud, people use _____ _____ to ensure that unwanted impulses will not intrude on conscious thought.

3. In dream interpretation, a psychoanalyst must learn to distinguish between the _____ content of a dream, which is what appears on the surface, and the _____ content, its underlying meaning.

4. Which of the following treatments deals with phobias by gradual exposure to the item producing the fear?
   a. Systematic desensitization
   b. Partial reinforcement
   c. Behavioural self-management
   d. Aversion therapy

Answers to Evaluate Questions

1. 1-c; 2-a; 3-d; 4-b 2. defence mechanisms 3. manifest; latent 4. a

Rethink

1. In what ways are psychoanalysis and cognitive therapy similar, and how do they differ?
2. How might you examine the reliability of dream interpretation?

Humanistic Approaches to Therapy

As you know from your own experience, it is impossible to master the material covered in a course without some hard work, no matter how good the teacher and the textbook are. *You* must take the time to study, to memorize the vocabulary, to learn the concepts. Nobody else can do it for you. If you choose to put in the effort, you'll succeed; if you don't, you'll fail. The responsibility is primarily yours.

Humanistic therapy draws upon this philosophical perspective of self-responsibility in developing treatment techniques. The many different types of therapy that fit into this category have a similar rationale: We have control of our own behaviour; we can make choices about the kinds of lives we want to live; and it is up to us to solve the difficulties that we encounter in our daily lives.

Instead of being the directive figures seen in some psychodynamic and behavioural approaches, humanistic therapists view themselves as guides or facilitators. Therapists using humanistic techniques seek to lead people to realizations about themselves and help them find ways to come closer to the ideal they hold for themselves. In this view, psychological disorders are the result of people's inability to find meaning in life and of feeling lonely and unconnected to others.

Humanistic approaches have produced a number of therapeutic techniques. Among the most important are client-centred therapy and gestalt therapy.

Prepare

What are humanistic approaches to treatment?

How does group therapy differ from individual types of therapy?

How effective is therapy, and which kind of therapy works best in a given situation?

Organize

Humanistic Approaches to Therapy

Group Therapy

Evaluating Psychotherapy

humanistic therapy: Therapy in which the underlying assumption is that people have control of their behaviour, can make choices about their lives, and are essentially responsible for solving their own problems.

Client-Centred Therapy

Consider the following therapy session excerpt:

Alice: I was thinking about this business of standards. I somehow developed a sort of a knack, I guess, of—well—habit—of trying to make people feel at ease around me, or to make things go along smoothly. . . .

Therapist: In other words, what you did was always in the direction of trying to keep things smooth and to make other people feel better and to smooth the situation.

Alice: Yes. I think that's what it was. Now the reason why I did it probably was—I mean, not that I was a good little Samaritan going around making other people happy, but that was probably the role that felt easiest for me to play. . . .

Therapist: You feel that for a long time you've been playing the role of kind of smoothing out the frictions or differences or what not. . . .

Alice: M-hm.

Therapist: Rather than having any opinion or reaction of your own in the situation. Is that it? (Rogers, 1951, pp. 152–153)

The therapist's comments are not interpretations or answers to questions that the client has raised. Instead, they tend to clarify or reflect back what the client has said (e.g., "In other words, what you did . . ."; "You feel that . . ."; "Is that it?"). This therapeutic technique is known as *nondirective counselling*. Nondirective counselling is at the heart of client-centred therapy, which was first practised by Carl Rogers (Rogers, 1951, 1980; Raskin & Rogers, 1989).

client-centred therapy: Therapy in which the goal is to reach one's potential for self-actualization.

The goal of **client-centred therapy** is to enable people to reach their potential for self-actualization. By providing a warm and accepting environment, therapists hope to motivate clients to air their problems and feelings. In turn, this enables clients to make realistic and constructive decisions about things that bother them in their current lives.

Instead of directing choices that clients make, therapists provide what Rogers calls *unconditional positive regard*—expressing acceptance and understanding, regardless of the feelings and attitudes the client expresses. In doing so, therapists hope to create an atmosphere in which clients are able to come to decisions that can improve their lives (Farber, Brink, & Raskin, 1996).

Furnishing unconditional positive regard does not mean that therapists must approve of everything their clients say or do. Rather, the assumption is that therapists need to communicate that they are caring, nonjudgmental, and *empathetic*—understanding of a client's emotional experience (Fearing & Clark, 2000).

It is relatively rare for client-centred therapy to be used today in its purest form. Contemporary approaches are apt to be somewhat more directive, with therapists nudging clients toward insights. Clients' insights are still seen as central to the therapeutic process.

Gestalt Therapy

PsychLink
Gestalt therapy
www.mcgrawhill.ca/college/feldman

Have you ever thought back to some childhood incident in which you were treated unfairly and again felt the rage that you experienced at that time? To therapists working in a gestalt perspective, the healthiest thing for you to do psychologically might be to act out that rage—by hitting a pillow, kicking a chair, or yelling in frustration. This sort of activity is an important part of what goes on in gestalt therapy sessions, in which the client is encouraged to act out past conflicts and difficulties.

gestalt therapy: An approach to therapy that attempts to integrate a client's thoughts, feelings, and behaviour into a unified whole.

The rationale for this treatment approach is the idea that people need to integrate their thoughts, feelings, and behaviours into a *gestalt,* the German term for "whole" (as we discussed in reference to perception in Chapter 3). In **gestalt therapy,** people are led to examine their earlier experiences and complete any "unfinished business" from their past that might still affect and colour present-day relationships. Gestalt therapy typically includes reenactments of specific conflicts that clients experienced earlier. For instance, a client might first play the part of his angry father and then play himself when his father yelled at him. Such reenactments are assumed to promote better understanding of the source of psychological disorders, as clients broaden their perspective on their situation. Ultimately, the goal of gestalt therapy is to experience life in a more unified and complete way (Perls, 1970; Perls, Hefferline, & Goodman, 1994; Serok, 2000).

Humanistic Approaches in Perspective

The notion that psychological disorders are the consequence of restricted growth potential is philosophically appealing to many people. Furthermore, humanistic therapists' acknowledgment that the freedom we possess can lead to psychological difficulties provides an unusually supportive environment for therapy. In turn, this atmosphere can help clients find solutions to difficult psychological problems.

On the other hand, the lack of specificity of the humanistic treatments has troubled critics. Humanistic approaches are not very precise and are probably the least scientifically and theoretically developed type of treatment. Moreover, this form of treatment is best suited for the same type of highly verbal client who profits most from psychoanalytic treatment.

Group Therapy

Although most treatment takes place between a single individual and a therapist, some forms of therapy involve groups of people seeking treatment. In **group therapy**, several unrelated people meet with a therapist to discuss some aspect of their psychological functioning.

group therapy: Therapy in which people discuss problems in a group.

People typically discuss their problems with the group, which is often centred around a common difficulty, such as alcoholism or a lack of social skills. For example, in one such instance, young offenders convicted of physical and sexual assaults participated in a group therapy program to gain self-knowledge regarding their maladaptive behaviours and develop empathy for their victims (Mamabolo, 1996).

Groups vary greatly in terms of the particular model they employ; there are psychoanalytic groups, humanistic groups, and groups corresponding to the other therapeutic approaches. Furthermore, groups also differ in the degree of guidance the therapist provides. In some, the therapist is quite directive; in others, the members of the group set their own agenda and determine how the group will proceed (Spira, 1997; Early, 1999).

Because several people are treated simultaneously in group therapy, it is a much more economical means of treatment than individual psychotherapy. On the other hand, critics argue that group settings do not afford the individual attention inherent in one-to-one therapy, and that in a group setting especially shy and withdrawn individuals might not receive the attention they need.

family therapy: An approach that focuses on the family and its dynamics.

Family Therapy

One specialized form of group therapy is family therapy. As the name implies, **family therapy** involves two or more members of the same family, one (or more) of whose problems led to treatment. By meeting with the entire family simultaneously, family therapists attempt to obtain a sense of how the family members interact with one another (Rolland & Walsh, 1996; Cooklin, 2000).

Family therapists view the family as a "system," and they assume that the separate individuals in the family cannot improve without understanding the conflicts that are to be found in the interactions of the family members. Thus each member is expected to contribute to the resolution of the problem being addressed.

Many family therapists assume that family members fall into rigid roles or set patterns of behaviour, with one person

In group therapy, people with psychological difficulties meet with a therapist to discuss their problems.

acting as the scapegoat, another as a bully, and so forth. In their view, family disturbances are perpetuated by this system of roles. One goal of this type of therapy, then, is to get the family members to adopt new, more constructive roles and patterns of behaviour (Minuchin & Nichols, 1992; Sprenkle & Moon, 1996).

Evaluating Psychotherapy: Does Therapy Work?

Your best friend, Ben, comes to you because he just hasn't been feeling right about things lately. He's upset because he and his girlfriend aren't getting along, but his difficulties go beyond that. He can't concentrate on his studies, has a lot of trouble getting to sleep, and—this is what really bothers him—he's begun to think that people are ganging up on him, talking about him behind his back. It just seems that no one really cares about or understands him or makes any effort to see why he's become so miserable.

Ben is aware that he ought to get *some* kind of help, but he is not sure where to turn. He is fairly skeptical of psychologists, thinking that a lot of what they say is just mumbo-jumbo, but he's willing to put his doubts aside and try anything to feel better. He also knows there are many different types of therapy, and he doesn't have a clue as to which would be best for him. He turns to you for advice, because he knows you are taking a psychology course. He asks, "Which kind of therapy works best?"

Is Therapy Effective?

Such a question requires a complex response, for there is no easy answer. In fact, identifying which form of treatment is most appropriate is a controversial, and still unresolved, task for psychologists specializing in psychological disorders. For example, even before considering whether any one form of therapy works better than another, we need to determine whether therapy in *any* form is effective in alleviating psychological disturbances.

Until the 1950s, most people simply assumed that therapy was effective. But in 1952 psychologist Hans Eysenck published what became a classic article that challenged this assumption. He claimed that people who received psychodynamic treatment and related therapies were no better off at the end of treatment than people who were placed on a waiting list for treatment but never received it. According to his analysis, about two-thirds of the people who reported suffering from "neurotic" symptoms believed that those symptoms had disappeared after two years, regardless of whether or not they had been in therapy. Eysenck concluded that people would go into **spontaneous remission**, recovery without treatment, if they were simply left alone—certainly a cheaper and simpler process.

Although Eysenck's conclusions were quickly challenged, his review stimulated a continuing stream of better controlled, more carefully crafted studies on the effectiveness of psychotherapy, and today most psychologists agree: Therapy does work. Several comprehensive reviews indicate that therapy brings about greater improvement than no treatment at all, with the rate of spontaneous remission being fairly low. In most cases, then, the symptoms of abnormal behaviour do not go away by themselves if left untreated—although the issue continues to be hotly debated (Bergin & Garfield, 1994; Seligman, 1996; Sohn, 1996).

Which Kind of Therapy Works Best?

Although most psychologists feel confident that psychotherapeutic treatment *in general* is more effective than no treatment at all, the question of whether any specific form of treatment is superior to any other has yet to be answered definitively (Barber & Lane, 1995; Pratt & Moreland, 1996).

For instance, one classic study comparing the effectiveness of various approaches found that although there is some variation among the success rates of the various treatment forms, most treatments have about the same success rate. As Figure 13-2 indicates, the success rates ranged from about 70 to 85 percent greater success for treated than

PsychLinks

Effectiveness of psychotherapy
www.mcgrawhill.ca/college/feldman

spontaneous remission: Recovery without treatment.

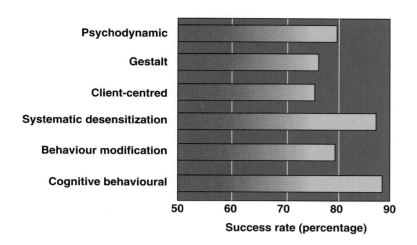

Figure 13-2 Estimates of the effectiveness of different types of treatment, in comparison to control groups of untreated people (Smith, Glass, & Miller, 1980). The percentile score shows how much more effective a particular type of treatment is for the average patient than is no treatment. For example, people given psychodynamic treatment score, on average, more positively on outcome measures than about three-quarters of untreated people.

for untreated individuals. There was a slight tendency for behavioural approaches and cognitive approaches to be more successful, but this result might have been due to differences in the severity of cases treated (Smith, Glass, & Miller, 1980; Orwin & Condray, 1984).

Other research, relying on *meta-analysis,* in which data from a large number of studies are statistically combined, yields similar general conclusions. Furthermore, a large-scale survey of 186 000 individuals found that although survey respondents felt they had benefited substantially from psychotherapy (see Figure 13-3), there was little difference in "consumer satisfaction" based on the specific type of treatment they had received ("Mental Health," 1995; Seligman, 1995; Strupp, 1996).

In short, converging evidence allows us to draw several conclusions about the effectiveness of psychotherapy (Strupp & Binder, 1992; Seligman, 1996):

- *For most people, psychotherapy is effective.* This conclusion holds over different lengths of treatment, specific kinds of psychological disorders, and types of treatment. Thus, the question "Does psychotherapy work?" appears to be convincingly answered: It does (Lipsey & Wilson, 1993; Seligman, 1996; Spiegel, 1999).
- *On the other hand, psychotherapy doesn't work for everyone.* As many as 10 percent of people show no improvement or actually deteriorate following treatment (Lambert, Shapiro, & Bergin, 1986; Luborsky, 1988).
- *Certain specific types of treatments are somewhat, although not invariably, better for specific types of problems.* For example, cognitive therapy works particularly well for panic disorders, and systematic desensitization relieves specific phobias quite effectively. However, there are many exceptions, and often the differences in success rates for different types of treatment are not substantial (Hubble, Duncan, & Miller, 1999; Miller & Magruder, 1999).
- *No single form of therapy works best on every problem.* Consequently, there is no definitive answer to the question "Which therapy works best?"

Because no one type of psychotherapy is invariably effective, eclectic approaches to therapy have become increasingly popular. In an **eclectic approach to therapy,** a therapist uses a variety of techniques, integrating several perspectives, to treat a person's problems. The eclectic therapist can choose a mix of treatment procedures appropriate to the specific needs of the individual.

In selecting and using specific therapeutic techniques, it is important to acknowledge influences of the broader social context of everyday life. For instance, in treating depressed women, it is important to understand how social and cultural factors shape and regulate their lives. This knowledge will help the therapist and client avoid the problem of disempowerment associated with drug

eclectic approach to therapy: An approach to therapy that uses techniques taken from a variety of treatment methods, rather than just one method.

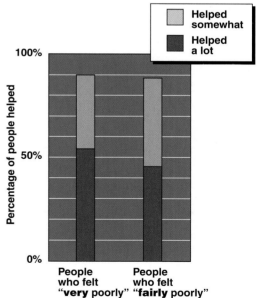

Figure 13-3 A large-scale survey of 186 000 individuals found that while the respondents had benefited substantially from psychotherapy, there was little difference in "consumer satisfaction" based on the specific type of treatment they had received.

Pathways Through Psychology

Janet Stoppard

Professor, Psychology Department, University of New Brunswick

Education: Ph.D. (Queen's University, Kingston); M.Sc. (Queen's University, Belfast, Northern Ireland); B.Sc. (Exeter University, UK)

Home: Fredericton, New Brunswick

Janet Stoppard

I became interested in psychology as a teenager after reading a book about "altered states of consciousness." I decided then to study psychology at university. After completing my undergraduate degree, I moved to Belfast in Northern Ireland to do a master's degree in clinical psychology. This was followed by several years working in child psychological services. Around this time (early 1970s), Belfast was becoming a difficult place to live because of the "troubles," and I made the decision to emigrate to Canada. I applied for a position as a clinical psychologist in Halifax, Nova Scotia, and once there, soon realized that having a Ph.D. would increase my career options. Less than two years after coming to Canada, I was a doctoral student in clinical psychology at another Queen's University, this time in Kingston, Ontario.

The early 1970s in Canada was an exciting time to be a graduate student in psychology. The "Women's Movement" was raising issues about the social and economic conditions of women's lives and feminist concerns were receiving increased attention with the 1970 report of the Royal Commission on the Status of Women. As a student, I was involved in the Kingston Women's Centre and debates about the status of women were a regular feature of campus life. The study of gender issues in psychology was a new and burgeoning research area. The appearance in 1972 of Phyllis Chesler's book "Women and Madness" inspired feminist critiques of mainstream clinical psychology. Gender bias in clinical practice became an important topic for research; feminist approaches to therapy began to be developed; and psychology of women emerged as a legitimate field of study. It was in this climate that I carried out my thesis research on the social psychology of gender stereotypes. By this time, my career goals had shifted toward academia. With an academic job in mind, I spent 1976–77 as a postdoctoral clinical fellow at UBC, based at the Health Sciences Centre Hospital, where my work focused on treatment of depression. I was struck by the preponderance of women among the depressed patients I saw. This observation stayed with me and

when I moved back to the Maritimes, and my current position at UNB, I pursued my interests in women's mental health and began to explore issues surrounding women's vulnerability to depression.

Since 1979, I have been a psychology professor at UNB, where I'm involved with the graduate program in Clinical Psychology and the undergraduate Women's Studies program. I helped to establish the Women's Studies program and was the program's first coordinator. I also teach a course on women and mental health that is part of the Women's Studies program. During the 1980s, I was involved with the Canadian Mental Health Association (CMHA) and in 1985–86, while on sabbatical in Toronto, coordinated a group that prepared a report for CMHA entitled "Women and Mental Health in Canada: Strategies for Change" (1987). This report, which documented ways in which women's mental health is disadvantaged, attracted considerable media attention and stimulated a number of national conferences on women's mental health. At the same time, I was researching explanations for gender-related differences in depression and this led to an evaluation of cognitive-behavioural theories of depression. My paper on this work, "An Evaluation of the Adequacy of Cognitive/Behavioural Theories for Understanding Depression in Women," was published in 1989 in *Canadian Psychology*. Most recently, my research has been focused on the contributions of qualitative research for understanding women's depression. In 1999, I was guest editor (with Linda McMullen, University of Saskatchewan) for a special theme issue of *Canadian Psychology*, which contained papers describing qualitative studies of women's experiences with depression. As well, my book *Understanding Depression: Feminist Social Constructionist Approaches* was published recently (Routledge, 2000). Writing this book gave me an opportunity to bring together ideas about women's depression that I've been developing over the last few years.

Source: Janet Stoppard, Ph.D., University of New Brunswick. <www.unb.ca/psychology/faculty/stoppard.htm>

How does Dr. Stoppard study depression in women?

therapy. Gammell and Stoppard (1999) point out that women experience the loss of a sense of power and control over their lives when their depression "is attributed to disorders of bodily biochemistry while their social situations are ignored" (p. 125). Taking into account the social context of women's lives may also help them deal with inappropriate beliefs about the self and the experience of depression that may arise in cognitive therapy (Stoppard, 1999; Hurst, 1999; Hurst & Genest, 1995). See the *Pathways Through Psychology* box to read about Janet Stoppard and her work on women and depression.

Treatment for psychological disorders must take into account the individual's environmental, cultural, and socioeconomic background.
What are the potential dangers in not considering these factors when providing treatment?

Can you think of specific examples of problems caused by cultural differences in psychotherapeutic settings?

EXPLORING DIVERSITY

Clinical Practice and Training in a Multicultural Society

Canadians are typically proud of being part of a multicultural society. We like to believe that we welcome immigrants and encourage them to honour their cultural roots. The Canadian view of multiculturalism corresponds to an integration strategy in which people maintain their own culture and interact with people from other cultures (Berry, 1999). Clinical psychologists are required by the Canadian Psychological Association Code of Ethics to respect cultural differences.

In recent years ethnic diversity in Canada has greatly increased. Before 1961, most immigrants came from Europe and the British Isles; currently most come from Asia. More than half of the immigrants to this country belong to a visible minority group, the two largest of which are Chinese and South Asians (Statistics Canada, 1996b). Most immigrants settle in large cities, primarily Toronto, Vancouver, and Montreal. Canadian Aboriginals also contribute to our diversity. There are about half as many Aboriginals as immigrants, and most of them live in Ontario and British Columbia. The far northern parts of Canada are mainly populated by Aboriginals.

The home language of many immigrants and Aboriginals is neither English nor French. Cree is the Aboriginal language used most frequently. In cities with large immigrant populations, the most common home languages are English, Chinese, and Punjabi in Vancouver; English, Chinese, Italian, and Portuguese in Toronto; and French, English, Italian, and Spanish in Montreal. This diversity in home languages is mirrored by cultural diversity.

Our cultural diversity presents significant challenges to clinical psychology. To provide effective treatment, psychologists need to understand how clients view their situation and make decisions within their culture. In a recent study about adapting community mental health services to the needs of immigrant families in Quebec, the researchers found that culturally relevant knowledge is essential. It underlies appropriate attitudes, cultural sensitivity, and the ability to engage clients in a productive relationship (Legault et al., 1997).

Diversity must also be taken into account in clinical research and training. Meyen Hertzsprung and Keith Dobson of the University of Calgary investigated diversity training in clinical psychology using a survey sent to the Directors of Clinical Training in 20 Canadian universities (Hertzsprung & Dobson, 2000). They found that all of the programs included discussion of diversity issues in the training of testing, diagnosis, and intervention. Also, more than half of the programs discussed diversity issues in relation to research, and encouraged research in diversity. However, only six programs had specific learning objectives for diversity training. The lack of learning objectives for diversity training was interpreted as an indication that the concept of a culturally competent psychologist is not clearly understood.

PsychLinks
Minorities and psychotherapy
www.mcgrawhill.ca/college/feldman

According to Marilyn Bowman of Simon Fraser University, differences in diversity between Canada and the United States create problems for Canadian clinical psychology training (Bowman, 2000). For example, visible minorities in Canada are composed mainly of non-English speakers who were foreign born; in the United States they are mostly English-speaking blacks who were native born. In terms of including students from diverse backgrounds in clinical psychology programs in Canada, competence in the language of instruction is often an obstacle. Bowman also discusses complications in the process of accreditation for programs by the American Psychological Association arising from American models of diversity being inappropriately applied in Canada.

In summary, our cultural diversity in Canada raises issues on many levels for clinical training and practice in psychology.

Evaluate

1. Match each of the following treatment strategies with the statement you might expect to hear from a therapist using that strategy.

   1. Gestalt therapy

   2. Group therapy

   3. Unconditional positive regard

   4. Behavioural therapy

   5. Nondirective counselling

   a. "In other words, you don't get along with your mother because she hates your girlfriend, is that right?"

   b. "I want you all to take turns talking about why you decided to come, and what you hope to gain from therapy."

   c. "I can understand why you wanted to wreck your friend's car after she hurt your feelings. Now, tell me more about the accident."

   d. "That's not appropriate behaviour. Let's work on replacing it with something else."

   e. "Remember the anger you felt and scream until you feel better."

2. _____ therapies assume people should take responsibility for their lives and the decisions they make.

3. _____ therapy emphasizes the integration of thoughts, feelings, and behaviours.

4. One of the major criticisms of humanistic therapies is that:

   a. they are too imprecise and unstructured.

   b. they treat only the symptom of the problem.

   c. the therapist dominates the patient–therapist interaction.

   d. it works well only on clients of lower socioeconomic status.

5. In a controversial study, Eysenck found that some people go into _____ _____, or recovery without treatment, if they are simply left alone instead of treated.

6. Treatments that combine techniques from all the theoretical approaches are called _____ procedures.

Rethink

1. How can people be successfully treated in group therapy when individuals with the "same" problem are so different? What advantages might group therapy offer over individual therapy?

2. List some examples of behaviour that might be considered abnormal by members of one cultural or economic group and normal by members of a different cultural or economic group. Suppose that most therapies had been developed by psychologists from minority culture groups and lower socioeconomic status; how might they differ from current therapies?

Answers to Evaluate Questions

1. 1-e; 2-b; 3-c; 4-d; 5-a 2. Humanistic 3. Gestalt 4. a 5. spontaneous remission 6. eclectic

Biomedical Therapy: Biological Approaches to Treatment

If you get a kidney infection, you're given an antibiotic and, with luck, about a week later your kidney is as good as new. If your appendix becomes inflamed, a surgeon removes it and soon your body functions normally once more. Could a comparable approach, focusing on the body's physiology, be taken with psychological disturbances?

According to biological approaches to treatment, the answer is yes. Biomedical therapies are used routinely. The approach suggests that rather than focusing on a patient's psychological conflicts or past traumas, or on environmental factors that might produce abnormal behaviour, it can be more appropriate to focus treatment on brain chemistry and other neurological factors directly. This can be done through the use of drugs, electric shock, or surgery (in places where psychosurgery is legal).

Prepare

How are drug, electroconvulsive, and psychosurgical techniques used today in the treatment of psychological disorders?

Organize

Biomedical Therapy
  Drug Therapy
  Electroconvulsive Therapy (ECT)
  Psychosurgery
  Biomedical Therapies in Perspective
  Community Psychology

Drug Therapy

Drug therapy, the control of psychological disorders through drugs, works by altering the operation of neurotransmitters and neurons in the brain. Some drugs operate by inhibiting neurotransmitters or receptor neurons, thus reducing activity at particular synapses, the sites where nerve impulses travel from one neuron to another (as first discussed in Chapter 2). Other drugs do just the opposite: They increase the activity of certain neurotransmitters or neurons, allowing particular neurons to fire more frequently. The major drugs are described below and summarized in Table 13-2.

drug therapy: Control of psychological problems through drugs.

Table 13-2 Drug Treatments

Class of Drug	Effects of Drug	Primary Action of Drug	Examples
ANTIPSYCHOTIC DRUGS	Reduction in loss of touch with reality, agitation	Block dopamine receptors	Chlorpromazine (Thorazine) Clozapine (Clozaril)
ANTIDEPRESSANT DRUGS			
Tricyclic antidepressants	Reduction in depression	Permits rise in neurotransmitters such as norepinepherine	Trazodone (Desyrel), Amitriptyline (Elavil), Desipramine (Norpamin)
MAO inhibitors	Reduction in depression	Prevent MAO from breaking down neurotransmitters	Phenelzine (Nardil)
Selective serotonin reuptake inhibitors	Reduction in depression	Inhibit reuptake of serotonin	Fluoxetine (Prozac), Luvox, Paxil, Celexa, Zoloft, Nefazodone (Serzone)
MOOD STABILIZERS			
Lithium	Mood stabilizer	Can alter transmission of impulses within neurons	Lithium (Lithonate), Depakote, Tegretol
ANTIANXIETY DRUGS	Reduction in anxiety	Increase activity of neurotransmitter GABA	Benzodiazepines (Valium, Xanax)

Antipsychotic Drugs

Probably no greater change has occurred in mental hospitals than the successful introduction in the mid 1950s of **antipsychotic drugs**—drugs used to reduce severe symptoms of disturbance, such as loss of touch with reality and agitation. Previously, the typical mental hospital fulfilled all the stereotypes of the insane asylum, with screaming, moaning, clawing patients displaying the most bizarre behaviours. Suddenly, in just a matter of days, the hospital wards became considerably calmer environments in which professionals could do more than just try to get the patients through the day without causing serious harm to themselves or others.

This dramatic change was brought about by the introduction of a drug called *chlorpromazine*. This drug, and others of a similar nature, rapidly became the most popular and successful treatment for schizophrenia. Today drug therapy is the preferred treatment for most cases of severely abnormal behaviour and, as such, is used for most hospitalized patients with psychological disorders. For instance, the drug *clozapine* represents the current generation of antipsychotics (Wallis & Willwerth, 1992; Rosenheck et al., 1997).

How do antipsychotic drugs work? Most operate by blocking the dopamine receptors at the brain's synapses. Some newer drugs, like clozapine, increase dopamine levels in certain parts of the brain, such as those related to planning and goal-directed activity (Mrzljak et al., 1996; Moghaddam & Adams, 1998).

Despite the effectiveness of antipsychotic drugs, they do not produce a "cure" in the same way that, say, penicillin cures an infection. As soon as the drug is withdrawn, the original symptoms tend to reappear. Furthermore, such drugs can have long-term side effects, such as dryness of the mouth and throat, dizziness, and sometimes tremors and loss of muscle control that might continue even after drug treatments are stopped (Shriqui & Annable, 1995).

Antidepressant Drugs

As you might guess from the name, **antidepressant drugs** are a class of medications used in cases of severe depression to improve patients' mood. They were discovered quite by accident: It was found that patients suffering from tuberculosis who were given the drug iproniazid suddenly became happier and more optimistic. When the same drug was tested on people suffering from depression, a similar result occurred, and drugs became an accepted form of treatment for depression (Shuchter, Downs, & Zisook, 1996).

Most antidepressant drugs work by changing the concentration of particular neurotransmitters. For example, *tricyclic drugs* increase the availability of norepinepherine at the synapses of neurons, whereas *MAO inhibitors* prevent the enzyme monoamine oxidase (MAO) from breaking down neurotransmitters. Norman Endler (described in the chapter prologue) was prescribed tricyclic antidepressants, and later, MAO inhibitors. Newer antidepressants, *selective serotonin reuptake inhibitors (SSRIs),* target the neurotransmitter serotonin, permitting it to linger at the synapse. One of the latest antidepressants, Nefazodone (Serzone), blocks serotonin at some receptor sites but not others (see Figure 13-4; Berman, Krystal, & Charney, 1996; J. W. Williams et al., 2000).

Although antidepressant drugs can produce side effects such as drowsiness and faintness, their overall success rate is quite good. Unlike antipsychotic drugs, antidepressants can produce lasting, long-term recoveries from depression. In many cases, even after patients stop taking the drugs, their depression does not return (Spiegel, 1989; Julien, 1995; Zito, 1993).

Antidepressant drugs have become some of the most heavily prescribed of all drugs. Billions of dollars are spent each year on antidepressants. In particular, the antidepressant *Fluoxetine,* sold under the trade name *Prozac,* is widely used.

Despite its high cost—each daily dose costs more than $2—Prozac has significantly improved the lives of thousands of depressed individuals. Compared to other antidepressants, Prozac (along with its cousins Luvox, Paxil, Celexa, and Zoloft) has relatively few side effects. Furthermore, many people who do not respond to other types of antidepressants do

antipsychotic drugs: Drugs that temporarily reduce psychotic symptoms such as agitation, overactivity, hallucinations, and delusions.

PsychLink
Information on medications
www.mcgrawhill.ca/college/feldman

antidepressant drugs: Medication that improves a depressed patient's mood and feeling of well-being.

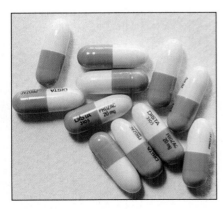

Prozac is a widely prescribed—but still controversial—antidepressant.

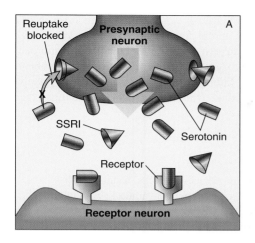 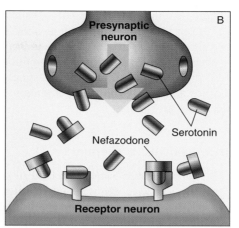

Figure 13-4 In (a), selective serotonin reuptake inhibitors (SSRIs) reduce depression by permitting the neurotransmitter serotonin to remain in the synapse. In (b), a newer antidepressant, Nefazodone (Serzone), operates more selectively, blocking serotonin at certain sites but not others, helping to reduce the side effects of the drug.

well on Prozac. On the other hand, like all drugs, Prozac does not agree with everyone. For example, 20 to 30 percent of users report experiencing nausea and diarrhea, and a smaller percentage report sexual dysfunctions (Kramer, 1993; Glenmullen, 2000).

In Europe, *St. John's wort,* an herb that has been likened to a "natural" antidepressant, is widely used. The substance is considered a natural health product in Canada and therefore is available without a prescription. Despite its popularity, the jury is still out on the effectiveness of St. John's wort. Although the American College of Physicians has supported the use of the herb in treating mild, short-term depression, the most recent and carefully designed study found the drug useless in treating depression, making its use problematic (Nierenberg, 1998b; Maidment, 2000; J. W. Williams et al., 2000; Shelton et al., 2001). In April 2000, Health Canada issued a warning about potentially harmful interactions between St. John's wort and some prescription drugs (for example, oral contraceptives, some heart drugs, and antidepressants).

lithium: A mineral salt used to treat bipolar disorders.

antianxiety drugs: Drugs that can reduce a person's level of anxiety, essentially by reducing excitability and increasing feelings of well-being.

Lithium

Lithium, a mineral salt, is a drug that has been used very successfully to treat bipolar disorder. Although no one knows definitely why, it and other drugs such as *Depakote* and *Tegretol* are effective in reducing manic episodes. However, they are not effective in treating depressive phases of bipolar disorder, and antidepressants are usually prescribed during these phases (Dubovsky, 1999).

Lithium and drugs similar to it have a quality that sets them apart from other drug treatments: They can be a *preventive* treatment, blocking future episodes of bipolar disorder. Many people who have had episodes of bipolar disorder in the past can prevent a recurrence of their symptoms by taking a daily dose of lithium. In contrast, most other drugs are useful only after symptoms of psychological disturbance occur.

Antianxiety Drugs

As the name implies, **antianxiety drugs** reduce the level of anxiety a person experiences, essentially by reducing excitability and increasing feelings of well-being. They are used not only to reduce general tension in people who are experiencing temporary difficulties but also to aid in the treatment of more serious anxiety disorders (Zito, 1993). Antianxiety drugs such as Xanax and Valium are among the medications most frequently prescribed by physicians.

Although the popularity of antianxiety drugs suggests that they hold few risks, they can produce a number of potentially serious side effects.

St. John's wort is available without a prescription.

This man is drinking tea containing kava (an herb marketed to treat anxiety). Health Canada has recently advised Canadians not to use kava because of concerns about liver toxicity.

electroconvulsive therapy (ECT): A procedure in which an electric current of 70 to 150 volts is briefly administered to a patient's head.

PsychLink

Information on ECT
www.mcgrawhill.ca/college/feldman

psychosurgery: Brain surgery once used to reduce symptoms of mental disorder.

For instance, they can cause fatigue, and long-term use can lead to dependence. Moreover, taken in combination with alcohol, some antianxiety drugs can become lethal. But a more important issue concerns their use to suppress anxiety. Almost every therapeutic approach to psychological disturbance views continuing anxiety as a signal of some sort of problem. Thus, drugs that mask anxiety can simply be hiding difficulties. Consequently, people who use antianxiety drugs might simply be hiding from, rather than confronting, their underlying problems.

Electroconvulsive Therapy (ECT)

> Martha Manning had contemplated all kinds of suicide—by pills, hanging, even guns. Her depression was so deep that she lived each minute "afraid I [wouldn't] make it to the next hour." But she balked when her therapist recommended electroconvulsive therapy, commonly known as "shock treatment." Despite her training and practice as a clinical psychologist, Manning immediately flashed to scenes from *One Flew Over the Cuckoo's Nest,* "with McMurphy and the Chief jolted with electroshock, their bodies flailing with each jolt." (Guttman, 1995, p. 16)

When Norman Endler was a graduate student, he observed a patient being given ECT by a much less humane and more dangerous procedure than the one used today. Fortunately for both Endler and Manning, receiving ECT was very different from what they had expected.

First introduced in the 1930s, **electroconvulsive therapy (ECT)** is a procedure in which an electric current of 70 to 150 volts is briefly administered to a patient's head, causing a loss of consciousness and often seizures. Today the patient is sedated by means of a general anaesthetic and is given muscle relaxants prior to administration of the current in order to reduce seizures and the intensity of muscle contractions produced during ECT. The typical patient receives about 10 such treatments in the course of a month, but some patients continue with maintenance treatments for months afterward (Nierenberg, 1998a; Fink, 1999).

ECT is a controversial technique. Apart from the obvious distastefulness of a treatment that evokes images of electrocution, ECT has frequent side effects. For instance, following treatment patients often experience disorientation, confusion, and sometimes memory loss that can last for months. Furthermore, many patients fear ECT, even though they are anesthetized during the treatment and thus experience no pain. Finally, we still do not know why ECT works, and critics suggest that the treatment can produce permanent brain damage (Fisher, 1985; Valente, 1991). However, the Canadian Psychiatric Association has concluded that ECT is safe and effective if it is used properly (Enns & Reiss, 1992).

Given the drawbacks to ECT, why is it used at all? The basic reason is that for many severe cases of depression it is the only quickly effective treatment. For instance, it can prevent depressed, suicidal individuals from committing suicide, and it can act more quickly than antidepressive medications. Still, ECT tends to be used only when other treatments have proved ineffective (American Psychiatric Association, 1990; Sackheim et al., 1996; Fink, 2000).

Psychosurgery

If ECT strikes you as a questionable procedure, the use of **psychosurgery**—brain surgery in which the object is to reduce symptoms of mental disorder—is likely to appear even more so. A technique that has not been used in Canada for many years, psychosurgery was first introduced as a "treatment of last resort" in the 1930s.

The first form of psychosurgery, *prefrontal lobotomy,* consisted of surgically destroying or removing parts of a patient's frontal lobes that were thought to control emotionality. In the 1930s and 1940s, the procedure was performed on thousands of patients, often with little precision (Miller, 1994).

Such psychosurgery often did improve a patient's behaviour—but not without drastic side effects. For along with remission of symptoms of mental disorder, some patients suffered personality changes, becoming bland, colourless, and unemotional. Other patients became aggressive and unable to control their impulses. In the worst cases, treatment killed the patient.

With the introduction of effective drug treatments—and the obvious ethical questions regarding the appropriateness of forever altering someone's personality—psychosurgery became obsolete. Although psychosurgery is no longer performed in this country, it continues to be done in rare instances elsewhere, and remains highly controversial (Baer et al., 1995; Jenike, 1998).

Biomedical Therapies in Perspective: Can Abnormal Behaviour Be Cured?

In some respects, there has been no greater revolution in the field of mental health than that represented by the biological approaches to treatment. As previously violent, uncontrollable patients have been calmed by the use of drugs, mental hospitals have been able to concentrate more on actually helping patients and less on custodial functions. Similarly, patients whose lives have been disrupted by depression or bipolar episodes have been able to function normally, and other forms of drug therapy have also shown remarkable results.

On the other hand, biomedical therapies are not without their detractors. For one thing, critics charge that they merely provide relief from the *symptoms* of mental disorder; as soon as the drugs are withdrawn, the symptoms return. Biomedical treatment might not solve the underlying problems that led a patient to therapy in the first place. Moreover, biomedical therapies can produce side effects, ranging from physical reactions to the development of *new* symptoms of abnormal behaviour. For these reasons, then, biologically based treatment approaches are not a cure-all for psychological disorders.

Community Psychology: A Focus on Prevention

Each of the treatments that we have reviewed in this chapter has a common element: It is a "restorative" treatment, aimed at alleviating psychological difficulties that already exist. However, an approach known as **community psychology** is geared toward a different aim: to prevent or minimize the incidence of psychological disorders.

Community psychology came of age in the 1960s, when plans were developed for a nationwide network of community mental health centres in the United States. These centres were meant to provide low-cost mental health services, including short-term therapy and community educational programs. With the development of effective drug therapy, the population of mental hospitals and psychiatric wards has decreased substantially in the United States and Canada during the past 30 years. In Canada, 78 percent of the in-patient beds were closed (Freeman, 1994). This change has been accompanied by a shift from institutional-based care to private practice on the part of clinical psychologists (Goodman, 2000). The influx of former mental patients into the community, known as **deinstitutionalization**, further spurred the community psychology movement.

In Canada, the recent need to control rising costs in health care has led to government restructuring of health care systems. This restructuring has been a factor in deinstitutionalization. To address the needs of those with mental health problems, the Canadian Mental Health Association has developed a national framework for mental health policy (Trainor et al., 1999; Pomeroy et al., 2002). This framework is based on the use of mental health services and a community resource base. The goal is sufficient development of community supports to ensure that the person has access to housing, work, income, and education.

A positive outcome of community psychology is telephone "hotlines" and crisis centres. In many North American cities, people experiencing acute stress can dial a telephone number at any time of the day or night and talk to a trained, sympathetic listener

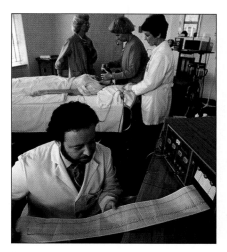
Dr. Richard B. Weiner of Duke University Medical Center reads a patient's electroencephalogram as technicians administer electroconvulsive therapy. ECT is a controversial treatment, but it does help some people whose severe depression has not responded to other approaches.

community psychology: A branch of psychology that focuses on the prevention and minimization of psychological disorders in the community.
deinstitutionalization: The transfer of former mental patients from institutions into the community.

While deinstitutionalization has had many successes, it has also contributed to the release of mental patients into the community with little or no support. As a result many have become homeless.

(Boehm et al., 1995; Twine & Barraclough, 1998; Blewett, 2000). Even in remote areas of the Canadian North, people can contact a crisis line: the Baffin Crisis Line, a service provided in three languages by northerners who understand the culture, setting, and problems of the North (Levy & Fletcher, 1998). Many cities have crisis centres and drop-in centres. Colleges and universities frequently offer crisis counselling to their students.

Unfortunately, the original goals of community psychology (the treatment and protection of deinstitutionalized patients) have not been met. Many people do not get the care they need (Kiesler & Simpkins, 1991, 1993; Torrey, 1996, 1997; Hwang, 2000).

BECOMING AN INFORMED CONSUMER OF PSYCHOLOGY

What are some basic guidelines for choosing a therapist who's right for you?

Choosing the Right Therapist

If you make the decision to seek therapy, you're faced with a daunting task. If you start therapy, the following general guidelines can help you determine whether you've chosen the right therapist:

- *You and your therapist should agree on the goals for treatment.* They should be clear, specific, and attainable.
- *You should feel comfortable with your therapist.* You should not be intimidated by, or in awe of, a therapist. Instead, you should trust the therapist and feel free to discuss even the most personal issues without fearing a negative reaction. In sum, the "personal chemistry" should feel right.
- *The therapist should have appropriate training and credentials and should be registered.* The Canadian Psychological Association recently affirmed the doctorate as the minimum requirement for registration (Goodman, 2000). Currently, in some Canadian jurisdictions there is some master's-level registration, usually with the designation "Psychological Associate." Check the therapist's membership in professional associations, and at the initial consultation, query her or him about the cost and billing practices.
- *You should feel that you are making progress after therapy has begun, despite occasional setbacks.* If you have no sense of improvement after repeated visits, this issue should be frankly discussed. Although there is no set timetable, the most obvious changes resulting from therapy tend to occur relatively early in the course of treatment. For instance, half of patients in psychotherapy improve by the eighth session and three-fourths by the twenty-sixth session (see Figure 13-5). The average number of sessions with college students is just five (Crits-Cristoph, 1992; "Brief Psychodynamic Therapy," 1994; Lazarus, 1997).

"Looking good!"

You should be aware that you will have to put in a great deal of effort in therapy. Although ours is a culture that promises quick cures for any problem, the reality is that solving difficult problems is not easy. People must be committed to making therapy work and should know that it is they, and not the therapist, who must do most of the work to resolve their problems. The potential is there for the effort to pay off handsomely—therapy can lead to a more positive, fulfilling, and meaningful life.

PsychLink

Choosing a therapist
www.mcgrawhill.ca/college/feldman

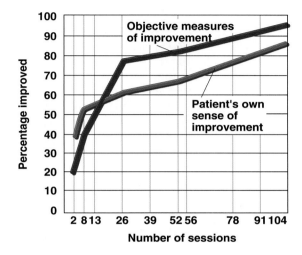

Figure 13–5 For most patients, improvements in psychological functioning occur relatively early after therapy has begun.
Source: Howard et al., 1986.

Evaluate

1. Antipsychotic drugs have provided effective, long-term, and complete cures for schizophrenia. True or false?
2. One of the most effective biomedical treatments for psychological disorders, used mainly to arrest and prevent manic-depressive episodes, is
   a. chlorpromazine.
   b. lithium.
   c. Librium.
   d. Valium.
3. Psychosurgery has grown in popularity as a method of treatment as surgical techniques have become more precise. True or false?
4. The trend toward releasing more patients from mental hospitals into the community is known as _____.

Answers to Evaluate Questions

1. False: schizophrenia can be controlled, but not cured, by medication. 2. b 3. False 4. deinstitutionalization

Rethink

1. One of the main criticisms of biological therapies is that they treat the symptoms of mental disorders without uncovering and treating the underlying problems from which people are suffering. Do you agree with this criticism or not? Why?
2. If a dangerously violent person could be "cured" of violence through a new psychosurgical technique, would you approve the use of this technique? What if the person agreed to—or requested—the technique? What sort of policy would you develop for the use of psychosurgery?

Looking Back

What are the goals of psychologically and biologically based treatment approaches?

- Psychotherapy (psychologically based therapy) and biomedical therapy (biologically based therapy) share the goal of resolving psychological problems by modifying people's thoughts, feelings, expectations, evaluations, and ultimately their behaviour. (p. 430)

What are the basic kinds of psychotherapies?

- Psychoanalytic treatment, based on Freud's psychodynamic theory, seeks to bring unresolved past conflicts and unacceptable impulses from the unconscious into the conscious, where the problems can be dealt with more effectively. This involves using techniques such as free association and dream interpretation. (p. 431)
- Behavioural approaches to treatment view abnormal behaviour itself as the problem, rather than viewing the behaviour as a symptom of some underlying cause. To bring about a "cure," according to this view, the outward behaviour must be changed. To do this, behavioural approaches use aversive conditioning, systematic desensitization, observational learning, token systems, and contingency contracting. (p. 433)
- Cognitive approaches to treatment see the goal of therapy as a restructuring of a person's belief system into a more realistic, rational, and logical view of the world. (p. 436)

What are humanistic approaches to treatment?

- Humanistic therapy is based on the premise that people have control over their behaviour, that they can make choices about their lives, and that it is up to them to solve their own problems. Humanistic therapies, which take a nondirective approach, include client-centred therapy and gestalt therapy. (p. 439)

How does group therapy differ from individual types of therapy?

- In group therapy, several people meet with a therapist to discuss some aspect of their psychological functioning, often centring on a common problem. (p. 441)

How effective is therapy, and which kind of therapy works best in a given situation?

- Most research suggests that, in general, therapy is more effective than no therapy, although how much more effective is not known. (p. 442)
- The answer to the more difficult question of which therapy works best is even less clear. However, particular kinds of therapy are more appropriate for some problems than for others. (p. 442)

How are drug and electroconvulsive techniques used today in the treatment of psychological disorders?

- Biological treatment approaches focus on the physiological causes of abnormal behaviour, rather than considering psychological factors. Drug therapy, the best example of biomedical treatments, has dramatically reduced the symptoms of mental disturbance. (p. 447)
- Antipsychotic drugs such as chlorpromazine are very effective in reducing psychotic symptoms. Antidepressant drugs, such as Prozac, reduce depression so successfully that they are very widely used. The antianxiety drugs, or minor tranquilizers, are among the most frequently prescribed medications. (p. 448)

- In electroconvulsive therapy (ECT), used only in severe cases of depression, an electric current of 70 to 150 volts is briefly administered to a patient. (p. 450)
- Community psychology was the stimulus for deinstitutionalization, in which previously hospitalized mental patients were released into the community. (p. 451)

Key Terms and Concepts

psychotherapy (p. 430)
biomedical therapy (p. 430)
psychodynamic therapy (p. 430)
psychoanalysis (p. 431)
behavioural treatment approaches (p. 433)
systematic desensitization (p. 434)
cognitive treatment approaches (p. 436)
cognitive-behavioural approach (p. 436)
rational-emotive behaviour therapy (p. 436)
humanistic therapy (p. 439)
client-centred therapy (p. 440)
gestalt therapy (p. 440)

group therapy (p. 441)
family therapy (p. 441)
spontaneous remission (p. 442)
eclectic approach to therapy (p. 443)
drug therapy (p. 447)
antipsychotic drugs (p. 448)
antidepressant drugs (p. 448)
lithium (p. 449)
antianxiety drugs (p. 449)
electroconvulsive therapy (ECT) (p. 450)
psychosurgery (p. 450)
community psychology (p. 451)
deinstitutionalization (p. 451)

Psychology on the Web

1. Find out about computer-assisted psychotherapy on the Web. Locate (1) a computerized therapy program, such as ELIZA, that offers "therapy" over the Internet, and (2) a report on "cybertherapy," by which therapists use the Web to interact with patients. Compare the two, describing how each one works.
2. Find more information on the Web about deinstitutionalization. Try to find pro and con arguments for it and summarize the arguments, including your judgment of the effectiveness and advisability of deinstitutionalization.

Epilogue

In this chapter we have examined how psychological professionals treat people with psychological disorders. We considered a range of approaches, including both psychologically based and biologically based therapies. It is clear that substantial progress has been made in recent years, both in terms of treating the symptoms of mental disorders and in understanding their underlying causes.

Before we leave the topic of psychological disorders, turn back to the prologue of this chapter, which describes Norman Endler's experience with depression, and consider the following questions.

1. Many people with bipolar disorder must take drugs such as lithium for the rest of their lives in order to avoid the symptoms of depression. Do you think these people are truly cured or not?
2. How and why has the social climate changed so that people who suffer from depression no longer feel compelled to hide the fact that they are taking drugs for the disorder?
3. In what respects do you think Norman Endler's experience with depression would be both easier and more difficult because of his psychological knowledge and experience?

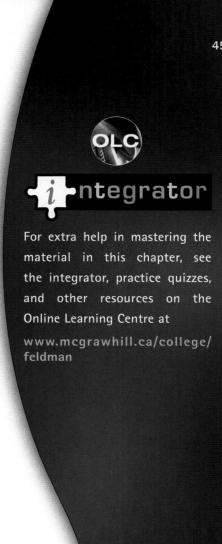

OLC

*i*ntegrator

For extra help in mastering the material in this chapter, see the integrator, practice quizzes, and other resources on the Online Learning Centre at

www.mcgrawhill.ca/college/feldman

Chapter Fourteen

Social Psychology

Prologue

...And They Brought Roses

In Ottawa, some 60 000 mourners stood patiently in line for many hours to pay their final respects to Pierre Elliott Trudeau, many bringing with them Trudeau's trademark red rose. Thousands more would gather on station platforms as the train bearing his body went by; others stood outside Notre-Dame Basilica in Montreal for the funeral service.

A family and a country united in grief at the death of Pierre Elliott Trudeau (1919–2000), former Prime Minister of Canada.

It was an outpouring of grief unprecedented in Canada for a political figure, paralleled only, some thought, by the public's grief at the death of Princess Diana in 1997. The diversity of the mourners in terms of age, ethnicity, language, and culture mirrored the population of the most culturally diverse country in the world. This was a most fitting tribute for the man who became Canada's Prime Minister in 1968 and held that position for most of the next 16 years. Trudeau was a charismatic and intellectual man with a vision of a just society, under whose leadership Canada's constitution was repatriated from Britain, bilingualism and multiculturalism were protected, and programs for youth were given prominence.

Looking Ahead

The extraordinary response to Trudeau's death raises many interesting questions. Why the outpouring of grief from people too young to remember the man? What made him such a powerful communicator? What drew international politicians like Jimmy Carter (an American President) and Cuba's Fidel Castro to count him as a friend? Will Trudeau's red rose become a symbol for renewed commitment to multiculturalism and a just society?

Each of these questions can be answered only by taking into account findings from the field of social psychology, the branch of psychology that focuses on those aspects of human behaviour that unite—and separate—us from one another. **Social psychology** is the study of how people's thoughts, feelings, and actions are affected by others. Social psychologists consider the nature and causes of individual behaviour in social situations.

The broad scope of social psychology is conveyed by the kinds of questions social psychologists ask, such as these: How can we convince people to change their attitudes or to adopt new ideas and values? How do we come to understand what others are like? How are we influenced by what others do and think? Why do some people display such violence, aggression, and cruelty toward others that people throughout the world live in fear of annihilation at their hands? And why, on the other hand, do some people place their own lives at risk to help others?

In this chapter, we explore social psychological approaches to these and other issues. Not only do we examine the processes that underlie social behaviour, we also discuss strategies for confronting and solving a variety of problems and issues that all of us face—ranging from achieving a better understanding of persuasive tactics to forming more accurate impressions of others.

We begin with a look at how our attitudes shape our behaviour, and how we form judgments about others. We'll discuss how we are influenced by others, and we will consider prejudice and discrimination, focusing on their roots and how they can be reduced. After examining what social psychologists have learned about the ways people form friendships and relationships, the chapter concludes with a look at the determinants of aggression and helping.

social psychology: The study of how people's thoughts, feelings, and actions are affected by others.

attitudes: Learned predispositions to respond in a favourable or unfavourable manner to a particular person, behaviour, belief, or thing.

Prepare

What are attitudes and how are they formed, maintained, and changed?

How do we form impressions of what others are like and of the causes of their behaviour?

What biases influence how we view others' behaviour?

Organize

Attitudes and Social Cognition
    Persuasion
    Social Cognition

PsychLink
Attitudes
www.mcgrawhill.ca/college/feldman

Attitudes and Social Cognition

What do Wayne Gretzky, Tiger Woods, and Rosie O'Donnell have in common?

Each appears in television commercials designed to mould or change our attitudes. Such commercials are part of the barrage of messages we receive each day—from sources as varied as politicians, sales staff in stores, and celebrities—all meant to influence us.

Persuasion: Changing Attitudes

Persuasion is the process of changing attitudes, one of the central concepts of social psychology. **Attitudes** are learned predispositions to respond in a favourable or unfavourable manner to a particular person, behaviour, belief, or thing (Eagly & Chaiken, 1993, 1995; Petty et al., 1997).

The ease with which attitudes can be changed depends on a number of factors, including these:

- *Message source.* The characteristics of a person who delivers a persuasive message, known as the *attitude communicator,* have a major impact on the effectiveness of that message. Communicators who are physically and socially attractive produce greater attitude change than those who are less attractive. Moreover, the expertise and trustworthiness of a communicator are related to the impact of a message—except when the communicator is believed to have an ulterior motive (Hovland, Janis, & Kelly, 1953; Priester & Petty, 1995).

- *Characteristics of the message.* It is not just *who* delivers a message but *what* the message is like that affects attitude and behaviour change. One-sided arguments—in which only the communicator's side is presented—are probably best if the communicator's message is initially viewed favourably by the target (recipient) of the message. But if the target receives a message presenting an unpopular viewpoint, two-sided messages—which include both the communicator's position and the one he or she is arguing against—are more effective, probably because they are seen as more precise and thoughtful. In addition, fear-producing messages ("If you don't practise safer sex, you'll get AIDS") are generally effective, although not always. For instance, if the fear aroused is too strong, such messages can arouse people's defence mechanisms and be ignored (Karlins & Abelson, 1979; Perloff, 1993; L. H. Rosenthal, 1997).
- *Characteristics of the target.* Once a message has been communicated, characteristics of the *target* of the message can determine whether the message will be accepted. For example, intelligent people are more resistant to persuasion than those who are less intelligent. There also seem to be gender differences in persuasibility. However, the magnitude of the difference between men and women is not large (Eagly, 1989; Rhodes & Wood, 1992; Wood & Stagner, 1994).

Companies use sports stars like Tiger Woods to persuade consumers to buy their products.
Can celebrities really affect the purchasing habits of consumers? How?

Whether recipients will be receptive to persuasive messages depends on the type of information processing they use. Social psychologists have discovered two primary information-processing routes to persuasion: central-route and peripheral-route processing. **Central-route processing** occurs when the recipient thoughtfully considers the issues and arguments involved in persuasion. **Peripheral-route processing**, in contrast, occurs when people are persuaded on the basis of factors unrelated to the nature or quality of the content of a persuasive message. Instead, they are influenced by factors that are irrelevant or extraneous to the attitude topic or issue, such as who is providing the message or how long the arguments are (Petty & Cacioppo, 1986; Petty et al., 1994).

In general, central-route processing occurs when targets are highly involved and motivated to comprehend the message. However, if central-route processing is not employed because the target is uninvolved, unmotivated, bored, or distracted, then the nature of the message becomes less important, and peripheral factors more critical (see Figure 14-1). Although both central-route and peripheral-route processing lead to attitude change, central-route processing generally leads to stronger, more lasting attitude change.

central–route processing: Message interpretation characterized by thoughtful consideration of the issues and arguments used to persuade.

peripheral–route processing: Message interpretation characterized by consideration of the source and related general information rather than of the message itself.

 PsychLink

Dual process persuasion
www.mcgrawhill.ca/college/feldman

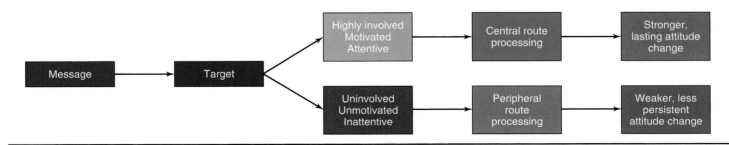

Figure 14-1 Routes to persuasion. Targets who are highly involved, motivated, and attentive use central-route processing when considering a persuasive message, and central-route processing leads to more lasting attitude change. In contrast, uninvolved, unmotivated, and inattentive targets are more likely to use peripheral-route processing, and attitude change is likely to be less enduring. Can you think of particular advertisements that try to produce central-route processing?

The Link Between Attitudes and Behaviour

Not surprisingly, attitudes influence behaviour. The strength of the link between particular attitudes and behaviour varies, of course, but generally people strive for consistency between their attitudes and their behaviour. Furthermore, people are fairly consistent in their attitudes. You would probably not hold the attitude that eating meat is immoral and still have a positive attitude toward hamburgers (Kraus, 1995).

Interestingly, not only do our attitudes influence our behaviour, but sometimes our behaviour shapes our attitudes. Consider, for instance, the following situation:

> You've just spent what you feel is the most boring hour of your life, turning pegs for a psychology experiment. Just as you're finally finished and about to leave, the experimenter asks you to do him a favour. He tells you that he needs a helper for future experimental sessions to introduce subsequent participants to the peg-turning task. Your specific job would be to tell them that turning the pegs is an interesting, fascinating experience. Each time you tell this tale to another participant, you'll be paid $1.

If you agree to help out the experimenter, you could be setting yourself up for a state of psychological tension that is known as cognitive dissonance. According to a major social psychologist, Leon Festinger (1957), **cognitive dissonance** occurs when a person holds two attitudes or thoughts (referred to as *cognitions*) that contradict each other.

A participant in the situation just described is left with two contradictory thoughts: (1) I believe the task is boring; and (2) I said it was interesting with little justification ($1). This should arouse dissonance. How can such dissonance be reduced? One cannot deny having said that the task was interesting without breaking with reality. Relatively speaking, it is easier to change one's attitude toward the task—and thus the theory predicts that participants will reduce dissonance by adopting more positive attitudes toward the task (Johnson, Kelly, & LeBlanc, 1995).

This prediction was confirmed in a classic experiment (Festinger & Carlsmith, 1959). The experiment followed essentially the same procedure outlined earlier. A participant was offered $1 to describe a boring task as interesting. In addition, as a control, other participants were offered $20 to say that the task was interesting. The reasoning behind this condition was that $20 was so much money that participants in this condition had a good reason to be conveying incorrect information; dissonance would *not* be aroused, and *less* attitude change would be expected. The results supported this notion. Participants who were paid $1 changed their attitudes more (becoming more positive toward the peg-turning task) than participants who were paid $20.

We now know that dissonance explains a number of everyday occurrences involving attitudes and behaviour. For example, a smoker who knows that smoking leads to lung cancer holds contradictory cognitions: (1) I smoke; and (2) Smoking leads to lung cancer. The theory predicts that these two thoughts will lead to a state of cognitive dissonance. More important, it predicts that the individual will be motivated to reduce such dissonance by one of the following methods: (1) modifying one or both of the cognitions; (2) changing the perceived importance of one cognition; (3) adding cognitions; or (4) denying that the two cognitions are related to each other. Hence the smoker might decide that he really doesn't smoke all that much (modifying the cognition), that the evidence linking smoking to cancer is weak (changing the importance of a cognition), that the amount of exercise he gets compensates for the smoking (adding cognitions), or that there is no evidence linking smoking and cancer (denial). Whatever technique is used, the result is a reduction in dissonance (see Figure 14-2).

Social Cognition: Understanding Others

We all know people, whether they be public figures or personal friends, with whom we disagree, and who do things of which we may disapprove. However, rather than allow ourselves to feel negatively towards these people, for whom we may feel genuine liking, we may ignore the offending behaviour. Cases like this illustrate the power of our impressions and attest to the importance of determining how people develop an

---

cognitive dissonance: The conflict that occurs when a person holds two attitudes or thoughts (referred to as *cognitions*) that contradict each other.

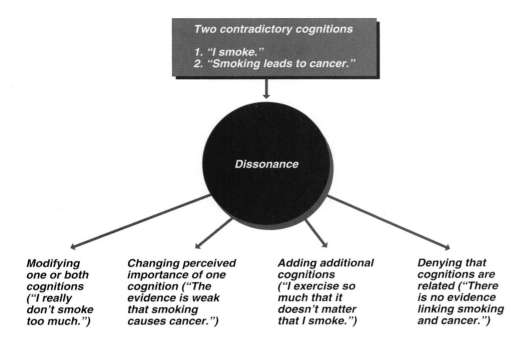

Figure 14-2 The simultaneous presence of two contradictory cognitions ("I smoke" and "Smoking leads to cancer") produces cognitive dissonance, which can be reduced through several methods. *What are additional ways that dissonance can be reduced?*

understanding of others. One of the dominant areas of study in social psychology during the last few years has been learning how we come to understand what others are like and how we explain the reasons underlying others' behaviour (Fiske & Taylor, 1991; Kunda, 1999).

Understanding What Others Are Like

Consider for a moment the enormous amount of information about other people to which we are exposed. How are we able to decide what is important and what is not, and to make judgments about the characteristics of others? Social psychologists interested in this question study **social cognition**—the processes that underlie our understanding of the social world. They have learned that individuals have highly developed **schemas**, sets of cognitions about people and social experiences (see Chapter 6). These schemas organize information stored in memory, represent in our minds the way the social world operates, and give us a framework to categorize, store, remember, and interpret information relating to social stimuli (Fiske & Taylor, 1991; Fiske, 1992a, 1992b).

We typically hold schemas for particular types of people. Our schema for "teacher," for instance, generally consists of a number of characteristics: knowledge of the subject matter he or she is teaching, a desire to impart that knowledge, and an awareness of the student's need to understand what is being said. Our schema for "mother" might include the characteristics of warmth, nurturance, and caring. Regardless of their accuracy, schemas are important because they organize the way in which we recall, recognize, and categorize information about others. Moreover, they allow us to predict what others are like on the basis of relatively little information, because we tend to fit people into schemas even if we don't have much concrete evidence to go on (Bargh et al., 1995).

social cognition: The processes that underlie our understanding of the social world.

schemas: Sets of cognitions about people and social experiences.

Impression Formation

How do we decide that Gail is a flirt, Andy is obnoxious, or Hector is a really nice guy? The earliest work on social cognition was designed to examine *impression formation,* the process by which an individual organizes information about another person to form an overall impression of that person. In one classic study, for instance, students were told that they were about to hear a guest lecturer (Kelley, 1950). One group of students was told that the lecturer was "a rather warm person, industrious, critical, practical, and determined"; a second group was told that he was "a rather cold person, industrious, critical, practical, and determined."

Impression formation
www.mcgrawhill.ca/college/feldman

Psychology at Work

Ann Altman

Advertising Executive

Education: B.A., psychology/philosophy, University of Florida at Gainesville; M.A., clinical psychology, University of Florida at Gainesville; further work toward an M.B.A., Florida State University

Home: Palm Harbor, Florida

Ann Altman

It is not surprising that over the years the field of advertising has looked to psychology as an important source of ideas for fine-tuning its promotion of products and services and for communicating with potential customers. Nor is it surprising to find people with psychology backgrounds becoming interested in and pursuing careers in advertising. Such is the case with Ann Altman.

Initially Altman pursued a doctorate, spending time in Holland researching the development of language in children with epilepsy. Eventually her interest in communication led her to the international business world of advertising, where her academic background and strengths in research have proved highly useful in the 15 years she has spent as an advertising executive.

"I apply psychology to everything I do," says Altman, who is the founder and president of the Altman Meder Lawrence Hill Advertising firm. "Advertising is a field of communication that mediates an essential interaction between a company and the audience it is trying to reach. Interestingly enough, my psychology background has given me the ability to step back and analyze what the client is truly saying, and to understand what the client needs."

Altman cites as an example a West German pharmaceutical company that approached her

> "Interestingly enough, my psychology background has given me the ability to step back and analyze what the client is truly saying, and to understand what the client needs."

---

central traits: The major traits considered in forming impressions of others.

The simple substitution of "cold" for "warm" was responsible for drastic differences in the way the students in each group perceived the lecturer, even though he gave the same talk in the same style in each condition. Students who had been told he was "warm" rated him considerably more positively than students who had been told he was "cold."

The findings from this experiment led to additional research on impression formation that focused on how people pay particular attention to certain unusually important traits—known as **central traits**—to help them form overall impressions of others. According to this work, the presence of a central trait alters the meaning of other traits. Hence the description of the lecturer as "industrious" presumably meant something different according to which central trait it was associated with—"warm" or "cold" (Asch, 1946; Widmeyer & Loy, 1988).

Other work on impression formation has used information-processing approaches (see Chapter 7) to develop mathematically oriented models of how individual personality traits are combined to create an overall impression. Generally, the results of this research suggest that in forming an overall judgment of a person, we use a psychological "average" of the individual traits we see, in a manner that is analogous to finding the mathematical average of several numbers (Kaplan, 1975; Anderson, 1996).

Of course, as we gain more experience with people and observe them in a variety of situations, our impressions of them become more complex. They may also become more accurate (Paulhus & Bruce, 1992). However, because there usually are gaps in our knowledge of others, we still tend to fit them into personality schemas that represent particular "types" of people. For instance, we might have a schema of "gregarious person" that includes the traits of friendliness, aggressiveness, and openness. The presence of just one or two of the associated traits might be sufficient to make us assign a person to a particular schema (Anderson & Klatzky, 1987; Sherman & Klein, 1994).

However, our schemas are susceptible to error. For example, our mood affects how we perceive others. People who are happy form more favourable impressions and make more positive judgments than people who are in a bad mood (Kenny, 1994; Bernieri et al., 1994).

Even when schemas are not entirely accurate, they serve an important function: They allow us to develop expectations about how others will behave. These expectations permit us to plan our interactions with others more easily, and they simplify a complex social world. (To see how work on social cognition is used in applied settings, see the *Psychology at Work* box.)

firm needing help in promoting a natural tooth-paste in the United States. The company had tried and failed several times to bring the product to the U.S. market, according to Altman.

"We began by establishing focus groups around the product, involving dental professionals, general users, and other groups we thought would be our target audience. We began to see certain patterns," she notes. "We found that the audience of greatest interest was female, aged 35 to 40, and of a certain educational level. Based on that finding, we set up targeted television, newspaper, and direct mail promotions.

"In the first research we did, 9 out of 10 people who tried the product said they would never touch it again because it wasn't foamy or sweet, but we were able to turn that around by finding out more about our participants' expectations

and reactions," says Altman. "We have to be accountable to our clients in establishing effective communications between them and their potential customers. Research—practical and targeted, but psychological research nonetheless— plays a big role. It is important that we know what our typical buyers are thinking and expecting. Then we have to prepare them for what we are delivering."

> "Research—practical and targeted, but psychological research nonetheless— plays a big role. It is important that we know what our typical buyers are thinking and expecting."

Attribution Processes: Understanding the Causes of Behaviour

Consider the following case:

> When Barbara Washington, a new employee at the Ablex Computer Company, completed a major staffing project two weeks early, her boss, Yolanda, was delighted. At the next staff meeting, she announced how pleased she was with Barbara and explained that *this* was an example of the kind of performance she was looking for in her staff. The other staff members looked on resentfully, trying to figure out why Barbara had worked night and day to finish the project not just on time, but two weeks early. She must be an awfully compulsive person, they decided.

Most of us, at one time or another, have puzzled over another person's behaviour. Perhaps it was in a situation similar to the one above, or it may have been under more formal circumstances, such as serving as a judge on a student judiciary board in a cheating case. In contrast to work on social cognition, which describes how people develop an overall impression about others' personality traits, **attribution theory** seeks to explain how we decide, on the basis of samples of an individual's behaviour, what the specific causes of that person's behaviour are (Weiner, 1985a, 1985b; Jones, 1990; White, 1992).

The general process we use to determine the causes of behaviour and other social occurrences proceeds in several steps, illustrated in Figure 14-3. After first noticing that a behavioural event has occurred, we must interpret the meaning of the event. This leads to the formulation of an initial explanation. Depending on the time available, the cognitive resources on hand (such as the attention we can give to the matter), and our motivation (determined in part by how important the event is to us), we might choose to accept our initial explanation or seek to modify it. If we have the time, cognitive resources, and motivation, the event becomes the trigger for deliberate problem solving as we seek a fuller explanation. During the problem formulation and resolution stage,

attribution theory: The theory of personality that seeks to explain how we decide, on the basis of samples of an individual's behaviour, what the specific causes of that person's behaviour are.

Is this youngster shy or is he just taking a break from a vigorous game of basketball? In the fundamental attribution error, people over-attribute behaviour to dispositional causes, and minimize the importance of situational causes.

Do you think something similar can occur between nations?

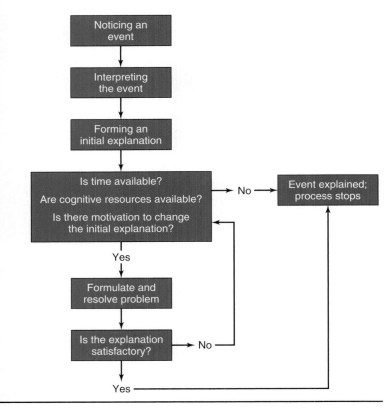

Figure 14-3 The general process we use to determine the causes of others' behaviour and social occurrences proceeds in several steps. The kind of explanation we come up with depends on the time available to us, our cognitive resources, and our degree of motivation to come up with an accurate explanation. If time, cognitive resources, and motivation are limited, we'll make use of our first impression, which can be inaccurate.

situational causes (of behaviour): A perceived cause of behaviour that is based on environmental factors.

dispositional causes (of behaviour): A perceived cause of behaviour that is based on internal traits or personality factors.

fundamental attribution error: A tendency to attribute others' behaviour to dispositional causes and the tendency to minimize the importance of situational causes.

halo effect: A phenomenon in which an initial perception of a person as having positive traits produces the expectation that the person has other uniformly positive characteristics.

assumed-similarity bias: The tendency to think of people as being similar to oneself, even when meeting them for the first time.

we might try out several possibilities before determining that we have reached a solution (Krull & Anderson, 1997).

In seeking an explanation for behaviour, one central question we must answer is whether the cause is situational or dispositional (Heider, 1958). **Situational causes** are elements of the environment. For instance, someone who knocks over a quart of milk and then cleans it up is probably doing so not because he or she is necessarily a terribly neat person, but because the *situation* requires it. In contrast, a person who spends hours shining the kitchen floor is probably doing so because he or she *is* a neat person—hence, the behaviour has a **dispositional cause**, prompted by the person's disposition (her or his internal traits or personality characteristics).

In our example involving Barbara, her fellow employees attributed her behaviour to her disposition rather than to the situation. But from a logical standpoint, it is equally plausible that there was something about the situation that caused the behaviour. If asked, Barbara might attribute her accomplishment to situational factors, explaining that she had so much other work to do that she just had to get the project out of the way, or that the project was not all that difficult and so it was easy to complete ahead of schedule. To her, then, the reason for her behaviour might not be dispositional at all; it could be situational.

Biases in Attribution: To Err Is Human

If we always processed information in the rational manner that attribution theory suggests, the world might run a lot more smoothly. Unfortunately, although attribution theory generally makes accurate predictions, people do not always process information about others in such a logical fashion. In fact, research reveals consistent biases in the ways people make attributions. Among the most typical are these:

- *The fundamental attribution error.* One of the most common biases in people's attributions is the tendency to over-attribute others' behaviour to dispositional causes, and the corresponding failure to recognize the importance of situational causes. Known as the **fundamental attribution error**, this tendency is quite prevalent in Western cultures. We tend to exaggerate the importance of personality characteristics (dispositional causes) in producing others' behaviour, minimizing the influence of the environment (situational factors). For example, we are more likely to jump to the conclusion that someone who is often late to work is too lazy to take an earlier bus (a dispositional cause) than to assume that the cause is due to situational factors, such as the bus always running late. (Ross, 1977; Ross & Nisbett, 1991; Gilbert & Malone, 1995).

- *The halo effect.* Harry is intelligent, kind, and loving. Is he also conscientious? If you were to guess, your response probably would be yes. Your guess reflects the **halo effect**, a phenomenon in which an initial understanding that a person has positive traits is used to infer other uniformly positive characteristics. The opposite would also hold true. Learning that Harry is unsociable and argumentative would probably lead you to assume he is lazy as well. However, few people have uniformly positive or uniformly negative traits, so the halo effect leads to misperceptions of others (Petzold, 1992; Larose & Standing, 1998).

- *Assumed-similarity bias.* How similar to you—in terms of attitudes, opinions, and likes and dislikes—are your friends and acquaintances? Most people believe that their friends and acquaintances are fairly similar to themselves. But this feeling goes beyond just people we know; there is a general tendency—known as the **assumed-similarity bias**—to think of people as being similar to oneself, even when meeting them for the first time. Given the range of people in the world, this means we're often wrong (Ross, Greene, & House, 1977; Hoch, 1987; Marks & Miller, 1987).

EXPLORING DIVERSITY

Ethnicity in the Twenty-First Century

How does multiculturalism help ensure greater tolerance of ethnic diversity?

"Ethnicity is likely to be to the twenty-first century what class was to the twentieth—a major source of social tensions and political conflicts; hence it will be a major focus of attention for an academia that will be asked to provide facts, explanations, and theories" (Berry & Laponce, 1994, p. 3). Berry and Laponce also point out that ethnicity will be a source of creative energy.

The importance of ethnicity is already becoming apparent in Canada. Since 1971, Canada has had an official multicultural policy. In 1982, multiculturalism and equality rights became a part of the Canadian constitution under the Charter of Rights and Freedoms.

Multiculturalism is a strategy designed to manage cultural diversity. The multicultural hypothesis suggests that when individuals maintain their unique ethnic identity they feel more secure. This security then translates into positive feelings about other ethnic groups, allowing for peaceful and productive coexistence and fair treatment for all.

Canadian social psychologists have become world leaders in research into bilingualism, multiculturalism, immigrant acculturation, ethnic identity, prejudice, stereotypes, and discrimination (Alcock, Carment, & Sadava, 2000). To social psychologists falls the role of analysis and research, often commissioned and funded by the government, which may translate into public policy (Tepper, 1994). Applied social psychology therefore extends knowledge in order " ...to understand and, perhaps solve contemporary social problems" (Sadava, 1997, p. 8).

One area in which social psychological research is influential is the study of attitudes. According to Kalin and Berry (1994), if multicultural policies are to be successful, they must have the support of individuals in the society. Personal attitudes are a key element to understanding and avoiding conflict. Although a match between policy and public views will contribute to the success of that policy, public policy may also be designed to encourage attitude change. Research projects are often designed to monitor such change (Berry, 1999).

In a test of the multicultural hypothesis, Berry and others (Kalin & Berry, 1994) found that those who scored as insecure on measures of cultural and economic security were less favourable in their attitudes towards other ethnic groups. Those who scored higher on security were more tolerant of others. This research appears to support the multicultural hypothesis, which states that fostering higher measures of economic and cultural security may lead to greater multicultural tolerance in a given society.

Evaluate

1. A learned predisposition to respond in a favourable or an unfavourable manner to a particular object is called a(n) _____.
2. One brand of peanut butter advertises its product by describing its taste and nutritional value. It is hoping to persuade customers through _____-route processing. In ads for a competing brand, a popular actor happily eats the product—but does not describe it. This approach hopes to persuade customers through _____-route processing.
3. Cognitive dissonance theory suggests that we commonly change our behaviour to keep it consistent with our attitudes. True or false?
4. Sopan was happy to lend his textbook to a fellow student who seemed bright and friendly. He was surprised when his classmate did not return it. His assumption that the bright and friendly student would also be responsible reflects the _____ effect.

Rethink

1. Suppose you were assigned to develop a full advertising campaign for a product, including television, radio, and print ads. How might the theories in this chapter guide your strategy to suit the different media?
2. Joan sees Annette, a new coworker, act in a way that seems abrupt and curt. Joan concludes that Annette is unkind and unsociable. The next day Joan sees Annette acting kindly to another worker. Is Joan likely to change her impression of Annette? Why or why not? Finally, Joan sees several friends of hers laughing and joking with Annette, treating her in a very friendly fashion. Is Joan likely to change her impression of Annette? Why or why not?

Answers to Evaluate Questions

1. attitude 2. central; peripheral 3. False; we typically change our attitudes, not our behaviour, to reduce cognitive dissonance. 4. halo

Pathways Through Psychology

James Alcock

Professor of Psychology and Director of the Graduate Program in Psychology at York University, Toronto, Ontario

Education: B.Sc., McGill University; Ph.D., McMaster University

Home: Toronto, Ontario

James Alcock

Most of my research and writing activity has had to do with the psychology of belief. I first became interested in this as a graduate student, when I became puzzled by the explosion of interest in putative psychic phenomena such as extrasensory perception. As I began to study both the extent of such belief and the factors that give rise to it, I became more and more aware that belief in paranormal and supernatural phenomena is often held with great tenacity, even though it may be at odds with other important beliefs of the individual.

My work has consisted of such things as presenting to subjects "impossible" demonstrations, assessing the extent to which their beliefs are affected by experiences that seem to defy common sense, and trying to understand how it is that "irrational" beliefs become part of their larger belief system. For example, in one study, subjects were asked if one could increase the area of a piece of paper by cutting it up and rearranging the order of the pieces. Subjects who were certain that this was impossible were then shown a demonstration in which such an event actually seemed to occur. Half of the subjects switched their belief from being certain that this could not happen to being certain that it could. The other half maintained their earlier belief despite the evidence of their eyes. I became interested in how and why some individuals stick with "theory" and ignore the "data," while others go with the data, and forget the theory.

In later years, I became more involved internationally. I was part of a group that was invited to China to give lectures, and to examine possible instances of psychic phenomena. Under test conditions these claims were not substantiated. I was asked by the National Research Council in the United States to prepare a comprehensive review of all research involving so-called human operator influence over the output of random number generators, in light of claims made by some scientists that they had demonstrated that thought could influence such devices. I found that there was no evidence for such a phenomenon and that the various research studies backing such claims suffered from serious methodological flaws.

Over the years, my interest in psychology has been sustained through work with both students and colleagues and by my research and writing. Bill Carment, Stan Sadava and I continue with our collaboration on *A Textbook of Social Psychology*. In 1981, *Parapsychology: Science or Magic?* was published. In it, I set out to show how ordinary psychological processes can't account for the many weird and seemingly paranormal experiences that people report. This marked a highlight of my continued interest in the paranormal research, as did the invitation to publish a target article, outlining my criticisms of parapsychological research, in *Behavioural and Brain Sciences*. The article was accompanied by the responses to my arguments by a large group of scholars from around the world.

These things are important to me, both professionally and personally, because I believe that as psychologists, we need to study the experiences that are important to people, and supposed psychic experiences typically are seen as very important. It is not enough simply to reject the psychic interpretation out of hand. We need to understand the nature of the experience, even if, as I personally believe, these experiences do not actually involve anything paranormal or supernatural, because they are so important to people. By understanding them we widen our knowledge of the human psyche, and the propensity in some circumstances to believe things that run quite counter to our logic.

Source: James Alcock, Ph.D., York University
<jalcock@glendon.yorku.ca>

Why does James Alcock believe that the study of the paranormal is important to psychology?

Social Influence

You have just transferred to a new college and are attending your first class. When the professor enters, your fellow classmates instantly rise, bow to the professor, and then stand quietly, with their hands behind their backs. You've never encountered such behaviour, and it makes no sense to you. Is it more likely that you will (1) jump up to join the rest of the class or (2) remain seated?

Based on what research has told us about **social influence**, the process by which the actions of an individual or group affect the behaviour of others, the answer to the question would almost always be the first option. As you undoubtedly know from your own experience, pressures to conform can be painfully strong, and they can bring about changes in behaviour that, when considered in perspective, otherwise never would have occurred.

Conformity: Following What Others Do

Conformity is a change in behaviour or attitudes brought about by a desire to follow the beliefs or standards of other people. The classic demonstration of pressure to conform comes from a series of studies carried out in the 1950s by Solomon Asch (Asch, 1951). In the experiments, participants thought they were participating in a test of perceptual skills with a group of six other participants. The participants were shown one card with three lines of varying length and a second card that had a fourth line that matched one of the first three (see Figure 14-4). The task was seemingly straightforward: The participants had to announce aloud which of the first three lines was identical in length to a "standard" line. Because the correct answer was always obvious, the task seemed easy to the participants.

Indeed, since the participants all agreed on the first few trials, the procedure appeared to be quite simple. But then something odd began to happen. From the perspective of the participant in the group who got to answer last, all of the first six participants' answers seemed to be wrong—in fact, unanimously wrong. And this pattern persisted. Over and over again, the first six participants provided answers that contradicted what the last participant believed to be correct. The dilemma that this situation posed for the last participant was whether to follow his or her own perceptions or to follow the group and repeat the answer that everyone else was giving.

As you might have guessed, this experiment was more contrived than it first appeared. The first six participants were actually confederates (paid employees of the experimenter) and had been instructed to give unanimously erroneous answers in many of the trials. And the study had nothing to do with perceptual skills. Instead, the issue under investigation was conformity.

What Asch found was that in about one-third of the trials, participants conformed to the unanimous but erroneous group answer, with about 75 percent of all participants conforming at least once. However, there were strong individual differences. Some participants conformed nearly all the time, whereas others never did so.

Since Asch's pioneering work, literally hundreds of studies have examined the factors affecting conformity, and we now know a great deal about the phenomenon (Moscovici, 1985; Tanford & Penrod, 1984; Wood et al., 1994). Among the most important variables producing conformity are the following:

- *The characteristics of the group.* The more attractive a group is to its members, the greater its ability to produce conformity (Hogg & Hardie, 1992). Furthermore, a person's relative **status**, the social rank held within a group, is critical: The lower a person's status in the group, the greater the power of the group over that person's behaviour.
- *The situation in which the individual is responding.* Conformity is considerably higher when people must make a response publicly than when they can respond privately, as our political leaders noted when they authorized secret ballots in voting.

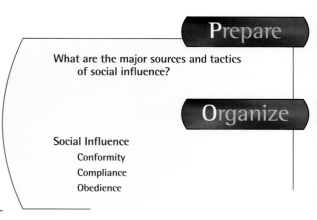

Prepare

What are the major sources and tactics of social influence?

Organize

Social Influence
Conformity
Compliance
Obedience

social influence: The process by which the actions of an individual or group affect the behaviour of others.

conformity: A change in behaviour or attitudes brought about by a desire to follow the beliefs or standards of other people.

status: Social rank within a group.

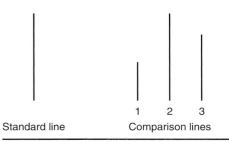

Figure 14-4 Which of the three comparison lines is the same length as the "standard" line? In Asch's conformity experiment, there was always a clear, correct answer, yet participants often conformed to the answers of the other group members. *What are some ways that participants in the study could have avoided being influenced by the pressure from the group?*

social supporter: A person who shares an unpopular opinion or attitude of another group member, thereby encouraging nonconformity.

 **PsychLink**

Persuasion and control
www.mcgrawhill.ca/college/feldman

compliance: Conforming behaviour that occurs in response to direct social pressure.

- *The kind of task.* People working on tasks and questions that are ambiguous (having no clear answer) are more susceptible to social pressure. Asked to give an opinion, such as on what type of clothing is fashionable, a person is more likely to yield to conformist pressures than if asked a question of fact. In addition, tasks at which an individual is less competent relative to the group create conditions in which conformity is more likely.
- *Unanimity of the group.* Conformity pressures are most pronounced in groups that are unanimous in their support of a position. But what of the case in which people with dissenting views have an ally in the group, known as a **social supporter**, who agrees with them? Having just one person present who shares the unpopular point of view is sufficient to reduce conformity pressures (Allen, 1975; Levine, 1989).

Compliance: Submitting to Direct Social Pressure

Conformity is a phenomenon in which the social pressure is subtle or indirect. But in some situations social pressure is much more obvious, and there is direct, explicit pressure to endorse a particular point of view or to behave in a certain way. Social psychologists call the type of conforming behaviour that occurs in response to direct social pressure **compliance**.

Several specific sales tactics are intended to gain compliance. The following are some of the most common:

- *The foot-in-the-door technique.* A salesperson comes to your door and asks you to accept a small sample. You agree, thinking you have nothing to lose. A little later comes a larger request, which, because you have already agreed to the first one, you have a harder time turning down.

  The salesperson in this case is employing a tried-and-true strategy that social psychologists call the *foot-in-the-door technique:* You first ask a person to agree to a small request and later ask them to comply with a more important one; compliance with the later request increases significantly when the person first agrees to the smaller favour.

  The foot-in-the-door phenomenon was first demonstrated in a study in which a number of experimenters went door-to-door asking residents to sign a petition in favour of safe driving (Freedman & Fraser, 1966). Almost everyone complied with this small, benign request. However, a few weeks later, different experimenters contacted the residents again and made a much larger request: that the residents erect a huge sign reading "Drive Carefully" on their front lawns. The results were clear: 55 percent of those who had signed the petition agreed to the request, whereas only 17 percent of people in a control group who had not been asked to sign the petition agreed.

  Why does the foot-in-the-door technique work? One reason is that involvement with the small request leads to an interest in an issue, and taking an action—any action—makes the individual more committed to the issue, thereby increasing the likelihood of future compliance. Another explanation revolves around people's self-perceptions. By complying with the initial request, individuals might come to see themselves as the kind of person who provides help when asked. Then, when confronted with the larger request, they agree in order to maintain the kind of consistency in attitudes and behaviour that we described earlier. Although we don't know which of these two explanations is more accurate, it is clear that the foot-in-the-door strategy is effective (Burger, 1999).
- *The door-in-the-face technique.* A fund raiser asks for a $500 contribution. You laughingly refuse, telling her that the amount is way out of your league. She then asks for a $10 contribution. What do you do? If you are like most people, you'll probably be a lot more compliant than if she hadn't asked for the huge contribution first. The reason lies in the *door-in-the-face technique,* in which a large request, refusal of which is expected, is followed by a smaller one. This

strategy, which is the opposite of the foot-in-the-door approach, has also proved to be effective (Dillard, 1991; Reeves et al., 1991; Abrahams & Bell, 1994).

One example of its success was shown in a field experiment in which college students were stopped on the street and asked to agree to a substantial favour—acting as unpaid counsellors for juvenile delinquents two hours a week for two years (Cialdini et al., 1975). Not surprisingly, no one agreed to make such an enormous commitment. But when they were later asked the considerably smaller favour of taking a group of delinquents on a two-hour trip to the zoo, half the people complied. In comparison, only 17 percent of a control group of participants who had not first received the larger request agreed.

The use of this technique is widespread. You may have used it at some point yourself, perhaps by asking your parents for a very large increase in your allowance and later settling for less. Similarly, television writers sometimes sprinkle their scripts with obscenities that they know will be cut by network censors, hoping to keep other key phrases intact (Cialdini, 1988).

- *The that's-not-all technique.* In this technique, you're offered a deal at an inflated price. But immediately following the initial offer, the salesperson offers an incentive, discount, or bonus to clinch the deal.

  Although it sounds transparent, such a practice can be quite effective. In one study, the experimenters set up a booth and sold cupcakes for 75 cents each. In one condition, customers were told directly that the price was 75 cents. But in another condition, they were told the price was $1, but had been reduced to 75 cents. As the that's-not-all technique would predict, more cupcakes were sold at the "reduced" price—even though it was identical to the price in the other experimental condition (Burger, 1986).

- *The not-so-free sample.* If you're ever given a free sample, keep in mind that it comes with a psychological cost. Salespeople provide samples to potential customers in order to instigate the norm of reciprocity. The *norm of reciprocity* is the well-accepted societal standard dictating that we should treat other people as they treat us. Receiving a not-so-free sample, then, suggests the need for reciprocation—in the form of a purchase, of course (Cialdini, 1988).

The techniques devised by social psychologists for promoting compliance are often used by companies seeking to sell their products to consumers, but they are also used by employers to bring about compliance and raise productivity of employees in the workplace. In fact, a branch of psychology, **industrial-organizational (I/O) psychology**, considers such issues as worker motivation, satisfaction, safety, and productivity. I/O psychologists also focus on the operation and design of organizations, asking such questions as how can decision making be improved in large organizations, and how can the fit between workers and their jobs be maximized. Furthermore, as we discuss in the *Applying Psychology in the 21st Century* box, one of the newest frontiers for industrial-organizational psychologists is tracking and targeting consumers virtually.

"*It's macaroni. We call it pasta as a marketing ploy.*"

industrial-organizational (I/O) psychology: The branch of psychology that focuses on work and job-related issues, including productivity, job satisfaction, decision making, and consumer behaviour.

Obedience: Obeying Direct Orders

Compliance techniques try to gently lead people toward agreement with a request. In some cases, however, requests are geared toward producing **obedience**, a change in behaviour in response to the commands of others. Although obedience is considerably less common than conformity and compliance, it does occur in several specific kinds of relationships. For example, we might show obedience to our boss, teacher, or parent, merely because of the power they hold to reward or punish us.

To acquire an understanding of obedience, consider for a moment how you might respond if a stranger said to you:

obedience: Conforming behaviour in reaction to the commands of others.

Applying Psychology in the 21st Century

Reading Your Mind, Reaching Your Wallet: Using Computer Technology to Increase Compliance

Jennifer Zweben has a weakness: she loves to buy CDs. Her studio apartment in San Jose, California, is littered with new purchases, everything from hip-hop to alternative, classical to techno. She's also a frequent online shopper, usually ringing up an order for CDs or books at least once a month. Indeed, just the other day, Zweben dropped by www.cdnow.com, an online music store, to check the price for her latest must-have. . . . While reading about the album, she noticed that the Web site had generated a list of other CDs for her to consider. One stood out: "Mermaid Avenue" by Billy Bragg and Wilco. Zweben, Webmaster at IBM Research, had heard a few songs from the album on the radio and liked them. "I'm always scouting for new music," she says, "but I wouldn't have remembered to look for this title on my own." She . . . plunked "Mermaid Avenue" into her virtual shopping cart (Lach, 1998, p. 39).

Welcome to the world of virtual persuasion, where compliance pressures are carefully addressed to the specific attitudes and prior behaviour of individuals like Jennifer Zweben. Such targeting of Web site visitors represents the newest use by industrial-organization psychologists of psychographics, a technique that divides people into lifestyle profiles related to purchasing patterns. Psychographics considers such characteristics as a target's age, race, ethnicity, religion, income, marital status, and buying patterns. The technique also examines leisure activities of consumers of particular products. For instance, auto manufacturers know that buyers of minivans are more likely to participate in conversations with friends, go to family gatherings, read, and attend church functions than owners of sport utility vehicles. On the other hand, sport utility vehicle owners are more likely to go to sporting events, work out, hunt, and go out to clubs than minivan owners (Bradsher, 2000; Binkley, 2000).

Web-based persuasion techniques employ past purchasing history and previously stated preferences to build profiles of individuals, permitting sellers to target offers that are most likely to be of interest to given individuals. For example, if someone expresses an interest online

in a new 'N Sync CD, a Web supplier might search its database to see what other CDs were purchased by those who bought 'N Sync CDs. Once it has found this information, it will create a screen on the computer, offering a list of CDs of potential interest—a process called *collaborative filtering*.

Such technology might well move beyond the Web and spawn other persuasion techniques. Consider this scenario: you load up your shopping cart at the supermarket with a week's worth of groceries. After scanning your purchases into the cash register, the clerk reads a message that pops up on a computer screen and says to you, "Do you need dog food today?" You nod and rush back for the dog food, knowing that your buying habits—and the fact that you buy dog food every month or so—lie in the database of the supermarket's computers (Lach, 1998).

Do you think psychographics and collaborative filtering are basically helpful tools for consumers, or are they invasions of privacy? Is there any downside to being led to make purchases that are entirely consistent with what you and others with similar purchasing habits have bought in the past?

I've devised a new way of improving memory. All I need is for you to teach people a list of words and then give them a test. The test procedure requires only that you give learners a shock each time they make a mistake on the test. To administer the shocks you will use a "shock generator" that gives shocks ranging from 30 to 450 volts. You can see that the switches are labelled from "slight shock" through "danger: severe shock" at the top level, where there are three red X's. But don't worry; although the shocks may be painful, they will cause no permanent damage.

Presented with this situation, you would be likely to think that neither you nor anyone else would go along with the stranger's unusual request. Clearly, it lies outside the bounds of what we consider good sense.

Or does it? Suppose the stranger asking for your help were a psychologist conducting an experiment. Or suppose it were your teacher, your employer, or your military commander—all people in authority with some seemingly legitimate reason for their request.

If you still believe it unlikely that you would comply—think again. For the situation presented above describes a now-classic experiment conducted by social psychologist Stanley Milgram in the 1960s (Milgram, 1974). In the study, participants were placed in a situation in which they were told by an experimenter to give increasingly stronger shocks to another person as part of a study on learning (see Figure 14-5). In reality, the experiment had nothing to do with learning; the real issue under consideration was the degree to which participants would comply with the experimenter's requests. In fact, the "learner" supposedly receiving the shocks was actually a confederate who never really received any shocks.

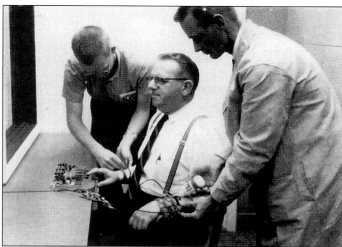

Figure 14-5 This impressive-looking "shock generator" was used to lead participants to believe they were administering electric shocks to another person, who was connected to the generator by electrodes that were attached to the skin.

Most people who hear a description of the experiment feel that it is unlikely that *any* participant would give the maximum level of shock—or, for that matter, any shock at all. Even a group of psychiatrists to whom the situation was described predicted that fewer than 2 percent of the participants would fully comply and administer the strongest shocks.

However, the actual results contradicted both experts' and nonexperts' predictions. Some 65 percent of the participants eventually used the highest setting on the shock generator, 450 volts, to shock the learner. This obedience occurred even though the learner, who had mentioned at the start of the experiment that he had a heart condition, demanded to be released, screaming "Let me out of here! Let me out of here! My heart's bothering me. Let me out of here!" Still, despite the learner's pleas, most participants continued to administer the shocks.

Why did so many individuals comply with the experimenter's demands? Extensive interviews were carried out with participants following the experiment. They showed that participants were obedient primarily because they believed that the experimenter would be responsible for any potential ill effects that befell the learner. The experimenter's orders were accepted, then, because the participants thought that they personally could not be held accountable for their actions—they could always blame the experimenter (Darley, 1995; Blass, 1996).

The Milgram experiment has been criticized for creating an extremely trying set of circumstances for the participants, thereby raising serious ethical concerns. (Undoubtedly, the experiment could not be conducted today because of ethical considerations.) Other critics have suggested that the conditions in Milgram's experiment did not mirror real-world obedience (Miller, Collins, & Brief, 1995; Blass, 2000).

Despite these concerns, Milgram's research remains one of the strongest laboratory demonstrations of obedience. We need only consider actual instances of obedience to authority to witness some frightening real-life parallels. For instance, a major defence offered after World War II by Nazi officers to excuse their participation in atrocities during the war was that they were "only following orders." Milgram's experiment, which was motivated in part by his desire to explain the behaviour of everyday Germans during World War II, forces each of us to ask ourselves this question: Would we be able to withstand the intense power of authority?

Perils of obedience
www.mcgrawhill.ca/college/feldman

1. A _____ _____, or person who agrees with the dissenting viewpoint, is likely to reduce conformity.
2. Who pioneered the study of conformity?
   a. Skinner
   b. Asch
   c. Milgram
   d. Fiala
3. Which of the following techniques asks a person to comply with a small initial request to enhance the likelihood that the person will later comply with a larger request?
   a. Door-in-the-face
   b. Foot-in-the-door
   c. That's-not-all
   d. Not-so-free sample
4. The _____-_____-_____-_____ technique begins with an outrageous request which then makes a smaller request seem reasonable.
5. _____ is a change in behaviour that is due to another person's orders.

Answers to Evaluate Questions

1. social supporter 2. b 3. b 4. door-in-the-face 5. Obedience

1. Given that persuasive techniques like those described in this section are so powerful, should there be laws against the use of such techniques? Should people be taught defences against such techniques? Is the use of such techniques ethically and morally defensible?
2. Why do you think the Milgram experiment is so controversial? What sorts of effects might the experiment have had on participants? Do you think the experiment would have had similar results if it had been conducted not in a laboratory setting, but among members of a social group (such as a fraternity or sorority) with strong pressures to conform?

Prepare

What are stereotypes, prejudice, and discrimination?
How can we reduce prejudice and discrimination?

Organize

Prejudice and Discrimination
   The Foundations of Prejudice
   Working to End Prejudice and Discrimination

stereotypes: Generalized beliefs and expectations about social groups and their members.
prejudice: The negative (or positive) evaluations of groups and their members.

discrimination: Negative behaviour toward members of a particular group.

Prejudice and Discrimination

What do you think of when someone says, "He's an immigrant," or "She's homeless," or "woman driver"? Most people automatically form an impression of what that individual is like. These views create **stereotypes**, generalized beliefs and expectations about groups and their members. Stereotypes, which can be negative or positive, allow us to handle vast amounts of information. We oversimplify the world by attending to broad generalizations and ignoring individual characteristics (Jussim et al., 1996; Macrae, Stangor, & Hewstone, 1996).

Stereotypes can lead to **prejudice**, the negative (or positive) evaluations of people based on group membership. Most commonly, but not exclusively, we label and evaluate people based on race, religion, and ethnicity.

Victoria Esses, of the University of Western Ontario, whose research interests include stereotypes, prejudice, and discrimination, has found that our attitudes about groups are affected by the labels we use to identify them. In a study using the labels "Aboriginal Peoples," "Native Indians," "First Nations people," "Native Canadians," and "Native Peoples," findings indicated that people reacted with less favourable attitudes to some labels than to others (Donakowski & Esses, 1996). Since all these labels refer to the same group—Aboriginal Canadians—it is the label and not the groups to which subjects were responding.

Although usually backed by little or no evidence, stereotypes often have harmful consequences. When people act on negative stereotypes, the result is **discrimination**—negative behaviour toward members of a particular group. Discrimination can lead to exclusion from jobs, neighbourhoods, or educational opportunities, and can result in members of particular groups receiving lower salaries and benefits.

High profile cases of restitution for discrimination involving, for example, Aboriginal Canadians, Japanese-Canadians, or those labelled "mentally defective" and sterilized by eugenics boards, might suggest that prejudice and discrimination are a thing of the past.

In Canada the law prohibits overt discrimination, but the reality may be somewhat different. Although in the minority, white supremacist groups that have chapters in Canada continue to draw members, and promote racial hatred and harm (Alcock, Carment & Sadava, 2000). At the societal level, black and Aboriginal people continue to be overrepresented in the criminal justice system (*Report of the Commission on Systemic Racism in the Ontario Criminal Justice System*, 1995).

Stereotyping not only leads to overt discrimination; it can actually *cause* members of stereotyped groups to behave in ways that reflect the stereotype, through a phenomenon known as the *self-fulfilling prophecy*. Self-fulfilling prophecies are expectations about the occurrence of a future event or behaviour that act to increase the likelihood that the event or behaviour *will* occur. For example, if people think that members of a particular group lack ambition, they might treat them in a way that diminishes their ambition (Harris-Kern & Perkins, 1995; Madon, Jussim, & Eccles, 1997).

The Foundations of Prejudice

No one has ever been born disliking a particular racial, religious, or ethnic group. People learn to hate, in much the same way that they learn the alphabet.

According to *social learning approaches* to stereotyping and prejudice, people's feelings about members of various groups are shaped by the behaviour of parents, other adults, and peers. *Right-wing authoritarianism* (RWA) is a term used to describe a highly prejudiced personality type. Research by Bob Altemeyer of the University of Manitoba (1981, 1994) suggests that three traits underlie this personality type: submission (to authority figures), aggression (against those they believe threaten the system) and conventionalism (adherence to perceived established norms). People who measure as high on the RWA are highly bigoted and may commend their children for expressing prejudices. Likewise, young children learn prejudice by imitating the behaviour of adult models. Such learning starts at an early age; children as young as 3 years of age begin to show preferences for members of their own race (Katz, 1976; Yenerall, 1995).

The mass media also provide a major source of information about stereotypes, not just for children, but for adults as well. Even today, some television shows and movies portray Italians as Mafia-like mobsters. Other media may portray Aboriginal people as dependent, uneducated, deviant, and alcoholic. A study done by Claxton-Oldfield and Keefe (1999) did a content analysis of a daily newspaper to examine potential stereotypes of the Innu of Labrador and found most stories depicted the Innu as dependent, in conflict with authority, or deviant. The authors found these stereotypes reflected in research on student's impressions of the Innu people. When such inaccurate portrayals are the primary source of information about minority groups, they can lead to the development and maintenance of unfavourable stereotypes (Herrett-Skjellum & Allen, 1996; Coltraine & Messineo, 2000).

Social learning theory does not provide the full story of stereotyping and prejudice. For instance, some psychologists argue that prejudice results when there is perceived competition for scarce societal resources such as jobs or housing (Simpson & Yinger, 1985). This type of prejudice has more to do with belief about the impact of a group on one's life rather than any negative stereotypes one may hold. Mark Zanna, of the University of Waterloo (1994), has proposed that prejudice may be based on affect and symbolic belief as well as on stereotypes. *Affect prejudice* is based on emotions or feelings towards another group. *Symbolic belief prejudice* is based on beliefs about how a group helps or hinders the attainment of goals.

Further, Zanna's research shows that we may be prejudiced against different groups for different reasons and that these reasons may change with circumstances. So, if a group is believed to be taking jobs away or using other scarce resources, prejudice towards that group may have a high symbolic belief component.

Other explanations of prejudice focus on mood states and their relationship to prejudice. When individuals are dissatisfied with their life circumstances they may look to blame someone or something. This behaviour is known as *scapegoating*. A series of five studies on the relationship between mood and prejudice were carried out by Esses,

PsychLink
Testing hidden prejudice
www.mcgrawhill.ca/college/feldman

Haddock, and Zanna (1994). Using both males and females and members of a number of ethnic groups, they found that when people were in a negative (bad) mood they were extremely likely to evaluate other ethnic groups in a highly unfavourable way.

Working to End Prejudice and Discrimination

According to Jane Elliott, a former fourth grade school teacher from Iowa and now a diversity trainer who travels the world with her message about how we learn to be prejudiced, "you can create racism. And, as with anything, if you can create it, you can destroy it" (Coronel, 1996). Her interest in racism began when she questioned her students about their knowledge of African Americans. They provided her with many negative stereotypes, which they had heard or been taught, since none of them had ever met a black person.

That experience set Elliott on a path to fight prejudice by teaching her students and others that we learn to adopt prejudiced attitudes. Since the 1960s, Elliott has used the simple technique of dividing the groups she works with into those with blue eyes and those with brown eyes and then proceeding to discriminate against those with blue eyes. It takes no time at all before the people with brown eyes take a dominant role and begin to treat the blue-eyed participants as inferior. Interestingly, even self-confident blue-eyed participants begin to lose confidence and act out the inferior stereotype that has been attached to them. Elliott found that her all-white class of fourth graders got the message very fast and began to examine their prejudices against people of other races. They also began to challenge parents who had taught them these attitudes (Kral, 2000).

Elliott's work sheds light on how we become prejudiced and how we can counteract it. Psychologists who work in this area have developed other strategies that have proven effective in diminishing the effects of prejudice and discrimination, including these:

PsychLink
Teaching tolerance project
www.mcgrawhill.ca/college/feldman

- *Increasing contact between the target of stereotyping and the holder of the stereotype.* Research has shown that increasing the amount of interaction between people from different groups can reduce negative stereotyping. But only certain kinds of contact are likely to foster a reduction in prejudice and discrimination. Situations where there is relatively intimate contact, where the individuals are of equal status, or where participants must cooperate with one another or are dependent on one another are most likely to reduce stereotyping (Gaertner et al., 1996; Pettigrew, 1997; Oskamp, 2000).

- *Making positive values and norms against prejudice more conspicuous.* It is not always necessary to rely on contact to reduce prejudice and discrimination. Another approach is to demonstrate to people the inconsistencies between values they hold regarding equality and fair treatment of others, and negative stereotyping. For instance, people who are made to understand that their values regarding equality and fairness are inconsistent with their negative perceptions of minority group members are more likely to work actively against prejudice in the future. Similarly, people who hear others vehemently condemn racism are subsequently more likely to strongly condemn racism (Rokeach, 1971; Blanchard, Lilly, & Vaughn, 1991).

- *Educating for tolerance.* Probably the most direct means of changing stereotypical and discriminatory attitudes is through education. Studies have shown that even 5-year-olds can display high levels of prejudice (Aboud, 1988; Doyle & Aboud, 1995). Efforts that could make use of the formal education system to reduce prejudice would be valuable. For example, studies done in Toronto (Reich & Purbhoo, 1975; Ziegler, 1981) showed that students in more ethnically heterogeneous settings were more tolerant of diversity.

Two Quebec researchers studied white third and fourth grade students to see if conversations between dyads of high-prejudice and low-prejudice students would affect their levels of tolerance. High-prejudice children did in fact become more tolerant after listening to their partners express a balanced and more tolerant attitude (Aboud & Doyle, 1996).

Another strategy is teaching people to be more aware of the positive characteristics of targets of stereotyping. For instance, when the meaning of puzzling behaviour is explained to people holding stereotypes, they may come to appreciate its true significance—even though it may still appear foreign and perhaps even threatening. Furthermore, training in statistical reasoning, which illustrates various logical fallacies, can inhibit the formation of certain stereotypes (Landis et al., 1976; Langer, Bashner, & Chanowitz, 1985; Schaller et al., 1996).

An area of education that has been found to reduce prejudice is bilingual education. Extensive research on second-language learning has been carried out by researchers at McGill University in Montreal (see Chapter 7). In general, findings from Canada and other parts of the world show that people who acquire a second language are less prejudiced. This is particularly true if the language is acquired out of interest in the other culture rather than simply to seek employment (Noels & Clément, 1998; Alcock, Carment, & Sadava, 2000).

Evaluate

1. Any expectation—positive or negative—about an individual based solely on that person's membership in a group can be a stereotype. True or false?
2. A negative (or positive) evaluation of a group and its members is called:
   a. stereotyping
   b. prejudice
   c. self-fulfilling prophecy
   d. discrimination
3. Paul is a store manager who does not expect women to succeed in business. He therefore offers important, high-profile responsibilities only to men. If the female employees fail to move up in the company, this could be an example of a _____-_____ prophecy.

Answers to Evaluate Questions

1. True 2. b 3. self-fulfilling

Rethink

1. How are stereotypes, prejudice, and discrimination related? In a society committed to equality, which of the three should be changed first? Why?
2. Do you think women can be victims of stereotype vulnerability? In what topical areas might this occur? Can men be victims of stereotype vulnerability?

Positive and Negative Social Behaviour

Are people basically good or bad?

Like philosophers and theologians, social psychologists have pondered the basic nature of humanity. Is it represented by the violence and cruelty we see throughout the world, or is there something special about human nature that permits loving, considerate, unselfish, and even noble behaviour?

We turn to two routes that social psychologists have followed in seeking answers to these questions. We first consider what they have learned about the sources of our attraction to others, and we end this chapter with a look at two sides of the coin of human behaviour: aggression and helping.

Prepare

Why are we attracted to certain people, and what progression do social relationships generally follow?

What factors underlie aggression and prosocial behaviour?

Organize

Positive and Negative Social Behaviour
  Liking and Loving
  Aggression and Prosocial Behaviour

Liking and Loving: Interpersonal Attraction and the Development of Relationships

There is nothing more central in most people's lives than their feelings for others, and consequently it is not surprising that liking and loving have become a major focus of interest for social psychologists. Known more formally as the study of **interpersonal attraction** or **close relationships**, this area addresses the factors that lead to positive feelings for others.

interpersonal attraction (or close relationships): Positive feelings for others; liking and loving.

How Do I Like Thee? Let Me Count the Ways

By far the greatest amount of research has focused on liking, probably because it is easier for investigators conducting short-term experiments to produce states of liking for strangers one has just met than to instigate and observe loving relationships over long periods of time. Hence traditional studies have given us a good deal of knowledge about the factors that initially attract two people to each other (Berscheid, 1985; Simpson & Harris, 1994). Among the most important factors considered by social psychologists are the following:

PsychLink
Study of relationships
www.mcgrawhill.ca/college/feldman

- *Proximity.* If you live in a dormitory or an apartment, consider the friends you made when you first moved in. Chances are you became friendliest with those who lived geographically closest to you. In fact, this is one of the most firmly established findings in the interpersonal attraction literature: *Proximity* leads to liking (Festinger, Schachter, & Back, 1950; Nahome & Lawton, 1975).
- *Mere exposure.* Repeated exposure to a person is often sufficient to produce attraction. Interestingly, repeated exposure to *any* stimulus—a person, picture, compact disc, or virtually anything—usually makes us like the stimulus more. Becoming familiar with a stimulus can evoke positive feelings; the positive feelings stemming from familiarity are then transferred to the stimulus itself. There are exceptions, though. When the initial interactions are strongly negative, repeated exposure is unlikely to cause us to like another person more. Instead, the more we are exposed to him or her, the more we might dislike the individual (Bornstein & D'Agostino, 1994; Kruglanski, Freund, & Bar Tal, 1996).
- *Similarity.* Folk wisdom tells us that birds of a feather flock together. Unfortunately, it also maintains that opposites attract. Social psychologists have come up with a clear verdict regarding which of the two statements is correct: We tend to like those who are similar to us. Discovering that others are similar to us in terms of attitudes, values, or traits promotes our liking them. Furthermore, the more similar others are, the more we like them (Byrne, 1969; Glaman, Jones, & Rozelle, 1996).

    One reason similarity increases the likelihood of interpersonal attraction is that we assume that people with similar attitudes will evaluate us positively. Because there is a strong **reciprocity-of-liking effect** (a tendency to like those who like us), our knowledge that another person evaluates us positively promotes our attraction to that person. In addition, we assume that when we like someone else, that person likes us in return (Condon & Crano, 1988; Metee & Aronson, 1974; Tagiuri, 1958).

reciprocity-of-liking effect: A tendency to like those who like us.

- *Physical attractiveness.* For most people, the equation *beautiful = good* is quite true. As a result, people who are physically attractive are more popular than those who are physically unattractive, if all other factors are equal. This finding, which contradicts the values that most people say they hold, is apparent even in childhood—with nursery-school-age children rating popularity on the basis of attractiveness—and continues into adulthood. Indeed, physical attractiveness might be the single most important element promoting initial liking in college dating situations, although its influence eventually decreases when people get to know each other better (Hadjistavropoulos & Genest, 1994; Keller & Young, 1996; Langlois et al., 2000; Sangrador & Yela, 2000).

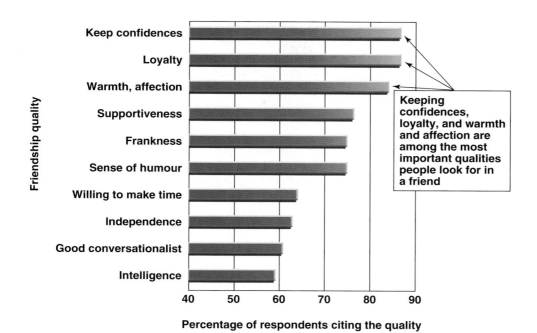

Figure 14-6 These are the key qualities looked for in a friend according to some 40 000 respondents to a questionnaire.

The factors we have discussed are not, of course, the only constituents of liking. For example, surveys have sought to identify the factors critical in friendships. In a questionnaire answered by some 40 000 respondents, the qualities that were most valued in a friend were the ability to keep confidences, loyalty, and warmth and affection, followed closely by supportiveness, frankness, and a sense of humour (Parlee, 1979). The results are summarized in Figure 14-6.

How Do I Love Thee? Let Me Count the Ways

Whereas our knowledge of what makes people like one another is extensive, our understanding of love is more limited in scope and recently acquired. For some time, many social psychologists believed that love was a phenomenon too difficult to observe and study in a controlled, scientific way. However, love is such a central issue in most people's lives that, in time, social psychologists could not resist its allure and became infatuated with the topic (Aron et al., 1997).

As a first step, researchers tried to identify the characteristics that distinguish between mere liking and full-blown love. They discovered that love is not simply liking of a greater quantity, but a qualitatively different psychological state. For instance, at least in its early stages, love includes relatively intense physiological arousal, an all-encompassing interest in another individual, fantasizing about the other, and relatively rapid swings of emotion. Similarly, love, unlike liking, includes elements of passion, closeness, fascination, exclusiveness, sexual desire, and intense caring. Partners are idealized; we exaggerate their good qualities and minimize their imperfections (Murray & Holmes, 1997). Karen and Ken Dion of the University of Toronto (1991, 1993, 1996) study romantic love. They are particularly interested in the role of personality and culture in love relationships.

Other researchers have theorized that there are two main types of love: passionate love and companionate love. **Passionate (or romantic) love** is a state of intense absorption in another person. It includes intense physiological arousal, psychological interest, and caring for the needs of the other. In contrast, **companionate love** is the strong affection we have for those with whom our lives are deeply involved. The love we feel for our parents, other family members, and even some close friends falls into the category of companionate love (Singelis, Choo, & Hatfield, 1995; Baumeister & Bratslavsky, 1999; Regan, 2000).

 **PsychLink**

Definition of love
www.mcgrawhill.ca/college/feldman

passionate (or romantic) love: A state of intense absorption in someone that includes intense physiological arousal, psychological interest, and caring for the needs of another.

companionate love: The strong affection we have for those with whom our lives are deeply involved.

According to psychologist Robert Sternberg (1986, 1988), an even finer differentiation between types of love is in order. He proposes that love is made up of three components: an *intimacy component,* encompassing feelings of closeness and connectedness; a *passion component,* made up of the motivational drives relating to sex, physical closeness, and romance; and a *decision/commitment component,* encompassing the initial cognition that one loves someone and the longer-term feelings of commitment to maintain love. These three components combine to produce the possible different types of love (see Figure 14-7).

Is love a necessary ingredient of a good marriage? Yes, if you live in Canada. On the other hand, it's considerably less important in other cultures. Although mutual attraction and love are the first or second most important characteristics desired in a mate for women and men in Canada, men in China rated good health as most important, and women there rated emotional stability and maturity as most important. In Zulu, South Africa, women rated dependable character first and men rated emotional stability first (Buss et al., 1990; see Table 14-1 and Chapter Activity 14-1).

Aggression and Prosocial Behaviour: Hurting and Helping Others

School shootings, carjackings, and road rage are just some of the examples of violence that seem all too common today. Yet we also find examples of generous, unselfish, thoughtful behaviour that suggest a more optimistic view of humankind. Consider, for instance, people like Mother Teresa, who ministered to the poor in India. Or contemplate the simple kindnesses of life: lending a valued compact disc, stopping to help a child who has fallen off her bicycle, or merely sharing a candy bar with a friend. Such instances of helping are no less characteristic of human behaviour than the distasteful examples of aggression. In this last part of the chapter, we explore how social psychologists have sought to explain instances of aggressive behaviour and helping behaviour (A. G. Miller, 1999).

PsychLink

Driver aggression/road rage
www.mcgrawhill.ca/college/feldman

aggression: The intentional infliction of injury or harm on another person.

Hurting Others: Aggression

We need look no farther than our daily paper or the nightly news to be bombarded with examples of aggression, both on a societal level (war, invasion, assassination) and on an individual level (crime, child abuse, and the many petty cruelties that humans are capable of inflicting on one another). Is such aggression an inevitable part of the human condition? Or is aggression primarily a product of particular circumstances that, if changed, could lead to its reduction?

The difficulty of answering such knotty questions becomes quickly apparent as soon as we consider how best to define the term *aggression.* Depending on the definition, examples of inflicted pain or injury might or might not qualify as aggression. It is clear, for instance, that a rapist is acting with aggression toward his victim. On the other hand, it is less certain that a physician who causes extreme pain to a patient by carrying out an emergency medical procedure with no available anesthetic should be considered aggressive.

Most social psychologists define aggression in terms of the intent and purpose behind the behaviour. **Aggression** involves intentionally inflicting injury or harm on another person (Berkowitz, 1993). Under this definition, it is clear that the rapist in our example is acting aggressively, whereas the physician causing pain during a medical procedure is not.

We turn now to several explanations for aggressive behaviour developed by social psychologists (Berkowitz, 1993; Geen & Donnerstein, 1998).

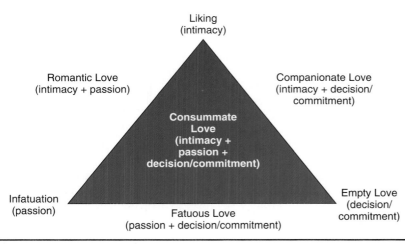

Figure 14-7 According to Sternberg, there are three main components of love: intimacy, passion, and decision/commitment. Different combinations of these components can create other various types of love. Nonlove contains none of the components.

Table 14-1 Rank Ordering of Desired Characteristics in a Mate

	CHINA		SOUTH AFRICA ZULU		CANADA ENGLISH		CANADA FRENCH	
	Males	Females	Males	Females	Males	Females	Males	Females
Mutual attraction—love	4	8	10	5	1	1	2	2
Emotional stability and maturity	5	1	1	2	3	3	1	1
Dependable character	6	7	3	1	2	2	6	4
Pleasing disposition	13	16	4	3	4	4	3	5
Education and intelligence	8	4	6	6	6	8	7	7
Good health	1	3	5	4	5	5	8	9
Good looks	11	15	14	16	7	6	5	6
Sociability	12	9	11	8	8	9	9	11
Desire for home and children	2	2	9	9	11	12	4	3
Refinement, neatness	7	10	7	10	10	7	10	8
Ambition and industriousness	10	5	8	7	9	13	11	15
Similar education	15	12	12	12	13	11	14	14
Good cook and housekeeper	9	11	2	15	15	10	13	10
Favourable social status or rating	14	13	17	14	12	15	12	12
Similar religious background	18	18	16	11	14	14	15	13
Good financial prospect	16	14	18	13	16	16	16	16
Chastity (no prior sexual intercourse)	3	6	13	18	17	18	17	18
Similar political background	17	17	15	17	18	17	18	17

Source: Buss et al., 1990. (1 indicates most desirable characteristic)

Chapter Activity 14–1
Create a Questionnaire

Create a questionnaire based on the characteristics listed in Table 14-1. Give this questionnaire to classmates and or friends. Are your results similar to the results found in the survey done by Buss et al? If your findings differ, what might the reasons be?

Instinct Approaches: Aggression as a Release If you have ever punched an adversary in the nose, you might have experienced a certain satisfaction, despite your better judgment. Instinct theories, noting the prevalence of aggression not only in humans but in animals as well, propose that aggression is primarily the outcome of innate—inborn—urges.

Sigmund Freud was one of the first to suggest, as part of his theory of personality, that aggression is a primary instinctual drive (see Chapter 10). Konrad Lorenz, an ethologist (a scientist who studies animal behaviour), expanded on Freud's notions by arguing that humans, along with members of other species, have a fighting instinct, which in earlier times ensured protection of food supplies and weeded out the weaker of the species (Lorenz, 1966, 1974). The controversial notion arising from Lorenz's instinct approach is that aggressive energy is constantly being built up within an individual until it is finally discharged in a process called **catharsis**. The longer the energy is built up, says Lorenz, the greater will be the amount of the aggression displayed when it is discharged.

Probably the most controversial idea to come out of instinct theories of aggression is Lorenz's proposal that society ought to provide acceptable means of catharsis

catharsis: The process of discharging built-up aggressive energy.

through, for instance, participation in sports and games, in order to prevent its discharge in less socially desirable ways. Although the notion makes logical sense, there is no possible way to devise an adequate experiment to test it. Relatively little support exists for instinct theories in general, because of the difficulty in finding evidence for any kind of pent-up reservoir of aggression (Berkowitz, 1993; Geen & Donnerstein, 1983). Most social psychologists suggest that we should look to other approaches to explain aggression.

Frustration–Aggression Approaches: Aggression as a Reaction to Frustration
Suppose you've been working on a paper that is due for a class early the next morning, and your printer runs out of ink just before you can print out the paper. You rush to the store to buy a new ink cartridge, only to find the salesclerk locking the door for the day. Even though the clerk can see you gesturing and literally begging him to open the door, he refuses, shrugging his shoulders and pointing to a sign that indicates when the store will open the next day. At that moment, the feelings you experience toward the salesclerk probably place you on the verge of real aggression, and you are undoubtedly seething inside.

> **frustration:** The thwarting or blocking of some ongoing, goal-directed behaviour.

Frustration-aggression theory tries to explain aggression in terms of events like this one. When first put forward, the theory said flatly that frustration *always* leads to aggression of some sort, and that aggression is *always* the result of some frustration, where **frustration** is defined as the thwarting or blocking of some ongoing, goal-directed behaviour (Dollard et al., 1939). More recent formulations, however, have modified the original one, suggesting instead that frustration produces anger, leading to a *readiness* to act aggressively. Whether or not actual aggression occurs depends on the presence of *aggressive cues,* stimuli that have been associated in the past with actual aggression or violence and that will trigger aggression again (Berkowitz, 1984). In addition, frustration is assumed to produce aggression only to the extent that the frustration produces negative feelings (Berkowitz, 1989, 1990).

What kinds of stimuli act as aggressive cues? They can range from the most overt, such as the presence of weapons, to the subtlest, such as the mere mention of the name of an individual who has behaved violently in the past. For example, in one experiment, angered participants behaved significantly more aggressively when in the presence of a rifle and revolver than in a comparable situation in which no guns were present (Berkowitz & LePage, 1967). Similarly, frustrated participants in an experiment who had viewed a violent movie were more physically aggressive toward a confederate with the same name as the star of the movie than toward a confederate with a different name (Berkowitz & Geen, 1966). It appears, then, that frustration does lead to aggression, at least when aggressive cues are present (Carlson, Marcus-Newhall, & Miller, 1990).

Observational Learning Approaches: Learning to Hurt Others   Do we learn to be aggressive? The observational learning (sometimes called social learning) approach to aggression says we do. Taking a view almost the opposite of instinct theories, which focus on innate explanations of aggression, observational learning theory (see Chapter 5) emphasizes that social and environmental conditions can teach individuals to be aggressive. Aggression is seen not as inevitable, but rather as a learned response that can be understood in terms of rewards and punishments.

Violence on television
www.mcgrawhill.ca/college/feldman

Observational learning theory pays particular attention not only to direct rewards and punishments that individuals themselves receive, but to the rewards and punishments that models—individuals who provide a guide to appropriate behaviour—receive for their aggressive behaviour. According to observational learning theory, people observe the behaviour of models and the subsequent consequences of the behaviour. If the consequences are positive, the behaviour is likely to be imitated when observers find themselves in a similar situation.

Suppose, for instance, that a girl hits her younger brother when he damages one of her new toys. Whereas instinct theory would suggest that the aggression had been pent up and was now being discharged, and frustration-aggression theory would examine the girl's frustration at no longer being able to use her new toy, observational learning theory would look to previous situations in which the girl had viewed others being rewarded for their aggression. For example, perhaps she had watched a friend get to play with a toy after he painfully twisted it out of the hand of another child.

Observational learning theory has received wide research support. For example, nursery-school-age children who have watched an adult model behave aggressively and then receive reinforcement for the aggression later display similar behaviour themselves, if they have been angered, insulted, or frustrated after exposure (Bandura, 1973, 1983; Anderson & Dill, 2000).

Helping Others: The Brighter Side of Human Nature

Turning away from aggression, we move now to the opposite—and brighter—side of the coin of human nature: helping behaviour. Helping behaviour, or **prosocial behaviour** as it is more formally known, has been considered under many different conditions. However, the question that psychologists have looked at most closely relates to bystander intervention in emergency situations. What are the factors that lead someone to help a person in need?

prosocial behaviour: Helping behaviour.

As we noted in Chapter 1 in the case of Kitty Genovese, one critical factor is the number of others present. When more than one person is witness to an emergency situation, a sense of diffusion of responsibility can arise among bystanders. **Diffusion of responsibility** is the tendency for people to feel that responsibility for acting is shared, or diffused, among those present. The more people present in an emergency, then, the less personally responsible each of them feels—and therefore the less help they provide (Latané & Nida, 1981; Kalafat, Elias, & Gara, 1993; Bickman, 1994; Markey, 2000).

diffusion of responsibility: The tendency for people to feel that responsibility for acting is shared, or diffused, among those present.

Although the majority of research on helping behaviour supports the diffusion-of-responsibility formulation, other factors are clearly involved in helping behaviour. According to a model developed by Latané and Darley (1970), the process of helping involves four basic steps (see Figure 14-8):

- *Noticing a person, event, or situation that might require help.*
- *Interpreting the event as one that requires help.* Even if an event is noticed, it could be sufficiently ambiguous to be interpreted as a nonemergency situation (Shotland, 1985; Harrison & Wells, 1991). It is here that the presence of others first affects helping behaviour. The presence of inactive others could indicate to the observer that a situation does not require help— a judgment the observer might not necessarily make if she or he were the lone observer.
- *Assuming responsibility for taking action.* It is at this point that diffusion of responsibility is likely to occur if others are present. Moreover, a bystander's particular expertise is likely to play a role in determining whether she or he helps. For instance, if people with training in medical aid or lifesaving techniques are present, untrained bystanders are less likely to intervene because they feel they have less expertise. This point was well illustrated in a study by Jane and Irving Piliavin (1972), who conducted a field experiment in which an individual seemed to collapse in a subway car with blood trickling out of the corner of his mouth. The results of the experiment showed that bystanders were less likely to help when a person (actually a confederate) appearing to be an intern was present than when the "intern" was not present.
- *Deciding on and implementing the form of assistance.* After an individual assumes responsibility for helping, he or she must decide how to provide assistance. Helping can range from very indirect forms of intervention, such as calling the police, to more direct forms, such as giving first aid or taking the victim to a hospital. Most social psychologists use a *rewards-costs approach* to predict the nature of assistance a bystander will choose to provide. The general notion is that the rewards of helping, as perceived by the bystander, must

Figure 14-8 The basic steps of helping.

Altruism is often the only bright side of a natural disaster. In response to the massive flooding that hit the U.S. Midwest, thousands of volunteers came from other areas of the country to pile sandbags, distribute donated food, and otherwise lend a helping hand.

altruism: Helping behaviour that is beneficial to others but clearly requires self-sacrifice.

Why is it so important to develop strategies to deal with anger?

outweigh the costs if helping is to occur, and most research tends to support this notion (Bell et al., 1995).

After the nature of assistance is determined, one step remains: the actual implementation of the assistance. A rewards-costs analysis suggests that the least costly form of implementation is the most likely to be used. However, this is not always the case: In some situations, people behave altruistically. **Altruism** is helping behaviour that is beneficial to others but clearly requires self-sacrifice. For example, an instance in which a person runs into a burning house to rescue a stranger's child might be considered altruistic, particularly when compared with the alternative of simply calling the fire department (Batson, 1991; Shapiro & Gabbard, 1994).

Some research suggests that people who intervene in emergency situations tend to possess certain personality characteristics that differentiate them from nonhelpers. For example, helpers are more self-assured, sympathetic, and emotionally understanding, and they have greater *empathy* (a personality trait in which someone observing another person experiences the emotions of that person) than nonhelpers (Batson et al., 1995; Sibicky, Schroeder, & Dovidio, 1995).

Still, most social psychologists agree that no single set of attributes differentiates helpers from nonhelpers. For the most part, temporary situational factors (such as the mood we're in) determine whether we will intervene in a situation requiring aid (Eisenberg, 1991; Knight et al., 1994; Bersoff, 1999).

BECOMING AN INFORMED CONSUMER OF PSYCHOLOGY

Dealing with Anger Effectively

At one time or another, almost everyone feels angry. The anger might result from a frustrating situation, or it could be due to the behaviour of another individual. How we deal with such anger might determine the difference between a promotion and a lost job or a broken relationship and one that mends itself.

Social psychologists who have studied the topic suggest that there are several good ways to deal with anger, strategies that maximize the potential for positive consequences (Deffenbacher, 1988, 1996; Bass, 1996; Nelson & Finch, 2000). Among the most useful strategies are the following:

- *Look again at the anger-provoking situation from the perspective of others.* By taking others' point of view, you might be able to understand the situation better, and with increased understanding you might become more tolerant of the apparent shortcomings of others.
- *Minimize the importance of the situation.* Does it really matter that someone is driving too slowly and that you'll be late to an appointment as a result? Reinterpret the situation in a way that is less bothersome.
- *Fantasize about getting even—but don't act on it.* Fantasy provides a safety valve. In your fantasies, you can yell at that unfair professor all you want and suffer no consequences at all. However, don't spend too much time brooding: Fantasize, but then move on.
- *Relax.* By teaching yourself the kind of relaxation techniques used in systematic desensitization (see Table 13-2 in the previous chapter), you can help reduce your reactions to anger. In turn, your anger might dissipate.

No matter which of these strategies you try, above all, don't ignore your anger. People who always strive to suppress their anger can experience a variety of unhappy consequences, such as self-condemnation, frustration, and even physical illness (Engebretson & Stoney, 1995; Sharma, Ghosh, & Spielberger, 1995).

Evaluate

1. We tend to like people who are similar to us. True or false?
2. Which of the following sets are the three components of love proposed by Sternberg?
   a. Passion, closeness, sexuality
   b. Attraction, desire, complementarity
   c. Passion, intimacy, decision/commitment
   d. Commitment, caring, sexuality
3. Based on the research evidence, which of the following might be the best way to reduce the amount of fighting a young boy does?
   a. Take him to the gym and let him work out on the boxing equipment.
   b. Take him to see *The Matrix* several times in the hope that it will provide catharsis.
   c. Reward him if he doesn't fight during a certain period.
   d. Ignore it and let it die out naturally.
4. If a person in a crowd does not help in an apparent emergency situation because many other people are present, that person is falling victim to the phenomenon of _____ ___ _____.

Answers to Evaluate Questions

1. True 2. c 3. c 4. diffusion of responsibility

Rethink

1. Can love be studied scientifically? Is there an elusive quality to love that makes it at least partially unknowable? How would you define "falling in love"? How would you study it?
2. How would the aggression of a Marc Lepine, who at the age of 25 took an automatic gun to the University of Montreal and killed 14 young women engineering students and himself, be interpreted by each of the three main approaches to the study of aggression: the instinct approach, the frustration-aggression approach, and the observational learning approach? Do you think any of these approaches fits the Lepine case better than the others?

Looking Back

What are attitudes and how are they formed, maintained, and changed?

- Social psychology is the study of the ways in which people's thoughts, feelings, and actions are affected by others, and the nature and causes of individual behaviour in social situations. (p. 458)
- Attitudes are learned predispositions to respond in a favourable or unfavourable manner to a particular object. (p. 458)
- Cognitive dissonance occurs when two cognitions—attitudes or thoughts—contradict each other and are held simultaneously by an individual. To resolve the contradiction, the person might modify the cognition, change its importance, or deny a link, thereby bringing about a reduction in dissonance. (p. 460)

How do we form impressions of what others are like and of the causes of their behaviour?

- Social cognition involves the processes that underlie our understanding of the social world. Schemas help us organize information about people and social experiences in memory and allow us to interpret and categorize information about others. (p. 460)
- People form impressions of others in part through the use of central traits, personality characteristics that are given unusually heavy weight when an impression is formed. (p. 461)
- Information-processing approaches have found that we tend to average sets of traits to form an overall impression. (p. 462)
- Attribution theory tries to explain how we understand the causes of behaviour, particularly with respect to situational or dispositional factors. (p. 463)

What biases influence how we view others' behaviour?

- Even though logical processes are involved, attribution is still prone to error. For instance, the fundamental attribution error is the tendency to over-attribute others' behaviour to dispositional causes, and the corresponding failure to recognize the importance of situational causes. (p. 464)
- Other biases include the halo effect and the assumed-similarity bias. (p. 464)

What are the major sources and tactics of social influence?

- Social influence is the area of social psychology concerned with situations in which the actions of an individual or group affect the behaviour of others. (p. 467)
- Conformity refers to changes in behaviour or attitudes that occur as the result of a desire to follow the beliefs or standards of others. (p. 467)
- Compliance is behaviour that occurs as a result of direct social pressure. Tactics for eliciting compliance include the foot-in-the-door, door-in-the-face, that's-not-all, and not-so-free-sample techniques. (p. 468)
- Obedience is a change in behaviour in response to the commands of others. (p. 469)

What are stereotypes, prejudice, and discrimination?

- Stereotypes are generalized beliefs and expectations about social groups and their members. (p. 472)
- Prejudice is the negative (or positive) evaluation of groups and their members. (p. 472)
- Stereotyping and prejudice can lead to discrimination, negative behaviour toward members of a particular group. (p. 472)

- Self-fulfilling prophecies are expectations about the occurrence of future events or behaviours that increase the likelihood that the events or behaviours will actually occur. (p. 473)
- According to social learning approaches, people learn stereotyping and prejudice by observing the behaviour of parents, other adults, and peers. (p. 473)

How can we reduce prejudice and discrimination?

- Ways to reduce prejudice and discrimination include increasing contact, making positive values against prejudice apparent, and providing positive information about the target of the attribution or stereotype. (p. 474)
- Education is an important factor in combatting intolerance. Extensive research done in Canada on second-language learning has demonstrated that people who learn a second language tend to be tolerant of diversity. (p. 474)

Why are we attracted to certain people, and what progression do social relationships generally follow?

- Among the primary determinants of liking are proximity, mere exposure, similarity, and physical attractiveness. (p. 476)
- Loving is distinguished from liking by the presence of intense physiological arousal, an all-encompassing interest in the other, fantasies about the other, rapid swings of emotion, fascination, sexual desire, exclusiveness, and strong feelings of caring. (p. 477)
- Love can be categorized into two types (passionate and companionate). In addition, the components of love—intimacy, passion, and decision/commitment—combine to form seven different types of love. (p. 477)

What factors underlie aggression and prosocial behaviour?

- Aggression is intentional infliction of injury or harm on another person. (p. 478)
- Explanations of aggression include instinct approaches, frustration-aggression theory, and observational learning. (p. 478)
- Helping behaviour in emergencies is determined in part by the phenomenon of diffusion of responsibility, which results in a lower likelihood of helping when more people are present. (p. 481)
- Deciding to help is the outcome of a four-stage process consisting of noticing a possible need for help, interpreting the situation as requiring aid, assuming responsibility for taking action, and deciding on and implementing a form of assistance. (p. 481)

Key Terms and Concepts

social psychology (p. 458)

attitudes (p. 458)

central-route processing (p. 459)

peripheral-route processing (p. 459)

cognitive dissonance (p. 460)

social cognition (p. 461)

schemas (p. 461)

central traits (p. 462)

attribution theory (p. 463)

situational causes (of behaviour) (p. 464)

dispositional causes (of behaviour) (p. 464)

fundamental attribution error (p. 464)

halo effect (p. 464)

assumed-similarity bias (p. 464)

social influence (p. 467)

conformity (p. 467)

status (p. 467)

social supporter (p. 468)

compliance (p. 468)

industrial-organizational (I/O) psychology (p. 469)

obedience (p. 469)

Psychology on the Web

1. Find examples on the Web of advertisements or other persuasive messages using central-route processing and peripheral-route processing. What type of persuasion appears to be more prevalent on the Web? For what type of persuasion does the Web appear to be most suited? Is there a difference between Web-based advertising and other forms of advertising?

2. Is "hate crimes legislation" a good idea? Use the Web to find at least two discussions of hate crimes legislation—one in favour and one opposed—and summarize in writing the main issues and arguments presented. Using your knowledge of prejudice and aggression, evaluate the arguments for and against hate crimes legislation. State your opinion about whether this type of legislation is advisable.

Epilogue

In this chapter we have touched on some of the major ideas, research topics, and experimental findings of social psychology. We have examined how people form, maintain, and change attitudes; and how they form impressions of others and assign attributions to them. We have also seen how groups, through conformity and tactics of compliance, can influence individuals' actions and attitudes. Finally, we discussed interpersonal relationships, including both liking and loving, and we looked at the two sides of a coin that represent the extremes of social behaviour: aggression and prosocial behaviour.

Turn back to the prologue of this chapter, which describes reactions to the death of Pierre Trudeau. Use your understanding of social psychology to consider the following questions.

1. Trudeau was a powerful advocate for bilingualism and multiculturalism. Can you discuss, in terms of the findings regarding persuasion, the renewed attention that these matters received following his death?

2. To which biases, if any, do you think people's attitudes toward Pierre Trudeau might have been subject?

3. Trudeau's son Justin delivered a powerful and very personal eulogy for his father. How would the discussion on impression formation explain why people were suggesting that he would follow his late father into politics?

Glossary

a

absolute threshold The smallest intensity of a stimulus that must be present for the stimulus to be detected (Ch. 3)

accommodate To alter existing schemas to allow for new knowledge or experience (Ch. 9)

achievement test A test designed to determine a person's level of knowledge in a given subject area (Ch. 7)

action potential An electric nerve impulse that travels through a neuron when it is set off by a "trigger," changing the neuron's charge from negative to positive (Ch. 2)

activation-synthesis theory Hobson's theory that the brain produces random electrical energy during REM sleep that stimulates memories lodged in various portions of the brain (Ch. 4)

activity theory of aging A theory that holds that the elderly who age most successfully are those who maintain the interests and activities they had during middle age (Ch. 9)

adaptation An adjustment in sensory capacity following prolonged exposure to stimuli (Ch. 3)

addictive drugs Drugs that produce a biological or psychological dependence in the user; withdrawal from them leads to a craving for the drug that in some cases can be nearly irresistible (Ch. 4)

adolescence The developmental stage between childhood and adulthood (Ch. 9)

age of viability The point at which the fetus can survive if born prematurely (Ch. 9)

aggression The intentional infliction of injury or harm on another person (Ch. 14)

algorithm A rule that, if applied appropriately, guarantees a solution to a problem (Ch. 7)

all-or-none law The rule that neurons are either on or off (Ch. 2)

altruism Helping behaviour that is beneficial to others but clearly requires self-sacrifice (Ch. 14)

anal stage According to Freud, a stage from 12 to 18 months to 3 years of age, in which a child's pleasure is centred on the anus (Ch. 10)

androgens Male sex hormones secreted by the testes (Ch. 8)

anorexia nervosa A severe eating disorder in which people may refuse to eat, while denying that their behaviour and appearance—which can become skeletonlike—are unusual (Ch. 8)

antianxiety drugs Drugs that can reduce a person's level of anxiety, essentially by reducing excitability and increasing feelings of well-being (Ch. 13)

antidepressant drugs Medication that improves a depressed patient's mood and feeling of well-being (Ch. 13)

antipsychotic drugs Drugs that temporarily reduce psychotic symptoms such as agitation, overactivity, hallucinations, and delusions (Ch. 13)

antisocial personality disorder A disorder in which individuals tend to display no regard for the moral and ethical rules of society or the rights of others (Ch. 12)

anxiety disorder Anxiety with no obvious external cause that impairs daily functioning (Ch. 12)

aptitude test A test designed to predict a person's ability in a particular area or line of work (Ch. 7)

archival research Research in which existing data, such as census documents, college records, or newspaper clippings, are examined to test a hypothesis (Ch. 1)

arousal approaches to motivation The belief that we try to maintain a certain level of stimulation and activity, increasing or reducing them as necessary (Ch. 8)

assimilate To interpret new information by assigning it to existing schemas (Ch. 9)

association areas One of the major areas of the brain; the site of the higher mental processes such as thought, language, memory, and speech (Ch. 2)

associative models of memory Models of memory as consisting of mental representations of clusters of interconnected information (Ch. 6)

assumed-similarity bias The tendency to think of people as being similar to oneself, even when meeting them for the first time (Ch. 14)

attachment The positive emotional bond that develops between a child and a particular individual (Ch. 9)

attention deficit hyperactivity disorder (ADHD) A learning disability marked by inattention, impulsiveness, a low tolerance for frustration, and a great deal of inappropriate activity (Ch. 12)

attitudes Learned predispositions to respond in a favourable or unfavourable manner to a particular person, behaviour, belief, or thing (Ch. 14)

attribution theory The theory of personality that seeks to explain how we decide, on the basis of samples of an individual's behaviour, what the specific causes of that person's behaviour are (Ch. 14)

authoritarian parents Parents who are rigid and punitive and value unquestioning obedience from their children (Ch. 9)

authoritative parents Parents who are firm, set clear limits, reason with their children, and explain things to them (Ch. 9)

autobiographical memories Our recollections of circumstances and episodes from our own lives (Ch. 6)

autonomic division The part of the nervous system that controls involuntary movement (the actions of the heart, glands, lungs, and other organs) (Ch. 2)

autonomy-versus-shame-and-doubt stage The period during which, according to Erikson, toddlers (ages 18 months to 3 years) develop independence and autonomy if exploration and freedom are encouraged, or shame and self-doubt if they are restricted and overprotected (Ch. 9)

axon The part of the neuron that carries messages destined for other neurons (Ch. 2)

b

babble Speechlike but meaningless sounds made by children from the ages of around 3 months through 1 year (Ch. 7)

background stressors ("daily hassles") Everyday annoyances, such as being stuck in traffic, that cause minor irritations that can have long-term ill effects if they continue or are compounded by other stressful events (Ch. 11)

basic skills approach An approach to early reading instruction that emphasizes the recognition of words in isolation (Ch. 7)

basilar membrane A vibrating structure that runs through the centre of the cochlea, dividing it into a upper and a lower chamber, and containing sense receptors for sound (Ch. 3)

behaviour modification A formalized technique for promoting the frequency of desirable behaviours and decreasing the incidence of unwanted ones (Ch. 5)

behavioural assessment Direct measures of an individual's behaviour used to describe characteristics indicative of personality (Ch. 10)

behavioural genetics The study of the effects of heredity on behaviour (Ch. 2)

behavioural perspective The perspective that looks at the behaviour itself as the problem (Ch. 1, 12)

behavioural treatment approaches Treatment approaches that build upon the basic processes of learning, such as reinforcement and extinction (Ch. 13)

biofeedback A procedure in which a person learns to control through conscious thought internal physiological processes such as blood pressure, heart and respiration rate, skin temperature, sweating, and constriction of particular muscles (Ch. 2)

biological and evolutionary approaches to personality The theory that important components of personality are inherited (Ch. 10)

biological perspective The approach that views behaviour from the perspective of biological functioning (Ch. 1)

biomedical therapy   Therapy that relies on drugs and other medical procedures to improve psychological functioning (Ch. 13)

biopsychologists (or behavioural neuroscientists)   Psychologists who specialize in considering the ways in which biological structures and functions of the body affect behaviour (Ch. 2)

bipolar disorder   A disorder in which a person alternates between periods of euphoric feelings of mania and periods of depression (Ch. 12)

bisexuals   Persons who are sexually attracted to people of the same sex and people of the opposite sex (Ch. 8)

borderline personality disorder   A disorder in which individuals have difficulty developing a secure sense of who they are (Ch. 12)

bottom-up processing   Perception that consists of recognizing and processing information about the individual components of the stimuli (Ch. 3)

Broca's aphasia   Impaired speech function of language resulting from injury to the brain's association areas (Ch. 2)

bulimia   A disorder in which a person binges on incredibly large quantities of food, then purges by vomiting or by using laxatives (Ch. 8)

c

Cannon-Bard theory of emotion   The belief that both physiological and emotional arousal are produced simultaneously by the same nerve stimulus (Ch. 8)

case study   An in-depth, intensive investigation of an individual or small group of people (Ch. 1)

cataclysmic events   Strong stressors that occur suddenly, affecting many people at once (e.g., natural disasters) (Ch. 11)

catharsis   The process of discharging built-up aggressive energy (Ch. 14)

central core   The "old brain," which controls such basic functions as eating and sleeping and is common to all vertebrates (Ch. 2)

central nervous system (CNS)   The system that includes the brain and spinal cord (Ch. 2)

central-route processing   Message interpretation characterized by thoughtful consideration of the issues and arguments used to persuade (Ch. 14)

central traits   The major traits considered in forming impressions of others (Ch. 14)

cerebellum (ser uh BELL um)   The part of the brain that controls bodily balance (Ch. 2)

cerebral cortex   The "new brain," responsible for the most sophisticated information processing in the brain; contains the lobes (Ch. 2)

chromosomes   Rod-shaped structures that contain the basic hereditary information (Ch. 9)

chunk   A meaningful grouping of stimuli that can be stored as a unit in short-term memory (Ch. 6)

circadian rhythms   Biological processes that occur repeatedly on approximately a 24-hour cycle (Ch. 4)

classical conditioning   A type of learning in which a neutral stimulus comes to bring about a response after it is paired with a stimulus that naturally brings about that response (Ch. 5)

client-centred therapy   Therapy in which the goal is to reach one's potential for self-actualization (Ch. 13)

cochlea (KOKE lee uh)   A coiled tube in the ear filled with fluid that vibrates in response to sound (Ch. 3)

cognitive approaches of motivation   The theory suggesting that motivation is a product of people's thoughts and expectations—their cognitions (Ch. 8)

cognitive-behavioural approach   An approach used by cognitive therapists that attempts to change the way people think through the use of basic principles of learning (Ch. 13)

cognitive development   The process by which a child's understanding of the world changes as a function of age and experience (Ch. 9)

cognitive dissonance   The conflict that occurs when a person holds two attitudes or thoughts (referred to as cognitions) that contradict each other (Ch. 14)

cognitive map   A mental representation of spatial locations and directions (Ch. 5)

cognitive perspective   The approach that focuses on how people think, understand, and know about the world (Ch. 1)

cognitive perspective   The perspective that people's thoughts and beliefs are a central component of abnormal behaviour (Ch. 12)

cognitive psychology   The branch of psychology that focuses on the study of mental processes (Ch. 7)

cognitive learning theory   The study of the thought processes that underlie learning (Ch. 5)

cognitive treatment approaches   Approaches to treatment that teach people to think in more adaptive ways by changing their dysfunctional cognitions about the world and themselves (Ch. 13)

collective unconscious   A set of influences we inherit from our own particular ancestors, the whole human race, and even animal ancestors from the distant evolutionary past (Ch. 10)

community psychology   A branch of psychology that focuses on the prevention and minimization of psychological disorders in the community (Ch. 13)

companionate love   The strong affection we have for those with whom our lives are deeply involved (Ch. 14)

compliance   Conforming behaviour that occurs in response to direct social pressure (Ch. 14)

compulsion   An irresistible urge to repeatedly carry out some act that seems strange and unreasonable (Ch. 12)

concepts   Categorizations of objects, events, or people that share common properties (Ch. 7)

concrete operational stage   According to Piaget, the period from 7 to 12 years of age, which is characterized by logical thought and a loss of egocentrism (Ch. 9)

conditioned response (CR)   A response that, after conditioning, follows a previously neutral stimulus (e.g., salivation at the ringing of a bell) (Ch. 5)

conditioned stimulus (CS)   A once-neutral stimulus that has been paired with an unconditioned stimulus to bring about a response formerly caused only by the unconditioned stimulus (Ch. 5)

cones   Cone-shaped, light-sensitive receptor cells in the retina that are responsible for sharp focus and colour perception, particularly in bright light (Ch. 3)

conformity   A change in behaviour or attitudes brought about by a desire to follow the beliefs or standards of other people (Ch. 14)

consciousness   The awareness of the sensations, thoughts, and feelings being experienced at a given moment (Ch. 4)

constructive processes   Processes in which memories are influenced by the meaning we give to events (Ch. 6)

continuous reinforcement schedule   Reinforcement of behaviour every time it occurs (Ch. 5)

control group   A group that receives no treatment in an experiment (Ch. 1)

convergent thinking   The ability to produce responses that are based primarily on knowledge and logic (Ch. 7)

conversion disorder   A major somatoform disorder that involves an actual physical disturbance, such as the inability to use a sensory organ or the complete or partial inability to move an arm or leg (Ch. 12)

coping   Efforts to control, reduce, or learn to tolerate the threats that lead to stress (Ch. 11)

correlational research   Research that examines the relationship between two sets of variables to determine whether they are associated, or "correlated" (Ch. 1)

creativity   The combining of responses or ideas in novel ways (Ch. 7)

cross-sectional research   A research method in which people of different ages are compared at the same point in time (Ch. 9)

crystallized intelligence   The accumulation of information, skills, and strategies learned through experience and that can be applied in problem-solving situations (Ch. 7)

culture-fair IQ test   A test that does not discriminate against members of any minority group (Ch. 7)

d

daydreams   Fantasies that people construct while awake (Ch. 4)

decay   The loss of information in memory through its nonuse (Ch. 6)

declarative memory   Memory for factual information: names, faces, dates, and the like (Ch. 6)

defence mechanisms   Unconscious strategies people use to reduce anxiety by concealing the source of the anxiety from themselves and others (Ch. 10, 11)

deinstitutionalization   The transfer of former mental patients from institutions into the community (Ch. 13)

dendrites   A cluster of fibres at one end of a neuron that receive messages from other neurons (Ch. 2)

dependent variable   The variable that is measured and is expected to change as a result of changes caused by the experimenter's manipulation (Ch. 1)

depressants   Drugs that slow down the nervous system (Ch. 4)

developmental psychology   The branch of psychology that studies the patterns of growth and change occurring throughout life (Ch. 9)

Diagnostic and Statistical Manual of Mental Disorders, Fourth Edition (DSM-IV)   The manual of the American Psychiatric Association that presents the diagnostic system used by most Canadian and U.S. mental health professionals to diagnose and classify abnormal behaviour (Ch. 12)

difference threshold   The smallest level of stimulation required to sense that a change in stimulation has occurred (Ch. 3)

diffusion of responsibility   The tendency for people to feel that responsibility for acting is shared, or diffused, among those present (Ch. 14)

discrimination   Negative behaviour toward members of a particular group (Ch. 14)

disengagement theory of aging   A theory that holds that aging is a gradual withdrawal from the world on physical, psychological, and social levels (Ch. 9)

dispositional causes (of behaviour)   A perceived cause of behaviour that is based on internal traits or personality factors (Ch. 14)

dissociative amnesia   A disorder in which the person has significant, selective memory loss (Ch. 12)

dissociative disorder   Psychological dysfunctions characterized by the separation of critical personality facets that are normally integrated, allowing stress avoidance by escape (Ch. 12)

dissociative fugue   A form of amnesia in which people take sudden, impulsive trips, sometimes assuming a new identity (Ch. 12)

dissociative identity disorder (multiple personality)   A disorder in which a person displays characteristics of two or more distinct personalities (Ch. 12)

divergent thinking   The ability to generate unusual, yet appropriate, responses to problems or questions (Ch. 7)

double standard   The view that premarital sex is permissible for males but not for females (Ch. 8)

dreams-for-survival theory   The theory that dreams permit information that is critical for our daily survival to be reconsidered and reprocessed during sleep (Ch. 4)

drive   Motivational tension, or arousal, that energizes behaviour in order to fulfill some need (Ch. 8)

drive-reduction approaches to motivation   A theory suggesting that when people lack some basic biological requirement such as water, a drive to obtain that requirement (in this case, the thirst drive) is produced (Ch. 8)

drug therapy   Control of psychological problems through drugs (Ch. 13)

e

eardrum   The part of the ear that vibrates when sound waves hit it (Ch. 3)

echoic memory   Memory of auditory information coming from the ears (Ch. 6)

eclectic approach to therapy   An approach to therapy that uses techniques taken from a variety of treatment methods, rather than just one method (Ch. 13)

ego   The part of the personality that provides a buffer between the id and the outside world (Ch. 10)

egocentric thought   A way of thinking in which the child views the world entirely from his or her own perspective (Ch. 9)

ego-integrity-versus-despair stage   According to Erikson, a period from late adulthood until death during which we review our life's accomplishments and failures (Ch. 9)

electroconvulsive therapy (ECT)   A procedure in which an electric current of 70 to 150 volts is briefly administered to a patient's head, causing a loss of consciousness and often seizures (Ch. 13)

embryo   A developed zygote that has a rudimentary heart, brain, and other organs (Ch. 9)

emotional intelligence   The ability to understand emotions in oneself and others and to regulate emotions in order to make life better (Ch. 7)

emotions   Feelings that generally have both physiological and cognitive elements and that influence behaviour (Ch. 8)

endocrine system   A chemical communication network that sends messages throughout the nervous system via the bloodstream (Ch. 2)

episodic memory   Memory for the biographical details of our individual lives (Ch. 6)

estrogen   A female sex hormone (Ch. 8)

evolutionary psychology   The branch of psychology that seeks to identify behaviour patterns that result from our genetic inheritance from our ancestors (Ch. 2)

excitatory message   A chemical message that makes it more likely that a receiving neuron will fire and an action potential will travel down its axons (Ch. 2)

experiment   The investigation of the relationship between two (or more) variables by deliberately producing a change in one variable in a situation and observing the

effects of that change on other aspects of the situation (Ch. 1)

experimental bias   Factors that distort how the independent variable affects the dependent variable in an experiment (Ch. 1)

experimental group   Any group receiving a treatment in an experiment (Ch. 1)

experimental manipulation   The change that an experimenter deliberately produces in a situation (Ch. 1)

explicit memory   Intentional or conscious recollection of information (Ch. 6)

extinction   The decrease in frequency, and eventual disappearance, of a previously conditioned response; one of the basic phenomena of learning (Ch. 5)

extramarital sex   Sexual activity between a married person and someone who is not his or her spouse (Ch. 8)

f

family therapy   An approach that focuses on the family and its dynamics (Ch. 13)

feature analysis   A theory of perception according to which we perceive a shape, pattern, object, or scene by reacting first to the individual elements that make it up (Ch. 3)

feature detection   The activation of neurons in the cortex by visual stimuli of specific shapes or patterns (Ch. 3)

fetus   A developing child, from 8 weeks after conception until birth (Ch. 9)

fixation   Conflicts or concerns that persist beyond the developmental period in which they first occur (Ch. 10)

fixed-interval schedule   A schedule that provides reinforcement for a response only if a fixed time period has elapsed, making overall rates of response relatively low (Ch. 5)

fixed-ratio schedule   A schedule whereby reinforcement is given only after a certain number of responses are made (Ch. 5)

flashbulb memories   Memories of a specific, important, or surprising event that are so vivid, they are like a snapshot of the event (Ch. 6)

fluid intelligence   Intelligence that reflects information-processing capabilities, reasoning, and memory (Ch. 7)

formal operational stage   According to Piaget, the period from age 12 to adulthood, which is characterized by abstract thought (Ch. 9)

frequency theory of hearing   The theory that the entire basilar membrane acts like a microphone, vibrating as a whole in response to a sound (Ch. 3)

frustration   The thwarting or blocking of some ongoing, goal-directed behaviour (Ch. 14)

functional fixedness   The tendency to think of an object only in terms of its typical use (Ch. 7)

functionalism   An early approach to psychology that concentrated on what the mind does—the functions of mental activity—

and the role of behaviour in allowing people to adapt to their environments (Ch. 1)

fundamental attribution error A tendency to attribute others' behaviour to dispositional causes and the tendency to minimize the importance of situational causes (Ch. 14)

g

g or g-factor The single, general factor for mental ability that was assumed to underlie intelligence in some early theories of intelligence (Ch. 7)

gate-control theory of pain The theory that a gate-like mechanism in the spinal column controls the flow of pain stimulation to the brain (Ch. 3)

general adaptation syndrome (GAS) A theory developed by Selye that suggests that a person's response to stress consists of three stages: alarm and mobilization, resistance, and exhaustion (Ch. 11)

generalized anxiety disorder Long-term, persistent anxiety and worry (Ch. 12)

generativity-versus-stagnation stage According to Erikson, a period in middle adulthood during which we take stock of our contributions to family and society (Ch. 9)

genes The parts of the chromosomes through which genetic information is transmitted (Ch. 9)

genetic preprogramming theories of aging Theories that hold that there is a built-in time limit to the reproduction of human cells, and that after a certain time they are no longer able to divide (Ch. 9)

genital stage According to Freud, the period from puberty until death, marked by mature sexual behaviour (i.e., sexual intercourse) (Ch. 10)

gestalt laws of organization A series of principles that describe how we organize bits and pieces of information into meaningful wholes (Ch. 3)

gestalt (geh SHTALLT) psychology An approach to psychology that focuses on the organization of perception and thinking in a "whole" sense, rather than on the individual elements of perception (Ch. 1)

gestalt therapy An approach to therapy that attempts to integrate a client's thoughts, feelings, and behaviour into a unified whole (Ch. 13)

glial cells Cells that nourish and insulate neurons (Ch. 2)

grammar The system of rules that determine how our thoughts can be expressed (Ch. 7)

group therapy Therapy in which people discuss problems in a group (Ch. 13)

h

habituation The decrease in the response to a stimulus that occurs after repeated presentations of the same stimulus (Ch. 9)

hair cells Tiny cells covering the basilar membrane that, when bent by vibrations entering the cochlea, transmit neural messages to the brain (Ch. 3)

hallucinogen A drug that is capable of producing hallucinations, or changes in the perceptual process (Ch. 4)

halo effect A phenomenon in which an initial perception of a person as having positive traits produces the expectation that the person has other uniformly positive characteristics (Ch. 14)

hardiness A personality characteristic associated with a lower rate of stress-related illness, consisting of three components: commitment, challenge, and control (Ch. 11)

health psychology The branch of psychology that investigates the psychological factors related to wellness and illness, including the prevention, diagnosis, and treatment of medical problems (Ch. 11)

hemispheres The two symmetrical left and right halves of the brain; each controls the side of the body opposite to it (Ch. 2)

heritability A measure of the degree to which a characteristic is related to genetic, inherited factors (Ch. 7)

heterosexuality Sexual attraction and behaviour directed to the opposite sex (Ch. 8)

homeostasis The body's tendency to maintain a steady internal state (Ch. 8)

homosexuals Persons who are sexually attracted to people of their own sex (Ch. 8)

hormones Chemicals that circulate through the blood and affect the functioning or growth of other parts of the body (Ch. 2)

humanistic approaches to personality The theory that people are basically good and tend to grow to higher levels of functioning (Ch. 10)

humanistic perspective The approach that suggests that all individuals naturally strive to grow, develop, and be in control of their lives and behaviour (Ch. 1)

humanistic perspective The perspective that emphasizes people's responsibility for their own behaviour, even when such behaviour is abnormal (Ch. 12)

humanistic therapy Therapy in which the underlying assumption is that people have control of their behaviour, can make choices about their lives, and are essentially responsible for solving their own problems (Ch. 13)

hypnosis A trancelike state of heightened susceptibility to the suggestions of others (Ch. 4)

hypochondriasis A disorder involving having a constant fear of illness and a preoccupation with one's health (Ch. 12)

hypothalamus A tiny part of the brain, located below the thalamus of the brain, that maintains homeostasis and produces and regulates vital, basic behaviour such as eating, drinking, and sexual behaviour (Ch. 2)

hypothesis A prediction, stemming from a theory, stated in a way that allows it to be tested (Ch. 1)

i

iconic memory Memory of information from our visual system (Ch. 6)

id The raw, unorganized, inborn part of personality, whose sole purpose is to reduce tension created by primitive drives related to hunger, sex, aggression, and irrational impulses (Ch. 10)

identical twins Twins who are genetically identical (Ch. 9)

identification The process of trying to be like another person as much as possible, imitating that person's behaviour and adopting similar beliefs and values (Ch. 10)

identity The distinguishing character of the individual: who each of us is, what our roles are, and what we are capable of (Ch. 9)

identity-versus-role-confusion stage According to Erikson, a time in adolescence of major testing to determine one's unique qualities (Ch. 9)

implicit memory Memories people are not consciously aware of, but that can affect their subsequent performance and behaviour (Ch. 6)

incentive approaches to motivation The theory suggesting that motivation stems from the desire to obtain valued external goals, or incentives (Ch. 8)

independent variable The variable that is manipulated by an experimenter (Ch. 1)

industrial-organizational (I/O) psychology The branch of psychology that focuses on work and job-related issues, including productivity, job satisfaction, decision making, and consumer behaviour (Ch. 14)

industry-versus-inferiority stage According to Erikson, the last stage of childhood, during which children ages 6 to 12 years either develop positive social interactions with others or feel inadequate and become less sociable (Ch. 9)

inferiority complex According to Adler, a complex developed by adults who have not been able to overcome the feelings of inferiority they developed as children, when they were small and limited in their knowledge about the world (Ch. 10)

information processing The way people take in, use, and store information (Ch. 9)

informed consent A document signed by participants affirming that they have been told the basic outlines of a research study and are aware of what their participation will involve (Ch. 1)

inhibitory message A chemical message that prevents a receiving neuron from firing (Ch. 2)

initiative-versus-guilt stage According to Erikson, the period during which children ages 3 to 6 years experience conflict between independence of action and the sometimes negative results of that action (Ch. 9)

insight A sudden awareness of the relationships among various elements that had previously appeared to be independent of one another (Ch. 7)

instincts Inborn patterns of behaviour that are biologically determined rather than learned (Ch. 8)

intellectual disability An impaired ability to learn (Ch. 7)

intellectually gifted Having an IQ score above 130; about 2 to 4 percent of the population (Ch. 7)

intelligence The capacity to understand the world, think rationally, and use resources effectively when faced with challenges (Ch. 7)

intelligence quotient (IQ) A score that takes into account an individual's mental and chronological ages (Ch. 7)

intelligence tests Tests devised to identify a person's level of intelligence (Ch. 7)

interference The phenomenon by which information in memory displaces or blocks out other information, preventing its recall (Ch. 6)

interneurons Neurons that connect sensory and motor neurons, carrying messages between the two (Ch. 2)

interpersonal attraction (or close relationships) Positive feelings for others; liking and loving (Ch. 14)

intimacy-versus-isolation stage According to Erikson, a period during early adulthood that focuses on developing close relationships (Ch. 9)

introspection A procedure used to study the structure of the mind, in which subjects are asked to describe in detail what they are experiencing when they are exposed to a stimulus (Ch. 1)

j

James-Lange theory of emotion The belief that emotional experience is a reaction to bodily events occurring as a result of an external situation ("I feel sad because I am crying") (Ch. 8)

just noticeable difference The minimum stimulation required to detect the difference between two stimuli (Ch. 3)

l

language The communication of information through symbols arranged according to systematic rules (Ch. 7)

language acquisition device A hypothesized neural system of the brain for understanding language (Ch. 7)

latency period According to Freud, the period between the phallic stage and puberty during which children temporarily put aside their sexual interests (Ch. 10)

latent content of dreams According to Freud, the "disguised" or real meanings of dreams, hidden by more obvious subjects (Ch. 4)

latent learning Learning in which a new behaviour is acquired but is not demonstrated until reinforcement is provided (Ch. 5)

lateralization The dominance of one hemisphere of the brain in specific functions (Ch. 2)

learned helplessness A state in which people conclude that unpleasant or aversive stimuli cannot be controlled—a view of the world that becomes so ingrained that they cease trying to remedy their aversive circumstances, even if they actually could exert some influence on them (Ch. 11)

learning A relatively permanent change in behaviour brought about by experience (Ch. 5)

learning-theory approach The theory suggesting that language acquisition follows the principles of reinforcement and conditioning (Ch. 7)

levels-of-processing theory The theory of memory that emphasizes the degree to which new material is mentally analyzed (Ch. 6)

life review The process in which people in late adulthood examine and evaluate their lives (Ch. 9)

limbic system The part of the brain located outside the "new brain" that controls eating, aggression, and reproduction (Ch. 2)

lithium A mineral salt used to treat bipolar disorders (Ch. 13)

lobes The four major sections of the cerebral cortex: frontal, parietal, temporal, and occipital (Ch. 2)

long-term memory Memory that stores information on a relatively permanent basis (Ch. 6)

m

major depression A severe form of depression that interferes with concentration, decision making, and sociability (Ch. 12)

mania An extended state of intense, wild elation (Ch. 12)

manifest content of dreams According to Freud, the overt story line of dreams (Ch. 4)

masturbation Sexual self-stimulation (Ch. 8)

means-end analysis Repeated testing for differences between the desired outcome and what currently exists (Ch. 7)

medical perspective The perspective that the root cause of abnormal behaviour will be found in a physical examination of the individual, which might reveal a hormonal imbalance, a chemical deficiency, or a brain injury (Ch. 12)

meditation A learned technique for refocusing attention that brings about an altered state of consciousness (Ch. 4)

memory The process by which we encode, store, and retrieve information (Ch. 6)

memory trace A physical change in the brain that occurs when new material is learned (Ch. 6)

menopause The point at which women stop menstruating and are no longer fertile (Ch. 9)

mental age The average age of individuals who achieve a particular level of performance on a test (Ch. 7)

mental images Representations in the mind of an object or event (Ch. 7)

mental retardation Having significantly below-average intellectual functioning and limitations in at least two areas of adaptive functioning (Ch. 7)

mental set The tendency for old patterns of problem solving to persist (Ch. 7)

metabolism The rate at which food is converted to energy and expended by the body (Ch. 8)

metacognition An awareness and understanding of one's own cognitive processes (Ch. 9)

Minnesota Multiphasic Personality Inventory-2 (MMPI-2) A test used to identify people with psychological difficulties as well as to predict such behaviour as job performance (Ch. 10)

mood disorder Disturbances in emotional feelings strong enough to interfere with everyday living (Ch. 12)

motivation The factors that direct and energize the behaviour of humans and other organisms (Ch. 8)

motor area The part of the cortex that is largely responsible for the voluntary movement of particular parts of the body (Ch. 2)

motor (efferent) neurons Neurons that communicate information from the nervous system to muscles and glands of the body (Ch. 2)

myelin sheath Specialized cells of fat and protein that wrap themselves around the axon, providing a protective coating (Ch. 2)

n

narcissistic personality disorder A personality disturbance characterized by an exaggerated sense of self-importance (Ch. 12)

narcotics Drugs that increase relaxation and relieve pain and anxiety (Ch. 4)

naturalistic observation Research in which an investigator simply observes some naturally occurring behaviour and does not make a change in the situation (Ch. 1)

nature-nurture issue The issue of the degrees to which environment and heredity influence behaviour and development (Ch. 9)

need for achievement A stable, learned characteristic in which satisfaction is obtained by striving for and attaining a level of excellence (Ch. 8)

need for affiliation An interest in establishing and maintaining relationships with other people (Ch. 8)

need for power A tendency to seek impact, control, or influence over others, and to be seen as a powerful individual (Ch. 8)

negative reinforcer An unpleasant stimulus whose removal leads to an increase in the probability that a preceding response will occur again in the future (Ch. 5)

neo-Freudian psychoanalysts Psychoanalysts who were trained in traditional Freudian theory but who later rejected some of its major points (Ch. 10)

neonate A newborn child (Ch. 9)

neurons Nerve cells that transmit messages to and from the brain and spinal cord (Ch. 2)

neurotransmitters   Chemicals that carry messages across the synapse to the dendrite (and sometimes the cell body) of a receiver neuron (Ch. 2)

neutral stimulus   A stimulus that, before conditioning, does not naturally bring about the response of interest (Ch. 4)

norms   Standards of test performance that permit the comparison of one person's score on the test to the scores of others who have taken the same test (Ch. 7)

O

obedience   Conforming behaviour in reaction to the commands of others (Ch. 14)

obesity   The state of being more than 20 percent above the average weight for a person of one's height (Ch. 8)

object permanence   The awareness that objects—and people—continue to exist even if they are out of sight (Ch. 9)

observational learning   Learning through observing the behaviour of another person called a model (Ch. 5)

obsession   A persistent, unwanted thought or idea that keeps recurring (Ch. 12)

obsessive-compulsive disorder   A disorder characterized by obsessions or compulsions (Ch. 12)

Oedipus conflict   A child's sexual interest in his or her opposite-sex parent, typically resolved through identification with the same-sex parent (Ch. 10)

operant conditioning   Learning in which a voluntary response is strengthened or weakened, depending on its favourable or unfavourable consequences (Ch. 5)

operationalization   The process of translating a hypothesis into specific, testable procedures that can be measured and observed (Ch. 1)

opponent-process theory of colour vision   The theory that receptor cells are linked in pairs, working in opposition to each other (Ch. 3)

optic nerve   A bundle of ganglion axons that carry visual information from the eye to the brain (Ch. 3)

oral stage   According to Freud, a stage from birth to 12 to 18 months, in which an infant's centre of pleasure is the mouth (Ch. 10)

otoliths   Tiny, motion-sensitive crystals within the semicircular canals that sense body acceleration (Ch. 3)

overgeneralization   The phenomenon whereby children apply rules even when their application results in an error (Ch. 7)

overweight   Having a Body Mass Index of 27 or higher (Ch. 8)

ovulation   The point at which an egg is released from the ovaries (Ch. 8)

p

panic disorder   Anxiety that reveals itself in the form of panic attacks that last from a few seconds to as long as several hours (Ch. 12)

parasympathetic division   The part of the autonomic division of the nervous system that acts to calm the body after the emergency situation is resolved (Ch. 2)

partial reinforcement schedule   Reinforcement of behaviour some but not all of the time (Ch. 5)

passionate (or romantic) love   A state of intense absorption in someone that includes intense physiological arousal, psychological interest, and caring for the needs of another (Ch. 14)

perception   The sorting out, interpretation, analysis, and integration of stimuli involving our sense organs and brain (Ch. 3)

peripheral nervous system   The part of the nervous system that includes the autonomic and somatic subdivisions; made up of long axons and dendrites, it branches out from the spinal cord and brain and reaches the extremities of the body (Ch. 2)

peripheral-route processing   Message interpretation characterized by consideration of the source and related general information rather than of the message itself (Ch. 14)

permissive parents   Parents who give their children lax or inconsistent direction and, although warm, require little of them (Ch. 9)

personal stressors   Major life events, such as the death of a family member, that have immediate negative consequences that usually fade with time (Ch. 7)

personality   The pattern of enduring characteristics that differentiates a person—the patterns of behaviours that make each individual unique (Ch. 10)

personality disorder   A mental disorder characterized by a set of inflexible, maladaptive personality traits that keep a person from functioning properly in society (Ch. 12)

phallic stage   According to Freud, a period beginning around age 3 during which a child's interest focuses on the genitals (Ch. 10)

phobias   Intense, irrational fears of specific objects or situations (Ch. 12)

phonemes   The smallest basic sound units (Ch. 7)

phonology   The study of the sound system in language (Ch. 7)

pituitary gland   The "master gland," the major component of the endocrine system, which secretes hormones that control growth (Ch. 2)

place theory of hearing   The theory that different areas of the basilar membrane respond to different frequencies (Ch. 3)

placebo   A false treatment, such as a pill, "drug," or other substance, that has no significant chemical properties or active ingredient (Ch. 1)

plasticity   The capacity of the brain to reorganize following injury (most common in children) (Ch. 2)

positive reinforcer   A stimulus added to the environment that brings about an increase in a preceding response (Ch. 5)

posttraumatic stress disorder (PTSD)   A phenomenon in which people who have been exposed to traumatic events reexperience the original stress event and associated feelings in a variety of ways, including vivid flashbacks or dreams (Ch. 11)

practical intelligence   Intelligence related to overall success in living (Ch. 7)

prejudice   The negative (or positive) evaluations of groups and their members (Ch. 14)

preoperational stage   According to Piaget, the period from 2 to 7 years of age which is characterized by language development (Ch. 9)

priming   A phenomenon in which exposure to a word or concept (called a prime) later makes it easier to recall related information, even when one has no conscious memory of the word or concept (Ch. 6)

principle of conservation   The knowledge that the quantity of a substance remains the same even though its shape or other aspects of its physical appearance might change (Ch. 9)

procedural memory   Memory for skills and habits, such as riding a bike or hitting a baseball (Ch. 6)

progesterone   A female sex hormone (Ch. 8)

projective personality test   A test in which a person is shown an ambiguous stimulus and asked to describe it or tell a story about it (Ch. 10)

prosocial behaviour   Helping behaviour (Ch. 14)

prototypes   Typical, highly representative examples of a concept (Ch. 7)

psychoactive drugs   Drugs that influence a person's emotions, perceptions, and behaviour (Ch. 4)

psychoanalysis   Psychodynamic therapy that involves frequent sessions and can last for many years (Ch. 13)

psychoanalytic perspective   The perspective that abnormal behaviour stems from childhood conflicts over opposing wishes regarding sex and aggression (Ch. 12)

psychoanalytic theory   Freud's theory that unconscious forces act as determinants of personality (Ch. 10)

psychodynamic perspective   The approach based on the belief that behaviour is motivated by unconscious inner forces over which the individual has little control (Ch. 1)

psychodynamic therapy   First suggested by Freud, therapy based on the premise that the primary sources of abnormal behaviour are unresolved past conflicts and the possibility that unacceptable unconscious impulses will enter consciousness (Ch. 13)

psychological tests   Standard measures devised to assess behaviour objectively and used by psychologists to help people make decisions about their lives and understand more about themselves (Ch. 10)

psychology   The scientific study of behaviour and mental processes (Ch. 1)

psychoneuroimmunology (PNI)   The study of the relationships among psychological factors, the immune system, and the brain (Ch. 11)

psychophysics   The study of the relationship between the physical aspects of stimuli and our psychological experience of them (Ch. 3)

psychophysiological disorders Medical problems influenced by an interaction of psychological, emotional, and physical difficulties (Ch. 4)

psychosocial development Development of individuals' interactions and understanding of each other and of their knowledge and understanding of themselves as members of society (Ch. 9)

psychosurgery Brain surgery once used to reduce symptoms of mental disorder (Ch. 13)

psychotherapy Treatment in which a trained professional—a therapist—uses psychological techniques to help someone overcome psychological difficulties and disorders, resolve problems in living, or bring about personal growth (Ch. 13)

puberty The period during which maturation of the sexual organs occurs, beginning at about age 11 or 12 for girls and 13 or 14 for boys (Ch. 9)

punishment A stimulus that decreases the probability that a previous behaviour will occur again (Ch. 5)

r

random assignment to condition A procedure in which participants are assigned to different experimental groups or "conditions" on the basis of chance and chance alone (Ch. 1)

rational-emotive behaviour therapy A form of therapy that attempts to restructure a person's belief system into a more realistic, rational, and logical set of views (Ch. 13)

reactance A negative emotional and cognitive reaction to a restriction of one's freedom that can be associated with medical regimens (Ch. 11)

reciprocity-of-liking effect A tendency to like those who like us (Ch. 14)

reflexes Automatic, involuntary responses to incoming stimuli (Ch. 2)

reflexes Unlearned, involuntary responses that occur automatically in the presence of certain stimuli (Ch. 9)

rehearsal The repetition or elaboration of information that has entered short-term memory (Ch. 6)

reinforcement The process by which a stimulus increases the probability that a preceding behaviour will be repeated (Ch. 5)

reinforcer Any stimulus that increases the probability that a preceding behaviour will occur again (Ch. 5)

reliability A test's measuring consistently what it is supposed to measure (Ch. 7)

REM sleep Sleep stage characterized by increased heart rate, blood pressure, and breathing rate; decreased muscle tone; rapid eye movements; and the experience of dreaming (Ch. 4)

replication The repetition of research, sometimes using other procedures, settings, and other groups of participants, in order to increase confidence in prior findings (Ch. 1)

resting state The state in which there is a negative electrical charge of about −70 millivolts within the neuron (Ch. 2)

reticular formation The part of the brain from the medulla through the pons made up of groups of nerve cells that can immediately activate other parts of the brain to produce general bodily arousal (Ch. 2)

retina The part of the eye that converts the electromagnetic energy of light into useful information for the brain (Ch. 3)

reuptake The reabsorption of neurotransmitters by a terminal button (Ch. 2)

rods Thin, cylindrical receptor cells in the retina that are highly sensitive to light (Ch. 3)

Rorschach test A test by developed by Swiss psychiatrist Hermann Rorschach that consists of showing a series of symmetrical stimuli to people and then asking them to say what the figures represent to them (Ch. 10)

S

Schachter-Singer theory of emotion The belief that emotions are determined jointly by a nonspecific kind of physiological arousal and its interpretation, based on environmental cues (Ch. 8)

schedules of reinforcement The frequency and timing of reinforcement following desired behaviour (Ch. 5)

schemas Organized bodies of information stored in memory that bias the way new information is interpreted, stored, and recalled (Ch. 6)

schemas Concepts that allow us to organize and make sense of our world (Ch. 9)

schemas Sets of cognitions about people and social experiences (Ch. 14)

schizophrenia A class of disorders involving severe distortions of reality (Ch. 12)

self-actualization A state of self-fulfillment in which people realize their highest potential in their own unique way (Ch. 8)

self-actualization According to Rogers, a state of self-fulfillment in which people realize their highest potential (Ch. 10)

self-report measures A method of gathering data about people by asking them questions about a sample of their behaviour (Ch. 10)

semantic memory Memory for general knowledge and facts about the world, as well as memory for the rules of logic that are used to deduce other facts (Ch. 6)

semantics The rules governing the meaning of words and sentences (Ch. 7)

semicircular canals Three tubelike structures of the inner ear containing fluid that sloshes through them when the head moves, signalling rotational or angular movement to the brain (Ch. 3)

sensation The processes by which our sense organs receive information from the environment (Ch. 3)

sensorimotor stage According to Piaget,

the stage from birth to 2 years, during which a child has little competence in representing the environment using images, language, or other symbols (Ch. 9)

sensory (afferent) neurons Neurons that transmit information from the perimeter of the body to the central nervous system (Ch. 2)

sensory area The site in the brain of the tissue that corresponds to each of the senses, with the degree of sensitivity relating to the amount of tissue (Ch. 2)

sensory memory The initial, momentary storage of information, lasting only an instant (Ch. 6)

shaping The process of teaching a complex behaviour by rewarding closer and closer approximations to the desired behaviour (Ch. 5)

short-term memory Memory that holds information for 15 to 25 seconds (Ch. 6)

significant outcome Meaningful results that make it possible for researchers to feel confident that they have confirmed their hypotheses (Ch. 1)

situational causes (of behaviour) A perceived cause of behaviour that is based on environmental factors (Ch. 14)

skin senses The senses that include touch, pressure, temperature and pain (Ch. 3)

social cognition The processes that underlie our understanding of the social world (Ch. 14)

social cognitive approaches to personality The theory that emphasizes the influence of a person's cognitions—thoughts, feelings, expectations, and values—in determining personality (Ch. 10)

social influence The process by which the actions of an individual or group affect the behaviour of others (Ch. 14)

social psychology The study of how people's thoughts, feelings, and actions are affected by others (Ch. 14)

social support A mutual network of caring, interested others (Ch. 11)

social supporter A person who shares an unpopular opinion or attitude of another group member, thereby encouraging nonconformity (Ch. 14)

sociocultural perspective The perspective that people's behaviour—both normal and abnormal—is shaped by the kind of family group, society, and culture in which they live (Ch. 12)

somatic division The part of the nervous system that specializes in the control of voluntary movements and the communication of information to and from the sense organs (Ch. 2)

somatoform disorder Psychological difficulties that take on a physical (somatic) form, but for which there is no medical cause (Ch. 12)

sound The movement of air molecules brought about by the vibration of an object (Ch. 3)

spinal cord A bundle of nerves that leaves the brain and runs down the length of the back and is the main means for transmitting messages between the brain and the body (Ch. 2)

split-brain patient   A person who suffers from independent functioning of the two halves of the brain, as a result of which the sides of the body work in disharmony (Ch. 2)

spontaneous recovery   The reemergence of an extinguished conditioned response after a period of rest (Ch. 5)

spontaneous remission   Recovery without treatment (Ch. 13)

stage 1 sleep   The state of transition between wakefulness and sleep, characterized by relatively rapid, low-voltage brain waves (Ch. 4)

stage 2 sleep   A sleep deeper than that of stage 1, characterized by a slower, more regular wave pattern, along with momentary interruptions of "sleep spindles" (Ch. 4)

stage 3 sleep   A sleep characterized by slow brain waves, with greater peaks and valleys in the wave pattern (Ch. 4)

stage 4 sleep   The deepest stage of sleep, during which we are least responsive to outside stimulation (Ch. 4)

status   Social rank within a group (Ch. 14)

stimulants   Drugs that affect the central nervous system by causing a rise in heart rate, blood pressure, and muscular tension (Ch. 4)

stimulus   Energy that produces a response in a sense organ (Ch. 3)

stimulus discrimination   The ability to differentiate between stimuli (Ch. 5)

stimulus generalization   A response to a stimulus that is similar to but different from a conditioned stimulus; the more similar the two stimuli, the more likely generalization is to occur (Ch. 5)

stress   The response to events that are threatening or challenging (Ch. 11)

structuralism   Wundt's approach, which focuses on the basic elements that form the foundation of thinking, consciousness, emotions, and other kinds of mental states and activities (Ch. 1)

subjective well-being   People's evaluations of their lives in terms of both their thoughts and their emotions; how happy people are (Ch. 11)

superego   According to Freud, the final personality structure to develop; it represents society's standards of right and wrong as handed down by a person's parents, teachers, and other important figures (Ch. 10)

survey research   Research in which people chosen to represent some larger population are asked a series of questions about their behaviour, thoughts, or attitudes (Ch. 1)

sympathetic division   The part of the autonomic division of the nervous system that acts to prepare the body in stressful emergency situations, engaging all the organism's resources to respond to a threat (Ch. 2)

synapse   The space between two neurons where the axon of a sending neuron communicates with the dendrites of a receiving neuron using chemical messages (Ch. 2)

syntax   The rules that indicate how words and phrases can be combined to form sentences (Ch. 7)

systematic desensitization   A behavioural technique in which gradual exposure to anxiety-producing stimuli is paired with relaxation in order to extinguish the response of anxiety (Ch. 13)

t

telegraphic speech   Sentences that sound as if they were part of a telegram, in which words not critical to the message are left out (Ch. 7)

temperament   A basic, innate disposition that emerges early in life (Ch. 9, 10)

teratogens   Environmental agents such as drugs, chemicals, viruses, or other factors that produce birth defects (Ch. 9)

terminal buttons   Small bulges at the end of axons that send messages to other neurons (Ch. 2)

test standardization   A technique used to validate questions in personality tests by studying the responses of people with known diagnoses (Ch. 10)

thalamus   The part of the brain located in the middle of the central core that acts primarily as a busy relay station, mostly for information concerning the senses (Ch. 2)

Thematic Apperception Test (TAT)   A test consisting of a series of ambiguous pictures about which the person is asked to write a story (Ch. 10)

theories   Broad explanations and predictions concerning phenomena of interest (Ch. 1)

thinking   The manipulation of mental representations of information (Ch. 7)

tip-of-the-tongue phenomenon   The inability to recall information that one realizes one knows—a result of the difficulty of retrieving information from long-term memory (Ch. 6)

top-down processing   Perception that is guided by higher-level knowledge, experience, expectations, and motivations (Ch. 3)

trait theory   A model of personality that seeks to identify the basic traits necessary to describe personality (Ch. 10)

traits   Enduring dimensions of personality characteristics along which people differ (Ch. 10)

treatment   In an experiment, the manipulation implemented by the experimenter (Ch. 1)

trichromatic theory of colour vision   The theory that there are three kinds of cones in the retina, each of which responds primarily to a specific range of wavelengths (Ch. 3)

trust-versus-mistrust stage   According to Erikson, the first stage of psychosocial development, occurring from birth to 18 months of age, during which time infants develop feelings of trust or lack of trust (Ch. 9)

Type A behaviour pattern   A pattern of behaviour characterized by competitiveness, impatience, tendency toward frustration, and hostility (Ch. 11)

Type B behaviour pattern   A pattern of behaviour characterized by cooperation, patience, noncompetitiveness, and nonaggression (Ch. 11)

u

unconditional positive regard   An attitude of acceptance and respect on the part of an observer, no matter what the other person says or does (Ch. 10)

unconditioned response (UCR)   A response that is natural and needs no training (e.g., salivation at the smell of food) (Ch. 5)

unconditioned stimulus (UCS)   A stimulus that brings about an automatic or unlearned response (Ch. 5)

unconscious wish fulfillment theory   Sigmund Freud's theory that dreams represent unconscious wishes that dreamers desire to fulfill (Ch. 4)

unconscious   A part of the personality of which a person is not aware, and which is a potential determinant of behaviour (Ch. 10)

uninvolved parents   Parents who show little interest in their children and are emotionally detached from them (Ch. 9)

uplifts   Minor positive events that make one feel good (Ch. 16)

v

validity   A test's actually measuring what it is supposed to measure (Ch. 7)

variable-interval schedule   A schedule whereby the time between reinforcements varies around some average rather than being fixed (Ch. 5)

variable-ratio schedule   A schedule whereby reinforcement occurs after a varying number of responses rather than after a fixed number (Ch. 5)

variables   Behaviours, events, or other characteristics that can change, or vary, in some way (Ch. 1)

visual illusions   Physical stimuli that consistently produce errors in perception (Ch. 3)

w

wear-and-tear theories of aging   Theories that hold that the mechanical functions of the body simply stop working efficiently when we are old (Ch. 9)

Weber's law   One of the basic laws of psychophysics, that a just noticeable difference is in constant proportion to the intensity of an initial stimulus (Ch. 3)

weight set point   The particular level of weight that the body strives to maintain (Ch. 8)

Wernicke's aphasia   Impaired understanding of language resulting from injury to the brain's association areas (Ch. 2)

whole language approach   An approach to early reading instruction that stresses the use of whole and meaningful materials (Ch. 7)

working memory An active "workspace" in which information is retrieved and manipulated, and in which information is held through rehearsal (Ch. 6)

Z

zone of proximal development (ZPD) According to Vygotsky, the range between what a child is able to accomplish unaided and what he or she is able to accomplish with the help of a more advanced peer or teacher (Ch. 9)

zygote The new cell formed by the union of an egg and sperm (Ch. 9)

References

*denotes Canadian research

Abi-Dargham, A., Laruelle, M., Aghajanian, G. K., Charney, D., et al. (1997). The role of serotonin in the pathophysiology and treatment of schizophrenia. *Journal of Neuropsychiatry and Clinical Neurosciences, 9,* 1–17.

Aboud, F. E. (1988). *Children and prejudice.* New York: Blackwell.*

Aboud, F. E. & Doyle, A. B. (1996). Does talk of race foster prejudice or tolerance in children? *Canadian Journal of Behavioural Science, 28,* 161–170.*

Abrahams, M. F., & Bell, R. A. (1994). Encouraging charitable contributions: An examination of three models of door-in-the-face compliance. *Communication Research, 21,* 131–153.

Abt, S. (1999, July 26). Armstrong wins tour and journey. *New York Times,* pp. D1, D4.

Adams, B., & Parker, J. D. (1990). Maternal weight gain in women with good pregnancy outcome. *Obstetrics and Gynecology, 76,* 1–7.

Adlaf, E. M., & Paglia, A. (2001). *Drug use among Ontario students: Finding from the OSDUS, 1977–2001.* Toronto: CAMH.*

Adler, J. (1984, April 23). The fight to conquer fear. *Newsweek,* pp. 66–72.

Adler, P. A., & Adler, P. (1994). Observational techniques. In N. K. Denzin & Y. S. Lincoln (Eds.), *Handbook of qualitative research.* Thousand Oaks, CA: Sage.

Advances in telepsychology/telehealth. (2000). *Professional Psychology: Research and Practice, 31* (2).

Affleck, G., Tennen, H., Urrows, S., & Higgins, P. (1994). Person and contextual features of daily stress reactivity: Individual differences in relations of undesirable daily events with mood disturbance and chronic pain intensity. *Journal of Personality and Social Psychology, 66,* 329–340.

Aghajanian, G. K. (1994). Serotonin and the action of LSD in the brain. *Psychiatric Annals, 24,* 137–141.

Agras, W. S., & Berkowitz, R. I. (1996). Behavior therapy. In R. E. Hales & S. C. Yudofsky (Eds.), *The American Psychiatric Press synopsis of psychiatry.* Washington, DC: American Psychiatric Press.

Ahissar, M., Ahissar, E., Bergman, H., & Vaadia, E. (1992). Encoding of sound-source location and movement: Activity of single neurons and interactions between adjacent neurons in the monkey auditory cortex. *Journal of Neurophysiology, 67,* 203–215.

Ahrons, C. (1995). *The good divorce: Keeping your family together when your marriage comes apart.* New York: HarperPerennial.

Aiken, L. R. (1996). *Assessment of intellectual functioning* (2nd ed.). New York: Plenum Press.

Aiken, L. R. (1997). *Psychological testing and assessment* (9th ed.). Boston: Allyn & Bacon.

Aiken, L. R. (2001). *Dying, death, and bereavement* (4th ed.). Mahwah, NJ: Erlbaum.

Aikman, P. (n.d.) Female genital mutilation: Human rights abuse or protected cultural practice? Available: <http://meds.queensu.ca/hsj/vol1-1/fgm.html>. Accessed February 13, 2001.*

Ainsworth, M. D. S., Blehar, M. C., Waters, E., & Wall, S. (1978). *Patterns of attachment: A psychological study of the strange situation.* Hillsdale, NJ: Erlbaum.

Ainsworth, M. D. S., Bowlby, J. (1991). An ethological approach to personality development. *American Psychologist, 46,* 333–341.

Akbarian, S., Kim, J. J., Potkin, S. G., Hetrick, W. P., et al. (1996). Maldistribution of interstitial neurons in prefrontal white matter of the brains of schizophrenic patients. *Archives of General Psychiatry, 53,* 425–436.

Akil, H., & Morano, M. I. (1996). The biology of stress: From periphery to brain. In S. J. Watson (Ed.), *Biology of schizophrenia and affective disease.* Washington, DC: American Psychiatric Press.

Akmajian, A., Demers, R. A., & Harnish, R. M. (1984). *Linguistics.* Cambridge, MA: MIT Press.

Akutsu, P. D., Sue, S., Zane, N. W. S., & Nakamura, C. Y. (1989). Ethnic differences in alcohol consumption among Asians and Caucasians in the United States: An investigation of cultural and physiological factors. *Journal of Studies on Alcohol, 50,* 261–267.

Alcock, J. E. (1981). *Parapsychology: Science or magic?* London: Pergamon.*

Alcock, J. E. (1987). The status of parapsychology in the world of science. *Behaviour and Brain Sciences, 10,* 553–564.*

Alcock, J. E. (1998). Science, pseudoscience and anomaly. *Behaviour and Brain Sciences, 21,* 303.*

Alcock, J. E., Carment, D. W., & Sadava, S. W. (2000). *A textbook of social psychology* (5th ed.). Scarborough, Ontario: Pearson Education Canada.*

Alford, B. A., & Beck, A. T. (1997) *The integrative power of cognitive therapy.* New York: Guilford Press.

Allen, M. (1999, September 19). Help wanted: The not-too-high-Q standard. *New York Times,* p. 3.

Allen, V. L. (1975). Social support for nonconformity. In L. Berkowitz (Ed.), *Advances in experimental and social psychology* (Vol. 8). New York: Academic Press.

Alliger, G. M., Lilienfeld, S. O., & Mitchell, K. E. (1996). The susceptibility of overt and covert integrity tests to coaching and faking. *Psychological Science, 7,* 32–39.

Alloy, L. B., Abramson, L. Y., & Francis, E. L. (1999). Do negative cognitive styles confer vulnerability to depression? *Current Directions in Psychological Science, 8,* 128–132.

Allport, G. W. (1961). *Pattern and growth in personality.* New York: Holt, Rinehart & Winston.

Allport, G. W. (1966). Traits revisited. *American Psychologist, 21,* 1–10.

Allport, G. W., & Postman, L. J. (1958). The basic psychology of rumor. In E. D. Maccoby, T. M. Newcomb, & E. L. Hartley (Eds.), *Readings in social psychology* (3rd ed.). New York: Holt, Rinehart & Winston.

Almer, E. (2000, April 22). Online therapy: An arm's length approach. *New York Times,* pp. A1, A11.

Altemeyer, B. (1981). *Right-wing authoritarianism.* Winnipeg: University of Manitoba Press.*

Altemeyer, B. (1994). Reducing prejudice in right-wing authoritarians. In M. P. Zanna & J. M. Olson (Eds.), *The psychology of prejudice: The Ontario Symposium (Vol. 7).*

Altman, N. (1996). The accommodation of diversity in psychoanalysis. In R. P. Foster, M. Moskowitz, & R. A. Javier (Eds.), *Reaching across boundaries of culture and class: Widening the scope of psychotherapy.* Northvale, NJ: Jason Aronson.

American Academy of Pediatrics. (1999a, July 26). *Circumcision: Information for parents.* Available on the World Wide Web at http://www.aap.org/family/circ.htm.

American Academy of Pediatrics. (1999b). Media education (RE9911). *Pediatrics, 104,* 341–343.

American Association on Mental Retardation (AAMR). (1992). *Mental retardation: Definition, classification, and systems of support.* Washington, DC: Author.

American Psychiatric Association. (1994). *Diagnostic and statistical manual of mental disorders* (4th ed.). Washington, DC: Author.

American Psychiatric Association, Task Force on Electroconvulsive Therapy. (1990). *The practice of electroconvulsive therapy: Recommendations for treatment, training, and privileging.* Washington, DC: American Psychiatric Association.

American Psychiatric Association. (1996). The Insanity Defense. Available <www.psych.org/public_info/insanity.cfm>. Accessed November 1, 2002.

American Psychological Association (APA). (1988). *Behavioral research with animals.* Washington, DC: Author.

American Psychological Association (APA). (1992). *Ethical principles of psychologists and code of conduct.* Washington, DC: Author.

American Psychological Association (APA). (1993, January/February). Subgroup norming and the Civil Rights Act. *Psychological Science Agenda, 5,* 6.

American Psychological Association (APA). (1999). *Talk to someone who can help.* Washington, DC: American Psychological Association.

Amnesty International. (1998). Female genital mutilation–A human rights information package. Available: <http://www. Amnesty.org/ailib/intcam/femgen/fgm3.htm>. Accessed December 12, 2002.

Anastasi, A. (1988). *Psychological testing* (6th ed.). New York: Macmillan.

Anastasi, A., & Urbina, S. (1997). *Psychological testing* (7th ed.). Englewood Cliffs, NJ: Prentice Hall.

Andersen, B. L., Kiecolt-Glaser, J.K., & Glaser, R. (1994). A biobehavioral model of cancer stress and disease course. *American Psychologist, 49,* 389–404.

Anderson, C. A., & Dill, K. E. (2000). Video games and aggressive thoughts, feelings, and behavior in the laboratory and in life. *Journal of Personality and Social Psychology, 78,* 772–790.

Anderson, J. R. (1981). Interference: The relationship between response latency and response accuracy. *Journal of Experimental*

Psychology: Human Learning and Memory, 7, 311–325.

Anderson, J. R., & Bower, G. H. (1972). Recognition and retrieval processes in free recall. *Psychological Review, 79,* 97–123.

Anderson, K. B., Cooper, H., & Okamura, L. (1997). Individual differences and attitudes toward rape: A meta-analytic review. *Personality and Social Psychology Bulletin, 23,* 295–315.

Anderson, N. H. (1996). *A functional theory of cognition.* Mahwah, NJ: Erlbaum.

Anderson, S. M., & Klatzky, R. L. (1987). Traits and social stereotypes: Levels of categorization in person perception. *Journal of Personality and Social Psychology, 53,* 235–246.

Anderson, T., & Magnusson, D. (1990). Biological maturation in adolescence and the development of drinking habits and alcohol abuse among young males: A prospective longitudinal study. *Journal of Youth and Adolescence, 19,* 33–42.

Andreasen, N. C., Arndt, S., Swayze II, V., Cizadlo, T., Flaum, M., O'Leary, D., Ehrhardt, J. C., & Yuh, W. T. C. (1994, October 14). Thalamic abnormalities in schizophrenia visualized through magnetic resonance image averaging. *Science, 266,* 294–298.

Angier, N. (1991, January 22). A potent peptide prompts an urge to cuddle. *New York Times,* p. C1.

Angier, N. (1999, May 16). Baby in a box. *New York Times Magazine,* p. 86.

Ansburg, P. I., & Dominowski, R. L. (2000). Promoting insightful problem solving. *Journal of Creative Behavior, 34,* 30–60.

Antony, M. M., Brown, T. A., & Barlow, D. H. (1992). Current perspectives on panic and panic disorder. *Current Directions in Psychological Science, 1,* 79–82.

Antony, M. M., & Swinson, R. P. (1996). Anxiety disorders: Future directions for research and treatment. Ottawa: Health Canada.*

Aponte, J. F., & Wohl, J. (2000). *Psychological intervention and cultural diversity.* Needham Heights, MA: Allyn & Bacon.

Apter, A., Galatzer, A., Beth-Halachmi, N., & Laron, Z. (1981). Self-image in adolescents with delayed puberty and growth retardation. *Journal of Youth and Adolescence, 10,* 501–505.

Archambault, D. L. (1992). Adolescence: A physiological, cultural, and psychological no man's land. In G. W. Lawson & A. W. Lawson (Eds.), *Adolescent substance abuse: Etiology, treatment, and prevention.* Gaithersburg, MD: Aspen.

Archer, S. L., & Waterman, A. S. (1994). Adolescent identity development: Contextual perspectives. In C. B. Fisher & R. M. Lerner (Eds.), *Applied developmental psychology.* New York: McGraw-Hill.

Arena, J. M. (1984, April). A look at the opposite sex. *Newsweek on Campus,* p. 21.

Ariel, S. (1999). *Culturally competent family therapy: A general model.* Westport, CT: Greenwood Press.

Armstrong, S. (1998, Nov/Dec). Not my daughter. *Homemaker's,* 66–83.*

Aron, A., Melinat, E., Aronon, E. N., Vallone, R. D., & Bator, R. J. (1997). The experimental generation of interpersonal closeness: A procedure and some preliminary findings. *Personality and Social Psychology Bulletin, 23,* 363–377.

Aronow, E., Reznikoff, M., & Moreland, K. (1994). *The Rorschach technique: Perceptual basics, content interpretation, and applications.* Boston: Longwood.

Aronson, E. (1988). *The social animal* (3rd ed.). San Francisco: Freeman.

Arvanitogiannis, A. (1999). Resetting the rat circadian clock by ultra-short light flashes. *Neuroscience Letters, 261,* 159–162.*

Asch, S. E. (1946). Forming impressions of personality. *Journal of Abnormal and Social Psychology, 41,* 258–290.

Asch, S. E. (1951). Effects of group pressure upon the modification and distortion of judgments. In H. Guetzkow (Ed.), *Groups, leadership, and men.* Pittsburgh: Carnegie Press.

Asher, S. R., & Parker, J. G. (1991). Significance of peer relationship problems in childhood. In B. H. Schneider, G. Attili, J. Nadel, & R. P. Weissberg (Eds.), *Social competence in developmental perspective.* Amsterdam: Kluwer Academic.

Ashton, M. C., Jackson, D. N., Helmes, E., & Paunonen, S. V. (1998). Joint factor analysis of the Personality Research Form and the Jackson Personality Inventory: Comparisons with the Big Five. *Journal of Research in Personality, 32,* 243–250.*

Ashton, M. C., Jackson, D. N., Paunonen, S. V., Helmes, E., & Rothstein, M. G. (1995). The criterion validity of broad factor scales versus specific trait scales. *Journal of Research in Personality, 29,* 432–442.*

Ashton, M. C., & Lee, K. (2001). A theoretical basis for the major dimensions of personality. *European Journal of Personality, 15,* 327–353.*

Ashton, M. C., Lee, K., & Son, C. (2000). Honesty as the sixth factor of personality: Correlations with Machiavellianism, primary psychopathy, and social adroitness. *European Journal of Personality, 14,* 359–368.*

Ashton, M. C., Paunonen, S. V., & Lee, K. (2002). What is the central feature of extraversion? Social attention versus reward sensitivity. *Journal of Personality and Social Psychology, 83,* 245–252.*

Aspinwall, L. G., & Taylor, S. E. (1997). A stitch in time: Self-regulation and proactive coping. *Psychological Bulletin, 121,* 417–436.

Assanand, S., Pinel, J. P. J., & Lehman, D. R. (1998). Personal theories of hunger and eating. *Journal of Applied Social Psychology, 28,* 998–1015.*

Atkinson, H. (Ed.). (1997, January 21). Understanding your diagnosis. *HealthNews,* p. 3.

Atkinson, J. (1995). Through the eyes of an infant. In R. L. Gregory, J. Harris, P. Heard, & D. Rose (Eds.), *The artful eye.* Oxford: Oxford University Press.

Atkinson, J. W., & Feather, N. T. (1966). *Theory of achievement motivation.* New York: Krieger.

Atkinson, J. W., & Raynor, J. O. (Eds.). (1974). *Motivation and achievement.* Washington, DC: Winston.

Atkinson, J. W., & Shiffrin, R. M. (1971, August). The control of short-term memory. *Scientific American,* pp. 82–90.

Atkinson, R. C., & Shiffrin, R. M. (1968). Human memory: A proposed system and its control processes. In K. W. Spence and J. T. Spence (Eds.), *The psychology of learning and motivation: Advances in research and theory* (Vol. 2, pp. 80–195). New York: Academic Press.

Averill, J. R. (1975). A semantic atlas of emotional concepts. *Catalog of Selected Documents in Psychology, 5,* 330.

Averill, J. R. (1994). Emotions are many splendored things. In P. Ekman & R. J. Davidson (Eds.), *The nature of emotion: Fundamental questions.* New York: Oxford University Press.

Averill, J. R. (1997). The emotions: An integrative approach. In R. Hogan, J. Johnson, & S. Briggs (Eds.), *Handbook of personality psychology.* Orlando: Academic Press.

Aycan, Z. (2000). Cross-cultural industrial and organizational psychology: Contributions, past developments, and future directions. *Journal of Cross-Cultural Psychology, 31,* 110–128.

Baddeley, A. D. (1992, January 31). Working memory. *Science, 255,* 556–559.

Baddeley, A. D. (1993). Working memory and conscious awareness. In A. F. Collins, S. E. Gathercole, M. A. Conway, & P. E. Morris (Eds.), *Theories of memory.* Hillsdale, NJ: Erlbaum.

Baddeley, A. D. (1995a). The psychology of memory. In A. D. Baddeley, B. A. Wilson, & F. N. Watts (Eds.), *Handbook of memory disorders.* Chichester, England: John Wiley.

Baddeley, A. D. (1995b). Working memory. In M. S. Gazzaniga (Ed.), *The cognitive neurosciences.* Cambridge, MA: MIT Press.

Baddeley, A. D. (1996). Exploring the central executive. *Quarterly Journal of Experimental Psychology, Human Experimental Psychology, 49A,* 5–28.

Baddeley, A. D., Gathercole, S., & Papagno, C. (1998). The phonological loop as a language learning device. *Psychological Review, 105,* 158–173.

Baddeley, A. D., & Wilson, B. (1985). Phonological coding and short-term memory in patients without speech. *Journal of Memory and Language, 24,* 490–502.

Baer, J. (1993). *Creativity and divergent thinking: A task-specific approach.* Hillsdale, NJ: Erlbaum.

Baer, L., Rauch, S. L., Callantine, T., Martuza, R., et al. (1995). Cingulotomy for intractable obsessive-compulsive disorder: Prospective long-term follow-up of 18 patients. *Archives of General Psychiatry, 52,* 384–392.

Bahrick, H. P., Hall, L. K., & Berger, S. A. (1996). Accuracy and distortion in memory for high school grades. *Psychological Science, 7,* 265–269.

Bailey, J. M. (1995). Biological perspectives on sexual orientation. In A. R. D'Augelli & C. J. Patteson (Eds.), *Lesbian, gay, and bisexual identities over the lifespan: Psychological perspectives.* New York: Oxford University Press.

Bailey, M., & Pillard, R. C. (1994, January). The innateness of homosexuality. *Harvard Mental Health Letter, 10,* pp. 4–6.

Bailey, J. M., Pillard, R. C., Kitzinger, C., & Wilkinson, S. (1997). Sexual orientation: Is it determined by biology? In M. R. Walsh (Ed.), *Women, men, and gender: Ongoing debates.* New Haven, CT: Yale University Press.

Bailey, J. M., & Zucker, K. J. (1995). Childhood sex-typed behavior and sexual orientation: A conceptual analysis and quantitative review. *Developmental Psychology, 31,* 43–55.

Baird, J. C. (1997). *Sensation and judgment: Complementarity theory of psychophysics.* Mahwah, NJ: Erlbaum.

Baker, R. A. (1998, February). A view of hypnosis. *Harvard Mental Health Letter,* pp. 5–6.

Baker, S. P., Lamb, M. W., Li, G., & Dodd, R. S. (1993). Human factors in crashes of commuter airplanes. *Aviation, Space, and Environmental Medicine, 64,* 63–68.

Ball, E. M., Simon, R. D., Tall, A. A., Banks, M. B., Nino-Murcia, G., & Dement, W. C. (1997, February 24). Diagnosis and treatment of sleep apnea within the community. *Archive of Internal Medicine, 157,* 419–424.

Ballinger, C. B. (1981). The menopause and its syndromes. In J. G. Howells (Ed.), *Modern perspectives in the psychiatry of middle age* (pp. 279–303). New York: Brunner/Mazel.

Bandura, A. (1973). *Aggression: A social learning analysis.* Englewood Cliffs, NJ: Prentice Hall.

Bandura, A. (1977). *Social learning theory.* Englewood Cliffs, NJ: Prentice Hall.

Bandura, A. (1983). Psychological mechanisms of aggression. In R. G. Geen & E. I. Donnerstein (Eds.), *Aggression: Theoretical and empirical reviews, Vol. 1: Theoretical and methodological issues.* New York: Academic Press.

Bandura, A. (1986). *Social foundations of thought and action: A social cognitive theory.* Englewood Cliffs, NJ: Prentice Hall.

Bandura, A. (1988). Self-regulation of motivation and action through goal systems. In V. Hamilton & H. Gordon (Eds.), *Cognitive perspectives on emotion and motivation.* Dordrecht, Netherlands: Kluwer Academic.

Bandura, A. (1994). Social cognitive theory of mass communication. In J. Bryant & D. Zillmann (Eds.), *Media effects: Advances in theory and research.* Hillsdale, NJ: Erlbaum.

Bandura, A. (1997). *Self-efficacy: The exercise of control.* New York: W. H. Freeman.

Bandura, A. (1999). Social cognitive theory of personality. In D. Cervone & Y. Shod (Eds.), *The coherence of personality.* New York: Guilford.

Bandura, A. (2000). Self-efficacy: The foundation of agency. In W. J. Perrig & A. Grob (Eds.), *Control of human behavior, mental processes, and consciousness: Essays in honor of the 60th birthday of August Flammer.* Mahwah, NJ: Erlbaum.

Bandura, A., Grusec, J. E., & Menlove, F. L. (1967). Vicarious extinction of avoidance behavior. *Journal of Personality and Social Psychology, 5,* 16–23.

Bandura, A., Ross, D., & Ross, S. (1963a). Imitation of film-mediated aggressive models. *Journal of Abnormal and Social Psychology, 66,* 3–11.

Bandura, A., Ross, D., & Ross, S. (1963b). Vicarious reinforcement and imitative learning. *Journal of Abnormal and Social Psychology, 67,* 601–607.

Banich, T., & Heller, W. (1998). Evolving perspectives on lateralization of function. *Current Directions in Psychological Science, 7,* 1–2.

Baranowsky, A., Young, M., Johnson-Douglas, S., Williams-Keeler, L., & McCarrey, M. (1998). PTSD transmission: A review of secondary traumatization in Holocaust survivor families. *Canadian Psychology, 39,* 247–256.*

Barber, J. (Ed.). (1996). *Hypnosis and suggestion in the treatment of pain: A clinical guide.* New York: W. W. Norton.

Barber, S., & Lane, R. C. (1995). Efficacy research in psychodynamic therapy: A critical review of the literature. *Psychotherapy in Private Practice, 14,* 43–69.

Barceló, A., Jones, B., & Grobe, C. (1998). *Provincial student drug use survey highlights.* Fredericton: Provincial Epidemiology Service, New Brunswick Department of Health and Community Services.*

Bargh, J., & Pietromonaco, P. (1982). Automatic information processing and social perception: The influence of trait information presented outside of conscious awareness on impression formation. *Journal of Personality and Social Psychology, 43,* 437–449.

Bargh, J. A., Raymond, P., Pryor, J. B., & Strack, F. (1995). Attractiveness of the underling: An automatic power sex association and its consequences for sexual harassment and aggression. *Journal of Personality and Social Psychology, 68,* 768–781.

Barinaga, M. (1997, May 30). How much pain for cardiac gain? *Science, 276,* 1324–1327.

Barinaga, M. (1999, July 23). Mapping smells in the brain. *Science, 285,* 508.

Barkley, R. A. (1998a, September). Attention-deficit hyperactivity disorder. *Scientific American,* pp. 66–71.

Barkley, R. A. (1998b). *Attention-deficit hyperactivity disorder: A handbook for diagnosis and treatment.* New York: Guilford Press.

Barnard, N. D., & Kaufman, S. R. (1997, February). Animal research is wasteful and misleading. *Scientific American,* pp. 80–82.

Barrera, M. E. & Maurer, D. (1981). Discrimination of strangers by the three-month-old. *Child Development, 52(2),* 558–563.*

Barrett, M. C., King, A., Lévy, J., Maticka-Tyndale, E., McKay, A. (1997). Canada. In R. T. Francoeur (Ed.), *The international encyclopedia of sexuality (Vol. 1): Argentina to Greece.* New York: Continuum.*

Barrett, M. (1999). *The development of language.* Philadelphia: Psychology Press.

Barron, F. (1990). *Creativity and psychological health: Origins of personal vitality and creative freedom.* Buffalo, NY: Creative Education Foundation.

Bartecchi, C. E., MacKenzie, T. D., & Schrier, R. W. (1995, May). The global tobacco epidemic. *Scientific American,* pp. 44–51.

Bartlett, F. (1932). *Remembering: A study in experimental and social psychology.* Cambridge, England: Cambridge University Press.

Bartoshuk, L. (2000, July/August). The bitter with the sweet. *APS Observer, 11,* 33.

Bartoshuk, L., & Beauchamp, G. K. (1994). Chemical senses. *Annual Review of Psychology, 45,* 419–449.

Bartoshuk, L., & Drewnowski, A. (1997, February). Symposium presented at the annual meeting of the American Association for the Advancement of Science, Seattle.

Basch, M. F. (1996). Affect and defense. In D. L. Nathanson (Ed.), *Knowing feeling: Affect, script, and psychotherapy.* New York: W. W. Norton.

Bass, A. (1996, April 21). Is anger good for you? *Boston Globe Magazine,* pp. 20–41.

Batista, A. P., Buneo, C. A., Snyder, L. H., & Anderson, R. A. (1999, July 9). Reach plans in eye-centered coordinates. *Science, 285,* 257–260.

Batson, C. D. (1991). *The altruism question: Toward a social-psychological answer.* Hillsdale, NJ: Erlbaum.

Batson, C. D., Batson, J. G., Todd, R. M., & Brummett, B. H. (1995). Empathy and the collective good: Caring for one of the others in a social dilemma. *Journal of Personality and Social Psychology, 68,* 619–631.

Bauer, P. J. (1996). What do infants recall of their lives? Memory for specific events by one- to two-year-olds. 102nd Annual Convention of the American Psychological Association. (1994, Los Angeles, California, US) *American Psychologist, 51,* 29–41.

Baum, A. (1994). Behavioral, biological, and environmental interactions in disease processes. In S. Blumenthal, K. Matthews, and S. Weiss (Eds.), *New research frontiers in behavioral medicine: Proceedings of the National Conference.* Washington, DC: NIH Publications.

Baum, A., Cohen, L., & Hall, M. (1993). Control and intrusive memories as possible determinants of chronic stress. *Psychosomatic Medicine, 55,* 274–286.

Baum, A. S., Revenson, R. A., & Singer, J. E. (Eds.). (2000). *Handbook of health psychology.* Mahwah, NJ: Erlbaum.

Baumeister, R., & Bratslavsky, E. (1999). Passion, intimacy, and time: Passionate love as a function of change in intimacy. *Personality and Social Psychology Review, 3,* 49–67.

Baumeister, R. F. (1998). The self. In D. T. Gilbert & S. T. Fiske (Eds.), *The handbook of social psychology* (4th ed., Vol. 1). New York: McGraw-Hill.

Baumeister, R. F., Bushman, B. J., & Campbell, W. K. (2000). Self-esteem, narcissism, and aggression: Does violence result from low self-esteem or from threatened egotism? *Current Directions in Psychological Science, 9,* 26–29.

Baumrind, D. (1971). Current patterns of parental authority. *Developmental Psychology Monographs, 4* (1, pt. 2).

Baumrind, D. (1980). New directions in socialization research. *Psychological Bulletin, 35,* 639–652.

Bayer, D. L. (1996). Interaction in families with young adults with a psychiatric diagnosis. *American Journal of Family Therapy, 24,* 21–30.

Baynes, K., Eliassen, J. C., Lutsep, H. L., & Gazzaniga, M. S. (1998, May 8). Modular organization of cognitive systems marked by interhemispheric integration. *Science, 280,* 902–905.

Bazell, B. (1998, August 25). Back pain goes high-tech. *Slate.msn.com,* 1–4.

Bear, M. F., Connors, B. W., & Paradiso, M. A. (2000). *Neuroscience: Exploring the brain.* Philadelphia: Lippincott Williams & Wilkins.

Beatty, J. (2000). *The human brain: Essentials of behavioral neuroscience.* Thousand Oaks, CA: Sage.

Beck, A. T. (1991). Cognitive therapy: A 30-year perspective. *American Psychologist, 46,* 368–375.

Beck, A. T. (1995). Cognitive therapy: Past, present, and future. In M. J. Mahoney (Ed.), *Cognitive and constructive psychotherapies: Theory, research, and practice.* New York: Springer.

Beck, M. (1992, May 25). Menopause. *Newsweek,* pp. 71–79.

Beckham, E. E., & Leber, W. R. (Eds.). (1997). *Handbook of depression* (2nd ed.). New York: Guilford Press.

Beckman, H. B., & Frankel, R. M. (1984). The effect of physician behavior on the collection of data. *Annals of Internal Medicine, 101,* 692–696.

Bedard, W. W., & Persinger, M. A. (1995). Prednisolone blocks extreme intermale social aggression in seizure-induced, brain-damaged rats: Implications for the amygdaloid central nucleus, corticotrophin-releasing factor, and electrical seizures. *Psychological Reports, 77,* 3–9.

Begley, S. (1998b, July 13). You're OK, I'm terrific: "Self-esteem" backfires. *Newsweek,* p. 69.

Begley, S. (2000, April 10). Decoding the human body. *Newsweek,* pp. 50–62.

Beilin, H. (1996). Mind and meaning: Piaget and Vygotsky on causal explanation. *Human Development, 39,* 277–286.

Belicki, K., Correy, B., Cuddy, M., Dunlop, A., & Boucock, A. (1993). Examining the authenticity of reports of sexual abuse. *Canadian Psychology, 34,* 284.*

Bell, A., & Weinberg, M. S. (1978). *Homosexuality: A study of diversities among men and women.* New York: Simon & Schuster.

Bell, A. H., Corneil, B. D., Meredith, M. A., & Munoz, D. P. (2001). The influence of stimulus properties on multisensory processing in the awake primate superior colliculus. *Canadian Journal of Experimental Psychology, 55,* 123–132.*

Bell, J., Grekul, J., Lamba, N., & Minas, C. (1995). The impact of cost on student helping behavior. *Journal of Social Psychology, 135,* 49–56.

Bell, S. M., & Ainsworth, M. D. S. (1972). Infant crying and maternal responsiveness. *Child Development, 43,* 1171–1190.

Bellack, A. S., Hersen, M., & Kazdin, A. E. (1990). *International handbook of behavior modification and therapy.* New York: Plenum Press.

Bellezza, F. S., Six, L. S., & Phillips, D. S. (1992). A mnemonic for remembering long strings of digits. *Bulletin of the Psychonomic Society, 30,* 271–274.

Belsky, J., & Rovine, M. (1988). Nonmaternal care in the first year of life and infant-parent attachment security. *Child Development, 59,* 157–167.

Bem, D. J. (1996). Exotic becomes erotic: A developmental theory of sexual orientation. *Psychological Review, 103,* 320–335.

Bem, D. J., & Honorton, C. (1994). Does psi exist? Replicable evidence for an anomalous process of information transfer. *Psychological Bulletin, 115,* 4–18.

Benjamin, J., Li, L., Patterson, C., Greenberg, B. D., Murphy, D. L., & Hamer, D. H. (1996). Population and familial association between the D4 dopamine receptor gene and measures of novelty seeking. *Nature and Genetics, 12,* 81–84.

Benjamin, L. T., Jr. (1997). The psychology of history and the history of psychology: A historiographical introduction. In L. T. Benjamin (Ed.), *A history of psychology: Original sources and contemporary research* (2nd ed.). New York: McGraw-Hill.

Benjamin, L. T., Jr., & Shields, S. A. (1990). Foreword. In H. Hollingworth, *Leta Stetter Hollingworth: A biography.* Bolton: Anker.

Bennett, A. (1992, October 14). Lori Schiller emerges from the torments of schizophrenia. *Wall Street Journal,* pp. A1, A10.

Bennett, M. R. (2000). The concept of transmitter receptors: 100 years on. *Neuropharmacology, 39,* 523–546.

Bennett, W., & Gurin, J. (1982). *The dieter's dilemma: Eating less and weighing more.* New York: Basic Books.

Benoit, D., & Parker, K. (2000). Stability and transmission of attachment across three generations. In D. Muir & A. Slater (Eds.), *Infant development: The essential readings.* Oxford: Blackwell Publishers.*

Benson, H. (1993). The relaxation response. In D. Goleman & J. Guerin (Eds.), *Mind-body medicine: How to use your mind for better health.* Yonkers, NY: Consumer Reports.

Benson, H., & Friedman, R. (1985). A rebuttal to the conclusions of Davis S. Holme's article, "Meditation and somatic arousal reduction." *American Psychologist, 40,* 725–726.

Benson, H., Kornhaber, A., Kornhaber, C., LeChanu, M. N., et al. (1994). Increases in positive psychological characteristics with a new relaxation-response curriculum in high school students. *Journal of Research and Development in Education, 27,* 226–231.

Bentall, R. P. (1992). The classification of schizophrenia. In D. J. Kavanagh (Ed.), *Schizophrenia: An overview and practical handbook.* London: Chapman & Hall.

Bergin, A. E., & Garfield, S. L. (1994). (Eds.). *Handbook of psychotherapy and behavior change* (4th ed.). New York: Wiley.

Berkowitz, L. (1984). Aversive conditioning as stimuli to aggression. In R. J. Blanchard & C. Blanchard (Eds.), *Advances in the study of aggression* (Vol. 1). New York: Academic Press.

Berkowitz, L. (1989). Frustration-aggression hypothesis. *Psychological Bulletin, 106,* 59–73.

Berkowitz, L. (1990). On the formation and regulation of anger and aggression: A cognitive-neoassociationistic analysis. *American Psychologist, 45,* 494–503.

Berkowitz, L. (1993). *Aggression: Its causes, consequences, and control.* New York: McGraw-Hill.

Berkowitz, L., & Geen, R. G. (1966). Film violence and the cue properties of available targets. *Journal of Personality and Social Psychology, 3,* 525–530.

Berkowitz, L., & LePage, A. (1967). Weapons as aggression-eliciting stimuli. *Journal of Personality and Social Psychology, 7,* 202–207.

Berlyne, D. (1967). Arousal and reinforcement. In D. Levine (Ed.), *Nebraska symposium on motivation.* Lincoln: University of Nebraska Press.

Berman, R. M., Krystal, J. H., & Charney, D. S. (1996). Mechanism of action of antidepressants: Monoamine hypotheses and beyond. In S. J. Watson (Ed.), *Biology of schizophrenia and affective disease.* Washington, DC: American Psychiatric Press.

Bernard, L. L. (1924). *Instinct: A study in social psychology.* New York: Holt.

Bernieri, F. J., Zuckerman, M., Koestner, R., & Rosenthal, R. (1994). Measuring person perception accuracy: Another look at self-other agreement. *Personality and Social Psychology Bulletin, 20,* 367–378.

Berquier, A., & Ashton, R. (1992). Characteristics of the frequent nightmare sufferer. *Personality and Social Psychology, 101,* 246–250.

Berrettini, W. H. (2000). Genetics of psychiatric disease. *Annual Review of Medicine, 51,* 465–479.

Berrios, G. E. (1996). *The history of mental symptoms: Descriptive psychopathology since the nineteenth century.* Cambridge, England: Cambridge University Press.

Berry, J. W. (1999). Intercultural relations in plural societies. *Canadian Psychology, 40,* 12–21.*

Berry, J. W., & Laponce, J. A. (Eds.). (1994). *Ethnicity and culture in Canada: The research landscape.* Toronto: University of Toronto Press.*

Berry, J. W., Poortinga, Y. H., Segall, M. H., & Dasen, P. R. (1992). *Cross-cultrual psychology: Research and applications.* New York: Cambridge University Press.*

Berscheid, E. (1985). Interpersonal attraction. In G. Lindzey & E. Aronson (Eds.), *Handbook of social psychology* (3rd ed.). New York: Random House.

Bersoff, D. N. (1995). *Ethical conflicts in psychology.* Washington, DC: American Psychological Association.

Bersoff, D. N. (1999). Why good people sometimes do bad things: Motivated reasoning and unethical behavior. *Personality and Social Psychology Bulletin, 25,* 28–39.

Beyene, Y. (1989). *From menarche to menopause: Reproductive lives of peasant women in two cultures.* Albany: State University of New York Press.

Bialystok, E. (1997). Effects of bilingualism and biliteracy on children's emerging concepts of print. *Developmental Psychology, 33,* 429–440.*

Bialystok, E., & Herman, J. (1999). Does bilingualism matter for early literacy? *Bilingualism: Language and Cognition, 2,* 35–44.*

Bickman, L. (1994). Social influence and diffusion of responsibility in an emergency. In B. Puka (Ed.), *Reaching out: Caring, altruism, and prosocial behavior. Moral development: A compendium, Vol. 7.* New York: Garland.

Bieber, I., et al. (1962). *Homosexuality: A psychoanalytic study.* New York: Basic Books.

Biederman, I. (1981). On the semantics of a glance at a scene. In M. Kubovy and J. R. Pomerangtz (Eds.), *Perceptual organization.* Hillsdale, NJ: Erlbaum.

Biederman, I. (1987). Recognition-by-components: A theory of human image understanding. *Psychological Review, 94,* 115–147.

Biederman, I. (1990). Higher-level vision. In D. N. Osherson, S. Kosslyn, & J. Hollerbach (Eds.), *An invitation to cognitive science: Visual cognition and action.* Cambridge, MA: MIT Press.

Binet, A., & Simon, T. (1916). *The development of intelligence in children (the Binet-Simon scale).* Baltimore: Williams & Wilkins.

Binkley, C. (2000, May 4). Casion chain mines data on its gamblers, and strikes pay dirt. *Wall Street Journal,* pp. A1, A10.

Binstock, R., & George, L. K. (Eds.). (1996). *Handbook of aging and the social sciences* (4th ed.). San Diego: Academic Press.

Birbaumer, N., Ghanayim, N., Hinterberger, T., Iversen, I., Kotchoubey, B., Kubler, A., Perelmouter, J., Taub, E., & Flor, H. (1999, March 25). A spelling device for the paralysed [letter]. *Nature, 398,* 297–298.

Bird, G., & Melville, K. (1994). *Families and intimate relationships.* (1994). New York: McGraw-Hill.

Birren, J. E. (Ed.). (1996). *Encyclopedia of gerontology: Age, aging and the aged.* San Diego: Academic Press.

Bjork, D. W. (1993). *B. F. Skinner: A life.* New York: Basic Books.

Bjork, E. L., & Bjork, R. A. (Eds.). (1996). *Memory.* New York: Academic Press.

Bjork, R. A., & Richardson-Klarehn, A. (1989). On the puzzling relationship between environmental context and human memory. In C. Izawa (Ed.), *Current issues in cognitive processes: The Tulane-Floweree symposium on cognition.* Hillsdale, NJ: Erlbaum.

Bjorklund, D. F. (1985). The role of conceptual knowledge in the development of organization in children's memory. In C. J. Brainerd & M. Pressley (Eds.), *Basic process in memory development.* New York: Springer-Verlag.

Bjorklund, D. F. (1997). In search of a metatheory for cognitive development (or, Piaget is dead and I don't feel so good myself). *Child Development, 68,* 144–148.

Blake, J., & de Boysson-Bardies, B. (1992). Patterns in babbling: A cross-linguistic study. *Journal of Child Language, 19,* 51–74.*

Blake, J., Quartaro, G., & Onorati, S. (1993). Evaluating quantitative measures of grammatical complexity in spontaneous speech samples. *Journal of Child Language, 20,* 139–152.*

Blakeslee, S. (1992, August 11). Finding a new messenger for the brain's signals to the body. *New York Times,* p. C3.

Blakeslee, S. (2000, January 4). A decade of discovery yields a shock about the brain. *New York Times,* D1.

Blanchard, F. A., Lilly, R., & Vaughn, L. A. (1991). Reducing the expression of racial prejudice. *Psychological Science, 2,* 101–105.

Blanck, P. D. (Ed.). (1993). *Interpersonal expectations: Theory, research and applications.* Cambridge, England: Cambridge University Press.

Bland, R. C., Newman, S. C., & Orn, H. (1988). Period prevalence of psychiatric disorders in Edmonton. *Acta Psychiatrica Scandanvica, 77,* 33–42.*

Blank, M., & White, S. J. (1999). Activating the zone of proximal development in school: Obstacles and solutions. In P. Lloyd & C. Fernyhough (Eds.), *Lev Vygotsky: Critical assessments: The zone of proximal development, Vol. 3.* New York: Routledge.

Blascovich, J. J., & Katkin, E. S. (Eds.) (1993). *Cardiovascular reactivity to psychological stress and disease.* Washington, DC: American Psychological Association.

Blass, T. (1996). Attribution of responsibility and trust in the Milgram obedience experiment. *Journal of Applied Social Psychology, 26,* 1529–1535.

Blass, T. (Ed.). (2000). *Obedience to authority: Current perspectives on the Milgram paradigm.* Mahwah, NJ: Erlbaum.

Blau, Z. S. (1973). *Old age in a changing society.* New York: New Viewpoints.

Blewett, A. E. (2000). Help cards for patients. *Psychiatric Bulletin, 24,* 276.

Blume, S. B. (1998, March). Alcoholism in women. *Harvard Mental Health Letter,* pp. 5–7.

Boakes, R. A., Popplewell, D. A., & Burton, M. J. (Eds.). (1987). *Eating habits: Food, physiology, and learned behaviour.* New York: Wiley.

Bochner, S. (1996). The learning strategies of bilingual versus monolingual students. *British Journal of Educational Psychology, 66,* 263–268.*

Boehm, K. E., Schondel, C. K., Marlowe, A. L., & Rose, J. S. (1995). Adolescents calling a peer-listening phone service: Variations in calls by gender, age, and season of year. *Adolescence, 30,* 863–871.

Bolla, K. I., Cadet, J. L., & London, E. D. (1998). The neuropsychiatry of chronic cocaine abuse. *Journal of Neuropsychiatry and Clinical Neurosciences, 10,* 280–289.

Booth, D. A. (1994). *Psychology of nutrition.* London: Taylor & Francis.

Bornstein, M. H. & Arterberry, M. (1999). Perceptual development. In M. Bornstein & M. Lamb, *Developmental psychology.* Mahwah, NJ: Erlbaum.

Bornstein, M. H., & Bruner, J. S. (Eds.). (1989). *Interaction on human development: Crosscurrents in contemporary psychology services.* Hillsdale, NJ: Erlbaum.

Bornstein, R. F. (1996). Construct validity of the Rorschach Oral Dependency Scale: 1967–1995. *Psychological Assessment, 8,* 200–205.

Bornstein, R. F., & D'Agostino, P. R. (1994). The attribution and discounting of perceptual

fluency: Preliminary tests of a perceptual fluency/attributional model of the mere exposure effect. *Social Cognition, 12,* 103–128.

Botting, J. H., & Morrison, A. R. (1997, February). Animal research is vital to medicine. *Scientific American, 276,* 83–86.

Bouchard, C., & Bray, G. A. (Eds.). (1996). *Regulation of body weight: Biological and behavioral mechanisms.* New York: Wiley.

Bouchard, C., Rhéaume, J., & Ladouceur, R. (1999). Responsibility and perfectionism in OCD: An experimantal study. *Behavior Research and Therapy, 37,* 239–248.*

Bouchard, C., Tremblay, A., Despres, J. P., Nadeau, A., et al. (1990, May 24). The response to long-term overfeeding in identical twins. *New England Journal of Medicine, 322,* 1477–1482.

Bourne, L. E., Dominowski, R. L., Loftus, E. F., & Healy, A. F. (1986). *Cognitive processes* (2nd ed.). Englewood Cliffs, NJ: Prentice Hall.

Bower, G. H., Thompson, S. S., & Tulving, E. (1994). Reducing retroactive interference: An interference analysis. *Journal of Experimental Psychology Learning, Memory, and Cognition, 20,* 51–66.

Bowman, M. L. (2000). The diversity of diversity: Canadian-American differences and their implications for clinical training and APA accreditation. *Canadian Psychology, 41,* 230–243.*

Bradsher, K. (2000, July 17). Was Freud a minivan or S.U.V. kind of guy? *New York Times,* pp. A1, A16.

Braff, D. L. (1993). Information processing and attention dysfunctions in schizophrenia. *Schizophrenia Bulletin, 19,* 233–259.

Brandimonte, M. A., Hitch, G. J., & Bishop, D. V. (1992). Manipulation of visual mental images in children and adults. *Journal of Experimental Child Psychology, 53,* 300–312.

Braun, A. R., Balkin, T. J., Wesensten, N. J., Gwadry, F., Carson, R. E., Varga, M., Baldwin, P., Belenky, G., & Herscovitch, P. (1998). Dissociated pattern of activity in visual cortices and their projections during human rapid eye movement sleep. *Science, 279,* 91–95.

Brazelton, T. B. (1969). *Infants and mothers: Differences in development.* New York: Dell.

Brehm, J. W., & Self, E. A. (1989). The intensity of motivation. *Annual Review of Psychology, 40,* 109–131.

Brehm, S. S., & Brehm, J. W. (1981). *Psychological reactance.* New York: Academic Press.

Breland, K., & Breland, M. (1961). Misbehavior of organisms. *American Psychologist, 16,* 681–684.

Brendgen, M., Vitaro, F., & Bukowski, W. M. (2000). Deviant friends and early adolescents' emotional and behavioral adjustment. *Journal of Research on Adolescence, 10,* 173–189.

Brewer, J. B., Zhao, Z., Desmond, J. E., Glover, G. H., & Gabrieli, J. D. E. (1998, August 21). Making memories: Brain activity that predicts how well visual experience will be remembered. *Science, 281,* 1185–1187.

Brief psychodynamic therapy, Part I. (1994, March). *Harvard Mental Health Letter,* p. 10.

Brislin, R. (1993). *Understanding culture's influence on behavior.* Fort Worth, TX: Harcourt Brace Jovanovich.

Brodbeck, D. R., and Shettleworth, S. J. (1995). Memory for the location and color of a compound stimulus: Comparison of a food-storing and a non-storing bird species. *Journal of Experimental Psychology: Animal Behaviour Processes, 21,* 64–77.*

Brody, N. (1990). Behavior therapy versus placebo: Comment on Bowers and Clum's meta-analysis. *Psychological Bulletin, 107,* 106–109.

Bromm, B., & Desmedt, J. E. (Eds.). (1995). *Pain and the brain: From nociception to cognition.* New York: Raven Press.

Brookhiser, R. (1997, January 13). Lost in the weed. *U.S. News and World Report,* p. 9.

Broughton, R. J., & Ogilvie, R. D. (Eds.). (1992). *Sleep, arousal and performance: Problems and promises.* Boston: Birkhauser.*

Brown, A. S., Susser, E. S., Butler, P. D., Andrews, R. R., et al. (1996). Neurobiological plausibility of prenatal nutritional deprivation as a risk factor for schizophrenia. *Journal of Nervous and Mental Disease, 184,* 71–85.

Brown, L. S., & Pope, K. S. (1996). *Recovered memories of abuse: Assessment, therapy, forensics.* Washington, DC: American Psychological Association.

Brown, M. B. (2000). Diagnosis and treatment of children and adolescents with attention-deficit/hyperactivity disorder. *Journal of Counseling and Development, 78,* 195–203.

Brown, R. (1958). How shall a thing be called? *Psychological Review, 65,* 14–21.

Brown, R. (1986). *Social psychology* (2nd ed.). New York: Macmillan.

Brown, S. I., & Walter, M. I. (Eds.). (1993). *Problem posing: Reflections and applications.* Hillsdale, NJ: Erlbaum.

Bruce, B., & Wilfley, D. (1996). Binge eating among the overweight population: A serious and prevalent problem. *Journal of the American Dietetic Association, 96,* 58–61.

Bruce, D., Dolan, A., & Phillips-Grant, K. (2000). On the transition from childhood amnesia to the recall of personal memories. *Psychological Science, 11,* 360–364.*

Bruce, V., Green, P. R., & Georgeson, M. (1997). *Visual perception: Physiology, psychology and ecology* (3rd ed.). Mahwah, NJ: Erlbaum.

Bruner, J. (1983). *Child's talk: Learning to use language.* Oxford: Oxford University Press.

Brunet, A., Boyer, R., Weiss, D. S., & Maarmar, C. R. (2001). The effects of initial trauma exposure on the symptomatic response to a subsequent trauma. *Canadian Journal of Behavioural Science, 33,* 97–102.*

Brunner, H. G., Nelen, M., Breakefield, X. O., Ropers, H. H., & van Oost, B. A. (1993, October 22). Abnormal behavior associated with a point mutation in the structural gene for monoamine oxidase A. *Science, 262,* 578–580.

Brzustowicz, L. M., Hodgkinson, K. A., Chow, E. W. C., Honer, W. G., & Bassett, A. S. (2000, April 28). Location of major susceptibility locus for familial schizophrenia on chromosome 1q21–q22. *Science, 288,* 678–682.

Buck, L., & Axel, R. (1991, April 5). A novel multigene family may encode odorant receptors: A molecular basis for odor recognition. *Cell, 65,* 167–175.

Bujold, A., Ladouceur, R., Sylvain, C., & Boisvert, J. (1994). Treatment of pathological gamblers: An experimental study. *Journal of Behaviour Therapy and Experimental Psychiatry, 25,* 275–282.*

Bukowski, W. M., Newcomb, A. F., & Hartup, W. W. (Eds.). (1996). *The company they keep: Friendship in childhood and adolescence.* New York: Cambridge University Press.

Burack, J. A., Hodapp, R. M., & Zigler, E. (Eds.). (1998). *Handbook of mental retardation and development*. New York: Cambridge University Press.

Burchinal, M. R., Roberts, J. E., Riggins, R., Jr., Zeisel, S. A., Neebe, E., & Bryant, D. (2000). Relating quality of center-based child care to early cognitive and language development longitudinally. *Child Development, 71,* 338–357.

Burger, J. M. (1986). Increasing compliance by improving the deal: The that's-not-all technique. *Journal of Personality and Social Psychology, 51,* 277–283.

Burger, J. M. (1999). The foot-in-the-door compliance procedure: A multiple-process analysis and review. *Personality and Social Psychology Review, 3,* 303–325.

Burgess, N., Becker, S., King, J., & O'Keefe, J. (2001). Memory for events and their spatial context: Models and experiments. *Philosophical Transactions of the Royal Society of London B, 356,* 1493–1503.*

Burnham, D. K. (1983). Apparent relative size in the judgment of apparent distance. *Perception, 12,* 683–700.

Burns, A., & Scott, C. (1994). *Mother-headed families and why they have increased.* Hillsdale, NJ: Erlbaum.

Burstyn, L. (1995, October). Female circumcision comes to America. *Atlantic Monthly, 276,* 28–35.

Bush, P. J., & Osterweis, M. (1978). Pathways to medicine use. *Journal of Health and Social Behavior, 19,* 179–189.

Bushman, B. J. (1993). Human aggression while under the influence of alcohol and other drugs: An integrative research review. *Current Directions in Psychological Science, 2,* 148–152.

Bushman, B. J., & Baumeister, R. F. (1998). Threatened egotism, narcissism, self-esteem, and direct and displaced aggression: Does self-love or self-hate lead to violence? *Journal of Personality and Social Psychology, 75,* 219–229.

Buss, D. M. (1999). Human nature and individual differences: The evolution of human personality. In L. A. Pervin & O. P. John (Eds.), *Handbook of personality: Theory and research* (2nd ed.). New York: Guilford Press.

Buss, D. M., et al. (1990). International preferences in selecting mates: A study of 37 cultures. *Journal of Cross-Cultural Psychology, 21,* 5–47.

Butcher, J. N. (1995). Interpretation of the MMPI-2. In L. E. Beutler & M. R. Berren (Eds.), *Integrative assessment of adult personality.* New York: Guilford Press.

Butcher, J. N. (1999). *A beginner's guide to the MMPI-2.* Washington, DC: American Psychological Association.

Butcher, J. N., Graham, J. R., Dahlstrom, W. G., & Bowman, E. (1990). The MMPI-2 with college students. *Journal of Personality Assessment, 54,* 1–15.

Butler, R., Oberlink, M. R., & Schechter, M. (Eds.). (1990). *The promise of productive aging: From biology to social policy.* New York: Springer.

Byne, W. (1996). Biology and homosexuality: Implications of neuroendocrinological and neuroanatomical studies. In R. P. Cabaj & T. S. Stein (Eds.), *Textbook of homosexuality and mental health.* Washington, DC: American Psychiatric Press.

Byrne, D. (1969). Attitudes and attraction. In L. Berkowitz (Ed.), *Advances in experimental social psychology* (Vol. 4, pp. 35–89). New York: Academic Press.

Cabeza, R., Mangels, J. A., Nyberg, L., Habils, R., Houle, S., McIntosh, A. R., & Tulving, E. (1997). Brain regions differentially involved in remembering what and when. *Neuron, 19,* 863–870.*

Caldwell, J. P. (2001). *Sleep, the complete guide to sleep disorders and a better night's sleep.* Toronto: Key Porter Books.*

Calmes, J. (1998, March 5). Americans retain puritan attitudes on matters of sex. *Wall Street Journal,* p. A12.

Campbell, J. D., Trapnell, P. D., Heine, S. J., Katz, I. M., Lavallee, L. F., & Lehman, D. R. (1996). Self-concept clarity: Measurement, correlates, and cultural boundaries. *Journal of Personality and Social Psychology, 70,* 141–156.*

Campbell, J. J., Lamb, M. E., & Hwang, C. P. (2000). Early child-care experiences and children's social competence between 1.5 and 15 years of age. *Applied Developmental Science, 4,* 166–175.

Campfield, L. A., Smith, F. J., Rosenbaum, M., & Hirsch, J. (1996). Human eating: Evidence for a physiological basis using a modified paradigm. [Special Issue: Society for the Study of Ingestive Behavior, Second Independent Meeting.] *Neuroscience and Biobehavioral Reviews, 20,* 133–137.

Canadian Centre for Substance Abuse. (1995). *Alcohol and drug use: Results from the 1993 General Society Survey.* Ottawa: CCSA.*

Canadian Institute for Health Information (2002). A Report on Mental Illnesses in Canada.* Available <http://secure.cihi.ca/cihiweb/dispPage.jsp?cw_page=reports_mental_illness_e>. Accessed December 11, 2002.

Canadian Psychological Association. (1991). *Canadian code of ethics for psychologists.* Revised. Ottawa: Author.*

Canadian Psychological Association. (1996). *Guidelines for the use of animals in research and instruction in psychology: Commentary and elaboration.* Ottawa: Author.*

Canadian Study of Health and Aging Working Group. (1994). Canadian study of health and aging: Study methods and prevalence of dementia. *Canadian Medical Association Journal, 150,* 899–913.*

Cannon, T. D. (1998). Genetic and perinatal influences in the etiology of schizophrenia: A neurodevelopmental model. In M. F. Lenzenweger & R. H. Dworkin (Eds.), *The origins and development of schizophrenia: Advances in experimental psychopathology.* Washington, DC: American Psychological Association.

Cannon, W. B. (1929). Organization for physiological homeostatics. *Physiological Review, 9,* 280–289.

Cantor, C., & Fallon, B. A. (1996). *Phantom illness: Shattering the myth of hypochondria.* Boston: Houghton Mifflin.

Capaldi, E. D. (Ed.) (1996). *Why we eat what we eat: The psychology of eating.* Washington, DC: American Psychological Association.

Carlson, M., Marcus-Newhall, A., & Miller, N. (1990). Effects of situational aggression cues: A quantitative review. *Journal of Personality and Social Psychology, 58,* 622–633.

Carney, R. N., & Levin, J. R. (1998). Coming to terms with the keyword method in introductory psychology: A "neuromnemonic" example. *Teaching of Psychology, 25,* 132–135.

Carney, R. N., Levin, J. R., Levin, M. E. & Schoen, L. M. (2000). Improving memory. In M. E. Ware & D. E. Johnson et al. (Eds.), *Handbook of demonstrations and activities in the teaching of psychology: Physiological-comparative, perception, learning, cognitive, and developmental* (2nd ed., Vol. 2). Mahwah, NJ: Erlbaum.

Carroll, J. M., & Russell, J. A. (1997). Facial expressions in Hollywood's portrayal of emotion. *Journal of Personality and Social Psychology, 72,* 164–176.

Carson, R. C., Butcher, J. N., & Coleman, J. C. (1992). *Abnormal psychology and modern life* (9th ed.). New York: HarperCollins.

Carter, A. S., Pauls, D. L., & Leckman, J. F. (1995). The development of obsessionality: Continuities and discontinuities. In D. Cicchetti & D. J. Cohen (Eds.), *Developmental psychopathology: Vol. 2. Risk, disorder, and adaptation.* New York: Wiley.

Carver, C. S., Harris, S. D., Lehman, J. M., Durel, L. A., Antoni, M. H., Spencer, S. M., & Pozo-Kaderman, C. (2000). How important is the perception of personal control? Studies of early stage breast cancer patients. *Personality and Social Psychology Bulletin, 26,* 139–149.

Case, R., & Okamoto, Y. (1996). The role of central conceptual structures in the development of children's thought. *Monographs of the Society for Research in Child Development, 61,* v-265.

Caspi, A., Henry, B., McGee, R. O., Moffitt, T. E., & Silva, P. A. (1995). Temperamental origins of child and adolescent behavior problems: From age three to age fifteen. *Child Development, 66,* 55–68.

Cattell, R. B. (1965). *The scientific analysis of personality.* Chicago: Aldine.

Cattell, R. B. (1967). *The scientific analysis of personality.* Baltimore: Penguin.

Cattell, R. B. (1987). *Intelligence: Its structure, growth, and action.* Amsterdam: North-Holland.

Cattell, R. B., Cattell, A. K., & Catell, H. E. P. (1993). *Sixteen personality factor questionnaire (16PF)* (5th ed.). San Antonio: Harcourt Brace.

Cattell, R. B., Eber & Tatsuoka (1970). *Handbook for the 16PF.* Champaign, IL: Institute for Personality and Ability Testing.

CBC News Online. (2002, June 12). *Obese children facing health 'crisis'.* Available: <http://cbc.ca/stories/2002/06/12/kids_obese020612>. Accessed December 12, 2002.

Cenoz, J., & Genesee, F. (1998). *Beyond bilingualism: Multilingualism and multilingual education.* Clevedon, England: Multilingual Matters.*

Centers for Disease Control. (1992). *Most students sexually active: Survey of sexual activity.* Atlanta: Author.

Centers for Disease Control and Prevention. (1994). Cigarette smoking among adults—United States, 1993. *Morbidity and Mortality Weekly Report, 43,* 925–930.

Chamberlain, K., & Zika, S. (1990). The minor events approach to stress: Support for the use of daily hassles. *British Journal of Psychology, 81,* 469–481.

Chandler, M., & Lalonde, C. (1996). Shifting to an interpretive theory of mind: 5- to 7-year-olds' changing conceptions of mental life. In A. J. Sameroff & M. M. Haith (Eds.), *The five to seven year shift: The age of reason and responsibility.* Chicago: University of Chicago Press.

Chandler, M. J. (1976). Social cognition and life-span approaches to the study of child development. In H. W. Reese & L. P. Lipsitt (Eds.), *Advances in child development and behavior* (Vol. 11). New York: Academic Press.

Chapman, L. J., & Chapman, J. P. (1973). *Disordered thought in schizophrenia.* New York: Appleton-Century-Crofts.

Chastain, G., & Landrum, R. E. (Eds.). (1999). *Protecting human subjects: Departmental subject pools and institutional review boards.* Washington, DC: American Psychological Association.

Cheakalos, C., & Heyn, E. (1998, November 2). Mercy mission. *People Weekly,* pp. 149–150.

Chen, J., & Gardner, H. (1997). Alternative assessment from a multiple intelligences theoretical perspective. In D. P. Flanagen, J. L. Genshaft, & P. L. Harrison (Eds.), *Contemporary intellectual assessment: Theories, tests, and issues.* New York: Guilford Press.

Cheney, C. D. (1996). Medical nonadherence: A behavior analysis. In J. R. Cautela & W. Ishaq (Eds.), *Contemporary issues in behavior therapy: Improving the human condition: Applied clinical psychology.* New York: Plenum Press.

Cheng, H., Cao, Y., & Olson, L. (1996, July 26). Spinal cord repair in adult paraplegic rats: Partial restoration of hind limb function. *Science, 273,* 510–513.

Cherlin, A. (1993). *Marriage, divorce, remarriage.* Cambridge, MA: Harvard University Press.

Cherry, B. J., Buckwalter, J. G., & Henderson, V. W. (1996). Memory span procedures in Alzheimer's disease. *Neuropsychology, 10,* 286–293.

Chess, S. (1997, November). Temperament: Theory and clinical practice. *Harvard Mental Health Letter,* pp. 5–7.

Cheston, S. E. (2000). A new paradigm for teaching counseling theory and practice. *Counselor Education and Supervision, 39,* 254–269.

Cheung, F. M., & Leung, K. (1998). Indigenous personality measures: Chinese examples. *Journal of Cross-Cultural Psychology, 29,* 233–248.*

Chi-Ching, Y., & Noi, L. S. (1994). Learning styles and their implications for cross-cultural management in Singapore. *Journal of Social Psychology, 134,* 593–600.

Childcare Resource and Research Unit, University of Toronto. (1998).* Available: <http://www.childcarecanada.org/resources/CRRUpubs/benefits/bctoc.html>. Accessed December 12, 2002.

Chin, S. B., & Pisoni, D. B. (1997). *Alcohol and speech.* New York: Academic Press.

Cho, A. (2000, June 16). What's shakin' in the ear? *Science, 288,* 1954–1955.

Chodorow, N. (1978). *The reproduction of mothering.* Berkeley: University of California Press.

Chomsky, N. (1968). *Language and mind.* New York: Harcourt Brace Jovanovich.

Chomsky, N. (1969). *The acquisition of syntax in children from five to ten.* Cambridge, MA: MIT Press.

Chomsky, N. (1978). On the biological basis of language capacities. In G. A. Miller & E. Lennenberg (Eds.), *Psychology and biology of language and thought* (pp. 199–220). New York: Academic Press.

Chomsky, N. (1991). Linguistics and cognitive science: Problems and mysteries. In A. Kasher (Ed.), *The Chomskyan turn.* Cambridge, MA: Blackwell.

Churchland, P. S., & Ramachandran, V. S. (1995). Filling in: Why Dennett is wrong. In B. Dahlbom (Ed.), *Dennett and his critics: Demystifying mind: Philosophers and their critics.* Oxford, England: Basil Blackwell.

Cialdini, R. B. (1988). *Influence: Science and practice* (2nd ed.). Glenview, IL: Scott, Foresman.

Cialdini, R. B. (1997). Professionally responsible communication with the public: Giving psychology a way. *Personality and Social Psychology Bulletin, 31,* 206–215.

Cialdini, R. B., Schaller, M., Houlihan, D., Arps, K., Fultz, J., & Beaman, A. L. (1975). Reciprocal concessions procedure for inducing compliance: The door-in-the-face technique. *Journal of Personality and Social Psychology, 31,* 206–215.

Clancy, S. A., Schacter, D. L., McNally, R. J, & Pitman, R. K. (2000). False recognition in women reporting recovered memories of sexual abuse. *Psychological Science. 11,* 26–31.

Clark, L., & Watson, R. (1999). Temperament. In L. A. Pervin & O. P. John (Eds.), *Handbook of personality: Theory and research* (2nd ed.). New York: Guilford Press.

Clark, R., Anderson, N. B., Clark, V. R., & Williams, D. R. (1999). Racism as a stressor for African Americans: A biopsychosocial model. *American Psychologist, 54,* 805–816.

Clark, R. E., & Squire, L. R. (1998, April 3). Classical conditioning and brain systems: The role of awareness. *Science, 280,* 77–81.

Clarke-Stewart, K. A., & Friedman, S. (1987). *Child development: Infancy through adolescence.* New York: Wiley.

Clarke-Stewart, K. A., Vandell, D. L., McCartney, K., Owen, M. T., & Booth, C. (2000). Effects of parental separation and divorce on very young children. *Journal of Family Psychology, 14,* 304–326.

Clarkin, J. F., & Lenzenweger, M. F. (Ed.). (1996). *Major theories of personality disorder.* New York: Guilford Press.

Claxton-Oldfield, S., & Keefe, S. M. (1999). Assessing stereotypes about the Innu of Davis Inlet, Labrador. *Canadian Journal of Behavioural Science, 31,* 86–91.*

Clay, R. A. (January, 2000). Psychotherapy *is* cost effective. *Monitor on Psychology,* pp. 39–41.

Cloud, J. (2000, June 5). The lure of ecstasy. *Time,* pp. 60–68.

Coates, T. J., & Collins, C. (1998, July). Preventing HIV infection. *Scientific American,* pp. 96–97.

Coffey, C. E., Saxton, J. A., Ratcliff, G., Bryan, R. N., & Lucke, J. F. (1999). Relation of education to brain size in normal aging: Implications for the reserve hypothesis. *Neurology, 53,* 198–207.

Cohen, D. (1993). *The development of play* (2nd ed.). London: Routledge.

Cohen, D. (1996). Law, social policy, and violence: The impact of regional cultures. *Journal of Personality and Social Psychology, 70,* 961–978.

Cohen, S. (1996, June). Psychological stress, immunity, and upper respiratory infections. *Current Directions in Psychological Science, 5,* 86–90.

Cole, M., & Gay, J. (1972). Culture and memory. *American Anthropologist, 74,* 1066–1084.

Coles, R. (1997). *The moral intelligence of children.* New York: Random House.

Collins, A. F., Gathercole, S. E., Conway, M. A. & Morris, P. E. (Eds.). (1993). *Theories of memory.* Hillsdale, NJ: Erlbaum.

Collins, A. M., & Loftus, E. F. (1975). A spreading-activation theory of semantic processing. *Psychological Review, 82,* 407–428.

Collins, A. M., & Quillian, M. R. (1969). Retrieval times from semantic memory. *Journal of Verbal Learning and Verbal Behavior, 8,* 240–247.

Coltraine, S., & Messineo, M. (2000). The perpetuation of subtle prejudice: Race and gender imagery in 1990s television advertising. *Sex Roles, 42,* 363–389.

Compas, B. E., Ey, S., & Grant, K. E. (1993). Taxonomy, assessment, and diagnosis of depression during adolescence. *Psychological Bulletin, 114,* 323–344.

Comuzzie, A. G., & Allison, D. B. (1998, May 29). The search for human obesity genes. *Science, 280,* 1374–1377.

Condon, J. W., & Crano, W. D. (1988). Inferred evaluation and the relation between attitude similarity and interpersonal attraction. *Journal of Personality and Social Psychology, 54,* 789–797.

Conoley, J. C., & Impara, J. C. (Eds.). (1997). *The 12th mental measurements yearbook.* Lincoln, NE: Buros Institute.

Conte, H. R., & Plutchik, R. (Eds.). (1995). *Ego defenses: Theory and measurement.* New York: Wiley.

Conway, M. A. (Ed.). (1997). *Cognitive models of memory.* Cambridge, MA: MIT Press.

Cooklin, A. (2000). Therapy, the family and others. In H. Maxwell (Ed.), *Clinical psychotherapy for health professionals.* London: Whurr.

Cooper, J., & Mackie, D. (1986). Video games and aggression in children. *Journal of Applied Social Psychology, 16,* 726–744.

Cooper, L. A., & Shepard, R. N. (1984, December). Turning something over in the mind. *Scientific American.* pp. 106–114.

Cooper, N. R., Kalaria, R. N., McGeer, P. L., & Rogers, J. (2000). Key issues in Alzheimer's disease inflammation. *Neurobiology of Aging, 21,* 451–453.

Cooper, S. H. (1989). Recent contributions to the theory of defense mechanism: A comparative view. *Journal of the American Psychoanalytic Association, 37,* 865–892.

Coren, S. (1992). The moon illusion: A different view through the legs. *Perceptual and Motor Skills, 75,* 827–831.

Coren, S. (1996). *Sleep thieves: An eye-opening exploration into the science and mysteries of sleep.* New York: Free Press.*

Coren, S., & Aks, D. J. (1990). Moon illusion in pictures: A multimechanism approach. *Journal of Experimental Psychology: Human Perception and Performance, 16,* 365–380.

Coren, S., & Hewitt, P. L. (1998). Is anorexia nervosa associated with elevated rates of suicide? *American Journal of Public Health, 88,* 1206–1207.*

Coren, S., & Ward, L. M. (1989). *Sensation and perception* (3rd ed.). San Diego: Harcourt Brace Jovanovich.

Coren, S., Ward, L. M., & Enns, J. T. (1999). *Sensation and perception* (5th ed.). Fort Worth: Harcourt Brace.*

Cornelius, S. W., & Caspi, A. (1987). Everyday problem solving in adulthood and old age. *Psychology and Aging, 2,* 144–153.

Cornell, T. L., Fromkin, V. A., & Mauner, G. (1993). A linguistic approach to language processing in Broca's aphasia: A paradox resolved. *Current Directions in Psychological Science, 2,* 47–52.

Coronel, M. (1996). Interview with Jane Elliott. Available: <http://www.magenta.nl/EyetoEye/contraste.html>. Accessed November 2, 2002.

Cote, K. A., & Campbell, K. B. (2000). The role of the sleep spindle in human information processing of high-intensity stimuli during sleep. *Journal of Sleep Research, 9,* 19–26.*

Cote, K. A., de Lugt, D. R., & Campbell, K. B. (2002). Changes in the scalp topography of event-related potentials and behavioural responses during the sleep onset period. *Psychophysiology, 39,* 29–37.*

Cote, K. A., Etienne, L., & Campbell, K. B. (2001). Neurophysiological evidence for the detection of external stimuli during sleep. *Sleep, 24,* 1–13.*

Cotterell, J. (1996). *Social networks and social influences in adolescence.* London: Routledge.

Cotton, P. (1993, July 7). Psychiatrists set to approve DSM-IV. *Journal of the American Medical Association, 270,* 13–15.

Cowley, G. (2000, January 31). Alzheimer's: Unlocking the mystery. *Time,* pp. 46–54.

Cox, B. J., Endler, N. S., & Swinson, R. P. (1995). An examination of levels of agoraphobic severity in panic disorder. *Behavior Research and Therapy, 33,* 57–62.*

Cox, B. J., Swinson, R. P., Endler, N. S. & Norton, G. R. (1994). The symptom structure of panic attacks. *Comprehensive Psychiatry, 35,* 349–353.*

Craig, I. W., McClay, J., Plomin, R., & Freeman, B. (2000). Chasing behaviour genes into the next millennium. *Trends in Biotechnology, 18,* 22–26.

Craig, R. J. (1999). *Interpreting personality tests: A clinical manual for the MMPI-2, MCMI-III, CPI-R, and 16PF.* New York: Wiley.

Craik, F. I. (1990). Levels of processing. In M. E. Eysenck (Ed.), *The Blackwell dictionary of cognitive psychology,* London: Blackwell.

Craik, F. I., & Lockhart, R. S. (1972). Levels of processing: A framework for memory research. *Journal of Verbal Behavior, 11,* 671–684.

Craik, F. I. M., & Tulving, E. (1975). Depth of processing and the retention of words in episodic memory. *Journal of Experimental Psychology, 104,* 268–294.*

Cramer, J. A. (1995). Optimizing long-term patient compliance. *Neurology, 45,* s25–s28.

Cramer, P. (1996). *Storytelling, narrative, and the Thematic Apperception Test.* New York: Guilford Press.

Crapo, L. (1985). *Hormones, the messengers of life.* New York: Freeman.

Crews, F. (1996). The verdict on Freud. *Psychological Science, 7,* 63–68.

Crick, N. R., & Dodge, K. A. (1994). A review and reformulation of social information-processing mechanisms in children's social adjustment. *Psychological Bulletin, 115,* 74–101.

Crits-Christoph, P. (1992). The efficacy of brief dynamic psychotherapy: A meta-analysis. *American Journal of Psychiatry, 149,* 151–158.

Crouter, A. C., Bumpus, M. F., Maguire, M. C., & McHale, S. M. (1999). Linking parents' work pressure and adolescents' well-being: Insights into dynamics in dual-earner families. *Developmental Psychology, 35,* 1453–1461.

Crow, T. J. (1995). A theory of the evolutionary origins of psychosis. *European Neuropsychopharmacology, 5,* 59–63.

Croyle, R. T., & Hunt, J. R. (1991). Coping with health threat: Social influence processes in reactions to medical test results. *Journal of Personality and Social Psychology, 60,* 382–389.

Csikszentmihalyi, M. (1997). *Creativity: Flow and the psychology of discovery and invention.* New York: Basic Books.

Culbertson, F. M. (1997, January). Depression and gender: An international review. *American Psychologist, 52,* 25–31.

Cummings, E., & Henry, W. E. (1961). *Growing old.* New York: Basic Books.

Cwikel, J., Behar, L., & Rabson-Hare, J. (2000). A comparison of a vote count and a meta-analysis review of intervention research with adult cancer patients. *Research on Social Work Practice, 10,* 139–158.

Czeisler, C. A., Duffy, J. F., Shanahan, T. L., Brown, E. N., Mitchell, J. F., Rimmer, D. W., Ronda, J. M., Silva, E. J., Allan, J. S., Emens, J. S., Dijk, D. J., & Kronauer, R. E. (1999, June 25). Stability, precision, and near-24-hour period of the human circadian pacemaker. *Science, 284,* 2177–2181.

Dabbs, J. M., Jr., Hargrove, M. F., & Heusel, C. (1996). Testosterone differences among college fraternities: Well-behaved vs. rambunctious. *Personality and Individual Differences, 20,* 157–161.

Damasio, A. (1999). *The feeling of what happens: Body and emotion in the making of consciousness.* New York: Harcourt Brace.

Damasio, H., Grabowski, T., Frank, R., Galaburda, A. M., & Damasio, A. R. (1994, May 20). The return of Phineas Gage: Clues about the brain from the skull of a famous patient. *Science, 264,* 1102–1105.

Damon, W. (1999, August). The moral development of children. *Scientific American,* pp. 72–78.

Daneman, M. & Hannon, B. (2001). Using working memory theory to investigate the construct validity of multiple-choice reading comprehension tests such as the SAT. *Journal of Experimental Psychology: General, 130,* 208–223.*

Daniels, H. (Ed.). (1996). *An introduction to Vygotsky.* London: Routledge.

Darley, J. M. (1995). Constructive and destructive obedience: A taxonomy of principal-agent relationships. *Journal of Social Issues, 51,* 125–154.

Darwin, C. J., Turvey, M. T., & Crowder, R. G. (1972). An auditory analogue of the Sperling partial-report procedure: Evidence for brief auditory storage. *Cognitive Psychology, 3,* 255–267.

Davidson, J. E., Deuser, R., & Sternberg, R. J. (1994). The role of metacognition in problem solving. In J. Metcalfe & A. P. Shimamura (Eds.), *Metacognition: Knowing about knowing.* Cambridge, MA: MIT Press.

Davidson, J. R. T. (2000). Trauma: The impact of post-traumatic stress disorder. *Journal of Psychopharmacology, 14,* S5–S12.

Davidson, R. J. (1994). Complexities in the search for emotion-specific physiology. In P. Ekman & R. J. Davidson (Eds.), *The nature of emotion.* New York: Oxford University Press.

Davidson, R. J., Gray, J. A., LeDoux, J. E., Levenson, R. W., Panksepp, J., & Ekman, P. (1994). Is there emotion-specific physiology? In P. Ekman & R. J. Davidson (Eds.), *The nature of emotion.* New York: Oxford University Press.

Davidson, R. J., Putnam, K. M., & Larson, C. L. (2000, July 28). Dysfunction in the neural circuitry of emotion regulation—a possible prelude to violence. *Science, 289,* 591–594.

DeAngelis, T. (2000, April). Is Internet addiction real? *APA Monitor,* pp. 24–27.

Deary, I. J., & Stough, C. (1996). Intelligence and inspection time: Achievements, prospects, and problems. *American Psychologist, 51,* 599–608.

de Boysson-Bardies, B., & Halle, P. A. (1994). Speech development: Contributions of cross-linguistic studies. In A. Vyt, H. Bloch, & M. H.

Bornstein (Eds.), *Early child development in the French tradition: Contributions from current research.* Hillsdale, NJ: Erlbaum.

deCharms, R. C., Blake, D. T., & Merzenich, M. M. (1998, May 29). Optimizing sound features for cortical neurons. *Science, 280,* 1439–1440.

Deci, E. L., Koestner, R., & Ryan, R. M. (1999). A meta-analytic review of experiments examining the effects of extrinsic rewards on intrinsic motivation. *Psychological Bulletin, 125,* 627–668.

DeCourville, N. H., & Sadava, S. W. (1997). The structure of problem drinking in adulthood: A confirmatory approach. *Journal of Studies on Alcohol, 58,* 146–154.*

Deffenbacher, J. L. (1988). Cognitive relaxation and social skills treatments of anger: A year later. *Journal of Consulting Psychology, 35,* 309–315.

Deffenbacher, J. L. (1996). Cognitive-behavioral approaches to anger reduction. In K. S. Dobson & K. D. Craig (Eds.), *Advances in cognitive-behavioral therapy* (Vol. 2). Thousand Oaks, CA: Sage.

deGroot, A. D. (1966). Perception and memory versus thought: Some old ideas and recent findings. In B. Kleinmuntz (Ed.), *Problem solving: Research, method, and theory,* New York: Wiley.

Delahanty, D., & Baum, A. (2000). Stress and breast cancer. In A. S. Baum, R. A. Revenson, & J. E. Singer (Eds.), *Handbook of health psychology.* Mahwah, NJ: Erlbaum.

Delaney, C. H. (1995). Rites of passage in adolescence. *Adolescence, 30,* 891–897.

Delgado, P. L., & Moreno, F. A. (2000). Role of norepinephrine in depression. *Journal of Clinical Psychiatry, 61,* 5–12.

Della Sala, S., Baddeley, A. D., Papagno, C., & Spinnler, H. (1995). Dual-task paradigm: A means to examine the central executive. In J. Grafman, K. J. Holyoak, & F. Boller (Eds.), *Structure and functions of the human prefrontal cortex.* [Annals of the New York Academy of Sciences, Vol. 769.] New York: New York Academy of Sciences.

Delprato, D. J., & Midgley, B. D. (1992). Some fundamentals of B. F. Skinner's behaviorism. *American Psychologist, 47,* 1507–1520.

DeLuca, R. V., Grayston, A. G., & Romano, E. (1999). Time-limited group therapy for sexually abused boys. In C. Schaefer (Ed.), *Short-term psychotherapy groups for children.* New York: Aronson.*

Dement, W. C. (1976). *Some must watch while some must sleep.* New York: Norton.

Dement, W. C. (1979). Two kinds of sleep. In D. Goleman & R. J. Davidson (Eds.), *Consciousness: Brain, states of awareness, and mysticism* (pp. 72–75). New York: Harper & Row.

Dement, W. C. (1989). Circadian rhythms and sleeping cycles. In D. F. Dinges and R. J. Broughton (Eds.), *Sleep and alertness: Chrono-biological, behavioral and medical aspects of napping.* New York: Lippincott, Williams & Wilkins.

Dement, W. C., & Wolpert, E. A. (1958). The relation of eye movements, body mobility, and external stimuli to dream content. *Journal of Experimental Psychology, 55,* 543–553.

Dempster, F. N. (1981). Memory span: Sources of individual and developmental differences. *Psychological Bulletin, 89,* 63–100.

Denis, M., & Greenbaum, C. (Trans.). (1991). *Image and cognition.* London, England: Harverster Wheatsheaf.

Denmark, F. L. (1994). Engendering psychology. *American Psychologist, 49,* 329–334.

Denmark, G. L., & Fernandez, L. C. (1993). Historical development of the psychology of women. In F. L. Denmark & M. A. Paludi (Eds.), *A handbook of issues and theories.* Westport, CT: Greenwood Press.

Dent, J. (1984, March). *Reader's Digest,* p. 38.

Dentzer, S. (1986, May 5). Can you pass the job test? *Newsweek,* pp. 46–53.

Deregowski, J. B. (1973). Illusion and culture. In R. L. Gregory & G. H. Combrich (Eds.), *Illusion in nature and art* (pp. 161–192). New York: Scribner's.

Desimone, R. (1992, October 9). The physiology of memory: Recordings of things past. *Science, 258,* 245–255.

Detterman, D. K., Gabriel, L. T., & Ruthsatz, J. M. (2000). Intelligence and mental retardation. In R. J. Sternberg et al. (Eds.), *Handbook of intelligence.* New York: Cambridge University Press.

de Valois, R. L., & de Valois, K. K. (1993). A multi-stage color model. *Vision Research, 33,* 1053–1065.

de Waal, F. B. M. (1999, December). The end of nature versus nurture. *Scientific American,* pp. 94–99.

Diaz-Guerrero, R. (1979). Culture and personality revisited. *Annals of the New York Academy of Sciences, 285,* 119–130.

DiChiara, T. J., & Reinhart, P. H. (1997). Redox modulation of hslo Ca^{2+}-activated K$^+$ channels. *Journal of Neuroscience, 17,* 4942–4955.

Diener, E. (2000). Subjective well-being: The science of happiness and a proposal for a national index. *American Psychologist, 55,* 34–43.

Diener, E., & Diener, C. (1996). Most people are happy. *Psychological Science, 7,* 181–185.

Diener, E., Suh, E. M., Lucas, R. E., & Smith, H. L. (1999). Subjective well-being: Three decades of progress. *Psychological Bulletin, 125,* 276–302.

Dietz, T. L. (1998). An examination of violence and gender role portrayals in video games: Implications for gender socialization and aggressive behavior. *Sex Roles, 38,* 425–442.

DiFranza, J. R., & Lew, R. A. (1995, April). Effect of maternal cigarette smoking on pregnancy complications and sudden infant death syndrome. *Journal of Family Practice, 40,* 385–394.

DiGiovanna, A. G. (1994). *Human aging: Biological perspectives.* New York: McGraw-Hill.

Dillard, J. P. (1991). The current status of research on sequential-request compliance techniques. [Special issue: Meta-analysis in personality and social psychology.] *Personality and Social Psychology Bulletin, 17,* 283–288.

DiMatteo, M. R. (1997). Health behaviors and care decisions: An overview of professional-patient communications. In D. S. Gochman (Ed.), *Handbook of health behavior research.* New York: Plenum Press.

Dinges, D. F., Pack, F., Williams, K., Gillen, K. A., Powell, J. W., Ott, G. E., Aptowicz, C., & Pack, A. I. (1997). Cumulative sleepiness, mood disturbance, and psychomotor vigilance performance decrements during a week of sleep restricted to 4–5 hours per night. *Sleep, 20,* 267–273.

Dion, K. K., & Dion, K. L. (1991). Psychological individualism and love. *Journal of Social Behaviour and Personality, 6,* 17–33.*

Dion, K. K., & Dion, K. L. (1993). Individualistic and collectivistic perspectives on gender and the cultural context of love and intimacy. *The Journal of Social Issues, 49,* 53–69.*

Dion, K. K., & Dion, K. L. (1996). Cultural perspectives on romantic love. *Personal Relationships, 3,* 5–17.*

Dishman, R. K. (1997, January). Brain monoamines, exercise, and behavioral stress: animal models. *Medical Science Exercise, 29,* 63–74.

Dobbins, A. C., Jeo, R. M., Fiser, J., & Allman, J. M. (1998, July 24). Distance modulation of neural activity in the visual cortex. *Science, 281,* 552–555.

Dobelle, W. H. (2000). Artificial vision for the blind by connecting a television camera to the visual cortex. *ASAIO Journal, 46,* 3–9.

Dobson, K. S. (1995). Psychology in Canada: The future is not the past. *Canadian Psychology, 36(1),* 1–11.*

Doi, T. (1990). The cultural assumptions of psychoanalysis. In J. W. Stigler, R. A. Shweder, & G. Herdt (Eds.), *Cultural psychology: Essays on comparative human development.* New York: Cambridge University Press.

Dollard, J., Doob, L., Miller, N., Mower, O. H., & Sears, R. R. (1939). *Frustration and aggression.* New Haven, CT: Yale University Press.

Domhoff, G. W. (1996). *Finding meaning in dreams: A quantitative approach.* New York: Plenum Press.

Donakowski, D. W. & Esses, V. M. (1996). Native Canadians, First Nations, or Aboriginals: The effect of labels on attitudes toward Native Peoples. *Canadian Journal of Behavioural Science, 28,* 86–91.*

Dorion, A. A., Chantome, M., Hasboun, D., Zouaoui, A., Marsault, C., Capron, C., & Duyme, M. (2000). Hemispheric asymmetry and corpus callosum morphometry: A magnetic resonance imaging study. *Neuroscience Research, 36,* 9–13.

Dortch, S. (1996, October). Our aching heads. *American Demographics,* pp. 4–8.

Doty, R. L., Green, P. A., Ram, C., & Yankell, S. L. (1982). Communication of gender from human breath odors: Relationship to perceived intensity and pleasantness. *Hormones and Behavior, 16,* 13–22.

Doyle, A. B. & Aboud, F. E. (1995). A longitudinal study of white children's racial prejudice as a social cognitive development. *Merrill-Palmer Quarterly, 41(2),* 210–229. *

Dozois, D. J. A., & Dobson, K. (2001). Information processing and cognitive organization in unipolar depression: Specificity and comorbidity issues. *Journal of Abnormal Psychology, 110,* 236–246.*

Dressler, W. W., & Oths, K. S. (1997). Cultural determinants of health behavior. In D. S. Gochman (Ed.), *Handbook of health behavior research.* New York: Plenum Press.

Drew, M. L., Dobson, K. S., & Stam, H. J. (1999). The negative self-concept in clinical depression: discourse analysis. *Canadian Psychology, 40,* 192–204.*

Dreyer, P. H. (1982). Sexuality during adolescence. In B. B. Wolman (Ed.), *Handbook of developmental psychology.* Englewood Cliffs, NJ: Prentice Hall.

Druckman, D., & Bjork, R. A. (1991). *In the mind's eye: Enhancing human performance.* Washington, DC: National Academy Press.

Drummond, D. C., Tiffany, S. T., Glautier, S., & Remington, B. (Eds.). (1995). *Addictive behaviour: Cue exposure theory and practice.* Chichester, England: Wiley.

Dryden, W. (1999). *Rational emotive behavior therapy: A training manual.* New York: Springer.

Dubovsky, S. (1999, February 25). Tuning in to manic depression. *HealthNews, 5,* p. 8.

Dugas, M. J., Ladouceur, R., Boisvert, J. M., & Freeston, M. H. (1996). Le trouble d'anxiété généralisée: Éléments fondamentaux et interventions psychologiques. *Canadian Psychology, 37,* 40–53.*

Dugger, C. W. (1996, December 28). Tug of taboos: African genital rite vs. U.S. law. *New York Times,* pp. 1, 9.

Dunbar, J. (1998). A critical history of CPA's various codes of ethics for psychologists (1939–1986). *Canadian Psychology, 39(3).**

Duncan, P. D., et al. (1985). The effects of pubertal timing on body image, school behavior, and deviance. [Special Issue: Time of maturation and psychosocial functioning in adolescence: I.] *Journal of Youth and Adolescence, 14,* 227–235.

Duncker, K. (1945). On problem solving. *Psychological Monographs, 58* (5, whole no. 270).

Dunham, R. M., Kidwell, J. S., & Wilson, S. M. (1986). Rites of passage at adolescence: A ritual process paradigm. *Journal of Adolescent Research, 1,* 139–153.

Dupre, D., Miller, N., Gold, M., & Rospenda, K. (1995). Initiation and progression of alcohol, marijuana, and cocaine use among adolescent abusers. *American Journal on Addictions, 4,* 43–48.

Durkin, M. S., & Stein, Z. A. (1996). Classification of mental retardation. In J. W. Jacobson & J. A. Mulick (Eds.), *Manual of diagnosis and professional practice in mental retardation.* Washington, DC: American Psychological Association.

Durrant, J. E. (1996). Public attitudes toward corporal punishment in Canada. In D. Frehsee, W. Horn, & K. D. Bussman (Eds.), *Family violence against children: A challenge for society.* Berlin: de Gruyter.*

Dutton, D. G., & Aron, A. P. (1974). Some evidence for heightened sexual attraction under conditions of high anxiety. *Journal of Personality and Social Psychology, 30,* 510–517.

Eagly, A. (1989, May). *Meta-analysis of sex differences.* Paper presented at the annual conference on adversity, University of Massachusetts, Amherst.

Eagly, A. H., & Chaiken, S. (1993). *The psychology of attitudes.* Fort Worth, TX: Harcourt Brace Jovanovich.

Eagly, A. H., & Chaiken, S. (1995). Attitude strength, attitude structure, and resistance to change. In R. E. Petty & J. A. Krosnick (Eds.), *Attitude strength: Antecedents and consequences.* Mahwah, NJ: Erlbaum.

Earley, J. (1999). *Interactive group therapy: Integrating interpersonal, action-oriented and psychodynamic approaches.* New York: Brunner/Mazel.

Eating disorders, Part II. (1997, November). *Harvard Mental Health Letter,* pp. 1–5.

Ebbinghaus, H. (1885/1913). *Memory: A contribution to experimental psychology* (H. A. Roger & C. E. Bussenius, Trans.). New York: Columbia University Press.

Ebomoyi, E. (1987). Prevalence of female circumcision in two Nigerian communities. *Sex Roles, 17,* 13–152.

Eccles, J. S., Lord, S. E., & Roeser, R. W. (1996). Round holes, square pegs, rocky roads, and sore feet: The impact of stage-environment fit on young adolescents' experiences in schools and families. In D. Cicchetti & S. L. Toth (Eds.), *Adolescence: Opportunities and challenges.* Rochester, NY: University of Rochester Press.

Eccleston, C., & Crombez, G. (1999). Pain demands attention: A cognitive-affective model of the interruptive function of pain. *Psychological Bulletin, 125,* 356–366.

Ecenbarger, W. (1993, April 1). America's new merchants of death. *Reader's Digest,* p. 50.

Edgette, J. H., & Edgette, J. S. (1995). *The handbook of hypnotic phenomena in psychotherapy.* New York: Brunner/Mazel.

Eich, E., Macaulay, D., Loewenstein, R. J., & Dihle, P. H. (1997). Memory, amnesia, and dissociative identity disorder. *Psychological Science, 8,* 417–421.

Eichenbaum, H. (1993, August 20). Thinking about brain cell assemblies. *Science, 261,* 993–994.

Eichenbaum, H. (1997). Declarative memory: Insights from cognitive neurobiology. *Annual Review of Psychology, 48,* 547–572.

Eisen, L., Field, T. M., & Larson, S. K. (1991). Environmental effects on the fetus: The examples of alcohol, cocaine, and exercise. In L. Diamant (Ed.), *Mind-body maturity: Psychological approaches to sports, exercise, and fitness.* New York: Hemisphere.

Eisenberg, N. (1991). Meta-analytic contributions to the literature on prosocial behavior. *Personality and Social Psychology Bulletin, 17,* 273–282.

Eisenberger, R., Pierce, W. D., & Cameron, J. (1999). Effects of reward on intrinsic motivation—negative, neutral, and positive: Comment on Deci, Koestner, and Ryan (1999). *Psychological Bulletin, 125,* 677–691.

Ekman, P. (1994a). All emotions are basic. In P. Ekman & R. J. Davidson (Eds.), *The nature of emotion: Fundamental questions.* New York: Oxford University Press.

Ekman, P., & Davidson, R. J. (1994). *The nature of emotion: Fundamental questions.* New York: Oxford University Press.

Elkind, D. (1967). Egocentrism in adolescence. *Child Development, 38,* 1025–1034.

Elkind, D. (1985). Cognitive development and adolescent disabilities. *Journal of Adolescent Health Care, 6,* 84–89.

Elkind, D. (1988). *Miseducation.* New York: Knopf.

Elkins, I. J., McGue, M., & Iacono, W. G. (1997). Genetic and environmental influences on parent-son relationships: Evidence for increasing genetic influence during adolescence. *Developmental Psychology, 33,* 351–363.

Elliot, A. J., & Church, M. A. (1997). A hierarchical model of approach and avoidance achievement motivation. *Journal of Personality and Social Psychology, 72,* 218–232.

Ellis, A. (1974). *Growth through reason.* Hollywood, CA: Wilshire Books.

Ellis, A. (1999). Why rational emotive to rational emotive behavior therapy? *Psychotherapy, 36,* 154–159.

Ellis, A., & Dryden, W. (1997). *The practice of rational emotive behavior therapy* (2nd ed.). New York: Springer.

Embretson, S. E. (1996). Multidimensional latent trait models in measuring fundamental aspects of intelligence. In I. Dennis & P. Tapsfield (Eds.), *Human abilities: Their nature and measurement.* Mahwah, NJ: Erlbaum.

Endler, N. S. (1982). *Holiday of darkness.* New York: John Wiley & Sons.*

Endler, N. S. (1997). Stress, anxiety and coping: The multidimensional interaction model. *Canadian Psychology, 38,* 136–153.*

Endler, N. S., & Parker, J. D. (1993). The multidimensional assessment of coping: Concepts, issues, and measurement. In G. L. Van Heck, & P. Bonaiuto (Eds.), *Personality psychology in Europe* (Vol. 4). Tilburg, Netherlands: Tilburg University Press.*

Endler, N. S., & Speer, R. L. (1998). Personality psychology: Research trends for 1993–1995. *Journal of Personality, 66,* 621–669.*

Engebretson, T. O., & Stoney, C. M. (1995). Anger expression and lipid concentrations. *International Journal of Behavioral Medicine, 2,* 281–298.

Engen, T. (1987, September–October). Remembering odors and their names. *American Scientist, 75,* 497–503.

Engle-Friedman, M., Baker, A., & Bootzin, R. R. (1985). Reports of wakefulness during EEG identified stages of sleep. *Sleep Research, 14,* 152.

Engler, J., & Goleman, D. (1992). *The consumer's guide to psychotherapy.* New York: Simon & Schuster.

Enns, M. W., & Reiss, J. P. R. (1992). Electroconvulsive therapy. *Canadian Journal of Psychiatry, 37,* 671–678.*

Enserink, M. (1999, April 9). Can the placebo be the cure? *Science, 284,* 238–240.

Enserink, M. (2000a, April 21). Are placebo-controlled drug trials ethical? *Science, 288,* 416.

Enserink, M. (2000b, July 28). The violence of the lambs. *Science, 289,* 580–581.

Epstein, R. (1987). The spontaneous interconnection of four repertoires of behavior in a pigeon. *Journal of Comparative Psychology, 101,* 197–201.

Erickson, M. H., Hershman, S., & Secter, I. I. (1990). *The practical application of medical and dental hypnosis.* New York: Brunner/Mazel.

Erikson, E. H. (1963). *Childhood and society* (2nd ed.). New York: W. W. Norton.

Erlandson, D. A., Harris, E. L., Skipper, B. L., & Allen, S. D. (1993). *Doing naturalistic inquiry: A guide to methods.* Newbury Park, CA: Sage.

Esses, V. M., Haddock, G., Zanna, M. (1994). The role of mood in the expression of intergroup stereotypes. In M. P. Zanna & J. M. Olson (Eds.), *The psychology of prejudice: The Ontario Symposium* (Vol. 7, pp. 77–101). Hillsdale, NJ: Erlbaum.*

Estes, W. K. (1991). Cognitive architectures from the standpoint of an experimental psychologist. *Annual Review of Psychology, 42,* 1–28.

Estes, W. K. (1997). Significance testing in psychological research: Some persisting issues. *Psychological Science, 8,* 18–19.

Eveleth, P., & Tanner, J. (1976). *World-wide variation in human growth.* New York: Cambridge University Press.

Everly, G. S. (1989). *A clinical guide to the treatment of the human stress response.* New York: Plenum.*

Everly, G. S., & Mitchell, J. T. (1992). The prevention of work-related post traumatic stress: The critical incident stress debriefing process (CSID). Paper presented at the second APA-NIOSH conference on occupational stress, Washington, DC.*

Eysenck, H. J. (1975). *Eysenck on extroversion.* New York: Wiley.

Eysenck, H. J. (1990). Biological dimensions of personality. In L. A. Pervin (Ed.), *Handbook of personality: Theory and research* (p. 246). New York: Guilford Press.

Eysenck, H. J. (1994a). The Big Five or giant three: Criteria for a paradigm. In C. F. Halverson, Jr., G. A. Kohnstamm, & R. P. Martin (Eds.), *The developing structure of temperament and*

personality from infancy to adulthood. Hillsdale, NJ: Erlbaum.

Eysenck, H. J., Barrett, P., Wilson, G., & Jackson, C. (1992). Primary trait measurement of the 21 components of the P-E-N system. *European Journal of Psychological Assessment, 8,* 109–117.

Falk, D., Forese, N., Sade, D. S., & Dudek, B. C. (1999). Sex differences in brain/body relationships of Rhesus monkeys and humans. *Journal of Human Evolution, 36,* 233–238.

Farber, B. A., Brink, D. C., & Raskin, P. M. (Eds.). (1996). *The psychotherapy of Carl Rogers: Cases and commentary.* New York: Guilford Press.

Farley, F. (1986, May). The big T in personality. *Psychology Today,* pp. 44–52.

Faulkner, H. J., & Levy, B. A. (1994). How text difficulty and reader skill interact to produce differential reliance on word and content overlap in reading transfer. *Journal of Experimental Child Psychology, 58,* 1–24.*

Fearing, V. G., & Clark, J. (Eds.). (2000). *Individuals in context: A practical guide to client-centered practice.* Chicago: Slack.

Federal, Provincial and Territory Advisory Committee on Population Health. (1999). *Toward a healthy future: Second report on the health of Canadians.* Ottawa: Health Canada.*

Feightner, J. W. (1994). Early detection of depression. In Canadian Task Force on the Periodic Health Examination, *Canadian Guide to Clinical Preventive Health Care.* Ottawa: Health Canada, 450–454.*

Feldman, R. S. (Ed.). (1982). *Development of nonverbal behavior in children.* New York: Springer-Verlag.

Feldman, R. S. (Ed.). (1993). *Applications of nonverbal behavioral theories and research.* Hillsdale, NJ: Erlbaum.

Feldman, R. S., Coats, E. J., & Schwartzberg, S. (1994). *Case studies and critical thinking about psychology.* New York: McGraw-Hill.

Fenton, W. S., & McGlashan, T. H. (1991). Natural history of schizophrenia subtypes: II. Positive and negative symptoms and long-term course. *Archives of General Psychiatry, 48,* 978–986.

Ferguson, G. A. (1993). Psychology in Canada 1939–1945. *Canadian Psychology, 33(4),* 697–705.*

Festinger, L. (1957). *A theory of cognitive dissonance.* Stanford, CA: Stanford University Press.

Festinger, L., & Carlsmith. J. M. (1959). Cognitive consequences of forced compliance. *Journal of Abnormal and Social Psychology, 58,* 203–210.

Festinger, L., Schachter, S., & Back, K. W. (1950). *Social pressure in informal groups.* New York: Harper.

Fields-Meyer, T. (1995, September 25). Having their say. *People,* pp. 50–60.

Fields-Meyer, T. (1999, October 25). The whiz kids. *People,* pp. 59–63.

Figueiras, M. J., & Marteau, T. M. (1995). Experiences of the menopause: A comparison between Portugal and the United Kingdom. *Analise Psicologica, 13,* 163–171.

Fine, L. (1994). Personal communication on cultural rituals.

Fink, A. & Kosecoff, J. (1998). *How to conduct surveys: A step-by-step guide.* Thousand Oaks, CA: Sage.

Fink, M. (1999). *Electroshock: Restoring the mind.* New York: Oxford University Press.

Fink, M. (2000). Electroshock revisited. *American Scientist, 88,* 162–167.

Finke, R. A. (1995). Creative insight and preinventive forms. In R. J. Sternberg & J. E. Davidson (Eds.), *The nature of insight.* Cambridge, MA: MIT Press.

Firestein, B. A. (Ed.). (1996). *Bisexuality: The psychology and politics of an invisible minority.* Thousand Oaks, CA: Sage.

Fischer, K. W., Shaver, P. R., & Carnochan, P. (1990). How emotions develop and how they organize development. *Cognition and Emotion, 4,* 81–127.

Fisher, C. B., & Fyrberg, D. (1994). Participant partners: College students weigh the costs and benefits of deceptive research. *American Psychologist, 49,* 417–427.

Fisher, K. (1985, March). ECT: New studies on how, why, who. *APA Monitor,* pp. 18–19.

Fiske, S. T. (1992a). Stereotypes work . . . but only sometimes: Comment on how to motivate the "unfinished mind." *Psychological Inquiry, 3,* 161–162.

Fiske, S. T. (1992b). Thinking is for doing: Portraits of social cognition from daguerreotype to laserphoto. *Journal of Personality and Social Psychology, 63,* 877–889.

Fiske, S. T., & Taylor, S. E. (1991). *Social cognition* (2nd ed.). New York: McGraw-Hill.

Flam, F. (1991, June 14). Queasy riders. *Science, 252,* 1488.

Flavell, J. H. (1993). Young children's understanding of thinking and consciousness. *Current Directions in Psychological Science, 2,* 40–43.

Fleming, R., Baum, A., & Singer, J. E. (1984). Toward an integrative approach to the study of stress. *Journal of Personality and Social Psychology, 46,* 939–949.

Folkhard, S., Arendt, J., & Clark, M. (1993). Can melatonin improve shift-workers' tolerance of the night shift? Some preliminary findings. *Chronobiology International, 10,* 315–320.*

Folkman, S., Lazarus, R. S., Dunkel-Schetter, C., DeLongis, A., & Green, R. J. (1986). Dynamics of a stressful encounter: Cognitive appraisal, coping, and encounter outcome. *Journal of Personality and Social Psychology, 50,* 992–1003.

Folkman, S., & Moskowitz, J. T. (2000). Stress, positive emotion, and coping. *Current Directions in Psychological Science, 9,* 115–118.

Ford, J. G. (1991). Rogers's theory of personality: Review and perspectives. *Journal of Social Behavior and Personality, 6,* 19–44.

Forer, B. (1949). The fallacy of personal validation: A classroom demonstration of gullibility. *Journal of Abnormal and Social Psychology, 44,* 118–123.

Foreyt, J. P., & Goodrick, G. K. (1994). *Living without dieting.* New York: Warner.

Forrester, M. A. (1996). *Psychology of language: A critical introduction.* Thousand Oaks, CA: Sage.

Fox, R. E. (1994). Training professional psychologists for the twenty-first century. *American Psychologist, 49,* 200–206.

Frances, A., First, M. B., & Pincus, H. A. (1995). *DSM-IV guidebook.* Washington, DC: American Psychiatric Press.

Franks, D. D., & Smith, T. S. (Eds.). (1999). *Mind, brain, and society: Toward a neurosociology of emotion* (Vol. 5). Stamford, CT: Jai Press.

Franzek, E., & Beckmann, H. (1996). Gene-environment interaction in schizophrenia: Season-of-birth effect reveals etiologically different subgroups. *Psychopathology, 29,* 14–26.

Frasure-Smith, N., Lesperance, F., & Talajic, M. (2000). The prognostic importance of depression, anxiety, anger, and social support following myocardial infarction: Opportunities for improving survival. In P. M. McCabe, N. Schneiderman. T. M. Field, & A. R. Wellens (Eds.), *Stress, coping, and cardiovascular disease.* Mahwah, NJ: Erlbaum.

Free, M. L. (2000). *Cognitive therapy in groups: Guidelines and resources for practice.* New York: Wiley.

Freedman, D. S. (1995). The importance of body fat distribution in early life. *American Journal of the Medical Sciences, 310,* S72–S76.

Freedman, J. L., & Fraser, S. C. (1966). Compliance without pressure: The foot-in-the-door technique. *Journal of Personality and Social Psychology, 4,* 195–202.

Freeman, S. J. (1994). An overview of Canada's mental health system. In L. L. Bachrach, P. Goering, & D. Wasylenki (Eds.), *Mental health care in Canada: New directions for mental health services.* San Fransisco: Jossey-Bass.*

French, H. W. (1997, February 2). Africa's culture war: Old customs, new values. *New York Times,* pp. 1E, 4E.

Freud, S. (1922/1959). *Group psychology and the analysis of the ego.* London: Hogarth Press.

Friedman, A. F., Lewak, R., Nichols, D. S., & Webb, J. T. (2000). *Psychological assessment with the MMPI-2.* Mahwah, NJ: Erlbaum.

Friedman, M. J., & Marsella, A. J. (1996). Posttraumatic stress disorder: An overview of the concept. In A. J. Marsella, M. J. Friedman, E. T. Gerrity, & R. M. Scurfield (Eds.), *Ethnocultural aspects of posttraumatic stress disorder: Issues, research, and clinical applications.* Washington, DC: American Psychological Association.

Fritsch, J. (1999, October 5). Scientists unmask diet myth: Willpower. *New York Times,* pp. D1, D9.

Fromkin, V. A. (2000). On the uniqueness of language. In K. Emmorey & H. Lane, et al. (Eds.), *The signs of language revisited: An anthology to honor Ursula Bellugi and Edward Klima.* Mahwah, NJ: Erlbaum.

Fromm, E., & Nash, M. (Eds.). (1992). *Contemporary hypnosis research.* New York: Guilford Press.

Funder, D. C. (1991). Global traits: A neo-Allportian approach to personality. *Psychological Science, 2,* 31–39.

Funder, D. C. (1997). *The personality puzzle.* New York: W. W. Norton.

Furnham, A. (1995). The relationship of personality and intelligence to cognitive learning style and achievement. In D. H. Saklofske & M. Zeidner (Eds.), *International handbook of personality and intelligence: Perspectives on individual differences.* New York: Plenum Press.

Furst, P. T. (1977). "High states" in culture-historical perspective. In N. E. Zinberg (Ed.), *Alternate states of consciousness.* New York: Free Press.

Gaertner, S. L., Rust, M. C., Dovidio, J. F., Bachman, B. A., et al. (1996). The contact hypothesis: The role of a common ingroup identity on reducing intergroup bias among majority and minority group members. In J. L. Nye & A. M. Brower (Eds.), *What's social about social cognition? Research on socially shared cognition in small groups.* Thousand Oaks, CA: Sage.

Galanter, E. (1962). Contemporary psychophysics. In R. Brown, E. Galanter, E. Hess, & G. Maroler (Eds.), *New directions in psychology* (pp. 87–157). New York: Holt.

Galanter, M. (Ed.). (1995). *Recent developments in alcoholism: Vol. 12. Alcoholism and women.* New York: Plenum Press.

Galanter, M., & Kleber, H. D. (Eds.). (1999). *The American Psychiatric Press textbook of substance abuse: Abuse treatment* (2nd ed.). Washington, DC: American Psychiatric Press.

Galatzer-Levy, R. M., & Cohler, B. J. (1997). *Essential psychoanalysis: A contemporary introduction.* New York: Basic Books.

Galavotti, C., Saltzman, L. E., Sauter, S. L., & Sumartojo, E. (1997, February). Behavioral science activities at the Center for Disease Control and Prevention: A selected overview of exemplary programs. *American Psychologist, 52,* 154–166.

Gale, N., Golledge, R. G., Pellegrino, J. W., & Doherty, S. (1990). The acquisition and integration of route knowledge in an unfamiliar neighborhood. *Journal of Environmental Psychology, 10,* 3–25.

Gallagher, M., & Rapp, R. R. (1997). The use of animal models to study the effects of aging on cognition. *Annual Review of Psychology, 48,* 339–370.

Galt, V. (2001a, June 6). Think you're overworked? Think again. *The Globe and Mail,* pp. A1, A14.*

Galt, V. (2001b, June 13). Happiness is work without housework. *The Globe and Mail,* pp. A1, A7.*

Gammell, D. J., & Stoppard, J. M. (1999). Women's experiences of treatment of depression: Medicalization or empowerment? *Canadian Psychology, 40,* 112–128.*

Gannon, P. J., Holloway, R. L., Broadfield, D. C., & Braun, A. R. (1998, January 9). Asymmetry of chimpanzee planum temporale: Humanlike pattern of Wernicke's brain language area homolog. *Science, 279,* 220–222.

Ganong, L. H. & Coleman, M. (1999). *Changing families, changing responsibilities: Family obligations following divorce and remarriage.* Mahwah, NJ: Erlbaum.

Gao, J., Parsons, L. M., Bower, J. M., Xiong, J., Li, J., & Fox, P. T. (1996, April 26). Cerebellum implicated in sensory acquisition and discrimination rather than motor control. *Science, 272,* 545–547.

Garcia, J. (1990). Learning without memory. *Journal of Cognitive Neuroscience, 2,* 287–305.

Garcia, J., Hankins, W. G., & Rusiniak, K. W. (1974). Behavioral regulation of the milieu intern in man and rat. *Science, 185,* 824–831.

Garcia-Andrade, C., Wall, T. L., & Ehlers, C. L. (1997). The firewater myth and response to alcohol in Mission Indians. *Journal of Psychiatry, 154,* 983–988.

Gardner, H. (1975). *The shattered mind: The person after brain damage.* New York: Knopf.

Gardner, H. (1997). *Extraordinary minds.* New York: Basic Books.

Gardner, H. (1999). *Intelligence reframed: Multiple intelligences for the 21st century.* New York: Basic Books.

Gardner, R. A., & Gardner, B. T. (1969). Teaching sign language to a chimpanzee. *Science, 165,* 664–672.

Garling, T. (1989). The role of cognitive maps in spatial decisions. *Journal of Environmental Psychology, 9,* 269–278.

Garrison, D. W., & Foreman, R. D. (1994). Decreased activity of spontaneous and noxiously evoked dorsal horn cells during transcutaneous electrical nerve stimulation (TENS). *Pain, 58,* 309–315.

Gass, C. S., Luis, C. A., Meyers, T. L., & Kuljis, R. O. (2000). Familial Creutzfeldt-Jakob disease: A neuropsychological case study. *Archives of Clinical Neuropsychology, 15,* 165–175.

Gatchel, R. J., & Turk, D. C. (Eds.). (1996). *Psychological Approaches to Pain Management: A Practitioner's Handbook.* New York: Guilford Press.

Gatchel, R. J., & Weisberg, J. N. (Eds.). (2000). *Personality characteristics of patients with pain.* Washington, DC: American Psychological Association.

Gathercole, S. E., & Baddeley, A. D. (1993). *Working memory and language processing.* Hillsdale, NJ: Erlbaum.

Gauthier, J. G. (1999). Bridging the gap between biological and psychological perspectives in the treatment of anxiety disorders. *Canadian Psychology, 40,* 1–11.*

Gauthier, J. G. & Phillips, A. G. (Eds.). (1997) *National conference on psychology as a science, May 8–11, 1997: Final report.* Canadian Psychological Association.*

Gazzaniga, M. S. (1998, July). The split brain revisited. *Scientific American,* pp. 50–55.

Ge, X., Conger, R. D., & Elder, G. H., Jr. (1996). Coming of age too early: Pubertal influences on girls' vulnerability to psychological distress. *Child Development, 67,* 3386–3400.

Geary, D. C., & Bjorklund, D. F. (2000). Evolutionary developmental psychology. *Child Development, 71,* 57–65.

Geen, R. G. (1984). Human motivation: New perspectives on old problems. In A. M. Rogers & C. J. Scheirer (Eds.), *The G. Stanley Hall Lecture Series* (Vol. 4). Washington, DC: American Psychological Association.

Geen, R. G. (1995). *Human motivation: A social psychological approach.* Pacific Grove, CA: Brooks/Cole.

Geen, R. G., & Donnerstein, E. (1983). *Aggression: Theoretical and empirical reviews.* New York: Academic Press.

Geen, R. G., & Donnerstein, E. (Eds.). (1998). *Human aggression: Theories, research and implications for social policy.* Orlando, FL: Academic Press.

Geiselman, R. E., Fisher, R. P., MacKinnon, D. P., & Holland, H. L. (1985). Eyewitness memory enhancement in the police interview: Cognitive retrieval mnemonics versus hypnosis. *Journal of Applied Psychology, 70,* 401–412.

Gelfand, M. M. (2000). Sexuality among older women. *Journal of Women's Health and Gender-Based Medicine, 9* (Suppl. 1), S15–S20.

Gelman, R., & Au, T. K.-F. (Eds.). (1996). *Perceptual and cognitive development.* New York: Academic Press.

Gelman, R., & Baillargeon, R. (1983). A review of some Piagetian concepts. In J. H. Flavell & E. M. Markman (Eds.). *Handbook of child psychology: Vol. 3. Cognitive development* (4th ed.). New York: Wiley.

Genesee, F. (1984). Beyond bilingualism: Social psychological studies of French immersion programs in Canada. *Canadian Journal of Behavioural Science, 16,* 338–352.*

Gentry, W. D., & Kobasa, S. C. O. (1984). Social and psychological resources mediating stress-illness relationships in humans. In W. D. Gentry (Ed.), *Handbook of behavioral medicine.* New York: Guilford Press.

Genuis, M., & Violato, C. (2000). Attachment security to mother, father, and the parental unit. In C. Violato & E. Oddone-Paolucci (Eds.), *The changing family and child development.* Aldershot, England: Ashgate.

George, M. S., Wassermann, E. M., Williams, W. A., Callahan, A., et al. (1995). Daily repetitive transcranial magnetic stimulations (rTMS) improves mood in depression. *Neuroreport: An International Journal for the Rapid Communication of Research in Neuroscience, 6,* 1853–1856.

George, T. P. (1999). Design, measurement, and analysis in developmental research. In M. Bornstein & M. Lamb, *Developmental psychology.* Mahwah, NJ: Erlbaum.

Gescheider, G. A. (1997). *Psychophysics: The fundamentals* (3rd ed.). Mahwah, NJ: Erlbaum.

Getner, D., & Holyoak, K. J. (1997, January). Reasoning and learning by analogy. *American Psychologist, 52,* 32–34.

Gibbons, A. (1990, July 13). New maps of the human brain. *Science, 249,* 122–123.

Gibbs, M. E., O'Dowd, B. S., Hertz, L., Robinson, S. R., et al. (1996). Inhibition of glutamine synthetase activity prevents memory consolidation. *Cognitive Brain Research, 4,* 57–64.

Gibbs, W. W. (1996, August). Gaining on fat. *Scientific American,* pp. 88–94.

Gibson, H. B. (1995). A further case of the misuse of hypnosis in a police investigation. *Contemporary Hypnosis, 12,* 81–86.

Gilbert, B. (1996). New ideas in the air at the National Zoo. *Smithsonian,* pp. 32–43.

Gilbert, D. G. (1995). *Smoking: Individual differences, psychopathology, and emotion.* Philadelphia: Taylor & Francis.

Gilbert, D. T., & Malone, P. S. (1995). The correspondence bias. *Psychological Bulletin, 117,* 21–38.

Gilbert, D. T., McNulty, S. E., Guiliano, T. A., & Benson, J. E. (1992). Blurry words and fuzzy deeds: The attribution of obscure behavior. *Journal of Personality and Social Psychology, 62,* 18–25.

Gilbert, D. T., Miller, A. G., & Ross, L. (1998). Speeding with Ned: A personal view of the correspondence bias. In J. M. Darley & J. Cooper (Eds.), *Attribution and social interaction: The legacy of Edward E. Jones.* Washington, DC: American Psychological Association.

Gilbert, P. (2000). Varieties of submissive behavior as forms of social defense: Their evolution and role in depression. In L. Sloman & P. Gilbert (Eds.), *Subordination and defeat: An evolutionary approach to mood disorders and their therapy.* Mahwah, NJ: Erlbaum.

Gilger, J. W. (1996). How can behavioral genetic research help us understand language development and disorders? In M. L. Rice (Ed.), *Toward a genetics of language.* Mahwah, NJ: Erlbaum.

Gilligan, C. (1982). *In a different voice: Psychological theory and women's development.* Cambridge, MA: Harvard University Press.

Gilligan, C. (1987). Adolescent development reconsidered. *New Directions for Child Development, 37,* 63–92.

Gilligan, C. (1993). Woman's place in man's life cycle. In A. Dobrin (Ed.), *Being good and doing right: Readings in moral development.* Lanham, MD: University Press of America.

Gilligan, C., Lyons, N. P., & Hanmer, T. J. (Eds.). (1990). *Making connections.* Cambridge, MA: Harvard University Press.

Gilligan, C., Ward, J. V., & Taylor, J. M. (Eds.). (1988). *Mapping the moral domain: A contribution of women's thinking to psychological theory and education.* Cambridge, MA: Harvard University Press.

Gillyatt, P. (1997, February). When the nose doesn't know. *Harvard Health Letter,* pp. 6–7.

Gladue, B. A. (1995). The biopsychology of sexual orientation. *Current Directions in Psychological Science, 3,* 150–154.

Gladwin, T. (1964). Culture and logical process. In N. Goodenough (Ed.), *Explorations in cultural anthropology: Essays in honor of George Peter Murdoch.* New York: McGraw-Hill.

Glaman, J. M., Jones, A. P., & Rozelle, R. M. (1996). The effects of co-worker similarity on the emergence of affect in work teams. *Group and Organization Management, 21,* 192–215.

Glassman, A. H., & Koob, G. F. (1996, February 22). Neuropharmacology: Psychoactive smoke. *Nature, 379,* 677–678.

Glenmullen, J. (2000). *Prozac backlash: Overcoming the dangers of Prozac, Zoloft, Paxil, and other antidepressants with safe, effective alternatives.* New York: Simon & Schuster.

Gliksman, L., Demers, A., Adlaf, E. M., Newton-Taylor, B., & Schmidt, K. (2000). *Canadian campus survey 1998.* Toronto: CAMH.*

Gobet, F., & Simon, H. A. (1996). Recall of random and distorted chess positions: Implications for the theory of expertise. *Memory and Cognition, 24,* 493–503.

Goldberg, C. (1999, October 27). Just another girl, unlike any other. *New York Times,* p. A14.

Goldsmith, H. H., & Harman, C. (1994). Temperament and attachment: Individuals and relationships. *Current Directions in Psychological Science, 3,* 53–56.

Goldstein, E. B. (1984). *Sensation and perception* (2nd ed.). Pacific Grove, CA: Brooks/Cole.

Goldstein, G., Beers, S. R., Longmore, S., & McCue, M. (1996). Efficacy of memory training: A technological extension and replication. *Clinical Neuropsychologist, 10,* 66–72.

Goldstein, I. (2000, August). Male sexual circuitry. *Scientific American,* pp. 70–75.

Goleman, D. (1988, January 21). Physicians may bungle key part of treatment: The medical interview. *New York Times,* p. B16.

Goleman D. (1993, July 21). "Expert" babies found to teach others. *New York Times,* p. C10.

Goleman, D. (1995). *Emotional intelligence: Why it can matter more than IQ.* New York: Bantam Books.

Goleman, D. (1998). *Working with emotional intelligence.* New York: Bantam.

Golledge, R. G., Klatzyy, R. L., Loomis, J. L., Speigle, J., & Tietz, J. (1998). A geographical information system for a GPS based personal guidance system. *International Journal of Geographical Information Science, 12,* 727–749.

Golombok, S., & Tasker, F. (1996). Do parents influence the sexual orientation of their children? Findings from a longitudinal study of lesbian families. *Developmental Psychology, 32,* 3–11.

Goode, E. (1999b, April 13). If things taste bad, "phantoms" may be at work. *New York Times,* pp. C1–C2.

Goodglass, H. (1993). *Understanding aphasia.* San Diego: Academic Press.

Goodman, J. T. (2000). Three decades of professional psychology: Reflections and future challenges. *Canadian Psychology, 41,* 25–33.*

Goodman, W. K., Rudorfer, M. V., & Maser, J. D. (1999). *Obsessive-compulsive disorder: Contemporary issues in treatment*. Mahwah, NJ: Erlbaum.

Gordon, J. W. (1999, March 26). Genetic enhancement in humans. *Science, 283*, 2023–2024.

Gortner, E., Gollan, J. K., Dobson, K. S., & Jacobson, N. S. (1998). Cognitive-behavioural treatment for depression: Relapse prevention. *Journal of Consulting and Clinical Psychology, 66*, 377–384.*

Gottesman, I. I. (1991). *Schizophrenia genesis: The origins of madness*. New York: Freeman.

Gottesman, I. I. (1997, June 6). Twin: En route to QTLs for cognition. *Science, 276*, 1522–1523.

Gottesman, I. I., & Moldin, S. O. (1998). Genotypes, genes, genesis, and pathogenesis in schizophrenia. In M. F. Lenzenweger & R. H. Dworkin (Eds.), *The origins and development of schizophrenia: Advances in experimental psychopathology*. Washington, DC: American Psychological Association.

Gottlieb, G., Wahlsten, D., & Lickliter, R. (1998). The significance of biology for human development: A developmental psychobiological systems view. In W. Damon (Ed.), *Handbook of child psychology* (5th ed.). New York: Wiley.*

Gould, R. L. (1978). *Transformations*. New York: Simon & Schuster.

Gouras, P. (1991). Color vision. In E. R. Kandel, J. H. Schwartz, & T. M. Jessell (Eds.), *Principles of neural science* (3rd ed.). New York: Elsevier.

Graf, P. (1990). Life-span changes in implicit and explicit memory. *Bulletin of the Psychonomic Society, 28*, 353–358.

Graf, P., & Masson, M. E. J. (Eds.). (1993). *Implicit memory: New directions in cognition, development, and neuropsychology*. Hillsdale, NJ: Erlbaum.

Graffin, N. F., Ray, W. J., & Lundy, R. (1995). EEG concomitants of hypnosis and hypnotic susceptibility. *Journal of Abnormal Psychology, 104*, 123–131.

Graham, R., & Cabeza, R. (2001). Dissociating the neural correlates of item and context memory: An ERP study of face recognition. *Canadian Journal of Experimental Psychology, 55*, 154–161.*

Grammer, K. (1996, June). *Sex and olfaction*. Paper presented at the annual meeting of the Human Behavior and Evolution Society, Evanston, Illinois.

Grandin, L. & Lupri, E. (1997). Intimate violence in Canada and the United States: A cross-national comparison. *Journal of Domestic Violence, 12(4)*, 417–443.*

Greenberg, L. S., & Paivio, S. C. (1997). *Working with emotions in psychotherapy*. New York: Guilford.*

Greenberg, R. L. (2000). The creative client in cognitive therapy. *Journal of Cognitive Psychotherapy, 14*, 163–174.

Greenberg, S. H. (1997, Spring/Summer). The loving ties that bond. *Newsweek*, pp. 68–72.

Greene, B., & Herek, G. (1994). *Lesbian and gay psychology: Theory, research, and clinical applications*. Newbury Park, CA: Sage.

Greene, R. L., & Clopton, J. R. (1994). Minnesota Multiphasic Personality Inventory–2. In M. E. Maruish (Ed.), *The use of psychological tests for treatment planning and outcome assessment*. Hillsdale, NJ: Erlbaum.

Greenfield, D. N. (1999, August). *Nature of Internet addiction: Psychological factors in compulsive Internet use*. Paper presented at the annual

meeting of the American Psychological Association, Boston.

Greeno, J. G. (1978). Natures of problem-solving abilities. In W. K. Estes (Ed.), *Handbook of learning and cognitive processes*. Hillsdale, NJ: Erlbaum.

Greenwald, A. G., Draine S. C., & Abrams, R. L. (1996, September 20). Three cognitive markers of unconscious semantic activation. *Science, 272*, 1699–1702.

Greenwald, A. G., Spangenberg, E. R., Pratkanis, A. R., & Eskenzai, J. (1991). Double-blind tests of subliminal self-help audiotapes. *Psychological Science, 2*, 119–122.

Greenwood, C. R., Carta, J. J., Hart, B., Kamps, D., Terry, B., Arreaga-Mayer, C., Atwater, J., Walker, D., Risley, T., & Delquadri, J. C. (1992). Out of the laboratory and into the community: 26 years of applied behavior analysis at the Juniper Gardens children's project. *American Psychologist, 47*, 1464–1474.

Gregory, R. L. (1978). *The psychology of seeing* (3rd ed.). New York: McGraw-Hill.

Gregory, S. (1856). *Facts for young women*. Boston.

Gregory, S. S. (1994, March 21). At risk of mutilation. *Time*, pp. 45–46.

Griffiths, M. (1997). Video games and aggression. *Psychologist, 10*, 397–401.

Grigorenko, E. L. (2000). Heritability and intelligence. In R. J. Sternberg et al. (Eds.), *Handbook of intelligence*. New York: Cambridge University Press.

Grillner, S. (1996, January). Neural networks for vertebrate locomotion. *Scientific American*, pp. 64–69.

Grimsley, D. L., & Karriker, M. W. (1996). Bilateral skin temperature, handedness, and the biofeedback control of skin temperature. *Journal of Behavioral Medicine, 19*, 87–94.

Grimson, W. E. L., Kikinis, R., Jolesz, F. A., & Black, P. M. (1999, June). Image-guided surgery. *Scientific American*, pp. 62–69.

Grohol, J. M. (1997). *The insider's guide to health resources online*. New York: Guilford Press.

Gross, J. (1991, June 16). More young single men hang onto apron strings. *New York Times*, pp. 1, 18.

Grossi, G., Samenza, C., Corazza, S., & Volterra, V. (1996). Hemispheric specialization for sign language. *Neuropsychologia, 34*, 737–740.

Groth-Marnat, G. (1990). *Handbook of psychological assessment* (2nd ed.). New York: Wiley.

Grube, J. W., Rokeach, M., & Getzlaf, S. B. (1990). Adolescents' value images of smokers, ex-smokers, and nonsmokers. *Addictive Behaviors, 15*, 81–88.

Gruneberg, M. M., & Pascoe, K. (1996). The effectiveness of the keyword method for receptive and productive foreign vocabulary learning in the elderly. *Contemporary Educational Psychology, 21*, 102–109.

Guilford, J. P. (1985). *The analysis of intelligence*. New York: McGraw-Hill.

Gullotta, T., Adams, G., & Markstrom, C. (1999). *The adolescent experience*. Orlando, FL: Academic Press.

Gur, R. C. (1996, March). Paper presented at the annual meeting of the American Association for the Advancement of Science, Baltimore, Maryland.

Gur, R. C., Gur, R. E., Obrist, W. D., Hungerbuhler, J. P., Younkin, D., Rosen, A. D., Skilnick, B. E., & Reivich, M. (1982). Sex and handedness differences in cerebral blood flow during rest and cognitive activity. *Science, 217*, 659–661.

Gur, R. C., Mozley, L. H., Mozley, P. D., Resnick, S. M., Karp, J. S., Alavi, A., Arnold, S. E., & Gur, R. E. (1995, January 27). Sex differences in regional cerebral glucose metabolism during a resting state. *Science, 267*, 528–531.

Gur, R. C., Turetsky, B. I., Matsui, M., Yan, M., Bilker, W., Hughett, P., & Gur, R. E. (1999). Sex differences in brain gray and white matter in healthy young adults: Correlations with cognitive performance. *Journal of Neuroscience, 19*, 4065–4072.

Gurin, J. (1989, July). Leaner, not lighter. *Psychology Today*, pp. 32–36.

Gurman, E. B. (1994). Debriefing for all concerned: Ethical treatment of human subjects. *Psychological Science, 5*, 139.

Gustavson, C. R., Garcia, J., Hankins, W. G., & Rusniak, K. W. (1974). Coyote predation control by aversive conditioning. *Science, 184*, 581–583.

Guttman, M. (1995, March 3–5). She had electroshock therapy. *USA Weekend*, p. 16.

Gwynn, M. I., & Spanos, N. P. (1996). Hypnotic responsiveness, nonhypnotic suggestibility, and responsiveness to social influence. In R. G. Kunzendorf, N. P. Spahos, & B. Wallace (Eds.), *Hypnosis and imagination*. Amityville, NY: Baywood.

Haber, R. N. (1983). Stimulus information processing mechanisms in visual space perception. In J. Beck, B. Hope, & A. Rosenfeld (Eds.), *Human and machine vision*. New York: Academic Press.

Hadjistavropoulos, T., & Genest, M. (1994). The underestimation of the role of physical attractiveness in dating preferences: Ignorance or taboo? *Canadian Journal of Behavioural Science, 26*, 298–318.*

Hafner, H., & Maurer, K. (1995). Epidemiology of positive and negative symptoms in schizophrenia. In C. L. Shriqui & H. A. Nasrallah (Eds.), *Contemporary issues in the treatment of schizophrenia*. Washington, DC: American Psychiatric Press.

Hagen, E., Sattler, J. M., & Thorndike, R. L. (1985). *Stanford-Binet test*. Chicago: Riverside.

Haimov, I., & Lavie, P. (1996). Melatonin: A soporific hormone. *Current Directions in Psychological Science, 5*, 106–111.

Hakuta, K. U., & Garcia, E.E. (1989). Bilingualism and education. *American Psychologist, 44*, 374–379.

Hall, G. C. N., & Barongan, C. (1997). Prevention of sexual aggression: Sociocultural risk and protective factors. *American Psychologist, 52*, 5–14.

Halling, S., & Goldfarb, M. (1996). The new generation of diagnostic manuals (*DSM-III, DSM-III-R,* and *DSM-IV*): An overview and a phenomenologically based critique. *Journal of Phenomenological Psychology, 27*, 49–71.

Halpern, D. F. (1998). Teaching critical thinking for transfer across domains. *American Psychologist, 53*, 449–455.

Hamer, D. H., Hu, S., Magnuson, V. L., Hu, N., & Pattatucci, A. M. L. (1993, July 16). A linkage between DNA markers on the X chromosome and male sexual orientation. *Science, 261*, 321–327.

Hamilton, C. E. (2000). Continuity and discontinuity of attachment from infancy through adolescence. *Child Development, 71*, 690–694.

Hammond, S. L., & Lambert, B. L. (1994a). Communicating about medications: Directions for research [Special Issue: Communicating with patients about their medications]. *Health Communication, 6,* 247–251.

Hammond, S. L., & Lambert, B. L. (Eds.). (1994b). *Communicating with patients about their medications.* Mahwah, NJ: Erlbaum.

Hannigan, J. H., Spear, L. P., Spear, N. E., & Goodlett, C. R. (Eds.). (1999). *Alcohol and alcoholism: Effects on brain and development.* Mahwah, NJ: Erlbaum.

Hannon, B., & Daneman, M. (2001a). Susceptibility to semantic illusions: An individual-difference perspective. *Memory and Cognition, 29,* 449–461.*

Hannon, B., & Daneman, M. (2001b). A new tool for measuring and understanding individual differences in the component processes of reading comprehension. *Journal of Educational Psychology, 93,* 103–128.*

Harden, B. (2000, January 9). Very young, smart, and restless. *New York Times Education Life,* pp. 28–31.

Hare, R. D. (1993). *Without conscience.* New York: The Guildford Press.*

Hare, R. D., Hart, S. D., & Harpur, T. J. (1991). Psychopathy and the *DSM-IV* criteria for antisocial personality disorder. *Journal of Abnormal Psychology, 100,* 391–398.

Harlow, H. F., & Zimmerman, R. R. (1959). Affectional responses in the infant monkey. *Science, 130,* 421–432.

Harlow, J. M. (1869). Recovery from the passage of an iron bar through the head. *Massachusetts Medical Society Publication, 2,* 329–347.

Harlow, R. E., & Cantor, N. (1996). Still participating after all these years: A study of life task participation in later life. *Journal of Personality and Social Psychology, 71,* 1235–1249.

Harold, G. T., Fincham, F. D., Osborne, L. N., & Conger, R. D. (1997). Mom and dad are at it again: Adolescent perceptions of marital conflict and adolescent psychological distress. *Developmental Psychology, 33,* 333–350.

Harper, T. (1978, November 15). It's not true about people 65 or over. *Green Bay Press-Gazette.* (Wisconsin), p. D1.

Harris-Kern, M. J., & Perkins, R. (1995). Effects of distraction on interpersonal expectancy effects: A social interaction test of the cognitive busyness hypothesis. *Social Cognition, 13,* 163–182.

Harris Poll. (2000 February 2). *The power of tobacco addiction.* New York: Harris Interactive.

Harrison, J. A., & Wells, R. B. (1991). Bystander effects on male helping behavior: Social comparison and diffusion of responsibility. *Representative Research in Social Psychology, 19,* 53–63.

Harrison, P. J., Everall, I. P., & Catalan, J. (1994). Is homosexual behaviour hard-wired? Sexual orientation and brain structure. *Psychological Medicine, 24,* 811–816.

Hart, B., & Risley, T. R. (1997). *Use of language by three-year-old children.* Courtesy of Drs. Betty Hart, University of Kansas, Lawrence, and Todd Risley, University of Alaska, Anchorage.

Hartung, C. M., & Widiger, T. A. (1998). Gender differences in the diagnosis of mental disorders: Conclusions and controversies of the *DSM-IV. Psychological Bulletin, 123,* 260–278.

Harvey, E. (1999). Short-term and long-term effects of early parental employment on children of the National Longitudinal Survey of Youth. *Developmental Psychology, 35,* 445–459.

Haseltine, W. A. (1997, March). Discovering genes for new medicines. *Scientific American,* pp. 92–97.

Hass, N. (1994, March 21). Fighting and switching. *Newsweek,* pp. 52–53.

Hauri, P. J. (Ed.). (1991). *Case studies in insomnia.* New York: Plenum Press.

Haviland-Jones, J., & Chen, D. (1999, April 17). *Human olfactory perception.* Paper presented at the Association for Chemoreception Sciences, Sarasota, Florida.

Hayflick, L. (1994). *How and why we age.* New York: Ballantine.

Health Canada (1996). Surveillance of congenital rubella syndrome and other rubella-associated adverse pregnancy outcomes. *Canada communicable disease report, Volume 22–5.** Available: <http://www.hc-sc.gc.ca/pphb-dgspsp/publicat/ccdr-rmtc/96vol22/dr2205eb.html>. Accessed December 14, 2002.

Health Canada. (1999). Statistical report on the health of Canadians.* Available: <http://www.hc-sc.gc.ca/hppb/phdd/report/stat/eng/index.html>. Accessed May 9, 2000.

Health Canada. (2001). *Canadian tobacco use monitoring survey.** Available: <http:www.hc-sc.gc.ca/hecs-sesc/tobacco/research/ctums/>. Accessed December 12, 2002.

Heath, A. C., & Madden, P. A. F. (1995). Genetic influences on smoking behavior. In J. R. Turner, L. R. Cardon, & J. K. Hewitt (Eds.), *Behavior genetic approaches in behavioral medicine: Perspectives on individual differences.* New York: Plenum Press.

Heatherton, T. F., Herman, C. P., & Polivy, J. (1992). Effects of distress on eating: The importance of ego-involvement. *Journal of Personality and Social Psychology, 62,* 801–803.

Heatherton, T. F., & Polivy, J. (1992). Chronic dieting and eating disorders: A spiral model. In J. Crowther, S. E. Hobfau, M. A. P. Stephens, D. L. Tennenbaum (Eds.), *The etiology of bulimia: The individual and familial context* (pp. 133–135). Washingotn, DC: Hemisphere Publishers.*

Hebl, M. R. & Hetherton, T. F. (1998). The stigma of obesity in women: The difference is black and white. *Personality and Social Psychology Bulletin, 24,* 417–426.

Heckhausen, H., Schmalt, H. D., & Schneider, K. (1985). *Achievement motivation in perspective* (M. Woodruff & R. Wicklund, Trans.). Orlando, FL: Academic Press.

Heider, F. (1958). *The psychology of interpersonal relations.* New York: Wiley.

Heine, S. J., & Lehman, D. R. (1997). Culture, dissonance, and self-affirmation. *Personality and Social Psychology Bulletin, 23,* 389–400.*

Heine, S. J., Kitayama, S., & Lehman, D. R. (2001a). Cultural differences in self-evaluation: Japanese readily accept negative self-relevant information. *Journal of Cross-Cultural Psychology, 32,* 434–443.*

Heine, S. J., Kitayama, S., Lehman, D. R., et al.[7 authors]. (2001b). Divergent consequences of success and failure in Japan and North America: An investigation of self-improving motivations and malleable selves. *Journal of Personality and Social Psychology, 81,* 599–615.*

Heine, S. J., Lehman, D. R., Greenholtz, J., & Peng, K. (2002). What's wrong with cross-cultural comparisons of subjective Likert scales? The reference-group effect. *Journal of Personality and Social Psychology, 82,* 903–918.*

Heine, S. J., Lehman, D. R., Markus, H. R., & Kitayama, S. (1999). Is there a universal need for positive self-regard? *Psychological Review, 106,* 766–794.*

Heinrichs, R. W. (1993). Schizophrenia and the brain: Conditions for neuropsychology of madness. *American Psychologist, 48,* 221–233.

Heishman, S. J., Kozlowski, L. T., & Henningfield, J. E. (1997). Nicotine addiction: Implications for public health policy. *Journal of Social Issues, 53,* 13–33.

Helmuth, L. (2000, August 25). Synapses shout to overcome distance. *Science, 289,* 1273.

Herek, G. M. (1993). Sexual orientation and military service: A social science perspective. *American Psychologist, 48,* 538–549.

Herholz, K. (1995). FDG PET and differential diagnosis of dementia. *Alzheimer Disease & Associated Disorders, 9,* 6–16.

Hermann, C., Kim, M., & Blanchard, E. B. (1995). Behavioral and prophylactic pharmacological intervention studies of pediatric migraine: An exploratory meta-analysis. *Pain, 60,* 239–255.

Herrett-Skjellum, J., & Allen, M. (1996). Television programming and sex stereotyping: A meta-analysis. In B. R. Burleson (Ed.), *Communication yearbook* (Vol. 19). Thousand Oaks, CA: Sage.

Hermann, D., McEvoy, C., Hertzog, C., Hertel, P., & Johnson, M. (Eds.). (1996). *Basic and applied research. Volume 1: Theory and context. Volume 2: Practical applications.* Mahwah, NJ: Erlbaum.

Hertzsprung, E. A. M., & Dobson, K. S. (2000). Diversity training: Conceptual issues. *Canadian Psychology, 41,* 184–191.*

Hetherington, E. M. (Ed.). (1999). *Coping with divorce, single parenting, and remarriage: A risk and resiliency perspective.* Mahwah, NJ: Erlbaum.

Hewlett, K. (2001). Memory is key to cross-cultural math differences. *Monitor on Psychology, 32,* 14.*

Heyward, W. L., & Curran, J. W. (1988, October). The epidemiology of AIDS in the U.S. *Scientific American,* pp. 72–81.

Hilgard, E. R. (1975). Hypnosis. *Annual Review of Psychology, 26,* 19–44.

Hill, J. O., & Peters, J. C. (1998). Environmental contributions to the obesity epidemic. *Science, 280,* 1371–1374.

Hinshaw, S. P., Zupan, B. A., Simmel, C., Nigg, J. T., & Melnick, S. (1997). Peer status in boys with and without attention-deficit hyperactivity disorder: Predictions from overt and covert antisocial behavior, social isolation, and authoritative parenting beliefs. *Child Development, 68,* 880–896.

Hipkiss, R. A. (1995). *Semantics: Defining the discipline.* Mahwah, NJ: Erlbaum.

Hirsh, I. J., & Watson, C. S. (1996). Auditory psychophysics and perception. *Annual Review of Psychology, 47,* 461–484.

Hobfoll, S. E., Freedy, J. R., Green B. L., & Solomon, S. D. (1996). Coping in reaction to extreme stress: The roles of resource loss and resource availability. In M. Zeidner & N. S. Endler (Eds.), *Handbook of coping: Theory, research, applications.* New York: Wiley.

Hobson, J. A. (1996, February). How the brain goes out of its mind. *Harvard Mental Health Letter,* pp. 3–5.

Hobson, J. A., & Silverstri, L. (1999, February). Parasomnias. *Harvard Mental Health Letter,* pp. 3–5.

Hoch, S. J. (1987). Perceived consensus and predictive accuracy: The pros and cons of projection. *Journal of Personality and Social Psychology, 53,* 221–234.

Kapur, S., & Remington, G. (1996). Serotonin-dopamine interaction and its relevance to schizophrenia. *American Journal of Psychiatry, 153,* 466–476.

Karlins, M., & Abelson, H. I. (1979). *How opinions and attitudes are changed.* New York: Springer-Verlag.

Karni, A., Tanne, D., Rubenstein, B. S., Askenazy, J. J. M., & Sagi, D. (1992, October). No dreams—no memory: The effect of REM sleep deprivation on learning a new perceptual skill. *Society for Neuroscience Abstracts, 18,* 387.

Karni, A., Tanne, D., Rubenstein, B. S., Askenasy, J. J. M., & Sagi, D. (1994, July 29). Dependence on REM sleep of overnight improvement of a perceptual skill. *Science, 265,* 679–682.

Karp, D. A. (1988). A decade of remembrances: Changing age consciousness between fifty and sixty years old. *Gerontologist, 28,* 727–738.

Karp, D. A. (1991). A decade of reminders: Changing age consciousness between fifty and sixty years old. In B. B. Hess & E. W. Markson (Eds.), *Growing old in America* (4th ed.). New Brunswick, NJ: Transaction.

Katz, A. N. (1989). Autobiographical memory as a reconstructive process: An extension of Ross's hypothesis. *Canadian Journal of Psychology, 43,* 512–517.

Katz, P. A. (Ed.). (1976). *Towards the elimination of racism.* New York: Pergamon Press.

Katz, S., Lautenschlager, G. J., Blackburn, A. B., & Harris, F. H. (1990). Answering reading comprehension items without passages on the SAT. *Psychological Science, 1,* 122–127.

Kaufman, A. S., & Lichtenberger, E. O. (1999). *Essentials of WISC-III and WPPSI-R assessment.* New York: Wiley.

Kausler, D. H. (1994). *Learning and memory in normal aging.* San Diego: Academic Press.

Kawachi, I., Colditz, G. A., Speizer, F. E., Manson, J. E., Stampger, M. J., Willett, W. C., & Hennekens, C. H. (1997). A prospective study of passive smoking and coronary heart disease. *Circulation, 95,* 2374–2379.

Kawasaki, C., Nugent, J. K., Miyashita, H., Miyahara, H., et al. (1994). The cultural organization of infants' sleep [Special issue: Environments of birth and infancy]. *Children's Environment, 11,* 135–141.

Kazdin, A. E. (1994). *Behavior modification in applied settings* (5th ed.). Pacific Grove, CA: Brooks/Cole.

Keating, D. P., & Clark, L. V. (1980). Development of physical and social reasoning in adolescence. *Developmental Psychology, 16,* 23–30.

Keefe, F. J., & France, C. R. (1999). Pain: Biopsychosocial mechanisms and management. *Current Directions in Psychological Science, 8,* 137–141.

Keehn, J. D. (1996). *Master builders of modern psychology: From Freud to Skinner.* New York: New York University Press.

Keller, M. C., & Young, R. K. (1996). Mate assortment in dating and married couples. *Personality and Individual Differences, 21,* 217–221.

Kelley, H. (1950). The warm-cold variable in first impressions of persons. *Journal of Personality and Social Psychology, 18,* 431–439.

Kelly, A. L. (1999, June 13). For employed moms, the pinnacle of stress comes after work ends. *New York Times,* p. 18.

Kelly, D. D. (1991). Sexual differentiation of the nervous system. In E. R. Kandel, J. H.

Schwartz, & T. M. Jessell (Eds.), *Principles of neural science* (3rd ed.). New York: Elsevier.

Kelly, F. D. (1997). *The assessment of object relations phenomena in adolescents: TAT and Rorschach measures.* Mahwah, NJ: Erlbaum.

Kemble, E., Filipi, T., & Gravlin, L. (1985). Some simple classroom experiments on cerebral lateralization. *Teaching of Psychology, 12(2),* 81–83.

Kemeny, A. (2002). Driven to excel: A portrait of Canada's workaholics. *Canadian Social Trends, 64 (Spring 2002).* Available: <http://www.statcan.ca/english/indepth/11-008/feature/stfeat.htm>. Accessed December 12, 2002.*

Kendler, K. S. (1996). Parenting: A genetic-epidemiologic perspective. *American Journal of Psychiatry, 153,* 11–20.

Kenny, D. A. (1994). *Interpersonal perception.* New York: Guilford Press.

Kidwell, J. S., Dunham, R. M., Bacho, R. A., Pastorino, E., et al. (1995). Adolescent identity exploration: A test of Erikson's theory of transitional crisis. *Adolescence, 30,* 785–793.

Kienker, P. K., Sejnowski, T. J., Hinton, G. E., & Schumacher, L. E. (1986). Separating figure from ground with a parallel network. *Perception, 15,* 197–216.

Kiesler, C. A., & Simpkins, C. (1991, June). The de facto national system of psychiatric inpatient care. *American Psychologist, 46,* 579–584.

Kiesler, C. A., & Simpkins, C. G. (1993). *The unnoticed majority in psychiatric inpatient care.* New York: Plenum Press.

Kiesler, D. J. (1999). *Beyond the disease model of mental disorders.* Westport, CT: Praeger.

Kiesler, S., & Kraut, R. (1999, September). Internet use and ties that bind. *American Psychologist, 15,* 783–784.

Kihlstrom, J. F. (1999). Unconscious. In L. A. Pervin & O. P. John (Eds.), *Handbook of personality: Theory and research* (2nd ed.). New York: Guilford Press.

Kihlstrom, J. F., Schacter, D. L., Cork, R. C., Hurt, C. A., & Behr, S. E. (1990). Implicit and explicit memory following surgical anesthesia. *Psychological Science, 1,* 303–306.

Kimble, G. A. (1989). Psychology from the standpoint of a generalist. *American Psychologist, 44,* 491–499.

Kimmel, A. J. (1996). *Ethical issues in behavioral research: A survey.* Oxford, England: Blackwell.

Kimura, D. (1992, September). Sex differences in the brain. *Scientific American,* pp. 119–125.

Kirk, S. A. (1992). *The selling of DSM: The rhetoric of science in psychiatry.* Hawthorne, New York: Aldine de Gruyter.

Kirsch, I. (Ed.). (1999). *How expectancies shape experience.* Washington, DC: American Psychological Association.

Kirsch, I., & Lynn, S. J. (1995). The altered state of hypnosis: Changes in the theoretical landscape. *American Psychologist, 50,* 846–858.

Kirsch, I., & Lynn, S. J. (1998). Dissociating the wheat from the chaff in theories of hypnosis: Reply to Kihlstrom (1998) and Woody and Sadler (1998). *Psychological Bulletin, 123,* 198–202.

Kirschstein, R. L. (2000). Parkinson's disease research agenda. National Institute of Neurological Disorders and Stroke Web site. Available: <http://www.ninds.nih.gov/about_ninds/nihparkinsons_agenda.htm>. Accessed December 12, 2002.

Kirsh, G. A., & Kuiper, N. A. (2002). Individualism and relatedness themes in the context of depression, gender and a self-schema model of emotion. *Canadian Psychology, 43,* 76–90.*

Kirshner, H. S. (1995). Alexias. In H. S. Kirshner (Ed.), *Handbook of neurological speech and language disorders: Neurological disease and therapy* (Vol. 33). New York: Marcel Dekker.

Kislevsky, B. S., Muir, D. W., Low, J. A., (2000). Maturation of human fetal responses to vibroacoustic stimulation. In D. Muir & A. Slater (Eds.), *Infant development: The essential readings.* Oxford: Blackwell Publishers.*

Kitterle, F. L. (Ed.). (1991). *Cerebral laterality: Theory and research.* Hillsdale, NJ: Erlbaum.

Klein, M. (1998, February). Family chats. *American Demographics,* p. 37.

Kleinman, A. (1996). How is culture important for *DSM-IV?* In J. E. Mezzich, A. Kleinman, H. Fabrega, Jr., & D. L. Parron (Eds.), *Culture and psychiatric diagnosis: A DSM-IV perspective.* Washington, DC: American Psychiatric Press.

Kleinman, A., & Cohen, A. (1997, March). Psychiatry's global challenge. *Scientific American,* pp. 86–89.

Klinke, R., Kral, A., Heid, S., Tillein, J., & Hartmann, R. (1999, September 10). Recruitment of the auditory cortex in congenitally deaf cats by long-term cochlear electrostimulation. *Science, 285,* 1729–1733.

Klinkenborg, V. (1997, January 5). Awakening to sleep. *New York Times,* pp. 26–31, 41, 51, 55.

Kluft, R. P. (1996). Dissociative identity disorder. In L. K. Michelson & W. J. Ray (Eds.), *Handbook of dissociation: Theoretical, empirical, and clinical perspectives.* New York: Plenum Press.

Kmiec, E. B. (1999). Gene therapy. *American Scientist, 87,* 240–247.

Knight, G. P., Johnson, L. G., Carlo, G., & Eisenberg, N. (1994). A multiplicative model of the dispositional antecedents of prosocial behavior: Predicting more of the people more of the time. *Journal of Personality and Social Psychology, 66,* 178–183.

Kobasa, S. C. (1979). Stressful life events, personality, and health: An inquiry into hardiness. *Journal of Personality and Social Psychology, 37,* 1–11.

Kobasa, S. C. O., Maddi, S. R., Puccetti, M. C., & Zola, M. A. (1994). Effectiveness of hardiness, exercise and social support as resources against illness. In A. Steptoe & J. Wardle (Eds.), *Psychosocial processes and health: A reader.* Cambridge, England: Cambridge University Press.

Kohlberg, L. (1984). *The psychology of moral development: Essays on moral development* (Vol. 2). San Francisco: Harper & Row.

Kohlberg, L., & Ryncarz, R. A. (1990). Beyond justice reasoning: Moral development and consideration of a seventh stage. In C. N. Alexander & E. J. Langer (Eds.), *Higher stages of human development: Perspectives on adult growth.* New York: Oxford University Press.

Köhler, W. (1927). *The mentality of apes.* London: Routledge & Kegan Paul.

Kolata, G. (1998). *Clone: The road to Dolly and the path ahead.* New York: William Morrow.

Konishi, M. (1993, April). Listening with two ears. *Scientific American,* pp. 66–73.

Konrad, W. (1994, April). Ten things your doctor won't tell you. *Smart Money,* p. 76.

Koocher, G. P., & Keith-Spiegel, P. (1998). *Ethics in psychology: Professional standards and cases* (2nd ed.). New York: Oxford University Press.

Koop, C. B. (1994). Infant assessment. In C. B. Fisher & R. M. Lerner (Eds.), *Applied developmental psychology*. New York: McGraw-Hill.

Koss, M. P. (1993). Rape: Scope, impact, interventions, and public policy responses. *American Psychologist, 48,* 1062–1069.

Kosslyn, S. M. (1981). The medium and the message in mental imagery. *Psychological Review, 88,* 46–66.

Kosslyn, S. M., Seger, C., Pani, J. R., & Hillger, L. A. (1990). When is imagery used in everyday life? A diary study. *Journal of Mental Imagery, 14,* 131–152.

Kosslyn, S. M., & Shin, L. M. (1994). Visual mental images in the brain: Current issues. In M. J. Farah & G. Ratcliff (Eds.), *The neuropsychology of high-level vision: Collected tutorial essays*. Hillsdale, NJ: Erlbaum.

Kotler-Cope, S., & Camp, C. J. (1990). Memory interventions in aging populations. In E. A. Lovelace (Ed.), *Aging and cognition: Mental processes, self-awareness, and interventions*. Amsterdam, Netherlands: North-Holland.

Kotre, J., & Hall, E. (1990). *Seasons of life*. Boston: Little, Brown.

Koval, J. J., Pederson, L. L., Mills, C. A., McGrady, G. A., & Carvajal, S. C. (2000). Models of the relationship of stress, depression, and other psychosocial factors to smoking behavior: A comparison of a cohort of students in Grades 6 and 8. *Preventive Medicine, 30,* 463–477.

Koveces, Z. (1987). *The container metaphor of emotion*. Paper presented at the University of Massachusetts, Amherst.

Kozma, A., Stones, M. J., & McNeil, J. K. (1991). *Psychological well-being in later life*. Toronto: Butterworths Canada.*

Kral, B. (2000). The eyes of Jane Elliott. *Horizon: People and Possibilities*. Available <http://www.horizonmag.com/4/jane-elliott.asp>. Accessed November 2, 2002.

Kramer, P. (1993). *Listening to Prozac*. New York: Viking.

Kraus, S. J. (1995, January). Attitudes and the prediction of behavior: A meta-analysis of the empirical literature. *Personality and Social Psychology Bulletin, 21,* 58–75.

Kravitz, E. A. (1988). Hormonal control of behavior: Amines and the biasing of behavioral output in lobsters. *Science, 241,* 1775–1782.

Kremer, J. M. D., & Scully, D. M. (1994). *Psychology in sport*. London, England: Taylor & Francis.

Kreuger, L. E. (1989). *The world of touch*. Hillsdale, NJ: Erlbaum.

Kriz, J. (1995). Naturwissenschaftliche Konzepte in der gegenwartigen Diskussion zum Problem der Ordnung (The contribution of natural science concepts to the current discussion of order). *Gestalt Theory, 17,* 153–163.

Krohne, H. W. (1996). Individual differences in coping. In M. Zeidner & N. S. Endler (Eds.), *Handbook of coping: Theory, research, applications*. New York: Wiley.

Kruglanski, A. W., Freund, T., & Bar Tal, D. (1996). Motivational effects in the mere-exposure paradigm. *European Journal of Social Psychology, 26,* 479–499.

Krull, D. S., & Anderson, C. A. (1997). The process of explanation. *Current Directions in Psychological Science, 6,* 1–5.

Kübler-Ross, E. (1969). *On death and dying*. New York: Macmillan.

Kuhl, P. K., Williams, K. A., Lacerda, F., Stevens, K. N., & Lindblom, B. (1992, January 31).

Linguistic experience alters phonetic perception in infants by 6 months of age. *Science, 255,* 606–608.

Kulynych, J. J., Vladar, K., Jones, D. W., & Weinberger, D. R. (1994). Gender differences in the normal lateralization of the supratemporal cortex: MRI surface-rendering morphometry of Heschl's gyrus and the planum temporale. *Cerebral Cortex, 4,* 107–118.

Kumpfer, K. L., & Alvarado, R. (1995). Strengthening families to prevent drug use in multiethnic youth. In G. J. Botvin, S. Schinke, & M. A. Orlandi (Eds.), *Drug abuse prevention with multiethnic youth* (pp. 255–294). Thousand Oaks, CA: Sage.*

Kunda, Z. (1999). *Social cognition: Making sense of people*. Cambridge, MA: MIT Press.

Kupfer, D. J., Reynolds, C. F., III. (1997, January 30). Management of insomnia. *New England Journal of Medicine, 336,* 341–346.

Kurtines, W., & Gewirtz, J. (1995). *Moral development: An introduction*. Boston: Allyn & Bacon.

Kvale, S. (1996). *Interviews: An introduction to qualitative research interviewing*. Newbury Park, CA: Sage.

Kwan, V. S. Y., Bond, M. H., & Singelis, T. M. (1997). Pancultural explanations for life satisfaction: Adding relationship harmony to self-esteem. *Journal of Personality and Social Psychology, 73,* 1038–1051.

Lach, J. (1998, November). Reading your mind, reaching your wallet. *American Demographics,* pp. 39–42.

Ladouceur, R. (1996). The prevalence of pathological gambling in Canada. *Journal of Gambling Studies, 12,* 129–142.*

Ladouceur, R., Boisvert, J., & Dumont, J. (1994). Cognitve-behavioural treatment for adolescent gamblers. *Behaviour Modification, 18,* 230–242.*

Ladouceur, R., & Mireault, C. (1988). Gambling behaviours among high-school students in the Quebec area. *Journal of Gambling Behaviour, 4,* 3–12.*

Ladouceur, R., Sylvain, C., Letarte, H., Giroux, I., & Jacques, C. (1998). Cognitive treatment of pathological gamblers. *Behaviour Research and Therapy, 36,* 1111–1119.*

Laird, J.D., & Bressler, C. (1990). William James and the mechanisms of emotional experience. *Personality and Social Psychology Bulletin, 16,* 636–651.

Lamb, M. (1982). The bonding phenomenon: Misinterpretations and their implications. *Journal of Pediatrics, 101,* 555–557.

Lamb, M. E. (1996). Effects of nonparental child care on child development: An update. *Canadian Journal of Psychiatry, 41,* 330–342.

Lambert, G., Johansson, M., Agren, H., & Friberg, P. (2000). Reduced brain norepinephrine and dopamine release in treatment-refractory depressive illness. *Archives of General Psychiatry, 57,* 787–793.

Lambert, M. J., Shapiro, D. A., & Bergin, A. E. (1986). The effectiveness of psychotherapy. In S. L. Garfield & A. E. Bergin (Eds.), *Handbook of psychotherapy and behavior change* (3rd ed.). New York: Wiley.

Lambert, W. E., & Anisfeld, E. (1969). A note on the relationship of bilingualism and intelligence. *Canadian Journal of Behavioural Science, 1,* 123–128.*

Lambert W. E., & Peal, E. (1972). The relation of bilingualism to intelligence. In A. S. Dil (Ed.), *Language, psychology, and culture*. Stanford, CA: Stanford University Press.*

Lambert, W. E., & Tucker, G. R. (1972). *Bilingual education in children: The St. Lambert experiment*. Rowley, MA: Newbury House.*

Lamerson, C. D., & Kelloway, E. K. (1996). Towards a model of peacekeeping stress: Traumatic and contextual influences. *Canadian Psychology, 37,* 195–204.*

Landis, D., Day, H. R., McGrew, P. L., Thomas, J. A., & Miller, A. B. (1976). Can a black "culture assimilator" increase racial understanding? *Journal of Social Issues, 32,* 169–183.

Landry, D. W. (1997, February). Immunotherapy for cocaine addiction. *Scientific American,* pp. 41–45.

Langer, E., Bashner, R. S., & Chanowitz, B. (1985). Decreasing prejudice by increasing discrimination. *Journal of Personality and Social Psychology, 49,* 113–120.

Langer, E., & Janis, I. (1979). *The psychology of control*. Beverly Hills, CA: Sage.

Langlois, J. H., Kalakanis, L., Rubenstein, A. J., Larson, A., Hallam, M., & Smoot, M. (2000). Maxims or myths of beauty? A meta-analytic and theoretical review. *Psychological Bulletin, 126,* 390–423.

Langreth, R. (2000, May 1). Every little bit helps: How even moderate exercise can have a big impact on your health. *Wall Street Journal,* p. R5.

Langs, G., Quehenberger, F., Fabisch, K., Klug, G., Fabisch, H., & Zapotoczky, H. G. (2000). The development of agoraphobia in panic disorder: A predictable process? *Journal of Affective Disorders, 58,* 43–50.

Larose, H., & Standing, L. (1998). Does the halo effect occur in the elderly? *Social Behavior and Personality, 26,* 147–150.

Larson, R. K. (1990). Semantics. In D. N. Osherson & H. Lasnik (Eds.). *Language*. Cambridge, MA: MIT Press.

Larson, R. W., Richards, M. H., & Perry-Jenkins, M. (1994). Divergent worlds: The daily emotional experience of mothers and fathers in the domestic and public spheres. *Journal of Personality and Social Psychology, 67,* 1034–1046.

Lask, B., & Bryant-Waugh, R. (Eds.). (1999). *Anorexia nervosa and related eating disorders in childhood and adolescence*. New York: Brunner/Mazel.

Lasnik, H. (1990). Syntax. In D. N. Osherson & H. Lasnik (Eds.), *Language,* Cambridge, MA: MIT Press.

Latané, B., & Darley, J. M. (1970). *The unresponsive bystander: Why doesn't he help?* New York: Appleton-Century-Crofts.

Latané, B., & Nida, S. (1981). Ten years of research on group size and helping. *Psychological Bulletin, 89,* 308–324.

Lautenbacher, S. & Rollman, G.B. (1999). Somatization, hypochondriasis, and related conditions. In A. R. Block, E. F. Kremer, & E. Fernandez (Eds.), *Handbook of pain syndromes: Biopsychosocial perspectives*. Mahwah, NJ: Erlbaum.*

Lazarus, A. A. (1997). *Brief but comprehensive psychotherapy: The multimodal way*. New York: Springer.

Lazarus, R. S. (1991a). Cognition and motivation in emotion. *American Psychologist, 46,* 352–367.

Lazarus, R. S. (1991b). *Emotion and adaptation.* New York: Oxford University Press.

Lazarus, R. S. (1994). Appraisal: The long and short of it. In P. Ekman & R. J. Davidson (Eds.), *The nature of emotion: Fundamental questions.* New York: Oxford University Press.

Lazarus, R. S. (1995). Emotions express a social relationship, but it is an individual mind that creates them. *Psychological Inquiry, 6,* 253–265.

Lazarus, R. S. (1999). *Stress and emotion: A new synthesis.* New York: Springer.

Lazarus, R. S., & Cohen, J. B. (1977). Environmental stress. In I. Altman & J. F. Wohlwill (Eds.), *Human behavior and the environment: Current theory and research* (Vol. 2). New York: Plenum Press.

Lee, K., Ashton, M. C., Hong, S., & Park, K. (2000). Psychometric properties of the nonverbal personality questionnaire in Korea. *Educational and Psychological Measurement, 60,* 131–141.*

Lefcourt, H. M. (2001). Humor: The psychology of living buoyantly. New York: Kluwer Academic/Plenum.*

Legault, G., Gravel, S., Fortin, S., Henneman, B., & Cardinal, M. (1997) Adaptation of services to new immigrant families: Perceptions of families and practitioners. *Canadian Journal of Community Mental Health, 16,* 67–83.*

Lehman, D. R., Lempert, R. O., & Nisbett, R. E. (1988). The effects of graduate training on reasoning: Formal discipline and thinking about everyday-life events. *American Psychologist, 43,* 431–442.

Lehman, D. R., & Taylor, S. E. (1988). Date with an earthquake: Coping with a probable, unpredictable disaster. *Personality and Social Psychology Bulletin, 13,* 546–555.

Lehrer, P. M. (1996). Recent research findings on stress management techniques. In Editorial Board of Hatherleigh Press, *The Hatherleigh guides series.* Vol. 4: *The Hatherleigh guide to issues in modern therapy.* New York: Hatherleigh Press.

Leibel, R. L., Rosenbaum, M., & Hirsch, J. (1995, March 9). Changes in energy expenditure resulting from altered body. *New England Journal of Medicine, 332,* 621–628.

Leibovic, K. N. (Ed.). (1990). *Science of vision.* New York: Springer-Verlag.

Leigh, H., & Reiser, M. F. (1980). *The patient.* New York: Plenum Press.

Leland, J. (2000, May 29). The science of women and sex. *Newsweek,* pp. 48–54.

Lenzenweger, M. F. & Dworkin, R. H. (Eds.). (1998). *The origins and development of schizophrenia: Advances in experimental psychopathology.* Washington, DC: American Psychological Association.

Leonard, B. E. (2000). Evidence for a biochemical lesion in depression. *Journal of Clinical Psychiatry, 61,* 12–17.

Leong, F. L., & Blustein, D. L. (2000). Toward a global vision of counseling psychology. *Counseling Psychologist, 28,* 5–9.

Lepore, S. J., Ragan, J. D., & Jones, S. (2000). Talking facilitates cognitive-emotional processes of adaptation to an acute stressor. *Journal of Personality and Social Psychology, 78,* 499–508.

Lepper, M. R., & Greene, D. (Eds.). (1978). *The hidden costs of reward.* Hillsdale, NJ: Erlbaum.

Lepper, M. R., Henderlong, J., & Gingras, I. (1999). Understanding the effects of extrinsic rewards on intrinsic motivation—Uses and abuses of meta-analysis: Comment on Deci, Koestner, and

Ryan (1999). *Psychological Bulletin, 125,* 669–676.

Lerner, R. M., Fisher, C. B., & Weinberg, R. A. (2000). Toward a science for and of the people: Promoting civil society through the application of developmental science. *Child Development, 71,* 11–20.

Lesch, K.-P., Bengel, D., Heils, A., Sabol, S. Z., Greenberg, B. D., Petri, S., Benjamin, J., Muller, C. R., Hamer, D. H., & Murphy, D. L. (1996, November 29). Association of anxiety-related traits with a polymorphism in the serotonin transporter gene regulatory region. *Science, 274,* 1527–1531.

LeVay, S. (1991) A difference in hypothalamic structure between heterosexual and homosexual men. *Science, 253,* 1034–1037.

LeVay, S. (1993). *The sexual brain.* Cambridge, MA: MIT Press.

Levenson, R. W. (1992). Autonomic nervous system differences among emotions. *Psychological Science, 3,* 23–27.

Levenson, R. W. (1994). The search for autonomic specificity. In P. Ekman & R. J. Davidson (Eds.), *The nature of emotion: Fundamental questions.* New York: Oxford University Press.

Levenson, R. W., Ekman, P., Heider, K., & Friesen, W. V. (1992). Emotion and autonomic nervous system activity in the Minangkabau of West Sumatra. *Journal of Personality and Social Psychology, 62,* 972–988.

Leventhal, H., & Cleary, P. D. (1980). The smoking problem: A review of the research and theory in behavioral risk modification. *Psychological Bulletin, 88,* 370–405.

Leventhal, H., & Tomarken, A. J. (1986). Emotion: Today's problems. *Annual Review of Psychology, 37,* 565–610.

Levine, J. M. (1989). Reaction to opinion deviance in small groups. In P. B. Paulus (Ed.), *Psychology of group influence* (2nd ed.). Hillsdale, NJ: Erlbaum.

Levinson, D. J. (1990). A theory of life structure development in adulthood. In C. N. Alexander & E. J. Langer (Eds.), *Higher stages of human development: Perspectives on adult growth.* New York: Oxford University Press.

Levy, B. (1996). Improving memory in old age through implicit self-stereotyping. *Journal of Personality and Social Psychology, 71,* 1092–1107.

Levy, B. A. (2000). Text processing: Memory representations mediate fluent reading. In M. Neveh-Benjamin, M. Moscovitch, & H. L. Roediger (Eds.), *Perspectives on human memory and cognitive aging: Essays in honor of Fergus Craik.* New York: Psychology Press.*

Levy, B. A., Abello, B., & Lysynchuk, L. (1997). Transfer from word training to reading in context: Gains in reading fluency and comprehension. *Disabilities Quarterly, 20,* 173–188.*

Levy, B. A., & Lysynchuk, L. (1997). Beginning word recognition: Benefits of training by segmentation and whole word methods. *Scientific Studies of Reading, 1,* 359–387.*

Levy, B. L., & Langer, E. (1994). Aging free from negative stereotypes: Successful memory in China and among the American deaf. *Journal of Personality and Social Psychology, 66,* 989–997.

Levy, D. H. (2000, August 20). Are you ready for the genome miracle? *Parade,* pp. 8–10.

Levy, S. (1997, May 19). Big Blue's hand of God. *Newsweek,* p. 72.

Levy, S., & Fletcher, E. (1998). Kamatsiaqtut, Baffin Crisis Line: Community ownership of support in a small town. In A. A. Leenaars, S. Wenckstern, I. Sakinofsky, R. J. Dyck, M. J. Kral, & R. C. Bland (Eds.), *Suicide in Canada* (pp. 353–366). Toronto: University of Toronto Press.*

Levy, S. M., Lee, J., Bagley, C., & Lippman, M. (1988). Survival hazards analysis in first recurrent breast cancer patients: Seven-year follow-up. *Psychosomatic Medicine, 50,* 520–528.

Lewis, M., Feiring, C., McGuffog, C., & Jaskir, J. (1984). Predicting psychopathology in six-year-olds from early social relations. *Child Development, 55,* 123–136.

Lewis, M., Feiring, C., & Rosenthal, S. (2000). Attachment over time. *Child Development, 71,* 707–720.

Lewis, M., & Haviland-Jones, J. M. (2000). *Handbook of emotions* (2nd ed.). New York: Guilford Press.

LeWitt, P. A. (2000). The challenge of managing mild Parkinson's disease. *Pharmacotherapy, 20,* 2S–7S.

Li, S. (1995). (A comparative study of personality in supernormal children and normal children.) *Psychological Science—China, 18,* 184–186.

Li, Y., Xu, J., Shi, X., & Yan, Y. (1999). Intelligence, memory, and event-related potential in patients with motor neuron disease. *Chinese Mental Health Journal, 13,* 180–181.

Liebert, R. M., & Sprafkin, J. (1988). *The early window: Effects of television on children and youth* (3rd ed.). New York: Pergamon Press.

Lindsay, P. H., & Norman, D. A. (1977). *Human information processing* (2nd ed.). New York: Academic Press.

Lindsay, R. C. L. (1994). Expectations of eyewitness performance: Jurors' verdicts do not follow from their beliefs. In D. F. Ross, J. D. Read, & M. P. Toglia (Eds.), *Adult eyewitness testimony: Current trends and developments* (pp. 362–384). New York: Cambridge University Press.*

Linszen, D. H., Dingemans, P. M., Nugter, M. A., Van der Does, A. J. W., et al. (1997). Patient attributes and expressed emotion as risk factors for psychotic relapse. *Schizophrenia Bulletin, 23,* 119–130.

Lipsey, M. W., & Wilson, D. B. (1993). The efficacy of psychological, educational, and behavioral treatment: Confirmation from meta-analysis. *American Psychologist, 48,* 1181–1209.

Loewenstein, G. (1994). The psychology of curiosity: A review and reinterpretation. *Psychological Bulletin, 116,* 75–98.

Loftus, E. F. (1979). *Eyewitness testimony.* Cambridge: Harvard University Press.

Loftus, E. F. (1997). Memory for a past that never was. *Current Directions in Psychological Science, 6,* 60–65.

Loftus, E. F. (1998, November). The memory police. *APA Observer,* pp. 3, 14.

Loftus, E. F., & Palmer, J. C. (1974). Reconstruction of automobile destruction: An example of the interface between language and memory. *Journal of Verbal Learning and Verbal Behavior, 13,* 585–589.

Logie, R. H., & Gilhooly, K. J. (1998). *Working memory and thinking.* Philadelphia: Psychology Press.

Long, A. (1987, December). What is this thing called sleep? *National Geographic, 172,* 786–821.

Long, G. M., & Beaton, R. J. (1982). The case for peripheral persistence: Effects of target and background luminance on a partial-report task.

Journal of Experimental Psychology: Human Perception and Performance, 8, 383–391.

Loomis, J. M., Golledge, R. G., & Klatzky, R. L. (in press). Navigation system for the blind: Auditory display modes and guidance. In *Presence: Teleoperators and Virtual Environments.*

Loomis, J. M., Klatzky, R. L., Golledge, R. G., Cicinelli, J. G., Pellegrino, J. W., & Fry, P. A. (1993). Nonvisual navigation by blind and sighted: Assessment of path integration ability. *Journal of Experimental Psychology: General, 122,* 73–91.

Looy, H. (1995). Born gay? A critical review of biological research on homosexuality. *Journal of Psychology and Christianity, 14,* 197–214.

Lorenz, K. (1966). *On aggression.* New York: Harcourt Brace Jovanovich.

Lorenz, K. (1974). *Civilized man's eight deadly sins.* New York: Harcourt Brace Jovanovich.

Lowe, M. R. (1993). The effects of dieting on eating behavior: A three-factor model. *Psychological Bulletin, 114,* 100–121.

Lown, B. (1999). *The lost art of healing.* New York: Ballantine.

Luborsky, L. (1988). *Who will benefit from psychotherapy?* New York: Basic Books.

Lucas, R. E., Diener, E., Grob, A., Suh, E. M., & Shao, L. (2000). Cross-cultural evidence for the fundamental features of extraversion. *Journal of Personality and Social Psychology, 79,* 452–468.

Luce, R. D. (1993). *Sound and hearing.* Hillsdale, NJ: Erlbaum.

Luchins, A. S. (1946). Classroom experiments on mental set. *American Journal of Psychology, 59,* 295–298.

Lucy, J. A. (1992). *Language diversity and thought: A reformulation of the linguistic relativity hypothesis.* Cambridge, England: Cambridge University Press.

Lucy, J. A. (1996). The scope of linguistic relativity: An analysis and review of empirical research. In J. J. Gumperz & S. C. Levinson (Eds.), *Rethinking linguistic relativity. Studies in the social and cultural foundations of language,* No. 17. Cambridge, England: Cambridge University Press.

Ludwig, A. M. (1996, March). Mental disturbances and creative achievement. *Harvard Mental Health Letter,* pp. 4–6.

Luria, A. R. (1968). *The mind of a mnemonist.* Cambridge, MA: Basic Books.

Ly, D. H., Lockhart, D. J., Lerner, R. A., & Schultz, P. G. (2000, March 31). Mitotic misregulation and human aging. *Science, 287,* 2486–2492.

Lykken, D. T. (1995). *The antisocial personalities.* Mahwah, NJ: Erlbaum.

Lykken, D. T., McGue, M., Tellegen, A., & Bouchard, T. J., Jr. (1993). Emergenesis: Genetic traits that may not run in families. *American Psychologist, 47,* 1565–1577.

Lykken, D. T., & Tellegen, A. (1996). Happiness is a stochastic phenomenon. *Psychological Science, 7,* 181–185.

Lynn, S. J., Lock, T. G., Myers, B., & Payne, D. G. (1997). Recalling the unrecallable: Should hypnosis be used to recover memories in psychotherapy? *Current Directions in Psychological Science, 6,* 79–83.

Lynn, S. J., Neufeld, V., Green, J. P., Sandberg, D., et al. (1996). Daydreaming, fantasy, and psychopathology. In R. G. Kunzendorf, N. P. Spanos, & B. Wallace (Eds.), *Hypnosis and imagination.* Amityville, NY: Baywood.

Lynn, S. J., & Rhue, J. W. (1988). Fantasy-proneness: Hypnosis, developmental antecedents, and psychopathology. *American Psychologist, 43,* 35–44.

Macaluso, E., Frith, C. D., & Driver, J. (2000, August 18). Modulation of human visual cortex by crossmodal spatial attention. *Science, 289,* 1206–1208.

MacDonald, T. K., Zanna, M. P., & Fong, G. T. (1996). Why common sense goes out the window: The effects of alcohol on the intentions to use condoms. *Personality and Social Psychology Bulletin, 22,* 763–775.*

MacDougall, J. C. (2001). Access to justice for deaf Inuit in Nunavut: The role of "Inuit Sign Language." *Canadian Psychology, 42,* 61–73.*

Mackay, R., & Myles, L. (1995). A major challenge for the education system: Aboriginal retention and dropout. In M. Battiste & J. Barman (Eds.), *First Nations education in Canada: The circle unfolds.* Vancouver: UBC Press.*

MacKenzie, B. (1984). Explaining race differences in IQ: The logic, the methodology, and the evidence. *American Psychologist, 39,* 1214–1233.

Mackintosh, N. J. (1998). *IQ and human intelligence.* Cambridge, England: Oxford University Press.

MacLean, P. (1990). *The triune brain in evolution.* New York: Plenum Press.

Macmillan, M. (1991). *Freud evaluated: The completed arc.* Amsterdam: North-Holland.

Macrae, C. N., Stangor, C., & Hewstone, M. (1996). *Stereotypes and stereotyping.* New York: Guilford Press.

MacTavish, J. (2001). *Bravo! Miss Brown: A world without sight and sound.* Toronto: Cavu Inc.*

Mader, S. (2000). *Human biology,* 6th Edition. New York: McGraw-Hill.

Madon, S., Jussim, L., & Eccles, J. (1997). In search of the powerful self-fulfilling prophecy. *Journal of Personality and Social Psychology, 72,* 791–809.

Mahoney, J. (2001, June 26). Lung illness rampant in Inuit children. *The Globe and Mail,* p. A4.*

Maidment, I. (2000). The use of St John's Wort in the treatment of depression. *Psychiatric Bulletin, 24,* 232–234.

Mairs, D. A. E. (1995). Hypnosis and pain in childbirth. *Contemporary Hypnosis, 12,* 111–118.

Malott, R. W., Whaley, D. L., & Malott, M. E. (1993). *Elementary principles of behavior* (2nd ed.). Englewood Cliffs, NJ: Prentice Hall.

Mamabolo, L. M. (1996). Group treatment program for sexually and physically assaultive young offenders in a secure custody facility. *Canadian Psychology, 37,* 154–160.*

Mann, D. (1997). *Psychotherapy: An erotic relationship.* New York: Routledge.

Manstead, A. S. R. (1991). Expressiveness as an individual difference. In R. S. Feldman & B. Rime (Eds.), *Fundamentals of nonverbal behavior.* Cambridge, England: Cambridge University Press.

Mapes, G. (1990, April 10). Beating the clock: Was it an accident Chernobyl exploded at 1:23 in the morning? *Wall Street Journal,* pp. A1, A16.

Marcus, G. F. (1996). Why do children say "breaked"? *Current Directions in Psychological Science, 5,* 81–85.

Margolis, E., & Laurence, S. (Eds.). (1999). *Concepts: Core readings.* Cambridge, MA: MIT Press.

Marijuana as medicine: How strong is the science? (May, 1997). *Consumer Reports,* pp. 62–63.

Markey, P. M. (2000). Bystander intervention in computer-mediated communication. *Computers in Human Behavior, 16,* 183–188.

Marks, G., & Miller, N. (1987). Ten years of research on the false-consensus effect: An empirical and theoretical review. *Psychological Bulletin, 102,* 72–90.

Markus, H. R., & Kitayama, S. (1991). Culture and the self: Implications for cognition, emotion, and motivation. *Psychological Review, 98,* 224–255.

Martin, A., Haxby, J. V., Lalonde, F. M., Wiggs, C. L., & Ungerleider, L. G. (1995, October 6). Discrete cortical regions associated with knowledge of color and knowledge of action. *Science, 270,* 102–105.

Martin, R. A. (1996). Humour as therapeutic play: Stress-moderating effects of humour. *Journal of Leisurability, 23,* 8–15.*

Marxsen, D., Yuille, J. C., & Nisbett, M. (1995). The complexities of eliciting and assessing children's statements. *Psychology, Public Policy and the Law, 1,* 450–460.*

Maslow, A. H. (1970). *Motivation and personality* (2nd ed.). New York: Harper & Row.

Maslow, A. H. (1987). *Motivation and personality* (3rd ed.). New York: Harper & Row.

Masters, W. H., & Johnson, V. E. (1979). *Homosexuality in perspective.* Boston: Little, Brown.

Mastropieri, M. A., & Scruggs, T. E. (1991). *Teaching students ways to remember: Strategies for learning mnemonically.* Cambridge, MA: Brookline Books.

Matarazzo, J. D. (1992). Psychological testing and assessment in the 21st century. *American Psychologist, 47,* 1007–1018.

Matthews, D. B., Best, P. J., White, A. M., Vandergriff, J. L., & Simson, P. E. (1996). Ethanol impairs spatial cognitive processing: New behavioral and electrophysiological findings. *Current Directions in Psychological Science, 5,* 111–115.

Matute, H. (1994). Learned helplessness and superstitious behavior as opposite effects of uncontrollable reinforcement in humans. *Learning and Motivation, 25,* 216–232.

Matute, H. (1995). Human reactions to uncontrollable outcomes: Further evidence for superstitions rather than helplessness. *Quarterly Journal of Experimental Psychology Comparative and Physiological Psychology, 48,* 142–157.

Maurer, D., Lewis, T. L., Brent, H. P., & Levin, A. V. (1999, October 1). Rapid improvement in the acuity of infants after visual input. *Science, 286,* 108–110.

Mawhinney, T. A. (1983). A picture vocabulary test for the Eastern James Bay Cree. In S. H. Irvine & J. W. Berry (Eds.), *Human assessment and cultural factors.* New York: Plenum.*

May, R. (1989). *Love and will.* New York: Norton.

Mayer, J. D., & Salovey, P. (1997). What is emotional intelligence? In P. Salovey & D. J. Sluyter (Eds.), *Emotional development and emotional intelligence.* New York: Basic Books.

Mayr, U., Kliegl, R., & Krampe, R. T. (1996). Sequential and coordinative processing dynamics in figural transformations across the life span. *Cognition, 59,* 61–90.

McAdams, D. P., Diamond, A., de St. Aubin, E., & Mansfield, E. (1997). Stories of commitment: The psychosocial construction of generative lives. *Journal of Personality and Social Psychology, 72,* 678–694.

McCabe, P. M., Schneiderman, N., Field, T., & Wellens, A. R. (Eds.). (2000). *Stress, coping, and cardiovascular disease.* Mahwah, NJ: Erlbaum.

McCain, N. L., & Smith, J. (1994). Stress and coping in the context of psychoneuroimmunology: A holistic framework for nursing practice and research. *Archives of Psychiatric Nursing, 8,* 221–227.

McCann, U. D., Mertl, M., Eligulashvili, V., & Ricaurte, G. A. (1999). Cognitive performance in (±) 3,4-methylenedioxymethamphetamine (MDMA, "Ecstasy") users: A controlled study. *Psychopharmacology, 143,* 417–425.

McClearn, G. E., Johansson, B., Berg, S., Pedersen, N. L., Ahern, F., Petrill, S. A., & Plomin, R. (1997, June 6). Substantial genetic influence on cognitive abilities in twins 80 or more years old. *Science, 276,* 1560–1583.

McClelland, D. C. (1985). How motives, skills, and values determine what people do. *American Psychologist, 40,* 812–825.

McClelland, D. C. (1993). Intelligence is not the best predictor of job performance. *Current Directions in Psychological Research, 2,* 5–8.

McClelland, D. C., Atkinson, J. W., Clark, R. A., & Lowell, E. L. (1953). *The achievement motive.* New York: Appleton-Century-Crofts.

McClintock, M. K., & Herdt, G. (1996). Rethinking puberty: The development of sexual attraction. *Current Directions in Psychological Science, 5,* 178–183.

McCormick, C. M., & Witelson, S. F. (1994). Functional cerebral asymmetry and sexual orientation in men and women. *Behavioural Neuroscience, 108,* 525–531.*

McCrae, R. R., & Costa, P. T., Jr. (1999). A five-factor theory of personality. In L. A. Pervin & O. P. John (Eds.), *Handbook of personality: Theory and research* (2nd ed.). New York: Guilford Press.

McCreary, D. R., & Sadava, S. W. (1998). Stress, drinking, and the adverse consequences of drinking in two samples of young adults. *Psychology of Addictive Behaviours, 12,* 247–261.*

McCullough, J. P., Jr. (1999). *Treatment for chronic depression: Cognitive behavioral analysis system of psychology (CBASP).* New York: Guilford Press.

McDonald, C., & Murray, R. M. (2000). Early and late environmental risk factors for schizophrenia. *Brain Research Reviews, 31,* 130–137.

McDonald, H. E., & Hirt, E. R. (1997). When expectancy meets desire: Motivational effects in reconstructive memory. *Journal of Personality and Social Psychology, 72,* 5–23.

McDonald, J. W. (1999, September). Repairing the damaged spinal cord. *Scientific American,* pp. 65–73.

McDougall, W. (1908). *Introduction to social psychology.* London: Methuen.

McDowell, D. M., & Spitz, H. I. (1999). *Substance abuse.* New York: Brunner/Mazel.

McEwen, B. S. (1998, January 15). Protective and damaging effects of stress mediators [Review article]. *New England Journal of Medicine, 338,* 171–179.

McFadyen, R. G. (1996). Gender, status and "powerless" speech: Interactions of students and lectures. *British Journal of Social Psychology, 35,* 353–367.

McFarlane, T., Polivy, J., & McCabe, R. (1999). Help, not harm: Psychological foundation for a nondieting approach toward health. *Journal of Social Issues, 55,* 256–276.*

McGaugh, J. L. (2000, January 14). Memory—A century of consolidation. *Science, 287,* 248–251.

McGaugh, J. L., Weinberger, N. M., & Lynch, G. (Eds.). (1990). *Brain organization and memory: Cells, systems, and circuits.* New York: Oxford University Press.

McGue, M. (1999). The behavioral genetics of alcoholism. *Current Directions in Psychological Science, 8,* 109–115.

McGuire, P. K., Shah, G. M. S., & Murray, R. M. (1993, September 18). Increased blood flow in Broca's area during auditory hallucinations in schizophrenia. *Lancet, 342,* 703–706.

McGuire, W. J. (1997). Creative hypothesis generating in psychology: Some useful heuristics. *Annual Review of Psychology, 48,* 1–30.

McKim, M. K., Cramer, K. M., Stuart, B., & O'Conner, D., L. (1999). Infant care decisions and attachment security: The Canadian transition to child care study. *Canadian Journal of Behavioural Science, 31(2),* 92–106.*

McLaughlin, S., & Margolskee, R. F. (1994). The sense of taste: The internal molecular workings of the taste bud help it distinguish the bitter from the sweet. *American Scientist, 82,* 538–454.

McManus, F., & Waller, G. (1995). A functional analysis of binge-eating. *Clinical Psychology Review, 15,* 845–863.

McMullin, R. E. (2000). *The new handbook of cognitive therapy techniques.* New York: Norton.

McWhirter, D. P., Sanders, S., & Reinisch, J. M. (1990). *Homosexuality, heterosexuality: Concepts of sexual orientation.* New York: Oxford University Press.

Mead, M. (1949). *Male and female.* New York: Morrow.

Mednick, A. (1993). World's women familiar with a day's double shift. *APA Monitor,* p. 32.

Meier, R. P., & Willerman, R. (1995). Prelinguistic gesture in deaf and hearing infants. In K. Emmorey & J. S. Reilly (Eds.), *Language, gesture, and space.* Hillsdale, NJ: Erlbaum.

Mel'nikov, K. S. (1993, October–December). (On some aspects of the mechanistic approach to the study of processes of forgetting.) *Vestnik Moskovskogo Universiteta Seriya 14 Psikhologiya,* 64–67.

Melton, G. B., & Garrison, E. G. (1987). Fear, prejudice, and neglect: Discrimination against mentally disabled persons. *American Psychologist, 42,* 1007–1026.

Meltzer, H. Y. (2000). Genetics and etiology of schizophrenia and bipolar disorder. *Biological Psychiatry, 47,* 171–173.

Meltzoff, A. N. (1996). The human infant as imitative generalist: A 20-year progress report on infant imitation with implications for comparative psychology. In C. M. Heyes & B. G. Galef, Jr. (Eds.), *Social learning in animals: The roots of culture.* San Diego: Academic Press.

Melzack, R., & Wall, P. D. (1965). Pain mechanisms: A new theory. *Science, 150,* 971–979.*

Mendez, F. J., & Garcia, M. J. (1996). Emotive performances: A treatment package for children's phobias. *Child and Family Behavior Therapy, 18,* 19–34.

Mental health: Does therapy help? (1995, November). *Consumer Reports,* pp. 734–739.

Mentzer, S. J., & Snyder, M. L. (1982). The doctor and the patient: A psychological perspective. In G. S. Sanders and J. Suls (Eds.), *Social psychology of health and illness* (pp. 161–181). Hillsdale, NJ: Erlbaum.

Merikle, P. M., & Daneman, M. (1996). Memory for unconsciously perceived events: Evidence from anesthetized patients. *Consciousness and Cognition, 5,* 525–541.*

Merikle, P. M., & Daneman, M. (1998). Psychological investigations of unconscious perception. *Journal of Consciousness Studies, 5,* 5–18.*

Merlin, D. (1993). Origins of the modern mind: Three stages in the evolution of culture and cognition. *Behavioral and Brain Sciences, 16,* 737–791.

Mesquita, B., & Frijda, N. H. (1992). Cultural variations in emotions: A review. *Psychological Bulletin, 112,* 179–204.

Metcalfe, J. (1986). Premonitions of insight predict impending error. *Journal of Experimental Psychology: Learning, Memory, and Cognition, 12,* 623–634.

Metee, D. R., & Aronson, E. (1974). Affective reactions to appraisal from others. In T. L. Huston (Ed.), *Foundations of interpersonal attraction* (pp. 235–283). New York: Academic Press.

Meyer, G. J. (2000). Incremental validity of the Rorschach Prognostic Rating scale over the MMPI Ego Strength Scale and IQ. *Journal of Personality Assessment, 74,* 356–370.

Meyer, R. G., & Osborne, Y. V. H. (1987). *Case studies in abnormal behavior* (2nd ed.). Boston: Allyn & Bacon.

Michael, R. T., Gagnon, J. H., Laumann, E. O., & Kolata, G. (1994). *Sex in America: A definitive survey.* Boston: Little, Brown.

Middlebrooks, J. C., Clock, A. E., Xu, L., & Green, D. M. (1994, May 6). A panoramic code for sound location by cortical neurons. *Science, 264,* 842–844.

Middlebrooks, J. C., & Green, D. M. (1991). Sound localization by human listeners. *Annual Review of Psychology, 42,* 135–159.

Mifflin, L. (1998, January 14). Study finds a decline in TV network violence. *New York Times,* p. A14.

Mikamo, K., Takao, Y., Wakutani, Y., & Nishikawa, S. (1994). Effects of mecobalamin injection at acupoints on intractable headaches. *Current Therapeutic Research, 55,* 1477–1485.

Miles, R. (2000, January 14). Diversity in inhibition. *Science, 287,* 244–246.

Milgram, R. M., Dunn, R. S., & Price, G. E. (Eds.). (1993). *Teaching and counseling gifted and talented adolescents: An international learning style perspective.* Westport, CT: Praeger/Greenwood.

Milgram, S. (1974). *Obedience to authority.* New York: Harper & Row.

Millar, W. (1996). Chronic pain. In Statistics Canada, *Health Reports, 7,* (pp. 447–52). Ottawa: Statistics Canada.*

Miller, A. G. (1999). Harming other people: Perspectives on evil and violence. *Personality and Social Psychology Review, 3,* 176–178.

Miller, A. G., Collins, B. E., & Brief, D. E. (1995). Perspectives on obedience to authority: The legacy of the Milgram experiments. *Journal of Social Issues, 51,* 1–19.

Miller, D. W. (2000, February 25). Looking askance at eyewitness testimony. *Chronicle of Higher Education,* pp. A19–A20.

Miller, G. A. (1956). The magical number seven, plus or minus two: Some limits on our capacity for processing information. *Psychology Review, 63,* 81–97.

Miller, J. G. (1999). Cultural psychology: Implications for basic psychological theory. *Psychological Science, 10,* 85–91.

Miller, K. J., & Mizes, J. S. (Eds.). (2000). *Comparative treatments for eating disorders.* New York: Springer.

Miller, L. T., & Vernon, P. A. (1997). Developmental changes in speed of information processing in young children. *Developmental Psychology, 33,* 549–554.

Miller, N. E. (1985, February). Rx: Biofeedback. *Psychology Today,* pp. 54–59.

Miller, N. E., & Magruder, K. M. (Eds.). (1999). *Cost-effectiveness of psychotherapy: A guide for practitioners, researchers, and policymakers.* New York: Oxford University Press.

Millon, T., & Davis, R. (1996). *Disorders of personality: DSM-IV and beyond* (2nd ed.). New York: Wiley.

Millon, T., & Davis, R. (1999). *Personality disorders in modern life.* New York: Wiley.

Millon, T., Davis, R., Millon, C., Escovar, L., & Meagher, S. (2000). *Personality disorders in modern life.* New York: Wiley.

Mills, J. L. (1999). Cocaine, smoking, and spontaneous abortion. *New England Journal of Medicine, 340,* 380–381.

Milner, A. D., & Goodale, M. A. (1995). *The visual brain in action.* New York: Oxford.*

Milner, B. (1966). *Amnesia following operation on temporal lobes.* In C. W. M. Whitty & P. Zangwill (Eds.), *Amnesia.* London: Butterworth.

Milner, B., Petrides, M., & Smith, M. L. (1985). Frontal lobes and the temporal organization of memory. *Human Neurobiology, 4,* 137–142.*

Milton, J., & Wiseman, R. (1999). Does psi exist? Lack of replication of an anomalous process of information transfer. *Psychological Bulletin, 125,* 387–391.

Mind over matter. (1999). *Discover, 20,* p. 2.

Mineka, S., & Henderson, R. W. (1985). Controllability and predictability in acquired motivation. *Annual Review of Psychology, 36,* 495–529.

Mingo, C., Herman, C. J., & Jasperse, M. (2000). Women's stories: Ethnic variations in women's attitudes and experiences of menopause, hysterectomy, and hormone replacement therapy. *Journal of Women's Health and Gender-Based Medicine, 9* (Suppl. 2), S27–S38.

Ministry of the Solicitor General of Canada. (1994, August 23). Weapons in schools study.* Available at <http://www.sgc.gc.ca/publications/news/19940823_e.asp>. Accessed December 14, 2002.

Minuchin, S., & Nichols, M. P. (1992). *Family healing.* New York: Free Press.

Miserando, M. (1991). Memory and the seven dwarfs. *Teaching of Psychology, 18,* 169–171.

Mistlberger, R. E. (1991). Scheduled daily exercise or feeding alters the phase of photic entrainment in syrian hamsters. *Physiology and Behaviour, 50,* 1257–1260.*

Mittleman, M. A., Maclure, M., Sherwood, J. B., Mulry, R. P., Tofler, G. H., Jacobs, S. C., Friedman, R., Benson, H., & Muller, J. E. (1995, October 1). Triggering of acute myocardial infarction onset by episodes of anger. *Circulation, 92,* 1720–1725.

Miyake, K., Chen, S., & Campos, J. J. (1985). Infant temperament, mother's mode of interaction, and attachment in Japan: An interim report. *Monographs of the Society for Research in Child Development, 50,* 276–297.

Miyashita, Y. (1995, June 23). How the brain creates imagery: Projection to primary visual cortex. *Science, 268,* 1719–1720.

Moghaddam, B., & Adams, B. W. (1998, August 28). Reversal of phencyclidine effects by a group II metabotropic glutamate receptor agonist in rats. *Science, 281,* 1349–1352.

Molfese, V. J. & Molfese, D. L. (2000). *Temperament and personality development across the life span.* Mahwah, NJ: Erlbaum.

Molitor, F., & Hirsch, K.W. (1994). Children's toleration of real-life aggression after exposure to media violence: A replication of the Drabman and Thomas studies. *Child Study Journal, 24,* 191–207.

Moody, H.R. (2000). *Aging.* Thousands Oaks, CA: Sage Publications.

Moore-Ede, M. (1993). *The twenty-four hour society.* Boston: Addison-Wesley.

Moretti, M. M., & Higgins, E. T. (1990). The development of self-system vulnerabilities: Social and cognitive factors in developmental psychopathology. In R. J. Sternberg & J. Kolligian, Jr. (Eds.), *Competence considered.* New Haven, CT: Yale University Press.

Morrow, J., & Wolff, R. (1991, May). Wired for a miracle. *Health,* pp. 64–84.

Moscovici, S. (1985). Social influence and conformity. In G. Lindzey & E. Aronson (Eds.), *Handbook of social psychology* (3rd ed.). New York: Random House.

Moscovitch, M. (1992). Memory and working with memory: A component process model based on modules and central systems. *Journal of Cognitive Neuroscience, 4,* 257–267.*

Moscovitch, M. (1994). Models of consciousness and memory. In M. Gazzaniga (Ed.), *The cognitive neurosciences* (pp. 1341–1356). Cambridge, MA: MIT Press.*

Motley, M. T. (1987, February). What I meant to say. *Psychology Today,* pp. 25–28.

Moutoussis, K., & Zeki, S. (1997). A direct demonstration of perceptual asynchrony in vision. *Proceedings of the Royal Society of London, B., Biological Sciences, 264,* 393–399.

Movshon, J. A., & Newsome, W. T. (1992). Neural foundations of visual motion perception. *Current Directions in Psychological Science, 1,* 35–39.

Mroczek, D. K., & Kolarz, C. M. (1998). The effect of age on positive and negative affect: A developmental perspective on happiness. *Journal of Personality and Social Psychology, 75,* 1333–1349.

Mrzljak, L., Bergson, C., Pappy, M., Huff, R., et al. (1996). Localization of dopamine D4 receptors in GABAergic neurons of the primate brain. *Nature, 381,* 245–248.

Mueser, K. T., Bellack, A. S., Wade, J. H., Sayers, S. L., Tierney, A., & Haag, G. (1993). Expressed emotion, social skill, and response to negative affect in schizophrenia. *Journal of Abnormal Psychology, 102,* 339–351.

Mufson, M. J. (1999, September). What is the role of psychiatry in the management of chronic pain? *Harvard Mental Health Letter,* pp. 8–10.

Muir, D. W., Humphrey, D. E., & Humphrey, G. K. (1994). Pattern and space perception in young infants. *Spatial Vision 8(1),* 141–165.*

Mukerjee, M. (1997, February). Trends in animal research. *Scientific American,* pp. 86–93.

Muller, R.T., & Diamond, T. (1999). Father and mother physical abuse and child aggressive behaviour in two generations. *Canadian Journal of Behavioural Science, 31(4),* 221–228.*

Mumme, D. L., Fernald, A., & Herrera, C. (1996). Infants' responses to facial and vocal emotional signals in a social referencing paradigm. *Child Development, 67,* 3219–3237.

Murdock, B. B. Jr. (1974). *Human memory: Theory and data.* Hillsdale, NJ: Erlbaum.*

Murdock, B. B. Jr. (1999). The buffer 30 years later: Working memory in a theory of distributed associative model (TODAM). In C. Izawa (Ed.), *On human memory.* Mahwah, NJ: Erlbaum.*

Murphy, S. T., & Zajonc, R. B. (1993). Affect, cognition, and awareness: Affective priming with optimal and suboptimal stimulus exposures. *Journal of Personality and Social Psychology, 64,* 723–739.

Murray, D. J., Kilgour, A. R., & Wasylkiw, L. (2000). Conflicts and missed signals in psychoananlysis, behaviourism, and Gestalt psychology. *American Psychologist, 55,* 422–426.*

Murray, J. B. (1990). Nicotine as a psychoactive drug. *Journal of Psychology, 125,* 5–25.

Murray, J. B. (1995). Evidence for acupuncture's analgesic effectiveness and proposals for the physiological mechanisms involved. *Journal of Psychology, 129,* 43–461.

Murray, S. L., & Holmes, J. G. (1997). A leap of faith? Positive illusions in romantic relationships. *Personality and Social Psychology Bulletin, 23,* 586–604.

Myerhoff, B. (1982). Rites of passage: Process and paradox. In V. Turner (Ed.), *Celebration: Studies in festivity and ritual.* Washington, DC: Smithsonian Institution Press.

Myers, D. G. (2000). The funds, friends, and faith of happy people. *American Psychologist, 55,* 56–67.

Myers, D. G., & Diener, E. (1996, May). The pursuit of happiness: New research uncovers some anti-intuitive insights into how many people are happy—And why. *Scientific American,* pp. 70–72.

Nahome, L., & Lawton, M. P. (1975). Similarity and propinquity in friendship formation. *Journal of Personality and Social Psychology, 32,* 205–213.

Nathan, P. E., & Gorman, J. M. (Eds.). (1997). *A guide to treatments that work.* New York: Oxford University Press.

Nathans, J., Davenport, C. M., Maumenee, I. H., Lewis, R. A., et al. (1989, August 25). Molecular genetics of human blue cone monochromacy. *Science, 245,* 831–838.

National Center for Health Statistics (1994). *Report on obesity in the United States.* Washington, DC: Author.

National Institute on Drug Abuse. (2000). *Principles of Drug Addiction Treatment: A research-based guide.* Washington, DC: National Institute on Drug Abuse.

National Institutes of Health. (1996). Integration of behavioral and relaxation approaches into the treatment of chronic pain and insomnia. NIH Technology Assessment Panel on Integration of Behavioral and Relaxation Approaches into the Treatment of Chronic Pain and Insomnia. *Journal of the American Medical Association, 276,* 313–318.

Navon, R., & Proia, R. L. (1989, March 17). The mutations in Ashkenazi Jews with adult G(M2) Gangliosidosis, the adult form of Tay-Sachs disease. *Science, 243,* 1471–1474.

Negrin, G., & Capute, A. J. (1996). Mental retardation. In R. H. A. Haslam & P. J. Valletutti (Eds.). *Medical problems in the classroom: The teacher's role in diagnosis and management* (3rd ed.). Austin, TX: PRO-ED.

Neher, A. (1991). Maslow's theory of motivation: A critique. *Journal of Humanistic Psychology, 31,* 89–112.

Neisser, U. (1982). *Memory observed.* San Francisco: Freeman.

Neisser, U. (1996, April). *Intelligence on the rise: Secular changes in IQ and related measures.* Paper presented at a conference at Emory University, Atlanta.

Neitz, J., Neitz, M., & Kainz, P. M. (1996, November 1). Visual pigment gene structure and the severity of color vision defects. *Science, 274,* 801–804.

Nelson, G., Prilleltensky, I., Laurendeau, M., & Powell, B. (1996). The prevention of mental health problems in Canada: A survey of provincial policies, structures and programs. *Canadian Psychology, 37,* 161–172.*

Nelson, M. (1992, February 3). Too tough to die. *People Weekly,* pp. 30–33.

Nelson, W. M., III, & Finch, A. J., Jr. (2000). Managing anger in youth: A cognitive-behavioral intervention approach. In P. C. Kendall (Ed.), *Child and adolescent therapy: Cognitive-behavioral procedures* (2nd ed.). New York: Guilford Press.

Ness, R. B., Grisso, J. A., Hirschinger, N., Markovic, N., Shaw, L. M., Day, N. L., & Kline, J. (1999). Cocaine and tobacco use and the risk of spontaneous abortion. *New England Journal of Medicine, 340,* 333–339.

Nesse, R. M. (2000). Is depression an adaptation? *Archives of General Psychiatry, 57,* 14–20.

A new approach to test-taking. (1994, November 15). *New York Times,* p. B9.

Newcombe, N. S., Drummey, A. B., Fox, N. A., Lie, E., & Ottinger-Alberts, W. (2000). Remembering early childhood: How much, how, and why (or why not). *Current Directions in Psychological Science, 9,* 55–58.

Newell, A., & Simon, H. (1972). *Human problem solving.* Englewood Cliffs, NJ: Prentice Hall.

NICHD Early Child Care Research Network. (1999). Child care and mother-child interaction in the first 3 years of life. *Developmental Psychology, 35,* 1399–1413.

Nickerson, R. S., & Adams, M. J. (1979). Long-term memory for a common object. *Cognitive Psychology, 11,* 287–307.

Nierenberg, A. (1998a, February 17). The physician's perspective. *HealthNews,* pp. 3–4.

Nierenberg, A. (1998b, April 20). Should you take St. John's Wort? *HealthNews,* p. 4.

Nigg, J. T., & Goldsmith, H. H. (1994). Genetics of personality disorders: Perspectives from personality and psychopathology research. *Psychological Bulletin, 115,* 346–380.

Nikles, C. D., II, Brecht, D. L., Klinger, E., & Bursell, A. L. (1998). The effects of current concern- and nonconcern-related waking suggestions on nocturnal dream content. *Journal of Personality and Social Psychology, 75,* 242–255.

Nisbett, R. E. (1968). Taste, deprivation, and weight determinants of eating behavior. *Journal of Personality and Social Psychology, 10,* 107–116.

Nisbett, R. E. (1972). Hunger, obesity and the ventromedial hypothalamus. *Psychological Review, 79,* 433–453.

Nisbett, R. E. (1994, October 31). Blue genes. *New Republic, 211,* 15.

Nisbett, R. E., Krantz, D. H., Jepson, D., & Kunda, Z. (1993). The use of statistical heuristics in everyday reasoning. In R. E. Nisbett (Ed.), *Rules for reasoning.* Hillsdale, NJ: Erlbaum.

Noble, H. B. (1999, March 12). New from the smoking wars: Success. *New York Times,* pp. D1–D2.

Noels, K.A., & Clément, R. (1998). Language in education: Bridging educational policy and social psychological research. In J. Edwards (Ed.), *Language in Canada.* Cambridge: Cambridge University Press.*

Nolen-Hoeksema, S., Larson, J., & Grayson, C. (1999). Explaining the gender differences in depressive symptoms. *Journal of Personality and Social Psychology, 77,* 1061–1072.

Novak, M. A., & Petto, A. J. (1991). *Through the looking glass: Issues of psychological well-being in captive nonhuman primates.* Washington, DC: American Psychological Association.

Noyes, R., Kathol, R. G., Fisher, M. M., Phillips, B. M., et al. (1993). The validity of *DSM-III-R* hypochondriasis. *Archives of General Psychiatry, 50,* 961–970.

Nunn, K. P. (1996). Personal hopefulness: A conceptual review of the relevance of the perceived future to psychiatry. *British Journal of Medical Psychology, 69,* 227–245.

Nyberg, L., & Tulving, E. (1996). Classifying human long-term memory: Evidence from converging dissociations. *European Journal of Cognitive Psychology, 8,* 163–183.

Oatley, K. (1992). *Best laid schemes: The psychology of emotions.* Cambridge, MA: Cambridge University Press.

Oatley, K., & Duncan, E. (1994). The experience of emotions in everyday life. *Cognition and Emotion, 8,* 369–381.*

Oatley, K., & Jenkins, J. M. (1996). *Understanding emotions.* Oxford, England: Blackwell.

Oatley, K., & Johnson-Laird, P. N. (1987). Toward a cognitive theory of emotions, *Cognition and Emotion, 1,* 29–50.*

O'Brien, C. P., Childress, A. R., McLellan, A. T., & Ehrman, R. (1992). Classical conditioning in drug-dependent humans. In P. W. Kalivas & H. H. Samson (Eds.). *The neurobiology of drug and alcohol addiction. Annals of the New York Academy of Sciences, Vol. 654.* New York: New York Academy of Sciences.

O'Connor, S. C., & Rosenblood, L. K. (1996). Affiliation motivation in everyday experience: A theoretical comparison. *Journal of Personality and Social Psychology, 70,* 513–522.

Ogilvie, R., & Harsh, J. (Eds.). (1994). *Sleep onset: Normal and abnormal processes.* Washington, DC: American Psychological Association.

Ogilvie, R. D. (1995). Sleep onset. In Carskadon, M. A. (Ed.), *Encyclopedia of sleep and dreaming* (pp. 566–569). New York: Macmillan.*

O'Grady, W. D., & Dobrovolsky, M. (Eds.). (1996). *Contemporary linguistic analysis: An introduction* (3rd ed.). Toronto: Copp Clark Pitman.

O'Hara, J. (2000, December 25/2001, January 1). Public pillow talk. *Maclean's, 113,* 38–40.*

O'Hare, D., & Roscoe, S. (1990). *Flightdeck performance: The human factor.* Ames: Iowa State University Press.

Okun, B. F. (1996). *Understanding diverse families: What practitioners need to know.* New York: Guilford Press.

Olds, J., & Milner, P. (1954). Positive reinforcement produced by electrical stimulation of septal area and other regions of rat brain. *Journal of Comparative and Physiological Psychology, 47,* 411–427.

Oliver, M. B., & Hyde, J. S. (1993). Gender differences in sexuality: A meta-analysis. *Psychological Bulletin, 114,* 29–51.

Olshansky, S. J., Carnes, B. A., & Cassel, C. (1990, November 2). In search of Methuselah: Estimating the upper limits to human longevity. *Science, 250,* 634–639.

Ontario Ministry of Health. (1994). Ontario Health Survey: Mental health supplement. Catalogue No. 2224153. Toronto, ON: Queen's Printer for Ontario.*

Oren, D. A., & Terman, M. (1998, January 16). Tweaking the human circadian clock with light. *Science, 279,* 333–334.

Ornstein, R. (1998). *The right mind: Making sense of the hemispheres.* New York: Harcourt Brace.

Orth-Gomer, K., Chesney, M. A., & Wenger, N. K. (Eds.). (1996). *Women, stress and heart disease.* Mahwah, NJ: Erlbaum.

Orth-Gomer, K., & Schneiderman, N. (Eds.). (1995). *Behavioral medicine approaches to cardiovascular disease prevention.* Mahwah, NJ: Erlbaum.

Ortony, A., & Turner, T. J. (1990). What's basic about basic emotions? *Psychological Review, 97,* 315–331.

Orwin, R. G., & Condray, D. S. (1984). Smith and Glass' psychotherapy conclusions need further probing: On Landman and Dawes' re-analysis. *American Psychologist, 39,* 71–72.

Orzack, M. S. (1999). Computer addiction: Is it real or virtual? *Harvard Mental Health Letter,* p. 8.

Oskamp, S. (Ed.) (2000). *Reducing prejudice and discrimination.* Mahwah, NJ: Erlbaum.

Oster, M. I. (1994). Psychological preparation for labor and delivery using hypnosis. *American Journal of Clinical Hypnosis, 37,* 12–21.

Owens, R. E., Jr. (2001). *Language development: An introduction* (5th ed.). Boston: Allyn & Bacon.

Paivio, A. (1971). *Imagery and verbal processes.* New York: Holt, Rinehart & Winston.

Paivio, A. (1975). Perceptual comparison through the mind's eye. *Memory and Cognition, 3,* 635–647.

Palermo, G. B. (1995). Adolescent criminal behavior: Is TV violence one of the culprits? *International Journal of Offender Therapy and Comparative Criminology, 39,* 11–22.

Paniagua, F. A. (2000). *Diagnosis in a multicultural context: A casebook for mental health professionals.* Thousand Oaks, CA: Sage.

Parke, R. D. (1996). *Fatherhood.* Cambridge, MA: Harvard University Press.

Parlee, M. B. (1979, October). The friendship bond. *Psychology Today,* pp. 43–45.

Parrott, R., Duncan, V., & Duggan, A. (2000). Promoting patients' full and honest disclosure during conversations with health caregivers. In S. Petronio (Ed.), *Balancing the secrets of private disclosures.* Mahwah, NJ: Erlbaum.

Patton, D., Brown, D., Broszeit, B., & Dhaliwal, J. (2001). *Substance use among Manitoba high school students.* Winnipeg: Addictions Foundation of Manitoba.*

Patzwahl, D. R., Zanker, J. M., & Altenmuller, E. O. (1994). Cortical potentials reflecting motion processing in humans. *Visual Neuroscience, 11,* 1135–1147.

Paulhus, D. L., & Bruce, M. N. (1992). The effects of acquaintanceship on the validity of personality impressions: A longitudinal study. *Journal of Personality and Social Psychology, 63,* 816–824.*

Paunonen, S. V., & Ashton, M. C. (2001a). Big Five Factors and facets and the prediction of behaviour. *Journal of Personality and Social Psychology, 81,* 524–539.*

Paunonen, S. V., & Ashton, M. C. (2001b). Big Five predictors of academic achievement. *Journal of Research in Personality, 35,* 78–90.*

Paunonen, S. V., Ashton, M.C., & Jackson, D. N. (2001). Nonverbal assessment of the Big Five personality factors. *European Journal of Personality,* 15, 3–18.*

Paunonen, S. V., Jackson, D. N., & Keinonen, M. (1990). The structured nonverbal assessment of personality. *Journal of Personality, 58,* 481–502.*

Paunonen, S. V., Jackson, D. N., Trzebinski, J., & Forsterling, F. (1992). Personality structure across cultures: A multimethod evalution. *Journal of Personality and Social Psychology, 62,* 447–456.*

Paunonen, S. V., Keinonen, M., Trzebinski, J., Forsterling, F., et al. [7 authors] (1996). The structure of personality in six cultures. *Journal of Cross-Cultural Psychology, 27,* 339–353.*

Pavlides, C., & Winson, J. (1989). Influences of hippocampal place cell firing in the awake state on the activity of these cells during subsequent sleep episodes. *Journal of Neuroscience, 9,* 2907–2918.

Pavlov, I. P. (1927). *Conditioned reflexes.* London: Oxford University Press.

Payne, D. G. (1986). Hyperamnesia for pictures and words: Testing the recall level hypothesis. *Journal of Experimental Psychology: Learning, Memory, and Cognition, 12,* 16–29.

Peirce, R. S., Frone, M. R., Russell, M., & Cooper, M. L. (1996). Financial stress, social support, and alcohol involvement: A longitudinal test of the buffering hypothesis in a general population survey. *Health Psychology, 15,* 38–47.

Peled, E., Jaffe, P. G., Edleson, J. L. (Eds.). (1995). *Ending the cycle of violence: Community responses to children of battered women.* Thousand Oaks, CA: Sage Publications.

Pelletier, M. H., Gauthier, J., Bouchard, S., & Côté, G. (1995). Cognitive-behavioural treatment of panic disorder with agoraphobia: One-year and five-year follow-ups. *Canadian Psychology, 36,* 80.*

Penfield, W., & Rasmussen, T. (1950). *The cerebral cortex of man.* New York: Macmillan.

Peng, K., & Nisbett, R. E. (1997). Cultural differences in preferences for linear vs. non-linear proverbs. Unpublished manuscript, University of Michigan.

Penn, D. L., Corrigan, P. W., Bentall, R. P., Racenstein, J. M., & Newman, L. (1997). Social cognition in schizophrenia. *Psychological Bulletin, 121,* 114–132.

Penney, J. B., Jr. (2000). Synopsis of neuropsychiatry. In B. S. Fogel, R. B. Schiffer, et al. (Eds.). *Neurochemistry.* Philadelphia: Lippincott-Raven.

Pennisi, E. (1997a, October 24). Enzyme linked to alcohol sensitivity in mice. *Science, 278,* 573.

Pennisi, E. (1997b, August 15). Schizophrenia clues from monkeys. *Science, 277,* 900.

Pennisi, E. (1997c, August 1). Transgenic lambs from cloning lab. *Science, 277,* 631.

Pennisi, E. (2000, May 19). And the gene number is . . . ? *Science, 288,* 1146–1147.

Perez, R. M., DeBord, K. A., & Bieschke, K. J. (Eds.). (2000). *Handbook of counseling and psychotherapy with lesbian, gay, and bisexual clients.* Washington, DC: American Psychological Association.

Perloff, R. M. (1993). *The dynamics of persuasion.* Hillsdale, NJ: Erlbaum.

Perls, F. S. (1970). *Gestalt therapy now: Therapy, techniques, applications.* Palo Alto, CA: Science & Behavior Books.

Perls, F. S., Hefferline, R., & Goodman, P. (1994). *Gestalt therapy: Excitement and growth in the human personality* (2nd ed.). New York: New York Journal Press.

Perry-Jenkins, M. (1993). Family roles and responsibilities: What has changed and what has remained the same? In J. Frankel (Ed.), *The employed mother and the family context.* New York: Springer.

Pervin, L. A. & John, O. P. (Eds.) (1999). *Handbook of personality: Theory and research* (2nd ed.). New York: Guilford Press.

Petersen, S. E., & Fiez, J. A. (1993). The processing of single words studied with positron emission tomography. *Annual Review of Neuroscience, 16,* 509–530.

Peterson, A. (1985). Pubertal development as a cause of disturbance: Myths, realities, and unanswered questions. *Genetic, Social and General Psychology Monographs, 111,* 205–232.

Peterson, C. (1999). Children's memory for medical emergencies: 2 years later. *Developmental Psychology, 35,* 1493–1506.*

Peterson, C. (2000). The future of optimism. *American Psychologist, 55,* 44–55.

Peterson, C. (2001). Children's long-tem memory for autobiographical events. *Developmental Review.* In press.*

Peterson, C., Maier, S. F., & Seligman, M. E. P. (1993). *Learned helplessness: A theory for the age of personal control.* New York: Oxford University Press.

Peterson, C., & Whalen, N. (2001). Five years later: Children's memory for medical emergencies. *Applied Cognitive Psychology, 15,* 7–24.*

Peterson, L. R., & Peterson, M. J. (1959). Short-term retention of individual items. *Journal of Experimental Psychology, 58,* 193–198.

Peterzell, D. H. (1993). Individual differences in the visual attention of human infants: Further evidence for separate sensitization and habituation processes. *Developmental Psychobiology, 26,* 207–218.

Petitto, L. A. (1993). On the ontogenetic requirements for early language acquisition. In B. de Boysson-Bardies, S. de Schonen, P. W. Jusczyk, P. McNeilage, & J. Morton (Eds.), *Developmental neurocognition: Speech and face processing in the first year of life.* Dordrecht, Netherlands: Kluwer Academic.

Petitto, L. A. (2000). The acquisition of natural signed languages: Lessons in the nature of human language and its biological foundations. In J. P. Chamberlain , J. Morford, & R. I. Mayberry (Eds.), *Language acquisition by eye,* New Jersey: Lawrence Erlbaum Associates.*

Petitto, L. A., & Marentette, P. F. (1991, March 22). Babbling in the manual mode: Evidence for the ontogeny of language. *Science, 251,* 1493–1496.

Petri, H. L. (1996). *Motivation: Theory, research, and applications* (4th ed.). Pacific Grove, CA: Brooks/Cole.

Petronis, A., & Kenedy, J. L. (1995). Unstable genes—unstable mind? *American Journal of Psychiatry, 152,* 164–172.

Pettigrew, T. F. (1997, February). Generalized intergroup contact effects on prejudice. *Personality and Social Psychology Bulletin, 23,* 173–185.

Pettingale, K. W., Morris, T., Greer, S., & Haybittle, J. L. (1985). Mental attitudes to cancer: An additional prognostic factor. *Lancet,* p. 750.

Petty, R. E., & Cacioppo, J. T. (1986). The elaboration likelihood model of persuasion. In L. Berkowitz (Ed.), *Advances in experimental social psychology* (Vol. 10). New York: Academic Press.

Petty, R. E., Cacioppo, J. T., Strathman, A. J., & Priester, J. R. (1994). To think or not to think: Exploring two routes to persuasion. In S. Savitt & T. C. Brock (Eds.), *Persuasion: Psychological insights and perspectives.* Boston: Allyn & Bacon.

Petty, R. E., Wegener, D. T., & Fabrigar, L. R. (1997). Attitudes and attitude change. *Annual Review of Psychology, 48,* 609–647.*

Petzold, P. (1992). Context effects in judgments of attributes: An information-integration approach. In H. G. Geissler, S. W. Link, & J. T. Townsend (Eds.), *Cognition, information processing, and psychophysics: Basic issues.* Scientific psychology series. Hillsdale, NJ: Erlbaum.

Pezdek, K., & Banks, W. P. (Eds.). (1996). *The recovered memory/false memory debate.* New York: Academic Press.

Piaget, J. (1970). Piaget's theory. In P. H. Mussen (Ed.), *Carmichael's manual of child psychology* (3rd ed., Vol. 1). New York: Wiley.

Piaget, J., & Inhelder, B. (1958). *The growth of logical thinking from childhood to adolescence* (A. Parsons & S. Seagrin, Trans.). New York: Basic Books.

Piasecki, T. M., Kenford, S. L., Smith, S. S., Fiore, M. C., & Baker, T. B. (1997). Listening to nicotine: Negative affect and the smoking withdrawal conundrum. *Psychological Science, 8,* 184–189.

Picard, A. (2001, June 11). Five Quebec teens dead after car crash in quarry. *The Globe and Mail,* p. A8.*

Picard, A. (2002, August 19). Antismoking campaign 'ineffective'. *The Globe and Mail,* p. A6.*

Pich, E. M., Pagliusi, S. R., Tessari, M., Talabot-Ayer, D., Hooft van Huijsduijnen, R., & Chiamulera, C. (1997, January 3). Common neural substrates for the addictive properties of nicotine and cocaine. *Science, 275,* 83–86.

Pihlgren, E. M., Gidycz, C. A., & Lynn, S. J. (1993). Impact of adulthood and adolescent rape experiences on subsequent sexual fantasies. *Imagination, Cognition and Personality, 12,* 321–339.

Piliavin, J. A., & Piliavin, I. M. (1972). Effect of blood on reactions to a victim. *Journal of Personality and Social Psychology, 23,* 353–362.

Pillard, R. C. (1996). Homosexuality from a familial and genetic perspective. In R. P. Cabaj & T. S. Stein (Eds.), *Textbook of homosexuality and mental health.* Washington, DC: American Psychiatric Press.

Pillitteri, G. (2002). Protecting Canadians and their families: Measures to deal with high risk offenders. Available: <http://www.garypillitterimp.on.ca/protectingdoc.htm>. Accessed November 1, 2002.*

Pinel, J. P. J., Assanand, S., & Lehman, D. R. (2000). Hunger, eating, and ill health. *American Psychologist, 55,* 1105–1116.*

Pinker, S. (1990). Language acquisition. In D. N. Osherson & H. Lasnik (Eds.), *Language.* Cambridge, MA: MIT Press.

Pledge, D. S. (1992). Marital separation/divorce: A review of individual responses to a major life stressor. *Journal of Divorce and Remarriage, 17,* 151–181.

Plomin, R. (1990, April 13). The role of inheritance in behavior. *Science, 248,* 183–188.

Plomin, R., & Caspi, R. (1999). Behavioral genetics and personality. In L. A. Pervin & O. P. John (Eds.), *Handbook of personality: Theory and research* (2nd ed.). New York: Guilford Press.

Plomin, R., & McClearn, G. E. (Eds.) (1993). *Nature, nurture and psychology.* Washington, DC: American Psychological Association.

Plomin, R., & Neiderhiser, J. M. (1992). Genetics and experience. *Current Directions in Psychological Science, 1,* 160–163.

Plomin, R., & Petrill, S. A. (1997). Genetics and intelligence: What's new? *Intelligence, 24,* 53–77.

Plous, S. (1996a). Attitudes toward the use of animals in psychological research and education: Results from a national survey of psychologists. *American Psychologist, 51,* 1167–1180.

Plous, S. (1996b). Attitudes toward the use of animals in psychological research and education: Results from a national survey of psychology majors. *Psychological Science, 7,* 352–358.

Plumert, J. M., Carswell, C., De Vet, K., & Ihrig, D. (1995). The content and organization of communication about object locations. *Journal of Memory and Language, 34,* 477–498.

Plummer, W., & Pick, G. (1996, October 10). Beating the blitz. *People Weekly,* pp. 129–132.

Plutchik, R. (1980). *Emotion: A psychorevolutionary synthesis.* New York: Harper & Row.

Polivy, J., & Herman, C. P. (1985). Dieting and bingeing: A causal analysis. *American Psychologist, 40,* 193–201.*

Polivy, J., & Herman, C. P. (1991). Good and bad dieters: Self-perception and reaction to a dietary challenge. *International Journal of Eating Disorders, 10,* 91–99.

Polivy, J. & Herman, C. P. (2002). Causes of eating disorders. *Annual Review of Psychology, 53,* 187–213.*

Polk, N. (1997, March 30). The trouble with school testing systems. *New York Times,* p. CN3.

Pollack, A. (2000, May 30). Neural cells, grown in labs, raise hopes on brain disease. *New York Times,* pp. D1, D6.

Pollack, M. H., & Marzol, P. C. (2000). Panic: Course, complications and treatment of panic disorder. *Journal of Psychopharmacology, 14,* S25–S30.

Pomerlau, O. F. (1995). Individual differences in sensitivity to nicotine: Implications of genetic research on nicotine dependence [Special Issue: Genetic, environmental, and situational factors mediating the effects of nicotine]. *Behavior Genetics, 25,* 161–177.

Pomeroy, E., Trainor, J., & Pape, B. (2002). Citizens shaping policy: The Canadian Mental Health Association's Framework for Support Project. *Canadian Psychology, 43,* 11–20.*

Ponterotto, J. G., Casas, J. M., Suzuki, L. A., & Alexander, C. M. (Eds.). (2001). *Handbook of multicultural counseling.* Thousand Oaks, CA: Sage.

Porkka-Heiskanen, T., Strecker, R. E., Thakkar, M., Bjorkum, A. A., Greene, R. W., & McCarley, R. W. (1997, May 23). Adenosine: A mediator of the sleep-inducing effects of prolonged wakefulness. *Science, 276,* 1265–1268.

Porte, H. S., & Hobson, J. A. (1996). Physical motion in dreams: One measure of three theories. *Journal of Abnormal Psychology, 105,* 329–335.

Porter, R. H., Cernich, J. M., & McLaughlin, F. J. (1983). Maternal recognition of neonates through olfactory cues. *Physiology and Behavior, 30,* 151–154.

Potheraju, A., & Soper, B. (1995). A comparison of self-reported dream themes for high school and college students. *College Student Journal, 29,* 417–420.

Pottieger, A. E., Tressell, P. A., Inciardi, J. A., & Rosales, T. A. (1992). Cocaine use patterns and overdose. *Journal of Psychoactive Drugs, 24,* 399–410.

Powell, D. H., & Whitla, D. K. (1994, February). Normal cognitive aging: Toward empirical perspectives. *Current Directions in Psychological Science, 3,* 27–31.

Powell, L. H., Shaker, L. A., & Jones, B. A. (1993). Psychosocial predictors of mortality in 83 women with premature acute myocardial infarction. *Psychosomatic Medicine, 55,* 426–433.

Pratt, S. I., & Moreland, K. L. (1996). Introduction to treatment outcome: Historical perspectives and current issues. In S. I. Pfeiffer (Ed.), *Outcome assessment in residential treatment.* New York: Haworth Press.

Pressley, M. (1987). Are keyword method effects limited to slow presentation rates? An empirically based reply to Hall and Fuson (1986). *Journal of Educational Psychology, 79,* 333–335.

Pressman, M. R., & Orr, W. C. (1997). *Understanding sleep: The evaluation and treatment of sleep disorders.* Washington, DC: American Psychological Association.

Preston, J. M. (1998). From mediated environments to the development of consciousness. In J. Gackenbach (Ed.), *Psychology and the Internet: Intrapersonal, interpersonal, and transpersonal implications.* San Diego: Academic Press.*

Pribram, K. H. (1984). Emotion: A neurobehavioral analysis. In K. R. Scherer & P. Ekman (Eds.), *Approaches to emotion.* Hillsdale, NJ: Erlbaum.

Priester, J. R. & Petty, R. E. (1995). Source attributions and persuasion: Perceived honesty as a determinant of message scrutiny. *Personality and Social Psychology Bulletin, 21,* 637–654.

Prince, R. J., & Guastello, S. J. (1990). The Barnum effect in a computerized Rorschach interpretation system. *Journal of Personality, 124,* 217–222.

Pulvirenti, L., & Koob, G. F. (1994). Lisuride reduces intravenous cocaine self-administration in rats. *Pharmacology, Biochemistry and Behavior, 47,* 819–822.

Purves, D., Augustine, G. J., Fitzpatrick, D., Katz, L. C., LaMantia, A., & McNamara, J. O. (Eds.). (1997). *Neuroscience.* Sunderland, MA: Sinauer.

Putnam, F. W. (1995a). Development of dissociative disorders. In D. Cicchetti & D. J. Cohen (Eds.), *Developmental psychopathology: Vol. 2. Risk, disorder, and adaptation.* New York: Wiley.

Putnam, F. W. (1995b). Traumatic stress and pathological dissociation. In G. P. Chrousos, R. McCarty, et al. (Eds.), *Stress: Basic mechanisms and clinical implications.* New York: New York Academy of Sciences.

Rachman, S., & deSilva, P. (1996). *Panic disorder.* Oxford, England: Oxford University Press.

Rachman, S., & Hodgson, R. (1980). *Obsessions and compulsions.* Englewood Cliffs, NJ: Prentice Hall.

Rachman, S. J. (1990). The determinants of treatment of simple phobias. *Advances in Behaviour Research and Therapy, 12,* 1–30.*

Rachman, S. J. (1991). Neo-conditioning and the classical theory of fear acquisition. *Clinical Psychological Review, 11,* 155–173.*

Rachman, S. J. (1994). Psychological treatment of panic: Mechanisms. In B. E. Wolfe & J. D. Maser (Eds.), *Treatment of panic disorder: A consensus development conference.* (pp. 133–148). Washington, DC: American Psychiatric Press.*

Rachman, S. J. (1997). A cognitive theory of obsessions. *Behaviour Research and Therapy, 35,* 793–802.*

Rakoff, V. M. (1995). Trauma and adolescent rites of initiation. In R. C. Marohn & S. C. Feinstein (Eds.), *Adolescent psychiatry: Developmental and clinical studies.* Hillsdale, NJ: Analytic Press.

Ralph, M. R., & Lehman, M. N. (1991). Transplantation: A new tool in the analysis of the mammalian hypothalamic circadian pacemaker. *Trends in Neuroscience, 14,* 362–366.*

Ramachandran, V. S. (1995). Filling in gaps in logic: Reply to Durgin et al. *Perception, 24,* 841–845.

Raskin, N. J., & Rogers, C. R. (1989). Person-centered therapy. In R. J. Corsini & D. Wedding (Eds.), *Current psychotherapies* (4th ed.). Itasca, IL: F. E. Peacock.

Ratcliff, R., & McKoon, G. (1989). Memory models, text processing, and cue-dependent retrieval. In H. L. Roediger III & F. I. M. Craik (Eds.), *Varieties of memory and consciousness: Essays in honour of Endel Tulving.* Hillsdale, NJ: Erlbaum.

Rau, H., Weitkunat, R., Brody, S., Buhrer, M., et al. (1996). Biofeedback of R-wave to pulse interval produces differential learning of blood pressure control. *Scandinavian Journal of Behaviour Therapy, 25,* 17–25.

Rawsthorne, L. J., & Elliot, A. J. (1999). Achievement goals and intrinsic motivation: A meta-analytic review. *Personality and Social Psychology Review, 3,* 326–344.

Ray, W. J. (2000). *Methods: Toward a science of behavior and experience* (6th ed.). Belmont, CA: Wadsworth.

Rector, N. A., Segal, Z. V., Gemar, M. (1998). Schema research in depression: A Canadian perspective. *Canadian Journal of Behavioural Science, 30,* 213–224.*

Redding, G. M., & Hawley, E. (1993). Length illusion in fractional Müller-Lyer stimuli: An object-perception approach. *Perception, 22,* 819–828.

Reeves, R. A., Baker, G. A., Boyd, J. G., & Cialdini, R. B. (1991). The door-in-the-face technique: Reciprocal concessions vs. self-presentational explanations. *Journal of Social Behavior and Personality, 6,* 545–558.

Regan, D. (Ed.). (1991). *Binocular vision.* New York: Macmillan.*

Regan, P. C. (2000). Love relationships. In L. T. Szuchman & F. Muscarella (Eds.), *Psychological perspectives on human sexuality.* New York: Wiley.

Reich, C., & Purbhoo, M. (1975). The effect of cross-cultural contact. *Canadian Journal of Behavioural Science, 7,* 313–327.*

Reichman, W. E., & Rabins, P. V. (1996). Schizophrenia and other psychotic disorders. In W. E. Reichman & P. R. Katz (Eds.),

Psychiatric care in the nursing home. New York: Oxford University Press.

Reisberg, D. (1997). *Cognition: Exploring the science of the mind.* New York: W. W. Norton.

Reisenzein, R. (1983). The Schachter theory of emotion: Two decades later. *Psychological Bulletin, 94,* 239–264.

Report of the Commission on Systemic Racism in the Ontario Criminal Justice System. (1995). Toronto: Queen's Printer for Ontario.*

Rescorla, R. A. (1988). Pavlovian conditioning: It's not what you think it is. *American Psychologist, 43,* 151–160.

Resnick, S. M. (1992). Positron emission tomography in psychiatric illness. *Current Directions in Psychological Science, 1,* 92–98.

Reyna, V. F. (1997). Conceptions of memory development with implications for reasoning and decision making. In R. Vasta (Ed.), *Annals of child development: A research annual* (Vol. 12, pp. 87–118). London: Kingsley.

Reynolds, R. I., & Takooshian, H. (1988, January). Where were you August 8, 1985? *Bulletin of the Psychonomic Society, 26,* 23–25.

Rhodes, N., & Wood, W. (1992). Self-esteem and intelligence affect influenceability: The mediating role of message reception. *Psychological Bulletin, 111,* 156–171.

Rhodewalt, F., & Fairfield, M. (1991). An alternative approach to Type A behavior and health: Psychological reactance and medical noncompliance. In M. J. Strube (Ed.), *Type A behavior.* Newbury Park, CA: Sage.

Rhue, J. W., Lynn, S. J., & Kirsch, I (Eds.). (1993). *Handbook of clinical hypnosis.* Washington, DC: American Psychological Association.

Ricciuti, H. N. (1993). Nutrition and mental development. *Current Directions in Psychological Science, 2,* 43–46.

Rice, G., Anderson, C., Risch, N., & Ebers, G. (1999, April 23). Male homosexuality: Absence of linkage to microsatellite markers at Xq28. *Science, 284,* 665–667.

Rice, V. H. (Ed.). (2000). *Handbook of stress, coping and health.* Thousand Oaks, CA: Sage.

Richie, J. (1994, April). Paper presented at the annual meeting of the American Association for Cancer Research, San Francisco.

Rieder, R. O., Kaufmann, C. A., & Knowles, J. A. (1996). Genetics. In R. E. Hales & S. C. Yudofsky (Eds.), *The American Psychiatric Press synopsis of psychiatry.* Washington, DC: American Psychiatric Press, Inc.

Riefer, D. M., Keveri, M. K., & Kramer, D. L. F. (1995). Name that tune: Eliciting the tip-of-the-tongue experience using auditory stimuli. *Psychological Reports, 77,* 1379–1390.

Risch, N., & Merikangas, K. (1996, September 13). The future of genetic studies of complex human diseases. *Science, 273,* 1516–1517.

Risley, R. C., & Rescorla, R. A. (1972). Associations in higher order conditioning and sensory pre-conditioning. *Journal of Comparative and Physiological Psychology, 81,* 1–11.

Ritzler, B., & Rosenbaum, G. (1974). Proprioception in schizophrenics and normals: Effects of stimulus intensity and interstimulus interval. *Journal of Abnormal Psychology, 83,* 106–111.

Robbins, T. W. (1988). Arresting memory decline. *Nature, 336,* 207–208.

Roberts, G., McCall, D., Stevens-Lavigne, A., et al., [8 authors]. (2001). *Preventing substance use problems among young people: A compendium of best practices.* Ottawa: Minister of Public Works and Government Services Canada.*

Roberts, S. M. (1995). Applicability of the goodness-of-fit hypothesis to coping with daily hassles. *Psychological Reports, 77,* 943–954.

Robertson, L. C., & Ivry, R. (2000). Hemispheric asymmetries: Attention to visual and auditory primitives. *Current Directions in Psychological Science, 9,* 59–63.

Robins, R. W., Gosling, S. D., & Craik, K. H. (1999). An empirical analysis of trends in psychology. *American Psychologist, 54,* 117–128.

Robins, R. W., & Paulhus, D. L. (2001). The character of self-enhancers: Implications for organizations. In B. W. Roberts & R. Hogan (Eds.), *Personality psychology in the workplace* (pp. 193–222). Washington, DC: American Psychological Association.*

Robinson, B. A. (1998). Female and intersexual genital mutilation in North America and Europe. Available: <http://www.religioustolerance.org/fem_cira.htm>. Accessed December 12, 2002.

Rock, A. (1999, January). Quitting time for smokers. *Money,* pp. 139–141.

Rodin, J. (1985). Insulin levels, hunger, and food intake: An example of feedback loops in body-weight regulation. *Health Psychology, 4,* 1–18.

Rodin, J. (1986, September 19). Aging and health: Effects of the sense of control. *Science, 233,* 1271–1276.

Roffwarg, H. P., Muzio, J. N., & Dement, W. C. (1996). Ontogenic development of the human sleep-dream cycle. *Science, 152,* 604–619.

Rogers, C. R. (1951). *Client-centered therapy,* Boston: Houghton-Mifflin.

Rogers, C. R. (1971). A theory of personality. In S. Maddi (Ed.), *Perspectives on personality.* Boston: Little, Brown.

Rogers, C. R. (1980). *A way of being.* Boston: Houghton Mifflin.

Rogers, P., & Eftimiades, M. (1995, July 24). Abner Louima. *People Weekly,* pp. 42–43.

Rogler, L. H. (1999). Methodological sources of cultural insensitivity in mental health research. *American Psychologist, 54,* 424–433.

Rokeach, M. (1971). Long-range experimental modification of values, attitudes, and behavior. *American Psychologist, 26,* 453–459.

Rolland, J. S., & Walsh, F. (1994). Family therapy: Systems approaches to assessment and treatment. In R. E. Hales & S. C. Yudofsky (Eds.), *The American Psychiatric Press synopsis of psychiatry.* Washington, DC: American Psychiatric Press.

Rolls, E. T. (1994). Neural processing related to feeding in primates. In C. R. Legg & D. A. Booth (Eds.). *Appetite: Neural and behavioural bases.* Oxford, England: Oxford University Press.

Root-Bernstein, R., & Root-Bernstein, M. (1999). *Sparks of genius: The thirteen thinking tools of the world's most creative people.* New York: Houghton Mifflin.

Rorschach, H. (1924). *Psychodiagnosis: A diagnostic test based on perception.* New York: Grune & Stratton.

Roseman, I. J., Wiest, C., & Swartz, T. S. (1994). Phenomenology, behaviors, and goals differentiate discrete emotions. *Journal of Personality and Social Psychology, 67,* 206–221.

Rosen, D. (1999, May 10). Dieting disorder: A physician's perspective. *Harvard Mental Health Newsletter,* p. 4.

Rosen, H. (2000). The creative evolution of the theoretical foundations for cognitive therapy. *Journal of Cognitive Psychotherapy, 14,* 123–134.

Rosenhan, D. L. (1973). On being sane in insane places. *Science, 179,* 250–258.

Rosenheck, R., Cramer, J., Xu, W., Thomas, J., Henderson, W., Frisman, L., Fye, C., & Charney, D. (1997). A comparison of clozapine and haloperidol in hospitalized patients with refractory schizophrenia. *New England Journal of Medicine, 337,* 809–815.

Rosenman, R. H. (1990). Type A behavior pattern: A personal overview. *Journal of Social Behavior and Personality, 5,* 1–24.

Rosenman, R. H., Brand, R. J., Sholtz, R. I., & Friedman, M. (1976). Multivariate prediction of coronary heart disease during 8.5 year follow-up in the Western collaborative group study. *American Journal of Cardiology, 37,* 903–910.

Rosenstein, D. S., & Horowitz, H. A. (1996). Adolescent attachment and psychopathology. *Journal of Consulting and Clinical Psychology, 64,* 244–253.

Rosenthal, A. M. (1993, July 27). The torture continues. *New York Times,* p. A13.

Rosenthal, E. (1996, January 10). From Lives Begun in a Lab, Brave New Joy. *The New York Times,* A2, B8.

Rosenthal, E. (1999, December 9). China's chic wasitline: Convex to concave. *New York Times,* pp. A1, A4.

Rosenthal, L. H. (1997). *A new perspective on the relation between fear and persuasion: The application of dual-process models.* Unpublished doctoral dissertation, Dept. of Psychology. University of Massachusetts, Amherst.

Rosenthal, R. (1994). Science and ethics in conducting, analyzing, and reporting psychological research. *Psychological Science, 5,* 127–134.

Rosenzweig, M. R. (1999). Continuity and change in the development of psychology around the world. *American Psychologist, 54,* 252–259.

Rosnow, R. L., & Rosenthal, R. (1997). *Turn away influences that undermine scientific experiments.* New York: Freeman.

Rosnow, R. L., Rotheram-Borus, M. J., Ceci, S. J., Blanck, P. D., & Koocher, G. P. (1993). The institutional review board as a mirror of scientific and ethical standards. *American Psychologist, 48,* 821–826.

Ross, C.A. (1994). *The Osiris complex: Case-studies in multiple personality disorder.* Toronto: University of Toronto Press.*

Ross, C. A. (1996). *Dissociative identity disorder: Diagnosis, clinical features, and treatment of multiple personality.* Somerset, NJ: Wiley.

Ross, C. A., Miller, S. D., Reagor, P., Bjornson, L., Fraser, G. A., & Anderson, G. (1990). Structured interview data on 102 cases of multiple personality disorder from four centers. *American Journal of Psychiatry, 147,* 596–601.

Ross, L. (1977). The intuitive psychologist and his shortcomings: Distortions in the attribution process. In L. Berkowitz (Ed.), *Advances in experimental social psychology* (Vol. 10, pp. 174–221). New York: Academic Press.

Ross, L., Greene, D., & House, P. (1977). The false consensus effect: An egocentric bias in social perception and attribution processes. *Journal of Experimental Social Psychology, 13,* 279–301.

Ross, L., & Nisbett, R. E. (1991). *The person and the situation.* New York: McGraw-Hill.

Ross, M., & Newby, I. R. (1996). Distinguishing memory from fantasy. *Psychological Inquiry, 7,* 173–177.

Roth, A., & Fonagy, P. (1996). *What works for whom? A critical review of psychotherapy research.* New York: Guilford Press.

Rothblum, E. D. (1990). Women and weight: Fad and fiction. *Journal of Psychology, 124,* 5–24.

Roush, W. (1995, September 1). Can "resetting" hormonal rhythms treat illness? *Science, 269,* 1220–1221.

Routtenberg, A., & Lindy, J. (1965). Effects of the availability of rewarding septal and hypothalamic stimulation on bar pressing for food under conditions of deprivation. *Journal of Comparative and Physiological Psychology, 60,* 158–161.

Rovee-Collier, C. (1993). The capacity for long-term memory in infancy. *Current Directions in Psychological Science, 2,* 130–135.

Rowe, J. B., Toni, I., Josephs, O., Frackowiak, R. S. J., & Passingham, R. E. (2000, June 2). The prefrontal cortex: Response selection or maintenance within working memory? *Science, 288,* 1656–1660.

Rozin, P. (1977). The significance of learning mechanisms in food selection: Some biology, psychology and sociology of science. In L. M. Barker, M. R. Best, & M. Donijan (Eds.), *Learning mechanisms in food selection.* Waco, TX: Baylor University Press.

Rozin, P. (1990). The importance of social factors in understanding the acquisition of food habits. In E. D. Capaldi & T. L. Powley (Eds.), *Taste, experience, and feeding.* Washington, DC: American Psychological Association.

Rubenstein, C. (1982, July). Psychology's fruit flies. *Psychology Today,* pp. 83–84.

Rubin, D. C. (1985, September). The subtle deceiver: Recalling our past. *Psychology Today,* pp. 39–46.

Rubin, D. C. (1995). *Memory in oral traditions.* New York: Oxford University Press.

Rubin, D. C. (1999). *Remembering our past: Studies in autobiographical memory.* New York: Cambridge University Press.

Ruble, D. N., Fleming, A. S., Hackel, L. S., & Stangor, C. (1988). Changes in the marital relationship during the transition to first-time motherhood: Effects of violated expectations concerning division of household labor. *Journal of Personality and Social Psychology, 55,* 78–87.

Rukavina, I., & Daneman, M. (1996). Integration and its effect on acquiring knowledge about competing scientific theories from text. *Journal of Educational Psychology, 88,* 272–287.*

Runco, M. A., & Sakamoto, S. O. (1993). Reaching creatively gifted students through their learning styles. In R. M. Milgram, R. S. Dunn, & G. E. Price (Eds.), *Teaching and counseling gifted and talented adolescents: An international learning style perspective.* Westport, CT: Praeger/Greenwood.

Ruppin, E., Reggia, J. A., & Horn, D. (1996). Pathogenesis of schizophrenic delusions and hallucinations: A neural model. *Schizophrenia Bulletin, 22,* 105–123.

Russell, J. A. (1980). A circumplex model of affect. *Journal of Personality and Social Psychology, 39,* 1161–1178.*

Russell, J. A. (1991a). Culture and the categorization of emotion. *Psychological Bulletin, 110,* 426–450.

Russell, J. A. (1991b). In defense of a prototype approach to emotion concepts. *Journal of Personality and Social Psychology, 60,* 37–47.*

Russell, J. A., & Fehr, B. (1994). Fuzzy concepts and the perception of emotion in facial expressions. *Social Cognition, 4,* 309–341.*

Russell, J. A., & Sato, K. (1995). Comparing emotion words between languages. *Journal of Cross Cultural Psychology, 26,* 384–391.

Russo, N. (1981). In L. T. Benjamin, Jr., & K. D. Lowman (Eds.), *Activities handbook for the teaching of psychology.* Washington, DC: American Psychological Association.

Russo, R., & Parkin, A. J. (1993). Age differences in implicit memory: More apparent than real. *Memory & Cognition, 21,* 73–80.

Ryan, R. M., & Deci, E. L. (1996). When paradigms clash: Comments on Cameron and Pierce's claim that rewards do not undermine intrinsic motivation. *Review of Educational Research, 66,* 33–38.

Saarni, C. (1999). *The development of emotional competence.* New York: Guilford Press.

Sacco, W. P., & Beck, A. T. (1995). Cognitive theory and therapy. In E. E. Beckham & W. R. Leber (Eds.), *Handbook of depression* (2nd ed.). New York: Guilford Press.

Sack, R. L., Lewy, A. J., White, D. M., Singer, C. M., Fireman, M. J., & Vandiver, R. (1990). Morning vs. evening light treatment for winter depression: Evidence that the therapeutic effects of light are mediated by circadian phase shift. *Archives of General Psychiatry, 47,* 343–351.

Sackheim, H. A., Luber, B., Katzman, G. P., et al. (1996, September). The effects of electroconvulsive therapy on quantitative electroencephalograms. *Archives of General Psychiatry, 53,* 814–824.

Sadava, S. W. (1987). Interaction theory. In H. T. Blane & K. E. Leonard (Eds.), *Psychological theories of drinking and alcoholism.* New York: Guilford.*

Sadava, S. W. (1997). Applied social psychology: An introduction. In S. W. Sadava & D. R. McCreary (Eds.), *Applied social psychology.* Upper Saddle River, New Jersey: Prentice Hall.*

Sadava, S. W., O'Connor, R., & McCreary, D. R. (2000). Employment status and health in young adults: Economic and behavioural mediators? *Journal of Health Psychology, 5,* 549–560.*

Sadava, S. W., & Pak, A. W. (1994). Problem drinking and close relationships during the third decade of life. *Psychology of Addiction, 8,* 251–258.*

Saggino, A. (2000). The Big Three or the Big Five? A replication study. *Personality and Individual Differences, 28,* 879–886.

Salovey, P., & Mayer, J. D. (1990). Emotional intelligence. *Imagination, Cognition, and Personality, 9,* 185–211.

Salovey, P., Rothman, A. J., Detweiler, J. B., & Steward, W. T. (2000). Emotional states and physical health. *American Psychologist, 55,* 110–121.

Salovey, P., & Sluyter, D. J. (Eds.). (1997). *Emotional development and emotional intelligence.* New York: Basic Books.

Salthouse, T. A. (1996, July). The processing-speed theory of adult age differences in cognition. *Psychological Review, 103,* 403–428.

Sams, M., Hari, R., Rif, J., & Knuutila, J. (1993). The human auditory memory trace persists about 10 sec: Neuromagnetic evidence. *Journal of Cognitive Neuroscience, 5,* 363–370.

Samuda, R. J. (1998). *Psychological testing of American minorities: Issues and consequences.* Thousand Oaks, CA: Sage.

Sandoval, J., Frisby, C. L., Geisinger, K. F., Scheuneman, J. D., & Grenier, J. R. (Eds.). (1998). *Test interpretation and diversity: Achieving equity in assessment.* Washington, DC: American Psychological Association.

Sanes, J. N., Donoghue, J. P., Thangaraj, V., Edelman, R. R., & Warach, S. (1995, June 23). Shared neural substrates controlling hand movements in human motor cortex. *Science, 268,* 1775–1777.

Sangrador, J. L., & Yela, C. (2000). "What is beautiful is loved": Physical attractiveness in love relationships in a representative sample. *Social Behavior and Personality, 28,* 207–218.

Sansone, C., & Harackiewicz, J. M. (Eds.). (2000). *Intrinsic and extrinsic motivation.* Orlando, FL: Academic Press.

Sapolsky, R. M. (1996, August 9). Why stress is bad for your brain. *Science, 273,* 749–750.

Saudino, K. J. (1997). Moving beyond the heritability question: New directions in behavioral genetic studies of personality. *Current Directions in Psychological Science, 6,* 86–90.

Saudino, K. J., & Plomin, R. (1996). Personality and behavioral genetics: Where have we been and where are we going? *Journal of Research in Personality, 30,* 335–347.

Savage-Rumbaugh, E. S., Murphy, J., Sevcik, R. A., Williams, S., Brakke, K., & Rumbaugh, D. M. (1993). Language comprehension in ape and child. *Monographs of the Society for Research in Child Development, 58* (3, 4).

Savage-Rumbaugh, S., & Brakke, K. E. (1996). Animal language: Methodological and interpretive issues. In M. Bekoff & D. Jamieson (Eds.), *Readings in animal cognition.* Cambridge, MA: MIT Press.

Saxe, L. (1994). Detection of deception: Polygraphy and integrity tests. *Current Directions in Psychological Science, 3,* 69–73.

Sayette, M. A. (1993). An appraisal disruption model of alcohol's effects on stress responses in social drinkers. *Psychological Bulletin, 114,* 459–476.

Scarr, S. (1992). Developmental theories for the 1990s: Development and individual differences. *Child Development, 63,* 1–19.

Scarr, S. (1993). Genes, experience, and development. In D. Magnusson, P. Jules, & M. Casaer (Eds.), *Longitudinal research on individual development: Present status and future perspectives.* Cambridge, England: Cambridge University Press.

Scarr, S. (1996). Behavior genetics and socialization theories of intelligence: Truce and reconciliation. In R. J. Sternberg & E. Grigorenko (Eds.), *Intelligence, heredity, and environment.* New York: Cambridge University Press.

Scarr, S., & Weinberg, R. A. (1976). I.Q. test performance of black children adopted by white families. *American Psychologist, 31,* 726–739.

Schab, F. R. (1991). Odor memory: Taking stock. *Psychological Bulletin, 109,* 242–251.

Schab, F. R., & Crowder, R. G. (Eds.). (1995). *Memory for odors.* Mahwah, NJ: Erlbaum.

Schacter, D. L. (1994). Implicit knowledge: New perspectives on unconscious processes. In O. Sporns & G. Tononi (Eds.), *Selectionism and the brain. International review of neurobiology, Vol. 37.* San Diego: Academic Press.

Schacter, D. L. (1995). Implicit memory: A new frontier for cognitive neuroscience. In M. S. Gazzaniga (Ed.), *The cognitive neurosciences.* Cambridge, MA: MIT Press.

Schacter, D. L. (1996). *Searching for memory: The brain, the mind, and the past.* New York: Basic Books.

Schacter, D. L. (1998, April 3). Memory and awareness. *Science, 280,* 59–60.

Schacter, D. L. (1999a). *The cognitive neuropsychology of false memories.* Philadelphia: Psychology Press.

Schacter, D. L., Chiu, C.-Y. P., & Ochsner, K. N. (1993). Implicit memory: A selective review. *Annual Review of Neuroscience, 16,* 159–182.

Schacter, D. L., Wagner, A. D., & Buckner, R. L. (2000). Memory systems of 1999. In E. Tulving, F. I. Craik, I. M. Fergus, et al. (Eds.). *The Oxford handbook of memory.* New York: Oxford University Press.

Schachter, S. (1971). Some extraordinary facts about obese humans and rats. *American Psychologist, 26,* 129–144.

Schachter, S., & Singer, J. E. (1962). Cognitive, social, and physiological determinants of emotional state. *Psychological Review, 69,* 379–399.

Schaie, K. W. (1991). Developmental designs revisited. In S. H. Cohen & H. W. Reese (Eds.), *Life-span developmental psychology: Methodological innovations.* Hillsdale, NJ: Erlbaum.

Schaie, K. W. (1993). The Seattle longitudinal studies of adult intelligence. *Current Directions in Psychological Science, 2,* 171–175.

Schaie, K. W. (1994). The course of adult intellectual development. *American Psychologist, 49,* 304–313.

Schaller, M., Asp, C. H., Rosell, M. C., & Heim, S. J. (1996). Training in statistical reasoning inhibits the formation of erroneous group stereotypes. *Personality and Social Psychology Bulletin, 22,* 829–844.

Schapira, A. H. V. (1999). Clinical review: Parkinson's disease. *British Medical Journal, 318,* 311–314.

Scharf, M. (1999, October 1). A new option for insomnia. *HealthNews,* p. 4.

Schedlowski, M., & Tewes, U. (Eds.) (1999). *Psychoneuroimmunology: An interdisciplinary introduction.* New York: Plenum Press.

Scheff, T. J. (1999). *Being mentally ill: A sociological theory* (3rd ed.). Hawthrone, NY: Aldine de Gruyter.

Scheier, M. F., & Carver, C. S. (1992). Effects of optimism on psychological and physical well-being: Theoretical overview and empirical update. [Special issue: Cognitive perspectives in health psychology.] *Cognitive Therapy and Research, 16,* 201–228.

Scherer, K. R. (1984). Les motions: Fonctions et composantes. [Emotions: Functions and components.] *Cahiers de psychologie cognitive, 4,* 9–39.

Scherer, K. R. (1994). Emotion serves to decouple stimulus and response. In P. Ekman & R. J. Davidson (Eds.), *The nature of emotion: Fundamental questions.* New York: Oxford University Press.

Schickedanz, J. A., Shickedanz, D. I., & Forsyth, P. D. (1982). *Toward understanding children.* Boston: Little, Brown.

Schizophrenia Society of Canada. (1998). *Recognizing schizophrenia for what it really is: A call to action* (Discussion Paper). Toronto: Author.* Available: <http://www.schizophrenia.ca/call2act.pdf>. Accessed December 12, 2002.

Schkade, D. A., & Kahneman, D. (1998). Does living in California make people happy? A focusing illusion in judgments of life satisfaction. *Psychological Science, 9,* 340–346.

Schmidt, D. (1999). Stretched dream science: The essential contribution of long-term naturalistic studies. *Dreaming, 9,* 43–69.

Schneider, E. L., & Rowe, J. W. (Eds.). (1996). *Handbook of the biology of aging* (4th ed.). San Diego: Academic Press.

Schneider, K. S. (1996, June 3). Mission impossible. *People,* pp. 65–74.

Schneider, K. S., & Gold, T. (1998, December 7). After the tears. *People,* pp. 126–136.

Schoen, L. M. (1996). Mnemopoly: Board games and mnemonics. *Teaching of Psychology, 23,* 30–32.

Schretlen, D., Pearlson, G. D., Anthony, J. C., Aylward, E. H., Augustine, A. M., Davis, A., & Barta, P. (2000). Elucidating the contributions of processing speed, executive ability, and frontal lobe volume to normal age-related differences in fluid intelligence. *Journal of the International Neuropsychological Society, 6,* 52–61.

Schwarz, N., Bless, H., Strack, F., Klumpp, G.,et al. (1991). Ease of retrieval as information: Another look at the availability heuristic. *Journal of Personality and Social Psychology, 61,* 195–202.

Schwartz, B. L., Travis, D. M., Castro, A. M., & Smith, S. M. (2000). The phenomenology of real and illusory tip-of-the-tongue states. *Memory & Cognition, 28,* 18–27.

Searleman, A., & Herrmann, D. (1994). *Memory from a broader perspective.* New York: McGraw-Hill.

Sears, D. O. (1986). College sophomores in the laboratory: Influences of a narrow data base on social psychology's view of human nature. *Journal of Personality and Social Psychology, 51,* 515–530.

Sears, R. R. (1977). Sources of life satisfaction of the Terman gifted men. *American Psychologist, 32,* 119–128.

Sebel, P. S., Bonke, B., & Winograd, E. (Eds.). (1993). *Memory and awareness in anesthesia.* Englewood Cliffs, NJ: Prentice Hall.

Seeley, R., Stephens, T., & Tate, P. *Anatomy & physiology,* 5th Edition. New York: McGraw-Hill.

Seeman, P. (1993). Schizophrenia as a brain disease: The dopamine receptor story. *Archives of Neurology, 50,* 1093–1095.

Segal, N. L. (1993). Twin, sibling, and adoption methods: Tests of evolutionary hypotheses. *American Psychologist, 48,* 943–956.

Segal, Z. V., Gemar, M., Truchon, C., Guirguis, M., & Horowitz, L. M. (1995). A priming methodology for studying self-representation in major depressive disorder. *Journal of Abnormal Psychology, 104,* 205–213.

Segal, Z. V., & Vella, D. D. (1990). Self-schema in major depression: Replication and extension of a priming methodology. *Cognitive Therapy and Research, 14,* 161–176.*

Segall, M. H., Campbell, D. T., & Herskovits, M. J. (1966). *The influence of culture on visual perception.* New York: Bobbs-Merrill.

Segalowitz, N. (1997). Individual differences in second language acquisition. In A. de Groot & J. Kroll (Eds.), *Tutorials in bilingualism.* Mahwah, NJ: Erlbaum.*

Seidenberg, M. S., & Petitto, L. A. (1987). Communication, symbolic communication, and language: Comment on Savage-Rumbaugh, McDonald, Sevcik, Hopkins, & Rupert (1986). *Journal of Experimental Psychology: General, 116,* 279–287.

Seligman, M. E. P. (1975). *Helplessness: On depression, development, and death.* San Francisco: Freeman.

Seligman, M. E. P. (1995, December). The effectiveness of psychotherapy: The *Consumer Reports* study. *American Psychologist, 50,* 965–974.

Seligman, M. E. P. (1996, October). Science as an ally of practice. *American Psychologist, 51,* 1072–1079.

Selikowitz, M. (1997). *Down syndrome: The facts* (2nd ed.). New York: Oxford University Press.

Selkoe, D. J. (1997, January 31). Alzheimer's disease: Genotypes, phenotype, and treatments. *Science, 275,* 630–631.

Sells, R. (1994, August). *Homosexuality study.* Paper presented at the annual meeting of the American Statistical Association, Toronto.

Selsky, A. (1997, February 16). African males face circumcision rite. *Boston Globe,* p. C7.

Seltzer, L. (1986). *Paradoxical strategies in psychotherapy.* New York: Wiley.

Selye, H. (1976). *The stress of life.* New York: McGraw-Hill.

Selye, H. (1993). History of the stress concept. In L. Goldberger & S. Breznitz (Eds.), *Handbook of stress: Theoretical and clinical aspects* (2nd ed.). New York: Free Press.

Seppa, N. (1996, May). A multicultural guide to less spanking and yelling. *APA Monitor,* p. 37.

Seppa, N. (1997, June). Children's TV remains steeped in violence. *APA Monitor,* p. 36.

Serok, S. (2000). *Innovative applications of gestalt therapy.* New York: Krieger.

Sesser, S. (1993, September 13). Opium war redux. *New Yorker,* pp. 78–89.

Seyfarth, R. M., & Cheney, D. L. (1992, December). Meaning and mind in monkeys (vocalizations and intent). *Scientific American, 267,* 122–128.

Seyfarth, R. M., & Cheney, D. L. (1996). Inside the mind of a monkey. In M. Bekoff & D. Jamieson (Eds.), *Readings in animal cognition.* Cambridge, MA: MIT Press.

Shadish, W. R., Cook, T. D., & Campbell, D. T. (2002). *Experimental and quasi-experimental designs for generalized causal inference.* New York: Houghton Mifflin.

Shapiro, A. P. (1996). *Hypertension and stress: A unified concept.* Mahwah, NJ: Erlbaum.

Shapiro, Y., & Gabbard, G. O. (1994). A reconsideration of altruism from an evolutionary and psychodynamic perspective. *Ethics and Behavior, 4,* 23–42.

Sharma, J., Angelucci, A., & Sur, M. (2000). Induction of visual orientation modules in auditory cortex. *Nature, 404,* 841–847.

Sharma, S., Ghosh, S. N., & Spielberger, C. D. (1995). Anxiety, anger expression and chronic gastric ulcer. *Psychological Studies, 40,* 187–191.

Sharps, M. J., Price, J. L., & Williams, J. K. (1994). Spatial cognition and gender: Instructional and stimulus influences on mental image rotation performance. *Psychology of Women Quarterly, 18,* 413–425.

Shatz, C. J. (1992, September). The developing brain. *Scientific American,* pp. 60–67.

Shaughnessy, J. J., Zechmeister, E. B., & Zechmeister, J. S. (2000). *Research methods in psychology* (5th ed.). New York: McGraw-Hill.

Shawver, L. (1995). *And the flag was still there: Straight people, gay people, and sexuality in the U.S. military.* New York: Harrington Park Press/Haworth Press.

Shaywitz, B. A., Shaywitz, S. E., Pugh, K. R., Constable, R. T., et al. (1995). Sex differences in the functional organization of the brain for language. *Nature, 373,* 607–609.

Shear, J. (Ed.). (1997). *Explaining consciousness: The hard problem.* Cambridge, MA: MIT Press.

Shelton, R. C., Keller, M. B., Gelenberg, A., Dunner, D. L., Hirschfeld, R., Thase, M. E., Russell, J., Lydiard, B., Crits-Cristoph, P., Gallop, R., Todd, L., Hellerstein, D., Goodnick, P., Keitner, G., Stahl, S. M., & Halbreich, U. (2001, April 18). Effectiveness of St. John's Wort in major depression. *Journal of the American Medical Association, 285,* 1978–1986.

Shepard, R., & Metzler, J. (1971). Mental rotation of three dimensional objects. *Science, 171,* 701–703.

Shepard, R. N., Metzler, J., Bisiach, E., Luzzati, C., Kosslyn, S. M., Thompson, W. L., Kim, I., & Alpert, N. M. (2000). Part IV: Imagery. In M. S. Gazzaniga et al. (Eds.), *Cognitive neuroscience: A reader.* Malden, MA: Blackwell.

Sherman, J. W., & Klein, S. B. (1994). Development and representation of personality impressions. *Journal of Personality and Social Psychology, 67,* 972–983.

Shettleworth, S. J., & Hampton, R. R. (1998). Adaptive specialization of spatial cognition in food-storing birds? Approaches to testing a comparative hypothesis. In R. P. Balda, I. M. Pepperberg, & A. C. Kamil (Eds.), *Animal cognition in nature: The convergence of psychology and biology in laboratory and field.* San Diego: Academic Press.*

Shiels, P. G., Kind, A. J., Campbell, K. H., Waddington, D., Wilmut, I., Colman, A., & Schnieke, A. E. (1999, May 27). Analysis of telomere lengths in cloned sheep [letter]. *Nature, 399,* 316–317.

Shier, D., Butler, J., & Lewis, R. (2000). *Hole's essentials of human anatomy and physiology* (7th ed.). New York: McGraw-Hill.

Shnek, Z. M., Foley, F. W., LaRocca, N. G., Smith, C. R., et al. (1995). Psychological predictors of depression in multiple sclerosis. *Journal of Neurologic Rehabilitation, 9,* 15–23.

Shotland, R. L. (1985, June). When bystanders just stand by. *Psychology Today,* pp. 50–55.

Shoulder, K. (1992, August). The empire returns. *Sky,* pp. 40–44.

Shrique, C. L., & Annable, L. (1995). Tardive dyskinesia. In C. L. Shriqui & H. A. Nasrallah (Eds.), *Contemporary issues in the treatment of schizophrenia.* Washington, DC: American Psychiatric Press.

Shuchter, S. R., Downs, N., & Zisook, S. (1996). *Biologically informed psychotherapy for depression.* New York: Guilford Press.

Shurkin, J. N. (1992). *Terman's kids: The groundbreaking study of how the gifted grow up.* Boston: Little, Brown.

Shweder, R. A. (1994). "You're not sick, you're just in love": Emotion as an interpretive system. In P. Ekman & R. J. Davidson (Eds.), *The nature of emotion: Fundamental questions.* New York: Oxford University Press.

Sibicky, M. E., Schroeder, D. A., & Dovidio, J. F. (1995). Empathy and helping: Considering the consequences of intervention. *Basic and Applied Social Psychology, 16,* 435–453.

Siegel, J. M. (1990). Stressful life events and use of physician services among the elderly: The moderating role of pet ownership. *Journal of Personality and Social Psychology, 58,* 1081–1086.

Siegel, J. M. (1993). Companion animals: In sickness and in health. *Journal of Social Issues, 49,* 157–167.

Siegel, J. M. (2000, January). Narcolepsy. *Scientific American,* pp. 76–81.

Siegel, R. K. (1989). *Life in pursuit of artificial paradise.* New York: Dutton.

Siegler, R. S. (1994). Cognitive variability: A key to understanding cognitive development. *Current Directions in Psychological Science, 3,* 1–5.

Siegler, R. S. (1998). *Children's thinking* (3rd ed.). Upper Saddle River, NJ: Prentice Hall.

Sigman, M. (1995). Nutrition and child development: More food for thought. *Current Directions in Psychological Science, 4,* 52–55.

Silver, L. B. (1999). *Attention-deficit/hyperactivity disorder: A clinical guide to diagnosis and treatment for health and mental health professionals.* Washington, DC: American Psychiatric Press.

Silver, R. L., & Wortman, C. B. (1980). Coping with undesirable life events. In J. Barber & M. E. P. Seligman (Eds.), *Human helplessness: Theory and application.* New York: Academic Press.

Silverman, K., Evans, S. M., Strain, E. C., & Griffiths, R. R. (1992, October 15). Withdrawal syndrome after the double-blind cessation of caffeine consumption. *New England Journal of Medicine, 327,* 1109–1114.

Silverman, K., Mumford, G. K., & Griffiths, R. R. (1994). Enhancing caffeine reinforcement by behavioral requirements following drug ingestion. *Psychopharmacology, 114,* 424–432.

Silverstein, B., Perdue, L., Peterson, B., Vogel, L., et al. (1986). Possible causes of the thin standard of bodily attractiveness for women. *International Journal of Eating Disorders, 5,* 907–916.

Simmons, R., & Blyth, D. (1987). *Moving into adolescence.* New York: Aldine de Gruyter.

Simonoff, E., Bolton, P., & Rutter, M. (1996). Mental retardation: Genetic findings, clinical implications and research agenda. *Journal of Child Psychology and Psychiatry and Allied Disciplines, 37,* 259–280.

Simpson, G. E., & Yinger, J. M. (1985). *Racial and cultural minorities: An analysis of prejudice and discrimination* (5th ed.). New York: Harper & Row.

Simpson, J. A., & Harris, B. A. (1994). Interpersonal attraction. In A. L. Weber & J. H. Harvey (Eds.), *Perspectives on close relationships.* Boston: Allyn & Bacon.

Sinclair, J. D. (1990). Drugs to decrease alcohol drinking. *Annals of Medicine, 22,* 357–362.

Singelis, T., Choo, P., & Hatfield, E. (1995). Love schemas and romantic love. *Journal of Social Behavior and Personality, 10,* 15–36.

Singer, J. L. (1975). *The inner world of daydreaming.* New York: Harper & Row.

Single, E., Van Truong, M., Adlaf, E., & Ialomiteanu, A. (1999). *Canadian profile 1999: Alcohol, tobacco and other drugs.* Ottawa: CCSA, Toronto: CAMH.*

Sinha, B. K., Willson, L. R., & Watson, D. C. (2000). Stress and coping among students in India and Canada. *Canadian Journal of Behavioural Science, 32,* 218–225.*

Sippola, L. K., Bukowski, W. M., & Noll, R. B. (1997). Dimensions of liking and disliking underlying the same-sex preference in early childhood and early adolescence. *Merrill-Palmer Quarterly, 43(4),* 591–609.*

Sizemore, C. C. (1989). *A mind of my own: The woman who was known as Eve tells the story of her triumph over multiple personality disorder.* New York: Morrow.

Skinner, B. F. (1957). *Verbal behavior.* New York: Appleton-Century-Crofts.

Slater, A. (1996). The organization of visual perception in early infancy. In F. Vital-Durand, J. Atkinson, & O. J. Braddick (Eds.), *Infant vision.* Oxford, England: Oxford University Press.

Slater, A., Mattock, A., & Brown, E. (1990). Size constancy at birth: Newborn infants' responses to retinal and real size, *Journal of Experimental Child Psychology, 49,* 314–322.

Sleek, S. (1995, November). Online therapy services raise ethical question. *APA Monitor,* p. 9.

Sleek, S. (1998, June). Psychologists debate merits of the polygraph. *APA Monitor,* p. 30.

Sloan, E. P., Hauri, P., Bootzin, R., Morin, C., et al. (1993). The nuts and bolts of behavioral therapy for insomnia. *Journal of Psychosomatic Research, 37* (Suppl), 19–37.

Slovic, P., Fischoff, B., & Lichenstein, S. (1976). Cognitive processes and societal risk taking. In J. S. Carroll & J. W. Payne (Eds.), *Cognition and social behavior.* Mahwah, NJ: Erlbaum.

Smith, E. (1988, May). Fighting cancerous feelings. *Psychology Today,* pp. 22–23.

Smith, E. E. (2000). Neural bases of human working memory. *Current Directions in Psychological Science, 9,* 45–49.

Smith, E. E., & Jonides, J. (1999, March 12). Storage and executive processes in the frontal lobes. *Science, 283,* 1657–1661.

Smith, K. A., Williams, C., & Cowen, P. J. (2000). Impaired regulation of brain serotonin function during dieting in women recovered from depression. *British Journal of Psychiatry, 176,* 72–75.

Smith, M. L., & Bigel, M. G. (2000). The temporal lobes and memory. In F. Boller and J. Grafman (Eds.), *Handbook of neuropsychology* (2nd Ed.), (pp. 49–65). Amsterdam: Elsevier.*

Smith, M. L., Glass, G. V., & Miller, T. J. (1980). *The benefits of psychotherapy.* Baltimore: Johns Hopkins.

Smith, M. V. (1996). Linguistic relativity: On hypotheses and confusions. *Communication and Cognition, 29,* 65–90.

Smith, M., & Lin, K. M. (1996). Gender and ethnic differences in the pharmacogenetics of psychotropics. In M. F. Jensvold, U. Halbreich, & J. A. Hamilton, (Eds.), *Psychopharmacology and women: Sex, gender, and hormones.* Washington, DC: American Psychiatric Press.

Smith, S. M. (1994). Frustrated feelings of imminent recall: On the tip of the tongue. In J. Metcalfe & A. P. Shimamura (Eds.), *Metacognition: Knowing about knowing.* Cambridge, MA: MIT Press.

Snyder, C. R. (1999). *Coping: The psychology of what works.* New York: Oxford University Press.

Snyder, F. (1970). The phenomenology of dreaming. In L. Madow & L. H. Snow (Eds.), *The psychodynamic implications of the physiological studies on dreams.* Springfield, IL: Thomas.

Sohn, D. (1996). Publication bias and the evaluation of psychotherapy efficacy in reviews of the research literature. *Clinical Psychology Review, 16,* 147–156.

Solcova, I., & Tomanek, P. (1994). Daily stress coping strategies: An effect of hardiness. *Studia Psychologica, 36,* 390–392.

Solomon, C. (1993, December 21). Having nightmares? Chances are, they are about your job. *Wall Street Journal,* pp. A1, A4.

Solomon, J. (1996, May 20). Breaking the silence. *Newsweek,* pp. 20–21.

Sommer, B. B., & Sommer, R. (1997). *A practical guide to behavioral research: Tools and techniques* (4th ed.). New York: Oxford University Press.

Sommerhof, G. (2000). *Understanding consciousness: Its function and brain processes.* Thousand Oaks, CA: Sage.

Sorrentino, R. M., Hewitt, E. C., & Raso-Knott, P. A. (1992). Risk-taking in games of chance and skill: Informational and affective influences on choice behavior. *Journal of Personality and Social Psychology, 62,* 522–533.

Spangler, W. D. (1992). Validity of questionnaire and TAT measures of need for achievement: Two meta-analyses. *Psychological Bulletin, 112,* 140–154.

Spanos, N. P., Burgess, C. A., Roncon, V., Wallace-Capretta, S., et al. (1993). Surreptitiously observed hypnotic responding in simulators and in skill-trained and untrained high hypnotizables. *Journal of Personality and Social Psychology, 65,* 391–398.

Spearman, C. (1927). *The abilities of man.* London: Macmillan.

Spence, C., Shore, D. I., Gazzaniga, M. S., Soto-Faraco, S., & Kingstone, A. (2001). Failure to remap visuotactile space across the midline in the split-brain. *Canadian Journal of Experimental Psychology, 55,* 133–140.*

Spence, J. T. (1985, August). *Achievement American style: The rewards and costs of individualism.* Presidential address, 93rd annual convention of the American Psychological Association, Los Angeles.

Spence, M. J., & DeCasper, A. J. (1982, March). *Human fetuses perceive maternal speech.* Paper presented at the meeting of the International Conference on Infant Studies, Austin, TX.

Spencer, R. (2000, May 3). Wanna piece of me? *The Globe and Mail,* p. R1.*

Sperling, G. (1960). The information available in brief visual presentation. *Psychology Monographs, 74* (whole no. 498).

Sperry, R. (1982). Some effects of disconnecting the cerebral hemispheres. *Science, 217,* 1223–1226.

Spetch, M. L. (1995). Overshadowing in landmark learning: Touch-screen studies with pigeons and humans. *Journal of Experimental Psychology: Animal Behavior Processes, 21,* 166–181.*

Spetch, M. L., Cheng, K. & MacDonald, S. E. (1996). Learning the configuration of a landmark array, I: Touch-screen studies with pigeons and humans. *Journal of Comparative Psychology, 110,* 55–68.*

Spetch, M. L., Cheng, K. & MacDonald, S. E., Linkenhoker, B. A., Kelly, D. M. & Doerkson, S. R. (1997). Learning the configuration of a landmark array in pigeons and humans, II: Generality across search tasks. *Journal of Comparative Psychology, 111,* 14–24.*

Spiegel, D. (1993). Social support: How friends, family, and groups can help. In D. Goleman & J. Gurin (Eds.), *Mind-body medicine.* Yonkers, NY: Consumer Reports Books.

Spiegel, D. (1996a, July). Cancer and depression. *British Journal of Psychiatry, 168,* 109–116.

Spiegel, D. (1996b). Dissociative disorders. In R. E. Hales & S. C. Yudofsky (Eds.), *The American Psychiatric Press synopsis of psychiatry.* Washington, DC: American Psychiatric Press, Inc.

Spiegel, D. (1996c). Hypnosis. In R. E. Hales & S. C. Yudofsky (Eds.), *The American Psychiatric Press synopsis of psychiatry.* Washington, DC: American Psychiatric Press.

Spiegel, D. (Ed.). (1999). *Efficacy and cost-effectiveness of psychotherapy.* New York: American Psychiatric Press.

Spiegel, D., & Cardena, E. (1991). Disintegrated experience: The dissociative disorders revisited. *Journal of Abnormal Psychology, 100,* 366–378.

Spiegel, D., Frischholz, E. J., Fleiss, J. L., & Spiegel, H. (1993). Predictors of smoking abstinence following a single-session restructuring intervention with self-hypnosis. *American Journal of Psychiatry, 150,* 1090–1097.

Spiegel, R. (1989). *Psychopharmacology: An introduction.* New York: Wiley.

Spielman, D. A., & Staub, E. (2000). Reducing boys' aggression: Learning to fulfill basic needs constructively. *Journal of Applied Developmental Psychology, 21,* 165–181.

Spillmann, L., & Werner, J. (Eds.). (1990). *Visual perception: The neurophysiological foundations.* San Diego: Academic Press.

Spira, J. (Ed.). (1997). *Group therapy for medically ill patients.* New York: Guilford Press.

Spitz, H. H. (1987). Problem-solving processes in special populations. In J. G. Borkowski & J. D. Day (Eds.), *Cognition in special children: Comparative approaches to retardation, learning disabilities, and giftedness.* Norwood, NJ: Ablex.

Sprecher, S., & McKinney, K. (1993). *Sexuality.* Newbury Park, CA: Sage.

Sprenkle, D. H., & Moon, S. M. (Eds.). (1996). *Research methods in family therapy.* New York: Guilford Press.

Squire, L. R. (1993). The hippocampus and spatial memory. *Trends in Neurosciences, 6,* 56–57.

St. Onge, S. (1995a). Modeling and role-playing. In M. Ballou (Ed.), *Psychological interventions: A guide to strategies.* Westport, CT: Praeger/Greenwood.

St. Onge, S. (1995b). Systematic desensitization. In M. Ballou (Ed.), *Psychological interventions: A guide to strategies.* Westport, CT: Praeger/Greenwood.

Stairs, A. (1995). Learning processes and teaching roles in Native education: Cultural base and cultural brokerage. In M. Battiste & J. Barman (Eds.), *First Nations education in Canada: The circle unfolds.* Vancouver: UBC Press.*

Stanton, A. L., & Franz, R. (1999). Focusing on emotions: An adaptive coping strategy? In C. R. Snyder (Ed.), *Coping: The psychology of what works.* New York: Oxford University Press.

Stanton, H. E. (1994). Sports imagery and hypnosis: A potent mix. *Australian Journal of Clinical and Experimental Hypnosis, 22,* 119–124.

Stark, C. (1998). Ethics in the research context: Misinterpretations and misplaced misgivings. *Canadian Psychology 39(3),* 202–211.*

Statistics Canada. (1996a). 1996 census family statistics.* Available: <http://www.statcan.ca/english/census96/june9/social.htm>. Accessed December 12, 2002.

Statistics Canada. (1996b). 1996 census population statistics.* Available: <http://www.statcan.ca/english/Pgdb/People/Population>. Accessed June 11, 2000.

Statistics Canada. (1996c). 1996 census language statistics.* Available: <http://www.statcan.ca/english/Pgdb/People/popula.hmt#lan>. Accessed June 1, 2000.

Statistics Canada. (1998a). *National public health survey.* Ottawa: Statistics Canada.*

Statistics Canada. (1999a). *Canada yearbook 1999.* Ottawa: Statistics Canada.*

Statistics Canada. (1999b). How healthy are Canadians? A special issue. *Statistics Canada Health Reports, Winter 99, (Vol.11), 3.* Ottawa: Statistics Canada.*

Statistics Canada. (2000). *Canadian community health survey. 2000/01.* Ottawa: Statistics Canada.*

Statistics Canada. (2001). Health indicators. *Available: <http://www.statcan.ca:80/english/freepub/82-221-XIE/00401/high/sever.htm>. Accessed December 12, 2002.

Statistics Canada. (2002a, May 7). Deaths 1999. *The Daily.** Available: <http://www.statcan.ca/Daily/English/020507/d020507b.htm>. Accessed December 12, 2002.

Statistics Canada. (2002b). Fact-sheet on gambling. *Perspectives on Labour and Income, 3(7)* [Online Edition].* Available: <http://www.statcan.ca/english/indepth/75-001/online/0070275-001-XIE.html>. Accessed December 12, 2002.

Staub, E. (1996). Cultural-societal roots of violence. *American Psychologist, 51,* 117–132.

Staudinger, U. M., Fleeson, W., & Baltes, P. B. (1999). Predictors of subjective physical health and global well-being: Similarities and differences between the United States and Germany. *Journal of Personality and Social Psychology, 76,* 305–319.

Steele, C. M., & Josephs, R. A. (1990). Alcohol myopia: Its prized and dangerous effects. *American Psychologist, 45,* 921–933.

Steele, C. M., & Southwick, L. (1985). Alcohol and social behavior I: The psychology of drunken excess. *Journal of Personality and Social Psychology, 48,* 18–34.

Steen, R. G. (1996). *DNA and destiny: Nature and nurture in human behavior.* New York: Plenum Press.

Stein, N. L., Brainerd, C., Ornstein, P. A., & Tversky, B. (Eds.). (1996). *Memory for everyday and emotional events.* Mahwah, NJ: Erlbaum.

Stein, N. L., Ornstein, P. A., Tversky, B., & Brainerd, C. (Eds.). (1997). *Memory for everyday and emotional events.* Mahwah, NJ: Erlbaum.

Stein, S. J., & Book, H. E. (2000). *The EQ edge: Emotional intelligence and your success.* Toronto: Stoddart.*

Steinberg, L. (1989). *Adolescence* (2nd ed.). New York: Knopf.

Steinberg, L. (1993). *Adolescence* (3rd ed.). New York: McGraw-Hill.

Steinberg, L., & Dornbusch, S. (1991). Negative correlates of part-time employment during adolescence: Replication and elaboration. *Developmental Psychology, 27,* 304.

Stephens T. (1998). Population mental health in Canada. Ottawa: Mental Health Promotion Unit, Health Canada.*

Stern, R. M., & Koch, K. L. (1996). Motion sickness and differential susceptibility. *Current Directions in Psychological Science, 5,* 115–120.

Sternberg, R. J. (1982). Reasoning, problem solving, and intelligence. In R. J. Sternberg (Ed.), *Handbook of human intelligence* (pp. 225–307). New York: Cambridge University Press.

Sternberg, R. J. (1990). *Metaphors of mind: Conceptions of the nature of intelligence.* New York: Cambridge University Press.

Sternberg, R. J. (1998). *Successful intelligence: How practical and creative intelligence determine success in life.* New York: Plume.

Sternberg, R. J. (2000). Intelligence and wisdom. In R. J. Sternberg (Ed.), *Handbook of intelligence.* New York: Cambridge University Press.

Sternberg, R. J., & Beall, A. E. (1991). How can we know what love is? An epistemological analysis. In G. J. O. Fletcher & F. D. Fincham (Eds.), *Cognition in close relationships.* Hillsdale, NJ: Erlbaum.

Sternberg, R. J., & Frensch, P. A. (1991). *Complex problem solving: Principles and mechanisms.* Hillsdale, NJ: Erlbaum.

Sternberg, R. J., & Grigorenko, E. (1997). Are cognitive styles still in style? *American Psychologist, 52,* 700–712.

Sternberg, R. J., & O'Hara, L. A. (2000). Intelligence and creativity. In R. J. Sternberg (Ed.), *Handbook of intelligence.* New York: Cambridge University Press.

Sternberg, R. J., Wagner, R. K., Williams, W. M., Horvath, J. A., et al. (1995). Testing common sense. *American Psychologist, 50,* 912–927.

Stevens, G., & Gardner, S. (1982). *The women of psychology: Pioneers and innovators* (Vol. 1). Cambridge, MA: Schenkman.

Stevenson, H. W. (1992, December). Learning from Asian schools. *Scientific American,* pp. 70–75.

Steward, E. P. (1995). *Beginning writers in the zone of proximal development.* Hillsdale, NJ: Erlbaum.

Stewart, D. W., & Kamins, M. A. (1993). *Secondary research: Information sources and methods.* (2nd ed.). Newbury Park, CA: Sage.

Stier, H., & Lewin-Epstein, N. (2000). Women's part-time employment and gender inequality in the family. *Journal of Family Issues, 21,* 390–410.

Stix, G. (1996, January). Listening to culture. *Scientific American,* pp. 16–17.

Stone, R., & Kelner, K. (2000, July 28). Violence: No silver bullet. *Science, 289,* 569.

Stoppard, J. M. (1999). Why new perspectives are needed for understanding depression in women. *Canadian Psychology, 40,* 79–90.*

Strauss, E. (1998, May 8). Writing, speech separated in split brain. *Science, 280,* 827.

Streissguth, A. P., Barr, H. M., Bookstein, F. L., Sampson, P. D., & Olson, H. C. (1999). The long-term neurocognitive consequences of prenatal alcohol exposure: A 14-year study. *Psychological Science, 10,* 186–190.

Strickland, B. R. (1992). Women and depression. *Current Directions in Psychological Science, 1,* 132–135.

Stroebe, M. S., Stroebe, W., & Hansson, R. O. (Eds.). (1993). *Handbook of bereavement: Theory, research, and intervention.* Cambridge, England: Cambridge University Press.

Strube, M. (Ed.). (1990). Type A behavior [Special issue]. *Journal of Social Behavior and Personality, 5.*

Strupp, H. H. (1996, October). The tripartite model and the *Consumer Reports* study. *American Psychologist, 51,* 1017–1024.

Strupp, H. H., & Binder, J. L. (1992). Current developments in psychotherapy. *Independent Practitioner, 12,* 119–124.

Sue, D. (1979). Erotic fantasies of college students during coitus. *Journal of Sex Research, 15,* 299–305.

Sue, D. W., & Sue, D. (1990). *Counseling the culturally different: Theory and practice* (2nd ed.). New York: Wiley.

Sue, D. W., Sue, D., & Sue, S. (1990). *Understanding abnormal behavior* (3rd ed.). Boston: Houghton-Mifflin.

Sue, S. (1998). In search of cultural competence in psychotherapy and counseling. *American Psychologist, 53,* 440–448.

Sulzer-Azaroff, B., & Mayer, R. (1991). *Behavior analysis and lasting change.* New York: Holt.

Sundin, O., Ohman, A., Palm, T., & Strom, G. (1995). Cardiovascular reactivity, Type A behavior, and coronary heart disease: Comparisons between myocardial infarction patients and controls during laboratory-induced stress. *Psychophysiology, 32,* 28–35.

Super, C. M. (1980). Cognitive development: Looking across at growing up. In C. M. Super & S. Harakness (Eds.), *New directions for child development: Anthropological perspectives on child development* (pp. 59–69). San Francisco: Jossey-Bass.

Supiano, M. A., & Hogikyan, R.V. (in press). Catecholamines and aging. In H. G. Ambrecht, R. M. Coe and J. E. Morley (Eds.), *The science of geriatric medicine.* Baltimore, MD: Johns Hopkins University Press.

Suzuki, K. (1991). Moon illusion simulated in complete darkness: Planetarium experiment reexamined. *Perception and Psychophysics, 49,* 349–354.

Svarstad, B. (1976). Physician-patient communication and patient conformity with medical advice. In D. Mechanic (Ed.), *The growth of bureaucratic medicine.* New York: Wiley.

Swan, S. W. (1997). Hormone replacement therapy and the risk of reproductive cancers. *Journal of Psychosomatic Obstetrics and Gynecology, 18,* 165–174.

Swanson, J. (Ed.). (1999). *Sleep disorders sourcebook.* New York: Omnigraphics, Inc.

Swets, J. A., & Bjork, R. A. (1990). Enhancing human performance: An evaluation of "new age" techniques considered by the U.S. Army. *Psychological Science, 1,* 85–96.

Swindle, R., Jr., Heller, K., Pescosolido, B., & Kikuzawa, S. (2000). Responses to nervous breakdowns in America over a 40-year period. *American Psychologist, 55,* 740–749.

Sylvain, C., Ladouceur, R., & Boisvert, J. (1997). Cognitive and behavioural treatment of pathological gambling: A controlled study. *Journal of Consulting and Clinical Psychology, 65,* 727–732.*

Szasz, T. S. (1961). *The myth of mental illness.* New York: Harper & Row.

Szasz, T. (1982). The psychiatric will: A new mechanism for protecting persons against "psychosis" and psychiatry. *American Psychologist, 37,* 762–770.

Szasz, T. S. (1994). *Cruel compassion: Psychiatric control of society's unwanted.* New York: Wiley.

Tabakoff, B., & Hoffman, P. L. (1996). Effect of alcohol on neurotransmitters and their receptors and enzymes. In H. Begleiter & B. Kissin (Eds.), *The pharmacology of alcohol and alcohol dependence. Alcohol and alcoholism, No. 2.* New York: Oxford University Press.

Tafarodi, R. W., & Swann, W. B. Jr. (1996). Individualism, collectivism, and global self-esteem: Evidence for a cultural trade-off. *Journal of Cross-Cultural Psychology, 27,* 651–672.*

Tagiuri, R. (1958). Social preference and its perception. In R. Tagiuri & L. Petrullo (Eds.), *Person, perception, and interpersonal behavior* (pp. 316–336). Stanford, CA: Stanford University Press.

Tan, V. L., & Hicks, R. A. (1995). Type A-B behavior and nightmare types among college students. *Perceptual and Motor Skills, 81,* 15–19.

Tandon, R. (1995). Neurobiological substrate of dimensions of schizophrenic illness. *Journal of Psychiatric Research, 29,* 255–260.

Tanford, S., & Penrod, S. (1984). Social influence model: A formal integration of research on majority and minority influence processes. *Psychological Bulletin, 95,* 189–225.

Tanner, J. M. (1990). *Foetus into man: Physical growth from conception to maturity (rev. ed.).* Cambridge, MA: Harvard University Press.

Taubes, G. (1998, May 29). Weight increases worldwide? *Science, 280,* 1368.

Taylor, A. (1991, April 8). Can Iacocco fix Chrysler—again? *Fortune,* pp. 50–54.

Taylor, H. (2000, January 29). *Harris Poll #5: Political trends.* New York: Harris Poll Interactive.

Taylor, M. (1996). A theory of mind perspective on social cognitive development. In R. Gelman & T. K-F. Au (Eds.), *Perceptual and cognitive development: Handbook of perception and cognition* (2nd ed.). San Diego: Academic Press.

Taylor, S. E. (1995). Quandary at the crossroads: Paternalism versus advocacy surrounding end-of-treatment decisions. *American Journal of Hospital Palliatory Care, 12,* 43–46.

Taylor, S. E., & Aspinwall, L. G. (1996). Mediating and moderating processes in psychosocial stress: Appraisal, coping, resistance, and vulnerability. In H. B. Kaplan (Ed.), *Psychosocial stress: Perspectives on structure, theory, life-course, and methods.* San Diego: Academic Press.

Tellegen, A., Lykken, D. T., Bouchard, T. J., Jr., Wilcox, K. J., Segal, N. L., & Rich, S. (1988). Personality similarity in twins reared apart and together. *Journal of Personality and Social Psychology, 54,* 1031–1039.

Tepper, E. L. (1994). Immigration policy and multiculturalism. In J. W. Berry & J. A. Laponce (Eds.), *Ethnicity and culture in Canada: The research landscape.* Toronto: University of Toronto Press.*

Terman, L. M., & Oden, M. H. (1947). *Genetic studies of genius, IV: The gifted child grows up.* Stanford, CA: Stanford University Press.

The World Psychiatric Association Program to Fight Stigma Due to Schizophrenia. (2002). Available <http://www.openthedoors.com/english/ 03_06.html>. Accessed December 11, 2002.

Thombs, D. L. (1999). *Introduction to addictive behaviors* (2nd ed.). New York: Guilford Press.

Thompson, A. (2000, April 13). Dallaire's last battle. *The Toronto Star,* p. A3.*

Thomson, A.M. (1997, January 10). More than just frequency detectors? *Science, 275,* 179–180.

Thorndike, E. L. (1932). *The fundamentals of learning.* New York: Teachers College Press.

Thorndike, R. L., Hagen, E., & Sattler, J. (1986). *Stanford-Binet* (4th ed.). Chicago: Riverside Press.

Thune, I., Brenn, T., Lund, E., & Gaard, M. (1997, May 1). Physical activity and the risk of breast cancer. *New England Journal of Medicine, 336,* 1269–1275.

Thurstone, L. L. (1938). *Primary mental abilities.* Chicago: University of Chicago Press.

Tolman, E. C., & Honzik, C. H. (1930). Introduction and removal of reward and maze performance in rats. *University of California Publications in Psychology, 4,* 257–275.

Torrey, E. F. (1996). *Out of the shadows: Confronting America's mental illness crisis.* New York: Wiley.

Torrey, E. F. (1997, June 13). The release of the mentally ill from institutions: A well-intentioned disaster. *Chronicle of Higher Education,* pp. B4–B5.

Toth, J. P., & Reingold, E. M. (1996). *Beyond perception: Conceptual contributions to unconscious influences of memory.* Oxford, England: Oxford University Press.

Trainor, J., Pomeroy, E., & Pape, B. (1999). *Building a framework for support: A community development approach to mental health policy.* Toronto: Canadian Mental Health Association.*

Treisman, A. (1988). Features and objects: The Fourteenth Bartlett Memorial Lecture. *Quarterly Journal of Experimental Psychology, 40,* 201–237.

Treisman, A. (1993). The perception of features and objects. In A. D. Baddeley & L. Weiskrantz (Eds.), *Attention: Selection, awareness, and control: A tribute to Donald Broadbent.* Oxford, England: Oxford University Press.

Tremblay, S. (1999). Crime statistics in Canada, 1998. *Juristat 19(9).* Ottawa: Canadian Centre for Justice Statistics, Statistics Canada.*

Tsunoda, T. (1985). *The Japanese brain: Uniqueness and universality.* Tokyo: Taishukan.

Tucker, J. A., Donovan, D. M., & Marlatt, G. A. (Eds.). (1999). *Changing addictive behavior: Bridging clinical and public health strategies.* New York: Guilford Press.

Tulving, E. (1985). How many memory systems are there? *American Psychologist, 40,* 385–398.*

Tulving, E. (1993). What is episodic memory? *Current Directions in Psychological Science, 2,* 67–70.

Tulving, E. (2000). Concepts of memory. In E. Tulving & F. I. M. Craik (Eds.), *The Oxford handbook of memory.* New York: Oxford University Press.

Tulving, E., & Craik, F. M. (2000). *The Oxford handbook of memory.* Cambridge, England: Oxford University Press.

Tulving, E., Hayman, C., & McDonald, C. (1991). Long-lasting perceptual and semantic priming in amnesia: A case experiment. *Journal of Experimental Psychology: Learning, Memory, and Cognition, 17,* 595–617.*

Tulving, E., & Psotka, J. (1971). Retroactive inhibition in free recall: Inaccessibility of information available in the memory store. *Journal of Experimental Psychology, 87,* 1–8.

Tulving, E., & Schacter, D. L. (1990, January 19). Priming and human memory systems. *Science, 247,* 301–306.

Tulving, E., & Thompson, D. M. (1973). Encoding specificity and retrieval processes in episodic memory. *Psychological Review, 80,* 352–373.

Turk, D. C. (1994). Perspectives on chronic pain: The role of psychological factors. *Current Directions in Psychological Science, 3,* 45–49.

Turk, D. C., & Nash, J. M. (1993). Chronic pain: New ways to cope. In D. Goleman & J. Guerin (Eds.), *Mind-body medicine: How to use your mind for better health.* Yonkers, NY: Consumer Reports.

Turkewitz, G. (1993). The origins of differential hemispheric strategies for information processing in the relationships between voice and face perception. In B. de Boysson-Bardies et al. (Eds.), *Developmental neurocognition: Speech and face processing in the first year of life.* Dordrecht, Netherlands: Kluwer Academic.

Turner, W. J. (1995). Homosexuality, Type 1: An Xq28 phenomenon. *Archives of Sexual Behavior, 24,* 109–134.

Tversky, A., & Kahneman, D. (1987). Rational choice and the framing of decisions. In R. Hogarth & M. Reder (Eds.), *Rational choice: The contrast between economics and psychology.* Chicago: University of Chicago Press.

Twine, N., & Barraclough, N. (1998). Crisis lines, telephone technology, and confidentiality. In A. A. Leenaars, S. Wenckstern, I. Sakinofsky, R. J. Dyck, M. J. Kral, & R. C. Bland (Eds.), *Suicide in Canada* (pp. 342–352). Toronto: University of Toronto Press.*

Ubell, E. (1993, January 10). Could you use more sleep? *Parade,* pp. 16–18.

Uchino, B. N., Uno, D., & Holt-Lunstad, J. (1999). Social support, physiological processes, and health. *Current Directions in Psychological Science, 8,* 145–148.

Udolf, R. (1981). *Handbook of hypnosis for professionals.* New York: Van Nostrand.

Ullman, S. (1996). *High-level vision: Object recognition and visual cognition.* Cambridge, MA: MIT Press.

Underwood, G. D. M. (Ed.). (1996). *Implicit cognition.* Oxford, England: Oxford University Press.

Vaillant, G. E., & Vaillant, C. O. (1990). Natural history of male psychological health: XII. A 45-year study of predictors of successful aging at age 65. *American Journal of Psychiatry, 147,* 31–37.

Valente, S. M. (1991). Electroconvulsive therapy. *Archives of Psychiatric Nursing, 5,* 223–228.

Valentiner, D. P., Foa, E. B., Riggs, D. S., & Gershuny, B. S. (1996). Coping strategies and posttraumatic stress disorder in female victims of sexual and nonsexual assault. *Journal of Abnormal Psychology, 105,* 455–458.

Vallis, M. (2000, April 28). Researchers narrow schizophrenia gene link search. *National Post,* p. A10.*

Van De Graaff, K. (2000). *Human anatomy* (5th ed.). New York: McGraw-Hill.

van Eck, M., Nicolson, N. A., & Berkhof, J. (1998). Effects of stressful daily events on mood states: Relationship to global perceived stress. *Journal of Personality and Social Psychology, 75,* 1572–1585.

Van Ginkel, R. (1990). Fishermen, taboos, and ominous animals: A comparative perspective. *Anthrozoos, 4,* 73–81.

Vanier Institute of the Family. (1997). *From the kitchen table to the boardroom table: The Canadian family and the work place.* Ottawa, Author.*

VanLehn, K. (1996). Cognitive skill acquisition. *Annual Review of Psychology, 47,* 513–539.

van Wel, F., Linssen, H., & Abma, R. (2000). The parental bond and the well-being of adolescents and young adults. *Journal of Youth and Adolescence, 29,* 307–318.

Velichkovsky, B. M., & Rumbaugh, D. M. (Eds.). (1996). *Communicating meaning: The evolution and development of language.* Mahwah, NJ: Erlbaum.

Velmans, M. (2000). *Understanding consciousness.* New York: Psychology Press.

Verhaeghen, P., Marcoen, A., & Goossens, L. (1992). Improving memory performance in the aged through mnemonic training: A meta-analytic study. *Psychology and Aging, 7,* 242–251.

Vernon, P. A., Jang, K. L., Harris, J. A., & McCarthy, J. M. (1997). Environmental predictors of personality differences: A twin and sibling study. *Journal of Personality and Social Psychology, 72,* 177–183.*

Victor, S. B., & Fish, M. C. (1995). Lesbian mothers and the children: A review for school psychologists. *School Psychology Review, 24,* 456–479.

Vihman, M. M. (1996). *Phonological development: The origins of language in the child.* London, England: Blackwell.

Vital-Durand, F., Atkinson, J., & Braddick, O. J. (Eds.). (1996). *Infant vision.* Oxford, England: Oxford University Press.

Vogel, G. (13 October, 2000). New brain cells prompt new theory of depression. *Science, 290,* 258–259.

von Restorff, H. (1933). Über die wirking von bereichsbildungen im Spurenfeld. In W. Kohler & H. von Restorff, *Analyse von vorgangen in Spurenfeld: I. Psychologische forschung, 18,* 299–342.

Vygotsky, L. S. (1926/1997). *Educational psychology.* Delray Beach, FL: St. Lucie Press.

Wachtel, P. L., & Messer, S. B. (Eds.). (1997). *Theories of psychotherapy: Origins and evolution.* Washington, DC: American Psychological Association.

Wagner, D. A. (1981). Culture and memory development. In H. C. Triandis & A. Heron (Eds.), *Handbook of cross-cultural psychology: Vol. 4. Developmental psychology.* Boston: Allyn & Bacon.

Wagner, E. F., & Atkins, J. H. (2000). Smoking among teenage girls. *Journal of Child and Adolescent Substance Abuse, 9,* 93–110.

Wagner, R. K. (1997). Intelligence, training, and employment. *American Psychologist, 52,* 1059–1069.

Wagner, R. K. (2000). Practical intelligence. In R. J. Sternberg (Ed.), *Handbook of intelligence.* New York: Cambridge University Press.

Waid, W. M., & Orne, M. T. (1982). The physiological detection of deception. *American Scientist, 70,* 402–409.

Walcott, D. M. (2000). Repressed memory still lacks scientific reliability. *Journal of the American Academy of Psychiatry and the Law, 28,* 243–244.

Waldrop, M. W. (1989, September 29). NIDA aims to fight drugs with drugs. *Science, 245,* 1443–1444.

Walker, L. J. (1984). Sex differences in the development of moral reasoning: A critical review. *Child Development, 55,* 677–691.*

Walker, L. J., & Hennig, K. H. (1997). Parent/child relationships in single-parent families. *Canadian Journal of Behavioural Science, 29(1),* 63–75.*

Wall, P. D., & Melzack, R. (1989). *Textbook of pain* (2nd ed.). New York: Churchill Livingstone.

Wallace, R. K., & Benson, H. (1972, February). The physiology of meditation. *Scientific American,* pp. 84–90.

Wallerstein, J. S., Lewis, J., Blakeslee, S., & Lewis, J. (2000). *The unexpected legacy of divorce.* New York: Hyperion.

Wallis, C., & Willwerth, J. (1992, July 6). Schizophrenia: A new drug brings patients back to life. *Time,* pp. 52–57.

Walsh, B. T., & Devlin, M. J. (1998, May 29). Eating disorders: Progress and problems. *Science, 280,* 1387–1390.

Walsh, D. M., Liggett, C., Baxter, D., & Allen, J. M. (1995). A double-blind investigation of the hypoalgesic effects of transcutaneous electrical nerve stimulation upon experimentally induced ischaemic pain. *Pain, 61,* 39–45.

Walter, H. J., Vaughan, R. D., & Wynder, E. L. (1994). Primary prevention of cancer among children: Changes in cigarette smoking and diet after six years of intervention. In A. Steptoe & J. Wardle (Eds.), *Psychosocial processes and health: A reader.* Cambridge, England: Cambridge University Press.

Ward, T. B., Smith, S. M., & Vaid, J. (1997). *Creative thought: An investigation of conceptual structures and processes.* Washington, DC: American Psychological Association.

Ward, W. C., Kogan, N., & Pankove, E. (1972). Incentive effects in children's creativity. *Child Development, 43,* 669–677.

Warner, R. E. (1991). A survey of theoretical orientations of Canadian clinical psychologists. *Canadian Psychology, 32,* 525–528.*

Wasserman, E. A., & Miller, R. R. (1997). What's elementary about associative learning? *Annual Review of Psychology, 48,* 573–607.

Waters, E., Hamilton, C. E., & Weinfield, N. S. (2000). The stability of attachment security from infancy to adolescence and early adulthood: General introduction. *Child Development, 71,* 678–683.

Watson, J. B. (1924). *Behaviorism.* New York: Norton.

Watson, J. B., & Rayner, R. (1920). Conditioned emotional reactions. *Journal of Experimental Psychology, 3,* 1–14.

Watson, M., Haviland, J. S., Greer, S., Davidson, J., & Bliss, J. M. (1999, October 16). Influence of psychological response on survival in breast cancer: A population-based cohort study. *Lancet, 354,* 1331–1336.

Webb, W. B. (1992). *Sleep: The gentle tyrant* (2nd ed.). Boston: Anker.

Weber, K. & Bennett, S. (1999). *Special education in Canadian schools.* Thornhill, ON: Highland Press.*

Wechsler, D. (1975). Intelligence defined and undefined. *American Psychologist, 30,* 135–139.

Week, D., & James, J. (1995). *Eccentrics: A study of sanity and strangeness.* New York: Villard Books.

Weinberg, M. S., Williams, C. J., & Pryor, D. W. (1991, February 27). Personal communication. Indiana University, Bloomington.

Weinberg, R. A., Scarr, S., & Waldman, I. D. (1992). The Minnesota Transracial Adoption Study: A follow-up of IQ test performance at adolescence. *Intelligence, 16,* 117–135.

Weiner, B. (1985a). *Human motivation.* New York: Springer-Verlag.

Weiner, B. (1985b). "Spontaneous" casual thinking. *Psychological Bulletin, 97,* 74–84.

Weiner, I. B. (1998). *Principles of Rorschach interpretation.* Mahwah, NJ: Erlbaum.

Weiner, J. (2000, February 7). Curing the incurable. *New Yorker,* pp. 64–73.

Weintraub, M. (1976). Intelligent noncompliance and capricious compliance. In L. Lasagna (Ed.), *Patient compliance.* Mt. Kisco, NY: Futura.

Weisberg, H. F., Krosnick, J. A., & Bowen, B. D. (1996). *An introduction to survey research, polling, and data analysis.* Newbury Park, CA: Sage.

Weisman, A., Lopez, S. R., Karno, M., & Jenkins, J. (1993). An attributional analysis of expressed emotion in Mexican-American families with schizophrenia. *Journal of Abnormal Psychology, 102,* 601–606.

Weiss, A. S. (1991). The measurement of self-actualization: The quest for the test may be as challenging as the search for the self. *Journal of Social Behavior and Personality, 6,* 265–290.

Weissman, M. M., Bland, R. C., Canino, G. J., et al. (1996, July 24–31). Cross-national epidemiology of major depression and bipolar disorder. *Journal of the American Medical Association, 276,* 293–299.

Weissman, M. W., & Olfson, M. (1995, August 11). Depression in women: Implications for health care research. *Science, 269,* 799–801.

Weitzenhoffer, A. M. (1999). *The practice of hypnotism* (2nd ed.). New York: Wiley.

Welder, A. N. (2000). Sexual abuse victimization and the child witness in Canada: Legal, ethical, and professional issues for psychologists. *Canadian Psychology, 41,* 160–173.*

Wells, G. L., Malpass, R. S., Lindsay, R. C. L., Fisher, R. P., Turtle, J. W., & Fulero, S. M. (2000). From the lab to the police station: A successful application of eyewitness research. *American Psychologist, 55,* 581–598.

Werker, J. F. (1989). Becoming a native listener. *American Scientist, 77,* 54–59.*

Wertheimer, M. (1923). Untersuchungen zur Lehre von der Gestalt. II. *Psychol. Forsch., 5,* 301–350. In Beardsley and M. Wertheimer (Eds.), *Readings in perception* (New York: Van Nostrand, 1958).

West, R. L. (1995). Compensatory strategies for age-associated memory impairment. In A. D. Baddeley, B. A. Wilson, & F. N. Watts (Eds.), *Handbook of memory disorders.* Chichester, England: Wiley.

Westen, D. (1998). The scientific legacy of Sigmund Freud: Toward a psychodynamically informed psychological science. *Psychological Bulletin, 124,* 333–371.

Westen, D., & Gabbard, G. O. (1999). Psychoanalytic approaches to personality. In L. A. Pervin & O. P. John (Eds.), *Handbook of personality: Theory and research* (2nd ed.). New York: Guilford Press.

Westera, D. A., & Bennett, L. R. (1994). Population-focused research: A broad-based survey of teens' attitudes, beliefs, and behaviours. *International Journal of Nursing Studies, 31,* 521–531.

Wetter, D. W., Fiore, M. C., Gritz, E. R., Lando, H. A., Stitzer, M. L., Hasselblad, V., & Baker, T. B. (1998). The Agency for Health Care Policy and Research. Smoking cessation clinical practice guideline: Findings and implications for psychologists. *American Psychologist, 53,* 657–669.

Whaley, B. B. (Ed.). (2000). *Explaining illness: Research, theory, and strategies.* Mahwah, NJ: Erlbaum.

Whitbourne, S. K. (1999). Physical changes. In J. C. Cavanaugh & S. K. Whitbourne (Eds.). *Gerontology: An interdisciplinary perspective.* New York: Oxford University Press.

Whitbourne, S. K., & Wills, K. (1993). Psychological issues in institutional care of the aged. In S. B. Goldsmith (Ed.), *Long-term care.* Gaithersburg, MD: Aspen Press.

Whitbourne, S. K., Zuschlag, M. K., Elliot, L. B., & Waterman, A. S. (1992). Psychosocial development in adulthood: A 22-year sequential study. *Journal of Personality and Social Psychology, 63,* 260–271.

White, P. A. (1992). The anthropomorphic machine: Causal order in nature and the world view of common sense. *British Journal of Psychology, 83,* 61–96.

Whorf, B. L. (1956). *Language, thought, and reality.* New York: Wiley.

Wickelgren, I. (1998a, September 11). The cerebellum: The brain's engine of agility. *Science, 281,* 1588–1590.

Wickelgren, I. (1998b, June 26). Teaching the brain to take drugs. *Science, 280,* 2045–2047.

Wickens, C. D. (1984). *Engineering psychology and human performance.* Columbus, OH: Merrill.

Widmeyer, W. N., & Loy, J. W. (1988). When you're hot, you're hot! Warm-cold effects in first impressions of persons and teaching effectiveness. *Journal of Educational Psychology, 80,* 118–121.

Widom, C. S. (1989). Does violence beget violence? A critical examination of the literature. *Psychological Bulletin, 106,* 3–28.

Wiebe, D. J. (1991). Hardiness and stress moderation: A test of proposed mechanisms. *Journal of Personality and Social Psychology, 60,* 89–99.

Wiehe, V. R., & Richards, A. L. (1995). *Intimate betrayal: Understanding and responding to the trauma of acquaintance rape.* Thousand Oaks, CA: Sage.

Wielgosz, A. T., & Nolan, R. P. (2000). Biobehavioral factors in the context of ischemic cardiovascular diseases. *Journal of Psychosomatic Research, 48,* 339–345.

Wigfield, A., & Eccles, J. S. (2000). Expectancy-value theory of achievement motivation. *Contemporary Educational Psychology, 25,* 68–81.

Wiggins, J. S. (1997). In defense of traits. In R. Hogan, J. Johnson, & S. Briggs, (Eds.), *Handbook of personality psychology.* Orlando, FL: Academic Press.

Wiggins, J. S., & Pincus, A. L. (1992). Personality: Structure and assessment. In M. R. Rosenzweig & L. W. Porter (Eds.), *Handbook of personality psychology,* (Vol. 43). Palo Alto: Annual Reviews Inc.*

Wileman, R., & Wileman, B. (1995). Towards balancing power in domestic violence relationships. *Australian and New Zealand Journal of Family Therapy, 16,* 165–176.

Wilgoren, J. (1999, October 22). Quality day care, early, is tied to achievements as an adult. *New York Times,* p. A16.

Wilkie, D. M., Carr, J. A. R., Galloway, J., Parker, K. J., & Yamamoto, A. (1997). Conditional time-place learning. *Behavioural Processes, 40,* 165–170.*

Williams, J. E., Paton, C. C., Siegler, I. C., Eigenbrodt, M. L., Nieto, F. J., & Tyroler, H. A. (2000). Anger proneness predicts coronary heart disease risk: Prospective analysis from the Atherosclerosis Risk in Communities (ARIC) study. *Circulation, 101,* 2034–2039.

Williams, J. W., Mulrow, C. D., Chiquette, E., Noel, P. H., Aguilar, C., & Cornell, J. (2000). A systematic review of newer pharmacotherapies for depression in adults: Evidence report summary. *Annals of Internal Medicine, 132,* 743–756.

Williams, S. W., & McCullers, J. C. (1983). Personal factors related to typicalness of career and success in active professional women. *Psychology of Women Quarterly, 7,* 343–357.

Willis, S. L., & Nesselroade, C. S. (1990). Long-term effects of fluid ability training in old-old age. *Developmental Psychology, 26,* 905–910.

Willis, S. L., & Schaie, K. W. (1994). In C. B. Fisher & R. M. Lerner (Eds.), *Applied developmental psychology.* New York: McGraw-Hill.

Willson, R. J., & Wilkie, D. M. (1993). Pigeons remember briefly trained spatial location-food associations over extended time periods. *Journal of Experimental Psychology: Animal Behaviour Processes, 19(4),* 373–379.*

Wilson, G. T., & Agras, W. S. (1992). The future of behavior therapy. *Psychotherapy, 29,* 39–43.

Wilson, J. P., & Keane, T. M. (Eds.). (1996). *Assessing psychological trauma and PTSD.* New York: Guilford Press.

Windholz, G. (1997, September). Ivan P. Pavlov: An overview of his life and psychological work. *American Psychologist, 52,* 941–946.

Winner, E. (1997). *Gifted children: Myths and realities.* New York: Basic Books.

Winner, E. (2000). The origins and ends of giftedness. *American Psychologist, 55,* 159–169.

Winningham, R. G., Hyman, I. E., Jr., & Dinnel, D. L. (2000). Flashbulb memories? The effects of when the initial memory report was obtained. *Memory, 8,* 209–216.

Winson, J. (1990, November). The meaning of dreams. *Scientific American,* pp. 86–96.

Winter, D. G. (1973). *The power motive.* New York: Free Press.

Winter, D. G. (1987). Leader appeal, leader performance, and the motive profile of leaders and followers: A study of American presidents and elections. *Journal of Personality and Social Psychology, 52,* 196–202.

Winter, D. G. (1988). The power motive in women—and men. *Journal of Personality and Social Psychology, 54,* 510–519.

Winter, K. A., & Kuiper, N. A. (1997). Individual differences in the experiences of emotions. *Clinical Psychology Review, 17,* 798–821.*

Witelson, S. F. (1995). Neuroanatomical bases of hemispheric functional specialization in the human brain: Possible developmental factors. In F. L. Kitterle (Ed.), *Hemispheric communication: Mechanisms and models.* Hillsdale, NJ: Erlbaum.

Wixted, J. T., & Ebbesen, E. B. (1991). On the form of forgetting. *Psychological Science, 2,* 409–415.

Wolpe, J. (1990). *The practice of behavior therapy.* Boston: Allyn & Bacon.

Wolters, G. (1995). Het geheugen. Functie, structuur en processen (Memory: Its function, structure, and processes). *Psycholoog, 30,* 369–374.

Wonderlic. (2000, March 7). Wonderlic Personnel Test. Available on the World Wide Web at *http://www.wonderlic.com/wpt.html.*

Wong, M. M., & Csikszentmihalyi, M. (1991). Affiliation motivation and daily experience: Some issues on gender differences. *Journal of Personality and Social Psychology, 60,* 154–164.

Wood, D., Bruner, J. & Ross, G. (1976). The role of tutoring in problem solving. *Journal of Child Psychology and Psychiatry, 17,* 89–100.

Wood, J. M., & Bootzin, R. (1990). The prevalence of nightmares and their independence from anxiety. *Journal of Abnormal Psychology, 99,* 64–68.

Wood, W., Lundgren, S., Ouellette, J. A., Busceme, S., & Blackston, T. (1994). Minority influence: A meta-analytic review of social influence processes. *Psychological Bulletin, 115,* 323–345.

Wood, W., & Stagner, B. (1994). Why are some people easier to influence than others? In S. Savitt & T. C. Brock (Eds.), *Persuasion: Psychological insights and perspectives.* Boston: Allyn & Bacon.

Woodruff-Pak, D. S. (1999). New directions for a classical paradigm: Human eyeblink conditioning. *Psychological Science, 10,* 1–7.

Woods, S. C., Schwartz, M. W., Baskin, D. G., & Seeley, R. J. (2000). Food intake and the regulation of body weight. *Annual Review of Psychology, 51,* 255–277.

Woods, S. C., Seeley, R. J., Porte, D., Jr., & Schwartz, M. W. (1998, May 29). Signals that regulate food intake and energy homeostasis. *Science, 280,* 1378–1383.

World Health Organization. (n.d.) *Tobacco Free Initiative.* Available: <www5.who.int/tobacco/>. Accessed December 12, 2002.

Wozniak, R. H., & Fischer, K. W. (Eds.). (1993). *Development in context: Acting and thinking in specific environments.* Hillsdale, NJ: Erlbaum.

Wright, J. H., & Beck, A. T. (1996). Cognitive therapy. In R. E. Hales & S. C. Yudofsky (Eds.), *The American Psychiatric Press synopsis of psychiatry.* Washington, DC: American Psychiatric Press.

Wright, M. J. (1993). Women groundbreakers in Canadian psychology: World War II and its aftermath. *Canadian Psychology, 33(4),* 675–682.*

Wright, M. J., & Myers, C. R. (1982). *History of academic psychology in Canada.* Toronto: C.J. Hogrefe.*

Wright, S. J. (1999). Human embryonic stem-cell research: Science and ethics. *American Scientist, 87,* 352–361.

Wynn, K. (1995). Infants possess a system of numerical knowledge. *Current Directions in Psychological Science, 4,* 172–177.

Wynn, K. (2000). Addition and subtraction by human infants. In D. Muir & A. Slater (Eds.), *Infant development: The essential readings.* Malden, MA: Blackwell.

Wyshak, G., & Barsky, A. (1995). Satisfaction with and effectiveness of medical care in relation to anxiety and depression: Patient and physician ratings compared. *General Hospital Psychiatry, 17,* 108–114.

Yalom, I. D. (1997). *The Yalom reader: On writing, living, and practicing psychotherapy.* New York: Basic Books.

Yan, H., Kinzler, K. W., & Vogelstein, B. (2000, September 15). Genetic testing—present and future. *Science, 289,* 1890–1892.

Yarmey, D.A. (2001). Expert testimony: Does eyewitness memory research have probative value for the courts? *Canadian Psychology, 42,* 92–100.*

Yenerall, J. D. (1995). College socialization and attitudes of college students toward the elderly. *Gerontology and Geriatrics Education, 15,* 37–48.

Yik, M. S. M., Bond, M. H., & Paulhus, D. L. (1998). Do Chinese self-enhance or self-efface? It's a matter of domain. *Personality and Social Psychology Bulletin, 24,* 399–406.*

Yost, W. A. (1992). Auditory perception and sound source determination. *Current Directions in Psychological Science, 1,* 179–184.

Young, M. W. (2000, March). The tick-tock of the biological clock. *Scientific American,* 64–71.

Yuille, J. C. (1988). The systematic assessment of children's testimony. *Canadian Psychology, 29,* 247–262.*

Yuille, J. C. (1997). Interviewing children is a complex task. *Contemporary Psychology, 42,* 803–804.*

Yuskauskas, A. (1992). Conflict in the developmental disabilities profession: Perspectives on treatment approaches, ethics, and paradigms. *Dissertation Abstracts International, 53,* 1870.

Zajonc, R. B. (1985). Emotion and facial efference: A theory reclaimed. *Science, 228,* 15–21.

Zajonc, R. B., & McIntosh, D. N. (1992). Emotions research: Some promising questions and some questionable promises. *Psychological Science, 3,* 70–74.

Zamarra, J. W., Schneider, R. H., Besseghini, I., Robinson, D. K., & Salerno, J. W. (1996). Usefulness of the transcendental meditation program in the treatment of patients with coronary artery disease. *American Journal of Cardiology, 77,* 867–870.

Zanna, M. P. (1994). On the nature of prejudice. *Canadian Psychology, 35,* 11–23.*

Zautra, A. J., Reich, J. W., & Guarnaccia, C. A. (1990). Some everyday life consequences of disability and bereavement for older adults. *Journal of Personality and Social Psychology, 59,* 550–561.

Zeidner, M., & Endler, N. S. (Eds.). (1996). *Handbook of coping: Theory, research, applications.* New York: Wiley.

Zeidner, M., & Saklofske, D. (1996). Adaptive and maladaptive coping. In M. Zeidner & N. S. Endler (Eds.), *Handbook of coping: Theory, research, applications* (pp. 505–531). New York: Wiley.*

Zevon, M., & Corn, B. (1990). Paper presented at the annual meeting of the American Psychological Association, Boston.

Zhdanova, I. V., Lynch, H. J., & Wurtman, R. J. (1997). Melatonin: A sleep-promoting hormone. *Sleep, 20,* 899–907.

Ziegler, S. (1981). The effectiveness of cooperative learning teams for increasing cross-ethnic friendship: Additional evidence. *Human Organization, 40,* 264–267.*

Zito, J. M. (1993). *Psychotherapeutic drug manual* (3rd ed., rev.). New York: Wiley.

Zuckerman, M. (1978). The search for high sensation. *Psychology Today,* pp. 30–46.

Zuckerman, M. (1991). One person's stress is another person's pleasure. In C. D. Spielberger, I. G. Sarason, Z. Kulczar, & G. L. Van Heck (Eds.), *Stress and emotion: Anxiety, anger, and curiosity.* New York: Hemisphere.

Zuckerman, M. (1994). *Behavioral expression and biosocial expression of sensation seeking.* Cambridge, England: Cambridge University Press.

Zuger, A. (1998, June 2). The "other" drug problem: Forgetting to take them. *New York Times,* pp. C1, C5.

Acknowledgments

Chapter 1

Cartoon by Roz Chast, page 22: © The New Yorker Collection 1998 Roz Chast from cartoonbank.com. All Rights Reserved. **Cartoon, page 24:** © The New Yorker Collection 1993 J. B. Handelsman from cartoonbank.com. All Rights Reserved.

Chapter 2

Figure 2-1: From K. Van de Graaff, *Human Anatomy,* 2000. Copyright © 2000 by the McGraw-Hill Companies, Inc. Reproduced with permission of the McGraw-Hill Companies. **Figure 2-4a:** From S. S. Mader, *Biology,* 2000. Copyright © 2000 by the McGraw-Hill Companies, Inc. Reproduced with permission of the McGraw-Hill Companies. **Figure 2-4b:** From G. B. Johnson, *The Living World,* 2000. Copyright © 2000 by the McGraw-Hill Companies, Inc. Reproduced with permission of the McGraw-Hill Companies. **Figure 2-6:** From E. Loftus & C. Wortmann, *Psychology,* 1989. Copyright © 1989 by the McGraw-Hill Companies, Inc. Reproduced with permission of the McGraw-Hill Companies. **Figure 2-9:** From R. Seeley et al., *Anatomy and Physiology.* Copyright © by the McGraw-Hill Companies, Inc. Reproduced with permission of the McGraw-Hill Companies. **Figure 2-10:** From G. B. Johnson, *The Living World,* 2000. Copyright © 2000 by the McGraw-Hill Companies, Inc. Reproduced with permission of the McGraw-Hill Companies. **Figure 2-11a:** From A. Schneider and B. Tarshih, *Elements of Physiological Psychology.* Copyright © by the McGraw-Hill Companies, Inc. Reproduced with permission of the McGraw-Hill Companies. **Figure 2-13:** From Penfield, W. & Rasmussen, T. (1950). *The cerebral cortex of man.* New York: Macmillan Publishing. **Figure 2-15:** From S. S. Mader, *Biology,* 2000. Copyright © 2000 by the McGraw-Hill Companies, Inc. Reproduced with permission of the McGraw-Hill Companies.

Chapter 3

Figure 3-1: From R. Seeley et al., *Anatomy and Physiology.* Copyright © by the McGraw-Hill Companies, Inc. Reproduced with permission of the McGraw-Hill Companies. **Figure 3-3:** From D. Shier, et al., *Hole's Human Anatomy and Physiology,* Copyright © 2000 by the McGraw-Hill Companies, Inc. Reproduced with permission of the McGraw-Hill Companies. **Figure 3-5:** From S. S. Mader, *Biology,* 2000. Copyright © 2000 by the McGraw-Hill Companies, Inc. Reproduced with permission of the McGraw-Hill Companies. **Figure 3-7:** Used with permission of Michael L. Atkinson from *Psychology: Alternate Edition for Canada* by Camille B. Wortman, Elizabeth F. Loftus, Charles Weaver and Michael L. Atkinson (Toronto: McGraw-Hill Ryerson, 2000). **Figure 3-8:** From R. Seeley et al., *Anatomy and Physiology.* Copyright © by the McGraw-Hill Companies, Inc. Reproduced with permission of the McGraw-Hill Companies. **Figure 3-9:** From R. Seeley et al., *Anatomy and Physiology.* Copyright © by the McGraw-Hill Companies, Inc. Reproduced with permission of the McGraw-Hill Companies. **Figure 3-10:** The Olfactory System. **Figure 3-12a &c:** From *Mind Sights* by R. C. Shepard, © 1990 by W. H. Freeman. Reprinted by permission of Henry Holt and Company LLC. **Figure 3-15:** Adapted from Figure 7.38, *Sensation and Perception,* by E. Goldstein, 1984, Wadsworth Group. **Figure 3-16:** From I. Biederman, "Higher Level Vision," in D. N. Osherson, S. Kosslyn and J. Hollerbach (eds.). *An Invitation to Cognitive Science: Visual Cognition and Action,* 1990. Copyright © 1990 MIT Press. Reprinted with permission. **Figure 3-18:** From S. Coren and L. Ward, *Sensation and Perception,* 3rd edition. Copyright © 1989 by John Wiley & Sons, Inc. This material is used by permission of John Wiley & Sons, Inc. **Figure 3-19:** From S. Coren and L. Ward, *Sensation and Perception,* 3rd edition. Copyright © 1989 by John Wiley & Sons, Inc. This material is used by permission of John Wiley & Sons, Inc. **Figure 3-22:** From Gregory & Gombich, *Illusions in Nature and Art,* 1973. **Table 3-1:** Copyright © 1998 Better Hearing Institute, Washington, DC. All Rights Reserved. **Cartoon by Ian Falconer, page 106:** © The New Yorker Collection 1996 Ian Falconer from cartoonbank.com. All Rights Reserved.

Chapter 4

Figure 4-1: From *Sleep* by J. Allen Hobson, © 1989, 1995 by Scientific American Library. Reprinted by permission of Henry Holt and Company, LLC. **Figure 4-3:** From *Secrets of Sleep* by Alexander Borbely. English translation copyright © 1986 by Basic Books, Inc. Copyright © 1984 by Deutsche Verlag-Anstalt GmbH, Stuttgart. Reprinted by permission of Basic Books, a member of Perseus Books, L.L.C. **Figure 4-4:** Reprinted with permission from H. P. Roffwarg, J. N. Munzio and W. C. Dement, "Ontogenic Development of the Human Sleep-Dream Cycle," *Science,* 152, 1996, pp. 604–619. Copyright 1996 American Association for the Advancement of Science. **Figure 4-5:** Dr. Allen R. Braun, N.I.D.C.D., N.I.H. **Figure 4-6:** From W. C. Dement, in D. F. Dinges and Broughton (eds.), *Sleep and Alertness: Chronobiological, Behavioral, and Medical Aspects of Napping,* 1989. Reprinted with permission of Lippincott, Williams and Wilkins Publishers. **Figure 4-7:** From *The Relaxation Response* by Herbert Benson, M.D., with Miriam Z. Klipper. Copyright © 1975 by William Morrow & Company, Inc. Reprinted by permission of HarperCollins Publishers, Inc. **Figure 4-8:** Percentages of Canadian university undergraduates reporting use of various drugs at least once (based on Gliksman et al., 2000). **Figure 4-9:** From S. S. Mader, *Biology,* 2000. Copyright © 2000 by the McGraw-Hill Companies, Inc. Reproduced with permission of the McGraw-Hill Companies. **Figure 4-10:** From Blakeslee, "Levels of Caffeine in Various Foods," *New York Times,* August 7, 1991. **Figure 4-11: Cartoon by Mischa Richter, page 137:** © The New Yorker Collection 1993 Mischa Richter from cartoonbank.com. All Rights Reserved.

Chapter 5

Figure 5-5: E. C. Tolman and C. H. Honzik, 1930, *Introduction and Removal of Reward and Maze Performance in Rats,* University of California Publications in Psychology, 4, 257–275. **Cartoon by Tom Cheney, page 164:** © The New Yorker Collection 1993 Tom Cheney from cartoonbank.com. All Rights Reserved. **Cartoon by Gahan Wilson, page 175:** © The New Yorker Collection 1995 Gahan Wilson from cartoonbank.com. All Rights Reserved.

Chapter 6

Figure 6-2: Figure from "Human Memory: A Proposed System and Its Control Processes," by R. C. Atkinson and R. M. Shiffrin, from *The Psychology of Learning and Motivation: Advances in Research and Theory,* Volume 2, edited by K. W. Spence and J. T. Spence, copyright © 1968 by Academic Press, reproduced by permission of the publisher. **Figure 6-3:** From A. D. deGroot, "Perception and Memory Versus Thought: Some Old Ideas and Recent Findings," in B. Kleinmuntz, (ed.), *Problem Solving: Research, Method and Theory.* Copyright © 1966 John Wiley & Sons, Inc. This material is used by permission of John Wiley & Sons, Inc. **Figure 6-4:** Adapted from S. E. Gathercole and A. D. Baddeley, 1993, *Working Memory and Language Processing,* Taylor and Francis, Inc. **Figure 6-6:** Figure from "Retrieval Times from Semantic Memory," by A. M. Collins and M. R. Quillian in *Journal of Verbal Learning and Verbal Behavior,* Volume 8, 240–247. Copyright © 1969 by Academic Press. Reproduced by permission of the publisher. **Figure 6-7:** Courtesy of Dr. Steven E. Peterson, Washington University. **Figure 6-8:** From K. Van De Graaff, *Human Anatomy.* Copyright © by the McGraw-Hill Companies, Inc. Reproduced with permission of the McGraw-Hill Companies. **Figure 6-11:** From D. C. Rubin, "The Subtle Deceiver Recalling," *Psychology Today,* September 1995. Reprinted with permission from *Psychology Today* Magazine. Copyright © 1995 Sussex Publishers, Inc. **Figure 6-12:** Figure from "Reconstruction of Automobile Destruction," by E. F. Loftus and J. C. Palmer in *Journal of Verbal Learning and Verbal Behavior,* Volume 13, 585–589. Copyright © 1974 by Academic Press. Reproduced by permission of the publisher. **Figure 6-13:** From H. P. Bahrick, L. K. Hall, and S. A. Berger, "Accuracy and Distortion in Memory for High School Grades," *Psychological Science,* 7, 1996, 265–269. Reprinted with permission of Blackwell Publishers. **Cartoon by Roz Chast, page 193:** © The New Yorker Collection 1994 Roz Chast from cartoonbank.com. All Rights Reserved. **Cartoon by Mick Stevens, page 208:** © The New Yorker Collection 1998 Mick Stevens from cartoonbank.com. All Rights Reserved.

Chapter 7

Figure 7-1: Reprinted with permission from R. Shepard and J. Metzler, "Mental Rotation of Three Dimensional Objects," *Science,* 171, pp. 701–703, 1971. Copyright © 1971 American Association for the Advancement of Science. **Figure 7-8:** Data from "A Neural Basis for General Intelligence," by Duncan, *Science,* 289, July 21, 2000, p. 399. **Figure 7-9:** Adaptation of sample items from *Wechsler Intelligence Scales for Children (WISC-III).* The Psychological Corporation. **Figure 7-10:** Reprinted with permission of Wonderlic, Inc., Libertyville, Illinois. **Figure 7-11:** From Robert J. Sternberg, and Richard K. Wagner (eds.), *Practical Intelligence: Nature and Origins of Competence in the Everyday World,* 1986. Reprinted with permission of Cambridge University Press. **Figure 7-12:** Reprinted with permission from R. J. Sternberg, "The Holey Grail of General Intelligence," *Science,* 289, pp. 399–401, 2000. Copyright © 2000 American Association for the Advancement of Science. **Figure 7-13:** Adapted from "Familial Studies of Intelligence: A Review, " by T. J. Bouchard and M. McGue, *Science,* 212, 1981, p. 1055–1059. **Cartoon by James Stevenson, page 232:** © The New Yorker Collection 1989 James Stevenson from cartoonbank.com. All Rights Reserved. **Cartoon by Roz Chast, page 240:** © The New Yorker Collection 1998 Roz Chast from cartoonbank.com. All Rights Reserved. **Cartoon by W. B. Park, page 243:** © The New Yorker Collection 1983 W. B. Park from cartoonbank.com. All Rights Reserved.

Chapter 8

Table 8-1: From M. Zuckerman, "The Search for High Sensation," *Psychology Today,* February 1978. Reprinted with permission from *Psychology Today* Magazine, Copyright © 1978 Sussex Publishers, Inc. **Figure 8-1:** From A. Maslow, *Motivation and Personality, 3/e,* Copyright © 1970. Reproduced by permission of Pearson Education, Inc., Upper Saddle River, New Jersey. **Figure 8-3:** From K. W. Fischer, P. R. Shaver and P. Carnochan, "How Emotions Develop and How They Organize Development," *Cognition and Emotion,* Vol. 4. Copyright © 1990 by Psychology Press Ltd. Reprinted by permission of Psychology Press Ltd., Hove, UK. **Cartoon by Michael Maslin, page 267:** © The New Yorker Collection 1999 Michael Maslin from cartoonbank.com. All Rights Reserved.

Chapter 9

Figure 9-2: Adapted from Frankenburg, et al., 1992, "The Denver II: A Major Revision and Restandardization of the Denver Developmental Screening Test," *Pediatrics,* 89, 91–97. **Figure 9-4:** Adapted from W. J. Robbins, *Growth,* 1929. Yale University Press. **Figure 9-6:** From Judith A. Schickedanz, et al., *Understanding Children and Adolescents, Fourth Edition.* Copyright © 2001 by Allyn & Bacon. Reprinted by permission. **Figure 9-7:** Adapted from F. N. Dempster, "Memory Span: Sources for Individual and Developmental Differences," *Psychological Bulletin,* 89, 63–100. **Table 9-5:** From L. Kohlberg, "State and Sequence: The Cognitive-Developmental Approach to Socialization." In D. Goslin (ed.) *Handbook of Socialization Theory and Research,* 1969. Reprinted with permission of David Goslin. **Figure 9-9:** From K. W. Schaie, "The Course of Adult Intellectual Development," *American Psychologist,* 49, 304–313. Copyright © 1984 by the American Psychological Association. Reprinted with permission. **Cartoon by Lee Lorenz, page 305:** © The New Yorker Collection 1985 Lee Lorenz from cartoonbank.com. All Rights Reserved. **Cartoon by Roz Chast, page 321:** © The New Yorker Collection 1993 Roz Chast from cartoonbank.com. All Rights Reserved.

Cartoon by Roz Chast, page 330: © The New Yorker Collection 1993 Roz Chast from cartoonbank.com. All Rights Reserved.

Chapter 10

Figure 10-2: From Cattell, Eber & Tatsuoka, *Handbook for the 16PF.* Copyright © 1970 by the Institute for Personality and Ability Testing. Printed with permission. **Figure 10-3:** From H. J. Eysenck, "Biological Dimensions of Personality," in L. A. Pervin ed., *Handbook of Personality: Theory and Research.* Copyright © Guilford Publications, Inc. Reprinted with permission. **Figure 10-6:** From Tellegen, et al., "Personality Similarity in Twins Reared Apart and Together," *Journal of Personality and Social Psychology,* 54, pp. 1031–1039, 1989. Copyright © 1988 by the American Psychological Association. Reprinted with permission. **Figure 10-8:** Based on R. P. Halgin and S. K. Whitbourne, *Abnormal Psychology,* 1994, Harcourt Brace, and Minnesota *Multiphasic Personality Inventory* 2, University of Minnesota. **Figure 10-9 left:** From L. B. Alloy, N. S. Jackson and J. Acocella, *Abnormal Psychology* 8th ed., 1999. Copyright © 1999 The McGraw-Hill Companies, Inc. Reprinted with permission of The McGraw-Hill Companies Inc. **Table 10-3:** From L. A. Pervin ed., *Handbook of Personality: Theory & Research.* Copyright © Guilford Publications, Inc. Reprinted with permission. **Cartoon by Sidney Harris, page 339:** Copyright © by Sidney Harris. **Cartoon by Robert Mankoff, page 353:** © The New Yorker Collection 1991 Robert Mankoff from cartoonbank.com. All Rights Reserved.

Chapter 11

Figure 11-1: Adapted from Baum, A., "Behavioral, Biological and Environmental Interactions in Disease Processes," In S. Blumenthal, K. Matthews, and S. Weiss (eds.), *New Research Frontiers in Behavioral Medicine: Proceedings of the National Conference,* NIH Publications, 1994. **Figure 11-2:** Reprinted with permission from Elsevier Science, *The Lancet,* 1985, Vol. 750. **Figure 11-3:** *Morbidity and Mortality Weekly Report,* July 9, 1993. Center for Disease Control. **Figure 11-4:** US Department of Agriculture, 1998. **Chapter Activity 11-1:** From S. Cohen, T. Kamarck and R. Mermelstein, "A Global Measure of Perceived Stress," *Journal of Health and Social Behavior,* 24. Copyright © American Sociological Association. Reprinted with permission. **Chapter Activity 11-2:** From Jenkins, Zyzsndki & Rosenman, "Coronary-Prone Behavior: One Pattern or Several?" *Psychosomatic Medicine,* 40, 25–43, 1979. Reprinted with permission of Lippincott, Williams & Wilkins. **Quote, page 380:** From P. Jaret, "Mind Over Malady," *Health,* November/December 1992, p. 87. Reprinted with permission of Peter Jaret. © 1992. **Cartoon by Edward Koren, page 378:** © The New Yorker Collection 1995 Edward Koren from cartoonbank.com. All Rights Reserved.

Chapter 12

Chapter Activity 12-1: Personal communication with W. Hill, 1992. Public Affairs Network Coordinator for the American Psychiatric Association. **Figure 12-2:** From Jamison, "The Number of Pieces Written by Composer Robert Schumann," *New York Times,* October 10, 1993. Copyright © 1993 by the New York Times Co. Reprinted by permission. **Table 12-5:** From *Schizophrenia Genesis: The Origins of Madness* by I. I. Gottesman, © 1991 by W. H. Freeman. Reprinted by permission of Henry Holt

and Company, LLC. **Quote, page 396:** From *Wall Street Journal,* Eastern Edition by A. Bennett. Copyright © 1992 Dow Jones & Co., Inc. Reproduced by permission of Dow Jones & Co., Inc. via Copyright Clearance Center. **Quote, page 404:** From M. M. Antony, T. A. Brown, and D. H. Barlow, "Current Perspectives on Pain and Panic Disorder," *Current Directions in Psychological Science,* 1, 1992, page 79. Reprinted with permission of Blackwell Publishers. **Figure 12-5:** Adapted from Canadian Institute for Health Information data. **Figure 12-6:** Health Canada; **Cartoon by Arnie Levin, page 401:** © The New Yorker Collection 2000 Arnie Levin from cartoonbank.com. All Rights Reserved.

Chapter 13

Figure 13-2: Smith, Mary Lee, Gene V. Glass, and Thomas I. Miller, *The Benefits of Psychotherapy,* Copyright 1980 The Johns Hopkins University Press. Reprinted by permission of The Johns Hopkins University Press. **Figure 13-3:** Copyright © 1995 by Consumers Union of U.S., Inc. Yonkers, NY 10703-1057, a nonprofit organization. Reprinted with permission from the November 1995 issue of *Consumer Reports* for educational purposes only. No commercial use or photocopying permitted. To learn more about Consumers Union, log onto www.ConsumerReports.org. **Figure 13-4:** From D. Mischoulon, "Antidepressants: Choices and Controversy," *Health News,* Copyright © 2000 Massachusetts Medical Society. All rights reserved. **Figure 13-5:** From Howard, et al., "The Changing Face of American Psychology: A Report from the Committee on Employment and Human Resources," *American Psychologist,* 41, pp. 1311–1327, 1986. Copyright © 1986 by the American Psychological Association. Reprinted with permission. **Chapter Activity 13-1:** Reprinted by permission of Dr. Herbert Benson, Beth Israel Deaconess Medical Center, Boston, Massachusetts. **Quote, p. 432:** From D. Sue, D. Sue and S. Sue, *Understanding Abnormal Behavior,* Third Edition. Copyright © 1990 by Houghton Mifflin Company. Used with permission. **Cartoon by Donald Reilly, page 437:** © The New Yorker Collection 1994 Donald Reilly from cartoonbank.com. All Rights Reserved. **Cartoon by Gahan Wilson, page 452:** © The New Yorker Collection 1994 Gahan Wilson from cartoonbank.com. All Rights Reserved.

Chapter 14

Figure 14-3: Adapted from Anderson, Krull & Weiner, "Explanations: Processes and Consequences," in Higgins & Kruglanski (eds.), *Social Psychology: Handbook of Basic Principles,* 1996, p. 274. **Figure 14-6:** From M. B. Parlee, "The Friendship Bond," *Psychology Today,* October 1979. Reprinted with permission from *Psychology Today* Magazine. Copyright 1979 Sussex Publishers, Inc. **Figure 14-7:** From R. J. Sternberg, "A Triangular Theory of Love," *Psychological Review,* 93, pp. 119–135, 1986. Copyright © 1986 by the American Psychological Association. Reprinted with permission. **Figure 14-8:** Based on B. Latané and J. M. Darley, 1970. *The Unresponsive Bystander: Why Doesn't He Help?* Appleton-Century-Crofts. **Table 14-1:** From D. M. Buss, et al., "International Preferences in Selecting Mates: A Study of 37 Cultures," *Journal of Cross-Cultural Psychology,* 21, pp. 5–47. Copyright © 1990 by Sage Publications. Reprinted by permission of Sage Publications, Inc. **Cartoon by Robert Weber, page 469:** © The New Yorker Collection 1989 Robert Weber from cartoonbank.com. All Rights Reserved.

PHOTOS

Table of Contents

p. vii: © Jon Riley/GETTY IMAGES; **p. viii top:** © Alexander Tsiaras/Stock Boston; **p. viii bottom:** © Martine Mouchy/GETTY IMAGES; **p. ix top:** © Nicholas Devore III/Network Aspen; **p. ix bottom:** © Joanna B. Penneo/Aurora/PictureQuest; **p. x:** CP Picture Archive/Tom Hanson; **p. xi top:** © Dwayne Newton/Photo Edit; **p. xi bottom:** © Michael Schwarz/Getty Images; **p. xii:** © Look GMBH/eStock Photography/PictureQuest; **p. xiii:** © Jill Sabella/GETTY IMAGES; **p. xiv top:** © Seth Resnick/Stock Boston; **p. xiv bottom:** © Vanessa Vick/Photo Researchers; **p. xv top:** © Zigy Kaluzny/GETTY IMAGES; **p. xv bottom:** CP Picture Archive/Chuck Stoody

Chapter 1

OPENER: © Jon Riley/GETTY IMAGES; **p. 3:** © Monika Graff/Image Works; **p. 7 top:** © Laura Dwight/Photo Edit; **p. 7 bottom:** © Ann Chwatsky/Phototake/PictureQuest; **p. 11:** © Bettmann/Corbis Images; **p. 12 top:** © The Granger Collection; **p. 12 bottom and p. 13 top:** Canadian Psychological Association; **p. 14:** Bettmann/Corbis Images; **p. 15:** © Culver Pictures; **p. 16:** CP/Eckehard Schulz; **p. 19 left:** © Richard T. Nowitz/National Geographic Image Collection; **p. 19 right:** © Frank Herholdt/GETTY IMAGES; **p. 20:** © Robert Brenner/Photo Edit; **p. 24:** © Robert I. M. Campbell/National Geographic Image Collection; **p. 26:** © Bill Aron/Photo Edit; **p. 27:** © James Wilson/Woodfin Camp; **p. 28 top:** Courtesy, Bibb Latane; **p. 28 bottom:** Courtesy, John Darley, Princeton University; **p. 30:** Courtesy Wendy Josephson; **p. 33:** © Tom Stewart/Corbis Stock Market; **p. 34 top:** © Dan McCoy/Rainbow; **p. 34 bottom:** © Douglas Faulkner/Photo Researchers; **p. 36:** Courtesy Alexandra Kitty

Chapter 2

OPENER: © Alexander Tsiaras/Stock Boston; **p. 43:** © AP/Wide World Photos; **p. 46:** © John D. Cunningham/Visuals Unlimited; **p. 55:** From Deloukas, et al. October 23, 1998. "A physical map of 30,000 human genes." *Science* 282(5389), 744–746. © 1998 American Association for the Advancement of Science. http://www.ncbi.nlm.nih.gov/genemap/; **p. 56:** Courtesy Julien Doyon; **p. 57:** © Leonard Lessin/Peter Arnold; **Fig. 2.8a–b:** © Science Photo Library/Science Source/Photo Researchers; **Fig. 2.8c:** © Mehau Kulyk/Science Photo Library/Photo Researchers; **Fig. 2.8d:** © Dan McCoy/Rainbow; **Fig. 2.8e:** © Roger Ressmeyer/Corbis Images; **p. 58 bottom:** Artificial Intelligence Laboratory, MIT. Image courtesy of Michael Leventon; **p. 60:** © Gavin Smith/FSP/Getty Images; **Fig. 2.14:** Courtesy, Trustees of the British Museum, Natural History; **p. 66:** From: Damasio H., Grabowski T., Frank R., Galaburda A. M., Damasio A. R. 1994. "The return of Phineas Gage: Clues about the brain from the skull of a famous patient." *Science,* 264:1102–1105, 1994. © 1994 American Association for the Advancement of Science. Department of Neurology and Image Analysis Facility, University of Iowa; **Fig. 2.15:** B. A. Shaywitz et al., 1995. NMR/Yale Medical School

Chapter 3

OPENER: © Martine Mouchy/GETTY IMAGES; **p. 79:** Courtesy University of Toronto Archives/Robert Lansdale Photography Ltd.; **p. 81:** © Curtis Myers/Stock Connection/Picturequest; **p. 84 both:** © Biophoto Associates/Photo Researchers; **Fig. 3.6 (all):** © Joe Epstein/Design Conceptions; **p. 91:** © AP/Wide World Photos; **p. 94:** © Video-Surgery/Photo Researchers; **p. 98 top:** Courtesy, Julie Mennella; **p. 98 bottom:** © Prof. P. Motta/Dept. of Anatomy/University "La Sapienza," Rome/SPL/Photo Researchers; **p. 99:** © Omikron/Photo Researchers; **p. 100:** Courtesy Patrick J. McGrath; **p. 101:** © Lisa M. McGeady/Corbis Images; **Fig. 3.17 both:** Courtesy, Bela Julesz; **p. 109:** © Cary Wolinsky/Stock Boston; **p. 111 top:** Courtesy Darren Hick; **p. 111 bottom left:** Jeff Greenberg/Stock Boston; **p. 111 bottom right:** Eyewire; **Fig. 3.19a:** © John G. Ross/Photo Researchers; **Fig. 3.20b–c:** © Innervisions

Chapter 4

OPENER: © Nicholas Devore III/Network Aspen; **p. 121:** CP/Sherbrooke La Tribune; **p. 123:** CP/Halifax Daily News/Darrell Oake; **p. 125:** Dick Hemmingway/Sleep Disorders Centre of Metropolitan Toronto; **p. 126:** Courtesy Robert D. Ogilvie; **p. 130:** © Stock Portfolio/Stock Connection/PictureQuest; **p. 133:** © Jose Carrillo/Stock Boston; **p. 135:** © AP, Midland Daily News/Wide World Photos; **p. 142 top:** Stone/Robert E. Daemmrich; **p. 142 bottom:** © Corbis Images; **p. 144 bottom:** © Dr. Dennis Kunkel/PhotoTake; **p. 145 left:** © Bob Daemmrich/Stock Boston; **p. 145 right:** © IT Int'l/eStock Photography/PictureQuest; **p. 147 top:** © Andrew Brookes/Corbis Stock Market; **p. 147 bottom:** © Lawrence Migdale/Stock Boston; **p. 148:** © Kal Muller/Woodfin Camp

Chapter 5

OPENER: © Joanna B. Penneo/Aurora/PictureQuest; **p. 155:** Heritage Studio; **p. 157:** © Culver Pictures; **p. 160:** © Pictor International/PictureQuest; **p. 161 both:** © Stuart Ellins; **p. 163:** © Nina Leen/TimePix; **p. 165:** Courtesy, Lynne Calero; **p. 170:** © Chris Stanford/Allsport; **p. 171:** Courtesy, Dr. Marian Bailey; **p. 172:** Courtesy Catharine Rankin; **p. 176 top:** © Spencer Grant/Stock Boston; **p. 176 bottom:** Courtesy, Albert Bandura; **p. 177 top:** © Michael Newman/Photo Edit; **p. 177 bottom:** From Meltzoff, A.N. (1988.) "Imitation of Televised Models by Infants," *Child Development, 59,* 1221–1229. Photo Courtesy of A. N. Meltzoff & M. Hanak

Chapter 6

OPENER: Saskatchewan First Nations Grand Chief Howard Anderson commemorates the Tomb of the Unknown Soldier in Ottawa (May 28, 2000)—CP Picture Archive/Tom Hanson; **p. 187:** Eyewire; **p. 190:** © Bob Wallace/Stock Boston; **p. 191:** © F. Dewey Webster/Sovfoto/Eastfoto/PictureQuest; **p. 195 top:** © Arthur Tilley/GETTY IMAGES; **p. 195 bottom:** © Susan Werner/PictureQuest; **Fig. 6.7:** © Dr. Steven E. Peterson/Washington University. From *Scientific American,* 12/93; **p. 200:** © Tom McCarthy/Index Stock Imagery; **Fig. 6.9:** © Disney Enterprises, Inc; **p. 205:** © Shahn Kermani/Getty Images; **p. 206:** © Joseph Nettis/Photo Researchers; **Fig. 6.16:** © Cecil Fox/Science Source/Photo Researchers; **p. 210:** Courtesy, Holly Tuokko

Chapter 7

OPENER: © Dwayne Newton/Photo Edit; **p. 217:** NASA; **p. 225 (all):** © Superstock; **p. 231:** Courtesy, Dr. Laura Ann Pettito © 1991/photo by Robert LaMarche; **p. 234:** Courtesy, Fred Genesee; **Fig. 7.11(1):** © TimePix; **Fig. 7.11(2-4):** © Bettmann/Corbis Images; **Fig. 7.11(5):** © Corbis/Vol. #80

Chapter 8

OPENER: © Michael Schwarz/GETTY IMAGES; **p. 257:** CP/Adrian Wyld; **p. 264:** Courtesy Tara K. MacDonald; **p. 267:** © Peter Menzel/Stock Boston; **p. 268:** © Tony Freeman/PhotoEdit; **p. 273:** © Bob Daemmrich/Stock Boston; **p. 274:** CP/Anthony Peters; **Fig. 8.2:** Reprinted by permission of the publisher from THEMATIC APPERCEPTION TEST by Henry A. Murray, Cambridge, Mass.: Harvard University Press, Copyright © 1943 by the Presidents and Fellows of Harvard College, © 1971 by Henry A. Murray; **p. 282:** Courtesy of Donald G. Dutton, Ph.D.; **Fig. 8.5:** George, M. S., et al. "Brain activity during transient sadness and happiness in healthy women." *American Journal of Psychiatry,* 152:341–351, 1995. © 1995, The American Psychiatric Association. Reprinted by permission.

Chapter 9

OPENER: © Look GMBH/eStock Photography/PictureQuest; **p. 289:** © Evan Richman/New York Times Pictures; **p. 291:** © Peter Byron; **Fig. 9.1a:** © D. W. Fawcett/Photo Researchers; **Fig. 9.1b:** © L. Willatt, East Anglian Regional Genetics Service/SPL/Photo Researchers; **Fig. 9.1c:** © Kenneth Eward/Photo Researchers; **Fig. 9.1d:** © Biophoto Associates/Science Source/Photo Researchers; **p. 295:** © AP/Wide World Photos; **p. 296 left:** Photo Lennart Nilsson/Albert Bonniers Forlag, A CHILD IS BORN, Dell Publishing Company; **p. 296 right:** © Petit Format/Science Source/Photo Researchers; **Fig. 9.3:** From: A. N. Meltzoff & M. K. Moore. 1977. "Imitation of facial and manual gestures by human neonates." *Science,* 198: 75–78. © 1977 American Association for the Advancement of Science; **Fig. 9.5:** Harlow Primate Laboratory, University of Wisconsin; **p. 310:** © Laura Dwight/Peter Arnold; **p. 312:** © Farrell Grehan/Corbis Images; **p. 315:** © Najlah Feanny/Saba; **p. 316:** © Danny Lehman/Corbis Images; **p. 318:** © C/B Productions/Corbis Stock Market; **p. 319:** © Julie Houck/Stock Boston; **p. 320:** Courtesy Lorrie K. Sippola; **p. 323:** © Stephen Simpson/GETTY IMAGES; **p. 327:** © Bob Daemmrich/Stock Boston; **p. 328:** Courtesy Kevin Sweryd; **p. 329:** © Lori Grinker/Contact Press Images/PictureQuest

Chapter 10

OPENER: © Jill Sabella/GETTY IMAGES; **p. 337:** Courtesy Jordan S. Dill; **p. 341:** © Tony Freeman/Photo Edit; **p. 343 both:** © Kobal Collection/Lucas-Film/20th Century Fox; **p. 349:** CP/Andrew Vaughan; **p. 354:** Courtesy Romin Tafarodi; **p. 362:** © Laura Dwight/Corbis Images

Chapter 11

OPENER: © Seth Resnick/Stock Boston; **p. 369:** Eyewire; **p. 374:** Courtesy Kavita Prakash; **p. 375:** CP/Adrian Wyld; **p. 376:** © Corbis/Vol. #62; **p. 378:** Courtesy Jo-Anne Trigg; **p. 382:** © Bob Daemmrich/Stock Boston; **p. 383:** © Prof. S. H. E. Kaufmann & Dr. J. R. Golecki/SPL/Photo Researchers; **p. 384:** © 2001 Buttout.com, Photo by Toni Michaels; **p. 389:** © David Toerge/Black Star

Chapter 12

OPENER: © Vanessa Vick/Photo Researchers; **p. 395:** Courtesy, Lori Schiller; **p. 397:** CP Picture Archive/Ian Macalpine; **p. 384:** Courtesy, Margaret Coggins; **p. 405:** CP/Toronto Star/David Cooper; **p. 409:** CP Picture Archive/Jacques Boissinot; **p. 410:** © Susan Greenwood/Getty Images; **p. 413:** © Wellcome Dept. of Cognitive Neurology/SPL/ Photo Researchers; **Fig. 12.3 (all):** © Derek Bayes/ TimePix; **Fig. 12.4 (both):** Courtesy, Nancy Andreasen, University of Iowa Hospitals & Clinics; **p. 418:** Courtesy Sylvia Geist

Chapter 13

OPENER: © Zigy Kaluzny/GETTY IMAGES; **p. 429:** Courtesy Norman Endler; **p. 432:** © Bruce Ayres/GETTY IMAGES; **p. 433:** © Jonathan Nourok/PhotoEdit; **p. 435:** © Rick Freedman/ Black Star; **p. 438:** CP/Tony Caldwell; **p. 441:** © Jon Bradley/GETTY IMAGES; **p. 445:** © Paul Chesley/Photographers/Aspen/PictureQuest; **p. 448:** © Custom Medical Stock Photo; **p. 449:** Corbis Images; **p. 450:** CP/Rick Rycroft; **p. 451:** © Will & Deni McIntyre/Photo Researchers; **p. 451:** © Phyllis Picard/Stock South/PictureQuest

Chapter 14

OPENER: Protestors March on the APEC conference in Vancouver (November 23, 1998)—CP Picture Archive/Chuck Stoody; **p. 457:** CP Picture Archive/ Frank Gunn; **p. 459:** © AP/Wide World Photos; **p. 462:** Courtesy, Ann Altman; **p. 463:** © Myrleen Ferguson Cate/PhotoEdit; **p. 466:** Courtesy James Alcock; **Fig. 14.4:** © William Vandivert/TimePix; **Fig. 14.5 (both):** From the film OBEDIENCE © 1965 by Stanley Milgram and distributed by Penn. State Media Sales. Permission granted by Alexandra Milgram; **p. 482:** © AP/Wide World Photos

Name Index

Subject Index

Note: Page numbers in *italics* indicate figures and illustrations; page numbers followed by *t* indicate tables.